STATUTORY HISTORY
OF THE
UNITED STATES

INCOME SECURITY

STATUTORY HISTORY
OF THE
UNITED STATES

INCOME SECURITY

Editor
Robert B. Stevens
Yale University

CHELSEA HOUSE PUBLISHERS
In Association with
McGRAW-HILL BOOK CO.
New York   Toronto   London   Sydney

PREFACE

I was delighted when Chelsea House invited me to produce a legislative history of income security. From a purely selfish point of view, it was an opportunity for reading in some sort of coherent pattern a great deal of material which I had either read at great speed or had, with that well-meaning enthusiasm so common in academic life, put aside to read at some later date.

At a less selfish level, anyone interested in social legislation must be concerned with the paucity of available published documents and the reluctance of publishers to cover any one area like income security in depth. Lawyers' works on social legislation meander through apparently unrelated areas, from consumer protection to workmen's compensation. Moreover, lawyers' casebooks tend to overemphasize litigation and underemphasize legislation, interspersing unrelated snippets from different statutes between far larger extracts from either judicial or administrative decisions.

The primary purpose of this volume is to present the political and legislative history of income security. Possibly I have overcompensated for some of the defects I discovered in other collections. For instance, I have included decisions in the courts only when I thought they related to the structure of the acts themselves. Decisions on the meaning of "employment," "disability," "insured," "partially disabled," and a multitude of other points exist in profusion in decisions from administrative bodies and the courts; hence, the thirteen Commerce Clearing House loose-leaf volumes entitled *Unemployment Insurance Reports* (there are twenty more volumes for individual states) and the seven Prentice-Hall volumes entitled *Social Security*. I am not for one moment denying that these decisions are important. They most certainly are; indeed it would be eminently desirable if they generated a far more sophisticated literature than has appeared so far. But including even a limited selection of such decisions here would detract from the coherence of the story which this book is attempting to cover.

This book is an effort to use official documents to tell a crucial aspect of social history: the story of governmental involvement in income security. In a period when the social scientists appear to have decided that it is unfashionable to discuss anything so mundane and potentially useful as social policy, it is perhaps the duty of that low-visibility technician, the lawyer, to attempt to fill this vacuum. Fulfillment of such a duty has an eminently practical aim. Without a clear grasp of modern social history—the whys and wherefores in their proper context—it is unlikely that the social relevance of present legislation will be fully understood, or that appropriate alternative policies will be developed for the future.

It has, of course, not been easy to decide what to include and what to exclude, and space limitations have prevented me from reproducing the various acts in full. When it comes to messages, hearings, debates, regulations, and litigation, I am fully aware that others would have made totally, or at least substantially, different selections. In dealing with legislation which was not passed, I have no doubt that my subjectivity is particularly noticeable since, with the usual academic license, I have generally stressed areas of particular interest to me.

In general, I have let documents speak for themselves. By this I mean that I have not provided commentary where I felt it unnecessary. Again I have obviously applied subjective standards. In linking different views in hearings, I have not hesitated to give running commentaries. But at the same time I have steered away from detailed introductions to statutes, preferring to rely on the direct evidence of committee reports to establish, insofar as possible, congressional intent. At the same time, with very few exceptions, reliance has been placed solely on documents emanating from the Federal Government. If this at times gives a special view of the problems or programs, it does, I hope, emphasize what this series is seeking to achieve.

Since this book is an attempt to examine in depth one segment of that field which lawyers broadly term social legislation, it is perhaps appropriate to consider this wider area for a moment. It is, however, difficult to obtain any agreement on the definition of the whole field, or on just what "social legislation" involves. In its purest meaning social legislation probably covers all those areas into which government has moved other than the ones which Adam Smith in the eighteenth century determined were legitimate activities for government. At least in this pure form, the term ought to cover situations where the market is no longer left to operate on its own.

We should therefore have to include in this definition federal regulation of railroads, aviation, airlines, trucking, telephones, radio and television, public utilities, and the rest. We should also have to include federal control over the distribution of goods represented by the activities of the Food and Drug Administration, the Federal Trade Commission, and the different safety bureaus, and no doubt some would even include certain aspects of the anti-trust laws. All these foregoing examples consist of attempts by Congress to implement a social policy of protecting consumers from the full force of the private enterprise system.

Congress has also legislated to protect different parts of the private enterprise system from the effect of market forces. Examples of this might range from tariff legislation to anti-chain-store laws like the Robinson-Patman Act. But many perhaps less obvious examples also exist. The Federal Government will spend over $4 billion in 1968 subsidizing the farming industry. The Post Office is another source of subsidy to industry: by carrying various categories of mail used by industry at less than cost; by subsidizing certain airlines and railroads for the services they provide; and by being forbidden to compete on equal terms with private parcel carriers. With the perennially high military budgets and the rapid growth of the space program, the amount of research and development funds poured into industry by government has swelled almost immeasurably; and where an

industry is sick, like the New Haven Railroad, or beset by foreign competition, like the merchant marine, operating and construction subsidies are the
order of the day.

While such an immense infusion of federal funds is not generally catego-
rized under the heading of social legislation, where is the line to be drawn?
The income tax acts and related legislation, imposing as they do (at least in
theory) a system of progressive taxation, provide the most obvious example of *social* policy in any legislation. Yet lawyers have consciously played
down their social policy aspects. For instance, the incentives to home
ownership through mortgage deductions, and the encouragement of private
medical care through the medical deductions, are not traditionally treated as
part of social legislation.

Rather than being defined through its impact on the structures of society,
"social legislation" has taken to itself areas which, for one reason or another, have been identified with the development of the welfare state. Tradition, attitudes, and history are thus the "test" for determining what is regarded as social legislation and what — being less controversial — is usually
not. Even Adam Smith regarded the provision of courts as a legitimate
exercise of the governmental function; they clearly are a social service
provided by the State and, some would argue, no more necessary than
hospitals. Yet the provision of medical care — particularly where federally
subsidized — is identified with elements of the welfare state, while court
structure, even where funded out of tax revenues, is generally not. Free
education for all, regarded as an ideal (often unrealized) in most countries describing themselves as socialist states, is treated as an elementary aspect of
the American way of life. A national park system, often an important plank
in the platforms of European socialist parties, was in this country largely
the creation of a breed of Republican who would have had little time for
the welfare state.

Tradition, therefore, is important in what we categorize as pertinent to
the welfare state. Moreover, it is not only political tradition which is important, but also legal tradition, for the categories assigned by lawyers to
different pieces of legislation often affect the view taken of them by later
generations of political commentators. Many of the important social policies concerning industry are subsumed under such headings as public law,
regulation of industry, or some such rubric. That area of legislation dealing
with the unions, with its many and often contradictory policies, is compart-
mentalized as labor law. Even civil rights, while included in the Public Welfare Title of the United States Code, is treated by lawyers as a definable
area within constitutional law.

Historical accident, together with the lawyer's obsession with categories,
make social legislation an unsatisfactory term. Whether one approves of
them or not, the deviations in our society from the presumed norm of market conditions is now so great that it leaves us with an amorphous and
largely unrelated series of acts. Some more easily definable description is

needed to identify those areas of the law which we now think of as relating to the welfare state. Perhaps there comes a point where the only solution is to be idiosyncratic. The trend over the last fifty years has been towards a welfare state, which I define as a concern by the electorate that the state become involved (or more involved) with four essentials—housing, education, health, and income security. For the purposes of this volume, then, those four areas will be treated as the scope of social legislation. Income security is thus one major plank in the development of interlocking programs for individual health, self-improvement, shelter, and well-being.

This volume will be concerned primarily with income security, that is to say, cash benefits, By this, at a federal level, is meant social security (covering old-age, survivors, disability, and now health insurance), the various grants-in-aid programs under public assistance provisions (old-age assistance, aid to dependent children, aid to families with dependent children, aid to the blind, aid to the permanently and totally disabled, and grants to states for medical assistance programs), and the system of unemployment compensation. The final section deals with new approaches to income security, ranging from the economic opportunity legislation to those many variations of the guaranteed income or the negative income tax.

Those conversant with the field will recognize that with the exception of the last section the book is concerned primarily with the various titles of the much amended Social Security Act. It thus steers entirely clear of education and housing. On the one hand, it does deal directly with health problems where they impinge most obviously on income security—such as Medicaid and health insurance for the elderly—since these particular "kind" services have historically been treated as an integral part of the "cash" services. On the other hand, this book does not treat public health programs dealing with such matters as rehabilitation and maternal and child welfare. No attempt is made other than to sketch their barest history before 1935, and after that date they are dealt with only where their comprehensiveness is essential to the understanding of other programs. Also not included are the other major federal programs in the field of health, ranging from grants for hospital building under the Hill-Burton Act to the ever-increasing scope of public health activities. For similar reasons, grants for mental retardation under Title XVII of the Social Security Act are omitted.

The centrality of income security through direct cash payments has thus been the standard for inclusion or exclusion. But even this rough-and-ready test is not uniformly applied. In order to make this a manageable volume, the federal programs for special groups—railroad social insurance, public employee programs, and veterans benefits—have also been excluded. Only when reference to these programs is an integral part of some core legislation are they dealt with even peripherally. Nevertheless, for the sake of completeness, a short statement of their present scope is included in the closing section.

The other qualification to be made to the claim of centrality of income security is that this is a book about federal legislation. Before 1935 it is fair to say that the states were exclusively responsible for any governmental concern there might be about income security. Since then the Federal Government has increasingly provided a system of social insurance for those who qualify; in fact it now shares its power with the states only in the case of unemployment insurance. There has also been a gradual federalization of public assistance programs, there being today four categories of programs for which federal grants-in-aid are available: old-age assistance (OAA), aid to families with dependent children (AFDC), aid to the blind (AB), and aid to the permanently and totally disabled (APTD). Federal aid is also available for paying the medical care of persons in these four categories and to the medically indigent generally under the 1965 amendments. But despite this federalization, public assistance of all varieties is still administered by the states and, of course, any public assistance outside these specific categories — general assistance (GA) — is financed solely by state and local money. Some idea of the relative federal-state-local expenditures under these different heads is provided in Part VII, which also includes an outline of workmen's compensation — the first, most legalistic, and therefore, not surprisingly, the most archaic of the attempts to develop an income security program. It has remained solely the concern of the states. The Federal Government has intervened only with respect to its own employees, the District of Columbia, and the longshoremen and harbor workers.

It is a matter of common knowledge that books produced by aging professors are not in fact written by them. I can freely admit that most of the succeeding pages contain the ideas, often revised and re-edited, of Presidents, congressmen (and their staffs), civil servants, lobbyists, and those concerned with the public interest. (And these categories are not always mutually exclusive.) But in addition to such public servants, I must and do readily concede that this volume would never have reached a publishable state had I not had the invaluable assistance of Edward Lyman of the George Washington Law School, class of 1968. I must also thank Jeffrey Radowitz and Richard Tropp of the Yale Law School, classes of 1969 and 1971 respectively.

Much of the work for these volumes was undertaken in New Haven, and I must thank librarian Arthur Charpentier of the Yale Law School, and my secretary Rosann Laroche. Both were remarkably helpful in answering my persistent demands. Some of the work was done at the Brookings Institution, where I owe thanks to Miss Virginia Whitney, the librarian, Mrs. M. S. Magg, the reference librarian, and the other members of the staff who filled my repeated requests.

It is not easy to thank all those who influenced my approach and attitudes to social legislation generally and income security in particular. But my primary interest in the field springs from a series of discussions with my former colleague Richard Titmuss, Professor of Social Administration at the London School of Economics. His perceptiveness in all fields of social policy is widely known, but only those who have been privileged to be befriended by him fully appreciate the breadth of his vision. I must similarly thank Professor Brian Abel-Smith, also of the London School of Economics.

In this country, I am obliged to those in Washington who have sharpened my understanding of the matters investigated here. At Brookings I must thank especially Joe Pechman and Gil Steiner. Among those who explained various political and social problems to me were Pat Connell Shakow, and Joe Chubb — former students — now moved to loftier heights on Capitol Hill. I also received great help from many persons in the Executive Branch, especially in the Department of Health, Education, and Welfare. To all such persons I offer my sincere thanks.

This is a legislative history and, as such, it should be the embodiment of that principle espoused by the patron saint of lawyers, Coke, who advised us not to turn *ad stirpes* but to look *ad fontes*. Since I have attempted to include at least a reasonable collection of the *fontes*, I have not sought to provide any systematic list of the *stirpes*. Yet, as a common lawyer, conscience has encouraged me at times to add a somewhat eclectic list of references.

In an attempt to justify my general position of refusing to include detailed references, I would argue that it is not difficult to find further readings. *The Social Security Bulletin* and *Welfare in Review* provide not only a sort of official commentary on current legislation in the field, but they also refer to articles in related fields by academic authors. For a survey development of income security itself, we are fortunate in having the writings of Witte and Altmeyer, at least for the earlier years, while the *Congressional Quarterly* is a useful mode of keeping matters up to date since that time.

For more general readings there are the writings of scholars like Haber, Burns, and Meyers. There are also various symposia which provide stimulating papers in most of the areas covered by this volume. Medical care has, of course, its own extensive bibliography, while the writings on poverty and its cures (the negative income tax being currently the most fashionable) threaten to engulf us all.

I thus put my conscience still further at rest, with the feeling that the serious student, anxious to use this book as the basis of research, will not be long in finding the interpretative articles he may feel he wants.

Robert B. Stevens
Professor of Law

Yale University
August 30, 1969

CONTENTS

II. THE SOCIAL SECURITY ACT
1935

VII. THE GREAT SOCIETY
1964–1968

INTRODUCTION:
THE FEDERAL ROLE IN INCOME SECURITY

THE FEDERAL ROLE IN INCOME SECURITY

In historical terms, the federal involvement with income security is very recent indeed. For all practical purposes, it has been just over thirty years since the Congress first undertook to organize such programs itself or to provide federal subsidies for programs which were the responsibility of the states. From this perspective, whatever one's political views, it is difficult not to be impressed at least by the magnitude of what has been accomplished.

Moreover, when one considers that the approach to income security was the work of one piece of legislation — the Social Security Act of 1935 — the story becomes even more remarkable. Why did this nation suddenly change course, at least with respect to federal intervention? How far has the approach and its specific provisions been altered over the years, and how far do the various programs fit the needs of the United States as it approaches the 1970's? This introductory essay is intended to offer some preliminary answers to these three questions.

The previously ascendent philosophy of rugged individualism assumed that a man would be best served if he served himself. Such a man, unemployed in a Boston slum, would in theory take himself to some frontier area and homestead the land or perhaps move to an area where there was still a demand for factory hands. He saved or insured to provide for injury, old age, or ill health; and if he failed to make the provisions which prudent Americans made, then he could rely on family, community, or private charity. Voluntarism was the order of the day.

It is easy to overdraw this picture of what later seemed to some an ideal period. Perhaps it was merely a figment of nostalgic memory, but the outlook of many observers over the past forty years has been premised on the assumption that it had indeed existed. Certainly legal provisions encouraged the old values to survive as long as possible. Each of the states had some variation of the English poor-law systems with either indoor (poor farms, workhouses) or outdoor (general assistance) relief. It was this relief which was available to a citizen who had failed to make provision for age or disability (either for himself or his survivors), or who lacked the courage to move in response to market pressures, or who could not take advantage of (or had exhausted) the provisions of private charity. Social stigma attached to what the state did provide. It was intended to. The "good" poor did not need to rely on any state assistance, while the "bad" poor were to be treated as akin to criminals. Indeed, it is arguable that the approach to criminals and the causes of crime showed far more enlightenment between 1800 and 1900 than did the approach to paupers and to the causes of poverty.

But changes were coming. The Civil War could barely have failed to have some effect on the attitude towards potential governmental power and authority. The Industrial Revolution, coming later on this side of the Atlantic, had already made its mark. Each successive wave of immigrants found it increasingly difficult to assimilate, with fewer community supports to rely on in their hour of need. If the early Germans and Irish had appeared to have grave difficulties, these were nothing compared with the difficulties faced by the Poles and Italians, who, in turn, had a far easier time than the Chinese or the emancipated Negroes.

Thus, by the turn of this century, at least in a few states, the attitude towards welfare services was changing. There was increasing hostility towards indoor relief; there was even a willingness to extend outdoor relief. For the aged who had suddenly fallen on hard times, some states were prepared to talk in terms of an old-age pension. To the widow with small children, there was by then the mother's pension. The blind man too gained increasing sympathy and help. It is true that such programs, established in a minority of states, were both discretionary and discriminatory, and covered but a small portion of the population who might be thought to need them, yet at least by 1900 they were heard of.

It was not long too before the more industrialized states began to respond to the carnage of modern industry (and the growing power of the unions) by enacting workmen's compensation legislation. World War I accelerated trends in this direction. It again exhibited the potential power of the Federal Government, which could not only provide welfare services during the war, but had the power and inclination to act in a paternalistic way to veterans after the war. A country that could and did do that could scarcely stop short when there was an economic collapse, and it was the economic collapse during the presidency of Herbert Hoover which ultimately led to the breakup of the established system.

Never before had vast numbers of provident members of the middle class or lower middle class found themselves without work. What minority groups had once had to suffer in silence was now the fate of many white middle-class Americans of North European stock. The system of private charity could no longer take the strain; the existing poor law system could not be allowed to. Indoor relief had largely disappeared in the 1920's. Now was the time to revise outdoor relief. After the Federal Emergency Relief Administration (FERA) the welfare system could never be quite the same again.

Even in its context the 1935 social security legislation was radical. Traditionally regarded by advocates of social security as decades behind all other countries, the United States found itself considered one of the most innovative nations in the field. Such a profound change gives some measure of the significance of the 1935 act and the depth of the crisis which spawned it. Moreover, the 1935 act set up a tripartite system of income security, an arrangement which has acted as the basis of the system from that day to this. The distinction between social security, public assistance, and unemployment compensation was settled by this one act.

The social security program (here used in its narrow sense) was to be solely a federal program of compulsory old-age insurance, with an appropriate reserve financed by contributions from both employers and employees. The public assistance provisions were to remain basically a state function. There was not to be (and there has not been) any federalization of the provision of public assistance or any contribution to general assistance — the core of the local welfare programs. In 1935 the Federal Government assumed one-half of the responsibility for funding certain types of public assistance such as old-age assistance and aid to the blind, and a one-third (50 per cent in 1939) share in funding aid to dependent children — in return for the imposition of limited federal standards on state programs. The third prong of the 1935 legislation — unemployment compensation — provided another method of federal-state cooperation. Strong federal tax and federal accounting procedures were provided, but all states ultimately took full advantage of the provisions allowing a rebate of all but a small percentage of the employers' tax. As a result, except in periods of recession, the states remained in exclusive control of their own programs.

Of course neither the scope nor the reputation of these three major programs remained static. In particular, social security has moved in the last three decades from being regarded as a dangerous socialistic invasion of American life to an almost sacrosanct institution. Social insurance has also come of age. Throughout the years its coverage has steadily increased. Beginning as an old-age insurance program (OAI) in 1935, it was expanded to cover survivors (OASI) in 1939 even before the first payments had been made under the program. At the same time there was a movement to include more and more persons under the plan. In 1950, for instance, farm workers and household employers were included, as were most categories of self-employed persons, and during the 1950's farming and self-employed groups were covered. During the 1960's social security coverage became almost universal, and those categories formerly not included on a compulsory basis were at last brought in (as were physicians in 1965), or, as in the case of employees of local and state governments, were allowed to join on a voluntary basis.

It was also during the 1950's that social security expanded into the area of disability, a move first seriously considered in 1939 but violently opposed by that most formidable of lobbies — the American Medical Association. In 1954 a disability freeze was introduced whereby during periods of disability those covered by OASI could retain their rights under the program even though they were no longer able to contribute. In 1956 the program actually undertook disability insurance, thus becoming OASDI, although only those between fifty and sixty-four were covered. In 1960 the age limit was abandoned and in 1965 the definition of disability was extended. Most important of all in the 1960's was the addition of both compulsory insurance for hospital and related expenses for those over sixty-five, and a voluntary insurance program for physicians and other medical services. Both these health programs were added in 1965, making social security a program of OASDHI from then on.

At the same time, there has been a slow change in the concept of social security as an insurance program, represented by the changes in the method of computing benefits and the amount of work required before benefits were payable. Thus, in the 1935 legislation the assumption was that benefits would be related to a lifetime's earnings, but as early as 1939 the basis was changed to reflect average earnings in covered employment as well as its length. This was further relaxed after 1950, when subsequent years could be treated as the base for computing benefits. Changes in 1954 and 1956 allowed any five years to be dropped for the purpose of computing benefits. At the same time, the length of time a potential beneficiary was required to work in covered employment was slowly reduced, despite the rapid expansion of covered employment. The 1935 legislation, using private insurance as a model, had assumed that the employee would have to remain in covered employment indefinitely. The 1939 act, which did much to change the philosophy of the program, only required that half the time between 1936 and the age of sixty-five be in covered employment (with a minimum of six quarters). In the 1950's each extension of covered employment categories was accompanied by relaxations in the number of quarters expected of those who had just been included, normally coupled with some compensating liberalization for those already in. The 1960 act defined insured status at one out of three post-1950 quarters, while the basic one out of four post-1950 calendar quarters formula was provided by the 1961 amendments.

In keeping with this evolution from insurance to social insurance, moves to increase this "blanketing in" approach have continued. In 1966, for instance, persons over seventy-two became eligible for old-age benefits even if they had less than six quarters of coverage, a development which brought general funds into the OASDI program. The 1965 medical care provisions provided financing from general revenues to pay the expenses of those over sixty-five not eligible for social security under the compulsory part of the scheme. Under the voluntary part of the legislation, the contributions of all the participants were matched by an equal amount from the central government.

Naturally there have been changes in both the tax base and the benefits which are payable under the program. The 1935 legislation established a tax base of $3,000 and a maximum contribution of 3 per cent by both employers and potential beneficiaries. The 1967 amendments—covering survivors, disability, and hospital insurance as well—provided for a tax base of $7,800 in 1968, with an ultimate contribution of 5.9 per cent from both employers and participants. The program had thus become a significant source of taxation as well as an important source of income for a major sector of the population.

Thus OAI grew to OASDHI in thirty years. But the two other prongs of social security—using that term in its broader sense—also developed. In public assistance, two of the programs—old-age assistance (OAA) and aid to the blind (AB) were much as they had been in 1935, except that the financing provisions had been changed. For AB, Washington meets the first $31 out of $37 spent per recipient and above that it pays between 50 and 65 per cent depending on the per capita income of the state. The average maximum federal contribution per recipient is $75 per month. These money payments may also include vendor payments for the cost of medical care. In OAA, the formula is similar except that medical costs are added above and beyond the $75 average.

The aid to dependent children program has changed more radically and is now, in many ways, the most important of the public assistance programs. Originally conceived of to care for the child who had lost one of its parents (ADC), after 1950 the program began to emphasize the need of the parent or person looking after the child (AFDC). In 1961, the federal grants were first used to cover situations where one of the parents was unemployed (AFDC-UP), and the following year states were given encouragement to establish programs where both parents were living but only one was incapacitated or unemployed. The 1967 act ensured that ultimately every state would have an AFDC-UP program. The federal contribution to AFDC is related to a global pool, with an average maximum of $32 per month, including money and vendor payments for medical and related programs. Washington pays $15 of the first $18, and sums in excess of that are paid according to a formula, ranging from 50 to 65 per cent depending on the per capita income of that state.

These then were the three basic public assistance programs begun in 1935. Their relative importance and scope have changed significantly. AB remained small: it covered 73,000 in 1940 and 82,800 in 1967, during which period the average monthly payment rose from $25.28 a month to $89.45, and its cost (including both federal and state participation) ran from $22 million to $85,614,000. The pattern was not dissimilar for OAA although the numbers involved were larger to begin with. But the 2,066,000 recipients, with average monthly payments of $20.26, for a total cost of $475 million in 1940 became, twenty-seven years later, 2,074,000 recipients, with an average payment of $69.70, and an annual cost of $1,-633,675,000. These figures exclude the cost of vendor payments. It was the ADC/AFDC program, however, which produced the most dramatic statistics. During the same period, the number of recipients rose from 1,261,000 to 5,207,000, with the average payment per family rising from $32.38 to $160.15 per month, and with the cost of the program rising from $133 million, to $2,256,629,000.

During these same years a number of other programs emerged. In 1950 aid to the permanently and totally disabled (APTD) was established, with federal participation along the lines of AB. More important, however, has been the growth of programs concerned with medical care. In 1960 Congress enacted medical assistance for the aged (MAA), popularly known as Kerr-Mills. It was available not only to those covered by OAA, but also to those over sixty-five who were "medically indigent," with the Federal Government paying between 50 and 83 per cent, depending on the per capita income of the state. The 1965 amendments (Title XIX) went even further and encouraged the states not only to establish medical care programs for all those covered by any of their public assistance programs, but also to encourage the establishment of medical programs for all those of any age who, while not covered by public assistance programs, were nevertheless "medically indigent." (This is commonly called Medicaid.) The federal participation formula was established at the same level as that under MAA, except that the 1967 amendments imposed a ceiling on medical indigency related to the average welfare eligibility in any state offering the program.

Such a change underlines the fact that, unlike OASDHI, all public assistance programs are state programs. Indeed general assistance still exists in every state and it is entirely funded from state and local taxes (although general assistance now accounts for only 7 per cent of public assistance). So too, while all states have OAA, AB, and AFDC programs, Nevada has no APTD program, a number of states currently have no AFDC-UP (unemployed parents) program, and by 1965 only forty-five states had the MAA program. The essentially local nature of these programs is also reflected in the size of average payments and the differing qualifications imposed. In OAA the average recipient in November, 1967, received $69.70, but that varied from $38.55 in Mississippi to $108.05 in New Hampshire. The average for AFDC was $160.15 per family and $39.15 per recipient, with the average recipient receiving $8.35 in Mississippi and $59.70 in New York. The financial involvement of the Federal Government also varied. In 1964 it paid nothing towards general assistance and 64.2 per cent towards OAA. Overall it paid 54.5 per cent of the $5.6 billion spent on public assistance in that year.

The third part of social security in the broader sense — unemployment compensation — was rapidly adopted in the different states. (Since all employers had to pay the 3 per cent federal tax there was a great incentive to the states to pass unemployment insurance laws entitling employers to offset up to 90 per cent of the federal tax for contributions paid into the state scheme.) Although the Federal Government administers the trust fund (maintaining separate accounts for each state) and imposes other minimum standards, the unemployment programs are very much state enterprises.

Thus some states seek to go beyond federal standards and cover domestic employees, others attempt to cover employers with only one or two employees (the federal standard only requires coverage of those with four or more), while some others cover local state employees. In the same way the states vary in their requirements for the base period on which the actual compensation is based. Most states, if the applicant has worked long enough, will ultimately pay about 50 per cent of the average weekly wage over the base period, with a maximum which varied in 1964 from $72 a week in Michigan to $30 in Mississippi. (In Puerto Rico it is $20.) The minimum can be as low as $5 in Hawaii and $3 in Missouri. There are normally also provisions for compensation during partial unemployment and a number of states provide additional payments for dependents. Most states require a waiting period before payments can begin.

Presumably because there was no employee contribution, and because employers had strong lobbies in state legislatures, unemployment compensation has proved to be by far the least expansive of the three prongs of social security. Also, many of the pressures at the federal level, such as the McCormack Amendment of 1939, have been designed to help those paying the taxes rather than those whom the system was designed to protect. And when there has been a fear of recession, as at the end of World War II, or an actual recession as in 1958 and 1961, only temporary improvement has been made. But attempts to rework the whole system, such as those pushed by Senator John F. Kennedy, has made virtually no progress. Such concepts as the experience rating seem impregnable.

So far this essay has sought to explain how the basic 1935 Social Security Act came to be passed, what it provided, and the changes which have been made in the three basic programs over the years. At the same time, it is impossible not to attempt to evaluate what has been achieved or to discuss how relevant the programs are to the needs of the 1970's.

It is a rash generalization, but one which contains more than a grain of truth, that governmental programs, however laudable their objects, tend to freeze organizational structures and outlooks. The whole area of social security is no exception. The three basic income security programs were designed to cope with the problems of the 1930's. Some of those problems still remain, but new ones have also arisen and attempts to adapt the programs have not been entirely successful. There is still a strong aura of the New Deal clinging to the approach of all these programs.

As has been seen the OASDHI program, as initially conceived, was a response to a crisis facing working- and middle-class America. The original OAI program has most of the marks of a publicly-run private insurance program. The persons it was intended to serve were those thrifty members of society who had seen their savings disappear in the collapse of the stock market or of their insurance company, or whose bank deposits had evaporated with the Great Crash of 1929. It was for this reason that the OAI program, as originally explained, talked of annuities rather than benefits, looked to a conservatively run trust fund along the lines of a private insurance company, and merged the two with its picture of the diligent worker slowly buying his way into an annuity program, with his annuity actuarily related to his contributions. (In addition, as the bill was originally drafted, the government would also have been able to sell annuities to those who retired.) The "something-for-nothing, leftist" programs of the Townsend and Lundeen movements were rejected out of hand, although in keeping with a philosophy which gripped all shades of the political and economic spectrum in the post-Depression days, annuitants were not to receive their annuities until they had stopped working.

In the same way, the public assistance provisions of the 1935 legislation were creatures of their time. Their approaches have to be viewed in the light of the bankruptcy or near-bankruptcy of many states, and the massive FERA programs. It seemed probable that the old poor law would never return and in this regard public assistance was retained partially as a transitional measure. It was assumed that as OAI gathered strength, OAA—at that time the most important and expensive of the public assistance programs—would simply "wither away." Likewise, unemployment compensation was expected to take much of the demand out of other forms of assistance. Overall then, the 1935 act seemed calculated to overturn a system born of the worse excesses of *laissez-faire* capitalism.

"What went wrong?" would not be a fair question. In one sense nothing went wrong. OASDHI is regarded by voters as an unqualified success and is therefore treated by most politicians as sacrosanct. Many decision-makers feel that unemployment compensation is a satisfactory program. Yet it is difficult to deny that in the last few years—at least since 1960—there has been an increasing feeling that all is not well. Indeed, there has been a growing call for a new beginning to the whole concept of income security coupled with a surfeit of programs designed to achieve this. But rather than asking "What went wrong?" perhaps the fairer question would be "What changed?"

The answer is that almost everything changed. To reread the population predictions in 1935 is like reading a fairy story. Not only has the population increased far beyond all projections, but the country has become urbanized and industrialized at rates not remotely conceived of thirty-three years ago. At the same time there have been equally inconceivable breakthroughs in technology and a staggering rise in gross national product.

At first sight these changes might seem to favor the eradication of those conditions with which income security programs are concerned. In some countries this might have been their effect; but social conditions in the United States have been such that, in many respects, the problems have been exacerbated. Rapid urbanization, World War II, and the constant turmoil of the Cold War have had an unsettling effect on what used to be known as the stability of society. This, together with the change from passive docility of minority groups, gratefully accepting welfare as a form of charity, to militancy, demanding that they be given a right to join in the prosperity of their own country, has changed the nature of public assistance. Nowhere are the effects of these social changes clearer than in AFDC, a program thought of as peripheral in 1935, but now in many ways at the core of public assistance, with battles over social security swirling about its borders.

It would be wrong, however, to regard the changed place of public assistance as a part of the civil rights movement. The change goes much deeper than that. A rapid rise in the real standard of living, coupled with greater awareness of disparities in the distribution of wealth, accounts for the growing sympathy towards the elderly person whose means are outstripped by inflation. Similarly, a reawakening social conscience points to the widening gap between poor and middle-class America, explaining new attempts to reach the hard-core unemployed, for whom the 1935 concept of unemployment compensation is totally irrelevant.

What exists today, then, is an income security program designed primarily to cope with the problems which faced the (largely white) urban lower middle class of the 1930's. The OAI and unemployment compensation programs were geared specifically to their needs; and the public assistance provisions were regarded as transitional: that is, they were based on the assumption that by the 1960's they would largely have withered away. But the two basic programs, for reasons partly outlined above, never did settle the problem of the 20 per cent of Americans about whom Michael Harrington wrote in his book, *The Other America*. The welfare mother and the hard-core unemployed were not envisioned by the Congress of 1935, and they are scarcely the darlings of the Congresses of the late 1960's.

It would be wrong, of course, to suggest that nothing has been done. The open-ended financing of the public assistance provisions, until partially curbed by the 1967 amendments, virtually ensured some minimal support for everyone on the growing welfare rolls. The OAI program also made changes, which gradually weakened its insurance character and turned it towards a more genuine income security program. Beginning in 1939, its benefits were based less on contributions than on average earnings, and those who had a limited number of contributions were treated as if they were fully paid up. The process of relating benefits to need and blanketing in those who needed the benefits but had not contributed their fair share was accelerated in the 1950's and 1960's. In keeping with this process, the trust fund was treated less and less as an insurance type of trust fund and increasingly as if it were a contingency fund. This is not to suggest, as some journalists are wont to do, that social security benefits were in jeopardy. While the U.S. Treasury is solvent there is no reason to doubt that all benefits will be met in full. Indeed, while the number of persons in the program continues to increase, and while the GNP continues to expand, there is every reason to suppose that the size and coverage of benefits will increase. What is suggested here is that the concept of "actuarial soundness" has shifted in meaning from the standards of private insurance to the standards required by political necessity.

If OAI failed to help bridge the ever widening gap between the social security-protected middle class and the minimally- or non-protected bottom fifth of the nation, it was partly because the advocates of OAI refused to admit that the program was far less like the public scheme of private insurance, and much more a compulsory income security mechanism. In this they were greatly aided by the existence, after 1939, of the trust funds which insulated OASDI from the remainder of the federal budget. It may be true that if the typical congressman (or at least his constituents) appreciated how far the program had moved towards providing benefits on the basis of need, there might have been trouble for the Social Security Administration. As it was, they were able to convince Congress to increase benefits in line with the cost of living and the growth rate of the nation by continuing to sell the program in terms of a retirement fund. In one sense those who are receiving benefits have contributed, but more often the cost of the benefits is borne by those yet to receive them.

That does not mean that the program is fiscally unsound; its political strength ensures its fiscal soundness. But it does mean that the mythology of contribution, carefully fostered by the Administration, prevents the program from fulfilling its potential. It also leads the advocates of the program into dangerous semantic battles about insurance and social insurance — with the result that in recent years we have witnessed the embarrassing plight of Administration spokesmen resorting to a defense with definitions from *Encyclopaedia Britannica*.

The aspect of social security as a "tax and transfer system" is less true of disability and of survivors' insurance. In theory, the hospital provisions (at least under Title XVIII A) should phase out the financing from general funds for those who have never contributed, but in practice the story may be very different. Thus there seems every chance that the whole system will retain or expand the redistributive element inherent to social insurance. At this stage what is perhaps most surprising is that the basic inconsistency between the various aims of the OAI program are so poorly understood. It is true that there are annual demands from those who still look on the program as a true form of insurance for which they have paid in full, that they be allowed to earn (or earn more) while receiving benefits. In addition, many know that a federal employee, who does not pay OASDI but who contributes under the federal scheme, may retire from government service at fifty-five and take full benefits under that scheme, and then work for ten years paying social security, thereby entitling himself to social security benefits as well — benefits, moreover, which may be at the maximum level. Perhaps he comes from the wrong social class to be accused of looking for something-for-nothing, but he could barely be said to have "bought an annuity." Such situations are the price which must be paid for the Social Security Administration's unflinching commitment to "actuarial soundness" — the apparent key to congressional affection.

If the program were admitted to be a tax and transfer arrangement, it should not be difficult to merge OAA with OAI, or APTD and AB with the disability provisions of OASDHI. Indeed, in the case of the latter two programs, there already has been some limited assimilation. But the rigid classification prevents, apparently irretrievably, the unmarried mother or other recipients of AFDC from ever being brought even within the most extended form of social security while it rests on its present assumptions or lives under its present mythology. The results are therefore likely to continue to be similar to those in 1967. By the social security amendments of that year, those who had "contributed" to OASDHI were rewarded with a minimum 13 per cent increase in benefits. AFDC recipients were rewarded by having their rolls frozen, and the possibility of being forced to work against their will. In the same way those same amendments drew a clear distinction in the health field. Title XVIII, based on "contributions," was extended, while Title XIX, the "something-for-nothing" program, was vigorously cut back. Indeed, Congress, it seemed, was drawing some of the distinctions drawn by the legislators of Elizabethan England who had provided different modes of treatment for the "good" poor and the "bad" poor.

To draw such distinctions is not to be original. The potential inequities were well appreciated by both the Lundeen and Townsend Movements in the mid-1930's. The distinction offended the progressive Republicanism of Senator La Follette in 1939 and the conservative Republicanism of Senator Robert Taft in the late 1940's and early 1950's. During the 1960's the differences have irritated not only civil rights groups but economists of many persuasions. Even lawyers and the courts have become involved and have attempted to establish a "right" to both OASDHI and public assistance.

While the heat generated about income security (and it is difficult to write without absorbing some of that heat) has centered on the partially spurious distinction between OASDHI and the public assistance programs, the unemployment compensation program must not be ignored entirely. It too suffered from many of the faults of absorbing too much of the philosophy of the New Deal. It was a program primarily designed for fully employed workers who lost their jobs for one reason or another. It did not begin to cover the hard-core unemployed—a basic social phenomenon of the 1960's. And even within its own framework it had increasing deficiencies. The absence of contributions from employees helped to keep benefits low (although single men in most states still fared reasonably well), reinforcing the point previously made about social security—if the beneficiaries can be made to appear to be "paying" for the program, they can lobby effectively for higher benefits. And whenever there was a major recession the twenty-six-week maximum period for benefits in most states proved pitiably short. At the same time the system had failed to provide the national uniformity its sponsors had sought in 1935, while the state bureaucracies it had spawned made radical change impossible.

The unemployment compensation scheme also exemplified the fragmentation process which had occurred in the area of income security legislation. As already suggested, there was a needlessly large artificial gap between public assistance and OASDHI, but the different framework

established for unemployment compensation meant that it was not fully
co-ordinated with the other two major programs either. It was scarcely to be
expected that the federal, federal-state, and state programs would all mesh
neatly, but the overlapping in the field of income security has been particularly noticeable.

In relative terms, however, the three major 1935-vintage programs are
well coordinated compared with the programs which existed before or
which have been added since. Only in very recent years has any effort been
made to bring workmen's compensation (an exclusively state-run program)
into the general scheme of income security. Moreover, an increasing number of programs have been growing up, which, by serving one sector of the
community, make rationalization even more difficult. Some, like the railroad retirement scheme, have meshed in with other income security provisions; while others, like the various programs of veterans' benefits, have
existed in a sort of blue-ribboned world where, surrounded by an aura of
unimpeachable patriotism, a socially acceptable form of public assistance is
dispensed with only the minimum of questions asked.

Such fragmentation has an important effect on the attitude towards the
less fashionable of the income maintenance programs. The $8 billion spent
during 1968 on veterans' programs, both cash and kind, caused barely a
ripple. While the hostility towards public assistance, and particularly
AFDC, lapped over from 1967 to 1968, farm subsidies—calling for almost
as much federal expenditure as the public assistance programs and representing an important income maintenance program in many rural areas
—were specifically exempted by Congress from the federal program cutback which was part of the tax surcharge package. Part of this inconsistency
results from such gross fragmentation of income maintenance programs that
some of them, such as farm subsidies, are not easily recognized as such. This
camouflage causes the same problem as that raised by the inability of many
middle-class taxpayers to appreciate that deductions for children or mortgage payments provide, in economic terms, subsidies little different from
low-cost public housing or direct cash payments by way of children's
allowances.

So far the discussion has centered on income security primarily as a
means of direct cash benefits. But the combined effect of fragmented
programs and a fragmented bureaucracy has meant that a great deal now
given by way of income security is in kind rather than in cash. Health
and hospital benefits have already been discussed since historically they
have been treated as part of cash programs. However, there are many more:
the food stamp and food surplus programs; the many programs to subsidize
housing—public housing, rent supplementation, s. 221(d)(3) housing, and
the like; the increasing programs in education—from public primary and
secondary schools to state universities and NDEA fellowships; and the
rapid increase in the number and type of work training programs under

either the aegis of OEO or the Department of Labor. All these to a greater or lesser extent may affect the life of the person in need of income security.

In response to these problems of fragmentation in cash and related kind programs, and so often to their growing inflexibility, a new approach to income security has been emerging. In some way it is a looking back to the approaches of Lundeen and Townsend. It normally calls for unification of income security programs and for their financing openly from general funds. It takes various forms — from the negative income tax and family allowances to a guaranteed income. If these programs abandon concepts of self-reliance based on the contributory theory of funding, they normally look to reliance based on individual choice, for these programs would leave to the individual rather than the social worker or his equivalent the decision about how the money provided was to be spent.

While such programs are still under consideration (and they have received remarkably wide support), a number of programs have come into existence, designed to strike at the roots of the kind of poverty which causes the need for income security provisions. The best known of these are the various poverty programs established under the Economic Opportunity Act of 1964, designed to retrain the hard-core unemployed. But within the last two years, there have been other changes. The 1967 amendments introduced mandatory work-training provisions. The New Dealish minimum wage legislation (fortunately outside the scope of this book) has been falling into disfavor with everyone but the unions, and in its place there is increasing talk of the government as an employer of the last resort.

The political system of this country is such that change does not come overnight. The basic programs of social security have such wide acceptance — and justifiably so — that their immediate overthrow would border on the unreal. But that they will increasingly be questioned cannot be doubted. The work of the Joint Economic Committee may slowly undermine the rigid discipline of the House Ways and Means Committee, which has exercised the House's power in income maintenance since 1935. The Senate may one day undermine the House's conservatism in this field as it did with medical care. It may well be in these areas that the present structure of income security will be challenged. It would be a pity, however, if it were challenged without a clear understanding of its origins and development.

PRE-NEW DEAL DEVELOPMENTS
1789–1934

PRE-NEW DEAL DEVELOPMENTS
1789 – 1934

If one limits discussion of governmental involvement in income security to the federal level, there is remarkably little to record during the hundred and fifty years before the passage of the Social Security Act of 1935. There were, it is true, certain medical programs for specialized groups, such as seamen. During the Progressive Era there was some purposeful federal involvement through the Children's Bureau, but the government's role was at best something less than dramatic.

Thus one must turn to the states to discover how those not able, or no longer able, to support themselves in fact fared; and there can be no denying that the provision of support by the states was rudimentary in the extreme. In part, this is understandable. Life was assumed to be somewhat brutish and it was considered to be the order of the day that some would be homeless and without medical care, while others would be sacrificed to the machine or malnutrition. Even seventy-five years ago there was almost no feeling that the states should be concerned with anything which today might be included in concepts of income security or medical care. As a collective social conscience developed, however, private charities emerged which coped with the problem in a way which, in relative terms, would be totally beyond their capacities today. Perhaps too, the traditional notions that the frontier was open to those who were deprived but able-bodied and that the family or community should accept greater responsibility in illness or old age may have had more than an element of truth in them.

In providing a background to the post-1935 federal involvement, this section looks first at the situation in the states, second at the early federal concerns, and third at workmen's compensation—the first viable governmental program attempting to cope with any aspect of income security.

THE ROLE OF THE STATES

The systems of public assistance in the different states, as they existed in the early 1930's, followed the pattern of the Elizabethan poor laws—with concepts of both indoor and outdoor relief. Attempted changes had been grafted on to what was essentially a system of parish relief. (Only workmen's compensation had moved appreciably beyond this point.) At the same time, the attempts to ameliorate the rather harsh system in the early part of this century were to shape not only the legislation of the 1930's but also the system of income security (and ultimately medical care) as it exists today.

Provision for the Aged

Throughout American history care of old persons was one of a few areas where serious efforts toward improvement had been made. But even that was essentially a product of the twentieth century. The Commission on Economic Security, which was to be responsible for the shape of the 1935 legislation, reported:

Social Security in America
(p. 156)

Until 10 years ago the only permanent provision for the needy aged in nearly all the States was through the medium of the so-called "almshouse" or "poor farm." The shocking conditions existing in the majority of these institutions were described in a book by Harry Carroll Evans, published in 1926 by a group of fraternal organizations.[1] This book summarized the findings of the surveys of American almshouses conducted by these organizations, with the aid of special examiners from the United States Department of Labor. Insufficient and unfit food, filth, and unhealthful discomfort characterized most of them. Even in institutions with sanitary and physically suitable buildings, it was found that feeble-minded, diseased, and defective inmates were frequently housed with the dependent aged.

The cost of maintaining old people in these institutions, as was revealed by a financial survey of almshouses made by the Federal Department of Labor in 1925, was high, principally because of inefficient "overhead."[2]

Stimulated by the facts disclosed in these two reports, the drive for regular noninstitutional aid for needy old people made more progress. A series of measures variously described as "old-age pensions," "old-age assistance," "old-age relief," and "old-age security" were passed by State after State, beginning with Montana in 1923, totaling 18 by the middle of 1931, and 28, with two additional Territorial laws, by January 1, 1935. These measures offer citizens of long residence, who have small assets and no financially competent relatives, monthly grants to enable them to maintain themselves outside institutions. The maximum monthly sums authorized range from $15 to $30 (the latter being the commonest figure).

*   *   *

The first State law was passed in Arizona in 1915 by an initiative act, which abolished almshouses and established provisions for old-age assistance and aid to dependent children in their stead. However, it was worded so loosely that it was declared unconstitutional on account of its vagueness. In the same year Alaska passed a law providing assistance to its aged

---

[1]Evans, Harry C., *The American Poor-Farm and Its Inmates* (Des Moines, 1926).
[2]Stewart, Estelle M., "The Cost of American Almshouses", *Bulletin of the U.S. Bureau of Labor Statistics No. 386* (U.S. Government Printing Office, Washington, D.C., 1925).

pioneers. This law, though it has been amended on different occasions, is still in effect at the present time.

No action was taken by any State until 8 years later, in 1923. In that year three States (Montana, Pennsylvania, and Nevada) passed old-age assistance laws, but only one of them, that of Montana, has remained on the statute books. In 1925 the Nevada State Legislature passed a bill repealing the 1923 law and putting another one in its place. The Pennsylvania law was declared unconstitutional in 1924 on the ground that it was in conflict with a provision in the State constitution, which prohibited the legislature from making appropriations for charitable, benevolent, and educational purposes. A movement was started immediately to amend the constitution, but it was not until 1931 that the amendment passed the legislature. Since this amendment had to be repassed in 1933 and then submitted to a referendum vote for approval, it was not until 1934 that Pennsylvania secured action. Thus, the decision of the court deferred legislation for 10 years in Pennsylvania.

Ohio, too, took some first steps in the year 1923. The question of old-age assistance was submitted to a referendum vote, but it was decided adversely by a vote of almost 2 to 1.

By 1925 the movement had gained considerable impetus. Although only Wisconsin enacted a law in that year, there was much activity in a number of the States. California passed a law, which, however, was vetoed by the Governor. Bills were introduced in the legislative sessions of Illinois, Indiana, Kansas, Maine, Michigan, Minnesota, New Jersey, Ohio, and Texas. In Indiana and Illinois the bills passed the lower house but were not acted upon by the upper chamber. In four States (Colorado, Minnesota, Pennsylvania, and Utah) commissions were appointed.

In 1926 one law was added, that of Kentucky. In the same year the Washington State Legislature approved a bill, which was vetoed by the Governor. In 1927 Maryland and Colorado enacted old-age assistance laws.

At the end of 1928, after 6 years of agitation, there were only six States and one Territory which had made provision for their aged. They were Colorado, Kentucky, Maryland, Montana, Nevada, Wisconsin, and Alaska. All the State laws were of the optional type, i. e., they left the adoption or rejection of an old-age assistance system to the discretion of the counties. For this reason these laws had very limited effect. In these six States there were slightly more than 1,000 recipients of old-age assistance grants, and these were found almost exclusively in Montana and Wisconsin, the former having 884, the latter 295 old people on their old-age assistance rolls. The total amount spent by the six States in 1928 was, in round numbers, $200,000.

From 1929 on the trend in legislation has been toward making the adoption of the old-age assistance systems mandatory upon the counties. This type of legislation proved much more effective, especially when it was ac-

Old Age Assistance Laws: Principal Features

State	Date enacted	Date amended	In effect	Nature of law	Administration — State	Administration — Local	Degree of State supervision	Allocation of expenses — State	Allocation of expenses — County	Allocation of expenses — Town
Alaska	1915	1917, 1919, 1925, 1929	1915	Mandatory	Alaska Pioneers Home	No local administration	Territory administration	All	None	None
Arizona	1933		1933	...do.	State auditor	County old-age pension commission	Duplicate certificate to auditor; annual report	67 percent	33 percent	None
California	1929	1931, 1933	1929	...do.	Department of social welfare, Division of State aid for the aged	County board of supervisors, local department of public welfare	Complete supervision; monthly reports	One-half	One-half	None
Colorado	1927	1931, 1933	1927	...do.	Right of appeal to district court and supreme court	County court; board of county commissioners, trustees	Annual report to Secretary of State	State fund allocated to counties in proportion to population.		None
Delaware	1931	1933	1931	...do.	State old-age welfare commission	County commissioners, trustees	State administration	All	None	None
Hawaii	1933	1933	1934	Optional	Territorial auditor	Old-age pension commission	Annual report to Territorial auditor	None	Shared by county and city	None
Idaho	1931		1931	Mandatory	Department of public welfare	...do.	Annual report only	None	All	None
Indiana	1933		1934	...do.	State auditor	Board of county commissioners	Annual report; duplicate certificate to auditor	One-half	One-half	None
Iowa	1934		1934	...do.	Old-age assistance commission	Old-age assistance boards	Complete supervision	All	None	None
Kentucky	1926		1926	Optional	None	County commissioners	None	None	All	None
Maine	1933		(6)	Mandatory	Department of health and welfare	Old-age pension boards	Complete supervision	One-half	One-half cities, towns, plantations	None
Maryland	1927	1931, 1932, 1933	1927	Optional	None	County commissioners	Annual report to Governor	One-third	Two-thirds	None
Massachusetts	1930	1932, 1933	1931	Mandatory	State department of public welfare	Bureau of old-age assistance	Complete supervision	None	None	cities and towns
Michigan	1933	1931, 1933	1933	...do.	State welfare department, old-age pension bureau	Old-age pension board	...do.	All	All	None
Minnesota	1929	1931, 1933	1929	Optional	None	Board of county commissioners	None	None	All	Reimburse county
Montana	1923		1923	...do.	None	...do.	None	None	All	None
Nebraska	1933		1933	Mandatory	Auditor of public accounts	...do.	Annual report to State auditor	None	All	None
Nevada	1925		1925	Optional	None	Board of county commissioners	...do.	None	All	None
New Hampshire	1931		1931	Mandatory	None	County commissioners	Annual report to Governor	None	All	Reimburse county
New Jersey	1931	1932, 1933	1932	...do.	Department of institutions and agencies, division of old-age relief	County welfare board	Complete supervision	Three-fourths	One-fourth	None
New York	1930	1934	1930	...do.	State department of social welfare	Public welfare district official	One-half public welfare district	One-half	One-half public welfare district	None
North Dakota	1933		1933	...do.	Secretary of agriculture and labor	Board of county commissioners	...do.	All	None	None
Ohio	1933		1934	...do.	Department of public welfare, division of aid for the aged	Board of aid for the aged	...do.	All	None	None
Oregon	1933		1934	...do.	State board of control	Old-age pension commission	Annual report to State board of control	Part of State liquor tax distributed to counties, balance paid by counties.		None
Pennsylvania	1934		1934	...do.	Department of welfare	Board of trustees of old-age assistance fund	Complete supervision	State fund allocated to counties according to number of people on pension rolls.		
Utah	1929		1929	...do.	None	Board of county commissioners	None	None	All	None
Washington	1933		1933	...do.	None	...do.	None	None	All	None
West Virginia	1931		1931	Optional	None	County court	Annual audit by tax commissioner	None	All	None
Wisconsin	1925	1929, 1931, 1933	1925	(9)	State board of control	County judge	Annual report	One-third	Two-thirds	Reimburse county
Wyoming	1929	1931	1929	Mandatory	None	Old-age pension commission	Annual report to State auditor	None	All	None

care of her children, releasing her from the inadequacies of the old type of poor relief and the uncertainties of private charity. The assurance of a definite amount of aid, not subject to change from week to week or month to month unless conditions in the family change, is one of the chief advantages of this form of assistance. The enactment of laws for aid to dependent children was evidence of public recognition of the fact that long-time care must be provided for those children whose fathers are dead, are incapacitated, or have deserted their families; that security at home is an essential part of a program for such care; and that this security can be provided for this whole group of children only by public provision for care in their own homes.

This program was accepted promptly in State after State because experience had shown that unless the mother who was left with young children to support belonged to the highly skilled or professional group her contribution in the home was greater than her earnings outside the home. Before the adoption of these laws it frequently and even usually happened that either her children were taken from her and cared for at greater cost in institutions or foster homes, or she was encouraged to make the attempt to be both homemaker and wage earner, with the result in such cases that the home was broken up after she had failed in her dual capacity and the children had become delinquent or seriously neglected.

Although legislative approval of this principle has been given by nearly all the States, in many States a large proportion of the counties have not provided the benefits which the laws contemplated. This is explained by the fact that (1) the majority of these statutes, unlike most of the recently enacted old-age assistance laws, were permissive rather than mandatory, and in all but a few States the costs were borne entirely by the county or town, with the result that in many counties grants were never made or were inadequate in amount; and (2) the numbers of dependent children have greatly increased during the depression, because more widowed mothers have been left without sufficient funds to care for their children, and no commensurate expansion of public funds for this type of care has occurred.

State laws for aid to dependent children were intended to afford assistance to families without male breadwinners, and all such laws apply to children of widows. In the laws and in administrative practice great variation is found in the definitions of persons eligible for aid — variations with respect to marital status of the mother, residence and citizenship, ages of children, and other items. In practice, in 1931, 82 percent of the families receiving aid to dependent children for which marital status was ascertained were families of widows. Information available in 1934 shows that in 36 States, the District of Columbia, Alaska, and Hawaii aid may be extended to mothers whose husbands have deserted (frequently granted only under specified conditions as to attempts to secure support and as to duration of the father's desertion) and in 21 States, the District of Columbia, and Alaska, to divorced mothers. The laws of these 21 States, the District of Columbia, and Alaska are very liberal, permitting aid to any mother with dependent children, or to a dependent family in which the father is dead, divorced, physically or mentally incapacitated, imprisoned, or where he has deserted his family. According to 1934 information, in 29 states, the District of Columbia, Alaska, and Puerto Rico aid may be granted for children up to 16 years of age, and in 2 States for children up to 17 or 18 years. . . . [See table on pages 28–29.]

Legislative authorization for public aid to mothers with dependent children has been provided by all the States except Alabama,[2] Georgia, and South Carolina, by the Territories of Alaska and Hawaii, and by Puerto Rico. Alabama has authorized home care of dependent children under a law comparable to poor relief. Information obtained in 1934 indicates that, although authorized by law, aid to dependent children was not granted anywhere in Arkansas, Mississippi, or New Mexico.

Except in New England, where the local administrative unit is the city or town, the county is the local unit responsible for granting aid to dependent children. Information obtained by the Children's Bureau in 1931 indicated that of the 2,723 counties in the United States authorized to give this form of aid, 1,490 (55 percent) were actually doing so, and in 1934 reports received from 25 States indicated that at least 171 counties in these States had discontinued aid. It is probable that less than half the counties with legal authority to aid dependent fatherless children in their own homes in 1934 were actually giving aid. Table 50 shows the information available on the extent to which aid to dependent children is provided in the United States. The great diversity in the present coverage of various State laws is illustrated by the fact that the percentage of counties within a State granting aid ranges from less than 1 percent to 100 percent, and the per-capita expenditures within a State range from less than one-half of 1 cent per capita to 93 cents. The total local and State expenditures now being made under statutes for aid to dependent children, about $37,500,000, not only fail to reach more than half of the counties authorized to grant aid, but in many instances afford a very small amount of aid per family. For example, the average amounts actually granted in 1933 or 1934 ranged from about $9 per month per family to about $51 per month per family, although the laws permitted much more, . . .

Aid to the Blind

Special provisions for the blind were yet another way in which the states had introduced an element of categorization into the provision of general assistance. In many senses the blind were treated more humanely than

---

[2]Alabama in 1935 enacted a law providing aid to dependent children that is comparable to the laws previously enacted in other States for this purpose.

any other group in part because the numbers involved were relatively small. In the 1930 Census it was reported that, nationwide, 63,489 persons were blind, and this estimate may in fact have been low. Yet even in this relatively small program, the disparity between the provisions in the different states shows the depth of the problem which any federalization of public assistance programs faced: The following section from Social Security in America *describes various types of state legislation.*

Social Security in America
(p. 301)

State Legislation for the Blind

State legislation for the blind has taken four principal forms: (1) educational and vocational training, principally of blind children; (2) workshops for the adult blind, maintained with State assistance; (3) field work in locating the blind, extending to them medical and similar assistance, help in procuring employment, and assistance in the marketing of products produced by the blind; and (4) cash grants to the blind.

Educational and vocational training is carried on principally in State schools for the blind and in special day classes established in connection with the public-school system, particularly in urban centers. There are also a considerable number of private institutions of this character.

Workshops for the blind have long been maintained as State institutions, and are also conducted by private organizations. In these workshops adult blind people carry on some occupations for which they have training, particularly basket weaving, rug making, etc. The number of blind people employed in such special workshops has never exceeded a few thousand.

All but 10 States (Arizona, Arkansas, Georgia, Idaho, Montana, Nebraska, Nevada, New Mexico, North Dakota, South Dakota) carry on some field work for the blind. In 13 States (Alabama, Florida, Iowa, Kansas, Minnesota, Mississippi, North Carolina, Oklahoma, South Carolina, Tennessee, Texas, Washington, West Virginia), however, expenditures for this purpose are less than $5 per year for each blind person in the State. A minimum expenditure of $25 per blind person per year is generally regarded as necessary, but only six States (Connecticut, Delaware, Massachusetts, Missouri, New Hampshire, and New York) expended this amount for this purpose in the latest year for which data are available.

   *   *   *

As of August 1, 1935, 27 States had laws providing for cash payments to the blind. These are Arkansas, California, Colorado, Connecticut, Idaho, Illinois, Indiana, Iowa, Kansas, Kentucky, Louisiana, Maine, Maryland, Missouri, Minnesota, Nebraska, Nevada, New Hampshire, New Jersey,

Conditions under which aid to dependent children may be granted and limitations on amount of aid (1934)

State	Age under which aid may be given	Conditions under which family deprived of father's support is eligible for aid	Years of residence		Maximum grant for family of 3 children
			State	County or town	
Alabama[1]	....	....	....	....	.....
Alaska	16	Father dead, deserting, divorced, incapacitated, in penal institution.[2]	1	....	$55.00
Arizona	16	Father dead, deserting, incapacitated	[3] 1	....	(4)
Arkansas	15	Father dead, deserting, incapacitated, in penal institution.	....	[3] 1	20.00
California	16	Father dead, incapacitated,[2] in institution (penal or other).	2	....	60.00
Colorado	18	Any mother[2]	....	....	(4)
Connecticut	16	Father dead	[3] 4	....	69.33
Delaware	16	Father dead, deserting, incapacitated,[2] in penal institution.	3	....	28.00
District of Columbia.	16	Any mother[2]	....	[3] 1	(4)
Florida	[5] 16	Law broadly inclusive[2,6]	2	1	41.00
Georgia[1]	....	....	....	....	.....
Hawaii	(7)	Father dead, deserting, in institution (penal or other).[2]	....	1	(4)
Idaho	15	Father dead, in institution (penal or other)[2].	2	6 mos.	20.00
Illinois	16	Father dead, deserting, incapacitated	....	[3] 3	[8] 35.00
Indiana	[9] 16	Any mother[10]	....	....	67.50
Iowa	16	Father dead, in State institution (penal or other).	....	1	32.50
Kansas	14	Law broadly inclusive[6]	2	1	50.00
Kentucky	[5] 14	Any mother[2]	....	2	(4)
Louisiana[11]	[5] 16	Father dead, incapacitated, in penal institution.	....	1	35.00
Maine	16	Any mother	5	....	(4)
Maryland	[5] 14	Father dead, incapacitated	....	3	(4)
Massachusetts	16	Any mother	2	....	(4)
Michigan	17	Law broadly inclusive[6]	....	1	60.67
Minnesota	16	Father dead, deserting, incapacitated, in State institution (penal or other).[2]	[3] 2	1	50.00
Mississippi	16	Any mother[2]	....	1	(4)
Missouri	16	Law broadly inclusive[6]	....	1	32.00
Montana	16	Father dead, incapacitated, in State institution (penal or other).	....	[3] 1	30.00
Nebraska	16	Law broadly inclusive[6]	....	2	30.00
Nevada	[5] 16	Any mother	....	2	55.00
New Hampshire	16	Any mother[2]	2	....	31.00
New Jersey	[5] 16	Father dead, deserting, incapacitated, in institution (penal or other).	....	5	(4)
New Mexico	16	Law broadly inclusive[6]	2	1	40.00

[1] No law for aid to dependent children.
[2] May be granted to other person having care of the child.
[3] Citizenship or application for such required (in New York under certain conditions only).
[4] Amount of grant not limited.
[5] Extension possible under specified conditions, usually invalidity or during school attendance.
[6] Includes families in which parent is divorced, deserting, physically or mentally incapacitated, imprisoned.
[7] Age not specified in law.
[8] Maximum grant in Cook County, $55.
[9] Granted to girls under 17; aid may be continued during minority.
[10] Court must commit children to administrative agency.
[11] Provisions of 1920 law. A law broader in scope was enacted in 1930, but funds have not been available to carry out its provisions.

Conditions under which aid to dependent children may be granted and limitations on amount of aid (1934)—Continued

State	Age under which aid may be given	Conditions under which family deprived of father's support is eligible for aid	Years of residence State	Years of residence County or town	Maximum grant for family of 3 children
New York	16	Father dead, deserting, incapacitated, in institution (penal or other).	[3] 2	....	([4])
North Carolina	14	Law broadly inclusive[6]	3	1	$30.00
North Dakota	15	Father dead, deserting, incapacitated, in penal institution.	....	[3] 1	45.00
Ohio	[5] 16	...do...	....	2	55.00
Oklahoma	14	Father dead, in State institution (penal or mental).	....	1	20.00
Oregon	[5] 14	Father dead, incapacitated, in institution (penal or other).	3	1	52.00
Pennsylvania	[5] 14	Father dead, in hospital for insane	2	1	40.00
Puerto Rico	16	Father dead	[3] 3	....	25.00
Rhode Island	[5] 14	Any mother[2]	[3] 3	1	([4])
South Carolina[1]	....	....	....	....	......
South Dakota	16	Law broadly inclusive[2,6]	1	6 mos.	42.50
Tennessee	17	Father dead, deserting, incapacitated, in penal institution.	2	2	35.00
Texas	16	Father dead, deserting, divorced, in institution (penal or mental).	....	2	27.00
Utah	16	Law broadly inclusive[6]	....	2	40.00
Vermont	16	Father dead, deserting, incapacitated, in institution (penal or other).[10]	....	....	26.00
Virginia	16	Law broadly inclusive[2,6]	2	1	([4])
Washington	15	Any mother	3	1	25.00
West Virginia	[5] 14	Father dead, deserting, incapacitated	[3] 2	1	45.00
Wisconsin	[5] 16	Law broadly inclusive[2,6]	1	....	([4])
Wyoming	14	Father dead, deserting, incapacitated, in penal institution.	....	1	40.00

New York, Ohio, Oklahoma, Pennsylvania, Utah, Washington, Wisconsin, and Wyoming. No complete data are at hand regarding the expenditures in these States for aid to the blind. From the latest reports it would appear, however, that in 24 of these States there was a total of 31,909 recipients of grants at the end of 1934, or 68.4 percent of the total blind population of the 24 States in 1930. The total expenditures for blind persons in these States amounted to $6,880,015 in 1934. The average grant paid was $19.96 per month, with a range from $0.83 in Arkansas to $33.12 in California.

* * *

The acts of 10 States (California, Indiana, Kentucky, Maryland, Minnesota, Missouri, Oklahoma, Utah, Washington, and Wisconsin) refuse aid to professional beggars, and in Missouri benefits are denied persons who refuse training or other measures designed to make them self-supporting.

Aid to the blind is discontinued in New York if a recipient of aid marries another blind or partially blind person, and in Minnesota a limit of $30 a month is set as the maximum joint grant to blind persons who contracted marriage after passage of the act.

Data on the operation of systems for aid to the blind in the United States, 1934

State	Recipients of grants	Blind population, census, 1930	Recipients as percent of 1930 blind population	Amount disbursed in 1934			Monthly grants paid		
				Total	State funds	County funds	Average	Maximum payable	Range of individual grants
Total........	31,909	39,675	68.4	$6,880,015	$3,397,219	$3,482,796	$19.96	......	....
Arkansas........	1,165	1,101	105.8	11,650	11,650	....	0.83	$25.00	$0.83
California.......	3,179	2,597	122.4	1,085,408	542,704	542,704	33.12	50.00	5.00–50.00
Colorado........	701	751	93.3	140,287	65,000	75,287	15.47	25.00	(1)
Connecticut......	374	581	64.4	22,820	22,820	....	5.09	30.00	(1)
Idaho..........	86	156	55.1	16,989	....	16,989	16.46	20.00	10.00–25.00
Illinois..........	4,484	4,490	99.9	2 1,309,745	2 486,402	2 823,343	25.75	30.42	1.00–30.42
Iowa...........	956	1,577	60.6	158,562	....	158,562	13.89	25.00	4.00–25.00
Kansas.........	66	1,246	5.3	8,996	....	8,996	11.36	50.00	5.00–25.00
Kentucky........	383	1,977	19.4	42,129	....	42,129	9.17	20.83	1.33–20.83
Louisiana........	420	1,252	33.5	63,000	....	63,000	12.50	25.00	(1)
Maine..........	922	626	147.3	148,317	148,317	....	13.33	25.00	(1)
Maryland........	62	799	7.8	7,817	....	7,817	11.84	20.83	3.33–20.00
Minnesota.......	442	1,049	23.7	147,203	147,203	....	27.75	(3)	(1)
Missouri.........	4,336	3,879	111.8	4 1,265,831	4 1,265,831	....	24.33	25.00	(1)
Nebraska........	325	552	59.0	45,103	....	45,103	11.77	25.00	5.00–25.00
Nevada..........	3	64	4.7	600	....	600	16.67	50.00	(1)
New Hampshire..	79	251	31.4	8,797	6,064	2,733	9.28	12.50	8.00–12.50
New Jersey......	372	1,222	30.4	91,090	....	91,090	21.98	40.00	(1)
New York.......	2,200	5 4,418	5 16.1	583,670	....	583,670	21.93	25.00	(1)
Ohio...........	5,152	4,154	124.0	620,393	....	620,393	10.04	33.33	1.25–35.00
Pennsylvania.....	4,142	4,373	94.7	651,228	651,228	....	23.30	30.00	(1)
Utah...........	21	238	8.8	2,105	....	2,105	8.35	50.00	3.00–20.00
Washington......	185	792	23.4	25,808	....	25,808	11.63	33.33	3.00–10.00
Wisconsin.......	1,854	1,530	121.2	422,467	50,000	372,467	19.40	30.00	(1)

1 No data.
2 Data are for 60 counties which reported as to amounts furnished by State and counties.
3 No limit; except for married couples, both blind, in which case not over $30 per month.
4 Includes oculists' fees.
5 Exclusive of New York City.
SOURCE: "Public Provision for Pensions for the Blind in 1934", *Monthly Labor Review*, vol. 41, no. 3, September 1935, pp. 584–601.

Only five State laws specify the method to be used in raising State funds for aid to the blind: Arkansas, by a tax on billiard and pool rooms; Illinois, Missouri, and Wisconsin by a property tax; and Wyoming by taxes on liquor. In the other States which provide for State financial participation the appropriations are presumably made from general funds.

Counties in eight States are authorized to pay blind allowances from general county funds (Idaho, Illinois, Kentucky, Louisiana, New Hampshire, New Jersey, Ohio, and Oklahoma); and in Iowa, counties may use either general funds or poor funds for this purpose. Five States authorize counties to levy special property taxes for revenue for aid to the blind (California, Maryland, Nevada, Utah, and Washington).

[The above table] indicates the administrative authority for aid to the blind in the 27 States which have blind pension laws. As a rule applications for grants are first passed upon by the designated county authorities, such as the commissioners or local courts. In some of the States a State office is charged with ultimate supervision and control, but in 10 States (Illinois, Kansas, Kentucky, Nebraska, Nevada, New Hampshire, Ohio, Utah,

Washington, and Wisconsin) the county commissioners, and in Iowa the county board of supervisors, have entire charge of the system. In Idaho the authority for the system is the judge of the county probate court. In Arkansas, California, Colorado, Louisiana, Maryland, Missouri, Pennsylvania, and Wyoming the decision of the local authority is subject to review by a State agency; whereas in Connecticut, Maine, Minnesota, New Jersey, and New York the entire authority is placed in a special commission for the blind or in some other State office.

Unemployment Compensation

Least developed of all these programs in the states was the one which was to appear as the most important in the 1930's — unemployment compensation. Its very limited scope up to the introduction of the Wagner-Lewis Bill in 1934 is described below.

Social Security in America
(p. 91–92)

Consideration of legislation for unemployment compensation in the United States began many years before the appointment of the Committee on Economic Security. As far back as 1916 an unemployment insurance bill was introduced in the Massachusetts Legislature. Five years later, Wisconsin followed with a second bill, the well-known Huber bill, drafted by Prof. John R. Commons. Although it never passed, it was reintroduced, regularly, with some modifications, in each Wisconsin Legislature during the following 10 years.

Meanwhile, interest in unemployment compensation was growing. Bills were introduced in Connecticut, Massachusetts, Minnesota, and New York in the twenties, but apart from the establishment of a small number of voluntary plans, little progress was made. Although the number of unemployment insurance bills increased considerably in the depression years after 1929, the Wisconsin law, passed in 1932, was the only legislation enacted. Many factors accounted for this record of almost complete failure, but the most important was the fear of the States that passage of an unemployment compensation law would put their employers at a competitive disadvantage with employers in States which had no similar law.

Because of this block to State action proponents of unemployment compensation began to feel that the Federal Government should take some action. Meyer London, a representative from New York, had introduced a resolution in Congress in 1916 to create a committee to draft a bill for a national unemployment insurance plan, but not till 12 years later, in 1928, did the subject come up again. In that year Senator Couzens introduced a resolution for an investigation of unemployment insurance by the committee on labor. After hearings, the committee reported that legislation for compulsory unemployment insurance was premature, but it favored the voluntary establishment of unemployment reserve funds by employers.

Little voluntary activity resulted. Under a resolution introduced by Senator Wagner in 1931, an investigation of foreign experience with unemployment insurance was conducted. The committee endorsed compulsory unemployment insurance but felt that the Federal Government's role should be limited to allowing credit against Federal income taxes for contributions by employers to State unemployment reserve funds. Although Senator Wagner introduced several bills embodying this principle, none of them ever came to a vote.

THE FEDERAL INVOLVEMENT

While the states provided limited funds for public assistance, the Federal Government remained outside the general area of income security. Yet, at an early date Congress came to take an interest in providing medical care for specialized groups. While these programs are technically beyond the narrow scope of income security, they remain important to our topic in that at least they showed the potential of federal intervention.

Provision for Sick and Disabled Seamen

Building in the traditions of Britain and other European maritime nations, in 1798 Congress passed legislation to provide what, in modern terms, might be regarded as a specialized form of compulsory health insurance for merchant seamen. (The states already had, as early as 1705, provided hospitals for sick seamen, and as early as 1790 Congress had legislated to ensure that at least minimum medical supplies were provided on every vessel.) Moreover, all the services were to be provided by the Federal Government.

An Act for the Relief of Sick and Disabled Seamen
(July 16, 1798, ch. 77, 1 Statutes at Large 635)

Section 1. Be it enacted by the Senate and House of Representatives of the United States of America in Congress assembled, That from and after the first day of September next, the master or owner of every ship or vessel of the United States, arriving from a foreign port into any port of the United

States, shall, before such ship or vessel shall be admitted to an entry, render to the collector a true account of the number of seamen, that shall have been employed on board such vessel since she was last entered at any port in the United States,—and shall pay to the said collector, at the rate of twenty cents per month for every seaman so employed; which sum he is hereby authorized to retain out of the wages of such seamen.

Sec. 2. And be it further enacted, That from and after the first day of September next, no collector shall grant to any ship or vessel whose enrolment or license for carrying on the coasting trade has expired, a new enrolment or license before the master of such ship or vessel shall first render a true account to the collector, of the number of seamen, and the time they have severally been employed on board such ship or vessel, during the continuance of the license which has so expired, and pay to such collector twenty cents per month for every month such seamen have been severally employed, as aforesaid; which sum the said master is hereby authorized to retain out of the wages of such seamen. And if any such master shall render a false account of the number of men, and the length of time they have severally been employed, as is herein required, he shall forfeit and pay one hundred dollars.

Sec. 3. And be it further enacted, That it shall be the duty of the several collectors to make a quarterly return of the sums collected by them, respectively, by virtue of this act, to the Secretary of the Treasury; and the President of the United States is hereby authorized, out of the same, to provide for the temporary relief and maintenance of sick or disabled seamen, in the hospitals or other proper institutions now established in the several ports of the United States, or, in ports where no such institutions exist, then in such other manner as he shall direct: *Provided,* that the monies collected in any one district, shall be expended within the same.

Sec. 4. And be it further enacted, That if any surplus shall remain of the monies to be collected by virtue of this act, after defraying the expense of such temporary relief and support, that the same, together with such private donations as may be made for that purpose (which the President is hereby authorized to receive) shall be invested in the stock of the United States, under the direction of the President; and when, in his opinion, a sufficient fund shall be accumulated, he is hereby authorized to purchase or receive cessions or donations of ground or buildings, in the name of the United States, and to cause buildings, when necessary, to be erected as hospitals for the accommodation of sick and disabled seamen.

Sec. 5. And be it further enacted, That the President of the United States be, and he is hereby authorized to nominate and appoint, in such ports of the United States, as he may think proper, one or more persons, to be called directors of the marine hospital of the United States, whose duty it shall be to direct the expenditure of the fund assigned for their respective ports, according to the third section of this act; to provide for the accommodation of sick and disabled seamen, under such general instructions as shall be given by the President of the United States, for that purpose, and also subject to the like general instructions, to direct and govern such hospitals as the President may direct to be built in the respective ports: and that the said directors shall hold their offices during the pleasure of the President, who is authorized to fill up all vacancies that may be occasioned by the death or removal of any of the persons so to be appointed. And the said directors shall render an account of the monies received and expended by them, once in every quarter of a year, to the Secretary of the Treasury, or such other person as the President shall direct; but no other allowance or compensation shall be made to the said directors, except the payment of such expenses as they may incur in the actual discharge of the duties required by this act.

Approved, July 16, 1798.

The following year the program was extended to the officers and men of the regular Navy. Thus, by 1800, the forerunners of the medical services of the armed services were already in existence, as were the foundations of the Public Health Service. There was further legislation to protect seamen in 1803 and 1843, and in 1811, a separate board—The Commissions of Naval Hospitals—was established. The Public Health Service grew in importance and constituted the principal means by which the Federal Government expanded in the area of medical care. It assumed responsibility for federal hospitals established for minority groups (e.g. Indians) and specific diseases, responsibility for quarantine and the growing problems arising from increased immigration, and, as the nineteenth century progressed, public health laboratories assisting local authorities.

Children's Bureau

By 1912 the long-term direction of federal involvement was becoming clearer. It was in that year that the Public Health Service was authorized to "study and investigate the diseases of man and conditions influencing the propagation and spread thereof." That was also the year of the establishment of the Children's Bureau, a creation whose long-term impact was considerable. The Bureau was later to be a model for the establishment of the social security organization, and to serve as one of the bases for the Federal Security Administration, which ultimately became the Department of Health, Education, and Welfare.

An Act to Establish in the Department of Commerce and Labor a Bureau to be Known as the Children's Bureau
(April 9, 1912, ch. 73, 37 Statutes at Large, Part 1, 79)

Be it enacted by the Senate and House of Representatives of the United States of America in Congress assembled, That there shall be established in the Department of Commerce and Labor a bureau to be known as the Children's Bureau.

Sec. 2. That the said bureau shall be under the direction of a chief, to be appointed by the President, by and with the advice and consent of the Senate, and who shall receive an annual compensation of five thousand dollars. The said bureau shall investigate and report to said department upon all matters pertaining to the welfare of children and child life among all classes of our people, and shall especially investigate the questions of infant mortality, the birth rate, orphanage, juvenile courts, desertion, dangerous occupations, accidents and diseases of children, employment, legislation affecting children in the several States and Territories. But no official, or agent, or representative of said bureau shall, over the objection of the head of the family, enter any house used exclusively as a family residence. The chief of said bureau may from time to time publish the results of these investigations in such manner and to such extent as may be prescribed by the Secretary of Commerce and Labor.

Sec. 3. That there shall be in said bureau, until otherwise provided for by law, an assistant chief, to be appointed by the Secretary of Commerce and Labor, who shall receive an annual compensation of two thousand four hundred dollars; one private secretary to the chief of the bureau, who shall receive an annual compensation of one thousand five hundred dollars; one statistical expert, at two thousand dollars; two clerks of class four; two clerks of class three; one clerk of class two; one clerk of class one; one clerk, at one thousand dollars; one copyist, at nine hundred dollars; one special agent, at one thousand four hundred dollars; one special agent, at one thousand two hundred dollars, and one messenger at eight hundred and forty dollars.

Sec. 4. That the Secretary of Commerce and Labor is hereby directed to furnish sufficient quarters for the work of this bureau at an annual rental not to exceed two thousand dollars.

Sec. 5. That this Act shall take effect and be in force from and after its passage.

Approved, April 9, 1912.

It was in the presidential election of 1912, that serious discussion of the state provision of medical care began. The previous year Lloyd George had pushed through the national insurance program in Britain, and in 1912 the Progressive Party in this country included a similar program as part of its platform. It was not an idle dream. In 1916 Congress held hearings on a bill which covered much of the ground of Lloyd George's social insurance; in 1917 the American Medical Association endorsed compulsory health insurance; and in 1919 a bill to establish such a scheme passed one house of the New York legislature. Although by 1920 the AMA had reversed its stand, the precedent was important.

Even during the 1920's, not normally noted for great advances in social legislation, there was at least one important example of federal involvement in this field—namely the Shepard-Towner Act of 1921. This legislation increased still further the federal administration role in child and maternal health. The funds appropriated to the several states were small, but the creation of a new federal bureaucracy was an important step.

Although the 1921 act died in 1929—partly as the result of the AMA's opposition—it had forcibly shown the potential of federal involvement in health care. The act had also raised the issue of how far the courts might be prepared to question the distribution of federal funds to the states in connection with social legislation. In Massachusetts v. Mellon, Frothingham v. Mellon, 262 U.S. 447 (1923), *the Supreme Court refused to accept jurisdiction on the ground that individual taxpayers could not inquire into the disposition of federal moneys in this area.*

Thus, shortly after the country had been established, Congress found itself dealing with special minorities, and legislating with respect to matters which today are regarded as a part of income security. During the 1910's and 1920's Congress experimented with legislation which opened up new areas of federal responsibility, and their establishment, both politically and constitutionally, was vital in establishing the shape of a more general federal responsibility when it finally emerged. (A parallel development should also perhaps be noted. In 1920 the Federal Government established a pension plan for its own employees.)

Old-Age Pensions

With the Great Depression, however, a new type of federal concern appeared. At the time the concern could barely have seemed particularly significant; in retrospect, it cannot easily be underestimated. In 1931, for instance, Senator Clarence C. Dill, of Washington introduced S. 3257, which would have provided federal matching grants for state old-age pensions. Sections 2 and 6 of this bill follow:

**A Bill (S.3257) to Encourage and Assist the States
in Providing for Pensions to the Aged**
71st Cong., 2d Sess. (1931)

*   *   *

Sec. 2. That in order to provide for the promotion of pensions for old age and for disabled persons by the various States there is hereby authorized to be appropriated out of the Treasury of the United States for the use of the States, subject to the provisions of this act, for the purpose of cooperating with them in the payment of old-age pensions and pensions to disabled persons for each fiscal year ending June 30 of each year thereafter for a period of three years, the sum of $10,000,000, said sum to be allotted to the States in the proportion which their population bears to the total population in the United States, not including the Territories, outlying possessions, and the District of Columbia according to the last preceding United States census.

All money expended under the provisions of this act from appropriations hereby authorized shall be upon condition (1) that for each dollar of Federal money expended there shall be expended in the State under the supervision and control of the State board at least an equal amount for the same purpose: *Provided,* That no portion of any money authorized to be appropriated by this act shall be used to purchase, preserve, or repair any buildings, or for the purchase or rental of any lands.

*   *   *

Sec. 6. The director shall not approve any plan submitted by the State authority which does not provide that—

(1) An old person entitled to relief under it: (a) Has been a citizen of the United States for at least twenty years and resident of the State for a period of years determined by the State law providing old-age assistance, but in no case for less than five years; (b) is sixty years old or over; (c) does not possess real and/or personal property of a value in excess of $5,000; (d) has no child or other person responsible under the law of the State for his support and able to support him; (e) has not disposed of any property during the five years prior to his application for relief, unless the State authority has, under a power granted by the State statute, waived this requirement; (f) has been decided by the State authority to be of good moral character; and (g) so much of any sum paid as assistance, which shall be equivalent to the share paid from the allotment under this act, shall be a lien on the estate of the assisted person and upon his death shall be collected by the State and reported to the bureau provided in this act.

While the bill gave rise to only limited hearings, as did its successor the following year, they represented important straws in the wind. The landslide presidential election of 1932 harnessed these earlier efforts. The year

1934 saw not only the establishment of FERA (the Federal Emergency Relief Administration), later found unconstitutional, but the introduction of comprehensive proposals (e.g. the Wagner-Lewis Bill on unemployment compensation) and the passage of the Railroad Retirement Act. These trends were to be translated into the basic legislation of 1935, but before looking at that we must first examine the one major innovation in income security in the twentieth century.

Workmen's Compensation

Workmen's compensation can claim to have been the first program in income security in this country. But it emerged out of technical legal concepts and remains today an aloof and legalistic addition to basic income security provisions.

The legislation emerged, partially at least, in reaction to those principles such as the fellow servant rule, contributory negligence, and volenti non fit inuria developed during the nineteenth century by the courts, which, among other things, prevented workmen from recovering for injuries suffered in their employment. All of these principles can be traced back to the English judges—for in the nineteenth century most state benches slavishly followed the English precedents. When, beginning in 1880, Parliament began to limit these doctrines, most state legislatures in this country followed, and in 1908, with the Federal Employers' Liability Act, Congress moved to protect railroad workers from the worst excesses of the fellow servant rule.

But by this time, the English Parliament had gone still further. It had been found that, even with the weakening of common law defenses, workmen were still not being compensated for injuries, either because they could not afford the time or money to litigate, or because they were unable to prove negligence. Thus, by the Workmen's Compensation Acts of 1897, 1900, and 1906, a system of compensating workers irrespective of negligence, and theoretically outside the courts, was established. For rather the same reasons, there was a demand for similar legislation in this country.

On this occasion it was the Federal Government which set the pace, by passing rudimentary legislation in 1908, for certain federal employees.

An Act Granting to Certain Employees of the United States the Right to Receive from it Compensation for Injuries Sustained in the Course of their Employment
(May 30, 1908, ch. 236, 35 Statutes at Large 556)

Be it enacted by the Senate and House of Representatives of the United States of America in Congress assembled, That when, on or after August first, nineteen hundred and eight, any person employed by the United

States as an artisan or laborer in any of its manufacturing establishments, arsenals, or navy-yards, or in the construction of river and harbor or fortification work or in hazardous employment on construction work in the reclamation of arid lands or the management and control of the same, or in hazardous employment under the Isthmian Canal Commission, is injured in the course of such employment, such employee shall be entitled to receive for one year thereafter, unless such employee, in the opinion of the Secretary of Commerce and Labor, be sooner able to resume work, the same pay as if he continued to be employed, such payment to be made under such regulations as the Secretary of Commerce and Labor may prescribe: *Provided,* That no compensation shall be paid under this Act where the injury is due to the negligence or misconduct of the employee injured, nor unless said injury shall continue for more than fifteen days. All questions of negligence or misconduct shall be determined by the Secretary of Commerce and Labor.

Sec. 2. That if any artisan or laborer so employed shall die during the said year by reason of such injury received in the course of such employment, leaving a widow, or a child or children under sixteen years of age, or a dependent parent, such widow and child or children and dependent parent shall be entitled to receive, in such portions and under such regulations as the Secretary of Commerce and Labor may prescribe, the same amount, for the remainder of the said year, that said artisan or laborer would be entitled to receive as pay if such employee were alive and continued to be employed: *Provided,* That if the widow shall die at any time during the said year her portion of said amount shall be added to the amount to be paid to the remaining beneficiaries under the provisions of this section, if there be any.

Sec. 3. That whenever an accident occurs to any employee embraced within the terms of the first section of this Act, and which results in death or a probable incapacity for work, it shall be the duty of the official superior of such employee to at once report such accident and the injury resulting therefrom to the head of his Bureau or independent office, and his report shall be immediately communicated through regular official channels to the Secretary of Commerce and Labor. Such report shall state, first, the time, cause, and nature of the accident and injury and the probable duration of the injury resulting therefrom; second, whether the accident arose out of or in the course of the injured person's employment; third, whether the accident was due to negligence or misconduct on the part of the employee injured; fourth, any other matters required by such rules and regulations as the Secretary of Commerce and Labor may prescribe. The head of each Department or independent office shall have power, however, to charge a special official with the duty of making such reports.

Sec. 4. That in the case of any accident which shall result in death, the persons entitled to compensation under this Act or their legal representatives shall, within ninety days after such death, file with the Secretary of Commerce and Labor an affidavit setting forth their relationship to the deceased and the ground of their claim for compensation under the provisions of this Act. This shall be accompanied by the certificate of the attending physician setting forth the fact and cause of death, or the nonproduction of the certificate shall be satisfactorily accounted for. In the case of incapacity for work lasting more than fifteen days, the injured party desiring to take the benefit of this Act shall, within a reasonable period after the expiration of such time, file with his official superior, to be forwarded through regular official channels to the Secretary of Commerce and Labor, an affidavit setting forth the grounds of his claim for compensation, to be accompanied by a certificate of the attending physician as to the cause and nature of the injury and probable duration of the incapacity, or the nonproduction of the certificate shall be satisfactorily accounted for. If the Secretary of Commerce and Labor shall find from the report and affidavit or other evidence produced by the claimant or his or her legal representatives, or from such additional investigation as the Secretary of Commerce and Labor may direct, that a claim for compensation is established under this Act, the compensation to be paid shall be determined as provided under this Act and approved for payment by the Secretary of Commerce and Labor.

Sec. 5. That the employee shall, whenever and as often as required by the Secretary of Commerce and Labor, at least once in six months, submit to medical examination, to be provided and paid for under the direction of the Secretary, and if such employee refuses to submit to or obstructs such examination his or her right to compensation shall be lost for the period covered by the continuance of such refusal or obstruction.

Sec. 6. That payments under this Act are only to be made to the beneficiaries or their legal representatives other than assignees, and shall not be subject to the claims of creditors.

Sec. 7. That the United States shall not exempt itself from liability under this Act by any contract, agreement, rule, or regulation, and any such contract, agreement, rule, or regulation shall be pro tanto void.

Sec. 8. That all Acts or parts of Acts in conflict herewith or providing a different scale of compensation or otherwise regulating its payment are hereby repealed.

Approved, May 30, 1908.

Within a short space of time support for workmen's compensation laws grew rapidly. On September 7, 1916, a much more comprehensive bill for federal employees was passed. Public Law Number 267 provided, in general, that the United States shall pay compensation to civil employees or their dependents for "the disability or death of an employee resulting from a personal injury sustained while in the performance of duty." Between 1910 and 1915, some thirty states also produced workmen's compensation legislation. Almost immediately there were constitutional challenges in the courts as the early acts took effect in 1911; and while the Supreme Court of the State of Washington upheld that state's law under the police power, the far more influential Court of Appeals in New York struck down its state law in Ives *v.* S. Buffalo Rly. Co., *201 N.Y. 271 (1911).*

But Congress had already turned its attention once again to such legislation. By a joint resolution of Congress passed in June, 1910, a Congressional Commission to Investigate the Matter of Employer's Liability and Workmen's Compensation was established. The Commission had been created to examine the possibility of a federal workmen's compensation act for certain employers engaged in interstate commerce; and the extensive hearings it stimulated provided an early demonstration of a lobbying clash between organized labor and employers' associations. Despite the clash, the Commission reported in favor of a strong bill, which was subsequently endorsed by President Taft in the following message to Congress.

Presidential Message of February 20, 1912 on Workman's Compensation
(Sen. Doc. 338, 62d Cong., 2d Sess.)

To the Senate and House of Representatives:

I have the honor to transmit herewith the report of the Employers' Liability and Workmen's Compensation Commission, authorized by joint resolution No. 41, approved June 25, 1910, "To make a thorough investigation of the subject of Employers' Liability and Workmen's Compensation, and to submit a report through the President to the Congress of the United States."

The commission recommends a carefully drawn bill, entitled "A bill to provide an exclusive remedy and compensation for accidental injuries resulting in disability or death, to employees of common carriers by railroads engaged in interstate or foreign commerce, or in the District of Columbia, and for other purposes." This bill works out in detail a compensation for accidental injuries to employees of common carriers in interstate railroad business, on the theory of insuring each employee against the results of injury received in the course of the employment, without reference to his contributory negligence, and without any of the rules obtaining in the common law limiting the liability of the employer in such cases. The only case in which no compensation is to be allowed by the act is where the injury or death of the employee is occasioned by his willful intention to bring about the injury or death of himself or of another, or when the injury results from his intoxication while on duty.

It is unnecessary to go into the details of the bill. They are, however, most admirably worked out. They provide for a medical and hospital service for the injured man, for a notice of the injury to the employer, where such notice is not obviously given by the accident itself; for the fixing of the recovery by agreement, if not by agreement, by an official adjuster, to be confirmed by the court, and, if a jury is demanded, to be passed on by a jury. The amount of recovery is regulated in proportion to the wages received, and the more or less serious character of the injury where death does not ensue, specific provision being made for particular injuries in so far as they can be specified. The compensation is to be made in the form of annual payments for a number of years or for life. The fees to be paid to attorneys are specifically limited by the act. The remedies offered are exclusive of any other remedies. The statistical investigation seems to show that under this act the cost to the railroads would be perhaps 25 per cent more than the total cost which they now incur.

The report of the commission has been very able and satisfactory, the investigations have been most thorough, and the discussion of the constitutional questions which have arisen in respect to the validity of the bill is of the highest merit.

Three objections to the validity of the bill of course occur:

In the first place, the question arises whether under the provisions of the commerce clause the bill could be considered to be a regulation of interstate and foreign commerce. That seems to be already settled by the decision of the Supreme Court in the employers' liability case.

The second question is whether the making of these remedies exclusive and the compelling of the railroad companies to meet obligations arising from injuries, for which the railroad would not be liable under the common law, is a denial of the due process of law which is enjoined upon Congress by the fifth amendment to the Constitution in dealing with the property rights. This question the report takes up, and in an exhaustive review of the authorities makes clear, as it seems to me, the validity of the act. This is the question which in the Court of Appeals of the State of New York was decided adversely to the validity of the compensation act adopted by the legislature of that State. How far that act and the one here proposed differ it is unnecessary to state. It is sufficient to say that the argument of the commission is most convincing to show that the police power of the Government exercised in the regulation of interstate commerce is quite sufficient to justify the imposition upon the interstate railroad companies of the liability for the injuries to its employees on an insurance basis.

The third objection is that the right of trial by jury, guaranteed by the seventh amendment, is denied. As a matter of fact, the right is preserved in this act by permitting a jury to pass on the issue when duly demanded, in accordance with the limitation of the act.

I sincerely hope that this act will pass. I deem it one of the great steps of progress toward a satisfactory solution of an important phase of the controversies between employer and employee that has been proposed within the last two or three decades. The old rules of liability under the common law were adapted to a different age and condition and were evidently drawn by men imbued with the importance of preserving the employers from burdensome or unjust liability. It was treated as a personal matter of each employee, and the employer and the employee were put on a level of dealing, which, however it may have been in the past, certainly creates injustice to the employee under the present conditions.

One of the great objections to the old common-law method of settling questions of this character was the lack of uniformity in the recoveries made by injured employees, and by the representatives of those who suffered death. Frequently meritorious cases that appealed strongly to every sense of human justice were shut out by arbitrary rules limiting the liability of the employer. On the other hand, often by perjured evidence and the undue emotional generosity of the jury, recoveries were given far in excess of the real injury, and sometimes on facts that hardly justified recovery at all. Now, under this system the tendency will be to create as nearly a uniform system as can be devised; there will be recoveries in every case, and they will be limited by the terms of the law so as to be reasonable.

The great injustice of the present system, by which recoveries of verdicts of any size do not result in actual benefit to the injured person because of the heavy expense of the litigation and the fees charged by the counsel for the plaintiff, will disappear under this new law, by which the fees of the counsel are limited to a very reasonable amount. The cases will be disposed of most expeditiously under this system, and the money will be distributed for the support of the injured person over a number of years, so as to make its benefit greater and more secure.

Of course the great object of this act is to secure justice to the weaker party under existing modern conditions, but a result hardly less important will follow from this act that I can not fail to mention.

The administration of justice to-day is clogged in every court by the great number of suits for damages for personal injury. The settlement of such cases by this system will serve to reduce the burden of our courts one-half by taking the cases out of court and disposing of them by this short cut. The remainder of the business in the courts will thus have greater attention from the judges, and will be disposed of with much greater dispatch. In every way, therefore, the act demands your earnest consideration, and I sincerely hope that it may be passed before the adjournment of this session of Congress.

There accompanies the letter of transmittal of Senator Sutherland not only the report of the commission but also the hearings of witnesses by the commission, all of which is herewith submitted.

Wm. H. Taft

The White House
February 20, 1912

The issue of constitutionality, which had dominated the Commission's hearings, continued to plague the future of workmen's compensation, and despite Taft's endorsement, the bill died. The immediate results of Taft's efforts in 1912 were two-fold: The Panama Canal Act, providing a method for the determination and adjustment of claims arising out of injuries to employees working on the canal or the Panama Railroad; and amendments to the act of 1908 to extend coverage to those engaged in hazardous work under the Bureau of Mines and the Forestry Service. The next few years saw a series of legal moves designed to produce legislation which was constitutional, moves ranging from the amendment of constitutions to various schemes for voluntary coverage. Finally, however, in 1917 the U.S. Supreme Court upheld all of the three major types of workmen's compensation legislation: compulsory, elective, and even those where there was an exclusive state fund. Within a few years nearly every state had some form of workmen's compensation.

New York Central Realty Co. v. White
243 U.S. 188 (1917)

Mr. Justice Pitney delivered the opinion of the court:

A proceeding was commenced by defendant in error before the Workmen's Compensation Commission of the State of New York, established by the Workmen's Compensation Law of that state,[1] to recover compensation from the New York Central & Hudson River Railroad Company for the death of her husband, Jacob White, who lost his life September 2, 1914, through an accidental injury arising out of and in the course of his employment under that company. The Commission awarded compensation in accordance with the terms of the law; its award was affirmed, without opinion, by the appellate division of the supreme court for the third judicial department, whose order was affirmed by the court of appeals, without opinion. 169 App. Div. 903, 152 N. Y. Supp. 1149, 216 N. Y. 653, 110 N. E. 1051. Federal questions having been saved, the present writ of error was sued out by the New York Central Railroad Company, successor, through a consolidation of corporations, to the rights and liabilities of the employing company. The writ was directed to the appellate division, to which the record and proceedings had been remitted by the court of appeals. Sioux Remedy Co. v. Cope, 235 U. S. 197, 200, 59 L. ed. 193, 196, 35 Sup. Ct. Rep. 57.

The errors specified are based upon these contentions: (1) that the liability, if any, of the railroad company for the death of Jacob White, is defined and limited exclusively by the provisions of the Federal Employers' Liabil-

[1] Chap. 816, Laws 1913, as re-enacted and amended by chap. 41, Laws 1914, and amended by chap. 316, Laws 1914.

ity Act of April 22, 1908, chap. 149, 35 Stat. at L. 65, Comp. Stat. 1913, § 8657, and (2) that to award compensation to defendant in error under the provisions of the Workmen's Compensation Law would deprive plaintiff in error of its property without due process of law, and deny to it the equal protection of the laws, in contravention of the 14th Amendment.

*   *   *

We turn to the constitutional question. The Workmen's Compensation Law of New York establishes forty-two groups of hazardous employments, defines "employee" as a person engaged in one of these employments upon the premises, or at the plant, or in the course of his employment away from the plant of his employer, but excluding farm laborers and domestic servants; defines "employment" as including employment only in a trade, business, or occupation carried on by the employer for pecuniary gain, "injury" and "personal injury" as meaning only accidental injuries arising out of and in the course of employment, and such disease or infection as naturally and unavoidably may result therefrom; and requires every employer subject to its provisions to pay or provide compensation according to a prescribed schedule for the disability or death of his employee resulting from an accidental personal injury arising out of and in the course of the employment, without regard to fault as a cause, except where the injury is occasioned by the wilful intention of the injured employee to bring about the injury or death of himself or of another, or where it results solely from the intoxication of the injured employee while on duty, in which cases neither the injured employee nor any dependent shall receive compensation. By § 11 the prescribed liability is made exclusive, except that, if an employer fail to secure the payment of compensation as provided in § 50, an injured employee, or his legal representative, in case death results from the injury, may, at his option, elect to claim compensation under the act, or to maintain an action in the courts for damages, and in such an action it shall not be necessary to plead or prove freedom from contributory negligence, nor may the defendant plead as a defense that the injury was caused by the negligence of a fellow servant, that the employee assumed the risk of his employment, or that the injury was due to contributory negligence. Compensation under the act is not regulated by the measure of damages applied in negligence suits, but, in addition to providing medical, surgical, or other like treatment, it is based solely on loss of earning power, being graduated according to the average weekly wages of the injured employee and the character and duration of the disability, whether partial or total, temporary or permanent; while in case the injury causes death, the compensation is known as a death benefit, and includes funeral expenses, not exceeding $100, payments to the surviving wife (or dependent husband) during widowhood (or dependent widowerhood) of a percentage of the average wages of the deceased, and if there be a surviving child or children under the age of eighteen years an additional percentage of such wages for each child until that age is reached. There are provisions invalidating agreements by employees to waive the right to compensation, prohibiting any assignment, release, or commutation of claims for compensation or benefits except as provided by the act, exempting them from the claims of creditors, and requiring that the compensation and benefits shall be paid only to employees or their dependents. Provision is made for the establishment of a Workmen's Compensation Commission[2] with administrative and judicial functions, including authority to pass upon claims to compensation on notice to the parties interested. The award or decision of the Commission is made subject to an appeal, on questions of law only, to the appellate division of the supreme court for the third department, with an ultimate appeal to the court of appeals in cases where such an appeal would lie in civil actions. A fund is created, known as "the state insurance fund," for the purpose of insuring employers against liability under the law, and assuring to the persons entitled the compensation thereby provided. The fund is made up primarily of premiums received from employers, at rates fixed by the Commission in view of the hazards of the different classes of employment, and the premiums are to be based upon the total pay roll and number of employees in each class at the lowest rate consistent with the maintenance of a solvent state insurance fund and the creation of a reasonable surplus and reserve. Elaborate provisions are laid down for the administration of this fund. By § 50, each employer is required to secure compensation to his employees in one of the following ways: (1) By insuring and keeping insured the payment of such compensation in the state fund; or (2) through any stock corporation or mutual association authorized to transact the business of workmen's compensation insurance in the state; or (3) "by furnishing satisfactory proof to the Commission of his financial ability to pay such compensation for himself, in which case the Commission may, in its discretion, require the deposit with the Commission of securities of the kind prescribed in § 13 of the Insurance Law, in an amount to be determined by the Commission, to secure his liability to pay the compensation provided in this chapter." If an employer fails to comply with this section, he is made liable to a penalty in an amount equal to the pro rata premium that would have been payable for insurance in the state fund during the period of noncompliance; besides which, his injured employees or their dependents are at liberty to maintain an action for damages in the courts, as prescribed by § 11.

In a previous year, the legislature enacted a compulsory compensation law applicable to a limited number of specially hazardous employments, and requiring the employer to pay compensation without regard to fault. Laws 1910, chap. 674. This was held by the court of appeals in Ives v. South Buffalo R. Co. 201 N. Y. 271, 34 L.R.A.(N.S.) 162, 94 N. E. 431, Ann. Cas. 1912B, 156, 1 N. C. C. A. 517, to be invalid because in conflict

[2]By chap. 674, Laws 1915, §§ 2 and 8, this Commission was abolished and its functions were conferred upon the newly created Industrial Commission.

with the due process of law provisions of the state Constitution and of the 14th Amendment. Thereafter, and in the year 1913, a constitutional amendment was adopted, effective January 1, 1914, declaring:

"Nothing contained in this Constitution shall be construed to limit the power of the legislature to enact laws for the protection of the lives, health, or safety of employees; or for the payment, either by employers, or by employers and employees or otherwise, either directly or through a state or other system of insurance or otherwise, of compensation for injuries to employees or for death of employees resulting from such injuries without regard to fault as a cause thereof, except where the injury is occasioned by the wilful intention of the injured employee to bring about the injury or death of himself or of another, or where the injury results solely from the intoxication of the injured employee while on duty; or for the adjustment, determination and settlement, with or without trial by jury, of issues which may arise under such legislation; or to provide that the right of such compensation, and the remedy therefor shall be exclusive of all other rights and remedies for injuries to employees or for death resulting from such injuries; or to provide that the amount of such compensation for death shall not exceed a fixed or determinable sum, provided that all moneys paid by an employer to his employees or their legal representatives, by reason of the enactment of any of the laws herein authorized shall be held to be a proper charge in the cost of operating the business of the employer."

In December, 1913, the legislature enacted the law now under consideration (Laws 1913, chap. 816), and in 1914 re-enacted it (Laws 1914, chap. 41) to take effect as to payment of compensation on July 1 in that year. The act was sustained by the court of appeals as not inconsistent with the 14th Amendment in Jensen v. Southern P. Co. 215 N. Y. 514, L.R.A.1916A, 403, 109 N. E. 600, Ann. Cas. 1916B, 276; and that decision was followed in the case at bar.

The scheme of the act is so wide a departure from common-law standards respecting the responsibility of employer to employee that doubts naturally have been raised respecting its constitutional validity. The adverse considerations urged or suggested in this case and in kindred cases submitted at the same time are: (a) That the employer's property is taken without due process of law, because he is subjected to a liability for compensation without regard to any neglect or default on his part or on the part of any other person for whom he is responsible, and in spite of the fact that the injury may be solely attributable to the fault of the employee; (b) that the employee's rights are interfered with, in that he is prevented from having compensation for injuries arising from the employer's fault commensurate with the damages actually sustained, and is limited to the measure of compensation prescribed by the act; and (c) that both employer and employee are deprived of their liberty to acquire property by being prevented from making such agreement as they choose respecting the terms of the employment.

In support of the legislation, it is said that the whole common-law doc-trine of employer's liability for negligence, with its defenses of contributory negligence, fellow servant's negligence, and assumption of risk, is based upon fictions, and is inapplicable to modern conditions of employment; that in the highly organized and hazardous industries of the present day the causes of accident are often so obscure and complex that in a material pro-portion of cases it is impossible by any method correctly to ascertain the facts necessary to form an accurate judgment, and in a still larger propor-tion the expense and delay required for such ascertainment amount in effect to a defeat of justice; that, under the present system, the injured workman is left to bear the greater part of industrial accident loss, which, because of his limited income, he is unable to sustain, so that he and those dependent upon him are overcome by poverty and frequently become a burden upon public or private charity; and that litigation is unduly costly and tedious, encouraging corrupt practices and arousing antagonisms be-tween employers and employees.

In considering the constitutional question, it is necessary to view the matter from the standpoint of the employee as well as from that of the em-ployer. For, while plaintiff in error is an employer, and cannot succeed without showing that its rights as such are infringed (Plymouth Coal Co. v. Pennsylvania, 232 U.S. 531, 544, 58 L. ed. 713, 719, 34 Sup. Ct. Rep. 359; Jeffrey Mfg. Co. v. Blagg, 235, U. S. 571, 576, 59 L. ed. 364, 368, 35 Sup. Ct. Rep. 167, 7 N. C. C. A. 570), yet, as pointed out by the court of appeals in the Jensen Case (215 N. Y. 526), the exemption from further liability is an essential part of the scheme, so that the statute, if invalid as against the employee, is invalid as against the employer.

The close relation of the rules governing responsibility as between em-ployer and employee to the fundamental rights of liberty and property is, of course, recognized. But those rules, as guides of conduct, are not beyond alteration by legislation in the public interest. No person has a vested inter-est in any rule of law, entitling him to insist that it shall remain unchanged for his benefit. Munn v. Illinois, 94 U. S. 113, 134, 24 L. ed. 77, 87; Hurta-do v. California, 110 U. S. 516, 532, 28 L. ed. 232, 237, 4 Sup. Ct. Rep. 111, 292; Martin v. Pittsburg & L. E. R. Co. 203 U. S. 284, 294, 51 L. ed. 184, 191, 27 Sup. Ct. Rep. 100, 8 Ann. Cas. 87; Second Employers' Lia-bility Cases (Mondou v. New York, N. H. & H. R. Co.) 223 U. S. 1, 50, 56 L. ed. 327, 346, 38 L.R.A.(N.S.) 44, 32 Sup. Ct. Rep. 169, 1 N. C. C. A. 875; Chicago & A. R. Co. v. Tranbarger, 238 U. S. 67, 76, 59 L. ed. 1204, 1210, 35 Sup. Ct. Rep. 678. The common law bases the employer's liability for injuries to the employee upon the ground of negligence; but negligence is merely the disregard of some duty imposed by law; and the nature and extent of the duty may be modified by legislation, with corre-sponding change in the test of negligence. Indeed, liability may be imposed for the consequences of a failure to comply with a statutory duty, irrespective of negligence in the ordinary sense; safety appliance acts being a familiar instance. St. Louis, I. M. & S. R. CO. v. Taylor, 210 U. S. 281, 295, 52 L. ed. 1061, 1068, 28 Sup. Ct. Rep. 616, 21 Am. Neg. Rep. 464; Texas & P. R. Co. v. Rigsby, 241 U. S. 33, 39, 43, 60 L. ed. 874, 877, 878, 36 Sup. Ct. Rep. 482.

The fault may be that of the employer himself, or — most frequently — that of another for whose conduct he is made responsible according to the maxim respondeat superior. In the latter case the employer may be entirely blameless, may have exercised the utmost human foresight to safeguard the employee; yet, if the alter ego, while acting within the scope of his duties, be negligent, — in disobedience, it may be, of the employer's positive and specific command, — the employer is answerable for the consequences. It cannot be that the rule embodied in the maxim is unalterable by legislation.

The immunity of the employer from responsibility to an employee for the negligence of a fellow employee is of comparatively recent origin, it being the product of the judicial conception that the probability of a fellow workman's negligence is one of the natural and ordinary risks of the occupation, assumed by the employee and presumably taken into account in the fixing of his wages. The earliest reported cases are Murray v. South Carolina R. Co. (1841) 1 McMull. L. 385, 398, 36 Am. Dec. 268; Farwell v. Boston & W. R. Corp. (1842) 4 Met. 49, 57, 38 Am. Dec. 339, 15 Am. Neg. Cas. 407; Hutchinson v. York, N. & B. R. Co. (1850) L. R. 5 Exch. 343, 351, 19 L. J. Exch. N. S. 296, 299, 14 Jur. 837, 840, 6 Eng. Ry. & C. Cas. 580; Wigmore v. Jay (1850) L. R. 5 Exch. 354, 19 L. J. Exch. N. S. 300, 14 Jur. 838, 841; Bartonshill Coal Co. v. Reid (1858) 3 Macq. H. L. Cas. 266, 284, 295, 4 Jur. N. S. 767, 6 Week. Rep. 664, 19 Eng. Rul. Cas. 107. And see Randall v. Baltimore & O. R. Co. 109 U. S. 478, 483, 27 L. ed. 1003, 1005, 3 Sup. Ct. Rep. 322; Northern P. R. Co. v. Herbert, 116 U. S. 642, 647, 29 L. ed. 755, 758, 6 Sup. Ct. Rep. 590. The doctrine has prevailed generally throughout the United States, but with material differences in different jurisdictions respecting who should be deemed a fellow servant and who a vice principal or alter ego of the master, turning sometimes upon refined distinctions as to grades and departments in the employment. See Knutter v. New York & N. J. Teleph. Co. 67 N. J. L. 646, 650–653, 58 L.R.A. 808, 52 Atl. 565, 12 Am. Neg. Rep. 109. It needs no argument to show that such a rule is subject to modification or abrogation by a state upon proper occasion.

The same may be said with respect to the general doctrine of assumption of risk. By the common law the employee assumes the risks normally incident to the occupation in which he voluntarily engages; other and extraordinary risks and those due to the employer's negligence he does not assume until made aware of them, or until they become so obvious that an ordinarily prudent man would observe and appreciate them; in either of which cases he does assume them, if he continues in the employment without obtaining from the employer an assurance that the matter will be remedied; but if he receive such an assurance, then, pending performance of the promise, the employee does not, in ordinary cases, assume the special risk. Seaboard Air Line R. Co. v Horton, 233 U. S. 492, 504, 58 L. ed. 1062, 1070, L.R.A.1915C, 1, 34 Sup. Ct. Rep. 635, Ann. Cas. 1915B, 475, 8 N. C. C. A. 834, 239 U. S. 595, 599, 60 L. ed. 458, 461, 36 Sup. Ct. Rep. 180. Plainly, these rules, as guides of conduct and tests of liability, are subject to change in the exericse of the sovereign authority of the state.

So, also, with respect to contributory negligence. Aside from injuries intentionally self-inflicted, for which the statute under consideration affords no compensation, it is plain that the rules of law upon the subject in their bearing upon the employer's responsibility, are subject to legislative change; for contributory negligence, again, involves a default in some duty resting on the employee, and his duties are subject to modification.

It may be added, by way of reminder, that the entire matter of liability for death caused by wrongful act both within and without the relation of employer and employee, is a modern statutory innovation, in which the states differ as to who may sue, for whose benefit, and the measure of damages.

But it is not necessary to extend the discussion. This court repeatedly has upheld the authority of the states to establish by legislation departures from the fellow-servant rule and other common-law rules affecting the employer's liability for personal injuries to the employee. Missouri P. R. Co. v. Mackey, 127 U. S. 205, 208, 32 L. ed. 107, 108, 8 Sup. Ct. Rep. 1161; Minneapolis & St. L. R. Co. v. Herrick, 127 U. S. 210, 32 L. ed. 109, 8 Sup. Ct. Rep. 1176; Minnesota Iron Co. v. Kline, 199 U. S. 593, 598, 50 L. ed. 322, 325, 26 Sup. Ct. Rep. 159, 19 Am. Neg. Rep. 625; Tullis v. Lake Erie & W. R. Co. 175 U. S. 348, 44 L. ed. 192, 20 Sup. Ct. Rep. 136: Louisville & N. R. Co. v. Melton, 218 U. S. 36, 53, 54 L. ed. 921, 928, 47 L.R.A.(N.S.) 84, 30 Sup. Ct. Rep. 676; Chicago, I. & L. R. Co. v. Hackett, 228 U. S. 559, 57 L. ed. 966, 33 Sup. Ct. Rep. 581; Wilmington Star Min. Co. v. Fulton, 205 U. S. 60, 73, 51 L. ed. 708, 715, 27 Sup. Ct. Rep. 412; Missouri P. R. Co. v. Castle, 224 U. S. 541, 544, 56 L. ed. 875, 878, 32 Sup. Ct. Rep. 606. A corresponding power on the part of Congress, when legislating within its appropriate sphere, was sustained in Second Employers' Liability Cases (Mondou v. New York, N. H. & H. R. Co.) 223 U. S. 1, 56 L. ed. 327, 38 L.R.A.(N.S.) 44, 32 Sup. Ct. Rep. 169, 1 N. C. C. A. 875. And see El Paso & N. E. R. Co. v. Gutierrez, 215 U. S. 87, 97, 54 L. ed. 106, 111, 30 Sup. Ct. Rep. 21; Baltimore & O. R. Co. v. Interstate Commerce Commission, 221 U. S. 612, 619, 55 L. ed. 878, 883, 31 Sup. Ct. Rep. 621.

It is true that in the case of the statutes thus sustained there were reasons rendering the particular departures appropriate. Nor is it necessary, for the purposes of the present case, to say that a state might, without violence to the constitutional guaranty of "due process of law," suddenly set aside all common-law rules respecting liability as between employer and employee, without providing a reasonably just substitute. Considering the vast industrial organization of the state of New York, for instance, with hundreds of thousands of plants and millions of wage earners, each employer, on the one hand, having embarked his capital, and each employee, on the other, having taken up his particular mode of earning a livelihood, in reliance upon the probable permanence of an established body of law governing the relation, it perhaps may be doubted whether the state could abolish all rights of action, on the one hand, or all defenses, on the other, without setting up something adequate in their stead. No such question is here presented, and we intimate no opinion upon it. The statute under consideration sets aside one body of rules only to establish another system in its place. If the employee is no longer able to recover as much as before in case of being injured through the employer's negligence, he is entitled to moderate compensation in all cases of injury, and has a certain and speedy remedy without the difficulty and expense of establishing negligence or proving the amount of the damages. Instead of assuming the entire consequences of all ordinary risks of the occupation, he assumes the consequences, in excess of the scheduled compensation, of risks ordinary and extraordinary. On the other hand, if the employer is left without defense respecting the question of fault, he at the same time is assured that it goes directly to the relief of the designated beneficiary. And just as the employee's assumption of ordinary risks at common law presumably was taken into account in fixing the rate of wages, so the fixed responsibility of the employer, and the modified assumption of risk by the employee under the new system, presumably will be reflected in the wage scale. The act evidently is intended as a just settlement of a difficult problem, affecting one of the most important of social relations, and it is to be judged in its entirety. We have said enough to demonstrate that, in such an adjustment, the particular rules of the common law affecting the subject-matter are not placed by the 14th Amendment beyond the reach of the lawmaking power of the state; and thus we are brought to the question whether the method of compensation that is established as a substitute transcends the limits of permissible state action.

We will consider, first, the scheme of compensation, deferring for the present the question of the manner in which the employer is required to secure payment.

Briefly, the statute imposes liability upon the employer to make compensation for disability or death of the employee resulting from accidental personal injury arising out of and in the course of the employment, without regard to fault as a cause except where the injury or death is occasioned by the employee's wilful intention to produce it, or where the injury results solely from his intoxication while on duty; it graduates the compensation for disability according to a prescribed scale based upon the loss of earning power, having regard to the previous wage and the character and duration of the disability; and measures the death benefits according to the dependency of the surviving wife, husband, or infant children. Perhaps we should add that it has no retrospective effect, and applies only to cases arising some months after its passage.

Of course, we cannot ignore the question whether the new arrangement is arbitrary and unreasonable, from the standpoint of natural justice. Respecting this, it is important to be observed that the act applies only to disabling or fatal personal injuries received in the course of hazardous employment in gainful occupation. Reduced to its elements, the situation to be dealt with is this: Employer and employee, by mutual consent, engage in a common operation intended to be advantageous to both; the employee is to contribute his personal services, and for these is to receive wages, and, ordinarily, nothing more; the employer is to furnish plant, facilities, organization, capital, credit, is to control and manage the operation, paying the wages and other expenses, disposing of the product at such prices as he can obtain, taking all the profits, if any there be, and, of necessity, bearing the entire losses. In the nature of things, there is more or less of a probability that the employee may lose his life through some accidental injury arising out of the employment, leaving his widow or children deprived of their natural support; or that he may sustain an injury not mortal, but resulting in his total or partial disablement, temporary or permanent, with corresponding impairment of earning capacity. The physical suffering must be borne by the employee alone; the laws of nature prevent this from being evaded or shifted to another, and the statute makes no attempt to afford an equivalent in compensation. But, besides, there is the loss of earning power,—a loss of that which stands the employee as his capital in trade. This is a loss arising out of the business, and, however it may be charged up, is an expense of the operation, as truly as the cost of repairing broken machinery or any other expense that ordinarily is paid by the employer. Who is to bear the charge? It is plain that, on grounds of natural justice, it is not unreasonable for the state, while relieving the employer from responsibility for damages measured by common-law standards and payable in cases where he or those for whose conduct he is answerable are found to be at fault, to require him to contribute a reasonable amount, and according to a reasonable and definite scale, by way of compensation for the loss of earning power incurred in the common enterprise, irrespective of the question of negligence, instead of leaving the entire loss to rest where it may chance to fall,—that is, upon the injured employee or his dependents. Nor can it be deemed arbitrary and unreasonable, from the standpoint of the employee's interest, to supplant a system under which he assumed the entire risk of injury in ordinary cases, and in others had a right to recover an amount more or less speculative upon proving facts of negligence that often were difficult to prove, and substitute a system under which, in all ordinary cases of accidental injury, he is sure of a definite and easily ascertained compensation, not being obliged to assume the entire loss in any case, but in all cases assuming any loss beyond the prescribed scale.

Much emphasis is laid upon the criticism that the act creates liability without fault. This is sufficiently answered by what has been said, but we may add that liability without fault is not a novelty in the law. The common-law liability of the carrier, of the innkeeper, or him who employed fire or other dangerous agency or harbored a mischievous animal, was not dependent altogether upon questions of fault or negligence. Statutes imposing liability without fault have been sustained. St Louis & S. F. R. Co. v. Mathews, 165 U.S. 1, 22, 41 L. ed. 611, 619, 17 Sup. Ct. Rep. 243; Chicago, R. I. & P. R. Co. v. Zernecke, 183 U.S. 582, 586, 46 L. ed. 339, 340, 22 Sup. Ct. Rep. 229.

We have referred to the maxim, respondeat superior. In a well-known English case, Hall v. Smith, 2 Bing. 156, 160, 130 Eng. Reprint, 265, 9 J. B. Moore, 226, 2 L. J. C. P. 113, this maxim was said by Best, Ch. J., to be "bottomed on this principle, that he who expects to derive advantage from an act which is done by another for him, must answer for any injury which a third person may sustain from it." And this view has been adopted in New York. Cardot v. Barney, 63 N.Y. 281, 287, 20 Am. Rep. 533. The provision for compulsory compensation, in the act under consideration, cannot be deemed to be an arbitrary and unreasonable application of the principle, so as to amount to a deprivation of the employer's property without due process of law. The pecuniary loss resulting from the employee's death or disablement must fall somewhere. It results from something done in the course of an operation from which the employer expects to derive a profit. In excluding the question of fault as a cause of the injury, the act in effect disregards the proximate cause and looks to one more remote,—the primary cause, as it may be deemed,—and that is, the employment itself. For this, both parties are responsible, since they voluntarily engage in it as coadventurers, with personal injury to the employee as a probable and foreseen result. In ignoring any possible negligence of the employee producing or contributing to the injury, the lawmaker reasonably may have been influenced by the belief that, in modern industry, the utmost diligence in the employer's service is in some degree inconsistent with adequate care on the part of the employee for his own safety; that the more intently he devotes himself to the work, the less he can take precautions for his own security. And it is evident that the consequences of a disabling or fatal injury are precisely the same to the parties immediately affected, and to the community, whether the proximate cause be culpable or innocent. Viewing the entire matter, it cannot be pronounced arbitrary and unreasonable for the state to impose upon the employer the absolute duty of making a moderate and definite compensation in money to every disabled employee, or, in case of his death, to those who were entitled to look to him for support, in lieu of the common-law liability confined to cases of negligence.

This, of course, is not to say that any scale of compensation, however insignificant, on the one hand, or onerous, on the other, would be supportable. In this case, no criticism is made on the ground that the compensation prescribed by the statute in question is unreasonable in amount, either in general or in the particular case. Any question of that kind may be met when it arises.

But, it is said, the statute strikes at the fundamentals of constitutional freedom of contract; and we are referred to two recent declarations by this court. The first is this: "Included in the right of personal liberty and the right of private property—partaking of the nature of each—is the right to make contracts for the acquisition of property. Chief among such contracts is that of personal employment, by which labor and other services are exchanged for money or other forms of property. If this right be struck down or arbitrarily interfered with, there is a substantial impairment of liberty in the long-established constitutional sense." Coppage v. Kansas, 236 U.S. 1, 14, 59 L. ed. 441, 446, L. R. A. 1915C, 960, 35 Sup. Ct. Rep. 240. And this is the other: "It requires no argument to show that the right to work for a living in the common occupations of the community is of the very essence of the personal freedom and opportunity that it was the purpose of the [14th] Amendment to secure." Truax v. Raich, 239 U.S. 33, 41, 60 L. ed. 131, 135, L.R.A. 1916D, 545, 36 Sup. Ct. Rep. 7.

It is not our purpose to qualify or weaken either of these declarations in the least. And we recognize that the legislation under review does measurably limit the freedom of employer and employee to agree respecting the terms of employment, and that it cannot be supported except on the ground that it is a reasonable exercise of the police power of the state. In our opinion it is fairly supportable upon that ground. And for this reason: The subject-matter in respect of which freedom or contract is restricted is the matter of compensation for human life or limb lost or disability incurred in the course of hazardous employment, and the public has a direct interest in this as affecting the common welfare. "The whole is no greater than the sum of all the parts, and when the individual health, safety, and welfare are sacrificed or neglected, the state must suffer." Holden v. Hardy, 169 U.S. 366, 397, 42 L. ed. 780, 793, 18 Sup. Ct. Rep. 383. It cannot be doubted that the state may prohibit and punish self-maiming and attempts at suicide; it may prohibit a man from bartering away his life or his personal security; indeed, the right to these is often declared, in bills of rights, to be "natural and inalienable;" and the authority to prohibit contracts made in derogation of a lawfully-established policy of the state respecting compensation for accidental death or disabling personal injury is equally clear. Chicago, B. & Q. R. Co. v McGuire, 219 U.S. 549, 571, 55 L. ed. 328, 340, 31 Sup. Ct. Rep. 259; Second Employers' Liability Cases (Mondou v.

New York, N. H. & H. R. Co.) 223 U.S. 1, 52, 56 L. ed. 327, 347, 38 L.R.A.(N.S.) 44, 32 Sup. Ct. Rep. 169, 1 N. C. C.A. 875.

We have not overlooked the criticism that the act imposes no rule of conduct upon the employer with respect to the conditions of labor in the various industries embraced within its terms, prescribes no duty with regard to where the workmen shall work, the character of the machinery, tools, or appliances, the rules or regulations to be established, or the safety devices to be maintained. This statute does not concern itself with measures of prevention, which presumably are embraced in other laws. But the interest of the public is not confined to these. One of the grounds of its concern with the continued life and earning power of the individual is its interest in the prevention of pauperism, with its concomitants of vice and crime. And, in our opinion, laws regulating the responsibility of employers for the injury or death of employees, arising out of the employment, bear so close a relation to the protection of the lives and safety of those concerned that they properly may be regarded as coming within the category of police regulations. Sherlock v. Alling, 93 U.S. 99, 103, 23 L. ed. 819, 820; Missouri P. R. Co. v. Castle, 224 U.S. 541, 545,56 L. ed. 875, 879, 32 Sup. Ct. Rep. 606.

No question is made but that the procedural provisions of the act are amply adequate to afford the notice and opportunity to be heard required by the 14th Amendment. The denial of a trial by jury is not inconsistent with "due process." Walker v. Sauvinet, 92 U.S. 90, 23 L. ed. 678; Frank v. Mangum, 237 U. S. 309, 340, 59 L. ed. 960, 985, 35 Sup. Ct. Rep. 582.

The objection under the "equal protection" clause is not pressed. The only apparent basis for it is in the exclusion of farm laborers and domestic servants from the scheme. But, manifestly, this cannot be judicially declared to be an arbitrary classification, since it reasonably may be considered that the risks inherent in these occupations are exceptionally patent, simple, and familiar. Missouri, K. & T. R. Co. v. Cade, 233 U. S. 642,650, 58 L. ed. 1135, 34 Sup. Ct. Rep. 678, and cases there cited.

We conclude that the prescribed scheme of compulsory compensation is not repugnant to the provisions of the 14th Amendment, and are brought to consider, next, the manner in which the employer is required to secure payment of the compensation. By § 50, this may be done in one of three ways: (a) State insurance; (b) insurance with an authorized insurance corporation or association; or (c) by a deposit of securities. The record shows that the predecessor of plaintiff in error chose the third method, and with the sanction of the Commission, deposited securities to the amount of $300,000, under § 50, and $30,000 in cash as a deposit to secure prompt and convenient payment, under § 25, with an agreement to make a further deposit if required. This was accompanied with a reservation of all contentions as to the invalidity of the act, and had not the effect of preventing plaintiff in error from raising the questions we have discussed.

The system of compulsory compensation having been found to be within the power of the state, it is within the limits of permissible regulation, in aid of the system, to require the employer to furnish satisfactory proof of his financial ability to pay the compensation, and to deposit a reasonable amount of securities for that purpose. The third clause of § 50 has not been, and presumably will not be, construed so as to give an unbridled discretion to the Commission; nor is it to be presumed that solvent employers will be prevented from becoming self-insurers on reasonable terms. No question is made but that the terms imposed upon this railroad company were reasonable in view of the magnitude of its operations, the number of its employees, and the amount of its pay roll (about $50,000,000 annually); hence no criticism of the practical effect of the third clause is suggested.

This being so, it is obvious that this case presents no question as to whether the state might, consistently with the 14th Amendment, compel employers to effect insurance according to either of the plans mentioned in the first and second clauses. There is no such compulsion, since self-insurance under the third clause presumably is open to all employers on reasonable terms that it is within the power of the state to impose. Regarded as optional arrangements, for acceptance or rejection by employers unwilling to comply with that clause, the plans of insurance are unexceptionable from the constitutional standpoint. Manifestly, the employee is not injuriously affected in a constitutional sense by the provisions giving to the employer an option to secure payment of the compensation in either of the modes prescribed, for there is no presumption that either will prove inadequate to safeguard the employee's interests.

Judgment affirmed.

THE SOCIAL SECURITY ACT
1935

THE SOCIAL SECURITY ACT
1935

THE SETTING

As has been seen, federal legislation in the area of income security was practically nonexistent before 1934, and federal concern with the area was miniscule. And in the states that had developed some philosophy in this area, the vast majority had not considered income security—or indeed almost any aspect of social welfare—as a legitimate responsibility of government. In the eyes of other industrialized societies, the United States appeared to be lagging dramatically behind in state guarantees of income security.

Faced, however, with eighteen million persons dependent on emergency relief and ten million workers unemployed, President Roosevelt could no longer be satisfied with temporary expedients. The Federal Emergency Relief Administration, established in 1933, virtually took over the relief operations of the states. Charitable resources had been exhausted by the dimensions of the Depression. Moreover, the results of the economic collapse were felt in segments of society which had never experienced destitution or unemployment before. A considerable segment of white lower middle-class America was brought face to face with the remnants of the Elizabethan poor laws. While the FERA softened the blow, the situation could not be allowed to occur again. Some long-term solution outside the poor laws had to be developed for those gainfully employed, and public assistance itself had to be radically revised.

Executive Action

The genesis of the 1935 legislation could be seen in 1934. In February of that year the Wagner-Lewis (unemployment compensation) Bill, based on a Brandeis theory encouraged by the Raushenbushes, had been introduced. It provided for a 5 per cent tax on the payrolls of those who employed ten or more persons, against which could be offset payments made to state unemployment funds which met certain federal standards. The bill was endorsed not only by organized labor, but also by the new Secretary of Labor, Frances Perkins, and effectively, in March, by the President. There was, however, vigorous opposition from various employers' groups, and the bill was subjected to hostility by reason of Senator Wagner's interest in the trade disputes legislation. Thus the bill was reported out of committee without recommendations. Ultimately, the President was convinced that further study was needed and perhaps a more comprehensive social welfare measure was justified. The bill therefore died.

Also during 1934 there had been a move in Congress to bring the Federal Government into the field of old-age security. Abraham Epstein and his group (then still called the Association for Old-Age Security) lobbied for a policy whereby the Federal Government would give grants-in-aid to state governments, covering one-third of what they spent by way of old-age assistance. This formula was incorporated in the Dill-Connery Bill, which authorized an appropriation of $10 million a year. Although the bill was not formally supported by the President it was given a favorable report by the House Labor and Senate Pensions Committees. But, increasingly, the President's advisers, such as Rex Tugwell, were advocating caution in general and further study in particular. By May, 1934, the President had apparently decided that it would be best to delay the legislation until the next session in order to use the intervening period to undertake the needed research.

It was this decision which led to the President's sending to Congress his famous message of June 8, 1934:

Presidential Message to the Congress Reviewing the Broad Objectives and Accomplishments of the Administration (June 8, 1934)
(H. R. Doc. 397, 73d Cong., 2d Sess.)

To the Congress:

You are completing a work begun in March, 1933, which will be regarded for a long time as a splendid justification of the vitality of representative government. I greet you and express once more my appreciation of the cooperation which has proved so effective. Only a small number of the items of our program remain to be enacted and I am confident that you will pass on them before adjournment. Many other pending measures are sound in conception, but must, for lack of time or of adequate information, be deferred to the session of the next Congress. In the meantime, we can well seek to adjust many of these measures into certain larger plans of governmental policy for the future of the Nation.

You and I, as the responsible directors of these policies and actions, may, with good reason, look to the future with confidence, just as we may look to the past fifteen months with reasonable satisfaction.

On the side of relief we have extended material aid to millions of our fellow citizens.

On the side of recovery we have helped to lift agriculture and industry from a condition of utter prostration.

But in addition to these immediate tasks of relief and recovery we have properly, necessarily and with overwhelming approval determined to safeguard these tasks by rebuilding many of the structures of our economic life and of reorganizing it in order to prevent a recurrence of collapse.

It is childish to speak of recovery first and reconstruction afterward. In the very nature of the processes of recovery we must avoid the destructive influences of the past. We have shown the world that democracy has within it the elements necessary to its own salvation.

Less hopeful countries where the ways of democracy are very new may revert to the autocracy of yesterday. The American people can be trusted to decide wisely upon the measures taken by the Government to eliminate the abuses of the past and to proceed in the direction of the greater good for the greater number.

Our task of reconstruction does not require the creation of new and strange values. It is rather the finding of the way once more to known, but to some degree forgotten, ideals and values. If the means and details are in some instances new, the objectives are as permanent as human nature.

Among our objectives I place the security of the men, women and children of the Nation first.

This security for the individual and for the family concerns itself primarily with three factors. People want decent homes to live in; they want to locate them where they can engage in productive work; and they want some safeguard against misfortunes which cannot be wholly eliminated in this man-made world of ours.

In a simple and primitive civilization homes were to be had for the building. The bounties of nature in a new land provided crude but adequate food and shelter. When land failed, our ancestors moved on to better land. It was always possible to push back the frontier, but the frontier has now disappeared. Our task involves the making of a better living out of the lands that we have.

So, also, security was attained in the earlier days through the interdependence of members of families upon each other and of the families within a small community upon each other. The complexities of great communities and of organized industry make less real these simple means of security. Therefore, we are compelled to employ the active interest of the Nation as a whole through government in order to encourage a greater security for each individual who composes it.

With the full cooperation of the Congress we have already made a serious attack upon the problem of housing in our great cities. Millions of dollars have been appropriated for housing projects by Federal and local authorities, often with the generous assistance of private owners. The task thus begun must be pursued for many years to come. There is ample private money for sound housing projects; and the Congress, in a measure now before you, can stimulate the lending of money for the modernization of existing homes and the building of new homes. In pursuing this policy we are working toward the ultimate objective of making it possible for American families to live as Americans should.

In regard to the second factor, economic circumstances and the forces of nature themselves dictate the need of constant thought as to the means by which a wise Government may help the necessary readjustment of the population. We cannot fail to act when hundreds of thousands of families live where there is no reasonable prospect of a living in the years to come. This is especially a national problem. Unlike most of the leading Nations of the world, we have so far failed to create a national policy for the development of our land and water resources and for their better use by those people who cannot make a living in their present positions. Only thus can we permanently eliminate many millions of people from the relief rolls on which their names are now found.

The extent of the usefulness of our great natural inheritance of land and water depends on our mastery of it. We are now so organized that science and invention have given us the means of more extensive and effective attacks upon the problems of nature than ever before. We have learned to utilize water power, to reclaim deserts, to recreate forests and to redirect the flow of population. Until recently we have proceeded almost at random, making many mistakes.

There are many illustrations of the necessity for such planning. Some sections of the Northwest and Southwest, which formerly existed as grazing land, were spread over with a fair crop of grass. On this land the water table lay a dozen or twenty feet below the surface, and newly arrived settlers put this land under the plow. Wheat was grown by dry farming methods. But in many of these places today the water table under the land has dropped to fifty or sixty feet below the surface and the top soil in dry seasons is blown away like driven snow. Falling rain, in the absence of grass roots, filters through the soil, runs off the surface, or is quickly reabsorbed into the atmosphere. Many million acres of such land must be restored to grass or trees if we are to prevent a new and man-made Sahara.

At the other extreme, there are regions originally arid, which have been generously irrigated by human engineering. But in some of these places the hungry soil has not only absorbed the water necessary to produce magnificent crops, but so much more water that the water table has now risen to the point of saturation, thereby threatening the future crops upon which many families depend.

Human knowledge is great enough today to give us assurance of success in carrying through the abandonment of many millions of acres for agricultural use and the replacing of these acres with others on which at least a living can be earned.

The rate of speed that we can usefully employ in this attack on impossible social and economic conditions must be determined by business-like procedure. It would be absurd to undertake too many projects at once or to do a patch of work here and another there without finishing the whole of an individual project. Obviously, the Government cannot undertake national projects in every one of the 435 Congressional districts, or even in every one of the 48 States. The magnificent conception of national realism and national needs that this Congress has built up has not only set an example of large vision for all time, but has almost consigned to oblivion our ancient habit of pork-barrel legislation; to that we cannot and must not revert. When the next Congress convenes I hope to be able to present to it a carefully considered national plan, covering the development and the human use of our natural resources of land and water over a long period of years.

In considering the cost of such a program it must be clear to all of us that for many years to come we shall be engaged in the task of rehabilitating many hundreds of thousands of our American families. In so doing we shall be decreasing future costs for the direct relief of destitution. I hope that it will be possible for the Government to adopt as a clear policy to be carried out over a long period, the appropriation of a large, definite, annual sum so that work may proceed year after year not under the urge of temporary expediency, but in pursuance of the well-considered rounded objective.

The third factor relates to security against the hazards and vicissitudes of life. Fear and worry based on unknown danger contribute to social unrest and economic demoralization. If, as our Constitution tells us, our Federal Government was established among other things "to promote the general welfare," it is our plain duty to provide for that security upon which welfare depends.

Next winter we may well undertake the great task of furthering the security of the citizen and his family through social insurance.

This is not an untried experiment. Lessons of experience are available from States, from industries and from many Nations of the civilized world. The various types of social insurance are interrelated; and I think it is difficult to attempt to solve them piecemeal. Hence, I am looking for a sound means which I can recommend to provide at once security against several of the great disturbing factors in life — especially those which relate to unemployment and old age. I believe there should be a maximum of cooperation between States and the Federal Government. I believe that the funds necessary to provide this insurance should be raised by contribution rather than by an increase in general taxation. Above all, I am convinced that social insurance should be national in scope, although the several States should meet at least a large portion of the cost of management, leaving to the Federal Government the responsibility of investing, maintaining and safeguarding the funds constituting the necessary insurance reserves.

I have commenced to make, with the greatest of care, the necessary actuarial and other studies for the formulation of plans for the consideration of the 74th Congress.

These three great objectives — the security of the home, the security of livelihood, and the security of social insurance — are, it seems to me, a mini-

mum of the promise that we can offer to the American people. They constitute a right which belongs to every individual and every family willing to
work. They are the essential fulfillment of measures already taken toward
relief, recovery and reconstruction.

This seeking for a greater measure of welfare and happiness does not
indicate a change in values. It is rather a return to values lost in the course
of our economic development and expansion.

Ample scope is left for the exercise of private initiative. In fact, in the
process of recovery, I am greatly hoping that repeated promises of private
investment and private initiative to relieve the Government in the immediate
future of much of the burden it has assumed, will be fulfilled. We have not
imposed undue restrictions upon business. We have not opposed the incentive of reasonable and legitimate private profit. We have sought rather to
enable certain aspects of business to regain the confidence of the public
We have sought to put forward the rule of fair play in finance and industry.

It is true that there are few among us who would still go back. These
few offer no substitute for the gains already made, nor any hope for making
future gains for human happiness. They loudly assert that individual liberty
is being restricted by Government, but when they are asked what individual liberties they have lost, they are put to it to answer.

We must dedicate ourselves anew to a recovery of the old and sacred
possessive rights for which mankind has constantly struggled — homes, livelihood, and individual security. The road to these values is the way of progress. Neither you nor I will rest content until we have done our utmost to
move further on that road.

The first step on that road was taken within the month.

Executive Order Establishing the Committee on Economic Security
and the Advisory Council on Economic Security
(June 29, 1934)*

By virtue of and pursuant to the authority vested in me by the National
Industrial Recovery Act (ch. 90, 48 Stat. 195), I hereby establish (1) the
Committee on Economic Security (hereinafter referred to as the Commit-
tee) consisting of the Secretary of Labor, chairman, the Secretary of the
Treasury, the Attorney General, the Secretary of Agriculture, and the
Federal Emergency Relief Administrator, and (2) the Advisory Council
on Economic Security (hereinafter referred to as the Advisory Council),
the original members of which shall be appointed by the President and

*Executive Order 6757, United States Presidents [Roosevelt, F. D.], Executive Orders,
March 1, 1934 – February 28, 1935.

additional members of which may be appointed from time to time by the Committee.

The Committee shall study problems relating to the economic security of individuals and shall report to the President not later than December 1, 1934, its recommendations concerning proposals which in its judgment will promote greater economic security.

The Advisory Council shall assist the Committee in the consideration of all matters coming within the scope ot its investigations.

The Committee shall appoint (1) a Technical Board on Economic Security consisting of qualified representatives selected from various departments and agencies of the Federal Government, and (2) an executive director who shall have immediate charge of studies and investigations to be carried out under the general direction of the Technical Board, and who shall, with the approval of the Technical Board, appoint such additional staff as may be necessary to carry out the provisions of this order.

Franklin D. Roosevelt

The White House
June 29, 1934

Findings of the Committee on Economic Security

The Committee on Economic Security was set an almost impossible task. In five months it was to recommend a system of nationwide social security for a country which had so far virtually ignored legislation in the field. In retrospect, the committee, composed of the Secretaries of Labor (Frances Perkins), the Treasury (Henry Morgenthau, Jr.), and Agriculture (Henry A. Wallace), together with the Attorney-General Homer S. Cummings and the Emergency Relief Administrator Harry L. Hopkins, performed a herculean task with what was remarkable efficiency. Perhaps Wisconsin, with its progressive tradition, can take some of the credit, for Wisconsin men were appointed executive director (Edwin E. Witte) and chairman of the Technical Board (Arthur J. Altmeyer).

In some ways the most telling part of the committee's work was its research, which indicated the magnitude of the various problems. While the staff reports were the basis of the new legislation, the following tables are taken from the summarized versions of the most relevant staff reports published after the passage of the 1935 act, found in Social Security in America.

The committee saw the problems to be tackled as essentially those caused by unemployment, the failure of family support(whether that was children failing to support their aged relatives, or husbands who failed to support their families) or physical afflictions like blindness. Of these there

Estimate of average nonagricultural employment

State	Average number of gainful workers			
	1930	1931	1932	1933
United States...............	38,505,000	38,575,000	38,570,000	38,735,000
Alabama......................	540,000	529,000	519,000	510,000
Arizona......................	127,000	127,000	129,000	131,000
Arkansas.....................	283,000	276,000	265,000	258,000
California....................	2,189,000	2,210,000	2,226,000	2,252,000
Colorado.....................	297,000	293,000	296,000	298,000
Connecticut...................	643,000	648,000	652,000	657,000
Delaware.....................	81,000	81,000	80,000	81,000
District of Columbia.............	243,000	245,000	246,000	247,000
Florida.......................	469,000	472,000	473,000	478,000
Georgia......................	660,000	642,000	632,000	615,000
Idaho........................	96,000	93,000	94,000	94,000
Illinois.......................	2,843,000	2,862,000	2,871,000	2,886,000
Indiana.......................	1,003,000	1,004,000	998,000	997,000
Iowa.........................	583,000	579,000	573,000	568,000
Kansas.......................	466,000	464,000	461,000	459,000
Kentucky.....................	553,000	543,000	533,000	525,000
Louisiana.....................	521,000	520,000	515,000	515,000
Maine........................	258,000	258,000	258,000	257,000
Maryland.....................	590,000	591,000	592,000	595,000
Massachusetts..................	1,762,000	1,773,000	1,780,000	1,787,000
Michigan.....................	1,691,000	1,710,000	1,722,000	1,739,000
Minnesota....................	691,000	690,000	686,000	685,000
Mississippi...................	294,000	279,000	265,000	254,000
Missouri.....................	1,089,000	1,089,000	1,083,000	1,083,000
Montana.....................	137,000	132,000	133,000	132,000
Nebraska.....................	310,000	309,000	309,000	304,000
Nevada......................	34,000	34,000	34,000	34,000
New Hampshire................	171,000	172,000	172,000	172,000
New Jersey...................	1,657,000	1,677,000	1,693,000	1,711,000
New Mexico..................	85,000	83,000	85,000	84,000
New York.....................	5,279,000	5,328,000	5,366,000	5,412,000
North Carolina.................	642,000	637,000	633,000	632,000
North Dakota..................	107,000	105,000	102,000	102,000
Ohio.........................	2,311,000	2,324,000	2,327,000	2,336,000
Oklahoma....................	525,000	524,000	518,000	517,000
Oregon.......................	329,000	331,000	332,000	334,000
Pennsylvania..................	3,479,000	3,495,000	3,505,000	3,597,000
Rhode Island..................	289,000	292,000	293,000	295,000
South Carolina.................	341,000	331,000	323,000	316,000
South Dakota..................	117,000	116,000	114,000	113,000
Tennessee.....................	587,000	577,000	568,000	560,000
Texas........................	1,374,000	1,379,000	1,371,000	1,376,000
Utah.........................	129,000	128,000	130,000	130,000
Vermont......................	103,000	103,000	102,000	102,000
Virginia......................	608,000	599,000	592,000	586,000
Washington...................	562,000	565,000	566,000	568,000
West Virginia.................	454,000	454,000	455,000	456,000
Wisconsin....................	841,000	841,000	836,000	833,000
Wyoming.....................	62,000	61,000	62,000	62,000

and unemployment, by States 1930-1933

					Percent of gainful workers				
Employed					Unemployed				
1930-33 average	1930	1931	1932	1933	1930-33 average	1930	1931	1932	1933
74.2	87.9	76.8	65.5	66.8	25.8	12.1	23.2	34.5	33.2
76.8	89.6	79.8	66.1	70.9	23.2	10.4	20.2	33.9	29.1
72.3	88.3	75.8	64.3	61.4	27.7	11.7	24.2	35.7	38.6
74.4	90.5	81.5	63.1	60.8	25.6	9.5	18.5	36.9	39.2
76.0	87.3	76.1	71.1	70.8	24.0	12.7	23.9	29.9	29.2
74.9	88.3	79.3	67.2	64.7	25.1	11.7	20.7	32.8	35.3
73.6	88.0	75.7	62.5	68.3	26.4	12.0	24.3	37.5	31.7
81.7	90.7	79.1	73.7	83.3	18.3	9.3	20.9	26.3	16.7
86.8	94.2	87.3	80.9	85.0	13.2	5.8	12.7	19.1	15.0
72.9	87.8	77.0	63.6	63.4	27.1	12.2	23.0	36.4	36.6
83.0	91.0	81.7	71.9	87.4	17.0	9.0	18.3	28.1	12.6
78.2	89.5	81.0	70.7	71.5	21.8	10.5	19.0	29.3	28.5
72.0	86.2	75.2	62.5	64.3	28.0	13.8	24.8	37.5	35.7
73.4	87.7	76.4	62.7	66.6	26.6	12.3	23.6	37.3	33.4
78.2	91.5	81.5	70.5	69.0	21.8	8.5	18.5	29.5	31.0
79.0	90.7	80.1	72.0	73.1	21.0	9.3	19.9	28.0	26.9
79.2	88.3	79.2	71.6	77.3	20.8	11.7	20.8	28.4	22.7
75.9	88.8	77.7	67.5	69.4	24.1	11.2	22.3	32.5	30.6
78.2	88.0	76.6	68.4	79.7	21.8	12.0	23.4	31.6	20.3
76.6	90.4	78.6	78.6	70.6	23.4	9.6	21.4	33.0	29.4
73.0	86.8	75.3	65.0	65.2	27.0	13.2	24.7	35.0	34.8
65.7	82.0	70.3	56.9	54.1	34.3	18.0	29.7	43.1	45.9
76.6	88.5	77.9	70.2	69.7	23.4	11.5	22.1	29.8	30.3
80.6	90.0	83.5	72.3	74.9	19.4	10.0	16.5	27.7	25.1
75.8	88.9	78.2	67.5	68.5	24.2	11.1	21.8	32.5	31.5
71.6	86.3	77.0	59.3	63.6	28.4	13.7	23.0	40.7	36.4
78.5	91.2	81.3	71.5	69.8	21.5	8.8	18.7	28.5	30.2
72.2	86.5	73.8	64.3	64.6	27.8	13.5	26.2	35.7	35.4
78.2	88.0	76.0	70.2	78.7	21.8	12.0	24.0	29.8	21.3
71.2	86.8	74.5	62.9	61.2	28.8	13.2	25.5	37.1	38.8
73.8	89.3	79.3	65.2	61.7	26.2	10.7	20.7	34.8	38.3
72.2	87.6	65.2	63.6	61.9	27.8	12.4	24.0	36.4	38.1
78.7	88.2	77.4	67.7	81.6	21.3	11.8	22.6	32.3	18.4
81.1	90.6	82.2	78.2	72.7	18.9	9.4	17.8	21.8	27.3
73.1	86.7	75.2	62.7	67.8	26.9	13.3	24.8	37.3	32.2
75.8	88.8	76.7	66.8	70.8	24.2	11.2	23.3	33.2	29.2
78.3	86.5	75.7	72.2	78.7	21.7	13.5	24.3	27.8	21.3
71.7	88.2	76.5	62.7	59.8	28.3	11.8	23.5	37.3	40.2
70.3	84.7	73.0	60.6	63.4	29.7	15.3	27.0	39.4	36.6
82.8	91.4	81.7	70.7	87.1	17.2	8.6	18.3	29.3	12.9
82.5	93.0	83.4	76.1	77.3	17.5	7.0	16.6	23.9	22.7
79.6	90.2	80.3	70.2	77.4	20.4	9.8	19.7	29.8	22.6
76.0	89.8	78.6	67.2	68.4	24.0	10.2	21.4	32.8	31.6
74.3	88.2	77.3	66.1	65.7	25.7	11.8	22.7	33.9	34.3
75.9	88.8	77.0	68.7	69.1	24.1	11.2	23.0	31.3	30.9
78.9	90.8	80.6	69.3	74.4	21.1	9.2	19.4	30.7	25.6
75.6	87.9	76.9	68.6	69.3	24.4	12.1	23.1	31.4	30.7
76.8	89.9	78.7	68.0	70.6	23.2	10.1	21.3	32.0	29.4
76.2	88.4	77.1	67.8	71.2	23.8	11.6	22.9	32.2	28.8
75.8	90.7	80.9	65.6	66.1	24.2	9.3	19.1	34.4	33.9

is little doubt that the issue of unemployment dominated the thinking of the committee — and understandably so in view of the magnitude of the problem.

Even such dramatic figures failed to give the full story. There was considerable part-time employment and harsh seasonable variations in employment in certain industries. The length of unemployment caused great hardship in certain areas and on certain age groups. It was, thus, perhaps natural for a committee so concerned with employment to see the issue of old age as primarily one of the inability of the older worker to obtain employment. The number of old persons was rising both absolutely and proportionately.

Social Security in America
(p. 141)

Actual and estimated number of persons aged 65 and over compared to total population, 1860-2000

Year	Number aged 65 and over	Total population	Percent aged 65 and over	Year	Number aged 65 and over	Total population	Percent aged 65 and over
1860......	849,000	31,443,000	2.7	1940.....	8,311,000	132,000,000	6.3
1870......	1,154,000	38,558,000	3.0	1950.....	10,863,000	141,000,000	7.7
1880......	1,723,000	50,156,000	3.4	1960.....	13,590,000	146,000,000	9.3
1890......	2,424,000	62,622,000	3.9	1970.....	15,066,000	149,000,000	10.1
1900......	3,089,000	75,995,000	4.1	1980.....	17,001,000	150,000,000	11.3
1910......	3,958,000	91,972,000	4.3	1990.....	19,102,000	151,000,000	12.6
1920......	4,940,000	105,711,000	4.7	2000.....	19,338,000	151,000,000	12.7
1930......	6,634,000	122,775,000	5.4				

SOURCE: Data for years 1860 to 1930 from the United States censuses. Estimates for subsequent years by the actuarial staff of the Committee on Economic Security. These forecasts are made on the assumption of a net immigration of 100,000 annually in years 1935-39, and 200,000 annually in 1940 and thereafter.

Persons with previous work experience at nonrelief employment seeking work, classified by length of time since last nonrelief employment of 4 weeks or more and by age[1]

Time since last non-relief employment	Age											
	All ages		16-24		25-44		45-54		55-64		65 and over	
	Number	Percent	Number	Percent	Number	Percent	Number	Percent	Number	Percent	Number	Percent
Total..........	10,058	100.0	1,854	100.0	4,958	100.0	1,934	100.0	972	100.0	340	100.0
Under 6 months.....	1,609	16.1	467	25.4	788	16.0	230	12.0	98	10.1	26	7.7
6 to 11 months.......	1,611	16.1	414	22.5	803	16.2	252	13.1	105	10.8	37	10.9
12 to 23 months......	1,873	18.7	378	20.6	943	19.1	333	17.3	172	17.8	47	13.9
24 to 35 months......	1,809	18.1	269	14.6	906	18.3	385	20.0	182	18.8	67	19.8
36 to 47 months......	1,364	13.6	165	9.0	654	13.2	320	16.6	168	17.3	57	16.9
48 months and over..	1,750	17.4	146	7.9	851	17.2	405	21.0	244	25.2	104	30.8
Unknown[2]..........	42	.....	15	.....	13	.....	9	.....	3	.....	2	.....

[1] Based on 5-percent sample of "Survey of Occupational Characteristics of Persons Receiving Relief" May 1934, furnished by the Research Section, Division of Research, Statistics, and Finance, Federal Emergency Relief Administration.
[2] Unknown distributed in computation of percentage.

It was harder for older persons to find work. Thus, old age and employment could be seen as directly related problems. But the committee research revealed other problems. Rural America was giving way to urban America. And the city was less hospitable to the elderly than life on the farm had been. Already there were signs that the family and private charity could not bear all the problems of old-age dependency.

Social Security in America
(p. 152)

Old-age dependency in the State of New York, July 1, 1929

Catagory	Percentage distribution	
	Persons 65 and over	Persons 70 and over
Self-dependent:		
Public pensioners..	8.3	11.0
Private pensioners..	1.8	3.0
Self-support on current earnings............................	28.5	17.0
Self-support on income....................................	5.0	5.0
Total..	43.6	36.0
Dependent:		
On private homes for the aged.............................	1.0	1.5
On relatives and friends....................................	49.4	55.6
On public and private charity..............................	3.5	4.5
Confined by Government....................................	2.5	2.4
Total..	56.4	64.0

SOURCE: New York State Commission on Old Age Security, *op cit.*, p. 39.

Economic status of aged studied in the District of Columbia, 1934

Status	Percentage distribution		
	White	Negro	Total
Independent.......................................	63	30	52
Supported by relatives.............................	30	50	37
Other means of support (friends, public or private relief)...	2	15	6
Dependent, but source of support not reported..........	1	2.5	1
Status not reported................................	4	2.5	4
Total..	100	100	100

SOURCE: "Study of the Aged in the District of Columbia", *Monthly Labor Review*, vol. 39, no. 2, August 1934, p. 328.

For those who could look into the future, it was clear that the issue of dependency would also become crucial where families with children broke up. Considering the potential scope of the need, the number of families receiving "mothers' pensions" at the time the committee sat was minuscule.

Social Security in America
(p. 240, 243)

*Marital status of families with female heads and number of children
under 21 years and under 10 years: United States population census, 1930
(unpublished figures)*

Number of children	Families with female heads						
	Total	Families with white or Negro female heads for which marital status was tabulated					Families with female heads for whom marital status was unknown[1]
		Total	Marital status				
			Married, husband not present	Widowed	Di-vorced	Single	
Number of children under 21 years							
Total families.........	3,792,902	3,742,432	400,695	2,534,630	235,893	571,214	50,470
Families tabulated.........	3,742,432	3,742,432	400,695	2,534,630	235,893	571,214	....
No children.............	2,250,624	2,250,624	159,851	1,479,577	106,340	504,856	....
1 child.................	640,302	640,302	91,710	447,209	60,342	41,041	....
2 children..............	382,756	382,756	64,625	267,502	36,724	13,905	....
3 or more children......	468,750	468,750	84,509	340,342	32,487	11,412	....
Families not tabulated......	50,470	....	....	....	....	....	50,470
Number of children under 10 years							
Total families.........	3,792,902	3,742,432	400,695	2,534,630	235,893	571,214	50,470
Families tabulated.........	3,742,432	3,742,432	400,695	2,534,630	235,893	571,214	....
No children under 10.....	3,108,734	3,108,734	275,180	2,103,206	179,619	550,729	....
1 child.................	364,147	364,147	66,630	249,468	35,274	12,775	....
2 children..............	162,500	162,500	33,735	109,963	14,038	4,764	....
3 children..............	69,190	69,190	15,805	46,698	4,786	1,901	....
4 or more children......	37,861	37,861	9,345	25,295	2,176	1,045	....
Families not tabulated......	50,470	....	....	....	....	....	50,470

[1] Includes 10,022 families with white and Negro female heads for whom marital status was not reported and 40,448 families with female heads of other races for which information was not tabulated.

The Politics of the Committee on Economic Security

*The different problems and the limited legislative provisions for handling
them in the states have already been seen. But this was only a beginning of
the task which faced the staff of the Committee on Economic Security.
Fortunately, it is now possible to piece together the politics of the committee from the writings of Witte and Altmeyer. (See E. E. Witte,* The Development of the Social Security Act [*Wisconsin 1963*] *and A. J. Altmeyer,* The
Formative Years of Social Security [*Wisconsin, 1966*])

Distribution of widowed and separated or divorced women heads of relief families in urban areas with children under the age of 16 years, based on 5-percent sample study of occupational characteristics of relief families in 79 cities, May 1934[1]

| Characteristics | Total | | White | Colored |
	Number	Percent distribution		
Total women..............................	973	100	545	428
Marital status:				
Widowed...................................	429	44	237	192
Separated.................................	454	47	237	217
Divorced..................................	90	9	71	19
Number of dependent children:				
1...	474	49	266	208
2...	269	28	157	112
3...	124	13	63	61
4...	55	6	31	24
5 or more.................................	51	5	28	23
Employment status:				
Employed at nonrelief job.................	119	12	51	68
Unemployed, but seeking work..............	556	57	278	278
Unemployed, but not seeking work..........	297	31	215	82
Housework and unpaid care of dependents...	194	20	159	35
Chronic illness or physical disability....	85	9	47	38
Feeble-mindedness or insanity.............	1	[2]	1	0
Old age or general disability.............	14	1	5	9
Other.....................................	3	[2]	3	0
Not reported..............................	1	[2]	1	0
Occupational status:				
No usual occupation.......................	316	32	230	86
Servant classes...........................	360	37	93	267
Semiskilled workers in manufacturing......	127	13	95	32
Other semiskilled workers.................	59	6	33	26
Clerks and kindred workers................	83	9	77	6
Wholesale and retail dealers..............	6	1	5	1
Professional persons......................	9	1	7	2
Other.....................................	13	1	5	8

[1] Data supplied by the Federal Emergency Relief Administration.
[2] Less than 1 percent.

The Executive Order of June 29, 1934, provided for four agencies. First was the Committee on Economic Security itself, the composition of which has already been discussed. The President included thereon the Secretary of Agriculture, rather than the Secretary of Commerce, who had appeared in the draft order apparently prepared by Mrs. Perkins, Dr. Altmeyer, and Mr. Hopkins. Second, there was to be an Advisory Council on Economic Security; third, a Technical Board on Economic Security; and fourth, an executive director.

Different studies were undertaken and some of the results have already been discussed. Research on unemployment insurance was headed by Dr. Bryce Stewart, that on old-age security by Professor Barbara Armstrong. Dr. Edgar L. Sydenstricker led the research on health insurance and medical care, while Mr. Emerson Ross directed the studies in public em-

*ployment and relief. Dr. Meredith B. Givens was in charge of the study of
employment opportunity and the U.S. Children's Bureau handled research
on security for children. Some work on the security of farmers was done in
conjunction with the Department of Agriculture, while the studies in
connection with reserve funds and other financial and administrative matters were often shared between the different departments. There were various statistical and actuarial services to complement these various studies.*

*The President was in constant touch with the committee and its execu-
tive staff and, while insisting that both staff and committee should have a
free hand, he clearly shaped much of the legislation. He made it clear that
he wanted comprehensive legislation, in the sense that it should cover both
old-age security and unemployment insurance. Indeed, he was anxious that
the committee consider the possibility of establishing a system of social
insurance which would protect every citizen from all economic misfortunes
throughout his life. (The same idea was put forward in Britain seven years
later in the Beveridge Report.) Roosevelt also made it clear that he preferred state as opposed to federal administration of the various schemes
contemplated, and he had a decided preference for programs based on insurance rather than plans which would require financing out of general funds.*

*By September, the preliminary reports from the staff studies were avail-
able, and the executive director wrote an introduction setting out preliminary recommendations for the plan of economic security. The core of the
preliminary report, (now found in the National Archives) was as follows:*

Preliminary Report of the Staff of the Committee on Economic Security
September, 1934
(p. 415)

*   *   *

(b) *General Outline of a Tentative, Comprehensive Program for Personal Economic Security.*

(1) The program for economic security should, as far as possible, stress
employment as the best cure for unemployment. Federal funds available
for use in connection with such a program should be used primarily (a) to
stimulate private employment, and (b) to provide supplemental public employment.

(2) If financially possible, the government should undertake an extensive
public employment program by next summer at the latest. This will necessarily have to be financed from general federal funds, with such additional
funds as may be made available by the state and local governments. All
federal construction work and the funds appropriated therefor should become an integral part of this employment program. Employment provided
under this program should be carried on, as nearly as possible, on an em-

ployment, rather than a relief, basis. The persons employed should be selected primarily on the basis of their fitness for jobs, but in the present emergency preference must necessarily be given to the people in the need and the amount of money that anyone can earn kept considerably below the earnings on a full time employment basis.

(3) As a permanent policy, the federal government, without guaranteeing employment, should continuously interest itself in maintaining a high level of employment. To this end it should consistently study the employment situation in all industries and throughout the country, and should develop plans for meeting emergencies which can be forecast or anticipated before they arise. It should adopt longtime programs for the economic development of the country and make advance plans, but, as far as possible, should concentrate the actual work in periods and places when and where private employment is seriously impaired. Included in such planning for employment should be programs for vocational training and re-training and for moving stranded populations. To make this policy successful the federal government should utilize its entire construction expenditures for the provision of work to supplement private employment and should try to get the state and local governments to do likewise, through encouraging planning on their part and subsidizing public works undertakings by state and local governments in periods when there is great need for additional public employment, (along the general lines of the P.W.A. subsidies and loans).

(4) A system of unemployment insurance should be launched on a nation-wide basis at the earliest date possible. This should be supported entirely from contributions of the employers, or of the employers and employees jointly. Unemployment insurance should be on a strictly contractual basis, without any means test. It should give limited benefits only, serving as a first line of defense. After exhaustion of the benefits to which any individual is entitled under the unemployment insurance plan, he shall receive no extended benefits but shall be entitled to work or relief on the same basis as uninsured workers.

(5) Old people without means of support who do not need institutional care should be granted old age pensions, in an amount sufficient to enable them to live in decency and dignity in their homes. To this end the federal government should subsidize state old age pension laws which meet prescribed federal standards. As 28 states now have such laws and all of these are non-contributory, it is assumed that such pensions for old people in need will be given on a non-contributory basis, entirely from public funds.

(6) A contributory pension system should, as soon as practicable, be set up as a supplement to the existing non-contributory system and in course of time should replace the non-contributory pensions except for persons who can not be brought under the contributory system. Contributory pensions should be based upon contract rather than need. In the long run they should be self-supporting, but governmental aid is necessary initially to

give a reasonable pension to people who are already well along toward old age.

(7) At an early date provisions should be made for the application of insurance principles against the economic risks arising out of ill health among the people in low income groups. Loss of wages due to illness — the smaller part of the total economic risk arising out of ill health — should be compensated, along with loss of income due to unemployment. A special system should be instituted for provision of medical and hospital care, and at least ultimately, also of dental and nursing care. The funds for such protection should come primarily from contributions of the employers and employees, with possible governmental subsidies to make such protection available to self-employed persons in the low income group.

(8) The large number of "young" families in which there is no breadwinner now on relief lists should be granted mothers' pensions instead of relief. To make this possible the federal government should subsidize the state mothers' pension laws, subject to compliance with standards to be prescribed in the federal act.

(9) As a further measure of protection for the large number of children included in the relief group and particularly for those in rural areas, a health program for mothers and children should be inaugurated similar to that which was carried on under the Shepard-Towner act. This involves cooperation between the state and federal governments, and is possible only with a federal subsidy.

(10) So long as the present critical situation continues, the federal government will probably have to continue to shoulder the bulk of the relief costs, particularly if it is not possible to carry out the recommendation for the immediate launching of an extensive public employment program. As a permanent policy, however, relief ought to be regarded as primarily a responsibility of the state and local governments, except in periods of great emergency.

(11) The entire program outlined should be considered and developed as a unified national program for economic security. Under the governmental system which exists in this country, however, such a program will require the cooperation of the national, state, and local governments. The national government should lay down the general standards and encourage and promote state and local cooperation. The actual administration of the several social insurance measures proposed, however, will have to be vested in the states (except that it may be possible, if a contributory old age insurance system is launched, to have this administered directly by the federal government); but the federal government should assume the responsibility for developing truly national systems of unemployment insurance, public provisions for medical care, etc. This can be most effectively accomplished through a device like the Wagner-Lewis bill in the last Congress. It is suggested that an excise tax be levied upon industry to be computed at a

specified percentage of payroll, and that as an offset a credit be allowed for payments made under state unemployment insurance, health insurance and old age insurance systems. Supplemental to such an excise tax, federal subsidies should be granted for non-contributory old age pensions, mothers' pensions, and child health work.

(12) All funds collected in connection with parts of this program which involve the accumulation of reserves (unemployment insurance and contributory old age pensions) should be deposited with and invested by the federal reserve banks. The control of the investment and liquidation of such funds should be vested in the Federal Reserve Board or any successor responsible for the credit policies of the country. At the outset, these funds should be invested largely, if not exclusively, in securities of the U.S. government or in securities guaranteed by the Government.

(13) The federal end of the entire program for economic security (except possibly relief in emergencies) should be centralized in a single federal department with, however, proper departmentalization. A large part of the administration should center in the public employment offices. These should select the people to be given public employment, collect and disburse the unemployment insurance funds, and undertake vocational training and re-training programs in cooperation with the local school system.

The program above outlined will give fairly adequate protection to the great majority of the persons employed in industry and at least some protection also to persons engaged in agriculture and self-employed people. Its cost at this stage can only be very roughly estimated. A fairly adequate system of unemployment insurance can be financed on about 4½% on payroll, which it is suggested in Appendix B should come 3% from industry and 1½% from the employees. The cost of such a system can be somewhat reduced, but only through reducing the benefits. A contributory old age pension system such as outlined in Appendix C, will cost 4% of the wages of eligible employees, but the major part of this will not be charged upon industry, in addition to which there will have to be, for many years to come, substantial government subsidies. Insurance against loss of wages due to illness costs about 1% of payroll; a complete system of the provision of medical care, hospital care, dental and nursing care, about 4 or 4½% of payroll (approximately 1/2 of which would come from industry); a partial system, embracing only general medical and hospital care, about 2% of payroll. The subsidies contemplated for old age pensions and mothers' pensions are not likely to cost in excess of $100,000,000; the subsidies proposed in connection with the medical care program, probably about the same amount.

With the production of the preliminary reports, influence largely passed from the staff to the different committees. For instance, in unemployment insurance, the staff recommended a national system, administered exclusively by the Federal Government, with employer, employee, and govern-

mental contributions, but also with a provision allowing industries and some employers to handle their own funds. The Technical Board referred the staff report to its Committee on Unemployment Insurance which, while favoring a national plan, made many important changes. In turn, the full Technical Board had reservations about a national system. The issues were being opened up.

Report of the Committee on Unemployment Insurance
(Submitted to Executive Committee of the Technical Board
of the Committee on Economic Security)
(September 26, 1934)

The committee considered only the major issues involved in the structure of a plan of unemployment insurance, feeling that the more detailed phases of plan structure would have to wait upon decision in the more fundamental points. The recommendations of the committee are as follows:

(1) The Federal Government should establish a national system and administer the plan in preference to the Wagner-Lewis procedure or any procedure involving state administration. (Unanimous)

(2) In the first instance, at least all contributions should be pooled. (Unanimous)

(3) Industries should be allowed to contract out and to establish approved industrial schemes. (One member dissenting)

(4) House funds should not be permitted. (1 Dissent; 1 Partial Dissent)

(5) If there is any breakdown of the general pooled fund into separate funds, a proportion of all contributions should be set aside in a national reinsurance fund to guarantee the ordinary benefits contracted for by the separate funds. (Unanimous)

(6) Provision should be made in emergency unemployment situations for the payment of extended benefits from Federal government funds to workers who have exhausted their right to ordinary benefit. (One vote reserved)

(7) Contributions from employers and employees to unemployment insurance should in no case be utilized to finance public works. (Unanimous)

(8) It is fundamental to the success of a plan of unemployment insurance that both employers and employees should contribute. (Unanimous)

Preliminary Report of the Technical Board
(Submitted to the Committee on Economic Security)
October 1, 1934

Compulsory Unemployment Insurance. On this subject the present trend of thought (subject to change) of the Board runs along the following lines:

(a) Unemployment insurance is an essential measure for the economic security of the most stable part of our industrial population, but is not a complete, all sufficient solution of the problem.

(b) Unemployment insurance should be strictly contractual, divorced from any means test. Unemployment insurance funds should not be used for relief or any other purposes other than the payment of ordinary benefits.

(c) Unemployment insurance should be supported by contributions from the employers and probably also from the employees. There should be no public contributions.

(d) All contributions should at the outset be pooled in a single fund but there should be further exploration of the advisability of permitting "contracting out" by separate industrial and house funds under restrictions adequately safeguarding the employees.

(e) Benefits should be paid in cash for a limited period only, in proportion to the claimant's period of employment, and should be sufficient to support the family while being paid.

(f) If constitutional, a nationally administered system of unemployment insurance is to be preferred to a state system, but the Committee should be satisfied that a nationally administered system is constitutional before commitments in favor of such a system are made to the public.

(g) If unemployment insurance is to be developed under a system of state administration or if industrial or house funds are permitted, a portion of all contributions should be set aside in a national reinsurance fund to guarantee payment of the contractual benefits from the separate funds.

At a meeting on October 1, 1934, the Committee on Economic Security generally approved the scope of the staff studies, but made few final decisions about the difficulties and disputes which had arisen. On unemployment, the disputes in fact grew wider rather than narrower. Not only was there disagreement about whether employment should be handled federally or at the state level, but also, if by the latter method, whether the Wagner-Lewis formula should be used (by which the Federal Government levied a tax against which payments made to approved state unemployment schemes could be offset) or a federal-state "subsidy" plan (returning the federal tax directly to the state). Ultimately, the Unemployment Insurance Com-

*mittee of the Technical Board voted for the former arrangement, following
the lines of the Wagner-Lewis Bill.*

While the committee was now agreed, the Technical Board remained divided, and Dr. Witte set out the alternatives available:

Report of the Technical Board
(Submitted to the Committee on Economic Security)
November 9, 1934

I. Three major alternative plans for the administration of unemployment insurance are worthy of consideration:

(1) *An exclusively Federal System.* — Under such a system the Federal Government would levy a tax on employers and possibly also on employees, the proceeds of which would be appropriated for unemployment insurance purposes. In this act it would set up a complete system for the administration of unemployment insurance specifying all conditions for benefits. The Federal Government would directly administer these benefits through the Employment Service and Federal record offices, which would probably be set up on a regional basis.

(2) *A cooperative Federal-State system on the subsidy plan.* — Under such a system the Federal Government would, likewise, levy and collect a pay-roll tax on employers and possibly also on employees. It would provide further for subsidies to States which enact unemployment insurance laws satisfying standards specified in the Federal act. These subsidies would be a stated percentage of the tax actually collected from the respective States, which would be set up as a credit in the Federal Reserve banks to the account of the State. A specified percentage (say, 20 percent) might be appropriated to the supervisory Federal department and used to finance the Employment Service, to create a reinsurance fund and/or a fund for payment of benefits to employees who lose their jobs soon after they have migrated into a new State after still having unused credits in another State. Under this system the States would likewise have to pass unemployment insurance laws which would have to satisfy the standards prescribed by Federal law, but might vary in other respects from the laws of other States. All funds would be held at all times by the Federal Government but the benefits would be administered by the States, presumably through the employment offices and central record offices.

(3) *A cooperative Federal-State system on the Wagner-Lewis principle.* — Under this system the Federal Government would impose an excise tax on employers against which there would be allowed as a credit (up to the full amount of the tax or any stated percentage thereof) the amounts paid by such employers into unemployment insurance or reserve funds established pursuant to State laws meeting standards prescribed in the Feder-

al law. The cooperating States would collect the contributions from employers (and, if they so determined also from employees) and deposit these in the Federal Reserve banks to be held to their credit and to be invested and liquidated under regulations to be made by the Federal Reserve Board. Under this plan, as well as under the subsidy plan, a percentage of the amounts collected by the States might be withheld by the Federal Government to be used as a reinsurance fund. The administration of benefits under this plan would be a State responsibility, but could be controlled to some (probably a limited) extent by Federal legislation.

II. Which of these three plans should be adopted should be decided primarily on practical and fundamental policy considerations, rather than on the issue of constitutionality. All three of these proposals are new and some arguments can be made both in favor and opposed to the constitutionality of each of them. What the Supreme Court might hold is largely conjecture and is likely to depend upon the detailed development of these respective plans. Among the people consulted there seems to be a quite general impression that the Federal-State subsidy plan is the least likely to be overthrown on constitutional grounds, but there are some uncertainties even as to this plan, depending upon how it is worked out in detail.

Fundamental in a decision between these plans is the question of the desirable extent of national control in this field. The exclusively national system would insure uniformity throughout the country, not only with regard to contributions but also benefits. It would ignore State lines and, thus, make it a relatively simple matter to protect the benefit rights of employees when they move from State to State. It would also make possible a pooled fund for the entire country and thereby automatically meet the problem presented by unusual unemployment in particular industries and States, without necessity for any reinsurance fund. It would also have the advantage of whatever degree of increased efficiency there may be in Federal as compared with State administration. It would be put into operation more quickly than any Federal-State plan and would come into effect at one and the same time throughout the entire country.

The major considerations on the other side concern the same fundamental question of the desirable extent of national control. An exclusively national system would necessitate decisions at the very outset on all points which could not be left to administrative discretion, such as employee contributions, industrial and plant funds, incentives to regularization, etc. Even among the people who strongly believe in unemployment insurance and who have given the most thought to this subject there are wide differences of opinion on many of the most fundamental questions arising in the preparation of an actual bill. Under a national system no experimentation on a relatively small scale would be possible and mistakes made initially would have much more serious consequences than under State system. Moreover, "all the eggs would be in one basket", with the result that if the national law should be held unconstitutional, there would be no State unemployment insurance laws which remained intact.

III. As between a Federal-State system on a subsidy plan and a Federal-State system along the lines of the Wagner-Lewis bill, the only absolutely necessary difference is that under the former all taxes (contributions) levied on industry would be collected by the Federal Government, while under the latter the contributions under the State unemployment insurance laws would be collected by the States. In practice, however, it seems almost certain that a greater degree of national control will be developed under the former than in the latter system.

The subsidy system provides a simpler method for the collection of contributions (pay-roll taxes) than the Wagner-Lewis device. It would have at least some tendency toward higher standards of administration—a most important matter. It probably would facilitate the setting up of reinsurance and transfer funds. From the point of view of expediency it has the advantage of being a brand-new proposal. Clearly it is superior to the Wagner-Lewis plan if extensive national control is desired at this time in unemployment insurance.

The Wagner-Lewis plan has the advantage over the subsidy plan that it will make it unnecessary to reach decisions under the Federal act on the most controversial questions in connection with unemployment insurance: Whether plant funds shall be permitted and whether employees shall be required to contribute. It may be that these questions could be left to the decisions of the States even under the subsidy plan but certainly not as easily as under the Wagner-Lewis device. Another important consideration is that under this plan there would be no pressure on Congress to use sources of revenue other than contributions for unemployment-insurance purposes, which is likely to become very strong under both the straight national and (Federal-State) subsidy plans. Finally, under the Wagner-Lewis bill, many States would doubtless pass unemployment insurance laws before the Federal tax became effective and could be litigated. In the event that the Federal law should then be held unconstitutional, the State laws would continue to operate. Under the subsidy plan, in contrast, while the States would also be required to pass legislation, their laws would include no revenue-raising features, so that they would become inoperative if the Federal act should for any reason be held invalid or if the Federal appropriation is discontinued.

IV. After extended consideration of these three major alternative plans for the administration of unemployment insurance, the executive committee board finds that it is divided regarding which of these systems is to be preferred. The unemployment insurance committee of the technical board, as well as the executive director, believe that the exclusively national system should be definitely rejected. Many of the members of the staff, on the other hand, favor a national system.

The unemployment insurance committee also holds the view that of the two alternative cooperative Federal-State systems the Wagner-Lewis plan is distinctly preferable to the subsidy system.

In view of the differences of opinion on the respective merits of the three major alternative systems of administration, a decision between these systems must be made by the Committee on Economic Security. An early decision is not only vital to the work of the staff but to the entire development of unemployment insurance legislation in this country. At this time unemployment insurance study commissions are functioning in nine states, charged with the duty of making recommendations on this subject to the incoming legislatures. In several other States unemployment insurance legislation was pledged in the platform of the party which won the recent election or has been promised by the successful candidate for Governor. And not only in these but many other States there is wide-spread interest in unemployment insurance legislation with good prospects for its enactment in the coming winter when 43 State legislatures will be in session. In all States, however, there is at present great uncertainty as to what the Federal Government is going to do, which is holding up all plans for State legislation.

Whether the Committee on Economic Security believes that an exclusively national system is or is not desirable, announcement of its decision upon this point at the forthcoming national conference on economic security would be most appropriate and valuable. The States would then know whether they are to be in the picture and could make their plans accordingly. In view of the near approach of the sessions of Congress and the State legislatures an early decision on the issue of an exclusively national versus a cooperative State-Federal system would seem imperative.

A decision regarding the type of a cooperative Federal-State system which is desired (if such a system is preferred over an exclusively national system) is less urgent. If the committee, however, has decided preferences as between the subsidy plan and the Wagner-Lewis plan, it will facilitate the work of the staff and the technical board if this question also is promptly decided.

Submitted in behalf of the executive committee.

Edwin E. Witte
Executive Director

The preceding memorandum was the main topic of discussion at the meeting of the Committee on Economic Security itself on November 9. That meeting finally settled that an exclusively federal system was out of the question, and it also favored, without settling, the Wagner-Lewis system over the subsidy plan. The President, in his speech to the National Committee on Economic Security on November 14, endorsed a federal-

state arrangement, although the conference itself voted in favor of an entirely federal system.

As has been seen, the staff and members of the Committee on Economic Security regarded unemployment as by far the most important issue before it. Yet the public continued to consider old-age problems as more pressing. The same presidential message referred to above was poorly received where it concerned old-age programs.

Presidential Address to National Conference on Economic Security
November 14, 1934*

I am glad to welcome you to the White House and to tell you that I am happy that there is so much interest in the problem of economic security. Last June I said that this winter we might well make a beginning in the great task of providing social insurance for the citizen and his family. I have not changed my opinion. I shall have recommendations on this subject to present to the incoming Congress.

Many details are still to be settled. The Committee on Economic Security was created to advise me on this matter. It will bring to me, not any preconceived views, but a mature judgment after careful study of the problem and after consultation with the Advisory Conference and the cooperating committees.

On some points it is possible to be definite. Unemployment insurance will be in the program. I am still of the opinion expressed in my message of June eighth that this part of social insurance should be a cooperative Federal-State undertaking. It is important that the Federal Government encourages States which are ready to take this progressive step. It is no less important that all unemployment insurance reserve funds be held and invested by the Federal Government, so that the use of these funds as a means of stabilization may be maintained in central management and employed on a national basis. Unemployment insurance must be set up with the purpose of decreasing rather than increasing unemployment. It is, of course, clear that because of their magnitude the investment and liquidation of reserve funds must be within control of the Government itself.

For the administration of insurance benefits, the States are the most logical units. At this stage, while unemployment insurance is still untried in this country and there is such a great diversity of opinion on many details, there is room for some degree of difference in methods, though not in principles. That would be impossible under an exclusively national system. And so I can say to you who have come from all parts of the country that not only will there have to be a Federal law on unemployment insurance, but

*3 *Public Papers and Addresses of Franklin D. Roosevelt, 1934*, p. 452.

State laws will also be needed. In January the great majority of the State Legislatures will convene, as well as Congress. You who are interested in seeing that unemployment insurance is established on a nationwide basis should make your plans accordingly.

We must not allow this type of insurance to become a dole through the mingling of insurance and relief. It is not charity. It must be financed by contributions, not taxes.

What I have said must not be understood as implying that we should do nothing further for the people now on relief. On the contrary, they must be our first concern. We must get them back into productive employment and as we do so we can bring them under the protection of the insurance system. Let us profit by the mistakes of foreign countries and keep out of unemployment insurance every element which is actuarially unsound.

There are other matters with which we must deal before we shall give adequate protection to the individual against the many economic hazards. Old age is at once the most certain, and for many people the most tragic of all hazards. There is no tragedy in growing old, but there is tragedy in growing old without means of support.

As Governor of New York, it was my pleasure to recommend passage of the Old-Age Pension Act which, I am told, is still generally regarded as the most liberal in the country. In approving the bill, I expressed my opinion that full solution of this problem is possible only on insurance principles. It takes so very much money to provide even a moderate pension for everybody, that when the funds are raised from taxation only a "means test" must necessarily be made a condition of the grant of pensions.

I do not know whether this is the time for any Federal legislation on old-age security. Organizations promoting fantastic schemes have aroused hopes which cannot possibly be fulfilled. Through their activities they have increased the difficulties of getting sound legislation; but I hope that in time we may be able to provide security for the aged—a sound and a uniform system which will provide true security.

There is also the problem of economic loss due to sickness—a very serious matter for many families with and without incomes, and therefore, an unfair burden upon the medical profession. Whether we come to this form of insurance soon or later on, I am confident that we can devise a system which will enhance and not hinder the remarkable progress which has been made and is being made in the practice of the professions of medicine and surgery in the United States.

In developing each component part of the broad program for economic security, we must not lose sight of the fact that there can be no security for the individual in the midst of general insecurity. Our first task is to get the economic system to function so that there will be a greater general security. Everything that we do with intent to increase the security of the individual will, I am confident, be a stimulus to recovery.

At this time, we are deciding on long-time objectives. We are developing a plan of administration into which can be fitted the various parts of the security program when it is timely to do so. We cannot work miracles or solve all our problems at once. What we can do is to lay a sound foundation on which we can build a structure to give a greater measure of safety and happiness to the individual than any we have ever known. In this task you can greatly help.

In retrospect the staff felt the National Conference was not a success. In its effort to engage the attention and support of as large a constituency as possible, it largely failed. But whereas the National Conference was an idea conceived by the Committee on Economic Security, the Advisory Council on Economic Security had been created in the original executive order. It held its first meeting on the following day, November 15, 1934. Although the council met for two days, once again it did not get further than unemployment insurance. It formed its own subcommittee on unemployment, which made oral reports to the Committee on Economic Security early in December. Some of its members revived once more the idea of a purely federal system.

In addition to the Advisory Council and Technical Board there were also a series of advisory committees, mainly in the health field (medical, public health, hospital, dental, child welfare, nursing). There was also the Advisory Committee on Public Employment and Public Assistance. This committee attempted to redress the overemphasis on unemployment insurance.

Informal Report of a Special Committee Advisory to the President's Committee on Economic Security
November 24, 1934

The Committee wishes to point out that the common social hazards which are present at all times but which become distorted in depression periods include, in addition to unemployment:

    (a) unemployability due to age, physical or mental disability or handicap, and occupational dislocation, and

    (b) lack of a wage earner, as found in broken families, widowhood, unattached children, etc.

Work provided by private industry or by the government through public works and emergency work programs would be the most effective methods of dealing with the problems of those without employment.

This Committee, however, believes that the social hazards to which millions of persons and families are subjected, are too varied and too complicated to make it safe to assume that work would remove the need for other security measures.

The FERA estimates that some member of the family is physically able to work in from 75 to 80 per cent of the families now on the relief rolls. This estimate is based on the number of families in which some member is physically able to work. The Committee believes that an allowance of another 20 to 25 per cent should be made, leaving from 40 to 50 per cent of the present number cared for, to be dealt with by other general or special measures. Health problems, the social and personal results of long continued unemployment, lack of adaptability to work available, and other problems would make it unsafe, the committee believes, to assume that a work program could, for a long time, absorb more than 60 to 50 per cent.

The second point which the Committee wishes to emphasize, is that the problems of these families and persons will not fall into well formed or easily recognized categories. If, for instance, the program included only old age pensions and mothers' assistance, the needs of a great bulk of the families would be left to the present relief system, the evils of which are well recognized. It is also true that mothers' assistance and old age pension systems usually require supplementary services of general or special relief agencies, because the operation of any categorical program requires simplification and clarification of issues of eligibility which result in waiting periods, disallowed claims, etc.

The Committee believes that it is of great importance that the federal government should lend its assistance to wiping out completely the poor law system of outdoor relief. A plan is advocated for a federal department or administration through which equalization funds would be administered to the states. This would be a powerful influence in building up state and local agencies which would be able in turn to do away with the evils of the present relief system. Strong state and local departments of public welfare well organized on a permanent rather than an emergency basis should be encouraged to provide assistance according to the varying needs of families and individuals in such a way as to apply the best known methods to counteract the demoralization and insecurity which result from the social hazards encountered. Such assistance should be adequate, timely, certain and well administered and the state and local administrations developed on a permanent basis should be encouraged to give most careful attention to the selection and training of qualified personnel.

Such was the tempo of the committee and its many satellites. But the committee itself was, in theory, to be guided chiefly by the Advisory Council. Meeting again on December 8 and 15, that council produced its report, rapidly followed by four supplementary reports, again raising major disagreements about unemployment insurance. Once more the staff apparently felt that the council had, on balance, been a failure.

Meanwhile, the Committee on Economic Security had also been meeting, holding its crucial drafting sessions two or three days before Christmas. An oral version of its report was given to the President by Secretary

Perkins on Christmas Eve, 1934. A final draft of the report was then pro-duced, revised at least twice, and presented to the President on January 15, 1935. Although the report was ultimately unanimous, there was consid-erable disharmony throughout the meetings. Secretary of Agriculture Henry Wallace still favored a solely federal system of unemployment in-surance. More crucial were the objections of Treasury Secretary, Henry Morgenthau, Jr. who preferred employee contributions in unemployment insurance and had severe reservations about the funding of the old-age insurance scheme. Both Wallace and Morgenthau were, however, ulti-mately persuaded to sign by Mrs. Perkins.

On January 16, there was an even more severe crisis. The President no-ticed that there would be a large deficit in the old-age insurance program, beginning in 1965. Roosevelt insisted that the program be changed and the relevant tables were omitted. (Hence although dated January 15 the report was in fact not delivered until January 17.)

Letter of Transmittal with the Report of the Committee on Economic Security
January 15, 1935

Dear Mr. President: In your message of June 8, 1934, to the Congress you directed attention to certain fundamental objectives in the great task of reconstruction; an indistinguishable and essential aspect of the immediate task of recovery. You stated, in language that we cannot improve upon:

> Our task of reconstruction does not require the creation of new and strange values. It is rather the finding of the way once more to known, but to some degree forgotten, ideals and values. If the means and details are in some instances new, the objectives are as permanent as human nature.
> Among our objectives I place the security of the men, women, and children of the Nation first.
> This security for the individual and for the family concerns itself primarily with three factors. People want decent homes to live in; they want to locate them where they can engage in productive work; and they want some safe-guard against misfortunes which cannot be wholly eliminated in this man-made world of ours.

Subsequent to this message you created, by Executive order, this Com-mittee on Economic Security to make recommendations to you on the third of the aspects of security which you outlined—that of safeguards "against misfortunes which cannot be wholly eliminated in this man-made world of ours."

In the brief time that has intervened, we have sought to analyze the haz-ards against which special measures of security are necesary, and have tried to bring to bear upon them the world experience with measures de-signed as safeguards against these hazards. We have analyzed all proposed safeguards of this kind which have received serious consideration in this country. On the basis of all these considerations, we have tried to formulate a program which will represent at least a substantial beginning toward the realization of the objective you presented.

We have had in our employ a small staff, which included some of the outstanding experts in this field. This staff has prepared many valuable studies giving the factual background, summarizing American and foreign experience, presenting actuarial calculations, and making detailed suggestions for legislation and administration.

We have also had the assistance of the Technical Board on Economic Security, provided for in your Executive order, and composed of 20 people in the Government service, who have special interest and knowledge in some or all aspects of the problem you directed us to study. The Technical Board, functioning as a group, through subcommittees, and as individuals, has aided the staff and the committee during the entire investigation. Many of the members have devoted much time to this work and have made very important contributions, indeed. Plus these, many other people in the Government service have unstintingly aided the committee with special problems on which their advice and assistance has been sought.

The Advisory Council on Economic Security, appointed by you and constituted of citizens outside of the Government service, representing employers, employees, and the general public, has assisted the committee in weighing the proposals developed by the staff and the Technical Board, and in arriving at a judgment as to their practicability. All members of the Council were people who have important private responsibilities, and many of them also other public duties, but they took time to come to Washington on four separate occasions for meetings extending over several days.

In addition to the Council, this committee found it advisable to create seven other advisory groups: A committee of actuarial consultants, a medical advisory board, a dental advisory committee, a hospital advisory committee, a public-health advisory committee, a child welfare committee, and an advisory committee on employment and relief. All of these committees have contributed suggestions which have been incorporated in this report. The medical advisory board, the dental advisory committee, and the hospital advisory committee are still continuing their consideration of health insurance, but joined with the public health advisory committee in endorsement of the program for extended public-health services which we recommend.

Finally, many hundreds of citizens and organization in all parts of the country have contributed ideas and suggestions. Three hundred interested citizens, representing practically every State, at their own expense, attended the National Conference on Economic Security, held in Washington on November 14, which was productive of many very good suggestions.

The responsibility for the recommendations we offer is our own. As was inevitable in view of the wide differences of opinion which prevail regarding the best methods of providing protection against the hazards leading to destitution and dependency, we could not accept all of the advice and suggestions offered, but it was distinctly helpful to have all points of view presented and considered.

To all who assisted us or offered suggestions, we are deeply grateful.

In this report we briefly sketch the need for additional safeguards against "the major hazards and vicissitudes of life." We also present recommendations for making a beginnning in the development of safeguards against these hazards, and with this report submit drafts of bills to give effect to these recommendations. We realize that some of the measures we recommend are experimental and, like nearly all pioneering legislation, will, in course of time, have to be extended and modified. They represent, however, our best judgment as to the steps which ought to be taken immediately toward the realization of what you termed in your recent message to the Congress "the ambition of the individual to obtain for him and his a proper security, a reasonable leisure, and a decent living throughout life."

Respectfully submitted.

> *Frances Perkins,*
> Secretary of Labor (Chairman).
> *Henry Morgenthau, Jr.,*
> Secretary of the Treasury.
> *Henry A. Wallace,*
> Secretary of Agriculture.
> *Harry L. Hopkins,*
> Federal Emergency Relief
> Administrator.

Report of the Committee on Economic Security
January 15, 1935

Need For Security

The need of the people of this country for "some safeguard against misfortunes which cannot be wholly eliminated in this man-made world of ours" is tragically apparent at this time, when 18,000,000 people, including children and aged, are dependent upon emergency relief for their subsistence and approximately 10,000,000 workers have no employment other than relief work. Many millions more have lost their entire savings, and there has occurred a very great decrease in earnings. The ravages of probably the worst depression of all time have been accentuated by greater urbanization, with the consequent total dependence of a majority of our people on their earnings in industry.

As progress is made toward recovery, this insecurity will be lessened, but it is not apparent that even in the "normal times" of the prosperous twenties, a large part of our population had little security. From the best estimates which are obtainable, it appears that in the years 1922 to 1929 there was an average unemployment of 8 percent among our industrial workers. In the best year of this period, the number of the unemployed averaged somewhat less than 1,500,000.

Unemployment is but one of many misfortunes which often result in destitution. In the slack year of 1933, 14,500 persons were fatally injured in American industry and 55,000 sustained some permanent injury. Nonindustrial accidents exacted a much greater toll. On the average, 2.25 percent of all industrial workers are at all times incapacitated from work by reason of illness. Each year above one-eighth of all workers suffer one or more illnesses which disable them for a week, and the percentage of the families in which some member is seriously ill is much greater. In urban families of low incomes, above one-fifth each year have expenditures for medical and related care of above $100 and many have sickness bills of above one-fourth and even one-half of their entire family income. A relatively small but not insignificant number of workers are each year prematurely invalided and 8 percent of all workers are physically handicapped. At least one-third of all our people, upon reaching old age, are dependent upon others for support. Less than 10 percent leave an estate upon death of sufficient size to be probated.

There is insecurity in every stage of life.

For the largest group, the people in middle years, who carry the burden of current production from which all must live, the hazards with which they are confronted threaten not only their own economic independence but the welfare of their dependents.

For those now old, insecurity is doubly tragic, because they are beyond the productive period. Old age comes to everyone who does not die prematurely and is a misfortune only if there is insufficient income to provide for the remaining years of life. With a rapidly increasing number and percentage of the aged, and the impairment and loss of savings, this country faces, in the next decades, an even greater old-age security problem than that with which it is already confronted.

For those at the other end of the life cycle—the children—dependence is normal, and security is best provided through their families. That security is often lacking. Not only do the children under 16 constitute above 40 percent of all people now on relief, as compared to 28 percent in the entire population, but at all times there are several millions in need of special measures of protection. Some of these need individual attention to restore, as fully as may be, lives already impaired. More of them—those who have been deprived of a father's support—need only financial aid which will make it possible for their mothers to continue to give them normal family care.

Most of the hazards against which safeguards must be provided are similar in that they involve loss of earnings. When earnings cease, dependency is not far off for a large percentage of our people. In 1929, at the peak of the stock-market boom, the average per capita income of all salaried employees at work was only $1,475. Eighteen million gainfully employed persons, constituting 44 percent of all those gainfully occupied, exclusive of farmers, had annual earnings of less than $1,000; 28,000,000 or nearly 70 percent, earnings of less than $1,500. Many people lived in straitened circumstances at the height of prosperity; a considerable number live in chronic want. Throughout the twenties, the number of people dependent upon private and public charity steadily increased.

With the depression, the scant margin of safety of many others has disappeared. The average earnings of all wage earners at work dropped from $1,475 in 1929 to $1,199 in 1932. Since then, there has been considerable recovery, but even for many who are fully employed there is no margin for contingencies.

The one almost all-embracing measure of security is an assured income. A program of economic security, as we vision it, must have as its primary aim the assurance of an adequate income to each human being in childhood, youth, middle age, or old age—in sickness or in health. It must provide safeguards against all of the hazards leading to destitution and dependency.

A piecemeal approach is dictated by practical considerations, but the broad objectives should never be forgotten. Whatever measures are deemed immediately expedient should be so designed that they can be embodied in the complete program which we must have ere long.

To delay until it is opportune to set up a complete program will probably mean holding up action until it is too late to act. A substantial beginning should be made now in the develoopment of the safeguards which are so manifestly needed for individual security. As stated in the message of June 8, these represent not "a change in values" but "rather a return to values lost in the course of our economic development and expension." "The road to these values is the way to progress." We will not "rest content until we have done our utmost to move forward on that road."

Summary Of Major Recommendations

In this report we discuss briefly all aspects of the problem of economic security for the individual. On many phases our studies enable us only to call attention to the importance of not neglecting these aspects of economic security and to give endorsement to measures and policies which have been or should be worked out in detail by other agencies of the Government.

Apart from these phases of a complete program for economic security with which we deal only sketchily, we present the following major recommendations:

Employment Assurance

Since most people must live by work, the first objective in a program of economic security must be maximum employment. As the major contribution of the Federal Government in providing a safeguard against unemployment we suggest employment assurance—the stimulation of private employment and the provision of public employment for those able-bodied workers whom industry cannot employ at a given time. Public-work programs are most necessary in periods of severe depression, but may be needed in normal times, as well, to help meet the problems of stranded communities and over-manned or declining industries. To avoid the evils of hastily planned emergency work, public employment should be planned in advance and coordinated with the construction and developmental policies of the Government and with the State and local public-works projects.

We regard work as preferable to other forms of relief where possible. While we favor unemployment compensation in cash, we believe that it should be provided for limited periods on a contractual basis and without governmental subsidies. Public funds should be devoted to providing work rather than to introduce a relief element into what should be strictly an insurance system.

Unemployment Compensation

Unemployment compensation, as we conceive it, is a front line of defense, especially valuable for those who are ordinarily steadily employed, but very beneficial also in maintaining purchasing power. While it will not directly benefit those now unemployed until they are reabsorbed in industry, it should be instituted at the earliest possible date to increase the security of all who are employed.

We believe that the States should administer unemployment compensation, assisted and guided by the Federal Government. We recommend as essential the imposition of a uniform pay-roll tax against which credits shall be allowed to industries in States that shall have passed unemployment compensation laws. Through such a uniform pay-roll tax it will be possible to remove the unfair competitive advantage that employers operating in States which have failed to adopt a compensation system enjoy over employers operating in States which give such protection to their wage earners.

We believe also that it is essential that the Federal Government assume responsibility for safeguarding, investing, and liquidating all reserve funds, in order that these reserves may be utilized to promote economic stability and to avoid dangers inherent in their uncontrolled investment and liquidation. We believe, further, that the Federal act should require high administrative standards, but should leave wide latitude to the States in other respects, as we deem experience very necessary with particular provisions of unemployment compensation laws in order to conclude what types are most practicable in this country.

Old-Age Security

To meet the problem of security for the aged we suggest as complementary measures noncontributory old-age pensions, compulsory contributory annuities, and voluntary contributory annuities, all to be applicable on retirement at age 65 or over.

Only noncontributory old-age pensions will meet the situation of those who are now old and have no means of support. Laws for the payment of old-age pensions on a needs basis are in force in more than half of all States and should be enacted everywhere. Because most of the dependent aged are now on relief lists and derive their support principally from the Federal Government and many of the States cannot assume the financial burden of pensions unaided, we recommend that the Federal Government pay one-half the cost of old-age pensions but not more than $15 per month for any individual.

The satisfactory way of providing for the old age of those now young is a contributory system of old-age annuities. This will enable younger workers, with matching contributions from their employers, to build up a more adequate old-age protection than it is possible to achieve with noncontributory pensions based upon a means test. To launch such a system we deem it necessary that workers who are now middle-aged or older and who, therefore, cannot in the few remaining years of their industrial life accumulate a substantial reserve be, nevertheless, paid reasonably adequate annuities upon retirement. These Government contributions to augment earned annuities may either take the form of assistance under old age pension laws on a more liberal basis than in the case of persons who have made no contributions or by a Government subsidy to the contributory annuity system itself. A portion of these particular annuities will come out of Government funds, but because receipts from contributions will in the early years greatly exceed annuity payments, it will not be necessary as a financial problem to have Government contributions until after the system has been in operation for 30 years. The combined contributory rate we recommend is 1 percent of pay roll to be divided equally between employers and employees, which is to be increased by 1 percent each 5 years, until the maximum of 5 percent is reached in 10 years.

There still remains, unprotected by either of the two above plans, professional and self-employed groups, many of whom face dependency in old age. Partially to meet their problem, we suggest the establishment of a voluntary Government annuity system, designed particularly for people of small incomes.

Security for Children

A large group of the children at present maintained by relief will not be aided by employment or unemployment compensation. There are the fatherless and other "young" families without a breadwinner. To meet the problems of the children in these families, no less than 45 States have enacted children's aid laws, generally called "mothers' pension laws." However, due to the present financial difficulty in which many States find themselves, far more of such children are on the relief lists than are in receipt of children's aid benefits. We are strongly of the opinion that these families should be differentiated from the permanent dependents and unemployables, and we believe that the children's aid plan is the method which will best care for their needs. We recommend Federal grants-in-aid on the basis of one-half the State and local expenditures for this purpose (one-third the entire cost).

We recommend also that the Federal Government give assistance to States in providing local services for the protection and care of homeless, neglected, and delinquent children and for child and maternal health services especially in rural areas. Special aid should be given toward meeting a part of the expenditures for transportation, hospitalization, and convalescent care of crippled and handicapped children, in order that those very necessary services may be extended for a large group of children whose only handicaps are physical.

Risks Arising Out of Ill Health

As a first measure for meeting the very serious problem of sickness in families with low income we recommend a Nation-wide preventive public-health program. It should be largely financed by State and local governments and administered by State and local health departments, the Federal Government to contribute financial and technical aid. The program contemplates (1) grants in aid to be allocated through State departments of health to local areas unable to finance public-health programs from State and local resources, (2) direct aid to States in the development of State health services and the training of personnel for State and local health work, and (3) additional personnel in the United States Public Health Service to investigate health problems of interstate or national concern.

The second major step we believe to be the application of the principles of insurance to this problem. We are not prepared at this time to make recommendations for a system of health insurance. We have enlisted the cooperation of advisory groups representing the medical and dental professions and hospital management in the development of a plan for health insurance which will be beneficial alike to the public and the professions concerned. We have asked these groups to complete their work by March 1, 1935, and expect to make a further report on this subject at that time or shortly thereafter. Elsewhere in our report we state principles on which our study of health insurance is proceeding, which indicate clearly that we contemplate no action that will not be quite as much in the interests of the members of the professions concerned as of the families with low incomes.

Conclusion

The program for economic security we suggest follows no single pattern. It is broader than social insurance and does not attempt merely to copy European methods. In placing primary emphasis on employment rather than unemployment compensation, we differ fundamentally from those who see social insurance as an all-sufficient program for economic security. We recommend wide application of the principles of social insurance, but not without deviation from European models. Where other measures seemed more appropriate to our background or present situation, we have not hesitated to recommend them in preference to the European practices. In doing so we have recommended the measures at this time which seemed best calculated under our American conditions to protect individuals in the years immediately ahead from hazards which plunge them into destitution and dependency. This, we believe, is in accord with the method of attaining the definite goal of the Government, social justice, which was outlined in the message of January 4, 1935. "We seek it through tested liberal traditions, through processes which retain all of the deep essentials of that republican form of government first given to a troubled world by the United States."

We realize that these measures we recommend will not give complete economic security. As outlined in the messages of June 8, 1934, and January 4, 1935, the safeguards to which this report relates represent but one of three major aspects of economic security for men, women, and children. Nor do we regard this report and our recommendations as exhaustive of the particular aspect which this committee was directed to study — "the major hazards and vicissitudes of life." A complete program of economic security "because of many lost years, will take many future years to fulfill."

The initial steps to bring this program into operation should be taken now. This program will involve considerable cost, but this is small as compared with the enormous cost of insecurity. The measures we suggest should result in the long run in material reduction in the cost to society of destitution and dependency, and we believe, will immediately be helpful in allaying those fears which open the door to unsound proposals. The program will promote social and industrial stability and will operate to enlarge and make steady a widely diffused purchasing power upon which depends the high American standard of living and the internal market for our mass production, industry, and agriculture.

THE ECONOMIC SECURITY BILL AND HEARINGS

Presidential Action

On January 17, 1935, the President sent his message to Congress, recommending legislation on economic security, and transmitting the report of the Committee on Economic Security.

Presidential Message of January 17, 1935 on Economic Security
(H. Doc. 81, 74th Cong., 1st Sess.)

To the Congress of the United States:

In addressing you on June 8, 1934, I summarized the main objectives of our American program. Among these was, and is, the security of the men, women, and children of the Nation against certain hazards and vicissitudes of life. This purpose is an essential part of our task. In my annual message to you I promised to submit a definite program of action. This I do in the form of a report to me by a Committee on Economic Security, appointed by me for the purpose of surveying the field and of recommending the basis of legislation.

I am gratified with the work of this Committee and of those who have helped it; the Technical Board on Economic Security drawn from various departments of the Government, and Advisory Council on Economic Security, consisting of informed and public-spirited private citizens and a number of other advisory groups, including a committee on actuarial consultants, a medical advisory board, a dental advisory committee, a hospital advisory committee, a public-health advisory committee, a child-welfare committee and an advisory committee on employment relief. All of those who participated in this notable task of planning this major legislative proposal are ready and willing, at any time, to consult with and assist in any way the appropriate congressional committees and members with respect to detailed aspects.

It is my best judgment that this legislation should be brought forward with a minimum of delay. Federal action is necessary to and conditioned upon the actions of States. Forty-four legislatures are meeting or will meet soon. In order that the necessary State action may be taken promptly it is important that the Federal Government proceed speedily.

The detailed report of the Committee sets forth a series of proposals that will appeal to the sound sense of the American people. It has not attempted the impossible nor has it failed to exercise sound caution and consideration of all of the factors concerned, the national credit, the rights and responsibilities of States, the capacity of industry to assume financial responsibilities and the fundamental necessity of proceeding in a manner that will merit the enthusiastic support of citizens of all sorts.

It is overwhelmingly important to avoid any danger of permanently discrediting the sound and necessary policy of Federal legislation for economic security by attempting to apply it on too ambitious a scale before actual experience has provided guidance for the permanently safe direction of such efforts. The place of such a fundamental in our future civilization is too precious to be jeopardized now by extravagant action. It is a sound idea—a sound ideal. Most of the other advanced countries of the world have already adopted it and their experience affords the knowledge that social insurance can be made a sound and workable project.

Three principles should be observed in legislation on this subject. In the first place, the system adopted, except for the money necessary to initiate it, should be self-sustaining in the sense that funds for the payment of insurance benefits should not come from the proceeds of general taxation. Second, excepting in old-age insurance, actual management should be left to the States subject to standards established by the Federal Government. Third, sound financial management of the funds and the reserves, and protection of the credit structure of the Nation should be assured by retaining Federal control over all funds through trustees in the Treasury of the United States.

At this time, I recommend the following types of legislation looking to economic security:

1. Unemployment compensation.
2. Old-age benefits, including compulsory and voluntary annuities.
3. Federal aid to dependent children through grants to States for the support of existing mother's pension systems and for services for the protection and care of homeless, neglected, dependent, and crippled children.
4. Additional Federal aid to State and local public-health agencies and the strengthening of the Federal Public Health Service. I am not at this time recommending the adoption of so-called "health insurance," although groups representing the medical profession are cooperating with the Federal Government in the further study of the subject and definite progress is being made.

With respect to unemployment compensation, I have concluded that the most practical proposal is the levy of a uniform Federal payroll tax, 90 percent of which should be allowed as an offset to employers contributing under a compulsory State unemployment compensation act. The purpose of this is to afford a requirement of a reasonably uniform character for all States cooperating with the Federal Government and to promote and encourage the passage of unemployment compensation laws in the States. The 10 percent not thus offset should be used to cover the costs of Federal and State administration of this broad system. Thus, States will largely administer unemployment compensation, assisted and guided by the Federal Government. An unemployment compensation system should be constructed in such a way as to afford every practicable aid and incentive toward the larger purpose of employment stabilization. This can be helped by the intelligent planning of both public and private employment. It also can be helped by correlating the system with public employment so that a person who has exhausted his benefits may be eligible for some form of public work as is recommended in this report. Moreover, in order to encourage the stabilization of private employment, Federal legislation should not foreclose the States from establishing means for inducing industries to afford an even greater stabilization of employment.

In the important field of security for our old people, it seems necessary to adopt three principles—first, noncontributory old-age pensions for those who are now too old to build up their own insurance; it is, of course, clear that for perhaps 30 years to come funds will have to be provided by the States and the Federal Government to meet these pensions. Second, compulsory contributory annuities which in time will establish a self-supporting system for those now young and for future generations. Third, voluntary contributory annuities by which individual initiative can increase the annual amounts received in old age. It is proposed that the Federal Government assume one-half of the cost of the old-age pension plan, which ought ultimately to be supplanted by self-supporting annuity plans.

The amount necessary at this time for the initiation of unemployment compensation, old-age security, children's aid, and the promotion of public health, as outlined in the report of the Committee on Economic Security, is approximately $100,000,000.

The establishment of sound means toward a greater future economic security of the American people is dictated by a prudent consideration of the hazards involved in our national life. No one can guarantee this country against the dangers of future depressions but we can reduce these dangers. We can eliminate many of the factors that cause economic depressions, and we can provide the means of mitigating their results. This plan for economic security is at once a measure of prevention and a method of alleviation.

We pay now for the dreadful consequence of economic insecurity—and dearly. This plan presents a more equitable and infinitely less expensive means of meeting these costs. We cannot afford to neglect the plain duty before us. I strongly recommend action to attain the objectives sought in this report.

Franklin D. Roosevelt

The White House
January 17, 1935

H.R. 4120

Already, by January 15, 1935, Thomas Eliot, the assistant solicitor in the Department of Labor, had drafted a bill. Indeed, he had been drafting throughout the previous three months, although the frequent changes in both the political climate and the views of the Committee on Economic Security, as well as the constitutional hurdles prevented a carefully drawn document.

Senator Robert F. Wagner (Dem., N.Y.) introduced the bill in the Senate and Representatives Robert L. Doughton (Dem., N.C.) (Chairman of Ways and Means) and David L. Lewis (Dem., Md.) (of the Wagner-Lewis Bill) introduced it in the House; the structure of H.R. 4120 became the basis of all subsequent income maintenance legislation. The first two titles established federal grants-in-aid for two categories of public assistance — old-age and aid to dependent children. Title III then established two forms of tax — an earnings tax and an employment excise tax (see also Title VI) clearly (although largely by implication) designed to fund old-age annuities (insurance) to be paid by, and unemployment insurance payments to be administered by, the Social Insurance Board (Title IV). The board was also authorized to sell old-age annuities (Title V). Later titles dealt with maternal and child health (Title VII), public health (Title VIII), and other matters basically outside the scope of this book.

Both titles I (OAA) and II (ADC) provided federal guidelines for state programs. These controls have remained the crux of federal-state battles in the area of income security. Even the definitional sections were to produce conflict in 1935 and in the following decades.

A Bill (H. R. 4120) to Alleviate the Hazards of Old Age, Unemployment, Illness and Dependency
74th Cong., 1st Sess. (1935)

*   *   *

Definition of Old-Age Assistance

Sec. 3. As used in this title, "old-age assistance" shall mean financial assistance assuring a reasonable subsistence compatible with decency and health to persons not less than sixty-five years of age who, at the time of receiving such financial assistance, are not inmates of public or other charitable institutions.

*   *   *

Definition of Dependent Children

Sec. 203. As used in this title, "dependent children" shall mean children under the age of sixteen in their own homes, in which there is no adult person, other than one needed to care for the child or children, who is able to work and provide the family with a reasonable subsistence compatible with decency and health.

But as well as definitions there were detailed criteria for state plans.

Approval of State Old-Age Plans

Sec. 4. A State plan for old-age assistance offered by the State authority for approval, shall be approved by the Administrator only if such plan —

(a) Is State-wide, includes substantial financial participation by the State, and, if administered by subdivisions of the State, is mandatory upon such subdivisions; and

(b) Establishes or designates a single State authority to administer or supervise the administration of the plan and insures methods of administration which are approved by the Administrator; and

(c) Grants to any person whose claim for assistance is denied the right to appeal to such State authority; and

(d) Provides that such State authority shall make full and complete reports to the Federal Emergency Relief Administration in accordance with rules and regulations to be prescribed by the Administrator; and

(e) Furnishes assistance at least great enough to provide, when added to the income of the aged recipient, a reasonable subsistence compatible with decency and health; and, whether or not it denies assistance to any aged persons, at least does not deny assistance to any person who

(1) Is a United States citizen; and

(2) Has resided in the State for five years or more within the ten years immediately preceding application for assistance; and

(3) Has an income which when joined with the income of such person's spouse, is inadequate to provide a reasonable subsistence compatible with decency and health; and

(4) Is sixty-five years of age or older: *Provided.* That until January 1, 1940, but not thereafter, assistance may be denied to otherwise eligible persons who are less than seventy years of age; and

(f) Provides that so much of the sum paid as assistance to any aged recipient as represents the share of the United States Government in such assistance shall be a lien on the estate of the aged recipient which, upon his death, shall be enforced by the State, and that the net amount realized by the enforcement of such lien shall be deemed to be part of the State's allotment from the United States Government for the year in which such lien was enforced: *Provided,* That no such lien shall be enforced against any real estate of the recipient while it is occupied by the recipient's surviving spouse, if the latter is not more than fifteen years younger than the recipient, and does not marry again.

Similar provisions appeared in the ADC Title.

Approval of State Plans for aid to Dependent Children

Sec. 204. A State plan for aid to dependent children, offered by a State authority for approval, shall be approved by the Administrator only if such plan—

(a) Provides that not later than June 30, 1936, and thereafter, aid to dependent children shall be available, to persons in need of the same, in every political subdivision of the State, and that the State shall make substantial contributions to the payment thereof; and

(b) Provides that such State authority shall make full and complete reports to the Federal Emergency Relief Administration in accordance with rules and regulations to be prescribed by the Administrator; and

(c) Furnishes assistance at least great enough to provide, when added to the income of the family, a reasonable subsistence compatible with decency and health; and

(d) Establishes or designates a single State agency, to administer or supervise the administration of the plan and insures methods of administration and payment which are approved by the Administrator; and

(e) Does not impose a residence requirement, as a condition precedent to the granting of such aid, of longer than one year.

Both programs were to be under the FERA and the Administor had wide powers of control.

Sec. 6 (l) The Administrator may withdraw his approval of a State plan, if after his approval thereof such plan fails to comply with the conditions specified in section 3 of this Act. In case of such withdrawal of approval, the Administrator shall notify the State authority of his action and the reasons therefor, and shall notify the Secretary of the Treasury to withhold payments to such State.

The appropriations for the first fiscal years were $50 million for OAA and $25 million for ADC. Authorizations for later years were $125 million *and $25 million respectively, and from the first a formula emerged. In OAA Section 7 provided:*

That no such installment shall exceed one-half of the amounts expended in such State, in the quarter immediately preceding the payment of such installment for the payment of old-age assistance, nor shall it exceed $15 a month per person, and for the administration of the State plan, up to 5 per centum of the total amount expended under such plan in such quarter.

For ADC the arrangement was rather different.

Sec. 206. (a) The Administrator shall compute annually the amount to be allotted to such State at a sum equal to one-third of the amount reported under section 204 (a). If the sum of all allotments under this paragraph be in excess of the appropriations for the purpose, then the allotment to each State shall be diminished to that percentage which the appropriations bear to the sum of all such allotments.

In the OAI titles, the other leading concepts which have survived to this day were emerging. Already the "average monthly wage" was the basis of computation, with the annuity formula worked out in terms of such a concept. But at least at this time the concept was a relatively simple one.

Sec. 405 (5) As used in this section "average monthly wage" shall mean the total amount of wages upon which taxes were paid under section 301 of this Act on behalf of the employee and prior to his attaining the age of sixty-five years, such amount to be divided by the number of months in which such taxes were paid, except that such average monthly wage shall not exceed $150. For the purpose of calculating the average monthly wage, the Social Insurance Board shall adjust the various lengths of the periods for which wages were paid to a monthly basis.

With respect to unemployment compensation, the Board could also demand certain standards of the state. Section 407 gives this power by insuring that:

Sec. 407 (1) All positions in the administration of the unemployment compensation law of such State are filled by persons appointed on a non-partisan basis, and selected on the basis of merit under rules and regulations prescribed or approved by the Board; and

(2) Administrative regulations and practices are reasonably calculated to insure full payment of unemployment compensation when due; and

(3) Unemployment compensation is paid as a matter of right and in accordance with the terms of the State unemployment compensation law to all

persons eligible thereto under such law, and that all persons whose claims for compensation are denied are given a fair hearing, before an impartial tribunal; and

(4) All such unemployment compensation is paid through public employment offices of the State; . . .

But while the Board collected all the 3 per cent employer tax for unemployment compensation, most of it was destined to stay but a short while in the fund because of the offset formula which had been devised. (Section 601 also included a formula for reducing the tax as the economy recovered.) Section 602 allowed 90 per cent of the federal tax to be omitted by way of a credit for contributions made to approved state unemployment funds. Moreover, Section 608 went further still and allowed an "additional credit allowance" where states met certain standards in their pooled fund, or, with appropriate safeguards, allowed special ratings to certain employers.

Structure of the Hearings

The House hearings began on January 21, 1935, and the Senate hearings the following day. The main Administration spokesman in both hearings was Dr. E. E. Witte, who was responsible both for outlining the bill and answering committee questions. His performance was workmanlike, if at times uninspiring. In the House hearings, the most persuasive of the Administration witnesses was Secretary Perkins—although normally she was not a favorite of Congressmen.

Economic Security Act
Hearings on H. R. 4120 before the House Ways and Means Committee
74th Cong., 1st Sess. (1935)
(p. 175)

Statement of Secretary of Labor Frances Perkins

Therefore this bill and this report which are before you, in covering all of these forms of social and economic disaster, have recognized that it is not possible at this time to recommend a 100 percent system which is guaranteed to be a panacea against every form of social insecurity.

We have felt that it was right and proper at this time to recommend to you the basic plan which could be built upon and expanded in the future if and when experience accumulated under these rather small but substantial, orderly and systematic methods, indicated that there should be an extension.

In other words, I think that our American way of thought, and the way of carrying on our Government's business, is to try a few procedures where they can be kept under close supervision and where the results can be annually reported upon to Congress and to State bodies, and to submit those for the scrutiny of the people, and to build only as we know that there is demand and need and successful experience to guide us.

As I say, we are therefore conscious that this program is not 100 percent perfect, but we are fully of the belief that it covers the major hazards—the major social and economic hazards in American life today— and that it will provide a substantial basis of security to the families in the low-income group and that it will furnish an experience out of which we can gradually develop whatever further activities and appropriations are needed.

In other words, we have been glad to be able to find a small and reasonable method to recommend to you, rather than to ask you to plunge into too large a program before it can be adequately canvassed.

In the Senate, political muscle was added to the Administration's proposals by Senator Wagner.

Economic Security Act
Hearings on S. 1130 before the Senate Finance Committee
74th Cong., 1st Sess. (1935)
(p. 1)

Senator Wagner.   Mr. Chairman and members of the committee: The center around which revolves all the political and economic thinking of our times is the depression of the past 5 years. Even when we infuse concrete facts with the touch of imagination that gives them life, we cannot count the cost of this calamity to the people of the United States. The huge sum of money that has been spent to provide relief and promote revival is a mere bagatelle compared to the $45,000,000,000 decline in our annual income. And even if some financial wizard could ferret out these losses in all their obscure ramifications, he could not measure the broken hopes, the ruined lives, and the aftermath of suffering that will be visited upon a large part of the next generation. You gentlemen know the truth so far as it can be known—for your hearings since 1929 have constituted a panorama of a nation's woes.

Happily, the forces making for recovery have now been set in motion. But our bitter experience has fastened attention upon three main problems that we must start to solve now if recovery is not to be built upon a bed of quicksand.

First, what must we do to set up safeguards for those millions who suffer privation and neglect during so-called "good times"? This may be called the problem of those disinherited by our economic system.

Secondly, what must we do to protect those who are destroyed by even the slight and short downward dips of the business cycle that may occur in the future despite our best efforts? This may be called the problem of those who live on a narrow margin of security.

Thirdly, and most important, what can human ingenuity do to prevent economic disorder in its most widespread and virulent forms from leading to national disaster? This may be called the problem of industrial stabilization.

With such general statements out of the way, the respective committees set to work to examine the provisions of the legislation in depth. And while the tripartite concept of income security was already established (social insurance for old age, a federal-state program for unemployment, and federal grants-in-aid for OAA and ADC), it is perhaps logical to look first at the two (in the bill, three) programs designed to grapple with the problem of old age.

The Problem of Old Age

The problem and the alternatives suggested are probably best seen from the testimony of Professor J. G. Brown of Princeton, who had been associated with the Committee on Economic Security. But, as usual, it was Dr. Witte who handled the details of the different programs. With respect to OAA, perhaps the most significant predictions were the probable cost of such a program.

House Hearings
(p. 87)

Statement of Dr. E. E. Witte

The costs will mount; that has been the experience everywhere. If you start with a pension system, you can expect that gradually people will rely more and more on the pensions.

Likewise, we have to contemplate that this depression has created a tremendous havoc with peoples' savings. The people that are now middle-aged or more, or at least many of them, are completely wiped out. They have only a short period of life in which they can make adequate provision for their old age. The situation that we are facing in the immediate future certainly is a great deal worse because of the depression that we have been in.

Then, again, these figures will mount because you have this constantly growing number of the aged. Actuarial estimates which contemplate that in time 50 percent of all the aged will qualify for pensions, and which contemplate that there will be an average grant of $25 a month, are to the effect that by 1980 the Federal part of the cost of the pensions, if not supplemented by a contributory system will be approximately $1,300,000,000.

Now, again those may be guesses. In European countries the figure of 50 percent is being approximated; 50 percent of the total number of aged depending upon the public for support. In England it is higher than 50 percent, and I think that we can take these figures, which are the best estimates that the most competent actuaries can make, allowing for a margin of safety, but whether we take them as gospel truth or not, I think it is very evident that the cost of the pensions will become a very large cost in years to come.

Let me repeat, too, that whether you enact pension laws or not, that cost is there. This growing number of old people will have to be supported by the generation then living, and whether you do it in the form of pensions or in some other way, there is no way of escaping that cost.

In the Senate there was the same concern about cost. Perhaps the most prophetic exchange came between Senator Thomas Gore and Dr. Witte.

Senate Hearings
(p. 85-86)

Senator Gore. Have you ever figured, Mr. Witte, whether or not these appropriations, the expenditures by the States on old-age pensions, are limited by the fact that when people in the State pay taxes they know they are paying taxes, and they have a check on it, but when the Federal Government enters into this scheme, then they have no check on who is paying the taxes, they think nobody is paying the taxes, that it is just bounty coming from Santa Claus, or somebody else, there is no check on that?

Mr. Witte. Senator, that is the double check that we have in this bill. The great protection of the Federal Government is that the States pay at least half the cost.

Senator Gore. Yes.

Mr. Witte. That is the double check. We feel that this will protect the Federal Treasury and that this is ample protection.

Senator Gore. On that point now, you estimate that the total expenditure will be $1,300,000,000 by the year 1980. Would you be surprised if it would reach that figure by 1950?

Mr. Witte. I would be greatly surprised.

Senator Gore. I hope that some curious historian will then check the record of this day.

But OAA (old-age pensions) were of course only one part of the protection to be provided to the elderly. The contributory scheme (OAI), then normally called the annuity program and now colloquially known as social security, was the second major prong of the attack. The political, practical and psychological basis of OAI was explained by Professor Brown.

House Hearings
(p. 241)

Statement of J. G. Brown

I would like to use my time to explain briefly the reasons why those of us on the staff of the Committee on Economic Security concerned in the formulation of the old-age security program arrived at certain more important principles later incorporated in the recommendations and the bill. I shall confine myself to the compulsory old-age insurance plan, the second plan, and that incorporated in title III and title IV of the bill. I will state the main reasons for our recommendations in outline form but shall be glad to elaborate on these reasons if you desire me to do so.

The use of the contributory-contractual principle:

1. A contributory-contractual plan uses the method of thrift to protect workers in their old age rather than needs-test relief which may in time discourage thrift.
2. It affords a facility for saving for old age which, provided by the Government itself, avoids the dangers of bank failures, of losses on securities and real estate, or of other means of investment or of hoarding.
3. It makes savings regular and automatic with a return as a matter of right, with compound interest in regular installments covering the precise period of need; that is, during old age.
4. It avoids the prospect of dependence on children or other relatives, who may themselves be in need, or on public relief subject to a needs test.
5. It provides not only the security of old-age protection but of an increasing estate available to dependents in case of death; that is the workers's own contributions as he goes through life gradually mount up to a small estate, a death benefit, you may call it, which is returnable with interest on death.

The provision for worker contributions:

1. By contributing, the individual worker establishes an earned contractual right to his annuity through his own thrift.
2. Worker contributions increase greatly the amount of the annuity which can be paid, in fact, under the recommendations practically double the amount of annuity which can be paid. This follows closely laws of other countries and is being increasingly done in private industry.
3. Through increasing the amount of the annuities, worker contributions encourage the displacement of superannuated workers and of minor children and women supporting dependent old persons from the labor market, with resulting increase in wages and earlier promotion.

4. Encourages the development of an adequate system of retirement annuities independent of employer control.
5. Encourages, through providing a more adequate system of retirement annuities, the employment of middle-aged workers, since the employer is no longer faced with the need to continue employment after 65 or to pay a higher rate of contribution under a private pension system on account of the increased age of the employee.

I feel, sir, that that is very important. We are facing a tremendous problem in the older worker. This plan, by so much as it relieves the employer of the obligation of continuing the employee after 65, or the obligation of building up contributions under a private pension scheme at a higher rate in those later years, by so much lessens the handicap of the older worker in getting a job. It is only one slight advantage, I admit, over against the physical factors, the speed of industry, and the demand of large industry for young men to be trained in their own plants, but it is still a factor in encouraging to some extent the employment of older workers.

Third, employer contributions.
1. Provides an automatic method of meeting the depreciation charges on the human factor cooperating in production similar to the usual accounting charges for depreciation of plant and equipment.

   Industry recognizes this. You have a large number of important and progressive companies already doing this at a relatively higher cost than is provided in this bill.
2. Makes uniform throughout industry a minimum cost of providing old-age security and protects the more liberal employer now providing pensions from the competition of the employer who otherwise fires the old person without a pension when superannuated. These progressive employers have gone ahead at very considerable cost and are now meeting the competition of many other plants which have done nothing to protect their employees against old age.
3. Spreads the cost of old-age protection uniformly over concerns that employ older workers and those that employ younger workers.

Mr. Litchfield, of the Goodyear Tire & Rubber Co., made that point very strongly, that the concerns that now continue to employ older workers are at a disadvantage compared with their competitors who hire younger workers at the prime of life and lay them off. The concerns employing older workers, naturally, are more inclined to protect them as they are the people who have to lay them off in old age, and they are the concerns who have developed pension plans; whereas other concerns hire younger workers and lay them off long before they are susceptible to pressure to have a pension plan.

Fourth, Government contributions:
1. The final security of any social insurance plan is the guarantee of

the Government. To buttress the guarantee of security there must be financial strength and the taxing power of Government.

2. There are limits to the reasonable use of employment and earnings taxes when used for a purpose benefiting the public as a whole. The payment of annuities larger than can be earned in the earlier years of the plan may well be considered a public benefit and has been so considered in practically every important foreign plan.

3. To avoid large reserves. If contribution rates are raised sharply in the early years of the plan, huge reserves accumulate. The problem of investing and liquidating these reserves may be far greater economically than that of a Federal subsidy in later years. If contribution rates are raised sharply in later years, the worker then contributing may receive on retirement scarcely more than a return of his own contributions, since the employers' contributions will have been used to pay back the amounts expended to supplement earlier annuities.

One of the most difficult problems in our consideration of these problems was to meet several variables. One variable is the size of the reserve. If that reserve is permitted to rise to the height of $75,-000,000,000 or $100,000,000,000, since you are bringing in the savings of millions upon millions of workers, you have a huge investment problem. But far more than merely the investment problem, you are diverting consumer purchasing power from people who always spend practically all of their money to consume — the workers — and putting it into capital goods, into the debt of the United States Government, which is naturally more likely to be used for capital goods, thereby diverting from use for consumer goods funds to be invested in capital goods. We feel from an economic point of view that this is dangerous. Therefore it has been the recommendation of the staff to keep down the size of the reserve under this plan.

4. The shifting of the incidence of the employment tax to the consumer, which may take place — that is, the employer's share of this tax may be shifted to the consumer over a period of time — may become in time a regressive tax that may well be supplemented by the use of funds drawn from a progressive income tax. The best time to draw upon other taxes would, however, be in the later years of the plan.

Fifth, the payment of larger annuities than are earned in the early years of the plan.

This plan involves 15-percent and 10-percent minimum annuity rates and the payment of annuities in excess of those earned in the early years of the plan.

Our reasons:

1. To obtain the social and economic advantages of contractual annu-

ities as soon as possible in order to secure the "lift" of self-sufficing and self-respecting old age in our time and not wait until Kingdom Come to obtain assured economic security for the aged.

2. To avoid the ridiculously low annuities involved in paying earned annuities only in the early years, which for a time might not warrant the nuisance and collection costs of the tax.

3. To secure the displacement of superannuated workers from the labor markets as soon as possible.

4. To hold down reserves.

I might say that the great majority of foreign countries — all of those we have studied, which includes every country having such a plan — do precisely this; and not only that, every private concern of which I have knowledge in starting an industrial pension plan has paid a larger pension to those middle-aged or now old than they could secure by their own contributions, matched by the employer.

Sixth, the maintenance of the lowest reserve compatible with the safe operation of the system.

1. To avoid the undue diversion of funds from the flow of consumer purchasing power on the one hand to capital investment on the other.

2. The accumulation of a large reserve may involve serious complications not only in Federal financing through the necessity of selling and repurchasing Federal obligations in huge amounts at unpropitious times but may affect adversely the capital market.

3. Large reserves may encourage demands for increased rates of benefit or unwise use of funds for other purposes.

   We are afraid that if this reserve should accumulate to 50 billion, 75 billion, or 100 billion, it would be a very natural demand on the part of those coming under the pension contracts to say, "with that huge sum, why cannot our benefits be increased?" It has happened in almost every policemen's and almost every firemen's pension plan in the country. You permit large reserves and the popular demand is for increased benefits.

4. The accumulation of large reserves may necessitate the reduction of other Federal taxes in order to create new obligations and thus for a time relieve the rich through taxes on lower incomes.

We certainly do not object to relieving taxes on anybody, but in this case it would be the accumulation of such a large reserve that the Government would have to begin to use those funds and reduce other taxes. In order to find a use for it, and to set up obligations against that use may require the reduction of other taxes.

Seventh, the gradual stepping up of contribution rates.

1. The gradual raising of the rates of contribution softens the impact of the new charge on both the employer who has no pension plan at present and the worker and allows time for readjustments.

2. To hold down the income into the fund until disbursements are sufficient to avoid the accumulation of large reserves.
3. A lower initial rate of contribution aids in the enforcement of the tax since coverage is secured and public support gained while the cost of the tax is small.

Eighth, enforcement of the taxes involved.

1. To the worker, the plan is in essence a method of savings with his employer matching his deposits. An interruption in his record reduces the annuity on retirement not merely by the amount of money unpaid but also by the reduction of the number of contribution weeks in his record. Every employed worker by so much has an interest in the enforcement of the tax and in reporting evasion on the part of the unscrupulous employer.
2. The use of a stamp book, especially in the case of smaller plants, improves enforcement since each employee can watch his savings accumulate and can note and report omissions.
3. The employer who evades the tax is not only defrauding the worker of his old-age pension but might be subject to fines and reimbursement of the tax at penalty rates to the credit of the employee.
4. The inclusion of domestic and farm labor, while socially desirable, may increase the problem of administering the plan at the outset.

These and many other aspects of the proposed contributory insurance program have been carefully considered. The reasons here marshalled are for your consideration. I know that I speak for the technical staff which aided in the development of the recommendations in expressing our desire to be of any help possible to the individual members of your committee or the committee as a whole in your study of the problem of old-age security.

His evidence was also revealing about demographic and biometric assumptions.

House Hearings
(p. 227–28)

I wish to point out that until a system of this sort is started, all calculations as to costs and expenditures, and hence all the fundamental data on which a sound decision can be made, are based on assumptions which are open to a large margin of error. It may be of some value to enumerate briefly the type of assumptions which have been necessary to arrive at the actuarial estimates which have been submitted to this committee. These estimates have been made by competent actuaries and have been subject to the scrutiny of the advisory board, whose professional competence is beyond question. Other actuaries would perhaps arrive at somewhat different results. It is only fair to these actuaries to say that they realize the calculations contain assumptions which may prove wide of the mark, and that they are of a fundamentally different kind from those which actuaries are called upon to make in connection with fixing premium rates and making valuations for private insurance companies.

First of all, these estimates involve a projection of the total future population. This projection was taken largely from the studies of population experts such as Drs. Thompson and Whelpton, of the Scripp Foundation for Population Research, and Dr. O. E. Baker, of the Department of Agriculture. It has been assumed that the population will rise gradually to 150 million in 1975 (?). On the basis of this first assumption age distributions have been projected on the basis of the 1930 census, with the assumption that the mortality among white males in the population in the period 1920–29 will apply to the whole population in the future. This makes some slight allowance for improved mortality. It has been assumed that initially the insured population would be about 33 million and would rise by 1980 to approximately 48 millions of persons. It has been further assumed that in the early years of operation of the system, 33 percent of the population 65 and over would qualify for annuities under it, and that this proportion would rise gradually to 60 percent. It has been assumed that the changes in salaries and wages by age would be such that the cost calculations could be based on the assumption that salaries remained constant. It has been further assumed that the net immigration would be 100,000 per year, distributed as to age according to immigration in recent years, and that survivorship of these immigrants could be determined on the basis of the same mortality table as was used in the other calculations. And finally it has been assumed that interest would be earned at the rate of 3 percent per annum on any accumulated funds. All allowance for shifts in and out of insured occupations is implicit in these foregoing assumptions.

The calculations which have been presented could not have been made at all without some assumption, implicit or otherwise, on all these points; and there will be no serious disagreement as to their reasonableness. In the absence of a system of old-age insurance which would yield data permitting specific measurements of each of the factors involved, no better estimate could be made 5 years from now. But until the system of old-age insurance yields its own data there can be no competent final determination of the financial foundations for this or any other scheme of old-age insurance. We can proceed as soundly today on measures of this sort as we can 1 year or 5 years or 10 years in the future.

On the issue of whether the government should add a share to the OAI fund, the most articulate witness was Mr. Murray Latimer of the Railroad Retirement Board.

House Hearings
(p. 225)

Statement of Murray Latimer

A further set of considerations relate to the problem of whether the Government should make contributions to the support of the old age insurance system. The dangers which such contributions involve are well known. There is perhaps too constant a temptation to regard the system as a bottomless well from which all may draw irrespective of their rights in the fund. There is apt to be encouragement for the payment of annuities which are unreasonably high relative to the incomes being received by that part of the population which is producing the national income. Too little attention is likely to be paid to keeping the payments made by future beneficiaries in reasonable line with the benefits which they will be entitled to receive. Discriminations are likely to arise between various classes of beneficiaries, based not on rights arising out of contributions, but on extraneous considerations. Continuity of policy may be influenced by changing political influences.

There are, however, weighty factors on the other side. High contributions on the part of the employees will tend to reduce standards of living, particularly among persons receiving relatively low pay. Contributions by employers may be passed on either in the form of higher prices for their products or low wages or greater unemployment. The accumulation of funds may tend to direct to an undesirable degree streams of purchasing power from consumers goods industries into capital goods industries. Assuming the funds which the Government would contribute to be raised by socially desirable forms of progressive taxation, these undesirable consequences of levies on employers and employees would be mitigated provided no great reserves would be built up. Progressive taxation has tended to grow in disfavor in recent years on the ground that it is an unreliable yielder of revenue in periods of depression. Such an objection has no great weight in connection with old-age insurance funds if adequate contingency reserves are maintained since temporary decreases in current income will not seriously endanger the operation of the fund. Given adequate experience on which calculations could be based, projections of expenditures can be made so far in advance that a firm basis of planning for the future can at all times be maintained with a higher degree of accuracy than in almost any other field.

But there are still further considerations which would justify a Government subsidy. The introduction of a system of old-age insurance will, as has already been pointed out, for a considerable period of years result in great savings as compared to a straight system of old-age pensions. On the basis of figures as to costs which have already been submitted to this committee in connection with the old-age provisions of title IV, and in connection with what the expenditures would be under title I without the old-age insurance, I have calculated that if the savings up to the year 1970 were set aside in a fund and accumulated at 3 percent interest, the total accumulation would be in excess of 10 billions of dollars. A similar saving would be made by the States. These savings deserve to be recognized in any consideration of the contributions of the Government to the old-age-insurance scheme.

I submit that it is the experience of the great majority of foreign countries that the Government must support in part the old-age insurance system, and this experience ought to be given considerable weight. The standard contained in the draft convention formulated by the international Labour Office, to which this Government has recently adhered, provides that "the public authority shall contribute to the financial resources of the benefits of insurance schemes covering employed persons in general and manual workers." This standard was adopted after a most exhaustive study by the International Labour Office and after a long period of discussion by representatives of governments, employers, and workers.

Again, it is generally conceded that a major factor in insecurity is the maldistribution of wealth and income. Social insurance may not only contribute directly toward the provision of security, but indirectly by assisting toward the elimination of these inequities. Finally, if it is true that the existence of a sound social insurance scheme is essential to the maintenance of social peace, then the state, whose chief mission is to maintain peace within the nation, should obviously contribute largely to the support of insurance.

But the President saw OAI as a self-supporting scheme. This became abundantly clear when the Secretary of the Treasury testified on what became known as the Morgenthau Amendment.

House Hearings
(p. 897)

Secretary Morgenthau: The chief suggestions that we should like to make in connection with the economic security bill are the following: (1) The substitution in the contributory old-age annuity system of a scale of contributory taxes and benefit payments that will facilitate the continued operation of the system on an adequate and sound financial basis, without imposing heavy burdens upon future generations. . . .

Old-Age Provisions

1. By inaugurating a national contributory old-age annuity system, the Federal Government is undertaking very heavy responsibilities extending

from year to year into the indefinite future. Under the modification that we shall suggest, as well as under the plan now incorporated in the economic security bill, the sums to be paid out each year in benefit payments will rise to more than $4,000,000,000. It is obvious that we must make sure now that the provisions incorporated in the bill will enable the Federal Government continuously to meet the heavy and recurring liabilities that will be imposed upon it.

2. Under the provisions now embodied in the economic security bill, the Federal Government is called upon to defray, out of its general revenues, not only one-half the cost of the Federal-State system of noncontributory old-age assistance, but also the cost of substantial unearned gratuities that are provided under the contributory system for persons who will retire during the next 40 years. The benefits provided for such persons will be substantially in excess of the contributions, plus interest, made in their behalf. Such excess benefit payments would be borrowed from current contributions to the fund and repaid with compound interest in subsequent years. In consequence, under the present bill, by 1980 and forever after, the cost of the contributory system to the Federal Government is estimated at $1,500,000,000 a year. This burden is in addition to a Federal cost estimated at $504,000,000 a year in 1980 and thereafter for the noncontributory system.

3. The alteration that we recommend will make it possible, without the imposition of onerous burdens upon the future, to provide annuities ranging from $22.50 to $82.50 per month for individuals whose monthly wages have averaged $150 or more; $15 to $55 for those whose monthly wages have averaged $100; and $7.50 to $27.50 for those whose monthly wages have averaged $50—the monthly annuities in each case varying with the number of years of contributions. This scale of benefits is the same as that now incorporated in the economic security bill for those who retire during the first 10 years. Our scale is somewhat smaller than that now incorporated in the bill for those who retire between 10 and 30 years after the system goes into effect; and our scale is distinctly higher thereafter. The aggregate benefit payments under the plan that we propose are substantially identical with those now incorporated in the bill, as may be seen in the appended tables. The small number of individuals who receive very modest annuities under the scale that we recommend would be eligible to have these supplemented under the noncontributory system, precisely as is the case under provisions now incorporated in the bill.

4. Any actuarial computations extending indefinitely into the future, such as are necessary for the establishment of a national contributory old-age annuity system, inevitably rest upon assumptions and forecasts that are subject to a very considerable margin of error. Subject to this acknowledged limitation, it is our opinion that the national contributory system can be launched and maintained on a sound financial basis by establishing the com-

bined rate of pay roll and earnings taxes at 2 percent for the first 3 years, 3 percent for the next 3 years, 4 percent for the third 3-year period, 5 percent for the fourth 3-year period, and 6 percent thereafter; in substitution for the rates now incorporated in the bill, which start at 1 percent and are increased by 1 percent at the end of each 5 years until a permanent level of 5 percent is reached at the end of 20 years.

5. A combined, contributory tax rate of 5 percent is the minimum that will permit the payment of adequate annuities and at the same time maintain the financial integrity of the system under both the present economic security provisions and under our proposed alteration. But a 5 percent rate can do this only if it is imposed from the start. Under the present provisions of the economic security bill, a 5-percent rate does not go into effect for 20 years. Hence, under the bill a heavy deficit is accumulated in the early years, and the small sums paid on behalf of individuals now middle-aged or over are kept so low as to be far out of keeping with the benefit payments scheduled for them upon retirement—despite the fact that the majority of such individuals will have means of their own. Under our proposal, the 6-percent rate that goes into effect at the end of 12 years will make up for the deficiency created by the low rates that will be in effect during the earlier years of the system.

6. Under our proposal, the Federal Government would guarantee an investment return of 3 percent on all receipts from the pay-roll and earnings taxes that were not currently disbursed in benefit payments. Such sums would be used progressively to replace the outstanding public debt with the new liability incurred by the Federal Government for old-age annuities. To the extent that the receipts from the old-age annuity taxes are used to buy out present and future holders of Government obligations, that part of the tax revenues that is now paid out to private bond holders will be available for old-age annuity benefits; thereby minimizing the net additional burdens upon the future. Such accumulations and public debt retirement will, of course, be relatively small during the first 10 years by reason of the low tax rates with which we propose that the system should be inaugurated.

7. It should be emphasized that the Federal Government, by inaugurating a national contributory old-age annuity system, is undertaking responsibilities of the first magnitude. Not only is it committed to paying a 3-percent return upon all collections in excess of curent benefit payments involved, but it is also diverting for the purpose of old-age security a very large fraction of its possible tax revenues. But we recommend this deliberately, in view of the outstanding importance of objective. We know, moreover, that, even in the absence of the well-considered legislation, we cannot avoid important financial outlays for the care of the aged. Students of our population trends tell us that the proportion of the aged and of the dependent aged in our population gives promise of increasing very materially in the course of the next few generations.

8. There are some who believe that we can meet this problem as we go by borrowing from the future to pay the costs. They are willing to incur the large and growing new liability for old-age annuities without effecting any compensating reductions in the outstanding public debt, reductions that could be represented by a reserve account in the Treasury. They would place all confidence in the taxing power of the future to meet the needs as they arose.

We do not share this view. We have already cited the fact that the aggregate benefit payments under our proposal, as under that of the economic security bill, will eventually exceed $4,000,000,000 a year. We cannot safely expect future generations to continue to divert such large sums to the support of the aged unless we lighten the burdens upon the future in other directions. If we fail to do this, the $4,000,000,000 a year will be a net additional burden. Such a burden might well jeopardize the continued operation of the system. If, on the other hand, we are able to reduce the necessary outlays of future generations in other directions, as by retiring a large part of the public debt, and by the provision of useful public works, we can look forward with far more assurance to the continued support of the system. This, then, is the purpose of our proposal. We desire to establish this system on such sound foundations that it can be continued indefinitely in the future; and, at the same time, to meet the highly desirable social objective of providing an adequate annuity without a means test to all eligible workers upon retirement.

9. We recognize that the incidence of the pay-roll and earnings taxes appears to be largely upon the mass of our population. But it should be emphasized that the effect of these taxes is to provide a substitute form of savings from which our workers will receive far greater and more assured benefits than from many other forms of savings now in existence. These taxes, in other words, will not be a net deduction from workers' incomes. They will release funds, as well as relieve anxiety, hitherto directed toward the universal problem of providing against one's old age.

10. Further, it is entirely possible that improvements in our revenue system may permit us in the course of time to reduce various taxes on consumption goods; and thereby to return to the mass of our population in this form what is taken from it in the form of pay-roll and earnings taxes.

11. Appended hereto are tables presenting the character of the tax rates, net total contributions after deduction for administrative expenses, estimated benefit payments, Federal contributions, and reserves, under both the national contributory old-age provisions as now incorporated in the economic security bill and under our proposed alteration.

The other important issue, which was pressed with respect to OAI, was coverage. Was it possible to include farmers and domestic servants? Should charitable organizations be compelled to join in? Might employers with good pension plans be entitled to get out? Typical of the disputes on the first question was an exchange between Representative Carl Vinson (Dem., Ga.) and Dr. Witte.

House Hearings
(p. 112)

Mr. Vinson. Referring to the persons domestically employed, assume that they would be excluded from the operation of the act; what effect would it have upon the cost to the Federal Government?

Mr. Witte. There are about 4 million persons engaged in domestic service in this country. It is a large group. It is a group of employees whose wages are small. Many of them will be in need when they reach age 65. It will materially increase the pension costs, but I cannot give you any definite figures.

Mr. Vinson. Have you any figure that approximates that cost?

Mr. Witte. They represent approximately 15 per cent of the total number of employees.

Mr. Vinson. I know, but I am not talking about the total number of employees, I am talking about the pay roll. They certainly do not represent 15 percent of the pay rolls.

Mr. Witte. No. The extra cost to the Government, if any, comes through the pensions.

Mr. Vinson. That is what I am trying to get at now. I take it that would be after age 65 in your added cost. In your judgment, or if you care to guess, what would be the average cost per annum if you would exclude those engaged in domestic employment from the operation of this bill?

Mr. Witte. Under this plan, there probably would be no added cost, because while there would be a larger cost toward the pensions, there would be a lesser cost toward the unearned annuities, which would probably cancel out.

Mr. Vinson. Then in regard to those casually employed, it occurs to me that almost any method we might adopt would be hard to administer so far as those who are casually employed are concerned. Would there be added costs eventually if the casually employed were excluded from the operation of the law?

Mr. Witte. I think in the long run practically none. Their contributions would be slight. They would never build up much of an annuity.

Mr. Vinson. What about that situation in respect of those employed in farm work?

Mr. Witte. Again, a large group of people, earning rather low incomes, many of whom will need assistance at age 65. But you cannot estimate the net cost in the end. I think that under the plan set forth, while there will be an additional pension cost, there will be that much less cost in the annuity.

Mr. Vinson. Do you think that in respect of those three classes, the domestically employed, the farmer, and the casually employed, the cost would substantially balance itself?

Mr. Witte. If you make the annuity system self-sustaining, there would be a lesser cost.

Mr. Vinson. Under the plan as suggested in this bill, what would be your judgment?

Mr. Witte. My judgment is that it would not make any great difference. If, in your judgment, you wish to exclude those costs initially, it will not materially affect the cost either way.

Mr. Hill. Just what class do you have in mind?

Mr. Vinson. The domestics, farmers, and the casually employed.

Do you not think it would tend to better administration and be particularly beneficial in respect of the removal of the nuisance feature if these three groups were excluded?

Mr. Witte. It certainly would be easier of administration initially, there is no question about that. On the other hand, if you wish to solve the problem permanently, you will probably bring them in at some later date. But initially certainly it would be much easier of administration.

Mr. Vinson. But when you say "to solve the problem permanently", do you have in your mind a self-sustaining plan?

Mr. Witte. Yes.

The various "charity" lobbies scarcely covered themselves with glory in their efforts to take their employers out of OAI. The representative of the American Council on Education, Dr. Cloyd H. Marvin, defended the universities' position.

Senate Hearings
(p. 1076)

[Universities are] dedicated in the service of mankind and not engaged directly or indirectly in carrying on their activities for profit and sympathize deeply with the broad humanitarian purposes of the President's social-security program embodied in what is styled the "Economic Security Act." They wish, however, to point out to the Senate committee that, perhaps through inadvertence, this bill departs from a century-old public policy of English and American law and fails to exempt from the taxes imposed by the act, institutions organized and operated exclusively for religious, educational, and charitable purposes. The purposes of this memorandum are not in any respect to place these institutions in opposition to the objects of the bill, but to point out as earnestly as possible to the committee that the historic conception of public policy mentioned above operates as strongly in respect of the taxes imposed by this act as it does in respect of all other taxes from which, for centuries, institutions of this character have been exempted.

The American Hospital Association took a similar line. (Senate Hearings, p. 421). But in the long run it was perhaps the demand that employees with "good" pension plans be allowed to opt out of OAI that was to cause the biggest fight. (Senate Hearings, p. 63)

The third and final part of the old-age program was the voluntary annuity system. It was described by Dr. Witte.

House Hearings
(p. 99)

Statement of Dr. E. E. Witte

The intent of voluntary annuities is to make available to people who cannot be brought under the compulsory system the opportunity to make their own provisions for old age. The compulsory system as conceived, takes in all employees, substantially all people who are employed, but that still leaves 40 percent of the gainfully employed people outside of the annuity system; it leaves the housewives, the farmers, and the tradesmen—large numbers of our people, outside entirely of the compulsory annuity system.

Following the example of Canada, which has had a voluntary annuity system for some years, this bill proposes that a voluntary annuity system shall be started simultaneously, without governmental subsidies whatsoever, and the only limitation shall be that the annuity shall not exceed $100 per month.

Title V follows the War Savings Certificate Act. The provisions are substantially the same as those which were found to be workable in the War Savings Act of war time.

The voluntary annuities contemplated can be in any amounts that the social insurance board prescribes. The intent is to make them available in small sums, on something like the same plan as the war savings certificates. There is no governmental contribution.

This has to be frankly stated, that the cost probably will not be appreciably less than insurance company annuities. There may be a saving in operation costs. On the other hand, the insurance companies figure higher interest earnings than 3 percent, which is all that we feel safe to figure on a governmental basis.

On the other hand, this will be a system adaptable to people of small means, just as the war-savings certificates were. Insurance companies are not in the field of selling annuities to the people that are buying their annuities by contributions of $1 a month or less; they are not in that field at all, and it is in that field that we believe there is a place for voluntary annuities by the Government, to enable people of small means who can not be brought under the compulsory system to come in and create their own provisions for old age.

Unemployment Compensation

While in retrospect unemployment compensation or insurance has seemed the least important of the three major divisions of social security, in 1935 it appeared as the most important, although the Economic Security Bill's program did nothing to cope with those currently out of work. Certainly, the program's structure generated the most controversy. Some favored an all-federal program, others a grant-in-aid program along the lines of OAA and ADC. Both unionists and the more enlightened employers—many employers were bitterly opposed to any form of unemployment insurance— would have preferred a grant-in-aid or subsidy program to the one in the bill. One such person was A.F. of L. president, William Green. (House Hearings, p. 387)

Aid to Dependent Children (ADC)

Aid to dependent children has become the most important part of the public assistance program included in the social security legislation, but the Administration clearly saw the program as existing on a very limited scale. (E.g., testimony of Miss Katharine F. Lenrott, Chief of the Children's Bureau, Senate Hearings, p. 337.) This view was supported by those academics who had studied the problem. Professor Abbott, for instance, saw it as a program for "nice families" and "nice children." (Senate Hearings, p. 494)

Aid to the Blind (AB)

As the bill went to Congress there was no reference to aid to the blind. But representatives of groups organized on behalf of the blind appeared, to ask for old-age pensions at fifty and additional funds to augment the inadequate aid provided by the states. (House Hearings, p. 726)

Federal Standards

While OAI was exclusively a federal program and unemployment compensation a program of federal-state cooperation, OAA and ADC (and by

*the time of the act, AB) were federal-state programs in the sense that the
states would be spending federal money. To what extent could the piper
call the tune with respect to those categories of public assistance? As
drafted, the bill gave considerable power to the administrator which did not
please the state commissioners of social welfare. Worse still, it made many
legislators very unhappy indeed.*

*On the other hand, some social welfare groups thought the federal require-
ments too strict—for very different reasons. The National Committee on
the Care of Transient and Homeless believed that to require the states to
have minimum residence requirements was to court disaster. Their study
concluded that a more comprehensive federal program for transients was
needed (the FERA had established one in August, 1933). Dr. Potter, the
representative of the committee, concluded that:*

House Hearings
(p. 528)

If we take the President at his word, that groups of this sort are to be
handled by the States and local communities as they were previously, we
go back to a system of handling that was of neglect, cruel, and sometimes
punitive to these individuals, because local communities, particularly since
the depression has become so long and so acute, feel that they have wanted
to maintain their own people and did not welcome at all the stranger, even
though the stranger came looking for work, which was a legitimate thing in
our American system.

Some claim his words were prophetic.
*From the political point of view, Miss Lenroot was asked the crucial
question.*

Senate Hearings
(p. 342)

The Chairman. What I am trying to get at is, if the majority of the opinion
of Congress should be that the Federal Government should make reasonable appropriations to the States to help out this situation, but different from
those who have provided this legislation, that they should be in a position
to dictate the character of treatment given and aid administered to the dependent children, then what would be your position, whether it would be
better to go ahead and make the allocations, if you could not get the full
loaf, to take part of the loaf, that would be your idea?
Miss Lenroot. I want to say in the first place that I am speaking only for
myself. Of course the administration of this bill is placed in the Federal

Emergency Relief Administration, at least temporarily, and I do not feel that I ought to speak for the Administration or for the Cabinet committee or anything of that kind as to what modifications might be made in the bill. I think really the Federal Emergency Relief Administration should be asked to speak to that point.

Speaking entirely personally, I feel that it would be a grave mistake to make a Federal appropriation without any power vested in the Federal Government to insure certain minimum standards of efficiency. I am not sure of just the language that would have to be put in, but I think there ought to be some indication; it might be somewhat more general in character.

But more likely, the hostility arose out of the southern politicians' urge to retain segregation. The NAACP and church groups had no doubt that this was the real issue. The testimony of Mr. G. E. Hayes of the Federal Council of Churches voices this opinion. (House Hearings, p. 600) NAACP representative C. H. Houston was even blunter.

Senate Hearings
(p. 641)

Statement of C. H. Houston

In the first place, the old-age-assistance program does not become operative in any State until the State has first accepted the act and established a State old-age authority and a State old-age plan satisfactory to the Federal administrator. When we look at the States which now have old-age pension laws according to the supplemental report of the President's committee, we note that there is not a single Southern State with such a program. And as practical statesmen you know the difficulties there will be in getting any substantial old-age-assistance plan through the legislature of any Southern State if Negroes are to benefit from it in any large measure. If the Southern States do pass old-age-assistance laws under such circumstances, it will be more than they have done for Negro education or Negro public health or any of the other public services which benefit the Negro masses.

Therefore the national association favors a strictly Federal old-age-assistance program either with direct benefits or with Federal grants in aid to the States, and such guaranties against discrimination which will insure that every American citizen shall receive his fair and equal share of the benefits according to his individual need.

Such a program is entirely feasible and eliminates certain bad features now present in the bill. As it now stands, the bill makes the old-age-assistance program the football of national politics. The power in a Federal administrator to approve or reject State plans is a tremendous weapon for political favor or political punishment. Further, the citizens of the States which have not accepted the old-age-assistance plans are taxed for the benefit of the States which have accepted.

From the point of view of the Negro it would be much easier to get fair enforcement of a Federal law than to get a really effective old-age assistance law passed by southern legislatures. There are lots of decent, fair-minded people in the South; but in many States it would be political suicide for them to advocate a State old-age assistance law giving Negroes substantial benefits in large numbers.

The Chairman. How much would you say the amount should be if the Federal Government itself contributed and none of the States had to contribute?

Mr. Houston. There would be two things that I would say. In the first place, we advocate that the old-age system and the old-age annuity be merged. I will explain why later. Under that merged plan we would say that if you had Federal grants-in-aid to the States, so that the States administered it, we would then say that the workers should not get any less than what he has actually paid in—that that should be the minimum. On the other hand, if you have benefits paid directly by the Federal Government to the individual, we would then say cut down the Federal minimum to such a point that it would not disturb conditions in any State, with the idea that the States could add increments that they wanted according to their resources and according to the social needs in the particular States.

Mr. Houston. I understand that; and I will give you our suggestion as to raising the revenues in just a second.

I was saying that at the present time so far as the attempt to get a State old-age assistance program through the Southern legislatures, and I called your attention to the fact that we know as well as anybody else that there are plenty of decent people down South, but we also know from experience, in the Scotsboro case and Judge Wharton, for example, that it is the same as political suicide to take an advanced stand on racial issues in many cases, and that it would be political suicide for some of these people to advocate a State old-age-assistance plan in which Negroes would benefit in any large numbers, and therefore it is going to be for us to obtain a better enforcement under a Federal law than it would be to get the Southern law with the same protection so far as the Negro workers are concerned.

Next, we oppose the residence requirements of the bill, requiring a residence of 5 years out of the last 10 within the States. The President's own Committee on Economic Security has stated that residence requirements presuppose a degree of security and permanence of employment which has been conspicuously lacking in our skilled workers, whose labor is frequently of a highly migratory order. (Mimeographed release no. 3834, Old Age Pensions.) It is, of course, in the ranks of these unskilled workers that the need for old-age assistance is greatest, and it is the cruelest kind of an illusion to dangle in front of them an old-age-assistance provision, and then say they have to starve in one State 5 years out of 10 before they get it.

And lest the committees believe I am overdrawing the picture, let me refer to the report by our A. A. A. investigation of a survey of cotton regions west of Memphis, filed with the A. A. A. just 2 days ago. The investigator reported evicted tenant-farmer families straggling along highways, wandering hopelessly in search of shelter and employment; rough-boarded shacks in muck-mired fields, with gaping walls open to the winter winds; evicted Negroes standing in the road not knowing where to turn for succor. To say that these people must remain in a State for 5 years in order to qualify for old-age assistance is the height of injustice, and a virtual return to slavery.

Under a wholly Federal old-age assistance plan with direct benefits or with grants-in-aid to the State there would not be any necessity of a State residence requirement. If any residence requirement should be invoked, it should only be a national residential requirement.

If you have to have any residence requirement whatsoever, it would be sufficient to establish a national residence requirement.

*   *   *

As to title II, aid to fatherless, dependent children; and title VII, maternal and child health: We make a special plea that guaranties of no discrimination be written into the bill. The matter of Negro health is a concern not only of the Negro but to every white person he comes in contact with. You know from conditions in the South, where Negroes are used in the home and where they are in constant contact with the white population, that Negro health is a matter of concern to the white population itself, and we urge that it be written into the bill that, in those States which provide for the separation of the races in public places and under public institutions, fair and adequate provisions be made for them in institutions and personnel administration.

It appeared that Mr. Hayes' qualms were at least partially justified, or so one would think from the testimony of Virginia Representative Howard W. Smith.

House Hearings
(p. 974)

Statement of Representative Howard W. Smith

I think there ought to be a further provision in that bill. I think there ought to be a provision that would allow the States to differentiate between persons. Here is what I mean by that: The language of the bill authorizes somebody hereafter to be appointed in Washington to say that neither the State of Virginia nor any other State may participate in the benefits of this legislation unless they provide a pension at least great enough to provide a reasonable subsistence compatible with decency and health. That is a very broad term. It may mean a great many things. But it seems to me that it should allow the States to differentiate between persons in this way:

As we all know, $30 a month to one individual would be perhaps a mere pittance. To another individual who has lived in comparatively moderate circumstances, as they do in the rural districts, all his life, for 65 years, $30 a month would be affluence. You take the average laborer on the farm, let us say, all through the country districts, and his earning capacity on an average over the past times has been from $20 to $30 a month. To put him on a pension at 65 of $30 a month is not only going to take care of him, but a great many of his dependents, relatives, and so on, who could much better be employed working on a farm.

It perhaps may not meet with the approval of some of the folks who appear before this committee, but I think you are going to find with the States that this is a very practical proposition. I find that in my State the people are very sympathetic toward the proposition.

At the same time it would be unfair not to concede that at least some of the doubts raised were motivated by a genuine fear among the poorer states that they might not have enough money to comply with the requirements of "decency and health." Representative Wright Patman of Texas, supported by Representative Smith, thought that the Federal Government would have to assume the responsibility, at least for a limited period:

House Hearings
(p. 949)

Statement of Representative Wright Patman

This Government should not regard the boundary lines of States in dealing with or legislating for the benefit of its citizens coming within a designated class. If it is a gift, the grant should be made, insofar as the Federal Government is concerned, to every citizen alike who qualifies as to age and financial circumstances. This is equally true if it is considered as compensation, payment, or reward for services rendered.

The State of Arkansas is unable to provide additional taxes that will increase her revenues sufficiently to meet, in my judgment, to any substantial degree, the requirements contained in this bill. Approximately 75,000 citizens of my State are 65 years of age and older and would be eligible on that basis to share in the benefits of this laudable program. To raise adequate revenue for the State to be able to contribute $15 per month, in order to match the maximum amount allotted by the Government, it would be necessary by some form of taxation for Arkansas to increase her revenues $13,500,000 per year. This is impossible and exceeds the amount of the present State's revenues for all purposes. In order to provide $10 per month to match an equal amount by the Federal Government thereby providing for a pension of $20 per month for its citizens, her revenues would have to be increased $9,000,000 per annum, and so as to provide a pension of $10 per month for American citizens residing within her boundaries, it would require and increase of $4,500,000 per annum. This amount under prevailing conditions is likewise impossible.

The Arkansas Legislature is now in session and is having serious difficulty in finding a way to raise revenue to finance her public schools, nearly all of which are in extreme distress, and many of her charitable institutions are inadequately supported and provided for.

Under these circumstances, Arkansas cannot meet the responsibility this law imposes, and I am persuaded there are other States confronted with a similar situation, and whose citizens will derive no benefit whatever under the old-age security provisions of this measure.

Shall citizens of Arkansas and other States who are American citizens as well, be discriminated against in this fashion? Shall they be penalized because of the financial inability of their State to make an equal contribution? If so, the penalty is unjust and aggravates rather than relieves their misfortune and a righteous government should not inflict it.

In this program we are dealing not with property rights, but with human beings—with life itself, seeking to make it more secure and enable a class of our citizens to have and enjoy as they face the setting sun such comforts as humble necessities afford. Shall these benefits be offered and made possible to some and withheld and denied to others? Every principle of equity and justice forbids that such a policy be sanctioned.

If the Government is going to make a gift for the benefit of her citizens of a certain age who have no means of support or pay to them a merited compensation, it should be in the same proportion to every citizen who qualifies, irrespective of State boundaries or the political subdivision in which they reside.

In a national emergency American citizens are called on to make the same sacrifices irrespective of their State domicile. This is equally true with reference to supporting and maintaining the Government in time of peace. Let us not now discriminate against and penalize those of our citizens who may be so unfortunate as to reside in a State unable to match dollars with the National Government for this relief.

The Social Welfare Lobby

The hearings on the 1935 bill also witnessed the formation of the power groups which were to be generally known as the social welfare lobby. To classify them thus is perhaps unfair. They have never become as strong, for instance, as the employers' lobby on workmen's compensation. Nor is it fair to regard the operation as a monolith. Labor (at this point the A.F. of L.) lobbied strongly for the bill but was chiefly concerned with unemployment compensation. (The trade unions were later to have an increasing stake in old-age insurance.)

Similarly, some of the testimony came from social welfare organizations which had lobbied in the twenties and thirties for economic security. Perhaps the most famous was Abraham Epstein, executive secretary of the American Association for Social Security. While he had serious reservations about the unemployment compensation provisions in the bill, his basic reaction was ecstatic:

Senate Hearings
(p. 462)

Mr. Epstein. The bill before you, the omnibus bill, does represent to my mind and to any student of the problem, perhaps the most outstanding case of social legislation or any form of legislation that has ever been before Congress. I think we all ought to be grateful to the President for the courage and daring that he had to present a comprehensive message like he did. I would like to call your attention to the fact that no political leader in the history of the world ever really had the courage to present as comprehensive a program on this form of legislation as President Roosevelt did. Even Bismarck who stands out as the first leader in social insurance in Germany, adopted his program bit by bit and piecemeal. Lloyd George, who certainly did a remarkable job in England and was as daring and as courageous as anybody, never dared to embrace so many of these things at one time. And so I do feel that the President deserves the congratulations and the gratitude of all of the people who are interested in social welfare, for the mere courage and graciousness with which he has grasped the problem of seeing that after all this is a national problem and that it must be handled in this comprehensive manner.

Perhaps most significant for the future was the appearance of the social work lobby. While not a powerful lobby superficially, their professional concepts of the social worker strongly influenced the development of all social security programs. Since the programs were self-funding and did not require annual re-authorization, control passed to the professional social workers who naturally tended to favor the status quo. Already, as early as 1935, the American Association of Social Workers had given its imprimatur.

House Hearings
(p. 647)

Statement of Miss Dorothy Kahn, Philadelphia, Pa., representing the American Association of Social Workers

Mr. Chairman, in coming before this committee, the American Association of Social Workers desires to indicate its support of the general principles involved in this program. It believes that the bill in its intent affords a framework for economic security for people in whom we are interested, the like of which this country has never seen before.

We, of course, as social workers of the people who in the last analysis deal with the end results of insecurity, and so we think that we have a few things to contribute in connection with the details of this bill, that we would like to lay before you.

Their general approach was closely linked to future administration.

House Hearings
(p. 656)

Continued Federal aid to States for the purpose of helping the States to provide care for persons in need could be most appropriately given by grants-in-aid for general assistance programs of State and local governments, administered through a permanent bureau or department of the Federal Government, combining economically the administration of special grants-in-aid for particular classes of need, and providing a means through which collateral services of the Federal Government could cooperate most effectively in strengthening the Federal, State, and local programs to care for those in need.

The program of the Federal bureau should be broad enough to include the following:

(a) Old-age assistance grants-in-aid as provided in the security bill (S. 1130).

(b) Families and dependent children without breadwinners able to be employed in public or private employment. This would include the provision that is made for some of these families under title II of the security bill (S. 1130).

(c) Families whose wage earners, because of long periods of unemployment, have incurred disabilities due to physical disorders and mental strain.

(d) Those able to work but because of industrial dislocation or for other causes cannot be fitted into employment programs.

(e) Transient and homeless families and individuals who cannot be employed on a work program.

(f) The families, such as those now on relief rolls, who are on part-time nonrelief jobs but whose wages would need to be supplemented.

(g) Families and individuals in villages and semirural areas not accepted for rural rehabilitation and for whom no work program is available.

The county or regional assistance office would be the point of local administration served by a State public welfare department. Such a department would in turn be served by the Federal bureau.

Particular services to be performed might be the basis for divisions within the bureau, as follows:

(a) Division on family and child welfare: Through a field staff, this division would serve as the connecting link between Federal and State programs.

(b) Division of accounting, statistics, and research. This division would be responsible for providing national reports on the amount of assistance under various Federal appropriations, and responsible for collecting such data as was necessary for determining the amounts of grants-in-aid to the several States. The division would also be expected to develop a system of statistics concerning the extent of the problems and the functioning of the local, State, and national measures under which the various governments operated.

(c) Division on personnel and training: The character of public-assistance program would depend to a great extent upon the kind of persons employed to deal with those who were in need of assistance and with the administrators of the programs. In order that the personnel could be kept free from partisan politics and could be selected on a basis of qualifications which would assure the local administration being at the level of Federal standards, the division on personnel and training should be available to maintain standards of personnel selection and assist in the professional education of persons who would become eligible for positions in the assistance program. In view of the cooperative nature of the relationship between the Federal, State, and local programs, it is urged that the Federal Civil Service Commission be authorized to set the standards for the State and local merit selection of personnel.

The field staff of the Federal bureau would represent special provisions made by the Federal Government for any special categories of need, such as, old age, dependent children, and so forth, in relation to the State departments. The Federal bureau would be equipped with such specialists in the various kinds of public assistance as would be necessary and these specialists would work with the States through the general field staff. The operation of the bureau would be under a chief and an assistant chief in general charge of the various divisions and functions of the bureau.

The bureau should have, in addition to the authority to require certain standards regarding personnel to be employed by State and local governments, authority also to establish standards regarding adequacy of assistance and establish certain minimum policies regarding the functions of the Federal, State, and local assistance programs. In addition to its authority to allocate grants-in-aid from the Federal Government to the States, some provision for equalization should be included in its authorization in view of the varying degrees of need in the several States and the varying capacities of the States to meet these needs.

The Core Opposition

A large segment of the Republican Party was prepared to accept the Economic Security Bill, although no doubt most Republicans would have had reservations. To the extent that there was general opposition, it came from associations of manufacturers. The representative of the National Association of Manufacturers articulated the matter quite clearly.

Senate Hearings
(p. 940)

Statement of National Association of Manufacturers

Mr. Chairman, I may say that we have had a committee studying this problem for some time immediately this bill became public, and our association realizes, of course, that actual distress and indigency must be relieved.

To the extent that the pending bill, S. 1130, seeks to accomplish this objective we are in accord. But our universal deep desire to relieve immediate distress and indigency should not over-influence our judgment in discussing the present bill, which does not purport to be an emergency measure.

It is equally important that we do not accept proposals or methods as actually capable of accomplishing their objectives merely because advocates declare they will do so.

We must beware that we do not thus accept proposals which may possibly aggravate instead of relieve the evils they are designed to eradicate; that we do not create other serious problems as grave, if not even more so, than those we seek to correct.

We may, in this connection, profit by foreign experience, and be able to avoid their mistakes. We must, for example, use every effort to see that while actually providing sound security for aged indigents, we do not repeat the experiences of foreign old-age pension laws, where the possession of a legal right to pension funds has resulted in a universal tendency for a steadily increasing number and proportion of old persons to turn to the government pensions for support.

Legislation which from its very nature tends to increase dependency and indigency decreases individual energy and efficiency of individuals in attempting to take care of themselves. It would thereby decrease the sum total of national productive effort in the country, and in the long run thereby decrease the aggregate income available for distribution among the body of citizens; and hence inevitably lower the standard of living. Foreign experience and knowledge of economic matters should be sufficient to cause us to examine most seriously and carefully any type of legislation which carried with it any threat of decreasing productive activity with consequent impairment of our standard of living.

We must, likewise, use every possible care to see that in attempts to provide unemployment compensation we avoid, if possible, repeating the experience of foreign countries with unemployment insurance. In those countries the laws have actually tended to increase unemployment, by freezing or stabilizing such economic maladjustments as uneconomic wages rates, and maldistribution of both industries and workers.

I wish to reiterate the assertion made by the preceding speaker that the unemployment excise tax here proposed is a tax on employment—that every increase in wages, every job given an additional person, is penalized by being taxed. We must carefully consider whether such a tax on employment will decrease employment opportunities by penalizing those who provide employment.

Senators will recall that Mr. A. H. Hansen, chairman of the unemployment insurance subcommittee of the Economic Security Committee's technical board, stated (hearings, p. 452) that "the first immediate effect" of a pay-roll tax would be to decrease employment.

I respectfully suggest that you consider requesting submission to this committee of any technical report which may have been prepared, estimating the effect of a pay-roll tax upon the volume of employment which might be directly due to the tax itself.

We especially direct your attention to the following points, which will be amplified in the following remarks:

(1) The bill rejects the belief by President Roosevelt that the contributory pension system proposed should be actuarially sound;

(2) The bill rejects the belief by President Roosevelt that the unemployment-compensation system should provide for specific contributions by employees as well as employers;

(3) The Economic Security Committee rejected on at least 12 points, many of them important, the suggestions of its advisory council;

(4) The Economic Security Committee rejected the advice and judgment of its own actuaries;

(5) The bill should be carefully considered in the light of many fundamental changes it proposes in the relationship of citizens to the Federal Government;

(6) The bill raises questions of the utmost gravity as to both the raising and safeguarding of terrifically huge sums of money; and

(7) The bill in its present form is unacceptable because of numerous specific defects.

Local manufacturers were even more strongly opposed.

Senate Hearings
(p. 898)

Our principal concern in Connecticut is with the size of this load and its discouraging effect on private enterprise at a time when the forces of recovery have gotten such impetus that nothing can stop their progress—except a measure of this sort. The industrial employers of our State are concerned, of course, about the latent powers of Federal coercion that lie in the bill. We have gone far along the path of enlightened legislation for the protection of industrial workers, and when certain low-grade nomadic industries came over our borders a few years ago, and engaged in the premeditated practice of low wage and law evasion, the Manufacturers Association of Connecticut was in the vanguard of those who drafted and sponsored laws to cure the evil. We believe, therefore, that we have shown not only the disposition but the ability to handle such matters within our own borders, and we find it hard to stifle a feeling of disquiet when the Federal Government attempts to direct us along a path of action that our own legislators, closer to their constituencies and more familiar with our limitations, have not seen fit to launch upon as yet.

Beyond the employers were the extreme right-wing groups such as the Sentinels of the Republic, who saw the end of the United States in the legislation.

House Hearings
(p. 678)

Statement of Sentinels of the Republic

The proposed "social security" legislation, under which Congress, by so-called "Federal aid", will in effect subsidize or bribe the several States with the money of the taxpayers to adopt highly complex and experimental schemes of unemployment insurance, old-age pensions, help for mothers and infants, child welfare, and local public-health programs, presents in aggravated form the objections we long and successfully urged against less ambitious proposals and measures covering the same fields of purely local legislation. After a lengthy struggle we secured the repeal of the Sheppard-Towner Maternity Act, and we now are equally hostile to the principle therein embodied and now involved in the new program of social legislation. In a country so vast and diverse social reform can be wisely and successfully accomplished only by State or municipal legislation, which can easily be tested, repealed, or modified in accordance with local experience. Witness the successful abolition of child labor in industry by State laws, the adoption of workmen's compensation insurance in most of the industrial States, and the vast improvement in educational and public-health service, all under State legislation and administration and at the expense of the respective communities. The progress of social reform in the United States has been rapid and genuine under our system of community responsibility. It may easily become perverted by the meddling of an irresponsible directing bureaucracy. All these fields of State action involve private right and domestic problems, and were wisely withheld by the founders from Federal control. None of these matters involves recovery. The proposed Federal legislation is designed to be permanent, and if enacted will work a permanent and unwholesome dislocation of our scheme of government.

Congress has no power to legislate on these subjects. It can only, in fact, appropriate money for purposes for which it has no constitutional sanction to act at all. In so doing it will further weaken the sense of responsibility of the people, make confirmed beggars of our States and cities, and stimulate an unhealthy growth of doctrinaire schemes in place of the wholesome measures which an aroused public conscience will enact when the need becomes evident.

The Alternatives

While, in retrospect, the Social Security Act has dominated thinking about income security, in 1935 the Roosevelt legislation was significantly pressured by alternative schemes. Some economists would have preferred a thirty-hour week, but the serious political threats came from the Townsend Movement and the Lundeen Bill, introduced by Representative Ernest Lundeen of Minnesota.

The Townsend Movement—a strange revival of pseudo-populism—was an immensely powerful force in the country. While the Townsend bills went through various drafts, the only one extant during the hearings, the McGroarty Bill, was H.R. 3977 (January 16, 1935). The gist of the bill was in Sections 2 and 3.

A Bill (H. R. 3977) to Promote the General Welfare, to Assure Permanent Employment and Social Security, and to Stabilize Business Conditions
74th Cong., 1st Sess. (1935)

Sec. 2. That every citizen of the United States, sixty years of age and over, or who shall attain the age of sixty years after the passage of this Act, while actually residing in the United States, shall be entitled to receive, upon application and qualification, a pension in the sum of $200 per month during the life of the pensioner: *Provided,* That (a) the pensioner shall discontinue and refrain from all gainful competitive pursuits or salaried positions of any kind; (b) the pensioner shall covenant and agree that he or she will within thirty days of receipt of said pension expend all of the same for goods, commodities, or services within the jurisdiction of the United States; (c) proof of age and citizenship shall be according to the law and procedure of the State of residence of the pensioner; and (d) this pension shall be wholly exempt from attachment, garnishment, or execution.

Sec. 3. There is hereby levied a tax of 2 per centum on the gross dollar value of each business, commercial, and/or financial transaction done within the United States. The President of the United States is hereby empowered by Executive order to increase or decrease the 2 per centum tax by not more than 50 per centum, when in his discretion he deems it advisable, in order to adequately finance the said pension roll. This tax shall be levied in addition to any other Federal tax on goods or commodities. This tax so levied shall be paid by the seller once each calendar month, calculated on the seller's aggregate gross sales, in accordance with rules and regulations to be promulgated by the Secretary of the Treasury of the United States.

Dr. Witte, Secretary Perkins, and FERA Administrator Hopkins were all grilled about the Townsend plan. Eventually, on behalf of the Administration, Dr. Witte inserted a written defense.

House Hearings
(p. 896)

Final Appraisal of Townsend Plan

The Townsend advocates base practically their entire argument on the "revolving" feature of their plan. If there does not result from the plan a very great increase in incomes and in the money value of transactions, the promised pensions cannot possibly be paid for any length of time without wholesale inflation. The total income of all of the people of the United States in 1933 was only 46 billion dollars. The people who are over 69 years of age are less than 9 percent of the entire population of the country. The Townsend proposal, consequently, might be described as a plan under which more than half the national income is to be given to the less than 9 percent of the people who are over 60 years of age. Unless there is a very great increase in the national income, this could be done only through reducing the incomes of the people under 60 years of age by approximately one-half.

The Townsend advocates claim that such a result will not be produced because business will be enormously stimulated through placing such a large amount of money in the hands of the old people to spend within the month in which received. They say nothing about the fact that the people under 60 will have approximately the same amount less to spend, as they will have to pay in taxes the amount which the people over 60 will get in pensions.

The Townsend literature states that the United States Government would have to pay only the 2 billion dollars required for the first month's pensions and that the plan would thereafter be self-sustaining because it would create enough new business to return to the Government the entire pension costs, without burdening the taxpayers. As the rate of tax proposed is only 2 percent, it is manifest that the 2 billion dollars paid out in the first month would have to increase to 100 billion during that month, to justify the expectations of the Townsend advocates. The Townsend plan contemplates that pensioners shall spend their money within the month in which received — that is, that all of the pension money shall be turned over once during the month — but in order to produce sufficient revenue to pay the pensions of the second month, without burdening the people under 60, there must be 50 turnovers of the pension within the first month.

Even the Townsend advocates acknowledge that this is impossible, but they are reduced to the dilemma either of burdening the people under 60 with heavy taxes which will greatly reduce their incomes or of having the Government pay the pension costs for a much longer period than the first month. Since it is inconceivable that the people under 60 would submit to have their incomes reduced by one-half, the latter course is the only possibility. This will mean a rapid increase in the national dept and in effect pronounced inflation.

Through inflation it may be possible to keep up the pension payments for some time. The final result, however, cannot be in doubt. The inflation and duplicate taxation involved in the Townsend plan will cause prices to soar and soon, even with $200 per month, the pensioners will not be better off than they were before, while those below 60 will be immeasurably worse off. The Townsend plan is one which involves not only revolving pensions but revolving taxes. It is a plan which arouses great hopes but actually will give the old people little or nothing.

After this initial statement, Witte and his advisers were unimpressive in testimony; before the Senate committee Townsend was subject to severe cross-examination in connection with the political activists of the movement.

If the Townsend bills represented some form of right-wing radicalism, the Lundeen Bill represented a movement on the part of the radical left which was barely enthusiastic about the Economic Security Bill. Its spokes-

men claimed that of its three parts, two (unemployment compensation and OAI) could not be expected to have any effect until the "next" depression, and the third (OAA and ADC) perpetuated the system of outdoor relief. "The Workers' Unemployment, Old-Age, and Social Insurance Act," H. R. 2827, took a much broader step towards existing problems.

A Bill (H. R. 2827) to Provide for the Establishment of Unemployment, Old Age, and Social Insurance
74th Cong., 1st Sess. (1935)

*   *   *

Sec. 2. The Secretary of Labor is hereby authorized and directed to provide for the immediate establishment of a system of unemployment insurance for the purpose of providing compensation for all workers and farmers above eighteen years of age, unemployed through no fault of their own. Such compensation shall be equal to average local wages, but shall in no case be less than $10 per week, plus $3 for each dependent. Workers willing and able to do full-time work but unable to secure full-time employment shall be entitled to receive the difference between their earnings and the average local wages for full-time employment. The minimum compensation guaranteed by this Act shall be increased in conformity with rises in the cost of living. Such unemployment insurance shall be administered and controlled, and the minimum compensation shall be adjusted by workers and farmers under rules and regulations which shall be prescribed by the Secretary of Labor in conformity with the purposes and provisions of this Act through unemployment insurance commissions directly elected by members of workers' and farmers' organizations.

Sec. 3. The Secretary of Labor is hereby further authorized and directed to provide for the immediate establishment of other forms of social insurance for the purpose of providing compensation for all workers and farmers who are unable to work because of sickness, old age, maternity, industrial injury, or any other disability. Such compensation shall be the same as provided by section 2 of this Act for unemployment insurance and shall be administered in like manner. Compensation for disability because of maternity shall be paid to women during the period of eight weeks previous and eight weeks following childbirth.

Sec. 4. All moneys necessary to pay compensation guaranteed by this Act and the cost of establishing and maintaining the administration of this Act shall be paid by the Government of the United States. All such moneys are hereby appropriated out of all funds in the Treasury of the United States not otherwise appropriated. Further taxation necessary to provide funds for the purposes of this Act shall be levied on inheritances, gifts, and individual and corporation incomes of $5,000 a year and over. The benefits of this Act shall be extended to workers, whether they be industrial, agricultural, domestic, office, or professional workers, and to farmers, without discrimination because of age, sex, race, color, religious or political opinion or affiliation. No worker or farmer shall be disqualified from receiving the compensation guaranteed by this Act because of past participation in strikes, or refusal to work in place of strikers, or at less than average local or trade-union wages, or under unsafe or unsanitary conditions, or where hours are longer than the prevailing union standards of a particular trade or locality, or at an unreasonable distance from home.

The Lundeen Bill had supporters in Congress who gave it a forum. While the House Ways and Means Committee was holding hearings on the Economic Security Bill, the Labor Committee began hearings on the Lundeen Bill, which began with Lundeen's own justification for the approach of this bill.

Unemployment, Old Age, and Social Insurance
Hearings on H. R. 2827, H. R. 2829, H. R. 185, and H. R. 10
before a Subcommittee of the House Labor Committee
74th Cong., 1st Sess. (1935)
(p. 4,5)

Statement of Representative Ernest Lundeen

We much move forward along new lines. There are those who are greatly agitated about a new deal and who indulge in throwing stones at anything that would change the old order. Calling names will not accomplish anything. Constructive and progressive legislation is needed. If our old parties cannot meet the situation, they will be thrown aside like old and outworn garments. That has happened before in our history and it may happen again.

Adhere To American Principles

There is no necessity to strike down any great principles that have been laid down in our Declaration of Independence and in our Constitution. There is no necessity for hauling down the American flag and flying any other banner in our American skies. If we adhere to the fundamental principles laid down by Washington, Jefferson, Jackson, and Lincoln, and work along the lines laid down by our Revolutionary fathers and those who builded and saved the Nation, there is no limit to the progress we can make. Our Constitution is flexible, and our form of government is flexible, and our Supreme Court has shown that it is willing to adjust itself to the times, as shown in the Minnesota moratorium decision on mortgage foreclosures, recognizing then as that great Court does, our State and National emergencies.

The complacent, the self-satisfied, the smug and reactionary who refuse to move, would sit here in the midst of destitution and poverty, surrounded with an ocean of plenty — a spectacle of misery and lack of vision and planning to the outside world. There is no necessity for all this misery. America has solved every problem we have ever faced in all our history. We have never failed, and we are not going to fail now!

To those who say, "Where is the money coming from?" I say, the reports of our National Treasury show every bond issue many times oversubscribed. Billionaire fortunes exist, and millionaire salaries are still being paid in America today.

For years we have thrown huge sums into the laps of kings and emperors of Europe, and those of us who protested were brushed aside. I think we will somewhat delay our future expeditions and ventures to save the world. "He who will not first take care of his own is worse than an infidel."

When we return to the Americanism of Washington, Jefferson, Jackson, and Lincoln, we will conserve our immense financial reservoirs, and with vision, store food and finances for the evil day. Remember Joseph and the 7 fat years and the 7 lean years.

From now on, we are going to be just plain Americans. We have learned our lesson. We have drained the bitter cup. From now on, we have no time for those who want Uncle Sam to change to a European Santa Claus. From now on we are looking to red-blooded Americans who think in terms of America first.

The bill rapidly picked up the support of some of the more radical labor groups. Similar views were expressed by the Workers' Unemployed Union (House Hearings, p. 783) and the Communist Party proposed seven criteria for judging any legislation.

House Labor Subcommittee Hearings
(p. 1217)

Statement of Communist Party

Any proposed legislative enactment which claims to forward this aim of social security must be judged by the degree to which it embodies the following provisions:

1. It must maintain the living standards of the masses unimpaired. Anything less than this is not social security, but merely institutionalizing the insecurity, the degradation of the masses. It must provide for benefits equal to average normal wages, with a minimum below which no family is allowed to fall.

2. It must apply to all categories of useful citizens, all those who depend upon continued employment at wages for their livelihood.
3. Benefits must begin at once, when normal income is cut off, and continue until the worker has been reemployed in his normal capacity and reestablished his normal income.
4. The costs of social insurance must be paid out of the accumulated and current surplus of society, and not by further reducing the living standards of those still employed. That means that the financing of the insurance must come from taxation of incomes, beginning at approximately $5,000 per year, and sharply graduated upward, with further provisions for taxation of undistributed surpluses, gifts, inheritances, and so forth.
5. Social-insurance legislation must provide guarantees against being misued by discriminations against negroes, foreign-born, and the young workers never yet admitted into industry, and other groups habitually discriminated against within the existing social order.
6. Guaranties must be provided against the withholding of benefits from workers who have gone on strike against the worsening of their conditions, or to force workers to scab against strikers, or to force workers to leave their homes, or to work at places far removed from their homes.
7. Administration of insurance must be removed from the control of local political machines, to guarantee that the present scandalous use of relief funds to impress masses into support of the Democratic Party shall not be made permanent under pretext of "insurance"; this means, that administration must be through the elected representatives of the workers involved, making use of their existing mass organizations, relying upon democratic self-activity and organization.

There is no substitute, there is no way to avoid, the demand for full unemployment, old-age, and social insurance. Its denial will only accelerate the growing revolutionary mass unrest, intensify the social struggles. The Wagner-Lewis bill is a transparent attempt to sidetrack this demand. The new legislation against the Communist Party is only a futile attempt to silence the movement. Neither can succeed. Only the workers' unemployment, old-age, and social insurance bill can satisfy the aroused masses of the useful people, the working people, of the United States.

If some of this testimony could be dismissed as rather extreme, it was certainly not totally out of keeping with the temper of the times. The Labor Committee continued holdings its own hearings on the Lundeen Bill, and on March 15, H. R. 2827 was voted out 7 to 6.

THE BILL BECOMES AN ACT

The Committees in Executive Session

The hearings ended before the House Ways and Means Committee on February 12 and before the Senate Finance Committee on February 20. The Committee on Ways and Means immediately began executive session, redrafting the bill under the guidance of Mr. Beaman, the committee counsel. These deliberations were to have a permanent effect on the shape of the legislation. The thrust of these proceedings is summarized in a letter from Witte to Hopkins:

Letter of Edwin E. Witte to Harry Hopkins
(in National Archives)
February 26, 1935

I give you herewith, pursuant to your request, a brief statement of the changes which have tentatively been made in the Economic Security Bill by the House Ways and Means Committee, together with my reactions thereon. These several changes have been agreed to as a basis for a complete redraft of the bill, which will then again be considered by the Committee.

TITLE I—OLD-AGE ASSISTANCE.

In this Title the Committee has stricken out all administrative control from Washington. It has eliminated the requirement that pensions shall be paid in an amount which is adequate for "a reasonable subsistence compatible with decency and health". It has also transferred the administration of the Title to the Social Insurance Board.

The elimination of administrative control greatly weakens the bill but I doubt whether the Committee can be persuaded to restore these provisions. Members of the Committee consulted the President on these changes and reported that the President was agreeable to let the states determine what old-age pensions shall be paid, without any "dictation" from Washington.

I doubt whether it is wise to even raise the question of administrative control. I strongly feel, however, that it is desirable to amend further this Title to eliminate the $15.00 maximum per case which the Federal Government will pay under the bill as it now stands. Upon this matter I have written you a separate memorandum.

One amendment that has not yet been offered but which a member has told me he will offer when the redraft of the bill is discussed, is to the effect that the President may allot additional amounts for old-age assistance, beyond those which are matched, to states which are unable to provide adequate funds for old-age assistance. I would not be surprised if this amendment were adopted. A better suggestion, I believe, is your idea of a sliding scale for matching.

TITLE II – AID TO DEPENDENT CHILDREN.

In this Title the definition has been changed to make it absolutely certain that no aid will be paid for children taken care of in foster homes. This is an amendment desired by the Catholics and was stated by me to be acceptable.

The Committee adopted a maximum Federal grant of $6.00 for the first child and $4.00 for the second. This is a most illogical limitation, which will result in great havoc unless fundamentally altered. The allotment for the first child, of course, must also include the aid for the mother, so that there is a lower amount for the first two persons to be taken care of than for the additional members of the family. I do not see the necessity for any limitation whatsoever as the Federal Government pays only one- third of the cost. If there must be a per case limitation, there should either be an allotment of $6.00 additional for the mother or of $10.00 or $12.00 for the first child and $3.00 or $4.00 for the second and additional children.

The Committee eliminated nearly all administrative control and also transferred the administration of this Title from the Federal Emergency Relief Administrator to the Social Insurance Board.

TITLE III AND SECTION 405 – COMPULSORY ANNUITIES.

In this Title the Committee has tentatively adopted an exemption which excludes from the operation of this Title all agricultural workers, domestic servants employed in homes, and casual workers; also all educational, charitable and religious institutions and hospitals. These exclusions will take somewhere between 8,500,000 and 9,000,000 people who were covered in the original bill out of the scope of the act.

While these exemptions will take out approximately one-fourth of all persons covered in the original bill, I doubt whether the Committee will change its position on any of these exemptions. Attempts to compel them to do so may lead to votes against passage of the bill by some of the administrative members of the Committee.

The Committee adopted the so-called "Morgenthau Amendment", relating to contribution and benefit rates. Under this amendment the rates of contribution will be increased to an initial (combined) rate of 2 percent, which is to be increased by 1 percent each three years until it reaches a maximum of 6 percent in 1949 and thereafter. This is in lieu of the initial rate of 1 percent in the bill which is increased at five intervals until it reaches 5 percent in 1957 and thereafter. The effect of the change is to make the annuity system entirely self-supporting, while under the plan proposed in the bill, the Federal Government will have to make large contributions to this system after 1965. This amendment was submitted to the President prior to its presentation to the Committee by Secretary Morgenthau and was approved by him.

The Morgenthau Amendment also slightly changed the annuity benefit provisions in Section 405. The change made will give older workers the same annuities as in the original bill but avoids the gap between the temporary and permanent plan, which was pointed out in the New York Times and elsewhere immediately after the bill was introduced. The benefit schedule as proposed in the Morgenthau Amendment is entirely consistent.

TITLE IV – SOCIAL INSURANCE BOARD.

In this Title, relating to the Social Insurance Board, the major change was to make this Board an entirely independent agency. This action was taken by the almost unanimous vote of the Committee. It is very evident that this vote will not be reversed unless the president insists on the original provision.

In Section 402 (a), the Committee eliminated all reference to health insurance. It does not want the Social Insurance Board to even study this subject.

In Section 407, relating to allotments to states for unemployment compensation administration, the Committee completely struck out the requirement that the state employees connected with the administration of unemployment compensation shall be selected on a merit basis. It also weakened the administrative control of the Social Insurance Board in other respects.

The Committee tentatively agreed to the inclusion of an additional standard to the effect that the compensation payable to employees who work in more than one state shall be recoverable from the state in which the major part of their work was done but shall be based on their entire employment in all of the several states in which they worked.

TITLE V – VOLUNTARY ANNUITIES.

In this Title, the Committee has tentatively agreed to a complete revision prepared by attorneys of the Treasury Department. This involves no important changes in policy except that the administration is vested in the Secretary of the Treasury instead of the Social Insurance Board.

TITLE VI – UNEMPLOYMENT COMPENSATION.

In this Title, the Committee eliminated the provisions in Section 601 which make the payroll tax in the first two years dependent upon the index of production. Instead of a flexible scale, the Committee adopted a 1 percent rate for the year 1936, a 2 percent rate for 1937, and a 3 percent rate for 1938 and thereafter.

In Section 602, the Committee accepted a motion offered by the Chairman under which the taxes collected from each state shall be credited to that state if prior to January 1, 1938, it passes an acceptable unemployment compensation act. This amendment was adopted on the plea that many State Legislatures will have adjourned before Congress has passed this bill and will not again hold sessions until 1937.

In Section 606, the definition of "employer" was changed to exempt completely farm laborers, domestic servants employed in homes, employees of charitable, religious and educational institutions and hospitals, and all employees of employers employing less than 10 persons. In this connection, the Committee followed the provisions of the Wagner-Lewis Bill in the 73rd Congress. These exemptions eliminate about 3,500,000 employees from coverage (15% of the total). About 700,000 of these are employees on farms; about 200,000 domestic servants; and the balance employees in small establishments. The Committee may be willing to include employees in establishments employing six or more employees instead of ten or more, as now proposed, but will not reverse itself on agricultural workers or domestic servants.

In this Section, the Committee also increased the number of weeks during which an employer must have at least the minimum number of employees from thirteen to twenty. This amendment was adopted to exempt virtually all canning factories from the operations of the law.

The Committee completely struck out Section 608 of the bill providing for additional credit to employers who have built up adequate reserve funds under plant account systems or who have become entitled to lower rates of contribution under the merit rating provisions of pooled fund laws. The effect of this amendment is to eliminate largely the incentive for employers to maintain separate plant accounts. This amendment was adopted after extended discussion and the Committee is not likely to reverse its position thereon unless the President so insists.

TITLE VII — SECURITY FOR CHILDREN.

*   *   *

TITLE VIII — PUBLIC HEALTH.

*   *   *

As is apparent from the above, very little will be left of the original bill in the redraft to which the Committee has tentatively agreed. Most of the changes, however, do not go to fundamentals. The most serious are the changes relating to administration, in which the Committee has indicated its distrust of existing agencies and its strong objection to standards or discretion on the part of any Federal official.

The exemptions introduced in the old-age annuity and unemployment compensation parts of the bill leave many millions of workers without protection. On these exemptions, however, the Committee seems very set and it is doubtful whether it is wise to press the members to restore the original provisions.

The changes made in the Federal agencies which are to be charged with the administration of the several Titles of the bill seem to me to be illogical. If the original provisions are to be restored, the President will have to ask for such action as the Committee was practically unanimous in voting for these changes. Similarly, the desirable administrative control cannot be restored in any part of the bill without a specific request of the President, and perhaps not even then.

The limitation introduced in the amount of Federal grants-in-aid to dependent children is very bad and should be eliminated.

* * *

During the twenty executive hearings which the Ways and Means Committee held, the provision which aroused the greatest controversy was the old-age insurance provision. There was at one point a strong probability that OAI would be struck from the bill, but the precursor of OASDHI was saved by the Administration supporters' agreeing to remove the voluntary annuities. Overall the bill came out of the committee vastly altered. Even its name was changed from Economic Security to Social Security. But the Administration had reason to be pleased, for while the Beaman Bill looked very different the changes which were made had not altered the three-pronged structure of social security, although they had certainly weakened federal control.

With respect to OAI, there were several specific changes. A number of industries, such as shipping, agriculture, and domestic service were now excluded from the provisions of social security, in addition to the "arms of government" exclusion in the original bill. The bill had also been amended to cover only those who employed ten or more for twenty weeks of the taxable year (a change made primarily to exclude canneries), and all charitable organizations were excluded. The committee also changed the rate of the tax. Thus it was provided that the rate would be 1 per cent in 1936, 2 per cent in 1937, and would not reach the standard rate of 3 per cent until 1938. The committee also voted to make the Social Security Board an independent agency.

In unemployment insurance the committee eliminated the provisions allowing the states to give preferential treatment to firms with good employment records and reserves, as it was feared that such a provision might be unconstitutional. The committee also struck out the provision allowing an employer to have either a pooled-fund or an individual-employer account.

In the OAA Title, the committee's changes were chiefly aimed at weakening the federal standards. The bill, as reported out, allowed the states to impose any conditions they might wish with only the most basic exceptions. In addition, the methods by which the Administration might withdraw approval of state plans were made subject to various procedural safeguards.

With respect to OAI the committee version of the bill went even further than the Administration's and totally separated the tax provisions from the benefits provision. Indeed there was no mention of an old-age insurance fund; in its place the Treasury was to keep an old-age reserve account. There was also no reference to any contractual right to a benefit. Overall, the Ways and Means Committee did everything it could to escape from the appearance that OAI was in fact an insurance system. Partly for this reason the House committee struck out the requirement than an annuitant must retire in order to receive a benefit.

Ways and Means made considerable changes in ADC. Control was taken from the FERA and given to the Social Security Board. Most important of all, Congressman Vinson of Georgia put a monthly limit on the amount which the Federal Government could contribute—$6 for the first child and $4 for each succeeding child. The committee also rejected a suggestion that a new category of assistance be created—aid to the blind.

House Action

The bill was finally reported out of committee on April 5.

Economic Security Bill
House Report No. 615
74th Cong., 1st Sess.
(April 5, 1935)

Purpose and Scope

The need for legislation on the subject of social security is apparent at this time. On every hand the lack of such security is evidenced by human suffering, weakened morale, and increased public expenditures.

This situation necessitates two complementary courses of action: We must relieve the existing distress and should devise measures to reduce destitution and dependency in the future.

Thus far in the depression, we have merely attempted to relieve existing distress, but the time has come for a more comprehensive and constructive attack on insecurity. The foundations of such a program are laid in the present bill.

Work for the employables on relief is contemplated in the work-relief bill; a second vital part of the program for security is presented in this bill.

The bill is designed to aid the States in taking care of the dependent members of their population, and to make a beginning in the development of measures which will reduce dependency in the future. It deals with four major subjects: Old-age security, unemployment compensation, security for children, and public health. These subjects are all closely related, all being concerned with major causes of dependency. Together they constitute an important step in a well-rounded, unified, long-range program for social security.

Old-Age Security

There are now approximately 7,500,000 men and women over 65 years of age in the United States, and for decades the number and percentage of old people in the population have been increasing. This tendency is almost certain to continue throughout the century. Statisticians estimate that by 1970 there will be 15,000,000 people over 65 years of age and by the end of the century, about 19,000,000. In contrast with less than 6 percent of the entire population now over 65, more than 10 percent will fall in this age group in 1970, and above 12 percent by the end of the century. These, moreover, are minimum estimates, which may be greatly exceeded if cures are discovered for the major causes of death among old people.

*   *   *

Approximately 1,000,000 men and women over 65 years of age are dependent upon the public for support, the great majority of them on relief. This number is certain to increase in the future due to (1) the rapid increase of persons over 65 years of age, (2) the fact that many of the older workers now unemployed will never be steadily employed again, (3) the disappearance during the depression of the lifetime savings of many families approaching old age, and (4) the lessened ability of children to support their parents. The social problem of old age dependency, great as it is today, is certain to become more acute in the future unless adequate measures are taken now.

Experience, both in this country and in other lands, has demonstrated that the best way to provide for old people who are dependent upon the public for support is through old-age-assistance grants, more commonly called "old-age pensions." Twenty-nine States and the Territories of Alaska and Hawaii have old-age pension laws. Approximately 200,000 old people are now in receipt of old-age assistance under these laws, and while the grants are often inadequate, the lot of the pensioners is distinctly less hard than that of old people on relief. But due in part to restrictive provisions in the State laws, and still more to the financial embarrassment of many State and local governments, the old-age pension laws are limited in their application and do not provide adequately for all old people who are dependent upon the public for support.

To encourage States to adopt old-age pension laws and to help them carry the burden of providing support for their aged dependents, this bill proposes that the Federal government shall match the expenditures of the State and local governments for old-age pensions, except that the Federal share is not to exceed $15 per month per individual. A few standards are prescribed which the States must meet to entitle them to Federal aid, but these impose only reasonable conditions and leave the States free of arbitrary interference from Washington.

* * *

The provisions for Federal aid, included in title I, are designed for the support of people now old and dependent. They do not, however, furnish a completely satisfactory solution of the problem of old-age support, considered from a long-time point of view. If no other provisions are made, the cost of gratuitous old-age pensions is bound to increase very rapidly, due to the growing number of the aged and the probable increasing rate of dependency. Unless a Federal benefit system is provided, the cost of old-age pensions under title I, shared equally by the Federal Government and the States, would by 1960 amount annually to more than $2,000,000,000 and by 1980 to nearly $2,600,000,000, on the basis of an average monthly pension of $25.

To keep the cost of Federal-aided State pensions under title I from becoming extremely burdensome in future years, and to assure support for the aged as a right rather than as public charity, and in amounts which will insure not merely subsistence but some of the comforts of life, title II of the bill establishes a system of old-age benefits, paid out of the Federal Treasury, and administered directly by the Federal Government. The benefits provided for workers who have been employed during substantially all their working life, will probably be considerably larger than any Federal-aided State pensions could be. The benefits to be paid are related to the wages earned, but there are adjustments favoring the lower paid employees and those approaching old age. The minimum monthly benefit payable is $10, and the maximum is $85. An employee whose total wages, as defined in the act, prior to the age of 65 amount to less than $2,000 will not qualify for benefits, but he will receive 3½ percent of his wages in a lump sum at the age of 65. He may be eligible also for a Federal-aided State pension under title I.

The establishment of the Federal old-age benefit system will materially reduce the cost of Federal-aided State pensions under title I in future years. It will not entirely replace that system, because not all persons will be under the Federal old-age benefit plan. It will operate, however, to reduce the total cost of old-age pensions under title I to the Federal and State Governments in the future by more than $1,000,000,000 annually.

It is important to note that by the investment of the large reserve on hand in the old-age reserve account, the Treasury will be able to withdraw

Illustrative monthly Federal old-age benefits under title II

Average monthly salary	Years of employment								
	5	10	15	20	25	30	35	40	45
$25...........	(¹)	$15.00	$16.25	$17.50	$18.75	$20.00	$21.25	$22.50	$23.75
$50...........	$15.00	17.50	20.00	22.50	25.00	27.50	30.00	32.50	35.00
$75...........	16.25	20.00	23.75	27.50	31.25	35.00	38.75	42.50	46.25
$100..........	17.50	22.50	27.50	32.50	37.50	42.50	47.50	51.25	53.75
$125..........	18.75	25.00	31.25	37.50	43.75	50.00	53.13	56.25	59.38
$150..........	20.00	27.50	35.00	42.50	50.00	53.75	57.50	61.25	65.00
$175..........	21.25	30.00	38.75	47.50	53.13	57.50	61.88	66.25	70.63
$200..........	22.50	32.50	42.50	51.25	56.25	61.25	66.25	71.25	76.23
$225..........	23.75	35.00	46.25	53.75	59.38	65.00	70.63	76.25	81.88
$250..........	25.00	37.50	50.00	56.25	62.50	68.75	75.00	81.25	85.00

¹ Lump sum payment of $52.50.

Estimated appropriations, benefit payments, and reserves under title II
[In millions of dollars.]

Fiscal year ending June 30—	Appropriation	Interest on reserve	Benefit payments	Amount carried forward to reserve	Reserve
1937....................	255.5	0.0	1.8	253.6	253.6
1938....................	513.5	7.6	7.2	514.0	767.6
1939....................	518.5	23.0	14.4	526.9	1,294.5
1940....................	662.2	38.8	22.0	679.1	1,973.6
1941....................	807.2	59.2	29.7	836.7	2,810.3
1942....................	814.8	84.4	60.4	838.7	3,649.0
1943....................	970.0	109.5	114.2	965.3	4,614.3
1944....................	1,126.6	138.5	173.1	1,091.9	5,706.2
1945....................	1,137.0	171.2	231.4	1,076.4	6,782.6
1946....................	1,291.0	203.5	302.0	1,192.9	7,975.5
1947....................	1,447.1	239.3	381.2	1,305.2	9,280.7
1948....................	1,460.1	278.5	457.5	1,281.1	10,561.8
1949....................	1,621.0	316.8	535.8	1,402.1	11,963.9
1950....................	1,783.3	358.9	612.6	1,529.6	13,493.5
1955....................	1,861.3	579.3	1,076.0	1,364.5	20,672.6
1960....................	1,939.1	765.6	1,672.7	1,032.0	26,551.8
1965....................	2,016.9	896.0	2,235.1	677.8	30,543.8
1970....................	2,094.8	975.2	2,792.1	277.9	32,782.9

from the market outstanding Federal bonds and hold them in the account. Their withdrawal will prevent the loss in income-tax receipts, which is now annually incurred due to the presence of these tax-exempt bonds in the hands of private owners.

Unemployment Compensation

Unemployment is an even more prevalent cause of dependency than old age; in fact, it is the most serious of all hazards confronting industrial workers. During the years 1922 to 1929 an average of 8 percent of the industrial workers in this country were unemployed, and in the four depression years, 1930 to 1933, the unemployment rate was above 25 percent. Of all urban families now on relief, more than four-fifths are destitute because of unemployment.

Unemployment is due to many causes and there is no one safeguard that is all-sufficient. It can be dealt with in a reasonably adequate fashion only through a twofold approach, similar to that recommended for dealing with the old-age problem. Provisions must be made for the relief of those now unemployed, and there should also be devised a method for dealing with the unemployment problem in a less costly and more intelligent way in future years. It should be clearly understood that State unemployment compensation plans made possible by this bill cannot take care of the present problem of unemployment. They will be designed rather to afford security against the large bulk of unemployment in the future.

For those now unemployed the best measure of protection is to give them employment, as is contemplated in the work-relief bill. To provide something better than relief on a needs basis for the unemployed of the future, the establishment by the States of unemployment compensation systems is urgently to be desired. Titles III and IX seek to encourage States to set up such systems and to keep them from being handicapped if they do so.

The essential idea in unemployment compensation, more commonly but less accurately called "unemployment insurance" is the accumulation of reserves in times of employment from which partial compensation may be paid to workers who become unemployed and are unable to find other work. Unemployment insurance cannot give complete and unlimited compensation to all who are unemployed. Any attempt to make it do so confuses unemployment insurance with relief, which it is designed to replace in large part. It can give compensation only for a limited period and for a percentage of the wage loss.

Unemployment compensation, nevertheless, is of real value to the industrial workers who are brought under its protection. In normal times it will enable most workers who lose their jobs to tide themselves over, until they get back to their old work or find other employment, without having to resort to relief. Even in depressions it will cover a considerable part of all unemployment and will be all that many workers will need. Unemployed workmen who cannot find other employment within reasonable periods will have to be cared for through work relief or other forms of assistance, but unemployment compensation will greatly reduce the necessity for such assistance. Unemployment compensation is greatly preferable to relief because it is given without any means test. It is in many respects comparable to workmen's compensation, except that it is designed to meet a different and greater hazard.

Unemployment compensation is valuable to the public as well as to the industrial workers themselves. It is a measure tending to maintain purchasing power, upon which business and industry are dependent. Had there been a system of unemployment compensation throughout the country in the years from 1922 on, with a 3-percent contribution rate, not only would practically all unemployment of the prosperity period have been compensated, but it is estimated that $2,500,000,000 would have been available for payment of benefits with the beginning of the depression in 1929. Such an amount paid to unemployed workmen at that time would unquestionably have had a most wholesome, stabilizing effect upon business.

Unemployment compensation has behind it an extensive European experience. No country which had experimented with unemployment insurance has ever abandoned it. In this country it has been endorsed by numerous Federal and State commissions and committees, but prior to this year only one State enacted such a law, and this came into operation less than a year ago.

The failure of the States to enact unemployment insurance laws is due largely to the fact that to do so would handicap their industries in competition with the industries of other States. The States have been unwilling to place this extra financial burden upon their industries. A uniform, Nation-wide tax upon industry, thus removing this principal obstacle in the way of unemployment insurance, is necessary before the States can go ahead. Such a tax should make it possible for the States to enact this socially desirable legislation.

This is one of the purposes of title IX of this bill. In this title a tax is imposed upon employers throughout the country against which a credit is allowed of up to 90 percent of the tax for contributions made by employers to unemployment compensation funds established pursuant to State law.

That this tax is imposed on employers is indicative of the conviction that employers should bear at least a part of the cost of unemployment compensation, just as they bear the cost of workmen's compensation. Each State is, of course, free to assess not only employers but employees; and in this connection it may be noted that in European countries, and under the law recently passed by the State of Washington, employees are required to contribute.

The amount of benefits payable for unemployment from contributions amounting to 3 percent of pay roll would vary from State to State. The maximum period for which benefits may be paid depends not only upon the rate of unemployment, but also upon the percentage of wages paid as benefits, the length of the required waiting period, the ratio of weeks of employment to weeks of benefits, and other provisions. The scale of benefits which States will be able to pay from a 3-percent rate of contributions on pay rolls will carry the great majority of unemployed workers through normal years until they are able to secure employment again. While the Federal tax is limited to 3 percent (1 percent in 1936 and 2 percent in 1937), some States will probably increase the benefits payable by requiring also contributions from the employees or the State government. Under a reasonable scale of benefits, reserves would accumulate in normal years to carry the fund through minor depressions or the first years of a major depression.

The bill permits the States wide discretion with respect to the unemployment compensation laws they may wish to enact. The standards prescribed in this bill, which are described in part II of this report, are designed merely to insure that employers will receive credit aginast the Federal payroll tax only for payments made under genuine unemployment compensation laws.

Yet the Federal Government, under this bill, has important functions to perform in order to make it possible for the States to have unemployment insurance laws and to facilitate their operation. It equalizes competitive conditions through the imposition of the employment excise tax provided for in title IX. The bill further provides that the Social Security Board, which is created in title VII to administer all parts of the social security program other than aids coming within the scope of operation of existing bureaus, shall have the duty of studying and making recommendations with respect to the broad problems of economic security. This Board will be able to render important actuarial and scientific services to the States in connection with their unemployment insurance systems. In title III financial aid is given the States by the Federal Government to defray their costs in administering unemployment insurance. Finally, the Federal Government is to handle all unemployment reserve funds, in a trust account in the United States Treasury for the benefit of the States to which they belong.

This last provision will not only afford maximum safety for these funds but is very essential to insure that they will operate to promote the stability of business rather than the reverse. Unemployment reserve funds have the peculiarity that the demands upon them fluctuate considerably, being heaviest when business slackens. If, in such times, the securities in which these funds are invested are thrown upon the market for liquidation, the net effect is likely to be increased deflation. Such a result is avoided in this bill through the provision that all reserve funds are to be held by the United States Treasury, to be invested and liquidated by the Secretary of the Treasury in a manner calculated to promote business stability. When business conditions are such that investment in securities purchased on the open market is unwise, the Secretary of the Treasury may issue special nonnegotiable obligations exclusively to the unemployment trust fund. When a reverse situation exists and heavy drains are made upon the fund for payment of unemployment benefits, the Treasury does not have to dispose of the securities belonging to the fund in open market but may assume them itself. With such a method of handling the reserve funds, it is believed that this bill will solve the problem often raised in discussions of unemployment compensation, regarding the possibility of transferring purchasing power from boom periods to depression periods. It will in fact operate to sustain purchasing power at the onset of a depression without having any counteracting deflationary tendencies.

Security For Children

Titles IV and V of the bill deal with another important aspect of economic security, that of security for children. Children are, perhaps, the most tragic victims of the depression. More than 40 percent of all persons on relief—approximately 9,000,000 individuals—are children under 16, in contrast to 28 percent of the entire population falling in this age group. In less than a generation these children will constitute a large part of the adults who must carry the burdens of our social system and the responsibilities of our Government. As was well stated by the Committee on Economic Security, "the core of any social plan must be the child." And with so many children now growing up under the abnormal conditions involved in relief and the many hardships created through the depression, it is imperative that everything possible be done to offset the demoralizing and deteriorating effects of the great disaster that has befallen this country.

Dependent Children

One clearly distinguishable group of children, now cared for through emergency relief, for whom better provision should be made, are those in families lacking a father's support. Nearly 10 percent of all families on relief are without a potential breadwinner other than a mother whose time might best be devoted to the care of her young children. Last fall it was estimated that there were above 350,000 families on relief the head of which was a widowed, separated, or divorced mother and whose other members were children under 16. Above 700,000 children under 16 belong to such families, and, with the increase in relief lists since then, this number has probably increased proportionately.

It has long been recognized in this country that the best provision that can be made for families of this description is public aid with respect to dependent children in their own homes. Forty-five States now have laws providing such aid, but in many of these States the laws are only partially operative or not at all so. With the financial exhaustion of State and local governments a situation has developed in which there are more than three times as many families eligible for such aid as are actually in receipt of it, and they are now being supported by emergency relief.

. . . it is highly desirable that these families should be taken care of through public aid. This will not be possible, however, unless the Federal Government aids the States in carrying this burden. Such aid is proposed in title IV of this bill, under which the Federal Government will assume one-third of the cost of aid to dependent children paid under State laws. This does not involve any larger expenditures than the Federal government has been making for the support of these families on relief, but will very materially aid the States in caring for this group of their unemployables, for whom they must now assume responsibility.

*   *   *

Appropriations Authorized

Aside from amounts authorized for administrative expenses (amounting to a sum in the neighborhood of $3,500,000), appropriations authorized under this act for grants to the States amount to $91,491,000 for the fiscal year 1936.

Appropriations authorized for grants-in-aid to the States (exclusive of title III) for the fiscal year ending June 30, 1936

Old-age assistance	$49,750,000
Aid to dependent children	24,750,000
Maternal and child health	3,800,000
Crippled children	2,850,000
Child welfare	1,500,000
Vocational rehabilitation	841,000
Public health	8,000,000
Total	91,491,000

Note.—In future years the first two items will increase in accordance with the increasing cost of old-age assistance and aid to dependent children.

In addition to these sums, there are authorized annual appropriations to the old-age account, estimates for which are shown in table IV of this report. There is also authorized an appropriation of $4,000,000 for the fiscal year ending June 30, 1936, and $49,000,000 for each subsequent fiscal year to make the payments to States under title III for the cost of administering their unemployment insurance laws.

Taxes

There are three taxes imposed in the bill:

(1) An income tax on wage-earners, beginning in the year 1937 at a rate of 1 percent of wages, and increasing to 3 percent in 1949. Large groups of wage earners are, for administrative reasons, excluded from the operation of this tax, but more than one-half of the total number of gainful workers are covered.

Estimate of number of employees covered under the tax provided in title VIII

(Based upon 1930 Census)

Total number of gainful workers	48,830,000
Total number of owners, operators, self-employed (including the professions)	12,087,000
Total of workers excluded because of occupation (farm labor, domestics, teachers, and governmental and institutional workers)	9,389,000
Total number of workers in eligible occupations	27,354,000
Excluded:	
Casuals	500,000
Over 65	1,050,000
	1,550,000
Estimated coverage	25,804,000

(2) An excise tax on employers, with certain exemptions, based on wages paid. This tax, like the income tax imposed in this title, will become operative in 1937 at 1 percent of wages, increasing thereafter; and again, for administrative reasons, there are numerous exemptions.

Revenue estimates (from taxes on employees and employers imposed by title VIII, sections 801 and 804)[1]

Combined rate of tax	Fiscal year received into Treasury	Estimated fiscal year receipts	Combined rate of tax	Fiscal year received into Treasury	Estimated fiscal year receipts
2 percent....	1937	$278,800,000	4 percent....	1944	$1,185,900,000
2 percent....	1938	560,200,000	4 percent....	1945	1,196,900,000
2 percent....	1939	565,600,000	5 percent....	1946	1,359,400,000
3 percent....	1940	714,600,000	5 percent....	1947	1,523,300,000
3 percent....	1941	864,800,000	5 percent....	1948	1,536,900,000
3 percent....	1942	873,000,000	6 percent....	1949	1,706,300,000
4 percent....	1943	1,028,800,000	6 percent....	1950	1,877,200,000

[1] Each of the two taxes is estimated to produce one-half of the total receipts shown

(3) An excise tax on employers who maintain comparatively large establishments, levied in title IX and mentioned heretofore in this report, in connection with the discussion of unemployment compensation.

Estimate of number of employees covered under the tax provided in title IX

(Based upon 1930 Census)

Total number of gainful workers................................ 48,830,000

Total number of owners, operators, self-employed (including the professions)...................................... 12,087,000

Total of workers excluded because of occupation (farm labor, domestics, teachers, and governmental and institutional workers)............. 9,389,000

Total number of workers in eligible occupations............... 27,354,000

Estimated number of workers attached to establishments with nine or less employees... 5,400,000

Estimated number of workers attached to establishments of 10 and more employees (including unemployed) April 1930...... 21,954,000

Average 1936 (4 percent increase)................................ 22,858,000

The actual number of employees covered by the tax would be considerably smaller than 22,858,000 due to unemployment. All workers employed during a part of the year, however, in establishments covered by the tax, would be covered with respect to that employment.

Revenue estimates (from tax on employers of 10 or more under title IX, with no allowance for 90-percent credit)

Calendar year with respect to which tax is levied	Fiscal year received into Treasury	Estimated receipts	Rate of tax	Calendar year with respect to which tax is levied	Fiscal year received into Treasury	Estimated receipts	Rate of tax
			Per-cent				*Per-cent*
1936.....	1937	$228,000,000	1	1940.....	1941	$820,000,000	3
1937.....	1938	501,000,000	2	1942.....	1943	846,000,000	3
1938.....	1939	786,000,000	3	1945.....	1946	872,000,000	3
1939.....	1940	803,000,000	3	1950.....	1951	906,000,000	3

Note.—The tax levied by title IX is subject to a credit of 90 percent of the amount of such tax for contributions into State unemployment funds. Therefore the minimum amount of revenue each year from this tax will be 10 percent of the above amounts. What part of the above estimates, greater than 10 percent of same, will be retained by the Treasury is problematical, being dependent on the number of States enacting unemployment insurance laws, and the rates and coverage thereof.

Practically no objections have been made to the imposition of the taxes levied in this bill. What objections have been offered overlook the fact that the initial rates are very low. The only tax in the year 1936 (which is not payable until 1937) is the 1-percent excise tax on employers of 10 or more employees against which a credit is allowed for payments made under State unemployment compensation laws. In 1937 the other taxes will also come into operation, but only at the rate of 1 percent upon employers.

Excise taxes measured by pay roll will normally be added to prices. But again, the effects are often exaggerated. The direct labor cost of all manufactured commodities represents on the average about 21 percent of the value of the product. Taxes of 1, 2, and 3 percent, and even the ultimate 6 percent (not reached until 1949) will, thus, increase the selling price not by these percentages, but by much less than these figures.

Taxes on pay rolls and wages are imposed in all unemployment-compensation systems the world over. Taxes on pay rolls for this purpose are justified because unemployment compensation is a legitimate part of the costs of production, as has long been recognized in the case of workmen's compensation for industrial accidents (the costs of which are, likewise, always computed on a pay-roll basis). Unemployment compensation belongs in the same category with wages, and it is no more than right that the consumers should bear this cost, as is the case with all other costs of production.

In this connection it must not be forgotten that employers and consumers must ultimately foot a large part of the bill for the relief of destitution. Federal, State, and local taxes and public indebtedness have been greatly increased by the tremendous problem of relief. This program will necessarily reduce this great load for public taxes now required for relief purposes. If the measures we propose will reduce dependency, as we expect, the burden upon employers and consumers may well be smaller than it is at present.

Conclusion

The proposals in this bill are forward looking. This bill is not to be considered a cure-all, nor a complete measure for economic security. It will doubtless have to be supplemented in the course of time, as has been the history of all other major new legislation. But it makes a beginning toward economic security which has been long overdue.

This beginning is made along lines which are in accord with our American institutions and traditions. It is not class legislation, but a measure which will benefit the entire public. While humanely providing for those in distress, it does not proceed upon the destructive theory that the citizens should look to the Government for everything. On the contrary, it seeks to reduce dependency and to encourage thrift and self-support.

From the governmental point of view this bill contemplates a united attack upon economic insecurity by the Federal and State Governments. It does not vest dictatorial powers in any Federal officials.

Of all major countries the United States is the last to give serious consideration to a comprehensive system of social insurance and related measures for economic security. The experience of this country in the trying years of the depression has *amply* demonstrated the need for this legislation.

*   *   *

The Republican minority was less enthusiastic.

House Report No. 615
74th Cong., 1st Sess.
Minority Views

We, the undersigned members of the minority, submit the following statement showing in brief our attitude toward this proposed legislation, which is known as "the economic security bill":

I

The bill is separated into several titles, which readily and naturally segregate themselves into two categories:

(1) Those which spring from the desire of the Federal Government to provide economic assistance to those who need and deserve it.

(2) Those which are based upon the principle of compulsory insurance.

In the first group are —

Title I, granting aid to the States in meeting the cost of old-age pensions;

Title IV, granting aid to the States in caring for dependent children;

Title V, granting aid to the States in providing for maternal and child welfare; and

Title VI, granting aid to the States in providing for public health generally.

We favor the enactment of each of the foregoing titles, which in our opinion should have been incorporated in a separate bill.

Old-Age Pensions

We favor such legislation as will encourage States already paying old-age pensions to provide for more adequate benefits, and will encourage all other States to adopt old-age pension systems.

However, we believe the amount provided in the bill to be inadequate, and favor a substantial increase in the Federal contribution.

Grants for Child Welfare, Public Health, etc.

Title IV. Dependent children: We favor a vigorous and sympathetic program for the care and training of dependent children that will recognize the importance of a congenial family environment.

Title V. Maternal and child welfare: For years our Government has extended aid to the States to provide for maternal and child welfare. Title V continues this aid in an increased amount.

Title VI. Public health: For years our Government also has provided aid in the interest of the public health. Title VI increases the amount of this aid.

We may add that we would favor a stronger and more vigorous program than that provided in this proposed legislation for the benefit of those covered by these three titles.

II

In the group of titles which are based upon the principle of compulsory insurance are title II, with its related title VIII, and title III, with its related title IX.

Unemployment Insurance

Titles III and IX taken together provides for what is commonly known as "unemployment insurance." The incidental revenue collected under title IX is intended to offset the payments made under title III.

The ostensible purpose of title III is commendable. Any program that would supplant unemployment with employment would meet with great favor. Employers and employees would all welcome such a program; also the many millions who are now unemployed. The latter are neither employers nor employees. Therefore, there are three great groups vitally interested in unemployment insurance.

Because of the large number of persons vitally interested, the problem is one which reaches practically every citizen, and its solution involves practically all our people. A program which will not give employment to the unemployed will not solve the problem.

On account of the deplorable condition in which the employer finds his business at this time; the tragic condition in which the employee finds himself due to the ever-mounting cost of the necessaries of life and the failure of wages to keep pace with these costs; and the fact that the number of unemployed is constantly increasing, there is doubt in our minds that the legislation proposed in these two titles will result in a general national benefit at this time.

However, we favor the principle of unemployment insurance. These titles of the bill aid those States desiring to establish such insurance, and therefore we resolve all doubts in favor of this legislation.

Compulsory Old-Age Annuities

Title II provides for compulsory old-age annuities, and title VIII provides the method by which the money is to be raised to meet the expense thereof.

These two titles are interdependent, and neither is of any consequence without the other. Neither of them has relation to any other substantive title of the bill. Neither is constitutional. Therein lies one of the reasons for our opposition to them.

The Federal Government has no power to impose this system upon private industry.

The best legal talent that the Attorney General's office and the Brain Trust could marshal has for weeks applied itself to the task of trying to bring these titles within constitutional limitations. Their best effort is only a plain circumvention. They have separated the proposition into two titles. This separation is a separation in words only. There is no separation in spirit or intent. These two titles must stand or fall together.

The learned brief submitted by the Attorney General's Office contains in its summation the following weak, apologetic language:

> There may also be taken into consideration the strong presumption which exists in favor of the constitutionality of an act of the Congress, in the light of

which and of the foregoing discussion it is reasonably safe to assume that the social security bill, if enacted into law, will probably be upheld as constitutional.

We also oppose these two titles because they would not in any way contribute to the relief of present economic conditions, and might in fact retard economic recovery.

The original bill contained a title providing for voluntary annuities. This was another attempt to place the Government in competition with private business. Under fire, this title has been omitted. It was closely akin to title II. In fact, it had one virtue that title II does not possess in that it was voluntary while title II is compulsory.

These titles impose a crushing burden upon industry and upon labor.

They establish a bureaucracy in the field of insurance in competition with private business.

They destroy old-age retirement systems set up by private industries, which in most instances provide more liberal benefits than are contemplated under title II.

Appended hereto is a table showing the total taxes imposed under titles VIII and IX.

Total taxes on employers and employees under social-security bill

Effective date of tax	On employers					On employees (title VIII)		Grand total on employers and employees	
	For unemployment insurance (title IX)		For employees' annuities (title VIII)		Total on employers				
	Amount	Rate	Amount	Rate		Amount	Rate	Amount	Rate
	Mills. of dols.	*Per-cent*	*Mills. of dols.*	*Per-cent*	*Mills. of dols.*	*Mills. of dols.*	*Per-cent*	*Mills. of dols.*	*Per-cent*
Jan. 1, 1936....	228	1	...	...	228	...	...	228	1
Jan. 1, 1937....	501	2	279	1	780	279	1	1,059	4
Jan. 1, 1938....	786	3	280	1	1,066	280	1	1,346	5
Jan. 1, 1939....	803	3	283	1	1,086	283	1	1,369	5
Jan. 1, 1940....	820	3	357	1½	1,177	357	1½	1,534	6
Jan. 1, 1941....	833	3	432	1½	1,265	432	1½	1,697	6
Jan. 1, 1942....	846	3	437	1½	1,283	437	1½	1,720	6
Jan. 1, 1943....	855	3	514	2	1,369	514	2	1,883	7
Jan. 1, 1944....	863	3	593	2	1,456	593	2	2,049	7
Jan. 1, 1945....	872	3	598	2	1,470	598	2	2,068	7
Jan. 1, 1946....	879	3	680	2½	1,559	680	2½	2,239	8
Jan. 1, 1947....	886	3	762	2½	1,648	762	2½	2,410	8
Jan. 1, 1948....	892	3	768	2½	1,660	768	2½	2,428	8
Jan. 1, 1949....	899	3	853	3	1,752	853	3	2,605	9
Jan. 1, 1950....	906	3	939	3	1,845	939	3	2,784	9

Conclusion

The minority membership of the Ways and Means Committee have at no time offered any political or partisan opposition to the progress of this measure, but on the contrary have labored faithfully in an effort to produce a measure that would be constitutional and that would inure to the general welfare of all the people.

> *Allen T. Treadway.*
> *Isaac Bacharach.*
> *Frank Crowther.*
> *Harold Knutson.*
> *Daniel A. Reed.*
> *Roy O. Woodruff.*
> *Thomas A. Jenkins.*

Supplemental Views of Mr. Knutson

While I concur in a general way with the conclusions of my colleagues of the minority, there are certain provisions of the bill so obnoxious to me that I cannot support it. My reasons for voting against the measure are as follows:

1. It is obvious from the provisions of this bill that it cannot be made effective for several years, hence it will be a bitter disappointment to those who have looked hopefully to this administration for immediate relief.
2. The measure is wholly inadequate and therefore will not give the result sought to be obtained.
3. The age limit of 65 is too high to give the needed relief. The limit should be fixed at 60, which would help the unemployment situation materially and at the same time care for a large number now out of work and who by reason of age are unemployable.
4. The old-age pension to be granted under H. R. 7260 would be wholly inadequate in the relief of distress. The amount paid would be so small that its effect upon business would be negligible.
5. The administering of this law will result in discrimination. People living in States that are bankrupt, or nearly so, will receive absolutely no benefits from this legislation. These people must be taken care of by the National Government.
6. The two pay-roll taxes which the bill imposes will greatly retard business recovery by driving many industries, now operating at a loss, into bankruptcy, or by forcing them to close down entirely, thereby further increasing unemployment, which would greatly retard recovery.
7. Many small concerns having 12 or 15 employees would discharge enough employees to exempt them from the payment of the pay-roll taxes which would yet further aggravate the unemployment situation.
8. The proposal to establish a new bureau to administer this law is indefensible and a needless expense to the taxpayers. In the interest of

economy the administration of the law should be vested in the Veterans' Administration, which is equipped to handle this activity.

Harold Knutson

The 1935 legislation also established another basic principle of social security legislation. At least as far as the House was concerned, all important decisions were made in the Ways and Means Committee — and in this respect the chairman of that committee maintained almost dictatorial control over social security. (This control by committee and chairman was achieved in later years by sending a bill to the House under a closed rule, which effectively barred amendments although it allowed substitute bills to be offered.) The strategy in 1935 was somewhat different. An attempt was made to muster a majority on the committee to send the bill under a closed (gag) rule, but it failed. Although the committee sent the bill under a wide open rule, it limited amendments to "germane" areas. The maneuver was attacked at once.

Congressional Debates
79 Congressional Record, p. 5457–59
(April 11, 1935)

Mr. James W. Mott [Rep., Ore.] . . . The Constitution of the United States guarantees to its people the right of petition to the proper authority, which in this case is the Congress of the United States, and that right presupposes and carries with it the right to have their orderly petitions properly considered and passed upon by the Congress in an orderly manner. I am not contending that you must grant those petitions by enacting their proposals into law, because to say that would be to deny to Congress the right to legislate as the representatives of the whole people. But I do say to you that you have no right to refuse to allow the legislation prayed for in those petitions to be considered on the floor of this House. I do say that you have no right, figuratively speaking, to throw those petitions in the waste basket. And finally I say that although you may have the legal right you have no moral right to adopt any rule today which will render it impossible for the House to consider and act upon either the revised McGroarty bill, the Lundeen bill, or any other old-age-pension bill now before Congress which proposes a different old-age-pension plan than that proposed in the President's bill. And that, Mr. Speaker, is precisely what the majority of this House will do if it adopts this rule.

Mr. Vito Marcantonio. [Rep., N.Y.] Mr. Speaker, the press of the Nation has heralded this rule as wide open. I agree that it is a wide-open rule technically, but from a practical standpoint it is a rule which accomplishes the same purpose of a stringent gag rule. It provents this House from discussing and passing on genuine social-security plans.

*   *   *

Mr. Marcantonio. Exactly. The Labor Committee reported the Lundeen bill favorably. Why should not this House be given an opportunity to discuss and pass on this plan?

Mr. Speaker, you may call this "social security", you may call this a "new deal", you may call it what you please, but it is simply the same old stacked deck of cards that were sent to the laundry 2 years ago to be powdered and polished and are now being dealt out in the same old manner. You can call it "social security"; you can call it "the new deal." I say to you this is not social security, not a new deal, but it is just a new delusion. [Applause.]

The House, however, accepted the committee's limitation on amendment and debate, a decision which, in the long run, meant that power over social security had been delegated by the House to the committee.

Despite the committee's strategy, efforts were made to introduce both the Lundeen and Townsend (McGroarty) bills; these attempts were easily defeated. (Lundeen Bill, substitute attempt defeated 40–158; McGroarty Bill, defeated 56–296. 79 Congressional Record, p. 5856–5968.)

Essentially the House debates were an anti-climax. The amendments which came nearest to success were those of Mrs. Isabella Greenaway of Arizona. She proposed that old-age (OAA) pensions be paid at once by the Federal Government until the states had an opportunity to pass their own legislation. In connection with this she suggested higher maxima. This amendment eventually lost 87–165. Another amendment to reduce the age for old-age assistance to sixty was defeated 13–115. However, an attempt to increase the federal contribution to old-age assistance up to a maximum of $40, lost by only 149–253.

Attempts to require employees to contribute to unemployment insurance and to force the Federal Government to add a subsidy were ruled out of order. The House also considered and rejected the lower federal formula under aid to dependent children, strongly suggesting that the program had far less political appeal than attempts to help the elderly.

It was clear that once the committee had endorsed the proposal, the chances of a change in the House were minuscule. But, at least for the benefit of constituents, it was possible to make eulogistic speeches, or have them inserted in the Record. *Finally on April 19, the final vote was taken with the predictable result: yea 372, nay 33, not present 3, not voting 25.*

Senate Action

While the House debated, the Senate was not active, but some two weeks after passage of the House bill, the Senate once again considered the matter. The executive sessions in the Senate Finance Committee are reported to have been well conducted. Administration pressure was exerted primarily to see that responsibility for the act was left with the Labor Department—Congressional antipathy to Mrs. Perkins had generated action to remove it from that Department's control—and also to return to the states the right to allow either individual-employer accounts or pooled-fund accounts in the unemployment insurance provisions.

The committee solved the administrative problem by giving the Social Security Board back to Labor, without giving control of the staff to the Secretary. It unenthusiastically restored voluntary annuities to the bill and more readily allowed the states to experiment with unemployment compensation. Rather surprisingly the committee added a category of aid to the blind to the public assistance provisions, but showed no willingness to be more generous in ADC. Again old-age insurance was threatened and although it was kept in the bill by the committee, skillfully directed by Chairman Byron P. Harrison of Massachusetts, the opposing argument—that companies with sound pension plans should be able to contract out of social security altogether—was gaining ground.

The changes made by the committee were conveniently recorded.

Social Security Bill
Senate Report No. 628
74th Cong., 1st Sess.
(May 13, 1935)

H. R. 7260, passed by the House on April 19 of this year, is herewith reported with the following principal changes:

1. A new title has been added (title X) to provide Federal aid to the States for the blind.
2. A new title has been added (title XI) to authorize the issue of voluntary Federal old-age annuity bonds by the Treasury. This measure is designed to enable persons not covered by the system of Federal old-age benefits to build up old-age annuities.
3. Section 202 in title II is amended to make retirement from regular employment a condition for payment of old-age benefits. This will eliminate the anomaly that employees over 65 may draw old-age benefit while earning adequate wages in full-time employment.
4. The grants-in-aid to the States for aid to dependent children has been placed under the Children's Bureau, instead of the Social Security Board. The Children's Bureau is the agency of the Government concerned with matters relating to children.
5. The Social Security Board has been placed under the Department of Labor, instead of being created as an entirely independent agency. The reason for this change is the close relationship between the

functions of the Social Security Board and those of the Labor Department. This type of legislation the world over is almost invar-
iably under the direction or supervision of the labor department or
its equivalent. By placing the Social Security Board under the Labor
Department, considerable saving in administrative costs may be
anticipated. The committee regards it as inadvisable to create new
independent agencies, particularly where their functions are closely
related to the major functions of an existing department.

6. The coverage of the tax upon employers in title IX has been changed
   from employers having 10 or more employees, within 20 weeks during the year, to 4 or more employees, within 13 weeks during any
   any year. This change has been made to avoid substantial administrative problems in connection with employers who may attempt
   to avoid the tax, and also to extend its coverage.
7. The requirement that State unemployment compensation funds
   shall be of the "pooled" type, in which all funds are mingled and un-
   divided, as a condition to qualify for the credit against the Federal
   tax under title IX, has been stricken. This will permit States to enact whatever type of unemployment compensation law they desire.
8. Two new sections have been inserted (909 and 910) to give additional credit to employers who, under State laws, are permitted to
   lower their rates of compensation because of favorable employment
   experience. These sections are designed to permit States to give an
   incentive to employers to stabilize employment.

*The Finance Committee made less effort to restrict debate than had the
Ways and Means Committee—and for this reason the Senate floor was a
more fruitful source of amendments than the House. The bill reached the
floor on June 14, introduced by Chairman Harrison and stoutly defended
by Senator Wagner, but at least three major amendments were successful.*

*The first and most important was the Clark Amendment which threat-
ened to hold up the whole bill. It represented the fruit of Mr. Forster's
appearances before both committees, and allowed companies with acceptable retirement programs to opt out of OAI. It was strongly opposed by
the Administration and Senator Harrison sought to counter the amendment by presenting a memorandum prepared by Dr. Witte. More effective,
perhaps, was the speech of Senator Alben B. Barkley.*

Congressional Debates
79 Congressional Record, p. 9625
(June 14, 1935)

Senator Alben W. Barkley [Dem., Ky.] . . .

Mr. President, my objection to the Clark amendment is that it sets up
two competitive systems of old-age relief. I believe one of the wisest things

the Nation has done has been to recognize the duty of the Government toward indigents. Whether the indigent condition be brought about by unemployment or old age or ill health, there is no way by which the public can escape the burden. It is always present in one form or another. Those who work must support those who do not work. It has always been so, and it will always be so. With respect to reduction of hours of labor, my theory has been that if we must decide whether all our people should be allowed to work three-fourths of the time or three-fourths of them should be allowed to work all the time and the other one-fourth never work at all, I prefer the first alternative so as to divide whatever work is available among all the ablebodied men and women of the country who desire to work, so they may share it in proportion to their ability, rather than that we shall have a permanent condition in this country in which three-fourths of the people shall be allowed to work all the time and one-fourth never to work at all, and therefore become burdens upon the three-fourths who shall be allowed to work. That is the reason why I favor reduction in hours of labor, insofar as we can do that, in order to spread the work which is available among all the people capable of working.

I feel the same way with repect to the provisions for oldage pensions and unemployment insurance. That is why I believe in this measure, worked out by a commission appointed a year ago by the President at the time he sent his message to Congress announcing that at this session he would propose a constructive plan of legislation to deal with this complicated and interrelated situation. After months of investigation and months of labor that commission brought out a tentative plan, which was submitted to the Houses of Congress, and both Houses, through their committees, held exhaustive hearings on the subject. The House of Representatives finally passed a bill, I believe, in much modified form. Our Committee on Finance gave weeks and months of study to this problem, and has brought here a bill proposing a uniform and universal plan to apply to our country.

Abraham Lincoln once said this country cannot endure half slave and half free. I do not believe any old-age pension system we may inaugurate can long endure half public and half private, because if we have private insurance or annuity plans set up in opposition to the plan of the Federal Government, it is not difficult to see that the high-pressure salesmanship of annuity companies and of insurance companies will always be on the doorsteps of the employers to convince them that they can insure their employees in a private system more cheaply than they can by the payment of taxes into the Federal Government and a consequent dispensation of the benefits in an orderly and scientific fashion.

Therefore I believe the effect of the Clark amendment—and I am sure, of course, the Senator from Missouri was not actuated by any such design or desire—will be to disorganize and disarrange the reserve fund set up in the Treasury under the Federal plan, and that it will gradually and effectually undermine the Federal system which we are trying to set up.

We will then have our Government in competition with every annuity writer and every employer in the country who thinks he may be able to save a little money by insuring his employees or by adopting some private annuity plan which may be suggested to him by some private insurance company or annuity company which desires to obtain the business.

But even such pleas as these were not enough: the Clark Amendment passed 51–35. There were two other defeats for the Administration in the Senate. The reinserted voluntary annuity scheme was defeated by voice vote. Similarly, against the wishes of the President, the Russell Amendments allowing states to receive OAA until July 1, 1937, without providing matching funds, passed easily.

The Conference Committee was not all it might have been from the Administration point of view, for the majority of Senate conferees were far from enthusiastic supporters of the legislation. When consideration did begin, it proved virtually impossible to agree over the Clark Amendment. By July 16 there was agreement on all other matters, and the following day both houses accepted the conference reports with the exception of the Clark Amendment. Of course, this is not to suggest that the other compromises were unimportant. It was in the Conference Committee that agreements were reached which settled the tax applying to employers of eight or more, and which restored the requirement of retirement for OAI. All references to minimum standards of health and decency were excluded from OAA. States without any old-age pensions could receive OAA grants-in-aid without providing matching funds until 1937. Residence requirements in ADC were rendered slightly stricter, and so on—but the Clark Amendment remained unresolved. The report of the Conference Committee is reproduced in 79 Congressional Record (p. 1132).

The days dragged on but the lawyers representing the Administration and the proponents of the amendment made no progress. Eventually a compromise was worked out omitting the Clark Amendment from the 1935 act and establishing a special committee of the two houses to consider an appropriate amendment to be introduced the following year. With this reservation the Senate accepted the conference report by a vote of 77–6. The House had previously passed the report and on August 14, the President signed the bill into law.

Presidential Statement upon Signing the Social Security Act
(August 14, 1935)*

Today a hope of many years' standing is in large part fulfilled. The civilization of the past hundred years, with its startling industrial changes, has

Public Papers and Addresses of Franklin D. Roosevelt, 1935, p. 324–25.

tended more and more to make life insecure. Young people have come to wonder what would be their lot when they came to old age. The man with a job has wondered how long the job would last.

This social security measure gives at least some protection to thirty millions of our citizens who will reap direct benefits through unemployment compensation, through old-age pensions and through increased services for the protection of children and the prevention of ill health.

We can never insure one hundred percent of the population against one hundred percent of the hazards and vicissitudes of life, but we have tried to frame a law which will give some measure of protection to the average citizen and to his family against the loss of a job and against poverty-ridden old age.

This law, too, represents a cornerstone in a structure which is being built but is by no means complete. It is a structure intended to lessen the force of possible future depressions. It will act as a protection to future Administrations against the necessity of going deeply into debt to furnish relief to the needy. The law will flatten out the peaks and valleys of deflation and of inflation. It is, in short, a law that will take care of human needs and at the same time provide for the United States an economic structure of vastly greater soundness.

I congratulate all of you ladies and gentlemen, all of you in the Congress, in the executive departments and all of you who come from private life, and I thank you for your splendid efforts in behalf of this sound, needed and patriotic legislation.

If the Senate and the House of Representatives in this long and arduous session had done nothing more than pass this Bill, the session would be regarded as historic for all time.

Social Security Act
(August 14, 1935, ch. 531, 49 Statutes at Large 620)

An Act to provide for the general welfare by establishing a system of Federal old-age benefits, and by enabling the several States to make more adequate provision for aged persons, blind persons, dependent and crippled children, maternal and child welfare, public health, and the administration of their unemployment compensation laws; to establish a Social Security Board; to raise revenue; and for other purposes.

Be it enacted by the Senate and House of Representatives of the United States of America in Congress assembled,

TITLE I—GRANTS TO STATES FOR OLD AGE ASSISTANCE

Appropriation

Section 1. For the purpose of enabling each State to furnish financial assistance, as far as practicable under the conditions in such State, to aged needy individuals, there is hereby authorized to be appropriated for the fiscal year ending June 30, 1936, the sum of $49,750,000, and there is hereby authorized to be appropriated for each fiscal year thereafter a sum sufficient to carry out the purposes of this title. The sums made available under this section shall be used for making payments to States which have submitted, and had approved by the Social Security Board established by Title VII, State plans for old-age assistance.

State Old-Age Assistance Plans

Sec. 2. (a) A State plan for old-age assistance must (1) provide that it shall be in effect in all political subdivisions of the State, and, if administered by them, be mandatory upon them; (2) provide for financial participation by the State; (3) either provide for the establishment or designation of a single State agency to administer the plan, or provide for the establishment or designation of a single State agency to supervise the administration of the plan; (4) provide for granting to any individual, whose claim for old-age assistance is denied, an opportunity for a fair hearing before such State agency; (5) provide such methods of administration (other than those relating to selection, tenure of office, and compensation of personnel) as are found by the Board to be necessary for the efficient operation of the plan; (6) provide that the State agency will make such reports, in such form and containing such information, as the Board may from time to time require, and comply with such provisions as the Board may from time to time find necessary to assure the correctness and verification of such reports; and (7) provide that, if the State or any of its political subdivisions collects from the estate of any recipient of old-age assistance any amount with respect to old-age assistance furnished him under the plan, one-half of the net amount so collected shall be promptly paid to the United States. Any payment so made shall be deposited in the Treasury to the credit of the appropriation for the purposes of this title.

(b) The Board shall approve any plan which fulfills the conditions specified in subsection (a), except that it shall not approve any plan which imposes, as a condition of eligibility for old-age assistance under the plan—

(1) An age requirement of more than sixty-five years, except that the plan may impose, effective until January 1, 1940, an age requirement of as much as seventy years; or

(2) Any residence requirement which excludes any resident of the State who has resided therein five years during the nine years immediately preceding the application for old-age assistance and has resided therein continuously for one year immediately preceding the application; or

(3) Any citizenship requirement which excludes any citizen of the United States.

Payment to States

Sec. 3. (a) From the sums appropriated therefor, the Secretary of the Treasury shall pay to each State which has an approved plan for old-age assistance, for each quarter, beginning with the quarter commencing July 1, 1935, (1) an amount, which shall be used exclusively as old-age assistance, equal to one-half of the total of the sums expended during such quarter as old-age assistance under the State plan with respect to each individual who at the time of such expenditure is sixty-five years of age or older and is not an inmate of a public institution, not counting so much of such expenditure with respect to any individual for any month as exceeds $30, and (2) 5 per centum of such amount, which shall be used for paying the costs of administering the State plan or for old-age assistance, or both, and for no other purpose: *Provided*, That the State plan, in order to be approved by the Board, need not provide for financial participation before July 1, 1937 by the State, in the case of any State which the Board, upon application by the State and after reasonable notice and opportunity for hearing to the State, finds is prevented by its constitution from providing such financial participation.

(b) The method of computing and paying such amounts shall be as follows:

(1) The Board shall, prior to the beginning of each quarter, estimate the amount to be paid to the State for such quarter under the provisions of clause (1) of subsection (a), such estimate to be based on (A) a report filed by the State containing its estimate of the total sum to be expended in such quarter in accordance with the provisions of such clause, and stating the amount appropriated or made available by the State and its political subdivisions for such expenditures in such quarter, and if such amount is less than one-half of the total sum of such estimated expenditures, the source or sources from which the difference is expected to be derived, (B) records showing the number of aged individuals in the State, and (C) such other investigation as the Board may find necessary. . . .

TITLE II—FEDERAL OLD-AGE BENEFITS

Old-Age Reserve Account

Section 201. (a) There is hereby created an account in the Treasury of the United States to be known as the "Old-Age Reserve Account." . . .

Old-Age Benefit Payments

Sec. 202. (a) Every qualified individual shall be entitled to receive, with respect to the period beginning on the date he attains the age of sixty-five, or on January 1, 1942, whichever is the later, and ending on the date of his death, an old-age benefit (payable as nearly as practicable in equal monthly installments) as follows:

(1) If the total wages determined by the Board to have been paid to him, with respect to employment after December 31, 1936, and before he attained the age of sixty-five, were not more than $3,000, the old-age benefit shall be at a monthly rate of one-half of 1 per centum of such total wages;

(2) If such total wages were more than $3,000, the old-age benefit shall be at a monthly rate equal to the sum of the following:

(A) One-half of 1 per centum of $3,000; plus

(B) One-twelfth of 1 per centum of the amount by which such total wages exceeded $3,000 and did not exceed $45,000; plus

(C) One-twenty-fourth of 1 per centum of the amount by which such total wages exceeded $45,000.

(b) In no case shall the monthly rate computed under subsection (a) exceed $85. . . .

Payments Upon Death

Sec. 203. (a) If any individual dies before attaining the age of sixty-five, there shall be paid to his estate an amount equal to 3½ per centum of the total wages determined by the Board to have been paid to him, with respect to employment after December 31, 1936. . . .

Payments to Aged Individuals Not Qualified for Benefits

Sec. 204. (a) There shall be paid in a lump sum to any individual who, upon attaining the age of sixty-five, is not a qualified individual, an amount equal to 3½ per centum of the total wages determined by the Board to have been paid to him, with respect to employment after December 31, 1936, and before he attained the age of sixty-five.

(b) After any individual becomes entitled to any payment under subsection (a), no other payment shall be made under this title in any manner measured by wages paid to him, except that any part of any payment under subsection (a) which is not paid to him before his death shall be paid to his estate. . . .

Sec. 210. . . .

(b) The term "employment" means any service, of whatever nature, performed within the United States by an employee for his employer, except—

(1) Agricultural labor;

(2) Domestic service in a private home;

(3) Casual labor not in the course of the employer's trade or business;

(4) Service performed as an officer or member of the crew of a vessel documented under the laws of the United States or of any foreign country;

(5) Service performed in the employ of the United States Government or of an instrumentality of the United States;

(6) Service performed in the employ of a State, a political subdivision thereof, or an instrumentality of one or more States or political subdivisions;

(7) Service performed in the employ of a corporation, community chest, fund, or foundation, organized and operated exclusively for religious, charitable, scientific, literary, or educational purposes, or for the prevention of cruelty to children or animals, no part of the net earnings of which inures to the benefit of any private shareholder or individual. . . .

TITLE III—GRANTS TO STATES FOR UNEMPLOYMENT COMPENSATION ADMINISTRATION

Appropriation

Section 301. For the purpose of assisting the States in the administration of their unemployment compensation laws, there is hereby authorized to be appropriated, for the fiscal year ending June 30, 1936, the sum of $4,-000,000, and for each fiscal year thereafter the sum of 49,000,000, to be used as hereinafter provided.

Payments to States

Sec. 302. (a) The Board shall from time to time certify to the Secretary of the Treasury for payment to each State which has an unemployment compensation law approved by the Board under Title IX, such amounts as the Board determines to be necessary for the proper administration of such law during the fiscal year in which such payment is to be made. The Board's determination shall be based on (1) the population of the State; (2) an estimate of the number of persons covered by the State law and of the cost of proper administration of such law; and (3) such other factors as the Board finds relevant. The Board shall not certify for payment under this section in any fiscal year a total amount in excess of the amount appropriated therefor for such fiscal year. . . .

Provisions of State Laws

Sec. 303. (a) The Board shall make no certification for payment to any State unless it finds that the law of such State, approved by the Board under Title IX, includes provisions for—

(1) Such methods of administration (other than those relating to selection, tenure of office, and compensation of personnel) as are

found by the Board to be reasonably calculated to insure full payment of unemployment compensation when due; and

(2) Payment of unemployment compensation solely through public employment offices in the State or such other agencies as the Board may approve; and

(3) Opportunity for a fair hearing, before an impartial tribunal, for all individuals whose claims for unemployment compensation are denied; and

(4) The payment of all money received in the unemployment fund of such State, immediately upon such receipt, to the Secretary of the Treasury to the credit of the Unemployment Trust Fund established by section 904; and

(5) Expenditure of all money requisitioned by the State agency from the Unemployment Trust Fund, in the payment of unemployment compensation, exclusive of expenses of administration; and

(6) The making of such reports, in such form and containing such information, as the Board may from time to time require, and compliance with such provisions as the Board may from time to time find necessary to assure the correctness and verification of such reports; and

(7) Making available upon request to any agency of the United States charged with the administration of public works or assistance through public employment, the name, address, ordinary occupation and employment status of each recipient of unemployment compensation, and a statement of such recipient's rights to further compensation under such law.

(b) Whenever the Board, after reasonable notice and opportunity for hearing to the State agency charged with the administration of the State law, finds that in the administration of the law there is—

(1) a denial, in a substantial number of cases, of unemployment compensation to individuals entitled thereto under such law; or

(2) a failure to comply substantially with any provision specified in subsection (a);

the Board shall notify such State agency that further payments will not be made to the State until the Board is satisfied that there is no longer any such denial or failure to comply. Until it is so satisfied it shall make no further certification to the Secretary of the Treasury with respect to such State. . . .

TITLE IV—GRANTS TO STATES FOR AID TO DEPENDENT CHILDREN

Appropriation

Section 401. For the purpose of enabling each State to furnish financial assistance, as far as practicable under the conditions in such State, to needy dependent children, there is hereby authorized to be appropriated for the fiscal year ending June 30, 1936, the sum of $24,750,000, and there is hereby authorized to be appropriated for each fiscal year thereafter a sum sufficient to carry out the purposes of this title. The sums made available under this section shall be used for making payments to States which have submitted, and had approved by the Board, State plans for aid to dependent children. . . .

Payment to States

Sec. 403. (a) From the sums appropriated therefor, the Secretary of the Treasury shall pay to each State which has an approved plan for aid to dependent children, for each quarter, beginning with the quarter commencing July 1, 1935, an amount, which shall be used exclusively for carrying out the State plan, equal to one-third of the total of the sums expended during such quarter under such plan, not counting so much of such expenditure with respect to any dependent child for any month as exceeds $18, or if there is more than one dependent child in the same home, as exceeds $18 for any month with respect to one such dependent child and $12 for such month with respect to each of the other dependent children. . . .

Definitions

Sec. 406. When used in this title — (a) The term "dependent child" means a child under the age of sixteen who has been deprived of parental support or care by reason of the death, continued absence from the home, or physical or mental incapacity of a parent, and who is living with his father, mother, grandfather, grandmother, brother, sister, stepfather, stepmother, step brother, stepsister, uncle, or aunt, in a place of residence maintained by one or more of such relatives as his or their own home. . . .

TITLE V — GRANTS TO STATES FOR MATERNAL AND CHILD WELFARE

PART 1 — MATERNAL AND CHILD HEALTH SERVICES

Appropriation

Section 501. For the purpose of enabling each State to extend and improve, as far as practicable under the conditions in such State, services for promoting the health of mothers and children, especially in rural areas and in areas suffering from severe economic distress, there is hereby authorized to be appropriated for each fiscal year, beginning with the fiscal year ending June 30, 1936, the sum of $3,800,000. The sums made available under this section shall be used for making payments to States which have submitted, and had approved by the Chief of the Children's Bureau, State plans for such services.

Allotments to States

Sec. 502. (a) Out of the sums appropriated pursuant to section 501 for each fiscal year the Secretary of Labor shall allot to each State $20,000, and such part of $1,800,000 as he finds that the number of live births in such State bore to the total number of live births in the United States, in the latest calendar year for which the Bureau of the Census has available statistics.

(b) Out of the sums appropriated pursuant to section 501 for each fiscal year the Secretary of Labor shall allot to the States $980,000 (in addition to the allotments made under subsection (a)), according to the financial need for each State for assistance in carrying out its State plan, as determined by him after taking into consideration the number of live births in such State. . . .

Approval of State Plans

Sec. 503. (a) A State plan for maternal and child-health services must (1) provide for financial participation by the State; (2) provide for the administration of the plan by the State health agency or the supervision of the administration of the plan by the State health agency; (3) provide such methods of administration (other than those relating to selection, tenure of office, and compensation of personnel) as are necessary for the efficient operation of the plan; (4) provide that the State health agency will make such reports, in such form and containing such information, as the Secretary of Labor may from time to time require, and comply with such provisions as he may from time to time find necessary to assure the correctness and verification of such reports; (5) provide for the extension and improvement of local maternal and childhealth services administered by local child-health units; (6) provide for cooperation with medical, nursing, and welfare groups and organizations; and (7) provide for the development of demonstration services in needy areas and among groups in special need. . . .

PART 2—SERVICES FOR CRIPPLED CHILDREN APPROPRIATION

Sec. 511. For the purpose of enabling each State to extend and improve (especially in rural areas and in areas suffering from severe economic distress), as far as practicable under the conditions in such State, services for locating crippled children, and for providing medical, surgical, corrective, and other services and care, and facilities for diagnosis, hospitalization, and aftercare, for children who are crippled or who are suffering from conditions which lead to crippling, there is hereby authorized to be appropriated for each fiscal year, beginning with the fiscal year ending June 30, 1936, the sum of $2,850,000. The sums made available under this section shall be used for making payments to States which have submitted, and had approved by the Chief of the Children's Bureau, State plans for such services.

Allotments to States

Sec. 512. (a) Out of the sums appropriated pursuant to section 511 for each fiscal year the Secretary of Labor shall allot to each State $20,000, and the reminder to the States according to the need of each State as determined by him after taking into consideration the number of crippled children in such State in need of the services referred to in section 511 and the cost of furnishing such services to them.

PART 3—CHILD-WELFARE SERVICES

Sec. 521. (a) For the purpose of enabling the United States, through the Children's Bureau, to cooperate with State public-welfare agencies in establishing, extending, and strengthening, especially in predominantly rural areas, public-welfare services (hereinafter in this section referred to as "child-welfare services") for the protection and care of homeless, dependent, and neglected children, and children in danger of becoming delinquent, there is hereby authorized to be appropriated for each fiscal year, beginning with the fiscal year ending June 30, 1936, the sum of $1,500,000. Such amount shall be allotted by the Secretary of Labor for use by cooperating State public-welfare agencies on the basis of plans developed jointly by the State agency and the Children's Bureau, to each State, $10,000, and the remainder to each State on the basis of such plans, not to exceed such part of the remainder as the rural population of such State bears to the total rural population of the United States. The amount so allotted shall be expended for payment of part of the cost of district, county or other local child-welfare services in areas predominantly rural, and for developing State services for the encouragement and assistance of adequate methods of community child-welfare organization in areas predominantly rural and other areas of special need. . . .

PART 4—VOCATIONAL REHABILITATION

Sec. 531. (a) In order to enable the United States to cooperate with the States and Hawaii in extending and strengthening their programs of vocational rehabilitation of the physically disabled, and to continue to carry out the provisions and purposes of the Act entitled "An Act to provide for the promotion of vocational rehabilitation of persons disabled in industry or otherwise and their return to civil employment," approved June 2, 1920, . . . there is hereby authorized to be appropriated for the fiscal years ending June 30, 1936, and June 30, 1937, the sum of $841,000 for each such fiscal year in addition to the amount of the existing authorization, and for each fiscal year thereafter the sum of $1,938,000.

TITLE VI – PUBLIC HEALTH WORK

Appropriation

Section 601. For the purpose of assisting States, counties, health districts, and other political subdivisions of the States in establishing and maintaining adequate public-health services, including the training of personnel for State and local health work, there is hereby authorized to be appropriated for each fiscal year, beginning with the fiscal year ending June 30, 1936, the sum of $8,000,000 to be used as hereinafter provided.

State and Local Public Health Services

Sec. 602. (a) The Surgeon General of the Public Health Service, with the approval of the Secretary of the Treasury, shall, at the beginning of each fiscal year, allot to the States the total of (1) the amount appropriated for such year pursuant to section 601; and (2) the amounts of the allotments under this section for the preceding fiscal year remaining unpaid to the States at the end of such fiscal year. The amounts of such allotments shall be determined on the basis of (1) the population; (2) the special health problems; and (3) the financial needs; of the respective States. Upon making such allotments the Surgeon General of the Public Health Service shall certify the amounts thereof to the Secretary of the Treasury.

(b) The amount of an allotment to any State under subsection (a) for any fiscal year, remaining unpaid at the end of such fiscal year, shall be available for allotment to States under subsection (a) for the succeeding fiscal year, in addition to the amount appropriated for such year.

(c) Prior to the beginning of each quarter of the fiscal year, the Surgeon General of the Public Health Service shall, with the approval of the Secretary of the Treasury, determine in accordance with rules and regulations previously prescribed by such Surgeon General after consultation with a conference of the State and Territorial health authorities, the amount to be paid to each State for such quarter from the allotment to such State, and shall certify the amount so determined to the Secretary of the Treasury. Upon receipt of such certification, the Secretary of the Treasury shall through the Division of Disbursement of the Treasury Department and prior to audit or settlement by the General Accounting Office, pay in accordance with such certification.

(d) The moneys so paid to any State shall be expended solely in carrying out the purposes specified in section 601, and in accordance with plans presented by the health authority of such State and approved by the Surgeon General of the Public Health Service.

Investigations

Sec. 603. (a) There is hereby authorized to be appropriated for each fiscal year, beginning with the fiscal year ending June 30, 1936, the sum of $2,-000,000 for expenditure by the Public Health Service for investigation of disease and problems of sanitation. . . .

TITLE VII—SOCIAL SECURITY BOARD

Establishment

Section 701. There is hereby established a Social Security Board to be composed of three members to be appointed by the President, by and with the advice and consent of the Senate. During his term of membership on the Board, no member shall engage in any other business, vocation, or employment. Not more than two of the members of the Board shall be members of the same political party. Each member shall receive a salary at the rate of $10,000 a year and shall hold office for a term of six years, . . .

Duties of Social Security Board

Sec. 702. The Board shall perform the duties imposed upon it by this Act and shall also have the duty of studying and making recommendations as to the most effective methods of providing economic security through social insurance, and as to legislation and matters of administrative policy concerning old-age pensions, unemployment compensation, accident compensation, and related subjects. . . .

TITLE VIII—TAXES WITH RESPECT TO EMPLOYMENT

Income Tax on Employees

Section 801. In addition to other taxes, there shall be levied, collected, and paid upon the income of every individual a tax equal to the following percentages of the wages (as defined in section 811) received by him after December 31, 1936, with respect to employment (as defined in section 811) after such date:
  (1) With respect to employment during the calendar years 1937, 1938, and 1939, the rate shall be 1 per centum.
  (2) With respect to employment during the calendar years 1940, 1941, and 1942, the rate shall be 1½ per centum.
  (3) With respect to employment during the calendar years 1943, 1944, and 1945, the rate shall be 2 percentum.
  (4) With respect to employment during the calendar years 1946, 1947, and 1948, the rate shall be 2½ per centum.
  (5) With respect to employment after December 31, 1948, the rate shall be 3 per centum.

Deduction of Tax From Wages

Sec. 802. (a) The tax imposed by section 801 shall be collected by the employer of the taxpayer, by deducting the amount of the tax from the wages as and when paid. . . .

Excise Tax on Employers

Sec. 804. In addition to other taxes, every employer shall pay an excise tax, with respect to having individuals in his employ, equal to the following percentages of the wages (as defined in section 811) paid by him after December 31, 1936, with respect to employment (as defined in section 811) after such date:

(1) With respect to employment during the calendar years 1937, 1938, and 1939, the rate shall be 1 per centum.

(2) With respect to employment during the calendar years 1940, 1941, and 1942, the rate shall be 1½ per centum.

(3) With respect to employment during the calendar years 1943, 1944, and 1945, the rate shall be 2 per centum.

(4) With respect to employment during the calendar years 1946, 1947, 1948, the rate shall be 2½ per centum.

(5) With respect to employment after December 31, 1948, the rate shall be 3 per centum. . . .

Definitions

Sec. 811. When used in this title—. . . (b) The term "employment" means any service, of whatever nature, performed within the United States by an employee for his employer, except—

(1) Agricultural labor;

(2) Domestic service in a private home;

(3) Casual labor not in the course of the employer's trade or business;

(4) Service performed by an individual who has attained the age of sixty-five;

(5) Service performed as an officer or member of the crew of a vessel documented under the laws of the United States or of any foreign country;

(6) Service performed in the employ of the United States Government or of an instrumentality of the United States;

(7) Service performed in the employ of a State, a political subdivision thereof, or an instrumentality of one or more States or political subdivisions;

(8) Service performed in the employ of a corporation. community chest, fund, or foundation, organized and operated exclusively for religious, charitable, scientific, literary, or educational purposes, or for the prevention of cruelty to children or animals, no part of the net earnings of which inures to the benefit of any private shareholder or individual.

TITLE IX—TAX ON EMPLOYERS OF EIGHT OR MORE

Imposition of Tax

Section 901. On and after January 1, 1936, every employer shall pay for each calendar year an excise tax, with respect to having individuals in his employ, equal to the following percentages of the total wages payable by him with respect to employment during such calendar year:

(1) With respect to employment during the calendar year 1936 the rate shall be 1 per centum;

(2) With respect to employment during the calendar year 1937 the rate shall be 2 per centum;

(3) With respect to employment after December 31, 1937, the rate shall be 3 per centum. . . .

Certification of State Laws

Sec. 903. (a) The Social Security Board shall approve any State law submitted to it, within thirty days of such submission, which it finds provides that —

(1) All compensation is to be paid through public employment offices in the State or such other agencies as the Board may approve;

(2) No compensation shall be payable with respect to any day of unemployment occurring within two years after the first day of the first period with respect to which contributions are required;

(3) All money received in the unemployment fund shall immediately upon such receipt be paid over to the Secretary of the Treasury to the credit of the Unemployment Trust Fund. . . .

(5) Compensation shall not be denied in such State to any otherwise eligible individual for refusing to accept new work under any of the following conditions: (A) If the position offered is vacant due directly to a strike, lockout, or other labor dispute; (B) if the wages, hours, or other conditions of the work offered are substantially less favorable to the individual than those prevailing for similar work in the locality; (C) if as a condition of being employed the individual would be required to join a company union or to resign from or refrain from joining any bona fide labor organization.

Unemployment Trust Fund

Sec. 904. (a) There is hereby established in the Treasury of the United States a trust fund to be known as the "Unemployment Trust Fund, . . ."

(b) It shall be the duty of the Secretary of the Treasury to invest such portion of the Fund as is not, in his judgment, required to meet current withdrawals. Such investment may be made only in interest bearing obligations of the United States or in obligations guaranteed as to both principal and interest by the United States. . . .

Interstate Commerce

Sec. 906. No person required under a State law to make payments to an unemployment fund shall be relieved from compliance therewith on the ground that he is engaged in interstate commerce, or that the State law does not distinguish between employees engaged in interstate commerce and those engaged in intrastate commerce.

Definitions

Sec. 907. When used in this title — (a) The term "employer" does not include any person unless on each of some twenty days during the taxable year, each day being in a different calendar week, the total number of individuals who were in his employ for some portion of the day (whether or not at the same moment of time) was eight or more. . . .

TITLE X—GRANTS TO STATES FOR AID TO THE BLIND

Appropriation

Section 1001. For the purpose of enabling each State to furnish financial assistance, as far as practicable under the conditions in such State, to needy individuals who are blind, there is hereby authorized to be appropriated for the fiscal year ending June 30, 1936, the sum of $3,000,000, and there is hereby authorized to be appropriated for each fiscal year thereafter a sum sufficient to carry out the purposes of this title. The sums made available under this section shall be used for making payments to States which have submitted, and had approved by the Social Security Board, State plans for aid to the blind. . . .

THE ROOSEVELT YEARS
1933 – 1944

THE ROOSEVELT YEARS
1933–1944

IMPLEMENTING THE SOCIAL SECURITY ACT: 1935

After signing the Social Security Act on August 14, President Roosevelt sent the names of the three members of the Social Security Board to Congress. John G. Winant, a former Republican governor of New Hampshire, Arthur Altmeyer of Wisconsin, Assistant Secretary of Labor, and former secretary of the Wisconsin Industrial Commission, and Vincent M. Miles, lawyer and Democratic national committeeman from Arkansas, were confirmed on August 23.

The work of the Board did not start propitiously. A Huey Long filibuster prevented an appropriation in 1935, and so there were no funds. Fortunately, the comptroller-general agreed to a formula giving a project grant from the Federal Emergency Relief Administration to the Board's staff to finance their activities in setting up the social security system. The Board also profited by the misfortune of the National Industrial Recovery Administration and inherited the administration's office equipment after the Supreme Court had declared the National Recovery Act unconstitutional in May, 1935.

The Board had other advantages. It was new and independent of traditional departments. Its prestige attracted good personnel, although it also attracted the interest of Congressmen seeking jobs for friends and constituents. At the top, however, there is little doubt that the Board attracted first-rate applicants, and it adapted well to the particular federal-state nature of the various grant programs. From the first, moreover, the Board placed great emphasis on implementing the power to conduct research, granted by the 1935 act.

Public Assistance Provisions

The Social Security Board's main task here was to serve as a resource as the states passed their legislation to take advantage of the three possible federal grants under the 1935 act: old-age assistance (OAA) paying 50 per cent of grants up to $30 a month, aid to dependent children (ADC) paying 33⅓ per cent of grants up to $18 for the first child and $12 for each succeeding child, and aid to the blind (AB) with the same terms as OAA.

The Social Security Act, while it did not include all of the strong requirements which some liberals had hoped for, had a profound effect on the public assistance structure in most states nevertheless. As the research of the Committee on Economic Security had shown, the majority of states had the most rudimentary public assistance programs, and even the most widespread program, old-age assistance, was often optional on a county basis, with each county fixing its amounts on an ad hoc *basis.*

The Social Security Act changed this. Each state now had to ensure cash payments at a state-wide level, require or supply some element of state supervision, provide hearings, and maintain confidentiality. By June 30, 1936, no less than thirty-six states had qualified for grants-in-aid under at least one of the three public assistance programs, although many of the states provided extremely limited financial assistance. While the Board could not force states to provide adequate cash payments, it could (and did) ensure that no flat payments could be made and that all the programs were based on a means test.

Congress had not only deleted the Administration's provision that the assistance furnished should provide "a reasonable subsistance compatable with decency and health," but it had also considerably weakened the provision requiring the states to adopt a merit system in their public assistance departments. Although by September, 1938, all states, territories, and the District of Columbia had one or more of the federal programs, by April, 1939, only nineteen states had instituted the merit system. It was therefore not surprising that in some states public assistance was deeply embroiled in politics.

Ohio was a notorious example. Even before the passage of the Social Security Bill, the FERA had had problems in Ohio. On March 16, 1935, for instance, President Roosevelt wrote to the Director of FERA, Harry Hopkins, putting the matter crisply:

Letter of President Franklin D. Roosevelt to Harry Hopkins
(March 16, 1935)*

My dear Mr. Hopkins: I have examined the evidence concerning corrupt political interference with relief in the State of Ohio. Such interference cannot be tolerated for a moment. I wish you to pursue these investigations diligently and let the chips fall where they may. This Administration will not permit the relief population of Ohio to become the innocent victims of either corruption or political chicanery.

You are authorized and directed forthwith to assume entire control of the administration of Federal relief in the State of Ohio. . . .

The situation in Ohio was no better after the passage of the 1935 act. Governor Davey was clearly using OAA as a form of political bribery. As

*Public Papers and Addresses of Franklin D. Roosevelt, 1935, p. 108

the 1938 primary drew near, he ordered two increases. After a hearing by the Social Security Board, a finding of improper administration was handed down. Those state officials who tried to remedy the defects were dismissed by the governor. The Board therefore refused to certify Ohio to the Treasury for the payment of further grants with the result that the October, 1938 matching grant for old-age assistance was not paid to Ohio.

The Social Security Board was also stern in other respects. Despite Congress' omission of "need" from the act, the Board reintroduced it administratively and pressured the states to establish guides for case workers. Similarly the Board stood no nonsense about state-wide standards — and while some variations in grants might be justified in different parts of a state, the basic standards were rigorously enforced, and variation within a state was strictly limited. The wide variation in payments between states, of course, continued.

Unemployment Insurance

While the condition of state public assistance laws was rudimentary in 1934, in the field of unemployment insurance, state laws were virtually non-existent: only one state had an unemployment insurance law. Yet by 1937 all the states and territories had such a law, and at least some of the credit for this must go to the Social Security Board and its Bureau of Unemployment Compensation which furnished the technical assistance. (There was more incentive to request assistance in this area since the Social Security Act provided that the Federal Government bear 100 per cent of administrative costs of unemployment insurance in the states, rather than the 50 per cent for public assistance.) Perhaps the most difficult task the Board had was persuading the states to pay benefits only through offices affiliated with the U.S. Employment Service. But this was generally established by the beginning of 1938, when most states could expect to pay their first benefits. (The number of affiliated offices rose from 215 in June, 1935, to 1,263 in June, 1938.)

Certainly there was less difficulty about insuring a merit system and an absence of political pressures in unemployment insurance. In 1939, when only nineteen states had the merit system in their public assistance agencies, thirty-nine used it for their unemployment insurance programs. Nor were there unseemly battles with the Social Security Board about the rates and standards of payments — the scheme was self-financing within the states and benefits were geared to the employer's contribution, which was related to the employee's wages. The biggest danger arose from a lack of federal minimum payments, since there would be an incentive for those employers entitled to lower contributions because of good experience rating to exert pressure to maintain minimum payments.

Old-Age Insurance

Here the Board was concerned with a purely federal program; the taxes were scheduled to begin on January 1, 1937, although the payments would not start until five years later.

The first problem—how to collect the tax—was a responsibility of the Bureau of Internal Revenue. The Bureau refused to accept the Board's advice that the British or French system be followed and that some form of stamps be used. Even more pressing was the need to assign some identification number to the millions of people covered by the scheme. In this regard the Board was apparently hampered by administrative disputes of its own and in the end, it was the Postmaster General and the Post Office Department who solved the problem by making post offices throughout the country available to distribute social security numbers. By June, 1937, over thirty million applications for numbers had been received.

Politically, the assignment of numbers was a dangerous weapon. The 1936 presidential campaign was under way, and Governor Alf Landon of Kansas began an attack on social security—an attack which was rapidly expanded by those opposed to the tax and also by those who saw political capital in the very assigning of a number. While the assault led to the resignation of former Governor Winant from the Social Security Board so that he could lead a counter-attack, President Roosevelt probably gained politically by being able to publicly rebut the more absurd charges about social security. But as a result of the attacks, the Board committed itself to a policy of confidentiality.

Letter of President Franklin D. Roosevelt to John G. Winant
(September 29, 1936)*

Dear Governor Winant: Your letter tendering your resignation as a member of the Social Security Board greatly distresses me. You are, of course, right in regarding the Social Security Act as "America's answer" to the "great human need" of "effective social machinery for meeting the problems of dependency and unemployment."

Like you, also, "I have never assumed that the Social Security Act was without fault. I had assumed and even hoped that time and experience might dictate many and important changes."

The Act was conceived and passed by the Congress as a humanitarian measure. Its passage transcended party lines. The opposition in both houses was, practically speaking, negligible. I share your regret that the evanescent passions of a political campaign have fanned the flames of partisan hostility to this nonpartisan legislation.

*Public Papers and Addresses of Franklin D. Roosevelt, 1936, p. 392–93.

Equally right are you in recognizing the "intention of Congress to create a non-partisan board, with personnel protected under civil service, and to insure non-partisan administration of the Act." Your appointment was intended to insure that it would be so administered. And, as you state, "it has been so administered."

Under such conditions I should have thought that you might have felt free to correct any misconception of the purpose of the legislation or any misinterpretation of its details. Appropriate education of the public mind regarding public measures is one of the inherent duties of an administrator.

For that reason I have hesitated to accept your resignation. I did not wish to lose the benefit of your devoted and disinterested service in the administration of the social security program. Yet, upon reflection and after talking with you, I have come to appreciate your position and the sense of public duty which impelled your resignation and your wish to be free as a citizen, not simply to clear up misconceptions and misinterpretations of the Act, but actively to defend the "constructive provisions" of the Act and to oppose spurious substitutes.

It is, therefore, with the deepest regret that I yield to your wish and accept your resignation. My regret is tempered by the knowledge that you have resigned only in order the better to defend the great work which you have so well begun.

The work within the Board was handled by the Bureau of Old-Age Insurance, and by the time the first taxes were collected in 1937, there were some 175 local offices (327 by mid-1939). By September, 1937 the reports on some thirty-six million employees began to pour in. At the same time the economic and political implications of the huge reserves which would be accumulated, at least until 1980, were finally appreciated, and a resolution by Senator Vanderberg in January, 1937 ultimately led to the establishment of an Advisory Council on Social Security.

CONSTITUTIONAL CHALLENGES

In the meantime, in a series of three cases, the Supreme Court upheld the constitutionality of the 1935 legislation. In Steward Machine Co. v. Davis, *301 U.S. 548, the constitutionality of the tax under Title IX and the payments under Title III were directly assailed. Both were held constitutional in an opinion by Mr. Justice Cardozo, with four Justices dissenting:*

Steward Machine Co. v. Davis
301 U.S. 548 (1937)

Mr. Justice Cardozo delivered the opinion of the Court.

The validity of the tax imposed by the Social Security Act on employers of eight or more is here to be determined.

Petitioner, an Alabama corporation, paid a tax in accordance with the statute, filed a claim for refund with the Commissioner of Internal Revenue, and sued to recover the payment ($46.14), asserting a conflict between the statute and the Constitution of the United States. Upon demurrer the District Court gave judgment for the defendant dismissing the complaint, and the Circuit Court of Appeals for the Fifth Circuit affirmed. 89 F. (2d) 207. The decision is in accord with judgments of the Supreme Judicial Court of Massachusetts (*Howes Brothers Co. v. Massachusetts Unemployment Compensation Comm'n*, December 30, 1936, 5 N. E. (2d) 720), the Supreme Court of California (*Gillum v. Johnson*, 7 Cal. (2d) 744; 62 P. (2d) 1037), and the Supreme Court of Alabama (*Beeland Wholesale Co. v. Kaufman*, 174 So. 516). It is in conflict with a judgment of the Circuit Court of Appeals for the First Circuit, from which one judge dissented. *Davis v. Boston & Maine R. Co.*, 89 F. (2d) 368. An important question of constitutional law being involved, we granted certiorari.

The Social Security Act (Act of August 14, 1935, c. 531, 49 Stat. 620, 42 U. S. C., c. 7 (Supp.)) is divided into eleven separate titles, of which only Titles IX and III are so related to this case as to stand in need of summary.

The caption of Title IX is "Tax on Employers of Eight or More." Every employer (with stated exceptions) is to pay for each calendar year "an excise tax, with respect to having individuals in his employ," the tax to be measured by prescribed percentages of the total wages payable by the employer during the calendar year with respect to such employment. § 901. One is not, however, an "employer" within the meaning of the act unless he employs eight persons or more. § 907 (a). There are also other limitations of minor importance. The term "employment" too has its special definition, excluding agricultural labor, domestic service in a private home and some other smaller classes. § 907 (c). The tax begins with the year 1936, and is payable for the first time on January 31, 1937. During the calendar year 1936 the rate is to be one per cent, during 1937 two per cent, and three per cent thereafter. The proceeds, when collected, go into the Treasury of the United States like internal-revenue collections generally. § 905 (a). They are not earmarked in any way. In certain circumstances, however, credits are allowable. § 902. If the taxpayer has made contributions to an unemployment fund under a state law, he may credit such contributions against the federal tax, provided, however, that the total credit allowed to any taxpayer shall not exceed 90 per centum of the tax against which it is credited, and provided also that the state law shall have been certified to the Secretary of the Treasury by the Social Security Board as satisfying certain minimum criteria. § 902. The provisions of § 903 defining those criteria are stated in the margin.[1] Some of the conditions thus attached to the allowance of a credit are designed to give assurance that the state unemployment compensation law shall be one in substance as well as name. Others are designed to give assurance that the contributions shall be protected against loss after payment to the state. To this last end there are provisions that before a state law shall have the approval of the Board it must direct that the contributions to the state fund be paid over immediately to the Secretary of the Treasury to the credit of the "Unemployment Trust Fund." Section 904 establishing this fund is quoted below. For the moment it is enough to say that the Fund is to be held by the Secretary of the Treasury, who is to invest in government securities any portion not required in his judgment to meet current withdrawals. He is authorized and directed to pay out of the Fund to any competent state agency such sums as it may duly requisition from the amount standing to its credit. § 904 (f).

Title III, which is also challenged as invalid, has the caption "Grants to States for Unemployment Compensation Administration." Under this title, certain sums of money are "authorized to be appropriated" for the purpose of assisting the states in the administration of their unemployment compensation laws, the maximum for the fiscal year ending June 30, 1936 to be $4,000,000, and $49,000,000 for each fiscal year thereafter. § 301. No present appropriation is made to the extent of a single dollar. All that the title does is to authorize future appropriations. Actually only $2,250,000 of the $4,000,000 authorized was appropriated for 1936 (Act of Feb. 11, 1936, c. 49, 49 Stat. 1109, 1113) and only $29,000,000 of the $40,000,000 authorized for the following year. Act of June 22, 1936, c. 689, 49 Stat. 1597, 1605. The appropriations when made were not specifically out of the proceeds of the employment tax, but out of any moneys in the Treasury. Other sections of the title prescribe the method by which the payments are

[1]Sec. 903, and Sec. 904.

to be made to the state (§ 302) and also certain conditions to be established to the satisfaction of the Social Security Board before certifying the
propriety of a payment to the Secretary of the Treasury. § 303. They are
designed to give assurance to the Federal Government that the moneys
granted by it will not be expended for purposes alien to the grant, and will
be used in the administration of genuine unemployment compensation
laws.

The assault on the statute proceeds on an extended front. Its assailants
take the ground that the tax is not an excise; that it is not uniform throughout the United States as excises are required to be; that its exceptions are
so many and arbitrary as to violate the Fifth Amendment; that its purpose
was not revenue, but an unlawful invasion of the reserved powers of the
states; and that the states in submitting to it have yielded to coercion and
have abandoned governmental functions which they are not permitted to
surrender.

The objections will be considered seriatim with such further explanation
as may be necessary to make their meaning clear.

First. The tax, which is described in the statute as an excise, is laid with
uniformity throughout the United States as a duty, an impost or an excise
upon the relation of employment.

1. We are told that the relation of employment is one so essential to the
pursuit of happiness that it may not be burdened with a tax. Appeal is
made to history. From the precedents of colonial days we are supplied with
illustrations of excises common in the colonies. They are said to have been
bound up with the enjoyment of particular commodities. Appeal is also
made to principle or the analysis of concepts. An excise, we are told, im-
ports a tax upon a privilege; employment, it is said, is a right, not a privilege, from which it follows that employment is not subject to an excise.
Neither the one appeal nor the other leads to the desired goal.

As to the argument from history: Doubtless there were many excises in
colonial days and later that were associated, more or less intimately, with
the enjoyment or the use of property. This would not prove, even if no
others were then known, that the forms then accepted were not subject to
enlargement. Cf. *Pensacola Telegraph Co.* v. *Western Union*, 96 U.S. 1, 9;
In re Debs 158 U.S. 564, 591; *South Carolina* v. *United States*, 199 U.S.
437, 448, 449. But in truth other excises *were* known, and known since
early times. Thus in 1695 (6 & 7 Wm. III, c. 6), Parliament passed an act
which granted "to His Majesty certain Rates and Duties upon Marriage,
Births and Burials," all for the purpose of "carrying on the War against
France with Vigour." See *Opinion of the Justices*, 196 Mass. 603, 609; 85
N. E. 545. No commodity was affected there. The industry of counsel has
supplied us with an apter illustration where the tax was not different in
substance from the one now challenged as invalid. In 1777, before our
Constitutional Convention, Parliament laid upon employers an annual

"duty" of 21 shillings for "every male Servant" employed in stated forms of work.[3] Revenue Act of 1777, 17 George III, c. 39.[4] The point is made as a distinction that a tax upon the use of male servants was thought of as a tax upon a luxury. *Davis* v. *Boston & Maine R. Co., supra.* It did not touch employments in husbandry or business. This is to throw over the argument that historically an excise is a tax upon the enjoyment of commodities. But the attempted distinction, whatever may be thought of its validity, is inapplicable to a statute of Virginia passed in 1780. There a tax of three pounds, six shillings and eight pence was to be paid for every male tithable above the age of twenty-one years (with stated exceptions), and a like tax for "every white servant whatsoever, except apprentices under the age of twenty one years." 10 Hening's Statutes of Virginia, p. 244. Our colonial forbears knew more about ways of taxing than some of their descendants seem to be willing to concede.[5]

The historical prop failing, the prop or fancied prop of principle remains. We learn that employment for lawful gain is a "natural" or "inherent" or "inalienable" right, and not a "privilege" at all. But natural rights, so called, are as much subject to taxation as rights of less importance.[6] An excise is not limited to vacations or activities that may be prohibited altogether. It is not limited to those that are the outcome of a franchise. It extends to vocations or activities pursued as of common right. What the individual does in the operation of a business is amenable to taxation just as much as what he owns, at all events if the classification is not tyrannical or arbitrary. "Business is as legitimate an object of the taxing powers as property." *Newton* v. *Atchison*, 31 Kan. 151, 154 (per Brewer, J.); 1 Pac. 288. Indeed, ownership itself, as we had occasion to point out the other day, is only a bundle of rights and privileges invested with a single name. *Henneford* v. *Silas Mason Co.*, 300 U. S. 577. "A state is at liberty, if it pleases, to tax them all collectively, or to separate the faggots and lay the charge distributively." *Ibid.* Employment is a business relation, if not itself a

[3]The list of services is comprehensive. It included: "Maitre d'Hotel, House-steward, Butler, Under-butler, Clerk of the Kitchen, Confectioner, Cook, House-porter, Footman, Running-footman, Coachman, Groom, Postillion, Stable-boy, and the respective Helpers in the Stables of such Coachman, Groom, or Postillion, or in the Capacity of Gardener (not being a Day-labourer), Park-keeper, Gamekeeper, Huntsman, Whipper-in . . ."

[4]The statute, amended from time to time, but with its basic structure unaffected, is on the statute books today. Act of 1803, 43 George III, c. 161; Act of 1812, 52 George III, c. 93; Act of 1853, 16 & 17 Vict., c. 90; Act of 1869, 32 & 33 Vict., c. 14. 24 Halsbury's Laws of England, 1st ed., pp. 692 *et seq.*

[5]See also the following laws imposing occupation taxes: 12 Hening's Statutes of Virginia, p. 285, Act of 1786; Chandler, The Colonial Records of Georgia, vol. 19, Part 2, p. 88, Act of 1778; 1 Potter, Taylor and Yancey, North Carolina Revised Laws, p. 501, Act of 1784.

[6]The cases are brought together by Professor John MacArthur Maguire in an essay, "Taxing the Exercise of Natural Rights" (Harvard Legal Essays, 1934, pp. 273, 322).

The Massachusetts decisions must be read in the light of the particular definitions and restrictions of the Massachusetts Constitution. *Opinion of the Justices*, 282 Mass. 619, 622; 186 N. E. 490; 266 Mass. 590, 593; 165 N. E. 904. And see *Howes Brothers Co.* v. *Massachusetts Unemployment Compensation Comm'n, supra.* pp. 730, 731.

business. It is a relation without which business could seldom be carried on effectively. The power to tax the activities and relations that constitute a calling considered as a unit is the power to tax any of them. The whole includes the parts. *Nashville, C. & St. L. Ry. Co.* v. *Wallace*, 288 U.S. 249, 267, 268.

The subject matter of taxation open to the power of the Congress is as comprehensive as that open to the power of the states, though the method of apportionment may at times be different. "The Congress shall have power to lay and collect taxes, duties, imposts and excises." Art. 1, § 8. If the tax is a direct one, it shall be apportioned according to the census or enumeration. If it is a duty, impost, or excise, it shall be uniform throughout the United States. Together, these classes include every form of tax appropriate to sovereignty. Cf. *Burnet* v. *Brooks*, 288 U.S. 378, 403, 405; *Brushaber* v. *Union Pacific R. Co.*, 240 U.S. 1, 12. Whether the tax is to be classified as an "excise" is in truth not of critical importance. If not that, it is an "impost" (*Pollock* v. *Farmers' Loan & Trust Co.*, 158 U.S. 601, 622, 625; *Pacific Insurance Co.* v. *Soule*, 7 Wall. 433, 445), or a "duty" (*Veasie Bank* v. *Fenno*, 8 Wall. 533, 546, 547; *Pollock* v. *Farmers' Loan & Trust Co.*, 157 U.S. 429, 570; *Knowlton* v. *Moore*, 178 U.S. 41, 46). A capitation or other "direct" tax it certainly is not. "Although there have been from time to time intimations that there might be some tax which was not a direct tax nor included under the words 'duties, imposts and excises,' such a tax for more than one hundred years of national existence has as yet remained undiscovered, notwithstanding the stress of particular circumstances has invited thorough investigation into sources of powers," *Pollock* v. *Farmers' Loan & Trust Co.*, 157 U.S. 429, 557. There is no departure from that thought in later cases, but rather a new emphasis of it. Thus, in *Thomas* v. *United States*, 192 U.S. 363, 370, it was said of the words "duties, imposts and excises" that "they were used comprehensively to cover customs and excise duties imposed on importation, consumption, manufacture and sale of certain commodities, privileges, particular business transactions, vocations, occupations and the like." At times taxpayers have contended that the Congress is without power to lay an excise on the enjoyment of a privilege created by state law. The contention has been put aside as baseless. Congress may tax the transmission of property by inheritance or will, though the states and not Congress have created the privilege of succession. *Knowlton* v. *Moore, supra*, p. 58. Congress may tax the enjoyment of a corporate franchise, though a state and not Congress has brought the franchise into being. *Flint* v. *Stone Tracy Co.*, 220 U.S. 107, 155. The statute books of the states are strewn with illustrations of taxes laid on occupations pursued of common right.[7] We find no basis for a holding that the power in that regard which belongs by accepted practice

[7]Alabama General Acts, 1935, c. 194, Art. XIII (flat license tax on occupations); Arizona Revised Code, Supplement (1936) § 3138a *et seq.* (general gross receipts tax); Connecticut General Statutes, Supplement (1935) §§ 457c, 458c (gross receipts tax on unincorporated

to the legislatures of the states, has been denied by the Constitution to the Congress of the nation.

2. The tax being an excise, its imposition must conform to the canon of uniformity. There has been no departure from this requirement. According to the settled doctrine the uniformity exacted is geographical, not intrinsic. *Knowlton* v. *Moore, supra*, p. 83; *Flint* v. *Stone Tracy Co., supra*, p. 158; *Billings* v. *United States*, 232 U.S. 261, 282; *Stellwagen* v. *Clum*, 245 U.S. 605, 613; *LaBelle Iron Works* v. *United States*, 256 U.S. 377, 392; *Poe* v. *Seaborn*, 282 U.S. 101, 117; *Wright* v. *Vinton Branch Mountain Trust Bank*, 300 U.S. 440. "The rule of liability shall be the same in all parts of the United States." *Florida* v. *Mellon*, 273 U.S. 12, 17.

Second. The excise is not invalid under the provisions of the Fifth Amendment by force of its exemptions.

The statute does not apply, as we have seen, to employers of less than eight. It does not apply to agricultural labor, or domestic service in a private home or to some other classes of less importance. Petitioner contends that the effect of these restrictions is an arbitrary discrimination vitiating the tax.

The Fifth Amendment unlike the Fourteenth has no equal protection clause. *LaBelle Iron Works* v. *United States, supra; Brushaber* v. *Union Pacific R. Co., supra*, p. 24. But even the states, though subject to such a clause, are not confined to a formula of rigid uniformity in framing measures of taxation. *Swiss Oil Corp.* v. *Shanks*, 273 U.S. 407, 413. They may tax some kinds of property at one rate, and others at another, and exempt others altogether. *Bell's Gap R. Co.* v. *Pennsylvania*, 134 U.S. 232; *Stebbins* v. *Riley*, 268 U.S. 137, 142; *Ohio Oil Co.* v. *Conway*, 281 U.S. 146, 150. They may lay an excise on the operations of a particular kind of business, and exempt some other kind of business closely akin thereto. *Quong Wing* v. *Kirkendall*, 223 U.S. 59, 62; *American Sugar Refining Co.* v. *Louisiana*, 179 U.S. 89, 94; *Armour Packing Co.* v. *Lacy*, 200 U.S. 226, 235; *Brown-Forman Co.* v. *Kentucky*, 217 U.S. 563, 573; *Heisler* v. *Thomas Colliery Co.*, 260 U.S. 245, 255; *State Board of Tax Comm'rs* v. *Jackson*, 283 U.S. 527, 537, 538. If this latitude of judgment is lawful for the states, it is lawful, *a fortiori*, in legislation by the Congress, which is subject to restraints less narrow and confining. *Quong Wing* v. *Kirkendall, supra*.

The classifications and exemptions directed by the statute now in controversy have support in considerations of policy and practical convenience that cannot be condemned as arbitrary. The classifications and exemptions

---

businesses); Revised Code of Delaware (1935) §§ 192–197 (flat license tax on occupations); Compiled Laws of Florida, Permanent Supplement (1936) Vol. I. § 1279 (flat license tax on occupations); Georgia Laws, 1935, p. 11 (flat license tax on occupations); Indiana Statutes Ann. (1933) § 64–2601 *et seq.* (general gross receipts tax); Louisiana Laws, 3rd Extra Session, 1934, Act No. 15, 1st Extra Session, 1935, Acts Nos. 5, 6 (general gross receipts tax); South Dakota Laws, 1933, c. 184 (general gross receipts tax, expired June 30, 1935); Washington Laws, 1935, c. 180, Title II (general gross receipts tax); West Virginia Code, Supplement (1935) § 960 (general gross receipts tax).

would therefore be upheld if they had been adoped by a state and the provisions of the Fourteenth Amendment were invoked to annul them. This is held in two cases passed upon today in which precisely the same provisions were the subject of attack, the provisions being contained in the Unemployment Compensation Law of the State of Alabama. *Carmichael* v. *Southern Coal & Coke Co.*, and *Carmichael* v. *Gulf States Paper Corp., ante*, p. 495. The opinion rendered in those cases covers the ground fully. It would be useless to repeat the argument. The act of Congress is therefore valid, so far at least as its system of exemptions is concerned, and this though we assume that discrimination, if gross enough, is equivalent to confiscation and subject under the Fifth Amendment to challenge and annulment.

Third. The excise is not void as involving the coercion of the States in contravention of the Tenth Amendment or of restrictions implicit in our federal form of government.

The proceeds of the excise when collected are paid into the Treasury at Washington, and thereafter are subject to appropriation like public moneys generally. *Cincinnati Soap Co.* v. *United States, ante*, p. 308. No presumption can be indulged that they will be misapplied or wasted.[8] Even if they were collected in the hope or expectation that some other and collateral good would be furthered as an incident, that without more would not make the act invalid. *Sonzinsky* v. *United States*, 300 U.S. 506. This indeed is hardly questioned. The case for the petitioner is built on the contention that here an ulterior aim is wrought into the very structure of the act, and what is even more important that the aim is not only ulterior, but essentially unlawful. In particular, the 90 per cent credit is relied upon as supporting that conclusion. But before the statute succumbs to an assault upon these lines, two propositions must be made out by the assailant. *Cincinnati Soap Co.* v. *United States, supra*. There must be a showing in the first place that separated from the credit the revenue provisions are incapable of standing by themselves. There must be a showing in the second place that the tax and the credit in combination are weapons of coercion, destroying or impairing the autonomy of the states. The truth of each proposition being essential to the success of the assault, we pass for convenience to a consideration of the second, without pausing to inquire whether there has been a demonstration of the first.

To draw the line intelligently between duress and inducement there is need to remind ourselves of facts as to the problem of unemployment that are now matters of common knowledge. *West Coast Hotel Co.* v. *Parrish,*

---

[8]The total estimated receipts without taking into account the 90 per cent deduction, range from $225,000,000 in the first year to over $900,000,000 seven years later. Even if the maximum credits are available to taxpayers in all states, the maximum estimated receipts from Title IX will range between $22,000,000, at one extreme, to $90,000,000 at the other. If some of the states hold out in their unwillingness to pass statutes of their own, the receipts will be still larger.

300 U.S. 379. The relevant statistics are gathered in the brief of counsel
for the Government. Of the many available figures a few only will be mentioned. During the years 1929 to 1936, when the country was passing
through a cyclical depression, the number of the unemployed mounted to
unprecedented heights. Often the average was more than 10 million; at
times a peak was attained of 16 million or more. Disaster to the breadwinner meant disaster to dependents. Accordingly the roll of the unemployed,
itself formidable enough, was only a partial roll of the destitute or needy.
The fact developed quickly that the states were unable to give the requisite
relief. The problem had become national in area and dimensions. There
was need of help from the nation if the people were not to starve. It is too
late today for the argument to be heard with tolerance that in a crisis so
extreme the use of the moneys of the nation to relieve the unemployed and
their dependents is a use for any purpose narrower than the promotion of
the general welfare. Cf. *United States* v. *Butler*, 297 U.S. 1, 65, 66, *Hel-
vering* v. *Davis*, decided herewith, *post*, p. 619. The nation responded to
the call of the distressed. Between January 1, 1933 and July 1, 1936, the
states (according to statistics submitted by the Government) incurred obligations of $689,291,802 for emergency relief; local subdivisions an ad-
ditional $775,675,366. In the same period the obligations for emergency
relief incurred by the national government were $2,929,307,125, or twice
the obligations of states and local agencies combined. According to the
President's budget message for the fiscal year 1938, the national government expended for public works and unemployment relief for the three
fiscal years 1934, 1935, and 1936, the stupendous total of $8,681,000,000.
The *parens patriae* has many reasons—fiscal and economic as well as social and moral—for planning to mitigate disasters that bring these burdens
in their train.

In the presence of this urgent need for some remedial expedient, the
question is to be answered whether the expedient adopted has overlept the
bounds of power. The assailants of the statute say that its dominant end
and aim is to drive the state legislatures under the whip of economic pressure into the enactment of unemployment compensation laws at the bidding
of the central government. Supporters of the statute say that its operation
is not constraint, but the creation of a larger freedom, the states and the
nation joining in a coöperative endeavor to avert a common evil. Before
Congress acted, unemployment compensation insurance was still, for the
most part, a project and no more. Wisconsin was the pioneer. Her statute
was adopted in 1931. At times bills for such insurance were introduced
elsewhere, but they did not reach the stage of law. In 1935, four states
(California, Massachusetts, New Hampshire and New York) passed unemployment laws on the eve of the adoption of the Social Security Act, and
two others did likewise after the federal act and later in the year. The statutes differed to some extent in type, but were directed to a common end. In

1936, twenty-eight other states fell in line, and eight more the present year. But if states had been holding back before the passage of the federal law, inaction was not owing, for the most part, to the lack of sympathetic interest. Many held back through alarm lest, in laying such a toll upon their industries, they would place themselves in a position of economic disadvantage as compared with neighbors or competitors. See House Report, No. 615, 74th Congress, 1st session, p. 8; Senate Report No. 628, 74th Congress, 1st session, p. 11.[9] Two consequences ensued. One was that the freedom of a state to contribute its fair share to the solution of a national problem was paralyzed by fear. The other was that in so far as there was failure by the states to contribute relief according to the measure of their capacity, a disproportionate burden, and a mountainous one, was laid upon the resources of the Government of the nation.

The Social Security Act is an attempt to find a method by which all these public agencies may work together to a common end. Every dollar of the new taxes will continue in all likelihood to be used and needed by the nation as long as states are unwilling, whether through timidity or for other motives, to do what can be done at home. At least the inference is permissible that Congress so believed, though retaining undiminished freedom to spend the money as it pleased. On the other hand fulfilment of the home duty will be lightened and encouraged by crediting the taxpayer upon his account with the Treasury of the nation to the extent that his contributions under the laws of the locality have simplified or diminished the problem of relief and the probable demand upon the resources of the fisc. Duplicated taxes, or burdens that approach them, are recognized hardships that government, state or national, may properly avoid. *Henneford* v. *Silas Mason Co., supra; Kidd* v. *Alabama*, 188 U.S. 730, 732; *Watson* v. *State Comptroller*, 254 U.S. 122, 125. If Congress believed that the general welfare would better be promoted by relief through local units than by the system then in vogue, the coöperating localities ought not in all fairness to pay a second time.

Who then is coerced through the operation of this statute? Not the taxpayer. He pays in fulfilment of the mandate of the local legislature. Not the state. Even now she does not offer a suggestion that in passing the unemployment law she was affected by duress. See *Carmichael* v. *Southern Coal & Coke Co.*, and *Carmichael* v. *Gulf States Paper Corp., supra.* For

---

[9]The attitude of Massachusetts is significant. Her act became a law August 12, 1935, two days before the federal act. Even so, she prescribed that its provisions should not become operative unless the federal bill became a law, or unless eleven of the following states (Alabama, Connecticut, Delaware, Georgia, Illinois, Indiana, Iowa, Maine, Maryland, Michigan, Minnesota, Missouri, New Hampshire, New Jersey, New York, North Carolina, Ohio, Rhode Island, South Carolina, Tennessee, Vermont) should impose on their employers burdens substantially equivalent. Acts of 1935, c. 479, p. 655. Her fear of competition is thus forcefully attested. See also California Laws, 1935, 'c. 352, Art. I, § 2; Idaho Laws, 1936 (Third Extra Session) c. 12, § 26; Mississippi Laws, 1936, c. 176, § 2−a.

all that appears she is satisfied with her choice, and would be sorely disappointed if it were now to be annulled. The difficulty with the petitioner's contention is that it confuses motive with coercion. "Every tax is in some measure regulatory. To some extent it interposes an economic impediment to the activity taxed as compared with others not taxed." *Sonzinsky* v. *United States, supra.* In like manner every rebate from a tax when conditioned upon conduct is in some measure a temptation. But to hold that motive or temptation is equivalent to coercion is to plunge the law in endless difficulties. The outcome of such a doctrine is the acceptance of a philosophical determinism by which choice becomes impossible. Till now the law has been guided by a robust common sense which assumes the freedom of the will as a working hypothesis in the solution of its problems. The wisdom of the hypothesis has illustration in this case. Nothing in the case suggests the exertion of a power akin to undue influence, if we assume that such a concept can ever be applied with fitness to the relations between state and nation. Even on that assumption the location of the point at which pressure turns into compulsion, and ceases to be inducement, would be a question of degree,—at times, perhaps, of fact. The point had not been reached when Alabama made her choice. We cannot say that she was acting, not of her unfettered will, but under the strain of a persuasion equivalent to undue influence, when she chose to have relief administered under laws of her own making, by agents of her own selection, instead of under federal laws, administered by federal officers, with all the ensuing evils, at least to many minds, of federal patronage and power. There would be a strange irony, indeed, if her choice were now to be annulled on the basis of an assumed duress in the enactment of a statute which her courts have accepted as a true expression of her will. *Beeland Wholesale Co.* v. *Kaufman, supra.* We think the choice must stand.

In ruling as we do, we leave may questions open. We do not say that a tax is valid, when imposed by act of Congress, if it is laid upon the condition that a state may escape its operation through the adoption of a statute unrelated in subject matter to activities fairly within the scope of national policy and power. No such question is before us. In the tender of this credit Congress does not intrude upon fields foreign to its function. The purpose of its intervention, as we have shown, is to safeguard its own treasury and as an incident to that protection to place the states upon a footing of equal opportunity. Drains upon its own resources are to be checked; obstructions to the freedom of the states are to be leveled. It is one thing to impose a tax dependent upon the conduct of the taxpayers, or of the state in which they live, where the conduct to be stimulated or discouraged is unrelated to the fiscal need subserved by the tax in its normal operation, or to any other end legitimately national. The *Child Labor Tax Case,* 259 U.S. 20, and *Hill* v. *Wallace,* 259 U.S. 44, were decided in the belief that the statutes there condemned were exposed to that reproach. Cf. *United*

States v. *Constantine*, 296 U.S. 287. It is quite another thing to say that a tax will be abated upon the doing of an act that will satisfy the fiscal need, the tax and the alternative being approximate equivalents. In such circumstances, if in no others, inducement or persuasion does not go beyond the bounds of power. We do not fix the outermost line. Enough for present purposes that wherever the line may be, this statute is within it. Definition more precise must abide the wisdom of the future.

Florida v. *Mellon*, 273 U.S. 12, supplies us with a precedent, if precedent be needed. What was in controversy there was § 301 of the Revenue Act of 1926, which imposes a tax upon the transfer of a decedent's estate, while at the same time permitting a credit, not exceeding 80 per cent, for "the amount of any estate, inheritance, legacy, or succession taxes actually paid to any State or Territory." Florida challenged that provision as unlawful. Florida had no inheritance taxes and alleged that under its constitution it could not levy any. 273 U.S. 12, 15. Indeed, by abolishing inheritance taxes, it had hoped to induce wealthy persons to become its citizens. See 67 Cong. Rec., Part 1, pp. 735, 752. It argued at our bar that "the Estate Tax provision was not passed for the purpose of raising federal revenue" (273 U.S. 12, 14), but rather "to coerce States into adopting estate or inheritance tax laws." 273 U.S. 12, 13. In fact, as a result of the 80 per cent credit, material changes of such laws were made in 36 states.[10] In the face of the attack we upheld the act as valid. Cf. *Massachusetts* v. *Mellon*, 262 U.S. 447, 482; also Act of August 5, 1861, c. 45, 12 Stat. 292; Act of May 13, 1862, c. 66, 12 Stat. 384.

United States v. *Butler, supra*, is cited by petitioner as a decision to the contrary. There a tax was imposed on processors of farm products, the proceeds to be paid to farmers who would reduce their acreage and crops under agreements with the Secretary of Agriculture, the plan of the act being to increase the prices of certain farm products by decreasing the quantities produced. The court held (1) that the so-called tax was not a true one (pp. 56, 61), the proceeds being earmarked for the benefit of farmers complying with the prescribed conditions, (2) that there was an attempt to regulate production without the consent of the state in which production was affected, and (3) that the payments to farmers were coupled with coercive contracts (p. 73), unlawful in their aim and oppressive in their consequences. The decision was by a divided court, a minority taking the view that the objections were untenable. None of them is applicable to the situation here developed.

(a) The proceeds of the tax in controversy are not earmarked for a special group.

(b) The unemployment compensation law which is a condition of the credit has had the approval of the state and could not be a law without it.

[10]Perkins, State action under the Federal Estate Tax Credit Clause, 13 North Carolina L. Rev. 271, 280.

(c) The condition is not linked to an irrevocable agreement, for the state at its pleasure may repeal its unemployment law, § 903 (a) (6), terminate the credit, and place itself where it was before the credit was accepted.

(d) The condition is not directed to the attainment of an unlawful end, but to an end, the relief of unemployment, for which nation and state may lawfully coöperate.

Fourth. The statute does not call for a surrender by the states of powers essential to their quasi-sovereign existence.

Argument to the contrary has its source in two sections of the act. One section (903[11]) defines the minimum criteria to which a state compensation system is required to conform if it is to be accepted by the Board as the basis for a credit. The other section (904[12]) rounds out the requirement with complementary rights and duties. Not all the criteria or their incidents are challenged as unlawful. We will speak of them first generally, and then more specifically in so far as they are questioned.

A credit to taxpayers for payments made to a State under a state unemployment law will be manifestly futile in the absence of some assurance that the law leading to the credit is in truth what it professes to be. An unemployment law framed in such a way that the unemployed who look to it will be deprived of reasonable protection is one in name and nothing more. What is basic and essential may be assured by suitable conditions. The terms embodied in these sections are directed to that end. A wide range of judgment is given to the several states as to the particular type of statute to be spread upon their books. For anything to the contrary in the provisions of this act they may use the pooled unemployment form, which is in effect with variations in Alabama, California, Michigan, New York, and elsewhere. They may establish a system of merit ratings applicable at once or to go into effect later on the basis of subsequent experience. Cf. §§ 909,910. They may provide for employee contributions as in Alabama and California, or put the entire burden upon the employer as in New York. They may choose a system of unemployment reserve accounts by which an employer is permitted after his reserve has accumulated to contribute at a reduced rate or even not at all. This is the system which had its origin in Wisconsin. What they may not do, if they would earn the credit, is to depart from those standards which in the judgment of Congress are to be ranked as fundamental. Even if opinion may differ as to the fundamental quality of one or more of the conditions, the difference will not avail to vitiate the statute. In determining essentials Congress must have the benefit of a fair margin of discretion. One cannot say with reason that this margin has been exceeded, or that the basic standards have been determined in any arbitrary fashion. In the event that some particular condition shall be

[11]See note 1, *supra.*
[12]See note 2, *supra.*

found to be too uncertain to be capable of enforcement, it may be severed from the others, and what is left will still be valid.

We are to keep in mind steadily that the conditions to be approved by the Board as the basis for a credit are not provisions of a contract, but terms of a statute, which may be altered or repealed. § 903 (a) (6). The state does not bind itself to keep the law in force. It does not even bind itself that the moneys paid into the federal fund will be kept there indefinitely or for any stated time. On the contrary, the Secretary of the Treasury will honor a requisition for the whole or any part of the deposit in the fund whenever one is made by the appropriate officials. The only consequence of the repeal or excessive amendment of the statute, or the expenditure of the money, when requisitioned, for other than compensation uses or administrative expenses, is that approval of the law will end, and with it the allowance of a credit, upon notice to the state agency and an opportunity for hearing. § 903 (b) (c).

These basic considerations are in truth a solvent of the problem. Subjected to their test, the several objections on the score of abdication are found to be unreal.

Thus, the argument is made that by force of an agreement the moneys when withdrawn must be "paid through public employment offices in the State or through such other agencies as the Board may approve." § 903 (a) (1). But in truth there is no agreement as to the method of disbursement. There is only a condition which the state is free at pleasure to disregard or to fulfill. Moreover, approval is not requisite if public employment offices are made the disbursing instruments. Approval is to be a check upon resort to "other agencies" that may, perchance, be irresponsible. A state looking for a credit must give assurance that her system has been organized upon a base of rationality.

There is argument again that the moneys when withdrawn are to be devoted to specific uses, the relief of unemployment, and that by agreement for such payment the quasi-sovereign position of the state has been impaired, if not abandoned. But again there is confusion between promise and condition. Alabama is still free, without breach of an agreement, to change her system over night. No officer or agency of the national Government can force a compensation law upon her or keep it in existence. No officer or agency of that Government, either by suit or other means, can supervise or control the application of the payments.

Finally and chiefly, abdication is supposed to follow from § 904 of the statute and the parts of § 903 that are complementary thereto. § 903 (a) (3). By these the Secretary of the Treasury is authorized and directed to receive and hold in the Unemployment Trust Fund all moneys deposited therein by a state agency for a state unemployment fund and to invest in obligations of the United States such portion of the Fund as is not in his judgment required to meet current withdrawals. We are told that Alabama in consenting to that deposit has renounced the plenitude of power inherent in her statehood.

The same pervasive misconception is in evidence again. All that the state has done is to say in effect through the enactment of a statute that her agents shall be authorized to deposit the unemployment tax receipts in the Treasury at Washington. Alabama Unemployment Act of September 14, 1935, § 10 (i). The statute may be repealed. § 903 (a) (6). The consent may be revoked. The deposits may be withdrawn. The moment the state commission gives notice to the depositary that it would like the moneys back, the Treasurer will return them. To find state destruction there is to find it almost anywhere. With nearly as much reason one might say that a state abdicates its functions when it places the state moneys on deposit in a national bank.

There are very good reasons of fiscal and governmental policy why a State should be willing to make the Secretary of the Treasury the custodian of the fund. His possession of the moneys and his control of investments will be an assurance of stability and safety in times of stress and strain. A report of the Ways and Means Committee of the House of Representatives, quoted in the margin, develops the situation clearly.[13] Nor is there risk of loss or waste. The credit of the Treasury is at all times back of the deposit, with the result that the right of withdrawal will be unaffected by the fate of any intermediate investments, just as if a checking account in the usual form had been opened in a bank.

The inference of abdication thus dissolves in thinnest air when the deposit is conceived of as dependent upon a statutory consent, and not upon a contract effective to create a duty. By this we do not intimate that the conclusion would be different if a contract were discovered. Even sovereigns may contract without derogating from their sovereignty. *Perry* v. *United States*, 294 U.S. 330, 353; 1 Oppenheim, International Law, 4th ed., §§ 493, 494; Hall, International Law, 8th ed., § 107; 2 Hyde, Interna-

[13]"This last provision will not only afford maximum safety for these funds but is very essential to insure that they will operate to promote the stability of business rather than the reverse. Unemployment reserve funds have the peculiarity that the demands upon them fluctuate considerably, being heaviest when business slackens. If, in such times, the securities in which these funds are invested are thrown upon the market for liquidation, the net effect is likely to be increased deflation. Such a result is avoided in this bill through the provision that all reserve funds are to be held by the United States Treasury, to be invested and liquidated by the Secretary of the Treasury in a manner calculated to promote business stability. When business conditions are such that investment in securities purchased on the open market is unwise, the Secretary of the Treasury may issue special nonnegotiable obligations exclusively to the unemployment trust fund. When a reverse situation exists and heavy drains are made upon the fund for payment of unemployment benefits, the Treasury does not have to dispose of the securities belonging to the fund in open market but may assume them itself. With such a method of handling the reserve funds, it is believed that this bill will solve the problem often raised in discussions of unemployment compensation, regarding the possibility of transferring purchasing power from boom periods to depression periods. It will in fact operate to sustain purchasing power at the onset of a depression without having any counteracting deflationary tendencies." House Report, No. 615, 74th Congress, 1st session, p. 9.

tional Law, § 489. The states are at liberty, upon obtaining the consent of Congress, to make agreements with one another. Constitution, Art. I, § 10, par. 3. *Poole* v. *Fleeger*, 11 Pet. 185, 209; *Rhode Island* v. *Massachusetts*, 12 Pet. 657, 725. We find no room for doubt that they may do the like with Congress if the essence of their statehood is maintained without impairment.[14] Alabama is seeking and obtaining a credit of many millions in favor of her citizens out of the Treasury of the nation. Nowhere in our scheme of government—in the limitations express or implied of our federal constitution—do we find that she is prohibited from assenting to conditions that will assure a fair and just requital for benefits received. But we will not labor the point further. An unreal prohibition directed to an unreal agreement will not vitiate an act of Congress, and cause it to collapse in ruin.

Fifth. Title III of the act is separable from Title IX, and its validity is not at issue.

The essential provisions of that title have been stated in the opinion. As already pointed out, the title does not appropriate a dollar of the public moneys. It does no more than authorize appropriations to be made in the future for the purpose of assisting states in the administration of their laws, if Congress shall decide that appropriations are desirable. The title might be expunged, and Title IX would stand intact. Without a severability clause we should still be led to that conclusion. The presence of such a clause (§1103) makes the conclusion even clearer. *Williams* v. *Standard Oil Co.*, 278 U.S. 235, 242; *Utah Power & Light Co.* v. *Pfost*, 286 U.S. 165, 184; *Carter* v. *Carter Coal Co.*, 298 U.S. 238, 312.

The judgment is

Affirmed.

Separate opinion of Mr. Justice McReynolds.

That portion of the Social Security legislation here under consideration, I think, exceeds the power granted to Congress. It unduly interferes with the orderly government of the State by her own people and otherwise offends the Federal Constitution.

In *Texas* v. *White*, 7 Wall. 700, 725 (1869), a cause of momentous importance, this Court, through Chief Justice Chase, declared—

"But the perpetuity and indissolubility of the Union, by no means implies the loss of distinct and individual existence, or of the right of self-government, by the States. Under the Articles of Confederation each State retained its sovereignty, freedom, and independence, and every power, jurisdiction, and right not expressly delegated to the United States. Under the Constitution, though the powers of the States were much restricted, still, all powers not delegated to the United States, nor prohibited to the States, are reserved to the States respectively, or to the people. And we have already had occasion to remark at this term, that 'the people of each

[14]Cf. 12 Stat. 503; 26 Stat. 417.

State compose a State, having its own government, and endowed with all the functions essential to separate and independent existence,' and that 'without the States in union, there could be no such political body as the United States.' [*Lane County* v. *Oregon*, 7 Wall. 71, 76.] Not only, therefore, can there be no loss of separate and independent autonomy to the States, through their union under the Constitution, but it may be not unreasonably said that the preservation of the States, and the maintenance of their governments, are as much within the design and care of the Constitution as the preservation of the Union and the maintenance of the National government. The Constitution, in all its provisions, looks to an indestructible Union, composed of indestructible States."

The doctrine thus announced and often repeated, I had supposed was firmly established. Apparently the States remained really free to exercise governmental powers, not delegated or prohibited, without interference by the Federal Government through threats of punitive measures or offers of seductive favors. Unfortunately, the decision just announced opens the way for practical annihilation of this theory; and no cloud of words or ostentatious parade of irrelevant statistics should be permitted to obscure that fact.

The invalidity, also the destructive tendency, of legislation like the Act before us were forcefully pointed out by President Franklin Pierce in a veto message sent to the Senate May 3, 1854.[1] He was a scholarly lawyer of distinction and enjoyed the advice and counsel of a rarely able Attorney General—Caleb Cushing of Massachusetts. This message considers with unusual lucidity points here specially important. I venture to set out pertinent portions of it which must appeal to all who continue to respect both the letter and spirit of our great charter.

"To the Senate of the United States:

"The bill entitled 'An Act making a grant of public lands to the several States for the benefit of indigent insane persons,' which was presented to me on the 27th ultimo, has been maturely considered, and is returned to the Senate, the House in which it originated, with a statement of the objections which have required me to withhold from it my approval.

*   *   *

"If in presenting my objections to this bill I should say more than strictly belongs to the measure or is required for the discharge of my official obligation, let it be attributed to a sincere desire to justify my act before those whose good opinion I so highly value and to that earnestness which springs from my deliberate conviction that a strict adherence to the terms and purposes of the federal compact offers the best, if not the only, security for the preservation of our blessed inheritance of representative liberty.

"The bill provides in substance:

[1]"Messages and Papers of the President" by James D. Richardson, Vol. V, pp. 247–256.

"First. That 10,000,000 acres of land be granted to the several States, to be apportioned among them in the compound ratio of the geographical area and representation of said States in the House of Representatives.

"Second. That wherever there are public lands in a State subject to sale at the regular price of private entry, the proportion of said 10,000,000 acres falling to such State shall be selected from such lands within it, and that to the States in which there are no such public lands land scrip shall be issued to the amount of their distributive shares, respectively, said scrip not to be entered by said States, but to be sold by them and subject to entry by their assignees: Provided, That none of it shall be sold at less than $1 per acre, under penalty of forfeiture of the same to the United States.

"Third. That the expenses of the management and superintendence of said lands and of the moneys received therefrom shall be paid by the States to which they may belong out of the treasury of said States.

"Fourth. That the gross proceeds of the sales of such lands or land scrip so granted shall be invested by the several States in safe stocks, to constitute a perpetual fund, the principal of which shall remain forever undiminished, and the interest to be appropriated to the maintenance of the indigent insane within the several States.

"Fifth. That annual returns of lands or scrip sold shall be made by the States to the Secretary of the Interior, and the whole grant be subject to certain conditions and limitations prescribed in the bill, to be assented to by legislative acts of said States.

"This bill therefore proposes that the Federal Government shall make provision to the amount of the value of 10,000,000 acres of land for an eleemosynary object within the several States, to be administered by the political authority of the same; and it presents at the threshold the question whether any such act on the part of the Federal Government is warranted and sanctioned by the Constitution, the provisions and principles of which are to be protected and sustained as a first and paramount duty.

"It can not be questioned that if Congress has power to make provision for the indigent insane without the limits of this District it has the same power to provide for the indigent who are not insane, and thus to transfer to the Federal Government the charge of all the poor in all the States. It has the same power to provide hospitals and other local establishments for the care and cure of every species of human infirmity, and thus to assume all that duty of either public philanthropy or public necessity to the dependent, the orphan, the sick, or the needy which is now discharged by the States themselves or by corporate institutions or private endowments existing under the legislation of the States. The whole field of public beneficence is thrown open to the care and culture of the Federal Government. Generous impulses no longer encounter the limitations and control of our imperious fundamental law; for however worthy may be the present object in itself, it is only one of a class. It is not exclusively worthy of benevolent regard. Whatever considerations dictate sympathy for this particular object apply in like manner, if not in the same degree, to idiocy, to physical disease, to extreme destitution. If Congress may and ought to provide for any one of these objects, it may and ought to provide for them all. And if it be done in this case, what answer shall be given when Congress shall be called upon, as it doubtless will be, to pursue a similar course of legislation in the others? It will obviously be vain to reply that the object is worthy, but that the application has taken a wrong direction. The power will have been deliberately assumed, the general obligation will by this act have been acknowledged, and the question of means and expediency will alone be left for consideration. The decision upon the principle in any one case determines it for the whole class. The question presented, therefore, clearly is upon the constitutionality and propriety of the Federal Government assuming to enter into a novel and vast field of legislation, namely, that of providing for the care and support of all those among the people of the United States who by any form of calamity become fit objects of public philanthropy.

"I readily and, I trust, feelingly acknowledge the duty incumbent on us all as men and citizens, and as among the highest and holiest of our duties, to provide for those who, in the mysterious order of Providence, are subject to want and to disease of body or mind; but I can not find any authority in the Constitution for making the Federal Government the great almoner of public charity throughout the United States. To do so would, in my judgment, be contrary to the letter and spirit of the Constitution and subversive of the whole theory upon which the Union of these States is founded. And if it were admissible to contemplate the exercise of this power for any object whatever, I can not avoid the belief that it would in the end be prejudicial rather than beneficial in the noble offices of charity to have the charge of them transferred from the States to the Federal Government. Are we not too prone to forget that the Federal Union is the creature of the States, not they of the Federal Union? We were the inhabitants of colonies distinct in local government one from the other before the revolution. By that Revolution the colonies each became an independent State. They achieved that independence and secured its recognition by the agency of a consulting body, which, from being an assembly of the ministers of distinct sovereignties instructed to agree to no form of government which did not leave the domestic concerns of each State to itself, was appropriately denominated a Congress. When, having tried the experiment of the Confederation, they resolved to change that for the present Federal Union, and thus to confer on the Federal Government more ample authority, they scrupulously measured such of the functions of their cherished sovereignty as they chose to delegate to the General Government. With this aim and to this end the fathers of the Republic framed the Constitution, in and by which the independent and sovereign States united themselves for certain specified objects and purposes, and for those only, leaving all powers not therein set forth as conferred on one or another of the three great departments — the legislative, the executive, and the judicial — indubitably with the States. And when the people of the several States had in their State conventions, and thus alone, given effect and force to the Constitution, not content that any doubt should in future arise as to the scope and character of this act, they ingrafted thereon the explicit declaration that 'the powers not delegated to the United States by the Constitution nor prohibited by it to the States are reserved to the States respectively or to the people.'

"Can it be controverted that the great mass of the business of Government — that involved in the social relations, the internal arrangements of the body politic, the mental and moral culture of men, the development of local resources of wealth, the punishment of crimes in general, the preservation of order, the relief of the needy or otherwise unfortunate members of society — did in practice remain with the States; that none of these objects of local concern are by the Constitution expressly or impliedly prohibited to the States, and that none of them are by any express language of the Constitution transferred to the United States? Can it be claimed that any of these functions of local administration and legislation are vested in the Federal Government by any implication? I have never found anything in the Constitution which is susceptible of such a construction. No one of the enumerated powers touches the subject or has even a remote analogy to it. The powers conferred upon the United States have reference to federal relations, or to the means of accomplishing or executing things of federal relation. So also of the same character are the powers taken away from the States by enumeration. In either case the powers granted and the powers restricted were so granted or so restricted only where it was requisite for the maintenance of peace and harmony between the States or for the purpose of protecting their common interests and defending their common sovereignty against aggression from abroad or insurrection at home.

"I shall not discuss at length the question of power sometimes claimed for the General Government under the clause of the eighth section of the Constitution, which gives Congress the power 'to lay and collect taxes, duties, imposts, and excises, to pay debts and provide for the common defense and general welfare of the United States,' because if it has not already been settled upon sound reason and authority it never will be. I take the received and just construction of that article, as if written to lay and collect taxes, duties, imposts, and excises *in order* to pay the debts and *in order* to provide for the common defense and general welfare. It is not a substantive general power to provide for the welfare of the United States, but is a limitation on the grant of power to raise money by taxes, duties, and imposts. If it were otherwise, all the rest of the Constitution, consisting of carefully enumerated and cautiously guarded grants of specific powers, would have been useless, if not delusive. It would be impossible in that view to escape from the conclusion that these were inserted only to mislead for the present, and, instead of enlightening and defining the pathway of the future, to involve its action in the mazes of doubtful construction. Such a conclusion the character of the men who framed that sacred instrument will never permit us to form. Indeed, to suppose it susceptible of any other construction would be to consign all the rights of the States and of the people of the States to the mere discretion of Congress, and thus to clothe the Federal Government with authority to control the sovereign States, by which they would have been dwarfed into provinces or departments and all sovereignty vested in an absolute consolidated central power, against which the spirit of liberty has so often and in so many countries struggled in vain.

"In my judgment you can not by tributes to humanity make any adequate compensation for the wrong you would inflict by removing the sources of power and political action from those who are to be thereby affected. If the time shall ever arrive when, for an object appealing, however strongly, to our sympathies, the dignity of the States shall bow to the dictation of Congress by conforming their legislation thereto, when the power and majesty and honor of those who created shall become subordinate to the thing of their creation, I but feebly utter my apprehensions when I express my firm conviction that we shall see 'the beginning of the end.'

"Fortunately, we are not left in doubt as to the purpose of the Constitution any more than as to its express language, for although the history of its formation, as recorded in the Madison Papers, shows that the Federal Government in its present form emerged from the conflict of opposing influences which have continued to divide statesmen from that day to this, yet the rule of clearly defined powers and of strict construction presided over the actual conclusion and subsequent adoption of the Constitution. President Madison, in the Federalist, says:

" 'The powers delegated by the proposed Constitution are few and defined. Those which are to remain in the State governments are numerous and indefinite. . . . Its [the General Government's] jurisdiction extends to certain enumerated objects only, and leaves to the several States a residuary and inviolable sovereignty over all other objects.'

"In the same spirit President Jefferson invokes 'the support of the State governments in all their rights as the most competent administrations for our domestic concerns and the surest bulwarks against anti-republican tendencies;' and President Jackson said that our true strength and wisdom are not promoted by invasions of the rights and powers of the several States, but that, on the contrary, they consist 'not in binding the States more closely to the center, but in leaving each more unobstructed in its proper orbit.'

"The framers of the Constitution, in refusing to confer on the Federal Government any jurisdiction over these purely local objects, in my judgment manifested a wise forecast and broad comprehension of the true interests of these objects themselves. It is clear that public charities within the

States can be efficiently administered only by their authority. The bill before me concedes this, for it does not commit the funds it provides to the administration of any other authority.

"I can not but repeat what I have before expressed, that if the several States, many of which have already laid the foundation of munificent establishments of local beneficence, and nearly all of which are proceeding to establish them, shall be led to suppose, as, should this bill become a law, they will be, that Congress is to make provision for such objects, the foundations of charity will be dried up at home, and the several States, instead of bestowing their own means on the social wants of their own people, may themselves, through the strong temptation which appeals to states as to individuals, become humble suppliants for the bounty of the Federal Government, reversing their true relations to this Union.

*   *   *

"I have been unable to discover any distinction on constitutional grounds or grounds of expediency between an appropriation of $10,-000,000 directly from the money in the Treasury for the object contemplated and the appropriation of lands presented for my sanction, and yet I can not doubt that if the bill proposed $10,000,000 from the Treasury of the United States for the support of the indigent insane in the several States that the constitutional question involved in the act would have attracted forcibly the attention of Congress.

"I respectfully submit that in a constitutional point of view it is wholly immaterial whether the appropriation be in money or in land.

*   *   *

"To assume that the public lands are applicable to ordinary State objects, whether of public structures, police, charity, or expenses of State administration, would be to disregard to the amount of the value of the public lands all the limitations of the Constitution and confound to that extent all distinctions between the rights and powers of the States and those of the United States; for if the public lands may be applied to the support of the poor, whether sane or insane, if the disposal of them and their proceeds be not subject to the ordinary limitations of the Constitution, then Congress possesses unqualified power to provide for expenditures in the States by means of the public lands, even to the degree of defraying the salaries of governors, judges, and all other expenses of the government and internal administration within the several States.

"The conclusion from the general survey of the whole subject is to my mind irresistible, and closes the question both of right and of expediency so far as regards the principle of the appropriation proposed in this bill. Would not the admission of such power in Congress to dispose of the public domain work the practical abrogation of some of the most important provisions of the Constitution?

*   *   *

"The general result at which I have arrived is the necessary consequence of those views of the relative rights, powers, and duties of the States and of the Federal Government which I have long entertained and often expressed and in reference to which my convictions do but increase in force with time and experience."

No defense is offered for the legislation under review upon the basis of emergency. The hypothesis is that hereafter it will continuously benefit unemployed members of a class. Forever, so far as we can see, the States are expected to function under federal direction concerning an internal matter. By the sanction of this adventure, the door is open for progressive inauguration of others of like kind under which it can hardly be expected that the States will retain genuine independence of action. And without independent States a Federal Union as contemplated by the Constitution becomes impossible.

At the bar counsel asserted that under the present Act the tax upon residents of Alabama during the first year will total $9,000,000. All would remain in the Federal Treasury but for the adoption by the State of measures agreeable to the National Board. If continued, these will bring relief from the payment of $8,000,000 to the United States.

Ordinarily, I must think, a denial that the challenged action of Congress and what has been done under it amount to coercion and impair freedom of government by the people of the State would be regarded as contrary to practical experience. Unquestionably our federate plan of government confronts an enlarged peril.

*   *   *

Separate opinion of Mr. Justice Sutherland (in which Mr. Justice Van Devanter concurred).

*   *   *

Separate opinion of Mr. Justice Butler.

*   *   *

The unemployment compensation provisions were attacked in the second case, Carmichael v. Southern Coal Co., *301 U.S. 495 (1937), and again the Supreme Court rejected the challenge and upheld the legislation (Mr. Justice Butler dissenting.)*

Finally in Helverling v. Davis, *the old-age insurance provisions were upheld.*

Helvering v. Davis
301 U.S. 619 (1937)

Mr. Justice Cardozo delivered the opinion of the Court.

The Social Security Act (Act of August 14, 1935, c. 531, 49 Stat. 620, 42 U.S. C., c. 7, (Supp.)) is challenged once again.

*   *   *

Title II has the caption "Federal Old-Age Benefits." The benefits are of two types, first, monthly pensions, and second, lump sum payments, the payments of the second class being relatively few and unimportant.

*   *   *

This suit is brought by a shareholder of the Edison Electric Illuminating Company of Boston, a Massachusetts corporation, to restrain the corporation from making the payments and deductions called for by the act, which is stated to be void under the Constitution of the United States. The bill tells us that the corporation has decided to obey the statute, that it has reached this decision in the face of the complainant's protests, and that it will make the payments and deductions unless restrained by a decree. The expected consequences are indicated substantially as follows: The deductions from the wages of the employees will produce unrest among them, and will be followed, it is predicted, by demands that wages be increased. If the exactions shall ultimately be held void, the company will have parted with moneys which as a practical matter it will be impossible to recover. Nothing is said in the bill about the promise of indemnity. The prediction is made also that serious consequences will ensue if there is a submission to the excise. The corporation and its shareholders will suffer irreparable loss, and many thousands of dollars will be subtracted from the value of the shares. The prayer is for an injunction and for a declaration that the act is void.

*   *   *

We were asked to determine: (1) "whether the tax imposed upon employers by § 804 of the Social Security Act is within the power of Congress under the Constitution," and (2) "whether the validity of the tax imposed upon employees by § 801 of the Social Security Act is properly in issue in this case, and if it is, whether that tax is within the power of Congress under the Constitution." The defendant corporation gave notice to the Clerk that it joined in the petition, but it has taken no part in any subsequent proceedings. A writ of certiorari issued.

First. Questions as to the remedy invoked by the complainant confront us at the outset.

Was the conduct of the company in resolving to pay the taxes a legitimate exercise of the discretion of the directors? Has petitioner a standing to challenge that resolve in the absence of an adequate showing of irreparable injury? Does the acquiescence of the company in the equitable remedy affect the answer to those questions? Though power may still be ours to take such objections for ourselves, is acquiescence effective to rid us of the duty? Is duty modified still further by the attitude of the Government, its waiver of a defense under § 3224 of the Revised Statutes, its waiver of a defense that the legal remedy is adequate, its earnest request that we determine whether the law shall stand or fall? The writer of this opinion believes that the remedy is ill conceived, that in a controversy such as this a court must refuse to give equitable relief when a cause of action in equity is neither pleaded nor proved, and that the suit for an injunction should be dismissed upon that ground. He thinks this course should be followed in adherence to the general rule that constitutional questions are not to be determined in the absence of strict necessity. In that view he is supported by *Mr. Justice Brandeis, Mr. Justice Stone* and *Mr. Justice Roberts*. However, a majority of the court have reached a different conclusion. They find in this case extraordinary features making it fitting in their judgment to determine whether the benefits and the taxes are valid or invalid. They distinguish *Norman* v. *Consolidated Gas Co.*, 89 F. (2d) 619, recently decided by the Court of Appeals for the Second Circuit, on the ground that in that case, the remedy was challenged by the company and the Government at every stage of the proceeding, thus withdrawing from the court any marginal discretion. The ruling of the majority removes from the case the preliminary objection as to the nature of the remedy which we took of our own motion at the beginning of the argument. Under the compulsion of that ruling, the merits are now here.

Second. The scheme of benefits created by the provisions of Title II is not in contravention of the limitations of the Tenth Amendment.

Congress may spend money in aid of the "general welfare." Constitution, Art. I, section 8; *United States* v. *Butler*, 297 U. S. 1, 65; *Steward Machine Co.* v. *Davis, supra*. There have been great statesmen in our history who have stood for other views. We will not resurrect the contest. It is now settled by decision. *United States* v. *Butler, supra*. The conception of the spending power advocated by Hamilton and strongly reinforced by Story has prevailed over that of Madison, which has not been lacking in adherents. Yet difficulties are left when the power is conceded. The line must still be drawn between one welfare and another, between particular and general. Where this shall be placed cannot be known through a formula in advance of the event. There is a middle ground or certainly a penumbra in which discretion is at large. The discretion, however, is not confided to the courts. The discretion belongs to Congress, unless the choice is clearly wrong, a display of arbitrary power, not an exercise of judgment. This is now familiar law.

"When such a contention comes here we naturally require a showing that by no reasonable possibility can the challenged legislation fall within the wide range of discretion permitted to the Congress." *United States* v. *Butler, supra*, p. 67. Cf. *Cincinnati Soap Co.* v. *United States, ante*, p. 308; *United States* v. *Realty Co.*, 163 U.S. 427, 440; *Head Money Cases*, 112 U.S. 580, 595. Nor is the concept of the general welfare static. Needs that were narrow or parochial a century ago may be interwoven in our day with the well-being of the Nation. What is critical or urgent changes with the times.

The purge of nation-wide calamity that began in 1929 has taught us many lessons. Not the least is the solidarity of interests that may once have seemed to be divided. Unemployment spreads from State to State, the hinterland now settled that in pioneer days gave an avenue of escape. *Home Building & Loan Assn.* v. *Blaisdell*, 290 U.S. 398, 442. Spreading from State to State, unemployment is an ill not particular but general, which may be checked, if Congress so determines, by the resources of the Nation. If this can have been doubtful until now, our ruling today in the case of the *Steward Machine Co., supra*, has set the doubt at rest. But the ill is all one, or at least not greatly different, whether men are thrown out of work because there is no longer work to do or because the disabilities of age make them incapable of doing it. Rescue becomes necessary irrespective of the cause. The hope behind this statute is to save men and women from the rigors of the poor house as well as from the haunting fear that such a lot awaits them when journey's end is near.

Congress did not improvise a judgment when it found that the award of old age benefits would be conducive to the general welfare. The President's Committee on Economic Security made an investigation and report, aided by a research staff of Government officers and employees, and by an Advisory Council and seven other advisory groups.[2] Extensive hearings followed before the House Committee on Ways and Means, and the Senate Committee on Finance.[3] A great mass of evidence was brought together supporting the policy which finds expression in the act. Among the relevant facts are these: The number of persons in the United States 65 years of age or over is increasing proportionately as well as absolutely. What is even more important the number of such persons unable to take care of themselves is growing at a threatening pace. More and more our population is becoming urban and industrial instead of rural and agricultural.[4] The evidence is impressive that among industrial workers the younger men and women are preferred over the older.[5] In times of retrenchment the older are commonly the first to go, and even if retained, their wages are likely to be lowered. The plight of men and women at so low an age as 40 is hard, almost hopeless, when they are driven to seek for reëmployment. Statistics are in the brief.

*   *   *

The problem is plainly national in area and dimensions. Moreover, laws of the separate states cannot deal with it effectively. Congress, at least, had a basis for that belief. States and local governments are often lacking in the resources that are necessary to finance an adequate program of security for

[2]Report to the President of the Committee on Economic Security, 1935.

[3]Hearings before the House Committee on Ways and Means on H. R. 4120, 74th Congress, 1st session; Hearings before the Senate Committee on Finance on S. 1130, 74th Congress, 1st Session.

[4]See Report of the Committee on Recent Social Trends, 1932, vol. 1, pp. 8, 502; Thompson and Whelpton, Population Trends in the United States, pp. 18, 19.

[5]See the authorities collected at pp. 54–62 of the Government's brief.

the aged. This is brought out with a wealth of illustration in recent studies of the problem.[9] Apart from the failure of resources, states and local governments are at times reluctant to increase so heavily the burden of taxation to be borne by their residents for fear of placing themselves in a position of economic disadvantage as compared with neighbors or competitors. We have seen this in our study of the problem of unemployment compensation. *Steward Machine Co.* v. *Davis, supra.* A system of old age pensions has special dangers of its own, if put in force in one state and rejected in another. The existence of such a system is a bait to the needy and dependent elsewhere, encouraging them to migrate and seek a haven of repose. Only a power that is national can serve the interests of all.

Whether wisdom or unwisdom resides in the scheme of benefits set forth in Title II, it is not for us to say. The answer to such inquiries must come from Congress, not the courts. Our concern here, as often, is with power, not with wisdom. Counsel for respondent has recalled to us the virtues of self-reliance and frugality. There is a possibility, he says, that aid from a paternal government may say those sturdy virtues and breed a race of weaklings. If Massachusetts so believes and shapes her laws in that conviction, must her breed of sons be changed, he asks, because some other philosophy of government finds favor in the halls of Congress? But the answer is not doubtful. One might ask with equal reason whether the system of protective tariffs is to be set aside at will in one state or another whenever local policy prefers the rule of *laissez faire.* The issue is a closed one. It was fought out long ago.[10] When money is spent to promote the general welfare, the concept of welfare or the opposite is shaped by Congress, not the states. So the concept be not arbitrary, the locality must yield. Constitution, Art. VI, Par. 2.

Third. Title II being valid, there is no occasion to inquire whether Title VIII would have to fall if Title II were set at naught.

The argument for the respondent is that the provisions of the two titles dovetail in such a way as to justify the conclusion that Congress would have been unwilling to pass one without the other. The argument for petitioners is that the tax moneys are not earmarked, and that Congress is at liberty to spend them as it will. The usual separability clause is embodied in the act. § 1103.

We find it unnecessary to make a choice between the arguments, and so leave the question open.

Fourth. The tax upon employers is a valid excise or duty upon the relation of employment.

As to this we need not add to our opinion in *Steward Machine Co.* v. *Davis, supra,* where we considered a like question in respect of Title IX.

[9]Economic Insecurity in Old Age, *supra,* chap. VI, p. 184.
[10]IV Channing, History of the United States, p. 404 (South Carolina Nullification); 8 Adams, History of the United States (New England Nullification and the Hartford Convention).

Fifth. The tax is not invalid as a result of its exemptions.

Here again the opinion in *Steward Machine Co.* v. *Davis, supra,* says all that need be said.

Sixth. The decree of the Court of Appeals should be reversed and that of the District Court affirmed.

Reversed.

Mr. Justice McReynolds and *Mr. Justice Butler* are of opinion that the provisions of the act here challenged are repugnant to the Tenth Amendment, and that the decree of the Circuit Court of Appeals should be affirmed.

PRELUDE TO AMENDMENT

As early as December, 1937, the President had been persuaded that some changes were necessary in the 1935 legislation. He accordingly wrote to both Chairman Harrison (of the Senate Finance Committee) and Chairman Doughton (of the House Ways and Means Committee):

Letter of President Roosevelt to Pat Harrison and Robert L. Doughton
(December 14, 1937)*

Mr. Altmeyer, Chairman of the Social Security Board, has submitted to me some non-controversial amendments to the Social Security Act. In brief, they cover the points listed in the attached memorandum. I feel they are of sufficient importance to warrant their passage at the earliest possible date.

As these amendments will considerably improve the effectiveness of this important Act, I have asked Chairman Altmeyer to discuss this matter with you personally.

*Summary of Amendments to the Social Security Act, forwarded
    with the foregoing letter.*

1. To pay death claims direct to the wife or dependent children and save expense of probating estates — as in veterans' laws. This would save real money to the widow and to the Board.
2. To change "wages payable" in unemployment compensation to "wages paid" as in old-age insurance and permit a duplicate list of wage payments and so complete our efforts greatly to simplify employers' wage reports.
3. To enable "merit rating" to work by making technical changes. It becomes effective in Wisconsin, January 1, 1938.

*Public Papers and Addresses of Franklin D. Roosevelt, 1937, p. 542–43.

4. To permit earlier payment of unemployment compensation in states that passed their laws late. For two years funds have been built up in these states. With increasing unemployment this will get money earlier to those laid off.

5. To permit persons now 60 and over to continue working through 1941 to qualify upon retirement for monthly old-age annuities instead of receiving small lump sum payments. A great gain all around.

6. To increase coverage

   a. To seamen on American vessels. Approved by Maritime Commission and the International Seamen's Union and the National Maritime Union.

   b. To employees of national banks, state banks that are members of the Federal Reserve System, institutions that are members of the Home Loan Bank system, and the like. The American Bankers Association approves.

It became clear that to think in terms of amendments was still somewhat premature and therefore in the spring of 1938, the President wrote to the chairman of the Social Security Board:

Letter of President Franklin D. Roosevelt to Arthur J. Altmeyer
(April 28, 1938)*

I am very anxious that in the press of administrative duties the Social Security Board will not lose sight of the necessity of studying ways and means of improving and extending the provisions of the Social Security Act.

The enactment of the Social Security Act marked a great advance in affording more equitable and effective protection to the people of this country against widespread and growing economic hazards. The successful operation of the Act is the best proof that it was soundly conceived. However, it would be unfortunate if we assumed that it was complete and final. Rather, we should be constantly seeking to perfect and strengthen it in the light of our accumulating experience and growing appreciation of social needs.

I am particularly anxious that the Board give attention to the development of a sound plan for liberalizing the old-age insurance system. In the development of such a plan I should like to have the Board give consideration to the feasibility of extending its coverage, commencing the payment of old-age insurance annuities at an earlier date than January 1, 1942, paying larger benefits than now provided in the Act for those retiring during

*Public Papers and Addresses of Franklin D. Roosevelt, 1938, p. 300–301.

the earlier years of the system, providing benefits for aged wives and widows, and providing benefits for young children of insured persons dying before reaching retirement age. It is my hope that the Board will be prepared to submit its recommendations before Congress reconvenes in January.

By December, 1938, the time seemed ripe to consider amendments to the act. On December 10, the final report of the Advisory Council on Social Security was published. The report first traced its own establishment:

Final Report of the Advisory Council on Social Security
Sen. Doc. 4, 76th Cong., 1st Sess.
December 10, 1938

The Advisory Council on Social Security was appointed by the Senate Special Committee on Social Security (subcommittee of the Committee on Finance) and the Social Security Board in May 1937. The following announcement, which was issued at that time, explains the purposes for which the council was appointed and lists its members:

> At a hearing before the Committee on Finance of the United States Senate on February 22, 1937, it was agreed that the chairman of the Committee on Finance would appoint a special committee to cooperate with the Social Security Board to study the advisability of amending titles II and VIII of the Social Security Act. The chairman of the Committee on Finance has appointed such a special committee consisting of Senator Pat Harrison, Senator Harry Flood Byrd, and Senator Arthur H. Vandenberg. It was agreed that this special committee in cooperation with the Social Security Board would appoint an Advisory Council on Social Security to assist in studying the advisability of amending titles II and VIII of the Social Security Act.
>
> It is desired that the Advisory Council on Social Security cooperate with the Special Committee of the Committee on Finance of the United States Senate and with the Social Security Board in considering the following matters:
> (1) The advisability of commencing payment of monthly benefits under title II sooner than January 1, 1942;
> (2) The advisability of increasing the monthly benefits payable under title II for those retiring in the early years;
> (3) The advisability of extending the benefits in title II to persons who become incapacitated prior to age 65;
> (4) The advisability of extending the benefits of title II to survivors of individuals entitled to such benefits;
> (5) The advisability of increasing the taxes less rapidly under title VIII;
> (6) The advisability of extending the benefits under title II to include groups now excluded;
> (7) The size, character and disposition of reserves;
> (8) Any other questions concerning the Social Security Act about which either the Special Senate Committee or the Social Security Board may desire the advice of the Advisory Council.

It is understood that the Social Security Board will make all necessary studies and furnish all necessary technical assistance in connection with the consideration of the foregoing subjects. It is further understood that these subjects will be considered jointly by the Advisory Council, the Special Senate Committee, and the Social Security Board.

The Special Committee on Social Security of the Committee on Finance of the United States Senate and the Social Security Board join in appointing the following persons to serve as members of an Advisory Council on Social Security.

Then, after describing its members and their method of operation, it neatly summarized their recommendations.

Summary of Recommendations

A. Recommendations on Benefits

I. The average old-age benefits payable in the early years under title II should be increased.

II. The eventual annual cost of the insurance benefits now recommended, in relation to covered pay roll and from whatever source financed, should not be increased beyond the eventual annual disbursements under the 1935 act.

III. The enhancement of the early old-age benefits under the system should be partly attained by the method of paying in the case of a married annuitant a supplementary allowance on behalf of an aged wife equivalent to 50 percent of the husband's own benefit; *provided,* that should a wife after attaining age 65 be otherwise eligible to a benefit in her own right which is larger in amount than the wife's allowance payable to her husband on her behalf, the benefit payable to her in her own right will be substituted for the wife's allowance.

IV. The minimum age of a wife for eligibility under the provision for wives' supplementary allowances should be 65 years; provided, that marital status had existed prior to the husband's attainment of age 60.

V. The widow of an insured worker, following her attainment of age 65, should receive an annuity bearing a reasonable relationship to the worker's annuity; *provided,* that marital status had existed prior to the husband's attainment of age 60 and 1 year preceding the death of the husband.

VI. A dependent child of a currently insured individual upon the latter's death prior to age 65 should receive an orphan's benefit, and a widow of a currently insured individual, provided she has in her care one or more dependent children of the deceased husband, should receive a widow's benefit.

VII. The provision of benefits to an insured person who becomes permanently and totally disabled and to his dependents is socially desirable. On this point the council is in unanimous agreement. There is difference of opinion, however, as to the timing of the introduction of these benefits. Some members of the council favor the immediate inauguration of such benefits. Other members believe that on account of additional costs and administrative difficulties, the problem should receive further study.

VIII. In order to compensate in part for the additional cost of the additional benefits herein recommended, the benefits payable to individuals as single annuitants after the plan has been in operation a number of years should be reduced below those now incorporated in title II. If the national income should increase in future years, these reductions may not be necessary.

IX. The death benefit payable on account of coverage under the system should be strictly limited in amount and payable on the death of any eligible individual.

X. The payment of old-age benefits should be begun on January 1, 1940.

B. *Recommendations on Coverage*

I. The employees of private nonprofit religious, charitable, and educational institutions now excluded from coverage under titles II and VIII should immediately be brought into coverage under the same provisions of these titles as affect other covered groups.

II. The coverage of farm employees and domestic employees under titles II and VIII is socially desirable and should take effect, if administratively possible, by January 1, 1940.

III. The old-age insurance program should be extended as soon as feasible to include additional groups not included in the previous recommendations of the council and studies should be made of the administrative, legal, and financial problems involved in the coverage of self-employed persons and governmental employees.

C. *Recommendations on Finance*

I. Since the Nation as a whole, independent of the beneficiaries of the system, will derive a benefit from the old-age security program, it is appropriate that there be Federal financial participation in the old-age insurance system by means of revenues derived from sources other than pay-roll taxes.

II. The principle of distributing the eventual cost of the old-age insurance system by means of approximately equal contributions by employers, employees, and the Government is sound and should be definitely set forth in the law when tax provisions are amended.

III. The introduction of a definite program of Federal financial participation in the system will affect the consideration of the future rates of taxes on employers and employees and their relation to future benefit payments.

IV. The financial program of the system should embody provision for a reasonable contingency fund to insure the ready payment of benefits at all times and to avoid abrupt changes in tax and contribution rates.

V. The planning of the old-age insurance program must take full account of the fact that, while disbursements for benefits are relatively small in the early years of the program, far larger total disbursements are inevitable in the future. No benefits should be promised or implied which cannot be safely financed not only in the early years of the program but when workers now young will be old.

VI. Sound presentation of the government's financial position requires full recognition of the obligations implied in the entire old-age security program and treasury reports should annually estimate the load of future benefits and the probable product of the associated tax program.

VII. The receipts of the taxes levied in title VIII of the law, less the costs of collection, should through permanent appropriation be credited automatically to an old-age insurance fund and not to the general fund for later appropriation to the account, in whole or in part, as Congress may see fit. It is believed that such an arrangement will be constitutional.

VIII. The old-age insurance fund should specifically be made a trust fund, with designated trustees acting on the behalf of the prospective beneficiaries of the program. The trust fund should be dedicated exclusively to the payment of the benefits provided under the program and, in limited part, to the costs necessary to the administration of the program.

IX. The consideration of change in the tax schedule under title VIII of the law should be postponed until after the rates of 1½ percent each on employer and employee are in effect since information will not be available for some time concerning (*a*) tax collections under varying conditions, (*b*) effective coverage under taxes and benefits, (*c*) average covered earnings, period of coverage, time of retirement, and average amount of benefits, (*d*) the possibilities of covering farm labor, domestic employees or self-employed persons, and (*e*) the possibilities of introducing new types of benefits.

X. The problem of the timing of the contributions by the government, taking into account the changing balance between pay-roll-tax income and benefit disbursements, is of such importance as to require thorough study as information is available.

XI. Following the accumulation of such information, this problem should be restudied for report not later than January 1, 1942, as to the proper planning of the program of pay-roll taxes and governmental contributions to the old-age insurance system thereafter, since by that time experience on the basis of 5 years of tax collections and 2 years of benefit payments (provided the present act is amended to that effect) will be available. Similar studies should be made at regular intervals following 1942.

The recommendations hardly came as a surprise since President Roosevelt had already made his position clear. But at least the Board was able to use the Advisory Committee's views to strengthen its own case.

On December 30, 1938 the Social Security Board sent its recommenda-tions to the White House. It was with respect to OAI that the most radical changes were suggested, moving the program much further away from private insurance and towards social insurance by emphasizing "average wages" rather than "accrued benefits," a development which also made possible the acceleration of the payment of benefits.

The Board also suggested expanding the coverage of OAI by including survivors and disability insurance and by enlarging the categories of per-sons included. Funding and administration were to remain self-sufficient, at least for the next fifteen years. Similar changes, especially extension of coverage and improved federal-state relationships were foreseen in un-employment compensation and public assistance. Perhaps the most radical proposal was the idea of variable grants — a concept which had become increasingly attractive to the Board in the preceding months.

Advisory Council Report

Variable Grants

Federal grants-in-aid under the three public assistance provisions of the Social Security Act will total approximately a quarter of a billion dollars during the current fiscal year. These grants are made to all States on the same percentage basis, regardless of the varying capacity among the States to bear their portion of this cost. The result has been wide difference be-tween the States, both in number of persons aided and average payments to individuals. Thus, in the case of old-age assistance the number of persons being aided varies from 54 percent of the population over 65 years of age in the State with the highest proportion to 7 percent in that with the lowest proportion. Similarly State averages for payments to needy old people range from about $32 per month to $6. While these variations may be explained in part on other grounds, there is no question that they are due in very large measure to the varying economic capacities of the States.

The Board believes that it is essential to change the present system of uniform percentage grants to a system whereby the percentage of the total cost in each State met through a Federal grant would vary in accordance with the relative economic capacity of the State. There should, however, be a minimum and maximum limitation to the percentage of the total cost in a State which will be met through Federal agents. The present system of uniform percentage grants results at best in an unnecessarily large amount of money flowing in and out of the Federal Treasury, and at worst in in-creasing the inequalities which now exist in the relative economic capac-ities of the States.

The Board believes that, with such large sums involved, it would be de-sirable to establish an interdepartmental agency representing the various governmental departments which collect and analyze economic data having a bearing on the relative economic capacity of the various States. Such an agency could be given the responsibility of determining the relative economic capacity of the various States, upon the basis of which the varying percentages of Federal grants would be computed.

Another important recommendation concerned confidentiality.

Disclosure of Confidential Information

The Board recommends that State public assistance plans be required as one of the conditions for the receipt of Federal grants, to include reasonable regulations governing the custody and use of its records, designed to protect their confidential character. The Board believes that such a provision is necessary for efficient administration, and that it is also essential in order to protect beneficiaries against humiliation and exploitation such as resulted in some States where the public has had unrestricted access to official records. Efficient administration depends to a great extent upon enlisting the full cooperation of both applicants and other persons who are interviewed in relation to the establishment of eligibility; this cooperation can only be assured where there is complete confidence that the information obtained will not be used in any way to embarrass the individual or jeopardize his interests. Similar considerations are involved in safeguarding the names and addresses of recipients and the amount of assistance they receive. Experience has proved that publication of this information does not serve the avowed purpose of deterring ineligible persons from applying for assistance. The public interest is amply safeguarded if this information is available to official bodies.

The Presidential Message of January 16, 1939 endorsed all the major recommendations of the Board.

Presidential Message Transmitting to the Congress a Report of the Social Security Board Recommending Certain Improvements in the Law
(January 16, 1939)*

Four years ago I sent to the newly convened Congress a message transmitting a report of the Committee on Economic Security. In that message I urged that Congress consider the enactment into law of the program of protection for our people outlined in that report. The Congress acted upon that recommendation and today we have the Social Security Act in effect throughout the length and breadth of our country.

*Public Papers and Addresses of Franklin D. Roosevelt, 1939, p. 77–80.

This Act has amply proved its essential soundness.

More than two and one half million needy old people, needy blind persons, and dependent children are now receiving systematic and humane assistance to the extent of a half billion dollars a year.

Three and a half million unemployed persons have received out-of-work benefits amounting to $400,000,000 during the last year.

A Federal old age insurance system, the largest undertaking of its kind ever attempted, has been organized and under it there have been set up individual accounts covering 42,500,000 persons who may be likened to the policy holders of a private insurance company.

In addition there are the splendid accomplishments in the field of public health, vocational rehabilitation, maternal and child welfare and related services, made possible by the Social Security Act.

We have a right to be proud of the progress we have made in the short time the Social Security Act has been in operation. However, we would be derelict in our responsibility if we did not take advantage of the experience we have accumulated to strengthen and extend its provisions.

I submit for your consideration a report of the Social Security Board, which, at my direction and in accordance with the congressional mandate contained in the Social Security Act itself, has been assembling data, and developing ways and means of improving the operation of the Social Security Act.

I particularly call attention to the desirability of affording greater old age security. The report suggests a two-fold approach which I believe to be sound. One way is to begin the payment of monthly old age insurance benefits sooner, and to liberalize the benefits to be paid in the early years. The other way is to make proportionately larger Federal grants-in-aid to those states with limited fiscal capacities, so that they may provide more adequate assistance to those in need. This result can and should be accomplished in such a way as to involve little, if any, additional cost to the Federal Government. Such a method embodies a principle that may well be applied to other Federal grants-in-aid.

I also call attention to the desirability of affording greater protection to dependent children. Here again the report suggests a two-fold approach which I believe to be sound. One way is to extend our Federal old age insurance system so as to provide regular monthly benefits not only to the aged but also to the dependent children of workers dying before reaching retirement age. The other way is to liberalize the Federal grants-in-aid to the states to help finance assistance to dependent children.

As regards both the Federal old age insurance system and the Federal-state unemployment compensation system, equity and sound social policy require that the benefits be extended to all of our people as rapidly as administrative experience and public understanding permit. Such an extension is particularly important in the case of the Federal old age insurance system. Even without amendment the old age insurance benefits payable in the early years are very liberal in comparison with the taxes paid. This is necessarily so in order that these benefits may accomplish their purpose of forestalling dependency. But this very fact creates the necessity of extending this protection to as large a proportion as possible of our employed population in order to avoid unfair discrimination.

Much of the success of the Social Security Act is due to the fact that all of the programs contained in this act (with one necessary exception) are administered by the states themselves, but coordinated and partially financed by the Federal Government. This method has given us flexible administration, and has enabled us to put these programs into operation quickly. However, in some states incompetent and politically dominated personnel has been distinctly harmful. Therefore, I recommend that the states be required, as a condition for the receipt of Federal funds, to establish and maintain a merit system for the selection of personnel. Such a requirement would represent a protection to the states and citizens thereof rather than an encroachment by the Federal Government, since it would automatically promote efficiency and eliminate the necessity for minute Federal scrutiny of state operations.

I cannot too strongly urge the wisdom of building upon the principles contained in the present Social Security Act in affording greater protection to our people, rather than turning to untried and demonstrably unsound panaceas. As I stated in my message four years ago: "It is overwhelmingly important to avoid any danger of permanently discrediting the sound and necessary policy of Federal legislation for economic security by attempting to apply it on too ambitious a scale before actual experience has provided guidance for the permanently safe direction of such efforts. The place of such a fundamental in our future civilization is too precious to be jeopardized now by extravagant action."

We shall make the most orderly progress if we look upon social security as a development toward a goal rather than a finished product. We shall make the most lasting progress if we recognize that social security can furnish only a base upon which each one of our citizens may build his individual security through his own individual efforts.

THE SOCIAL SECURITY ACT: 1939

House Hearings

Presented with a bill including these recommendations, the Ways and Means Committee could proceed with hearings. On this occasion, the hearings were very different from those held four years earlier. OAI was on its way towards becoming a sacred cow, and presumably Congress still believed that public assistance would wither away. The hearings, therefore, were important not for what they disclosed about opposition to the new bill, but for what they told about the possibilities for change within such legislation.

It would be wrong, of course, to say there was no lobbying in the 1935 sense. Dr. Townsend was there, and was not without support. But the Townsend Movement had split, and support for flat pensions, when it did emerge in the Senate, came from a very different power bloc. Similarly, Dr. Epstein was less influential than he had been in 1935.

The hearings were important for what they told about the thinking of the Social Security Board. Dr. Altmeyer, chairman of the Board, appeared at some thirteen sessions of the House Ways and Means Committee, and he was eventually given most of what he had requested in his original statement. But it was a remarkable performance by any standard, particularly because the hearings stressed the most important change in social security, the violent swing by OAI from an annuity program to social insurance, as well as pointing to other important changes in public assistance and unemployment compensation.

OAI

Dr. Altmeyer began by outlining the studies made in OAI.

Social Security Act Amendments of 1939
Hearings before the House Ways and Means Committee
76th Cong., 1st Sess. (1939)
(p. 54)

Statement of Arthur J. Altmeyer

         *   *   *

At the close of 1937 over 36,600,000 social security account numbers had been issued. Over 6,000,000 more came in during 1938, bringing the total to date to about 12,600,000 account numbers.

The maintenance of the wage records for the millions who have active wage accounts constitutes the biggest bookkeeping job in the world. Use of modern mechanical methods in maintaining employee accounts has made it possible to carry operations forward rapidly and economically. The present cost of carrying a worker's account averages less than 20 cents a year and it is expected that this cost can be further reduced as time goes on.

Already the old-age benefit system is working effectively with respect to the provision dealing with lump-sum benefits. Beginning with 1937, lump-sum benefits have been paid to workers who had reached the age of 65 or to their estates in case of death. By the close of 1938, almost 270,000 claims, reaching a total of nearly $12,000,000 had been paid. Of these approximately 120,000 were made to workers who had reached the age of 65; the rest were made to the estates of workers who had died. The average amount for all claims certified by the end of 1938 was $44.

These sums are small, to be sure, but as the system grows older, and the total of wage accounts grow, the size of the lump-sum benefits will increase. Some idea of their growth can be gained in comparing the average lump-sum benefits paid in January 1938 and those paid in December 1938. The average for January was something over $31; for December of the same year it was something over $65.

Compared to the greater program of paying monthly benefits which will be adequate to keep a retired worker from want, these figures are insignificant. They are mentioned merely to indicate that the wheels of the system are moving smoothly and those provisions which are immediately active are functioning effectively.

Because the limited group of employments for which insurance was provided had been selected primarily upon the basis of administrative feasibility, it did not seem fair that uninsured persons should be taxed in order to provide old-age benefits as of right for the insured group. I therefore recommended to your committee in 1935 that the old-age-insurance system be made self-supporting from pay-roll taxes on insured employees and their employers.

Operation of the act has provided significant information bearing on this question. This information shows that the extent of migration, temporary or permanent, from uninsured to insured employment is far greater than was assumed by the President's Committee on Economic Security in 1935. In my last annual report I pointed out that the consequence of this migration was that the scheduled tax rates were insufficient to maintain the system on the actuarial reserve basis provided by the law.

There is, however, another and more cheerful result of this migration. As a consequence of the migration, a much larger proportion of the total population of the United States is qualifying under the contributory system to receive old-age benefits than had been expected. My latest annual report presented the estimate that, without extension of the coverage under the present law, 80 percent of the population of the United States ultimately will have qualified during their working life for at least the minimum annuity under title II of the act.

This experience throws new light on our original belief that the act ought to be self-supporting. Four years of experience have shown that the benefits of the act will be so widely diffused that supplemental funds from general tax revenues may be substituted — without substantial inequity — for a considerable proportion of the expected interest earnings from the large reserve contemplated by the present law. Therefore, it becomes apparent that the argument for a large reserve does not have the validity which 4 years ago it seemed to possess.

There is no need at the present time and, I believe, there will be no need in the near future, for supplementing pay-roll taxes from general revenue. For all classes of beneficiaries, the values of the benefits which the act provides are, and for a long time will be, substantially in excess of the contributions under the schedule provided in the law.

There is another reason for questioning the schedule of tax rates and the resultant reserve set-up in 1935. We adopted a gradual step-up in the tax rate in 1935 in order to give industry an opportunity to accustom itself to the new taxes and so avoid any undue restrictive effects. The trend of business conditions in specific future years could not, of course, then be accurately foreseen. In periods of incomplete business recovery like the present, the contributory old-age-insurance system should be so financed as to have the least possible deterring effect on business. It is, therefore, a pertinent question whether a substantial increase in the tax rate should be allowed to occur at the present stage of business recovery.

The depressing effect of the present disturbed state of world affairs upon the American economy makes it especially urgent that at this time we do not place any avoidable burdens on American productive enterprise.

Turning to amendments, Altmeyer proposed that payment of benefits begin in 1940 rather than 1942, and that those who worked on after sixty-five be allowed to go on paying social security taxes. More important were his other suggestions.

House Hearings
(p. 58)

. . . the monthly benefits payable to those retiring in the early years be increased. We believe that this can be done without increasing the eventual annual cost of the system. At this point we come to what is, in a very real sense, our basic problem in old-age insurance — how to make the protection offered more immediately effective, without jeopardizing the reasonable relationship between benefits and past earnings and without setting up a scale of benefits the cost of which would become intolerably burdensome in future years. It is essential that any plan meet both of these tests.

Even this change was probably less significant than the proposal to add dependents' benefits or the change basing benefits on "average wages" rather than "accrued annuities."

House Hearings
(p. 59)

Another proposal—to change the benefit base from total accumulated wages to average wages—would also increase the size of the benefits available in the early years. The present provision places a very real handicap on those who do not have many years left in which wages can accumulate. The average wage base would reduce this adverse differential. It would have the additional advantage of relating benefits more closely to the worker's normal wage during his productive years than is the case under the present formula.

$$* \qquad * \qquad *$$

But I think it is clear that utilizing average wages as the benefit base would give adequate protection to both long and short term participants and could at the same time be arranged so as to eliminate bonuses which would be unwarranted in the future.

This is not to say that length of service and of contributions should play no part in determining the size of the benefit. The Board believes that length of employment can be effectively recognized on a percentage basis —that is, for every year in which a worker was in covered employment, his basic benefit, as determined from his average wages, could be increased by a small percentage, and for every year in which he was out of covered employment his basic benefit could be decreased by a small percentage. This flexible arrangement would have definite advantage in that it would not put too heavy a penalty on those who spend only part of their working lives in covered employment while at the same time it would give proportionate recognition to those with long records as participants.

Although the Board was proposing extensive new coverage, it was the change from an annuity base to social insurance, together with the transformation of the reserve fund to a trust fund using a pay-as-you-go system which was to intrigue congressmen. Some even accepted the idea—totally unacceptable in 1935—that general tax powers might ultimately have to be used to support the OAI program. The full implications of all these developments were not easy to determine. Mr. Witte (who had returned to the University of Wisconsin) had already been recalled to testify about the reserve fund in particular. He attacked the calculations made by the Senate Finance Committee in 1935 that foresaw a $47 billion reserve by 1980. They were, he said, based on faulty assumptions, and in any event, the bill as finally passed in 1935 had not called for a formal reserve of this type. His general view called for a compromise.

House Hearings

(p. 1758)

. . . we must find a reasonable compromise between a pay-as-you-go plan and a full reserve plan, neither of which is at all practicable in a national old-age insurance system.

He was also sure that the future lay in increased social security tax rates rather than direct governmental contributions. Even the Secretary of the Treasury was now prepared to endorse the change in funding.

Altmeyer, however, was not prepared to accept a direct relationship between the move towards "average wage" and away from the funding concepts of a private insurance scheme.

House Hearings

(p. 2205)

Mr. Altmeyer. No sir. There is no connection between our recommendation concerning a different pattern of benefits and this question of whether you will stay on a so-called reserve plan or go to a pay-as-you-go plan. The two can be determined entirely separately. There is this relationship, Congressman, that to the extent that the different pattern of benefits calls for more immediate annual costs your excess contributions in the early years is reduced. Now, you could still, however, maintain a reserve system, in spite of that difference between the contributions and the benefit payments in the early years.

The reserve system, in essence, consists of two aspects: It is an attempt to show on the Government books the true situation as regards the operation of this old-age-insurance system; secondly, it is an attempt to budget the costs over a long period of years of this old-age insurance system.

I have said many times, and I say again, that I think both from a bookkeeping standpoint and from the budgeting standpoint, the reserve system is sound. That is entirely separate, however, from the question of the pattern of benefits and the question of how those benefits shall be paid. But because of misunderstanding concerning the reserve system, it has failed largely in its purpose of presenting to the American people a clear picture of the financial aspects of this old-age-insurance system, and it has failed, apparently, to impress many people with the sort of budgeting that is provided.

I have never said that I consider that the reserve system is the sole way that a system of old-age insurance can be constructed. There are other ways of showing on the books of the Government the true financial picture, and other ways of budgeting the cost of the old-age insurance system.

The 1939 proposals had in fact created a "credibility gap" which has endured to this day. The "average wage" was introduced so that benefits should be related to need, yet "need" was a word which could never be mentioned in the same breath as social insurance.

The Altmeyer position was readily supported, but the only important witness to take it to its logical conclusion was Dr. Abraham Epstein, who tried to connect the issue of funding as well.

House Hearings
(p. 1059)

Statement of Dr. Abraham Epstein

*   *   *

Instead of rushing into expansion of the scope the present social-security program, Congress cannot delay a moment considering amendments to basically change the direction of the old-age insurance program from one of insecurity to one of security. The present insurance system is supported solely by taxes on workers, which directly reduce the income of the very group which is supposed to benefit by the legislation, and by taxes on pay rolls which, because of their transfer to the price of goods and services, are in reality indirect taxes on the consuming public, of which the workers form the largest group. Although the only way in which the burden of old-age dependency can be shared equitably by all classes of the population is through a direct governmental contribution—a principle accepted for 50 years throughout the world—our system scrupulously avoids such a contribution. As a result our program will not only take out of the stream of purchasing power during the next generation considerably larger funds than are necessary to pay benefits but places the burden of the system primarily on the workers, especially the younger ones. Our system forces the workers, particularly the younger generation, and their employers not only to pay fully for their own annuities but also to pay a large portion of cost of the benefits to the older workers.

Indeed, not only do the workers bear an excessive load under our old-age insurance system but the withdrawal of sorely needed purchasing power is having devastating effects upon our national economy. From January 1, 1937, to June 30 of this year, the Federal Government collected in old-age insurance taxes no less than $708,752,000. Up to that date it has spent the totally insignificant sum of $5,431,000 in lump-sum payments to those insured persons who have reached the age of 65 and to the survivors of insured persons who died. This withdrawal of mass purchasing power has been an important factor in the present economic depression. This was not only the contention of the American Association for Social Security but is attested to by every index of labor and business conditions as well as by the chairman of the Federal Reserve System, who last May admitted that the

1937 depression was due partly to "the withdrawal of consuming power through social-security taxes and reduced governmental expenditures." Under our present program, this withdrawal of purchasing power over and above the benefits to be paid continue until almost 1970.

The burdens placed upon the workers and the resultant depressing effects upon the national economy make constructive changes along these lines the most imperative tasks of the next Congress. Most of the present evils could be overcome if the Federal Government would assume a share of the old-age insurance costs as is done by all other nations. Such Government participation is the only way to reverse the present trend of the system toward greater insecurity. Such a step would also offer us the best method of scrapping the utterly fantastic and dangerous reserve basis of our old-age insurance program. This reserve, which is to reach $47,000,000,000 by 1980, is totally unnecessary and inapplicable to a governmental social insurance program. Reserves held by a government are in fact nothing but a fiction as they constitute liabilities rather than assets. For, since it would be foolish for the Government to keep the funds buried in vaults and it cannot invest its moneys in private industry, governmental reserves are merely I O U's upon which the people who pay the original contributions also have to pay interest. The excess of contributions over benefits will never be returned by the Government as such reserves are returned by private insurance companies. The so-called reserves under our old age insurance system merely constitute a permanent forced gift to the National Treasury from the poorest sector of the population.

The dilemmas posed by the 1939 changes in benefit structures and funding have not been fully resolved, even today. Compared with the OAI proposals, those suggested for the other two branches of social security were less radical.

Unemployment Compensation

The unemployment compensation provisions for the most part became operative only in 1938, and Dr. Altmeyer was particularly pleased with this precaution.

House Hearings
(p. 48)

Statement of Arthur J. Altmeyer

*   *   *

The Federal act required each State to collect contributions for a period of 2 years before benefits could be paid in order to build up a sufficient reserve so that the system will remain solvent even when an emergency causes an unusually heavy drain. The soundness of this provision has been demonstrated by the experience of the 22 States which began to pay benefits in January 1938. The drain of several months' severe decline in employment was immediately thrust upon their funds. In the very first week these States were confronted with more than a million claims for benefits. As a result, in about half these States withdrawals for benefit payments exceeded current income for some months and they were compelled to dip into their reserves. But during the last few months, as business and employment have improved, States which were drawing on reserves have again begun to replenish their reserves.

Apart from calling for increased coverage, the Board was generally anxious to hold a financial line, but this proved unexpectedly difficult. The manufacturers of Massachusetts apparently put considerable pressure on Representative McCormack who was soon pressing for various devices to allow the states to lower the unemployment tax rates paid by manufacturers.

Public Assistance (PA)

With respect to public assistance Dr. Altmeyer reported himself satisfied, but he also called for certain changes. For example, the states should be forced to initiate the merit system for both public assistance and unemployment compensation (p. 67). In ADC he recommended that the federal share be made the same as it was in OAA and AB. For these programs Altmeyer, representing the Board, pressed for a radical change — variable grants.

House Hearings
(p. 68)

All of these changes . . . would not reach the most fundamental problem — that of varying economic capacity of the States. While other factors may have had some influence, there can be no doubt that the wide range in the adequacy of State programs is largely due to this cause. Since Federal grants are now made to all States on a uniform percentage basis, no consideration can be given either to the economic resources of the State, or to the extent of its burden of dependency. We believe it is desirable to change the present percentage formula to one which would allow — within maximum and minimum limitations — for variation in Federal grants in accordance with the relative economic capacity of the State. Since such large sums of money are involved, it might be desirable to establish an interdepartmental agency representing the various governmental departments which collect and analyze economic data having a bearing on the relative economic capacity of the various States. Such an agency could be given the responsibility of determining the relative economic capacity of the various States.

Considering the implications of variable grants, the questioning was not as hostile as it might have been. The committee seemed more interested in the powers of the Federal Government to cut off funds — as it had in Ohio and in the touchy question of confidentiality of public assistance records.

Committee Report

In retrospect, it was the decisions on OAI which stand out as the most significant events of the 1939 legislative year. There was no doubt that the arguments of the Social Security Board convinced the House Ways and Means Committee (and ultimately Congress) that many of the "private insurance" aspects of old-age annuities should be considerably weakened. While the Administration had rejected the argument that pensions should not be funded at all, but rather paid out of general revenues, it had conceded that the government need not maintain the type of reserve funds kept by an insurance company. More important still, the committee, by accepting that the average earnings, rather than accumulated credits, should be the basis of a retirement pension made "need" as much as "investment" the criterion for annuities. While the social security establishment was to defend the scheme as genuine insurance from that day to this, and although there may be disagreement about the definition of insurance, these aspects of the 1939 bill undercut their argument. The committee however, clearly accepted Altmeyer's reasoning.

Social Security Act Amendments of 1939
House Report No. 728
76th Cong., 1st Sess.
(May 14, 1939)

It is essential than that the contributory basis of our old-age insurance system be strengthened and not weakened. Contributory insurance is the best-known method of preventing dependency in old age by enabling wage earners to provide during their working years for their support after their retirement. By relating benefits to contributions or earnings, contributory old-age insurance preserves individual thrift and incentive; by granting benefits as a matter of right it preserves individual dignity. Contributory insurance therefore strengthens democratic principles and avoids paternalistic methods of providing old-age security. Moreover, a contributory basis facilitates the financing of a social-insurance scheme and is a safe-guard against excessive liberalization of benefits as well as a protection against reduction of benefits.

The Administration had planned little action on unemployment insurance, but a proposal which became known as the McCormack Amendment was put forth.

Provision is made so that the States may reduce their unemployment-insurance contributions if a certain reserve fund has been attained and minimum benefit standards have been provided. All except about five States will be able to take advantage of this change during 1940. This may save employers from $200,000,000 to $250,000,000 during 1940 if the States reduce their contribution rates from an average of 2.7 to 2 percent.

The committee accepted the Board's recommendation for ADC, namely, that the federal grant-in-aid for public assistance be increased from 33 1/3 per cent to 50 per cent. The committee also voted to increase the federal participation in AB but did not do so for OAA. There were two other proposals relating to all three of the public assistance programs (OAA, AB, and ADC) which the committee did accept, confidentiality of records and need as a criterion of eligibility.

In two respects, however, the committee refused to accept the Board's recommendations on public assistance. Despite the Ohio experience, it still refused to demand that the public assistance agencies in the states adopt the merit system. Moreover, it refused to accept the Board's notion of the variable grant. According to this plan the amount of the federal grant-in-aid would no longer be determined on a fixed percentage, but rather by a formula based on the economic condition of the state. Such a method of redistributing wealth within the Union did not appeal to the committee.

In 1939 other aspects of the bill seemed equally important. The system was already becoming something of a political football. The date of the first benefits were pushed forward to 1940 from 1942, while the amounts involved were increased. In addition, the tax was frozen at 1 per cent for another three years. The lump sum payments of social security were abolished in favor of the payment of survivors' benefits to widows and orphans, the first major addition to the program. The committee also accepted various administrative changes including the right to a fair hearing, but it refused to extend the coverage of social security, or to include disability coverage.

House Debates

The preliminary sparring in the House debates took place on June 6, with Mr. Robert L. Doughton [Dem., N.C.] outlining the provisions of the bill

*and Mr. Allen T. Treadway [Rep., Mass.] making a fighting speech based
on the minority report of the House committee. The speech is highly significant in some ways.*

Congressional Debates
84 Congressional Record, p. 6694
(June 6, 1939)

The $47 Billion Reserve

Mr. Treadway . . .

We of the Republican minority are particularly proud of the part we have
played in bringing about the abolition of the proposed mythical reserve
fund of $47,000,000,000 and the substitution of a modified pay-as-you-go
policy with respect to old-age insurance.

We have criticized from the very beginning this reserve fund hoax, under
which wage earners and employers were being taxed an excessive amount
on the theory that a $47,000,000,000 reserve was being built up to pay
retirement pensions in future years.

Of course, we all know that the money which is being raised by pay-roll
taxes does not actually go into the trust fund.

Appropriations are made to the fund by Congress, it is true, but the Secretary of the Treasury takes the cash and uses it for current expenditures,
and all that goes into the fund is the Government's IOU.

The Republican Party made an issue of this procedure in the 1936
campaign, but the people did not seem to be able to understand the devious
ways of high finance.

We kept hammering away, nevertheless.

In January 1937 a minority group which had been appointed to study the
question of old-age insurance in behalf of the Republicans in both branches,
made a report in which it recommended the abolition of the $47,000,000,000
reserve fund and the substitution of a pay-as-you-go policy with a small
contingent reserve.

*   *   *

The present pay-roll taxes are excessive.

Under a strict pay-as-you-go policy they would not even need to be
1 percent as they are at present.

There is absolutely no justification for collecting from business concern
and from the wage earners of the country more pay-roll taxes than are
necessary to support the system on a sound basis.

These pay-roll taxes directly reduce the consuming power of the workers
of the country and they increase the cost of goods and services because they
are a burden on production and distribution.

I am in hopes that some day some substitute form of taxation can be worked out, because in many respects the pay-roll tax is one of the worst forms of taxation yet devised.

As the debate continued it focused on funding, especially since the social security program was about to move from OAI to OASI.

Congressional Debates
84 Congressional Record, p. 6855

Mr. Frank B. Keefe [Rep., Wisc.] I would like a little information on that point. The gentleman stated that when the trustees needed money with which to meet their obligations or pay annuities, they called upon the Government to pay and the Government pays. When they make the demand on the Government to pay those obligations, I would like to know where the Government ultimately is going to get the money to pay those obligations except by the levy of taxes? If they do have to resort to the levying of taxes, then are not these same contributors, who have contributed to the creation of this fund, going to be taxed again in order to ultimately receive their annuities? That is the question that agitates the people all over the country and I would like to have it earnestly answered.

Mr. John W. McCormack [Dem., Mass.]. The special obligations are provided for in order to obtain the interest guaranteed, to prevent the Government bond market from fluctuating unreasonably against the interest, the Government, and the people.

When Congress provided that this fund shall earn 3-percent interest, guaranteed by the Government, and if bonds bearing that rate are not obtainable, it necessarily follows, unless the money is to be wholly idle, that some such provision had to be considered and enacted. In addition, it is a curb on governmental activities in its own bond market that would prevent Government bonds from fluctuating in the market in an adverse manner. Of course, when resorted to, indirectly, giving an answer to the gentleman of my own personal views, this constitutes an increase in the bonded indebtedness, but it is a situation provided by law, a situation that cannot be controlled if we are going to guarantee to this fund a stated rate of interest.

* * *

It does constitute an increase to the extent that we resort to special obligations of the bonded indebtedness of the Government. Does that answer the gentleman's inquiry? . . .

Mr. Jere Cooper [Dem., Tenn.]. Just to analyze the point of view of the gentleman, which I realize is a point of view that is entertained by many, what is the practical difference between levying the taxes now to provide funds for the Government, with these people having to pay their proportional part, and later levying taxes to provide funds when these people would then just pay their proportional part? Certainly there cannot be any practical difference.

Mr. Keefe. If these trustees were empowered as any other similar trustees would be empowered to invest, for instance, in the obligations of the H.O.L.C., obligations which are fully guaranteed by the Government but will be paid out of funds paid to the H.O.L.C. by the citizens of America, then the taxes would not have again to be levied upon those people who contributed to create this fund. That is the point I am trying to bring out.

Mr. McCormack. In answer to the gentleman, I have frankly stated my opinion. Congress provides a certain rate of interest. In order to meet that rate of interest under certain circumstances special obligations would be issued. Precedent has been established for this. These obligations occupy the same status as a bond. They are in the same category as a bond.

Mr. Keefe. I understand that.

Mr. McCormack. The characterization of these obligations as IOU's, of course, has no greater strength than if the same characterization were directed against a bond issued by the Government. Insofar as this committee is humanly able, we have provided in the pending bill a separate fund and provided for its administration by trustees, and insofar as we are humanly able we have directed those trustees to go into the open market when it is not inconsistent with the best interest of our Government and purchase bonds. In doing this, I submit to the gentleman from Wisconsin and my colleagues on both sides of the aisles, we are doing everything we can possibly do. My purpose in rising was to briefly answer what I believe to be the unwarranted statements, inconsistent with the facts of the gentleman from California.

*   *   *

Despite these claims and charges, the bill was eventually passed. Both Republicans and Democrats favored raising the federal contribution in ADC to 50 per cent, as well as increasing the maximum federal contribution in OAA from $15 to $20 a month. Both Republican and Democrat leadership showed a noted antipathy to the variable grant. The typical view was that of Representative Frank H. Buck from California.

Congressional Debates
84 Congressional Record, p. 6865

Mr. Buck . . .

Mr. Chairman, in conclusion I desire to discuss briefly the subject of the "liberalizing" amendments that have been suggested by some of the Representatives who come from States that are not matching the present Federal old-age assistance contribution. I have some hesitancy in going into this subject, because as has been pointed out, the State of California is the only State that is now fully matching the contributions that the Government makes. I am satisfied, however, that whether or not ours is the only State that can do that or will do it, the equal matching principle is the sound principle on which Federal contributions should be made. Once we start paying two-thirds of the first $15, as has been suggested, and half of the rest, or matching at the rate of 4 to 1 for the benefit of certain states, it will not be long until all the States will come to you and ask you for a flat, a uniform, and a universal pension of the kind you voted down here the other day. There are reasons, which I shall insert in the Record, for rejecting any such proposal of a uniform or universal basis.

Mr. Treadway. Mr. Chairman, will the gentleman yield?

Mr. Buck. I yield to the gentleman from Massachusetts.

Mr. Treadway. Is it not a fact that if a change in the ratio of 50-50 should be made it would simply add to the expense of the Government and in no way benefit the aged people we are expecting to aid?

Mr. Buck. That is my opinion. May I say that while this does not appear in the records, in the executive sessions Dr. Altmeyer stated that if we should adopt a proposal such as having the Federal Government pay two-thirds of the first $15 and half of the remainder it would increase the tax cost to the United States by from $40,000,000 to $100,000,000 a year.

This is on the basis of a $30 top matching. If we take the $40 top matching that the committee has recommended, the cost would be from $45,000,000 to $110,000,000 a year. The 4-to-1 matching proposal will cost the Federal Government an additional $220,000,000 per year.

Mr. Chairman, our committee is a hard-working committee. We have a great many things to consider, but, fundamentally, we are charged with raising the revenue for the country through taxation. When you vote on these so-called liberalizing proposals, remember that the next week you are going to be called upon to tax your people to pay for them. There is no alternative whatsoever. We cannot go on borrowing indefinitely; we will not do so, and we are going to have to bring in a tax bill that will wring the money out of the pockets of whom? Of those who are prepared to produce in the next generation and who are engaged in active business today in order to make these unreasonable pension payments to the States whose legislators themselves refuse to provide the funds which are necessary to take care of the States' responsibilities to their own aged. I am not insensible of the difficulties that some of our States have in providing for social aid, but I have noticed that whenever it is necessary for any State to match other Federal appropriations such as those made for roads, the States have always been able to find the necessary money. I am afraid that some of those who are urging these excessive payments are forgetting that after all it is the right of the State to determine how far it wants to go in social insurance. When the Federal Government holds up the standard, be it $30 a month or $40 a month, and says that it will match up to half that amount, any money that a State provides in my opinion, the Federal Government has extended an invitation sufficiently broad and sufficiently liberal, and until the time comes when the States take advantage of that invitation the Congress should not go further by authorizing larger subsidies which must be borne by the taxpayers on top of the already tremendous load of taxes under which they are staggering.

Such a position did not prevent the Colmer Amendment which required the Federal Government to provide four-fifths of the first $20 in the public assistance programs. Some southerners were prepared to go even farther. But with a gag rule no amendment had a serious chance, and even the Colmer Amendment was defeated. Similarly there was no possibility of weakening the McCormack Amendment which the committee had presented to the House as a fait accompli. *Under the guise of merit ratings, states could reduce the employees' contribution below 2.7 per cent in the unemployment compensation program. While the Board strongly opposed such a change, it was welcomed by the leadership of both parties. Indeed, with the exceptions noted here, the bill went through the House with a great deal of mutual admiration between the majority and minority leaders. It was now abundantly clear that, as far as the House was concerned, any changes in a social security bill had to be made in Ways and Means, and, once made, there was no real chance of altering them. In this spirit the House passed the bill.*

Senate Action — OAI

Hearings before the Senate were largely a repetition of the arguments made to the House, but certain matters were significant enough to justify special treatment. Once again it was the changes in the qualifications for beneficiaries and the abolition of the Reserve Fund which provoked the most discussion. It did not take long for the Senators to realize the point of the proposed changes. Dr. Altmeyer argued that the changes made OAI more responsive to need without requiring that the question of need be directly scrutinized, for that would have involved a violation of the insurance principle.

The toughest attack of all came from Senator Robert M. La Follette, Jr. of Wisconsin. Behind the scenes it was clear that suggestions of a flat pension scheme were gaining ground in both parties, and it seemed as if La Follette was the spokesman. Time and again La Follette showed the illogicalities of the proposed changes by producing examples of unfairness noted by Witte.

Social Security Act Amendments of 1939
Hearings on H.R. 6635 before the Senate Finance Committee
76th Cong., 1st Sess. (June, 1939)
(p. 53–54)

Senator La Follette. Is it true that no year counts toward meeting the qualification requirement at less than $200 wages received in it?

Mr. Altmeyer. That is right.

Senator La Follette. I would like to bring out what may happen on account of this slight difference in amount received by taking two examples. Take employee C and employee D who attained the age of 65 in the early part of 1938. Both earned $3,000 in wages in 1937 and employee C received $200 in 1938, before he attained age 65, but the prorata part of employee D's wages before 65 was only $199.99. Now, suppose they both ceased work before January 1, 1940. As I understand it, employee C would be entitled to benefit and employee D would not; is that correct, under the bill as it stands?

Mr. Altmeyer. I do not know whether I got all of the conditions.

Senator La Follette. There is a difference of 1 penny in the amount of wages received in the calendar year. So because he got 1 cent less he would be out, but the fellow who got 1 cent more would be in?

Mr. Altmeyer. Except, of course, in making the statement that these earnings do not count, I should correct my statement to say that they do count toward these total earnings that are mentioned here.

Senator La Follette. No; but assume that these two people, in one of the years for which they must have wages under covered employment, one of them got a cent less than $200; he would be out of any benefits, would he not?

Mr. Altmeyer. That is correct; however, by earning $200 in 1940, or later, he could qualify.

Senator La Follette. And the person who got a penny more would be in?

Mr. Altmeyer. That is true. Under the present act if a man earned $1,999.99 he would be out with no possibility of qualifying later, and a fellow who earned $2,000 would be in.

Senator La Follette. Now, employee B, in this example, would have a primary insurance benefit of $24.37, would he not?

Mr. Altmeyer. I imagine so.

Senator La Follette. So the difference of 1 penny in wages might make a difference of many thousands of dollars in benefits?

Mr. Altmeyer. Yes, sir; if the person suddenly quit working for all time.

In addition, Senator Altmeyer was required to answer a series of detailed written questions. He defended his position with a general statement.

Senate Hearings
(p. 62)

General Statement by Mr. Altmeyer

The questions submitted for the most part relate to the border-line situations arising in the early years of any contributory social-insurance system which does not cover all of the gainfully occupied persons. While many of these border-line situations could be eliminated or their effects modified by reducing the eligibility requirements in the early years, the cost would of course be greater in the early years and border-line situations would still arise.

The existing old-age insurance law has the same difficulties. Initially, its requirements are far more restrictive than those of the proposed amendments. In the first place, they exclude from coverage completely (except for a small lump-sum refund) all those who attain age 65 prior to January 2, 1941. In the second place, it is necessary that the wage earner shall secure $2,000 or more of wages, some part of which is earned in at least 5 different calendar years after 1936 and prior to attaining age 65.

The proposed amendments have substantially liberalized these provisions, making possible the coverage of those attaining age 65 prior to January 2, 1941, and reducing, as regards those at or close to age 65, the amount of wages which must be earned and the number of years in which wages must be earned. The fact that the present law excludes from coverage those attaining age 65 prior to January 2, 1941, greatly increases the problem of setting up satisfactory eligibility requirements for those retiring in the early years. These now excluded are the ones who are likely to retire soonest. However, their wages after age 65 are not reported to the Government since these wages do not count for either benefit or tax purposes. There are difficulties and disadvantages in attempting to give consideration to these wages just as there are difficulties and disadvantages in failing to take them into account.

As the system matures, the requirements in the proposed amendments for a fully insured status gradually increase, since the opportunity to qualify increases. However, there has been introduced what is known as a currently insured status, designed to provide benefits to survivors in the event of the death of an individual who has been working in covered employment approximately half of the time during the 3 years immediately preceding his death.

The fundamental problem that arises in the early years of any contributory social-insurance system is to provide benefits that are reasonably adequate and at the same time insure, as the system matures, a reasonable relationship between contributions and benefits. Obviously, if a social-insurance system is to be adequate it is necessary to pay benefits to those retiring in the early years which are in excess of the benefits which their contributions would purchase on an actuarial basis from a private insurance company. This is not in violation of sound principles of contributory social insurance, but rather an application of sound social-insurance principles. In other words, a social-insurance system should provide that the low-wage earners and the wage earners who have had an opportunity to contribute only a short time receive more in proportion to their contributions than high-wage earners and wage earners who have had an opportunity to contribute a long time. The old-age insurance system under consideration accomplishes this purpose by using a larger proportion of the employers' contributions for low-wage earners and wage earners who have had an opportunity to contribute only a short time, but at the same time provides protection to all persons at least as much as they could purchase with their own individual contributions on an actuarial basis from a private insurance company.

While the relationship between contributions and benefits cannot be exact, especially in the early years of the operation of a system, it is absolutely essential that the benefits bear a reasonable relationship to the wage loss that is sustained since protection against wage loss is the fundamental purpose of contributory social insurance. Because this is the fundamental purpose of contributory social insurance, it is of course necessary to have some earnings qualifications as a condition of eligibility for benefits. Just as in the case of contributions qualifications, these earnings qualifications cannot be as strict in the early years because those reaching retirement age in these years have had only limited opportunity to demonstrate their earnings record since the date that the system went into effect. However, as the system grows older and the opportunity to establish a contributions and earnings record increases, it is desirable that the contributions and earnings qualifications also be strengthened in order to make certain that benefits are reasonably related to contributions and loss of earnings. In this way it is possible to insure an automatic balance between contributions and benefits and to achieve maximum protection at minimum cost under a cooperative arrangement including employees, employers, and the Government.

It was thought that Altmeyer, as chairman of the Social Security Board, was able to speak for the President in the battle over "arbitraries."

Senate Action—Unemployment Compensation

Although the Social Security Board had simply intended to keep the unemployment compensation programs at their original level, those plans were upset by the McCormack Amendment. The Senate Finance Committee heard from several state unemployment commissions. In general, the poorer states were opposed to the McCormack Amendment while the wealthier ones favored it. Manufacturers' organizations supported the amendment

*and were also anxious to put a limit on the amount of wages subject to un-
employment compensation taxes.*

Senate Committee Report

*By the time the bill came out of committee it had been liberalized still
further in its OAI provision. In addition to a minimum-maximum of $10 –
$85 for the primary beneficiary, and an advance from January, 1942, to
January, 1940 for first payments, other suggestions were made.*

Social Security Act Amendments of 1939
Senate Report No. 734
76th Cong., 1st Sess.
(July 7, 1939).

*   *   *

The second major change proposed is the liberalization of benefits to insured workers retiring in the early years of the system. This liberalization is
effected by two important changes. First, the benefit base is changed from
total accumulated wages to average wages; second, supplementary benefits
are provided in those cases

The bill contains a third major change, designed to improve the long-run
effectiveness of our insurance system. This amendment proposes to establish monthly survivors benefits. The Social Security Act now provides a
certain amount of survivorship protection in the form of lump-sum payments. These are small and inadequate in the early years of the system and
entirely unrelated to the needs of the recipients. However they will eventually be rather costly and will not provide protection in those cases where
most needed. The new plan will eliminate most lump-sum benefits and will
substitute monthly benefits for those groups of survivors whose probable
need is greatest. These groups are widows over 65, widows with children,
orphans, and dependent parents over 65. The monthly benefits payable to
these survivors are related in size to the deceased individual's past monthly
benefit or the monthly benefit he would have received on attaining age 65.

In the case of a widow, the monthly benefit is three-fourths of the deceased's monthly benefit or prospective benefit. In the case of an orphan or
dependent parent, it is one-half of the deceased's monthly benefit or prospective benefit.

A monthly benefit will be payable to a parent only if no widow or unmarried child under age 18 survived, and only if the parent was wholly
dependent upon the deceased at time of death. While it would thus be necessary for a parent to prove dependency at the time of death, once that fact

had been established no subsequent showing of need would be required. Ample precedent for such provisions is found in the State workmen's compensation laws, which constitute the oldest form of social insurance in this country.

In addition to these OAI changes both unemployment compensation and public assistance were very much on the minds of the Finance Committee members. After looking at the average benefits in the different states and the current reserves in the different state funds, the committee eliminated the McCormack Amendment. It also accepted the House amendments to raise the 50 per cent federal share of OAA to a maximum of $40 a month and agreed to raise the ADC formula to 50 per cent as well, allowing the Federal Government to pay a maximum of $9 per child per month. During the executive sessions of the committee, Senator Connally suggested that in OAA programs the Federal Government should provide two-thirds of the first $15 and one-half of the remaining figure up to $40. Although it was rejected by the committee, the suggestion obviously had considerable support.

Debates

The most significant part of the Senate debates was the handling of the federal share of public assistance. Senator Tom Connally of Texas pressed his amendment vigorously, while Senator James F. Byrnes of South Carolina called for variable grants. The tone of the debates was set by the chairman of the committee.

Congressional Debates
84 Congressional Record, p. 8830
(July 11, 1939)

Mr. [Pat] Harrison, [Dem., Mass] . . .

About the only contest in the Finance Committee arose over the question of requiring the Federal Government to extend greater assistance to States for our elderly people. There were two proposals before the committee. One was suggested by the Senator from South Carolina who is chairman of the Unemployment and Relief Committee, which was appointed at the last session of the Congress to study the question of unemployment and relief and to try to solve that problem. He appeared before the committee and endeavored to have it carry out the recommendations of his committee and to make allocations to the States on the basis of the per capita income of residents of the State to the per capita income of the Nation as a whole. That would have assisted greatly many needy States. I may say to the Senate

I voted for that amendment not only as a member of the Byrnes committee on unemployment but I voted for it in the Finance Committee. I was very hopeful that it would be adopted, because there are many States in the Union that cannot respond even to the $15 maximum that is provided in the present law. My State is among the number of the States so situated. No man can get any glory from answering criticisms that the old people residing in his State receive only about $7 — half from the State and half from the Federal Government. I have an abiding conviction that some States have about reached the maximum of their ability to pay under present conditions and unless the Federal Government provides additional aid the old people who are in need will have to suffer.

Someone may say that the poorer States have spent a great deal of money for roads. Of course they have. They have spent money for roads because they wanted to get out of the mud; and they have also had to spend money for schools. There are many problems that affect some sections of the country that do not affect other sections; but the States have to carry those loads. So I felt that the amendment offered by the Senator from South Carolina was entirely justified. When it was defeated the distinguished Senator from Texas (*Mr. Connally*), a member of the committee, offered an amendment that up to $15 would require the Federal Government to put up $2 to the State's $1. That would have practically insured to every old person in need about $15. The increase would apply to the poorer States and the richer States, because all would have contributed alike up to $15, on the matching basis of $2 by the Federal Government and $1 by the State. The cost involved under the amendment of the Senator from Texas was estimated at about $80,000,000 per year, and under the Byrnes amendment the cost was estimated to be from $30,000,000 to $40,000,000 per year.

Those questions will come before the Senate during the further debate on the pending bill. I never like to vote against my committee — I always am a committee man — yet in this one case, I may say to the Senate, when these amendments are offered I shall vote for the proposals. I believe they are justified by the facts, and have advised the Finance Committee that I shall support them.

The two Senators carried their views to the Senate floor.

Congressional Debates
84 Congressional Record, p. 8648

Mr. Connally. If the Senator will permit me to state the effect of the amendment, I shall then be glad to yield.

Mr. President, the effect of this amendment is to provide that in the matter of old-age assistance or old-age pensions the Federal Government shall make a contribution of $2 to the State's $1, up to $15. Above $15 there shall be an equal contribution. The purpose of the amendment is to provide Federal benefits, or at least to offer encouragement to the weaker and poorer States, in order that they may make adequate contribution for old-age assistance.

I now yield to the Senator from South Carolina.

Mr. Byrnes. Mr. President, I presented to the committee for its consideration an amendment having in mind the same object as that now presented by the Senator from Texas. The amendment I offered was drafted in accordance with the suggestion which had been made by the officials of the Social Security Board and by others who have given thought to this subject, and provided that the contribution on the part of the States should be based upon a variable formula, so that the States with a low per capita income would contribute an amount related to the percentage that the per capita income of the State bore to the national income.

Mr. Connally. I suggest to the Senator that his amendment provided a two-thirds maximum.

Mr. Byrnes. Yes. In the amendment which I offered, as well as in the amendment of the Senator from Texas, as I understand, there is a provision that in no case shall the contribution by the Federal Government amount to more than two-thirds, nor shall the contribution of the State government amount to less than one-third.

The committee, after considering the amendment and also the amendment offered by the Senator from Texas failed to adopt either of them. It is my opinion that the amendment of the Senator from Texas will receive greater support than the amendment offered by me. Because I am in favor of the objective, I am, therefore, not going to offer the amendment I offered to the committee. Instead I am going to support the amendment of the Senator from Texas.

I desire to call the attention of the Senate to the situation confronting us. Under the existing law, though the Federal Government is contributing 50 percent of any amount not in excess of $30, the average amount paid by the various States of the Union as of December 31 was $19.55. The amount paid ranges all the way from $32.43 in California to $6.15 in Arkansas.

Under the circumstances, the provision of the bill as it passed the House and was reported by the committee increasing to $20 the contribution to be made by the Federal Government, conditioned upon the State appropriating $20, is, in my opinion, absolutely ineffective and can only result in misleading many of the aged who are in need throughout the country. Manifestly, if the States cannot now contribute one-half of $30, it will be impossible for them to contribute one-half of $40. When only one State in the Union contributes $15; namely, the State of California, I can see no justification for the hope that by merely increasing the maximum contribution of the Federal Government in the statute we can thereby bring about an increased payment to the needy old people throughout the country.

Today when we talk about $30 old-age assistance in the Congress, it is almost a hopeless task to explain the situation to the man in Arkansas who says, "I get an average of $6.15 a month," and so on, throughout the other States where the payment is less than $15 a month.

A revised version of the Connally Amendment eventually passed on July 12, 43-35.

Although the other amendments accepted had been recommended by the Finance Committee, some stirred heated debates nevertheless. The Social Security Board's wish to have the merit system apply in all states was at least partially gratified, and the bill itself was finally passed (57-8) on July 13.

The Conference Committee was able to agree on most points. The Senate reduced the ADC figures, fixing the new formula at a 50 per cent federal contribution, and similarly reached an agreement over the merit system in state administrations. The Senate even gave way readily on the McCormack Amendment, an action which was to have a profound effect on the development of unemployment compensation. Only the Connally Amendment was initially deadlocked, and after the President declared himself against variable or similar grants agreement was rapidly reached.

The Act

The act as it finally passed achieved most of the things the Board had set out to do. Title II, dealing with old-age insurance was totally rewritten. The new title revised and extended the provisions for old-age insurance benefits by establishing benefits for qualified wives and children of individuals entitled to old-age insurance benefits and by providing benefits for widows, children, and parents of deceased individuals, who, regardless of age at death, had fulfilled certain conditions. It also allowed a lump-sum payment on death where no monthly benefits were payable and advanced the date for initial monthly payment from 1942 to 1940, delaying the increase in tax (from 1 to 1 1/2 per cent) until 1943. In addition, the Federal Old-Age and Survivors Insurance Trust Fund was established, with provisions for a board of three trustees to manage the fund. Increased coverage, while it did not go so far as the Board would have liked, at least brought in maritime workers, those wage earners over sixty-five, and employees of certain governmental agencies. For the first time old persons were entitled to earn (up to $15 a month) without losing their pension. There were also various administrative changes, but most important of all, the basis for computing *benefits was changed from cumulative lifetime earnings after 1936 to average earnings in covered work.*

Social Security Act Amendments of 1939
(August 10, 1939, ch. 666, 53 Statutes at Large, Part 2, 1360)

TITLE II–AMENDMENT TO TITLE II OF THE SOCIAL SECURITY ACT

Sec. 201. Effective January 1, 1940, title II of such Act is amended to read as follows:

"TITLE II–FEDERAL OLD-AGE AND SURVIVORS INSURANCE BENEFITS

*   *   *

"(b) There is hereby created a body to be known as the Board of Trustees of the Federal Old-Age and Survivors Insurance Trust Fund (hereinafter in this title called the 'Board of Trustees') which Board of Trustees shall be composed of the Secretary of the Treasury, the Secretary of Labor, and the Chairman of the Social Security Board, all ex officio. The Secretary of the Treasury shall be the Managing Trustee of the Board of Trustees (hereinafter in this title called the 'Managing Trustee'). It shall be the duty of the Board of Trustees to—

"(1) Hold the Trust Fund;

"(2) Report to the Congress on the first day of each regular session of the Congress on the operation and status of the Trust Fund during the preceding fiscal year and on its expected operation and status during the next ensuing five fiscal years;

"(3) Report immediately to the Congress whenever the Board of Trustees is of the opinion that during the ensuing five fiscal years the Trust Fund will exceed three times the highest annual expenditures anticipated during the five-fiscal-year period, and whenever the Board of Trustees is of the opinion that the amount of the Trust Fund is unduly small.

The report provided for in paragraph (2) above shall include a statement of the assets of, and the disbursements made from, the Trust Fund during the preceding fiscal year, an estimate of the expected future income to, and disbursements to be made from, the Trust Fund during each of the next ensuing five fiscal years, and a statement of the actuarial status of the Trust Fund.

*   *   *

"OLD-AGE AND SURVIVORS INSURANCE BENEFIT PAYMENTS

"Primary Insurance Benefits

"Sec. 202. (a) Every individual, who (1) is a fully insured individual (as defined in section 209 (g)) after December 31, 1939, (2) has attained the age of sixty-five, and (3) has filed application for primary insurance benefits, shall be entitled to receive a primary insurance benefit (as defined in section 209 (e)) for each month, beginning with the month in which such individual becomes so entitled to such insurance benefits and ending with the month preceding the month in which he dies.

"Wife's Insurance Benefits

"(b) (1) Every wife (as defined in section 209 (i)) of an individual entitled to primary insurance benefits, if such wife (A) has attained the age of sixty-five, (B) has filed application for wife's insurance benefits, (C) was living with such individual at the time such application was filed, and (D) is not entitled to receive primary insurance benefits, or is entitled to receive primary insurance benefits each of which is less than one-half of a primary insurance benefit of her husband, shall be entitled to receive a wife's insurance benefit for each month, beginning with the month in which she becomes so entitled to such insurance benefits, and ending with the month immediately preceding the first month in which any of the following occurs: she dies, her husband dies, they are divorced a vinculo matrimonii, or she becomes entitled to receive a primary insurance benefit equal to or exceeding one-half of a primary insurance benefit of her husband.

"(2) Such wife's insurance benefit for each month shall be equal to one-half of a primary insurance benefit of her husband, except that, if she is entitled to receive a primary insurance benefit for any month, such wife's insurance benefit for such month shall be reduced by an amount equal to a primary insurance benefit of such wife.

"Child's Insurance Benefits

*   *   *

"DEFINITIONS

*   *   *

"Sec. 209. When used in this title—

*   *   *

"(f) The term 'average monthly wage' means the quotient obtained by dividing the total wages paid an individual before the quarter in which he died or became entitled to receive primary insurance benefits, whichever first occurred, by three times the number of quarters elapsing after 1936 and before such quarter in which he died or became so entitled, excluding any quarter prior to the quarter in which he attained the age of twenty-two during which he was paid less than $50 of wages and any quarter, after the quarter in which he attained age sixty-five, occurring prior to 1939.

"(g) The term 'fully insured individual' means any individual with respect to whom it appears to the satisfaction of the Board that—

"(1) He had not less than one quarter of coverage for each two of the quarters elapsing after 1936, or after the quarter in which he attained the age of twenty-one, whichever quarter is later, and up to but excluding the quarter in which he attained the age of sixty-five, or died, whichever first occurred, and in no case less than six quarters of coverage; or

"(2) He had at least forty quarters of coverage.

"As used in this subsection, and in subsection (h) of this section, the term 'quarter' and the term 'calendar quarter' mean a period of three calendar months ending on March 31, June 30, September 30, or December 31; and the term 'quarter of coverage' means a calendar quarter in which the individual has been paid not less than $50 in wages. When the number of quarters specified in paragraph (1) of this subsection is an odd number, for purposes of such paragraph such number shall be reduced by one. In any case where an individual has been paid in a calendar year $3,000 or more in wages, each quarter of such year following his first quarter of coverage shall be deemed a quarter of coverage, excepting any quarter in such year in which such individual dies or becomes entitled to a primary insurance benefit and any quarter succeeding such quarter in which he died or became so entitled.

"(h) The term 'currently insured individual' means any individual with respect to whom it appears to the satisfaction of the Board that he has been paid wages of not less than $50 for each of not less than six of the twelve calendar quarters, immediately preceding the quarter in which he died.

*   *   *

TITLE III—AMENDMENTS TO TITLE III OF THE SOCIAL SECURITY ACT

Sec. 302. Section 303 (a) of such Act is amended to read as follows:

"(a) The Board shall make no certification for payment to any State unless it finds that the law of such State, approved by the Board under the Federal Unemployment Tax Act, includes provision for—

"(1) Such methods of administration (including after January 1, 1940, methods relating to the establishment and maintenance of personnel standards on a merit basis, except that the Board shall exercise no authority with respect to the selection, tenure of office, and compensation of any individual employed in accordance with such methods) as are found by the Board to be reasonably calculated to insure full payment of unemployment compensation when due; and

"(2) Payment of unemployment compensation solely through public employment offices or such other agencies as the Board may approve; and

"(3) Opportunity for a fair hearing, before an impartial tribunal, for all individuals whose claims for unemployment compensation are denied; . . .

*   *   *

TITLE IV–AMENDMENTS TO TITLE IV OF THE SOCIAL SECURITY ACT

Sec. 401. (a) Clause (5) of section 402 (a) of such Act is amended to read as follows: "(5) provide such methods of administration (including after January 1, 1940, methods relating to the establishment and maintenance of personnel standards on a merit basis, except that the Board shall exercise no authority with respect to the selection, tenure of office, and compensation of any individual employed in accordance with such methods) as are found by the Board to be necessary for the proper and efficient operation of the plan."

*   *   *

TITLE VI–AMENDMENTS TO THE INTERNAL REVENUE CODE

Sec. 601. Section 1400 of the Internal Revenue Code is amended to read as follows:

"Sec. 1400. RATE OF TAX.

"In addition to other taxes, there shall be levied, collected, and paid upon the income of every individual a tax equal to the following percentages of the wages (as defined in section 1426 (a)) received by him after December 31, 1936, with respect to employment (as defined in section 1426 (b)) after such date:

"(1) With respect to wages received during the calendar years 1939, 1940, 1941, and 1942, the rate shall be 1 per centum.

"(2) With respect to wages received during the calendar years 1943, 1944, and 1945, the rate shall be 2 per centum.

"(3) With respect to wages received during the calendar years 1946, 1947, and 1948, the rate shall be 2½ per centum.

"(4) With respect to wages received after December 31, 1948, the rate shall be 3 per centum."

*   *   *

"Sec. 1600. RATE OF TAX.

"Every employer (as defined in section 1607 (a)) shall pay for the calendar year 1939 and for each calendar year thereafter an excise tax, with respect to having individuals in his employ, equal to 3 per centum of the total wages (as defined in section 1607 (b)) paid by him during the calendar year with respect to employment (as defined in section 1607 (c)) after December 31, 1938."

Sec. 609. Section 1601 of the Internal Revenue Code is amended to read as follows:

"Sec. 1601. CREDITS AGAINST TAX.

"(a) CONTRIBUTIONS TO STATE UNEMPLOYMENT FUNDS. —

"(1) The taxpayer may, to the extent provided in this subsection and subsection (c), credit against the tax imposed by section 1600 the amount of contributions paid by him into an unemployment compensation law of a State which is certified for the taxable year as provided in section 1603.

"(2) The credit shall be permitted against the tax for the taxable year only for the amount of contributions paid with respect to such taxable year. . . .

Presidential Statement on Signing Some Amendments
to the Social Security Act
(August 11, 1939)*

It will be exactly four years ago on the fourteenth day of this month that I signed the original Social Security Act. As I indicated at that time and on various occasions since that time, we must expect a great program of social legislation, such as is represented in the Social Security Act, to be improved and strengthened in the light of additional experience and understanding. These amendments to the Act represent another tremendous step forward in providing greater security for the people of this country. This is especially true in the case of the federal old age insurance system which has now been converted into a system of old age and survivors' insurance providing lifetime family security instead of only individual old age security to the workers in insured occupations. In addition to the worker himself, millions of widows and orphans will now be afforded some degree of protection in the event of his death whether before or after his retirement.

The size of the benefits to be paid during the early years will be far more adequate than under the present law. However, a reasonable relationship is retained between wage loss sustained and benefits received. This is a most important distinguishing characteristic of social insurance as contrasted with any system of flat pensions.

Payment of old age benefits will begin on January 1, 1940, instead of January 1, 1942. Increase in pay-roll taxes, scheduled to take place in January, 1940, is deferred. Benefit payments in the early years are substantially increased.

I am glad that the insurance benefits have been extended to cover workers in some occupations that have previously not been covered. However,

*Public Papers and Addresses of Franklin D. Roosevelt, 1939, p. 439.

workers in other occupations have been excluded. In my opinion, it is imperative that these insurance benefits be extended to workers in all occupations.

The Federal-State system of providing assistance to the needy aged, the needy blind, and dependent children, has also been strengthened by increasing the federal aid. I am particularly gratified that the Federal matching ratio to States for aid to dependent children has been increased from one-third to one-half of the aid granted. I am also happy that greater Federal contributions will be made for public health, maternal and child welfare, crippled children, and vocational rehabilitation. These changes will make still more effective the Federal-State cooperative relationship upon which the Social Security Act is based and which constitutes its great strength. It is important to note in this connection that the increased assistance the States will now be able to give will continue to be furnished on the basis of individual need, thus affording the greatest degree of protection within reasonable financial bounds.

As regards administration, probably the most important change that has been made is to require that State agencies administering any part of the Social Security Act coming within the jurisdiction of the Social Security Board and the Children's Bureau shall set up a merit system for their employees shall be selected on a non-political basis and shall function on a non-political basis.

In 1934 I appointed a committee called the Committee on Economic Security made up of Government officials to study the whole problem of economic and social security and to develop a legislative program for the same. The present law is the result of its deliberations. That committee is still in existence and has considered and recommended the present amendments. In order to give reality and coordination to the study of any further developments that appear necessary I am asking the committee to continue its life and to make active study of various proposals which may be made for amendments or developments to the Social Security Act.

Unemployment compensation coverage was extended to some two hundred thousand persons, mainly bank employees. (At the same time the redefinition of agricultural labor made an equally large number ineligible.) A maximum limit of $3000 was placed on the employee payment on which the tax was levied which brought employment insurance in line with old-age insurance. At the same time more non-profit organizations were taken out of the scheme. The McCormick Amendment had paved the way for states to possibly cut back on unemployment insurance expenditures.

In the various categories of public assistance, the variable grant was still not accepted, but in both AB and OAA the maximum amount covered by the 50 per cent federal grant was raised to $40. Thus, the states could claim up to $20 a month from the Federal Government for each recipient under these programs. At the same time the ADC formula was raised from

33 1/3 to 50 per cent, and children were covered to the age of eighteen if they were still attending school. In all three categories of public assistance, need and confidentiality were established criteria, and the Ohio fiasco resulted in an obligatory merit system for all participating public assistance agencies. (Incidentally, the battles about Ohio continued: The OAA federal share for October was cut back in 1938 because the Board had determined that the old-age pension was being used by the incumbent governor to bribe the electorate. In 1939, however, Congress passed H.R. 5118, which was vetoed by President Roosevelt, to restore the lost funds to Ohio.)

1939 was also significant for social security because in that year the Social Security Board, whose chairman now became Commissioner, was incorporated into the Federal Security Board. Autonomy and political power were by no means completely lost, but at least another layer of control was inserted.

Reorganization Act of 1939
(April 3, 1939, ch. 36, 53 Statutes at Large, Part 2, 501)

*   *   *

Section 201. Federal Security Agency. — (a) The United States Employment Service in the Department of Labor and its functions and personnel are transferred from the Department of Labor; the Office of Education in the Department of the Interior and its functions and personnel (including the Commissioner of Education) are transferred from the Department of the Interior; the Public Health Service in the Department of the Treasury and its functions and personnel (including the Surgeon General of the Public Health Service) are transferred from the Department of the Treasury; the National Youth Administration within the Works Progress Administration and its functions and personnel (including its Administrator) are transferred from the Works Progress Administration; and these agencies and their functions, together with the Social Security Board and its functions, and the Civilian Conservation Corps and its functions, are hereby consolidated under one agency to be known as the Federal Security Agency, with a Federal Security Administrator at the head thereof. The Federal Security Administrator shall be appointed by the President, by and with the advice and consent of the Senate, and shall receive a salary at the rate of $12,000 per annum. He shall have general direction and supervision over the administration of the several agencies consolidated into the Federal Security Agency by this section and shall be responsible for the coordination of their functions and activities.

(b) The Federal Security Administrator shall appoint an Assistant Federal Security Administrator, who shall receive a salary at the rate of $9,000 per annum, and he may also appoint such other personnel and make such expenditures as may be necessary.

(c) The Assistant Administrator shall act as Administrator during the absence or disability of the Administrator or in the event of a vacancy in that office and shall perform such other duties as the Administrator shall direct.

(d) The several agencies and functions consolidated by this section into the Federal Security Agency shall carry with them their personnel.

Section 202. Social Security Board. — The Social Security Board and its functions shall be administered as a part of the Federal Security Agency under the direction and supervision of the Federal Security Administrator. The Chairman of the Social Security Board shall perform such administrative duties as the Federal Security Administrator shall direct.

MOBILIZATION AND DEMOBILIZATION

The years between the 1939 amendments and the 1946 amendments are important not so much for the changes made or omitted in OASI, unemployment compensation, or public assistance, but for the debates engendered during that time. While in 1935 everyone insisted that the social security system was intended as a long-term solution to the problems it dealt with, and that its provisions were in no sense meant as ad hoc *solutions, as the country recovered economically it was clear that the 1935 assumptions would be subject to rigorous re-examination.*

Thus in each area there was reassessment. In OASI, the difference between social insurance and traditional forms of insurance rapidly became clear. It also slowly became apparent that the withering away of old-age assistance was by no means a forgone conclusion. As the amounts paid under OAA grew, the idea of a unified old-age pension, incorporating both old-age insurance and old-age assistance, became increasingly attractive from the political point of view. Indeed the principles which had underlain the unworkable Townsend Plan were temporarily government policy — at least in the White House and with the Federal Security Agency, if not at the Social Security Board. But if the Board was hostile to the federalization of old-age assistance (although increasingly prepared to consider the variable grant system), it was still captivated with the idea of a federal unemployment insurance system. It also committed itself far more clearly than the White House to governmental health care, preferably through insurance. Slowly emerging as the basic problem was the growth of such public assistance programs as ADC and, despite all the hopes for a bright new post-war world, of a hard-core of poor who were evidently largely unemployable.

Nineteen-hundred and forty was, of course, the year in which the first regular old-age and survivors' benefits were paid, and officially this was the highlight of the year. The Foreword to the Social Security Yearbook, 1940 *rightly reflected the respect in which the program was held.*

Social Security Yearbook, 1940
(p. 111)

During the course of a year, probably a majority of all families in the United States are in direct contact with one aspect or another of the social security program. Several million households are receiving, under the Social Security Act and related State legislation, the assistance payments which help to provide the means of subsistence of the needy aged, needy blind, and dependent children. In some of these households and in additional millions of households, persons of working age rely on the public employment services for help in getting work or in finding a better job or, when no suitable work is to be found, receive the unemployment compensation to which qualified workers are entitled. Many additional millions of families have the assurance that they are building up or have secured some means of livelihood in the event of the unemployment or death of the wage earner, and that protection is being built up against incapacity to earn in old age. Hundreds of thousands of retired workers and their dependents and the survivors of insured workers are already receiving monthly payments under the Federal old-age and survivors insurance system and other Federal retirement programs. It seems likely that few, if any, of the peace-time activities of government have had so widespread, intimate, and continuous a relationship to the lives of American families as the group of social insurance and assistance programs developed during recent years and especially since 1935, when the Social Security Act became law.

Presidential messages included the usual encouragement about extension of the program. The annual message on January 3, 1940 called for "the extension of social security to larger groups." In that year the most serious social security problem seemed to be the protection of the rights of those workers who were drawn into some form of national service as the nation responded to World War II, which by that time already ravaging Europe. In September, 1940, Roosevelt noted:

Presidential Message Recommending the Preservation of Benefit Rights of Workers Who are Called into Active Service
(September 14, 1940)*

The social gains of recent years, including insurance and other benefit rights, must be preserved unimpaired. The National Guard legislation, which I recently approved, contained provisions evidencing this policy in connection with benefit rights of workers who are called into active service, and a similar provision is contained in pending selective service legislation.

*Public Papers and Addresses of Franklin D. Roosevelt, 1940, p. 427.

I recommend to the Congress early consideration of the problems thus recognized, and enactment of the necessary legislation incident to preserving insurance protection under the Social Security Act, the Railroad Retirement Act, and the Railroad Unemployment Insurance Act, and to facilitate State action under the Federal-State unemployment insurance program.

The agencies administering the Federal acts have been considering the needed technical changes to meet these problems and are now ready to furnish recommendations to the Congress in this connection.

In fact nothing came of this particular message, and the problem was to remain a serious one for the next few years.

From the point of view of future income security legislation, however, the most important matter during these years was the dispute between the Federal Security Administrator, Paul V. McNutt, and the Commissioner for Social Security, Arthur Altmeyer. The Administrator, who had presidential aspirations in 1940, was interested in a uniform federal pension scheme, financed out of the progressive income tax and incorporating both old-age benefits under social security and old-age assistance programs. Such a plan was anathema to the Social Security Board, committed as it was to the idea of contributions and insurance. Dr. Altmeyer was able to persuade President Roosevelt to his side, but this was not enough. Within a few weeks, the Senate Finance Committee had appointed a special subcommittee to investigate the Old-Age Pension System.

The Board was prepared to come forward with a compromise proposal. Dr. Altmeyer proposed a "double-decker" system which included a basic flat federal pension of $20, superimposed by a supplementary pension based on contributions. While the Board did not favor such a scheme, it did realize that political necessity might force such a plan on the country. Indeed, in that year's election campaign, it seemed that the President was endorsing such a proposal.

Presidential Address at Teamsters Union Convention
(September 11, 1940)*

Yes, it is my hope that soon the United States will have a national system under which no needy man or woman within our borders will lack a minimum old-age pension that will provide adequate food, adequate clothing and adequate lodging to the end of the road and without having to go to the poorhouse to get it. I look forward to a system coupled with that, a system which, in addition to this bare minimum, will enable those who have faithfully toiled in any occupation to build up additional security for their old age which will allow them to live in comfort and in happiness.

Public Papers and Addresses of Franklin D. Roosevelt, 1940, p. 411.

Nothing more was heard of this from the Administration, but on August 28, 1941, the Senate subcommittee in effect called for a "double-decker" system.

Old Age Pension System
Senate Report No. 666
77th Cong., 1st Sess.
(August 28, 1941)
(p. 8)

Injustices of the Present System

The operation of our two systems of old-age insurance and assistance has resulted in creating serious injustices as between individual recipients within the insurance system, as between recipients of payments in the two different systems, and as between different States under both systems.

1. The essentially noncontributory nature of the insurance system results in the unjust weighting of benefit payments against the poorly paid worker.
2. The existence of two parallel yet different systems by which we attempt to care for our retired workers has created a series of absurd and anomalous situations which tend to undermine the value of both systems.
3. Both of the present systems of old-age assistance and insurance unfortunately operate to drain wealth from our least prosperous States to our most fortunate ones.

Proposal for a General Pension

The committee is of the opinion that the immediate passage of a law providing a general pension of $30 a month for persons without employment past 60 is imperative to the present well-being of our older citizens. The committee, however, wishes to emphasize that such a measure is designed solely for the immediate future, because the expanding and accelerating insurance system recommended by the committee would soon preempt the pension field. Thus, the number of recipients of pensions will steadily dwindle each year until at the end of the coming decade almost all payments will be made as benefits under the insurance system and only a limited number as general pensions.

Public Opinion on Old-Age Pensions

In the midst of the present national emergency, faced with the expenditure of billions of dollars for national defense, the people of America have expressed their almost unanimous conviction that the Government of the United States should provide more adequate pensions for our retired workers. In a recent scientific poll taken by the American Institute of Public Opinion, 91 percent of all voters sampled answered an unequivocal "yes" to the direct question: Are you in favor of Government old-age pensions? The committee believes that such unanimity of opinion, particularly in the face of the present emergency, demands that the Congress respond promptly to this undeniable popular mandate for the establishment of a national old-age pension system.

Recommendations of the Committee

This committee believes that fundamental changes in the Social Security Act of 1935, as amended in 1939, are an immediate necessity for the welfare of the older citizens of this Nation. In accordance with that belief, it submits the following recommendations:

A. Title II of the Social Security Act and the Federal Insurance Contributions Act (Formerly Title VIII of the Social Security Act)

1. (*a*) We recommend that the present system of old-age and survivors insurance as provided under title II of the Social Security Act and the Federal Insurance Contributions Act be retained and extended to provide for as universal coverage as possible. We recommend that all groups within the extended coverage shall begin to pay taxes as of January 1, 1943.

   (*b*) We recommend an immediate, detailed investigation into the best method of extending the coverage of the insurance system to all self-employed groups, farmers, and farm workers, employees of the Federal Government, of States, counties, and municipalities and all other employed individuals who are not now covered by the system. In the rare cases of those individuals who escaped tax responsibility through failure to engage in gainful employment during their lives it is recommended that equalization of the tax burden be effected in their cases through the instrumentality of the income tax.

2. We recommend that the benefits provided under the insurance system be made payable upon retirement from employment at the age of 60 rather than at the age of 65, as at present provided.

3. We recommend that a minimum benefit of $30 per month be established for all beneficiaries, including those now in receipt of payments, regardless of the size of their previous earnings.

4. We recommend that the combined employer-employee taxes on pay rolls in the then covered employments be raised to 4 percent on January 1, 1943, and that the taxes further be raised to 6 percent

on January 1, 1944, instead of on January 1, 1949, as contemplated in the present act.

5. We recommend the repeal of the present provision of the law requiring as a condition of eligibility for benefits that an individual be paid not less than $50 in wages in any quarter of coverage.

6. We recommend that wives' and widows' insurance benefits be increased from one-half and three-quarters, respectively, to the husband's primary insurance benefit to an amount equal to such primary benefit.

B. Title I of the Social Security Act

1. We recommend the abolition of the present Federal-State old-age assistance system based on the means test as provided in title I of the act, and recommend that title I be amended to provide for the payment by the Federal Government through the instrumentality of the several States of a general pension of $20 per month after July 1, 1942, and $30 per month after January 1, 1944, to every American citizen who has retired from gainful employment at or after the age of 60, unless he is in receipt of payments from the Federal Government under the old-age insurance system or under the provisions of the Railroad Retirement Act of 1940.

2. We recommend that such pensions be supported by general appropriations financed as far as possible by the utilization of those funds collected through the 6 percent employer-employee pay-roll tax provided by the Federal Insurance Contributions Act to the extent that they shall not be required for current payments under the insurance benefit provisions of title II of the act. In this connection we emphasize again our earlier recommendation that all employed persons be brought under the coverage of the insurance system at as early a date as is found to be feasible. Until such time as all, or nearly all, citizens will receive their benefits under the insurance system, it is the opinion of the committee that diversion of workers' contributions to the payment of a general pension should be balanced by an equally general tax program. This generally can be achieved directly (for workers) and indirectly (for wives and widows) by coverage of all gainfully employed persons under the insurance system.

In the light of this report it was not really surprising that when the Finance Committee began hearings on a derivative of the Townsend Plan, S. 1932, there should be surprisingly widespread support for a bill to pay flat old-age pension. The bill's sponsor, Senator Sheridan Downey of California, explained it.

Old Age Pensions
Hearings on S. 1932 before the Senate Finance Committee
77th Cong., 1st Sess. (December, 1941)
(p. 7, 14)

The bill that is now before this committee calls for a Federal contribution to everyone past 60 who is retired from gainful employment in the sum of $30 a month, with the expectation that every State would then add whatever it desired to that amount; and I might say that in the State of California I hope that the $30 will be raised to the sum of $60.

*   *   *

Mr. Chairman, it seems to me almost by a law of nature that 9 out of 10 families, the middle class of America, have had some major disaster strike at them, over a period of years, which has wiped out their savings; families with an income of $250 or $300 a month who might, during the past 10 or 20 years, have been able to save some of their income, almost without exception, have been met with unemployment, sickness, failure of a bank or insurance company, failure or disability of some relative. The patient hoarding of years has thus been wiped out by conditions almost always and entirely beyond the control of those people. Prominent in this sorry list is that sad and dreary record of lapsed insurance policies; the dreary record of families who have faithfully and diligently maintained policies for 5, 10, 15, 20 years and then had to borrow on them because of unemployment, sickness or some other terrible disaster.

From the hearings and the tone of presidential remarks, there was every reason to expect some fusion of the social security and public assistance provisions for the elderly. After only two days of hearings, however, the attack on Pearl Harbor occurred and for the next few years this particular debate was stilled.

History tells us that there is nothing like a major holocaust to concentrate the views of a nation on the kind of society it would like after the conflict. The Beveridge Report in England, published in 1942, was to act as a basis for the post-war welfare state. There was nothing so dramatic, or at least so well publicized, in this country, but during 1943 and 1944 it was clear that there was considerable thought about the type of economic security system that should be sought when peace returned.

Even while the war was on, President Roosevelt was prepared to harness the prevalent patriotic sentiments in order to push his view on economic imbalance in the community. His budget message of 1942 attacked various forms of tax avoidance available to the wealthy, and at the same time he assailed the disparity of living standards in different parts of the country. Although the President had torpedoed the "variable grant" system which had been suggested in 1939, he now appeared to have been converted to it.

Annual Budget Message of the President
(January 5, 1942)*

I favor an amendment to the Social Security Act which would modify matching grants to accord with the needs of the various States. Such legislation would probably not affect expenditures substantially during the next fiscal year.

Well, you know what we have been trying to do on that. It is going to be a hard thing to get through a State like Georgia, which hasn't got the taxable values in the State. And therefore, when they come to a matching program with the Federal Government, their total is very, very low, if judged on a per capita basis. That does not take care of their sick, and blind, and unemployed, and relief people, and so forth and so on, because the State hasn't got the taxable values.

In a State like New York, on the other hand, they have got the taxable values. They can put up much larger funds, again on a per capita basis, than the State of Georgia.

Now the objective is that the Federal grants will be so distributed as to help the poorer States more greatly than the richer States. And that would not be left to the discretion of the State legislature, because a lot of them might try to save money on that basis, but would be based on some kind of an index figure, which in turn would be based on the per capita income of the individuals in all of the States. The States that have the highest per capita income would get the least, and the States that have the lowest income would get the most. Well, that is something we are shooting for, and have been for the last year. . . .

Roosevelt also continued to be enthusiastic as well about an extension of social security coverage in the form of increases in old-age and survivors' insurance, hospitalization benefits, and unemployment compensation.

Already, in 1942, the National Resources Planning Board had produced a major study, Security, Work and Relief Policies, *which expressed a new national commitment to the problem regarded as sectional before the war. While the report of the NRPB went to Congress, the findings and recommendations of the study appeared as part of a ten-cent pamphlet.* After the War—Towards Security.

After the War—Towards Security
(p. 2)

*   *   *

The specific objectives of public-aid policy should be:
1. Increasing emphasis upon policies aiming at the prevention of

*Public Papers and Addresses of Franklin D. Roosevelt, 1942, p. 12.

economic insecurity through a fuller utilization of our productive resources, including labor, and by more comprehensive measures to improve the health of our people.

2. Government provision of work for all adults who are willing and able to work, if private industry is unable to provide employment.

3. Appropriate measures to equip young persons beyond the compulsory school-attendance age for assuming the full responsibilities of citizenship.

4. Assurance of basic minimum security through social insurance, so far as possible.

5. Establishment of a comprehensive underpinning general public-assistance system providing aid on the basis of need, to complete the framework of protection against economic insecurity.

6. Expansion of social services which are essential for the health, welfare, and efficiency of the whole population; this expansion should be as wide and as rapid as possible.

By 1943 the emphasis was clearly on what would happen when Germany and Japan were finally defeated. The Report of the Social Security Board for 1943, *for instance, pinpointed the defects in existing programs and offered a comprehensive program for the future.*

The Report of the Social Security Board for 1943
Social Security During and After the War
(p. 32)

*   *   *

Social Insurance

A comprehensive system of social insurance would include provisions to compensate part of the involuntary loss of earnings experienced by the working population for any common reason beyond the control of individual workers. Such reasons may be grouped into those which cause prolonged or permanent loss of earnings — old age, death, and permanent disability of the wage earner, and those which cause more or less temporary interruption of earnings — unemployment and sickness. An approach to both types of risks is made under the Social Security Act through the provisions for old-age and survivors insurance and for unemployment compensation. In the opinion of the Board, the existing measures need revision and extension. The act contains no provision for offsetting wage losses due to sickness and disability except those incurred in old age.

Old-age and survivors insurance. — The fundamental limitation of this Federal insurance program is its restriction of coverage, the extent and character of which have been outlined in earlier pages. The Board believes that the wartime situtation gives particular urgency to its recommendation that coverage be extended to agricultural workers, domestic workers in private homes, employees of nonprofit organizations, and self-employed persons. The high levels of current employment and earnings now would make it possible for many workers to pay contributions and thus gain insurance rights which they may not be able to acquire in future years, in particular the older workers who may be in need of retirement provision when the war ends and younger men return to civilian life. Extension of coverage would not entail serious administrative difficulties. For appropriate groups, it might be effective to use a stamp system, under which employers purchase stamps at post offices or from rural mail carriers to place in a book which evidences the contributions made by workers and employers. Extension of the basic protection of old-age and survivors insurance to public employees—Federal, State, and local—would also be feasible and would round out insurance protection of survivors, now lacking to nearly all these employees, and provisions for old-age retirement, now unavailable to many, and would assure continuity of rights. Extension should be made in such a way as not to endanger any rights of these workers under existing special systems and to increase, not lessen, the total insurance protection available to them.

An immediate problem related to coverage arises from the situation of the millions of persons now in the armed forces. Because of the eligibility provisions and the method of computing benefits under the program, the insurance protection which servicemen and women may have acquired before their induction will be partly or wholly used up, and the amount of potential benefits payable to them or to their survivors will diminish. Servicemen and women have protection against death while in service, or after service from service-connected causes, in the form of benefits provided under veterans' legislation; in some cases, survivors of veterans who die while in service will be eligible for both veterans' benefits and old-age and survivors insurance benefits. After discharge from service, however, many veterans will be without any survivorship protection in the event of death from non-service-connected causes. The problem with respect to veterans who live to retirement age is less acute, since very few who leave military service after the war will be ineligible for old-age and survivors insurance benefits because of their military service, and, though benefit amounts will be somewhat reduced in all cases, the amount of the reduction will be small. Moreover, the great majority of the present members of the armed forces will not reach retirement age for many years. As a solution to the problems with respect to the armed forces, the Board recommends the adoption of provisions which will equitably protect potential insurance rights developed before entrance into the armed forces and which will give equitable wage credits based on periods of national service in lieu of private employment.

Such provisions should be accompanied by appropriate arrangements to reimburse the insurance system out of general funds of the Treasury.

The Board is also prepared to offer recommendations with respect to changes in the present program which would strengthen its protection and remove certain anomalies, inequities, and administrative complexities. Among changes to improve adequacy are those which relate to the age at which benefits become payable to women, the amount and conditions for payment of parent's benefits, the conditions for payment of lump-sum death benefits, the maximum amount of all benefits payable with respect to the wages of an insured worker, and the recomputation of benefit amounts after an application for primary benefits has been filed.

Since wives are ordinarily younger than their husbands, the qualifying age of 65 for receipt of a wife's benefit often works hardship on aged couples when the husband must or wishes to give up work on reaching retirement age, while the benefit for his wife is not payable until several years later. There is little doubt that the proportion of women who are unable to engage in regular employment at age 60 is larger than the proportion of men at age 65. A minimum qualifying age of 60 years, rather than the present 65, would therefore be desirable for wives of primary beneficiaries, for women workers who claim benefits in their own right, and for widows of insured workers.

At present, benefits to children aged 16 and 17 must be suspended if the child fails to attend school regularly and attendance is feasible. Since ordinarily it is found that school attendance is not feasible for the older children who are not in school, the Board recommends deletion of this requirement, which results in a large number of fruitless investigations.

Unemployment insurance. — The course of events since Pearl Harbor has emphasized what had become increasingly evident in prior years — that employment and unemployment are no respecters of State lines. When the social security program first came under discussion, it was argued that establishment of State systems for unemployment compensation would afford an opportunity for experimenting in different types of unemployment insurance and for adapting State systems to the widely varying economic conditions of the different States. It was also pointed out that the Federal-State system itself should be regarded as an experiment. Both the present world situation and the results of 4 years' full operation of all State programs now make it urgent to evaluate experience.

Serious administrative complexities are inherent in the present basis of operation because of the duplication of effort on the part of various Federal and State agencies concerned with the collection of contributions and maintenance of wage records for social insurance purposes. The multiple system of tax collection is unduly costly in terms of public expenditures and expenses of employers for tax compliance. Nearly all establishments are subject to Federal contribution for old-age and survivors insurance, the Federal unemployment tax, and contributions under one or more State unemployment compensation laws. On the other hand, some small employers are not subject to the Federal unemployment tax, though liable for Federal old-age and survivors insurance contributions and unemployment contributions under State law. A few are subject only to the last and not to any Federal tax. When an employer is taxable by both Federal and State governments, the respective coverage does not necessarily relate to the same employees or the same amounts of wages. An interstate employer may be required to make reports to several different States on different forms, under different instructions, and at different rates. He may not be sure in which State a worker is covered. Triplicate tax collections must be made — by the Federal Government for the two Federal insurance taxes and by the State unemployment compensation agencies. Duplicating wage records are necessarily maintained by the Federal Government for purposes of old-age and survivors insurance and by the State unemployment compensation agencies.

Difficulties and conflicts in administration also result from the present division of responsibilities for unemployment insurance between the Federal Government and the States. Federal grants to States under the Social Security Act supply the total costs of "proper and efficient administration" of State laws. The State agency is responsible for administering the State law; it spends Federal money without responsibility for providing the funds. The Social Security Board must ascertain that the funds have been used in accordance with the terms of the Federal law, yet it lacks authority to prescribe methods which have proved economical and efficient without infringing on the responsibility of the State. Appropriate discharge of the responsibility of one agency almost inevitably conflicts with the responsibility possessed by the other.

Of greater importance is the increasing evidence that the Federal-State system results in great diversity in the protection afforded against the risk of unemployment. Development of unemployment insurance under the 51 separate laws of the States and Territories has resulted in serious discrepancies in the adequacy of the provisions for unemployed workers in various parts of the country. It has also resulted in a segregation of insurance reserves under which there is a possibility that some States may become insolvent while other States have unnecessarily large reserves. The variations in contribution rates now permissible under the Social Security Act through State provisions for experience rating place disproportionate burdens on employers in interstate competition and set a penalty on the efforts of any particular State to improve its benefit standards and a premium on measures to restrict payments to workers.

In the opinion of the Social Security Board, these and other discrepancies, complexities, and lacks in the existing Federal-State program all lead to a single conclusion — that the origin and character of mass unemployment and of measures to combat it are such that responsibility for unemployment insurance cannot safely be divided among 51 separate systems. Evidence accumulates daily on the extent to which the tides of employment and unemployment are governed by Nation-wide or world-wide conditions. The conditions of employment within the United States are and will be governed largely by circumstances which only the Federal Government can influence — for example, policies concerning the cancelation of war contracts and demobilization of the armed forces. Because of the differences in size and economic structure, the States are not equally sound financial units for unemployment insurance purposes. To ensure payments of benefits to qualified unemployed workers in any part of the country, reserves segregated in 51 funds must be far larger, in the aggregate, than would be necessary if the total were available to pay benefits wherever the claims originated.

The early discussion of adapting unemployment insurance to the particular conditions of a State overlooked the fact that variations in wage scales, types of industry, risks of unemployment, and other important factors are at least as great within States as among the 51 jurisdictions participating in the present program. A national system under which benefits are a proportion of wages, as is the case under the Federal old-age and survivors insurance system, effects an automatic adjustment of benefit payments to differences in pay scales in different areas. Present differences among the States in coverage, benefit provisions, and assets available for benefits bear little consistent relation to underlying economic differences.

The Board therefore is of the opinion that administration of unemployment insurance should be made a Federal responsibility in order to gear unemployment compensation effectively into a comprehensive national system of social security. Only Nation-wide measures to counter unemployment can be effective,when the need arises for swift and concerted action to harmonize insurance activities with national policy during the changeover of our economic system to peace. At that time, any need for quick and unforeseen changes obviously can be met far more effectively by Nationwide policy and by a single act of Congress, than through the action of 51 administrative agencies and the necessarily cumbersome process of amending as many separate laws.

Even if the special stresses of post-war years were not impending, the Federal-State basis of the unemployment compensation program would have merited reconsideration and revision at this time. The actual course of its operation during a relatively favorable period of years has given no indication, in the opinion of the Board, that it possesses the advantages which it was hoped thus to achieve; on the contrary, experience has marshaled impressive evidence of its flaws and shortcomings. Incorporation of unemployment insurance in a unified national system of social insurance would result, the Board believes, in a program far safer, stronger, and more nearly adequate from the standpoint of unemployed workers and the Nation, and would permit more economical and effective methods of administration.

Losses and costs of disability. — Loss of earnings from permanent and total disability has been widely accepted in other countries, and under retirement plans in this country, as a risk paralleling loss of earnings in old age. The worker who is permanently disabled in youth or middle age is in very much the same situation as the worker incapacitated by age, except that his need for insurance may be even greater because he has had less time to accumulate savings while his responsibilities for family support are likely to be greater. The Board recommends that insurance against permanent total disability be incorporated in the Federal system of old-age and survivors insurance and extended to all covered by that system under provisions, including benefits to dependents, which would follow the general pattern of this Federal program.

Cash benefits for temporary sickness and the early period of disabilities which may later prove permanent would strike at another serious cause of poverty and dependency. The Board believes that such provision is a feasible and needed adjunct to the social security program. Compensation of disability would be most effective and also most readily administered if provisions for both types of benefits were coordinated, so that the worker who had received the maximum number of weeks of benefits for temporary disability and was still incapacitated could continue to receive compensation, with appropriate adjustment of levels of benefits to the duration of disability. A unified system of disability compensation merits careful consideration.

Costs of medical care, as has been pointed out, are a peculiarly appropriate field for insurance provisions, since the problem does not lie in the average annual cost but in the uneven and unpredictable incidence of a risk to which nearly all the population is subject. These costs, as well as losses of earnings, constitute an important direct factor in causing dependency. Moreover, there is impressive evidence that the barrier of currently meeting costs of medical care keeps many individuals from receiving services which might prevent or cure sickness and disability and postpone death. From the standpoint of the general welfare and of safeguarding public funds for insurance, assistance, and public services provided in dependency, the Board believes that comprehensive measures can and should be undertaken to distribute medical costs and assure access to services of hospitals, physicians, laboratories, and the like to all who have need of them. For all groups ordinarily self-supporting, such a step would mean primarily a redistribution of existing costs through insurance devices. It should be effected in such a way as to preserve free choice of doctor or hospital and personal relationships between physicians and their patients, to maintain professional leadership, to ensure adequate remuneration—very probably, more nearly adequate than that in customary circumstances—to all practitioners and institutions furnishing medical and health services, and to guarantee the continued independence of nongovernmental hospitals.

A comprehensive unified system of social insurance.—The present recommendations of the Board would result in the establishment of a single comprehensive system of social insurance with provisions for compensating a reasonable portion of wage losses due to unemployment, sickness and disability, old age, and death, and a considerable part of the expense of hospital and medical services. It is believed that all these types of insurance should include specific provisions not only for the insured worker himself but also, as is now the case in old-age and survivors insurance, for his wife or widow and his dependent children. The system should cover all persons who work for others, including the large groups of agricultural and domestic workers now almost wholly without social insurance protection and, except probably for unemployment compensation and temporary disability insurance, farmers and other self-employed persons. It is difficult to extend insurance against unemployment or temporary disability to self-employed persons, because of the problem of determining whether interruption of work has resulted in loss of income.

A unified system which is comprehensive with respect to both the risks and the population included would close the gaps and obviate the overlaps that result from variations and restrictions in the multiplicity of existing Federal, State, and local provisions for social insurance purposes. This result would be of special importance not only in ensuring protection for workers who now lack any insurance coverage, but also for improving the levels of benefits for those whose employment has been partly outside the coverage of a given system and those whose covered employment has been interrupted by periods of unemployment or disability. It would be feasible to remedy the disparities and inequities in benefits of different types, gearing all benefits to levels of earnings and presumptive requirements, with respect both to the short or long-term character of the risk and the worker's family responsibilities.

A comprehensive national system, moreover, would make possible much greater simplicity and economy in operation. One system for collection of contributions would suffice. One employer report and one set of wage records would supply the information needed for computation of benefits. One local administrative office could maintain contacts with workers, claimants, and employers, with respect to all types of insurance. Administration of such a system should, in the opinion of the Board, be decentralized, with advisory councils and appeals boards in the several States.

The costs of a comprehensive system are not great in relation to the return to be anticipated in national and individual protection and the alternative costs now borne directly and indirectly by individuals, employers, and the general public. For at least the first decade, the current cost for all types of the benefits mentioned above would be more than met be a rate of 12 percent of covered earnings for employers and employees combined, as compared with the combined standard rate of 7 percent payable by employers and workers for insurance programs under the Social Security Act beginning January 1944. If the total is divided equally between employers and workers, there would be an increase from 5 percent to 6 percent in the basic employer rate and from 2 percent to 6 percent in the rate for employees.

The 4-percent increase for employees does not exceed the present average annual cost of medical care among wage-earning families, without allowance for the uncompensated wage losses they experience from such causes and other contingencies for which the system would provide. When account is taken of the increases already scheduled in the Federal Insurance Contributions Act by 1949, the proposed 12 percent would mean no increase in employer rates and an addition of 3 percent of wages for employees. If all employees were covered and, except for unemployment and temporary disability insurance, all self-employed persons, future costs of public assistance would be considerably lightened.

Since a rise in current expenditures for old-age and survivors benefits is to be anticipated for some decades to come and a similar cumulating increase would occur in long-term benefits for permanent total disability, the rate of 12 percent may become insufficient after a decade or more to meet total benefit expenditures under such a program. The Board recommends that any costs in excess of 12 percent should be met by a Federal contribution to the system, and that eventually employers, workers, and the Federal Government should each bear one-third of the cost.

The Board believes that social insurance is essentially national in character. In the course of a working lifetime, many individuals move from State to State. Congress determined that the maintenance of lifetime records of earnings, among other considerations, pointed to the desirability of a national system of old-age and survivors insurance. Similar problems would be involved in the long-term risk of permanent total disability. Experience in the operation of the Federal-State unemployment compensation system has made it clear that protection of current-risk programs is weakened by segregation of separate State funds and that administrative complexities and costs are increased by the existence of separate State systems. Since the cost of social insurance is met in considerable part from pay rolls, the presence or absence of particular insurance programs and differences in the rates of contributions for existing programs both serve to create unfair interstate competition when programs are on a State basis.

The Board is not unmindful that the program here proposed would entail modifications of many existing arrangements for social insurance and related programs as well as the establishment of new mechanisms in areas where none now exists. It has given study and thought to many of the particulars which would be involved in implementing this plan or some modification of it, and is prepared to offer more specific information and recommendations should these be desired by the Congress.

Public Assistance

In public assistance, as contrasted with social insurance, the Board believes that there is a strong presumption in favor of State programs. The costs of assistance are met from general revenues rather than on the basis of pay rolls, and payments are made on the basis of current individual need. Since, however, the Federal Government shares assistance costs under the Social Security Act, it must be concerned that the basis and extent of Federal participation are such as will effect the purpose of the social security program.

Special types of public assistance. — The most serious lack in operations under present provisions of the Social Security Act is that evidenced by inadequacies of assistance in many collaborating States. A major factor underlying this situation, as has been pointed out, is the uniform-matching basis of Federal grants for the needy aged, children, and the blind, in combination with the inequalities in State resources for assistance. The present basis of Federal financial participation has not served effectively to diminish State differences in the availability of assistance to needy persons; at its worst, it has heightened these differences in some respects. The Board therefore recommends consideration of a variable-matching basis, under which the Federal grant-in-aid would cover more than half the total cost in States which themselves have only small economic resources.

The studies made by the Board during the past 8 years lead to the conclusion that State per capita income, as indicated in annual estimates now prepared regularly by the Federal Government for other purposes, affords a reasonable basis for objective measurement of State differences in economic and fiscal capacity. It might be found feasible, for example, to continue the Federal grant at 50 percent of expenditures under an approved State assistance plan for States in which per capita income is at or above the national per capita. When average income in a State is below the national average, the Federal grant to the State might be increased accordingly. For example, if per capita income in a State is only half that in the country as a whole, the Federal share in assistance costs might be twice that of the State.

It would be appropriate to require, as a condition of Federal grants, that the States themselves make similar adjustments among localities which share assistance costs under Federal-State programs. The Board also believes that it would be reasonable to require, as a condition of approval of the State assistance plan, elimination of State residence requirements for recipients of assistance. Legal settlement in a locality has long been a characteristic condition of eligibility for older forms of public aid since, typically, all costs of relief were met by localities. The Social Security Act specifies maximum State residence requirements which may be imposed in a State plan that is approved by the Social Security Board, and that some State funds be provided even though there is local financial participation. If an increased part of the total assistance cost is borne by Federal funds, it would seem reasonable to eliminate State residence requirements.

Among the three assistance programs now maintained under the Social Security Act, the gravest inadequacies are in aid to dependent children. Studies of the Board lead to the conclusion that need among children is at least as great as that among the aged, while aid actually given for children is only a fraction of that for the aged in terms of either the number of recipients or the total amounts. Serious limitations in the availability of Federal funds for needy children arise under two conditions of the Federal act: the restriction in the situations in which Federal matching funds may be used and in the amounts of individual payments to be matched. The Social Security Board recommends that Federal funds under the Social Security Act be available for use under approved plans for children who are needy for any reason whatever, not merely, as at present, for those who have been deprived of parental care or support by reason of the death, absence, or incapacity of the parent. The Board also recommends elimination of the Federal maximums, under which matching Federal funds now can be used only within the limits of $18 a month for the first child and $12 for each additional child aided in the same home. States may and do provide larger amounts when they are able; in the latter half of 1942, total Federal funds for aid to dependent children represented only 67 cents per dollar of total State and local funds, in contrast to 99 cents for old-age assistance and 92 cents for aid to the blind. The limitation of Federal matching, however, has restricted aid to children in States which have been unable or unwilling to assume the whole cost of adequate payments; in many instances, these are the States with only small resources and relatively large numbers of children in their population.

At the present time, matching funds may not be used in payments to needy children aged 16 and 17 unless the child is attending school regularly. The Board believes that the requirement of school attendance should be eliminated. Suitable schools for older children are lacking in some areas, and for other reasons school attendance may not be feasible or even desirable.

Under all three assistance programs a serious lack arises from the fact that matching Federal funds may not be used to meet costs of medical care given to recipients, except as such costs can be included in the monthly payment to the recipient without restriction of any part of that payment for this particular purpose. The unpredictability and unevenness of medical costs and the maximum on the amount of Federal matching, as well as the limitations of State resources, necessitate a more flexible method of meeting medical needs of persons receiving assistance. In many instances, such care might aid recipients in regaining self-support and thus lessen or obviate their need for continued assistance; about one-third of the children accepted for aid are in need because of the physical or mental incapacity of the parent, and about one-fourth of the persons receiving aid to the blind in the 20 States for which this information is available could profit by some type of medical treatment to improve or conserve vision.

The Board recommends that matching Federal funds be made available to pay medical agencies and practitioners for the costs of medical services and supplies provided for recipients of assistance. Federal reimbursement might well be based on combined costs incurred within a State for medical services to recipients under all assistance programs. If arrangements are adopted for medical services to be provided through a comprehensive social insurance system, State assistance agencies could collaborate effectively with the insurance authorities by making equitable payments so that these services would be available to assistance recipients under whatever arrangements had been developed with physicians, hospitals, and others to furnish services for the insured population.

General assistance. — General assistance is now the only financial recourse for needy incapacitated adults other than the aged and the blind and for families which depend upon marginally employable persons, whose earnings are insufficient to meet unusual strains on family income and whose rights, if any, to unemployment benefits are usually meager. It is used to meet many types of need arising from inadequacy of individual payments for the special types of assistance, gaps in the coverage of social insurance programs or inadequacy in the amount or duration of individual benefits, and risks for which there still is no insurance provision. At present, general assistance is administered by some 10,000 local units and, in considerable part, from only local resources.

Any decline in levels of employment may be expected to squeeze out the workers with the least skill and experience and hence the least likelihood of having insurance rights or savings. Wartime activities have been developed in many areas which are without local resources to meet the needs of families and individuals who would be stranded by any curtailment of these activities. Other communities which have benefited little from present economic conditions will be called upon to meet the needs of families stranded elsewhere without jobs or returning without funds to weather the period of readjustment. The present financial structure of general assistance in the United States and the legal and administrative arrangements which necessarily have been erected on this structure have proved unable to cope with demonstrated needs in many parts of the country.

The Board believes that Federal participation in general assistance, through matching Federal grants to the States under certain general conditions such as those provided for the special types of assistance, would go far toward remedying present deficiencies and toward effecting a unity and flexibility in public assistance as a whole which will be needed in coming years and the more distant future. It therefore is recommended that such grants be authorized under the Social Security Act.

If the planners were enthusiastically looking to the future, those who were responsible for the Insurance Trust Funds (established by the 1939 legislation) were becoming increasingly alarmed, particularly by Congress' annual insistence on postponing the increase in the social security tax. The Report for 1942–43, *published in 1944, was typical.*

**Eighth Annual Report of the Social Security Board
for the Fiscal Year 1942 – 43**

*   *   *

Summary and Conclusion

The board of trustees has repeatedly emphasized in its annual reports that the primary consideration with respect to the size of the trust fund is its adequacy to assure the financial integrity of the old-age and survivors insurance program. There is a large measure of uncertainty with regard to economic developments in the next 5 years — particularly if a part of the period should be in the post-war phase. Neither the present nor the immediately prospective level of employment can be confidently considered representative of what is likely to be the long-term experience. The probable post-war level of benefit payments is high and the trend of such payments will be an ascending one over the next generation and longer. With present benefit payments in the magnitude of $180 million a year, over the period of several decades disbursements will increase some 25 to 30 times. Prudent management requires emphasis on the long-range relationship of income and disbursements.

It is estimated that the level premium cost of the benefits now provided by the system is between 4 and 7 percent of the covered pay roll. This means that if pay-roll taxes of this magnitude (employer tax and employee taxes combined) had been levied from the beginning, and were continued indefinitely, the system as a whole would be just self-supporting. But Congress has now maintained old-age and survivors insurance tax rates at 1 percent each on employees and employers for over 7 years instead of permitting the scheduled increases of the act to become effective, although in recent years economic conditions have imposed no obstacle in such increases. The tax rates maintained during this period have been equal to only one-half of the low estimate of the level premium cost of the system.

It is clear that the present rates of contributions even under the most favorable prospects are not more than half the minimum level premium cost of the system. Moreover, they are only one-third the ultimate maximum rates provided by statute. The board believes that since the existing rates of contribution are less than those necessary to support the system on a level-premium basis (or bear such proportion of the total cost as it is believed suitable to meet by employer and employee contributions), and general economic conditions are such that increased rates of contribution could be borne without injury to the economy, the rates of contribution should be raised. It is clear, in the opinion of the board, that, under present conditions, an increase in contribution rates would cause no hardship; but, on the contrary, would assist the economic stabilization program by the absorption of excess purchasing power. The board of trustees believes, therefore, that in the interest of the long-run welfare of the system and of the general economy, contribution rates should be immediately increased to 2 percent each for employers and employees.

Increasing concern about the fiscal integrity of the old-age and survivors' provisions did not stop the Social Security Board from thinking about expansion. As early as 1942, the President's budget message had talked in terms of a "uniform national system" of unemployment insurance, and it was barely a secret that the Social Security Board wanted to see the program federalized. The Annual Report of the Social Security Board 1943–44 (*contained in* The Annual Report of the Federal Security Agency, 1944) *seemed to foreshadow a more integrated national approach to all aspects of welfare.*

At the end of 1943 and throughout 1944, the President was calling for Congress to extend social security and particularly for returning veterans.

Annual Budget Message of the President
(January 10, 1944)*

Veterans' Legislation and Social Security

Last July I recommended to the Congress a minimum program to assist servicemen and servicewomen in meeting some of the problems they will face when discharged. This included mustering-out pay for every member of the armed forces sufficient to provide for a reasonable period after discharge. I also urged an educational and training program to enable those demobilized from the armed forces, to further their education and training and to prepare for peacetime employment. I am confident that the Congress will take early action along these lines.

The permanent program of social security initially adopted in 1935 provides a framework within which many of the problems of demobilization can be met. This framework of unemployment insurance and retirement benefits must be reinforced and extended so that we shall be better equipped for readjustment of the labor force and for the demobilization of the armed forces and civilian war workers.

Pressing economic need has forced many workers to continue in employment or seek work even when disability, old age, or care of young children would have made retirement from the labor force preferable. Extension at the present time of the coverage of the Federal old-age and survivors insurance system to many groups now denied protection, and expansion of the scope of the system to include disability benefits, would permit these workers to retire after the war. The old-age and survivors insurance system should

Public Papers and Addresses of Franklin D. Roosevelt, 1944–45, p. 17-18.

also be amended to give those in the armed forces credit for the period of their military service.

The proposed changes in the social security law would provide the necessary minimum protection for nearly all individuals and their families, including veterans of the present war. They would provide benefits additional to veterans' pensions, veterans' compensation, and national service life insurance in case of death or disability attributable to military service.

I repeat my recommendation that the present unemployment insurance system be strengthened so that we shall be able to provide the necessary protection to the millions of workers who may be affected by reconversion of industry. I prefer an extension of coverage and liberalization of enemployment benefits to any special legislation, such as that providing for dismissal payments through war contractors. I also recommend the adoption of a program of Federal unemployment allowances for members of the armed forces. Furthermore, I suggest Congress consider the establishment of unemployment insurance for maritime employees and a temporary system of unemployment allowances for those in Federal service who, because of their wartime employment, have been unable to build up rights under the existing system.

At least some of this was achieved with the G.I. Bill of Rights (Servicemen's Readjustment Act, 1944), and in the election campaign of that year, the President sought to give political substance to the somewhat academic programs for the future proposed by the Social Security Board. However, the President was still unable to persuade Congress to undertake that which the Board wanted so much—an increase in the social security tax.

MEDICAL CARE: 1934–1945

Executive Recommendations

While the original report of the Committee on Economic Security contained some general statements on health insurance, the final report on the subject was not available until well into 1935. In any event, the Committee on Economic Security had already decided that the inclusion of anything resembling health insurance would jeopardize passage of the 1935 legislation, a view which the President clearly shared. Such a fear was no doubt justified but, of course, this did not mean that there were not plans for some form of federal medical care provisions. The staff of the committee was aggressively committed to some such project. As early as September, 1934, the Director and Assistant Director of the Health Insurance Staff had produced a working paper, which became Appendix D *to the* Preliminary Report of the Staff of the Committee on Economic Security.

*This document was historic in its prophecies about the politics of medical
care, if slightly sanguine in its belief that a comprehensive program could
be undertaken within the immediate future, and it was to have a profound
effect on the future development of medical care in this country. The authors offered three basic principles to be followed, suggested by their study
of foreign health insurance schemes.*

Preliminary Report of the Staff of the Committee
on Economic Security
Appendix D
(p. 4)

(i) Adequate reorganization and responsibility to the medical professions
in respect to professional personnel, problems, and services;

(ii) Administrative separation, so far as is practical of responsibility for cash
and service benefits, so that the physician who is responsible for service is not
also responsible for the certification of disability to receive cash benefits.

(iii) Broad scope of the insured population to take in more than the poorest
classes in order that the system shall be able to afford fair accommodation of
those who furnish medical services.

*While it was decided that a health insurance program would not be part
of the 1935 legislation, interest in such a program remained strong among
members of the staff. During January and February of 1935, various advisory committees in the medical field were invited to discuss a report containing a detailed program of insurance — whose core consisted of an important provision of medical services:*

Report of Medical Advisory Committee
(p. 36)

*   *   *

V. Medical Benefits

Health and medical services should be provided as insurance benefits in
the form of services, and not in the form of cash with which to purchase
service.

The medical benefits provided through a system of compulsory insurance
may range from the services which a general practitioner of medicine of
ordinary skill and experience can furnish in his office up to a complete and
all-embracing program of all health and medical services which the needs of
the insured population may dictate. The one, as at first established in the
British system, is as inadequate to solve the economic problems as to meet
the needs for health service; the other is beyond the financial resources of

most population groups to be served and exceeds the resources of the facilities which exist in most communities. Somewhere between the two extremes lies the reasonable choice.

Keeping our attention focused upon the objectives of the insurance program, there are two paths which the argument may follow. The scope of medical benefits might be determined according to the nature of the need which is to be met or according to the kinds of service which might be provided. Study of these two lines of approach leads us to the conclusion that the first is impractical and that the second is both practical and flexible.

If we follow the argument in terms of the kinds of services which might be provided, the following six categories embrace all the important kinds:
1. The services of a general practitioner of medicine and the provision of such drugs and medicines as he prescribes;
2. The services of physicians who have attained special skill and competence in the recognized specialties of medicine;
3. The services ordinarily provided in general and special hospitals, clinics and laboratories;
4. Dental service;
5. Nursing service in the home;
6. Medical and surgical commodities (approved home remedies, eye glasses, orthopedic appliances, etc.)

While this report was to shape proposals for medical care during the next thirty years, the meetings which generated it were apparently stormy. Obviously the President was right in assuming that the presence of health insurance in the bill would insure its defeat.

As it was, the Economic Security Bill contained only the Public Health Title, and this was supported by the AMA, but some flavor of the potential hostility of the medical profession to anything more comprehensive is evident in this communication from the Illinois State Medical Society, presented by Representative Everett M. Dirksen of Illinois.

Economic Security Bill
Hearings on H. R. 4120 before the House Ways and Means Committee
74th Cong., 1st Sess. (January and February, 1935)
(p. 1139)

Statement of Illinois State Medical Society

Course of the Enterprise and Consequences

Ultimately the effort results in an enormous bureaucracy. In Germany there are 2,000 more insurance administrators than physicians in the Krankenkassen. The political control is injurious to the system, unfair to the patient, disheartening to the doctor, and destructive to the proper practice of medicine.

The conduct of a compulsory and often almost universal health and medical service placed in the hands of a lay board, or commission means that this vast project is entrusted to people wholly unfitted for the task and unfamiliar with its problems. Furthermore, such organizations soon become so powerful financially and politically that they cannot be altered or dislodged as welfare workers are well aware.

When benefits are distributed to individuals through an extensive administrative group with numerous employees the combination quickly becomes a gigantic and extremely powerful political machine, a plaything of politics.

This very natural result advances the directoral body in power but always affects the quality of medical service injuriously. Restrictions on scientific practice are imposed by lay administrators which benefit the politics and the treasury of the organization rather than the patient.

Effects of this Speculation upon the Patient

Sickness insurance is a source of degradation and mental degeneration to the insured.

The patient malingers, or is suspected of it, and his feelings are hurt by the inquiry or antagonized by discovery. Much time is wasted in bringing this fraud to light. Sickness insurance creates neuroses and prevents their proper and efficient treatment. The greed to get something back for money spent is always present among the insured and urges them to seek aid. Prescriptions, expensive and often not needed, are regularly demanded and either the patient is served or the doctor is criticized, even cashiered.

Sickness is often an economic problem rather than pathologic. Sickness insurance is a form of deadly infection which creates a constantly increasing amount of illness and emasculates the individual by depriving him of his courage, sense of responsibility and manhood. He becomes fundamentally a chronic and demoralized invalid.

In England 14 out of 100 claimed sickness benefits in 1921 and this grew to 23 in 1927. With unmarried women the proportion grew from 12 to 21 and for married women from 19 to 38 out of each 100 applicants.

According to estimates, from 60 to 75 percent of those who come for medical attention do not need it. If told so they are displeased and flock to quacks who must be paid for their services. In only 5 of 19 countries having national insurance were the patients satisfied with the service.

The occasional lack of adequate medical care furthermore results oftener from the indifference of the people than from economic stress. The Metropolitan Life Insurance Co. learned from a house-to-house canvass of several thousand families that the majority of parents who had failed to have their children inoculated against diphtheria recognized its benefit and believed in preventive medicine but neglected to have it done. Would health insurance correct such heedlessness?

The entire history of health insurance has proved that "sickness" is an indefinable condition which is often coveted by the insured person with no desire to get well.

Effects Upon the Practice of Medicine

The practice of medicine is mechanized unduly, personal responsibility diminished, diagnosis crippled, research hampered, and so much time wasted on the urgencies of the would-be sick that none is left for the really disabled.

The efforts of societies and lay boards are directed everywhere toward the destruction of the professional status and its replacement by an industrial contract.

The question of a free choice of physician is antagonized and restricted by the insurance administrator since only those doctors will be chosen, he contends, who are liberal with certificates of incapacity for work and generous with drugs, for all insurance schemes lead to expensive over-medication. German physicians report that the insured patients will use ten times as much medicine as the uninsured.

Effect Upon the Physicians

The insurance code demands constant expansion of medical service, while the management at the same time fights adequate medical compensation. The doctor is over busy. He has no time to renovate his ideas by consulting the monthly records of medical progress.

The personal relation of patient and physician is destroyed and a purely cash connection retained with the organization. Commercialism is rampant and professional control of the medical problem eliminated. Insurance service is always second class since the better practitioners will not apply. In only 6 of the 19 countries having national insurance were the doctors satisfied with the service.

In view of these facts, the medical profession of Illinois feels that more prolonged study is required for the proper solution of this medical problem and for the present, the members of this society desire opportunity to practice medicine as hitherto for the best interests of the public without domination by laymen, either social service workers, political appointees or any others who have no experience with difficulties inherent to medical practice.

In conclusion let it be emphasized by repetition that all available statistics demonstrate that health conditions prevailing in Illinois are distinctly superior to those in the nation at large, and that the latter, as previously pointed out, easily surpass those in nations where health insurance schemes have been adopted.

Respectfully submitted.

Illinois State Medical Society

The President, for various political and personal reasons, was anxious to placate the medical profession and during 1935 he appointed a Medical Advisory Committee composed of members of the medical establishment. When the Committee on Economic Security sent its report, Risks to Economic Security Arising out of Illness, *to the President on June 15, 1935, recommending that compulsory health insurance should ultimately be introduced, its reservation that that moment might not be appropriate was strongly endorsed by the Medical Advisory Committee. In August, 1935, an Interdepartmental Committee to Co-ordinate Health and Welfare Activities was established; and in January, 1936, the President asked the Social Security Board to undertake further research into the whole area of health insurance.*

By 1937 this interdepartmental committee was once again thinking in terms of a national program and it appointed a Technical Committee on Medical Care, which in 1938 developed a program including not only disability insurance, increased maternal and child health, public health services, and federal aid to hospital construction, but also federal grants-in-aid to the states for programs for the "medically needy" and for general medical care. (The AMA opposed disability insurance, hospital construction, and grants to the states for medical care.)

These series of suggestions became known as the National Health Program, and, as such, they were the center of focus at the 1938 National Health Conference—where they attracted considerable popular and some professional support. Supporting evidence of the need for a health program was supplied by the Bureau of Research and Statistics, which released a compilation of data reported to the Social Security Board by state agencies administering approved plans for old-age assistance. In December, 1938, the health program was formally endorsed by the Social Security Board and the President appeared willing to take some tentative steps.

A Request for Consideration of the Recommendations of the Interdepartmental Committee to Coordinate Health Activities with Respect to the National Health Program
(January 23, 1939)*

To the Congress:

In my annual message to the Congress I referred to problems of health security. I take occasion now to bring this subject specifically to your atten-

Public Papers and Addresses of Franklin D. Roosevelt, 1939, p. 97.

tion in transmitting the report and recommendations on national health prepared by the Interdepartmental Committee to Coordinate Health and Welfare Activities.

The health of the people is a public concern; ill health is a major cause of suffering, economic loss, and dependency; good health is essential to the security and progress of the Nation.

Health needs were studied by the Committee on Economic Security which I appointed in 1934 and certain basic steps were taken by the Congress in the Social Security Act. It was recognized at that time that a comprehensive health program was required as an essential link in our national defenses against individual and social insecurity. Further study, however, seemed necessary at that time to determine ways and means of providing this protection most effectively.

In August, 1935, after the passage of the Social Security Act, I appointed the Interdepartmental Committee to Coordinate Health and Welfare Activities. Early in 1938, this committee forwarded to me reports prepared by its technical experts. They had reviewed unmet health needs, pointing to the desirability of a national health program, and they submitted the outlines of such a program. These reports were impressive. I therefore suggested that a conference be held to bring the findings before representatives of the general public and of the medical, public health, and allied professions.

More than 200 men and women, representing many walks of life and many parts of our country, came together in Washington last July to consider the technical committee's findings and recommendations and to offer further proposals. There was agreement on two basic points: The existence of serious unmet needs for medical service; and our failure to make full application of the growing powers of medical science to prevent or control disease and disability.

I have been concerned by the evidence of inequalities that exist among the States as to personnel and facilities for health services. There are equally serious inequalities of resources, medical facilities and services in different sections and among different economic groups. These inequalities create handicaps for the parts of our country and the groups of our people which most sorely need the benefits of modern medical science.

The objective of a national health program is to make available in all parts of our country and for all groups of our people the scientific knowledge and skill at our command to prevent and care for sickness and disability; to safeguard mothers, infants and children; and to offset through social insurance the loss of earnings among workers who are temporarily or permanently disabled.

The committee does not propose a great expansion of Federal health services. It recommends that plans be worked out and administered by States and localities with the assistance of Federal grants-in-aid. The aim is a flexible program. The committee points out that while the eventual costs of the proposed program would be considerable, they represent a sound investment which can be expected to wipe out, in the long run, certain costs now borne in the form of relief.

We have reason to derive great satisfaction from the increase in the average length of life in our country and from the improvement in the average levels of health and well-being. Yet these improvements in the averages are cold comfort to the millions of our people whose security in health and survival is still as limited as was that of the Nation as a whole fifty years ago.

The average level of health or the average cost of sickness has little meaning for those who now must meet personal catastrophes. To know that a stream is four feet deep on the average is of little help to those who drown in the places where it is ten feet deep. The recommendations of the committee offer a program to bridge that stream by reducing the risks of needless suffering and death, and of costs and dependency, that now overwhelm millions of individual families and sap the resources of the Nation.

I recommend the report of the Interdepartmental Committee for careful study by the Congress. The essence of the program recommended by the Committee is Federal-State cooperation. Federal legislation necessarily precedes, for it indicates the assistance which may be made available to the States in a cooperative program for the Nation's health.

Congressional Action

Acting on the strength of this message, Senator Robert F. Wagner of New York introduced a bill (S. 1620) to implement the National Health Program.

A subcommittee (chaired by Senator James E. Murray of Montana) of the Senate Education and Labor Committee held hearings on the bill. Needless to say, the AMA opposed the bill rigorously—even those parts its House of Delegates had voted to support. In a tentative report, however, the subcommittee talked in terms of producing an amended bill the following year. Already S. 1620 prepared the way for future development.

Establishing a National Health Program
Senate Report No. 1139
76th Cong., 1st. Sess.
(1939)

Principal Provisions of the Bill
*   *   *

Maternal and Child Health

*   *   *

Public Health Work

*   *   *

Grants to the States for Hospitals and Health Centers

*   *   *

Grants to States for Medical Care

Section 4 of the bill further amends the Social Security Act by adding a new title (XIII) to provide Federal grants-in-aid to the States to enable them to extend and improve medical care, especially in rural areas and among individuals suffering from severe economic distress. The sum of $35,000,000 is authorized to be appropriated for the fiscal year 1940, and thereafter such sums as the Congress may consider necessary. Any sums authorized under these appropriations are to be distributed to the States submitting plans approved by the Social Security Board (sec. 1301).

If the sum appropriated for the fiscal year 1940 is insufficient to meet the total payments for that year, the total amount available is to be allotted among the States by the Social Security Board after taking into consideration the population, the number of individuals in need of the services, the special health problems, and the financial resources of the several States (sec. 1302).

The approval of State plans is conditioned upon stipulations like those already reviewed in connection with the preceding titles, except that administration of the State plan is not exclusively restricted to the State health agency (sec. 1303).

Payments to the States are to be made on the basis of the same variable matching formula applying to payments under other titles of the bill. No Federal grants are to be made in respect to so much of the State expenditures as are in excess of $20 a year per individual eligible for medical care under the proposed plan, or so much as are expenditures for the institutional care of cases of mental disease, mental defectiveness, epilepsy, and tuberculosis (sec. 1304).

Federal payments are to be suspended if any State fails to comply with requirements specified in the title (sec. 1305).

The administration of the title is vested in the Social Security Board. The Board is authorized to create a Federal advisory council (or councils) to advise it with respect to the administration of this title, and to make and publish rules and regulations necessary for efficient administration. One million dollars is authorized to be appropriated for the fiscal year 1940 to meet the administrative expenses of the Board, and for each fiscal year thereafter a sum sufficient for such purposes (Secs. 1306 – 1308).

Grants to States for Temporary Disability Compensation

Section 4 of the bill also adds a third new title to the Social Security Act, title XIV, to assist the States in the development, maintenance and administration of plans of temporary disability compensation. The appropriation of $10,000,000 is authorized for the fiscal year 1940, and of such sums for the fiscal years thereafter as may be necessary to carry out the purposes of the title. Sums appropriated by the Congress under these authorizations are to be distributed to the States having plans for temporary disability compensation approved by the Social Security Board (sec. 1401).

State plans to be approved for grants-in-aid under this title are required to be based upon State laws which meet a number of conditions explicitly laid down in the title. The State law must provide for: Administration and payment of disability compensation through a single State agency, or through more than one where this may be consistent with efficient administration of the State plan; methods of administration necessary for efficient operation; opportunity for fair hearing before an impartial tribunal for individuals whose benefit claims are denied; cooperation and working agreements with State agencies administering related programs or services; the making of such reports to the Social Security Board as may be required and necessary, etc. No plan for disability compensation is to be approved by the Social Security Board for any State which does not have a plan or plans, approved under other titles of the bill, such as will assure that reasonably adequate medical services, including preventive services, are available to minimize disability among persons covered by the temporary disability compensation plan of the State. Payments will cease when the plan fails to meet the stipulated conditions (sec. 1402).

Grants to the States which have approved plans would amount to one-third of the sums expended as temporary disability compensation plus one-third of the costs of administration found by the Board to be necessary for proper and efficient administration of the plan. The method of computing and paying such amounts is similar to the provisions of the assistance titles in the present Social Security Act (sec. 1403). The appropriation of $250,000 for the fiscal year 1940 is authorized to cover the Board's administrative expenses, and for each fiscal year thereafter a sum sufficient for such purposes (sec. 1404).

The report went on to consider a number of other matters: variable grants, the concept of "medically needy," medical education, the need for minority group protection, and the problem of coverage.

At this point the President seemed to lose interest in the National Health Program and early in 1940 he sent a message to Congress calling for a small program of federal aid for the construction of local hospitals. This seemed rather weak after the strong report of the interdepartmental committee and the Wagner Bill of 1939. Nevertheless, when Senators Wagner and George introduced the Hospital Construction Bill in the Senate it had bipartisan support. It did not, however, pass the House.

In the next few years, despite the Social Security Board's recommendations for permanent disability benefits, the issue of federal involvement in health care was relatively dormant, but two events in 1943 were to prove significant. In March of that year there began the first nationwide medical care program, EMIC (Emergency Maternal and Infant Care), to give medical services to the wives and children of enlisted men. 1943 was also the year of the first Murray-Wagner-Dingell Bill, providing a comprehensive medical care program. Organized labor supported the bill, but once again the AMA. vigorously opposed it and although it was drafted by the Social Security Board, the bill was not endorsed by the President. He remained neutral, and the proposal died in committee.

The bill (H.R. 2861) is important because, unlike the 1939 legislation, it emphasized health insurance rather than grants to the states for medical care programs. It was also significant in that it looked to a comprehensive social system, including permanent disability insurance, maternity benefits, and a more federalized system of unemployment compensation (Title VIII).

Title IX concerned medical care. It would have provided general medical and laboratory benefits and thirty days of hospitalization to covered individuals. The Surgeon General of the Public Health Service was to establish a system of enlisting doctors to provide services and otherwise to administer the plan.

Despite the fact that H.R. 2861 was not passed, the Board persisted and in 1944 published the Need for Medical Care Insurance. *In the annual report for that year, the Board clearly committed itself to health insurance.*

Ninth Annual Report of the Social Security Board for the Fiscal Year 1943–44

Methods of Paying Medical Costs

In an ordinary year the American people pay about $4 billion for all civilian health and medical services, including costs of hospital construction. Of this total, about four-fifths comes from private funds and one-fifth from public funds. The total expenditure, governmental and private, for all health and medical services is equivalent to about $30 a person a year. But in any year some families pay little or nothing to doctors and hospitals, while others pay hundreds or even thousands of dollars. The difficulty with medical costs is that no family can know how much or how costly medical care they will need or can limit their needs for care to what they can afford. If costs could be averaged for the types of medical services which are ordinarily bought individually, most self-supporting families could pay for adequate medical care without hardship.

Tax-supported care. — For certain major forms of medical care or care of certain groups in the population, much or all of the cost has been "averaged" through payment from the tax funds to which the whole community contributes, not merely the sick person or his family. In 1943, for example,

97 percent of all beds in hospitals for mental and nervous diseases were in publicly owned and operated hospitals, and 85 percent of all beds for tuberculous patients were in tax-supported hospitals. These types of long-continued care obviously are too costly for any but the richest families to bear individually. These diseases, moreover, have long been recognized as endangering public health and safety and leading to public costs for broken and dependent families.

The Federal Government, again for obvious reasons, has always been responsible for medical care of the armed forces. In addition to care of service-connected injuries and illnesses, moreover, by the end of the war some 16 million veterans will be able to receive publicly supported medical care for non-service-connected conditions through veterans' facilities.

From colonial times, care of the sick poor has been considered a public responsibility, though often provided very inadequately if at all. It is estimated that total public expenditures for medical care of the indigent and low income groups — including expenditures of the Federal Government, the States, and their localities — are at least $150 million a year.

Most of the care given under the arrangements outlined above is "state medicine" in the sense that it is financed from public funds, is given through publicly owned facilities, and is given for the most part by physicians or others paid directly by government agencies. It represents not only a method of financing costs but also a way of organizing medical and institutional practice. Since "state medicine" has ordinarily been used as a term of opprobrium, it should be pointed out that some of these areas of medical service, notably care of mental illness and prevention and care of tuberculosis and other communicable diseases, are those in which progress has been outstanding and for which the United States is known favorably throughout the world.

Insurance methods. — Another group of arrangements has been developed in the United States through which costs of medical care are distributed among employers or the individuals directly concerned, or both, without recourse to tax funds.

Costs of medical care for work-connected injuries, and in some States also of occupational disease, are insured under State or Federal workmen's compensation laws; only one State lacks such legislation. These laws make costs of industrial accident and disease a part of the cost of production.

In recent years a large number of middle-class families have been able to average some of their medical costs through membership in voluntary prepayment plans. The membership of Blue Cross plans, which cover certain hospital bills, includes about 15 million persons, or about 11 percent of the population. Voluntary prepayment plans for medical care, established by industry, medical societies, and community and other groups, probably cover about 4 or 5 million persons, about half of whom are counted in the number covered by Blue Cross plans. These families pay a regular fixed amount each month and know that, within limits fixed by the contract, their hospital or other medical bills will be paid if they become sick. Contracts are commonly restricted to surgical expenses or fix extra fees for some services. In addition, commercial insurance companies sell policies — usually to indemnify hospital or surgical expenses or both — on an individual and group basis. The scope of the protection is always limited and often is restricted to care of accidental injuries. All in all, possibly from 30 to 35 million persons have some protection against hospital and medical costs under the Blue Cross and other voluntary prepayment plans and commercial insurance. Comprehensive protection against medical and hospital costs is limited to a few million.

Workmen's compensation and the other arrangements mentioned above are forms of insurance. They are ways of distributing and paying costs, not forms of medical practice. In one way and another, they help to cut through the barrier of costs by distributing medical care expenses over the whole group of insured persons, the well and the sick, and by distributing the costs over periods of time — the years of earning as well as the weeks or months of sickness. In the usual voluntary prepayment plan, a patient picks his doctor or hospital from all participating in the plan; doctors and hospitals decide whether or not they wish to join such plans. These plans cause no change in the personal relationship between a doctor and his patient, except to wipe out misgivings of both about the bill and to lessen the other important failing in that relationship — that so many people have no relationship with any doctor.

All the voluntary forms of medical care insurance mentioned above are fulfilling valuable functions in their limited sphere. They are necessarily more costly than the arrangements which could be evolved with wider sharing of sickness risks and with the administrative economies feasible for larger units. Their great shortcoming is that they reach so small a part of the population and fail to reach those who have the greatest need of medical care insurance. From the standpoint of both the public and the families concerned, the great majority of the population must have some better way to pay medical costs if American families are to achieve the level of health and economic independence which our national resources should assure.

Compulsory social insurance. — Neither the course of present developments in this country nor experience in other countries which have tried voluntary health insurance gives any indication that comprehensive and adequate arrangements to insure medical costs can be made in any way except through a compulsory insurance system. In this aspect of health security the United States faces a situation not unlike that in old-age security a decade ago. At that time, many employers had established sound retirement systems for their workers; some persons had banded together to provide for themselves as a group or had made adequate individual pro-visions through annuities or other forms of commercial insurance. It was clear then, however, as it is clear now for medical care insurance, that these voluntary arrangements could not be expected to extend to even a majority of the population in need of insurance or to the groups whose needs were greatest.

Medical care insurance would enable self-supporting families to pay for and get needed medical services without any important alteration because of the insurance system in present forms or organization of medical practice. Moreover, families dependent on public funds could be covered through payment of contributions on their behalf by the agencies administering as-sistance. They thus would receive care in the same way in which others receive it; the stigma and, typically, the inadequacy of "poor-law medicine" could be wiped out.

Contributions equivalent to about 3 percent of annual earnings would pay for adequate basic medical and hospital services for both workers and their dependents. A more comprehensive system would cost the equi-valent of about 4 percent. These costs would be no more than now is spent by families on the average. They are less than the average expenditure by families in the low income groups, since, contrary to the general impression, low-income families spend, on the average, a larger proportion of their in-comes for medical care than families in better circumstances, though—be-cause of their more frequent and severe illness—they receive much less in relation to what they need.

Public discussion has centered around three alternative methods of pro-viding medical care insurance. It has been suggested that it could be estab-lished on a State-by-State basis, without participation by the Federal Government. It could follow the pattern of unemployment compensation, in which Federal legislation gave inducement to States to enact laws and establish insurance systems. Or, following the analogy of old-age and sur-vivors insurance, it could be established as a Federal system.

For reasons outlined in the following section of this report, the Board believes that it would be simplest, most economical, and most effective to establish comprehensive protection through Federal legislation, while providing authority to utilize State agencies and other facilities. In any event, administration of benefits should be so decentralized that all neces-sary arrangements with doctors, hospitals, and others would be worked out on a local basis. The general pattern of arrangements with hospitals and doctors should be developed with the collaboration of professional organiza-tions and with careful regard for regional, State, and local circumstances. In each area of administration—local, State, and Federal—policies and opera-tions should also be guided by advisory bodies representing those who pay the insurance contributions and those who provide the services.

The much-advertised fears of "socialized medicine," "regimentation" of doctors, hospitals, or patients, loss of the patient's freedom to choose his doctor, and deterioration of quality of care can be made wholly groundless. A system of medical care insurance can and should be so designed as to avoid these disadvantages. By making services readily available to those who need them, without fear of the costs, the quality and effectiveness of service may be improved, and the incomes of doctors and hospitals may be made better and more secure. If, at the same time, professional education, research, and the construction of needed facilities are financially aided, progress in medicine and improvement in national health can be greatly accelerated.

President Roosevelt was never a particularly reliable supporter of federal health insurance. As the 1944 election approached, the President seemed to be moving towards an endorsement of state provision of medical care, but once the election was over he seemed less committed to the idea. In the budget message of 1945, he did seem to envision medical care within social security; still, at the time of his death there had been no further move.

THE TRUMAN YEARS
1945–1952

THE TRUMAN YEARS
1945–1952

POST-WAR UNEMPLOYMENT

On January 3, 1945, in the annual budget message President Roosevelt called on Congress to "give early consideration to extension and improvement of our social security system" and to "re-examine the financial basis of the program," but on May 8 the President was dead. In some ways, his successor was likely to be even more sympathetic to welfare issues. At least regarding health care he was clearly more concerned than Roosevelt whose interest in the matter appeared to be directly related to Federal Security Administrator McNutt's political fortunes and his own family relationship with AMA President Harvey Cushing. At the same time, Truman was less likely to favor exclusively federal solutions, and he did not feel Roosevelt's direct tie to the Social Security Board. Perhaps even more significant was the fact that Truman was a man of action. And action appeared to be most needed in the area of unemployment compensation.

The war in Europe ended in May, and by August it had terminated in Asia as well. The Full Employment Bill which had been before Congress for most of the year made it clear that a general objective of the Truman Administration would be to achieve maximum employment. The President also realized the employment problems that would inevitably confront the workingman during the transition from wartime to peacetime production, so within a month of coming into office he sent a special message on unemployment compensation to Congress.

Special Presidential Message to the Congress
on Unemployment Compensation
(May 28, 1945)*

To the Congress of the United States:

The Congress and the Executive Branch of the Government have already moved to prepare the country for the difficult economic adjustments which the Nation will face during the transition from war to peace.

1. The Congress has created the Office of War Mobilization and Reconversion to coordinate the reconversion activities of all Federal agencies, and that Office has established basic reconversion policies.
2. Specific laws have been enacted by the Congress setting forth the policies and providing the administrative machinery for contract

Public Papers of the Presidents, Harry S. Truman, 1945, p. 72–75.

293

       termination, plant clearance, financial aid to business, and the disposition of surplus property.

3. Our military and civilian agencies have prepared themselves to expedite industrial reconversion and reemployment.

4. As part of an over-all program for returning veterans the GI Bill of Rights provides "readjustment allowances," weekly cash benefits to veterans until they are able to obtain jobs.

5. Congress has permitted business to carry back postwar losses against excess profits tax payments during the reconversion period.

6. Congress has established support prices for agricultural products so that farmers will be protected against a postwar collapse of income.

       There remains, however, a major gap in our reconversion program: the lack of adequate benefits for workers temporarily unemployed during the transition from war to peace. I urge the Congress to close this gap.

I am confident that, with appropriate measures, we can avoid large-scale and lengthy unemployment during the transition period. However, some temporary unemployment is unavoidable, particularly when total demobilization becomes possible. Even if reconversion proceeds rapidly, no amount of planning can make jobs immediately available for all displaced personnel. We must provide maximum security to those who have given so fully of themselves on the fighting and production fronts. The transition from war to peace is part and parcel of the war and we cannot shirk our obligation to those temporarily unemployed through no fault of their own.

To produce what is needed for the Pacific war, we must appeal to the workers to accept and remain in jobs which they ultimately must lose when munitions production ceases. The Government has thus incurred a moral obligation to these workers and to those who have stuck faithfully to their posts in the past.

To fulfill this obligation, we must rely principally upon our existing system of unemployment insurance. However, the existing State laws embrace three major defects:

1. Only about about 30 million of our 43 million non-agricultural workers are protected by unemployment insurance. The absence of protection for Federal Government employees — in Navy Yards, arsenals and Government offices — is particularly inequitable, since these workers are subject to risks of unemployment similar to the risks of those who work for private employers. Lack of protection for employees in small establishments and for maritime workers also constitutes a serious shortcoming in the present programs.

2. The weekly benefit payments provided under many of the State laws are inadequate to maintain purchasing power and to provide a reasonable measure of economic security for the workers. Most

States fix a maximum rate of $15 to $18 a week. This is clearly inadequate to protect unemployed workers against ruthless cuts in living standards, particularly if they have families.

3. The length of time for which benefits are paid is too short. In nearly one-third of the States, no worker can receive more than 16 weeks of benefits in any year, and many workers do not qualify even for this length of time.

Therefore, I recommend specifically that Congress take emergency action to widen the coverage of unemployment compensation and to increase the amount and duration of benefits—at least for the duration of the present emergency period of reconversion. Basically this can be accomplished only by amending the Social Security Act so as to induce State laws to provide more adequately for anyone who is unemployed.

To be sure, the States have large sums in the Unemployment Trust Fund. But since changes of State laws cannot be effected overnight, I propose that the Congress, during this emergency period, extend the coverage of unemployment compensation to include Federal employees, maritime workers, and other workers not now insured. Moreover, I see no feasible way to make benefits payable to such workers, unless they are financed entirely by the Federal Government during the present emergency. The benefits should appropriately be administered by the States.

I also recommend that Congress provide, through supplementary Federal emergency benefit payments, minimum standards for the weekly rate and duration of unemployment benefits. Every eligible worker should be entitled to 26 weeks of benefits in any one year, if his unemployment continues that long. The maximum payment, at least for the worker who has dependents, should be raised from present levels to not less than $25 per week. In this connection, Congress will no doubt wish to reexamine the readjustment allowance provisions of the GI Bill of Rights. All payments should be made through the existing unemployment compensation machinery of the several States, just as payments to veterans are now made.

These provisions are essential for the orderly reconversion of our wartime economy to peacetime production. They are badly needed for the duration of the reconversion emergency.

Decent unemployment benefits would serve as a bulwark against postwar deflation. By assuring workers of a definite income for a definite period of time, Congress will help materially to prevent a sharp decline in consumer expenditures which might otherwise result in a downward spiral of consumption and production. Adequate unemployment insurance is an indispensable form of prosperity insurance.

Congress will soon deal with the broader question of extending, expanding and improving our Social Security program, of which unemployment insurance is a part. Although such improvement is fundamental, congressional deliberations on the broad issues will take time. On the specific issue of unemployment benefits, we may not have time available. We are already entering the first phase of reconversion; we must be prepared immediately for the far larger problems of manpower displacement which will come with the end of the war in the Pacific.

I earnestly hope, therefore, that the appropriate Committees of Congress will undertake immediate consideration of the emergency problem.

Harry S. Truman

A bill to implement the President's basic proposal—that the Federal Government furnish funds for the states to provide $25 a week for up to twenty-six weeks—was proposed in the House on July 9 by Robert Doughton of North Carolina, chairman of the Ways and Means Committee; a more comprehensive bill (S. 1274) was introduced by Harley Kilgore of West Virginia on July 17 in the Senate. While the Finance Committee held hearings at the end of August and the beginning of September, opposition was growing rapidly outside the Congress, especially from manufacturers and the states. The hearings themselves revealed a remarkable reassertion of states' rights. Representatives of state unemployment agencies made clear their belief "that supplementation of present state benefits will ultimately lead to nationalization of the entire system, and to this we are opposed." During the hearings, a senior unemployment compensation official from Connecticut was even more dramatic, "We may be unconsciously building an atomic bomb under our system of government far more dangerous than the one that hit Japan."

With the collapse of Japan the President returned to the fray, and even before the Finance Committee had reported he sent another special message to the Congress detailing a program for the reconversion period.

Special Presidential Message to the Congress Presenting a 21-Point Program for the Reconversion Period
(September 6, 1945)*

1. Unemployment Compensation

The end of the war came more swiftly than most of us anticipated. Widespread cut-backs in war orders followed promptly. As a result, there has already been a considerable number of workers who are between jobs as war industries convert to peace. Other workers are returning to a 40-hour week and are faced with a corresponding reduction in take-home pay.

This has led to a natural feeling of uneasiness among the rank and file of our people. Let me emphasize that there will be no reason for undue

*Public Papers of the Presidents, Harry S. Truman, 1945, p. 267.

timidity. A vast backlog of orders may soon make possible the greatest peacetime industrial activity that we have ever seen. But this can happen only if the Congress and the administration move vigorously and courageously to deal with the economic problems which peace has created. Then there need be no reason to fear either the immediate future or the years that lie ahead of us.

Determined action now will create the atmosphere of confidence which is so vital to a rapid reconversion with a minimum of unemployment and hardship.

No matter how rapidly reconversion proceeds, however, no amount of effort or planning will be able immediately to provide a job for everyone displaced from war work. Obviously, displaced war workers cannot find jobs until industry has been regeared and made ready to produce peacetime goods. During this lag the Government should provide help. The cost of this transition from war to peace is as much a part of the cost of war as the transition from peace to war — and we should so consider it.

This course is recommended not only as a matter of justice and humanity, but also as a matter of sound business. Nothing would be more harmful to our economy than to have every displaced war worker stop buying consumer goods. And nothing would be more conducive to a large-scale cessation of buying than the feeling on the part of displaced war workers that all their income had stopped and that their remaining financial resources had to be hoarded.

For one group of those who may become unemployed in the near future — the demobilized veterans — the Congress has already made special provision. Any veteran who has satisfactorily completed 90 days of service is now entitled by law to a weekly unemployment allowance of $20 for as much as 52 weeks depending on the length of his service.

By contrast, there are more than 15,000,000 workers not protected under our present unemployment insurance laws. There are many millions more for whom protection is inadequate. Many of these have been unable to accumulate adequate savings.

On May 28, 1945, I recommended to the Congress that the Federal Government immediately supplement the unemployment insurance benefits now provided by the several States. That is the only feasible way to provide at least a subsistence payment in all parts of the United States during this coming unemployment period.

As I pointed out then, the existing State laws relative to unemployment insurance are inadequate in three respects:

(1) Only about 30,000,000 of our 43,000,000 nonagricultural workers are protected by unemployment insurance. Federal Government employees, for example, such as Federal shipyard and arsenal workers, are not covered. Nor are employees of small businesses and small industrial establishments. Nor are the officers and men of

the merchant marine who have braved enemy torpedoes and bombs to deliver supplies and the implements of war to our armed services and our allies.

(2) The weekly benefit payments under many of the State laws are now far too low to provide subsistence and purchasing power for the workers and their families. Almost half of the States have the clearly inadequate maximum of $15 to $18 a week.

(3) Many of the States pay benefits for too short a period. In more than one-third of the States, for example, 18 weeks is the maximum.

I recommended then, and I urgently renew my recommendation now, that the Congress take immediate action to make good these deficiencies for the present emergency period of reconversion.

Specifically, coverage should be extended to include Federal employees, maritime workers, and other workers not now insured. This additional compensation during the present emergency will have to be financed entirely by the Federal Government, but the benefits should appropriately be administered by the States.

I also recommended, and I now repeat that recommendation, that the Congress provide, through supplementary Federal emergency benefit payments, additional unemployment benefits so as to bring them up to adequate standards in all the States. All payments, however should be made through the existing unemployment compensation machinery of the several States.

During this emergency every eligible worker should be entitled to 26 weeks of unemployment benefits in any one year. The maximum weekly payment for those workers whose previous earnings were high enough, should be not less than $25 per week.

If the Congress decides to take this very necessary step, it will also wish to reconsider and increase the unemployment allowance provided for veterans.

There has been so much misrepresentation about this temporary proposal that I think I should categorically state what the bill does *not* do.

It does *not* give everyone $25 a week. Under it, an applicant must be ready, willing, and able to work and must have earned wages high enough so that the percentage rate will yield this maximum figure.

It does *not* federalize the unemployment compensation system. It leaves it with the States.

It is *not* intended to take the place of the permanent amendments to the unemployment compensation system which are now being studied by the Congress. It is an emergency measure designed to expand the present system without changing its principles. It is designed only to meet the immediate pressing human problems of reconversion.

This recommendation is *not* to be confused with the broader question of extending, expanding, and improving our entire social security program of which unemployment insurance is only a part. I expect to communicate with the Congress on this subject at a later date. But I sincerely urge that we do not wait for consideration of such a complex question before enacting this much needed emergency legislation.

*   *   *

Truman's explanations were to no avail. As reported out by the Senate Finance Committee, the bill retained the twenty-six-week provision, but evaded the $25 per week issue. Moreover the Senate report unequivocally emphasized the temporary nature of the solution.

Emergency Unemployment Compensation
Senate Report No. 565
79th Cong., 1st Sess.
(1945)

General Statement

This bill as reported by the committee provides three means for affording the protection to workers which is essential to an orderly transition from our wartime economy to a peacetime economy. For the period ending June 30, 1947, it provides for—
1. Supplementing the unemployment compensation payable under State laws so as to extend the duration of the period for which such compensation is payable.
2. Paying unemployment-compensation benefits to Federal employees and maritime workers.
3. Transportation allowances to assist persons who have been engaged in war work away from their homes to return to their homes or to go to places where new employment is available.

These are emergency measures to meet the problems of temporary unemployment and shifting employment during the reconversion period.

The cost of the benefits provided by the bill will be borne entirely by the Federal Government. This is entirely appropriate, as the problems which the bill seeks to meet arise as a result of our national war effort, and the cost of the bill should be regarded as a part of the cost of the war. No one can foretell the exact extent of the unemployment which will occur during the reconversion period or the extent to which it will be necessary to aid in redistributing the labor force to meet the needs of our postwar economy. However, it is clearly the obligation of the National Government to take all reasonable steps to protect individuals who have been engaged in war work by alleviating the hardships which they may incur by reason of the sudden termination of these activities.

*After three days of debate in the Senate the bill was passed by voice vote
basically as it had been reported out of committee. However, the bill was
never reported out of the House Ways and Means Committee. There, a
14 – 10 vote on September 24 decided that its consideration should be
"indefinitely postponed." The opportunity for even a short-term solution to
unemployment compensation had been lost and the long-term solution
was as evasive as ever.*

PROPOSED LEGISLATION

*The only legislation affecting social security that was passed by Congress
in 1945 postponed again the increase in the social security tax. But it was
apparent that some fundamental re-thinking was needed. In early May,
1945, Truman suggested that perhaps the Federal Security Agency had
outgrown its original purpose. He proposed extension of social security
to white collar workers and farmers, an expansion of public health, and the
creation of a cabinet level welfare department.*

*Shortly before President Roosevelt died, the House Ways and Means
Committee had appropriated money for a study to examine the need for extension of all social security programs. The report was published under the
title,* Issues in Social Security: *A Report to the House Committee on Ways
and Means by the Committee's Social Security Technical Staff on H.R. 204,
79th Cong., 1st Sess. (1946).*

*Meanwhile, the Social Security Board, devoted much of its 1945 report
to a section entitled "Facing Forward to Peace."*

Annual Report of the Federal Security Agency, 1945

Social Security Agency

In summary, the Social Security Board recommends the establishment of:

A comprehensive basic national system of social insurance, covering all
major risks to economic independence and all workers and their dependents
to whom such risks apply. Such a program would include insurance against
wage loss in periods of disability and against costs of medical care, as well
as old-age and survivors insurance unemployment insurance, relating benefits to past earnings with provision for additional benefits for dependents.
It would be designed to close existing gaps in the coverage of both persons
and risks, to remove present inequities in the protection of workers and the
financial burdens of employers, and to provide a consistent relationship

among insurance provisions for the various risks and between provisions of the basic system and of supplementary special systems for particular groups. As compared with separate programs to meet particular risks, such a system would reduce administrative costs and burdens and simplify arrangements as they affect workers, employers, and public agencies. It would greatly strengthen protection against want and dependency at a minimum cost. *A comprehensive program of public assistance,* on a State-Federal basis, under which payments financed from State and Federal funds would be available to any needy person in the United States irrespective of the reason for need or the place of residence. Such a program would be designed to remove the great disparities which now exist in the treatment of various classes of needy persons and in the treatment of persons who are in like circumstances but live in different parts of the country. It would also be designed to remove serious present inequities in the relative burdens borne by States and localities in financing public assistance.

For particular programs the recommendations of the Board include:

Old-Age and Survivors Insurance

Coverage of all gainful workers, including agricultural and domestic employees, public employees and employees of nonprofit organizations, and self-employed persons, including farmers.

Credit to servicemen for their period of service in the armed forces.

Reduction of the qualifying age for all women beneficiaries to 60 years, rather than 65.

Increase in benefit amounts, particularly for low-paid workers.

Increase from $3,000 to $3,600 a year in the amount of earnings subject to contribution and counted in computation of benefits.

Increase in the amount of earnings permitted a beneficiary without suspension of benefits, with a less severe penalty than at present for the first failure to report earnings in excess of the permitted amount.

Deletion of the requirement of school attendance as a condition of receipt of benefits by children aged 16 and 17.

Greater uniformity in defining, for purposes of the insurance system, family relations qualifying members of a worker's family for benefits.

Benefits during periods of extended or permanent disability, like those for old-age retirement.

Definition of good cause for voluntary leaving or for refusing suitable work to include good personal reasons, not merely causes attributable to the job or the employer.

If minimum benefit standards are adopted but the credit-offset feature of the present tax is retained, change in the additional credit provisions so that employers may obtain rate reductions either through experience rating, State-wide reduction, or some other method.

If minimum benefit standards are adopted, permanent provision through a reinsurance fund—rather than loans, as now temporarily provided—to States whose unemployment funds run low.

Additional Insurance Provision

Cash benefits to insured workers and their dependents during both temporary disability (less than 6 months) and extended disability (6 months and over).

Insurance against costs of medical care, including payments to physicians and hospitals, with provision for decentralization of administration and possible utilization of State administration.

Public Assistance

Federal grants-in-aid to States for general assistance to any needy person, irrespective of cause of need, as well as for old-age assistance, aid to the blind, and aid to dependent children.

Special Federal aid to low-income States, in addition to the equal-matching grant, to enable them to meet full need, as defined by the State, among all their needy population.

State distribution of available Federal and State assistance funds to localities in accordance with need in the locality and, where localities participate in financing assistance, also in relation to local fiscal capacity.

Federal financial participation in medical care payments made directly by the assistance agency to doctors, hospitals, or other agencies that furnish such care to needy persons under State public assistance programs.

Deletion of the Federal matching maximum for individual payments of aid to dependent children, and deletion or increase of such maximums for old-age assistance and aid to the blind.

Abolition of State residence requirements as a condition of eligibility for assistance under State plans approved under the Social Security Act.

Extension of Federal financial participation in aid to dependent children to include aid to any needy child, irrespective of the reason for need, who is living with a natural or adoptive parent, legal guardian, or relative. Substantially the same objective could be achieved through the Board's recommendation on Federal financial participation in general assistance. One or both changes, however, are urgently needed to assure more nearly adequate provision for needy children. In addition, appropriate provision under the Social Security Act for the care of a child who is in need of foster-home care.

Deletion of the requirement for Federal matching that, as a condition of eligibility for aid, children aged 16 and 17 must attend school.

Unification of the administration of State public assistance programs at both State and local levels as a condition of the Federal grant.

The Annual Report for 1946 contained an almost identical plea for a comprehensive program in social security. Only the introduction differed radically:

Annual Report of the Federal Security Agency, 1946

Social Security Administration

To attain the objectives of a social security program, the Board believes, social insurance and public assistance, separately or in combination, must provide against all common hazards to livelihood among all groups of the population. Our present provision for social security in the United States is seriously deficient in both these respects. Moreover, existing arrangements to safeguard or enhance the economic security of families and individuals have grown up at different times and places and for various separate groups. As a result, the character and extent of present protection, when it exists, differ greatly for persons in essentially similar circumstances. Our social and political traditions as a democracy and the continuing progress of our free competitive economy require, in the opinion of the Board, a broader, sounder, and more equitable basis for ensuring individual and national well-being.

Certainly the OASI program had achieved remarkable success. By 1945 there were over 41.5 million insured workers, but it was clear that any fundamental change depended on the publication of Issues in Social Security. *The report was submitted to the House Committee on Ways and Means in January, 1946, and its main themes were outlined in the* Digest of Issues in Social Security *(1947), which contained a succinct history of OASI and offered a blueprint for the future. With respect to public assistance it took an ambivalent position, assuming that "withering away" was still only a matter of time, but calling for expanded programs at the same time.*

SOCIAL SECURITY AMENDMENTS OF 1946

Issues in Social Security *was made available early in 1946 when the President had already spoken in favor of new legislation. In his State of the Union Message he announced:*

President Harry S. Truman
First Annual Message
(January 14, 1946)*

*   *   *

(j.) Social security and health

Our Social Security System has just celebrated its tenth anniversary. During the past decade this program has supported the welfare and morale

*Public Papers of the Presidents, Harry S. Truman 1947, p. 63–64.

of a large part of our people by removing some of the hazards and hardships of the aged, the unemployed, and widows and dependent children.

But, looking back over 10 years' experience and ahead to the future, we cannot fail to see defects and serious inadequacies in our system as it now exists. Benefits are in many cases inadequate; a great many persons are excluded from coverage; and provision has not been made for social insurance to cover the cost of medical care and the earnings lost by the sick and the disabled.

In the field of old-age security, there seems to be no adequate reason for excluding such groups as the self-employed, agricultural and domestic workers, and employees of nonprofit organizations. Since many of these groups earn wages too low to permit significant savings for old age, they are in special need of the assured income that can be provided by old-age insurance.

We must take urgent measures for the readjustment period ahead. The Congress for some time has been considering legislation designed to supplement at Federal expense, during the immediate reconversion period, compensation payments to the unemployed. Again I urge the Congress to enact legislation liberalizing unemployment compensation benefits and extending the coverage. Providing for the sustained consumption by the unemployed persons and their families is more than a welfare policy; it is sound economic policy. A sustained high level of consumer purchases is a basic ingredient of a prosperous economy.

Moreover, the importance attached to economic security was underlined when the Full Employment Act was signed on February 20, 1946.

The combination of presidential resolve and the publication of Issues in Social Security *virtually insured that some social security legislation would also be enacted during 1946. In connection with* Issues, *the Committee on Ways and Means held hearings on old-age and survivors' insurance during February, March, and April, on public assistance during April and May, and on unemployment compensation during May and June.*

Hearings on Issues in Social Security

Concerning old-age and survivors' insurance, much of the testimony considered to what extent the program was indeed an insurance program and the role of the trust fund. Once again, much of the burden of cross-examination fell on Dr. Altmeyer.

Social Security Act Amendments of 1946
Hearings before the House Ways and Means Committee
79th Cong., 2d Sess. (1946)
(p. 25)

Mr. Wasielewski. You make the statement, in your prepared paper, though, that there should be a correspondence between the benefits and the cost of living. Do you think as the cost of living goes up the benefits should go up, and as the cost of living comes down, they should be reduced? Is that the policy you think should be followed in reference to social security?

Mr. Altmeyer. No, I don't. I think we cannot work out any formula under an insurance system that would follow exactly the ups and downs of the cost of living.

Mr. Wasielewski. In 1939, when Congress brought in the survivorship end of the social-security program and expanded somewhat the benefits, without at the same time making any change in the contributions made, don't you think we may have fallen into some error there on the part of the actuaries, so far as the soundness of the system is concerned?

Mr. Altmeyer. No, for the reason that what was done in 1939 would increase the benefits in the early years of the system and smooth them out in the latter years of the system, so that the over-all cost over the developing lifetime of the system was no greater.

Mr. Wasielewski. Getting back to my earlier question, do you think we should attempt to maintain the social-security program on an insurance basis, or let it become a gratuity?

Mr. Altmeyer. I don't know what you mean by an insurance basis, or what you mean by gratuity. If you mean should we continue to finance it solely out of pay-roll contributions or also finance it partly out of general revenue, I would say to the extent this program is made all-inclusive the justification for financing partly out of general revenue increases.

Mr. Wasielewski. Was it the original intention in 1935 that the contributions paid out of taxes on the pay roll would be sufficient to maintain the system?

Mr. Altmeyer. Yes, and changes made in 1939 did not upset that principle.

Mr. Wasielewski. When the Social Security Act was first adopted there was never any mention that the social security benefits paid to any person under this act were to be sufficient of themselves to support him. It was merely to supplement what it was expected the individual would have in his own right.

Mr. Altmeyer. That is right.

Mr. Wasielewski. Do you think we should now change our policy and try to support them wholly on their benefits, or do you think it should still be the policy of the Government to merely have these benefits act as a supplement to what the person may have established in the way of savings for his old age?

Mr. Altmeyer. I think the latter is more nearly correct. My feelings is in a social-insurance system we ought to construct a benefit formula or an amount of benefits table in such a way that in the vast majority of cases, practically all cases, those benefits, added to private savings and other private provisions, are sufficient to maintain a person on a decent level. I don't think that it would be possible to construct a social-insurance system whereby the benefits payable in and of themselves would always be sufficient, in all cases, to cover the cost of living of the recipient, without increasing the cost beyond what would be considered a reasonable level.

Mr. Wasielewski. And if you don't take into account income a person may earn from investments or interest or other sources outside their taxable earnings from actual labor, it would lead to the conclusion that it was not the intention to encourage the saving of money by the people.

Mr. Altmeyer. That is right.

Mr. Carlson. Doctor, I would like to ask a question. Let us assume now that we do not change this coverage, nor do we change the present 2-percent tax, and using as a basis an annual average wage of $1,500 for men and $900 for women, which is one of the low estimates submitted to this committee, in what year will the benefits catch up with the receipts on the basis of that income?

Mr. Altmeyer. Would you repeat that question, please? I don't know whether I got it all.

Mr. Carlson. I probably didn't express it correctly. My thought is this: Using the low estimate submitted on average income of $1,500 for men, and $900 for women, and following through with the present tax, 1 percent on employer, and 1 percent on employee, in what year will the benefit payments catch up with the receipts?

Mr. Altmeyer. You mean if no changes were made in benefits at all?

Mr. Carlson. No changes at all.

Mr. Altmeyer. Well, I would assume probably in 10 years.

Mr. Carlson. That would be 1955.

Mr. Altmeyer. Yes.

Mr. Carlson. Could you give me an estimate as to how much the reserve fund would be at that time?

Mr. Altmeyer. I made an estimate running 5 years, and it would be about $11,000,000,000 at the end of 5 years, as I recall, at the present rate.

Mr. Carlson. Then we can legislate on the basis that if we do not increase the coverage, do not change the rates, that we will have in reserve in 1955, or approximately then, $11,000,000,000?

Mr. Altmeyer. I said 5 years from now. That would be 1952.

Mr. Carlson. In 1952?

Mr. Altmeyer. Yes.

Mr. Carlson. Is it your thought then that the line would cross the benefits?

Mr. Altmeyer. The lines would not cross, as I say, until possibly 10 years from now at the very earliest, so that the reserve would be higher than $11,000,000,000,000 before the lines crossed.

Mr. Carlson. What will it be, then, in 1955, if that is when the lines cross?

Mr. Altmeyer. I haven't made any calculations beyond 5 years, but it probably might increase another two to three billion, between 1952 and 1955.

The Social Security Board was also moving tentatively towards an increase in benefits and contributions as well as towards changes in the "average monthly wage" formula.

House Hearings
(p. 37)

Mr. Altmeyer. The next suggestion that is made is modification in the method of calculating the average monthly wage.

Under the present law, benefits are based on wages based on all months since January 1, 1937. The lack of wages in insured employment in any period reduces the average to an excessive degree when, as in the early years of the program, the period of coverage is short. To avoid this, the average wage could be determined by relating it only to those periods when the workers' earnings exceeded a certain amount. That is to say, do not count, in calculating your average, any quarter in which the earnings fell below a certain amount, so that your average would be higher.

In order to afford reasonable recognition of the length of time a person contributed to the system, the benefits might continue to be increased by 1 percent for each year of coverage, as is now the case, and reduced by 2 percent for each year the workers were out of covered employment. That is to say, instead of taking the whole period back to January 1, 1937, whether the persons were working or not working, as your divisor, you take as your divisor only those periods when he did work and earned a sizable amount of money. You would then get a fairer average wage.

But if you did that, and did not apply this 1 percent increase for every year that he was in the system, and reduced it 2 percent for every year that he was out of the system, you would have this inequitable results: That a person might be in the system only 4 or 5 years, and another person might be in the system 40 years, and they would draw the same benefit, because their average wage would be calculated only on those periods when they were working in employment under the system.

Therefore, what we are suggesting is, work out a truer average wage, but recognize the length of time under the system by this 1 percent increase for years in the system and the 2 percent decrease in the years out of the system.

At the same time Dr. Altmeyer was pressing for the establishment of disability insurance.

Perhaps in the first flush of post-war good feeling opposition to old-age and survivors' benefits was particularly muted. Certainly with the trust fund in increasing difficulty and the insurance aspect of the program becoming less and less clearly defined, it was surprising to find few serious attacks on the bases of the program. Probably the most constructive critic was Marion B. Folsom who made some telling points about the coverage of the act, but the House Ways and Means Committee apparently accepted far more readily than it had in 1939, that the system was one of social insurance.

When it came to public assistance, the Social Security Board was prepared to push for radical reforms, as long as the programs in that category were kept separate from the insurance program. In Issues *Dr. Altmeyer endorsed the suggestion that the only long-term solution to public assistance was a federal contribution on a non-categorical basis — i.e. a federal share in general assistance — coupled with a variable grant system.*

House Hearings
(p. 790)

The Board believes that, just as the Federal Government should vary its share of assistance according to the economic ability of the State, so the State should distribute Federal and State funds to localities in such a manner that need can be met in full in all parts of a State according to the standards the State establishes.

All these suggested changes in public assistance led the Board to reverse the stand on residence requirements for which it had lobbied in 1935 and to relax its requirements on support by relatives.

House Hearings
(p. 796)

Since adoption of the various recommendations made would substantially increase Federal financial participation in all States, the Board believes that this extension of Federal participation should be contingent on removal of State residence requirements for eligibility to public assistance.

*　　*　　*

It is recommended that a State plan, to be approved, may not deny assistance to an individual on the ground that relatives should support him, if in fact they are not doing so. The purpose of public assistance is to provide aid to persons who actually lack means of support.

In some ways the most interesting development in OASI and PA was the growth of what was later to be known as the Welfare Lobby. There was pressure not only from special interest groups like the American Foundation for the Blind, but also from the American Association of Social Workers and the American Public Welfare Association representing the social workers themselves.

H.R. 7037

During the hearings, a bill (H.R. 6911) including a provision allowing variable grants, was reported out, but after an acrimonious debate, it was abandoned. On July 15, a more modest bill (H.R. 7037) was introduced. In order to avoid the amendment of the eighty-seven pending social security bills, it was coupled with a rule allowing only one hour of debate and no amendments. The House Ways and Means Committee in this way consolidated the hold over social security matters which it had developed in the pre-war period. Although there was considerable heated dispute before the rule was adopted by a voice vote, the transfer of power from the House to the committee was settled.

The debate on the bill itself was mainly recorded disappointment that its provisions were not stronger. Even Chairman Doughton was apologetic.

Congressional Debates
92 Congressional Record, p. 9913
(July 24, 1946)

Mr. Doughton . . .

I appreciate very much the action of the House in making possible the consideration of this bill reported by the Ways and Means Committee, and that is said with no criticism whatever of those who took a different view. The matter of changing the social-security law and amending it is a controversial subject. As I stated previously, I have lived with this subject ever since 1935. I had the honor and privilege of being chairman of the Committee on Ways and Means when that committee reported to the House the first bill ever reported by any committee on social security and I have always felt very proud of that. At that time we set up the social-security system and, while the law has been amended from time to time since, while not yet perfect, it still retains its original framework as that has been tested and found sound. The present bill is the best we can get under the conditions that obtain today, the conditions under which we were compelled to work.

*   *   *

We began work on the social-security bill as early as we could and worked as continuously as it was reasonably possible. We realized that due to the early adjournment of Congress, the limited time, and the importance of the subject that it would be impossible to get anything enacted during the remainder of this session of the Congress that was of a controversial nature or upon which disagreement could not be reconciled by members of our committee. We proceeded all the way with that understanding; that is, that we would have to leave controversial matters for future study and future determination. We proceeded that way until we had completed our work, completed our hearings, completed our executive sessions, and got ready to report out our bill, and when we did that we found that there was a difference of opinion as to what we could get through, as to what should go in the bill. When we reported the bill out after extended executive sessions we had a minority which was unyielding and inflexible, but just as sincere as the majority. They believed that certain provisions the majority wanted should not go into the bill. But we reported the bill with these provisions. We thought perhaps we could reconcile those differences. The minority submitted a very strong minority report, so we could not reach an agreement on the bill as reported. Finally, to make possible enactment of legislation, we made changes in two titles of the bill. If we had not done this it would have been impossible to get through any legislation and we could not assume responsibility for it.

*   *   *

I share with many of you the feeling that both the insurance and the assistance provisions in the bill fall far short of what is desirable for permanent legislation. Public assistance recipients, particularly those in low-income States, receive inadequate assistance under existing law and there should be some basic changes to remedy this situation.

The debates, were not particularly enlightening. What was perhaps most interesting was the political support which social security—and especially OASI—had acquired since 1939. There was even increasing support for the variable grant in PA.

Senate Action

The Senate Finance Committee, however, was prepared to be more radical than the House. In general, it called for a major study by the Joint House and Senate Committee on Taxation, and in particular, accepted the variable grant in Title V.

Social Security Act Amendments of 1946
Senate Report No. 1862
79th Cong., 2d Sess.
(July 27, 1946)

TITLE V.—STATE GRANTS FOR OLD-AGE ASSISTANCE, AID TO DEPENDENT CHILDREN, AND AID TO THE BLIND

The purpose of title V is to increase Federal participation in old-age assistance, aid to the blind, and aid to dependent children and accordingly to increase the protection afforded by these programs. The title will result in additional Federal funds for all States.

The bill provides (1) an increase in the Federal share of assistance payments in States with per capita income below the average for the Nation; and (2) an increase in the Federal matching maximums.

Under the bill as passed by the House of Representatives, 11 States would not have received any additional Federal funds for the aged, 4 States would not have received anything additional for dependent children, and 13 States would not have received anything more for the blind. Under the bill as reported out by the committee, however, every State will receive additional Federal funds.

The committee is strongly of the opinion that raising the Federal matching maximums on individual payments as proposed in the House bill, without simultaneously providing special Federal aid to low-income States, will only serve to increase the very inequities we are seeking to minimize. Under the House bill, the already large disparity in payments between the high-and low-income States would be widened. Under the House bill, the richer States, i.e., most of those that are now making payments in excess of the present matching maximums on individual payments, will receive additional Federal funds to assist them in making such payments. The low-income States, on the other hand, for the most part are unable to make payments that even approach the present Federal matching maximums. Their limited resources are already strained to the utmost in taking care of the increased number of individuals who have sought aid since VJ-day; they have no margin of funds available to raise payments to take full advantage of even the present Federal maximums; in fact, in recent months some of these States have had to cut the payments of those receiving assistance so that new cases could be placed on the rolls.

*   *   *

Under the House bill, almost 60 percent of the additional Federal expenditures required to meet the cost of raising the maximums on individual payments as proposed, would flow to the 10 States with highest per capita income; in sharp contrast, the 10 lowest-income States would receive but 2 percent of the additional Federal funds. Three of the 10 States with lowest per capita income would receive no increase under the House bill. The committee believes that giving more money to those States which now have most, at the expense of those which have least, will not serve the best interests of the Nation.

In May 1946, average payments for old-age assistance ranged from a low of less than $20 in 11 States (Alabama, Arkansas, Delaware, Georgia, Kentucky, Mississippi, North Carolina, South Carolina, Tennessee, Virginia, and West Virginia) to highs of more than $40 in the States of California, Colorado, Connecticut, Massachusetts, and Washington. Of the 11 States in which average payments were less than $20, all but Delaware is among the States with per capita income lower than the national average. Similarly in aid to dependent children, average payments per family in May 1946 amounted to $75 or more in the States of California, Delaware, Massachusetts, New York, Oregon, Utah, and Washington. In sharp contrast average payments of less than $35 per month per family—which usually averages at least 3.5 members including the adult who cares for the children—were made in 13 States (Alabama, Arkansas, Florida, Georgia, Iowa, Kentucky, Mississippi, North Carolina, South Carolina, Tennessee, Texas, Virginia, and West Virginia). As in old-age assistance, the majority of States in which payments are lowest are those with low per capita income. The picture is essentially the same in aid to the blind.

To those who claim that these low payments reflect differences in living costs, the committee wishes to point out that though some difference in living costs exists between high- and low-income States, the differences in levels of assistance are far greater than can be justified on this ground alone. In support of this statement the difference in cost of living in certain cities included in the index of the Bureau of Labor Statistics was compared with the difference in average payments of old-age assistance. The cost of living in Boston, for example, was only 3 percent higher than that in Memphis. But the average payment of old-age assistance in Boston was more than two and a half times the average in Memphis. The cost of living in Los Angeles was only about 1 percent higher than that in Atlanta, but a recipient of old-age assistance in Los Angeles got nearly three times as much as a recipient in Atlanta.

A review of recent trends in some of the low-income States shows their immediate need for more funds for public assistance. In these States as in others the end of the war brought an upturn in the number of persons applying for assistance and an increase in the amount of money required to provide minimum necessities.

Some of the low-income States in the South have been able to add new persons to the rolls only if they reduced payments. One of these States has recently cut each payment by $3.35 per person. Several States, which have never been able to give 100 percent of the amounts which they found that recipients needed, have had to cut the fraction still further, especially for aid to dependent children. The common practice in the low-income States of making payments on the basis of only a fraction of the amount found to be needed is evidence of the fact that lower payments in these States result chiefly from less adequate assistance rather than from lower cost of living.

When they have insufficient funds, assistance agencies have to choose between aiding fewer persons more adequately although they refuse aid to other needy people, and making still smaller payments to more recipients.

In the fiscal year 1944–45, the 12 States with the lowest per capita income had 21 percent of the population of the country but received only 15 percent of the total amount granted by the Federal Government for public assistance.

Increase in Federal share in low-income States. — Federal grants-in-aid for public assistance are intended to help in aiding needy aged and blind persons and dependent children in all parts of the country and to some extent to equalize the financial burden throughout the Nation. The present system of equal matching, however, has not adequately fulfilled these objectives. The present 50-percent basis for Federal participation does not recognize differences in the ability of States to finance public assistance, nor does it recognize the greater incidence of poverty in States with low economic resources. To assist their needy people, the low-income States must make greater tax effort than States with larger resources where relatively fewer persons are in need. This is illustrated by the fact that, in 1942, the latest year for which complete information is available, two-thirds of the States with less than average per capita income appreciably exceeded the average for all States in tax effort to finance the special types of public assistance. In contrast, only one-sixth of the States with per capita income above the national average exerted above-average tax effort for this purpose.

In all but 2 of the 12 States with highest per capita income, the average old-age assistance payment in November 1945 exceeded $32. In all but 2 of the 12 States with lowest per capita income, the average payment was under $24. Similarly, in aid to dependent children, the 12 States with highest per capita income included only 1 with average payments per family below $60, while the 12 States with lowest resources all had average payments below $40. Some of the low-income States have in recent months been forced either to cut payments, despite rapidly rising living costs, or to refuse aid to eligible applicants.

For States with per capita income below the average for the Nation, the committee proposes an increase in the proportion of assistance costs borne by the Federal Government. The share of the cost to be paid by each low-income State will depend upon how its per capita income compares with that for the country as a whole. The State proportion will be equal to one-half the percentage which its per capita income is of the national per capita income. For example, a State whose per capita income is only 80 percent of the national per capita income would contribute 40 percent of its expenditures for assistance; the Federal share would be 60 percent in this State. All States whose per capita income falls below two-thirds of the national per capita income will pay 33⅓ percent of assistance costs from State and local funds and will receive 66⅔ percent of such costs from Federal funds.

No change in relative State and Federal shares of assistance payments is proposed for the States with per capita income equal to or greater than that for the Nation. In no State will the increased Federal share apply to individual payments in excess of $50 in old-age assistance and aid to the blind, and, in aid to dependent children, in excess of $27 for the first child in the home and $18 for each additional child. Though the Federal Government stands ready to pay a larger percentage of the cost of individual payments in low- than in high-income States, it will not contribute a larger sum to any payment in low-income States than in those with relatively more resource. . . .

Unlike members of the House, Senators were free to offer amendments. Senator Downey's attempt to offer the latest version of the Townsend Plan and support for variable grants vied with one another for attention. The Townsend Amendment was defeated by voice vote on July 30; the bill, including the provision for variable grants, passed (also by voice vote) on the same day.

When the committee met, those from the House vigorously opposed variable grants. Eventually the Senate conferees gave up their demands and variable grants were dropped, but the bill stipulated that the Federal Government would provide two-thirds of the first $15 for OAA and AB, and two-thirds of the first $9 for any child under ADC. Above those amounts the Federal Government would pay one-half of OAA and AB up to $45, and one-half of ADC up to $24 for a first child and $15 for additional children. At least the 50 per cent federal share had been revised, although the arrangements were to expire at the end of 1947, on the assumption that further legislation would have been enacted by then. The conference also eliminated the social security study which the Senate bill had demanded.

The report was accepted by voice vote in the Senate. In the House there was more debate, again focusing on the variable grant. But Representative Jenkins of Ohio reflected the view of several members when he declared, "If the people of the southern states are satisfied to pay small pensions, why should Congress be worried about it?"

THE EIGHTIETH CONGRESS
AND SOCIAL SECURITY

Although the issues of social security were well discussed in the years between 1939 and 1946, any resulting legislation was of a stop-gap nature.

Indeed, many of the provisions of the 1946 act were admittedly designed to be transitory; the act addressed itself to few of the major underlying themes of income security. The elections of that year did not bode well for the program. Social security, in its widest sense, was a Democratic measure, and the congressional election of 1946 gave the Republicans an edge of 245 – 188 in the House, and 51 – 45 in the Senate. It was scarcely surprising that the activities of the eightieth Congress were seen as an important factor in determining the outcome of the 1948 presidential elections.

1947

President Truman, however, was not easily awed. Early in the year he set forth his views quite clearly, and without apology.

The President's Economic Message to Congress
(January 8, 1947)*

Promoting welfare, health, and security

There are certain programs of Government which have come to be looked upon as "welfare programs" in a narrow sense. This has placed them in an insulated compartment. They have not been sufficiently related to the needs of the economy as a whole. In fact, they are a part of the problem of maximum employment, production, and purchasing power.

The Employment Act presents the opportunity to abandon this insulation, and to put these programs back in the economic setting from which they must draw their sustenance.

Unemployment insurance is designed to take care of the unemployed as a matter of right rather than of charity, but it also provides purchasing power as a cushion against recessions, and its tax features are of general economic significance. Retirement and pension systems exist to take care of workers who have given of their years in factory, field, or office. But these systems, both on the income and outgo side, have a profound effect upon volumes of purchasing power, and the retirement age needs to be adjusted to the size and composition of our labor force and the trend of improved technologies. Health insurance relates clearly to the efficiency of workers and thus to the productivity of industry and agriculture. And this is even more true of education, which must be reshaped continuously to meet the changing demands and job opportunities of the machine age — or, some day, of the atomic age.

The total amounts of public outlays for these and other purposes need to be measured against the total size of our economy — its wealth and resources

Ibid., p. 35 et seq.

today, and the trends and policies which shape its future. Many of these programs have been born of a depression psychology. They have proceeded from the assumption that our enterprise system will necessarily fail to employ given numbers of people from time to time, and that these other programs must be brought forward to prime the pump or fill in the gaps. Here, too, we need a restatement. We should regard them rather as an inescapable obligation of an enlightened people, and we should expand them as our resources permit.

The relationship between these welfare programs and general economic conditions has been inadequately explored. Proposals for maximum employment, production, and purchasing power, and proposals traditionally regarded as being in the general-welfare area, should be integrated because they are interrelated. Further studies will provide the basis for this integration.

Public health and education programs. — Among those whose income is less than the minimum necessary for a decent subsistence are those who cannot earn their living because of physical unfitness or lack of educational training.

A combination of public health, nutrition, education, and regional development programs would create additional job opportunities and supply workers fit to fill these jobs. Relatively small Government expenditures for health and education yield a high national dividend. It is more economical to prepare people to earn a decent living than to care for them through relief.

The Federal Government is now spending a large amount of money for health and education programs for war veterans, but general expenditures in these fields are relatively small. I urge the Congress to give early consideration to expanded peacetime programs of public health, nutrition, and education.

Social security. — Although maximum employment would protect wage earners generally from the effects of prolonged mass unemployment, the individual is still exposed to many hazards of economic insecurity.

Our social security program has not kept pace with the times, nor with our increase in general living standards. Many individuals are not covered by the present provisions of the Act, and the benefit payments to those covered are inadequate under today's conditions.

I recommend that the Congress, cooperating with the States, take action that will lead to increasing the amount and duration of unemployment benefits. Present unemployment reserve funds are ample to support such increases.

I recommend that the Congress amend the social-security laws to extend the benefits of old-age and survivors' insurance to the occupational groups now excluded, and to include under unemployment compensation the employees of all establishments, regardless of size, in the industries now covered by the Unemployment Compensation Tax Act. In expanding general social security, the Congress should not overlook the railway workers, whose protection is under separate laws.

While we compensate workers for loss of wages due to unemployment arising from lack of work opportunities, we do not insure them against the risks of loss of earnings from temporary or permanent disability, nor against the costs of medical care. This represents not only a heavy loss for the individual but a great waste of productive manpower.

There is an urgent need to spread the risks arising from sickness and disability by insuring workers against the loss of income and by providing, through social insurance, ready access to essential preventive and curative medical services. I have, in a previous message, presented recommendations for a program of medical care and disability benefits. I urge early consideration of this program.

Our present social insurance system is financed by employee and employer contributions. We must recognize, however, that the employees' contributions and the employers' pay-roll tax curtail mass purchasing power and increase businessmen's costs. From an economic point of view, it would be desirable to finance a part of the social security system out of the general budget. Therefore, I propose that the Congress, in working out a system of financing an expanded social security program, give full consideration to the economic as well as the social import of various methods of taxation for this purpose.

Despite this broad proposal, the legislation for 1947 was, perhaps not surprisingly, scarce. If the political scene was unproductive, the activities of the Social Security Administration were interesting. Once again it was considering the variable grant concept and during the year it published Bureau Memorandum No. 66 by B. L. Johnson.

The Principle of Equalization Applied to the Allocation of Grants-in-Aid
by B. L. Johnson

Conclusion

Close inspection of the operation of present Federal aids, especially those for public assistance, discloses that these grants are not conforming to the basic principle of direct relationship to need, State by State, and of *inverse* relationship to fiscal ability, State by State. Especially in open-end matching grant programs, where State ability to support the service seems to be the controlling factor, Federal aid seems to be offered on a basis quite the opposite of this principle.

If the twin goals of equal program levels for equal effort are to be realized, techniques for allocation and matching of Federal grants will need further analysis and revision to bring the results in line with the principles stated.

Even in a Republican-dominated Congress there was considerable support for the variable grant system in all three public assistance programs. A bill to this effect (S. 1355) was introduced in the Senate by Senator John Sherman Cooper of Kentucky and in the House by Representative Aime Joseph Forand of Rhode Island. The system was also endorsed by the Conference of Southern Governors.

Variable grants was only one of the issues in the continuing social security controversy. The President and the Social Security Administration also advocated disability insurance, but it was not a year for legislation in this or any other area of income security.

None of the thirty-odd bills introduced in 1947 to extend social security coverage made any substantial progress. The Townsend Plan, advocating a flat pension, was still alive, although bottled up in the House Ways and Means Committee, as were other bills to establish a federal pension. One of these—the Harris Bill—provided a monthly federal pension of $60 for anyone not paying federal income tax. The Wagner-Murray-McGrath-Dingell Bill sought to federalize unemployment insurance.

In fact, there was legislative change on only two fronts. First, Congress froze the social security tax again. (H.R. 3818 maintained the rate at 1 per cent until the end of 1949, at 1.5 per cent during 1950 and 1951, and at 2 per cent thereafter). This same bill also extended the public assistance formula, at the 1946 level, through June 30, 1950.

The only other social security bill passed by Congress in 1947, (H.R. 3997, designed to exclude news vendors from coverage under the Social Security Act) had the distinction of being vetoed by the President. The decision National Labor Relations Board *v.* Hearst Publications, Inc., *322 U.S. 111, had held that news vendors were covered by the National Labor Relations Act and in* Hearst Publications, Inc. *v.* United States, *70 F. Supp. 666 (N.D. Cal. 1946) a district court in San Francisco held that they were employees for the purposes of the employment tax (affirmed* per curiam *by the Ninth Circuit, 1948). It was this district court decision which provoked H.R. 3997—a bill passed in both houses by voice vote. The most noteworthy part of this legislation was the reaction of President Truman.*

Memorandum of Presidential Disapproval of Bill To Exclude Newspaper and Magazine Vendors From the Social Security System
(August 6, 1947)*

I am withholding my approval of H.R. 3997, a bill "To exclude certain

Public Papers of the Presidents, Harry S. Truman, 1947, p. 371–72.

vendors of newspapers or magazines from certain provisions of the Social Security Act and Internal Revenue Code".

This bill proceeds in a direction which is exactly opposed to the one our Nation should pursue. It restricts and narrows coverage under our social security law, while our objective should be to enlarge that coverage. The strength, security and welfare of the entire Nation, as well as that of the groups now excluded, demand an expanded social security system.

H.R. 3997 would remove social security protection from news vendors who make a full-time job of selling papers and who are dependent on that job for their livelihood. They and their families are exposed to the same risks of loss of income from old age, premature death, or unemployment as are factory hands or day laborers. They unquestionably fall in the group for whose protection our social security laws were devised.

Many, perhaps most, street vendors of newspapers are excluded even at present from coverage under the Social Security Act because they are independent contractors rather than employees of the publishers whose papers they sell. But some vendors work under arrangements which make them bona-fide employees of the publishers and, consequently, are entitled to the benefits of the Social Security Act. The standards used for determining whether or not the employer-employee relationship exists are the same in the newspaper business as they are in other enterprises. There is no justification for changing these standards so as to discriminate against employees in this particular industry.

It is said that the publishers have difficulty in keeping the necessary records and in collecting the employee contributions required by the social security system. In those cases where the vendors are so closely associated with the paper as to be its employees, the difficulties are no greater than those confronting many other employers of outside salesmen, or indeed employers of other kinds of labor. Certainly, it has not been shown that these difficulties are so formidable as to warrant a special rule of exclusion and the consequent destruction of benefit rights of insured persons and their dependents.

H.R. 3997 would invite other employers to seek exemptions whenever they can allege that the law is inconvenient or difficult for them to comply with. It would establish a precedent for special exemption, and the exclusion of one group would lead to efforts to remove social security protection from workers in other activities. Demands for further special legislation would be inevitable.

We must not open our social security structure to piece-meal attack and to slow undermining. We must, instead, devote our energies to expanding and strengthening that system.

Harry S. Truman

At the same time the Supreme Court in United States *v.* Silk, *331 U.S. 704 (1947) gave the impression that it was extending the coverage of OASI through judicial legislation. It greatly expanded the definition of "employee" within the meaning of the law, not restricting it to the common law meaning. Salesmen, taxicab drivers, miners, and others were held to be covered by the Social Security Act.*

1948

At a time when Congress was irritated by the President's veto of the News Vendors' Bill, United States v. Silk scarcely smoothed the troubled waters. As soon as Congress reconvened in 1948, there was another move to deal with the news vendors, and H.R. 5052 once again tried to exclude them from OASI. The bill was passed by the House without discussion by voice vote on March 4, and by the Senate without change on March 23. Although the President vetoed it, the House overrode the veto 308–28 as did the Senate 77–7.

In some ways, the News Vendors' Bill was now fairly unimportant. Congress had already turned its attention to Silk and to another Court decision which seemed to have abandoned the OASI common law definition of employee and substituted one of "economic reality."

Representative B. W. Gearhart of California had already sponsored House Joint Resolution 296, which prohibited the IRS from extending social security coverage to door-to-door salesmen, something it had attempted to do as of January 1, 1948. The measure overwhelmingly passed both houses, changed only by an amendment to raise federal contributions to OAA and AB by $5 a month and to ADC by $3 a month. The President took this amendment into account in vetoing the whole bill.

Presidential Veto of Resolution Excluding Certain Groups From Social Security Coverage
(June 14, 1948)*

To the House of Representatives:

I return herewith, without my approval, House Joint Resolution 296, "To maintain the status quo in respect of certain employment taxes and social-security benefits pending action by Congress on extended social-security coverage".

Despite representations to the contrary, sections 1 and 2 of this resolution would exclude from the coverage of the old age and survivors insurance and unemployment insurance systems up to 750,000 employees, consisting of a substantial portion of the persons working as commission salesmen, life insurance salesmen, piece workers, truck drivers, taxicab drivers, miners,

*Public Papers of the Presidents, Harry S. Truman, 1948, p. 344.

journeymen tailors, and others. In June, 1947, the Supreme Court held that these employees have been justly and legally entitled to social security protection since the beginning of the program in 1935. I cannot approve legislation which would deprive many hundreds of thousands of employees, as well as their families, of social security benefits when the need for expanding our social insurance system is so great.

Furthermore, if enacted into law, this resolution would overturn the present sound principle that employment relationships under the social security laws should be determined in the light of realities rather than on the basis of technical legal forms. In so doing, it would make the social security rights of the employees directly excluded, and many thousands of additional employees, depend almost entirely upon the manner in which their employers might choose to cast their employment arrangements. Employers desiring to avoid the payment of taxes which would be the basis for social security benefits for their employees could do so by the establishment of artificial legal arrangments governing their relationship with their employees. I cannot approve legislation which would permit such employers at their own discretion to avoid the payment of social security taxes and to deny social security protection to employees and their families.

It has been represented that the issue involved in this resolution is whether or not the legislative branch of the government shall determine what individuals are entitled to social security protection. This is not the issue at all. The real issue is whether the social security coverage of many hundreds of thousands of individuals should be left largely to the discretion of their employers. On this issue the proper course is obvious.

The expressed purpose of the sponsors of this resolution is to exclude from the coverage of the Social Security Act persons who have the status of independent contractors, rather than that of employees. But no legislation is needed to accomplish this objective. Under present law, as interpreted by the Supreme Court, only persons who are bonafide employees are covered by our social security system.

When all of the considerations regarding sections 1 and 2 of the resolution are sifted, two basic facts remain unrefuted. Hundreds of large employers are assured of an exemption from social security taxes, while hundreds of thousands of employees and their families are equally assuredly prevented from receiving the social security protection which the Supreme Court in June of last year clearly indicated was justly theirs. These two facts were minimized by the sponsors of the resolution who would have us believe, for example, that a travelling salesman who devotes full working time in the service of one company and depends completely upon that company for his livelihood is not an employee of that company but is an independent businessman and does not need social security protection.

Instead of clarifying the distinction between independent contractors and employees, which is a difficult legal issue in many cases, this resolution would revive the confusion which has plagued the administration of the

Social Security Act for so many years. Benefits which are now payable to thousands of persons would have to be withheld pending final determination of the new and complex legal problems raised by this resolution.

Moreover, the resolution purports to preserve the past coverage of employees who have already made contributions under this system. But in fact, under the terms of the Social Security Act, such coverage would expire in a few years, and previous contributions would be made worthless.

It has been asserted that it would be difficult for employers to keep the necessary records and meet other requirements of the law with respect to the employees affected by this resolution. This is reminiscent of the objections made in opposition to the original Social Security Act in 1935. If such objections had prevailed in 1935, our social security program never would have been enacted. To allow them to prevail now would threaten the very foundation of the system. I cannot believe that the mere convenience of employers should be considered more important than the social security protection of employees and their families.

It has also been urged that without this resolution some persons would receive credit toward old age and survivors benefits for three or four past years during which contributions were not collected. If the elimination of these credits had been the real purpose of the resolution, it could readily have been achieved without permanently excluding anyone from social insurance protection.

If our social security program is to endure, it must be protected against these piece-meal attacks. Coverage must be permanently expanded and no employer or special group of employers should be permitted to reverse that trend by efforts to avoid a tax burden which millions of other employers have carried without serious inconvenience or complaint.

Section 3 of this resolution contains provisions — completely unrelated to sections 1 and 2 — for additional public assistance of $5 per month to the needy aged and blind, and $3 per month to dependent children.

These changes fall far short of the substantial improvements in our public assistance program which I have recommended many times. Nevertheless, I am strongly in favor of increasing the amount of assistance payments. Were it not for the fact that the Congress still has ample opportunity to enact such legislation before adjournment, I would be inclined to approve the resolution in spite of my serious objections to sections 1 and 2. Speedy action on public assistance legislation is clearly possible. I note that section 3 of this resolution was adopted as an amendment on the floor of the Senate, and passed by both houses in a single afternoon. Accordingly, I am placing this matter before the Congress in adequate time so that the public assistance program will not suffer because of my disapproval of this resolution.

At the same time, I urge again that the Congress should not be satisfied at this session merely to improve public assistance benefits — urgent as that is. There are other equally urgent extensions and improvements in our social security system which I have repeatedly recommended. They are well understood and widely accepted and should be enacted without delay.

Because sections 1 and 2 of this resolution would seriously curtail and weaken our social security system, I am compelled to return it without my approval.

Harry S. Truman

The Congress overrode the veto the day it was applied and the bill therefore became P.L. 642.

The Eightieth Congress was certainly not afraid of the President, any more than the President was afraid of it. During its second session it not only passed two measures over the President's veto but also directly attacked the appropriation for the Social Security Administration. Such hostility barely fazed the President. Both his budget message and economic report anticipated extensions in the system and the report considered two programs in detail.

The President's Economic Message to Congress
(January 14, 1948)*

*   *   *

Old-age security. The retirement problem has economic as well as social aspects. Those who have withdrawn from productive activity because of age continue to require goods and services, and to make expenditures which flow into the general income stream. A systematic national program which provides for regularity and certainty in the basic income of those who have retired is a more efficient economic policy than the haphazard treatment of this problem which preceded the establishment of old-age insurance. Such a system has the further advantage that it helps to regularize the saving habits of workers during their productive years.

There are now more than 10 million people in the United States, about 8 percent of the total population, who have reached the age of 65. By 1960, about 15 million people, or about 9 percent of the population, will have reached that age. Our systems of protection against the economic hazards of old age and dependency are inadequate. There are now some 17 million jobs in which workers cannot build up wage credits for old-age retirement. The coverage of old-age and survivors' insurance should be extended, and benefits should be adjusted upward with a higher limit upon earnings which may be received after retirement without loss of benefits.

A lowering of the retirement age will be feasible in future years as we attain the levels of national ouput that sustained maximum employment and

Public Papers of the Presidents, Harry S. Truman, 1948, p. 87.

production will bring. At the same time, industry should provide opportunities for the efficient employment of these older people who are able and willing to work although they have earned the right to retire.

Public assistance. The social insurances are supplemented by public-assistance programs financed by States with the aid of Federal grants. The public-assistance programs are now more significant, both in terms of the number of people aided and in terms of total expenditures, than the social insurances. About 4 million people now depend on public assistance, in part because existing social insurances, particularly old age and survivors' insurance, are deficient and because there is no national health insurance program. Expansion of social insurance will decrease the need for public assistance expenditures, but those who must still rely on public assistance should receive adequate payments. The Federal Government should make grants to States to help them finance general-assistance payments, and all public-assistance grants should take account of variations in the ability of the States to finance adequate assistance programs.

Nor was the President prepared to let the matter drop with general statements. Congress itself was harangued.

Special Presidential Message to the Congress on Social Security
(May 24, 1948)*

To the Congress of the United States:

I wish to urge upon the Congress the necessity for action at this session to strengthen our system for the protection of our people from the hazards of economic insecurity. We must not let our concern with the pressing problems of post-war adjustment cause us to neglect the human needs of our people.

On several occasions during the past three years, I have recommended to the Congress the type of legislation which I believe should be enacted to strengthen our present social security system. The Congress has not acted on these recommendations. Instead, it is considering legislation which would actually remove the protection of our social security system from many persons now entitled to its benefits. I believe that instead of limiting coverage it should be expanded, and that a number of other improvements should be made.

I urge, therefore, that the Congress take early action on the following recommendations.

1. *More adequate benefits under old-age and survivors insurance.*

The benefits being paid under old-age and survivors insurance are seriously inadequate. They were adjusted last in 1939. Even then the benefits

Ibid., p. 272.

in most cases replaced only a small part of the income that the worker or his survivors had lost because of his retirement or death. Earnings and the cost of living have risen sharply since that time and cannot be expected to return to prewar levels. Consequently, further adjustments in benefit returns are imperative.

People whose sole income is from social security payments have just about reached the breaking point. Many of them are widows of workers who were insured under our social insurance system, and others are parents in families receiving aid to dependent children. Many have retired on old-age insurance benefits; others are receiving old-age assistance. All of them face a desperate struggle in trying to procure bare necessities at present prices.

The present average payment for a retired worker is about $25 a month, and is substantially less for dependents and survivors. If the insurance system is to prevent dependency upon public and private charity this amount is obviously far too low. I recommend that the Congress increase benefits by at least 50 percent.

I also recommend that women be made eligible for old-age benefits at 60 years, rather than the present 65 years. Wives are usually younger than their husbands. In most cases, therefore, an insured worker cannot retire at 65 because it will be some years before his wife becomes eligible for a wife's benefit, and both of them cannot live on his benefit alone. Lowering the eligibility age is also important for women insured in their own right, for widows, and for mothers who depended on the earnings of a deceased insured worker.

The present law also works hardship by denying benefits to any person who earns $15 in any month. I recommend that this limit be raised to $40, so that the law will permit more older workers to supplement his benefits by part-time employment.

At the same time that these changes in benefits are made, I recommend that the limit on earnings taxable under the law be raised from $3000 to $4800, and that the date for increasing the tax rate from one per cent to one-and-one-half per cent be moved forward from January 1, 1950, to January 1, 1949.

2. *Extended coverage for old-age and survivors insurance.*

The protection afforded by old-age and survivors benefits under our existing social insurance program is unfairly and unnecessarily restricted. More than 20 million persons at work in an average week are in jobs where they cannot earn any rights toward these benefits. People in these jobs are in at least as great need of insurance protection as those in jobs already covered. Many of them are in greater need because their earnings are low and uncertain or irregular.

These groups were originally excluded largely because of various special administrative problems. Simple procedures have now been worked out to collect contributions and pay benefits for these people without undue cost of administrative difficulty, and with little inconvenience to employers.

I strongly recommend that the protection of the Federal old-age and survivors insurance system be extended as rapidly as possible to the groups now excluded.

3. *Extended coverage for unemployment insurance.*

In the case of unemployment insurance, coverage is even more restricted than under old-age and survivors insurance. The principal difference is that under unemployment insurance employees of small firms (those firms employing less than eight persons) are not covered by the Federal law, whereas they are covered under old-age and survivors insurance.

Because of differences in the administrative problems under the two programs, it is more difficult to extend coverage under unemployment insurance. Nevertheless, we should extend coverage at this time to at least two important groups now excluded.

I recommend, therefore, that Federal legislation be amended to extend coverage to those persons who are now excluded merely because they are employed by small firms. These workers are already covered in many States, and I see no reason why they should not be covered in the others.

In addition, I recommend that legislation be enacted to provide unemployment compensation to persons employed by the Federal Government. It seems absurd that the Federal Government does not provide to its employees the same protection that private employers are required to furnish for their employees.

In unemployment insurance also, benefits should be more adequate, particularly for the unemployed person who has a family to support. Not all States have raised benefit amounts and extended duration to meet present conditions or to recognize the special needs of workers with dependents. I believe that all States should do so. In addition, the unduly harsh provisions of some State laws for disqualifying claimants should be eliminated.

4. *Insurance against loss of earnings due to illness or disability.*

I recommend that our social insurance system be broadened to include insurance against the loss of earnings due to temporary or extended disability.

Disability may have an even more serious effect on family income than old age or death. It may occur without warning in early or middle life when the worker has heavy responsibilities for family support and has had little time or chance to make individual savings. It usually involves medical costs as well as loss of wages.

On an average day sickness and disability keep out of the labor force three and a half to four million persons who otherwise would have been working or looking for work. Of these, more than a million and a half have been disabled for six months or longer.

Two States now provide insurance benefits against loss of income from temporary illness or disability. Other States are considering establishing such protection. I believe that the Federal Government should provide a strong financial inducement to all States to provide such insurance.

In the case of disability extending for six months or more, I recommend that insurance against loss of earnings be established in connection with the present old-age and survivors insurance program.

5. *Improved public assistance for the needy.*

All of the foregoing recommendations relate to measures to strengthen our contributory social insurance system. Social insurance is a practical and tested means by which individuals can join together for self protection. It does now, and should increasingly in the future, constitute our social security system's first line of defense against want. Our constant aim should be to extend and improve this means for providing protection through mutual efforts by employers and employees, on a basis which emphasises independence and self-reliance, rather than relief.

But we cannot neglect our second line of defense. Needy persons who are not as protected adequately by insurance have to fall back on public assistance. And we must expect that there will be some who will continue to need public aid even after the desirable expansion in our social insurance system becomes effective. We should therefore strive to make this assistance adequate throughout the United States.

The recent rise in living costs bears especially heavily on old people, fatherless children, and others who cannot earn and must depend on small fixed incomes or on savings. Those who can no longer make ends meet have been obliged to ask for public aid.

The aid now available to needy people is inadequate in many cases and in some areas in the country. This inadequacy stems in large part from three major deficiencies in the Federal Government's program for helping the States to finance public assistance.

The Social Security Act sets undesirably low maximum limits on the amount of the payment to an individual in which the Federal Government will share. The limits are even lower for aid to dependent children than for aid to the needy aged and the needy blind.

Even within the present maximum limits, the amount of the Federal grant to a State depends on the amount the State itself provides for the program. Where need is greatest, State resources are usually smallest. A needy person in a poor State therefore benefits less from Federal funds under the Social Security Act than a person in no greater need who happens to live in a rich State.

Moreover, Federal grants to States under the present Act may be used only for three groups of the needy—the aged, the blind, and dependent children. Other persons in equal need do not share in these funds. Nor is there any provision under which the Federal Government shares with the States the costs of welfare services which avert or reduce the need for continued assistance.

I recommend that the Act be amended to meet these deficiences (1) by permitting the Federal Government to match more fully the higher payments which many States find necessary to meet the needs of recipients; (2) by relating Federal grants more equitably to the financial resources and needs of each State; and (3) by providing Federal grants to help cover the cost of aid to persons not included in the present categories and the cost of essential welfare services which avert or reduce the need for assistance.

The measures I have recommended have had long and careful consideration, and I strongly urge their enactment without further delay.

It has long been recognized as an inescapable obligation of a democratic society to provide for every individual some measure of basic protection from hardship and want caused by factors beyond his control. In our own country, the obligation of the Federal Government in this respect has been recognized by the establishment of our social security system.

Under this system, most of our people now enjoy some degree of protection against the insecurity resulting from old age or unemployment or the death of heads of families. But the protection that is given them is far from adequate, and there are other millions of our people who are excluded from such protection altogether.

It is especially important to strengthen our social security system at this critical time, when the false claim is constantly being made that democratic societies cannot protect their people from the economic and social uncertainties of modern civilization. We have studied with care and at great length the manner in which the system should be strengthened and we have the knowledge now to take many specific steps for that purpose. We should act upon that knowledge without further delay.

The passage of the Social Security Act in 1935 marked a great advance in our concept of the means by which our citizens, through their Government, can provide against common economic risks. Although this Act is still under attack from some quarters, it is regarded by a vast majority of the American people as an essential and basic element of our democracy. A strong social security system is recognized as an essential part of our national program to insure maximum levels of production and employment and to insure fair distribution of the output of our economy.

The original Act was necessarily experimental in many respects, and was deliberately limited in its coverage and in the benefits provided until experience should permit its extension. In 1939, substantial amendments were made to improve the Act on the basis of the experience gained by that time.

Since 1939, we have gained much further experience. Furthermore, extensive study has been given to the problem, both by the Executive and Legislative Branches. From this experience and these studies has come a wide area of agreement concerning most of the steps needed to improve our social security system. Even where agreement has not been reached, the evidence and arguments have been so fully developed that nothing can be gained by further delay.

I wish to emphasize that, because of general economic conditions, this is a particularly opportune time for taking these steps. Now, when employment and earnings are at the highest levels on record, is the most favorable time for our working people to earn protection against serious economic risks which face them and their families as a result of unemployment, disability, old age, and death. Moreover, the increased coverage and higher contribution rates which I have proposed will result in a greater excess of income over expenditures in the social insurance trust funds than is at present the case. Even when the expanded public assistance program is taken into account, the net effect of my recommendations is still to increase substantially the excess of income over outgo. Such an excess of income over outgo is valuable to reduce present inflationary pressures and to store up purchasing power for future use.

The measures I have recommended will extend and broaden our social security system to provide protection to millions of our people now excluded and against risks now pressing heavily upon individual families. They will provide protection to our people more and more on an insurance basis, and reduce our reliance on relief and similar types of public aids. They will do much to prevent distress and to continue our progress toward the great goals of individual welfare and independence.

It would clearly be unfair to the millions of our people for whom we know how to provide better protection to delay longer these sound and practical measures.

Harry S. Truman

Meanwhile, Representative Daniel A. Reed of New York introduced H.R. 6777 which made it possible for employees not covered by social security to "contract in." The bill, based on a report of the Social Security Subcommittee of the House Ways and Means Committee (House Report No. 2168, 80th Cong., 2d Sess., passed the House, only to be stalled in the Senate.

The Advisory Council and Related Reports

Perhaps the most constructive development in social security during 1948 was the report of the Advisory Council on Social Security which had been appointed by the Senate Finance Committee in 1947.

Part I, dealing with OASI, still suggested that PA would wither away.

Proposed Changes in Old-Age and Survivors' Insurance:
Report of the Advisory Council on Social Security
(Submitted to the Senate Finance Committee)
(1948)

The Method of Social Insurance

The Council favors as the foundation of the social-security system the method of contributory social insurance with benefits related to prior earnings and awarded without a needs test. Differential benefits based on a work record are a reward for productive effort and are consistent with general economic incentives, while the knowledge that benefits will be paid — irrespective of whether the individual is in need — supports and stimulates his drive to add his personal savings to the basic security he has acquired through the insurance system. Under such a social insurance system, the individual earns a right to a benefit that is related to his contribution to production. This earned right is his best guaranty that he will receive the benefits promised and that they will not be conditioned on his accepting either scrutiny of his personal affairs or restrictions from which others are free.

Public-assistance payments from general tax funds to persons who are found to be in need have serious limitations as a way of maintaining family income. Our goal is, so far as possible, to prevent dependency through social insurance and thus greatly reduce the need for assistance. We recognize that, for a decade or two, public assistance will be necessary for many persons whose need could have been met by the insurance program if it had been in effect for a longer time and had covered all persons gainfully employed. The Council looks forward, however, to the time when virtually all persons in the United States will have retirement or survivorship protection under the old-age and survivors insurance program. If insurance benefits are of reasonable amount, public assistance will then be necessary only for those aged persons and survivors with unusual needs and for the few who, for one reason or another, have been unable to earn insurance rights through work. Under such conditions the Federal expenditure for public assistance can be reduced to a small fraction of its present amount.

The Council then turned its attention to deficiencies and recommendations.

Summary of Recommendations

1. *Self-employment.* — Self-employed persons such as business and professional people, farmers, and others who work on their own account should be brought under coverage of the old-age and survivors insurance system. Their contributions should be payable on their net income from self-

employment, and their contribution rate should be 1½ times the rate payable by employees. Persons who earn very low incomes from self-employment should for the present remain excluded.

2. *Farm workers.*—Coverage of the old-age and survivors insurance system should be extended to farm employees.

3. *Household workers.*—Coverage of the old-age and survivors insurance system should be extended to household workers.

4. *Employees of nonprofit institutions.*—Employment for nonprofit institutions now excluded from coverage under the old-age and survivors insurance program should be brought under the program, except that clergymen and members of religious orders should continue to be excluded.

5. *Federal civilian employees.*—Old-age and survivors insurance coverage should be extended immediately to the employees of the Federal Government and its instrumentalities who are now excluded from the civil-service retirement system. As a temporary measure designed to give protection to the short-term Government worker, the wage credits of all those who die or leave Federal employment with less than 5 years' service should be transferred to old-age and survivors insurance. The Congress should direct the Social Security Administration and the agencies administering the various Federal retirement programs to develop a permanent plan for extending old-age and survivors insurance to all Federal civilian employees, whereby the benefits and contributions of the Federal retirement systems would supplement the protection of old-age and survivors insurance and provide combined benefits at least equal to those now payable under the special retirement systems.

6. *Railroad employees.*—The Congress should direct the Social Security Administration and the Railroad Retirement Board to undertake a study to determine the most practicable and equitable method of making the railroad retirement system supplementary to the basic old-age and survivors insurance program. Benefits and contributions of the railroad retirement system should be adjusted to supplement the basic protection afforded by old-age and survivors insurance, so that the combined protection of the two programs would at least equal that under the Railroad Retirement Act.

7. *Members of the armed forces.*—Old-age and survivors insurance coverage should be extended to members of the armed forces, including those stationed outside the United States.

8. *Employees of State and local governments.*—The Federal Government should enter into voluntary agreements with the States for the extension of old-age and survivors insurance to the employees of State and local governments, except that employees engaged in proprietary activities should be covered compulsorily.

9. *Social security in island possessions.*—A commission should be established to determine the kind of social-security protection appropriate to the possessions of the United States.

10. *Inclusion of tips as wages.* — The definition of wages as contained in section 209 (a) of the Social Security Act, as amended, and section 1426 (a) of subchapter A of chapter 9 of the Internal Revenue Code should be amended to specify that such wages shall include all tips or gratuities customarily received by an employee from a customer of an employer.

11. *Insured status.* — To permit a larger proportion of older workers, particularly those newly covered, to qualify for benefits, the requirements for fully insured status should be 1 quarter of coverage for each 2 calendar quarters elapsing after 1948 or after the quarter in which the individual attains the age of 21, whichever is later, and before the quarter in which he attains the age of 65 (60 for women) or dies. Quarters of coverage earned at any time after 1936 should count toward meeting this requirement. A minimum of 6 quarters of coverage should be required and a worker should be fully and permanently insured if he has 40 quarters of coverage. In cases of death before January 1, 1949, the requirement should continue to be 1 quarter of coverage for each 2 calendar quarters elapsing after 1936 or after the quarter in which the age of 21 was attained, whichever is later, and before the quarter in which the individual attained the age of 65 or died.

12. *Maximum base for contributions and benefits.* — To take into account increased wage levels and costs of living, the upper limit on earnings subject to contributions and credited for benefits should be raised from $3,000 to $4,200. The maximum average monthly wage used in the calculation of benefits should be increased from $250 to $350.

13. *Average monthly wage.* — The average monthly wage should be computed as under the present law, except that any worker who has had wage credits of $50 or more in each of six or more quarters after 1948 should have his average wage based either on the wages and elapsed time counted as under the present law or on wages and elapsed time after 1948, whichever gives the higher result.

14. *Benefit formula.* — To provide adequate benefits immediately and to remove the present penalty imposed on workers who lack a lifetime of coverage under old-age and survivors insurance, the primary insurance benefit should be 50 percent of the first $75 of the average monthly wage plus 15 percent of the remainder up to $275. Present beneficiaries, as well as those who become entitled in the future, should receive benefits computed according to this new formula for all months after the effective date of the amendments.

15. *Increased survivor protection.* — To increase the protection for a worker's dependents, survivor benefits for a family should be at the rate of three-fourths of the primary insurance benefit for one child and one-half for each additional child, rather than one-half for all children as at present. The parent's benefit should also be increased from one-half to three-fourths. Widows' benefits should remain at three-fourths of the primary insurance benefit.

16. *Dependents of insured women.* — To equalize the protection given to the dependents of women and men, benefits should be payable to the young children of any currently insured woman upon her death or eligibility for primary insurance benefits. Benefits should be payable also (a) to the aged, dependent husband of a primary beneficiary who, in addition to being fully insured, was currently insured at the time she became eligible for primary benefits, and (b) to the aged, dependent widower of a woman who was fully and currently insured at the time of her death.

17. *Maximum benefits.* — To increase the family benefits, the maximum benefit amount payable on the wage record of an insured individual should be three times the primary insurance benefit amount or 80 percent of the individual's average monthly wage, whichever is less, except that this limitation should not operate to reduce the total family benefits below $40 a month.

18. *Minimum benefit.* — The minimum primary insurance benefit payable should be raised to $20.

19. *Retirement test.* — No retirement test (work clause) should be imposed on persons aged 70 or over. At lower ages, however, the benefits to which a beneficiary and his dependents are entitled for any month should be reduced by the amount in excess of $35 which he earns from covered employment in that month. Benefits should be suspended for any month in which such earnings exceed $35 but, each quarter, beneficiaries should receive the amount by which the suspended benefits exceeded earnings above the exemption.

20. *Qualifying age for women.* — The minimum age at which women may qualify for old-age benefits (primary, wife's, widow's, parent's) should be reduced to 60 years.

21. *Lump-sum benefits.* — To help meet the special expenses of illness and death, a lump-sum benefit should be payable at the death of every insured worker even though monthly survivor benefits are payable. The maximum payment should be four times the primary insurance benefit rather than six times as at present.

22. *Contribution schedule and Government participation.* — The contribution rate should be increased to $1\frac{1}{2}$ percent for employers and $1\frac{1}{2}$ percent for employees at the same time that benefits are liberalized and coverage is extended. The next step-up in the contribution rate, to 2 percent on employer and 2 percent on employee, should be postponed until the $1\frac{1}{2}$-percent rate plus interest on the investments of the trust fund is insufficient to meet current benefit outlays and administrative costs. There are compelling reasons for an eventual Government contribution to the system, but the Council feels that it is unrealistic to decide now on the exact timing or proportion of that contribution. When the rate of 2 percent on employers and 2 percent on employees plus interest on the investments of the trust fund is insufficient to meet current outlays, the advisability of an immediate Government contribution should be considered.

The section on permanent and total disability insurance was equally radical.

Permanent and Total Disability Insurance

Eligibility requirements. — To qualify for benefits, a disabled person would have to be incapable of self-support for an indefinite period — permanently and totally disabled. He would have to be unable, by reason of a disability medically demonstrable by objective tests, to perform any substantially gainful activity. This requirement would eliminate the problems involved in the adjudication of claims based solely on subjective symptoms.

We recommend that a waiting period of 6 months be required and that benefits be payable only in those cases in which, at the end of the waiting period, the disability appears likely to be of long-continued and indefinite duration. This requirement is much more exacting than the disability provisions of commercial insurance policies now being issued, which specify that a total disability that has persisted for 6 months will be presumed to be permanent. The definition as a whole constitutes a strict test of permanent and total disability, which would operate as a safeguard against unjustified claims.

To assure that disability benefits will be available only to workers who have suffered income loss by reason of disability, we recommend that strict eligibility requirements be adopted to test both the recency and long duration of an individual's attachment to the labor market. To be eligible, a worker would need a minimum of 40 quarters of coverage, would have to have one quarter of coverage for every 2 in his working lifetime after 1948 in covered employment, and would have to show employment during at least one-half the time within the period immediately preceding the onset of his disability.

Amount of benefits. — The same benefit formula recommended for old-age and survivors insurance is proposed for the disability insurance program. The Council does not recommend, however, that benefits be provided for dependents of the disabled worker. If these were provided, there is the possibility that disability benefits in some cases might prove attractive enough to discourage return to gainful work after recovery or rehabilitation. Thus the benefits under the disability program when the worker has dependents would be substantially less than those we propose for old-age and survivors benefits. They would be as much as one-half the average monthly wage only in the case of workers who averaged $75 a month or less, while the average benefit for all workers would be only about 30 percent of the average wage.

Provisions for rehabilitation of disabled workers. — The Council recommends that contributions be made from the Federal old-age and survivors insurance trust fund toward the expense of rehabilitating beneficiaries on the disability rolls. A substantial number of beneficiaries can be rehabilitated and become self-supporting. The national economy will benefit from the restoration of their earning capacity, and the cost of the insurance system will be reduced because the disability benefits of persons who have been rehabilitated will be terminated.

Termination or suspension of benefits. — Benefits should be denied when the beneficiary refuses to undergo a medical examination or reexamination and should be suspended when he refuses to cooperate in his rehabilitation. Payments should also be suspended for any period for which workmen's compensation is payable under a State or Federal program.

Integration with old-age and survivors insurance. — Permanent and total disability insurance and old-age and survivors insurance should be administered as a single system. Aside from the similarity of risks, considerations of administrative efficiency and economy make the integration logical. Integration would also facilitate the maintenance of the benefit rights of disabled workers for purposes of future old-age and survivors insurance payments.

If the administration of the two programs is integrated, the facilities already established under old-age and survivors insurance for maintaining individual wage records, the network of old-age and survivors insurance field offices, and the administrative machinery for awarding benefits and certifying claims could be adapted to the requirements of the disability program with relatively minor adjustments.

Summary of Recommendations

1. *Increased payments for aid to dependent children.* — The Federal Government's responsibility for aid to dependent children should be made comparable to the responsibility it has assumed for old-age assistance and aid to the blind. In determining the extent of Federal financial participation, the needs of adult members of the family as well as of the children should be taken into consideration. Federal funds should equal three-fourths of the first $20 of the average monthly payment per recipient (including children and adults) plus one-half the remainder, except that such participation should not apply to that part of payments to recipients in excess of $50 for each of two eligible persons in a family and $15 for each additional person beyond the second.

2. *Federal grants for general assistance.* — Federal grants-in-aid should be made available to the States for general assistance payments to needy persons not now eligible for assistance under the existing State-Federal public assistance programs. Federal financial participation should equal one-third of the expenditures for general assistance payments, except that such participation should not apply to that part of monthly payments to

recipients in excess of $30 for each of two eligible persons in a family and $15 for each additional person beyond the second. In addition, the Federal Government should match administrative expenses incurred by the States for general assistance on a 50–50 basis, in the same manner that it now shares in administrative expenses for the existing State-Federal public assistance programs. The proposed grants-in-aid for general assistance, however, should not be considered as a substitute for a program designed to deal with large-scale unemployment.

3. *Medical care for recipients.*— To help meet the medical needs of recipients of old-age assistance, aid to the blind, and aid to dependent children, the Federal Government should participate in payments made directly to agencies and individuals providing medical care, as well as in money payments to recipients as at present. The Federal Government should pay one-half the medical-care costs incurred by the States above the regular maximums of $50 a month for a recipient ($15 for the third and succeeding persons in a family receiving aid to dependent children) but should not participate in the medical costs above the regular maximums which exceed a monthly average of $6 per person receiving old-age assistance or aid to the blind and a monthly average of $3 per person receiving aid to dependent children.

State public-assistance agencies should be required to submit plans to the Social Security Administration for its approval, setting forth the conditions under which medical needs will be met, the scope and standards of care, the methods of payment, and the amount of compensation for such care.

4. *Care of the aged in medical institutions.*— The Federal Government should participate in payments made to or for the care of old-age-assistance recipients living in public medical institutions other than mental hospitals. Payments in excess of the regular $50 maximum made to recipients living in public or private institutions or made by the public-assistance agency directly to those institutions for the care of aged recipients should be included as a part of medical-care expenditures under recommendation 3. To receive Federal funds to assist aged persons in medical institutions under either public or private auspices, a State should be required to establish and maintain adequate minimum standards for the facilities and for the care of persons living in these facilities. These standards should be subject to approval by the Social Security Administration.

5. *Residence requirements.*— Federal funds should not be available for any public-assistance program in which the State imposes residence requirements as a condition of eligibility for assistance, except that States should be allowed to impose a 1-year residence requirement for old-age assistance.

6. *Study of child health and welfare services.*— A commission should be appointed to study current child health and welfare needs and to review the programs operating under title V of the Social Security Act relating to maternal and child health services, services for crippled children, and child

welfare services. The commission should make recommendations as to the proper scope of these services and the responsibilities that should be assumed by the Federal and State governments, respectively.

The Council discussed public assistance:

The Nature of the Program

Responsibility for public assistance in the United States is now shared by the local, State, and Federal Governments. Until 1936 this responsibility was entirely local and State, except for the emergency programs during the early thirties. Earlier still, the responsibility for relief was entirely local. Even now all expenditures for general assistance come from local funds in 15 States; half or more than half of the funds for general assistance come from the State in only 18 States; and in only 4 States are all expenditures for general assistance financed by the State. . . .

With the passage of the Social Security Act, the Federal Government assumed substantial responsibility on a continuing basis for public assistance to the aged, to the blind, and to dependent children. Within these areas the Federal Government has supplied large sums, at first on a 50–50 matching basis within maximums of $30 for old-age assistance and aid to the blind, while the basis was $1 for each $2 for aid to dependent children within maximums of $18 for the first child and $12 for each additional child aided in the family. In 1939 the Federal maximums for old-age assistance and aid to the blind were increased to $40 and Federal matching for aid to dependent children was established on a 50–50 basis. Since October 1, 1946, Federal funds have been paid under a matching formula which established the Federal share of assistance payments at two-thirds of the first $15 of the average monthly payment per recipient, plus one-half the remainder within maximums of $45 for old-age assistance and aid to the blind; in aid to dependent children the Federal share has been two-thirds of the first $9 of the average payment per child plus one-half of the remainder within maximums of $24 for the first child and $15 for each additional child aided.

In October 1948 the Federal participation in the three State-Federal programs will increase again under Public Law 642. The Federal Government will provide three-fourths of the first $20 of the average monthly payment plus one-half of the remainder within maximums of $50 for old-age assistance and aid to the blind; the Federal share for aid to dependent children will be three-fourths of the first $12 of the average payment per child plus one-half the remainder within the maximums of $27 for the first child and $18 for each additional child. Except for the emergency programs in the early thirties, no Federal funds have been made available for general assistance.

The Federal Government has not assumed responsibility for the operation of the three public-assistance programs for which Federal aid is provided.

Aside from sharing in the costs of assistance and administration, the role of the Federal Government has been limited to that of setting minimum standards and providing technical advice and consultation on problems of administration.

Because public assistance is essentially a State responsibility, considerable variation in operating policies and in eligibility requirements, including definitions of need, appears among the States. The wide range in the proportion of persons receiving assistance in the several States and the range in the amount of the average payment not only indicate State differences in the need to be met and ability to meet that need, but also reflect wide State diversity in standards and policies. The proportion of the population aged 65 or over who were in receipt of old-age assistance in December 1947 ranged from a high of 581 per 1,000 in Oklahoma, and more than 400 per 1,000 in Colorado, Georgia, and Texas, to a low of less than 100 per 1,000 in Delaware, the District of Columbia, Maryland, New Jersey, New York, and Virginia (appendix III-A, chart 3). The average payment per recipient for old-age assistance ranged from $84.72 a month in Colorado and $57.10 in California to $16.90 in Georgia and $15.87 in Mississippi (appendix III-A, chart 2). Similar variation occurs in the other programs. The Council does not regard an investigation of the policy decisions by the several States in connection with public assistance as part of its mandate. Nevertheless, the very wide variation among the States suggests that Congress might want to inform itself further concerning the effect of Federal grants-in-aid upon the policy decisions of the several States. A special investigation of this matter is worthy of consideration.

Wide differences are also apparent in the extent to which expenditures and case loads of the various public assistance programs have been affected by general economic conditions. The rise in employment brought about by the war and postwar boom was sharply reflected in rapidly declining expenditures for general assistance. Expenditures by the States and localities for the general assistance program dropped from $493,900,000 in 1940 to $104,800,000 in 1945 and rose to $168,200,000 in 1947. (See appendix III-A, table 13, for case loads and expenditures, 1936–47.) Although expenditures for aid to dependent children increased from $128,300,000 in 1940 to $151,400,000 in 1945 and $275,600,000 in 1947, a relationship between this program and business conditions is reflected in the changes in the number of families on the rolls. At the end of the 1940 fiscal year, 333,000 families were receiving aid as compared with 255,600 at the end of the 1945 fiscal year. The 1947 case load, however, exceeded the 1945 figure partly, no doubt, because the rise in the number of broken homes, in the birth rate, and in the cost of living made it necessary for families to seek aid to supplement income from other sources. (See appendix III-A, table 12.) Changes in the number of recipients of old-age assistance and aid to the blind have not reflected general economic conditions to the same extent as general assistance or aid to dependent children. Although the number of recipients on old-age assistance did decline somewhat in 1943, 1944, and 1945, the 1945 figure was somewhat more than 2,000,000 as compared with somewhat less than 2,000,000 in 1940. By June of 1947 there were 2.3 million persons on the old-age assistance rolls, the same number as were on the rolls in March 1948, the last date for which figures are available. Expenditures for old-age assistance and aid to the blind rose continually throughout this period since the level of assistance payments increased enough to offset the declining number of recipients in those years when the number did decline. (See appendix III-A, tables 10 and 11.)

The varying effect of general economic conditions on the different programs reflects the fact that general assistance and, to a less extent, aid to dependent children are available to persons who are employable in times of good business conditions. On the other hand, old-age assistance and aid to the blind are limited for the most part to persons unable to work regardless of economic conditions. A study conducted in 1944 in 21 States indicated that only about 20 percent of the old-age assistance recipients were under age 70 and about 45 percent were age 75 or over. To some extent, the differences in expenditures and case loads of the various programs may also reflect the absence of Federal participation in general assistance and the lower rate of Federal participation in aid to dependent children. States and localities have not been encouraged to put money into these programs to the same extent as in old-age assistance and aid to the blind.

Several other factors should be taken into account in seeking an explanation of the differences in expenditures from one year to the next and among the various programs. These factors include (1) the increase in the number of aged persons in the population from about 9 million in 1940 to about 10.8 million in 1947, (2) the long waiting lists of eligible applicants during the early years of the State-Federal programs, a fact which indicates that the number of recipients was lower in the early years because funds were not available to meet existing need (witness the 260,000 applications for old-age assistance pending in January 1940 as compared with 42,000 in January 1945), and (3) the increase in expenditures for assistance resulting from rising prices.

Major Defects in the System of Federal Grants-in-Aid for Public Assistance

The Council believes that the basic features of the present arrangements are sound. In particular, it believes that the diversity of conditions and traditions among the States makes it desirable that the States retain wide discretion in determining needs, eligibility, and administrative policies. The Council feels, however, that the present system of Federal grants-in-aid for public assistance has many gaps and inequities. Federal participation in aid to dependent children is far less adequate than in old-age assistance and aid to the blind. Needy persons who require medical attention cannot receive adequate medical services within the limits of the ceilings on Federal matching. Moreover, many persons who do not fall within the categories of the aged, the blind, or dependent children may be in dire need of public assistance. As now constituted, the Social Security Act ignores the needs of this group. In point of fact, the act has led some States to apply virtually all the State and local funds available for public assistance to the specific programs for which Federal reimbursement is available, leaving little or no money for so-called general assistance. State funds are thus concentrated on programs which have Federal grants-in-aid.

There is an immediate and imperative need to redress this imbalance by eliminating the existing gaps and correcting the inequities in the public assistance titles of the Social Security Act. More extensive Federal participation in such programs has been recommended because of the conviction that readjustments are urgently needed and cannot otherwise be achieved as expeditiously. The Council believes, however, that the total amount of Federal expenditure for assistance should decline as the insurance program becomes more fully operative.

In making recommendations to improve the present Federal policy in assistance, the Council has been guided by the following major considerations:

1. The public-assistance program should not interfere with the growth and improvement of the insurance program.

2. The Federal Government's participation in public assistance should be designed to encourage the best possible administration by the States and localities and promote adequate support of the needy by the States and the localities.

3. The Federal Government should continue its present practice of setting only minimum standards relating to conditions of eligibility and administration but, beyond the minimum, it should leave to the States wide discretion both in determining policies and in setting standards of need.

Finally, the Council took up unemployment compensation.

Recommendations for Improvement of the Program

A summary of the Council's recommendations follows:

1. *Employees of small firms.* — The size-of-firm limitation on coverage in the Federal Unemployment Tax Act should be removed, and employees of small firms should be protected under unemployment insurance just as they are now protected under old-age and survivors insurance.

2. *Employees of nonprofit organizations.* — The Federal Unemployment Tax Act should be broadened to include employment by all nonprofit organizations, except that services performed by clergymen and members of religious orders should remain excluded. The exclusion of domestic workers in college clubs, fraternities, and sororities by the 1939 amendments

to the Federal Unemployment Tax Act should be repealed so that these workers will again be protected under all State laws.

3. *Federal civilian employees.* — Employees of the Federal Government and its instrumentalities should receive unemployment benefits through the State unemployment insurance agencies in accordance with the provisions of the State unemployment insurance laws. The States should be reimbursed for the amounts actually paid in benefits based on Federal employment. If there is employment under both the State system and for the Federal Government during the base period, the wage credits should be combined and the States should be reimbursed in the proportion which the amount of Federal employment or wages in the base period bears to the total employment or wages in the base period. The special provisions for federally employed maritime workers should be extended until this recommendation for covering all Federal employees becomes effective.

4. *Members of the armed forces.* — Members of the armed forces who do not come under the servicemen's readjustment allowance program should be protected by unemployment insurance.

5. *Borderline agricultural workers.* — To afford protection to certain workers excluded by the 1939 amendments to the Federal Unemployment Tax Act, defining agricultural labor, coverage of that act should be extended to services rendered in handling, packing, packaging, and other forms of processing agricultural and horticultural products, unless such services are performed for the owner or tenant of the farm on which the products are raised and he does not employ five or more persons in such activities in each of four calendar weeks during the year. Coverage should also be extended to services now defined as agricultural labor by section 1607 (1) (3) of the Unemployment Tax Act.

6. *Inclusion of tips in the definition of wages.* — The definition of wages contained in section 1607 (b) of the Federal Unemployment Tax Act should be amended to specify that such wages shall include all tips or gratuities customarily received by an employee from a customer of an employer.

7. *Contributory principle.* — To extend to unemployment insurance the contributory principle now recognized in old-age and survivors insurance, a Federal unemployment tax should be paid by employees as well as employers. Employee contributions to a State unemployment-insurance fund should be allowed to offset the Federal employee tax in the same manner as employer contributions are allowed to offset the Federal tax on employers. The employee tax would be collected by employers and paid by them when they pay their own unemployment tax.

8. *Maximum wage base.* — To take account of increased wage levels and costs of living, and to provide the same wage base for contributions and benefits as that recommended for old-age and survivors insurance, the upper limit on earnings subject to the Federal unemployment tax should be raised from $3,000 to $4,200.

9. *Minimum contribution rate.* — The Federal unemployment tax should

be 0.75 percent of covered wages payable by employers and 0.75 percent payable by employees. The taxpayer should be allowed to credit against the Federal tax the amount of contributions paid into a State unemployment fund, but this credit should not exceed 80 percent of the Federal tax. Since no additional credit against the Federal tax should be allowed for experience rating, the States would, in effect, be required to establish a minimum rate of 0.6 percent on employers and 0.6 percent on employees.

10. *Loan fund.* — The Federal Government should provide loans to a State for the payment of unemployment-insurance benefits when a State is in danger of exhausting its reserves and covered unemployment in the State is heavy. The loan should be for a 5-year period and should carry interest at the average yield of all interest-bearing obligations of the Federal Government.

11. *Standards on experience rating.* — If a State has an experience rating plan, the Federal act should require that the plan provide: (1) a minimum employer contribution rate of 0.6 percent; (2) an employee rate no higher than the lowest rate payable by an employer in the State; and (3) a rate for newly covered and newly formed firms for the first 3 years under the program which does not exceed the average rate for all employers in the State.

12. *Combining wage credits earned in more than one State and processing interstate claims.* — The Social Security Administration should be empowered to establish standard procedures for combining unemployment-insurance wage credits earned in more than one State and for processing interstate claims. These procedures should be worked out in consultation with the administrators of the State programs and should provide for the combination of wage credits not only when eligibility is affected but also when such combination would sustantially affect benefit amount or duration. All States should be required to follow the prescribed procedures as a condition of receiving administrative grants. Similar procedures should be worked out, in cooperation with the Railroad Retirement Board, for combining wage credits earned under the State systems and under the railroad system.

13. *Financing administrative costs.* — Income from the Federal Unemployment Tax Act should be dedicated to unemployment-insurance purposes. One-half of any surplus over expenses incurred in the collection of the tax and the administration of unemployment insurance and the employment service should be appropriated to the Federal loan fund, and one-half of the surplus should be proportionately assigned to the States for administration or benefit purposes. A contingency item should be added to the regular congressional appropriation for the administration of the employment-security programs. The administrative standards in the Social Security Act should be applicable to the expenditure of the surplus funds as well as to expenditures of the funds originally appropriated.

14. *Clarification of Federal interest in the proper payment of claims.* — The Social Security Act should be amended to clarify the interest of the

Federal Government not only in the full payment of benefits when due, but also in the prevention of improper payments.

15. *Standards for disqualifications.* — A Federal standard on disqualifications should be adopted prohibiting the States from (1) reducing or canceling benefit rights as the result of disqualification except for fraud or misrepresentation, (2) disqualifying those who are discharged because of inability to do the work, and (3) postponing benefits for more than 6 weeks as the result of a disqualification except for fraud or misrepresentation.

16. *Study of supplementary plans.* — The Congress should direct the Federal Security Agency to study in detail the comparative merits in times of severe unemployment of (a) unemployment assistance, (b) extended unemployment-insurance benefits, (c) work relief, (d) other income-maintenance devices for the unemployed, including public works. This study should be conducted in consultation with the Social Security Administration's Advisory Council on Employment Security, the Council of Economic Advisers, and the State employment security agencies, and should make specific proposals for Federal measures to provide economic security for workers who do not have private or public employment during a depression and who are not adequately protected by unemployment insurance.

From the point of view of the future, the four parts of the Advisory Council report were, of course, significant, but so was the work of the Subcommittee on Low-Income Families of the Joint Committee on the Economy. Despite social security, programs of job training, vocational rehabilitation, the Full Employment Act, and minimum wage legislation — all of which had done much to help the typical worker — poverty had not disappeared. Indeed, a hard core of poverty was emerging more clearly than ever before, and it was a phenomenon which swelled the demands on public assistance programs. At least the staff of the subcommittee saw the implications of this, although, as was clear from their report, the Advisory Council on Social Security was not yet aware of these matters.

Low-Income Families and Economic Stability
Materials on the Problem of Low-Income Families
Assembled by the Staff of the Subcommittee on Low-Income Families
of the Joint Committee on the Economic Report
1949

Introduction and Summary

The Employment Act of 1946 sets forth as basic economic goals of the Nation the promotion of maximum employment, production, and purchasing power. One of the first essentials to the achievement of these goals is a thorough appraisal of the income and consumption of the population, to be followed by positive remedial action where needed to foster expanded production and consumption by all economic groups. That a part of our population is both underproducing and underconsuming is well known, but the size, needs, and economic circumstances of the low-income families in America have not been adequately appraised in recent years. Since the low purchasing power of these groups retards the future rate of economic progress of the Nation, their circumstances and the effect thereof on the national economy are currently being studied by the Joint Committee on the Economic Report.

To maintain maximum employment of the Nation's material and human resources, the economy must consume and invest the total quantity of goods and services produced. Demand for consumer goods, backed up by wartime accumulations of liquid funds, has kept investment and employment at high levels since the end of hostilities in 1945. High investment has increased industrial capacity, which has considerably increased the total flow of consumer goods. If there are to be ample employment opportunities, this flow of consumer goods must be steadily consumed. Old markets must be expanded and new markets developed. The unfilled wants of American families now living on inadequate incomes constitute a great underdeveloped economic frontier — a new and expansible market for the products of American industry. In an economic system geared to mass production, there must be mass consumption if severe economic dislocations are to be avoided.

The low-income families have been left behind in the economic progress of America. They do not have many of the products considered symbolic of the American standard of living. For example, in 1946 there were about two million nonfarm families living in houses without running water. Some low-income families live at levels below even the most conservative estimate of the minimum necessary for health and decency. These families would buy a larger quantity of the goods produced by the economic capacity of the Nation, if their needs were backed by ability to buy.

This point has been very effectively stated by Mr. Eric Johnston, former President of the United States Chamber of Commerce, in his book, America Unlimited (New York; 1944, pp. 116-118):

> America is a wealthy nation enjoying unprecedented levels of comfort and leisure, of course, when contrasted with other countries, or when contrasted with its own past. But these things are relative. We are still incredibly poor and shamefully backward when measured by the yardstick of our unexploited possibilities. The areas we have conquered, in the matter of living standards and general improvement, are pathetically small when compared with the uncharted spaces still to be conquered. The American people are well off from the vantage point of any European or Asiatic people. I submit, however, that they are far from well off from the vantage point of what we could produce and could consume   *   *   *
>
> We do not need statistics to confirm what our own eyes witness: Slums, substandard homes and diets, children deprived of the minimal conditions of civilized living, a thousand and one proofs that there is unlimited room for economic improvement   *   *   *

I certainly do not wish to join the ranks of those who focus attention only on shortcomings. But I do believe that we must correct them. As long as there are millions of American families existing on substandard levels, there are tasks to challenge our full energies as a nation. Not only must our whole population be brought above this subsistence line but the standards themselves must be raised. That, I say, is a challenge as grim as any war. We have what it takes to meet it.

How Many Low-Income Families?

This report concentrates attention on the numbers and circumstances of urban families having less than $2,000 of money income, and of farm families having less than $1,000 of money income. Information is also presented on the circumstances of families above these levels. The $2,000 and $1,000 figures are not intended to be, and must not be interpreted to be, a definition of "low" income. The boundary line on the income scale between want and sufficiency is difficult to determine, particularly when the determination is attempted for purposes of a national study. For example, the Bureau of Labor Statistics has estimated that in 1947 the minimum budget necessary for a family of four persons to maintain an "adequate standard of living" varied from a low of $3,004 in New Orleans to a high of $3,458 in Washington, D. C., in the 34 cities studied. Using similar methods, the Social Security Administration estimated that a budget for an elderly couple living at the same level would have required $1,365 a year in Houston, Tex., and $1,767 a year in Washington, D. C., in June 1947. The cash-income levels chosen for the present report were selected only to designate an income group for intensive study. An important consideration in making the choice was to use amounts which would be realistic in even the lowest cost areas of the country. It is improbable that there will be more than a minor proportion of families able to purchase all their requirements with incomes below these amounts.

The Bureau of the Census estimates that there were 38.5 million families and about 8 million "single individuals not in families" in the United States in 1948. Nearly 10 million of the families received total cash incomes of less than $2,000 in that year. This is one-fourth of the total number of families. The proportions and numbers of families at the different levels of income are depicted in the chart below.

The main purpose of this preliminary document is to provide information on the circumstances of the bottom groups in this distribution—and to state in broad terms the problems raised by the facts—for the subcommittee's study and recommendations. The salient points of the detailed information contained in the body of this document and in its appendixes are summarized here.[1]

[1]War and postwar changes in the inequality of incomes are summarized in appendix G, which compares the distribution of income in 1935–36 with the distribution in 1941 and in 1948. Rough estimates of changes in purchasing power are also presented.

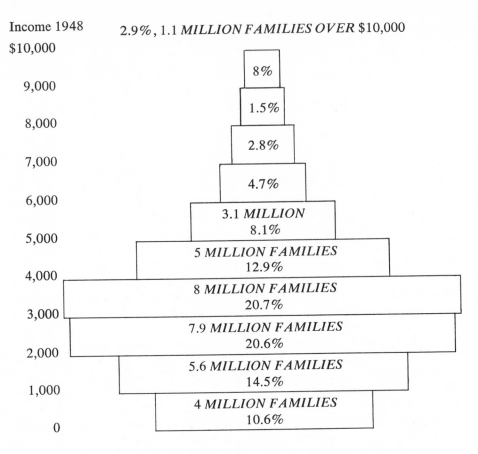

Distribution of money income of United States families,[1] 1948.

[1]Does not include single-person families.

Source: Prepared by the staff of the Joint Committee on the Economic Report from data provided by the Bureau of the Census.

Composition of the Low-Income Group

The nearly ten million families receiving less than $2,000 per year are composed of several groups and each group constitutes a separate problem requiring, in most instances, different remedial action.

First. Most of the families below the $2,000 level are urban or nonfarm families, but farm poverty is also a most important problem. Of the total of nearly ten million families, about 3.3 million lived on farms. Of this number, 1.7 million had incomes below $1,000 in 1948. Raising the level of living of low-income farmers calls for measures specifically designed for that purpose and differing sharply from measures to raise the production and consumption of urban workers. It also calls for measures quite different from the general agricultural price-support and soil-conservation programs. Continually depressed rural farm areas might best be helped by long-range area-development programs which would provide opportunities for industrial employment, and which would provide markets for special agricultural products, such as vegetables and milk.

Second. The problem of impoverished old age is one of the most difficult and one of the most important facing our society. It is a problem which is becoming more and more serious as the proportion of old people increases. Of the total of 6.3 million nonfarm families with incomes below $2,000 in 1948, more than one-fourth, or 1.7 million, were headed by persons over 65; they constitute one-half of all families in this age group. Many such people are able and want to continue to work, either on a full-time or part-time basis. And in a highly specialized economy such as ours it must be possible to find ways of prolonging their productive life; there seems to be no essential reason that worth-while tasks cannot be found for these people in an industrial economy, as were found for them in the simpler agricultural economy of former times. It is suggested that the subcommittee consider ways and means of helping these people to find a productive niche in our complex industrial system.

Third. There will always remain in our form of society a sizable group of individuals who for one reason or another cannot be made producing members. These nonearners, however, are still consumers, and their consumption is maintained, at least partially, through social insurance and public assistance programs. For a detailed description of what is now being done for these low-income groups see Joint Committee Print Selected Programs Which Aid the Unemployed and Low Income Families, Joint Committee on the Economic Report, Washington, 1949.

Fourth. When nonfarm low-income families are classified by occupation of the head of the family, the unskilled and the semiskilled service workers, laborers, and operatives are found to make up the hard core of the urban low-income group. They number about 2.2 million. Raising their level of living must involve raising their productivity, perhaps by long-range programs of vocational and academic education. The economic progress of America has greatly reduced the proportions of common-labor jobs. Wielders of pick and shovel have been gradually replaced by operators of excavating machinery. This movement must be fostered, not only by encouragement of progress on the technical side, but on the human side as well. The subcommittee may well wish to consider ways and means of broadening opportunities to learn skilled trades.

In this connection, the low incomes of unskilled workers in some industries may be partially explained as the result of their poor bargaining strength. Besides the problem of raising productivity, there exists in some industries and localities a separate problem of insuring that workers receive full compensation for their efforts. Minimum-wage legislation is, therefore, germane to the subcommittee's study.

Fifth. Nonwhite families make up a significant group of the low-income families. Of the nonfarm families with incomes below $2,000, about 800,000 — or one-eighth — were headed by nonwhite males. This proportion of nonwhites in the low-income group is considerably greater than the proportion of nonwhites in the general population, and indicates that broadening educational and vocational opportunities for the Negro may be a constructive method of attacking the low-income problem.

Sixth. Broken families, those headed by women because of widowhood, desertion, or divorce, are found in large numbers in the nonfarm low-income group. Of the total of 6.3 million urban families receiving incomes under $2,000, about 1.5 million were headed by women. Expansion of the program for aid to dependent children is a palliative of this problem.

Seventh. Low-income families are, as would be expected, headed by persons with little education. Sixty-four percent of the nonfarm families headed by persons between the ages of 25 and 64 years receiving incomes below $2,000 in 1946 had not progressed beyond the eighth grade. Only 6 percent had gone beyond high school. Lack of education for a better-paying occupation thus appears as an important cause of low income. More important than this, however, is the fact that educational opportunity in the United States, at least beyond the grade-school level, still greatly depends upon the income status of the child's family. Low incomes result from lack of education, and lack of education for the next generation results from the low incomes of the present, a process which tends to stratify the population. Broadening educational opportunities, both academic and vocational, for all qualified students regardless of present income status, is not only a most promising long-range attack on the low-income problem, but is also absolutely necessary to preserve the American tradition of equal opportunity for all.

Eighth. Disabled persons in need of vocational rehabilitation number about 1.5 million, and they are found in the low-income group. Much can be done to restore earning power to these people, and the expansion of existing programs of rehabilitation deserves consideration.

Living Conditions of Low-Income Families

A national study of expenditures of American families, by income level, has not been undertaken since the war. The older studies are largely invalidated by the radical changes in employment opportunities and living conditions which have occurred since they were made. This is one of the most important gaps in the available information, a gap which must be filled by new studies. However, some information is included in this report on particular items of expenditure of low-income families, which the following remarks summarize.

First. Food expenditure takes about half of the incomes of city families having less than $2,000 per year. The proportion decreases as income rises, amounting to 74 percent of total expenditures for those below $1,000 and to only 17 percent for those above $7,500. Dollar amounts per person averaged only $6 per week for families in the under-$2,000 income group. This compares with an average of $17 for families having incomes above that level. The poor use more grains, and less milk, meat, vegetables, and fruits than do the comparatively well-to-do.

Besides the great importance of improving American diets, these facts indicate that the domestic market for our agricultural surpluses could be greatly expanded by raising the incomes of the poor. Low-income families are a great underdeveloped market for America's farm production.

Second. The Bureau of the Census estimates that in 1946 about 2.3 million (44 percent) of the nonfarm families headed by persons 25 to 64 years old, who received less than $2,000 in annual income, owned their own homes. However, the implications of these data must be subjected to careful analysis before any conclusion may be drawn. Of those who rented their dwellings, about half paid rents of more than $20 per month, and one-eighth paid rents of more than $40. In the main, housing expenses account for a disproportionate share of the expenditures of urban families with incomes under $2,000. Among those who rented, approximately one-eighth of those with incomes under $1,000 paid 50 percent or more of their income for rent while those with incomes between $1,000 and $2,000 paid a minimum of 25 percent. In addition to being relatively too costly, a large share of the units are wholly inadequate in terms of physical condition, plumbing facilities, overcrowding and general environment.

Conclusion

This document, as its title indicates, is intended to be a convenient handbook of facts on the numbers and circumstances of that segment of the families of the Nation having incomes under $2,000 in urban areas and $1,000 in rural areas. The detailed material which follows is factual and descriptive; it endorses no prescriptions and suggests very few. Final recommendations await the hearings and deliberations of the subcommittee.

Two broad questions, one of fact and one of policy, are not answered in this report, though it lays the foundation for their consideration:

1. What is the effect of the low production and low purchasing power of the poorer families on the economy as a whole? Will their low production and purchasing power hinder the stabilization of the economy at levels of maximum production and employment? Does the prosperity and progress of all depend upon raising their level of living?

2. What can be done to increase the production and earning capacity of these families, thus making for a more prosperous national economy?

THE EIGHTY-FIRST CONGRESS

The elections of November, 1948 had not only returned President Truman to office, but also established a Democratic majority in both houses. The President had sought a broad mandate; his State of the Union Message for 1949 left no doubt about his views.

President Harry S. Truman
Fourth Annual Message
(January 5, 1949)*

*   *   *

The present coverage of the social security laws is altogether inadequate; the benefit payments are too low. One-third of our workers are not covered. Those who receive old-age and survivors insurance benefits receive an average payment of only $25 a month. Many others who cannot work because they are physically disabled are left to the mercy of charity. We should expand our social security program, both as to the size of the benefits and the extent of coverage, against the economic hazards due to unemployment, old age, sickness, and disability.

The annual budget message to Congress for the fiscal year 1950 was more specific.

Annual Budget Message of the President
(January 10, 1949)†

Social Welfare, Health, and Security

In the last 15 years the Federal Government has established a basic pattern of activities in the field of social welfare, health, and security. The national system of old-age and survivors insurance, the system of regular grants to States for public assistance payments to the needy aged and blind and to dependent children, the Federal-State system of unemployment insurance, and several grant programs for the promotion of public health and of children's welfare were established by the Social Security Act of 1935. More recent laws established the railroad retirement system and grants to States for the school lunch, hospital construction, and mental health programs. Also included in the Government's social welfare, health, and security programs are the older system of grants to States for vocational rehabilitation, and those Federal services directed toward the prevention of crime and the apprehension and detention of criminals.

*Public Papers of the Presidents, Harry S. Truman 1949, p. 5.
†*Ibid.*, p. 66.

Under the Social Security Act, the national policy contemplated that old-age and survivors insurance would be the primary Government measure affording economic protection to the needy aged and dependent children, and that unemployment compensation would provide temporary assistance to the unemployed. Other types of social insurance were to be added later to provide more adequate protection against major economic hazards of our society. Public assistance was designed as a backstop, a second line of defense, eventually to be replaced in large measure by social insurance benefits. We have not made progress toward this objective in the last decade. Individual benefit payments under public assistance now are substantially higher than under old-age and survivors insurance. They are more adequate, in many cases, than under unemployment insurance.

Three principal steps should be taken now to strengthen and complete the system of social insurance, and thereby to make our governmental programs consistent with the basic national policy in this field.

First, old-age and survivors insurance should be extended to nearly all the 25 million gainfully employed persons not now covered; the scale of benefits should be sharply raised; benefits should be provided for women at an earlier age; and higher part-time earnings should be permitted. (In addition, coverage under the unemployment compensation system should be extended and benefits made more adequate, as indicated in the "Labor" section of this Message.)

Second, disability insurance should be provided to protect against loss of earnings during illness or other temporary disability. . . .

Even the President's midyear economic report was reasonably specific.

Special Presidential Message to Congress
(July 11, 1949)*

Social Security

Although unemployment has not risen to the dangerous levels which would call for all-out emergency measures, there is an inescapable obligation of Government to take action when large numbers of people are unemployed through no fault of their own. Such action is important not only to the unemployed but also to business, since unemployment benefits maintain to some extent the purchasing power of those who have lost their jobs. Because these measures contribute toward isolating the consequences of unemployment and reducing its duration, it is not economical even by the measure of dollars alone to leave these protective devices in an inadequate state. The cost of such measures is determined not only by the extent of cover-

*Ibid., p. 364.

age or size of benefits but also by the extent and duration of unemployment.

Under current economic conditions, it is urgent that the unemployment compensation system be broadened and liberalized. I recommend that the Congress strengthen our Federal-State unemployment insurance system by establishing minimum benefit standards for all parts of the country and by broadening coverage. These minimum standards should provide benefits for 26 weeks ranging up to $30 a week for single individuals, with additional amounts for dependents.

Ample funds are available for this purpose in the trust accounts of most States. However, these increased benefits will require action by the State legislatures and it will obviously take some time before the laws of all States can be amended for this purpose. It will be necessary, therefore, to allow a reasonable period before the requirement for new standards takes effect.

To encourage the States to meet the new standards without waiting for this period to expire, I recommend that a Federal reinsurance fund be established for those States which meet the minimum standards to assure that the increased protection will not threaten the continued solvency of State unemployment funds. This would represent an extension and strengthening of the present legislation authorizing Federal loans to States whose unemployment funds run low, which expires on December 31, 1949.

I further recommend that the expiration date for unemployment benefits for veterans under the Servicemen's Readjustment Act be extended for one year, to July 25, 1950. Such benefits should not be available to those eligible for unemployment compensation under State laws, except where necessary to bring State payments up to the Federal level, or when State benefits are used up.

The improvements in the old-age and survivors' insurance system which I have recommended to the Congress are also badly needed. The present schedule for increasing pay roll taxes to 1½ percent each on employers and employees next January will provide the financial basis for such improvements without unduly reducing consumer purchasing power.

I have already recommended to the Congress that in addition to Federal aid to the States for the needy aged, for the blind, and for dependent children, such aid should be extended to other needy persons receiving general assistance. In most States, the programs now in operation are inadequate and in many localities there is no program at all. Recent economic developments have emphasized the need for aid and I again urge its favorable consideration by the Congress.

OASI and PA

All this White House pressure made the deliberations of the House Ways and Means Committee with respect to H.R. 2892 (to improve public welfare programs) and H.R. 2893 (to broaden the base of OASI) even more remarkable. Despite the projections made in 1935, public assistance had not withered away, and the social security establishment was slowly becoming aware of what had happened:

Social Security Act Amendments of 1949
Hearings on H.R. 2892 and H.R. 2893 before
the House Ways and Means Committee
81st Cong., 1st Sess. (June, 1949)
Part I — Public Assistance and Public Welfare
(p. 7 *et seq.*)

Dr. Altmeyer. Fourteen years have elapsed since this committee first considered the enactment of social-security legislation for this country. I believe this committee has a right to be proud of its handiwork. The Social Security Act has been successful in accomplishing its primariy immediate objective, and that is the abolition of the old-fashioned poorhouse. Today, throughout America, needy persons receive cash assistance which enables them to live in their own homes. Nevertheless the Social Security Act has not yet fully achieved its long-range objective of preventing destitution through the establishment of a comprehensive system of contributory social insurance, nor is all need now being met through the public-assistance system.

As a matter of fact, our social-security system has become decidedly lopsided. Today there are over 5,000,000 people in the United States receiving some form of public assistance. In contrast there are only about half that number receiving old-age and survivors' insurance benefits. As a Nation we are now spending at the rate of nearly $2,000,000,000 a year for public assistance. But we are paying out only $600,000,000 in old-age and survivors insurance benefits.

We have gained much in experience since this committee framed the original act of 1935 and amended the act in 1939. On the basis of this experience it should be possible to improve our social-security system by making contributory social insurance the basic program, while at the same time improving the public-assistance program as a second line of defense.

As this committee well knows, under a system of contributory social insurance, workers and their employers are enabled to pay in advance for protection against major economic hazards which are likely to cause destitution. Later on, it is my understanding this committee will consider changes in the contributory social insurance system with a view to making contributory social insurance a really effective first line of defense against destitution. But today we are discussing what, as I have suggested, should be considered only as the second line of defense, namely, a public-welfare program.

Public assistance should become less and less important as our first line of defense becomes more and more effective in preventing destitution.

Therefore, the recommendations that we are about to make to you are not presented with a view to establishing a vast new system of "home relief." On the contrary, our recommendations consist largely of revision of the present provisions in the Social Security Act to make them more effective and consistent in providing assistance to needy persons.

The following figures will give some idea of the scope of public assistance in this country today and the need for appraising the effectiveness of the present provisions of the Social Security Act relating to public assistance. Today, as I have said, there are over 5,000,000 needy persons receiving various forms of public assistance. Of these persons, 2,500,000 are old people, 1,700,000 persons in families receiving aid to dependent children, 86,000 are blind, and 800,000 are needy persons who do not fall within the first three categories. The Federal Government is now providing grants-in-aid to the States to help them meet the cost of providing assistance to the aged, dependent children, and the blind. However, no Federal grants are made to the States to help them bear the cost of providing assistance to needy persons who do not fall within these three categories.

Summary of Recommendations

Primary objective is a system of contributory social insurance.

We believe that our present programs of contributory social insurance should be greatly strengthened. With a really effective social-insurance system, the great majority of families could maintain their economic independence when they meet with common hazards against which they have little or no individual defense. However, even with complete coverage of the major economic risks of the working population, there will always be some individuals who will fail to qualify for insurance benefits and other individuals who will need a variety of services for which they will need to turn to the public welfare agency. For these persons, there should be constructive welfare programs, including public assistance and family and child welfare services. In addition to these provisions for safeguarding family income and family welfare, a comprehensive program of services for children should be developed. We therefore recommend in addition to the establishment of a comprehensive system of contributory social insurance the following:

A constructive program of public welfare, including public assistance and family- and child-welfare services. Under this program, on a Federal-State basis, payments and services financed from Federal and State funds would be available on a consistent basis to needy persons. The Federal financial contribution should be designed to remove the great disparities now existing in the treatment of various classes of needy persons and to reduce the disparities among different parts of the country. It should also be designed to remove serious present inequities in the relative burdens borne by States and localities in financing public assistance. The role of public welfare agencies should be strengthened by Federal participation on a State-wide basis in constructive social services for all adults and children.

The major legislative changes that would assist in the achievement of the objectives outlined above include:

Special Federal aid to low-income States to enable States with relatively low economic resources to develop adequate public-welfare programs.

As a condition of Federal aid, State apportionment of Federal and State funds among the localities in accordance with their need for funds.

Increase of the Federal maximums limiting Federal participation in individual monthly payments for aid to dependent children.

Federal grants to States for assistance to needy persons who are not now included in the three special types of assistance for the needy aged, blind, and dependent children.

Extension of Federal participation in aid to dependent children to include any needy child living with a parent, relative, or other person who assumes responsibility for parental care and support and who maintains a family home for the child.

Federal participation in the costs of medical services made available to needy persons under State public-assistance programs and in payments to needy sick persons who reside in public or private medical institutions other than mental hospitals and tuberculosis sanatoria.

Financial participation in welfare services administered by the staff of the public-welfare agency and designed to help families and individuals become self-supporting, to keep families together in their own homes, and to reduce the need for institutional care.

Explicit provision in the Federal act that a State, as a condition of plan approval, be required to establish the budget to be used in measuring the amount of assistance required by needy persons to supplement their own resources, if any; to develop standards that will assure equitable treatment of needy persons throughout the State; and to consider, in determining the amount of assistance, only resources actually available to the individual.

Unification of the administration of State public-assistance programs at both State and local levels as a condition of Federal grants.

Extension of Federal grants-in-aid for all public assistance programs to Puerto Rico and the Virgin Islands.

Various members of the House Ways and Means Committee were becoming anxious about the continuing need for public assistance.

House Hearings
(p. 35 *et seq.*)

Representative Richard M. Simpson [Rep., Penn.] . . . What I mean is this: Has OASI helped us cut down on the need for relief agencies?

Dr. Altmeyer. I get your point, and I think that the chart shows that the expenditures under old-age and survivors insurance are so relatively small that they have not taken up a considerable portion of the total expenditures.

Mr. Simpson. As the OASI payments have gone up; has also the general relief payment had to go up at the same time?

Dr. Altmeyer. They have not gone up so far, because of the existence of old-age and survivors insurance, but if old-age and survivors insurance had covered the entire population, and if the benefits under old-age and survivors insurance were larger, then your middle line would be much lower, and your lower line would be much higher. That is the point we have made.

Mr. Cooper. May I submit a question to that point?

To what extent old-age and survivors insurance payments have been made, that has had an effect on benefit payments?

Dr. Altmeyer. On assistance payments.

Mr. Cooper. Because, no doubt, there are thousands of these people who are receiving old-age and survivors insurance payments, if they did not get to that they would be reflected in the top line of the benefit payments.

Dr. Altmeyer. Yes; that is the point.

*   *   *

Mr. Reed. How many years do you think it would require for the old-age security insurance to take the load off the public assistance? The theory was that this OASI would sooner or later remove much of the need for old-age assistance. How many years do you anticipate will be required in order to lift that load?

Dr. Altmeyer. It depends, Mr. Congressman, on how far you extend the coverage of old-age and survivors insurance. I have a chart that shows that because of the present restricted coverage the agricultural States, particularly, are at a disadvantage and that coverage is a very important factor everywhere. The second important factor is the ease with which persons can qualify for social insurance, the so-called eligibility requirements, and the third factor is the amount of the insurance benefit. The more adequate the amount of insurance benefits the less the need for public assistance, of course.

*   *   *

Mr. Reed. Do you expect that OASI will ever absorb all of the OAS?

Dr. Altmeyer. I think it ought to absorb enough so that the Federal Government would not be required to participate in financing in public assistance because the residual load would be low enough so that the States ought to be able to carry it.

It was Dr. Altmeyer who bore the brunt of the questioning in the second part of the hearings, as he vigorously argued for: 1. the extension of coverage by the old-age and survivors' insurance program to practically all gainfully employed persons; 2. the raising of the level of benefits paid under the program; and 3. the expansion of the program to provide protection against disability as well as old age and death. Next to his extensive contribution, the most important Administration spokesman was G.J. Schoeneman of the Treasury, who explained how his department proposed to collect taxes from newly covered groups. Before then, administrative difficulties had always been cited as a justification for not extending the insurance programs under social security. In all, there were more than two hundred fifty persons testifying. In general, it was the Democrats who demanded an increase in social security, and the Republicans who wanted a more general program involving a merger of public assistance and insurance programs.

Finally, on August 22, the committee produced its own bill (H.R. 6000), incorporating many of the Administration proposals. There could be little doubt that the bill represented the first major changes in the social security system since 1939. In OASI, not only would there be a vast extension in the number of persons covered, (although not to the twenty million called for by Administration bills), but benefits would be radically increased. The committee accepted the Administration's demand for a minimum of $25 a month and a maximum of $180, and, continuing the trend of the 1939 amendments, the benefits would take greater notice of "average wages" —and less of number of years worked under the system. Although the Administration had wished to abolish the "1 per cent per year worked" increase in benefits, it was reduced only to ½ per cent and the committee left the assessment as it was, the period preceding retirement, rather than accepting an average of the worker's best five years. Nor would the committee lessen the requirement that a worker must have spent half this time in covered employment to qualify for a pension. Funding was finally set on a more satisfactory basis by raising both employers' and employees' contributions and lifting the taxable wage from $3,000 to $3,600 and disability insurance was added to the program.

In public assistance, a new category, aid to the totally disabled (ATD), was created although the committee refused to include those only partially affected or to create a new grouping for the "needy". The scope of ADC was also extended to support for parents of children covered by the program. Variable grants were rejected again, but a new formula was devised where the Federal Government paid four-fifths of the earlier matching funds. There were also important steps towards providing what became known as "vendor payments for medical services to those on public assistance." All these amendments, as well as the "insurance provisions" which in-creasingly upset the Republican minority, were included in Social Security Act Amendments of 1946, *House Report No. 1300, 81st Cong., 1st Sess. (p. 5 et seq.).*

After a bottle-neck in the Rules Committee, the bill was reported out with a closed (gag) rule. This refusal to allow amendments caused con-siderable debate, but discussion on the bill itself was understandably

uninspiring. The main speech in favor was made by Representative Dough-
ton, the chairman of the House Ways and Means Committee, but more
emotional support came from Representative George H. Christopher of
Missouri, "Do you know what this legislation is which we are considering
today? This legislation is the heart and soul of the New Deal. It is the
practical application of the Sermon on the Mount."

The main issue under insurance was coverage, and Representative
Reid F. Murray of Wisconsin gave a typical plea for the farmers.

Congressional Debates
81 Congressional Record, p. 13929
(October 5, 1949)

Mr. Murray . . . What do they have to look forward to? They can look
forward to the time when they get old, and believe me, when you get to be
65 years old you are not going to do too much farming. All they have to look
forward to is that they might have someone point a finger at them and call
them a reliefer, and yet it all comes out of the same pot, more or less. There
is no reason why rural people, not only the farmers, but the rural areas
everywhere should not be included under the social-security program.

The most debated issue was disability insurance, generally supported
by the Democrats but opposed by the Republicans, who saw it competing
unfairly with private insurance. Even more frightening was the thought of
"socialized medicine."

Congressional Debates
81 Congressional Record, p. 13845 *et seq.*

Mr. [Noah M.] Mason [Rep., Ill.]. . . . Mr. Chairman, H. R. 6000, in my
opinion, is a long step down the road to a welfare state. It is the initial or
preliminary step toward *socialized medicine* – a cradle-to-grave program
that will eventually cost the taxpayers of this Nation between fifteen and
twenty billion dollars per year.

*   *   *

Mr. Simpson of Pennsylvania. I have one other matter about which I want
to talk. I think it will strike an interesting chord in the mind of each of you,
at least from my viewpoint. I feel that this provision in the bill providing
for permanent-disability benefits is one that will lead inevitably to what each
of us thinks of as *socialized medicine*. I have told many a doctor and civilian
in my district that I am opposed to socialized medicine, and I do not want
to support legislation which in my opinion may lead to it. You look surprised, perhaps, because it is very true that this bill is written most carefully

to insure as far as possible that the benefits which a man who is totally and permanently disabled may receive will not be received until these safeguards have all been surmounted, and they are considerable. It must be a 6-month period within which the man is disabled, and there must be a finding by competent doctors.

For the most part the gag rule in the House meant that the debates consisted of speeches (given or inserted) rehashing the majority and minority reports, but it also insured that the bill would be passed in its original form by a comfortable margin. The President was then prepared to press the project to a conclusion in 1950 and both the State of the Union Message and the economic report called for prompt action. Even the annual budget message was detailed with respect to social security since, on January 1, 1950 the tax had finally been raised to 1.5 per cent.

Annual Budget Message of the President
(January 9, 1950)*

Social Welfare, Health, and Security

The coming year will be an extremely significant one for the Nation's social security program. The decisions of the Congress on pending legislation will determine the direction which this country will follow in providing basic protection against the major economic hazards of old age, unemployment, illness, and disability. It is my strong belief that it is a responsibility of the Government to provide this protection, and to provide it in a manner that is consistent with our ideals of independence and self-reliance — through the already established and tested principle of contributory social insurance. This was the basic philosophy of the Social Security Act, in which the major role was given to social insurance, financed mutually by employers and employees, with benefits available as a matter of right without a means test. Public assistance was given only a supplementary role to fill in the diminishing gaps in insurance protection.

The effects of our failure in recent years to carry out this philosophy are already dramatized by the increase in the public assistance rolls. Because the protection of social insurance is so limited and inadequate, far too many people have been forced to seek public relief. In some States, for example, half the aged people are on the relief rolls. Approximately 2,700,000 aged people and 1,500,000 dependent children now receive public assistance. By contrast, only 1,900,000 aged persons receive insurance benefits and 800,000 children and their mothers receive survivors benefits under the

*Public Papers of the Presidents, Harry S. Truman, 1950, p. 71–74.

old-age and survivors insurance system. Average old-age insurance benefits are only 26 dollars a month compared with average old-age public assistance benefits of 45 dollars.

Public demand for some form of basic financial protection against loss of earning power is evident in the keen interest of wage earners in industrial pension and insurance plans. There can be no question that our society can and should provide such protection. What I wish to emphasize is that the basic approach should be through a comprehensive public program of old-age, survivors, and disability insurance, rather than through a multiplicity of unrelated private plans, which would inevitably omit large numbers of the working population and treat others unequally. Private plans and voluntary insurance can then provide desirable supplemental protection.

I urge that the Congress enact legislation to expand and improve the old-age and survivors insurance system in accordance with the recommendations made last spring. Specifically, nearly all gainfully employed people, including farmers and the self-employed, should be covered; benefits should be increased sharply; and disability should be added to the risks covered. It is also important that the tax base be raised to the first 4,800 dollars of earned income, not only to reflect changes in wage levels since 1939, but also to bring both receipts and benefits to proper levels.

The recommended program will cover about 85 percent of all employed people, and will thus gradually reduce the need for public assistance. In the meantime, however, it is necessary to provide some help for those persons not yet protected by social insurance, as well as for those who would need public aid even with an adequate social insurance system. I therefore renew my recommendation of last year that the program of Federal grants to States for public assistance be extended and improved. The proposal that I submitted to the Congress last spring was designed to permit Federal sharing in the cost of aid to needy persons excluded from the present program, as well as in the cost of essential medical and welfare services. It was also designed to make Federal grants more responsive to the financial resources of each State. Within the framework of general policy under the Social Security Act, the States are responsible for determining the size of benefit payments and the eligibility of individuals for assistance. In adopting amendments to the present program, we should continue to rely on the States to bear a considerable share of the financial responsibility.

*   *   *

Assistance to the aged and other special groups. — Grants-in-aid to States for public assistance to the needy aged, the blind, and dependent children are expected to reach 1.2 billion dollars in 1951 under the present program, with the Federal share averaging about 52 percent of total payments by State and local governments to these groups. For some time, the number of recipients has been increasing and now exceeds 4,000,000 persons; it is expected to average 4,600,000 during 1951. Average benefits are also expected to continue their rise. As a result, Federal expenditures will exceed those for the current year by an estimated 55 million dollars. The Budget contains an additional 200 million dollars as the first-year expenditure estimated for proposed legislation to cover all the needy and to put the program on a variable grant basis. The revised formula which I have recommended would relate grants to the financial resources of the individual States and would also permit the Federal share to be held within reasonable limits.

The Senate Finance Committee began work on H.R. 6000 as soon as the second session got under way. As was now almost customary, the legislative outlook could best be judged by Dr. Altmeyer's opening presentation. He considered the legislative outlook as well as the suggestions of the Senate-appointed Advisory Council.

Social Security Act Amendments of 1946
Hearings on H.R. 6000 before the Senate Finance Committee
81st Cong., 2d Sess. (January, 1950)
Part I – Testimony and Recommendations
by the Social Security Administration
(p. 19)

Statement of Arthur Altmeyer

I believe that this committee has a right to be proud of the fact that the Social Security Act has been successful at least in accomplishing one primary objective, the abolition of the old fashioned "poor house." Nevertheless, I think we must all agree that the Social Security Act has not yet fully achieved its long-range objective of preventing destitution through the establishment of a comprehensive system of contributory social insurance. It is also unfortunately true that all residual need is not being met through the supplementary public assistance system that is incorporated in the Social Security Act.

*   *   *

In response to the request for our evaluation of the recommendations of the Senate Advisory Council, let me say that we are in complete agreement with the emphasis and the priority placed by the committee on its recommendation for the improvement of the social insurances and with the position of the Council that improvements in the social insurance program would "in the long run greatly reduce the need for public assistance." We are also in agreement that the public assistance system must be improved to carry the job of a "large scale transitional system during the relatively short period which will elapse before the comprehensive social insurance system becomes fully effective" and that moreover changes in the assistance program should be made with a recognition of the "function of public assistance in a mature social security system as a means of supplementing the basic insurance benefits and in filling in the gaps in insurance protection."

With these formalities out of the way, Dr. Altmeyer fought for Administration proposals which had been dropped from the bill. For example, he pressed for OASI coverage for farmers and professional persons, and for a $4,800 tax base.

Of the other Administration testimony, probably the most important concerned public assistance.

Senate Hearings
(p. 136 *et seq.*)

Statement of Jane M. Hoey, Director, Bureau of Public Assistance, Social Security Administration, Federal Security Agency.

Both the Advisory Council to the Senate Committee on Finance and the House Committee on Ways and Means considered the inadequacies of the present program for aiding dependent children. The present law limits the program to children under 18 years of age who are dependent because of the death, incapacity, or continued absence from home of a parent. Children in families which experience economic need but in which none of these factors are present also suffer acute privation and undergo destructive hardships. As a matter of fact, requiring that a parent be absent from the home before his children can receive assistance places a kind of financial premium on a broken home and exerts an influence exactly opposed to the purpose of the whole aid-to-dependent-children program; namely, to keep families together. We would therefore recommend that the definition of a dependent child be amended to include all children under the age of 18 living in families where there is economic need.

The Chairman. Would you pardon me, right there?

Miss Hoey. Yes Senator.

The Chairman. Would not that program tend to produce more trouble than it would cure? If here is a family, intact, where the mother and the father are there, should not assistance be given so that they may take care of the family, rather than having somebody come in under the father and the mother and take care of the children because the economic condition of the family is not good?

Miss Hoey. Senator, the assistance payments are made directly to the parents for the children. That is the primary purpose of the assistance. It is to give it to parents and they spend it as they please for the care of the children. It is given for the children, but through the parents.

The Chairman. There you have another problem. Perhaps the same habits would lead to the wastage of those funds, unless they were safeguarded by the parents, who had failed in the first instance to provide.

Miss Hoey. We are talking largely about the unemployed parent who is not covered by unemployment insurance and has no other resources, where the children are in need. Now, if he deserts the family, or if it is a case of separation and nonsupport, they are eligible.

The Chairman. You are going to add to the benefits of the father and mother because there are dependent children in a home which does not have the capacity to meet the needs of that home?

Miss Hoey. Yes. That would be a temporary measure, of course, and there would be conditions set up, I am sure, by the States, by which the father would be referred to the Employment Service, so that he could get a job. Usually the stay of employable people on general assistance is for a very short period.

The Chairman. I am afraid that would greatly swell the rolls of the unemployed.

In the "public" part of the hearings, the insurance industry made clear what it thought the relationship between private insurance and social security should be.

Senate Hearings
(p. 943)

Statement of M. Albert Linton, President, Provident Mutual Life Insurance Co.

The role of social security: The inflation brought on by World War II has left the benefits of the Social Security Act considerably short of what was originally intended to be provided. Accordingly, a realistic approach to social security indicates the need for an increase in OASI benefits. Incidentally, I should say that we are in favor of the extension of coverage to as wide an extent as is practicable.

Social security will become increasingly important in the future. Today there are in this country about eight persons aged 20 to 64, roughly the productive period of life, for each person over age 65. In a generation, using an average of estimates, the indications are that this figure will be reduced to five persons in the producing ages for each person over age 65, with further reduction continuing after that. The importance, therefore, of planning practicable and reasonable provision for the aged can hardly be overemphasized. Great care must be exercised lest larger benefits be promised than can be delivered without danger to the economy of the country and without undermining personal initiative and responsibility. Political considerations and the history of social welfare programs clearly indicate that it is exceedingly difficult to correct overgenerous benefit scales once a large number of persons acquire a personal interest in their continuation.

Under any form of organized society the producers among the population must provide goods and services for themselves and the nonproducers as well. Social-security expansion tends to accelerate the transfer of individuals from the producing to the nonproducing portion of the population and to fix minimum benefits for the latter. If the number of nonproducers and the level of benefits afforded them places an unacceptable burden on the producers, serious consequences are likely to follow. Benefits may be reduced, taxation may be imposed to such an extent that the enterprise system is endangered, or the dollar may be cheapened through deficit financing.

We strongly urge that your committee be constantly guided by fundamental considerations. (The Federal Government, through the Social Security Act, should provide no more than a *basic floor* of financial protection for its citizens.) If this sound principle is not kept in mind in establishing a new level of social security benefits, the most serious consequences will ultimately develop. To provide benefits large enough for comfortable living under the Social Security Act will cause tens of millions of people to rely on Government for their financial protection rather than on their own ambition and initiative. Should such an attitude toward the Central Government develop, the direct impact of Government upon the lives of individuals, already great, would increase. It would eventually produce a public attitude of undue dependence upon the state and lay the groundwork for the loss of our basic freedoms.

Not only must benefits be limited so as to preserve individual initiative and responsibility, but unwise liberality in social-security benefits must be avoided for the sake of the economy of the country. The danger of such liberality can readily be seen from estimates of the snowballing cost of benefits. The first-year cost of the revised program is estimated officially at about 1½ billion dollars. By the time persons now entering the labor market are eligible to retire, the estimated costs of these benefits, omitting provision for any total and permanent disability benefits, range from 5.5 percent to 9.5 percent of estimated pay rolls. In terms of dollars these represent costs ranging from 8.3 to 12.6 billion dollars a year. These costs are in addition to all the other costs of running the Government, the cost of maintaining our Military Establishment and any other welfare programs. Over-generous provision for social-security benefits will inevitably lead to a Federal budget of truly staggering dimensions, the load becoming heavier each year as more and more persons become eligible for benefits.

With these arguments representatives of the insurance industry opposed increases in the OASI tax base and benefits and any allowance for the number of years worked. Of course, they rejected the establishment of disability insurance as did the American Medical Association whose trustees had adopted a formal public position.

Senate Hearings
(p. 1324)

Statement of American Medical Association

In the past, the American Medical Association has made it a practice to take a stand on legislation involving medical care and the health of the American people. While H. R. 6000 is primarily a social-welfare proposal, it does contain one provision having serious medical implications; namely, that section on compulsory contributory permanent- and total-disability insurance.

The major benefits included in the present social-security system — old-age and unemployment — are adaptable to mass or objective administration from an office remote from the individual. This is not true of total- and permanent-disability benefits. Age is a condition over which the individual is unable to exercise any control, and unemployment is an occurrence over which the individual may have little or no control. Qualification for the benefits is categorical and not difficult to determine. In contrast, total and permanent disability is often a condition over which the individual who is disabled and his physician may exercise control.

This subjective control which may be exercised by the individual multiplies the opportunity for malingering and actually takes the program out of the insurance category. We must always oppose any program which places a brake on the incentive of the sick and disabled to desire recovery.

To initiate a Federal disability program would represent another step toward wholesale nationalization of medical care and the socialization of the practice of medicine. The program as now proposed would not accomplish the entire nationalization of medical care, but the inevitable expansion and liberalization of the program which would surely follow makes probable its eventual accomplishment. The steps in liberalization are not hard to visualize, such as payment of benefits to dependents of disabled covered persons, removal of the time lag of 6 months, and substitution of temporary-disability benefits, then eventually full cash sickness and disability provisions. We would then have nothing less than a total national compulsory sickness program.

During the hearings on this bill persons fully qualified in the field of economics and insurance and students of political science warned against the high additional percentage of national income to be committed to social programs by the enactment of extensions as proposed by H. R. 6000. Of this danger, we are aware.

The American Medical Association recognized the need for assistance to the disabled needy and feels that this aid should always be administered on a local level. Financial assistance to the locality should only be advanced from State or Federal sources when a need can be clearly shown.

The hearings were also concerned with the definition of "employee", and possible social security coverage for state and local government employees, professional persons, and employees of non-profit organizations. There was considerable disagreement on the wage base for social security—in general the unions wanted it as high as possible, while employers' groups wanted to keep it low.

After the hearings, the Senate Finance Committee spent over a month in executive session and finally produced a three hundred twenty-page report, together with a bill incorporating its changes.

H.R. 6000, as it came to the Senate floor, showed many differences from the bill which had been before the House. Compulsory coverage was smaller, although there was provision for voluntary coverage. Benefits were increased considerably, and eligibility was appreciably widened—a person now only had to be insured for one-half of the quarters since 1950. Disability insurance was eliminated, but certain new beneficiary categories were included and beneficiaries were allowed to earn up to $50 a month without losing their entitlement. The Senate also left the tax base at $3,000 and delayed raising the rate to 2 per cent until 1956.

In the public assistance programs, the Senate agreed to raise the ADC maximum to $30 for the first child and $20 for additional children, but would not alter the federal-state formula. The right to earn $50 a month was extended to AB, and states were authorized to pay directly for medical care furnished to public assistance recipients. In addition the provision allowing federal advances to state unemployment insurance accounts was extended.

The debates began on June 13. Senator Walter F. George, chairman of the Senate Finance Committee, introduced the bill which was vigorously supported by liberal Senators.

The most significant Republican speech came from Senator Robert A. Taft. He very cogently suggested that OASI and OAA should be merged in a single system. Under his plan, everyone would get a flat pension upon reaching the age of sixty-five and there would be no eligibility requirement except age. He also suggested that besides minimum subsistence pensions there should be graduated, increased benefits related to the amount of taxes paid during the worker's life.

Congressional Debates
81 Congressional Record, p. 8586
(June 13, 1949)

Mr. Taft . . . I feel that the bill carries out general pledges which have been made by both parties, and I also think it moves in the right direction. The only thing I do not like about the bill is the fact that it still adheres to the so-called social-insurance program. I do not believe it is insurance, and I think the sooner we recognize that old-age pensions are desired by the people on a pay-as-you-go basis, on a universal basis, the better off we shall be.

I think social insurance is not, in fact, insurance. It is not anything in the world but the taxing of people to provide free services to other people.

I do not like to have old-age pensions, which are popular and necessary, and of which I approve, used as a basis for extending so-called social insurance to all kinds of other fields of social welfare, and increasing the tremendous expense of welfare service beyond the present means of the people of the country. I do not believe the Federal Government ought to become more involved than it is in the general problem of providing welfare services and providing for the needy throughout the entire Nation.

As I say, this old-age system is not insurance. It started out to be an actuarily sound fund. The fund was to be established by the people who paid taxes in, and then when it reached the proper point they were to take out what they were entitled to as a result of having paid something into the fund. That was very soon abandoned, because the fund was impossible to administer.

If we should try to have an actuarily sound fund invested in good property, it would get up into the neighborhood of $100,000,000,000, and very soon the fund would own all the property, stocks, and bonds in the United States. It was soon recognized that that could not be done. We could not actually buy all those stocks, so the fund was to be invested in Government bonds. That was nothing but a collection of Government IOU's. We collected a tax, put the tax into the fund, then took the cash out of the fund and put it in Government bonds. Then the Treasury spends the money taken out of the fund. When we come to try to cash in on the fund, we have to tax the people again to pay the interest or the principal on the bonds in the fund. In the last analysis, the fact is that where we have a widely spread old-age pension system and undertake to pay persons over 65 years of age when they are not working, the sum is so large that it is impossible to handle on an actuarily sound basis. In the long run we have to recognize that the only way to pay those sums is for the people who are working at the time to pay the benefits for the people who are not working. There is no other way to do it. We may as well recognize that at the beginning. If we are going to pay old-age pensions, the only way to do it is to pay it out of contributions of the people who are earning money at the time.

Mr. Smith of New Jersey. Mr. President, will the Senator yield?

Mr. Taft. I yield.

Mr. Smith of New Jersey. I should like to ask the Senator if I correctly understand his position. Is the Senator proposing that hereafter those presently working will be taxed to pay benefits to those who are 65 and over, but at the same time those presently working will not be contributing to their own retirement benefits?

Mr. Taft. That is correct. I would favor a universal old-age pension system. At the same time, we might just as well recognize what we are doing. In the old days children were supposed to take care of their parents. That was sometimes done, and sometimes it was not done. Sometimes there were no children to assume the responsibility. For that system we should substitute a system under which all the people under 65 are undertaking to say they will pay old-age pensions to everyone over 65, hoping that when they reach the age of 65 the people who are at that time working will assume the same obligation.

Mr. Smith of New Jersey. I understand the Senator to take the position that the contributions made by individuals through the years have no relation to their ultimate pensions.

Mr. Taft. I think there is a slight relation, but the benefits which are paid have only a slight relation to what a man pays in.

I should like to read from a speech made by Representative Carl T. Curtis, of Nebraska, in the House of Representatives. He said:

Let us consider the case of a man who is now 40 years of age. Let us assume that he has been under old-age and survivors insurance since it started in 1937, that he and his wife are the same age, and that both will reach 65 at the same time. We will also assume that his average monthly wage has been $200. This man will have paid in in taxes according to the schedule in the present law a sum of $1,440, and his employer a like amount, or a total of $2,880.

This amount would have purchased him a monthly benefit of $14.10 on an actuarial basis. However, under existing law he would draw $47.95 a month, and his wife would draw $23.98, or a total of $71.93. In less than 3½ years he and his wife would draw out everything that he and his employer have paid in, even though he would have been covered for 37 long years. The actuaries say that the total value of all these benefits under existing law is $9,770. Under the pending measure his benefits will be raised to $71.10 a month, his wife's to $35.60 a month, or a total of $106.70 a month.

Mr. Smith of New Jersey. Mr. President, will the Senator yield further?

Mr. Taft. I yield.

Mr. Smith of New Jersey. Do I correctly understand that the Senator from Ohio would favor a flat pension for everyone, or would he favor a graduated pension?

Mr. Taft. I favor universal pensions, but the question of whether the pension should be flat or graduated should be studied by the committee which is proposed to be established under our proposal and which, as I understand, has been approved by the Finance Committee and will be considered by the Senate at about the same time we vote on the bill itself.

Mr. Smith of New Jersey. I am glad to hear the Senator refer to a committee for studying the question.

Mr. Taft. The Senator asked about a universal pension system. A flat pension system is in force in England today, but the conditions in England are much more uniform than they are in sections of the United States. I personally, at the moment, should be inclined to favor a flat minimum and then have an increased benefit as people have paid taxes during their life or as they have earned money during the 10 years prior to the time they retired. Under that rule there would be some relation to the amount paid in. I think some relation should be recognized. But it is not very close. Take the case of a man with an average wage of $50 a month. He pays in a tax matched by his employer. The total tax paid in is $60 by each, or $120 over a 10-year period. Under the pending bill he would receive retirement pay of $22 a month instead of $20. If he has a wife who is over 65 years of age, he would get $33 a month. On the other hand, a man earning $100 a month pays in $120, twice as much as does the man earning $50 a month. He retires on only $27.50 a month, instead of $22.50 a month which the other fellow gets. There is practically no relation between what he has paid in and what he gets.

Under the new bill, the same thing is roughly true. A man with $100 average monthly wage would pay $432 and would receive $50 a month on retirement. On the other hand, a man with $200 monthly average wage would pay, or have paid for him, twice as much, or $864, but his benefit would be only $65 a month. For the same payment the first man might get $75 a month for half the money paid in by the single man under the proposed bill.

What I want to point out is that this bill already has gone far toward recognizing the principle of paying to those over 65 years of age a pension, with little relation to what they paid in during their life. In other words, it is no longer insurance. It is something called social insurance. It is not insurance, and, at least up to date, this system has not been very social either, because it has covered only a very small portion of the total number of people who are over 65 years of age.

* * *

As I see it, the general problem of taking care of the unfortunate is primarily one for the States, and ought to be administered by them. We ought not to have a national system. In the case of old-age pensions, the people have thought that it should be a national program, and they have made it a national program. But the moment we use the insurance idea as an excuse to cover other benefits, we shall have the Federal Government take over the entire welfare activities of the United States. We shall be doing the whole thing in Washington, and we shall be administering it from here. It would cost us about three times as much as it would if we left it with the States and assisted them in those fields.

I am willing to consider the general problem of how far the Federal Government should help the States in the matter of permanent disability as a matter of State aid. However, permanent disability is a very minor factor. In total money, it is very small, and it is well within the financial capacity of the States to look after. I see no particular reason, on the basis of necessity, why the Federal Government should be invited in.

The point I have been trying to make is that this bill does not provide insurance, and the sooner we get back to the recognition that what we are doing is simply debating an old-age pension policy and not any general theory of social insurance, the better off we will be.

I regret that we are calling this a social insurance bill. The fact is that the changes that have been made show it is not insurance. Take one thing, for example. Take the fact that we are doubling these payments. If the payments under the old-age and survivors insurance program paid for the benefits, and were intended to pay for the benefits, then certainly we could not double the benefits and maintain that principle. Even if they paid in enough to get the benefit they are supposed to get under the old system, we are now going to give them twice as much. In other words, we are recognizing in this bill that we have an obligation to pay old-age pensions to people who are old, simply because they are old and not because they paid money into the fund.

The one thing I do like about the bill is that it does establish that principle. It destroys the whole idea of insurance even while it uses the term "insurance." It puts it on the basis of old-age pension, and therefore moves in the direction of universal pension for all over 65, which I think we ought to adopt. I might say that I believe the Committee on Finance would agree with that point of view. The argument which was made against it, and which prevailed, properly so, was that it required such a complete study and such a complete change in the present system that it could not possibly be done in 4 months. We are not going to stay here 4 months longer this year. We felt something ought to be done about the inequities of the present system. The House committee has not even considered plans of that kind, so far as I know. Therefore, they would have to consider the whole thing if we tried to change the system now. However, as I see it, the bill destroys the whole theory of insurance. It recognizes an obligation. Under the new start principle, a man who pays in practically nothing will get $70 a month. Why should we not give the man who does not pay in anything $70 a month, or at least $65 a month? As I see it, we have practically destroyed the theory of social insurance. All I regret is that we still use the name "insurance" when as a matter of fact there is no insurance about it.

$$* \qquad * \qquad *$$

I believe we should insist upon a commission to study the whole problem of a universal pension. I think it can be worked out. I think it can be worked out with very little additional expenditure by the Federal Government over what is being paid today. I think it can be worked out so as to relieve the Federal Government of the $900,000,000 a year which today we are paying to the States to make the old-age assistance payments. I am only guessing, but I should think that, whereas in 1952 the present program would cost us $3,200,000,000, for somewhere between $4,000,000,000 and $5,000,-000,000 a year we can provide a universal old-age pension.

$$* \qquad * \qquad *$$

*Such pay-as-you-go proposals were advocated by many Republicans in
1949–50, and were even seriously mentioned in the 1950 Republican Platform. Under one, backed by the U.S. Chamber of Commerce, all employed workers would be subject to the existing OASI payroll tax, all aged
persons would be eligible for the benefits (eliminating OAA), and future
benefits would be financed out of contributions that same year. The existing OASI trust fund reserves would have been used to meet heavy initial
costs of the new system.*

*These programs were opposed by organized labor and by most liberals.
In the short run, they argued, the payments to the aged would drain the existing trust fund reserves and preclude any increases in benefits in the future.
In the long run, a current financing system, necessitating yearly congressional action, would permit conservative groups seeking lower taxes to exert continual pressure (particularly in years of federal financial deficits) to
reduce old-age pension costs by keeping benefits low. Moreover, eliminating
old-age assistance altogether would shift the charity burden from general
revenues, raised by a progressive taxation, to payroll taxes levied only on
the bottom level of income. Thus, part of the cost of providing for indigents
would be borne, not by the wealthy, but by low income workers.*

*After a week of debate, the Senate voted to finance a two-year study of
pay-as-you-go pension proposals, and then began to consider amendments.
Although most failed, two important changes were made before the bill
passed. The tax base rose to $3,600, and the Knowland Amendment, was
added, preventing the Federal Government from curtailing its contribution
to state unemployment compensation funds for non-compliance with federal
rulings.*

*The House-Senate Conference dragged on for several weeks and the
report ultimately endorsed what had been done by the Senate. Those already receiving social security had their benefits boosted an average of
77 per cent. The payroll tax was to rise to 2 per cent in 1954 and then, over
twenty years, to 3.25 per cent. Disability insurance was abandoned, but aid
to the needy disabled was introduced as a new category of public assistance
with a federal share between 60 and 75 per cent of a $50 per month maxi-
mum. The conferees retained the Knowland Amendment and rejected the
House suggestion that under OASI there should be ½ per cent increment
in benefit for each year worked. Thus benefits were settled at the same figure
whether the worker had worked for ten or fifty years.*

*After an attempt to strike out the Knowland Amendment, the bill was
passed by both houses and signed by the President on August 28.*

Social Security Amendments of 1950
(August 28, 1950, ch. 809, 64 Statutes at Large, Part 1, 477)

"QUARTER AND QUARTER OF CONVERAGE

"Definitions

"*Sec. 213.* (a) For the purposes of this title —

"(1) The term 'quarter', and the term 'calendar quarter', means a period of three calendar months ending on March 31, June 30, September 30, or December 31. . . .

"(B) The term 'quarter of coverage' means, in the case of a quarter occurring after 1950, a quarter in which the individual has been paid $50 or more in wages or for which he has been credited (as determined under section 212) with $100 or more of self-employment income, except that —

"(i) no quarter after the quarter in which such individual died shall be a quarter of coverage;

"(ii) if the wages paid to any individual in a calendar year equal or exceed $3,600, each quarter of such year shall (subject to clause (i)) be a quarter of coverage;

"(iii) if an individual has self-employment income for a taxable year, and if the sum of such income and the wages paid to him during such taxable year equals $3,600, each quarter any part of which falls in such year shall be a quarter of coverage; and

"(iv) no quarter shall be counted as a quarter of coverage prior to the beginning of such quarter.

*   *   *

"INSURED STATUS FOR PURPOSE OF OLD-AGE AND SURVIVORS INSURANCE BENEFITS

"*Sec. 214.* For the purposes of this title —

"Fully Insured Individual

*   *   *

"(2) In the case of any individual who did not die prior to September 1, 1950, the term 'fully insured individual' means any individual who had not less than —

"(A) one quarter of coverage (whether acquired before or after such day) for each two of the quarters elapsing after 1950, or after the quarter in which he attained the age of twenty-one, whichever is later, and up to but excluding the quarter in which he attained retirement age, or died, whichever first occurred, except that in no case shall an individual be a fully insured individual unless he has at least six quarters of coverage; or

"(B) forty quarters of coverage.

"(3) When the number of elapsed quarters specified in paragraph (1) or (2) (A) is an odd number, for purposes of such paragraph such number shall be reduced by one.

"Currently Insured Individual

"(b) The term 'currently insured individual' means any individual who had not less than six quarters of coverage during the thirteen-quarter period ending with (1) the quarter in which he died, (2) the quarter in which he became entitled to old-age insurance benefits, or (3) the quarter in which he became entitled to primary insurance benefits under this title as in effect prior to the enactment of this section.

"COMPUTATION OF PRIMARY INSURANCE AMOUNT

"Sec. 215. For the purposes of this title—

"Primary Insurance Amount

"(a) (1) The primary insurance amount of an individual who attained age twenty-two after 1950 and with respect to whom not less than six of the quarters elapsing after 1950 are quarters of coverage shall be 50 per centum of the first $100 of his average monthly wage plus 15 per centum of the next $200 of such wage; except that if his average monthly wage is less than $50, his primary insurance amount shall be the amount appearing in column II of the following table on the line on which in column I appears his average monthly wage.

I Average Monthly Wage	II Primary Insurance Amount
$30 or less	$20
$31	$21
$32	$22
$33	$23
$34	$24
$35 to $49	$25

"Average Monthly Wage
*   *   *

"(b) (1) An individual's 'average monthly wage' shall be the quotient obtained by dividing the total of—

"(A) his wages after his starting date (determined under paragraph (2)) and prior to his wage closing date (determined under paragraph (3)), and

"(B) his self-employment income after such starting date and prior to his self-employment income closing date (determined under paragraph (3))

by the number of months elapsing after such starting date and prior to his divisor closing date (determined under paragraph (3)) excluding from such elapsed months any month in any quarter prior to the quarter in which he attained the age of twenty-two which was not a quarter of coverage, except that when the number of such elapsed months thus computed is less than eighteen, it shall be increased to eighteen.

*   *   *

TITLE III—AMENDMENTS TO PUBLIC ASSISTANCE AND MATERNAL AND CHILD WELFARE PROVISIONS OF THE SOCIAL SECURITY ACT

Part 1 — Old-Age Assistance

REQUIREMENTS OF STATE OLD-AGE ASSISTANCE PLANS

*   *   *

COMPUTATION OF FEDERAL PORTION OF OLD-AGE ASSISTANCE

Sec. 302. (a) Section 3 (a) of the Social Security Act is amended to read as follows:

"Sec. 3. (a) From the sums appropriated therefor, the Secretary of the Treasury shall pay to each State which has an approved plan for old-age assistance, for each quarter, beginning with the quarter commencing October 1, 1950, (1) in the case of any State other than Puerto Rico and the Virgin Islands, an amount, which shall be used exclusively as old-age assistance, equal to the sum of the following proportions of the total amounts expended during such quarter as old-age assistance under the State plan, not counting so much of such expenditure with respect to any individual for any month as exceeds $50—

"(A) three-fourths of such expenditures, not counting so much of any expenditure with respect to any month as exceeds the product of $20 multiplied by the total number of such individuals who received old-age assistance for such month; plus

"(B) one-half of the amount by which such expenditures exceed the maximum which may be counted under clause (A);

*   *   *

DEFINITION OF OLD-AGE ASSISTANCE

Sec. 303. (a) Section 6 of the Social Security Act is amended to read as follows:

"DEFINITION

"*Sec. 6.* For the purposes of this title, the term 'old-age assistance' means money payments to, or medical care in behalf of or any type of remedial care recognized under State law in behalf of, needy individuals who are sixty-five years of age or older, but does not include any such payments to or care in behalf of any individual who is an inmate of a public institution (except as a patient in a medical institution) or any individual (a) who is a patient in an institution for tuberculosis or mental diseases, or (b) who has been diagnosed as having tuberculosis or psychosis and is a patient in a medical institution as a result thereof."

*   *   *

Part 2 — Aid to Dependent Children

REQUIREMENTS OF STATE PLANS FOR AID TO DEPENDENT CHILDREN

*   *   *

COMPUTATION OF FEDERAL PORTION OF AID TO DEPENDENT CHILDREN

Sec. 322. (a) Section 403 (a) of the Social Security Act is amended to read as follows:

"*Sec. 403.* (a) From the sums appropriated therefor, the Secretary of the Treasury shall pay to each State which has an approved plan for aid to dependent children, for each quarter, beginning with the quarter commencing October 1, 1950, (1) in the case of any State other than Puerto Rico and the Virgin Islands, an amount, which shall be used exclusively as aid to dependent children, equal to the sum of the following proportions of the total amounts expended during such quarter as aid to dependent children under the State plan, not counting so much of such expenditure with respect to any dependent child for any month as exceeds $27, or if there is more than one dependent child in the same home, as exceeds $27 with respect to one such dependent child and $18 with respect to each of the other dependent children, and not counting so much of such expenditure for any month with respect to a relative with whom any dependent child is living as exceeds $27 —

"(A) three-fourths of such expenditures, not counting so much of the expenditures with respect to any month as exceeds the product of $12 multiplied by the total number of dependent children and other individuals with respect to whom aid to dependent children is paid for such month, plus

"(B) one-half of the amount by which such expenditures exceed the maximum which may be counted under clause (A); . . .

*   *   *

DEFINITION OF AID TO DEPENDENT CHILDREN

Sec. 323. (a) Section 406 of the Social Security Act is amended by striking out subsection (b) and inserting in lieu thereof the following:

"(b) The term 'aid to dependent children' means money payments with respect to, or medical care in behalf of or any type of remedial care recognized under State law in behalf of, a dependent child or dependent children, and (except when used in clause (2) of section 403 (a)) includes money payments or medical care or any type of remedial care recognized under State law for any month to meet the needs of the relative with whom any dependent child is living if money payments have been made under the State plan with respect to such child for such month;

"(c) The term 'relative with whom any dependent child is living' means the individual who is one of the relatives specified in subsection (a) and with whom such child is living (within the meaning of such subsection) in a place of residence maintained by such individual (himself or together with any one or more of the other relatives so specified) as his (or their) own home."

(b) The amendment made by subsection (a) shall take effect October 1, 1950.

*   *   *

Part 4—Aid to the Blind

REQUIREMENTS OF STATE PLANS FOR AID TO THE BLIND

*   *   *

COMPUTATION OF FEDERAL PORTION OF AID TO THE BLIND

Sec. 342. (a) Section 1003 (a) of the Social Security Act is amended to read as follows:

"*Sec. 1003.* (a) From the sums appropriated therefor, the Secretary of the Treasury shall pay to each State which has an approved plan for aid to the blind, for each quarter, beginning with the quarter commencing October 1, 1950, (1) in the case of any State other than Puerto Rico and the Virgin Islands, an amount, which shall be used exclusively as aid to the blind, equal to the sum of the following proportions of the total amounts expended during such quarter as aid to the blind under the State plan, not counting so much of such expenditure with respect to any individual for any month as exceeds $50—

"(A) three-fourths of such expenditures, not counting so much of any expenditure with respect to any month as exceeds the product of $20 multiplied by the total number of such individuals who received aid to the blind for such month, plus

"(B) one-half of the amount by which such expenditures exceed the maximum which may be counted under clause (A);

*   *   *

Part 5—Aid to the Permanently and Totally Disabled

Sec. 351. The Social Security Act is further amended by adding after title XIII thereof the following new title:

"TITLE XIV—GRANTS TO STATES FOR AID TO THE
PERMANENTLY AND TOTALLY DISABLED

"APPROPRIATION

*   *   *

*"STATE PLANS FOR AID TO THE PERMANENTLY AND
TOTALLY DISABLED*

"Sec. 1402. (a) A State plan for aid to the permanently and totally disabled must (1) provide that it shall be in effect in all political subdivisions of the State, and, if administered by them, be mandatory upon them; (2) provide for financial participation by the State; (3) either provide for the establishment or designation of a single State agency to administer the plan, or provide for the establishment or designation of a single State agency to supervise the administration of the plan; (4) provide for granting an opportunity for a fair hearing before the State agency to any individual whose claim for aid to the permanently and totally disabled is denied or is not acted upon with reasonable promptness; (5) provide such methods of administration (including methods relating to the establishment and maintenance of personnel standards on a merit basis, except that the Administrator shall exercise no authority with respect to the selection, tenure of office, and compensation of any individual employed in accordance with such methods) as are found by the Administrator to be necessary for the proper and efficient operation of the plan; (6) provide that the State agency will make such reports, in such form and containing such information, as the Administrator may from time to time require, and comply with such provisions as the Administrator may from time to time find necessary to assure the correctness and verification of such reports; (7) provide that no aid will

be furnished any individual under the plan with respect to any period with respect to which he is receiving old-age assistance under the State plan approved under section 2 of this Act, aid to dependent children under the State plan approved under section 402 of this Act, or aid to the blind under the State plan approved under section 1002 of this Act; (8) provide that the State agency shall, in determining need, take into consideration any other income and resources of an individual claiming aid to the permanently and totally disabled; (9) provide safeguards which restrict the use or disclosure of information concerning applicants and recipients to purposes directly connected with the administration of aid to the permanently and totally disabled; (10) provide that all individuals wishing to make application for aid to the permanently and totally disabled shall have opportunity to do so, and that aid to the permanently and totally disabled shall be furnished with reasonable promptness to all eligible individuals; and (11) effective July 1, 1953, provide, if the plan includes payments to individuals in private or public institutions, for the establishment or designation of a State authority or authorities which shall be responsible for establishing and maintaining standards for such institutions.

* * *

"PAYMENT TO STATES

Sec. 1403. (a) From the sums appropriated therefor, the Secretary of the Treasury shall pay to each State which has an approved plan for aid to the permanently and totally disabled, for each quarter, beginning with the quarter commencing October 1, 1950, (1) in the case of any State other than Puerto Rico and the Virgin Islands, an amount, which shall be used exclusively as aid to the permanently and totally disabled, equal to the sum of the following proportions of the total amounts expended during such quarter as aid to the permanently and totally disabled under the State plan, not counting so much of such expenditure with respect to any individual for any month as exceeds $50—

"(A) three-fourths of such expenditures, not counting so much of any expenditure with respect to any month as exceeds the product of $20 multiplied by the total number of such individuals who received aid to the permanently and totally disabled for such month, plus

"(B) one-half of the amount by which such expenditures exceed the maximum which may be counted under clause (A);

* * *

"DISCLOSURE OF INFORMATION IN POSSESSION OF AGENCY

"Sec. 1106. (a) No disclosure of any return or portion of a return (including information returns and other written statements) filed with the Commissioner of Internal Revenue under title VIII of the Social Security Act or under subchapter E of chapter 1 or subchapter A of chapter 9 of the

Internal Revenue Code, or under regulations made under authority thereof, which has been transmitted to the Administrator by the Commissioner of Internal Revenue, or of any file, record, report, or other paper, or any information, obtained at any time by the Administrator or by any officer or employee of the Federal Security Agency in the course of discharging the duties of the Administrator under this Act, and no disclosure of any such file, record, report, or other paper, or information, obtained at any time by any person from the Administrator or from any officer or employee of the Federal Security Agency, shall be made except as the Administrator may by regulations prescribe. Any person who shall violate any provision of this section shall be deemed guilty of a misdemeanor and, upon conviction thereof, shall be punished by a fine not exceeding $1,000, or by imprisonment not exceeding one year, or both.

*   *   *

PROVISIONS OF STATE UNEMPLOYMENT COMPENSATION LAWS

Sec. 405. (a) Section 1603 (c) of the Internal Revenue Code is amended (1) by striking out the phrase "changed its law" and inserting in lieu thereof "amended its law", and (2) by adding before the period at the end thereof the following: "and such finding has become effective. Such finding shall become effective on the ninetieth day after the Governor of the State has been notified thereof unless the State has before such ninetieth day so amended its law that it will comply substantially with the Secretary of Labor's interpretation of the provision of subsection (a), in which event such finding shall not become effective. No finding of a failure to comply substantially with the provision in State law specified in paragraph (5) of subsection (a) shall be based on an application or interpretation of State law with respect to which further administrative or judicial review is provided for under the laws of the State".

(b) Section 303 (b) of the Social Security Act is amended by inserting before the period at the end thereof the following: "*:Provided*, That there shall be no finding under clause (1) until the question of entitlement shall have been decided by the highest judicial authority given jurisdiction under such State law; *Provided further*, That any costs may be paid with respect to any claimant by a State and included as costs of administration of its law".

*   *   *

Presidential Statement
Upon Signing the Social Security Act Amendments
(August 28, 1950)*

I have today appoved H.R. 6000, the Social Security Act Amendments of 1950. These amendments greatly strengthen the old-age and survivors

*Ibid., p. 600.

insurance system and the public assistance programs originally established by the Social Security Act of 1935.

The passage of this legislation is an outstanding achievement. In this act the 81st Congress has doubled insurance benefits and brought 10 million more persons under old-age and survivors insurance — including those whose insurance rights were taken away by the 80th Congress. Millions of others will benefit from the new public assistance provisions giving help to the disabled and to dependent children. For the first time American citizens in Puerto Rico and the Virgin Islands will be covered under both the insurance and assistance programs. In addition, veterans of World War II will now receive wage credits for military service in computing their insurance benefits.

This act will help a great many people right away. Three million aged persons, widows, and orphans will receive increased insurance benefits beginning with the month of September. A million more will begin to receive increased payments within the next few months. Nearly 3 million needy persons will benefit from increased Federal aid to the States for public assistance purposes.

By making it possible for most families to obtain protection through the contributory insurance system, and by increasing insurance benefits, the act will ultimately reduce dependence on public charity. This measure demonstrates our determination to achieve real economic security for the American family. This kind of progressive, forward-looking legislation is the best possible way to prove that our democratic institutions can provide both freedom and security for all our citizens.

We still have much to do before our social security programs are fully adequate. While the new act greatly increases coverage, many more people still need to be brought into the old-age and survivors insurance system. Expanded coverage and increased benefits in old-age insurance should now be matched by steps to strengthen our unemployment insurance system. At the same time, we urgently need a system of insurance against loss of wages through temporary or permanent disability. These and other vital improvements in our social security laws are needed in addition to the act which I have signed today. I shall continue to urge action on this unfinished business and I know that the committees of Congress are now preparing to give these matters serious consideration.

There is one very unfortunate feature in the new law. This is the so-called Knowland amendment, tacked on as a rider in the Senate. It may result in undermining the safeguards enacted by the Congress to protect workers against loss of unemployment insurance benefits if they refused to accept employment at substandard wages or working conditions. This amendment has nothing whatever to do with old-age insurance or public assistance, the main subjects of the new law. While the other provisions of the bill were the product of thorough consideration in the committees of both Houses, neither committee ever had an opportunity to hold hearings on the Knowland amendment. I trust that the Congress will reconsider this ill-advised provision and will act promptly to remove it from the social security laws.

Both the House Committee on Ways and Means and the Senate Committee on Finance have already announced that they intend to study proposals for further improvement in our social security programs. Members of these committees have worked long and faithfully on the act which I have signed today. I am confident that their future efforts will be equally productive in advancing social security in this country.

Unemployment Compensation

President Truman was anxious both in 1949 and in 1950 to see some action on unemployment compensation and in the budget message for 1950 he discussed his proposals.

Annual Budget Message of the President
(January 17, 1950)*

Trust accounts and unemployment compensation legislation. — Last year's temporary but sharp rise in unemployment provided the first real test of the Federal-State unemployment insurance system since its establishment 15 years ago. The system was of great help in tiding workers over temporary unemployment and in sustaining markets for the products of employed workers. During the last 12 months, a total of 1.7 billion dollars in benefits was paid from the trust fund. At the same time, major shortcomings of the present system became painfully clear. It does not cover enough workers, and does not replace enough of the wages lost through unemployment. I shall submit proposals for legislation to overcome these and other defects by strengthening the present Federal-State system.

At present, only about two-thirds of the workers employed in nonagricultural industries are insured against the hazards of temporary unemployment. Coverage should be extended to employees of small establishments, of industries processing agricultural products, and of the Federal Government. This would raise coverage to about three-fourths of nonagricultural workers. Furthermore, legislation should include minimum Federal standards for eligibility and disqualifications, in order to remove some of the present inequalities in administration among the States.

Present weekly benefits now average about one-third of previously earned weekly wages. The insurance was originally intended to replace at least half of previous earnings — the minimum needed to pay for food and rent

*Public Papers of the Presidents, Harry S. Truman, 1950, p. 99.

—but benefits in many States have not kept up with price rises. In order to assure more nearly adequate benefits throughout the Nation, the Federal law should provide minimum standards for benefits paid from the State trust accounts. These standards should require benefits of 50 percent of previous wages up to 30 dollars a week for single workers, with additional amounts for dependents up to 42 dollars a week for a worker with three dependents. The legislation should also require that benefits be available to eligible claimants for at least 26 weeks.

In addition to these changes in coverage and benefit standards, I shall recommend amendments to the finanancing provisions of present legislation, including establishment of a reinsurance system to provide grants to States whose reserves for benefits become temporarily low, despite reasonable measures to maintain adequate funds. Although most States have sufficient reserves to pay higher benefits without increasing taxes, one or two States may need assistance by next autumn or shortly thereafter.

The proposed legislation will affect chiefly the trust fund rather than the appropriations for administration. For both the trust fund and the appropriations, the effect in the fiscal year 1951 will be slight because time will be required for the State legislatures to revise their laws to conform with new standards established by the Congress. Benefits for Federal workers will represent the principal continuing budgetary cost of my recommendations. (The estimated expenditures for these benefits in the fiscal year 1951 are shown under general government.) Estimates for proposed reinsurance appropriations are also included in the Budget. Expenditures from these appropriations will be necessary only if State reserves become inadequate to provide for temporarily high numbers of insured unemployed.

However, it soon became necessary for the President to reiterate his remarks about unemployment insurance.

Special Presidential Message to the Congress on the Unemployment Insurance System
(April 6, 1950)*

To the Congress of the United States:

One of the great advances in economic legislation made during the 1930's was to establish the Federal-State system of employment security. This system has two parts—first, a nation-wide employment service to help workers find jobs and employers find job-seekers, and, second, a nation-wide system of unemployment insurance to help tide workers over periods of unemployment.

Ibid., p. 244 *et seq.*

Finding a job is of more importance to an unemployed worker, of course, then receiving unemployment insurance benefits. Consequently, great emphasis has always been placed on strengthening and improving the employment service.

We cannot, however, completely eliminate unemployment; even in times of high employment, there will be turnover of jobs and numerous shifts and changes in job opportunities. Consequently, we must have a strong and steadily improving system of unemployment insurance.

Under our Federal-State unemployment insurance system, benefits are paid, in accordance with State laws, to workers who, while able and seeking to work, are unemployed through no fault of their own. These benefits are paid from the proceeds of State payroll taxes, which are deposited in reserve accounts—one for each State—in the Unemployment Trust Fund in the United States Treasury.

In the past twelve years, unemployment insurance has proved its worth not only as an invaluable source of support to unemployed workers and their families, but also as a means of maintaining purchasing power of great value to the entire economy. In 1949, for example, 1.7 billion dollars in benefits were paid to more than seven million individuals, the largest amount for any year in the history of the system. This was a significant factor in preventing serious dislocations during last year's period of economic readjustment.

Our experience with unemployment insurance has revealed weaknesses as well as strengths in the existing system. While many improvements have been made in the State laws since the program began, the system is far from adequate today.

Over 15 million workers—about one-third of all employees—are not protected by unemployment insurance. In 1949, only about one-fifth of the purchasing power lost through unemployment was replaced by unemployment insurance benefits. In 1949, weekly benefits averaged only about $20—not enough to preserve a minimum standard of living. Nearly 2 million workers used up their benefits entirely—showing that benefits were not available for a long enough period. While the unemployment reserve funds of the States have so far proved to be adequate, a few States may soon face financial difficulties because of local concentration of unemployment.

On several occasions in recent years, I have recommended that the system be improved, to extend protection to many workers not now covered; to provide, in every State, benefits for 26 weeks ranging up to $30 a week for single persons, with additional benefits for dependents; and to increase the financial stability of the system.

Action on these proposals has become more urgent as unemployment has increased somewhat in spite of the continuing high levels of business activity. While unemployment dropped over half a million between February and March, on the average nearly 4½ million persons were looking for work during the first three months of this year, as compared to 3 million in the same months of 1949, and nearly 2½ million in 1948. Furthermore, the length of time it takes people to find jobs is becoming longer. One million people—about one out of every four unemployed—have been out of work for 15 weeks or more. A year ago, only 420,000 were without jobs that long, and in 1948, only 330,000.

This gradual growth in unemployment over the last two years is not because there are fewer jobs. Employment has remained at high levels, along with industrial production, consumer incomes, and other indicators of the health of our economy.

But there are more people looking for work. In recent years, up to one million more people have come into the labor market each year, looking for work, than have left the labor market. Part of the new group entering the labor market this year will be the largest number of college graduates in our history—some 500,000 young people, including about 250,000 veterans. In addition, of course, a large number of high school graduates will also be looking for jobs.

Furthermore, as new plants and equipment have been added and supplies of raw materials have become more ample, businessmen have been able to produce more with the same number of workers.

Thus, our labor force has increased, our productivity has increased, but the number of jobs has not kept pace. This emphasizes the importance of expanding our economy so that new jobs will be created to use skills and energies that are now being wasted. It also emphasizes the importance of making better provision for those who are temporarily out of work.

The Congress now is well along toward completing action on legislation to improve the old-age and survivors' insurance and public assistance programs. Like those programs, the unemployment insurance system needs to be improved in the light of experience. Accordingly, I recommend that the Congress turn its attention as soon as possible to strengthening our Federal-State unemployment insurance system.

First, I recommend that coverage be extended to about 6 million workers not now covered. The first major deficiency in the present Federal-State system of unemployment insurance is that it excludes large numbers of workers.

Coverage should be extended to employees of small firms—those employing one to seven workers. Workers in firms employing fewer than eight workers were originally left out of the Federal law because of expected administrative difficulties. In fact, however, such employees have been satisfactorily covered for years under the Federal old-age and survivors' insurance system, and 17 States have already extended their unemployment compensation systems to cover them, without encountering any serious administrative difficulties. Many other States are waiting for the Federal Government to act, and have provisions in their laws which would cover these employees automatically when the coverage of the Federal Act is extended. No reason exists for discriminating longer in the Federal law against such workers.

Coverage should also be extended to Federal Government civilian employees. Although the Federal Government took the leadership in establishing a system of unemployment insurance for workers in private industry, it has not assumed the same obligation toward its own employees. Yet the rate at which Federal workers—especially manual workers—are separated from their jobs is approximately as high as in private industry. Federal workers should no longer be denied the protection of unemployment insurance.

I also propose extensions of coverage to about 500,000 persons who are employed on a commission basis, and about 200,000 workers in occupations of an industrial nature connected with agriculture, all of whom are excluded at present. Moreover, the Federal unemployment insurance legislation should be extended to Puerto Rico, subject to its acceptance by the Territorial Legislature.

Second, I recommend the establishment of nation-wide minimum levels for amounts and duration of unemployment benefits, in order to correct the second major deficiency in the present unemployment insurance system —the inadequacy of benefits.

At present, while the Federal law includes a number of standards which the States are required to meet, it does not establish minimum levels for benefit amounts or duration. Maximum weekly benefits in the various States now range from $15 to $27 for single persons; benefits are somewhat larger for persons with dependents in the 11 States providing dependents' allowances. With these maximum levels, average weekly benefits for the Nation as a whole were just over $20 in 1949.

The variations among States create serious inequities. They mean that workers who lose their jobs in identical circumstances are treated very differently because of the accident of geographical location. They mean that businessmen in some States suffer a greater loss in markets when unemployment occurs than do those in other States.

Furthermore, while the States generally have increased benefits in recent years, so that the situation is not nearly so bad as in the case of old-age and survivors' benefits, in most States the increases in benefits have lagged considerably behind increases in wages and costs of living. Thus, unemployment benefits today replace a smaller proportion of a worker's regular wages than was the case when the system was started.

For these reasons, I believe that nationwide minimums should be established by law which will assure adequate benefits in all States. The standards proposed are these: benefits for single persons should approximate 50 percent of normal earnings, up to a maximum of at least $30 a week. Additional allowances should be granted for individuals with dependents. The proportion of previous earnings replaced would vary with the number of dependents, up to a maximum of 70 percent of wages, or $42, whichever is lower, for an individual with three or more dependents.

These standards are not high. If they had been in effect, the national average weekly benefits in 1949 would have been just over $24. But this would be a substantial improvement in an income level which, at best, is intended to provide only for subsistence expenses. Furthermore, uniform standards would reduce present inequities in benefit levels among different States. Some variation in benefit amounts would and should remain, reflecting the differences in wage levels and costs of living in different parts of the country.

At present, the maximum duration of benefits varies among the States from 12 to 26 weeks. Like the variation in size of benefits, this is inequitable, and in many States simply represents a lag in reaching what was considered from the beginning to be a desirable standard, but which was originally set low because of actuarial uncertainties. With this wide range, the average duration of benefits in 1949 was less than 13 weeks. Because of the short duration of benefits, nearly 2 million workers exhausted their rights to benefits before finding another job.

Benefits should be available for at least 26 weeks in a year to all workers who are out of work that long. Experience in the States which have increased the duration of benefits is that while average duration does not rise very much, because most workers find a new job before using up benefits, the number who use up their benefits entirely is markedly decreased. It is estimated that, under my proposal, the number of workers who exhausted their benefits in 1949 would have been only half as large as it was.

The combined effect of my recommendations for extended coverage, higher benefits, and longer duration, would have resulted in about $850 million more in benefits—and in consumer demand—in 1949. The cost of these improvements would be moderate. At the same time that weekly benefits are raised, the upper limit to the amount of wages taxed should be raised from $3,000 to $4,800 per worker, in line with the increases in wage levels. On this basis, the combined cost of all benefits for all States under these proposals would have been about 1.2 percent of taxable payrolls in in 1948 and 2.5 percent in 1949—compared with actual costs (on the basis of the present $3,000 wage limit) of .9 percent of taxable payrolls in 1948 and 2.2 percent in 1949.

In most States, the rate of tax has been extremely low in recent years —many employers have had to pay no tax whatever. Some States have had to increase rates somewhat last year or this year, but in all but a few cases, taxes are still well below the rate of 2.7 percent contemplated when the system was started. Under my proposals, many States would not have to increase tax rates to cover all the increased costs, since they still have excess reserves. Most, if not all, States would find no trouble meeting the additional costs within the 2.7 percent tax rate.

Consequently, I believe that the standards I propose will achieve substantial improvement in the unemployment insurance system, benefiting both workers and businessmen, at very reasonable costs. As is the case at present with respect to coverage, the Federal law should not prevent the States from exceeding the minimum standards if they wish to do so.

Third, I recommend that adequate methods should be required to provide benefits for workers who move from one State to another.

Clearly a worker who is employed in two different States during a year is as entitled to unemployment insurance benefits when out of work as a worker who is employed in only one. The States have generally recognized this, and have attempted voluntarily to work out methods for paying benefits in such interstate cases. They have, however, been only partially successful. Interstate workers generally must wait much longer to receive benefits than intrastate workers. Furthermore, the benefits of many interstate workers are lower than if they had worked in only one State.

It is a difficult problem to develop adequate methods for paying benefits promptly and equitably to interstate workers in our Federal-State unemployment insurance system. Nevertheless, it is in the national interest to encourage the mobility of labor, since that is indispensable to economic expansion in a free society like ours. Consequently, I believe that the States should be required to adopt such methods as are necessary to provide fair and adequate protection for interstate workers.

Fourth, I recommend that both Federal and State laws concerning fraud and disqualifications should be revised and improved.

It was a weakness in the original Federal legislation that it did not clearly require the States to deal adequately with the question of fraud. Some States — without going to uneconomical extremes in inspection and policing — have instituted effective methods for preventing or detecting fraudulent claims. I believe, however, that the Federal law should be clarified so that all States can be required to have adequate means for dealing with those few individuals who attempt to obtain benefits through misrepresentation.

During the last few years, some States have considerably enlarged the number of reasons for disqualifying workers who seek unemployment benefits and have increased the severity of penalties for disqualification. These excessive disqualifications have operated to prevent persons who are genuinely out of work through no fault of their own from receiving benefits. These over-severe disqualification provisions, which penalize the innocent along with the guilty, should be corrected.

Fifth, I recommend, at this time, two improvements in the financing arrangements for unemployment insurance.

Since the beginning of the program, a small part of the unemployment tax has been collected by the Federal Government and included in general Federal revenues. The administrative costs of the program — both Federal and State — have been paid out of general Federal revenues, and have never been as large as the Federal unemployment tax collections. I propose that the Federal unemployment tax be paid into a special Federal unemployment account in the Unemployment Trust Fund (which now includes the separate State reserve accounts for the payment of benefits). This account would be used exclusively to pay the cost of State and Federal administration of the employment security program, and the cost of reinsurance grants, to be available to States who encounter temporarily severe financial difficulties.

Experience has demonstrated that the cost of unemployment insurance varies widely among the different States. This is mainly due to differences in each State's economic structure and in the incidence of unemployment in certain industries, which are beyond the control of the individual State. It has become evident that a few States, while able to finance an adequate system of unemployment insurance in normal periods, may not be able to maintain the solvency of their unemployment funds in a period of severe unemployment under the present financial provisions provided in the Federal legislation. So that these States will not be forced to increase their tax rates unduly during periods of declining employment and payrolls, the legislation should be amended to provide assistance to such States through reinsurance grants when their funds approach exhaustion. This will be a major step toward strengthening our Federal-State system of unemployment insurance, since it will, without detracting from the independence of State action, gain some of the advantages of pooled reserves.

A strengthened unemployment insurance system not only will furnish more adequate aid to those who become unemployed, but also will do more to maintain the high volume of consumer purchasing power so necessary to the welfare of the entire economy. Thus it is a strong element in our program to support growth and expansion in the economy.

Our essential economic problem is to put to sound, productive use our increasing technical knowledge and our growing labor force. To this end, we need imaginative and enterprising investment – in plant capacity, in new equipment, in basic resource development. To this end, we need vigorous competition and a growing number of new businesses. To this end, we need a stable agriculture, sensible wage-price-profit decisions, and mature labor-management relations. To this end, we need an expanding world economy, with a productive flow of international trade and investment.

Both private and public policies must be directed to these purposes, and I have recommended a series of measures to the Congress for Federal action. My present proposal to strengthen our unemployment insurance system is one of these measures.

I am particularly urging action at this session of Congress on unemployment insurance because State legislation must follow the Federal amendments. Action by the Congress this year would clear the way for State action in 1951, when practically all of the State legislatures will be meeting in regular session.

But the primary reason for Congressional action is the real need of those who are unemployed. The unemployment insurance system is a tried and proven means of assisting them. That system urgently needs strengthening. I therefore request favorable consideration of these recommendations at this session of Congress.

Harry S. Truman

It was not to be a successful year for unemployment compensation changes. Dr. Altmeyer did raise some new issues in his testimony and the Knowland Amendment was passed but these were the only results of the President's extensive campaign.

THE FINAL TWO YEARS: 1951–1952

1951

One trait has characterized the Social Security Administration from its inception: a belief that all social security legislation is only a prelude to more such legislation. However, in the public assistance programs and especially in ADC—things were getting worse. It was now questionable that the insurance provisions of social security would ultimately drive aid programs out of business and the existence of the hard-core poor had already become evident. The reports of the Subcommittee on Low Income Families made gloomy reading.

Low-Income Families and Economic Stability
Report of the Subcommittee on Low-Income Families
(Submitted to the Joint Committee on the Economic Report)
March 9, 1950
(p. 3)

Raising the incomes of the lowest third may be accomplished either by transferring wealth from the more fortunate members of the economy, that is, by taxation and subsidy, or by providing better opportunities for the members of the low-income group to develop their own productive capacities and so to become full partners in American prosperity. While the first method, the palliative of relief, may be necessary for a small proportion of the low-income families, we believe that most of them will rise by their own efforts—once they are given the traditional American fair field and no favor. To this end we have aimed our investigation and designed our recommendations. We believe that our study and our hearings have established three ruling principles to guide constructive plans to raise the productivity and incomes of the lowest third.

First, good employment opportunities are essential; the economy must be kept at high levels of employment and production. Our success in raising the productivity and incomes of the lower groups depends upon our success in solving the problems of investment, of monetary and fiscal policies, and of periodical unemployment. These problems are now being studied by other subcommittees of the Joint Committee on the Economic Report. Long-range policies such as we recommend can never succeed against a background of drastically fluctuating employment, for the lowest third suffers most in periods of deflation and depression.

The problem of low income and dependency is only in part a problem of unemployment and the business cycle; maintaining full employment is a necessary but not a sufficient condition for the solution of the problem. Even in times of good employment opportunities as in 1948, a large proportion of the Nation's families had low incomes. Of the 10,000,000 families with money incomes of less than $2,000 in 1948, only about 420,000, or 5 percent, reported their family head as "unemployed" when the census income survey was made.[8] Hence, long-run measures to increase productivity and incomes are necessary, and we have devoted our attention primarily to such recommendations.

Second, development of human resources should be fostered by providing equal opportunities for all to improve and use their own capacities. Initative can be encouraged and given room to work by calculated measures but simply passing a law will not do the job. No legislation or community action can guarantee a good living, but much can be done to provide equal opportunity to make a good living.[9]

Third, we believe there is a danger that poverty and dependency may tend to perpetuate themselves by a vicious circle process. Opportunities should be provided to break this circle.[10] For example, there is a clear tendency for low incomes to result in poor education for the children of poorer families. The committee on the objectives of a general education in a free society, of Harvard University, has estimated that the lower-income group sends only about 30 percent of its children through high school and about 5 percent to college. It is usually a sacrifice for parents in this group to keep their children even in high school and they cannot possibly pay money toward college.[11] In turn, deficient education tends to result in low incomes for the children, by disqualifying them for better-paying jobs.[12]

[8]Materials on the Problem of Low Income Families, table A-3, p. 62.
[9]Testimony of Msgr. L. G. Ligutti, executive director of the National Catholic Rural Life Conference. December 21, 1949.
[10]Testimony of Dr. Caroline F. Ware, December 14, 1949.
[11]Materials on the Problem of Low-Income Families, p. 17.
[12]Ibid., pp. 15–16, also appendix E-2, pp. 109-110.

Similar cycles can be traced in the relations between incomes and factors such as health, juvenile delinquency, geographical location, and housing. Thus, poverty and low living standards of the present generation tend to breed poverty and low living standards for the next. We believe that these vicious circles can be broken by measures calculated to enlarge and equalize opportunities for all our people. In the balance of this report, we have arranged our recommendations for such measures according to the principal categories of the low-income group; the rural low-income family, the unskilled, the broken family, the disabled, and the aged.

Conclusion

The two greatest economic (and social) problems of our time come within the field of inquiry and advice assigned to the Joint Committee on the Economic Report by act of Congress.

One problem is the maintenance of employment, production and consumption at high levels and without severe fluctuations. The other problem (to which this report addresses itself) is how to bring within this circle of high employment, production, and consumption the millions who fail to find entrance even in good times.

The comfortable thing to do is to assume deficiencies of inheritance, to this group of our citizens, to assume that they are just congenital morons. This leads to the conclusion that nothing can be done about it. Or, instead, we may assume that the difficulties of these people are due to moral delinquency and so assuming, we may view this national lesion with a warm, moral glow.

While the impoverished circumstances of some families may be associated with the elements of bad inheritance and moral degeneracy, we must not assume that they constitute the major part of the problem. Nor should we assume that such elements cannot be diminished or compensated for. Causes and cures of low incomes in America exist and they must be sought and found.

Our concern is a humanitarian one. But it is more than this. The area we have been studying is that which furnishes a fertile bed for the seeds of physical and social disease. It is a powerful instrument for the fomentation of political movements which seek to destroy our way of life. It is essential that this threat to our existence as a nation of free men and women be removed by bringing the majority of these low-income groups within our system of high employment, production, distribution, and consumption.

However, no one — least of all President Truman — was yet prepared to consider public assistance a permanent part of the social scene. His annual budget message in 1951 reinforced this position.

Annual Budget Message of the President
(January 15, 1951)*

*   *   *

Social Security, Welfare, and Health

Last year the Congress enacted important improvements in our social security program. Coverage under old-age and survivors insurance was extended to some 10 million additional workers. Eligibility requirements were relaxed for older people, so that many more will qualify for retirement annuities in the near future. The level of benefits was raised substantially and the taxable wage base was increased moderately, to make the benefits and the taxes more commensurate with earnings.

In taking this step, the Congress clearly decided that social insurance, rather than public assistance, is to be the primary vehicle for providing social security in this country. This accords fully with our American tradition of self-reliance. In the future, the great majority of American families will obtain, through their own and their employers' contributions, a considerable degree of insurance protection against poverty arising from the old age or death of the wage earner.

In spite of these far-reaching improvements, however, the Nation's social insurance program still does not measure up to the full needs or aspirations of the American people; nor has it by any means achieved the scope of protection that our economy can afford and should give. Millions of people, including self-employed farmers, many domestic and agricultural workers, many public employees, and members of the Armed Forces, still are not under social insurance. Our aim should be to establish for all employed people a minimum protection that each person takes with him wherever he works. Pension and insurance plans for special groups should supplement social security benefits, as industry pensions already do for several million workers. Moreover, we need to fill important gaps in our social insurance system by providing protection on a prepaid basis against the costs of medical care and the loss of family income in cases of disability. These measures will help to provide that material security which is essential to a vigorous democracy and a highly productive labor force.

All Federal programs of social security, welfare, and health are estimated to require expenditures of 2.6 billion dollars in the fiscal year 1952, an increase of 105 million dollars over the current year. Three-fourths of the expenditures are for public assistance, for accident compensation payments, and for the transfer of railroad payroll tax receipts to the railroad retirement trust account. The amounts of these expenditures are all determined by statutory requirements. The remaining one-fourth provides for all the public health activities of the Government, for aid to various special groups, and

Public Papers of the Presidents, Harry S. Truman, 1951, p. 96 et seq.

for the Federal Bureau of Investigation and other crime control and correction services.

Public assistance. — The same legislation which extended coverage of old-age and survivors insurance also made changes in the Federal-State public assistance program. It authorized Federal grants for assistance to totally and permanently disabled persons, extended the aid for dependent children to include a relative who takes care of such children, and provided for Federal sharing of payments made by the States to hospitals and doctors furnishing medical care for persons receiving public assistance.

With many more persons eligible now or in the near future for old-age and survivors insurance benefits, and with the increased employment opportunities of the defense economy, public assistance should conform more nearly to its intended purpose of filling gaps in social insurance. Thus, increases in expenditures resulting from the new public assistance legislation are expected to be largely offset by decreases resulting from a reduction in the number of children and old people on the public assistance rolls. The estimated expenditures of 1.3 billion dollars for public assistance in the fiscal year 1952 exceeds by 20 million dollars the amount for the current year.

Ironically, the main social security bill before Congress in 1951 was concerned with the federal contribution to public assistance programs. H.R. 2416, a tax measure, was amended in the Senate to increase the federal participation in OAA and AB by $5 a month and in ADC by $3 a month. After approval by voice vote, however, Senator Taft led a movement to send the bill back to committee, arguing that the increase in the federal share would not insure any increase for recipients. When the bill re-emerged from committee, the increases were limited to $3 and $2, but the McFarland Amendment insured that the whole increase would be passed on.

The President was far from happy with the work of the Senate:

Letter to the President of the Senate on a Pending Bill to Increase Public Assistance Payments
(July 18, 1951)*

Dear Mr. Vice President: I understand that the Senate Committee on Finance has reported to the Senate an amendment to H.R. 2416, a tax bill already passed by the House. This amendment is intended to increase by about three dollars per month the Federal share of State public assistance payments to needy individuals who are aged, blind, or disabled. A similar increase of about two dollars per month would be provided for dependent children. This amendment would add about $140 million per year to Federal expenditures for public assistance.

Ibid., p. 395–97.

It seems to me that any legislation to increase public assistance payments should take account of the relationship between those payments and the amounts paid under our old age and survivors insurance system.

In considering increases in public assistance payments, it is vitally important that we all keep clearly in mind the basic purpose of public assistance. Its purpose is and has always been to supplement our social insurance system. Our aim has been to expand coverage of social insurance and gradually reduce the need for supplementary public assistance programs. It is essential that a proper relationship be maintained between insurance benefits and assistance payments. At the very least, average benefits from insurance should be as high as average payments under public assistance. Today, the average payment in both programs is about forty-three dollars per month. An increase in public assistance alone would, therefore, result in an average insurance benefit lower than the average assistance payment.

This would be a highly undesirable result for the future of both programs. As the Senate Committee on Finance pointed out in its report on the Social Security Act Amendments of 1950:

> Your committee's impelling concern . . . has been to take immediate effective steps to cut down the need for further expansion of public assistance . . . Unless the insurance system is expanded and improved so that it in fact offers a basic security to retired persons and to survivors, there will be continual and irresistible pressure for putting more and more Federal funds into less constructive assistance programs. We consider the assistance methods to have serious disadvantages to the long-run approach to the Nation's social security problem.

The logic of this report certainly applies in the case of the present amendment. The relationship between the insurance and assistance programs established by the Social Security Act Amendments of 1950 should not now be upset to the detriment of insurance.

If public assistance payments are now to be increased, then old age and survivors insurance benefits should also be increased to at least an equal degree.

Fortunately, it is now possible to increase these insurance benefits without changing the actuarial status of the old age and survivors insurance system as calculated when the Social Security Act Amendments were adopted last year. This is true because the increases in wages which have since taken place will mean a greater increase in the income of the insurance fund than in the liabilities which that fund will be called upon to bear.

As for the increase in public assistance payments provided by the amendment now before the Senate, I believe that consideration should be given to including a provision which would make it entirely clear that the additional funds are actually to be passed along without delay, to the people who receive State aid.

Although practically all the States would receive additional Federal funds under the formula provided in this amendment, the amendment itself provides no assurance that these increases would be passed on promptly to individuals. When the Federal share in the public assistance program was increased in October 1948, the short-run effect was to substitute some Federal funds for State and local funds going into current programs. An immediate result was to make the average increase in payments to invididuals less, in many cases, than had been intended by the Congress. If new increases are now to be authorized, we should take care to avoid a repetition of this experience.

Harry S. Truman

The White House
Washington D.C.

The Senate went ahead to pass its version of H.R. 2416 by voice vote, but the House refused to hold a conference and, at the end of the session, the bill was still in the House Ways and Means Committee.

The only social security legislation passed in 1951 was an Administration-opposed provision, allowing states to open their relief rolls to public inspection without losing their right to federal grants-in-aid. This was a breach of the confidentiality requirements which early social security legislation had imposed. Introduced by Senator William E. Jenner of Indiana as an amendment to H.R. 2416, the provision was ultimately incorporated into the Revenue Act of 1951 (H.R. 4473, P.L. 183).

1952

In 1952 with an election pending and Democratic majorities in both houses, the President moved to improve the social security system. His report to Congress on January 16, 1952 set the tone.

Presidential Economic Report to Congress
(January 16, 1952)*

To meet urgent needs in the health field, programs for Federal aid to medical education and the strengthening of local public health services should be enacted promptly. I have recently appointed a Commission on the Health Needs of the Nation, composed of professional and lay persons, which will make an objective study of vital health problems, including the provision of adequate health care to all our people at prices they can afford to pay.

Certain extensions and changes in the old-age and survivors insurance program, in line with longer-range objectives, would, if undertaken promptly,

Public Papers of the Presidents, Harry S. Truman, 1952, p. 46.

yield the additional advantage of helping those groups who have been hit hardest by past inflation. Raising the level of benefit payments is especially desirable, and other improvements should include raising the taxable wage base, extending the coverage to farmers and certain other groups, and providing for permanent and total disability.

To provide more adequate protection against unemployment, I recommend the enactment of legislation to strengthen the present Federal-State unemployment insurance system, along the lines suggested in my message to the Congress on April 6, 1950. Legislation for this purpose is now pending before the Congress, providing specifically for extension of coverage to additional workers, establishment of nation-wide minimum levels for amounts and duration of unemployment benefits, establishment of adequate methods to assure payment of benefits to workers who move from one State to another, and improvements in administration of the system.

The details of the program were spelled out in the annual budget message on January 21, 1952.

At the beginning of the 1952 session of Congress, liberal Congressmen in both the House and Senate introduced bills to extend the social security system. The Administration bill, H.R. 7800, emerged on May 12 from the House Ways and Means Committee where no hearings had been held. Chairman Doughty took the view that the bill covered areas "extensively studied" in previous hearings.

The main features of the bill as it was introduced were a $20 increase in the amount an OASI beneficiary might earn without losing benefits, and an increase in the amounts of benefits. The provision which was to cause greatest trouble was one which froze the benefits of the disabled by preserving their insurance rights (OASI) without actually establishing disability insurance.

The bill was introduced on May 19, and the substantive debate took place amid a procedural discussion of the gag rule.

The Republican opposition naturally objected to the absence of any hearings and especially disliked disability provisions which generated considerable concern about "socialized medicine". For supporters of the bill the most cheering speech was Mr. Forand's who gradually established himself as a leading proponent of an espansive view of social security.

The "socialized medicine" scare resulted in a 151–141 vote in favor of the bill—forty-four votes short of the two-thirds majority needed to suspend the rules.

The bill came up again on June 16, again under a suspension of the rules. This time the Administration toned down the power of the Social Security Administrator to determine disability, the presumed basis of the AMA spectre of "socialized medicine."

The AMA was far from satisfied and filled the Congressional Record *with insertions of the Oath of Hippocrates, resolutions of the AMA House of*

Delegates, and cables from hundreds of county medical societies. This political pressure was answered most effectively by Representative John D. Dingell. Other Democrats used the opportunity to blast traditional Republican opposition to social security. This time the Ways and Means Committee had better control over the House and after Chairman Doughty had put his imprimatur on the bill, it passed easily.

The Senate Finance Committee also reported the bill out without holding any hearings, but the AMA was more successful there than it had been in the House. Therefore the provision freezing insurance rights during disability was omitted and the chief features of the bill as it came to the Senate floor were benefit increases and liberalization of the retirement test. However, it was the changes in public assistance rather than in OASI which aroused the most interest. Senator Ernest W. McFarland of Arizona, introduced an amendment which raised the federal share in all four PA programs by $5 a month. And the amendment was carried by a voice vote. The bill was generally supported by old line liberals like Senator Hubert H. Humphrey of Minnesota and Senator James E. Murray of Montana, but the Republicans continued their scepticism about the "insurance" aspect of OASI, and called for a re-examination of the old-age programs.

In conference the bill was subjected to one remarkable compromise: the disputed disability freeze provision was allowed, but unless legislation activated it in 1953, the provision was to be still-born. A sum of $75 a month was set as a maximum for earnings before social security benefits were lost. In general there was an overall increase in OASI benefits and a revision of the benefit formula (to a federal share of 55 per cent of the first $100 in average monthly wages and 15 per cent of the next $200) in OAA. In addition, the House accepted the Senate's changes in public assistance grants-in-aid on condition the increase had a two-year limitation. The President was pleased with the new bill except for the disability freeze compromise.

Presidential Statement Upon Signing the
Social Security Act Amendments
(July 18, 1952)*

I have today signed H.R. 7800, the Social Security Act Amendments of 1952. This is an important landmark in the progress of our social security system.

The new law increases old-age and survivors insurance benefits by an average of $6 per month. The new law also makes certain increases in the minimum benefits under the Railroad Retirement System. These increases become effective for the month of September and will add to the incomes of more than 4.5 million people now drawing benefits from these insurance systems.

*Ibid., p. 486–88.

Both systems are further improved by increasing from $50 to $75 per month the amount which a person can earn without losing his insurance benefit. In addition, members of the Armed Forces serving from 1947 through 1953, will now receive the same employment credit under the old-age and survivors insurance system that was granted servicemen during World War II.

The new law also increases by $250 million per year, the amount of the Federal contribution to the States for public assistance. This will make it possible for the States to increase assistance payments to the 5 million dependent children and aged, blind, and disabled citizens now receiving State help to meet their minimum financial needs. Increases will amount to about $3 per month for dependent children, and $5 per month for the rest, provided that the States use all the new Federal funds to increase total payments to the needy individuals. It is hoped and expected that this will be done.

The major features of this new law follow the recommendations which I made to the Congress last January. The Congress is to be congratulated for this prompt and effective action to strengthen the social security laws and to ease the pressure of living costs for so many millions of Americans.

A large share of the credit for this timely and constructive measure is due to Chairman Doughton of the House Ways and Means Committee, the sponsor of the great Social Security Act of 1935 and of every major improvement in social security since that time. Chairman Doughton has announced his retirement from the House of Representatives after 40 years of service. H.R. 7800 is his last legislative achievement for the American people and I am sure they will join with me in honoring him for it.

In this new law, otherwise so generally desirable, there is one drawback which I feel requires comment at this time. I deeply regret that the Congress failed to take proper action to preserve the old-age and survivors insurance rights of persons who become permanently and totally disabled. There is a provision in the act which purports, beginning July 1, 1953, to preserve an individual's rights in the event of disability—but, unfortunately, the act also includes a sentence, saying that this provision shall cease to be in effect on June 30, 1953. The net effect of this is that the provision will expire on the day before it can go into effect. Thus, in the act I have just signed, the Congress takes away with one hand what it appears to give with the other.

The provision thus nullified by this extraordinary effective date arrangement, is analogous to the waiver of premiums in private insurance policies. This provision would permit aged persons whose disability has forced them into early retirement to have their benefits recomputed so that lost time due to their disability would not count against them.

No fair-minded individual denies the justice of such a provision. No procedures would be involved that are not already a part of the daily routine of scores of private life insurance companies. No administrative methods would be required that are not already used by any one of several Government disability programs for veterans, railroad employees, and Government workers, including Members of the Congress themselves.

The way in which this provision was, in effect, defeated is such a revealing example of how the Republicans dance when a well-heeled lobbyist pipes a tune that I think it warrants being brought to the particular attention of the American people in this election year.

The disability provision was recommended to the House of Representatives by its Committee on Ways and Means. On May 19th, the bill was taken up on the House floor under a motion to suspend the rules, a procedure which permits quick action but requires a two-thirds favorable vote to pass a bill. This procedure was agreed to because no one foresaw any opposition to this sensible and reasonable piece of legislation.

At that point, the Washington lobbyist for the American Medical Association got the notion that here was a chance for him to attack what he chose to call a "socialistic" proposal. So he sent a letter or telegram to every Member of the House. There had been no other opposition to H.R. 7800.

There was, as Chairman Doughton stated on the floor of the House, "no more socialized medicine in . . . [this provision] . . . than there is frost in the sun." Yet, when the House voted on the measure, nearly 70 percent of the Republicans were against the bill. A great majority of the Democrats, to their credit, stood firm and voted for the bill, but with the solid Republican opposition, they were unable to muster the necessary two-thirds vote.

After that defeat, the bill was sent back to the Ways and Means Committee. Then the story began to get around as to what had really happened. A great number of Republicans apparently decided they couldn't take the heat when they got caught, for when the bill was again reported and again brought to the floor, only 12 percent of the Republicans persisted in their opposition.

On this second try, the bill passed the House, on June 17th. But the American Medical Association lobby had accomplished what it wanted just the same. For the month's delay in the House had created such a situation that the Senate could act before adjournment only by dispensing with hearings. It was then the strategy of the American Medical Association to put up a great demand to be heard on the disability provision. Faced with the Association's insistence, the Senate committee decided to drop this provision rather than schedule hearings which might consume the time before adjournment and thus lose the chance for Senate action on the bill.

The net result of the medical lobby's maneuvering was the impairment of insurance protection for millions of disabled Americans. What the lobby could not engineer outright, it won by delay. And be it noted that this victory for the lobby, at the people's expense, was accomplished by a great majority of the Republicans in the House. They were perfectly willing to deny to millions of Americans the benefits provided by this bill in order to satisfy the groundless whim of a special interest lobby — a lobby that purports to speak for, but surely fails to represent, the great medical profession in the United States.

I earnestly hope that the Congress next year will override the foolish objections of the medical lobby and put a proper disability provision in the law.

The new law as finally adopted omits one other good provision which was passed by the House. I refer to a section of the House bill which would have permitted State and local government employees who are covered by retirement systems, to hold a referendum as to whether they wish to come under the Federal insurance program. There is a widespread desire on the part of such employees to obtain the protection of the insurance program. I hope the Congress will enact this much-needed provision next year also.

In addition, I hope the Congress at that time will also consider the entire question of further extending and liberalizing the Social Security Act as a whole.

Unfinished Business

During these years there was a basic re-thinking about the relationship between old-age assistance and insurance aspects of social security. The Seventy-ninth Congress had established the Joint Committee on the Economic Report and in 1952 the report was ready, prepared by the National Planning Association. While Pensions in the United States *did not provide recommendations as clear as some would have wished, it did underscore the importance of correlating the different programs.*

Pensions in the United States
(p. 26)

I. The first principle of a constructive approach to the income maintenance needs of the aged is that there should be opportunity for productive employment for those who are able to and want to work.

II. There is widespread agreement that underlying anything the individual may do for himself or any arrangements made through collective bargaining or by an employer there should be a universally available public program directed to income maintenance for the aged.

III. There is widespread agreement that the means-test method is a less satisfactory way of providing income for retired persons than a non-means-test program, and that the basic public program should, therefore, not include a test of need. There is also recognition, however, that assistance to the aged will continue to be required to meet needs not otherwise met.

IV. There is considerable agreement in this country on the desirability of relating retirement pay to previous earnings and on the desirability of having the fundamental public program contributory.

V. There is widespread acceptance of the idea that private pension plans are desirable as supplements to the public program.

Unemployment compensation was the next pressing issue. Despite the economic fluctuations posed by recessions and the Korean War, unemployment insurance remained the stepchild of the social security system after 1945. During 1952, several bills on unemployment were presented. These called for federal supplementation of state unemployment insurance when workers, faced with industries moved into war work, were forced out of jobs. Hearings were held in both Houses with labor strongly for the legislation and employers' groups generally opposed. In the end neither the Senate Finance Committee nor the House Ways and Means Committee took action on the legislation. The more fundamental reforms in unemployment insurance, suggested since 1939 were not considered and the system was ill-equipped to face the economic crises which were to plague the incoming Republican Administration.

MEDICAL CARE: 1945–1952

1945–1948

President Roosevelt, as has been seen, was not prepared to become deeply involved in medical care and health insurance. His successor—to the surprise of many—was much more firmly committed.

Special Presidential Message to the Congress Recommending
a Comprehensive Health Program
(November 19, 1945)*

To the Congress of the United States:

In my message to the Congress of September 6, 1945, there were enumerated in a proposed Economic Bill of Rights certain rights which ought to be assured to every American citizen.

One of them was: "The right to adequate medical care and the opportunity to achieve and enjoy good health." Another was the "right to adequate protection from the economic fears of . . . sickness. . . ."

*   *   *

*Public Papers of the Presidents, Harry S. Truman 1945, p. 475.

As of April 1, 1945, nearly 5,000,000 male registrants between the ages of 18 and 37 had been examined and classified as unfit for military service. The number of those rejected for military service was about 30 percent of all those examined. The percentage of rejection was lower in the younger age groups, and higher in the higher age groups, reaching as high as 49 percent for registrants between the ages of 34 and 37.

In addition, after actual induction, about a million and a half men had to be discharged from the Army and Navy for physical or mental disability, exclusive of wounds; and an equal number had to be treated in the Armed Forces for diseases or defects which existed before induction.

Among the young women who applied for admission to the Women's Army Corps there was similar disability. Over one-third of those examined were rejected for physical or mental reasons.

These men and women who were rejected for military service are not necessarily incapable of civilian work. It is plain, however, that they have illnesses and defects that handicap them, reduce their working capacity, or shorten their lives.

It is not so important to search the past in order to fix the blame for these conditions. It is more important to resolve now that no American child shall come to adult life with diseases or defects which can be prevented or corrected at an early age.

Medicine has made great strides in this generation—especially during the last four years. We owe much to the skill and devotion of the medical profession. In spite of great scientific progress, however, each year we lose many more persons from preventable and premature deaths than we lost in battle or from war injuries during the entire war.

We are proud of past reductions in our death rates. But these reductions have come principally from public health and other community services. We have been less effective in making available to all of our people the benefits of medical progress in the care and treatment of individuals.

In the past, the benefits of modern medical science have not been enjoyed by our citizens with any degree of equality. Nor are they today. Nor will they be in the future—unless government is bold enough to do something about it.

People with low or moderate incomes do not get the same medical attention as those with high incomes. The poor have more sickness, but they get less medical care. People who live in rural areas do not get the same amount or quality of medical attention as those who live in our cities.

Our new Economic Bill of Rights should mean health security for all, regardless of residence, station, or race—everywhere in the United States.

We should resolve now that the health of this Nation is a national concern; that financial barriers in the way of attaining health shall be removed; that the health of all its citizens deserves the help of all the Nation.

The message went on to identify five problem areas "where we must attack vigorously if we would reach the health objectives of our Economic Bill of Rights": 1. The unequal distribution of medical personnel and facilities; 2. The need to develop prior health services and maternal and child care; 3. The potential for investment in medical research and professional education; 4. The high cost of individual medical care, endangering families with "economic disaster"; 5. Loss of earnings during sickness.

These then are the five important problems which must be solved, if we hope to attain our objective of adequate medical care, good health, and protection from the economic fears of sickness and disability.

To meet these problems, I recommend that the Congress adopt a comprehensive and modern health program for the Nation, consisting of five major parts — each of which contributes to all the others.

First: Construction of hospitals and related facilities

[Federal assistance for building new institutions and modernizing others, in order to meet existing deficiencies].

*   *   *

Second: Expansion of public health, maternal and child health services

[An enlarged program of federal grants to states].

*   *   *

Third: Medical education and research

[Federal grants-in-aid to public non-profit agencies for professional education and medical research].

*   *   *

Fourth: Prepayment of Medical Costs

Everyone should have ready access to all necessary medical, hospital and related services.

I recommend solving the basic problem by distributing the costs through expansion of our existing compulsory social insurance system. This is not socialized medicine.

Everyone who carries fire insurance knows how the law of averages is made to work so as to spread the risk, and to benefit the insured who actually suffers the loss. If instead of the costs of sickness being paid only by those who get sick, all the people — sick and well — were required to pay premiums into an insurance fund, the pool of funds thus created would enable all who do fall sick to be adequately served without overburdening anyone. That is the principle upon which all forms of insurance are based.

During the past fifteen years, hospital insurance plans have taught many Americans this magic of averages. Voluntary health insurance plans have been expanding during recent years; but their rate of growth does not justify the belief that they will meet more than a fraction of our people's needs. Only about 3% or 4% of our population now have insurance providing comprehensive medical care.

A system of required prepayment would not only spread the costs of medical care, it would also prevent much serious disease. Since medical bills would be paid by the insurance fund, doctors would more often be consulted when the first signs of disease occur instead of when the disease has become serious. Modern hospital, specialist and laboratory services, as needed, would also become available to all, and would improve the quality and adequacy of care. Prepayment of medical care would go a long way toward furnishing insurance against disease itself, as well as against medical bills.

Such a system of prepayment should cover medical, hospital, nursing and laboratory services. It should also cover dental care—as fully and for as many of the population as the available professional personnel and the financial resources of the system permit.

The ability of our people to pay for adequate medical care will be increased if, while they are well, they pay regularly into a common health fund, instead of paying sporadically and unevenly when they are sick. This health fund should be built up nationally, in order to establish the broadest and most stable basis for spreading the costs of illness, and to assure adequate financial support for doctors and hospitals everywhere. If we were to rely on state-by-state action only, many years would elapse before we had any general coverage. Meanwhile health service would continue to be grossly uneven, and disease would continue to cross state boundary lines.

Medical services are personal. Therefore the nation-wide system must be highly decentralized in administration. The local administrative unit must be the keystone of the system so as to provide for local services and adaptation to local needs and conditions. Locally as well as nationally, policy and administration should be guided by advisory committees in which the public and the medical professions are represented.

Subject to national standards, methods and rates of paying doctors and hospitals should be adjusted locally. All such rates for doctors should be adequate, and should be appropriately adjusted upward for those who are qualified specialists.

People should remain free to choose their own physicians and hospitals. The removal of financial barriers between patient and doctor would enlarge the present freedom of choice. The legal requirement on the population to contribute involves no compulsion over the doctor's freedom to decide what services his patient needs. People will remain free to obtain and pay for medical service outside of the health insurance system if they desire, even though they are members of the system; just as they are free to send their children to private instead of to public schools, although they must pay taxes for public schools.

Likewise physicians should remain free to accept or reject patients. They must be allowed to decide for themselves whether they wish to participate in the health insurance system full time, part time, or not at all. A physician may have some patients who are in the system and some who are not. Physicians must be permitted to be represented through organizations of their own choosing, and to decide whether to carry on in individual practice or to join with other doctors in group practice in hospitals or in clinics.

Our voluntary hospitals and our city, county and state general hospitals, in the same way, must be free to participate in the system to whatever extent they wish. In any case they must continue to retain their administrative independence.

Voluntary organizations which provide health services that meet reasonable standards of quality should be entitled to furnish services under the insurance system and to be reimbursed for them. Voluntary cooperative organizations concerned with paying doctors, hospitals or others for health services, but not providing services directly, should be entitled to participate if they can contribute to the efficiency and economy of the system.

None of this is really new. The American people are the most insurance-minded people in the world. They will not be frightened off from health insurance because some people have misnamed it "socialized medicine".

I repeat — what I am recommending is *not* socialized medicine.

Socialized medicine means that all doctors work as employees of government. The American people want no such system. No such system is here proposed.

Under the plan I suggest, our people would continue to get medical and hospital services just as they do now — on the basis of their own voluntary decisions and choices. Our doctors and hospitals would continue to deal with disease with the same professional freedom as now. There would, however, be this all-important difference: whether or not patients get the services they need would not depend on how much they can afford to pay at the time.

I am in favor of the broadest possible coverage for this insurance system. I believe that all persons who work for a living and their dependents should be covered under such an insurance plan. This would include wage and salary earners, those in business for themselves, professional persons, farmers, agricultural labor, domestic employees, government employees and employees of non-profit institutions and their families.

In addition, needy persons and other groups should be covered through appropriate premiums paid for them by public agencies. Increased Federal funds should also be made available by the Congress under the public assistance programs to reimburse the States for part of such premiums, as well as for direct expenditures made by the States in paying for medical services provided by doctors, hospitals and other agencies to needy persons.

Premiums for present social insurance benefits are calculated on the first $3,000 of earnings in a year. It might be well to have all such premiums, including those for health, calculated on a somewhat higher amount such as $3,600.

A broad program of prepayment for medical care would need total amounts approximately equal to 4% of such earnings. The people of the United States have been spending, on the average, nearly this percentage of their incomes for sickness care. How much of the total fund should come from the insurance premiums and how much from general revenues is a matter for the Congress to decide.

The plan which I have suggested would be sufficient to pay most doctors more than the best they have received in peacetime years. The payments of the doctors' bills would be guaranteed, and the doctors would be spared the annoyance and uncertainty of collecting fees from individual patients. The same assurance would apply to hospitals, dentists and nurses for the services they render.

Federal aid in the construction of hospitals will be futile unless there is current purchasing power so that people can use these hospitals. Doctors cannot be drawn to sections which need them without some assurance that they can make a living. Only a nation-wide spreading of sickness costs can supply such sections with sure and sufficient purchasing power to maintain enough physicians and hospitals.

We are a rich nation and can afford many things. But ill-health which can be prevented or cured is one thing we cannot afford.

Fifth: Protection against loss of wages from sickness and disability

[A cash benefit system as an integral part of social security]

*   *   *

I strongly urge that the Congress give careful consideration to this program of health legislation now.

Many millions of our veterans, accustomed in the armed forces to the best of medical and hospital care, will no longer be eligible for such care as a matter of right except for their service-connected disabilities. They deserve continued adequate and comprehensive health service. And their dependents deserve it too.

By preventing illness, by assuring access to needed community and personal health services, by promoting medical research, and by protecting our people against the loss caused by sickness, we shall strengthen our national health, our national defense, and our economic productivity. We shall increase the professional and economic opportunities of our physicians, dentists and nurses. We shall increase the effectiveness of our hospitals and public health agencies. We shall bring new security to our people.

We need to do this especially at this time because of the return to civilian life of many doctors, dentists and nurses, particularly young men and women.

Appreciation of modern achievements in medicine and public health has created widespread demand that they be fully applied and universally available. By meeting that demand we shall strengthen the Nation to meet future economic and social problems; and we shall make a most important contribution toward freedom from want in our land.

Harry S. Truman

To implement this Truman program, Senators Murray and Wagner and Representative Dingell introduced the National Health Bill of 1945.

National Health Bill of 1945
S. 1606, H.R. 4730
79th Cong., 2d Sess.

TITLE I—GRANTS TO STATES FOR HEALTH SERVICES

PART A—GRANTS TO STATES FOR PUBLIC HEALTH

*   *   *

*PART B—GRANTS TO STATES FOR MATERNAL AND
    CHILD HEALTH SERVICES*

*   *   *

*PART C—GRANTS TO STATES FOR MEDICAL CARE OF NEEDY
    PERSONS*

Appropriation

Sec. 131. For the purpose of enabling each State to provide medical care, as far as practicable under the conditions in such State, for needy persons, there is hereby authorized to be appropriated for the fiscal year ending June 30, 1946, the sum of $10,000,000, and there is hereby authorized to be appropriated for each fiscal year thereafter a sum sufficient to carry out the purpose of this part. The sums made available under this section shall be used for making payments to States which have submitted and had approved by the Social Security Board (hereinafter referred to as the "Board"), State plans for medical care of needy persons.

Approval of State Plans

Sec. 132. (a) A State plan for medical care must —
  (1) provide that it shall be in effect in all political subdivisions of the State, and if administered by them, be mandatory upon them;
  (2) provide for financial participation by the State, and for such distribution of funds, as to assure meeting in full the need of individuals for medical care throughout the State, as determined in accordance with standards established by the State;
  (3) (A) provide for the establishment or designation of a single State public assistance agency to administer or to supervise the administration of the plan for medical care; and (B) provide that there will not be more than one public assistance agency of a local subdivision of the State established or designated to administer the plan for medical care within such subdivision;
  (4) provide for granting to any individual, whose claim for medical care is denied, an opportunity for a fair hearing before such State agency;
  (5) provide such methods of administration (including methods relating to the establishment and maintenance of personnel standards on a merit basis, except that the Board shall exercise no authority with respect to the selection, tenure of office, and compensation of any individual employed in accordance with such methods) as are found by the Board to be necessary for the proper and efficient operation of the plan;
  (6) provide that the State agency will make such reports, in such form and containing such information, as the Board may from time to time require, and comply with such provisions as the Board may from time to time find necessary to assure correctness;
  (7) provide safeguards which restrict the use or and verification of such reports; disclosure of information concerning applicants and recipients to purposes directly connected with the administration of the plan; and
  (8) provide that the State agency shall, in determining need for medical care, take into consideration (A) the requirements of individuals claiming medical care under the plan, and (B) any income and resources of an individual claiming medical care under the plan, which must be taken into consideration with regard to an individual claiming assistance under a State plan approved under the Social Security Act, as amended.

  (b) The Board shall approve any plan which fulfills the conditions specified in subsection (a), except that it shall not approve any plan which imposes as a condition of eligibility for medical care under the plan any citizenship or residence requirement, or any requirement which excludes any recipient of public assistance under a State plan approved under the Social Security Act, as amended.

Payment to States

Sec. 133. (a) From the sums appropriated therefor under section 131, the Secretary of the Treasury shall pay to each State which has an approved plan for medical care, for each year or part thereof covered by such plan, amounts equal to the Federal proportion of the total amount of public funds expended under the State plan, during each year or part thereof covered by such plan, as is determined in accordance with section 135, not counting so much of such expenditures for medical care for any individual under the age of eighteen years who at the time of such expenditure is living in a public or private institution, or for any individual who has attained the age of eighteen years and at the time of such expenditure is living in a public institution, and not counting so much of such total expenditures by the State as are included in any other State plan aided by grants under any other part of this title, or any other Act of Congress. The amounts so paid to a State by the Secretary of the Treasury shall be used exclusively for carrying out the purposes of this title.

*   *   *

Administration

Sec. 136. (a) In carrying out the duties imposed upon it by this part, the Board is hereby authorized and directed, with the approval of the Federal Security Administrator, to enter into such agreements or cooperative working arrangements with the Surgeon General of the Public Health Service, and with the Chief of the Children's Bureau, as may be necessary to insure coordination in the administration of programs and services under this part with those under parts A and B of this title and with those under title II of this Act.

(b) Medical care under this part may be provided either (1) by the State or local public assistance agency administering the plan for medical care through (A) money payments to individuals claiming such care, or (B) payments to the persons or institutions furnishing such care or, (C) direct provision of such care; (2) in accordance with agreements (authorized in regulations by the Board) between such State or local agency and other agencies of the State or political subdivision thereof, by such other agencies; or, (3) through arrangments by a State or local public agency with the Surgeon General for services furnished under title II of this Act, on the basis of equitable payments to the Personal Health Services Account established under title II of this Act; or, (4) through such combination or modification of (1), (2), or (3) as the Board may approve.

TITLE II – PREPAID PERSONAL HEALTH
SERVICE BENEFITS

Primary Personal Health Service Benefits

Sec. 201. (a) Every individual, who is currently insured, and has been determined by the Board to be eligible for benefits under this title in a current benefit year, shall be entitled to receive personal health service benefits.

Dependent's Personal Health Service Benefits

(b) Every dependent (as defined in section 214 (1)) of an individual who is currently insured and who has been determined by the Board to be eligible for benefits under this title in a current benefit year, shall be entitled to receive personal health service benefits, if such dependent is not entitled to receive such benefits under subsection (a) of this section in the current benefit year.

Personal Health Service Benefits for Retired and Survivor Beneficiaries

Sec. 202. Every individual entitled for any period to monthly benefits under Title II of the Social Security Act, as amended, shall be entitled to receive personal health service benefits for the current benefit year, if such individual is not entitled to receive such benefits under section 201.

Administration

Sec. 203. (a) The Surgeon General of the Public Health Service shall perform the duties imposed upon him by this Act, under the supervision and direction of the Federal Security Administrator, and after consultations with the Advisory Council (hereinafter established) as to questions of general policy and administration, and in consultation with the Board shall also have the duty of studying and making recommendations as to the most effective methods of providing personal health service benefits, and as to legislation and matters of administrative policy concerning health and related subjects.

*　　*　　*

National Advisory Medical Policy Council

Sec. 204. (a) There is hereby established a National Advisory Medical Policy Council (herein referred to as the "Advisory Council") to consist of the Surgeon General as Chairman and sixteen members to be appointed without regard to the civil-service laws by the Surgeon General and with the approval of the Federal Security Administrator. The sixteen appointed members shall be selected from panels of names submitted by the professional and other agencies and organizations concerned with medical, dental, and nursing services and education and with the operation of hospitals and laboratories and from among other persons, agencies, or organizations informed on the need for or provision of medical, dental, nursing, hospital, laboratory, or related services and benefits. The membership of the Advisory Council shall include (1) medical and other professional representatives, and (2) public representatives, in such proportions as are likely to provide fair representation to the principal interested groups that furnish and receive personal health services, having regard for the functions of the Advisory Council. The Advisory Council shall meet not less frequently than twice a year and whenever at least four of the members request a meeting. Each appointed member shall hold office for a term of four years, except that any member appointed to fill a vacancy occurring prior to the expiration of the term for which his predecessor was appointed shall be appointed for the remainder of such term, and the terms of office of the members first taking office shall expire, as designated by the Surgeon General at the time of appointment, four at the end of the first year, four at the end of the second year, four at the end of the third year, and four at the end of the fourth year after the date of appointment. Each appointed member shall receive compensation at a rate not to exceed $25 per day during the time spent in attending meetings of the Advisory Council and for the time devoted to official business of the Advisory Council under this title, inclusive of travel time; and actual and necessary traveling expenses and per diem in lieu of subsistence, allowable in accordance with the Standardized Government Travel Regulations, while away from his place of residence upon official business under this Act. The Advisory Council, and each of its appointed members, shall be provided by the Surgeon General with such secretarial, clerical or other assistants as the Congress shall authorize and provide each year for carrying out the purposes of this section.

(b) The Advisory Council shall advise the Surgeon General with reference to questions of general policy and administration in carrying out the provisions of this title, including—

(1) professional standards of quality to apply to personal health service benefits;

(2) designation of specialists and consultants;

(3) methods and arrangements to stimulate and encourage the attainment of high standards through coordination of the services of general or family practitioners, specialists and consultants, laboratories, and other auxiliary services, and through the coordination of the services of physicians and dentists with those of educational and research institutions, hospitals and public-health centers, and through other useful means;

(4) standards to apply to participating hospitals, to the relations or coordination among hospitals, and to the establishment and maintenance of the list of participating hospitals;

(5) adequate and suitable methods and arrangements of paying for personal health service benefits;

(6) studies and surveys of personal health services and of the quality and adequacy of such services; and

(7) grants-in-aid for professional education and research projects.

(c) The Advisory Council shall establish special advisory, technical regional, or local committees or commissions, whose membership may include members of the Advisory Council or other persons or both, to advise upon general or special questions, professional and technical subjects, questions concerning administration, problems affecting regions or localities, and related matters.

Methods and Policies for Administration

Sec. 205. (a) Any physician, dentist, or nurse legally qualified by a State to furnish any services included as personal health service benefits under this title shall be qualified to furnish such services as benefits under this title (except as otherwise provided in subsection (c) of this section or in subsection (f) of section 214), and this provision shall extend to any group of physicians, dentists, or nurses or combinations thereof whose members are similarly qualified.

(b) Every individual entitled to receive general medical or general dental benefit shall be permitted to select, from among those designated in subsection (a) of this section, those from whom he shall receive such benefit, subject to the consent of the practitioner or group of practitioners selected, and every such individual and every group of such individuals shall be permitted to make such selection through a representative of his or their own choosing, and to change such selection.

(c) Services which shall be deemed to be specialist or consultant services, for the purposes of special rates of payment under this title, shall be those so designated by the Surgeon General, and the practitioners from among those included in subsection (a) of this section who shall be qualified as specialists or consultants and entitled to the special rates of compensation provided for specialists or consultants shall be those so designated by the Surgeon General as qualified to furnish such specialist or consultant services and only with respect to the particular class or classes of specialist or consultant services he shall determine for each such specialist or consultant, in accordance with general standards previously prescribed by him after consultation with the Advisory Council. In establishing such standards and in designating such specialists or consultants the Surgeon General shall utilize as far as is consistent with the purposes of this title standards and certifications developed by competent professional agencies and shall take into account the personnel resources and needs of regions and local areas.

(d) The services of a specialist or consultant shall ordinarily be available only upon the advice of the general or family practitioner or of a specialist or consultant attending the individual. The services of specialists and consultants shall also be available when requested by an individual entitled to specialist and consultant services as benefits and approved by a medical administrative officer appointed by the Surgeon General.

(e) The Surgeon General shall publish and otherwise make known in each local area to individuals entitled to benefit under this title the names of medical and dental practitioners and groups of practitioners who have agreed to furnish services as benefits under this title and to make such lists of names readily available to individuals entitled to benefits under this title. Such lists of names shall include general or family practitioners and qualified specialists and consultants, respectively, and with respect to qualified specialists and consultants the class or classes of specialist or consultant services for which each has been qualified.

(f) The methods of administration, including the methods of making payments to practitioners, shall —

(1) insure the prompt and efficient care of individuals entitled to personal health service benefits;

(2) promote personal relationships between physician and patient;

(3) provide professional and financial incentives for the professional advancement of practitioners and encourage high standards in the quality of services furnished as benefits under this title through the adequacy of payments to practitioners, assistance in their use of opportunities for postgraduate study, coordination among the services furnished by general or family practitioners, specialists and consultants, laboratory, and other auxiliary services, coordination among the services furnished by practitioners, hospitals, public-health centers, educational, research, and other institutions, and between preventive and curative services, and otherwise;

(4) aid in the prevention of disease, disability, and premature death; and

(5) insure the provision of adequate service with the greatest economy consistent with high standards of quality.

(g) Payments from the Account to general medical and family practitioners or to general dental practitioners, for services under this part, shall be made —

(1) on the basis of fees for services rendered to individuals entitled to benefits, according to a fee schedule;

(2) on a per capita basis, the amount being according to the number of individuals entitled to benefit who are on the practitioner's list;

(3) on a salary basis, whole time or part time; or

(4) on a combination or modification of these bases, as the Surgeon General may approve;

according in each local area as the majority of the general medical and family practitioners or of the general dental practitioners, respectively, to be paid for such services shall elect: *Provided*, That (1) the Surgeon General may also make payments by another method (from among the methods listed in this subsection) to those general medical and family practitioners or to those general dental practitioners who do not elect the method of such majority, especially when in the judgment of the Surgeon General such alternative method of making payments contributes to carrying out the provisions of subsection (f) of this section; (2) any of the methods of making payments (from among the methods listed in this subsection) may be used, according as the Surgeon General may approve, in making payments to groups of practitioners that contain designated specialists or consultants as well as general or family practitioners; and (3) nothing in this subsection shall prohibit the Surgeon General from negotiating agreements or cooperative working arrangements to utilize inclusive services of hospitals and their staffs and/or attending staffs, or from entering into contracts for such inclusive services, in accordance with the provisions of section 203.

(h) The methods of making payments from the account to designated specialists and consultants for services under this title, furnished as special medical or special dental benefit, may include payments on salary (whole time or part time), per session, fee-for-service, per capita, or other basis, or combinations thereof, as the Surgeon General and the specialists and consultants may agree.

(i) Rates or amounts of payment for particular services or classes of services furnished as benefits under this title may be nationally uniform or may be adapted to take account of relevant regional or local conditions and other factors. Payments shall be adequate, especially in terms of annual income or its equivalent and by reference to annual income customarily received among physicians, dentists, or nurses, having regard for age, specialization, and type of community; and payments shall be commensurate with skill, experience, and responsibility involved in furnishing service.

(j) In order to maintain high standards in the quality of services furnished as medical or dental benefit, the Surgeon General may prescribe maximum limits to the number of potential beneficiaries for whom a practitioner or group of practitioners may undertake to furnish general medical or general dental benefit, and such limits may be nationally uniform or may be adapted to take account of relevant factors.

(k) In any local area where payment for the services of a general or family practitioner is only on a per capita basis, the Surgeon General shall make per capita payments (subject to limits prescribed in accordance with subsection (j) of this section) on a pro rata basis among the practitioners and groups of practitioners of the local area on the list established pursuant to subsection (e) of this section with respect to those individuals in the local area who, after due notice, have failed to select a general or family practitioner or who having made one or more successive selections have been refused by the practitioner or practitioners selected.

(l) In each local area the provision of general medical or general dental benefit for all individuals entitled to receive such benefit shall be a collective responsibility of all qualified general medical or family practitioners or of all qualified general dental practitioners, respectively, in the area who have undertaken to furnish such benefit.

(m) Home-nursing benefit shall ordinarily be available only upon the advice of a legally qualified attending physician. Home-nursing benefit shall also be available when requested by an individual entitled to this benefit and approved by a medical officer designated by the Surgeon General.

Participating Hospitals

Sec. 206. (a) The Surgeon General shall publish a list of institutions which he finds to be participating hospitals, and shall from time to time revise such list to include thereon all institutions which he thereafter finds to be participating hospitals and to withdraw therefrom all institutions which he finds cease to meet the requirements of a participating hospital. Inclusion of an institution upon such list shall, unless and until withdrawn by the Surgeon General, be conclusive that such institution is a participating hospital for the purpose of this section.

(b) The Surgeon General is directed to make findings of fact and decisions as to the status of any institution as a participating hospital in accordance with general standards previously prescribed by him after consultation with the Advisory Council. Any institution which is not included by the Surgeon General in the list of participating hospitals, or having been included thereon has been withdrawn therefrom, may file with the Surgeon General a petition to be included in such list, which petition shall set forth such information as the Surgeon General may deem necessary to establish that such institution meets the requirements of a participating hospital. Whenever requested by any institution the petition of which has been denied, the Surgeon General shall give such institution reasonable notice and an opportunity for a fair hearing with respect to the decision denying such petition, and, if a hearing is held, shall, on the basis of evidence adduced at the hearing, affirm, modify, or reverse his findings of fact and such decision.

(c) The Surgeon General shall exercise no supervision or control over a participating hospital (which is not owned and operated, or leased and operated, by the United States), nor shall any requirement for participation by a hospital or any term or condition of any agreement under this part relating to, or on behalf of, any such hospital prescribe its administration, personnel, or operation.

Appeal; Judicial Review: Limitations upon the Powers of the Surgeon General

Sec. 207. (a) The Surgeon General is hereby authorized to establish necessary and sufficient appeal bodies to hear complaints from individuals entitled to benefits under this title, from practitioners who have entered into agreement for the provision of services as benefits under. . . .

Relation with Workmen's Compensation Benefits

Sec. 208. No individual shall be entitled to any benefit under this title with respect to any injury, disease, or disability on account of which any medical, dental, home nursing, laboratory, or hospitalization service is being received, or upon application therefor would be received, under a workmen's compensation plan of the United States or of any State. . .

Limitations on Benefits

Sec. 210. (a) The Surgeon General may, after consultation with the Advisory Council and with the approval of the Administrator, determine for any calendar year or part thereof that every individual entitled to general medical, general dental, or home-nursing benefit may be required by the physician, dentist, or nurse furnishing such benefit to pay a fee with respect to the first service or with respect to each service in a period of sickness or course of treatment. Such determination shall be made only after good and sufficient evidence indicates that such determination is necessary and desirable to prevent or reduce abuses of entitlement to any such benefit, and shall fix the maximum size of such fee at an amount estimated to be sufficient to prevent or reduce abuses and not such as to interpose a substantial financial restraint against proper and needed receipt of medical, dental, or home-nursing benefit. Such determination may also limit the application of such fees to home calls, to office visits, or to both, and may fix the maximum total amount of such fee payments in a period of sickness or course of treatment, and may also provide for differences in the maximum size of such fees or total amount of such fee payments for urban and rural areas and with regard for differences among States or communities. Each such determination shall be withdrawn as rapidly as the Surgeon General finds practical.

                    *   *   *

Report Concerning Dental, Nursing, and other Benefits; Care and Prevention for Chronic Sickness and Mental Diseases

Sec. 211. (a) The Surgeon General and the Social Security Board jointly shall have the duty of studying and making recommendations as to the most effective methods of providing dental, nursing, and other needed benefits not already provided or not currently furnished under this title . . .

Eligibility

Sec. 215. (a) An individual shall be deemed to be currently insured under this title if he (1) had during his eligibility period been paid wages of not less than $150, or (2) acquired not less than six quarters of coverage during the first twelve of the last fourteen completed calendar quarters immediately preceding the first day of a benefit year, not counting among such completed quarters any quarter in any part of which the individual was under a disability which lasted six consecutive months or more.

The National Health Bill was introduced in the fall of 1945. No hearings were held until April, 1946. In the meantime, however, Chairman Murray of the Senate Committee on Education and Labor issued a number of committee prints so that "members of the committee can be better informed prior to and during hearings on legislation." In Print No. 1 there was both a joint statement by the sponsors and a question-and-answers section. The second part was designed to rebut increasing criticism from organized medicine that the envisaged system was "socialized medicine", and an unnecessary interference with the physician's freedom to practice. Documentation of the AMA views was included in Print No. 2.

The President's National Health Program and the New Wagner Bill
[Editorial from the Journal of the American Medical Association, vol. 129, No. 14, December 1, 1945, pp. 950–53.]

Last week the Journal published the message sent to Congress on November 19 by President Harry S. Truman submitting a national health program. On the same day Senator Wagner, of New York, introduced for himself and Senator Murray Senate bill 1606, and Congressman Dingell introduced into the House the same version of the new Wagner-Murray-Dingell bill. Obviously a number of conferences between those interested must have preceded the coordinated action that occurred. Senator Wagner accompanied his introduction of the measure with another opening statement, a brief summary of the health provisions and a long series of questions and answers about the prepaid medical care provisions of the National Health Act of 1945. The language of the President in his message to the Congress and of Senator Wagner in his statement to the Senate and the language of the measure itself are the same trite locutions that the advocates of Federal compulsory sickness insurance have used for these many years in trying to force these proposals on the American people. According to Arthur Sears Henning, "the compulsory health insurance plan is chiefly the brain child of Isidore S. Falk, research director of the Social Security Board, and Michael M. Davis, a member of the CIO political action committee."

Elsewhere in this issue appears an analysis by the bureau of legal medicine of the American Medical Association of the changes in the latest version of the Wagner-Murray-Dingell bill from that introduced previously. Mr. Wagner in his opening statement again informs the Senate that this bill is the result of the constructive suggestions of many outstanding medical authorities and of labor, farm, consumer, and health organizations interested in improving the Nation's health. Neither the President nor Mr. Wagner nor the Social Security Board made the slightest attempt to consult any representatives of the American Medical Association, which now embraces in its membership more than 125,000 American physicians. Typical of the kind of government that the bureaucrats would force on the American people is this technique of consulting advisers who are known in advance to be in complete agreement with the persons whom they are supposed to advise and of studiously avoiding anyone who might offer a contrary opinion. This is government by minority with a vengeance.

The insidious strategy that has been employed in recent years, leading toward culmination by approval of the President of the United States, is clearly apparent to those with an understanding of what has been going on. Since the time when Michael Davis and his associates engineered the formation of the Committee on the Costs of Medical Care down to the present, a gradual enlistment has been secured in behalf of socialized medicine of every agency that could be induced to combine in a movement toward socialization of the American system of government. Around their banner have rallied the members of the so-called Boas' Physicians Forum, certain doctors of philosophy in the field of economics and sociology, the socialist element in the American Public Health Association and those employed in governmental health agencies who thirst for increased power and expansion of the bureaus that they serve. Let the people of our country realize that the movement for the placing of American medicine under the control of the Federal Government through a system of Federal compulsory sickness insurance is the first step toward a regimentation of utilities, of industries, of finance, and eventually of labor itself. This is the kind of regimentation that led to totalitarianism in Germany and the downfall of that nation. Its prime consideration is deduction from the pay of the worker and taxation of the employer so that the Government does for the people most of the things that our people in the United States have been accustomed to do for themselves. The time may yet come when the American worker, as was the case with the German worker, will have more deductions from his wages than "take home" pay.

"Socialized Medicine" and Free Choice

In the President's message to the Congress and in the material written for Mr. Wagner by those whom he employs and consults in the preparation of his proposals, constantly reiterated is the statement that these proposals are not "socialized medicine." The first of Mr. Wagner's questions and answers is concerned with this question in semantics. Worse than socialized medicine is "state medicine." In any system of state medicine the government collects the funds available, manages the service, and distributes the payments. Is not this what the Wagner-Murray-Dingell bill would accomplish? True, in the proposed legislation for a Federal system of compulsory sickness insurance, patients are told that they will have free choice of doctors; doctors are told that they will have the right to refuse any patients; but the bill provides that the Surgeon General can limit the number of patients that a physician will see, and that the Surgeon General will provide other physicians when too many patients select one or more of the physicians in a community. The measure mentions free choice of doctor for the patient, but it is free choice within limitations. It is free choice of the doctors who are willing to work under the system. It is free choice if the doctor is willing to work under a fee bill set up by the Government. It is free choice if the doctor is willing to accept a payment of so much per person per year for his services. It is free choice if the doctor is willing to work as a salaried member of a group. It is free choice if the doctor is willing to abide by a majority vote of the doctors licensed to practice in his community. What kind of free choice is that?

Senator Wagner has always insisted that compulsory health insurance — really sickness insurance — is not socialized medicine. Actually the proposals involve both socialized medicine and state medicine. The American people are entitled to straightforward, honest statements from their representatives as to what such proposed measures would do to them and to their physicians. They have not had such a straightforward statement either from the President in his message or from Senator Wagner in his statement to the Congress.

The exchange of views continued. A memorandum prepared by the Bureau of Research and Statistics of the Social Security Board, with an introduction by Bureau Director, I. S. Falk, was issued as a committee print in March, 1946 ("Need for Medical Case Insurance"). It documented disabling diseases, recognized and unrecognized diseases and defects, unpredictability of illness and costs and their uneven distribution gaps between need and receipt of care, inadequacy and unevenness in care being given, and maldistribution of medical personnel and hospitals, providing by far the most detailed study of medical case organization that had appeared in a public document until that date.

The memorandum was followed by a working blueprint from the bureau in support of the system of personal health insurance outlined in the National Health Bill. Its detailed suggestions traced their source to the research in health insurance conducted a decade earlier by the Committee on Economic Security, but the arguments were contemporary.

Medical Care Insurance:
A Social Insurance Program for Personal Health Services
Report from The Bureau of Research and Statistics
of the Social Security Board
(Submitted to the Senate Committee on Education and Labor)
July 8, 1946

*　　*　　*

Neither the course of present developments in this country nor experience in other countries which have tried voluntary health insurance gives any indication that comprehensive and adequate arrangements to insure medical costs can be made in any way except through a compulsory insurance system. The adoption of compulsory insurance by some 35 countries resulted not so much from the successes as from the failure of voluntary insurance to achieve comprehensive coverage, adequacy of benefits, or economy of costs. No country that adopted compulsory health insurance has ever given it up; on the contrary, the trend in each case has been to broaden the coverage and enlarge the scope of the benefits—toward the goal of complete coverage and comprehensive service.

*   *   *

While the series of committee prints and the continuing review of health insurance focused on the introduction of health insurance into the social security system, Issues in Social Security *emphasized public assistance elements which were relevant—with or without health insurance—to the adequate provision of medical care.*

Digest of Issues in Social Security
(p. 33–34)

Experience of State agencies suggests that maximums on payments to individuals are a special problem in meeting health requirements of needy individuals. Health care is a common requirement like food, shelter, and clothing. But unlike them, it often involves large expenditures, usually without previous warning.[11]

The need for medical care

According to the National Health Survey of 1934–36, a house-to-house canvass conducted by the United States Public Health Service, 172 out of each 1,000 persons during a 12-month period suffered disabling diseases either acute or chronic.[12] In contrast, families receiving public assistance experienced a disability rate of 234 out of each 1,000 persons. Average duration of disabling illness among the assistance group was 11.9 days as compared to 3.9 days per person in the group with incomes of $3,000 and over.

Adequate medical care may in some instances reduce the duration of assistance. The vision of some of the persons receiving aid to the blind may by proper medical care be conserved, in some instances, or even be restored.

[11]Details on the medical care programs of various public assistance agencies are presented on pp. 355–356 of Issues in Social Security. On pp. 352 to 354 are presented recommendations of various groups as to improving medical care provided under public assistance.
[12]U. S. Public Health Service, Illness and Medical Care in Relation to Economic Status, The National Health Survey: 1934–36, Bulletin No. 2, Washington, 1938, as quoted in National Resources Planning Board. Security Work, and Relief Policies, Washington 1942, pp. 118–120.

Effect of Federal maximums upon provision for medical care

[In States that] limit medical care to those costs which can be met within the maximum payment, the needy persons' requirements may not be met; if, on the other hand, these needs are met the burden will be passed on to the doctor, hospital, or other health agency. Most States make some provision for medical care either outside the money payment or in payments larger than those toward which the Federal Government can contribute. These States believe that the Federal Government should share in such assistance costs.

Federal payments are available at present only for those medical costs which can be budgeted to the recipient [of special assistance].

Maximums on grants limit the provision of adequate medical care, both because the maximums are low and because most medical needs cannot be planned for in regular budgeting. Although such costs can be estimated and averaged over a period for a group, as an insurance risk, this average cannot be budgeted to an individual, as can be done with the average cost of food or clothing. On the other hand, if the State or local agency budgets medical expenses for an individual at the time they arise, the individual payment may exceed Federal maximums and place a burden for the excess upon the State or local community. If a higher average were matchable with Federal funds, this would encourage States to remove or modify their own maximums and to expand or create medical-care programs.

Effect of Federal participation only in money payments to individuals

The requirement in the [Social Security Act] that all assistance be cash also limits the provision of adequate medical care. Unlike the provision of food, lodging, and clothing, medical care is usually rendered before payment is made. Further, the cost of a recipient's last illness may not be known until after his death. This can be a sizable problem since in the period of a year 1 old-age-assistance recipient in 14 dies. If the recipient dies before the medical bills are presented they cannot be met through money payments to the recipient. As a result, the cost of this care, if the recipient had no insurance or other estate, must be paid wholly from State or local funds.

Meeting health requirements

If Federal matching maximums are eliminated or if payments for medical care directly to doctors, hospitals, and other health agencies are exempted from the maximums, States would be encouraged to establish or improve medical-care programs. If Federal maximums are changed to an average-per-case basis, the excess cost of medical care to particular individuals could be spread over the entire group of recipients. If the Social Security Act is amended to adjust the maximums and/or permit matching of payments for medical care made to doctors, hospitals, and other agencies, the States will be encouraged to adopt the most effective type of plans for medical care, within their financial ability.

The hearings on the National Health Program began in the Senate in April, 1946. Chairman Murray outlined the procedure to be followed, and at once became embroiled in the dispute over socialism which seemed to be the most important issue at stake, and which provided a theme for the whole debate.

The argument between Senators Taft and Murray became more and more vehement until Senator Taft walked out. It was against this emotionally-charged background that Senator Wagner and other political witnesses presented their arguments. Proponents of the bill were forced to adopt a defensive posture.

In place of S. 1606, the AMA submitted its own ten-point plan endorsing federal aid for preventive and public health services, for hospital construction in needy areas, for the medical care of veterans, and for scientific research. However, it also advocated "the American system of individual initiative and freedom of enterprise" — the alleged antithesis of "socialized medicine" — in relation to the provision of health insurance. Thus, while the AMA favored certain sections of the National Health Program, and strongly endorsed voluntary health insurance, its opposition to compulsory health insurance as part of the social security system was unwavering.

S. 1606 was not voted out of committee and no hearings were held on the Taft-Smith-Ball Bill (S. 2143), which tried to establish a National Health Agency. On the other hand, 1946 did produce, with bipartisan support, the Hospital Survey and Construction Act (the Hill-Burton Act), providing for federal subsidy to hospitals in rural areas.

The elections that fall returned a Republican majority in both houses in 1947, and made a meaningful discussion of health insurance unlikely in the eightieth Congress. The President, however, remained undeterred and returned to the theme time and again.

Annual Budget Message of the President
(January 10, 1947)*

During the war, nearly 5 million men were rejected for military service because of physical or mental defects which in many cases might have been prevented or corrected. This is shocking evidence that large sections of the population are at substandard levels of health. The need for a program that will give everyone opportunity for medical care is obvious. Nor can

*Public Papers of the Presidents, Harry S. Truman, 1947, p. 63–64.

there by any serious doubt of the Government's responsibility for helping in this human and social problem.

The comprehensive health program which I recommended on November, 19, 1945, will require substantial additions to the Social Security System and, in conjunction with other changes that need to be made, will require further consideration of the financial basis for social security. The system of prepaid medical care which I have recommended is expected eventually to require amounts equivalent to 4 percent of earnings up to $3,600 a year, which is about the average of present expenditures by individuals for medical care. The pooling of medical costs, under a plan which permits each individual to make a free choice of doctor and hospital, would assure that individuals receive adequate treatment and hospitalization when they are faced with emergencies for which they cannot budget individually. In addition, I recommended insurance benefits to replace part of the earnings lost through temporary sickness and permanent disability.

Even without these proposed major additions, it would now be time to undertake a thorough reconsideration of our social security laws. The structure should be expanded and liberalized. Provision should be made for extending coverage credit to veterans for the period of their service in the armed forces. In the financial provisions we must reconcile the actuarial needs of social security, including health insurance, with the requirements of a revenue system that is designed to promote a high level of consumption and full employment.

Special Presidential Message to the Congress on Health and Disability Insurance
(May 19, 1947)*

To the Congress of the United States:

Healthy citizens constitute our greatest national resource. In time of peace, as in time of war, our ultimate strength stems from the vigor of our people. The welfare and security of our nation demand that the opportunity for good health be made available to all, regardless of residence, race or economic status.

At no time can we afford to lose the productive energies and capacities of millions of our citizens. Nor can we permit our children to grow up without a fair chance for a healthy life. We must not permit our rural families to suffer for lack of physicians, dentists, nurses and hospitals. We must not reserve a chance for good health and a long productive life to the well-to-do alone. A great and free nation should bring good health care within the reach of all its people.

*Ibid., p. 250 et seq.

In my message to the Congress on November 19, 1945, I said that every American should have the right to adequate medical care and to adequate protection from the economic threat of sickness. To provide this care and protection is a challenging task, requiring action on a wide front.

I have previously outlined the long-range health program which I consider necessary to the national welfare and security. I say again that such a program must include:

1. Adequate public health services, including an expanded maternal and child health program.
2. Additional medical research and medical education.
3. More hospitals and more doctors — in all areas of the country where they are needed.
4. Insurance against the costs of medical care.
5. Protection against loss of earnings during illness.

I am pleased to observe that important advances were made by the last Congress toward realization of some of the goals which I set forth in my earlier message. But we must not rest until we have achieved all our objectives. I urge this Congress to enact additional legislation to authorize the program I have outlined, even though the fulfillment of some aspects of it may take time.

Our public health services — federal, state and local — provide our greatest and most successful defense against preventable diseases. But in many states, cities and counties in America, limited funds reduce the work of our public health services to a dangerously inadequate level. Public services related to maternal and child health were expanded by the 79th Congress, through amendments to the Social Security Act. This action was gratifying, but the long-range need for additional health services for children and expectant mothers, and for care of crippled or otherwise physically handicapped children, should be carefully studied by the Congress.

The Nation's medical research programs must in the future be expanded so that we can learn more about the prevention and cure of disease. The Congress has already recognized this by providing for research into the causes of cancer and mental diseases and abnormalities. Further dividends will accrue to our Nation — and to our people — if research can point the way toward combatting and overcoming such major illnesses as arthritis and rheumatic fever, and diseases of the heart, kidneys and arteries.

We still face a shortage of hospitals, physicians, dentists and nurses. Those we have are unfairly distributed. The shortage of doctors, dentists and nurses can be met only through expanded educational opportunities. The shortage of hospitals will be met in part through the action of the last Congress which provided Federal aid for the construction of hospitals.

In the last analysis the patient's ability to pay for the services of physicians or dentists, or for hospital care, determines the distribution of doctors and the location of hospitals. Few doctors can be expected to practice today in sparsely settled areas or where prospective patients are unable to pay for their services. Doctors tend to concentrate in communities where hospitals and other facilities are best and where their incomes are most secure. The unequal distribution of doctors and hospitals will plague this nation until means are found to finance modern medical care for all of our people.

National health insurance is the most effective single way to meet the Nation's health needs. Because adequate treatment of many illnesses is expensive and its cost cannot be anticipated by the individual, many persons are forced to go without needed medical attention. Children do not receive adequate medical and dental care. Symptoms which should come early to the attention of a physician are often ignored until too late. The poor are not the only ones who cannot afford adequate medical care. The truth is that all except the rich may at some time be struck by illness which requires care and services they cannot afford. Countless families who are entirely self-supporting in every other respect cannot meet the expense of serious illness.

Although the individual or even small groups of individuals cannot successfully or economically plan to meet the cost of illness, large groups of people can do so. If the financial risk of illness is spread among all our people, no one person is overburdened. More important, if the cost is spread in this manner more persons can see their doctors, and will see them earlier. This goal can be reached only through a national medical insurance program, under which all people who are covered by an insurance fund are entitled to necessary medical, hospital and related services.

A national health insurance program is a logical extension of the present social-security system which is so firmly entrenched in our American democracy. Of the four basic risks to the security of working people and their families — unemployment, old age, death and sickness — we have provided some insurance protection against three. Protection against the fourth — sickness — is the major missing element in our national social insurance program.

An insurance plan is the American way of accomplishing our objective. It is consistent with our democratic principles. It is the only plan broad enough to meet the needs of all our people. It is — in the long run — far less costly and far more effective than public charity or a medical dole.

Under the program which I have proposed patients can and will be as free to select their own doctors as they are today. Doctors and hospitals can and will be free to participate or to reject participation. And a national health insurance plan can and should provide for administration through state and local agencies, subject only to reasonable national standards.

Finally, I should like to repeat to the Congress my earlier recommendation that the people of America be protected against loss of earnings due to illness or disability not connected with their work. Protection against temporary disability is already provided by two states and is being con-

sidered in others. Comprehensive disability insurance should exist throughout the Nation. It can and should be a part of our social insurance system.

The total health program which I have proposed is crucial to our national
welfare. The heart of that program is national health insurance. Until
it is a part of our national fabric, we shall be wasting our most precious national resource and shall be perpetuating unnecessary misery and human
suffering.

I urge the Congress to give immediate attention to the development and
enactment of national health and disability insurance programs.

Harry S. Truman

*This presidential pressure insured that there would be a pretense of action
in the medical care field despite an unfavorable political climate. Senators
Wagner and Murray sponsored a national health insurance bill (S. 1320)
and Senator Taft reintroduced his earlier legislation (S. 545).*

*Hearings on both bills (S. 1320 and S. 545) were held during May, June,
and July, 1947 and January, February, May, and June, 1948 with unfortunate results. At best, they seemed to harden the position of both opponents
and proponents and at worst, they became vitriolic attacks on the names of
many distinguished public servants.*

*The AMA was cautious, if not outwardly hostile, towards both bills, but
on this occasion there were some physicians prepared to support health
insurance. As time passed, the tone of the hearings degenerated completely,
and by 1948 the hearings were dominated by the testimony of Dr. Marjorie
Shearen, a violent opponent of "socialized medicine". Dr. Shearen alleged
that she had been muzzled while working for the Federal Security Agency
and then called on physicians to resist to the last ditch, something physicians, and particularly the AMA, were only too eager to do. Nor did the representatives of organized medicine limit their activities to the direct issue of
federally–funded medical care. They were also busily resisting any sort of
disability insurance which might entail the state funding of medical
diagnosis.*

*Compared to the optimism of Truman's first presidential health message
in 1945, the future of national health insurance seemed bleak. A stalemate
was rapidly being reached.*

*Two philosophies were in conflict. National health insurance, like other
aspects of the contributory social security program, would be a right for all
beneficiaries; no means test was involved. The assistance approach, on
the other hand, rejected blanket coverage through any compulsory system;
instead, publicly-supported medical care would be made available only to
those who could not afford to purchase it privately. This latter philosophy
permeated the Taft proposals and was later incorporated into the Kerr-
Mills Act (1960) and into Title XIX of the Social Security Amendments
of 1965.*

1949 – 1952

The year 1949 looked more promising for medical care legislation in view of the 1948 Republican defeat. Understandably the presidential messages strongly favored national health insurance and Truman declared that "national health insurance is the only workable way to assure that all individuals have access to the medical care they need. I recommend the enactment of such a program this year." The program was finally published in April.

The proposed "National Health Insurance and Public Health Act" (S. 1679) included a system of grants and scholarships for the education of health personnel (Title I), provision for the exchange of medical research through national research institutes (Title II), an enlarged hospital survey and construction program (Title III), special aid for rural and other shortage areas, particularly assistance to farmers' health cooperatives (Title IV), grants to states for public health work (Title V), and research grants for programs on child life, maternal and child health, and crippled children (Title VI). The core of the bill was the controversial Title VII "Prepaid Personal Health Insurance Benefits", the last serious attempt to introduce a comprehensive national health service into this country. Most provisions of the other titles were sooner or later enacted into law, but Title VII met too stiff an opposition.

The hearings were as acrimonious and inconclusive as they had been in the eightieth Congress, and they were distinguished only by the first appearance of health insurance testimony. The two sides were too far apart for any useful results. The AMA was merciless in its attacks on the Federal Security Agency, and the supporters of the bill did not hesitate to vigorously attack the AMA. Attempts to argue rationally were to no avail, although the AMA was pushed into supporting some program of vendor payments for public assistance recipients.

Meanwhile the Senate Labor and Public Welfare Committee was holding hearings. After a clash with Acting Administrator Kingsley, Senator Taft appeared to promote his own alternative.

National Health Program of 1949
Hearings on S. 1106, S. 1456, S. 1581, and S. 1679
before a Subcommittee of the Senate Labor and
Public Welfare Committee
81st Cong., 1st Sess. (May and June, 1949)
(p. 111)

Statement of Honorable Robert A. Taft

Senator Taft. Mr. Chairman and members of the committee, Senator Donnell and I appear here today to present to the committee and explain Senate bill 1581, which we introduced in common with Senator Smith of New Jersey. Senator Smith is, unfortunately, ill at home and is unable to appear with us at this time.

Mr. Chairman, I think we all realize the general situation and the problems which this committee has been trying to meet in a number of different ways. We have today a very extensive medical system in the United States. We feel that it is a good system and that the problems which arise out of it are problems which would arise under any circumstances and which should be met by constructive study and by the adoption of measures which may effect a steady improvement in that system, not by throwing away the system and beginning over again.

In the first place, of course, we have the problems of public health, research, and preventive medicine. That field has been and is today the field of Government primarily. There is, of course, some very important private research in that field, particularly in basic medical problems. There is a good deal of scattered work in the field of public health among private charitable institutions. But in general, of course, it cannot be done on a commercial basis at all and it is and should be the function of Government.

This function includes the diagnosis and inspection of the health of school children and other general measures directed to preventing the development of disease. The Government has a wide field in which those functions can be increased and improved. I think it is the first and primary function of Government to bring about that improvement.

The second feature of our general medical system is that of providing medical care. It has always been assumed in this country that those able to pay for medical care would buy their own medical service, just as under any system, except a socialistic system, they buy their own food, their own housing, their own clothing, and their own automobiles.

Obviously, many families have difficulty in providing food, housing, clothing, and automobiles, but no more difficulty, certainly, in providing medical care.

The general appeal in this country has always been for those who are unable to buy medical care, unable to pay for their own expenses in the medical field. We have brought about, in order to meet that situation, a great development of private charity throughout the United States. Those charities have then been supported by Community Chest organizations throughout the States, which lay a tremendous amount of their appeal to the people for funds on the necessity for providing adequate medical care for those who are unable to pay for it.

That work has been supplemented by the States and local communities through their general hospitals, free nursing and medical service in hospitals, services of preliminary and preventive nature through public health units, so that medical care has already been made available to a large proportion of those who are unable to pay for it in the United States.

Undoubtedly, in that system there are gaps, particularly in rural districts and poorer districts in the cities, and we have a very definite interest in trying to fill up those gaps.

There also developed the realization that illness may be concentrated; that illness in the case of families who can pay for medical care may be concentrated in a single year and, thus, assume the nature of a catastrophe.

This has ordinarily been met in the past by the furnishing of the same kind of free medical care as that furnished to those who could not pay for it at all. But it was conceived that that problem could be met by providing medical insurance that would take care of extreme cases of illness, just as fire insurance takes care of the destruction of a single building by fire and the tremendous loss, which may occur at one time but which through the insurance system can be spread over a great number of people and a great length of time. This insurance has been gradually developing on a private basis and a not-for-profit basis in the United States until it is fairly generally available to the people.

In general, we believe that the present system has done an excellent job. I disagree entirely with Mr. Kingsley's statement on page 7 of his report that:

> It appears to be agreed that our present system of payment for medical care is totally inadequate.

I do not think that is at all true, and I think we have in this system as good a system of medical care as they have in any country in the world, with the possible exception of one or two small countries where their health problems are much less complicated and much easier to deal with.

Last year, when our committee met here, that is the Subcommittee on Health, which had more or less these same measures before it, the Brookings Institution was requested to make a study, at the request of Senator Smith, who was then chairman of the Subcommittee on Health of this committee. That study was made by George W. Bachman and Lewis Meriam, with the support of the Brookings Institution, and I assume this report, entitled "The Issue of Compulsory Health Insurance," will be furnished to every member of the committee, and I hope every member of the committee will read it, if they have not already done so.

The conclusions of that report are stated on page 67, and I quote:

> The conclusions based on this foundation—

the foundation of the evidence which had been reviewed—

> are:
>
> 1. Probably no great nation in the world has among its white population better health than prevails in the United States. A few small homogeneous countries such as New Zealand with respect to its white population, are slightly ahead of the United States as a whole, but certain States of the United States with larger populations equal them.

2. It is apparent that the United States under its voluntary system of medical care has made greater progress in the application of medical and sanitary science than any other country. This progress is now reflected in low mortality and morbidity rates of infectious diseases and in increased life expectancy. There is every reason to believe that these trends will continue unabated under our present system of medical care.
3. The nonwhites in the United States have materially poorer health than the whites, but the evidence does not indicate that this condition is primarily or even mainly due to inadequacy of medical care.
4. The advances in health among both the whites and the nonwhites that have been made in the United States in the past four decades do not suggest basic defects in the American system.

There are various criticisms of the system in the other recommendations, although I will not read the entire recommendations, because it is available in its entirety to the committee, and there are, of course, many defects in the system, but I only want to question the basis on which we are asked to throw away the present system in the claim made that the present system is totally inadequate.

Several other bills were also presented but none was reported out of committee either that year or in 1950.

While the President still pressed publicly for health insurance, he obviously would have been satisfied with a less dramatic breakthrough. His annual message to Congress in 1950 foresaw the strengthening of medical care through public assistance as a result of the 1949 Social Security Amendments which had already passed the House and were waiting for Senate action.

However the promise of a national, compulsory health insurance system for the whole population was to remain unfulfilled for AMA opposition prevented any direct, federal, medical care program. Advocates of a federal insurance plan turned instead to hospital insurance, and concentrated on the plight of the aged. The new emphasis was reflected in the 1951 Annual Report of the Social Security Administration.

During 1951 and 1952 congressional fights were mainly over disability insurance. The AMA had effectively killed the disability freeze in the 1952 act through a meaningless compromise, but the establishment of vendor payments in PA and a possible health care program for the elderly still left some liberals hopeful. Certainly concern with the nation's health had not evaporated entirely. The Commission on the Health Needs of the Nation, appointed by the President early in 1952, favored an extension of federally-supported medical care in their December report.

Building America's Health
A Report to the President by the President's Commission
on the Health Needs of the Nation
Vol. 1 — Findings and Recommendations
(1952)

INTRODUCTION

The maintenance of health must now be added to food, shelter, and clothing as one of the necessities of living. Health means more than freedom from disease, freedom from pain, freedom from untimely death. It means optimum physical, mental, and social efficiency and well-being. The individual ranks health for himself, and for his family even more, high in the scale of human aspirations. For the State, health is the wellspring of a nation's strength, its provision and protection one of the first obligations.

Health reflects dynamically the measure of man's control over his environment and his ever-changing adjustment to it. Health makes possible the maximum self-expression and self-development of man. It is the first prerequisite for leading a full life. The degree to which individuals, voluntary groups, and the State cooperate successfully in providing for the health of all represents the maturity and level of civilization of the Nation.

Importance of Health Services

Failure to safeguard health, whether through ignorance, neglect, or the lack of means, exposes the individual to suffering, incapacity, or death. National neglect of proper measures for the preservation of health exposes the country to weakness and destruction. The goal of optimum physical, mental, and social efficiency and well-being justifies all prudent efforts for its attainment — whether these be social measures necessary for the promotion of health; application of technical skills in the prevention of disease, diagnosis, treatment and rehabilitation; training of specialized personnel; expansion of facilities; or the organization necessary to make health services available to all.

The increased importance of health services to the individual and the Nation, and the changed social viewpoint that has emerged as a result of the acquisition of procedures that are truly life-saving, necessitate a re-evaluation of our attitudes toward providing them. We need a set of principles which, while embodying due regard for the strong traditions and sound practices of the past, take cognizance of the epoch-making changes of the present and the potentialities of the future. There was a time, only a few decades back, when our state of medical knowledge was such that it severely limited endeavors to improve the health of the people through the extension of medical services. That day is past.

It is now abundantly clear that the provision of adequate health services profoundly affects the individual's chances of survival and the strength and happiness of the Nation as well. This fact imposes certain ethical and practical considerations upon us. When the very life of a man, or the lives of his family, may depend upon his receiving adequate medical services, society must make every effort to provide them. When this man knows that such health boons exist, available to some and denied to him, a free society will find the way to comply with the demand that he will surely make. These benefits sometimes can be obtained by the individual's own effort; but when these efforts fail, other means must be found. And democracy requires that the same high quality of service be made available to all men equally.

Individual and Social Responsibility

The individual effort of an informed person will do more for his health and that of his family than all the things which can be done for them. In the past, measures for health maintenance demanded individual responsibility only to a limited degree. The development of pure water supplies, pasteurization of milk, and other sanitary accomplishments were achieved through social action in which the individual may have participated as a citizen, but was required to take no further individual responsibility.

Future accomplishments, however, depend to an even greater degree upon the individual's assumption of responsibility for his own health. It is the individual who must consult his physician for early care, avoid obesity and alcholism, and drive his automobile safely. These things cannot be done for him. They require both information and motivation. Personal health practices which are determined by the individual's knowledge, attitude and decision have now become of paramount importance in gaining health. Effort by each person to improve his own health can be expected to pay great returns.

Recognition of the significance of individual responsibility for health does not discharge the obligation of a society which is interested in the health of its citizenry. Such recognition, in fact, increases social responsibility for health. Heretofore social effort in behalf of health has been limited largely to such measures as delivery of pure water to the individual's tap and the sanitary disposal of his sewage. Now it becomes necessary for a society which wishes to advance the health of its citizens to adopt measures which guarantee to the individual an opportunity to make appropriate decisions in behalf of his health. Society must assure its citizens access to professional services, education concerning personal health practices, and a reasonably safe physical environment. Only then can individual responsibility for health exercised through personal action reach its full potential.

As a matter of fact, for most of those who now lack comprehensive health services, the reason lies in large measure beyond individual control. The individual may not be sufficiently well informed to appreciate the benefit and hence does not actively demand it. In many other instances, the health personnel and facilities do not exist in the area in which he lives. Moreover, an individual may be fully convinced of the primary value of the best health service for himself and his family, yet not have available the money to purchase it or the arrangements to secure it.

Government and Health Services

Hence, the community — and particularly the most responsible community organization, government — must participate in the expansion of means to achieve health. In assuring the development of proper facilities and in seeing that comprehensive health services are made available to all, the local, State, and Federal governments have both separate and joint responsibilities.

The local community (or region) should be the focus for the administration of most of the direct medical services provided to the individual. Its local health unit should be adequate to the task of supplying community-wide sanitation and preventive services. Its citizens should supply much of the initiative needed to expand its medical plant and induce medical personnel to practice in the area. At public hearings across the country we were deeply impressed with the work of voluntary local health councils in stimulating imaginative community planning, leading to direct action in the health field.

State governments have many responsibilities in the health field in addition to giving both financial and advisory assistance to local community health services. They have the traditional responsibility of caring for the mentally ill and the tuberculous. State health departments have vast responsibilities in planning the expansion of health resources and in stimulating Statewide attacks on disease.

The Federal Government, first of all, is responsible for seeing that our Nation's military personnel and our veterans get the highest quality of medical care. It also must provide services to such special groups as merchant seamen and Indians.

Then, since the good health of our people is a national resource, the Federal Government has a major responsibility for promoting and stimulating a comprehensive health program for all our people. The Federal Government, therefore, must provide leadership and initiative in planning the development of our health resources. Of particular importance is the obligation of our Nation's Government to equalize the opportunities for health among the citizens of the various States through use of the Federal taxing power to overcome the disadvantages of low-income States. Grants-in-aid to State and local governments to help them carry out their responsibilities in the health field should continue as an important form of national assistance. One of the most important roles of the Federal Government in health is to act as a catalyst, to stimulate new programs and to expand existing ones. In this connection the grant-in-aid principle has already proved itself to be an effective mechanism for arousing state and local effort. Finally, the Federal Government must take whatever other steps prove necessary to safeguard what is probably our most important national resource—the health of our people.

Frequently, it is hard to draw the line where the responsibility of one segment of government leaves off and another begins. In reality, a feeling of partnership should pervade all levels of government for both the initiation and maintenance of health programs. Each level of government can perform certain functions in health with greatest effectiveness, and this should be the real criterion in assigning tasks.

In considering the roles of the individual and various elements of Government in securing health services, one must not lose sight of a most precious relationship for health. Throughout the whole history of civilized man the relationship between patient and physician has been a special thing. In days when scientific knowledge was scanty, this relationship yielded about all the benefits the patient received. Even today, all the complex arrangements that exist to provide medical care have not replaced it. The patient's confidence in his physician underlies most successful care. But now the physician needs more than knowledge of human nature and love of mankind. To be effective in the modern sense he must have the help that the modern hospital supplies, the assistance of trained helpers, and adequate facilities.

Comprehensive Health Services

The physician no longer makes his sole contribution to the health of individuals and the Nation by treating disease. Now, a broader view of health service is being developed—one that takes into account more than what a physician does in the diagnosis and treatment of disease. It includes things that are done in the absence of disease, namely, the promotion of health and prevention of disease; and what is done beyond the ordinary treatment of disease, namely, rehabilitation. This view, a spectrum of comprehensive health services, specifically includes the contribution of a variety of personnel and of community services. The physician leads the over-all effort, but as one member of a well-trained team comprised of dentists, nurses, technicians, and many other professional health workers. Only through such joint endeavor can the whole range of services be delivered.

To be most effective the health team, with community and national support, must achieve a smooth continuum of care—embracing promotion of health, prevention of diseases, diagnosis and treatment, and rehabilitation—all of which is constantly improved through education and research.

Health Principles

From such considerations the Commission has formulated these principles to be used as a guide in approaching our health problem.

WE BELIEVE THAT:

1. Access to the means for the attainment and preservation of health is a basic human right.
2. Effort of the individual himself is a vitally important factor in attaining and maintaining health.
3. The physician-patient relationship is so fundamental to health that everyone should have a personal physician.
4. The physician should have access to proper facilities and equipment, affiliation on some basis with a hospital, and the help of trained personnel in order to fulfill his part in providing comprehensive health services.
5. Comprehensive health service includes the positive promotion of health, the prevention of disease, the diagnosis and treatment of disease, the rehabilitation of the disabled — all supported by constantly improving education of personnel and a continuous program of research.
6. Comprehensive health service is the concern of society and is best insured when all elements of society participate in providing it.
7. Responsibility for health is a joint one, with the individual citizen and local, State, Federal governments each having major contributions to make toward its fuller realization.
8. The American people desire and deserve comprehensive health service of the highest quality and in our dynamic expanding economy the means can be found to provide it.
9. The same high quality of health services should be available to all people equally.
10. A health program must take into account the progress and experience of the past, the realities of the present, and must be flexible enough to cope with future changes.

We set as a goal for this Nation a situation in which adequate health personnel, facilities, and organization make comprehensive health services available for all, with a method of financing to make this care universally accessible. We are confident that many of the great plagues of the past can be eradicated; present knowledge makes possible the extermination of tuberculosis, syphilis, typhoid fever, diphtheria and other diseases. We look forward to the control of poliomyelitis, cancer, and many forms of heart disease. We expect to see a splendid hospital system with every area of the country provided with an adequate number of beds, and the obsolete structures of the past replaced by new facilities which embody all the modern advances. We seek the expansion of our educational system so that an adequate number of physicians and all other needed health personnel will be trained, with every qualified boy and girl having an equal opportunity to enter the professions. We favor continued research into health problems, including the training of an adequate number of scientific workers and providing them with facilities to carry out their work.

We believe it is well within the economic potential of this country to provide itself with the finest system of medical care in the world, that the American people desire this and deserve no less. We believe that it is true economy to invest in bigger and better health services, since the cost of adequate health promotion and protection is probably far less than the cost involved to the Nation through its neglect of health. The added contributions a healthier people could make to a better and more secure life for all justify increased expenditures for these purposes.

Apart from humanitarian considerations, the dollar-and-cents savings in the reduction of disease and disability more than justify increased expenditures for better health services.

Finally, we are convinced that the good health of the American people is a powerful democratic resource in our effort to build a united, free world. By the same token, our civil defense health services can be only as strong as the resources which underlie them. Constant planning and building of our basic health services, therefore, strengthen the ramparts of civil defense and increase the vitality of our leadership in the free world.

REORGANIZATION AND ADMINISTRATION
1945–1952

It was during 1946 that President Truman issued his second reorganization plan dealing with the Federal Security Agency. The plan was presumably a preparation for the establishment of the Department of Health, Education, and Welfare and, in general, strengthened the power of the Federal Security Agency in social policy. Under the Government Reorganization Act of 1945, the plan would go into effect on July 16, 1946 unless it were vetoed by both houses before then. The House voted down the plan but in spite of considerable hostility it was passed in the Senate and went into effect on July 16.

Special Presidential Message to the Congress
Transmitting Reorganization Plan 2 of 1946
(May 16, 1946)*

To the Congress of the United States:

The fundamental strength of a nation lies within its people. Military and industrial power are evidences, not the real source of strength. Over the years the prosperity of America and its place in the world will depend on

*Public Papers of the Presidents, Harry S. Truman 1946, p. 255.

the health, the education, the ingenuity, and the integrity of its people and on their ability to work together and with other nations.

The most basic and at the same time the most difficult task of any country is the conservation and development of its human resources. Under our system of government this is a joint responsibility of the Federal, State, and local governments, but in it the Federal Government has a large and vital role to play. Through its research, advice, stimulation, and financial aid, it contributes greatly to progress and to the equalization of standards in the fields of education, health, and welfare; and in the field of social insurance it also directly administers a major segment of the program.

To meet its full responsibilities in those fields, the Federal Government requires efficient machinery for the administration of its social programs. Until 1939, the agencies in charge of those activities were scattered in many parts of the Government. In that year President Roosevelt took the first great step toward effective organization in this area when he submitted Reorganization Plan I establishing the Federal Security Agency "to promote social and economic security, educational opportunity, and the health of the citizens of the nation."

The time has now come for further steps to strengthen the machinery of the Federal Government for leadership and service in dealing with the social problems of the country. Several programs closely bound up with the objectives of the Federal Security Agency are still scattered in other parts of the Government. As the next step, I consider it essential to transfer these programs to the Federal Security Agency and to strengthen its internal organization and management.

Broadly stated, the basic purpose of the Federal Security Agency is the conservation and development of the human resources of the nation. Within that broad objective come the following principal functions: child care and development, education, health, social insurance, welfare (in the sense of care of the needy and the defective), and recreation (apart from the operation of parks in the public domain).

These functions constitute a natural family of closely-related services, interwoven at many points and in many ways. For example, the development of day-care centers for children has involved joint planning and service by specialists of the Children's Bureau, the Office of Education, the Public Health Service, and several other agencies. The schools are both a major consumer of public health services and a leading vehicle for health education and for disseminating the results of research carried on by the Public Health Service. The promotion of social security involves a whole battery of activities, especially social insurance, public assistance, health and child welfare.

In order to proceed as promptly as possible with the development of the Federal Security Agency to meet the post-war responsibilities of the Government within its field of activity, I am transmitting herewith Reorganization Plan No. 2, which I have prepared in accordance with the provisions of section 3 of the Reorganization Act of 1945 (Public No. 263, 79th Congress, 1st Session), approved December 20, 1945; and I declare that, with respect to each reorganization made in this Plan, I have found that such reorganization is necessary to accomplish one or more of the purposes of section 2(a) of the Act:

(1) to facilitate orderly transition from war to peace;
(2) to reduce expenditures and promote economy;
(3) to increase efficiency;
(4) to group, coordinate, and consolidate agencies and functions according to major purposes;
(5) to reduce the number of agencies by consolidating those having similar functions, and to abolish such agencies or functions thereof as may not be necessary for the efficient conduct of the Government; and
(6) to eliminate overlapping and duplication of effort.

The Plan includes certain interagency transfers and several abolitions and changes in the internal organization of the Federal Security Agency.

The Plan transfers to the Federal Security Administrator the functions of the Children's Bureau, except those relating to child labor under the Fair Labor Standards Act. These child labor functions are transferred to the Secretary of Labor in order that they may be performed by, or in close relationship with, the Wage and Hour Division which administers the rest of the Act. The Plan continues the Children's Bureau within the Federal Security Agency to deal with problems of child life, but is flexible enough to enable the Administrator to gear in the Bureau's programs effectively with other activities of the Agency.

The child labor program is the only permanent program of the Children's Bureau that is properly a labor function. The other four—child welfare, crippled children, child and maternal health, and research in problems of child life—all fall within the scope of the Federal Security Agency. The transfer of the Children's Bureau will not only close a serious gap in the work of the Agency, but it will strengthen the child-care programs by bringing them into closer association with the health, welfare, and educational activities with which they are inextricably bound up.

The promotion of the education, health, welfare, and social security of the nation is a vast cooperative undertaking of the Federal, State, and local governments. It involves numerous grant-in-aid programs and complex inter-governmental relations. The transfer of the Children's Bureau will simplify these relations and make for better cooperation.

To illustrate, State welfare departments now depend on both the Bureau of Public Assistance in the Federal Security Agency and the Children's Bureau in the Labor Department for funds for child-care activities. Similarly, State health departments obtain grants from the Public Health Service for general public health work and from the Children's Bureau for child and maternal health activities. All of these grants involve the establishment of minimum standards and a measure of Federal supervision. The transfer of the Children's Bureau programs will make it possible to develop more consistent policies and procedures and to simplify dealings with the States. This will eliminate needless inconvenience for both parties and enable the State and Federal Governments to join more efficiently in their common objective of furthering the health and welfare of the American child.

Next, the Plan transfers the vital statistics functions of the Census Bureau to the Federal Security Administrator, to be performed through the Public Health Service or other facilities of the Federal Security Agency. In every State but one the State health department is in charge of vital statistics. The work in the States is partially financed from public health grants administered by the Public Health Service. This transfer will make the agency providing the grants also responsible for carrying on the Federal part of the vital statistics program. Furthermore, it will make for a better correlation of vital statistics with morbidity statistics, which are closely connected in nature and are already handled by the Public Health Service. In addition, the Federal Security Agency, more than any other Federal agency in peacetime, depends on vital statistics and vital records in the operation of its programs.

The Plan transfers the functions of the United States Employees Compensation Commission to the Federal Security Administrator, and provides for a three-member board of appeals to hear and finally decide appeals on claims of Government employees. By abolishing the Commission, the Plan eliminates a small agency and lightens the burden on the President. The Federal Security Administrator, as the head of the Federal agency with the greatest experience in insurance administration, is in the best position to guide and further the program of the Commission.

The abolition of the Commission as an administrative body and the creation of an appeals board will provide the advantages of a single official in charge of operations while affording claimants the protection of a three-member board for the final decision of appeals on claims. This arrangement has proved both administratively efficient and satisfactory to claimants in many similar programs. It is essentially the plan used in the administration of veterans' pensions and old-age and survivors insurance and employed by many States in their workmen's compensation programs. The board of appeals created by this Plan will deal only with claims of Government employees since appeals on other types of claims under the jurisdiction of the Commission—(a) longshoremen and harbor workers, and (b) private employees in the District of Columbia—are heard by the Federal District Courts rather than the Commission.

The Reorganization Plan which created the Federal Security Agency in 1939 provided that the Federal Security Administrator should direct and supervise the Social Security Board, and that he might assign administrative duties to the Chairman of the Board, rather than to the Board as a whole. Thus, it took the first step toward establishing a definite line of responsibility for the administration of social security functions in the Agnecy. The Plan I am now submitting further clarifies these lines of responsibility by providing for the normal type of internal organization used in Federal departments and agencies.

A full-time board in charge of a group of bureaus within an agency is at best an anomaly. The Social Security Board rendered an outstanding service in launching the social security program, and its members deserve the thanks of the nation for this achievement. The program, however, is now firmly established and its administration needs to be tied in more fully with other programs of the Federal Security Agency. The existence of a department within a department is a serious barrier to effective integration.

In order to obtain more expeditious and effective direction for the social security program and to further the development of the Federal Security Agency, this Plan transfers the functions of the Social Security Board to the Federal Security Administrator and provides for not more than two new assistant heads of the Agency for the administration of the program. Because of the additional functions transferred to the Administrator by this Plan, I have found that these officers will be needed to assist him in the general management of the Agency and to head the constituent unit or units which the Administrator will have to establish for the conduct of social security activities.

To permit a consolidation of work for the blind, the functions of the Office of Education as to the vending stand program for the blind are transferred to the Federal Security Administrator, in whom are vested other vocational rehabilitation functions. This transfer will permit the program to be assigned to the Office of Vocational Rehabilitation, where other vocational rehabilitation activities for the blind are now concentrated.

*   *   *

In order to enable the Administrator more adequately to coordinate the administration of the grant-in-aid programs vested by statute in the constituent units of the Federal Security Agency, the Plan provides that, insofar as practicable and consistent with the applicable legislation, he shall establish uniform standards and procedures for these programs and permit States to submit a single plan of operation for related grant-in-aid programs. Most of these programs involve the establishment of certain minimum standards on fiscal, personnel, and other aspects of administration in the States. In many cases, the same State Agency is operating under two or more grant-in-aid programs. Much needless inconvenience and confusion can be avoided for all concerned by unifying Federal standards and combining State plans for the operation of the programs in such cases.

After careful consideration of a number of other agencies and functions I have refrained from proposing in this Plan their transfer to the Federal Security Agency. Most of these involve activities which, though related to the functions of the Federal Security Agency, are incidental to the purpose of other agencies or are connected so closely with such agencies as to make transfer undesirable. A few are activities which should probably be shifted in whole or in part to the Federal Security Agency, but I believe such shifts can best be accomplished by interagency agreement or action in connection with appropriations.

The Reorganization Plan here presented is a second important step in building a central agency for the administration of Federal activities primarily relating to the conservation and development of human resources. But, while this step is important in itself, I believe that a third step should soon be taken. The time is at hand when that agency should be converted into an Executive department.

The size and scope of the Federal Security Agency and the importance of its functions clearly call for departmental status and a permanent place in the President's Cabinet. In number of personnel and volume of expenditures the Agency exceeds several of the existing departments. Much more important, the fundamental character of its functions—education, health, welfare, social insurance—and their significance for the future of the country demand for it the highest level of administrative leadership and a voice in the central councils of the Executive Branch.

Accordingly, I shall soon recommend to the Congress that legislation be promptly enacted making the Federal Security Agency an Executive department, defining its basic purpose, and authorizing the President to transfer to it such units and activities as come within that definition.

The people expect the Federal Government to meet its full responsibilities for the conservation and development of the human resources of the nation in the years that lie ahead. This Reorganization Plan and the legislation that I shall propose will provide the broad and firm foundation required for the accomplishment of that objective.

Harry S. Truman

The following year Truman submitted another reorganization plan, attempting, among other things, to transfer the U.S. Employment Service to the Department of Labor. Congress promptly rejected the plan but on January 19, 1948, Truman tried again. His reorganization plan of 1948 joined the U.S. Employment Service to the Federal Security Agency's Bureau of Employment Security, and then transferred the new agency to the Department of Labor. Thus, Truman was requesting changes in addition to those rejected the year before. The business community opposed the plan, fearing higher unemployment taxes if the Labor Department administered unemployment insurance benefits. The reorganization plan was subsequently rejected by both houses.

**Special Presidential Message to the Congress
Transmitting Reorganization Plan 1 of 1948**
(January 19, 1948)*

To the Congress of the United States:

I transmit herewith Reorganization Plan No. 1 of 1948, under the Reorganization Act of 1945, which transfers the United States Employment Service and the Bureau of Employment Security to the Department of Labor. The United States Employment Service is now in the Department of Labor by temporary transfer under authority of Title I of the First War Powers Act, 1941, while the Bureau of Employment Security is at present a constituent unit of the Federal Security Agency. This plan will place the administration of the employment service and unemployment compensation functions of the Federal Government in the most appropriate location within the Executive establishment and will provide for their proper coordination.

I find that this proposed reorganization is necessary to accomplish the following purposes of the Reorganization Act of 1945: (1) to group, coordinate, and consolidate agencies and functions of the Government according to major purposes, (2) to increase the efficiency of the operations of the Government, and (3) to promote economy to the fullest extent consistent with the efficient operation of the Government.

The United States Employment Service was established in the Department of Labor by the Wagner-Peyser Act in 1933. It was later transferred under Reorganization Plan No. 1, effective July 1, 1939, to the Social Security Board in the Federal Security Agency. After the creation of the War Manpower Commission, the United States Employment Service was placed under that Commission by Executive Order No. 9247 of September 17, 1942. Shortly after the Japanese surrender the Service was transferred to the Department of Labor by Executive Order No. 9617. Both of these transfers were made under the temporary authority of Title I of the First War Powers Act.

The provision of nation-wide system of public employment offices, which assists workers to get jobs and employers to obtain labor, belongs under the leadership of the Secretary of Labor. Within our Federal Government the Department of Labor is the agency primarily concerned with the labor market and problems of employment.

The Department of Labor already has within its organization many, but not all, of the resources needed for the full performance of this role. It has a broad understanding of working conditions and the factors in labor turnover. Through the Bureau of Labor Statistics, it develops extensive information on the long-term trends in employment and on the occupational

Public Papers of the Presidents, Harry S. Truman, 1948, p. 102.

characteristics of the labor force. Through the Apprentice Training Service it promotes the development of needed skills. I consider it necessary and desirable that these facilities of the Department of Labor should now be augmented by the other major operating agencies in the field of employment — the United States Employment Service and the Bureau of Employment Security. These agencies are concerned, as is the Department of Labor, with the full and proper employment of American workers.

The results achieved by the Employment Service after more than two years of operation within the Department of Labor strongly justify the decision to place these functions permanently within that Department. More employers are now using the facilities of the public employment offices than ever before in the history of the peace-time Employment Service. More services are being furnished employers by the public employment offices than ever before. Today the public employment office has become the central labor exchange in the community and the primary source of information of employment opportunities and immediate labor market trends.

The Bureau of Employment Security in the Federal Security Agency administers the Federal activities relating to the nationwide unemployment compensation system. As a practical matter these functions have proved to be intimately related to those of the United States Employment Service. Under existing state laws, claimants for unemployment compensation must register with the Employment Service before they may become eligible for benefits. In consequence nearly all states have assigned the administration of these two programs to the same agency.

Both the employment service and the unemployment compensation system are concerned with the worker as a member of the labor force. Both are concerned with shortening the periods of unemployment and with promoting continuity of employment. When the worker becomes unemployed, the alternatives are either to assist him in obtaining new employment or to pay him benefits. The proper emphasis is on employment rather than on benefit payments. This emphasis can best be achieved by having the two programs administered in the agency most concerned with the employment process — the Labor Department.

By reason of the reorganizations made by this plan, I find that the responsibilities and duties of the Secretary of Labor will be of such nature as to require the inclusion in the plan of provisions for the appointment and compensation of a Commissioner of Employment to coordinate the employment service and unemployment insurance activities within the Department. The plan also provides that the Federal Advisory Council, a group representative of labor, management and the public, authorized by the Wagner-Peyser Act, shall advise the Secretary and the Commissioner on the operation of both the unemployment compensation system and the United States Employment Service.

Harry S. Truman

After rejecting the President's plan, Congress attached a rider to the FSA supplemental funds bill, transferring the USES to the FSA's Bureau of Employment Security. The bill passed and then passed again over the President's veto.

In 1949 Truman again tried to move the employment security programs to the Department of Labor and this time he was successful. However even more radical reform was envisaged. As early as 1947, the President had called for the establishment of a Department of Welfare "to further our national program in the fields of health, education, and welfare." It was probably not surprising that the eightieth Congress refused to make the change, but the President tried again with the eighty-first.

Complicating the struggle for a new Department of Welfare were plans for still another department—one to coordinate all governmental medical and health programs. In 1947 the AMA appeared before a Senate subcommittee to support a bill creating an independent Department of Health. Their proposal was rejected by the committee, however.

In 1949 opponents of the Truman Plan instead urged unification of all governmental health and medical programs into a new semi-autonomous department, similar to the United Medical Administration recommended by the Hoover Commission. Truman rejected the proposal.

Senator Robert Taft then went before a Senate subcommittee to support the Hoover Commission's recommendation, which he had incorporated into a bill of his own. Taft did not object to the inclusion of a health administration in a Department of Health, Education, and Welfare, as did the AMA.

National Health Program of 1949
Hearings before a Subcommittee of the Senate
Labor and Public Welfare Committee
81st Cong., 1st Sess. (September, 1949)
(p. 114-16)

Senator [Claude] Pepper [Dem., Fla.]. . . . your bill would make the health agency have cabinet status, would it?

Senator Taft. No; it is an independent agency and I understand it is so under the Hoover Commission report. I personally have supported the idea of a Department of Health, Welfare, and Education, as you know, and I would not object to putting this health agency into such a department.

My only view is that if we did that, it should be a very distinct bureau of that agency and that the head of the health activity, the Health Bureau, should be responsible directly to the Secretary who sat in the Cabinet, that he should have direct access to that Secretary and not have some intermediate Under Secretary or others through whom he would have to go.

The bill I supported here last year had that provision, I think three Under Secretaries, one for Health, one for Education, and one for Welfare.

Various other parts of the bill cover this question of public health. Some of them are not before this committee, but we feel that the public health end of the bill and of the activities of this committee are just as important as the general problem of medical care. I think the authors of the bill have always favored the various bills for increased research in cancer, heart, psychiatry, dentistry; I cooperated with Senator Hill in rewriting the Hill-Burton bill after Senator Burton was appointed to the Court, and we have generally, all of us, favored the measures which gave Government aid in this general field of public health.

Taft's bill also was rejected.

After Truman failed in 1949, he tried offering a slightly modified plan in 1950, leaving the Public Health Service and the Office of Education semi-independent within the new department. The Senate Committee on Expenditures in the Executive Departments reported the bill unfavorably and the program failed. Other Taft proposals for a United Medical Administration met similar continued opposition.

President Truman finally gave up. After the 1950 congressional rejection his failure to elevate the FSA can partially be blamed on speculation that the first secretary would have been Oscar Ewing, the FSA Administrator and advocate of a national health insurance program.

For five years the Truman Administration had attempted to consolidate various health, education, and welfare programs within a single department on the cabinet level. All these plans failed, and it was up to Eisenhower to create a Department of Health, Education, and Welfare.

A survey of organization and administration between 1945 and 1952 must also include the battles between the Social Security Administration and Congress in 1948. Congress felt that Social Security was too independent and did not co-ordinate its activities with the remainder of the Federal Security Agency. In fact, there was probably little love lost between the Commissioner of Social Security and the Administrator of the Agency, but as a result of congressional hostility the SSA appropriation for independent services was drastically cut. (See Investigation of the Federal Security Agency, Hearings on the Department of Labor — Federal Security Agency Appropriation Bill for 1949 before House Appropriation's Subcommittee, 80th Cong., 2d Sess.)

THE EISENHOWER YEARS
1953 – 1960

THE EISENHOWER YEARS
1953 – 1960

After seventeen years of social security under a Democratic Administration, a Republican President was in the White House once again. Moreover, the Republicans had won both houses of Congress in the 1952 elections. If social security were to be cut down, 1953 would be the key year. For the outgoing Democrats it was the end of an era: the New Deal and the Fair Deal were over.

For the Social Security Administration the chief fear was a merger between contributory insurance and old-age assistance. Illogical as it may have been for the liberals to defend the contributory system, they saw the possible introduction of a flat old-age pension as the death of OASI.

The Republicans had rightly sensed that the amendments of 1939 and 1950 had moved the contributory system far from traditional notions of annuities financed by contributions. It is easy to see why Senator Taft and Representative Reed found that logically OASI must be merged with OAA. Liberal Democrats were less concerned with logic than with Republican motives.

They strongly suspected that some Republicans were hostile to OASI because it competed with private insurance and undermined private pension plans. They also assumed that once OASI was abolished, OAA would be used either as a political football to "bribe" the electorate; or as a means of manipulating the economic cycle rather than to help the poor. OAA also implied a means test, which seemed more sinister than OASI's limit on outside earnings.

For all these reasons those who had helped build up the system genuinely feared that the system as they knew it was about to be dismantled. The new President had declared, before he was a candidate, "If all Americans want is security, they can go to prison. They'll have enough to eat, a bed, and a roof over their heads". Specifically, it seemed as if the new Administration might try to merge OAA and OASI, a plan suggested by the 1952 Republican Platform. Even the U. S. Chamber of Commerce had specifically endorsed a merger of the two programs and the new Federal Security Administrator, Mrs. Oveta Culp Hobby, appointed leading members of that organization as her special advisers.

1953

Surprisingly, however, the early statements by the new President were not radically different from those of Democratic Presidents. President Eisenhower's first State of the Union Message advocated an extension of social security long called for by the Democrats, with only a hint of caution.

President Dwight D. Eisenhower
First Annual Message
(February 2, 1953)*

*   *   *

There is urgent need for greater effectiveness in our programs, both public and private, offering safeguards against the privations that too often come with unemployment, old age, illness, and accident. The provisions of the old-age and survivors insurance law should promptly be extended to cover millions of citizens who have been left out of the social-security system. No less important is the encouragement of privately sponsored pension plans. Most important of all, of course, is renewed effort to check the inflation which destroys so much of the value of all social-security payments.

*   *   *

To bring clear purpose and orderly procedure into this field, I anticipate a thorough study of the proper relationship among Federal, State, and local programs. I shall shortly send you specific recommendations for establishing such an appropriate commission, together with a reorganization plan defining new administrative status for all Federal activities in health, education, and social security.

This particular concern was reiterated a few days later.

Presidential Statement Concerning the Need for a
Presidential Commission on Federal-State Relations
(February 26, 1953)†

The development of the Federal Social Security system warrants study. This analysis should encompass not only the distribution of costs between the State and Federal government but also the operation and coverage of the system itself. It is a proper function of government to help build a sturdy floor over the pit of personal disaster, and to this objective we are all committed. However, we are equally committed to carrying out that great pro-

*Public Papers of the Presidents, Dwight D. Eisenhower, 1953, p. 32.
†Ibid., p. 71.

gram efficiently and with greatest benefit to those whom it is designed to help.

Those worried about possible federal involvement in medical care, however, remained unconcerned for the new President apparently shared the outlook of the AMA.

Presidential Remarks to the Members of the House of Delegates
of the American Medical Association
(March 14, 1953)*

* * *

I have found, in the past few years, that I have certain philosophical bonds with doctors. I don't like the word "compulsory." I am against the word "socialized." Everything about such words seems to me to be a step toward the thing that we are spending so many billions to prevent; that is, the overwhelming of this country by any force, power, or idea that leads us to foresake our traditional system of free enterprise.

Now, that is the doctrine of the administration. It is most certainly the doctrine of the Republican Party and those Republican leaders in Congress. They are here to speak for themselves, but I am sure they will allow me that one word. We live by it, and we intend to practice it.

Now, we thoroughly understand, also, the importance of your functions in our society. We also understand and are determined to meet the requirements of our population in the services that only you can provide. But we do have faith that Americans want to do the right thing, and the medical profession will provide the kind of services our country needs better, with the cooperation and the friendship of the administration, rather than its direction or any attempt on its part to be the big "poobah" in this particular field.

That is what I came to repeat. In many sections of the country, in every area, I have said these things before—and to some of you that are here today. I repeat them, and I tell you it is going to be the philosophy of this administration for the next 4 years, or as long as the good Lord allows me —all or part of it—to spend those 4 years.

Eisenhower's early statements somewhat calmed those who thought the system was about to be attacked root-and-branch, but two things shortly revived their qualms. In a special budget message on May 20, President Eisenhower recommended that a social security tax increase, originally scheduled for January 1, 1954 (imposing a 2 per cent rate on both employers and employees) be postponed for one year. This was interpreted by some as a hint of an OAA-OASI merger.

Ibid., p. 98.

There was little need for speculation in connection with the operations of the Curtis Subcommittee. On February 20, 1953, the new chairman of the House Ways and Means Committee, Daniel Reed of New York, appointed Representative Carl Curtis of Nebraska as chairman of a subcommittee to undertake a broad study of social security legislation. Curtis was a strong advocate of a pay-as-you-go plan, and according to his critics, the hearings were designed to publicize this approach.

The Curtis Hearings

The hearings stimulated controversy even before they began. When the subcommittee was assembled, there were allegations that Representative Curtis had hand-picked a staff of known critics of the existing social security programs. In any event, hearings were scheduled for late July, 1953, and the first major crisis for OASI had begun.

The hearings opened quietly with representatives of the Census Bureau offering recent statistics on the country's population trends. They pointed to significant alterations in the birth rate and, in addition, an unexpected increase in the number of aged persons. On the following day witnesses from the Internal Revenue Service explained the effects of the tax laws on income security. Thus far supporters of the status quo *had little to fear.*

The subcommittee hearings were not resumed until November, giving the staff several months to collect information and to plan the questioning of future witnesses. In November the first few days of the hearings were devoted to investigating various programs within the system. The chairman and some staff members were generally critical and indicated that a universal pay-as-you-go plan was the desirable alternative.

Although there were obvious differences of opinion between the Democratic and Republican members of the subcommittee, disagreements remained relatively quiet until November 27, when Arthur J. Altmeyer, the former Commissioner of Social Security, appeared to testify. Altmeyer had been subpoenaed by the chairman and Representative Dingell objected to that procedure, "Bringing a man like [him] under subpoena. Mr. Chairman, you ought to be ashamed of yourself . . . He has done more for social security, Mr. Chairman, than you ever imagined is possible . . ." (Analysis of the Social Security System, *Hearings before a Subcommittee of the House Ways and Means Committee, 83d Cong., 1st Sess., p. 891).*

Robert H. Winn, appointed by Representative Curtis as chief counsel of the subcommittee questioned Altmeyer on whether or not it was proper to refer to social security as insurance, and whether or not there existed any right to receive benefits. The chief counsel read quotes from statements allegedly made by the witness during the previous twenty years, and then requested a confirmation of the statements. Altmeyer and the two Demo-

cratic subcommittee members continually objected to the course of the proceedings.

Dr. Altmeyer appeared before the subcommittee unprepared to submit a formal statement and unaware of the questions which were to be asked. The point of the interrogation was not always clear but finally, the chairman revealed what counsel was trying to establish. Representative Curtis claimed that under the Social Security Act the United States issued no contracts and thus the recipients had no rights to their benefits. He added, "Our sole purpose here is to ascertain what are the facts, whether it is insurance or not, whether it is a contract or not" (House Hearings, p. 921).

When the subcommittee reconvened after the noon recess, the chairman informed Altmeyer that he could present a formal statement. Although he was unprepared, the witness commenced a review of the development of the act. Altmeyer's testimony was constantly interrupted and finally the chairman broke in, "Now Mr. Altmeyer, you did appear here and say you had a statement and suggested that you wanted about an hour to make it. You have had an hour and thirty-seven minutes . . . . Wind up your statement as quickly as you can" (House Hearings, p. 950).

Altmeyer completed the historical review and then asked if he could present his own views on improving the system.

House Hearings
(p. 953–55)

Mr. Altmeyer . . . Now, I haven't, Mr. Chairman, expressed my personal views as to what I think could be done to improve the law. I do not know whether that is going to be considered by this committee or not.

Chairman Curtis. Testimony for or against proposals will, of course, be heard by the full Ways and Means Committee, when they consider the legislation. We have not had any witnesses go into that.

Mr. Altmeyer. Then may I just make a brief concluding statement, if I am not permitted to make recommendations or suggestions or express my opinion as to improvements?

Chairman Curtis. I have no objection to you putting your recommendations in the record.

Mr. Altmeyer. Oh, no, Mr. Chairman. I would like to get them presented so that they could be discussed and questions asked to elucidate just exactly what the implications are.

Chairman Curtis. This is not a legislative committee, but at your request I set aside the questioning for you to make the statement which you said you had, the statement that you estimated would take about an hour. In just a few minutes, 2 hours will be up.

Now, what is it further that you want to read from the statement that you said you had?

Mr. Altmeyer. Well, I have a statement, Mr. Chairman—it would probably take me an hour and a quarter—as to my views and recommendations regarding improvement of the present social-security system. But, if you are not interested in learning about my views, I forego that privilege.

Chairman Curtis. You have used almost 2 hours. If you have something that you want to say in just 2 or 3 minutes, wind it up. The Chair has been more than liberal with you.

Mr. Altmeyer. May I make a brief statement, then, in conclusion, which I promise you will not take more than 10 minutes—perhaps 5 minutes?

Chairman Curtis. You may proceed. We will let you have the 2 full hours. You have about 5 minutes to go.

Mr. Altmeyer. How many?

Chairman Curtis. You have 5 minutes, and then it will be 2 hours that you have consumed.

*   *   *

Mr. Altmeyer. Thank you very much for that additional time.

Mr. Dingell. He can put the rest in the record.

Mr. Eberharter. He may not prefer to.

Mr. Altmeyer. May I then say, Mr. Chairman, that in the consideration of the development of a social security program, we ought to proceed upon the assumption that we want to develop a social security system based upon a free enterprise system, and designed so as to promote all of the values inherent in a free enterprise system.

May I also say that we must proceed upon the assumption that every effort will be made to make this free enterprise system as productive as possible and as just as possible to the participants thereof.

I believe that a social security system ought to be designed to provide a minimum basic protection upon which the individual may build a further degree of protection as desired by him and his family. I do not look upon that minimum basic protection as simply an animal level of subsistence. I look upon it as a level that permits some degree of gracious living to all of the American people, and I believe that there is no fixed amount that should be established as the limit of a decent, humane, minimum basic protection for all of the American people.

I believe that a system of social security ought to protect all of the people against all of the major economic hazards which lead to destitution I believe that a contributory social insurance system enabling people to help pay for their own protection ought to be the first line of defense against destitution, and the major element in any system of social security.

I believe that benefits should be related to income loss under this contributory social insurance system.

I believe that we must preserve both the principle of individual equity and he principle of social adequacy.

I believe that we should have a safe system of financing that looks to the future as well as the present and makes certain that we know where we are going and have set up an automatic system of financing so that these benefits that are provided as a matter of statutory right by the Congress of the United States may be preserved and protected and paid when due.

I believe that public assistance should be retained as the second line of defense against destitution.

I believe that every effort should be made to prevent the hazards causing destitution. I believe that there should be industrial accident prevention, that there should be employment offices to reduce the amount of unemployment to a minimum, that we ought to have hiring and firing practices that would permit persons in their fifties and sixties and seventies to continue to work if they want to and are able to do so. I think it is tragic and inhuman to throw them on the scrap heap just when they reach an arbitrary age limit, whether it is 65 or whether it is any other, and I believe that we should have rehabilitation programs of all sorts to enable people to continue to be productive, to restore their productive capacity if it has been lost or impaired.

Now, Mr. Chairman, I have very definite views as to how to accomplish these objectives but, since you have informed me that my time is at an end, I want to thank the committee for the privilege of appearing, and if at any future time I can be of any further assistance to the committee, I shall be glad to.

Having completed the brief summary of his recommendations, Altmeyer prepared to leave, but Representative Curtis had other ideas, and informed the witness that the morning questioning would be continued. An angry exchange again erupted.

House Hearings
(p. 955–56)

The Chairman. You are not through. We are going to proceed now with the questioning intended for this afternoon. It will probably take a night session.
Mr. Altmeyer. Then I was misled, Mr. Chairman, because you gave me to believe that the questioning had ended and I could proceed with my statement.
Chairman Curtis. I made no such statement.
Mr. Altmeyer. Again a misunderstanding.
Chairman Curtis. I made no such statement. The witness will not decide when his statement is going to be made and when questions are going to be asked.
Mr. Altmeyer. Then may I make a supplemental connected statement later.
Chairman Curtis. No; the counsel will proceed with the questioning.
Mr. Eberharter. Let the record show that the witness—
Chairman Curtis. The gentleman from Pennsylvania is out of order.
Mr. Eberharter. Is prevented from continuing to make a statement.

Chairman Curtis. The gentleman from Pennsylvania is out of order. I have given you people 2 hours.

Mr. Eberharter. Put that on the record, too.

Chairman Curtis. The gentleman from Pennsylvania is out of order.

Mr. Eberharter. That is all right. I am willing to be out of order. Put that on the record, too.

Tempers were strained after the long session, and when Altmeyer replied that he could not hear the question, the chief counsel shouted back, "Can you hear me now?" Both Democratic members objected to the treatment of the witness and Representative Herman P. Eberharter stated: "I do not think the witness can be browbeaten by your yelling at him, Mr. Counsel." Chairman Curtis responded by ruling the Pennsylvania Democrat out of order. Ultimately, Dr. Altmeyer lost his composure:

House Hearings
(p. 964)

Mr. Winn. In the study for the Joint Committee on the Economic Report by the National Planning Association, 82d Congress, 2d session, the so-called Ball report, entitled "Pensions in the United States," published in December of 1952, we find at pages 34 and 35 the following statement:

> The attitude which people have toward the payment which they will receive and the conditions under which they will receive it is a matter of the first importance; a security system does not give security, even if physical needs are met, unless people know they can count on the payment and feel good about the conditions under which the payment is made.

Do you subscribe to those statements?

Mr. Altmeyer. I do, and I think you are doing more to destroy the confidence of the American people in this system than anybody else except the chairman of the committee.

Mr. Dingell. That is correct.

Despite the late hour, examination of the witness continued. The chief counsel attempted to establish that social security proponents had deceived the public by calling the benefits a "right." Altmeyer simply stated that benefits were not based on a contractual right, but on a statutory right with the full influence and power of the government backing it. Before the chairman adjourned the subcommittee, he made the following statement.

House Hearings
(p. 1015)

Chairman Curtis. I am going to make a few remarks and then we are going to close this hearing.

Mr. Altmeyer, it is apparent that the people of the country have no insurance contract. That does not mean that I do not want to do my full part to do justice to them and to carry out and make good on the moral commitment that has been made to them. Yet, notwithstanding the fact that they had no insurance contract, it remains true that the agency under your direction repeatedly in public statements, by pamphlets, radio addresses, and by other means, told the people of the country that they had insurance.

I think a number of people were misled by that. I say that because I, myself, was mistaken when I wrote my minority report in 1949. I was of the opinion that the Government had a contractual obligation to fulfill all of these benefits. I still want them fulfilled.

However, there is no contract of insurance and the fact that upon your recommendation the word "insurance" was sprinkled around in the statute did not make it insurance. I believe that the 83d Congress will write some good social security legislation, that there will be some improvements in it, and that we will make good on what we say. In due time I will take my responsibility and state what I recommend in the way of amendments to improve the social security law. That is what I want to do.

However, as the record stands now, when the new administration took over, taxes had been collected from more than 90 million people. We have some 13½ million aged. Some 17 or 18 years after the program started, 6 out of 10 aged people are ineligible to draw benefits. They have been told that this is an insurance idea. That has been the answer given to old people who have waited for a benefit and that has been the anwer given to the young who were paying their money in.

In our previous hearings, we have charted the facts and figures about the income in the fund. We want those facts and figures to speak just for what they are.

I have not engaged in any loose remarks about the fund being in Government bonds and therefore was not good. We are not interested in those stock criticisms that might have been used in the past. I do not think there is any place to put the social-security fund except in Government bonds.

We have tried honestly and sincerely for several weeks to get the facts on the record so as to see what kind of system we have.

As I say, we have a system that has promised a lot to the American people. I do not know how many Congresses I will serve in, but in those that I serve I want to make good on those moral commitments.

However, I do not want to tell people that they have insurance policies when they do not.

We have collected all of this money from 90 or 100 million people, and 17 or 18 years later two-thirds of our aged problem is still unsolved so far as title II is concerned. The young people who are paying in money month after month only have a statutory right that a Congress 10 years, or 15 years, or any time might take away from them. Maybe it has to be that way. But certainly we should not tell them that it is insurance, because in the minds of the average American that is something valuable, it is an enforcible policy, and whoever in the Federal agency was responsible for conveying this misleading information to the American people and saying such things as "Your card constitutes a policy," certainly was mistaken.

I think that these facts, together with the other material that has been developed in the last 2 weeks, as well as material which has not been presented in public hearings, are important. It is my hope—and I believe that it will happen—that the 83d Congress will improve social security. In due time I will have my own statement as to what I believe should be done in the way of amendments in order that we may meet our obligation in our time toward a social problem, a situation that comes to every human being—that of age.

The committee will stand adjourned, and this ends our public hearings.

The committee will have a brief executive session.

Mr. Altmeyer, you are excused.

(Whereupon, at 6:55 p. m., Friday, November 27, 1953, the public hearings were concluded and the committee proceeded to executive session.)

After all the excitement, the subcommittee report was not quite as radical as had been expected. Published nine months after the close of hearings, it had no effect on the 1954 Social Security Amendments which Congress had already adopted.

The Administration Viewpoint

Despite Representative Curtis and his subcommittee, it slowly became clear that the Administration was not about to upset all the work of the New Deal and the Fair Deal. The Republicans apparently sided with the AMA on medical care, and in the long run, the President might rethink the basis of income security. In the short run, however, the new Administration dared not interfere with OASI.

Early in 1953 Eisenhower's Federal Security Administrator, Mrs. Oveta Culp Hobby, appointed an advisory group of five consultants to make recommendations on expansion of the system. Three of these original consultants, members of the U.S. Chamber of Commerce, advocated a full-scale pay-as-you-go plan. There was immediate speculation that the Administration wanted to merge OASI and OAA, but pressure from labor and farm organizations resulted in expansion of the advisory group to twelve members, an increase which made radical change unlikely.

The group's primary concern was expansion of OASI coverage and they finally agreed to bring about ten million additional employees and self-employed professionals into the program. Their report went to Mrs. Hobby who was now Secretary of the new Department of Health, Education and Welfare.

In his next message to Congress President Eisenhower discussed the report and emphasized a substantial increase in the types of covered employment.

Special Presidential Message to Congress
Transmitting Proposed Changes in the Social Security Program
August 1, 1953*

*   *   *

The Department of Health, Education, and Welfare, with the counsel and assistance of twelve outstanding consultants, has been carefully studying the difficult technical and administrative aspects of this effort.

The Secretary of that Department has now recommended the specific additional groups which, in the judgment of the Department and its consultants, should be covered under this program. The Secretary has also recommended the means by which these additional groups can be brought into the system most equitably, with full consideration for the new groups as well as those who have heretofore contributed to the insurance system. The Secretary's recommendations would effectively carry out the objectives that I expressed in my Message to the Congress on the State of the Union and I am pleased to transmit them to the Congress for its consideration.

The report's recommendations mentioned only this change and although the President mentioned other studies, there were no additional reports by the advisory group. The Administration's position on an OASI-OAA merger remained unclear, but as the months passed it seemed probable that the early fears of OASI supporters were unjustified.

Congress adjourned two days after receiving the President's recommendations and no legislative action resulted other than the introduction of H.R. 6812 by Representative Reed, chairman of the Ways and Means Committee. This was merely the formal introduction of the presidential proposals. However, the Curtis hearings and the Administration's firm commitment to the proposed increased coverage promised considerable congressional activity regarding social security in 1954.

Organization

Early in his Administration the new President scored a coup denied to his Democratic predecessor when he succeeded in elevating the Federal Security Administration into a Department of Health, Education, and Welfare. Truman attempted such a move on several ocassions but had been rebuffed each time by a Republican-southern Democratic coalition. This

*Public Papers of the Presidents, Dwight D. Eisenhower, 1953, p. 534.

same coalition offered little resistance to Eisenhower's plan, and the American Medical Association, which had actively opposed the earlier programs, also endorsed the new proposal.

On March 12, 1953 Eisenhower transmitted his reorganization plan to Congress, along with a special message on the plan.

Special Presidential Message to Congress
Transmitting the Reorganization Plan 1 of 1953
(March 12, 1953)*

I transmit herewith Reorganization Plan No. 1 of 1953, prepared in accordance with the provisions of the Reorganization Act of 1949, as amended.

In my message of February 2, 1953, I stated that I would send to the Congress a reorganization plan defining a new administrative status for Federal activities in health, education, and social security. This plan carries out that intention by creating a Department of Health, Education, and Welfare as one of the executive departments of the Government and by transferring to it the various units of the Federal Security Agency. The Department will be headed by a Secretary of Health, Education, and Welfare, who will be assisted by an Under Secretary and two Assistant Secretaries.

The purpose of this plan is to improve the administration of the vital health, education, and social security functions now being carried on in the Federal Security Agency by giving them departmental rank. Such action is demanded by the importance and magnitude of these functions, which affect the well-being of millions of our citizens. The programs carried on by the Public Health Service include, for example, the conduct and promotion of research into the prevention and cure of such dangerous ailments as cancer and heart disease. The Public Health Service also administers payments to the States for the support of their health services and for urgently needed hospital construction. The Office of Education collects, analyzes and distributes to school administrators throughout the country information relating to the organization and management of educational systems. Among its other functions is the provision of financial help to school districts burdened by activities of the United States Government. State assistance to the aged, the blind, the totally disabled, and dependent children is heavily supported by grants-in-aid administered through the Social Security Administration. The old age and survivors insurance system and child development and welfare programs are additional responsibilities of that Administration. Other offices of the Federal Security Agency are responsible for the conduct of Federal vocational rehabilitation programs and for the enforcement of food and drug laws.

*Ibid., p. 94–98.

There should be an unremitting effort to improve those health, education, and social security programs which have proved their value. I have already recommended the expansion of the social security system to cover persons not now protected, the continuation of assistance to school districts whose population has been greatly increased by the expansion of defense activities, and the strengthening of our food and drug laws.

But good intent and high purpose are not enough; all such programs depend for their success upon efficient, responsible administration. I have recently taken action to assure that the Federal Security Administrator's views are given proper consideration in executive councils by inviting her to attend meetings of the Cabinet. Now the establishment of the new Department provided for in Reorganization Plan No. I of 1953 will give the needed additional assurance that these matters will receive the full consideration they deserve in the whole operation of the Government.

This need has long been recognized. In 1923, President Harding proposed a Department of Education and Welfare, which was also to include health functions. In 1924, the Joint Committee on Reorganization recommended a new department similar to that suggested by President Harding. In 1932, one of President Hoover's reorganization proposals called for the concentration of health, education and recreational activities in a single executive department. The President's Committee on Administrative Management in 1937 recommended the placing of health, education and social security functions in a Department of Social Welfare. This recommendation was partially implemented in 1939 by the creation of the Federal Security Agency—by which action the Congress indicated its approval of the grouping of these functions in a single agency. A new department could not be proposed at that time because the Reorganization Act of 1939 prohibited the creation of additional executive departments. In 1949, the Commission on Organization of the Executive Branch of the Government proposed the creation of a department for social security and education.

The present plan will make it possible to give the officials directing the Department titles indicative of their responsibilities and salaries comparable to those received by their counterparts in other executive departments. As the Under Secretary of an executive department, the Secretary's principal assistant will be better equipped to give leadership in the Department's organization and management activities, for which he will be primarily responsible. The plan opens the way to further administrative improvement by authorizing the Secretary to centralize services and activities common to the several agencies of the Department. It also establishes a uniform method of appointment for the heads of the three major constituent agencies. At present, the Surgeon General and the Commissioner of Education are appointed by the President and confirmed by the Senate, while the Commissioner for Social Security is appointed by the Federal Security Administrator. Hereafter, all three will be Presidential appointees subject to Senate confirmation.

I believe, and this plan reflects my conviction, that these several fields of Federal activity should continue within the framework of a single department. The plan at the same time assures that the Office of Education and the Public Health Service retain the professional and substantive responsibilities vested by law in those agencies or in their heads. The Surgeon General, the Commissioner of Education and the Commissioner of Social Security will all have direct access to the Secretary.

There should be in the Department an Advisory Committee on Education, made up of persons chosen by the Secretary from outside the Federal Government, which would advise the Secretary with respect to the educational programs of the Department. I recommend the enactment of legislation authorizing the defrayal of the expenses of this Committee. The creation of such a Committee as an advisory body to the Secretary will help ensure the maintenance of responsibility for the public educational system in State and local governments while preserving the national interest in education through appropriate Federal action.

After investigation I have found and hereby declare that each reorganization included in Reorganization Plan No. 1 of 1953 is necessary to accomplish one or more of the purposes set forth in section 2(a) of the Reorganization Act of 1949, as amended. I have also found and hereby declare that by reason of these reorganizations, it is necessary to include in the reorganization plan provisions for the appointment and compensation of the new officers specified in sections 1, 2, 3, and 4 of the reorganization plan. The rates of compensation fixed for these officers are, respectively, those which I have found to prevail in respect of comparable officers in the executive branch of the Government.

Although the effecting of the reorganizations provided for in the reorganization plan will not in itself result in immediate savings, the improvement achieved in administration will in the future allow the performance of necessary services at greater savings than present operations would permit. An itemization of these savings in advance of actual experience is not practicable.

Dwight D. Eisenhower

Reorganization Plan No. 1 of 1953

DEPARTMENT OF HEALTH, EDUCATION, AND WELFARE

Section 1. Creation of Department; Secretary. — There is hereby established an executive department, which shall be known as the Department of Health, Education, and Welfare (hereafter in this reorganization plan referred to as the Department). There shall be at the head of the Department a Secretary of Health, Education, and Welfare (hereafter in this reorganization plan referred to as the Secretary), who shall be appointed by the President by and with the advice and consent of the Senate, and who shall receive compensation at the rate now or hereafter prescribed by law for the heads of executive departments. The Department shall be administered under the supervision and direction of the Secretary.

Sec. 2. Under Secretary and Assistant Secretaries. — There shall be in the Department an Under Secretary of Health, Education, and Welfare and two Assistant Secretaries of Health, Education, and Welfare, each of whom shall be appointed by the President by and with the advice and consent of the Senate, shall perform such functions as the Secretary may prescribe, and shall receive compensation at the rate now or hereafter provided by law for under secretaries and assistant secretaries, respectively, of executive departments. The Under Secretary (or, during the absence or disability of the Under Secretary or in the event of a vacancy in the office of Under Secretary, an Assistant Secretary determined according to such order as the Secretary shall prescribe) shall act as Secretary during the absence or disability of the Secretary or in the event of a vacancy in the office of Secretary.

Sec. 3. Special Assistant. — There shall be in the Department a Special Assistant to the Secretary (Health and Medical Affairs) who shall be appointed by the President by and with the advice and consent of the Senate from among persons who are recognized leaders in the medical field with wide non-governmental experience, shall review the health and medical programs of the Department and advise the Secretary with respect to the improvement of such programs and with respect to necessary legislation in the health and medical fields, and shall receive compensation at the rate now or hereafter provided by law for assistant secretaries of executive departments.

Sec. 4. Commissioner of Social Security. — There shall be in the Department a Commissioner of Social Security who shall be appointed by the President by and with the advice and consent of the Senate, shall perform such functions concerning social security and public welfare as the Secretary may prescribe, and shall receive compensation at the rate now or hereafter fixed by law for Grade GS – 18 of the general schedule established by the Classification Act of 1949, as amended.

Sec. 5. Transfers to the Department. — All functions of the Federal Security Administrator are hereby transferred to the Secretary. All agencies of the Federal Security Agency, together with their respective functions, personnel, property, records, and unexpended balances of appropriations, allocations, and other funds (available or to be made available), and all other functions, personnel, property, records, and unexpended balances of appropriations, allocations, and other funds (available or to be made available) of the Federal Security Agency are hereby transferred to the Department.

Sec. 6. Performance of Functions of the Secretary. — The Secretary may from time to time make such provisions as the Secretary deems appropriate authorizing the performance of any of the functions of the Secretary by any other officer, or by any agency or employee, of the Department.

Sec. 7. Administrative Services. — In the interest of economy and efficiency the Secretary may from time to time establish central administrative services in the fields of procurement, budgeting, accounting, personnel, library, legal, and other services and activities common to the several agencies of the Department; and the Secretary may effect such transfers within the Department of the personnel employed, the property and records used or held, and the funds available for use in connection with such administrative service activities as the Secretary may deem necessary for the conduct of any services so established: *Provided,* That no professional or substantive function vested by law in any officer shall be removed from the jurisdiction of such officer under this section.

Sec. 8. Abolitions. — The Federal Security Agency (exclusive of the agencies thereof transferred by section 5 of this reorganization plan), the offices of Federal Security Administrator and Assistant Federal Security Administrator created by Reorganization Plan No. I (53 Stat. 1423), the two offices of assistant heads of the Federal Security Agency created by Reorganization Plan No. 2 of 1946 (60 Stat. 1095), and the office of Commissioner for Social Security created by section 701 of the Social Security Act, as amended (64 Stat. 558), are hereby abolished. The Secretary shall make such provisions as may be necessary in order to wind up any outstanding affairs of the Agency and offices abolished by this section which are not otherwise provided for in this reorganization plan.

Sec. 9. Interim Provisions. — The President may authorize the persons who immediately prior to the time this reorganization plan takes effect occupy the offices of Federal Security Administrator, Assistant Federal Security Administrator, assistant heads of the Federal Security Agency, and Commissioner for Social Security to act as Secretary, Under Secretary, and Assistant Secretaries of Health, Education, and Welfare and as Commissioner of Social Security, respectively, until those offices are filled by appointment in the manner provided by sections 1, 2, and 4 of this reorganization plan, but not for a period of more than 60 days. While so acting, such persons shall receive compensation at the rates provided by this reorganization plan for the offices the functions of which they perform.

The Congress acted both quickly and favorably on the proposal.

1954

Administration support for congressional action came early in 1954 when the President, in his State of the Union Message, noted the need for "strengthened old-age and unemployment insurance measures. ·. . ." Later in the same speech, the President reaffirmed his recommendations for increased coverage of the OASI program and included general statements about improved public assistance programs, and additional unemployment protection.

President Dwight D. Eisenhower
Second Annual Message
(January 7, 1954)*

Our basic social security program, the Old-Age and Survivors Insurance system, to which individuals contribute during their productive years and receive benefits based on previous earnings, is designed to shield them from destitution. Last year I recommended extension of the social insurance system to include more than 10,000,000 additional persons. I ask that this extension soon be accomplished. This and other major improvements in the insurance system will bring substantial benefit increases and broaden the membership of the insurance system, thus diminishing the need for Federal grants-in-aid for such purposes. A new formula will therefore be proposed, permitting progressive reduction in such grants as the need for them declines.

* * *

Federal grant-in-aid welfare programs, now based on widely varying formulas, should be simplified. Concrete proposals on fourteen of them will be suggested to the appropriate Committees.

The program for rehabilitation of the disabled especially needs strengthening. Through special vocational training, this program presently returns each year some 60,000 handicapped individuals to productive work. Far more disabled people can be saved each year from idleness and dependence if this program is gradually increased. My more detailed recommendations on this and the other social insurance problems I have mentioned will be sent to the Congress on January 14th.

* * *

Protection against the hazards of temporary unemployment should be extended to some 6½ millions of workers, including civilian Federal workers, who now lack this safeguard. Moreover, the Secretary of Labor is making available to the states studies and recommendations in the fields of weekly benefits, periods of protection and extension of coverage. The Economic Report will consider the related matter of minimum wages and their coverage.

Although the President seemed fully committed to improving social security coverage and benefits, there was no doubt that the Administration

*Public Papers of the Presidents, Dwight D. Eisenhower 1954, p. 13-20.

was unalterably opposed to any federal program providing direct medical care.

Health

I am flatly opposed to the socialization of medicine. The great need for hospital and medical services can best be met by the initiative of private plans. But it is unfortunately a fact that medical costs are rising and already impose severe hardships on many families. The Federal Government can do many helpful things and still carefully avoid the socialization of medicine.

OASI and PA

On January 14, 1954, Eisenhower sent his special message on social security to Congress outlining specific provisions he sought to have enacted. The message was an amplification of earlier recommendations emphasizing a contributory system with benefits related to individual earnings and it finally quelled any fears about an OASI-OAA merger.

The President suggested that the public assistance federal matching program change as the increased OASI benefits became effective. The proposal was based on the premise—inherent in the original 1935 legislation—that as OASI coverage increased, the need for public assistance would necessarily decrease. At that point the Federal Government's obligations to the individual states would also be reduced.

Special Presidential Message to the Congress on
Old-Age and Survivors' Insurance and on Federal
Grants-in-Aid for Public Assistance Programs
(January 14, 1954)*

To the Congress of the United States:

I submit herewith for the consideration of the Congress a number of recommendations relating to the Old Age and Survivors Insurance System and the Federal grant-in-aid programs for public assistance.

The human problems of individual citizens are a proper and important concern of our government. One such problem that faces every individual is the provision of economic security for his old age and economic security for his family in the event of his death. To help individuals provide for that security—to reduce both the fear and the incidence of destitution to the minimum—to promote the confidence of every individual in the future—these

Ibid., p. 62.

are proper aims of all levels of government, including the Federal Government.

Private and group savings, insurance, and pension plans, fostered by a healthy, fully functioning economy, are a primary means of protection against the economic hazards of old age and death. These private savings and plans must be encouraged, and their value preserved, by sound tax and fiscal policies of the Government.

But in addition, a basic, nation-wide protection against these hazards can be provided through a government social insurance system. Building on this base, each individual has a better chance to achieve for himself the assurance of continued income after his earning days are over and for his family after his death. In response to the need for protection arising from the complexities of our modern society, the Old Age and Survivors Insurance system was developed. Under it nearly 70 million persons and their families are now covered, and some 6 million are already its beneficiaries. Despite shortcomings which can be corrected, this system is basically sound. It should remain, as it has been, the cornerstone of the government's programs to promote the economic security of the individual.

Under Old Age and Survivors Insurance (OASI), the worker during his productive years and his employer both contribute to the system in proportion to the worker's earnings. A self-employed person also contributes a percentage of his earnings. In return, when these breadwinners retire after reaching the age of 65, or if they die, they or their families become entitled to income related in amount to their previous earnings. The system is not intended as a substitute for private savings, pension plans and insurance protection. It is, rather, intended as the foundation upon which these other forms of protection can be soundly built. Thus the individual's own work, his planning, and his thrift will bring him a higher standard of living upon his retirement, or his family a higher standard of living in the event of his death, than would otherwise be the case. Hence the system both encourages thrift and self-reliance, and helps to prevent destitution in our national life.

In offering, as I here do, certain measures for the expansion and improvement of this system, I am determined to preserve its basic principles. The two most important are: (1) it is a contributory system, with both the worker and his employer making payments during the years of active work; (2) the benefits received are related in part to the individual's earnings. To these sound principles our system owes much of its wide national acceptance.

During the past year we have subjected the Federal social security system to an intensive study which has revealed certain limitations and inequities in the law as it now stands. These should be corrected.

1. *OASI Coverage Should Be Broadened.*

My message to the Congress on August 1, 1953, recommended legislation to bring more persons under the protection of the OASI system. The new groups that I recommended be covered—about ten million additional people—include self-employed farmers; many more farm workers and domestic workers; doctors, dentists, lawyers, architects, accountants, and other self-employed professional people; members of State and local retirement systems on a voluntary group basis; clergymen on a voluntary group basis; and several smaller groups. I urge the Congress to approve this extension of coverage.

Further broadening of the coverage is being considered by the Committee on Retirement Policy for Federal Personnel, created by the Congress. This Committee will soon report on a plan for expanding OASI to Federal employees not now protected, without impairing the independence of present Federal retirement plans. After the Committee has made its report, I shall make appropriate recommendations on that subject to the Congress.

Extension of coverage will be a highly important advance in our OASI system, but other improvements are also needed. People over 65 years of age who can work should be encouraged to do so and should be permitted to take occasional or part-time jobs without losing their benefits. The level of benefits should be increased. Certain defects in and injustices under the present law should be eliminated. I submit the following recommendations to further these purposes.

2. *The Present "Retirement Test" Should Be Liberalized and Its Discrimination Against the Wage Earner Should Be Removed.*

By depriving an OASI beneficiary of his benefit payment for any month in which he earns wages of more than $75, present law imposes an undue restraint on enterprise and initiative. Retired persons should be encouraged to continue their contributions to the productive needs of the nation. I am convinced that the great majority of our able-bodied older citizens are happier and better off when they continue in some productive work after reaching retirement age. Moreover, the nation's economy will derive large benefits from the wisdom and experience of older citizens who remain employed in jobs commensurate with their strength.

I recommend, therefore, that the first $1000 of a beneficiary's annual earnings be exempted under the retirement test, and that for amounts earned above $1000 only one month's benefit be deducted for each additional $80 earned.

To illustrate the effect of these changes: a beneficiary could take a $200 a month job for five months without losing any benefits, whereas under present law he would lose five months' benefits. He could work throughout the year at $90 a month and lose only one month's benefit, whereas under present law he would lose all twelve.

Approval of this recommendation will also remove the discriminatory treatment of wage earners under the retirement test. Self-employed persons already have the advantage of an exemption on an annual basis, with the right to average their earnings over the full year. The amendment I have proposed would afford this advantage, without discrimination, to all beneficiaries.

3. OASI Benefits Should Be Increased.

Today thousands of OASI beneficiaries receive the minimum benefit of twenty-five dollars a month. The average individual benefit for retired workers approximates fifty dollars a month. The maximum benefit for an individual is $85 a month. For OASI to fulfill its purpose of helping to combat destitution, these benefits are too low.

I recommend, therefore, that benefits now being received by retired workers be increased on the basis of a new formula to be submitted to the appropriate Committees by the Secretary of Health, Education, and Welfare. This formula should also provide increases for workers retiring in the future, raising both the minimum and the maximum benefits. These increases will further the objectives of the program and will strengthen the foundation on which its participants may build their own security.

4. Additional Benefit Credits Should Be Provided.

The maintenance of a relationship between the individual's earnings and the benefits he receives is a cornerstone of the OASI system. However, only a part of many workers' annual earnings are taken into account for contribution and benefit purposes. Although in 1938 only the first $3000 of a worker's annual earnings were considered for contribution and benefit purposes, statistical studies reveal that in that year 94% of full-time male workers protected by OASI had all of their earnings covered by the program. By 1950 less than half of such workers — 44% — had their full earnings covered by the program, so the Congress increased the earnings base to $3600.

Today, the earnings base of $3600 covers the full earnings of only 40% of our regular male workers. It is clear, therefore, that another revision of this base is needed to maintain a reasonable relationship between a worker's benefits and his earnings.

I recommend, therefore, that the earnings base for the calculation of OASI benefits and payroll taxes be raised to $4200, thus enabling 15,000,000 people to have more of their earnings taken into account by the program.

5. Benefits Should Be Computed on a Fairer Basis.

The level of OASI benefits is related to the average of a worker's past earnings. Under present law periods of abnormally low earnings, or no earnings at all, are averaged in with periods of normal earnings, thereby reducing the benefits received by the retired worker. In many instances, a worker may earn little or nothing for several months or several years because of illness or other personal adversity beyond his power of prevention or remedy. Thus the level of benefits is reduced below its true relation to the earning capabilities of the employee. Moreover, if the additional millions of persons recommended for inclusion under OASI are brought into the program in 1955 without modification of present law, their average earnings will be sharply lowered by including as a period of no earnings the period from 1951 to 1955 when they were not in the program. I recommend, therefore, that in the computation of a worker's average monthly wage, the four lowest years of earnings be eliminated.

  6. The Benefit Rights of the Disabled Should Be Protected.

One of the injustices in the present law is its failure to make secure the benefit rights of the worker who has a substantial work record in covered employment and who becomes totally disabled. If his disability lasts four years or less, my preceding recommendation will alleviate this hardship. But if a worker's earnings and contributions cease for a longer period, his retirement rights, and the survivor rights of his widow and children may be reduced or even lost altogether. Equity dictates that this defect be remedied. I recommend, therefore, that the benefits of a worker who has a substantial work record in covered employment and who becomes totally disabled for an extended period be maintained at the amount he would have received had he become 65 and retired on the date his disability began.

The injustice to the disabled should be corrected not simply by preserving these benefit rights but also by helping them to return to employment wherever possible. Many of them can be restored to lives of usefulness, independence and self-respect if, when they apply for the preservation of their benefit rights, they are promptly referred to the Vocational Rehabilitation agencies of the States. In the interest of these disabled persons, a close liaison between the OASI system and these agencies will be promptly established upon approval of these recommendations by the Congress. Moreover, in my message of January 18 to the Congress, I shall propose an expanded and improved program of Vocational Rehabilitation.

Costs

I am informed by the Secretary of Health, Education and Welfare that the net additional cost of the recommendations herein presented would be, on a long-term basis, about one-half of one percent of the annual payrolls subject to OASI taxes. The benefit costs will be met for at least the next fifteen to twenty-five years under the step-rate increases in OASI taxes already provided in the law.

Public Assistance

An important by-product of the extension of the protection of the OASI system and the increase in its benefit scale is the impact on public assistance programs. Under these programs States and localities provide assistance to the needy aged, dependent children, blind persons and the permanently and totally disabled, with the Federal Government sharing in the cost.

As broadened OASI coverage goes into effect, the proportion of our aged population eligible for benefits will increase from forty-five percent to seventy-five percent in the next five or six years. Although the need for some measure of public assistance will continue, the OASI program will progressively reduce, year by year, the extent of the need for public assistance payments by the substitution of OASI benefits. I recommend that the formula for Federal sharing in the public assistance programs for these purposes reflect this changing relationship without prejudicing in any manner the receipt of public assistance payments by those whose need for these payments will continue.

Under the present public assistance formula some States receive a higher percentage share of Federal funds than others. In the program of old-age assistance, for example, States making low assistance payments receive up to eighty percent Federal funds in defraying the costs of their programs. States making high assistance payments receive about sixty-five percent of Federal funds in that portion of the old-age assistance payments which is within the $55 maximum for Federal participation.

This variation in Federal participation is the result of a Congressional determination that the Federal sharing should be higher for States which, because of low resources, generally make low assistance payments. In order better to achieve this purpose, I recommend that a new formula be enacted. It should take into account the financial capacity of the several States to support their public assistance programs by adopting, as a measure of that capacity, their per capita income. Such a new formula will also facilitate the inclusion, in the old-age assistance program, of a factor reflecting the expansion of OASI.

The present formula for Federal sharing in public assistance programs requires adjustment from another standpoint. Under present law, the Federal Government does not share in any part of a monthly old-age assistance payment exceeding $55. Yet many of these payments must exceed this amount in order to meet the needs of the individual recipient, particularly where the individual requires medical care. I consider it altogether appropriate for the Federal Government to share in such payments and recommend, therefore, that the present $55 maximum be placed on an average rather than on an individual basis. Corresponding changes in the other public assistance programs would be made. This change in the formula would enable States to balance high payments in cases of acute need against low payments where the need is relatively minor. In addition, great administrative simplification would be achieved.

A new public assistance formula should not become effective until the States have had an opportunity to plan for it. Until such time, the 1952 public assistance amendments should be extended.

The recommendations I have here submitted constitute a coordinated approach to several major aspects of the broad problem of achieving economic security for Americans. Many other phases of this national problem exist and will be reflected in legislative proposals from time to time to the Congress. The effort to prevent destitution among our people preserves a greater measure of their freedom and strengthens their initiative. These proposals are constructive and positive steps in that direction, and I urge their early and favorable consideration by the Congress.

Dwight D. Eisenhower

Shortly after his special message to Congress, President Eisenhower transmitted his budget message and again urged adoption of his social security proposals. Meanwhile, on January 14, Representative Reed of New York had introduced two bills embodying the Eisenhower proposals, H.R. 7199, covering old-age insurance, and H.R. 7200, covering public assistance.

Congress was mainly concerned with proposed changes in OASI; the public assistance bill received little serious consideration. Since the Administration had separated itself from the "blanketing-in" proposals of the Curtis subcommittee, and the pay-as-you-go plan of the U.S. Chamber of Commerce, there seemed to be general support in both the executive and legislative branches for liberalization of the OASI program. The main difference between the Administration and congressional leaders concerned how many additional persons could be covered by the program.

Hearings before the Ways and Means Committee started on April 1, with Secretary Hobby as the first witness. Testifying with her were several subordinates from HEW who answered most of the committee's inquiries. The Secretary offered a general statement on the background of social security and the need to expand the program to cover an additional ten and a half million persons.

Secretary Hobby sounded surprisingly like her Democratic predecessors as she reaffirmed a basic commitment to the "contributory system". She then noted two deficiencies in the social security programs and suggested six major changes.

Social Security Act Amendments of 1954
Hearings on H.R. 7199
before the House Ways and Means Committee
83d Cong., 2d Sess. (April, 1954)
(p. 30 *et seq.*)

Statement of Secretary Oveta Culp Hobby

Social security has become one of the everyday phrases in the American language. Most people mean by "social security" the Federal system which Congress has named old-age and survivors insurance.

For millions, this program spells the hope of a secure basic income in future old age. For millions, also, it provides the present assurance that in case of the death of the family breadwinner money will be coming in to help keep the home intact. This program, as the President has said, is the "cornerstone of the Government's programs to promote the economic security of the individual."

* * *

The first conclusion that the Department came to in its study of the old-age and survivors insurance program was the soundness of its basic concepts, that contributions of the workers themselves, and their employers, should support the system and that benefits should have a relationship to the individual worker's past earnings. A system based on these principles is most conducive to the enhancement of the individual's sense of personal dignity and worth in a free society.

Our confirmation of the value of the basic principles of the OASI system led us to a thorough examination of its specific provisions. We found two general shortcomings: First, the system as presently constituted fails to include many occupations and classes of workers, and, second, the benefit provisions are, particularly under today's conditions, in certain respects inadequate and inequitable.

* * *

Then Secretary Hobby listed the six major changes suggested (at p. 37):

1. Extend coverage to 10½ million persons.
2. Drop 4 years of lowest earnings in computing benefits.
3. Raise earnings base to $4,200.
4. Increase benefit levels.
5. Improve retirement test.
6. Preserve benefit rights for the disabled.

One of the most controversial sections of the bill dealt with the preservation of benefit rights for the disabled, the disability freeze provision. (Its reappearance, incidentally, seems to suggest that Secretary Hobby had come under the sway of her Social Security Administration advisors.) Mr. Roswell B. Perkins, Assistant Secretary of HEW, discussed the bill's provisions for determining disability.

House Hearings
(p. 99)

Mr. Perkins. Now, the emphasis which H.R. 7199 places on rehabilitation is apparent, and one way that that would be done is the fact that H.R. 7199 directs the Secretary to enter into agreements with the States whereby this determination of disability would be made by the vocational rehabilitation agencies of the States.

A person who was disabled would apply to one of the 512 OASI field offices for preservation of his rights under this disability freeze. If he had the required work history, under the OASI system, he would be referred to the State vocational rehabilitation agency, where he would be given an examination by the counselor in the agency, who would call for a medical examination by one of the local doctors in the community, if needed, under the usual working relationships which exist between the State vocational rehabilitation agencies and the doctors today.

This disability examination would serve as the evidence as to whether his rights should be preserved under this proposal. At the same time, it would serve as the basis for the rehabilitation plan, which the State vocational rehabilitation agency would draw up for the worker, and the worker would be returned to work; that is, if the rehabilitation were successful.

This rehabilitation would be a part of the usual State-Federal vocational rehabilitation program and would be financed in the usual manner under that program.

Although the Ways and Means Committee was hearing testimony on both H.R. 7199 and H.R. 7200, Secretary Hobby made only one brief reference to public assistance during her testimony.

House Hearings
(p. 100)

Secretary Hobby. Although I am not testifying on H.R. 7200 at this time our discussion this morning would be incomplete without some further mention of public assistance and of H.R. 7200.

The administration believes that in the past there has been insufficient emphasis upon the close relationship between old-age and survivors insurance and the public assistance programs. Our review made in the past year has resulted in a new and integrated approach to these programs on the part of the administration.

OASI is moving gradually toward maturity. The broadened coverage proposed in H.R. 7199 will greatly accelerate this process. As OASI assumes more and more of the load of supporting our aged population, the need for old-age assistance payments by the States should diminish.

H.R. 7200, a closely related bill to H.R. 7199, would revise the old-age assistance formula to reflect this fact. The new formula would contain a factor reducing the Federal percentage share of old-age assistance expenditures gradually in any State as a larger and larger proportion of aged of that State become OASI beneficaries.

The action taken by this committee on H.R. 7199 will have an important bearing on the future of public assistance. We believe that the soundness of the approach taken in H.R. 7200 with respect to public assistance will be apparent upon the completion of your hearings on the bill before you today.

The American Medical Association led opposition to the bill although it objected to only two provisions. First, the AMA opposed compulsory coverage of physicians under social security. Dr. Francis Blasinghame spoke for the organization.

House Hearings
(p. 226)

Statement of Dr. Francis Blasinghame

We consider it absolutely incompatible with the free enterprise system for a group to be compulsorily covered under a governmental system of old-age benefits when that group strongly and with great force opposes such coverage.

Old age benefits under the act simply do not fit the economic pattern of the life of the self-employed physician. To compel him to come under the provisions of this portion of the Social Security Act would represent a failure to understand that physicians, like many other professional people, serve the citizens of their community best by following their traditional economic pattern of life. In making this comment, it is not my intention to make any inferences whatsoever regarding the applicability of old age survivors insurance program to the 50 million employed persons in the United States.

Secondly, the AMA opposed the disability freeze, stating that "it most definitely would become an entering wedge for the regimentation of the medical profession by creating the mechanism for the adoption of a federal cash permanent and total disability program, which in turn could lead to a full-fledged system of compulsory sickness insurance" (House Hearings, p. 228).

The AMA's position was attacked by an opposing medical organization, The Physicians Forum.

House Hearings
(p. 250)

Statement of the Physicians Forum

Our organization has been on record for more than 2 years in favor of the inclusion of doctors and other professionals under the Social Security Act, and we have endeavored to inform as many practicing physicians as possible of the benefits which they would receive from this coverage. We state our firm belief that, if a national poll were taken today, doctors would overwhelmingly favor inclusion. To bolster this contention, the membership of the medical society of the county of New York, the largest component of the American Medical Association, has twice voted for Federal social security. Similar resolutions, submitted by forum members, have been passed by the Kings, Queens, and Sullivan County societies of New York State. In New York Jersey, (sic) in polls of both the Bergen and Essex County membership, a significant majority of those replying wish these benefits.

Representatives of the National Grange and The National Farmer's Union both went on record supporting extension of OASI coverage to farmers and farm workers. Various labor organizations also supported the proposals, objecting only that the recommendation did not go far enough in liberalizing benefits, coverage, and the wage base. The life insurance industry testified against both liberalization of benefits and the recommended disability freeze, and the Townsendites appeared before the committee once again to offer a universal coverage bill as a substitute for the Administration's legislation.

The committee held executive sessions until May 28, when it reported out a bill including the major Administration provisions. The committee bill, H.R. 9366, made two significant modifications: (1) it excluded self-employed physicians from compulsory coverage, and (2) limited coverage to farm workers only sporadically employed. Also the existing public assistance formula was simply extended for an additional two years. The committee report summarized the major provisions of the bill.

Social Security Act Amendments of 1954
House Report No. 1698 on H.R. 9366
83d Cong., 2d Sess.
(May 28, 1954)

II. Summary of Principal Provisions of the Bill

A. Old-age and survivors insurance

1. Extension of coverage. — Old-age and survivors insurance coverage would be extended to approximately 10 million persons who work during the course of a year in jobs now excluded from the program. The groups brought into the program under the bill are as follows:

(a) Self-employed farm operators whose net earnings from farm self-employment total $400 or more in a year, with a special provision to make it easier for low-income farm operators to compute their net earnings (about 3.6 million).

(b) Professional self-employed persons now excluded, other than physicians, whose net earnings from professional self-employment total $400 or more in a year, including lawyers, dentists, architects, engineers, accountants, funeral directors, osteopaths, chiropractors, veterinarians, naturopaths, optometrists, ministers, and Christian Science practitioners (about 400,000).

(c) Employees of State and local governments who are covered by State and local retirement systems, other than policemen and firemen, under voluntary agreements between the State and the Federal Government, if a majority of the members of the system vote in a referendum and two thirds of those who vote favor coverage (about 3.5 million).

(d) Farmworkers who are paid at least $200 by a given employer in a calendar year, with special provisions to coordinate the annual earnings test with the quarterly insured status requirements (about 1.3 million).

(e) Domestic workers in private nonfarm homes (and others who perform work not in the course of the employer's trade or business) who are paid $50 in cash wages by an employer in a calendar quarter but who do not meet the 24-day test required in the present law (about 250,000).

(f) Ministers and members of religious orders employed by nonprofit organizations if the organization elects to cover them and if at least two-thirds of such individuals elect to be covered (about 250,000).

(g) Most Federal employees not covered by retirement systems, including temporary employees in the field service of the Post Office Department, census-taking employees of the Bureau of the Census, civilian employees of Coast Guard post exchanges, and certain other groups, and also employees of district Federal Home Loan Banks and the Tennessee Valley Authority, who have retirement systems (about 150,000).

(h) American citizens employed outside of the United States by foreign subsidiaries of American employers, under voluntary agreements between the Federal Government and the parent American company (about 100,000).

(i) Those homeworkers who are now excluded from employee coverage (although they may now be covered as self-employed persons) because the services they perform are not subject to State licensing laws (about 100,000).

(j) Certain employees engaged in fishing and related activities, either on vessels of 10 net tons or less or on shore (about 50,000).

(k) American citizens employed by American employers on vessels and aircraft of foreign registry (very few people involved).

2. *Computation of average monthly wage.* — Up to 5 years in which earnings were lowest (or nonexistent) could be dropped from the computation of the average monthly wage.

3. *Earnings base.* — The total annual earnings on which benefits would be computed and contributions paid is raised from $3,600 to $4,200.

4. *Increase in benefits.* — (a) More than 6.3 million persons now on the benefit rolls would have their benefits increased. The average increase for retired workers would be about $6 a month, with proportionate increases

for dependents and survivors. The range in primary insurance amounts would be $30 to $98.50 as compared to $25 to $85 under present law.

(b) Persons who retire or die in the future would, in general, have their benefits computed by the following new formula: (i) 55 percent of the first $110 of average monthly wage (rather than $100 as in present law) plus 20 percent of the next $240 (rather than 15 percent of the next $200); (ii) the minimum monthly benefit amount for a retired worker would be $30, and the minimum amount payable where only one survivor is entitled to benefits on the deceased insured person's earnings, would be $30; (iii) the maximum monthly family benefit of $168.75 would be increased to $200; (iv) the provision of existing law that total family benefits cannot exceed 80 percent of the worker's average monthly wage would not reduce total family benefits below 1½ times the insured worker's primary insurance amount or $50, whichever is the greater; and (v) lump-sum death payments would not exceed $255, the maximum under existing law.

5. *Limitation on earnings of beneficiaries.* — The earnings limitation on beneficiaries under age 75 would be made the same for wage earners and self-employed persons. A beneficiary could earn as much as $1,000 in a year in any employment, covered or noncovered. He would lose 1 month's benefit for each unit of $80 (or fraction thereof) of earnings (covered or noncovered) in excess of $1,000, but in no case would he lose benefits for months in which he neither earned more than $80 in wages nor rendered substantial services in self-employment. Beneficiaries residing in foreign countries would have their benefits suspended for any month in which they worked on 7 or more days.

6. *Eligibility for benefits.* — (a) As an alternative to the present requirements for fully insured status, an individual would be fully insured if all the quarters elapsing after 1954 and up to the quarter of his death or attainment of age 65 were quarters of coverage, provided he had at least 6 quarters of coverage after 1954.

(b) Benefits would be paid to the surviving aged widow, widowed mother, and children, or parents of any individual who died prior to September 1, 1950, and had at least 6 quarters of coverage.

7. *Preservation of benefit rights for disabled.* — The period during which an individual was under an extended total disability would be excluded in determining his insured status and the amount of benefits payable to him upon retirement or to his survivors in the event of his death. Only disabilities lasting more than 6 months would be taken into account. Determinations of disability would be made by State vocational rehabilitation agencies or other appropriate State agencies pursuant to agreements with the Secretary of Health, Education, and Welfare.

8. *Limitation on payments to persons outside the United States.* — Benefits to survivors or dependents would not be paid for any month in which such survivor or dependent resided outside the United States unless such

survivor or dependent met certain requirements of residence in the United States or the insured individual on whose record the benefit is based was currently insured on the basis of military service wage credits or earnings as an American citizen employed abroad by an American employer.

9. *Deportation, and periods of unlawful residence.* — All benefits payable on the basis of an individual's wage record would be terminated upon notification by the Attorney General that the individual has been deported from the United States for certain specified causes. Earnings derived during periods of unlawful residence in the United States as determined by the Attorney General could not be used in determination of insured status or benefit amount.

10. *Recomputation of benefits for work after entitlement.* — An individual may have his benefit recomputed to take into account additional earnings after entitlement if he has covered earnings of at least $1,000 in a calendar year after 1953 and after the year in which his benefit was last computed.

11. *Contribution rates.* — Employers and employees will continue to share equally, with the rates on each being as follows:

Calendar years:	Rate (percent)
1954 – 59	2
1960 – 64	2½
1965 – 69	3
1970 – 74	3½
1975 and after	4

The self-employed would pay 1½ times the above rates.

B. Public assistance

1. The provisions of the 1952 amendments, presently scheduled to expire on September 30, 1954, with respect to temporary increases in Federal payments to States for old-age assistance, aid to dependent children, aid to the blind, and aid to the permanently and totally disabled are extended through September 30, 1955.

2. The privisions of the 1950 amendments for approval of certain State plans for aid to the blind which did not meet the requirements of clause 8 of section 1002 (a) of the Social Security Act are extended from June 30, 1955, to June 30, 1957.

H.R. 9366 was at least a partial fulfillment of the Republican platform and consequently it met little opposition from members of that party. Since the majority of Democrats were traditionally committed to liberalization of benefits and coverage, there was not much serious debate in the House.

The House followed the traditional procedure for social security amendments; it adopted a closed rule allowing no amendments from the floor.

Representative Reed, the bill's author, introduced the major provisions of his proposal (Congressional Record, *Vol. 100, p. 7426*). *Compared with earlier bills, the debates were embarrassingly amicable, although there were odd moments of disagreement. For example, dentists complained of social discrimination since they were included under the extension of OASI while physicians were not.*

Representative Curtis, who directed the controversial hearings on social security the year before, urged passage of H.R. 9366, but continued to call for universal coverage.

The final House vote on H.R. 9366 was taken on June 1, and the bill was overwhelmingly adopted, representing the greatest bipartisan vote on social security since 1935 and indicating the political popularity of the system. This was also the first time a social security amendment had passed either house of Congress while the Republicans held a majority.

The adoption of the bill by the House increased pressure on the Senate to act before the fall elections. The Senate Finance Committee immediately scheduled public hearings for the last week of June and the early part of July. Once again Secretary Hobby was the first witness. She urged Senate approval of H.R. 9366, but also forcefully suggested that the House provisions deleting compulsory coverage for farm operators and farm workers, and exempting physicians from OASI coverage, be reversed, and the Administration's proposals restored. She also made a strong plea for the disability freeze which remained in the House bill, but was threatened in the Senate by the AMA. Her only reference to OAA was an endorsement of the "withering away" doctrine.

Social Security Amendments of 1954
Hearings on H.R. 1954 before the Senate Finance Committee
83d Cong., 2d Sess. (June, 1954)
(p. 217)

Statement of Secretary Oveta Culp Hobby

As old-age and survivors insurance assumes more and more of the load of supporting our aged population, the need for old-age assistance payments will diminish. By the end of 1955 the States will have saved about $15 million in their old-age assistance programs as a result of the improvements in old-age and survivors insurance. By 1960 these savings to the States will be at the rate of $75 million a year and by 1980, $130 million a year.

As the President stated in his message of January 14, transmitting his OASI recommendations to the Congress—

> As broadened OASI coverage goes into effect, the proportion of our aged population eligible for benefits will increase from 45 to 75 percent in the next

5 or 6 years. Although the need for some measure of public assistance will continue, the OASI program will progressively reduce, year by year, the extent of the need for public-assistance payments by the substitution of OASI benefits.

Under the present old-age assistance matching formula the general revenues of the Federal Government matched the States on a 50–50 basis on that part of old-age assistance payments which exceeds $25 up to the maximum of $55. If the present OASI bill is passed increasing benefits and making coverage virtually universal, it would seem reasonable in those old-age assistance cases where the individual is receiving a Federal OASI benefit that matching of any supplementary payment from the general revenues of the Federal Government be at the 50–50 rate, rather than at the higher rates applicable to the first $25 of an old-age assistance payment.

The remaining testimony offered to the Finance Committee closely duplicated what had been presented to the House Ways and Means Committee only three months earlier. No new issues were presented, and again the only controversies concerned the exemption of physicians from OASI coverage, the compulsory coverage of farm workers and operators, and the adoption of the disability freeze provisions. Only three important modifications distinguished the Finance Committee bill from the House version: (1) it excluded farmers and self-employed professionals from coverage; (2) it adopted the Administration's suggestion for broadened coverage of farm workers; and (3) it liberalized the retirement test.

The Senate debate was opened by the chairman of the Finance Committee, Senator Eugene D. Millikin of Colorado, who emphasized the presidential commitment to the OASI approach:

Congressional Debates
100 Congressional Record, p. 143831
(August 13, 1954)

Mr. Millikin. Mr. President, H.R. 9366, as amended by the Committee on Finance, is designed to improve the old-age and survivors insurance system—the system which President Eisenhower has called "the cornerstone of the Government's programs to promote the economic security of the individual."

In his message to Congress of January 14, 1954, the President recommended the expansion and improvement of old-age and survivors insurance and the preservation of the basic principles of the system. He cited two principles as the most important. These are:

First. The contributory aspect of the system under which the worker and his employer make payments during the years of active work, and

Second. The benefits received are related in part to the individual's earnings.

The provisions of the pending bill follow the President's recommendations.

Contributory social insurance continues to be basic in our governmental system for affording protection against the economic hazards resulting from old age and premature death. In my opinion, it is in the public interest for us to expand and improve the existing program which has been in operation since. 1937.

There was little debate on the proposed committee amendments which were adopted in toto. *At one point Senator Herbert Lehman of New York offered an even more liberal measure as a substitute for H.R. 9366, but later he withdrew his proposals. His purpose, however, was clearly to claim some Democratic credit for the legislation.*

Congressional Debates
100 Congressional Record, p. 14416
(August 13, 1954)

Mr. Lehman. But, Mr. President, while the administration may take the credit for recommending these improvements in the social-security program, I should like to point out that the credit for originally suggesting these improvements may properly be claimed by this side of the aisle.

A glance at the Congressional Record, volume 99, part 6, page 7750, of July 1, 1953, will show that on that date I introduced a bill, S. 2260, on behalf of myself and 10 other Senators, which contained almost all the provisions now contained in the bill being considered by the Senate. An identical bill was at that time introduced into the House by a number of Democratic Members of that body, including Representatives Dingell, of Michigan, and Celler and Roosevelt, of New York.

In order to let these provisions be brought to the attention of the Senate, I have revised my bill in a few minor respects and reintroduced it as an amendment in the nature of a substitute to H.R. 9366. As such I wish to discuss it and compare its provisions with those of the administration bill.

The Senate debate was more interesting than the House discussion had been. Senator John F. Kennedy proposed an amendment to raise the minimum payment under OASI from $30 to $35 a month. His move was rejected by voice vote after the Republican leadership had expressed fears for the "integrity" of the trust fund. Somewhat illogically, the same leadership also opposed an amendment by Senator John C. Stennis of Mississippi to exclude itinerant farm workers from coverage because it involved a group of workers who are most in need of the protection provided by the old-age and survivors' insurance scheme. "They have less opportunity to build up resources for their old age than do most members of the working force." (100 Congressional Record, p. 14434.)

Additional amendments liberalizing the bill were introduced by various Senate Democrats, but all the proposals were rejected by voice vote and on August 13 the Senate passed H.R. 9366 as it had been introduced.

Conferees were immediately appointed by both houses and one week later, the Conference Committee filed its report. Coverage for self-employed farmers was adopted, as well as extended to farm workers earning $100 in one quarter from a single employer. Certain professionals, funeral directors, accountants, architects, and engineers, were covered—physicians, lawyers, osteopaths, dentists, and veterinarians were not. The existing formula for federal aid to the states for public assistance was extended to September 30, 1956.

On the day the conference report was issued, both houses adopted the measure by voice vote. President Eisenhower signed H.R. 9366 into law in September, calling the legislation "one of the cornerstones of our program to build a better . . . America."

Presidential Statement Upon Signing
the Social Security Act Amendments of 1954
(September 1, 1954)*

I am very happy to sign the Social Security Amendments of 1954. By enabling some 10,000,000 more Americans to participate in the Old-Age and Survivors Insurance Program, it gives them an opportunity to establish a solid foundation of economic security for themselves and their families.

Beyond broadening the coverage of this program, this new law contains four other important provisions:

First, it raises payments to all retired workers by at least five dollars a month. It also raises—by $13.50 a month for retired workers and by $31.25 a month for families—the ceiling on payments to people now receiving monthly checks. People becoming eligible in the future will also receive higher payments, including increases that result from raising from $3,600 to $4,200 the maximum wage base from which the amount of their benefit checks is determined.

Second, the law eliminates the four or five lowest years of earnings from the computation of the OASI checks of workers who retire in the future. This provision is of great importance to many people whose years of unusually low earnings—for reasons of unemployment, illness, or otherwise—would sharply reduce their benefits.

Third, all retired workers under the program are permitted to earn more without forfeiting OASI checks. The amount of exempt earnings is increased to $1,200 a year, and this annual exemption is applied equally to wage earners and self-employed workers.

Ibid., p. 801–802.

Fourth, the Act preserves the benefits rights, under Old-Age and Survivors Insurance, of those workers regularly covered under the program who become totally disabled for long and indefinite periods.

This new law is an important part of the broad program of the Administration and the 83d Congress to improve the well-being of our people. In the past month I have signed into law a number of other Acts directly affecting the human problems of each family in the land.

*   *   *

These Acts and the Social Security amendments I have approved today will bolster the health and economic security of the American people. They represent one of the cornerstones of our program to build a better and stronger America.

Unemployment Compensation

While Congress was considering OASI and public assistance, the Administration was also urging adoption of unemployment legislation during the 1954 session.

Several bills attempting to modernize the federal-state unemployment insurance program were later introduced in the House. The Administration argued that such action was needed if economic stability was to be achieved and pointed mainly towards coverage for additional categories of employers and workers.

The House Ways and Means Committee scheduled hearings for June 8–11 on the twenty bills relating to unemployment compensation which had been introduced. Three days of testimony followed with business leaders generally opposing any increased coverage, and union groups urging even greater liberalization.

On June 29, the committee reported a "clean bill" incorporating provisions from several of the pending proposals. The committee bill, H.R. 9709, amended the Federal Unemployment Tax Act by extending the application of that act to employers of four or more workers in twenty weeks. (Existing law covered employers of eight or more persons). The bill also extended state unemployment insurance coverage to substantially all federal civilian employees. These two proposals would have added 1.3 million additional workers in the private sector, and 2.5 million federal civilian employees, to those already covered by unemployment insurance.

The greatest opposition came from Democrats such as Representative John A. Blatnik of Minnesota who alleged that the bill was a "phony". Since the bill was under closed rule and amendments were not allowed, a group of eighty-five Representatives, led by Representative Forand of Rhode Island, attempted to substitute H.R. 9430. Representative Blatnik spoke on behalf of this latter bill.

Congressional Debates
100 Congressional Record, p. 10088
(July 8, 1954)

Mr. Blatnik . . .

Anyone familiar with the facts of life as they relate to unemployment compensation must recognize that the provisions of the Forand bill offer logical solutions to repair the basic weaknesses of the present unemployment insurance system. What does the Forand bill propose? I will enumerate. Firstly, the Forand bill would extend the maximum duration of benefit payments under the unemployment insurance system to 39 weeks as against 26 weeks in about half the States today. Secondly, the Forand bill provides that the maximum primary benefit payable under State laws to unemployed workers shall be not less than two-thirds of the State's average weekly wage — this would mean a substantial increase over benefits payable under existing law; and finally, the Forand bill would extend the coverage of unemployed compensation to nearly every employee in America. In short, Mr. Chairman, the Forand bill proposes to extend the period during which unemployment compensation is payable, to substantially increase the amount of benefits payable, and to extend the coverage of the Federal-State unemployment system to virtually every worker in America.

The House rejected the alternative proposals and, on July 8, adopted H.R. 9709. The Senate Finance Committee held no hearings on the bill and reported it out on July 12 without amendment. Later, however, an amendment by Senator Johnson of Colorado was accepted, delaying for one year the extension of coverage to employers with four or more employees. The new effective date was to be December 31, 1955. On August 18, the day after Senate adoption of H.R. 9709, the House concurred in the Senate amendment by voice vote and the bill was sent to President Eisenhower for his signature.

On September 1, 1954, the same day he signed the social security amendments, President Eisenhower signed H.R. 9709.

Social Security Amendments of 1954
(September 1, 1954, ch. 1212, 68 Statutes at Large 1130)

Be it enacted by the Senate and House of Representatives of the United States of America in Congress assembled, That, effective with respect to services performed after December 31, 1955, section 3306 (a) of the Internal Revenue Code of 1954 is hereby amended by striking out "eight or more" and inserting in lieu thereof "4 or more".

Sec. 2. Effective with respect to rates of contributions for periods after December 31, 1954, section 3303 (a) of the Internal Revenue Code of 1954 is hereby amended by adding after paragraph (3) the following:

"For any person (or group of persons) who has (or have) not been subject to the State law for a period of time sufficient to compute the reduced rates permitted by paragraphs (1), (2), and (3) of this subsection on a 3-year basis, the period of time required may be reduced to the amount of time the person (or group of persons) has (or have) had experience under or has (or have) been subject to the State law, whichever is appropriate, but in no case less than 1 year immediately preceding the computation date."

Sec. 3. Effective with respect to the taxable year 1955 and succeeding taxable years, section 6152 (a) (3) of the Internal Revenue Code of 1954 is hereby repealed.

Sec. 4. (a) The Social Security Act, as amended, is further amended by adding after title XIV thereof the following new title:

"TITLE XV – UNEMPLOYMENT COMPENSATION FOR FEDERAL EMPLOYEES

*   *   *

"COMPENSATION FOR FEDERAL EMPLOYEES UNDER STATE AGREEMENTS

"Sec. 1502. (a) The Secretary is authorized on behalf of the United States to enter into an agreement with any State, or with the agency administering the unemployment compensation law of such State, under which such State agency (1) will make, as agent of the United States, payments of compensation, on the basis provided in subsection (b) of this section, to Federal employees, and (2) will otherwise cooperate with the Secretary and with other State agencies in making payments of compensation under this title.

"(b) Any such agreement shall provide that compensation will be paid by the State to any Federal employee, with respect to unemployment after December 31, 1954, in the same amount, on the same terms, and subject to the same conditions as the compensation which would be payable to such employee under the unemployment compensation law of the State if the Federal service and Federal wages of such employee assigned to such State under section 1504 had been included as employment and wages under such law.

"(c) Any determination by a State agency with respect to entitlement to compensation pursuant to an agreement under this section shall be subject to review in the same manner and to the same extent as determinations under the State unemployment compensation law, and only in such manner and to such extent.

"(d) Each agreement shall provide the terms and conditions upon which the agreement may be amended or terminated.

"COMPENSATION FOR FEDERAL EMPLOYEES IN ABSENCE OF STATE AGREEMENT

"Sec. 1503. (a) In the case of a Federal employee whose Federal service and Federal wages are assigned under section 1504 to a State which does

not have an agreement under this title with the Secretary, the Secretary, in accordance with regulations prescribed by him, shall, upon the filing by such employee of a claim for compensation under this subsection, make payments of compensation to him with respect to unemployment after December 31, 1954, in the same amounts, on the same terms, and subject to the same conditions as would be paid to him under the unemployment compensation law of such State if such employee's Federal service and Federal wages had been included as employment and wages under such law, except that if such employee, without regard to his Federal service and Federal wages, has employment or wages sufficient to qualify for any compensation during the benefit year under the law of such State, then payments of compensation under this subsection shall be made only on the basis of his Federal service and Federal wages.

"(b) In the case of a Federal employee whose Federal service and Federal wages are assigned under section 1504 to Puerto Rico or the Virgin Islands, the Secretary, in accordance with regulations prescribed by him, shall, upon the filing by such employee of a claim for compensation under this subsection, make payments of compensation to him with respect to unemployment after December 31, 1954, in the same amounts, on the same terms, and subject to the same conditions as would be paid to him under the unemployment compensation law of the District of Columbia if such employee's Federal service and Federal wages had been included as employment and wages under such law, except that if such employee, without regard to his Federal service and Federal wages, has employment or wages sufficient to qualify for any compensation during the benefit year under such law, then payments of compensation under this subsection shall be made only on the basis of his Federal service and Federal wages.

"(c) Any Federal employee whose claim for compensation under subsection (a) or (b) of this section has been denied shall be entitled to a fair hearing in accordance with regulations prescribed by the Secretary. Any final determination by the Secretary with respect to entitlement to compensation under this section shall be subject to review by the courts in the same manner and to the same extent as is provided in section 205 (g) with respect to final decisions of the Secretary of Health, Education, and Welfare under title II.

"(d) The Secretary may utilize for the purposes of this section the personnel and facilities of the agencies in Puerto Rico and the Virgin Islands cooperating with the United States Employment Service under the Act of June 6, 1933 (48 Stat. 113), as amended, and may delegate to officials of such agencies any authority granted to him by this section whenever the Secretary determines such delegation to be necessary in carrying out the purposes of this title. For the purpose of payments made to such agencies under such Act, the furnishing of such personnel and facilities shall be deemed to be a part of the administration of the public employment offices of such agencies.

Retrospect and Prospect

The year 1954 was a gratifying one for supporters of the traditional views of social security. That January it was doubtful whether social security, as it then existed, would survive the demands for change by individuals and groups, both in and out of government. The United States Chamber of Commerce was still promoting its pay-as-you-go plan, and the Curtis hearings supported those urging universal coverage. The position of the Administration was uncertain.

However, any doubts quickly subsided when the Republican Administration took the initiative. Congressional Republicans immediately followed the White House lead and pushed for adoption of liberalizing amendments to the OASI program and the unemployment insurance program. When the White House and congressional Republicans were joined by the northern Democrats, passage of the proposals was assured. For the first time, major social security legislation was adopted under a Republican Administration.

With the amendments in 1954, nine out of ten employed persons were covered by the OASI program. Workers were permitted to drop as many as five years of low earnings from their wage records in computing their average monthly pay. The wage base of annual earnings rose from $3600 to $4200, resulting also in higher maximum benefits. Disability was finally recognized as a factor in determining eligibility—the 1954 amendments preserved benefits for totally disabled workers by discounting wages lost through illness. The amount a retired person could earn before OASI payments were reduced was also increased and the age at which beneficiaries could receive full OASI payments regardless of other income was reduced from seventy-five to seventy-two. At the same time, another four million additional workers were included in the unemployment compensation program.

1954 brought about these changes, but many Congressmen and several powerful lobbies found the improvements far too limited. Nothing, for instance, had come of the Truman Commission on the Health Needs of the Nation. The AMA took a predictable negative stand.

Somewhat surprisingly, the President had proposed that the Federal Government reinsure private insurance companies to protect them against particularly heavy losses in health insurance. Hearings were held in both houses, (Health Reinsurance Legislation, *Hearings before the Senate Committee on Interstate and Foreign Commerce, 83d Cong., 2d Sess.;* President's Health Recommendations and Related Measures, *Hearings before the House Committee on Labor and Public Welfare, 83d Cong., 2d Sess.) and both committees rejected the bill. (See* Federal Reinsurance Service, Senate Report No. 1798.) *It had been supported by some insurance companies, but opposed by the AMA as "the opening wedge toward socialized medicine." The House debated and killed the bill, and it was not even discussed in the Senate.*

1955 – 1956

The 1954 congressional elections returned Democratic majorities to both houses. Although the Republicans had supported substantial changes in the social security system, the mood of the new Congress was to adopt additional liberalizing amendments.

Many Democrats in Congress had long been promoting the idea of including disability benefits within the basic structure of the OASI program. These same advocates had supported reduction of the eligibility age for women from sixty-five to sixty-two. With a majority in both houses, the time was ripe for the introduction of an omnibus bill instituting these various changes.

The Eisenhower Administration did not actively encourage or support major changes in the social security program during 1955. In his budget message, the President emphasized the achievements of the 1954 amendments rather than suggesting any new programs. He warned that federal programs in the area of social security were only supplemental to private and state and local programs, and called for only two recommended changes in the OASI program.

Annual Budget Message of the President
(January 17, 1955)*

In the last Congress, old-age and survivors insurance was extended to 10 million more persons and benefits were improved. Vocational rehabilitation grants to the States have been stepped up toward the objective for 1959 of helping 200,000 people a year to rehabilitate themselves. We have undertaken to aid the construction of medical diagnostic and treatment centers, rehabilitation facilities, nursing homes, and chronic disease hospitals, as well as general hospitals.

*   *   *

Welfare, Health, and Education

Major advances have been made in the past year in the fields of social security, health, and education, pursuant to recommendations which I made to the Congress. We have demonstrated that the well-being of our people can be strengthened without yielding to the dangers of centralized power in the Federal Government, and we shall continue firmly to resist any project which would seem to us to involve such dangers. We have found ways to provide greater human security and social opportunity, while restricting the Federal Government's role to that of assisting private action and State

*Public Papers of the Presidents, Dwight D. Eisenhower 1955, p. 141 et seq.

and local responsibility with research and technical assistance, social insurance, and grants-in-aid. We believe that these gains can be continued through cooperative action among all levels of American government together with private participation.

*   *   *

In connection with old-age and survivors insurance, I am recommending two legislative measures. One is the coordination of income and old-age insurance tax collection procedures to make reporting easier for wage earners and employers and at the same time to reduce Government costs for collecting taxes and paying benefits. The second is extension of this insurance to military personnel and to those Federal civilian personnel not now covered, as the basic part of improved systems of survivorship, disability, and retirement protection, with existing staff retirement systems retained as independent and separate entities. The military retirement pay system should remain unchanged. Certain adjustments in the present civilian personnel retirement systems will be needed.

In his budget message Eisenhower revealed that the Administration would, in the immediate future, send a special message to Congress recommending adoption of a coordinated health program. Among his proposals was a federally financed re-insurance program which would encourage private insurance carriers to broaden their benefits and extend coverage to more people. He also recommended separate federally matched vendor payments for medical care of welfare recipients under PA.

Special Presidential Message to the Congress
Recommending a Health Program
(January 31, 1955)*

To the Congress of the United States:

Because the strength of our nation is in its people, their good health is a proper national concern; healthy Americans live more rewarding, more productive and happier lives. Fortunately, the nation continues its advance in bettering the health of all its people.

Deaths from infectious diseases have diminished. During the past year, important progress has been made in dealing with such diseases as rheumatic fever, high blood pressure, poliomyelitis and tuberculosis. Intensified research has produced more knowledge than ever before about the scourges of heart disease and cancer.

The 83rd Congress, during the last legislative session, supported dramatic new strides in vocational rehabilitation. By 1959, consequently, we should be restoring to useful lives most persons who become disabled and who can

*Ibid., p. 216 et seq.

be rehabilitated and returned to employment. In human terms, this will be a heartwarming achievement.

The 1954 amendments to the Hospital Survey and Construction Act opened another new chapter in the national drive for better health. Under these amendments, further provision was made to help build health care facilities for the chronically ill; to aid in the construction of nursing and convalescent homes; to provide for more diagnostic and treatment centers for patients who do not need hospital care; and to help make centers available for the rehabilitation of the disabled.

These achievements represent a major gain for the immediate and future welfare of countless Americans—in the health of both mind and body. Recent advances do not, however, represent our full capacity to wage war on illness and disability throughout the land.

The Immediate Needs

As a nation, we are doing less than now lies within our power to reduce the impact of disease. Many of our fellow Americans cannot afford to pay the costs of medical care when it is needed, and they are not protected by adequate *health insurance.* Too frequently the local hospitals, clinics, or nursing homes required for the prevention, diagnosis and treatment of disease either do not exist or are badly out of date. Finally, there are critical shortages of the trained personnel required to study, prevent, treat and control disease.

The specific recommendations that follow are designed to meet this threefold deficiency.

Meeting the Costs of Medical Care

For most Americans, insurance—private, voluntary insurance—provides a sound and effective method of meeting unexpected hazards which may be beyond the capacity of the individual to bear. Risk sharing through group action is in the best tradition of vigorous and imaginative American enterprise.

The Government should cooperate with, and encourage, private carriers in the improvement of health insurance. Moreover, a great many people who are not now covered can be given its protection, particularly in rural areas where group enrollment is at present difficult.

Existing health insurance can also be improved by expanding the scope of the benefits provided. Not all private expenditures for medical care can or should be covered by insurance; nevertheless, many policies offered today are too limited in scope. They are principally for hospitalized illness and for relatively short periods of time.

I recommend, consequently, the establishment of a Federal health reinsurance service to encourage private health insurance organizations in offering broader benefits to insured individuals and families and coverage to more people.

In addition, to improve medical care for the aged, the blind, dependent children, and the permanently and totally disabled who are public assistance recipients, I recommend the authorization of limited Federal grants to match State and local expenditures.

Reinsurance. — The purpose of the reinsurance proposal is to furnish a system for broad sharing among health insurance organizations of the risks of experimentation. A system of this sort will give an incentive to the improvement of existing health insurance plans. It will encourage private, voluntary health insurance organizations to provide better protection — particularly against expensive illness — for those who now are insured against some of the financial hazards of illness. Reinsurance will also help to stimulate extension of private voluntary health insurance plans to millions of additional people who do not now have, but who could afford to purchase, health insurance.

The Department of Health, Education, and Welfare has been working with specialists from the insurance industry, with experts from the health professions, and with many other interested citizens, in its effort to perfect a sound reinsurance program — a program which involves no Government subsidy and no Government competition with private insurance carriers. The time has come to put such a program to work for the American people.

I urge the Congress to launch the reinsurance service this year by authorizing a reasonable capital fund and by providing for its use as necessary to reinsure three broad areas for expansion in private voluntary health insurance:

1. health insurance plans providing protection against the high costs of severe or prolonged illness,
2. health insurance plans providing coverage for individuals and families in predominantly rural areas,
3. health insurance plans designed primarily for coverage of individuals and families of average or lower income against medical care costs in the home and physician's office as well as in the hospital.

*   *   *

Medical care for public assistance recipients. — Nearly 5 million persons in the United States are now receiving public assistance under State programs aided by Federal grants. Present arrangements for their medical care, however, are far from adequate. Special provision for improving health services for these needy persons must be made.

I recommend to the Congress, therefore, that it authorize separate Federal matching of State and local expenditures for the medical care needed by public assistance recipients. The separate matching should apply to each of the four Federally-aided categories — the aged, the permanently and totally disabled, the blind and children deprived of parental care.

Democratic Extension of OASI

The recommendations of the Eisenhower Administration represented only a part of the tremendous volume of legislation proposed in Congress. More than one hundred bills were introduced in the House during the session, suggesting various methods of increasing benefits and extending coverage.

On June 17, 1955 Representative Jere Cooper of Tennessee, chairman of the Ways and Means Committee, sent a letter to the Secretary of the Department of Health, Education, and Welfare, Mrs. Oveta Culp Hobby, informing her that the committee would be holding executive sessions on the various proposals, and inviting testimony from her department. The Republican members of the committee, led by Representative Jenkins, argued that public hearings should be held, and strongly opposed the manner in which the legislation was being considered by the committee.

Responding to the chairman's request for the Administration's position on the proposed legislation, the Secretary also objected to the committee's decision to hold no public hearings.

However, the committee refused to change its position, and on July 11, after several weeks of closed hearings, Chairman Cooper introduced H.R. 7225, which embodied the committee's decisions. The bill was favorably reported out of the committee on July 14:

Social Security Act Amendments of 1955
House Report No. 1189
84th Cong., 1st Sess.
(July 14, 1955)

A. Principal Features of H.R. 7225

H.R. 7225, as reported by your committee, would strengthen the old-age and survivors insurance program by providing:

(1) *Disability benefits.* — Payment of monthly benefits at or after age 50 to workers who are totally and permanently disabled and who meet strict tests as to duration and recentness of old-age and survivors insurance coverage. It is estimated that in the first year disability insurance benefits would be payable to about 250,000 workers, amounting to $200 million in benefits, and that in 25 years 1 million workers would be receiving disability benefits amounting to about $850 million in benefits a year. The procedures for determining and for defining disability would be those now contained in present law with respect to the preservation of insurance rights of individuals with extended total disability.

(2) *Lowering of retirement age for women.* — Payment of monthly benefits at age 62 for women who are insured workers, wives of insured workers,

and widows and dependent mothers of deceased insured workers. It is estimated that in the first year benefits would be paid to almost 800,000 additional women, amounting to about $400 million in benefits, and that in about 25 years 1,800,000 additional women would be receiving benefits amounting to about $1.3 billion.

(3) *Children's disability benefits.* — Continuation of monthly benefits to children who become totally and permanently disabled before age 18. It is estimated that eventually 5,000 children and their mothers would be receiving benefits totaling $2 to $3 million per year.

(4) *Expanded old-age and survivors insurance coverage.* — Extension of coverage to the self-employed professional groups now excluded (except physicians), to certain farm owners who receive income under share-farming agreements, to turpentine and gum naval stores employees, and to certain employees of the Tennessee Valley Authority and of the Federal Home Loan Banks. It is expected that this extension of coverage will provide old-age and survivors insurance protection to an estimated additional 250,000 individuals and their families.

(5) *Adjustment of contribution schedule.* — Increases in the present schedule of contributions of one-half percent each on employers and employees and three-fourths percent on the self-employed, effective simultaneously with the improvement in the benefit provisions on January 1, 1956. The amendments recommended by your committee, including the revised contribution schedule, will place the system in a stronger actuarial position than it is under present law.

One week later the bill was debated by the House. As with previous social security legislation, it was brought up for floor debate under a suspension of the rules, but on this occasion not only were floor amendments barred but debate was limited to forty minutes and a two-thirds vote was required for passage. There was no time for full discussion of the important proposals in the bill and its opponents were limited to general statements attacking the disability benefits and lower eligibility age for women. Many of the speeches consisted of attacks on the procedural methods.

When the limited time for debate expired, the bill was overwhelmingly adopted — in a roll call vote 372-31. Since Congress was about to adjourn, there was no Senate action on the bill that year, but the Finance Committee did state that public hearings would be scheduled for early 1956.

The Administration and H. R. 7225

The Eisenhower Administration had opposed the House adoption of H.R. 7225 in 1955, and in his State of the Union Message on January 5, 1956, the President warned against amendments to OASI which were not actu-

arially sound. However, he also revealed that the Administration would support increases in some categories of the public assistance programs:

President Dwight D. Eisenhower
Fourth Annual Message
(January 5, 1956)*

Under the 1954 Amendments to the old-age and survivors' insurance program, protection was extended to some 10 million additional workers and benefits were increased. The system now helps protect 9 out of 10 American workers and their families against loss of income in old age or on the death of the breadwinner. The system is sound. It must be kept so. In developing improvements in the system, we must give the most careful consideration to population and social trends, and to fiscal requirements. With these considerations in mind, the Administration will present its recommendations for further expansion of coverage and other steps which can be taken wisely at this time.

*   *   *

Other needs in the area of social welfare include increased child welfare services, extension of the program of aid to dependent children, intensified attack on juvenile delinquency, and special attention to the problems of mentally retarded children.

Although the Administration remained opposed to a lower eligibility age for women and to reduction of the age limit for disabled individuals, a statement in the President's annual message transmitting the 1956 Economic Report to Congress indicated that Eisenhower would support efforts to include those professional groups not yet under OASI.

There was definite Administration support for changes in the public assistance programs. In his budget message, the President requested temporary extension of the existing federal matching formulas and called for an increase in the overall amount the Federal Government could reimburse the state, as well as changes designed to encourage the states to spend more money on medical care for welfare recipients.

Annual Budget Message of the President
(January 16, 1956)†

Public assistance and old-age and survivors insurance.—Grants to the States for old-age assistance and aid to dependent children, the blind, and the totally disabled are estimated at 1.5 billion dollars in the fiscal year

*Public Papers of the Presidents, Dwight D. Eisenhower, 1956, p. 21.
†Ibid, p. 118–19.

1957, the largest expenditure item in the welfare category of the Federal budget.

Our welfare policies have a twofold emphasis: To provide basic economic protection for older people and for widowed mothers and children through self-sustaining social insurance; and, where possible, to prevent need as well as to relieve it. My budget recommendations for both existing and proposed programs reflect this emphasis.

Old-age and survivors insurance—financed through a trust fund outside the regular budget—is now providing benefits at a rate of more than 5 billion dollars a year to more than 6 million persons over age 65 and to 1½ million mothers and children. The number of beneficiaries is growing. More than nine-tenths of all employed persons in the country are now insured. Legislation should be enacted to bring in the groups still excluded—for example, employees of the Federal Government.

For a large group of needy people not receiving OASI benefits, public assistance remains the only public resource. One out of every three people over 80 years of age is on the public assistance rolls, as compared with only about 1 in every 10 in the age group 65 to 69 which, for the most part, has the insurance protection. To avoid hardship to present public assistance recipients, I propose that the present formula for determining the Federal share of assistance payments be temporarily extended. This will allow time to reappraise the need for the present high level of the Federal contribution to public assistance as the effects of the recent strengthening of old-age and survivors insurance protection become more fully apparent. Meanwhile, to reflect the fact that more and more people are becoming eligible for old-age and survivors insurance benefits, I recommend legislation to fix at 50 percent the Federal share of supplementary old-age assistance payments by the States to beneficiaries of this insurance who are added to the assistance rolls after the fiscal year 1957.

The Federal Government should also do more to assist the States to adopt preventive measures which will reduce need and increase self-help among those who depend upon public welfare. Likewise, special provision should be made for improving medical care of public assistance recipients through legislation to permit separate Federal matching of State and local expenditures for this purpose.

The Senate Finance Committee scheduled hearings on H.R. 7225 beginning on January 25, 1956. The first witness was Robert Meyers, chief actuary of the Social Security Administration who had been with the program since its inception in 1935. He avoided discussion of the policy issues of the bill, and simply gave testimony about the effect of the proposed changes. At the request of the committee, Mr. Meyers submitted a cost estimate of the provisions in H.R. 7225.

The committee did not question the witness extensively. However, it was evident from the tone of many of the senators that the disability pro-

vision was a major obstacle. Whether this provision, and the proposal to reduce the eligibility age for women, would get out of the committee was certainly doubtful.

Since there were no public hearings on H.R. 7225 when it was considered in the House, spokesmen for many interest groups sought to testify before the Senate Finance Committee. Some of the opposition was directed against any increases or changes in the system; however, many groups appearing before the committee were actively against only certain parts of the bill.

The American Medical Association vigorously opposed the disability provisions in the bill, as it had opposed the disability freeze. It inserted a statement in the record of the hearings arguing primarily that the disability payments would eventually lead to Federal Government domination of the medical profession.

Since physicians were specifically excluded from OASI compulsory coverage, the AMA took no position on the inclusion of other professional groups. However, the American Bar Association did testify regarding compulsory or voluntary coverage for attorneys.

The life insurance companies, particularly those offering retirement and pension plans, opposed lowering the women's eligibility age. On the other hand, organized labor was prepared to support all the provisions of H.R. 7225, and was particularly delighted with the disability provisions. The U.S. Chamber of Commerce, whose pay-as-you-go proposals had been defeated in 1954, opposed the lower eligibility age for women, claiming that the changes would simply institute many new and expensive government programs and would adversely affect the trends toward private pension plans as well. The Chamber also opposed the provision extending benefits to totally and permanently disabled individuals at age fifty.

Not all the testimony heard by the committee concerned the two controversial provisions. The National Association of Manufacturers, while opposing both the disputed clauses, urged the committee to adopt the proposal for a permanent advisory council on social security. To balance these business community views, the committee heard various academics testifying in favor of the major changes.

On March 5, while the Finance Committee was still conducting public hearings on H.R. 7225, Senator Robert E. Kerr of Oklahoma introduced an amendment which would have added a food stamp plan designed to distribute surplus food to the aged, disabled, blind, dependent children, unemployed, and other needy persons. The proposal stimulated some favorable testimony, but the amendment failed to obtain the support of a majority of the committee, and did not appear in the version of the bill reported to the full Senate.

March 22 was the last day of public hearings on the bill. The committee heard testimony from the new Secretary of HEW, Marion Folsom, who voiced the Administration's opposition to two key provisions in the legis-

lation. The Secretary stated he was "deeply concerned over the effects these proposals would have now and in the long run" and warned against major changes in the program until complete studies had been made of their impact. The Secretary was adamant in his opposition to the lower eligibility age for women, and he reiterated his warnings of difficulties with the disability provisions.

On June 5, the Finance Committee reported out H.R. 7225 with the two key changed amendments: first, the disability provision and the related tax increase were eliminated; second, the lower eligibility age for women was restricted to widows only.

The report accompanying the bill stated that the change of the eligibility age for female employees might prove harmful to their welfare. Concerning the deletion of the disability benefit provisions, the report stated: "Monthly disability benefits have a completely different nature as compared with the present provisions for old-age benefits and survivors' benefits. Lack of objectivity in determination of disability makes it both easier for the claimant to maintain, and harder for the administration to deny the presence of qualifying disability. In many instances, physical disability does not necessarily produce economic disability, although this would in many cases, be the tendency if monthly benefits were available". (Senate Report No. 2133, accompanying H.R. 7225, June 5, 1956, p. 13.) The report also represented a conservative cost-estimate approach. It seemed as if the Administration, with the help of the AMA and the U.S. Chamber of Commerce, had convinced the majority of the committee that disability benefits would be extremely difficult to administer and would have an adverse effect on the entire social security system.

When H.R. 7225 passed the House in 1955, there had been no provisions in the bill regarding public assistance. As previously noted, however, President Eisenhower in his 1956 budget message requested that the federal matching ratios for public assistance be extended, and that there be an actual increase in the overall amount the Federal Government could reimburse the state. During the Finance Committee's hearings testimony was taken on a variety of public assistance proposals, and when H.R. 7225 was reported out, several public assistance sections were included:

Social Security Act Amendments of 1956
Senate Report No. 2133
84th Cong., 2d Sess.
(June 5, 1956)

* 　 * 　 *

The amendments in the committee bill to titles I, IV, VII, X, XI, and XIV of the Social Security Act would —

(1) Provide separate matching for medical-care expenditures on behalf of recipients of assistance;

(2) Make explicit that services to return recipients of aid to the blind and aid to the permanently and totally disabled to self-support or self-care are objectives of these programs and that services to strengthen family life are a major objective of the program of aid to dependent children;

(3) Make two small additional groups of children eligible for aid;

(4) Authorize grants for cooperative research; and for training of public-assistance personnel;

(5) Extend the present matching formulas to June 30, 1959.

Matching of Assistance Expenditures for Medical Care

In titles I, IV, X, and XIV of the Social Security Act, Federal participation in assistance is limited by maximums on the amount of monthly payments to or on behalf of an individual. These maximums are $55 for aged, blind, and disabled recipients and lesser amounts for recipients of aid to dependent children. Since medical expenses for an individual may be high in one month (sometimes running to several hundred dollars) and small or nonexistent in other months, and since many of the individuals with the largest medical needs also have maintenance needs of $55 or more, there is frequently little or no Federal participation in payments made by States for medical care. This has limited the amounts of medical care that many States have been able to make available to recipients, and has almost certainly discouraged many of the States with less than average per capita income from assuming substantial responsibility for the costs of medical care for needy people.

The bill would provide Federal matching of expenditures for payments to suppliers of medical care separate from money payments to assistance recipients and would use an average basis for determining Federal participation in payment to suppliers of medical care. Large expenditures of this kind made by a State on behalf of some recipients could be averaged with small expenditures or no expenditures for other recipients. The Federal Government would participate in one-half of the cost up to an average expenditure of $8 a month per adult receiving aid and $4 a month per child. This assurance of Federal participation on an averaging basis should stimulate States to secure necessary care for recipients, particularly in States with relatively limited resources. Under this legislation States would be free to purchase coverage from any medical insurance plan. Under the bill all payments to suppliers of medical care would be matched under the separate provision. States would still be able if they chose to do so to include in money payments to recipients amounts to meet medical needs within the maximums on money payments specified in titles I, IV, X, and XIV.

Self-Support and Self-Care

Individuals who receive assistance are materially affected by the extent to which appropriate welfare services are provided by assistance agencies. Services that assist families and individuals to attain the maximum economic and personal independence of which they are capable provide a more satisfactory way of living for the recipients affected. To the extent that they can remove or ameliorate the causes of dependency they will decrease the time that assistance is needed and the amounts needed. For these reasons the availability of such services to families and individuals is a part of effective administration of the public-assistance programs and therefore a proper administrative expenditure by States in which the Federal Government shares. Similarly, in the aid to dependent children program, services to strengthen family life are an investment in future citizens.

While some such welfare services have been provided effectively in many States, these amendments should stimulate States to expand their services. The bill would amend the titles for the blind and the disabled to make clear that the provision of welfare services to assist recipients to self-support and self-care are program objectives, along with the provision of income to meet current needs. Similarly, the aid to dependent children title would be amended to emphasize that services to strengthen family life are included in the programs' objectives. The amendments will also make explicit that the Federal Government shares in the States' cost in providing these services. These amendments, coupled with those for training and research, should do much to provide a more constructive emphasis in these programs.

No similar amendment has been included for title I for the needy aged. In view of the characteristics of the group of aged recipients as a whole, self-support or even self-care objectives are not as applicable to aged recipients as in the case of the recipients under the other State-Federal programs. Nonetheless, services to aged individuals have been provided under title I of present law. It is not the intent of your committee to alter present practices under which the cost of services for aged individuals are shared in by the Federal Government as administrative expenses.

Extension of Aid to Dependent Children

Two amendments have been made to the aid to dependent children title neither of which affects large numbers of children but both of which make some additional needy children eligible for aid. The first would permit Federal participation in assistance to needy children who are deprived of parental support or care for the reasons now listed in the law and who are living in the homes of first cousins, nieces, or nephews, thereby extending the degree of relationship slightly beyond the present law. This will permit additional children to have the advantages of life in a home maintained by close relatives. The second would eliminate the requirement that for a needy child between the ages of 16 and 18 to receive aid, he be in regular attendance at school. This would permit Federal sharing in assistance to such children unable to attend school because of illness or handicap, or because school facilities are not available.

Grants for Cooperative Research or Demonstration Projects

*　　*　　*

Grants for Training of Welfare Personnel

*　　*　　*

Extension of the Public Assistance Matching Formulas

The formulas for Federal matching of public-assistance payments are scheduled to revert to the pre-1952 levels on September 30, 1956. Until old-age and survivors insurance benefits are more generally received under the extensions of coverage made by the 1954 amendments, the number of aged persons needing assistance payments will remain high, particularly in rural States. Decreases in payments to recipients of old-age assistance, aid to the blind, aid to dependent children, and aid to the permanently and totally disabled would be likely in a substantial number of States if the Federal share of assistance payments is reduced. To avoid this the bill would extend the present formulas to June 30, 1959. This will permit time in which to study and determine what should be the appropriate share of public-assistance costs that should be borne by the Federal Government on a long-range basis. By that time the extensions of coverage under old-age and survivors insurance, particularly those affecting employment in agriculture, should be having more effect. Termination at the end of a fiscal year should facilitate both State and Federal fiscal planning.

Three Democratic committee members, Senator Walter F. George of Georgia, Senator Russell Long of Louisiana, and Senator Paul H. Douglas of Illinois filed a minority report, criticizing the committee for eliminating the disability provisions. It stated that existing state programs for disability benefits were wholly inadequate, and that there were a million disabled workers between fifty and sixty-five who were dependent on the state public assistance programs. The minority report also criticized the opponents of the disability provisions who were demanding additional studies, as merely blocking the program by tactical maneuvers. The same senators joined by Senator George A. Smathers of Florida also advocated setting the retirement age for all women at age sixty-two.

The Senate commenced debate on H.R. 7225 in early July, although no *key votes were taken until July 16 and 17. Senator Long introduced an amendment to the public assistance sections of the bill, although it had already been rejected by the Finance Committee. The Long Amendment, provided for revision of the federal matching formula for OAA, AB, and APTD. Under the existing formula, the Federal Government paid four-fifths of the first $25; Long proposed that this be increased to five-sixths of the first $30, arguing that his amendment merely followed the formula changes made in 1946, 1948, and 1952.*

There were the usual battles about which states would "really" benefit and it seemed that very little had been done to minimize the different average payments between the rich and the poor states. Senator Long attempted to refute his opponents' arguments.

Congressional Debates
102 Congressional Record, p. 12877
(July 12, 1956)

Mr. Long. Those opposing this amendment, not being content with arguing that the low-income States should not receive additional assistance, then turn around and say that the high-income States should not receive additional assistance.

As a matter of fact, they are wrong on both points. The fact is that the high-income States make very disproportionate contributions to the support of the general purposes of government. They have advanced the payments to aid recipients well beyond the point where the Federal Government will match the contributions. They feel that the fact that they make a high contribution to the general purposes of Government entitles them to expect that this amendment would also benefit them, which it would not do unless we advance the point at which the Federal matching payment ends.

Let us consider the 10 highest payment States, namely, Colorado, Connecticut, New York, Massachusetts, Washington, California, New Jersey, Minnesota, Kansas, and Oregon. Those States have 30 percent of the population. They pay 38.9 percent of the taxes, and would receive 33.3 percent of the benefit of the amendment.

Now let us consider the 10 low-payment States, namely, West Virginia, Mississippi, Arkansas, Alabama, North Carolina, South Carolina, Georgia, Kentucky, Tennessee, and Virginia. Those 10 low-payment States have 18.8 percent of the population. They pay 9.6 percent of the tax burden, and they would receive 19 percent of the benefits of this amendment.

Based upon those figures, Senators will see that the high-payment States are certainly entitled to expect that they would receive additional matching funds when they go beyond the point where the Federal Government would match.

On the afternoon of July 16, the Senate adopted the Long Amendment.

Although the Senate Finance Committee had eliminated the OASI disability insurance provisions and also the reduction of OASI eligibility age for women to age sixty-two, it was clear that there would be a major fight on the Senate floor to reinstate them.

Senator George introduced the first amendment concerning disability. Naturally, the AMA's hostility was vigorously attacked and fiscal responsibility was claimed because of a separate disability trust fund. The George Amendment narrowly passed, restoring disability insurance to the bill.

Senator Kerr introduced an amendment concerning the second controversial provision, lowering the minimum eligibility age for all women to sixty-two, and giving actuarily reduced benefits to wives and working women claiming benefits between ages sixty-two and sixty-five. Senator Martin of Iowa opposed the amendment, arguing that the increased benefits did not justify the costs which would be incurred, and that the proposal amounted to a discrimination against women. The proposal was also opposed by Senator Curtis almost exclusively on economic grounds. Nevertheless, the Senate overwhelmingly adopted the Kerr Amendment. Evidently, the suggestion of actuarily reduced benefits for women between the ages of sixty-two and sixty-five, eliminated much of the senatorial opposition voiced by the Finance Committee. Several other relatively minor amendments were adopted by the Senate before the surprisingly unanimous vote on bill.

The popularity of social security among voters, and the fact that congressional elections were less than four months away, undoubtedly influenced the result. Conferees were immediately appointed by both houses, and a conference report was soon ready, adopting, with only minor changes, the Senate version of the OASI sections. In other words, the House bill and the Senate amendments had triumphed. Women were now eligible for OASI at sixty-two and disability insurance (at least for those of fifty or over) had turned the program into OASDI.

The Conference Committee also increased the federal share of assistance to the aged, blind, and disabled to four-fifths of the first $30 and one-half of the next $30. On the other hand, the committee reduced the Senate provisions for medical care payments under PA to $6 a month for an adult and $3 for a child. The conferees also extended OASI coverage to osteopaths (as did the House bill) and eliminated the Senate provision providing for the establishment of a United States Commission on the Aging and Aged.

The House adopted the conference report with little debate and the following night, only hours before Congress adjourned, the Senate agreed as well.

The bill was then sent to the White House. President Eisenhower was expected to sign it into law even though he had consistently opposed the two key provisions in the bill.

Questioned on these sections at a news conference on August 1 the President responded, "Well, I think that certain parts of them were unwise and, therefore, I regret them to that extent—one of the things being that we are loading on the security system something I don't think should be there, and if it is going to be handled, should be handled another way."

Although dissatisfied with the congressional action, Eisenhower signed H.R. 7225 and issued the following statement, voicing concern over the continued actuarial balance of the system.

Presidential Statement on Signing H.R. 7225
(August 1, 1956)*

I have today signed H.R. 7225, the Social Security Amendments of 1956. The new law embraces a wide range of changes in old-age and survivors insurance, the public assistance programs, and child welfare services.

This Administration's strong support of the social security program was demonstrated by the broad expansion and improvements enacted in 1954 at my recommendation. The 1954 Amendments, which extended coverage of the program to millions of additional persons and included higher benefits for all who were then or who would become beneficiaries, have had a major impact in bringing greater security to our people.

The new law also contains certain major provisions which were recommended by the Administration. It extends social security coverage to about 600,000 additional farm owners or operators and about 225,000 self-employed lawyers, dentists, and others.

It provides for increased Federal funds to encourage better medical care for the needy aged, blind, disabled, and dependent children. This will help meet a critical problem for these groups.

Another Administration proposal placed increased emphasis, in public assistance programs, on services to help more needy people build toward independence. The law initiates new programs of grants to train more skilled social workers and to support research in ways of helping people overcome dependency. Another Administration proposal will increase funds for child welfare services.

The law also includes provisions about which the Administration had serious reservations in their initial form; these provisions were modified and improved before their final enactment and now meet, in part, some of the Administration's objections.

The original proposal to lower the retirement age for all women was changed to provide that employed women and wives may accept reduced benefits at an earlier age or obtain full benefits at age 65. I am hopeful that

*Public Papers of the Presidents, Dwight D. Eisenhower, 1956, p. 638.

this provision will now have no adverse effect on employment opportunities for older women. The law allows full benefits at age 62 for widows because of their special needs.

Congress also modified somewhat the original proposal to provide disability benefits at age 50 or above. A separate trust fund was established for the disability program in an effort to minimize the effects of the special problems in this field on the other parts of the program—retirement and survivors' protection. We will, of course, endeavor to administer the disability provisions efficiently and effectively, in cooperation with the States. I also pledge increasing emphasis on efforts to help rehabilitate the disabled so that they may return to useful employment.

The original proposal would have imposed a 25 percent increase in social security taxes on everyone covered by the system. I am pleased that the tax increase has now been cut in half. Our actuaries report that while they cannot estimate costs of the disability program with certainty, the tax increase should be adequate to finance the benefits, assuming effective administration.

Although there were differences of opinion over separate provisions, the final legislation was approved overwhelmingly by Congress. In signing this legislation, I am hopeful that this new law, on the whole, will advance the economic security of the American people.

Social Security Amendments of 1956
(August 1, 1956, 70 Statutes at Large 807)

TITLE I—AMENDMENTS TO TITLE II OF THE SOCIAL SECURITY ACT

*   *   *

RETIREMENT AGE FOR WOMEN

Section 216 (a) of the Social Security Act is amended to read as follows:

"Retirement Age

"(a) The term 'retirement age' means—
        "(1) in the case of a man, age sixty-five, or
        "(2) in the case of a woman, age sixty-two."

*   *   *

"Adjustment of Old-Age and Wife's Insurance Benefit Amounts in Accordance With Age of Female Beneficiary

"(q) (1) The old-age insurance benefit of any woman for any month prior to the month in which she attains the age of sixty-five shall be reduced by—

"(A) 5/9 of 1 per centum, multiplied by

"(B) the number equal to the number of months in the period beginning with the first day of the first month for which she is entitled to an old-age insurance benefit and ending with the last day of the month before the month in which she would attain the age of sixty-five.

"(2) The wife's insurance benefit of any wife for any month after the month preceding the month in which she attains the age of sixty-two and prior to the month in which she attains the age of sixty-five shall be reduced by—

"(A) 25/36 of 1 per centum, multiplied by

"(B) the number equal to the number of months in the period beginning with the first day of the first month for which she is entitled to such wife's insurance benefit and ending with the last day of the month before the month in which she would attain the age of sixty-five, except that in no event shall such period start earlier than the first day of the month in which she attains the age of sixty-two.

*　　*　　*

"DISABILITY INSURANCE BENEFIT PAYMENTS

"Disability Insurance Benefits

"Sec. 223. (a) (1) Every individual who—

"(A) is insured for disability insurance benefits (as determined under subsection (c) (1)),

"(B) has attained the age of fifty and has not attained the age of sixty-five,

"(C) has filed application for disability insurance benefits, and

"(D) is under a disability (as defined in subsection (c) (2) at the time such application is filed,

shall be entitled to a disability insurance benefit for each month, beginning with the first month after his waiting period (as defined in subsection (c) (3)) in which he becomes so entitled to such insurance benefits and ending with the month preceding the first month in which any of the following occurs: his disability ceases, he dies, or he attains the age of sixty-five.

"(2) Such individual's disability insurance benefit for any month shall be equal to his primary insurance amount for such month determined under section 215 as though he became entitled to old-age insurance benefits in the first month of his waiting period.

"Filing of Application

"(b) No application for disability insurance benefits which is filed more than nine months before the first month for which the applicant becomes entitled to such benefits shall be accepted as a valid application for purposes of this section.

"Definitions

"(c) For purposes of this section—

"(1) An individual shall be insured for disability insurance benefits in any month if—

"(A) he would have been a fully and currently insured individual (as defined in section 214) had he attained retirement age and filed application for benefits under section 202 (a) on the first day of such month, and

"(B) he had not less than twenty quarters of coverage during the forty-quarter period ending with the quarter in which such first day occurred, not counting as part of such forty-quarter period any quarter and part of which was included in a period of disability (as defined in section 216 (i)) unless such quarter was a quarter of coverage.

"(2) The term 'disability' means inability to engage in any substantial gainful activity by reason of any medically determinable physical or mental impairment which can be expected to result in death or to be of long-continued and indefinite duration. An individual shall not be considered to be under a disability unless he furnishes such proof of the existence thereof as may be required.

"(3) The term 'waiting period' means, in the case of any application for disability insurance benefits, the earliest period of six consecutive calendar months—

"(A) throughout which the individual who files such application has been under a disability, and

"(B) (i) which begins not earlier than with the first day of the sixth month before the month in which such application if filed if such individual is insured for disability insurance benefits in such sixth month, or (ii) if he is not so insured in such month, which begins not earlier than with the first day of the first month after such sixth month in which he is so insured.

*   *   *

(2) For purposes of determining entitlement to a disability insurance benefit for any month after June 1957 and before December 1957, an application for disability insurance benefits filed by any individual after July 1957 and before January 1958 shall be deemed to have been filed during the first month after June 1957 for which such individual would (without regard to this paragraph) have been entitled to a disability insurance benefit had he filed application before the end of such month.

*   *   *

FEDERAL OLD-AGE AND SURVIVORS INSURANCE TRUST FUND AND FEDERAL DISABILITY INSURANCE TRUST FUND

"*Sec. 201.* (a) There is hereby created on the books of the Treasury of the United States a trust fund to be known as the 'Federal Old-Age and Survivors Insurance Trust Fund'. The Federal Old-Age and Survivors Insurance Trust Fund shall consist of the securities held by the Secretary of the Treasury for the Old-Age Reserve Account and the amount standing to the credit of the Old-Age Reserve Account on the books of the Treasury on January 1, 1940, which securities and amount the Secretary of the Treasury is authorized and directed to transfer to the Federal Old-Age and Survivors Insurance Trust Fund, and, in addition, such amounts as may be appropriated to, or deposited in, the Federal Old-Age and Survivors Insurance Trust Fund as hereinafter provided.

*   *   *

"(b) There is hereby created on the books of the Treasury of the United States a trust fund to be known as the 'Federal Disability Insurance Trust Fund.' The Federal Disability Insurance Trust Fund shall consist of such amounts as may be appropriated to, or deposited in, such fund as provided in this section. There is hereby appropriated to the Federal Disability Insurance Trust Fund for the fiscal year ending June 30, 1957, and for each fiscal year thereafter, out of any moneys in the Treasury not otherwise appropriated, amounts equivalent to 100 per centum of—

"(1) $\frac{1}{2}$ of 1 per centum of the wages (as defined in section 3121 of the Internal Revenue Code of 1954) paid after December 31, 1956, and reported to the Secretary of the Treasury or his delegate pursuant to subtitle F of the Internal Revenue Code of 1954, which wages shall be certified by the Secretary of Health, Education, and Welfare on the basis of the records of wages established and maintained by such Secretary in accordance with such reports; and

(2) $\frac{3}{8}$ of 1 per centum of the amount of self-employment income as defined in section 1402 of the Internal Revenue Code of 1954) reported to the Secretary of the Treasury or his delegate on tax returns under subtitle F of the Internal Revenue Code of 1954 for any taxable year beginning after December 31, 1956, which self-employment income shall be certified by the Secretary of Health, Education, and Welfare on the basis of the records of self-employment income established and maintained by the Secretary of Health, Education, and Welfare in accordance with such returns.

*   *   *

COMPUTATION OF AVERAGE MONTHLY WAGE

Sec. 115. (a) Section 215 (b) (1) of the Social Security Act is amended to read as follows:

"(b) (1) An individual's 'average monthly wage' shall be the quotient obtained by dividing the total of his wages and self-employment income after his starting date (determined under paragraph (2)) and prior to his closing date (determined under paragraph (3)), by the number of months elapsing after such starting date and prior to such closing date, excluding from such elapsed months—

"(A) the months in any year prior to the year in which he attained the age of twenty-two if less than two quarters of such prior year were quarters of coverage, and

"(B) the months in any year any part of which was included in a period of disability except the months in the year in which such period of disability began if their inclusion in such elapsed months (together with the inclusion of the wages paid in and self-employment income credited to such year) will result in a higher primary insurance amount.

* * *

"*Sec. 3101.* RATE OF TAX.

"In addition to other taxes, there is hereby imposed on the income of every individual a tax equal to the following percentages of the wages (as defined in section 3121 (a)) received by him with respect to employment (as defined in section 3121 (b))—

"(1) with respect to wages received during the calendar years 1957 to 1959, both inclusive, the rate shall be 2¼ percent;

"(2) with respect to wages received during the calendar years 1960 to 1964, both inclusive, the rate shall be 2¾ percent;

"(3) with respect to wages received during the calendar years 1965 to 1969, both inclusive, the rate shall be 3¼ percent;

"(4) with respect to wages received during the calendar years 1970 to 1974, both inclusive, the rate shall be 3¾ percent; and

"(5) with respect to wages received after December 31, 1974, the rate shall be 4¼ percent."

(c) Section 3111 of such code is amended to read as follows:

"*Sec. 3111.* RATE OF TAX.

"In addition to other taxes, there is hereby imposed on every employer an excise tax, with respect to having individuals in his employ, equal to the following percentages of the wages (as defined in section 3121 (a)) paid by him with respect to employment (as defined in section 3121 (b))—

"(1) with respect to wages paid during the calendar years 1957 to 1959, both inclusive, the rate shall be 2¼ percent;

* * *

Part I — Matching of Assistance Expenditures for Medical Care

MEDICAL CARE FOR OLD-AGE ASSISTANCE RECIPIENTS

* * *

(c) Section 3(a) of such Act is further amended by inserting the following new clause immediately before the period at the end thereof: ", and (4) in the case of any State, an amount equal to one-half of the total of the sums expended during such quarter as old-age assistance under the state plan in the form of medical or other type of remedial care (including expenditures for insurance premiums for such care or the cost thereof), not counting so much of such expenditure for any month as exceeds the product of $6 multiplied by the total number of individuals who received old age assistance under the State plan for such month."

*   *   *

(c) Section 403 (a) of such Act is further amended by inserting the following new clause immediately before the period at the end thereof: "; and (4) in the case of any State, an amount equal to one-half of the total of the sums expended during such quarter as aid to dependent children under the State plan in the form of medical or any other type of remedial care (including expenditures for insurance premiums for such care or the cost thereof), not counting so much of such expenditure for any month as exceeds (A) the product of $3 multiplied by the total number of dependent children who received aid to dependent children under the State plan for such month plus (B) the product of $6 multiplied by the total number of other individuals who received aid to dependent children under the State plan for such month".

*   *   *

MEDICAL CARE FOR RECIPIENTS OF AID TO THE BLIND

*   *   *

MEDICAL CARE FOR RECIPIENTS OF AID TO PERMANENTLY AND TOTALLY DISABLED

*   *   *

Part II — Services in Programs of Old-Age Assistance, Aid to Dependent Children, Aid to the Blind, and Aid to the Permanently and Totally Disabled

OLD-AGE ASSISTANCE

*   *   *

AID TO DEPENDENT CHILDREN

Sec. 312. (a) The first sentence of section 401 of the Social Security Act is amended to read: "For the purpose of encouraging the care of dependent children in their own homes or in the homes of relatives by enabling each State to furnish financial assistance and other services, as far as practicable under the conditions in such State, to needy dependent children and the parents or relatives with whom they are living to help maintain and strengthen family life and to help such parents or relatives to attain the maximum self-support and personal independence consistent with the maintenance of continuing parental care and protection, there is hereby authorized to be appropriated for each fiscal year a sum sufficient to carry out the purposes of this title."

(b) Subsection (a) of section 402 of such Act is amended by striking out "and" before clause (11) thereof, and by striking out the period at the end of such subsection and inserting in lieu thereof a semicolon and the following new clause: "and (12) provide a description of the services (if any) which the State agency makes available to maintain and strengthen family life for children, including a description of the steps taken to assure, in the provision of such services, maximum utilization of other agencies providing similar or related services."

*   *   *

Part V — Amendments to Matching Formulas

*AMENDMENT TO MATCHING FORMULA FOR
OLD AGE ASSISTANCE*

Sec. 341. Section 3 (a) of the Social Security Act is amended to read as follows:

"(a) From the sums appropriated therefor, the Secretary of the Treasury shall pay to each State which has an approved plan for old-age assistance, for each quarter, beginning with the quarter commencing October 1, 1956, (1) in the case of any State other than Puerto Rico and the Virgin Islands, an amount equal to the sum of the following proportions of the total amounts expended during such quarter as old-age assistance under the State plan, not counting so much of such expenditure with respect to any individual for any month as exceeds $60—

"(A) four-fifths of such expenditures, not counting so much of any expenditure with respect to any month as exceeds the product of $30 multiplied by the total number of such individuals who received old-age assistance for such month; plus

"(B) one-half of the amount by which such expenditures exceed the maximum which may be counted under clause (A);

*   *   *

*AMENDMENT TO MATCHING FORMULA FOR AID TO DEPENDENT
CHILDREN*

Sec. 342. Section 403 (a) of the Social Security Act is amended to read as follows:

"(a) From the sums appropriated therefor, the Secretary of the Treasury shall pay to each State which has an approved plan for aid to dependent children, for each quarter, beginning with the quarter commencing October 1, 1956, (1) in the case of any State other than Puerto Rico and the Virgin Islands, an amount equal to the sum of the following proportions of the total amounts expended during such quarter as aid to dependent children under the State plan, not counting so much of such expenditure with respect to any dependent child for any month as exceeds $32, or if there is more than one dependent child in the same home, as exceeds $32 with respect to one such dependent child and $23 with respect to each of the other dependent children, and not counting so much of such expenditure for any month with respect to a relative with whom any dependent child is living as exceeds $32—

"(A) fourteen-seventeenths of such expenditures, not counting so much of the expenditures with respect to any month as exceeds the product of $17 multiplied by the total number of dependent children and other individuals with respect to whom aid to dependent children is paid for such month; plus

"(B) one-half of the amount by which such expenditures exceed the maximum which may be counted under clause (A);

*   *   *

AMENDMENT TO MATCHING FORMULA FOR AID TO THE BLIND

*   *   *

AMENDMENT TO MATCHING FORMULA FOR AID TO THE PERMANENTLY AND TOTALLY DISABLED

*   *   *

The most important change brought about by the 1956 amendments was the inclusion of disability protection in the basic scheme of the system. Old-age and survivors' insurance was now to be called old-age, survivors', and disability insurance and it would only be a matter of time before the age limitation (fifty) was eliminated altogether, extending coverage to everyone within the system. The mood of Congress favored these increased benefits and there were certain to be new attempts to liberalize the social security system when the eighty-fifth Congress convened.

1957–1958

August, 1956—just weeks after the passage of the omnibus social security amendments—was the month of the national party conventions. Social security, and OASDI in particular, was a very popular program after its twenty-one years of existence, and both parties included in their platform support for future increases in, and expansion of the system.

The Democratic platform, adopted on August 16, in Chicago, pledged the party to continued endorsement of social welfare programs. Referring specifically to OASDI, the Democrats claimed (Congressional Quarterly Almanac 1956, *p. 773*): *"By lowering the retirement age for women and for disabled persons, the Democratic Eighty-fourth Congress pioneered two great advances in Social Security, over the bitter opposition of the Eisenhower Administration. We shall continue our efforts to broaden and strengthen this program by increasing benefits to keep pace with improving standards of living; by raising the wage base upon which benefits depend; and by increasing benefits for each year of covered employment."*

The document also committed the party to continued support of public assistance programs: "We pledge improvements in the public assistance program even beyond those enacted by the Democratic Eighty-fourth Congress, through greater assistance for the aged, the blind, dependent children, the disabled and other needy persons who are not adequately protected by contributory insurance programs."

Finally, the party pledged its support to improvement of the third major program under the basic social security system, unemployment insurance: "We shall continue to work for a stronger unemployment insurance system, with broader coverage and increased benefits consistent with rising earnings. We shall also work for a floor to assure minimum level and duration of benefits and fair eligibility rules."

The Republican Party met in San Francisco and on August 21, 1956, adopted its platform promising (Congressional Quarterly Almanac 1956, *p. 781*) *"continuation of peace, prosperity and progress." The party stated its continued support for social security improvements simply: "We shall continue to seek extension and perfection of a sound social security system."*

Both parties, therefore, were on record as favoring continued improvement and expansion of the social security programs, when the Eighty-fifth Congress convened in January, 1957. (In the new body were 233 Democratic Congressmen and 200 Republicans; forty-nine Democratic Senators and forty-seven Republicans.) There was no attempt to make any major changes in the system. Rather, everyone seemed to be waiting to see the effect of these past amendments.

President Eisenhower, commencing his second term after re-election in November, made no major requests to Congress for changes in social security. In fact, he made no mention of social security at all in his State of the Union message, and only passing reference to it in his budget message to Congress.

Annual Budget Message of the President
(January 21, 1957)*

*   *   *

In recent years, a succession of legislative enactments has moved a long way toward the goal of universal social security coverage, but there are a number of collateral steps which will add much to the meaning of our social security system as a whole. In part, these steps can be taken by budgetary action, for example, by giving particular attention to the needs of the rapidly increasing number of older persons in our society. Other steps will require legislation. First, the unemployment insurance system should be extended and improved.

*   *   *

1957

While there was no major legislation proposed either by the President or by the Congress, there were a number of minor amendments adopted during 1957. The first of these was signed into law by President Eisenhower on April 25, and it simply provided for a two-year extension of the special provisions for state aid to the blind.

The President signed two more bills on July 17, both related to disability provisions under social security. The first of these amendments, H.R. 6191, made two changes. The deadline for disabled workers to file an application for a disability freeze was extended for one year until June 30, 1958. The "offset" provision was also modified, allowing veterans to keep disability benefits paid under social security as well as those received from any federal or state agency. The House committee reported out H.R. 6191 on March 27, 1957, and it was subsequently adopted by both House and Senate without change.

The second bill, H.R. 7238, gave each state the option of proceeding either under the provisions of the 1956 amendments or the earlier formula. The 1956 legislation had changed the basis of federal sharing in vendor payments for medical care PA programs and was to be effective July 1, 1957. Some states believed it advantageous to continue under the pre-1956 amendment formula, and H.R. 7238 made that possible. The bill was passed in both houses and a Conference Committee reported a compromise bill which was subsequently adopted by both houses.

On August 30, 1957, President Eisenhower signed a series of five bills which collectively made minor changes in the OASDI provisions of social security. Together these bills provided coverage for employees of interstate agencies and of some state and local governments; made benefits

*Public Papers of the Presidents, Dwight D. Eisenhower 1957, p. 53.

payable to alien survivors of members of the Armed Forces living outside the United States; allowed additional time for ministers to decide whether to be covered under OASDI as self-employed persons; and established standards for determining whether certain income of ministers was to be considered as earnings.

1958 — OASDI and PA

Since 1950 Congress had chosen to enact major changes in social security every other year, corresponding to the biennial congressional elections. During the first session of the eighty-fifth Congress, both houses again delayed any major social security action until the second session which coincided with an election year. These tactics are an indication both of the popularity of the program with the electors and of the potential for reform or persuasion available in government-run income maintenance schemes. The year 1958 was to provide a particularly tough test of this thesis, since the 1956 omnibus amendments had created an Advisory Council on Social Security Financing which was to report to Congress in 1959. Because the report would not be made for another year there was serious doubt whether Congress would pass any major social security amendments during 1958, despite the election.

President Eisenhower, therefore, made no requests for changes in OASDI programs other than to suggest in his budget message that technical provisions in the program should be simplified. However, in the same message, the President called for reductions in the federal share of public assistance grants to states.

Annual Budget Message of the President
(January 14, 1958)*

*   *   *

Although Federal old-age, survivors, and disability insurance provides an increasing share of economic security for the aged, the dependent, and the disabled, the Federal Government's expenditures for public assistance continue to mount because of the successive amendments increasing the Federal matching share. These programs are now well established and the individual States have gained experience as to appropriate levels of assistance. In line with my belief that the States should have greater responsibility for programs of this nature, proposals will be sent to the Congress for modernizing the formulas for public assistance with a view to gradually reducing Federal participation in its financing. This legislation should be

*Public Papers of the Presidents, Dwight D. Eisenhower, 1958, p. 52.

made effective starting in 1960 to assure that the States will have adequate opportunity to adjust their finances and their programs, thus preventing an adverse impact on needy recipients.

During the first half of 1958 the country experienced a recession, which convinced many congressional leaders that social security amendments could not be delayed until the Advisory Council Report was ready in 1959. On March 1, 1958, the Trustees of the Old-Age and Survivors' Insurance Trust Fund issued their annual report on the actuarial and financial stability of the fund showing that for the first time in its eighteen-year history the social security system would pay out more in benefits than it would receive in contributions.

Representative Wilbur Mills of Arkansas, chairman of the House Ways and Means Committee announced that his committee would hold two weeks of public hearings in June on all titles of the Social Security Act. The actuarial soundness of the Trust Fund was one of the subjects to be investigated. Administration spokesmen were invited to testify on any of their proposals and on any of the numerous bills then pending before the committee.

The hearings commenced with Secretary of Health, Education, and Welfare, Marion B. Folsom, as the first witness. The Secretary discussed the Administration's proposal to reduce the federal share of assistance programs.

Social Security Legislation
Hearings before the House Ways and Means Committee
85th Cong., 2d Sess. (June, 1958)
(p. 5)

*   *   *

Statement of Marion B. Folsom

Federal-State relations: In recent years, a steadily increasing portion of total public-assistance costs has been shifted from the States to the Federal Government. In 1946, State and local governments provided 60 percent of the costs of all public assistance.

In 1957, their share had decreased to 50 percent. Counting only those programs in which the Federal Government participates — aid to the needy aged, blind, disabled, and dependent children — the State and local share of the cost has declined from 55 percent in 1946 to 45 percent last year. Since 1946 the welfare appropriations of State and local governments have dropped from 10.8 percent to 8.6 percent of their total expenditures. In this same period the Federal Government's expenditures for public assistance have increased by more than $1 billion until they are now 3 times as large as in 1946.

The shifting of public-assistance costs to the Federal Government has been most pronounced in the high per capita income States which have greater ability to support their own programs. Several middle and low per capita income States have actually increased their effort in relation to their fiscal ability.

Not only has there been an increase in the overall Federal share, but the method by which this has been accomplished raises some serious questions. As you know, the formulas have been modified in 1946, 1948, 1952, and 1956, until today the Federal Government in the programs for aged, blind, and disabled persons, pays 80 percent of the first $30 of assistance payments on the average, and 50 percent of the remainder of each individual payment up to $60. If the monthly payment to an individual is $60, the Federal share in $39.

But if the monthly payment is $30, the Federal share is $24 and the State or local share is only $6. Thus, in the States where payments are lowest, the Federal share is highest. In some of these States, the Federal share in the federally aided programs is now between 75 and 80 percent.

It seems to me this approach results in some serious disparities and inequities. The proportion of Federal support in any particular State is not necessarily related to the fiscal ability of the State or the need of persons for public assistance. The Federal share may be high simply because a State chooses to make only a limited effort for welfare purposes, and sets a relatively low standard of payments to persons in need. Or the Federal share may be high because the State has a large number of persons on public assistance who also are receiving OASI benefits and, thus, need only small supplementary amounts from welfare funds. Certainly there is no justification for providing the highest Federal share of public-assistance payments in those very cases where the Federal OASI program already has substantially reduced the need.

We should bear in mind that from the outset one of the fundamental concepts of this program has been that the separate States, not the Federal Government, should determine the scope of the program, set standards of need and eligibility, and actually operate the program directly or in cooperation with local agencies. I believe that a further general expansion of the Federal Government's financial share in these present programs, and particularly any further expansion under the present formula for Federal matching, is undesirable.

I believe a more equitable and constructive approach, both from the point of view of sound Federal-State relations and the humanitarian objectives of this program, would be to set the Federal share of funds more in accord with the fiscal abilities and the needs of the States. This concept would tend to provide more adequate assistance in the low-income States where human needs are often greatest.

The Secretary then took up the OASDI program. He emphasized the Administration's position that the fund could not absorb any increased benefits without major changes to the entire system, and that those should be put off until the Advisory Council's report was ready in 1959.

In response to a question by Representative Aime J. Forand of Rhode Island, Secretary Folsom made it clear that the Administration opposed any action by this Congress relating to OASDI.

House Hearings
(p. 12)

Mr. Forand. Mr. Secretary, the general tenor of your statement, if I interpret it correctly, is that the administration feels that very little should be done by way of improvement of the social security system at this time. Is that a fair understanding of your statement?

Secretary Folsom. Yes, sir. We would like to await the reports of the Advisory Council on Financing first, and then have a study of the major questions.

Mr. Forand. You say that that report will not be ready before the end of the year.

Secretary Folsom. That is right. As I indicated, I asked the Council if they could make the report for use of this session of Congress, but they said it was not possible.

Mr. Forand. That seems to have been the case right along every time we have suggested improvements in the system. There is always a delay and procrastination and I, for one, feel that ample notice has been given over such a long period about several of these amendments to the system that have been recommended by Members of Congress that we ought to be able to get something more definite than the fact that we are going to have a report by the end of the year. When I say "you," please understand that I am not talking about you personally.

During the same exchange, the Secretary also made it clear that the Administration opposed Representative Forand's pending bill creating medical insurance under social security.

House Hearings
(p. 12–13)

You are representing the administration and, since the administration feels that no liberalization should be made at this time, would the administration object to a self-sustaining program for hospital and surgical needs like that which is incorporated in my bill, H.R. 9467?

Secretary Folsom. I would say that we would not favor that legislation.

Mr. Forand. In other words, the administration is opposed to that legislation?

Secretary Folsom. Yes.

Mr. Forand. I had heard some time ago that that would be the position but I had hoped that it would be a little more favorable. However, I was told that the administration was not too certain that it wanted to come out openly and oppose the legislation but rather would suggest further study which is a nice way of delaying action.

Several members of the committee questioned Secretary Folsom at length regarding the many proposals pending before the committee. One bill would have provided a 10 per cent across-the-board benefit increase, with a related tax increase sufficient to finance it. In response to questions by Representative Herlong of Florida the Secretary stated his opposition to such legislation.

The hearings followed their predictable course, with the usual organizations appearing. Mr. Nelson Cruikshank, on behalf of the AFL-CIO, called for overall increases in all social security programs. The U.S. Chamber of Commerce again sent its representative, Mr. A.D. Marshall, to testify before the committee against any increases in the basic programs. He stated that with the economy in a recession, 1958 was the wrong year to add any new employers' taxes.

Perhaps the most significant event in the hearings was the reintroduction of the health insurance issue. During 1957, Representative Forand had introduced H.R. 9467, providing a health insurance program for OASDI beneficiaries. There was no action on the bill in 1957, as Congress adjourned shortly after its introduction, but the bill remained before the Ways and Means Committee and Representative Forand asked that a description of it be inserted in the record. It was the medical care provisions of H.R. 9467 which ultimately culminated in Title XVIII of the Social Security Act of 1965.

House Hearings
(p. 881)

Statement of Representative Forand on H.R. 9647

*   *   *

2. Health Benefits for OASI Beneficiaries

The purpose of this new type of program, set forth in section 106 of H.R. 9467, is to provide aged persons and their dependents insured under old-age and survivors insurance and the survivors of deceased persons so insured, with insurance protection against the cost of hospitalization, subsequent skilled nursing home care, and surgical services; to achieve such insurance protection within the framework of the national system of old-age and survivors insurance; and to assure adequate and prompt payments to the physicians, hospitals, and nursing homes for services rendered to these individuals, utilizing the cooperation of voluntary nonprofit health associations when such cooperation will contribute to efficient and economical operation.

The program is proposed because (1) the present old-age and survivors insurance benefits are inadequate to meet the needs of insured aged persons and their dependents, and of the survivors of deceased insured persons, who require hospitalization and skilled nursing home care, (2) many of them are not able to obtain, to continue, or to pay for private insurance against the cost of such care which is more expensive for such individuals than employed groups, (3) many of them are forced to apply for public assistance to meet hospitalization, surgical, and nursing home costs, (4) many hospitals are constantly confronted with serious financial difficulties resulting from unpaid services furnished to these individuals, and (5) it is in the interest of the general welfare for financial burdens resulting from the hospital, nursing home, and surgical services required by these individuals to be relieved through old-age and survivors insurance rather than through expenditures financed from general tax revenues.

Through relying on the insurance program, the bill would work in the direction preferred by the Congress.

Eligibility for insurance

The bill provides for the payment of certain hospital, nursing home, and surgical costs for persons receiving old-age or survivors insurance benefits and for persons who would be eligible for such benefits if they applied. Twelve or thirteen million persons would thus receive the protection of such payments in the first year.

Whether or not they retired, men would be protected at age 65 if they had made sufficient contributions in covered employment or self-employment. Women would similarly be eligible at age 62 without having to take the actuarial reduction in benefits provided in present law. I have deliberately included persons who have not yet retired for several reasons. It is undesirable that aged persons should feel they have to stop working to receive the benefits of this program since their services will still prove constructive and since retirement may bring undesirable consequences. For the self-employed, retirement cannot be properly planned when illness has struck, so that a requirement that they retire before receiving these health benefits would involve great difficulties.

Duration of services covered

Up to 120 days of combined hospital and skilled nursing home services could be paid for in a 12-month period, but not more than 60 of these days could be days of hospital service.

Hospital services

Hospital services which would be paid for include the services, drugs, appliances, and medical care ordinarily furnished by the hospital to its bed patients. (The insurance would cover semiprivate accommodations if available unless other accommodations are required for medical reasons—in short, those services ordinarily provided in plans such as the Blue Cross.) Such services would be covered when provided by a licensed hospital which had entered into an agreement with the Secretary except that the costs would not be paid for care in: any tuberculosis or mental hospital; any Federal hospital, or any other hospital for hospital services which it is obligated by contract with the United States to furnish at the expense of the United States; or any hospital furnishing services at public expense, except when a person receiving such services must meet a means test.

Nursing-home services

Nursing-home services which would be paid for include the skilled nursing care, related medical and personal services and accompanying bed and board provided by a licensed nursing home which is operated in connection with a hospital or in which a person licensed to practice medicine or surgery in the State prescribes or directs the nursing care and medical services provided. Services provided by a nursing home would be covered by the insurance provided by the bill only if the individual has been transferred to the nursing home from the hospital on a doctor's certification that the services are necessary for an illness or condition connected with that for which the hospital was treating him.

Surgical services

Surgical services which would be paid for include those provided in a hospital and which are certified as necessary by a licensed physician. Oral surgery would be included when provided in a hospital and certified as necessary by a licensed physician or dentist. Surgical services provided in the outpatient department of a hospital or in a doctor's office would be included in case of an emergency or for minor surgery.

Medical and hospital services under workmen's compensation

Payment would not be made under these provisions for services required by reason of any injury, disease, or disability on account of which such services are being received or paid for under a workmen's compensation law or plan of the United States or of any State.

Agreements with hospitals, nursing homes, and providers of surgical services

Any hospital (other than a tuberculosis or mental hospital) or qualified nursing home licensed pursuant to the law of the State in which it is located would be eligible to enter into an agreement for payment from the Federal old-age and survivors insurance trust fund for the cost of hospital or nursing home services furnished to qualified individuals in accordance with the provisions of this bill. Each agreement would cover hospital services to be included and the basis for payment. The Secretary of Health, Education, and Welfare would enter into agreements with qualified providers of surgical services, either individually or with any association or organization authorized by the surgeons, physicians, or dentists to act on their behalf. These agreements would provide that the rate of payment agreed on would constitute full payment for services.

No control over institutions or physicians

The bill provides for the payment of specified costs from the OASI trust fund, not for governmental supervision of health care. Because of misunderstandings on this point, certain specific safeguards are worth quoting in full:

"Sec. 266 (d) (5). No supervision or control over the details of administration or operation, or over the selection, tunure, or compensation of personnel, shall be exercised under the authority of this section over any hospital or nursing home which has entered into an agreement under this section."

"Sec. 226 (d) (8). Nothing in such agreements or in this Act shall be construed to give the Secretary supervision or control over the practice of medicine or the manner in which medical services are provided."

Free choice by patient

A person who qualifies for hospitalization, nursing home services, or surgical services could select any qualified hospital or nursing home which has entered into an agreement and which admits him, provided he has been referred by a physician licensed by the State in which he resides or in which the hospital or nursing home is located. A person eligible for surgical services could freely select the surgeon of his choice, provided that the surgeon must be certified by the American Board of Surgery or must be a member of the American College of Surgeons (except in cases of emergency where the life of the patient would be endangered by delay or in cases where certification is not feasible for other reasons). This exception would make it possible for surgical services to be covered in rural areas where the types of surgeons mentioned are not available. In cases of oral surgery an eligible person could select a duly licensed dentist.

Payment to hospitals and nursing homes

Methods of determining payments to hospitals and nursing homes would be similar to those already developed in connection with many private insurance plans and certain Government programs.

The amount of the payments to any hospital or nursing home would be determined on the basis of the reasonable cost incurred by the hospital or nursing home for all bed patients, or, when use of such a basis is impractical for the hospital or nursing home or inequitable to the institution or to the Federal old-age and survivors insurance trust fund, on a reasonably equivalent basis which takes account of pertinent factors with respect to the services furnished to those persons for whom payment is made in accordance with the provisions of the bill.

Payments to physicians and dentists

The rates of payments to physicians and dentists would be set forth in the agreements, and such payments made would constitute full payment for the surgical services provided.

Utilization of private nonprofit organizations

To the extent that satisfactory agreements can be made and to the extent that the Secretary of Health, Education, and Welfare determines that the effective and economical administration of these provisions will be furthered, the bill provides that the Secretary may utilize the services of private nonprofit organizations which represent qualified providers of hospital, nursing home, or surgical services or which operate voluntary insurance plans under which agreements, similar to those provided by these provisions, are made with hospitals, nursing homes and physicians for paying for the costs of services . . . [which] would be specifically limited.

Administration by Secretary of Health, Education, and Welfare

The program is to be administered by the Secretary of the Department of Health, Education and Welfare. The OASDI system would use its existing record-keeping system to certify eligibility, to issue insurance cards, and the like. The Secretary would prescribe regulations under which the provisions of the program would be carried out.

Advisory Council

The Secretary would consult with a National Advisory Health Council. This Council would consist of the Commissioner of Social Security and eight members appointed by the Secretary. Four of the appointed members would be persons who are outstanding in fields pertaining to hospital and health activities and four would be appointed to represent the consumers of hospital, nursing home, and surgical services and be familiar with the need for such services by eligible groups.

Effective date

The bill provides that payment for hospital, nursing home, or surgical services, in accordance with these provisions, would be made for such services which are furnished on and after the 1st day of the 12th calendar month after the month in which this act is enacted.

The American Medical Association immediately labeled Representative Forand's bill "one that would propel us completely and irresponsibly into a federally controlled health-care program."

Meanwhile, public hearings before the Ways and Means Committee concluded on June 30, 1958, and the committee met in executive session during the next month to draft a "clean" bill, H.R. 13549. The legislation incorporated several pending suggestions with respect to OASDI primarily increasing benefits and their corresponding tax rate across the board.

But the most important changes proposed in the bill involved public assistance programs. It permitted the maximum federal share for old-age assistance, aid to the blind, and aid to the totally and permanently disabled to be increased to 70 per cent in those states whose average individual incomes were below the national per capita average. The bill also increased the Federal Government share of maximum coverage benefits and maximum monthly payments to dependent children.

As in the past, the House adopted a closed rule for the consideration of H.R. 13549, which meant floor debate would be limited and, more important, that no amendments were permitted from the floor. Apart from Chairman Mills' defense of the method, the most interesting speech came from Representative Noah M. Mason of Illinois who had cast the lone dissenting vote in the Ways and Means Committee. His opposition was based on a report by the Brookings Institution that social security should be organized on a pay-as-you-go basis.

Congressional Debates
102 Congressional Record, p. 15735–6
(July 31, 1958)

Mr. Mason. Mr. Chairman, I was the lone "no" vote in the Committee on Ways and Means against this bill. Everybody on the committee was out of step but me. At least that is the way it looked. I feel it is incumbent upon me to tell you why I voted "no" on that bill. In the first place, the bill is nothing but a stopgap bill. We have set up a Commission to make a complete report on the financial soundness of the social security fund, and that Commission will bring in a report this December telling us what is the matter with the fund, if anything is the matter. Pending that report, we cannot act intelligently over the whole situation bearing upon social security. So we decided for 2 reasons and 2 reasons only to act now with this stopgap bill and not wait for a complete overhaul next year. What are those two reasons? Well, first, and I agree with this reason: We did not think we should wait until next year to increase the soundness of the program. We did not think we could wait until next year at least to take one step toward making the program more sound. And on that I am in full accord with the committee. The other reason that we could not wait until next year is the fact that this is an election year and, naturally, in an election year we must, if we can, sweeten up the voters a little bit. So we did increase the benefits a little bit to sweeten up the voters. We also knew very well from a practical standpoint that we just could not vote increased taxes in social security without at least sweetening up the benefits a little bit. So we put the two together—and that is this bill.

I have always opposed the social security program, but I insist I am not against the social security objectives. I want to give the old people what they are entitled to in security, even a little more generous than what they are getting under this bill. So why is it then that I voted against this? Because I have always said that social security should be on a pay-as-you-go basis: That is, require each generation to take care of its own people and not push off to the next generation and to future generations the care of the old people of today. That is exactly what we are doing under this program. I have good authority for making that statement. I have looked over a Brookings Institute report, and the Brookings Institute has a good reputation all over the country. This is what the Brookings Institute says—

The Chairman. The time of the gentleman has expired.

Mr. Reed. Mr. Chairman, I yield the gentleman 5 additional minutes.

Mr. Mason. I quote from the Brookings Institute bearing on the present social-security program. This is what it said:

> We (the present generation) do the promising; you (all future generations) do the paying.

That is how the Brookings Institute characterizes this present social security setup.

The Brookings Institute report recommends that the present social security setup be abandoned entirely and a genuine pay-as-you-go system be established in its place. And a little more generous than this system is. They also say:

> Our generation should care for its own and trust future generations to do likewise.

That seems to me to be a sensible, practical and wise conclusion for them to reach. This bill does make the fund a little more sound—actuarially sound, as they say—and in that respect it is an improvement upon the present situation. But if we did away with the program, as the Brookings Institute recommends, it would remove all need for reserve; all need for level premiums; all need for costly and elaborate bookkeeping systems, such as the present law requires.

Once before, 8 or 10 years ago, when we had an amendment to the social-security law under consideration, I took the floor and I opposed it, and I said this: "The Townsend plan petition has been at the Speaker's desk for 12 years, and I have refused to sign it because I was still hoping to at least make this system sound, make it a program much better than the Townsend system. But I had given up hope." That was 8 or 10 years ago. "I am now going up and sign the petition, which I have refused to sign for 12 years." And I did it. I also said then, "In my opinion, after careful consideration, the Townsend plan is more equitable, more practical, more just, much easier and cheaper to administer and less costly in the long run." I still believe it, and because I believe it I voted "no" in committee and I will vote "no" on the floor.

The limited debate time was used primarily to allow members to make brief statements of their reasons for supporting the measure which could then be conveniently reproduced from the Congressional Record *for the benefit of constituents at home. The House vote overwhelmingly approved H.R. 13549 on a role call vote and the bill was sent to the Senate, where hearings were scheduled for the following week before the Senate Finance Committee.*

The Republican Administration was in the peculiar position of having a social security bill imposed on it by a Democratic Congress. On OASDI Secretary Flemming decided to compromise:

Social Security Amendments
Hearings on H.R. 13549 before the Senate Finance Committee
85th Cong., 2d Sess. (August, 1958)
(p. 110)

The administration would have preferred to await the report of this Advisory Council before recommending changes in the program of such magnitude as those proposed in H.R. 13549. We believe that both the administration and the Congress would have been in a better position to make major decisions after receiving the benefits of the study by the Advisory Council.

Nevertheless, this preference is based principally on questions of timing and procedure. From the information available to us now, we recognize that the major provisions of H.R. 13549 have considerable merit and do, in fact, meet certain real needs in this important program.

The proposed changes in the contribution rate would eliminate, after 1959, the estimated annual deficits over the next few years and would substantially strengthen the long-range financial condition of the program.

A 12 percent increase in wages since 1954, when the last major changes were made in benefit amounts and the tax base, justifies the proposed increase in the earnings base.

An 8 percent increase in prices since 1954 justifies some increase in benefits, particularly for the millions of persons who have been on the benefit rolls for several years or more and have had no adjustment to meet rising living costs since 1954.

On the whole, therefore, I believe the major changes in old-age and survivors insurance, which I have just discussed, are reasonable and desirable and I recommend their adoption.

Public Assistance was, however, a very different matter.

Senate Hearings
(p. 112)

On the whole, however, the administration is strongly opposed to the public assistance title of H.R. 13549 because these desirable principles would be applied in such a way as to substantially increase the Federal Government's share in the cost of this program and further reduce the relative role of the States.

In his budget message last January, the President stated his conviction that the States should have greater—not lesser—responsibility for programs of this nature. The President also stated:

> Proposals will be sent to the Congress for modernizing the formulas for public assistance with a view to gradually reducing Federal participation in its financing.

Former Secretary Folsom, in his testimony recently to the Committee on Ways and Means in the House of Representatives, recommended that no action be taken on public assistance at this time and stated that the administration would present recommendations to Congress early next year in time to permit adequate consideration by the Congress before the current financing formulas expire next June 30.

I believe that the philosophy expressed by the President is sound and I concur in the recommendation of former Secretary Folsom.

In recent years, a steadily increasing portion of total public assistance costs has been shifted from the States to the Federal Government. In 1937, State and local governments provided more than 80 percent of all public assistance expenditures.

In 1946, State and local governments provided 60 percent of the costs of all public assistance.

In 1957, their share had decreased to 50 percent. Counting only those programs in which the Federal Government participates—aid to the needy aged, blind, disabled, and dependent children—the State and local share of the cost has declined from 55 percent in 1946 to 45 percent last year.

While State expenditures for public assistance have doubled since 1946, the Federal Government's expenditures in this same period have increased by more than $1 billion and are now 3 times as large as in 1946.

In the face of this trend, the proposed bill would increase the Federal contribution by an additional $288 million in the first full year, and probably by more than $300 million in future years.

These programs are State programs, initiated by the States and administered by the States and communities. They are based on the sound concept that the States and local communities can best determine the actual needs of individuals and administer programs of assistance to them.

In the next session of Congress, I believe, it should be possible for the executive and legislative branches, working together, to develop a new formula which will have the effect of providing vigorous Federal support for the public assistance program without weakening the role of the States.

The proposed bill would further weaken the role of the States. In the long run, to continue such a trend might well prove to be a disservice rather than a service to those who are dependent on the program.

It should be emphasized that the administration's opposition is not directed against an increase in assistance payments to individuals but is directed only against an increase in the proportion of such payments that will be borne by the Federal Government.

I am impressed by this fact: If the States find that increased payments to individuals are needed, the Federal Government already is in a position under the existing law to match, on a 50–50 basis, State funds to increase payments for 60 percent of all the persons now receiving old-age assistance.

In many of the States where public-assistance payments are now the lowest, an even higher percentage of recipients could receive increased payments on a 50–50 matching basis.

It is also very important to consider the fiscal circumstances under which this increase in the Federal share of public-assistance expenditures is proposed. The members of this committee, I know, are already deeply concerned over the prospective $12 billion Federal deficit for this fiscal year. The proposed bill would, of course, increase the prospective deficit.

The Senate hearings were, in general, more lively and informative than the House hearings. Senator Paul Douglas of Illinois pressed the chief actuary of the Social Security Administration about the fiscal soundness of OASDI, suggesting that the built-in factor of an increase in earnings had not been considered when actuarial estimates had been made.

Executive opposition to establishing the variable grant in PA was the biggest problem. In an attempt to lessen Administration hostility, Senator Kerr of Oklahoma offered a committee amendment which reduced the maximum average federal payment to adult public assistance recipients from $66 to $65, and the maximum benefit payment for children from $33 to $30, reduced the maximum matching percentage from 70 per cent to 67 per cent and delayed implementation of the changes from October 31, 1958, to January 1, 1959. The committee accepted the amendment, except for the reduction in maximum matching percentage.

As usual, the Senate debate was more general than the House discussion. Senator Ralph Yarborough immediately offered an amendment raising OASDI benefits across the board by 10 per cent rather than 7 which was defeated.

There were other, important battles. There were fears that President Eisenhower would veto the entire measure if the bill went to the White House with a variable formula in the categorical public assistance program. To avoid this, Senator Smathers of Florida introduced two amendments which the Senate subsequently adopted.

The first Smathers amendment reduced the maximum matching percentage to 65 per cent. The second amendment reinstated the existing federal share of ADC payments. Together the two Smathers amendments reduced the total cost of the bill from $288 million annually to $197 million, and they passed the Senate with minimum disagreement.

Meanwhile, Representative Forand had submitted a bill to the House Ways and Means Committee which would have provided for medical and health insurance for beneficiaries under the OASDI program. That provision was not included in the House bill and consequently was of no importance in the Senate Finance hearings. However, on August 15, Senator Hubert Humphrey of Minnesota stated that he would introduce an amendment from the floor to provide hospital insurance for the aged under social security. No vote was recorded on this proposal since it was not formally introduced.

Senator Wayne Morse of Oregon offered an omnibus bill providing 25 per cent social security increases and creating a health insurance program as a substitute for H.R. 13549. Although there was some approval, the bill was rejected by a voice vote. Senator Long's amendment, changing the effective date of the public assistance provisions from January 1, 1959 to October 31, 1958, to agree with the House bill, was adopted by voice vote. On August 16, the second day of debate, the Senate unanimously approved H.R. 13549. Three days later, the House accepted the Senate version of the bill, clearing the way for presidential approval.

On August 29, 1958, President Eisenhower signed H.R. 13549.

Social Security Amendments of 1958
(August 28, 1958, 72 Statutes at Large 1013)

TITLE I—INCREASE IN BENEFITS UNDER TITLE II OF THE SOCIAL SECURITY ACT

INCREASE IN BENEFIT AMOUNTS

*   *   *

INCREASE IN EARNINGS BASE FROM $4,200 TO $4,800

Definition of Wages

* * *

(2) Section 209 (a) of such Act is further amended by adding at the end thereof the following new paragraph:

"(3) That part of remuneration which, after remuneration (other than remuneration referred to in the succeeding subsections of this section) equal to $4,800 with respect to employment has been paid to an individual during any calendar year after 1958, is paid to such individual during such calendar year;".

* * *

INSURED STATUS REQUIREMENTS

Disibility Freeze

Sec. 204. (a) Paragraph (3) of section 216 (i) of such Act is amended to read as follows:

"(3) The requirements referred to in clauses (A) and (B) of paragraphs (2) and (4) are satisfied by an individual with respect to any quarter only if—

"(A) he would have been a fully insured individual (as defined in section 214) had he attained retirement age and filed application for benefits under section 202 (a) on the first day of such quarter; and

"(B) he had not less than twenty quarters of coverage during the forty-quarter period which ends with such quarter, not counting as part of such forty-quarter period any quarter any part of which was included in a prior period of disability unless such quarter was a quarter of coverage;

except that the provisions of subparagraph (A) of this paragraph shall not apply in the case of any individual with respect to whom a period of disability would, but for such subparagraph, begin prior to 1951."

* * *

"SEC. 3101. RATE OF TAX.

"In addition to other taxes, there is hereby imposed on the income of every individual a tax equal to the following percentages of the wages (as defined in section 3121 (a)) received by him with respect to employment (as defined in section 3121 (b))—

"(1) with respect to wages received during the calendar year 1959, the rate shall be 2½ percent;

"(2) with respect to wages received during the calendar years 1960 to 1962, both inclusive, the rate shall be 3 percent;

"(3) with respect to wages received during the calendar years 1963 to 1965, both inclusive, the rate shall be 3½ percent;

"(4) with respect to wages received during the calendar years 1966 to 1968, both inclusive, the rate shall be 4 percent; and

"(5) with respect to wages received after December 31, 1968, the rate shall be 4½ percent."

Tax on Employers

(c) Section 3111 of such Code (relating to rate of tax on employers under the Federal Insurance Contributions Act) is amended to read as follows:

"SEC. 3111. RATE OF TAX.

"In addition to other taxes, there is hereby imposed on every employer an excise tax, with respect to having individuals in his employ, equal to the following percentages of the wages (as defined in section 3121 (a)) paid by him with respect to employment (as defined in section 3121 (b))—

"(1) with respect to wages paid during the calendar year 1959, the rate shall be 2½ percent; . . .

*   *   *

TITLE V—AMENDMENTS RELATING TO PUBLIC ASSISTANCE

OLD-AGE ASSISTANCE

Sec. 501. Subsection (a) of section 3 of the Social Security Act is amended to read as follows:

"(a) From the sums appropriated therefor, the Secretary of the Treasury shall pay to each State which has an approved plan for old-age assistance, for each quarter, beginning with the quarter commencing October 1, 1958, (1) in the case of any State other than Puerto Rico, the Virgin Islands, and Guam, an amount equal to the sum of the following proportions of the total amounts expended during such quarter as old-age assistance under the State plan (including expenditures for insurance premiums for medical or any other type of remedial care or the cost thereof)—

"(A) four-fifths of such expenditures, not counting so much of any expenditure with respect to any month as exceeds the product of $30 multiplied by the total number of recipients of old-age assistance for such month (which total number, for purposes of this subsection, means (i) the number of individuals who received old-age assistance in the form of money payments for such month, plus (ii) the number of other individuals with respect to whom expenditures were made in such month as old-age assistance in the form of medical or any other type of remedial care); plus

"(B) the Federal percentage of the amount by which such expenditures exceed the maximum which may be counted under clause (A), not counting so much of any expenditure with respect to any month as exceeds the product of $65 multiplied by the total number of such recipients of old-age assistance for such month; . . .

*   *   *

AID TO DEPENDENT CHILDREN

Sec. 502. Subsection (a) of section 403 of the Social Security Act is amended to read as follows:

"(a) From the sums appropriated therefor, the Secretary of the Treasury shall pay to each State which has an approved plan for aid to dependent children, for each quarter, beginning with the quarter commencing October 1, 1958, (1) in the case of any State other than Puerto Rico, the Virgin Islands, and Guam, an amount equal to the sum of the following proportions of the total amounts expended during such quarter as aid to dependent children under the State plan (including expenditures for insurance premiums for medical or any other type of remedial care or the cost thereof)—

"(A) fourteen-seventeenths of such expenditures, not counting so much of any expenditure with respect to any month as exceeds the product of $17 multiplied by the total number of recipients of aid to dependent children for such month (which total number, for purposes of this subsection, means (i) the number of individuals with respect to whom aid to dependent children in the form of money payments is paid for such month, plus (ii) the number of other individuals with respect to whom expenditures were made in such month as aid to dependent children in the form of medical or any other type of remedial care); plus

"(B) The Federal percentage of the amount by which such expenditures exceed the maximum which may be counted under clause (A), not counting so much of any expenditure with respect to any month as exceeds the product of $30 multiplied by the total number of recipients of aid to dependent children for such month; . . .

*   *   *

FEDERAL MATCHING PERCENTAGE

Sec. 505. Subsection (a) of section 1101 of the Social Security Act is amended by adding at the end thereof the following new paragraph:

"(8) (A) The 'Federal percentage' for any State (other than Puerto Rico, the Virgin Islands, and Guam) shall be 100 per centum less the State percentage; and the State percentage shall be that percentage which bears the same ratio to 50 per centum as the square of the per capita income of such State bears to the square of the per capita income of the continental United States (excluding Alaska); except that (i) the Federal percentage shall in no case be less than 50 per centum or more than 65 per centum, and (ii) the Federal percentage shall be 50 per centum for Alaska and Hawaii.

"(B) The Federal percentage for each State (other than Puerto Rico, the Virgin Islands, and Guam) shall be promulgated by the Secretary between July 1 and August 31 of each even-numbered year, on the basis of the average per capita income of each State and of the continental United States (excluding Alaska) for the three most recent calendar years for which satisfactory data are available from the Department of Commerce. Such promulgation shall be conclusive for each of the eight quarters in the period beginning July 1 next succeeding such promulgation: *Provided*, That the Secretary shall promulgate such percentages as soon as possible after the enactment of the Social Security Amendments of 1958, which promulgation shall be conclusive for each of the eleven quarters in the period beginning October 1, 1958, and ending with the close of June 30, 1961."

Presidential Statement Upon Signing the Social Security Amendments
(August 29, 1958)*

I have today approved H.R. 13549, "To increase benefits under the Federal Old-Age, Survivors, and Disability Insurance System, to improve the actuarial status of the Trust Funds of such System, and otherwise improve such System; to amend the public assistance and maternal and child health and welfare provisions of the Social Security Act; and for other purposes."

This act is a significant forward step in the old-age, survivors, and disability insurance program of the social security system. The increases in benefits and in the tax base are desirable in the light of changes in the economy since these provisions were last amended in 1954. The increase in social security contribution rates and the accelerated tax schedule in the bill will further strengthen the financial condition of this system in the years immediately ahead and over the long-term future. It is, of course, essential that the old-age, survivors, and disability insurance program, which is so vital to the economic security of the American people, remain financially sound and self-supporting.

The act also makes desirable changes which will permit Federal support for child welfare services where needed in urban areas and provides for State and local financial participation in the costs of this program on an improved basis.

In the public assistance programs the bill institutes the desirable principle of varying Federal matching of costs in accordance with the relative fiscal

*Public Papers of the Presidents, Dwight D. Eisenhower, 1958, p. 661.

capacity of each State as measured by per capita income. However, the effect of this change is very limited because the formula used results only in increases in the Federal share. In addition, the introduction of averaging of benefits on an overall basis provides increases in the Federal share, regardless of the fiscal ability of the State.

For the fifth time in twelve years legislation has been enacted providing an increase in the Federal share of the costs of these programs and a decrease in the relative financial contribution of the States and communities. These successive increases have raised the Federal share from about 45 percent in 1946 to an estimated 58.5 percent under this bill.

Increases in the proportion of the public assistance programs which are financed by the Federal Government can lead only to a weakening of the responsibility of the States and communities. I believe deeply in the concept that the States and communities can best determine the actual needs of individuals and best administer programs of assistance to them—and that State and local financial responsibility in these programs should be strengthened, not weakened.

I am, accordingly, asking the Secretary of Health, Education, and Welfare to deal specifically with this problem in the review of the public assistance programs which is now under way. It is my hope that the work of the Advisory Council on Public Assistance which is established by this bill will materially assist in the early development of constructive recommendations.

Dwight D. Eisenhower

Unemployment Compensation

The country was suffering a severe economic strain at the start of 1958, the result of the recession which had begun the year before. Unemployment was high, reaching a peak of 7.5 per cent in April and a large number of unemployed workers, covered by state unemployment compensation provisions, had exhausted their rights to benefits. They numbered 1.1 million in 1957, and in 1958 that figure jumped to 2.5 million. Congressional leaders went to Washington in January, 1958, realizing that immediate action was required, but whether there should be merely temporary provisions to relieve the immediate crisis or a complete rewriting of the existing federal-state unemployment programs under social security was a difficult question. Shortly after the second session of the eighty-fifth Congress convened, Seantor John Kennedy of Massachusetts introduced a comprehensive bill (S. 3244) extensively revising the existing unemployment system. Representative Eugene McCarthy of Minnesota introduced an identical bill in the House. These proposals, actively and forcefully supported by the AFL-CIO, called for a flat thirty-nine weeks of benefit payments in all states and extended coverage to millions not within the system at that time.

The Eisenhower Administration was aware of the acute situation, but thought much less drastic legislation was needed. On March 25 the President sent a special message to Congress embodying his recommendations for congressional action.

Special Presidential Message to Congress
on Extending Unemployment Compensation Benefits
(March 25, 1958)*

I recommend to the Congress the enactment of legislation to provide for the temporary continuation of unemployment compensation benefits to otherwise eligible individuals who have exhausted their benefits under State and Federal laws. I believe that these workers and their families should be enabled temporarily to receive weekly benefits for a longer period than is now in effect so that in the current economic situation they and their families can obtain a greater measure of security.

These recommendations reflect my strong conviction that we must act promptly, emphatically and broadly to temper the hardship being experienced by workers whose unemployment has been prolonged. They also reflect my conviction that the need for additional assistance to these workers will be of relatively brief duration.

Such legislation should not encroach upon the prerogatives which belong to the States, and matters of eligibility, disqualification, and benefit amounts should be left to the States. The legislation should provide, however, for the payment, to individuals who have exhausted their regular unemployment compensation benefits, of temporary benefits for an additional period equal to one-half of the duration of their regular benefits.

The State Employment Security agencies and the Railroad Retirement Board would administer the program. The Government would be reimbursed for the costs incurred by it for this program in each State through an increase, four years after the program's end, in the tax payments to the Federal Government by employers in that State under the Federal Unemployment Tax Act. Any State, however, that wished to avoid an increase in such tax on the payrolls of employers within the State, could provide for reimbursement to the Federal Government either by direct appropriation or by authorizing transfers from its credit in the Unemployment Trust Fund.

The temporary Federal assistance which this program provides, while of great immediate benefit, is in no sense a substitute for extending the coverage of unemployment compensation which I have previously recommended, or for appropriate State action extending the duration of benefits and increasing benefit amounts which I have previously urged upon the States.

Dwight D. Eisenhower

*Public Papers of the Presidents, Dwight D. Eisenhower, 1959, p. 229.

The Eisenhower proposals were mild compared with the Kennedy-McCarthy legislation. The President's plan required the states to extend temporarily the duration of eligibility for benefits by 50 per cent, and estimated the average extension at eight weeks with average payments of $29 per week. The plan was mandatory, providing for federal take-over in any state which balked at the extension and it allowed the additional benefits to be paid out of general federal revenues as loans, with the states obligated to pay back the money by 1963.

The Administration's proposals were introduced by Representative Daniel Reed of New York as H.R. 11679. The Democratic leaders also introduced a plan (H.R. 11326, 11327) containing most of the provisions subsequently adopted by the Ways and Means Committee in its bill, H.R. 12065.

The House Ways and Means Committee scheduled three days of public hearings, starting March 28. The Secretary of Labor, James Mitchell, was the first witness called and he inserted into the record an explanation of the President's legislative proposal.

Federal Unemployment Compensation Benefits
Hearings on H.R. 11326 before the House Ways and Means Committee
85th Cong., 2d Sess. (March, 1958)
(p. 14-16)

Statement of Secretary James Mitchell

This proposal is designed to carry out the President's recommendation for an additional period of unemployment compensation for workers who have exhausted their regular unemployment benefits.

This is a program for a limited period to assist the States in meeting an urgent and immediate need and not a proposal for supplementation of regular benefits on a prolonged basis. It would not impose any Federal standard on the States or change in any way the standards that the States have set in their unemployment compensation laws with respect to eligibility, disqualification, or benefit amount. Nor would it change the duration of benefits provided under the State law, but rather would provide additional temporary benefits for those who have exhausted their rights under State or Federal laws. The temporary program is designed to fit in with the existing system and to avoid creating problems of adjustment in the various States which could hamper, impair, or delay the effectiveness of this program.

In general, the proposal would provide workers who have run out of their regular unemployment benefits since the beginning of 1958 because of lengthy unemployment with additional benefits equal to one-half the total amount of their regular benefits. These temporary benefits would be payable for unemployment occurring from 30 days after enactment of the measure through March 31, 1959. No temporary additional benefits would be payable for unemployment occurring before this period, although eligibility to receive the benefits during the period may be based on exhaustion of regular benefits occurring on or after December 31, 1957.

Workers who have exhausted their rights to unemployment compensation under State laws and under the Federal programs providing unemployment compensation for railroad workers, Federal civilian employees, and Korean veterans would be covered by this proposal. The benefits would be paid by the State employment security agencies, as agents of the United States, or by the Railroad Retirement Board in the case of benefits to railroad workers. Provision is also made for payments to workers where no State agency agreement is in effect.

The unemployment for which the temporary additional benefits are provided in this period need not be continuous. If a worker becomes employed before he receives all his temporary benefits, but again loses his job during the period of the program, he could receive the remaining temporary benefits available to him.

The additional benefits provided by the bill would not be paid for any period of unemployment for which unemployment compensation under any State or Federal law is payable. If a worker, while receiving the additional benefits provided by the bill, again becomes entitled to regular benefits under a State or Federal law, the additional benefits would cease until he had exhausted these further regular benefits.

The provisions applicable to workers who have exhausted their regular benefit rights under State unemployment compensation laws and the Federal programs providing unemployment compensation for Federal civilian employees and Korean veterans are contained in title I of the bill. Title II of the bill applies to workers who have exhausted their regular benefit rights under the Railroad Unemployment Insurance Act.

The bill provides that if a worker's right to temporary additional benefits is first determined under either one of the titles of the bill, his rights to such compensation at any subsequent period will continue to be determined under the same title, even though after becoming entitled to such additional benefits he became entitled to regular benefits under the law or laws covered by the other title and exhausted them. This provision will avoid difficult and costly administrative problems and duplication of payments under the two titles of this proposal.

Title I

Under title I of the bill, the Secretary of Labor would be authorized to enter into agreements with the States whereby the States would act as agents of the United States in making the temporary benefit payments. Where no such agreement is in effect the Secretary is authorized to utilize other Government agencies for making the payments. He is also authorized to use the same procedures for payment of the temporary benefits to Federal civilian employees and Korean veterans in Puerto Rico and the Virgin Islands as are used to pay their regular benefits in those places.

The provisions of the last unemployment compensation law under which a worker used up his regular benefits before he makes his first claim for the temporary benefits would generally govern his drawing of the temporary benefits. The eligibility requirements of that State law, such as being available for work, and disqualification provisions, such as being suspended from benefits for a specified number of weeks for refusal to accept suitable work, and other conditions of the State law, would govern the receipt of the temporary benefits.

The total amount of temporary additional benefits payable is established by the law under which he last exhausted his regular benefits before he files his first claim for temporary benefits. This total would equal one-half the total regular benefits for total unemployment. For example, a worker to whom 26 times $30 a week was payable under such law, could receive one-half of 26 times $30 or $390 in temporary benefits. This total would be paid at the same weekly rate as was payable to him for his regular benefits.

However, if during the effective period of the bill, additional regular benefits under any unemployment compensation law referred to in this title become payable to an individual and are exhausted, the weekly rate at which such benefits were payable would apply to this remaining amount of temporary benefits payable to him. Suppose the worker above who was entitled to temporary benefits up to a maximum of $390 drew 9 weeks of temporary benefits at his $30 rate or a total of $270 and then became entitled to new regular benefits at a rate of $20 a week. After exhaustion of such new regular benefits, he could again draw temporary benefits but at a rate of $20 a week until he has received the difference between $390 and $270, that is $120. Were he totally unemployed he would thus receive temporary benefits of $20 a week for 6 weeks.

If a worker is partially unemployed, his weekly benefit amount would be the difference between his weekly benefit amount for total unemployment plus the partial earnings limit provided by the State law, minus his earnings. While the partially unemployed worker would receive temporary benefits in the same total amount as would a totally unemployed worker, he would receive less each week. As a result he would receive benefits for a longer period. This is what happens when a partially unemployed worker draws regular benefits. His incentive to accept part-time jobs while drawing benefits is thus not diminished.

The total cost incurred by the United States for benefits paid under this program (except the cost of benefits to Federal employees and Korean veterans) and all administrative expenses would be paid for through a temporary increase in the amount which employers covered under the Federal Unemployment Tax Act would be required to pay to the United States. Such an increase would be effected through a reduction in the tax credit afforded to employers covered by the Federal Unemployment Tax Act and would apply for taxable years beginning January 1, 1963, with respect to wages attributable to a State unless or until the total costs incurred by the United States with respect to such State have been restored.

Since it will not be possible to determine whether the additional tax has produced sufficient revenue with respect to a particular State until the tax is actually paid, about January 30 each year, there may be some excess collections with respect to some States. These excess collections would be returned to the account of the State with respect to which they were collected, and would be available solely for the payment of regular benefits under such State's law.

Title II

Under this title the Railroad Retirement Board would be authorized to pay temporary additional unemployment benefits during the same period to railroad workers who have exhausted their rights to regular benefits under the Railroad Unemployment Insurance Act on or after December 31, 1957. The provisions of that act would apply to the temporary benefits program to the same extent and in the same manner as to the payment of regular railroad unemployment benefits except where inconsistent with the provisions of this title. However, the maximum number of days for which temporary benefits would be payable under this title would be 65.

The rate of the daily benefit payable would be that which was payable to the employee under the Railroad Unemployment Insurance Act at the time he last exhausted his rights to benefits under that act prior to filing a claim under this title. The total amount of temporary additional unemployment compensation payable under this title would be 65 times the rate of the regular daily benefit payable before his first claim for additional benefits. Any subsequent change in his regular daily rate would not affect the total amount of temporary benefits payable to him.

Estimated cost for paying additional unemployment compensation to workers who exhaust their benefits under the State unemployment insurance laws, Jan. 1, 1958 – Apr. 1, 1959

Unemployment compensation benefit payments $560,000,000
Grants to States for administrative costs (4,780) 26,104,000
Salaries and expenses, Bureau of Employment Security (82) 625,000
Salaries and expenses, Office of the Solicitor (4) 28,000
Salaries and expenses, Office of the Secretary (Personnel) (2) 14,000
Total, Department of Labor 586,771,000

One of the fundamental differences between the Administration bill and the Democratic leadership bill was that the latter provided outright grants to the states, while the former made granted loans which were to be repaid. The Secretary of Labor was questioned on this difference.

House Hearings
(p. 16)

Mr. Forand. Mr. Secretary, do I understand that the whole idea here is a question of loans rather than grants?
Secretary Mitchell. As I said in my statement, Mr. Forand, this is a Federal program financed through Federal tax, financed through the operation of the present Federal tax. The recovery of the money by the Federal Government will be accomplished by an increase in the Federal tax, as I stated, beginning on wages paid after January 1, 1963.
Mr. Forand. Boiled down it means that this is a loan and not a grant?
Secretary Mitchell. No, sir. No, sir; this is a Federal program financed by the Federal Government and as a result of Federal taxes.
Mr. Forand. But you are going to get your money back under the plan, is that not right?
Secretary Mitchell. As the result of Federal taxation.

While Secretary Mitchell conceded that unemployment was rising rapidly, he saw no need to extend compensation to those not then covered. He was supported in this view by employers' groups. Mr. R. T. Compton, appearing on behalf of the National Association of Manufacturers, opposed any legislation extending benefits under the unemployment compensation program. He argued that the pending bills were merely "relief" measures being passed off as unemployment compensation, and claimed that such legislation would wreck the entire system.

Organized labor was represented by Nelson Cruikshank, who had testified before the Ways and Means Committee on numerous occasions in support of expanded social security programs. The AFL-CIO had been the moving force behind the Kennedy-McCarthy bill; thus much of Cruikshank's testimony was devoted to urging adoption of that measure. However, realizing that there was little chance for action on the Kennedy-McCarthy Bill, Mr. Cruikshank gave tacit approval of the Democratic leadership bill rather than the Administration's proposal.

Hearings were concluded on April 1, but no report was immediately forthcoming. On April 13, in an obvious attempt to encourage faster congressional action on his legislation, President Eisenhower issued a statement calling for Congress to "move as swiftly as possible on this vital problem" of unemployment compensation.

Ten days after the President's statement, the Ways and Means Committee reported out H.R. 12065. The committee bill, almost identical to the Democratic leadership's porposals, called for a flat sixteen-week extension of exhausted benefits to workers already insured under the unemployment compensation programs. The bill also gave sixteen weeks of benefits to workers not already covered by unemployment insurance: domestics, agricultural workers, state and local government employees, and employees of small firms not covered by the program. Funds for the temporary program, commencing retroactively on July 1, 1957, and extending through June 30, 1959, would be grants to coincide with state payments.

The committee report estimated the total additional cost to the Federal Government between $1 billion and $1.5 billion. It also advocated non-repayable federal grants rather than loans since this would avoid imposing an additional obligation on heavily burdened industrial states, which had the highest unemployment rates. Those opposing the committee bill maintained that the proposal destroyed the long-existing policy of having complete state responsibility for financing compensation programs.

At a news conference on April 23, President Eisenhower indicated that he might veto the bill as it was reported from the Ways and Means Committee. Later in the same news conference, responding to a question on Administration opposition to extension of benefits to uncovered workers, Eisenhower replied that such a provision would ruin the insurance aspects of the program and make it nothing but a dole.

The committee bill, H.R. 12065, was called for House debate on April 30, after adoption of a closed rule. Representative Wilbur D. Mills, chairman of the Ways and Means Committee, took the floor to explain the committee's action and to justify its rejection of the Administration's proposals. Stating that it was unrealistic to believe that the states would ever pay back the loans under the Administration bill, Chairman Mills said the committee was attempting to avoid the illusion of repayment by simply giving grants in the first place.

The Administration supporters in the House forcefully opposed the committee bill in debate, and on May 1, a substitute bill for H.R. 12065 was introduced by Representative Albert S. Herlong of Florida.

Congressional Debates
102 Congressional Record, p. 7878.

Mr. Herlong . . .

Mr. Chairman, the statement was made here yesterday that we should be honest about this whole matter and that the provision of the substitute which I shall offer that requires the States to repay amounts advanced to them by the Federal Government was just kidding the people; that as a matter of fact the Congress would come along in a few years and forgive any amounts the States might owe. I shall discuss that feature of my bill later, but let me say now that it seems to me honesty also would compel amendments in the terms of the committee bill. The title of the committee bill should be changed to that of an unemployment relief bill; it should be amended to include a "need" clause, and it should be administered by the machinery of the welfare department rather than by the unemployment compensation insurance department. This bill should not be used as an instrument to destroy, albeit unwittingly, what has been designed and working as a sound unemployment compensation insurance program.

Mr. Chairman, there is no question but that there is a need for extension of unemployment insurance benefits in some sections of our country. There are some areas where many perople who have had a longtime attachment to the labor market have been laid off and are still unable to find work due to existing economic conditions. Many of them have exhausted their entitlements under their State laws. Surely in those areas the machinery should be set up so that they could continue to receive payments a while longer. I submit that the substitute I shall offer accomplishes that result. Moreover, it does it in a sound way, without making a complete mockery of the entire unemployment compensation system.

The substitute bill was backed by a coalition of southern Democrats and Republicans and, with their combined votes, was ultimately adopted. The coalition bill was similar to the President's original proposal in that it extended the duration of benefits by 50 per cent and provided loans to those states needing additional funds to finance the extended benefits. After agreeing to substitute the coalition bill for the committee bill, the House then passed the measure by a roll call vote.

The first witness to testify before the Senate Finance Committee was Secretary of Labor Mitchell. The original Administration bill made the extension of benefits mandatory for the states. The coalition bill which was subsequently adopted by the House made the plan optional, and Administration support for this feature of the bill was in doubt. Secretary Mitchell, questioned on this issue, stated that the Administration was backing the bill in its present form, including the optional provision. Senator Douglas pointed out to Secretary Mitchell his inconsistent position. Before the Ways and Means Committee he had opposed the optional feature, now, before the Finance Committee, he was supporting it. The Secretary replied that his support grew out of expediency, in order to insure rapid approval of the bill.

Later Senator Douglas revealed the results of a private poll of state governors: Only two governors felt that their states could exercise the optional features of H.R. 12065 without special legislation. Secretary Mitchell replied that the poll had been "colored" by the use of unfair or prejudicial language in the questionnaire, and a vigorous exchange followed between Senators Douglas and Gore and Secretary Mitchell.

Senator John Kennedy appeared before the committee to testify on behalf of his bill, which would have completely changed the existing federal-state unemployment compensation program. Senator Kennedy said that

H.R. 12065 *"accomplishes nothing whatsoever,"* and he was also sceptical that states would be able to take advantage of its provisions.

In general, those appearing before the Senate committee offered more traditional advice. The Chamber of Commerce representative testified that his organization considered unemployment insurance strictly a state problem and was opposed to any federal action. However, if Congress decided to act, H.R. 12065 was the least offensive bill under consideration. The Finance Committee eventually reported the bill out in a form identical to that passed by the House.

From the time the bill was reported from the Finance Committee until it was called for debate, there were indications from the Administration that the President would sign the bill in its current form. It seemed that the President would rather have the optional provision in the bill than delay final passage by forcing a Conference Committee to work out the differences.

Senator Harry Byrd of Virginia spoke in favor of the bill on May 27, arguing that the economic difficulties of the times should not scare Congress into rewriting the whole unemployment compensation system. He defended not only the provisions of the bill itself, but also its funding. The opposite view was pressed by Senator Kennedy who, along with co-sponsors introduced an amendment to make three major changes in the existing unemployment compensation program. First, it broadened coverage of the unemployment compensation law by making it applicable to employers with one or more employees. Under the existing law, only those employed in establishments with four or more employees were covered. Second, the amendment increased benefits so that the minimum would equal 50 per cent of the worker's average weekly wage, or two-thirds the average weekly wage in the state, whichever was less. Kennedy argued that this approximated the same proportionate amount provided when the unemployment laws were first enacted. Finally, the Kennedy Amendment provided for a uniform duration of thirty-nine weeks of benefits.

Some Senators, such as Senator Charles E. Potter of Michigan, opposed the Kennedy Amendment because it would delay final legislation, while other Senators had more basic grievances. The amendment was defeated 21-63.

On the second day of debate (May 28), Senator Kennedy offered another amendment which would have extended benefit payments by a flat sixteen weeks. Financing would be similar to the Administration proposal but states were exempted from repayment if they liberalized their programs. This amendment was also defeated.

A final amendment was introduced on May 28 by Senator Douglas providing federal relief payments to workers not covered by the insurance program. During debate, Senator Douglas argued that the pending bill, H.R. 12065, gave no protection to a one and a half million of the presently unemployed. The Senator warned that the Senate could not *"sweep these people under the rug . . . ."* The Douglas Amendment also failed, and the same day H.R.

12065 was passed unanimously. Since it was identical to the House version, the bill could be sent directly to the White House.

The President signed H.R. 12065 on June 4, and one week later Congress completed action on the supplemental appropriations bill for the 1958 fiscal year, providing the Department of Labor with $665.7 million to administer the temporary program. The President signed the appropriations bill on June 13, and several states began immediate action to extend their benefits under the new provisions. By the end of September about one-third of the states had made arrangements to accept the full provisions of the act, and five additional states extended benefit payments with their own reserve funds.

That year President Eisenhower also requested that a permanent unemployment program similar to that adopted for federal civilian employees in 1954 be adopted for ex-servicemen. The proposal covered unemployed veterans who were not eligible for state unemployment compensation because the United States had been their employer and had made no contributions to the unemployment funds. However, veterans of the Korean War were not covered since programs were already available for them. There was no congressional opposition to the proposal which was easily passed by both houses and the bill was signed on August 28.

Throughout the hearings on the Temporary Unemployment Compensation Act there was pressure on Congress to attack the long-term problems needing reform in the system of unemployment compensation. Thus, while the Ways and Means Committee was at work on short-term bills, another House committee began public hearings on the problems of unemployment. The House Banking and Currency Committee began hearing testimony on April 14, and the list of witnesses was impressive. The first to appear was former President Harry S. Truman, who called for a massive federal stimulation of the economy so that the United States growth rate would match that of the Soviet Union. He recommended other measures.

Legislation to Relieve Unemployment
Hearings before the House Banking and Currency Committee
85th Cong., 2d Sess.
(p. 7)

Statement of former President Harry S. Truman

. . . other measures should be taken to meet the problems of the recession. One of the most important of these is to extend Federal aid to the State unemployment insurance systems to lengthen the period for the payment of insurance benefits. Also, as a long-range measure, unemployment insurance coverage should be extended and Federal standards should be established to bring about a greater degree of uniformity in the various laws.

This refrain was taken up by the several governors who appeared. Governor Averell Harriman of New York, for instance, talked of the need for a federal program.

House Hearings
(p. 242, p. 401)

Statement of Governor Averell Harriman

I want to stress today my conviction that the Federal Government must take measures to support a strong economy with maximum employment. This was laid down as a matter of national policy in the Employment Act of 1946, and it has distressed me to see that current national economic policies have abandoned responsibility for the maximum employment, production, and purchasing power objectives of this act.

*   *   *

Federal standards for unemployment insurance and minimum wages: Federal standards should be established for unemployment insurance at an adequate level in benefits and period of coverage, and the numbers eligible expanded. Not only would this lead to greater benefits for unemployed in many States, but would afford protection to States like New York which already have high standards. In addition we need an extension of the protection of Federal minimum wages to millions now unprotected. This is particularly important now to protect against exploitation of the unemployed seeking jobs.

Labor leaders, such as David J. McDonald, president of the United Steelworkers of America, were even more insistent that some long-term changes had to be made. However, Secretary of Labor Mitchell could not see the need for further reforms, and despite the bulk of the evidence and the eminent witnesses, no further action was taken. It seemed that long-term reform of the unemployment compensation programs was impossible.

1959

Pressing Problems

There had been congressional action on social security during every session of Eisenhower's Administration, although the major changes had occurred

---

*On several occasions President Eisenhower had urged the widening of the unemployment compensation program to include workers not then covered. The President was always cau-

*during election years. In 1959 the President followed that trend by making
no major proposals on social security.* By then the country was recovering
from an economic recession; the high unemployment rate and the consequent pressure for federal action on public assistance and unemployment
compensation had therefore been reduced.*

*The Administration continued to disapprove of the increased federal
share in public assistance programs, and in the budget message of 1959,
President Eisenhower called for its reduction. (It should be noted that
Eisenhower made this same recommendation in 1958 and Congress, ignoring his request had, in fact, increased the federal share in these programs.)
In the same message the President also referred to the Advisory Council
on Public Assistance which was authorized by the 1958 amendments.*

Annual Budget Message of the President
(January 19, 1959)*

While continuing to support programs necessary to stimulate greater
state and local effort in areas of critical national concern, this administration
has consistently endeavored to strengthen our system of government by
encouraging state and local governments to assume responsibility for many
public needs which they can provide well without relying on federal aid at
all, or by financing a larger share from their own revenue sources. Therefore, toward this objective, legislation is again recommended to: . . .

(c) Increase state and local participation in the financing of public assistance programs.

*   *   *

Under the authority of recent legislation, an advisory council is being
appointed by the Secretary of Health, Education, and Welfare to study the
whole structure and financing of our public assistance programs. I have
asked the Secretary to present to this council, at the earliest possible time,
the issue of what constitutes an appropriate Federal share in these programs.
I have also requested him to develop recommendations, after consulting the
council, which can be presented to the Congress to increase State and local

---

tious, however, to emphasize that the program should remain primarily the responsibility of the
states, and should not be taken over by the Federal Government.

Many congressional leaders favored extension of the temporary unemployment compensation program and on March 4, the House Majority Leader, John McCormack, and the Speaker
of the House, Sam Rayburn, revealed that the House Ways and Means Committee would report out a bill, H.R. 5640, to extend the duration of the 1958 temporary benefits provisions
through June 30, or longer if a state wished to fund the extension itself.

When H.R. 5640 was sent to the Senate, there was significant senatorial support to extend
the program for fifteen months rather than the three months provided in the bill. However, the
House version was finally adopted, extending additional benefits only to July 1, 1959. (P.L.
86-7)

**Public Papers of the Presidents, Dwight D. Eisenhower, 1959,* p. 97–98, p. 102–103.

participation in the cost of the public assistance programs beginning in 1961. In this connection, I believe we must keep in mind the fact that the Federal share of such expenditures has increased to more than 57% on an overall basis and runs as high as 80% in many cases. I believe that this trend is inconsistent with our American system of government. If it continues, the control of these programs will shift from our State and local governments to the Federal Government. We must keep the financing and control of these programs as close as we possibly can to the people who pay the necessary taxes and see them in daily operation.

A basic problem in the public assistance programs is achieving the goal of helping people to help themselves return to self-support. Solution of this problem requires studies into the causes of dependency and its prevention. It also requires better training of local case workers. This budget provides for cooperative work with the States in these two areas.

Nevertheless, as well as increasing the Federal Government's share of public assistance benefits, section 704 of the 1958 ammendments had provided that an Advisory Council on Public Assistance, composed of twelve individuals and the Commissioner of Social Security, be appointed early in 1959 to study the economic and social ramifications of the program, and to make suggestions for improvements in the system. On December 31, 1959, the report of the Advisory Council was released. Among its twenty specific recommendations was the suggestion that the federal share of PA not be reduced.

Similarly, one of the basic arguments which had been made against the adoption of the 1958 amendments relating to OASDI had been that any changes should have been delayed until the Report of the Advisory Council on Social Security Financing had been completed. Congress had ignored this argument and had adopted the changes without benefit of the report. However, the Advisory Council continued its investigation, and during the first week of 1959 issued its report, concluding that the basic financing scheme was actuarily sound, but that certain future changes would be necessitated by changes in the labor force, in wage levels, and in other variables.

Financing Old-Age, Survivors, and Disability Insurance, Report of the Advisory Council on Social Security Financing
February, 1959

The Major Finding

The method of financing the old-age, survivors, and disability insurance program is sound, and, based on the best estimates available, the contribution schedule now in the law makes adequate provision for meeting both short-range and long-range costs.

The Council finds that the present method of financing the old-age, survivors, and disability insurance program is sound, practical, and appropriate for this program. It is our judgment, based on the best available cost estimates, that the contribution schedule enacted into law in the last session of Congress makes adequate provision for financing the program on a sound actuarial basis.

The Council has studied the estimates of the short-range and long-range costs of the old-age and survivors insurance program, the various demographic and other assumptions on which they are based, and the basic techniques used in deriving the estimates.[1] The Council believes that the assumptions are a reasonable basis for forecasts extending into the distant future, and that the estimating techniques are appropriate and sound. The Council endorses the present practice under which both the estimating techniques and the assumptions are re-examined periodically to take account of emerging experience and changing conditions.

It is our judgment that the program is in close actuarial balance since the level-premium equivalent of the contribution rates varies from the estimated level-premium cost by no more than one-quarter of 1 percent of covered payroll.[2] There is no advantage in trying to achieve a closer balance between estimated long-range income and outgo, especially since those estimates are subject to periodic review and such review encompasses the testing of the adequacy of the schedule of contribution rates. If earnings should continue to rise in the future as they have in the past, the level-premium cost of the present benefits, expressed as a percentage of payroll, would be lower than shown in the cost estimates we have used.

---

[1]See sec. VII B for a discussion of the estimates. The estimates referred to throughout this report are the official estimates of the Social Security Administration. The latest estimates are contained in *Actuarial Cost Estimates and Summary of Provisions of the Old-Age, Survivors, and Disability Insurance System as Modified by the Social Security Amendments of 1958*. Washington: U. S. Government Printing Office, 1958. The Report of the Board of Trustees for the fiscal year 1958 will be submitted to the Congress by March 1, 1959, and will contain both the detail of the cost estimates and a reprint of this report of the Advisory Council.

[2]The "level-premium cost" is the percent of covered payroll that, if charged from now on indefinitely into the future, would produce enough contribution and interest income to the fund to meet the cost of the benefit payments and administrative expenses. The "level-premium equivalent of the contribution rates" is the percent of covered payroll that, if charged from now on indefinitely into the future, would produce the same amount of income to the fund over the long-range future as will be produced by the graded schedule of contribution rates. The level-premium cost of the OASI part of the program is 8.27 percent of payroll on the basis of the intermediate cost estimates; the level-premium equivalent of the contributions is 8.02 percent of payroll. The level-premium cost of the disability insurance part of the program is 0.49 percent of payroll; the level premium equivalent of the contributions is 0.50 percent of payroll.

The Council is also pleased to report that under the new schedule of contributions and benefits not only is the system in close actuarial balance for the long run, but also after 1959 the income to the system is estimated to exceed the outgo in every year for many years into the future. We believe that it is important that income exceed outgo during the early years of development of the system as well as that the system be in close actuarial balance over the long range.

We have no suggestions for basic changes in the present plan of financing. We do, however, have certain specific recommendations which we believe will strengthen the plan.

Summary of Other Findings and Conclusions

The Council's recommendations are designed to supplement, not to alter, the basic provisions of the existing financing plan. Specifically, the Council endorses the contributory principle, an interest-earning fund on a limited basis, investment of the funds solely in United States Government obligations, and the other major features of the present financial arrangements.

The Council anticipates that further changes in the social security program will be needed as changes occur in the labor force, wage levels, and doubtless in other factors that in a dynamic economy will affect the appropriateness of the program. Because of these changes and such changes as may occur in the factors which enter into the actuarial cost estimates, we believe there is a need for periodic scrutiny of all factors which in any way affect the financing of the program. These factors include the maximum earnings base for determining benefits and contributions. This maximum determines the proportion of the Nation's payrolls available to finance the program and is a major factor in determining the extent to which the program pays benefits reasonably related to the past earnings of the individual. As a whole, our recommendations look toward a continuing review of the financial arrangements so that they, along with the other provisions of the program, can be kept sound and workable in a changing economy.

At this time we recommend no change in the contribution schedule. It is not certain, however, that the ultimate rate should go into effect in 1969, as provided in the present law. A sound decision on whether there should be a change in the amount or timing of the increase scheduled for 1969 can best be made in the period just before 1969 after the advisory council then serving has evaluated the question.

The Council suggests that greater emphasis be given in the future to estimates of the probable course of the income and outgo of the system over the then ensuing 15 or 20 years. As the program reaches a greater degree of maturity and the contribution rate approaches the level of a reasonable minimum estimate of the costs over a period of many decades into the future, it will be appropriate, as it has not been in the past, to base financial decisions largely on what may be expected to take place during the period of 15 to 20 years thereafter. Estimates showing the relationship of income and outgo over the very long-range future have been and will continue to be important as a guide to policy and necessary as a brake against making commitments which, though inexpensive today, may have substantially greater costs in the long-run future. As the system matures, however, forecasts of what will happen during the shorter run will become progressively more significant and useful.

The Council recommends certain changes in the provisions governing the interest rate on the special obligations issued for purchase by the trust funds, and also certain other changes in the management of the funds that are designed to bring their earnings more nearly into line with earnings of private investors in long-term Government bonds.

Multi-Faceted Approach

In the end, there were no social security hearings during 1959, but in many ways the old divisions were breaking down. The Joint Economic Committee was concerned with all aspects of the economy, with income security among them. The Currency and Banking Committee had established an interest in unemployment compensation and in general, the Congress increasingly looked at causes of poverty, rather than temporary measures to fight it. In line with this trend the Senate Labor and Public Welfare Committee created a subcommittee to study the problems of the aged and aging. The subcommittee first solicited the views of a consultant panel of recognized authorities in the problems of the elderly, and then scheduled hearings in six major cities across the country, to obtain the views of local leaders and of the aged citizens themselves.

Hearings were held, for instance, in San Francisco, California with Senator Patrick V. McNamara of Michigan, the subcommittee chairman, and Senator Jennings Randolph of West Virginia representing the subcommittee. The views given by local leaders of national organizations were often simply restatements of congressional testimony given by their Washington representatives; the AFL-CIO spokesman in San Francisco called for the same programs the national organization was supporting: an increase in social security and related income maintenance programs, health care, etc. The president of the California Medical Association testified on problems facing the elderly, and suggested that many of these problems could be solved by private rather than public action. The doctor also said, "From an overall standpoint, one of the least of the potential needs of the aged is med-

ical care of their serious ailments and particularly of their serious remedial surgical needs" (The Aged and Aging in the United States, *Hearings before the Subcommittee on Problems of the Aged and Aging of the Senate Committee on Labor and Public Welfare, 86th Cong., 2d Sess., p. 877). He stated that the medical profession, through state and voluntary programs, was providing the necessary medical care required by senior citizens.*

After hearing formal testimony from the representatives of various groups and organizations, the subcommittee opened the rostrum to elder citizens who were in the audience. Their statements covered a wide range of problems, but it was clear that one of the greatest concerns of the aged was the problem of receiving adequate medical care. There were moving statements from many of the elderly and retired emphasizing exorbitant costs. The link between the elderly and the need for medical care was becoming ever more obvious.

The subcommittee concluded the hearings in the six cities by the middle of December, 1959, and returned to Washington with volumes of testimony and statistics. In addition, the subcommittee had hundreds of responses from individuals and organizations whose views on these problems had been solicited. Whether this material would become a basis for legislative recommendations remained uncertain. It was not until January 29, 1960, that the subcommittee issued its first report on the problems of the aged and aging in the United States, including twelve specific recommendations for congressional action. Leading the list of priorities was the proposal for a health insurance plan for the aged financed under the basic OASDI program.

The Federal Council on Aging also conducted a study and reported its findings to the President on September 30, 1959. (Members of the Council included the Secretaries of the Departments of Health, Education, and Welfare, of the Treasury, of Agriculture, of Commerce, and of Labor, and the Administrator of the Housing and Home Finance Agency.) The report discussed the various federal programs related to aged and aging citizens and also considered future needs and challenges.

While the Senate subcommittee was holding hearings on the problems of the aged, a House subcommittee of the Committee on Ways and Means held hearings in Washington on the administration of the disability program under social security. The basic issue before the subcommittee was whether the fifty-year-old age limit for disability insurance was essential or could be deleted without financially weakening the entire program.

The first two days of hearings were conducted in executive session; testimony was taken from HEW officials in the Bureau of Old-Age and Survivors Insurance. On the first day of public hearings, several of these same officials appeared to testify again. Among them was George Wyman, Deputy Commissioner of Social Security. He commenced his public testi-

mony by citing the recent study, made by the chief actuary of the Social Security Administration, which had concluded that the fifty-year-old age limit could be eliminated without increasing disability insurance tax rates.

Dr. S. Duffy Hancock, the chairman of the Medical Advisory Committee to the Social Security Administration, also appeared before the subcommittee to give a brief statement on the work of the advisory group. He concluded with the suggestion that there be further experience with the existing disability provisions before any changes were enacted. It was to prove a vain plea.

Medical Care

Many Democrats in Congress had continually urged adoption of some variation of a health insurance plan since President Truman introduced his major ideas in 1949. The Truman proposal had been embodied in bills sponsored by Senators Murray and Wagner and Representative Dingell; it had caused bitter controversy at hearings in 1949 and 1950. The bills failed to win congressional approval, and when President Eisenhower and the Republican Administration came into office there seemed to be little chance of any immediate action on comprehensive health insurance legislation. In fact, the Eisenhower Administration programs were rather limited. Small health insurance companies were allowed to pool their resources in order to spread the risk, and federal reinsurance was instituted to protect insurance companies from excessive losses from extended medical insurance coverage.

The health insurance issue remained almost dormant during the first Eisenhower term, but in 1957 Representative Aime Forand introduced a bill providing health insurance coverage for persons already covered by the basic OASDI programs. Hearings were held on the Forand Bill in 1958, but the House Ways and Means Committee rejected the proposal and reported out an omnibus social security bill containing no health insurance provision.

In 1959 Representative Forand again introduced his hospital and surgical insurance legislation (H.R. 4700), and the Ways and Means Committee scheduled public hearings on the measure for July. The Administration, however, remained opposed to any variety of the Forand Bill, and spokesmen for the President made various statements at the congressional hearings calling the proposals unnecessary and damaging to the basic social security system.

The first witness to testify was Arthur Flemming, Secretary of Health, Education, and Welfare, who stated on behalf of the Administration, "We are convinced that making adequate medical care reasonably available to our aged population should, as far as possible, be achieved through reliance upon and encouragement of individual and organized voluntary action," (Hospital, Nursing Home, and Surgical Benefits for OASI Beneficians, *Hearings before the House Ways and Means Committee, 86th Cong., 1st Sess., on H.R. 4700, p. 10).*

Information inserted into the record by the Secretary pointed up the much higher cost of commercial health insurance compared to non-profit Blue Cross-Blue Shield plans, and, by implication, over projected Federal Government programs.

**Hospital, Nursing Home, and Surgical Benefits for OASI Beneficians
Hearings on H.R. 4700 before the House Ways and Means Committee**
86th Cong., 1st Sess. (1959)
(p. 19)

* * *

(The information provided by the Department of Health, Education, and Welfare is as follows:)

Proportion of premium income (less dividends or earned income credits) returned as benefits by insurance carriers of different types in 1958

[Percent of income paid in benefits]

Nonprofit service-type plans:
Blue Cross — total business, all 79 plans in the United States 97.2
    Hospitalization only 97.6
Blue Shield total business, all 66 plans in the United States 89.6
    Blue Shield surgical-medical only 89.5

    Combined Blue Cross-Blue Shield operations 94.7

Cash indemnity accident and health insurance:
Group insurance business (United States) 85.2
Individual business (United States) 48.6
Noncancellable individual insurance business (United States) 40.8

    Combined insurance company business 71.2

In this situation, it was difficult not to conclude that attempting to provide medical care to the elderly through voluntary health insurance plans or through public assistance still left a gap in the middle. Many old people who were not on public assistance could not afford medical care, nor were comprehensive insurance schemes available to them at a price they could afford. It was this group which was causing the greatest concern, and which, in the absence of government health insurance, would have to be helped through other measures.

While Secretary Flemming seemed to be moving toward government subsidy of voluntary health insurance, the spokesmen for organized medicine remained firm advocates of the status quo. Dr. Herbert Berger, speaking on behalf of the New York State Society of Internal Medicine, branded the bill "communistic legislation." Representative Forand quickly responded to the charge.

House Hearings
(p. 43 – 45)

Mr. Forand. Dr. Berger, I direct your attention to last sentence in the first paragraph on page 2 of your statement. It reads:

> Does it not seem inconsistent that we should be fighting such communism in Geneva while introducing legislating supporting it in Washington?

Now, are you stating that this is Communist legislation, that I am a Communist or a Pinko? I resent this and I would like to have explanation of what you mean.

Dr. Berger. I will be glad to, Congressman. Perhaps your definition of communism and mine may differ. However, as I see communism and this is a personal point of view, it is the introduction of the State into the affairs of the individual to such an extent that the individual becomes a rather lesser person than the State. The rights of the individual are lost. I would say that if Government were to interfere in the health care of these aged people whose care properly belongs to themselves where possible or to their relatives, then this is actually an example of not what we see in Russia but an example of pure communism.

I feel that this is probably a mistake, that we would by such a mechanism break up normal family obligations and responsibilities. I recognize, of course, sir, that there are individuals who have no family and I would contend that such individuals are being cared for locally, so that I do not see that this problem exists. Certainly in my own community there is no one at any age who suffers from lack of medical care.

Mr. Forand. So in your mind I am introducing communistic legislation?

Dr. Berger. As I see communism; yes, sir, I am afraid I will have to come to that conclusion.

Mr. Forand. Well, it is the first time I have heard of the term "communism" being that broad. If it suits your purpose, of course, this is a free country, you can use it but I frankly resent it.

Dr. Berger. I am sorry, sir, there is nothing personal intended there.

Mr. Forand. I gather from your testimony that you work for the New York City Department of Welfare and attempt to provide good quality care for elderly patients. As I understand it you and private physicians on the welfare panel who care for these patients are paid from public funds. Is that not correct?

Dr. Berger. Yes, sir.

Mr. Forand. Do you feel that this type of provision for the care of patients is socialized medicine?

Dr. Berger. I feel that it is a proper activity of a community to care for its aged or for anybody else who is indigent.

Mr. Forand. You have not answered my question. Is that socialized medicine?

Dr. Berger. I would say that this is a small degree of socialized medicine, yes.

Mr. Forand. And you are taking part in it?

Dr. Berger. Yes, sir; I am.

Mr. Forand. Is it communism?

Dr. Berger. No, sir; because these people still have a considerable degree of free choice which I think would probably be lost in the legislation that you are proposing.

Mr. Forand. If the patients had contributed to a fund and the doctors and nursing homes were paid from this fund for care provided would you consider that to be socialized medicine?

Dr. Berger. No, sir.

Mr. Forand. What specific features of the Forand bill do you believe involves (sic) socialized medicine?

Dr. Berger. I think particularly the fact that it probably could not be managed economically by the individual, himself. His taxes to cover it are at best only half of it since the other half is passed on to the rest of the population. I recognize here, sir, that I am not speaking in a role that I would prefer to be in, that of a practicing physician. Economics is certainly not my forte. But I will try to answer the question and not avoid it.

Mr. Forand. But if the funds for this were coming from taxation generally, such as the public fund from which you are paid, for work in New York, it would be all right?

Dr. Berger. No, sir, I did not say that. What I feel is this, that the individual should, if possible provide for his future. If he does this by paying some part of his income to social security that is perfectly all right. At best he contributes half of this and the Secretary of Health, Education, and Welfare indicated that even this half would not cover the entire costs of this expense. Therefore, all other individuals are being taxed to cover this particular expense which the individual should have borne, himself.

Mr. Forand. Where did the money come from for the Welfare Department to pay for your services?

Dr. Berger. It comes from the taxes that are raised by the city of New York.

Mr. Forand. Is there any difference between that type of tax and the Federal Government's?

Dr. Berger. I think there is because of the nature of administration of a large organization originating here in Washington to handle a matter in some distant part of the country. I think on a local basis there are better opportunities to do this job properly. I recognize and I agree with you these are public funds raised by the public.

Mr. Forand. Are you aware of the fact that the public money that the city of New York uses to pay for your services in part is Federal money?

Dr. Berger. I am, sir.

Mr. Forand. Then what is the difference?

Dr. Berger. I personally would prefer frankly that there were no such source of revenue either city or Federal. Certainly I practiced medicine before either of these were available and old people in those days were cared for adequately. This is again one of the altruistic gestures of my profession. I think we would be perfectly willing to bear this burden alone without any tax setup.

Mr. Forand. Then why don't you render your services free?

Dr. Berger. We did for many years until these things became available.

Mr. Forand. I did not say in the past. Why don't you now?

Dr. Berger. For the most part they are when one considers the nature of the funds. For example, as a consultant in internal medicine a private patient might very well pay $50 or $100 for my services. I render these to the city of New York for $5. I am a consultant to the Department of Health, Education, and Welfare, Public Health Service, and render the services there for nothing.

Mr. Forand. If you are so much opposed to the payment of Federal or State funds for this purpose and you get so little, it is difficult to understand why you accept even that mite.

Dr. Berger. Perhaps you are right, I should not.

Mr. Forand. Now you imply that you would favor increasing social security benefits so that people can defray all of their expenses, medical and non-medical. Would you care to give us an estimate as to why the necessary increase would be on the average more or less than $10 a month?

Dr. Berger. I have no knowledge in this area at all. It is not that I favor this, sir, but I was trying to give you not a negative approach but some positive methods by which this problem could be met. One of the methods would be, of course, to provide these people with enough money so that they could meet all of their expenses.

Mr. Forand. Where would that money come from?

Dr. Berger. The money should come from the deductions from their own salaries during their working lifetime.

Mr. Forand. The employee and the employer as the system operates today; is that correct?

Dr. Berger. I would prefer that it be the employee, himself.

Mr. Forand. Just the employee?

Dr. Berger. Yes, sir.

Mr. Forand. Thank you. That is all, Mr. Chairman.

Dr. Leonard Larson, chairman of the Board of Trustees of the American Medical Association, told the committee that sustained progress had been made in developing voluntary health programs for the needy. The AMA was one of the leading groups against H.R. 4700. A representative for the Health Insurance and Life Insurance Associations of America, Mr. E. J. Faulkner, stated that these groups were also firmly opposed to H.R. 4700. In general, however, they took a more intellectual approach to the problem than had the AMA.

Despite the various hearings conducted by committees and subcommittees, there were no social security or health insurance bills reported to either the House or Senate during 1959. After its mid-year hearings the Ways and Means Committee took no further public action on the Forand Bill during the first session of the eighty-seventh Congress. However, the basic plan to include medical care among OASDI benefits had gained support from several key congressional leaders.

1960

While 1959 had been a year of discussion; 1960 was a year of decision. It was also, of course, a presidential election year and medical care was a key issue.

At a February press conference, President Eisenhower commented on proposed social security amendments: "There is under consideration a possible change to run up the taxes by a quarter of a per cent to make greater provision for the care of the aged." Because the Forand Bill was designed to provide medical care for the aged under the social security program, the Eisenhower statement led some to believe the Administration was considering support for some variation of a medical care program. However, such speculation was dispelled by another Eisenhower statement on March 30:

Presidential News Conference
(March 30, 1960)*

Q. J. F. Ter Horst, Detroit News: I'd like to jump, sir, from the youth to the aged, if I may.

Public Papers of the Presidents, Dwight D. Eisenhower, 1960–61, p. 324–25.

There has been a lot of controversy on Capitol Hill and we understand also within administration circles regarding what kind of medical care should be provided for senior citizens. And, some of the administration critics have even gone so far as to say the President does not understand this problem because he has never had to defray his own medical bills. I wonder, sir, if you could help us understand what your position and what your philosophy is toward what the Government should really do for senior citizens and what they should do on their own.

The President. Well, of course, I'll start off with this: you start off asking what the Government should do. There are lots of governments, and the thing I object to is putting everything on the Federal Government. I point out to you people all the time, if a city or a county or a State has to raise funds, if they have to do it even by borrowing, they have to go into the market with their bonds. The Federal Government tries to do that also, as long as it is fiscally responsible, but the Federal Government can print money. Nobody else can. So, it is always a little caution that you ought to tuck in the back of your minds when you think just of bringing in new responsibilities and new expenses in the Federal Government.

Now, to talk about this specific thing: I have, from the time this subject was discussed with me very thoroughly and exhaustively away back in 1951 and '52, I have been against compulsory insurance as a very definite step in socialized medicine. I don't believe in it, and I want none of it myself. I don't want any of it.

At the same time, there has been a great deal of progress made in this whole field. The number of people that have come under the voluntary health insurance programs has been very great, increasing rapidly. We still leave with ourselves, however, the problem of those people who are not indigent—taken care of under that State assistance act, I forget the name of it—but the people who are just too low incomed to take care of these catastrophic illnesses.

I think we have got to develop a voluntary program. As a matter of fact, in all our discussions inside the Cabinet, that is exactly what I've instructed the HEW Secretary to do: to get all the people that are interested —the insurance companies, the doctors, the older people, everybody that seems to have a real worthwhile opinion and conviction on this thing—get them in and work out what should be the responsibility of the individual and the city and the State and, finally, the Federal Government.

I want to point out at this time there is not a single State that has a program in this field. It seems to me that the problem does have enough of the local in its character that they should be just as interested as anybody else. Now, we are trying to develop a program that will show exactly where the Federal responsibility in this field should begin and where it should end.

Even though the Administration had taken a firm stand against the Forand Bill, political and congressional developments insured substantial controversy over the measure on Capitol Hill. Senator John Kennedy announced his candidacy for the Democratic nomination for President on January 2, 1960. Three weeks later he introduced a Senate bill corresponding to the proposal before the House. The interest of a prime presidential candidate in health insurance for the aged made the controversy a major political issue in the November election campaign. Moreover, in March, the Ways and Means Committee commenced three months of executive sessions to consider the Forand Bill and other medical care and social security programs.

The bitterness generated by the health insurance proposals diverted attention from several other possible changes in OASDI. The Ways and Means Committee was considering liberalization of the retirement test so that beneficiaries between the ages of sixty-five and seventy-two could earn a greater outside income. Other possible changes included lower work requirements to become eligible for benefits, no age requirement for disability insurance, and a .1 of 1 per cent increase in the unemployment tax on employers.

The Ways and Means Committee continued its executive session hearings and on March 22 Representative Forand introduced House Resolution 483 authorizing a special rule for consideration of H.R. 4700 by the whole House. It was the first step in a plan to get the bill out of the Ways and Means Committee by a discharge petition. The resolution failed to stimulate the committee into immediate action; indeed, on March 31, the committee tentatively voted not to include the Forand Bill in its general recommendations for amendments to the social security programs.

On May 3, President Eisenhower sent a special message to Congress urging action on several of his legislative proposals. Included in his message was the announcement that within the week HEW Secretary Flemming would present a new program for medical care for the aged to Congress. Apparently the Republicans were countering the Forand-Kennedy challenge.

The following day Secretary Flemming revealed the Administration's health care proposals before the Ways and Means Committee. The plan actually provided two separate programs, with the choice of alternative up to the individual. One possibility was a state-administered program with a $24 annual enrollment fee for each insured individual. With HEW approval the states could use commercial insurance companies as the administrators of the program. Direct grants would be available to encourage states to provide the necessary medical services for the aged but they would be required to pay 80 per cent of the cost of certain medical services specified in the act. (Secretary Flemming explained that the Federal Government would pay an average of 50 per cent of the costs as grants, but under an equalization formula this percentage would go as high as 80 per cent for the poorer states.)

The second alternative under the Administration's plan provided sub-

*sidization of private medical insurance policies. A combination of federal
and state funds would pay up to 50 per cent of the premiums on a private
policy, if the policy met minimum state-established criteria.*

*States would be required to adopt both programs and every person over
sixty-five whose adjusted gross income, social security benefits, railroad
retirement benefits, and veterans pensions did not total more than $2500
($3800 in case of a couple) during the preceding year, would have the option
of coverage by either program. Secretary Flemming estimated that 75 per
cent of all persons over sixty-five years of age would be eligible to participate in the plan.*

*The Administration's plan increased the congressional controversy on
the medical care issue, and the Ways and Means Committee simply continued its closed hearings. Feeling was intensified when it was revealed
that Vice-President Richard M. Nixon, certain to be the Republican presidential candidate, was a prime draftsman of the Administration's plan.*

*The House Ways and Means Committee eventually rejected both the
Forand Bill and the Administration's proposal, and instead reported H.R.
12580 to the House. It was another omnibus social security bill and included many substantial changes besides those dealing directly with
medical care for the aged. The medical care amendments were important
as a temporary restraint on the movement toward national health insurance
on the one hand, and federal subsidy of private insurance on the other. The
new bill embraced neither. Instead H.R. 12580, the Kerr-Mills Bill, created
a new category of federal grants to states (Title XVI of the Social Security
Act), keyed to help the elderly who were not on public assistance but who
faced ruin in the event of large medical bills. The bill also made changes in
OAA medical programs by increasing the federal share of old-age assistance
medical payments. H.R. 12580 also provided for increases in coverage and
benefits for several groups of OASDI recipients and raised the employer's
unemployment tax .1 of 1 per cent in order to increase the loan fund for
states with unemployment compensation emergencies. Among many other
changes, the age requirement for disability benefits was dropped. Only a
few years earlier the disability program had stimulated heated congressional
dispute; in 1960 the health care proposals received all the attention.*

Social Security Act Amendments of 1960
House Report No. 1799
86th Cong., 2d Sess.
(July 12, 1960)

The Committee on Ways and Means, to whom was referred the bill
(H.R. 12580) to extend and improve coverage under the Federal old-age,
survivors, and disability insurance system and to remove hardships and in-

equities, improve the financing of the trust funds, and provide disability benefits to additional individuals under such system; to provide grants to States for medical care for aged individuals of low income; to amend the public assistance and maternal and child welfare provisions of the Social Security Act; to improve the unemployment compensation provisions of such act; and for other purposes, having considered the bill, report favorably thereon without amendment and recommend that the bill do pass.

I. SCOPE OF THE BILL

The soundness and effectiveness of the programs encompassed in the Social Security Act are extremely important to every American family. Your committee believes it has an obligation to determine, from time to time, whether in a diverse and changing economy these programs are fulfilling their objectives within a framework of fiscal and actuarial soundness.

During this Congress your committee has given careful consideration to existing programs under the Social Security Act, and to changes which have been suggested.

As a result of this review and consideration, your committee is proposing in this bill a number of improvements in the programs contained in the Social Security Act, including old-age and survivors insurance, disability insurance, unemployment compensation, public assistance, and maternal and child welfare. In addition, the committee is recommending that a new title be added to the Social Security Act which will initiate a Federal-State grants-in-aid program of medical services to the low-income aged.

II. SUMMARY OF PRINCIPAL PROVISIONS OF THE BILL

A. Medical Care for the Aged

1. Medical services for the aged (title XVI)

Purpose. — A new title of the Social Security Act would be established (title XVI) which would initiate a new Federal-State grants-in-aid program to help the States assist low-income aged individuals who need assistance in meeting their medical expenses. Participation in the program can begin after June 1961, upon the submittal of a plan which meets the general requirements specified in the bill. This effective date is necessary in order to give many State legislatures time to consider and act on a program. Participation in the Federal-State program will be completely optional with the States, with each State determining the extent and character of its own program, including (within broad limits) standards of eligibility and scope of benefits. The limits of Federal participation are discussed later in this report.

Eligibility. — Persons 65 years of age and over, whose income and resources — taking into account their other living requirements as determined by a State—are insufficient to meet the cost of their medical services, will be eligible under the program. Persons eligible to participate under this program will not include those persons participating under the other Federal-State public assistance program.

Scope of benefits.—The scope of medical benefits and services provided will be determined by the States. The Federal Government, however, will participate under the matching formula in any program which provides any or all of the following services (where limits are applicable they are specified), provided both institutional and non-institutional services are available:

> (A) Inpatient hospital services up to 120 days per year;
> (B) Skilled nursing-home services;
> (C) Physicians' services;
> (D) Outpatient hospital services;
> (E) Organized home care services;
> (F) Private duty nursing services;
> (G) Therapeutic services;
> (H) Major dental treatment;
> (I) Laboratory and X-ray services up to $200 per year;
> (J) Prescribed drugs up to $200 per year.

Federal matching.—The Federal Government will provide funds for payments for medical benefits under an approved State plan in accordance with an equalization formula under which the Federal share will be between 50 percent and 65 percent of the costs depending upon the per capita income of the State. This is the same matching formula which applies now on that part of the average old-age assistance payments between $30 and $65 a month. A State's program under the new title cannot be more liberal than the medical program under the State's old-age assistance program, and there can be no reduction in existing public assistance programs to finance this new title.

The payments under this program will be made directly to providers of the medical services.

Number of persons affected and cost.—Under this new title State plans (with Federal matching funds) could provide potential protection to as many as 10 million persons age 65 and over whose financial resources are such that if they have extensive medical expenses, they will qualify. Each year an estimated one-half to 1 million persons among these 10 million become ill and require medical services such as are provided under this title.

An estimated $325 million in medical services will be provided in a full year of operation, after the States have had opportunity to develop these programs. The estimated Federal share is $165 million and the estimated State share is $160 million. (See table A in part III for State-by-State breakdown.)

2. Improvement of medical care for old-age assistance recipients

Contingent upon a showing of a significant improvement in their medical payment programs for old-age assistance recipients, States would get somewhat more favorable Federal matching, effective October 1960, for additional expenditures up to an average of $5 per recipient in medical payments. Over 2 million persons could be affected by this change. The cost in a full year of operation would total $16 million in additional medical payments. This would represent about $10½ million to the Federal Government and about $5½ million to the States.

As recommended by the Advisory Council on Public Assistance, appointed pursuant to the Social Security Amendments of 1958, the bill instructs the Secretary of Health, Education, and Welfare to develop guides or recommended standards for the information of the States as to the level, content, and quality of medical care for the public assistance medical programs. He would also prepare such guides and standards for use in the new programs of medical services for the low-income aged.

B. The Old-Age, Survivors, and Disability Insurance (OASDI) Provisions

1. The disability insurance program

(a) Removal of age 50 eligibility requirement. — An estimated 250,000 people — disabled insured workers under age 50 and their dependents — would qualify for benefits for the second month following the month of enactment of the bill through removal of the age 50 qualification for benefits in present law.

(b) Trial work period. — The bill would strengthen the rehabilitation aspects of the disability program by providing a 12-month period of trial work, during which benefits are continued for all disabled workers who attempt to return to work, rather than limiting this trial work period to those under the formal Federal-State vocational rehabilitation plan, as in existing law.

(c) Waiting period. — The bill would provide that the disabled worker who regains his ability to work and then within 5 years again becomes disabled will not be required to wait through a second 6-month waiting period before his benefits will be resumed, as is now required.

2. Insured status requirement

The bill would liberalize the insured status requirement by making eligible for benefits persons who have one quarter of coverage for every four calendar quarters elapsing after 1950 (or age 21) and before retirement age (65 for men, 62 for women), disability or death. Present law requires one quarter of coverage for each two quarters so elapsing. (No change would be made in the requirement that a person must have a minimum of 6 quarters of coverage or the provision giving permanent insured status to persons with 40 quarters of coverage.) The change makes the requirement in the short run comparable to that which will prevail in the long run (permanent insured status with 40 quarters of coverage in a working life). For example, a person reaching retirement age this year would need to have only 9 quarters of coverage to be insured, whereas under present law, he would need 18 or 19 quarters of coverage. About 600,000 people — workers, dependents, and survivors — would be eligible for benefits the month after the month of enactment as a result of this change.

3. Improved benefit protection for dependents and survivors of insured workers — wives, widows, children, husbands, and widowers

The committee's bill would increase the benefits payable to children in certain cases and would provide benefits for certain wives, widows, widowers, and children of insured workers who are not now eligible for benefits. Other than as noted below, these changes would be effective for benefits for the month following the month of enactment.

(a) *Survivors of workers who died before 1940.* — Survivors of workers who died before 1940, and who had at least six quarters of coverage, would qualify for benefit payments. About 25,000 people, most of them widows aged 75 or over, would be made eligible for benefits for the first time by this change.

(b) *Increase in children's benefits.* — The benefits payable to the children of deceased workers, which now can be somewhat less than 75 percent of the worker's benefit depending on the number of children in the family, would be made 75 percent for all children, subject to the family maximum of $254 a month, or 80 percent of the worker's average monthly wage if less. About 400,000 children would get some increase in benefits as a result of this change, effective for benefits for the third month after the month of enactment.

(c) *Other changes affecting wives, widows, children, husbands, and widowers.* — Certain dependents and survivors of insured workers would also benefit by provisions included in the bill which (1) authorize benefits on the basis of certain invalid ceremonial marriages contracted in good faith; (2) reduce from 3 years to 1 year the period required for marriage for a wife, husband, or stepchild of a retired or disabled worker to qualify for benefits; and (3) assure continuation of a child's right to a benefit based on the wage record of his father, which is now voided if a stepfather was supporting him at the time his father died or retired.

4. Increased coverage

The coverage of the program would be extended to about 300,000 additional people — self-employed physicians, domestic workers earning at least $25 but not as much as $50 in a calendar quarter from a single employer, parents who work for their sons and daughters in a trade or business, workers in Guam and American Samoa, American citizens employed in the United States by foreign governments and international organizations, and certain policemen and firemen under retirement systems in Virginia.

Another opportunity would be provided for an estimated 60,000 ministers to be covered under the program. If the States take advantage of the opportunity offered them, nearly 2½ million employees of State and local governments could obtain coverage for certain past years on a retroactive basis. Other provisions would facilitate coverage for some of the noncovered people employed in positions covered by State or local retirement systems and for the 100,000 noncovered employees of certain nonprofit organizations.

5. Investment of the trust funds

The bill would make certain changes in the investment provisions relating to the Federal Old-Age and Survivors Insurance Trust Fund and Federal Disability Insurance Trust Fund so as to make interest earnings on the Government obligations held by the trust funds more nearly equivalent to the rate of return being received by people who buy Government obligations in the open market.

These changes would make for more equitable treatment of the trust funds and are generally in line with the recommendations of the Advisory Council on Social Security Financing.

6. Technical and minor substantive changes

The bill would provide a number of amendments of a technical nature. These provisions will correct several technical flaws in the law, make for more equitable treatment of people, and simplify and improve the operation of the program.

7. Financing of the bill and actuarial status of the trust funds

These improvements provided under your committee's bill in the old-age, survivors, and disability insurance program will not necessitate an increase in social security taxes to keep the program actuarially sound. Both trust funds will remain in approximate actuarial balance.

* * *

D. The Unemployment Compensation Program

Your committee's bill contains provisions to improve and extend the existing Federal-State program of employment security.

Title V (1) raises the net Federal unemployment tax (the tax that may not be offset by a credit for taxes paid under a State program) from three-tenths to four-tenths of 1 percent on the first $3,000 of covered wages; (2) provides that the proceeds of this higher Federal tax after covering the administrative expenses of the employment security program will be available to build up a larger fund for advances to States whose reserves have been depleted; (3) makes additional improvements in the arrangements for administrative financing; and (4) improves the operation of the Federal unemployment account by tightening the conditions pertaining to eligibility for and repayment of advances.

Title V also extends the coverage of the unemployment compensation programs to several groups not presently covered. It is estimated that from 60,000 to 70,000 additional employees would be brought under the unemployment compensation system by this extension.

Title V, in addition, provides that Puerto Rico will be treated as a State for the purposes of the unemployment compensation program.

Five Republican menbers of the committee filed sharp dissents.

After adopting a closed rule prohibiting floor amendments, Representative Mills of Arkansas, sponsor of the bill, opened the House debate. His address indicated that a desire for actuarial soundness shaped the bill, although there was some compromise on how to achieve it.

The medical provisions of H.R. 12580 were attacked both by fiscal purists and proponents of other means of medical care. Representative Mason, of Illinois for example, opposed the medical care section (Title XVI), both in the committee and during the debate, but admitted that the proposal was superior to any of the other proposals presented to the committee. Representative Forand whose own comprehensive health care proposals had been rejected by the Ways and Means Committee, said he would vote for H.R. 12580 because the health provisions would do no harm to the aged, but no good either. He called the bill a sham. The House overwhelmingly passed H.R. 12580 on June 23.

While the House Ways and Means Committee had been holding executive sessions on the omnibus social security proposals, the Senate Subcommittee on the Problems of the Aged and Aging conducted public hearings. According to the report issued by the subcommittee in January, 1960 the main problem confronting the elderly in the United States was inadequate medical care. After recommending that the problem of medical care be given priority congressional attention, the subcommittee held its own hearings in April. Included in the record of the hearings was a statement by Walter Reuther calling for comprehensive legislative action on health care for the aged. On the other hand, an American Medical Association spokesman, Dr. James Z. Appel, opposed any Forand-type health insurance legislation and recounted the AMA's own efforts to improve the health of the elderly.

Another key witness to testify before the Senate subcommittee was Representative Forand who defended his own controversial proposal on the grounds that it would be financially self-sustaining and relatively inexpensive. He also criticized the delaying tactics of the Administration and the opposition of organized medicine.

Three weeks after the Senate subcommittee hearings ended, Chairman McNamara introduced a comprehensive bill (S. 3503) providing medical care for the aged through the social security system. There were fifteen Democratic co-sponsors, including Senator Kennedy, who had earlier introduced the Forand Bill in the Senate. Although this bill was not as broad as the earlier legislation it relied on the basic social security system and would have covered 1.7 million old-age assistance recipients who were not under OASDI.

After passage in the House the Kerr-Mills Bill went to the Senate where it was immediately assigned to the Finance Committee. Secretary Flemming opened the hearings which began the next week. He urged adoption of the Administration proposal rather than the House bill which was designed to supplement the health care provisions of H.R. 12580 (Kerr-Mills), not replace them. The Secretary also explained that his statements were in full accord with the position of President Eisenhower and the entire executive branch. Senator Leverett Saltonstall of Massachusetts soon formally introduced the Administration bill (S. 3784). Meanwhile, Senator McNamara who had presented his comprehensive medical care proposal (S. 3504) to the Senate on May 6, appeared before the Finance Committee to explain it. He urged that this be made an amendment to H.R. 12580.

While the Senate Finance Committee was holding hearings, the committee received a telegram from the governors attending the fifty-second annual Governor's Conference. By a vote of 30 to 13, the governors had adopted a resolution urging the establishment of a medical care program for the aged, financed and operated under the basic OASDI system. The political tempo for change was clearly accelerating.

Witnesses who had testified before the Ways and Means Committee returned to offer the same arguments to the Finance Committee. Among them was the newly elected president of the American Medical Association. In the tradition of that organization, he testified against any medical care proposals, but noted that if legislation were enacted the AMA preferred Title VI of H.R. 12580.

Mr. Nelson Cruikshank, of the AFL-CIO, testified on behalf of H.R. 12580, but he also urged that several changes be made, such as the addition of medical care for the aged under the basic OASDI system.

On June 30, the last day of public hearings before the Finance Committee, Senator Clinton Anderson of New Mexico offered a new social security medical plan. More moderate than the earlier Forand, Kennedy, and McNamara bills, it still used social security to finance the benefits. Co-sponsoring the Anderson plan were Senators Humphrey and McCarthy, both Minnesota Democrats. The amendment was a compromise measure by backers of a comprehensive medical care program under social security and stimulated the most heated debate during the executive sessions of the Finance Committee.

The proponents of the Anderson plan argued that it was actuarily sound since revenues derived from the amendment's tax increases covered the cost of the greater benefits. Therefore, one of the main sources of controversy over the Forand-Kennedy Bill was eliminated. The Anderson plan would also have reduced considerably the price of the program by eliminating or lowering some of the benefits provided in the earlier bills.

Congress recessed in July for the national party conventions after agreeing to reconvene in August to complete congressional action on many pending bills.

The Democrats met in Los Angeles the second week of July and nominated Senator John Kennedy as their presidential candiate and Senator Lyndon Johnson as their vice-presidential candidate. Since Kennedy was one of the Democratic leaders in the fight for a medical care plan, and Johnson was the majority leader in the Senate, the ticket insured a strong push for adoption of one of the medical care OASDI programs when Congress reconvened.

In order to reinforce their candidates' positions on social security and medical care for the aged, the Democratic Convention adopted strong planks in its party platform favoring health and welfare programs for the aged and aging. In particular, it criticized the "means" test for medical care in the Administration proposal and stressed instead the right to adequate medical care.

The Republican platform called for improved public assistance through abolition of the categories of aid and of the minimum age for disability insurance. Presidential candidate Richard Nixon split with his fellow Republicans on medical care, and therefore the Republican platform included only a general statement favoring medical care for the aged, without specifically supporting one particular plan. However, the plank emphasized medical benefits only for the aged who "needed" such financial assistance and thus supported inclusion of a means test in any health care plan.

When Congress reconvened in August, the Senate Finance Committee issued its report and the bill went to the full Senate. The committee had rejected the Anderson and McNamara proposals by identical votes of 12 to 5, but still the committee bill was more liberal than the House version and called for a federal-state medical care program. Basically the Federal Government's share in the matching grants plan was increased with the poorer southern states (whose senatorial votes were needed to defeat the Forand-Kennedy Bill) benefiting the most. The Kerr-Mills compromise legislation was taking shape.

In addition to the medical care revisions, the Finance Committee also made other changes in H.R. 12580. The committee again excluded physicians from the basic OASDI system and deleted several other groups included in the extended coverage in the House bill. In addition, the committee increased from $1200 to $1800 the amount a beneficiary could earn

each year without having benefits reduced and allowed men to retire at
sixty-two with reduced benefits.

Social Security Amendments of 1960
Senate Report No. 994
87th Cong., 1st Sess.
(August 15, 1960)

The Committee on Finance, to whom was referred the bill (H.R. 12580)
to extend and improve coverage under the Federal old-age, survivors, and
disability insurance system and to remove hardships, and inequities, improve the financing of the trust funds, and provide disability benefits to
additional individuals under such system; to provide grants to States for
medical care for aged individuals of low income; to amend the public assistance and maternal and child welfare provisions of the Social Security Act;
to improve the unemployment compensation provisions of such act; and
for other purposes, having considered the same, report favorably thereon
with amendments and recommend that the bill do pass.

I. SCOPE OF THE BILL

In this 25th anniversary year of the Social Security Act, the committee
has examined proposals relating to almost every title of the Social Security
Act. As a result of our consideration, the committee is reporting a bill which
makes changes and improvements in all of the programs encompassed by
this legislation.

The major issue presented to the committee this year has been the increasing cost of adequate medical care for older people. The evidence
presented to the committee indicated that these costs derive, to a large
extent, from the fact that impressive improvements have been made in
medicines and medical technology, which assist in better diagnosis and
treatment, and from improved hospital and other facilities and their wider
availability to the public. The knowledge that these costs are unpredictable,
and sometimes very heavy, especially for our older men and women living
on reduced retirement incomes, has been a matter of grave concern to this
committee.

As a result, we are recommending a program of Federal assistance in
providing, through the cooperation of the States, an expanded program of
medical care for persons aged 65 and over. Under this proposal the Federal
share of existing old-age assistance plans will be substantially increased to
encourage States to strengthen their medical programs for these people or
to initiate new programs. In addition, Federal money will be made available,
on a generous matching formula, to assist the States in aiding those aged

persons, many of them otherwise self-sufficient, who need help only in meeting the costs of medical care of a very expensive nature.

II. PRINCIPAL PROVISIONS OF THE BILL ON MEDICAL SERVICES FOR THE AGED

The amendment of the Committee on Finance is an improvement on the bill passed by the House of Representatives for a number of reasons. First, it can be made effective on October 1, 1960, whereas the effective date of the House bill is July 1, 1961. Second, the committee plan strengthens the House bill by adding an additional $130 million in Federal money for the medical vendor payments, in the form of more favorable Federal matching, to act as an incentive to the initiation or fuller development of State medical programs for the aged. Finally, the reported bill is a simplification and streamlining of the House bill, which will greatly facilitate its administration.

In summary, the bill as reported by the committee represents a realistic and workable plan. States can take advantage of its provisions in part or whole almost immediately upon enactment. The financial incentive in the plan should enable every State to improve and extend medical services to aged persons.

The Committee on Finance has made three basic changes in the existing old-age assistance provisions (title I) of the Social Security Act to encourage the States to improve and extend medical services to the aged:

(a) Increases Federal funds to the States for medical services for the 2.4 million aged persons on old-age assistance:

(b) Authorizes Federal grants to the States for payment of part or all of the medical services of a group of persons totaling about 10 million who may, at one time or another, be in need of assistance in paying their medical expenses;

(c) Instructs the Secretary of Health, Education, and Welfare to develop guides or recommended standards for the use of the States in evaluating and improving their programs of medical services for the aged.

The committee has given careful consideration to the subject of medical care for the aged. This has included review of the testimony presented in the extensive public hearings held by the House Committee on Ways and Means and the additional hearings by the Committee on Finance on the House bill and certain other health care proposals which have been advanced. As a result, the committee is cognizant of many problems which exist in this area. The committee is also cognizant of difficulties attendant upon various approaches which have been advanced.

Your committee has designed a Federal-State matching program based upon historic principles of Federal-State cooperation. This program is established under title I of the Social Security Act, thereby providing additional matching funds to the States to (1) establish a new or improve their existing medical care program for those on the old-age assistance rolls, and (2) add a new program designed to furnish medical assistance to those needy elderly citizens who are not eligible for old-age assistance but who are financially unable to pay for the medical and hospital care needed to preserve their health and prolong their life. This twofold plan would thus cover all medically needy aged 65 or over, whether or not they are eligible for old-age assistance, or whether or not they are eligible for the benefits under the social security or any other retirement program. It accomplishes this objective within the framework of a Federal-State program with broad discrimination allowed to the States as to the programs they will institute, improve, and administer in meeting the health needs of the aged when illness occurs or continues.

A. Medical Care for the Aged Receiving Old-Age Assistance

1. Purpose

The existing provisions of title I provide Federal funds to the States for medical services to aged individuals who are determined to be needy by the States. At the present time, States provide needy aged persons with "money payments" for medical services and also provide "vendor payments" to the suppliers of medical care (for instance, doctors, hospitals, and nurses). These provisions vary greatly. Some States have relatively adequate provisions for the medical care of needy aged persons; others have little or no provision. The increased Federal financial provisions in the bill are designed to encourage the States to extend comprehensive medical services to all needy persons receiving monthly assistance payments. Participation in the Federal-State program is completely optional with the States, with each State determining the extent and character of its own program, including the standards of eligibility and the nature and scope of benefits. The limits of Federal financial participation are discussed later in this report.

2. Effect of bill

At the present time, the Federal Government makes available to the States funds for medical services to needy aged persons. Federal financial participation is limited to a stated statutory proportion of average assistance expenditures up to $65 per month.

To encourage all States to develop a comprehensive medical care program, additional Federal funds would be available to the States, effective October 1, 1960, as follows: A provision is added to the existing law to provide for Federal financial participation in expenditures to vendors for medical services of up to $12 per month in addition to the existing $65 maximum provision. Where the State average payment is over $65 per month, the Federal share in respect to such medical-services costs would be a minimum of 50 percent and a maximum of 80 percent depending upon each State's per capita income. Where the State average payment is $65 a month or under, the Federal share, in respect to such medical-services costs, would be 15 percentage points in addition to the existing Federal percentage points (50 to 65 percent); thus, for these States the Federal percent applicable to such medical-services costs would range from 65 to 80 percent.

A State with an average payment of over $65 a month would never receive less in additional Federal funds in respect to such medical-services costs than if it had an average payment of $65. For example, if a State has an average payment of $67, including an average of $10 in such medical-services costs, and has a Federal medical percentage of 70 percent, it will receive an additional Federal payment per recipient of old-age assistance (over present law) of the larger of (a) 15 percent of $10, or $1.50, or (b) 70 percent of $2 (i.e., the excess of the average payment over $65), or $1.40.

As to Puerto Rico, Guam, and the Virgin Islands, their additional matching for vendor medical expenditures will be on up to an additional $6 a month per recipient rather than the additional $12 a month for the States and the District of Columbia. This was done because their matching maximum for old-age assistance is an average of $35 a month per recipient in contrast to $65 for the States. Under existing law there are also dollar maximums applicable to Guam, Puerto Rico, and the Virgin Islands for the public assistance programs, these are increased proportionately on condition that the additional increases are used for vendor medical expenditures under the old-age assistance.

The payments under this program would be made directly to providers of medical services.

3. Eligibility

Each State has the responsibility of determining the standard of eligibility for the medical care it provides aged persons. For aged persons receiving money payments the State must take into consideration any income and resources of the individual.

4. Scope of medical services

There is no Federal limitation on medical services provided under the bill. Each State may determine for itself the scope of medical services to be provided in its program.

5. Federal matching

The bill provides for an increase in Federal funds for medical services. The formula, as outlined above, would result in Federal funds in addition to those presently provided. Additional Federal funds may be obtained only for medical services, within the $12 per recipient maximum for payments, made directly to providers of the medical services. States have the option of transferring part or all of the money payments now made for medical services to vendor payments. The bill would give the States a financial incentive to establish such programs where they do not exist or to extend such programs where they are not adequate in coverage or comprehensive in the scope of benefits.

Under the provisions of the committee bill, a State desiring to establish a program for assisting low income individuals in meeting their medical expenses would submit an amendment of its old-age assistance plan which, if found by the Secretary of Health, Education, and Welfare to fulfill the requirements specified in this title, would be approved for Federal matching. A number of the plan requirements are substantially the same as those in the present public assistance titles. Other plan requirements are directed specifically to accomplishing the purposes of the new title, to assist aged persons who are able to meet their expenses other than their medical needs.

A State would have broad latitude in determining eligibility for benefits . . . as well as the scope and nature of the services to be provided. . . . Each State would determine the tests for eligibility and the medical services to be provided under the State program within the limitations described below. Federal financial participation would be governed by the establishment of an approved plan subject to the criteria and limitations prescribed in the law.   *   *   *

2. Eligibility

Benefits under a State program may be provided only for persons 65 years of age or over to the extent they are unable to pay the cost of their medical expenses. Under this program, it will be possible for States to provide medical services to individuals on the basis of an eligibility requirement that is more liberal than that in effect for the States' old-age assistance programs.

Section 1 of the Social Security Act, as it would be amended by the bill, provides that one of the objectives of the title is to furnish medical assistance to individuals who are not recipients of old-age assistance but whose income and resources are insufficient to meet the costs of necessary medical services.

It would cover all medically needy aged 65 or over; it would cover every such person including those under the social security system, railroad retirement system, civil service system, or any other public or private retirement system whether such person is retired or still working, subject only to the participation in the program by the State of which they are resident; it would cover the widows of such workers as well as their dependents who meet the age 65 requirement and are unable to provide for their medical care. There are many individuals who have not worked under the social security program or any other retirement program for a sufficient time to ever become eligible for retirement benefits; this is another needy group which would be able to receive medical assistance under the health plan endorsed by the Finance Committee.

A State may, if it wishes, disregard in whole or part, the existence of any income or resources, of an individual for medical assistance. An individual who applies for medical assistance may be deemed eligible by the State notwithstanding the fact he has a child who may be financially able to pay all or part of his care, or that he owns or has an equity in a homestead, or that he has some life insurance with a cash value, or that he is receiving an old-age insurance benefit, annuity, or retirement benefit. The State has wide latitude to establish the standard of need for medical assistance as long as it is a reasonable standard consistent with the objectives of the title. In establishing such standard a State must comply with all other applicable provisions of section 2 of the Social Security Act, as it would be amended by the bill.

This is based on the grounds that an aged individual who has adjusted his living standard to a low income, but who still has income and resources above the level applicable for old-age assistance, might be unable to deal with his medical expenses. The committee intends that States should set reasonable outer limits on the resources an individual may hold and still be found eligible for medical services. Individuals who are recipients of old-age assistance in any month would not be eligible for participation in the medical assistance program in that month.

3. Scope of benefits

The scope of medical benefits and services provided will be determined by the States. The Federal Government, however, will participate under the matching formula in any program which provides any or all of the following services, provided both institutional and noninstitutional services are available:

(1) Inpatient hospital services;
(2) Skilled nursing-home services;
(3) Physicians' services;
(4) Outpatient hospital services;
(5) Home health care services;
(6) Private duty nursing services;
(7) Physical therapy and related services;
(8) Dental services;
(9) Laboratory and X-ray services;
(10) Prescribed drugs, eye glasses, dentures, and prosthetic devices;
(11) Diagnostic, screening, and preventive services; and
(12) Any other medical care or remedial care recognized under State law.

The Federal Government will not participate as to services rendered in mental and tuberculosis hospitals.

The description of the care, services, and supplies provided with Federal financial participation which may be provided for recipients of medical assistance for the aged is intended to be as broad in scope as the medical and other remedial care which may be provided as old-age assistance under title I of the existing law with Federal financial participation. The various types of care and services have been enumerated primarily for informational purposes. Accordingly, a State may, if it wishes, include medical services provided by osteopaths, chiropractors, and optometrists and remedial services provided by Christian Science practitioners.

4. Federal matching

The Federal Government will share with the States in the cost of the new medical assistance program in accordance with the matching formula prescribed by the bill. The Federal share of the cost will be determined in the same general manner as now provided for the portion of the old-age assistance payments between $30 and $65 per month; that is, the Federal share will depend upon the per capita income of the State as related to the national average, but with a range from 50 to 80 percent. For Puerto Rico, Guam, and the Virgin Islands the matching will be on a 50–50 basis. There is no maximum upon the dollar amount of Federal participation in the new program. Appropriation requirements, therefore, would depend upon the programs developed by the States. Thus, the total cost would depend upon the scope of services offered and the number of persons found eligible by the States under the respective State plans.

The Federal Government will participate in the cost of administering these programs on a dollar-for-dollar basis, as is now true in the case of the four public assistance programs.

The committee, in recognition of the fact that some States could take advantage of the Federal funds for this program very quickly, has set the effective date for the new program as October 1, 1960.

5. Plan requirements

Although the requirements for the approval of the medical assistance for the aged in the State plan are generally comparable to those in the public assistance titles of the Social Security Act, the committee concluded that some changes are needed to carry out the intent of the new part of the program.

A State would not be permitted as a condition for medical assistance to impose a lien on the property of a recipient during his lifetime. An enrollment fee for recipients would not be permitted. However, the bill would permit the recovery from an individual's estate after the death of his spouse if one survives him. This provision was inserted in order to protect the individual and his spouse from the loss of their property, usually the home, during their lifetime.

The committee concluded also that in order to meet the practicalities of providing an effective medical benefit program for this low income group, a State should not be permitted to have as an eligibility requirement a durational residence requirement which excludes any individual who resides in the State. A State plan must also provide for inclusion, to the extent required by regulation prescribed by the Secretary of Health, Education, and Welfare, of provisions with respect to the furnishing of care to individuals who are residents of the State but are absent therefrom. It is the intent of the committee that the Secretary will promulgate regulations governing the provision of such assistance to residents outside of their States of residence in a reasonable manner with due regard to the traditional rights of the States under the public assistance programs to determine the scope of the medical care provided.

C. Medical Guides and Recommendations

As recommended by the Advisory Council on Public Assistance, appointed pursuant to the Social Security Amendments of 1958, the bill instructs the Secretary of Health, Education, and Welfare to develop guides or recommended standards for the information of the States as to the level, content, and quality of medical care for the public assistance medical programs. He would also prepare such guides and standards for use in the new programs of medical assistance for the medically needy aged.

D. Numbers of Persons Affected and Costs

Under the revised title I, State plans (with Federal matching funds) could provide potential protection under the new program of medical assistance for the aged to as many as 10 million persons aged 65 and over whose financial resources are such that, if they have sizable medical expenses, they will qualify. These 10 million persons would include the vast majority of the 12 million individuals aged 65 and over who are receiving old-age and survivors insurance benefits—as well as other aged persons, too. Each year, after all State plans are in full operation, an estimated one-half to 1 million persons among these 10 million may become ill and require medical services that will result in payments under this title. In the first year after enactment of the bill, when relatively few States will probably have had an opportunity to develop comprehensive plans (although it is expected that all States now not having comprehensive medical programs for their old-age assistance recipients will adopt or extend such programs) an estimated additional $60 million in Federal funds would be expended for medical assistance for the aged. In addition, increased Federal funds for matching vendor medical-care payments in respect to the 2.4 million old-age assistance recipients are estimated at about $140 million. Thus, under both programs combined, the cost would total about $200 million.

With respect to costs after the new programs have been in effect for several years, it must be considered that the old-age assistance roll is decreasing slowly, but that States with no vendor medical payments now (or with small payments of this type) will probably develop quite comprehensive medical-care programs for the old-age assistance recipients. The increased Federal funds for matching the vendor medical-care payments of old-age assistance recipients are estimated at about $175 million annually in the long run. In addition, an estimated $165 million in Federal funds for medical services for the aged may be provided in a full year of operation after the States have had opportunity to develop these programs (and this figure could even be somewhat higher if all States had relatively well developed and comprehensive plans). Thus, under both programs combined, the annual cost would total about $330 million.

III. SUMMARY OF OTHER PROVISIONS OF THE BILL

A. The Old-Age, Survivors, and Disability Insurance (OASDI) Provisions

1. The disability insurance program

(a) Removal of age 50 eligibility requirement. — An estimated 250,000 people — disabled insured workers under age 50 and their dependents — would qualify for benefits for the second month following the month of enactment of the bill through removal of the age 50 qualification for benefits in present law.

(b) Trial work period. — The bill would strengthen the rehabilitation aspects of the disability program by providing a 12-month period of trial work, during which benefits are continued for all disabled workers who attempt to return to work, rather than limiting this trial work period to those under the formal Federal-State vocational rehabilitation plan, as in existing law.

(c) Waiting period. — The bill would provide that the disabled worker who regains his ability to work and then within 5 years again becomes disabled will not be required to wait through a second 6-month waiting period before his benefits will be resumed, as is now required.

2. Retirement test (earnings limitation)

The committee's bill would liberalize the retirement test (earnings limitation) to allow annual earnings of $1,800 per year without loss of benefits. Under existing law a beneficiary under age 72 will lose 1 month's benefits for every $80 (or fraction thereof) by which his annual earnings exceed $1,200. Under the committee's bill a beneficiary would lose 1 month's benefits for every $80 (or fraction thereof) by which his annual earnings exceed $1,800. There would be no change in the provision of existing law which guarantees that no benefits will be lost for any month in which a beneficiary earns $100 or less and does not render substantial services in self-employment. The House bill would have made no change in the earnings limitation of present law.

3. Reduction of retirement age for men to 62

Under the bill as reported by the Committee on Finance, men workers and dependent husbands would be entitled to elect to retire at age 62, with actuarially reduced benefits, in the same way that women workers and wives can now make such an election. Likewise, dependent widowers and dependent fathers of deceased workers would qualify for full benefits at age 62 in the same manner as widows and dependent mothers of deceased workers now can qualify. Approximately 1.8 million men would be eligible to elect to retire immediately and receive these benefits.

4. Insured status requirement

The committee's bill deletes the provision of the House bill which would liberalize the fully insured status requirement by making eligible for benefits persons who have one quarter of coverage for every four calendar quarters elapsing after 1950 (or age 21), and before age 62 or, if earlier, disability or death. Present law requires one quarter of coverage for each two quarters so elapsing. The House provision would enable a rather substantial number of people to qualify for benefits on the basis of a very limited record in covered work, and a relatively small contribution to the system. The liberalization would also have caused a large drain on the trust fund, particularly within the next few years.

5. Improved benefit protection for dependents and survivors of insured workers —wives, widows, children, husbands, and widowers

The committee's bill, like the House bill, would increase the benefits payable to children in certain cases and would provide benefits for certain wives, widows, widowers, and children of insured workers who are not now eligible for benefits. Other than as noted below, these changes would be effective for benefits for the month following the month of enactment.

(a) Survivors of workers who died before 1940. — Survivors of workers who died before 1940, and who had at least six quarters of coverage, would qualify for benefit payments. About 25,000 people, most of them widows aged 75 or over, would be made eligible for benefits for the first time by this change.

(b) Increase in children's benefits. — The benefits payable to the children of deceased workers, which now can be somewhat less than 75 percent of the worker's benefit depending on the number of children in the family, would be made 75 percent for all children, subject to the family maximum of $254 a month, or 80 percent of the worker's average monthly wage if less. About 400,000 children would get some increase in benefits as a result

of this change, effective for benefits for the third month after the month of enactment.

(c) Other changes affecting wives, widows, children, husbands, and widowers. — Certain dependents and survivors of insured workers would also benefit by provisions included in the bill which (effective with the month of enactment) (1) authorize benefits on the basis of certain invalid ceremonial marriages contracted in good faith; and (2) assure continuation of a child's right to a benefit based on the wage record of his father, which is now voided if a stepfather was living with and supporting him at the time his father died, or, in a retirement or disability case, at the time when the child applied for benefit.

The House provision reducing from 3 years to 1 year the period required for marriage for a wife, husband, or stepchild of a retired or disabled worker to qualify for benefits was deleted, however, because there was insufficient evidence that the 3-year provision is not necessary to prevent payments to persons who marry for the primary purpose of qualifying for benefits.

6. Increased coverage

Another opportunity would be provided for an estimated 60,000 ministers to be covered under the program, in the same manner as is provided in the House bill. In addition, if the States take advantage of the opportunity offered them, nearly 2½ million employees of State and local governments could obtain coverage for certain past years on a retroactive basis. The provision of the House bill covering American citizens employed in the United States by foreign governments was also approved, as was the House provision making possible the coverage of certain policemen and firemen under retirement systems in Virginia. Other approved provisions would facilitate coverage for some of the noncovered people employed in positions covered by State or local retirement systems, and for the 100,000 non-covered employees of certain nonprofit organizations.

The provision in the House bill extending coverage to physicians has been deleted because of lack of definitive information on whether a majority of doctors wish to come under the program. The coverage of domestic and casual workers who earn between $25 and $50 a quarter from one employer, as provided in the House bill, was eliminated, together with the coverage of parents who work for their sons or daughters. In both of these instances it was not clear that the administrative problems which constituted the reasons for these exclusions had been completely eliminated. Also eliminated from the House bill were the extensions of coverage to American Samoa and Guam, to Americans employed in the United States by international organizations, and to certain American employees of labor organizations in the Panama Canal Zone. The committee believes that further examination and hearings should be undertaken before coverages should be extended to these groups of workers.

7. Investment of the trust funds

The bill would make certain changes in the investment provisions relating to the Federal Old-Age and Survivors Insurance Trust Fund and Federal Disability Insurance Trust Fund so as to make interest earnings on the Government obligations held by the trust funds more nearly equivalent to the rate of return being received by people who buy Government obligations in the open market.

These changes, which were made in the House bill, would make for more equitable treatment of the trust funds and are generally in line with the recommendations of the Advisory Council on Social Security Financing.

8. Technical and minor substantive changes

The bill would provide a number of amendments of a technical nature. These provisions will correct several technical flaws in the law, make for more equitable treatment of people, and simplify and improve the operation of the program.

B. Aid to the Blind Program of Public Assistance

The committee's bill liberalizes the exemption of earned income allowed for people receiving aid to the blind under State programs (now $50 per month) so that earnings of $1,000 per year, plus one-half of additional earnings, would be exempted under these plans. This provision is not in the House bill. The committee's bill, like that of the House, would extend to June 30, 1964 (now expires June 30, 1961), the temporary legislation which relates to the approval by the Secretary of Health, Education, and Welfare of certain State plans for aid to the blind which do not meet in full certain Federal requirements relating to the "needs" test.

C. The Maternal and Child Welfare Programs

*   *   *

D. The Unemployment Compensation Program

The committee's bill makes two changes affecting the so-called George-Reed loan fund which is used to make advances to States with depleted reserve accounts:

(1) The maximum amount authorized in the loan fund from Federal unemployment tax revenues is increased from $200 million to $500 million;

(2) More realistic eligibility requirements for States applying for advances are provided and also increases in the rate of repayment of advances.

The committee deleted the provisions contained in the House bill raising the Federal unemployment tax, establishing a new procedure for financing administrative expenses, extending coverage to several groups of workers, and including Puerto Rico in the unemployment compensation program.

The Finance Committee's report also included the minority views of five Democratic Senators; Anderson, Douglas, Gore, McCarthy, and Hartke. They stated their opposition to both the committee bill and the Administration's proposals and revealed their intention of offering the Anderson Bill as an amendment to H.R. 12580 when it was presented to the Senate for debate.

Two days before the report was actually issued, Senator Anderson offered his plan on the floor of the Senate, acting on behalf of himself, Senator Kennedy, and eight other Senators. On the same day, President Eisenhower stated at a news conference that he was opposed to "compulsory medicine," a clear reference to the threat of the Anderson Amendment to H.R. 12580 and an indication that adoption of an OASDI-based medical care program for the aged would end with a White House veto. (This threat of veto was one argument used on the Senate floor by opponents of the Anderson-Kennedy plan.)

Senator Byrd of Virginia, chairman of the Finance Committee, opened the floor debate on H.R. 12580 with an explanation of the committee's action and a summary of the bill's main provisions. The debate immediately polarized around the Anderson Amendment.

Congressional Debates
106 Congressional Record, p. 16916 *et seq.*
(August 20, 1960)

Mr. Byrd . . .

First, the amendment is offered as an addition to the bill reported by the Finance Committee. It is not a substitute for the Finance Committee bill or for any of its provisions. This amendment establishes a fully financed social insurance program on a contributory basis to cover the cost of certain types of health services for more than 9 million aged persons who are receiving OASDI benefits. This amendment plus the amendments reported by the Finance Committee would provide help to all of the aged — those who are under social security and those who are not.

Persons Eligible

Under this amendment all persons who have attained the age of 68 and who are entitled to receive old-age, survivors, or disability insurance benefits under the existing social security program would be eligible to receive lifetime protection without any means or income test against the cost of certain types of health services. There are now about 9,185,000 persons who are 68 years old and over, and who are receiving social security benefits. I ask unanimous consent to have printed at this point in the *Record*, a table prepared by the Actuarial Branch of the Bureau of Old-Age and Survivors Insurance which gives a State-by-State breakdown of these 9,185,000 aged persons.

*   *   *

Scope of Benefits

Mr. President, the cost of four essential types of health benefits would, subject to certain limits, be provided. These are:

First. Hospital inpatient services. The cost of inpatient hospital services for up to 120 days in a year in excess of the first $75 would be provided. This first $75 would have to be paid by the individual in each benefit year.

Inhospital services which are covered would include bed and board in the hospital in semiprivate accommodations and those ancillary services, such as laboratory, drugs, supplies, and nursing services, as are generally furnished to inpatients in a hospital.

Second. Skilled nursing home services: Skilled nursing home recuperative care for up to 240 days in a benefit year would be covered. The definition of "skilled nursing home services" is, however, quite limited. It is restricted to those services which are furnished in a nursing facility, after the individual has been transferred to such facility from a hospital and a physician has certified that such nursing home care is required in connection with the condition for which he was hospitalized. This limited definition is essential in order to keep costs within proper limits and to assure that the program will not merely pay for custodial care of aged individuals.

Third. Home health services: Nursing and other home health services are provided in an individual's home for up to 360 visits within a benefit year. These services, which would include both professional nursing care, practical nursing care, and specified homemaker's services, would have to be provided through a public or nonprofit agency.

The Blue Cross has issued a booklet entitled "Cost of Hospital Care in Indiana, 1956," which reached my office this morning. It deals with problems which have arisen. I think it interesting that on page 35 of the booklet it is pointed out that "this impact of the cost of health care takes on added significance when one realizes that fewer than 40 percent of those over 65 are now covered by some form of hospitalization insurance."

In other words, this writer of group insurance points out that despite the best it can do, there still are some gaps in that program. A more recent study might reveal slightly different figures.

While I indicated that inpatient hospital services would be provided for up to 120 days, skilled nursing home recuperative care for up to 240 days, and home health services for up to 365 visits, there is an overall ceiling on those benefits. Under the amendment, only 180 units of services are available to any individual within a single year. A unit of service is equal to 1 day of inpatient hospital care, 2 days of skilled nursing home care or three home health visits. This provision is intended to control the amount of services furnished to any individual and to encourage the use of facilities less expensive than the hospital. For example, if an individual received 120 days of hospital care, he would have only 60 units of service remaining. Those 60 units would entitle him to only 120 days of skilled nursing home care, or 180 home health visits, or a combination of the two. For each day less than the 120 days he remained in the hospital, however, he would be entitled to 2 additional days in a nursing home or three additional visits by a home health agency.

Fourth. Outpatient diagnostic hospital services: Outpatient hospital diagnostic services, such as diagnostic X-ray and laboratory services, are covered by this amendment. The inclusion of the cost of these services will be a great benefit to all individuals in encouraging the early diagnosis of an illness.

Payment for these services furnished to eligible individuals will be made only if such services are furnished after a physician has certified in writing that such hospital, nursing home, home health, or outpatient diagnostic services are necessary. Continued recertification by the physician may be required by the Secretary of Health, Education, and Welfare after the individual has been in the hospital or other institutions or has been receiving the home health services for an extended period of time. The amendment also provides that in the case of an individual who is in the hospital for a continuous period in excess of 30 days, the need for continued hospitalization shall be reviewed by a hospital committee that includes two or more physicians.

On August 22 Senator Jacob Javits of New York offered a revised edition of his original medical care proposal as a substitute for the pending Anderson Amendment. Senator Javits stated that his amendment, a compromise between his first plan and the Administration's program as introduced by Senator Saltonstall, had tacit Administration approval. It offered a wider range of benefits and deleted the deductible feature, but retained the required enrollment fee. It was similar to the Kerr plan embodied in the Finance Committee bill, except that under the Kerr formula the poorer states had a better matching ratio. In addition, the Javits plan specified a uniform range of benefits whereas the Kerr Bill left that determination to the individual states. Senator Javits urged adoption of his amendment on the grounds that any bill providing medical care for the aged under the OASDI system would be vetoed by President Eisenhower. His bill, while it went further than the Administration's plan, met the four basic criteria of that proposal and would thus receive presidential approval.

Senator Kerr addressed himself to both the bill and the Anderson Amendment. He claimed that the committee bill did not go far enough, but that political realities prevented any stronger measure in 1960. On August 23, the Senate voted on and rejected both the Anderson and Javits Amendments; They overwhelmingly approved H.R. 12580, virtually as it was reported from the Finance Committee. The only two opposing votes were cast by Senator Barry Goldwater of Arizona and Senator Strom Thurmond of South Carolina.

Because of the differences between the House and Senate versions of H.R. 12580, a Conference Committee was appointed. Eventually, Senator Edward Long's amendment, including tuberculosis and mental patients within the medical care program, was dropped, as were the optional retirement at age sixty-two (with reduced benefits) and the Senate amendment increasing the earnings limitation to $1800. The conferees devised a compromise allowing retirees to earn more than $1200 annually, and to receive partial benefits for income over $1200 but less than $1800. The committee dropped the House provision covering physicians under the basic OASDI program. The coverage increase and the new wide disability plan stood as passed.

Senator Russell Long, who sat on the Conference Committee, refused to sign the report and later urged rejection of the report during Senate debate. The Louisiana Democrat argued that the provisions in the bill, other than those for medical care, had been cut back 80 per cent from what they had been and urged that the bill be returned to conference.

However, the House accepted the conference report on August 26 and the Senate followed suit three days later. On September 13, 1960, President Eisenhower signed H.R. 12580 into law.

Social Security Amendments of 1960
(September 13, 1960, 74 Statutes as Large 924)

Fully Insured Status Sec. 204. (a) Section 214 (a) of the Social Security Act is amended to read as follows:

"Fully Insured Individual

"(a) The term 'fully insured individual' means any individual who had not less than—
   "(1) one quarter of coverage (whenever acquired) for each three of the quarters elapsing—
       "(A) after (i) December 31, 1950, or (ii) if later, December 31 of the year in which he attained the age of twenty-one, and
       "(B) prior to (i) the year in which he died, or (ii) if earlier, the year in which he attained retirement age,
   except that in no case shall an individual be a fully insured individual unless he has at least six quarters of coverage; or
   "(2) forty quarters of coverage; or

"(3) in the case of an individual who died prior to 1951, six quarters of coverage;

not counting as an elapsed quarter for purposes of paragraph (1) any quarter any part of which was included in a period of disability (as defined in section 216(i)) unless such quarter was a quarter of coverage. When the number of elapsed quarters referred to in paragraph (1) is not a multiple of three, such number shall, for purposes of such paragraph, be reduced to the next lower multiple of three."

(b) The primary insurance amount (for purposes of title II of the Social Security Act) of any individual who died after 1939 and prior to 1951 shall be determined as provided in section 215 (a) (2) of such Act.

(c) Section 109 (b) of the Social Security Amendments of 1954 is amended by inserting immediately before the period at the end of such subsection "and in or prior to the month in which the Social Security Amendments of 1960 are enacted".

(d) (1) The amendments made by subsections (a) and (b) of this section shall be applicable (A) in the case of monthly benefits under title II of the Social Security Act for months after the month in which this Act is enacted, on the basis of applications filed in or after such month, (B) in the case of lump-sum death payments under such title with respect to deaths occurring after such month, and (C) in the case of an application for a disability determination with respect to a period of disability (as defined in section 216(i) of the Social Security Act) filed after such month.

(2) For the purposes of determining (A) entitlement to monthly benefits under title II of the Social Security Act for the month in which this Act is enacted and prior months with respect to the wages and self-employment income of an individual and (B) an individual's closing date prior to 1960 under section 215(b) (3) (B) of the Social Security Act, the provisions of section 214(a) of the Social Security Act in effect prior to the date of the enactment of this Act and the provisions of section 109 of the Social Security Amendments of 1954 in effect prior to such date shall apply.

TITLE IV – DISABILITY INSURANCE BENEFITS AND THE DISABILITY FREEZE

ELIMINATION OF REQUIREMENT OF ATTAINMENT OF AGE FIFTY FOR DISABILITY INSURANCE BENEFITS

Sec. 401. (a) Section 223(a) (1) (B) of the Social Security Act is amended by striking out "has attained the age of fifty and".

(b) The last sentence of section 223(c) (3) of such Act is amended by striking out the semicolon and all that follows and inserting in lieu thereof a period.

(c) The amendments made by this section shall apply only with respect to monthly benefits under sections 202 and 223 of the Social Security Act for months after the month following the month in which this Act is enacted which are based on the wages and self-employment income of an individual who did not attain the age of fifty in or prior to the month following the month in which this Act is enacted, but only where applications for such benefits are filed in or after the month in which this Act is enacted.

*   *   *

ELIMINATION OF THE WAITING PERIOD FOR DISABILITY INSURANCE BENEFITS IN CERTAIN CASES

Sec. 402. (a) Section 223(a) (1) of the Social Security Act is amended by striking out "shall be entitled to a disability insurance benefit for each month, beginning with the first month after his waiting period (as defined in subsection (c) (3)) in which he becomes so entitled to such insurance benefits" and inserting in lieu thereof the following: "shall be entitled to a disability insurance benefit (i) for each month beginning with the first month after his waiting period (as defined in subsection (c) (3)) in which he becomes so entitled to such insurance benefits, or (ii) for each month beginning with the first month during all of which he is under a disability and in which he becomes so entitled to such insurance benefits, but only if he was entitled to disability insurance benefits which terminated, or had a period of disability (as defined in section 216(i)) which ceased, within the 60-month period preceding the first month in which he is under such disability,".

(b) Section 223(a) (2) of such Act is amended to read as follows:

"(2) Such individual's disability insurance benefit for any month shall be equal to his primary insurance amount for such month determined under section 215 as though he became entitled to old-age insurance benefits in—

"(A) the first month of his waiting period, or

"(B) in any case in which clause (ii) of paragraph (1) of this subsection is applicable, the first month for which he becomes so entitled to such disability insurance benefits."

(c) The first sentence of section 223(b) of such Act is amended to read as follows: "No application for disability insurance benefits shall be accepted as a valid application for purposes of this section (1) if it is filed more than nine months before the first month for which the applicant becomes entitled to such benefits, or (2) in any case in which clause (ii) of paragraph (1) of subsection (a) is applicable, if it is filed more than six months before the first month for which the applicant becomes entitled to such benefits; and any application filed within such nine months' period or six months' period, as the case may be, shall be deemed to have been filed in such first month."

(d) The second sentence of section 223(b) of such Act is amended by striking out "if he files application therefor" and inserting in lieu thereof "if he is continuously under a disability after such month and until he files application therefor, and he files such application".

(e) (1) The first sentence of section 216(i) (2) of such Act is amended to read as follows: "The term 'period of disability' means a continuous period (beginning and ending as hereinafter provided in this subsection) during which an individual was under a disability (as defined in paragraph (1)), but only if such period is of not less than six full calendar months' duration or such individual was entitled to benefits under section 223 for one or more months in such period."

(2) (A) The fifth sentence of such section 216(i) (2) is amended by inserting ", or, in any case in which clause (ii) of section 223(a) (1) is applicable, more than six months before the first month for which such applicant becomes entitled to benefits under section 223," after "(as determined under this paragraph)".

(B) Such section 216(i) (2) is further amended by adding at the end thereof the following new sentence: "Any application for a disability determination which is filed within such three months' period or six months' period shall be deemed to have been filed on such first day or in such first month, as the case may be."

(f) The amendments made by subsections (a) and (b) shall apply only with respect to benefits under section 223 of the Social Security Act for the month in which this Act is enacted and subsequent months. The amendment made by subsection (c) shall apply only in the case of applications for benefits under such section 223 filed after the seventh month before the month in which this Act is enacted. The amendment made by subsection (d) shall apply only in the case of applications for benefits under such section 223 filed in or after the month in which this Act is enacted. The amendment made by subsection (e) shall apply only in the case of individuals who become entitled to benefits under such section 223 in or after the month in which this Act is enacted.

* * *

TITLE VI – MEDICAL SERVICES FOR THE AGED

AMENDMENTS TO TITLE I OF THE SOCIAL SECURITY ACT

Sec. 601. (a) The heading of title I of the Social Security Act is amended to read as follows:

"TITLE I – GRANTS TO STATES FOR OLD-AGE ASSISTANCE AND MEDICAL ASSISTANCE FOR THE AGED"

(b) Sections 1 and 2 of such Act are amended to read as follows:

"APPROPRIATION

"Section 1. For the purpose (a) of enabling each State as far as practicable under the conditions in such State, to furnish financial assistance to aged

needy individuals and of encouraging each State, as far as practicable under such conditions, to help such individuals attain self-care, and (b) of enabling each State, as far as practicable under the conditions in such State, to furnish medical assistance on behalf of aged individuals who are not recipients of old-age assistance but whose income and resources are insufficient to meet the costs of necessary medical services, there is hereby authorized to be appropriated for each fiscal year a sum sufficient to carry out the purposes of this title. The sums made available under this section shall be used for making payments to States which have submitted, and had approved by the Secretary of Health, Education, and Welfare (hereinafter referred to as the 'Secretary'), State plans for old-age assistance, or for medical assistance for the aged, or for old-age assistance and medical assistance for the aged.

"STATE OLD-AGE AND MEDICAL ASSISTANCE PLANS

"*Sec. 2.* (a) A State plan for old-age assistance, or for medical assistance for the aged, or for old-age assistance and medical assistance for the aged must—

"(1) provide that it shall be in effect in all political subdivisions of the State, and, if administered by them, be mandatory upon them;

"(2) provide for financial participation by the State;

"(3) either provide for the establishment or designation of a single State agency to administer the plan, or provide for the establishment or designation of a single State agency to supervise the administration of the plan;

"(4) provide for granting an opportunity for a fair hearing before the State agency to any individual whose claim for assistance under the plan is denied or is not acted upon with reasonable promptness;

"(5) provide such methods of administration (including methods relating to the establishment and maintenance of personnel standards on a merit basis, except that the Secretary shall exercise no authority with respect to the selection, tenure of office, and compensation of any individual employed in accordance with such methods) as are found by the Secretary to be necessary for the proper and efficient operation of the plan;

"(6) provide that the State agency will make such reports, in such form and containing such information, as the Secretary may from time to time require, and comply with such provisions as the Secretary may from time to time find necessary to assure the correctness and verification of such reports;

"(7) provide safeguards which restrict the use or disclosure of information concerning applicants and recipients to purposes directly connected with the administration of the State plan;

"(8) provide that all individuals wishing to make application for assistance under the plan shall have opportunity to do so, and that such assistance shall be furnished with reasonable promptness to all eligible individuals;

"(9) provide, if the plan includes assistance for or on behalf of individuals in private or public institutions, for the establishment or designation of a State authority or authorities which shall be responsible for establishing and maintaining standards for such institutions:

"(10) if the State plan includes old-age assistance—

"(A) provide that the State agency shall, in determining need for such assistance, take into consideration any other income and resources of an individual claiming old-age assistance;

"(B) include reasonable standards, consistent with the objectives of this title, for determining eligibility for and the extent of such assistance; and

"(C) provide a description of the services (if any) which the State agency makes available to applicants for and recipients of such assistance to help them attain self-care, including a description of the steps taken to assure, in the provision of such services, maximum utilization of other agencies providing similar or related services; and

"(11) if the State plan includes medical assistance for the aged—

"(A) provide for inclusion of some institutional and some noninstitutional care and services;

"(B) provide that no enrollment fee, premium, or similar charge will be imposed as a condition of any individual's eligibility for medical assistance for the aged under the plan;

"(C) provide for inclusion, to the extent required by regulations prescribed by the Secretary, of provisions (conforming to such regulations) with respect to the furnishing of such assistance to individuals who are residents of the State but are absent therefrom;

"(D) include reasonable standards, consistent with the objectives of this title, for determining eligibility for and the extent of such assistance; and

"(E) provide that no lien may be imposed against the property of any individual prior to his death on account of medical assistance for the aged paid or to be paid on his behalf under the plan (except pursuant to the judgment of a court on account of benefits incorrectly paid on behalf of such individual), and that there shall be no adjustment or recovery (except, after the death of such individual and his surviving spouse, if any, from such individual's estate) of any medical assistance for the aged correctly paid on behalf of such individual under the plan.

"(b) The Secretary shall approve any plan which fulfills the conditions specified in subsection (a), except that he shall not approve any plan which imposes, as a condition of eligibility for assistance under the plan—

"(1) an age requirement of more than sixty-five years; or

"(2) any residence requirement which (A) in the case of applicants for old-age assistance, excludes any resident of the State who has resided therein five years during the nine years immediately preceding the application for old-age assistance and has resided therein continuously for one year immediately preceding the application, and (B) in the case of applicants for medical assistance for the aged, excludes any individual who resides in the State; or

"(3) any citizenship requirement which excludes any citizen of the United States.

"(c) Nothing in this title shall be construed to permit a State to have in effect with respect to any period more than one State plan approved under this title."

(c) Section 3(a) of such Act is amended to read as follows:

"*Sec. 3.* (a) From the sums appropriated therefor, the Secretary of the Treasury shall pay to each State which has a plan approved under this title, for each quarter, beginning with the quarter commencing October 1, 1960—

"(1) in the case of any State other than Puerto Rico, the Virgin Islands, and Guam, an amount equal to the sum of the following proportions of the total amounts expended during such quarter as old-age assistance under the State plan (including expenditures for insurance premiums for medical or any other type of remedial care or the cost thereof)—

"(A) four-fifths of such expenditures, not counting so much of any expenditure with respect to any month as exceeds the product of $30 multiplied by the total number of recipients of old-age assistance for such month (which total number, for purposes of this subsection, means (i) the number of individuals who received old-age assistance in the form of money payments for such month, plus (ii) the number of other individuals with respect to whom expenditures were made in such month as old-age assistance in the form of medical or any other type of remedial care); plus

"(B) the Federal percentage (as defined in section 1101(a)(8)) of the amount by which such expenditures exceed the maximum which may be counted under clause (A), not counting so much of any expenditure with respect to any month as exceeds the product of $65 multiplied by the total number of such recipients of old-age assistance for such month; plus

"(C) the larger of the following: (i) the Federal medical percentage (as defined in section 6(c) of the amount by which such expenditures exceed the maximum which may be counted under clause (B), not counting so much of any expenditure with respect to any month as exceeds (I) the product of $77 multiplied by the total number of such recipients of old-age assistance for such month, or (II) if smaller, the total expended as old-age assistance in the form of medical or any other type of remedial care with respect to such month plus the product of $65 multiplied by such total number of such recipients, or (ii) 15 per centum of the total of the sums expended during such quarter as old-age assistance under the State plan in the form of medical or any other type of remedial care, not counting so much of any expenditure with respect to any month as exceeds the product of $12 multiplied by the total number of such recipients of old-age assistance for such month; and

"(2) in the case of Puerto Rico, the Virgin Islands, and Guam, an amount equal to—

"(A) one-half of the total of the sums expended during such quarter as old-age assistance under the State plan (including expenditures for insurance premiums for medical or any other type of remedial care or the cost thereof), not counting so much of any expenditure with respect to any month as exeeds $35 multiplied by the total number of recipients of old-age assistance for such month; plus

"(B) the larger of the following amounts: (i) one-half of the amount by which such expenditures exceed the maximum which may be counted under clause (A), not counting so much of any expenditure with respect to any month as exceeds (I) the product of $41 multiplied by the total number of such recipients of old-age assistance for such month, or (II) if smaller, the total expended as old-age assistance in the form of medical or any other type of remedial care with respect to such month plus the product of $35 multiplied by the total number of such recipients, or (ii) 15 per centum of the total of the sums expended during such quarter as old-age assistance under the State plan in the form of medical or any other type of remedial care, not counting so much of any expenditure with respect to any month as exceeds the product of $6 multiplied by the total number of such recipients of old-age assistance for such month; and

"(3) in the case of any State, an amount equal to the Federal medical percentage (as defined in section 6(c)) of the total amounts expended during such quarter as medical assistance for the aged under the State plan (including expenditures for insurance premiums for medical or any other type of remedial care or the cost thereof); and

"(4) in the case of any State, an amount equal to one-half of the total of the sums expended during such quarter as found necessary by the Secretary of Health, Education, and Welfare for the proper and efficient administration of the State plan, including services which are provided by the staff of the State agency (or of the local agency administering the State plan in the political subdivision) to applicants for and recipients of old-age assistance to help them attain self-care."

(d) Section 3(b) (2) (B) of such Act is amended by striking out "old-age assistance" and inserting in lieu thereof "assistance".

(e) Section 4 of such Act is amended by striking out "State plan for old-age assistance which has been approved" and inserting in lieu thereof "State plan which has been approved under this title".

(f) (1) Section 6 of such Act is amended by striking out "but does not include" and all that follows and inserting in lieu thereof "but does not include—

"(1) any such payments to or care in behalf of any individual who is an inmate of a public institution (except as a patient in a medical institution) or any individual who is a patient in an institution for tuberculosis or mental diseases, or

"(2) any such payments to any individual who has been diagnosed as having tuberculosis or psychosis and is a patient in a medical institution as a result thereof, or

"(3) any such care in behalf of any individual, who is a patient in a medical institution as a result of a diagnosis that he has tuberculosis or psychosis, with respect to any period after the individual has been a patient in such an institution, as a result of such diagnosis, for forty-two days."

(2) Section 6 is further amended by inserting "(a)" immediately after "*Sec. 6.*" and by adding after such section 6 the following new subsections:

"(b) For purposes of this title, the term 'medical assistance for the aged' means payment of part or all of the cost of the following care and services for individuals sixty-five years of age or older who are not recipients of old-age assistance but whose income and resources are insufficient to meet all of such cost—

"(1) inpatient hospital services;

"(2) skilled nursing-home services;

"(3) physicians' services;

"(4) outpatient hospital or clinic services;

"(5) home health care services;

"(6) private duty nursing services;

"(7) physical therapy and related services;

"(8) dental services;

"(9) laboratory and X-ray services;

"(10) prescribed drugs, eyeglasses, dentures, and prosthetic devices;

"(11) diagnostic, screening, and preventive services; and

"(12) any other medical care or remedial care recognized under State law;

except that such term does not include any such payments with respect to —

"(A) care or services for any individual who is an inmate of a public institution (except as a patient in a medical institution) or any individual who is a patient in an institution for tuberculosis or mental diseases; or

"(B) care or services for any individual, who is a patient in a medical institution as a result of a diagnosis of tuberculosis or psychosis, with respect to any period after the individual has been a patient in such an institution, as a result of such diagnosis, for forty-two days.

"(c) For purposes of this title, the term 'Federal medical percentage' for any State shall be 100 per centum less the State percentage; and the State percentage shall be that percentage which bears the same ratio to 50 per centum as the square of the per capita income of such State bears to the square of the per capita income of the continental United States (including Alaska) and Hawaii; except that (i) the Federal medical percentage shall in no case be less than 50 per centum or more than 80 per centum, and (ii) the Federal medical percentage for Puerto Rico, the Virgin Islands, and Guam shall be 50 per centum. The Federal medical percentage for any State shall be determined and promulgated in accordance with the provisions of subparagraph (B) of section 1101(a) (8) (other than the proviso at the end thereof); except that the Secretary shall, as soon as possible after enactment of the Social Security Amendments of 1960, determine and promulgate the Federal medical percentage for each State —

"(1) for the period beginning October 1, 1960, and ending with the close of June 30, 1961, which promulgation shall be based on the same data with respect to per capita income as the data used by the Secretary in promulgating the Federal percentage (under section 1101(a) (8)) for such State for the fiscal year ending June 30, 1961 (which promulgation of the Federal medical percentage shall be conclusive for such period), and

"(2) for the period beginning July 1, 1961, and ending with the close of June 30, 1963, which promulgation shall be based on the same data with respect to per capita income as the data used by the Secretary in promulgating the Federal percentage (under section 1101(a) (8)) for such State for such period (which promulgation of the Federal medical percentage shall be conclusive for such period)."

INCREASE IN LIMITATIONS ON ASSISTANCE PAYMENT TO PUERTO RICO, THE VIRGIN ISLANDS, AND GUAM

Sec. 602. Section 1108 of the Social Security Act is amended by —

(1) striking out "$8,500,000" and inserting in lieu thereof

"$9,000,000, of which $500,000 may be used only for payments certified with respect to section 3(a) (2) (B)";

(2) striking out "$300,000" and inserting in lieu thereof "$315,000,
of which $15,000 may be used only for payments certified in respect
to section 3(a) (2) (B)";

(3) striking out "$400,000" and inserting in lieu thereof "$420,000,
of which $20,000 may be used only for payments certified in respect
to section 3(a) (2) (B)"; and

(4) striking out "titles I, IV, X, and XIV", and inserting in lieu
thereof "titles I (other than section 3(a) (3) thereof), IV, X, and XIV".

TECHNICAL AMENDMENT

Sec. 603. (a) Section 618 of the Revenue Act of 1951 (65 Stat. 569) is
amended by striking out "title I" and inserting in lieu thereof "title I
(other than section 3(a) (3) thereof)".

(b) The amendment made by subsection (a) shall take effect October 1, 1960.

EFFECTIVE DATES

Sec. 604. The amendments made by section 601 of this Act shall take
effect October 1, 1960, and the amendments made by section 602 shall
be effective with respect to fiscal years ending after 1960.

*   *   *

*Four days before leaving office President Eisenhower delivered his last
annual budget message to Congress. He referred to the comprehensive
gains made during his Administration in social security, welfare, and
medical care for the aged and rather surprisingly took the view that recent
medical care programs did not reach all the unprotected aged. He called
on the new Congress to extend medical coverage. (It is not clear what encouraged President Eisenhower to change his position on this. No doubt
the politics of the year had their effect. But he may also have been influenced
by* Goals for Americans, *the Report of the President's Commission on
National Goals, published in 1960.)*

President Dwight D. Eisenhower
Ninth Annual Message
(January 16, 1961)*

Social Insurance and Other Welfare

Since the Social Security Act first became law in 1935, the United States
has made great strides in its public income maintenance programs, both

Public Papers of the Presidents, Dwight D. Eisenhower, 1960–61, p, 1009–11.

under the social security system and other public retirement systems. Today 93% of our workers are protected under the basic old-age, survivors, and disability insurance program or under other Federal or State-local retirement systems. To assist the unemployed we also have the Federal-State unemployment insurance system, and the Federal Government further provides or helps finance assistance to needy groups through other programs.

In 10 years the benefit payments made because of loss of income due to old age, death, disability, or unemployment under Federal, State, and local programs have trebled, rising in the calendar year 1960 to approximately $26 billion, of which about $24 billion was paid from federally administered or federally aided programs. Benefits were paid during the calendar year 1960 to an average of more than 20 million families or single persons. The cost of these benefits, 6% of our national income, is funded from employee and employer contributions and taxes. Benefit payments and taxes under laws already in effect will increase greatly over the years.

Social insurance. — The Federal old-age, survivors, and disability insurance system now covers 9 out of 10 American workers and their families. In fiscal year 1962 it will pay $12.9 billion in benefits to an average of 16.5 million people of all ages, including 12 million persons aged 65 and over. Coverage should be extended to Federal civilian employees and self-employed physicians, the largest groups of regularly employed persons in our economy not now covered by this,system.

Benefit payments and administrative costs are paid from trust funds supported by payroll taxes shared equally by workers and employers and from contributions of the self-employed. The combined employer-employee rate is now 6% of covered payrolls. Under present law it will rise by steps to 9% in calendar year 1969. Expenditures for the administration of this vast insurance system will be increased in fiscal year 1962 to cope with the increased workloads resulting from extension of disability protection to workers below age 50 and from other amendments enacted by the last Congress.

Public assistance. — Total Federal expenditures for public assistance and medical aid in 1962 under existing law are estimated to increase by $128 million over 1961, largely reflecting the cost of the newly enacted medical assistance program for the aged. In 1962, the Federal share of payments for an average of 6.3 million recipients is estimated to be $2.3 billion, which is 58% of the total. Caseloads for old-age assistance and aid to the blind are declining moderately, while caseloads for aid to dependent children and aid to the permanently and totally disabled are increasing.

Medical care for the aged. — In recent years, the American people have greatly improved their ability to obtain and pay for medical care through private and nonprofit health organizations. This approach has produced excellent results and should be preserved.

However, some aged persons are finding it increasingly difficult to pay for the medical services which they require. Medical and institutional care for the aged financed by public funds (Federal, State, and local) is currently estimated to cost over $1 billion annually. The last Congress authorized substantial expansion in Federal assistance for medical care of the aged through (1) increased Federal participation under the regular old-age assisance program and (2) a new program of medical assistance for the aged who are not recipients of public assistance but who nevertheless require aid to pay their medical and hospital bills.

In the 1962 budget, $400 million is included in the amount shown for public assistance for the old and the new programs of medical care for the aged. There will be a substantial increase in these expenditures in future years under existing law as additional States participate in these programs.

Extension of medical care assistance to the aged through a voluntary program under Federal-State-local auspices—as authorized by the Congress —is sound national policy both from a fiscal standpoint and from the standpoint of encouraging the widest participation of private as well as public agencies in the improvement of medical care for this group. However, under the program approved by the Congress many of the aged will still not be able to obtain needed protection against catastrophic hospital and medical expenses even though under ordinary circumstances they are able to pay their normal medical bills. The Congress is therefore urged to broaden the existing program in keeping with the recommendations which were made by this administration last spring. This would further increase the number who receive assistance.

Public action in providing assistance for medical care and the sharply rising costs of hospital and medical care underline the need for more adequate information regarding medical costs and the best methods of organizing to meet them. This budget provides for augmented research in medical economics under the Department of Health, Education, and Welfare. Likewise, it expands the related program of research and demonstration projects on causes of dependency for which appropriations were first authorized last year.

Changes in unemployment compensation were less dramatic in 1960, but the report of the Senate's Special Committee on Unemployment Problems was published. The so-called Johnson Committee called for long-term changes in the unemployment program similar to earlier Kennedy recommendations such as national standards, including a minimum of thirty-nine weeks coverage. Moreover the Social Security Amendments of 1960 as ultimately passed did make some administrative changes (for details see the Report of the Finance Committee) and also included a limited extension of the unemployment compensation program (Title V).

However, during 1960 the Supreme Court did hand down a potentially significant decision interpreting a section of the Social Security Act, Flemming v. Nestor, 363 v.s. 603. The case itself was of little immediate significance, but the basic philosophy of the social security program was questioned.

The Court, in a 5 to 4 decision, held that receipt of social security bene-fits was not an accrued right, and that Congress had the power to limit or terminate benefits so long as the congressional action did not "manifest a patently arbitrary classification, utterly lacking in rational justification." Justice Harlan, writing for the majority, held that social security benefits were different from private insurance annuities, since the private an-nuity agreement imposed a contractual obligation which could not be avoided. The Court thus reached the same conclusions that Representative Carl T. Curtis' Special Subcommittee on Social Security had reached in 1953.

THE NEW FRONTIER
1961–1963

THE NEW FRONTIER
1961–1963

During the presidency of John F. Kennedy and the early years of the presidency of Lyndon B. Johnson great changes ocurred in all areas of social security. Programs like medical care, shelved for thirty years, easily passed. Social insurance was liberalized still further and even public assistance was, on the surface, given a new look. At the same time, a different approach to some of the problems which generated a need for income security was attempted—the Poverty Program, for example. There was also public discussion of other new approaches: in particular, a guaranteed income or some form of negative income tax. If the promise of these new programs horrified some and disappointed others, at least there was a sense that revised concepts were abroad. While many of these concepts were given legislative form during the Johnson Administration, their intellectual bases were established during the years of the New Frontier.

1961

Demands arose for congressional action on social security during 1961. President Kennedy's message of February 2, 1961 on economic recovery and growth set the pace of the new legislative agenda.

Special Presidential Message to the Congress
Program for Economic Recovery and Growth
(February 2, 1961)*

To the Congress of the United States:

America has the human and material resources to meet the demands of national security and the obligations of world leadership while at the same time advancing well-being at home. But our Nation has been falling further and further short of its economic capabilities. In the past 7 years, our rate of growth has slowed down disturbingly. In the past 3½ years, the gap between what we can produce and what we do produce has threatened to become chronic. And in the past year our economic problem has been aggravated by recession and by loss of gold. I shall shortly send to the Congress a separate message dealing with our international balance of payments and gold position.

The Nation cannot—and will not—be satisfied with economic decline and slack. The United States cannot afford, in this time of national need

Public Papers of the Presidents, John F. Kennedy, 1961, p. 41

and world crisis, to dissipate its opportunities for economic growth. We cannot expect to make good in a day or even a year the accumulated deficiencies of several years. But realistic aims for 1961 are to reverse the downtrend in our economy, to narrow the gap of unused potential, to abate the waste and misery of unemployment, and at the same time to maintain reasonable stability of the price level. For 1962 and 1963 our programs must aim at expanding American productive capacity at a rate that shows the world the vigor and vitality of a free economy. These are not merely fond hopes; they are realistic goals. We pledge and ask maximum effort for their attainment.

I am proposing today measures both to alleviate the distress arising from unsatisfactory performance of the economy and to stimulate economic recovery and growth. If economic developments in the first quarter of this year indicate that additional measures are needed, I will promptly propose such measures.

*   *   *

The number of persons out of work and seeking employment has been rising since the early summer of 1960 and has reached serious proportions in these rigorous winter months. In January 5.4 million persons were unemployed, more than 1.3 million have been continuously out of work for 15 weeks or longer, 600,000 for 6 months or more. In addition, workers involuntarily confined to part-time work numbered 1.7 million, a rise of 200,000 over December.

We have long since decided as a nation that we will not turn our backs upon workers and their families undergoing the hardships of unemployment. Furthermore, we know all too well that the loss of income of the unemployed inevitably depresses consumer spending, threatening to deepen the recession and delay recovery. The flow of wage and salary payments, measured at an annual rate, has fallen by $4 billion from August to December.

Our unemployment insurance system serves to mitigate, in some degree, the hardships of displaced employees and helps to strengthen the economy against the forces of contraction. The total number of persons drawing benefits under that system has risen sharply since the middle of 1960, and in mid-January stood at 3.4 million, 1 million higher than a year ago. Although average benefits amount to only $34 per week, total payments are estimated to have been $430 million in January, compared to $264 million in January a year ago. The number of persons exhausting unemployment benefits has also increased. About 500,000 persons who have exhausted their benefits are still unemployed. During the first 6 months of 1961, nearly 1½ million more persons will use up their unemployment benefits before finding jobs.

In these urgent circumstances, I shall ask the Congress to enact a temporary program for extending the duration of benefits. Under agreements voluntarily entered into between the States and the Federal Government, additional weeks of benefits would be authorized from Federal funds, during the 12 months following enactment, to persons who have exhausted regular benefits since October 31, 1960, and are still unemployed. These extended benefits would equal one-half — up to a maximum of 13 weeks — of the duration provided by the State. The duration of the benefits would be subject to an overall maximum, State and Federal, of 39 weeks. Where the State law already provides benefits for longer than 26 weeks, the Federal Government would pay, for the period of the emergency, for all weeks of benefits beyond 26, up to a maximum of 39, thus freeing State funds for much-needed increases in benefit amounts. The amount thus going into increased income and purchasing power will be advanced from general revenues and later repaid in full from increased insurance contributions obtained by raising the taxable payroll maximum per employee from $3,000 to $4,800 annually. This increase will maintain the self-supporting basis of the system and enhance its capacity to meet future emergencies.

Our permanent Federal-State unemployment insurance system, which has become an institution essential to the efficient functioning of our labor markets as well as a strong defense against economic contraction, is in need of permanent reform. As I said in 1958, I believe it would be a tragic mistake to embark on a Federal supplementation program geared to the present emergency without also strengthening the underlying system. A mere stop-gap approach ignores the role our permanent unemployment insurance system was intended to play, and establishes instead a precedent for falling back on temporary remedies whenever the system is really needed. The standards of the system have proven inadequate to deal with the recession problem.

This time, we must establish a permanent unemployment compensation system which can do the job it was intended to do. A program of Federal legislation designed to revise and strengthen the benefit and financing provisions of the system will therefore be recommended to the Congress by the end of March.

*   *   *

Under the aid to dependent children program, needy children are eligible for assistance if their fathers are deceased, disabled, or family deserters. In logic and humanity, a child should also be eligible for assistance if his father is a needy unemployed worker — for example, a person who has exhausted unemployment benefits and is not receiving adequate local assistance. Too many fathers, unable to support their families, have resorted to real or pretended desertion to qualify their children for help. Many other fathers are prevented by conscience and love of family from taking this route, thereby disqualifying their children under present law.

I recommend that the Congress enact an interim amendment to the aid to dependent children program to include the children of the needy unemployed. Temporary action is recommended pending completion of a study of a permanent program to aid needy children and certain other groups now excluded from the Federal-State public assistance programs.

*   *   *

The current softness of the economy underscores the inadequacy of social security benefits in relation to the needs of many present beneficiaries. The average retired worker's benefit is only $74 a month. A majority of these beneficiaries have no other significant income. The basic principle of our social insurance system is undermined when a substantial number of retired individuals must seek public assistance or else subsist below minimum standards of health and comfort. We must not permit the benefits of retired workers and their families to lag behind rises in living costs; we cannot decently exclude our older population from the general advances in standards of living enjoyed by employed workers.

I recommend that Congress enact five improvements in benefits, to become effective April 1. All are clearly justified in equity and decency. They will increase benefit payments for between 4 and 5 million people in the next 12 months. Besides meeting pressing social needs, the additional flow of purchasing power will be a desirable economic stimulus at the present time. Early enactment will serve this end.

The old-age, survivors, and disability insurance program is financed on a sound actuarial basis, with insurance contributions adjusted to scheduled benefit payments. The benefit improvements I am proposing can be covered by additions of one-fourth of 1 percent each to the employer's and employee's contributions, beginning at the next scheduled increase in contributions on January 1, 1963.

The five proposals are:

1. Raise the minimum monthly benefit for the retired worker from $33 per month to $43 per month, increasing benefits for more than 2,200,000 people in the first 12 months. We wish it could be raised higher—but surely we cannot continue benefits at such an unconscionably low minimum.

2. Improve retirement protection by paying actuarially reduced benefits to men beginning at age 62. Present law does not permit a man to become eligible for optional retirement benefits before age 65, although such benefits are available to women at age 62 on an actuarially reduced basis. Provision for paying reduced benefits to men beginning at age 62 would make benefits available to older unemployed workers at comparatively little additional program cost. The plight of the older unemployed man is particularly serious in areas of chronic unemployment. However, the difficulties older workers find in reentering the labor market after losing their jobs or after periods of illness exist in all parts of the country. Frequently, as persons approach age 65 they find it difficult to compete in their accustomed occupations because of physical incapacity which may not, however, have progressed to the point of total disability. Provision for actuarially reduced benefits at age 62 to men as well as women will provide income for 600,000 people, some of whom would otherwise have to turn to public assistance for support.

3. Provide benefits for 170,000 additional people by liberalizing the insured-status requirement. At present a person can receive benefits only if before retirement he was employed in jobs covered by the social security program for one out of every three quarters after 1950. The proposal is to reduce the required coverage to one quarter out of every four. This is only fair to our present generation of older people, as it brings their eligibility requirement into line with the one that present law contemplates for future generations, that is 10 years of coverage out of a working life of about 40 years.

4. Increase the aged widow's benefit from 75 percent to 85 percent of her husband's benefit amount, raising benefits for 1,550,000 widows. There is no justification either in equity or in the facts of family consumption for this size gap in the level of widows' benefits.

5. Broaden disability insurance protection. The social security program should provide disability insurance benefits for insured workers and their families after the workers have been totally disabled for 6 months. Under present law, disability benefits are available only if the disabled worker's condition is expected to result in death or to last for a long and indefinite period. The proposed change provides benefits in the first 12 months for 85,000 people (totally disabled workers and their dependents) many of whom otherwise have to resort to public assistance. Since it would no longer be necessary to determine that the disabled person is unlikely to recover, the change removes an important barrier to rehabilitation. It also speeds up determinations of disability. While the change has these desirable effects, it would in no sense be an innovation. Similar provisions are contained in many private insurance contracts and other disability programs.

Social Security Amendments

An Administration bill, H. R. 4571, embodying the proposals made by the President in his economic message, was introduced after a message to Congress on February 20 and limited executive hearings began before the House Ways and Means Committee on March 9.

The new Secretary of Health, Education, and Welfare, Abraham Ribicoff, called for a new minimum of $43 a month for OASDI retirement benefits. He also proposed that men should be eligible for reduced retirement benefits at sixty-two and requested that the requirements for insurance be reduced. Ribicoff also suggested increased widow's benefits and extended disability provisions.

Social Security Act Amendments of 1961
Executive Hearings on H.R. 4751 before the House Ways
and Means Committee
87th Cong., 1st Sess. (March, 1961)
(p. 16)

Statement of Secretary Abraham Ribicoff

We recommend that requirement for insured status be changed so that a worker will be fully insured if he has 1 quarter of coverage for every 4 calendar quarters elapsing after 1950 and up to the year of death or attainment of retirement age, instead of 1 for every 3. Under the proposal, about 170,000 people who are not now insured would become eligible for benefits in the first 12 months of operation. Taking into account the proposals to raise the minimum benefit to $43 and to pay actuarially reduced benefits to men as early as age 62, also being recommended at this time, the total amount that would be payable to these people in the first 12 months would be $65 million.

The committee will recall that this provision was passed by the House last year, but was deleted in the Senate; the provision that was finally enacted, calling for 1 quarter of coverage for every 3 elapsed quarters, was a compromise between the House provision and the 1-for-2 requirement then in the law.

The 1-for-4 provision would make the insured-status requirements for people who are now old comparable to those that will apply in the mature program for people who will attain retirement age at that time. People who were young when the program started and young people who began working after that time will need about 1 year of work for every 4 years elapsing after age 21 (10 years out of a possible 40 or more years in a working lifetime) in order to be insured at retirement age. Under the 1-for-3 requirement, people who are now old must meet a proportionally stricter test. People who were first covered in 1955, for example, and who reached age 65 in 1961 must have 3¼ years of coverage out of the 6 years prior to 65 in which they could possibly have been covered. For these people the present requirement is even more strict than the pre-1960 requirement of 1 quarter of coverage for every 2 elapsed quarters was for people generally.

The proposal would help many people who are uninsured, not because they worked irregularly over their lifetimes, but because the work they did in the prime of life was not covered. By the time their regular occupations were covered they were already so old that they could not work regularly enough to meet the insured status requirements in the law.

The level-premium cost of the proposal would be 0.02 percent of payroll.

The hearings continued on throughout March although only Administration witnesses appeared. On April 7 the House reported out a revised ver-

*sion of the bill increasing minimum benefits to $40 (rather than the re-
quested $43), beginning the increased taxes in 1962 instead of 1963, raising
the widow's pension to 82.5 per cent of retirement benefits from 75 per
cent, and rejecting a shorter period for establishment of total disability. The
committee outlined the scope of the new bill, H.R. 6027, in its report.*

Social Security Act Amendments of 1961
House Report No. 216
87th Cong., 1st Sess.
(April 7, 1961)

II. SUMMARY OF THE PRINCIPAL PROVISIONS OF THE BILL

A. Increase in the Minimum Benefit

The bill would increase from $33 to $40 the minimum monthly retirement
benefit payable under the program to persons retiring at or after age 65 and
the minimum monthly disability benefit, with proportionate increases in the
minimum benefits payable to dependents and survivors. This provision
would mean increased benefits for 2,175,000 people, amounting to $170 mil-
lion, during the first 12 months of operation.

B. Benefits at Age 62 for Men

The bill would make benefits available for men beginning at age 62, with
the benefits payable to men claiming benefits before age 65 reduced to take
account of the longer period over which the benefits will be paid. The effect
of this change would be that men electing to retire at age 62 will receive the
same total amount of benefits over the remainder of their lives as they would
have received had they waited to retire at age 65.

In the first year of operation, about 560,000 people would get benefits
amounting to $440 million under this proposed change.

The bill would liberalize the insured status requirements so that a worker
would be fully insured if he has one quarter of coverage for every year elapsing after 1950 (or after the year in which he attained age 21, if that was
later) and up to the year of disability, death, or attainment of age 65 for men
(62 for women). Under present law one quarter of coverage is required for
every three elapsed calendar quarters.

This change would bring about 160,000 people onto the benefit rolls in
the first year for a total of $65 million in benefits.

*　　　*　　　*

G. *Increase in Contribution Rates*

To meet the increased cost incurred as a result of the improvements in the old-age, survivors, and disability insurance program which would be made by the bill, provision is made for an increase in the scheduled contribution rates. Beginning in 1962, contribution rates would be raised by ⅛ of 1 percent each for employees and employers and by 3/16 of 1 percent for the self-employed. The level-premium increase in cost which would result from the bill is 0.25 percent of payroll and the level-premium equivalent of the income from the increase in the contribution rates is also 0.25 percent of payroll. This means that the improvements would be fully financed and the system would remain actuarially sound.

*   *   *

On the floor of Congress, Representative Thomas B. Curtis of Missouri questioned the bill's fiscal soundness.

Congressional Debates
107 Congressional Record, p. 6470
(April 20, 1961)

Mr. Chairman, the place where the discussion was left by our able chairman is a good place to pick up, and I refer to the point of actuarial soundness. That is, the practical use of the word "actuarial." In a sense it is actuarially sound, but when we go to the premises upon which this actuarial soundness is based, we begin to see that it is not actuarially sound in the sense that insurance programs in the private sector are actuarially sound.

Let us not "kid" ourselves. We are not voting our own money to pay for these benefits. We are voting the money of our children and our children's children because these benefits that we vote here today, if we do, and have in the past, are not going to be paid for by the taxes in our generation but, indeed, are going to be paid for by the labor force beginning in 1970, beginning in 1980, beginning in 1990. The actuarial soundness of the program is based on the assumption that the taxes we impose here in perpetuity, with the built-in increases that go on through 1969, will actually be imposed and that the laboring force will continue to increase and that this great economy of ours will not suffer a serious depression like it did in the thirties, because all of these throw out the actuarial soundness of this system. So one of the big problems that face us today, those of us who are deeply concerned about the future welfare of our society, the future generations and the heritage we are passing on, look to the impact of this thing right now.

The bill easily passed the House without amendments on April 20. During the next month the Senate Finance Committee conducted hearings and finally issued its report in late June. There were only two major additions to the House bill: federal aid to states was increased, allowing more generous assistance to the aged, the blind, and the disabled; temporary federal payments were offered to U.S. nationals returned from foreign countries. The committee report also re-examined the fiscal basis of the social insurance system and largely accepted the traditional assumptions.

On the Senate floor several adjustments were made. Senator Vance Hartke of Indiana offered a compromise solution to keep the earnings limit at $1200, but to set a 50 per cent formula for reduction between $1500 and $1700. This formula was accepted with little debate. The Senate then agreed that the new increases in social security taxes should occur in 1968 rather than 1969 and accepted Senator Jack R. Miller's amendment placing limitations on the right of returning nationals to obtain social security benefits. However, the amendment to liberalize the disability provisions was rejected.

The Conference Committee published its report on June 28. It accepted the new earnings limit, reduced the new Senate formula for public assistance, and limited the returning nationals program to a one-year period. Both houses accepted the report and it was signed by the President on June 30, 1961.

Social Security Amendments of 1961
(June 30, 1961, 75 Statutes at Large 131)

*   *   *

FULLY INSURED STATUS

Sec. 103. (a) Section 214 (a) of the Social Security Act is amended to read as follows:

"Fully Insured Individual

"(a) The term 'fully insured individual' means any individual who had not less than—

"(1) one quarter of coverage (whenever acquired) for each calendar year elapsing after 1950 (or, if later, the year in which he attained age 21) and before—

"(A) in the case of a woman, the year in which she died or (if earlier) the year in which she attained age 62,

"(B) in the case of a man who has died, the year in which he died or (if earlier) the year in which he attained age 65, or

"(C) in the case of a man who has not died, the year in which he attained (or would attain) age 65,

except that in no case shall an individual be a fully insured individual unless he has at least 6 quarters of coverage; or

"(2) 40 quarters of coverage; or

"(3) in the case of an individual who died before 1951, 6 quarters of coverage;

not counting as an elapsed year for purposes of paragraph (1) any year any part of which was included in a period of disability (as defined in section 216 (i))."

*   *   *

Tax on Employees

(b) Section 3101 of such Code (relating to rate of tax on employees under the Federal Insurance Contributions Act) is amended to read as follows: "*Sec. 3101. RATE OF TAX.* "In addition to other taxes, there is hereby imposed on the income of every individual a tax equal to the following percentages of the wages (as defined in section 3121 (a)) received by him with respect to employment (as defined in section 3121 (b))—

"(1) with respect to wages received during the calendar year 1962, the rate shall be $3\frac{1}{8}$ percent;

"(2) with respect to wages received during the calendar years 1963 to 1965, both inclusive, the rate shall be $3\frac{5}{8}$ percent;

"(3) with respect to wages received during the calendar years 1966 to 1967, both inclusive, the rate shall be $4\frac{1}{8}$ percent; and

"(4) with respect to wages received after December 31, 1967, the rate shall be $4\frac{5}{8}$ percent."

Tax on Employers

(c) Section 3111 of such Code (relating to rate of tax on employers under the Federal Insurance Contributions Act) is amended to read as follows: "*Sec. 3111. RATE OF TAX.* "In addition to other taxes, there is hereby imposed on every employer an excise tax, with respect to having individuals in his employ, equal to the following percentages of the wages (as defined in section 3121 (a)) paid by him with respect to employment (as defined in section 3121 (b))—

"(1) with respect to wages paid during the calendar year 1962, the rate shall be $3\frac{1}{8}$ percent;

"(2) with respect to wages paid during the calendar years 1963 to 1965, both inclusive, the rate shall be $3\frac{5}{8}$ percent;

"(3) with respect to wages paid during the calendar years 1966 to

1967, both inclusive, the rate shall be 4⅛ percent; and

"(4) with respect to wages paid after December 31, 1967, the rate shall be 4⅝ percent."

*   *   *

ADDITIONAL FEDERAL PARTICIPATION IN PUBLIC ASSISTANCE PAYMENTS

Sec. 303. (a) (1) Section 3(a) (1) of the Social Security Act is amended—

(A) by striking out "$30" and inserting in lieu thereof "$31";

(B) by striking out "$65" each place it appears therein and inserting in lieu thereof "$66"; and

(C) by striking out "$80" and inserting in lieu thereof "$81".

(2) Section 3(a) (2) of such Act is amended—

(A) by striking out "$35" each place it appears therein and inserting in lieu thereof "$35.50"; and

(B) by striking out "$42.50" and inserting in lieu thereof "$43".

(b) (1) Section 1003(a) (1) of such Act is amended—

(A) by striking out "$30" and inserting in lieu thereof "$31"; and

(B) by striking out "$65" and inserting in lieu thereof "$66".

(2) Section 1003(a) (2) of such Act is amended by striking out "$35" and inserting in lieu thereof "$35.50".

(c) (1) Section 1403(a) (1) of such Act is amended—

(A) by striking out "$30" and inserting in lieu thereof "$31"; and

(B) by striking out "$65" and inserting in lieu thereof "$66".

(2) Section 1403(a) (2) of such Act is amended by striking out "$35" and inserting in lieu thereof "$35.50".

(d) Effective only for the fiscal year ending June 30, 1962, section 1108 of the Social Security Act (as amended by section 6 of Public Law 87–31) is amended by striking out "$9,425,000", "$318,750", and "$425,000" and inserting in lieu thereof "$9,500,000", "$320,000", and "$430,000", respectively.

(e) The amendments made by subsections (a), (b), and (c) of this section shall apply only in the case of expenditures made after September 30, 1961, and before July 1, 1962, under a State plan approved under title I, X, or XIV, as the case may be, of the Social Security Act.

Medical Care in 1961

The medical care provisions of the new social security bill generated a great deal of interest. Senator Jacob Javits presented an amendment calling for additional medical care for the aged. He suggested federal support for extensive state programs of medical care for those over sixty-five whose in-

dividual incomes did not exceed $3000, or whose joint incomes did not exceed $4500. The amendment was eventually withdrawn, but a record in favor of medical care for the elderly through social security was being built up. Another part of the record for 1961 was the King-Anderson Bill designed to implement President Kennedy's proposals.

Although Chairman Mills opposed the program, the House Ways and Means Committee did hold hearings. Organized medicine continued to maintain a solid front against "socialized medicine".

Health Services for the Aged Under Social Security
Hearings on H.R. 4222 before the House Ways and Means Committee
87th Cong., 1st Sess. (February, 1961)
(p. 455)

Statement of Medical Society of New York

The Medical Society of the State of New York, therefore, holds, in summary, (1) that the social security approach to medical care for the aged as embodied in the proposed law, H.R. 4222, is not needed in New York State, and (2) that the Kerr-Mills law, as implemented in New York State through the Metcalf-McCloskey law, should be given ample opportunity to prove that it is capable of meeting the medical needs of the aged population of the State of New York.

The chairman of the Committee on Federal Legislation of that society was subjected to cross-examination.

House Hearings
(p. 539)

Mr. Stephen B. Derounian [Rep., N.Y.]. Dr. Lawrence, will you spell out a bit more why you think the quality of medical care will be reduced under the proposed bill?

Dr. Lawrence. Congressman Derounian, we feel in our State medical society that if the King bill were passed there would be a certain amount of control over the provision of services to our patients by the doctors in the hospitals who provide these services. We feel that there would be an opportunity to extend this control to such an extent that doctors would not be able to give what they thought was the best care in many instances. We feel that there would be restriction on the hospitals of certain services. We feel that rather than improve medical care to our patients this would decrease the excellent care that our patients are now receiving.

At this stage, there seemed little chance that a health care bill would pass Congress although it seemed to be needed. The assumption that the Kerr-Mills program had stemmed the demands for medical care was rapidly being disproved.

Aid to Dependent Children

One of the sixteen priority measures requested by President Kennedy in 1961 was to make unemployed workers temporarily eligible for aid to dependent children (ADC) programs. (Previously the program had been limited to situations where the father was dead, disabled, or absent). The Administration bill to achieve this (H.R. 3865) was introduced on February 6 by Representative Wilbur Mills of Arkansas, chairman of the House Ways and Means Committee.

**Extended Unemployment Compensation and Aid to Dependent
Children of Unemployed Parents
Hearings on H.R. 3864 and H.R. 3865 before the House Ways
and Means Committee**
87th Cong., 1st Sess. (February, 1961)
(p. 93–95)

Legislative Proposal

It is proposed to broaden the coverage of title IV of the Social Security Act, under which grants are made to States for aid to dependent children, so as to provide assistance with Federal help to children who are in need because of the unemployment of a parent. This proposal would—

(*a*) Enable the States to include in their Federal-State aid to dependent children program not only the children deprived of care and support because of death, continued absence, or incapacity of a parent, but also the families where a parent is unemployed.

(*b*) Provide that States desiring to extend their Federal-State aid to dependent children program to the families of the unemployed be required to enter into cooperative arrangements with the State employment service to assure maximum utilization of that service in returning the unemployed parent to work. These arrangements would include provision for appropriate registration with the public employment service.

(*c*) State the intent of Congress that the additional funds made available be used for assistance to needy unemployed families who are either ineligible for assistance or who receive inadequate amounts of assistance and that the additional Federal funds are not intended to replace State and local funds now aiding needy persons.

(d) Become effective as of April 1, 1961, and would expire June 30, 1962.

(e) Temporarily increase the limitations on Federal funds which may be paid to Puerto Rico for public assistance.

Reasons for Proposal

(a) Federal grants to States under present law provide assistance only to the needy aged, blind, and disabled, and to dependent children who are deprived of parental support or care solely because of the death, continued absence, or the physical or mental incapacity of a parent. Where a family is in need because the father is unemployed, the family cannot receive assistance under the federally aided program of aid to dependent children.

(b) Assistance to other needy persons, such as the unemployed, must come from State and local funds without Federal sharing in the cost of such assistance.

(c) States make varying provisions for needy persons not included under the four federally aided categories, and in many States assistance is not available to persons in need because of unemployment or is inadequate because State and local funds are limited.

(d) The proposed change in the Federal law to include children of unemployed parents would enable the States to provide assistance with Federal help to families in need because of a parent's unemployment.

(e) The provision for the establishment of cooperative arrangements with the public employment service will further the objective of helping these needy families to again become self-supporting.

(f) This measure will help meet the needs of a substantial number of unemployed families, including those not covered by the unemployment compensation program and those who have exhausted their benefits under that program.

(g) Without an increase in the existing limitation on public assistance funds Puerto Rico would not receive additional Federal funds.

Program data for aid to dependent children—Current data

Number of families receiving assistance, November 1960 . . .   795,012
Number of children receiving assistance, November 1960 . .   2,341,615
Federal expenditures for fiscal year 1960 . . . . $665,700,000

Increases under proposal to add unemployment (assuming passage by Apr. 1, 1961, and participation by all States)

Average monthly number of families, more than   250,000
Average monthly number of children, more than   750,000

Increase in Federal funds for the 15-month period Apr. 1, 1961,
    through June 30, 1962 . . . . $305,000,000

*At the hearings, which included testimony on the Extended Unemploy-
ment Compensation Bill, the Administration's position was forcefully put
by Secretary Ribicoff.*

House Hearings
(p. 95)

Secretary Ribicoff. Basically, we are here seeking an amendment to the
social security laws, and we respectfully ask this committee to include children of unemployed parents as eligible for aid to dependent children, as we
do at present the children of absent, deceased, and disabled parents.

Basically, there is no reason why a hungry child of an unemployed father
should not be fed, as well as a child in other unfortunate circumstances.

There is a grave need, here, because what we are trying to do with ADC
is keep families together. And certainly we should not, as a society, so conduct our programs as to discourage a family grouping or to encourage a parent to leave the home in order for his children to receive aid in their basic
needs.

Of course, this also would have economic benefits, as well as the humane,
by placing into circulation during the next 15 months some $305 million. It
is part of the President's program against the present recession.

*By February 27, the committee had reported out the bill changing only
the Administration's provision that ADC should be terminated if the parent
refused an offered job "without good cause." The House debated the new
ADC bill only briefly. Although some members were far from enthusiastic,
the majority was clearly favorable.*

Congressional Debates
107 Congressional Record, p. 3764
(March 10, 1961)

Mr. [Noah M.] Mason. Mr. Chairman, I yield myself such time as I may require.

Mr. Chairman, H.R. 4884, the bill before us, is another instance of the
Federal Government stepping over into State affairs and attempting to assume the responsibilities and the duties that properly and naturally belong to
the States; and because of that I am opposed to it.

Mr. Chairman, as our very able committee chairman has stated, the legislation before the Committee today would amend the aid to dependent chil-

dren title of the Social Security Act so that children of unemployed parents will be eligible for benefits paid in part with Federal matching funds on the same basis as children who have been deprived of parental support by the death, absence, or incapacity of a parent.

Mr. Chairman, the bill is represented as a temporary program which would be for the 15-month period beginning April 1, 1961, and ending June 30, 1962, but let us not fool ourselves that the Congress will not be urged to extend this program further next year. We all know that 90 percent of the temporary programs have a way of staying with us in perpetuity. The people who now advocate this program as a temporary measure will in the months ahead be before the committee urging that the program be extended. I predict that the rationale of their urging will be that while we are not then in a recession we are experiencing structural unemployment, which results from the fact that actual productivity is lagging behind potential productivity. Therefore, let us recognize that we are not talking about a program of a few months' duration, costing perhaps a few hundred million dollars.

If the present proponents of the temporary program have their way, we are talking about a long-term program costing our taxpayers on an accumulative basis many billions of dollars.

Will these billions tend to improve the care of needy children in America? I think not. I think instead we will increase the Federal funds used for public assistance purposes and we will reduce the State and local funds made available for those purposes with the result that we have not increased the well-being of the potential beneficiaries. It is another instance of the Federal Government taxing the citizens of the States, deducting the Federal bureaucracy brokerage fee, and then returning a lesser amount to the States to finance programs that the States are capable of taking care of themselves without massive Federal intervention. In this connection I would say that the proponents of the legislation have not demonstrated a need for the measure they advocate but they have demonstrated a shocking unawareness of what is done for our needy citizens on the State and local levels of government.

Mr. Chairman, I am not going to belabor this issue. There is no one who is more generally interested in the well-being of our children than I am. It is because of my interest in children and because of the very strong feeling that I have that State and local community care of needy children should not be interfered with by the Federal Government that prompt me to oppose this proposal now before us.

Congressional Debates
107 Congressional Record, p. 3768

Mr. [John W.] McCormack. Mr. Chairman, I rise to warmly and vigorously endorse the provisions and objectives of H.R. 4884. This legislation amends title IV of the Social Security Act by providing Federal grants and aid to dependent children of unemployed parents.

Title IV of the Social Security Act has, since 1935, provided assistance to children only if the wage earning parent were dead, were permanently disabled, or ill, or missing from home. Many thousands of children, whose parents are unemployed, or face temporary financial disaster because of temporary illness, have been deprived of both the financial assistance and services of the aid-to-the-dependent-children program because of this restrictive insistence on the absenteeism of the wage earner.

It is my considered opinion, which is shared by many social welfare leaders, that these restrictions have contributed to advance instability to synthetic desertion when such desertion represented the father's only means of getting adequate financial protection for his minor children.

Under present State public welfare laws, children of unemployed parents may receive assistance only under the category of general assistance; in some States there is not even such a program of general assistance. In a great majority, where such a program exists there is neither Federal nor State supervision of the county and city administrations, which administer general assistance. The standards of such assistance, even when granted, are concededly very low and inadequate for the preservation of health and the prevention of illness.

The present national recession has resulted in the highest count of unemployed wage earners since World War II. It is no secret that hundreds of thousands of wage earners have exhausted their unemployment compensation benefits. It is common knowledge that the population of the United States has accelerated rapidly and particularly for the school age and preschool age population of the United States. Hundreds of thousands of children of such wage earners are now without the basic necessities of adequate food, adequate fuel and shelter, and without adequate clothing. This legislation makes it possible for all of the States to extend their aid-to-the-dependent-children program to children and families of unemployed wage earners, to protect their health, to give adequate relief, and to provide protective child welfare services when and where needed.

I urge your support of H.R. 4884.

After House passage by a voice vote, the Finance Committee began working on H.R. 4884, making certain changes.

Social Security — Child Welfare
Senate Report No. 165
87th Cong., 1st Sess.
(March 22, 1961)

II. BRIEF ANALYSIS OF AMENDMENTS ADDED
BY THE COMMITTEE

The Committee on Finance added the following amendments to the House-passed bill:

(1) With respect to the program authorizing payments to needy children of unemployed parents, the Senate bill —

(a) changes the effective date from April 1, 1961, as in the House bill, to May 1, 1961, so that the program will run for 14 months through June 1962;

(b) eliminates the provision of the House bill which required the State welfare agency to enter cooperative arrangements with the State vocational education agency relative to the retraining of unemployed parents; and

(c) gives to the States the option to exclude such aid to children of an unemployed parent who is receiving unemployment compensation.

(2) Extends the effective date of the so-called Flemming ruling, regarding denial by certain States, pursuant to State statute, of benefits to children in unsuitable homes, until 60 days after the close of the next regular session of the legislature. If this amendment is not adopted, Federal matching funds would be withheld after June 30, 1961, from States who have terminated assistance to children in a home determined to be unsuitable unless the State made other provision for the children affected.

(3) Provides Federal matching funds for the 14-month period from May 1, 1961 through June 30, 1962, for State expenditures for children under the aid to dependent children program, who, because of a court determination that continuation in the family's home would be contrary to the child's welfare, are placed in foster-family homes. Under present law, Federal matching is restricted to children living with parents or certain specified relatives.

(4) Increases from 80 to 100 percent the Federal share of the existing authority for grants for the training of public welfare personnel during the period of July 1, 1961, through June 30, 1963.

(5) Increases by $3 the maximum amount with respect to which the Federal Government will participate financially in State programs carrying out the special medical care provision for recipients of old-age assistance. This amendment increases the special provision made in 1960 for this purpose from $12 to $15, and will be effective July 1, 1961.

(6) Changes the title of the "aid to dependent children" program to "aid to families with dependent children," to more adequately describe the program.

(7) Authorizes the use of moneys appropriated to the Department of Labor for its administration of the employment security program to pay costs involved in borrowing State employment security personnel to administer the recently enacted Temporary Extended Unemployment Compensation Act.

The bill was also passed in the Senate by voice vote with a cursory debate. This time, in the conference the House accepted most of the Senate's recommendations, and the bill was rapidly passed. ADC-UP had been added to the categories of public assistance.

An Act to Amend Title IV of the Social Security Act to Authorize Federal Financial Participation in Aid to Dependent Children of Unemployed Parents
(May 8, 1961, 75 Statutes at Large 75)

"DEPENDENT CHILDREN OF UNEMPLOYED PARENTS

"Sec. 407. Effective for the period beginning May 1, 1961, and ending with the close of June 30, 1962, the term 'dependent child' shall, notwithstanding section 406 (a), include a needy child under the age of eighteen who has been deprived of parental support or care by reason of the unemployment (as defined by the State) of a parent and who is living with any of the relatives specified in section 406 (a) in a place of residence maintained by one or more of such relatives as his (or their) own home, but only with respect to a State whose State plan approved under section 402 —

"(1) includes aid for such child, and

"(2) includes —

"(A) provision for entering into cooperative arrangements with the system of public employment offices in the State looking toward employment of the unemployed parents of such children, including appropriate provision for registration and periodic reregistration of the unemployed parent of any such child and for maximum utilization of the job placement services and other services and facilities of such offices, and

"(B) provisions to assure that aid to dependent children is not provided to any such child or relative if, and for as long as, the unemployed parent refuses without good cause to accept employment, in which he is able to engage, which (i) is offered through such public employment offices, or (ii) is otherwise offered by an employer if the offer is determined by the State or local agency administering the State plan, after notification by such employer, to be a bona fide offer of such employment, and

"(3) includes provision for entering into cooperative arrangements

> with the State agency responsible for administering or supervising the administration of vocational education in the State, looking toward maximum utilization of available public vocational education services and facilities in the State in order to encourage the retraining of individuals capable of being retrained.

For purposes of the preceding sentence, a State plan may, at the option of the State, provide for the denial of all (or any part) of the aid under the plan to which any child or relative might otherwise be entitled for any month, if the unemployed parent of such child receives unemployment compensation under an unemployment compensation law of a State or of the United States for any week any part of which is included in such month."

*   *   *

Unemployment

Much of the 1961 legislation was prompted by a need to get the country "moving again." This was especially true for unemployment compensation. (By March no less than 6.9 per cent of the work force was unemployed and 1,862,000 had been unemployed for fifteen weeks or more). After only three weeks in office the new President had the Temporary Extended Unemployment Bill (H.R. 4806) before Congress; seven weeks after that it had been signed by the President.

The main reason for new federal legislation was that several of the state programs were running into difficulties. The 1935 legislation had imposed a 3.1 per cent payroll tax on those employers who were covered. In practice, however, only .4 per cent of this actually went to the federal trust fund, since employers were entitled to a 2.7 per cent tax credit for payment by way of state unemployment taxes. In fact, what most employers paid was far less than that, for in addition to good "experience rating" reductions allowed under the 1935 legislation, employers saved money because of the frugal administration and low benefits of state programs. Thus, an extended recession put state funds in unexpected jeopardy and depleted several state accounts in the federal trust fund.

This difficult financial situation led to a radical legislative proposal in 1961: that the federal .4 per cent tax should be pooled in the trust fund, rather than separated in a series of state accounts. Under the proposed Kennedy Bill, nine "deficit" states (Alaska, Kentucky, Michigan, New Jersey, New York, Ohio, Oregon, Pennsylvania, and West Virginia) would draw more benefit money out of the fund than their employers paid. The Administration proposal also called for the extension of the wage base from $3000 to $4800.

The first witness before the House committee (in joint hearings on the ADC-UP bill) was Secretary of Labor Arthur J. Goldberg.

**Temporary Unemployment Compensation and Aid to Dependent
Children of Unemployed Parents
Hearings on H.R. 3864 and H.R. 3865 before the House Ways
and Means Committee**
87th Cong., 1st Sess. (February, 1961)
(p. 12)

Statement of Arthur J. Goldberg

I appreciate the opportunity to appear before this committee to urge prompt
and favorable consideration of a proposal, H.R. 3864, that would carry out a
part of the program recommended by the President earlier this month to alleviate the distress arising from unsatisfactory performance of our economy
and to stimulate economic recovery and growth.

The legislation embodied in H.R. 3864 was more specifically recommended by the President to the Congress in letters of February 6 transmitting the bill to the President of the Senate and the Speaker of the House.
It would establish a temporary Federal program that would operate during
the present recession period to provide extended unemployment benefits
for workers who have exhausted their rights under State laws and to assist
the States in meeting the exceptional problems currently posed by the rapid
rise in the number of long term unemployed.

While H.R. 3864 is of course only a part of a broader program, it is a very
crucial part of this program. In fact, I believe that I can scarcely overstate
its importance in meeting the needs of the unemployed and providing purchasing power to those who will use it. This program will quickly put into
circulation almost a billion dollars of purchasing power to buy the necessities
of life. And this purchasing power would be paid out to the largest number,
and therefore at its highest rate, during the early months of the program,
when it will be most beneficial to our economy.

The President recognized the importance of this program in his February
6 letters when he stated:

> * * * The costs and effects of mass unemployment arising from a national
> recession clearly reach across State lines. The problem is national in scope,
> and the Federal Government has the responsibility for taking action as soon as
> possible to meet it. That is why I propose this temporary program as a first
> step. The extension of the unemployment compensation program will permit
> 3 million workers to receive benefits totaling about $950 million.

It is unnecessary, I am sure, for me to belabor the need for this program.

As we all know, unemployment in this country has assumed serious dimensions. We are experiencing high levels of unemployment not only because we are now in a recession, but because we have had a gradual rise in
unemployment, apart from recessions over the last decade.

I am convinced that the enactment of H.R. 3864 would be an important
step in the right direction; it would on the one hand meet the needs of the

workers and their families, and, on the other, would help to create and sustain a demand for the goods and services available under our economy.

Briefly, H.R. 3864 provides for federally financed additional unemployment compensation to each unemployed worker who has exhausted his rights, equal to 50 percent of the benefits provided him by State law, up to a maximum of 13 times his weekly benefit amount, that is, 13 weeks for total unemployment. Where a State after the effective date of this program has paid unemployment benefits to the individual under its law in excess of 26 weeks for total unemployment, the Federal Government will reimburse the State. Whether by reimbursement to the State or by the payment of Federal benefits to the individual, the total payable out of Federal funds may not exceed a maximum of 13 times his weekly benefit amount for the duration of this program. Nor will Federal funds be used for payments with respect to an individual if any such payment would bring his total benefits (Federal and State) with respect to a benefit year, including extended duration, to more than 39 times his weekly benefit amount.

The provision for reimbursement is included in recognition of the action taken by some States in providing more than 26 weeks of normal or extended duration to some or all workers. Without such a provision, these States would be placed at a disadvantage, since they would have assumed the cost burden of long term unemployment that would in other States be met from Federal funds. In addition, reimbursement would help replenish the reserves of those States which have had heavy compensable unemployment.

The Federal extended benefits under the bill would be payable promptly; that is, for weeks of unemployment beginning as soon as 15 days after enactment of the legislation. Workers who had exhausted their benefit rights after October 31, 1960, and are still unemployed would be entitled to the temporary benefits. The program would remain in full effect for approximately a year, that is, until the end of March 1962. Individuals who had filed a claim and who had been found entitled to extended benefits by that date, however, could draw their benefits for weeks of unemployment beginning after April 1 but before July 1, 1962.

Benefits and reimbursement would be paid only in States which enter into an agreement with the Secretary of Labor. The State may choose to enter an agreement only to act as agent for the United States in the payment of the emergency Federal benefits; it may enter into an agreement providing only for reimbursement to the State for benefits paid by it in excess of 26 weeks; or it may enter into an agreement providing for both. The agreement will be very simple, designed to assure that the statute is complied with and that the Federal funds are safeguarded. It will, in fact, be very much like the agreements now in effect between the State employment security agencies and the Department of Labor under which Federal benefits are paid to Federal employees and exservicemen.

If all the States enter into agreements the costs of this program, it is estimated, would be about $950 million. These costs would be financed initially out of general funds of the Treasury. Ultimately, however, they would be financed out of proceeds of the Federal unemployment tax, which would be returned to the general funds of the Treasury. Thus, the cost of financing the program would be spread among employers in all the States. Since no State is a self-contained economic unit, we should not expect a State to carry alone the crushing burden of long duration unemployment. This is especially so when the causes of prolonged unemployment cross State lines. The proposed financing would pool the risk and costs of recessionary unemployment, which is more a national than a State problem.

There is another advantage to financing the program in the manner proposed by the bill; namely, that Federal benefits can be paid promptly in all States, since no State legislative action would be necessary in order to do so. Speed in putting the money made available by the program into the hands of the unemployed is a significant factor in the program's value as an emergency antirecession measure.

The cost of the program proposed by the bill would be substantially met out of the increased revenues resulting from the proposed increase in the wages taxable under the Federal Unemployment Tax Act. At present the taxable wage base under this act is $3,000. It is proposed to increase it to $4,800, effective January 1, 1962. This would produce additional Federal revenues through fiscal year 1966 of about $695 million, or an annual average approximating $172 million. These receipts, combined with the additional revenues resulting from the recent 0.1 percent increase in the Federal unemployment tax will make it possible to cover the cost of the program proposed by H.R. 3864 by the end of fiscal year 1966. The total Federal unemployment tax income, after paying all employment security administrative costs, Federal and State, including the costs of the proposed program, would be sufficient also to build up a balance in the Federal unemployment account for advances under title XII to States which are in financial difficulty. The balance would be increased by the $225 million of outstanding title XII advances to the States which will have been repaid by then.

Apart from its role in financing the emergency program, an increase in the taxable wage base has the further advantage of being a long overdue improvement that would assist in augmenting the capacity of our present unemployment insurance system to do a better job. Only about 60 percent of covered wages are now being taxed. Compare this with the 100 percent subject to tax when the system was established, and the 97 percent . . . when the $3,000 limit was established in 1939 for the purpose of achieving the technical advantages of conforming the wage base of the Federal unemployment tax to the wage base of the old-age and survivors insurance tax. . . .

By February 23 the committee had voted out a bill, which raised the effective federal tax from .4 per cent to .8 per cent for a two year period, but left the tax base unchanged. Somewhat surprisingly the pooling arrangements were retained.

Temporary Unemployment Compensation Act of 1961
House Report No. 271
87th Cong., 1st Sess.
(March, 1961)

IV. GENERAL EXPLANATION OF THE BILL

A. Compensation and Reimbursement Provisions of Bill

There are two kinds of Federal payments provided by the bill.

First, an unemployed worker could receive 50 percent of the number of weeks provided under the State program by way of Federal temporary unemployment compensation (subject to a maximum of 13 weeks). In determining the number of weeks on which to base the 50-percent extended duration, the number of weeks provided in the State's "regular" compensation program, as well as the number of weeks provided under any "additional" unemployment compensation program which the State has established for periods of high unemployment, will be taken into account in determining payments to the unemployed worker. For example, if a State's "regular" unemployment compensation program provides 12 weeks of benefits and such State also has an additional unemployment compensation program which provides 6 weeks of benefits, the Federal payment to the unemployed worker would be 50 percent of this amount, or 9 weeks. The weekly benefit amount would be determined in accordance with the various State benefit formulas and benefits would be payable subject to the terms and conditions of the various State laws. To be entitled to benefits, a worker must be registered with a State employment office and must be able to work and available for work.

Second, in a State which provides more than 26 weeks' duration of benefits, the State would be reimbursed for the number of weeks paid in excess of 26. If, for example, the State pays 30 weeks of benefits to an individual, the State would be reimbursed for 4 weeks. The individual would then be eligible for temporary extended unemployment compensation for an additional 9 weeks of total unemployment, reaching the maximum of 13 weeks provided under the bill.

The bill provides that the total payments and reimbursements that can be made with respect to an unemployed person will be fixed at the time of his first claim for temporary extended unemployment compensation or for his first week for which reimbursement is made under the bill, whichever is earlier. Once this total is fixed, the individual may not establish any additional entitlement to Federal payments by again qualifying for State benefits and again exhausting his State entitlement.

The bill provides that Federal payments may not be made if they would bring the total to which an individual is entitled (State and Federal) to more than 39 weeks of benefits for total unemployment without his establishing a new benefit year under State law. Thus, if an individual receives, prior to the effective date of this bill, 30 weeks of benefits under a State law, there would be no reimbursement, since these weeks occurred prior to the effective date. If the individual were still unemployed after the effective date, he would be entitled to 13 additional weeks of temporary extended unemployment compensation but he could not obtain benefits for more than 9 weeks without establishing a new benefit year.

Nine States now have provisions in their permanent law for the payment of unemployment compensation for more than 26 weeks in a benefit year. A benefit year is usually the 12-month period which begins when the worker first becomes unemployed and files a claim. Six States have adopted provisions for temporarily extending their benefit duration during periods of high unemployment. In these States the temporary extended benefits are "triggered" during periods of high unemployment by reaching the percentage of unemployment specified in the State law. In five of the six States, temporary extended benefits are now being paid or are expected to be paid in the very near future.

B. Financing Provisions of the Bill

The bill provides that the estimated cost of $927 million for temporary Federal extended unemployment payments and reimbursements is to be financed through a temporary increase in the Federal unemployment tax. This would be accomplished by raising the net amount of this tax which comes to the Federal Government from four-tenths of 1 percent to eight-tenths of 1 percent on the present taxable wage base of $3,000. This increase of four-tenths of 1 percent would be effective for calendar years 1962 and 1963 and, it is estimated, will produce $984 million. This increase in the tax would apply to all employers taxable under the Federal Unemployment Tax Act.

Under existing law the Federal unemployment tax is applied to employers who have four or more employees at the rate of 3.1 percent on the first $3,000 paid to each employee. A credit of not to exceed 2.7 percent for State unemployment taxes is provided for employers against this 3.1 percent tax, accounting for the net Federal tax of four-tenths of 1 percent. The rates of tax imposed by the various States vary. Within a State the tax rates vary under the "experience rating" provisions of its law.

The bill increases the Federal unemployment tax to 3.5 percent for taxable years 1962 and 1963. The 2.7 percent credit against this 3.5 percent would still apply. Thus, for the 2 years involved the net additional Federal tax would be 0.4 percent for the purposes of financing the program provided by the bill.

The machinery which would be established for financing these temporary Federal payments would be the setting up of a separate account in the unemployment trust fund to be called the "Federal extended compensation account." Initially, the cost of these payments will be met by advances from the general fund of the Treasury to the Federal extended compensation account. These advances (excluding the cost of extended benefits for Federal employees and ex-servicemen) will be repaid out of the proceeds from the temporary increase of four-tenths of 1 percent in the net Federal unemployment tax. Any excess revenues which may be developed from this temporary increase above the amounts necessary to repay the Treasury advances will be distributed to the States on a pro rata basis determined by the proportion for 1962 and 1963 of taxable wages in a particular State to the total taxable wages for all States.

C. Period Covered by the Bill

Temporary Federal unemployment compensation (or reimbursement) may be paid for weeks of unemployment beginning 15 days after the date of enactment of this legislation. As noted earlier, these payments and reimbursements will be made only in the case of States which choose to enter agreements with the Secretary of Labor and only after the agreements are entered into. Payments may be made with respect to individuals who have exhausted their benefits under applicable State law after June 30, 1960, and before April 1, 1962. A person who has begun to receive benefits provided by the bill (or benefits reimbursed under the bill) by April 1, 1962, can continue to receive such payments for weeks of unemployment which began on or before June 30, 1962, the termination date for the program.

The temporary increase in the Federal unemployment tax from 3.1 to 3.5 percent (an increase of four-tenths of 1 percent in the net Federal tax) will apply for the calendar years 1962 and 1963 only.

The bill easily passed the House and a week later hearings began before the Senate Finance Committee. Once again Secretary Goldberg pressed for the legislation, strongly opposing any amendment to exclude or reduce benefits of those who were receiving other assistance.

The Finance Committee made several major changes including the highly significant Byrd Amendment. Basically, this attempted two things: tax changes were put on a pay-as-you-go basis by moving the tax increases forward from 1962–63 to 1961–62; pooling in the federal trust fund was not allowed, but states could increase taxes to repay loans from the fund. Its other major purpose was to impose a means test for unemployment payments, including the reduction of benefits if the recipient was receiving other private or public assistance funds. The committee also extended moneys available for administration of programs by the states and suggested a survey of the additional persons covered by the bill.

The opponents of the Byrd Amendment waged a successful attempt to have it defeated on the floor. However, the 'pay-as-you-go' provisions were retained in a close vote. The amendment for reduced benefits was finally accepted, as were the survey and the increase for administrative costs.

In conference, opposition to the pooling system diminished when it was pointed out that seventeen states had failed thus far to repay their loans under the 1958 legislation. The Senate demand for reductions because of other assistance was weakened and the pay-as-you-go provision was rejected. The survey was accepted, as well as the increase for state administrative costs, and in this form, the bill was approved by both houses on March 22.

Temporary Extended Unemployment Compensation Act of 1961
(March 24, 1961, 75 Statutes at Large 8)

* * *

Eligibility

Sec. 3. (a) Payment of temporary extended unemployment compensation shall be made, for any week of unemployment which begins in the covered period specified in section 6, to individuals who have, after June 30, 1960, exhausted (within the meaning prescribed by the Secretary by regulations) all rights under the State law and title XV and who have no rights to unemployment compensation with respect to such week under any such law or under any other Federal or State unemployment compensation law.

Weekly Benefit Amount ₁

(b) The temporary extended unemployment compensation payable to an individual for a week of total unemployment shall be the weekly benefit amount (including allowances for dependents) for total unemployment which was payable to him pursuant to the State law or title XV under which he last exhausted his rights before making his first claim under this Act. The temporary extended unemployment compensation payable to an individual for a week of less than total unemployment shall be computed on the basis of such weekly benefit amount, except that in such computation allowances for dependents shall be taken into account in the manner provided by the applicable State law with respect to such a week of less than total unemployment.

* * *

LIMITATION ON TOTAL PAYMENTS AND REIMBURSEMENTS

Overall Limitation

Sec. 5. (a) The sum of the temporary extended unemployment compensation payable to any individual, plus the State unemployment compensation paid to such individual with respect to which any State is entitled to re-imbursement under this Act (or would be entitled to such reimbursement but for the fact that such compensation is paid under title XV), shall not exceed whichever of the following amounts is the smaller:

(1) An amount equal to 50 percent of the total amount of State un-employment compensation (including allowances for dependents) which was payable to him for his first compensation period, or

(2) An amount equal to 13 times his weekly benefit amount for his first compensation period.

*   *   *

Compensation To Be Reduced by Certain Retirement Pensions and Annuities

(e) (1) Any agreement under this Act shall provide that temporary ex-tended unemployment compensation payable to an individual with respect to a week shall be reduced, under regulations prescribed by the Secretary, by any amount received with respect to such week as a retirement pension or annuity under a public or private retirement plan or system provided, or contributed to, by any base period employer. An amount received with re-spect to a period other than a week shall be prorated by weeks. No reduction shall be made under this paragraph for (A) any retirement pension or annuity received by reason of disability, or (B) any amount received until title II of the Social Security Act.

(2) For purposes of this subsection, the term "base period employer" means, in the case of any individual, any person who paid such individual any remuneration for employment which was taken into account in com-puting the amount or duration of any State unemployment compensation which was payable to such individual at any time during the compensation period.

(3) For purposes of section 3(c), so much of any State law as provides a disqualification for, or a reduction in, State unemployment compensation for amounts received as retirement pensions or annuities (or for amounts received under title II of the Social Security Act) shall be deemed to be in-consistent with the provisions of this Act relating to the payment of tem-porary extended unemployment compensation.

1962

The "New" Approach to Public Welfare: Genesis

By 1962, the idea that with the growth of OASDI, the need for public as-sistance would wither away, was patently a fallacy. It was time for "the great re-examination." Groundwork for such a reconsideration had been laid even before President Kennedy took office in 1960. A task force under Wilbur Cohen, then at the University of Michigan, began work on the general problems of public assistance, and in September, 1961, their Report of the Ad Hoc Committee on Public Welfare *called for both short- and long-term changes.*

Report of the Ad Hoc Committee on Public Welfare
Department of Health, Education, and Welfare
September, 1961

Recommendation 1. Strengthening Aid to Dependent Children
(ADC) Families

Measures should be adopted for the immediate initiation of an accelerated, intensive program, throughout all welfare departments, of rehabilitative services to ADC families by trained personnel. Adequate financial support should be provided to states and localities to enable them to help individuals and families receiving ADC become self-supporting, and to correct or prevent the family disruptions which result from absence of a father or his unemployment.

Recommendation 2. ADC Legislation—Recent Amendments and
Proposals for Changes

The amendments to Title IV in the Social Security Act passed in 1961 should be extended to continue (a) assistance to children of unemployed parents, and (b) assistance to children in foster homes. (c) A new amendment should be adopted to provide for federal participation in meeting the needs of physically or mentally incapacitated or unemployed fathers residing in the home, on the same basis as participation now is available for others in the household. (d) Compliance by all states with the suitable homes requirement should become effective by September 1, 1962, as provided by legislation subsequent to the ruling of the previous Secretary of Health, Education, and Welfare.

Recommendation 3. Measures for Studying and Dealing with
the Problem of Illegitimacy

Because of the disturbing rate of growth of illegitimacy in all segments of society in this country, and its impact as one of the major causes of dependency in ADC, it is recommended that (a) a comprehensive national study of the social causes of illegitimacy in the total population and of effective measures of prevention and treatment be undertaken by the Department of Health, Education, and Welfare and (b) there be federal encouragement and financial support for special projects by state and local public welfare agencies to provide intensive preventive and treatment service for mothers and their children born out of wedlock.

Recommendation 4. Federal Participation in Community Work Programs

The major line of defense against joblessness should be programs of training and retraining, unemployment insurance and public works programs. To the extent that these do not meet the problem, federal participation should be permitted in payments of public assistance to persons engaged in community work programs under federally approved state plans. These should include provision for training and retraining; standards to protect the health and safety of the workers; provision for payment at not less than prevailing wages; and avoidance of replacement of regular jobs in private or public employment. Development of community work programs by localities should be optional, but in accordance with state standards.

Recommendation 5. Improvement of Care for Children

Child welfare appropriations should be raised to the authorized amount of $25,000,000 to improve the adequacy of preventive and protective children's services. A supplemental appropriation of $5,000,000 should be made to provide essential day care services for children.

Recommendation 6. Earnings of Youth on ADC

Deduction of all of the earnings of an employed child in the household should not be required. Legislation should be enacted which will permit exemption of such earnings from deduction from the amount of assistance granted the family.

Recommendation 7. Removal of Residence Requirements
for Assistance

All restrictions based on length of residence should be eliminated as eligibility requirements for public assistance and there should be a system of financial incentives to states to encourage them to move in this direction, with the option of taking such steps in one assistance category at a time.

Recommendation 8. Safeguarding the Principle of Cash Payment
Through Limited Use of Vouchers

For those persons who are found to have severe problems of money management, but who do not require a court-appointed guardian, special provision should be made for payment of assistance by voucher, provided that proper safeguards are maintained, and provided further that no more than one percent of federal funds granted to the States for assistance is used for voucher payments.

Recommendation 9. Extension of Aid to the Disabled

The Aid to the Permanently and Totally Disabled program should be extended to include persons who are temporarily or partially disabled. This would permit assistance to persons whose ability to provide for their own needs is interrupted by temporary sickness or injury, which may be no less disruptive in its immediate effects on themselves and their families than the problems of those permanently and totally disabled.

Recommendation 10. Experimentation and Progress in Research
and Demonstration

A sharply increased program of research and demonstration should be supported by the federal government to stimulate the development of new knowledge of the complex problems relating to dependency and family breakdown, and to provide for experimental approaches to meet these problems.

Recommendation 11. Assistance and Rehabilitation Services to Families

A new approach to reducing social problems by serving the family through a single category of assistance with intensified rehabilitative services, supported by special federal grants under federally approved state plans, is urgently recommended.

Recommendation 12. Improving Personnel for Rehabilitative Purposes

To make possible the rehabilitative services so strongly advocated, the goal should be established that within 10 years, one-third of all persons engaged in social work capacities in public welfare should hold masters' degrees in social work. This should be sought through an augmented program of grants to states, as well as continuation of federal support to accredited schools of social work. There should also be support for a stepped-up emphasis on upgrading staff through in-service training in state and local welfare agencies.

Recommendation 13. Improvement of Child Welfare Services

It is imperative that the resources, professional competence and range of coverage of the public child welfare services be brought to a level that will enable them: (a) to deal effectively with the hazards that jeopardize the well-being of too many of the nation's children; and (b) to give greater emphasis to protection of children living in their own family homes. For these purposes, federal child welfare services grants to States should be broadened to provide for federal participation in the cost of the total on-going child welfare services. They should be on a variable formula basis.

Recommendation 14. Provisions for Continuing Program of
Research and Special Demonstration Projects

A long-range program of support for research and demonstration programs should be developed through two channels: (a) grants to states for efforts to determine facts affecting the needs in the state for assistance and rehabilitative services and to evaluate the effectiveness of administration; and (b) grants to other social agencies or institutions of higher learning for projects to shed light on the basic causes of social problems and special approaches to services which promise benefit.

During 1961, Secretary Ribicoff also appointed George Wyman to make a report on the administrative aspects of the Children's Bureau and the Bureau of Public Assistance. This report was similarly strong.

Action

By December, 1961, HEW had finished its study and President Kennedy announced proposals for major legislative changes early in 1962.

Special Presidential Message to the Congress on Public Welfare Programs
(February 1, 1962)*

To the Congress of the United States:

Few nations do more than the United States to assist their least fortunate citizens—to make certain that no child, no elderly or handicapped citizen, no family in any circumstances in any State, is left without the essential needs for a decent and healthy existence. In too few nations, I might add, are the people aware of the progressive strides this country has taken in demonstrating the humanitarian side of freedom. Our record is a proud one — and it sharply refutes those who accuse us of thinking only in the materialistic terms of cash registers and calculating machines.

Our basic public welfare programs were enacted more than a quarter century ago. Their contribution to our national strength and well-being in the intervening years has been remarkable.

But the times, the conditions, the problems have changed — and the nature and objectives of our public assistance and child welfare programs must be changed, also, if they are to meet our current needs.

The impact of these changes should not be underestimated:

— People move more often—from the farm to the city, from urban centers to the suburbs, from the East to the West, from the South to the North and Midwest.

— Living costs, and especially medical costs, have spiraled.

— The pattern of our population has changed. There are more older people, more children, more young marriages, divorces, desertions and separations.

— Our system of social insurance and related programs has grown greatly: in 1940 less than 1% of the aged were receiving monthly old age insurance benefits; today over 2/3rds of our aged are receiving these benefits. In 1940

*Public Papers of the Presidents, John F. Kennedy, 1962, p. 98.

only 21,000 children, in families where the breadwinner had died, were getting survivor insurance benefits; today such monthly benefits are being paid to about 2 million children.

All of these changes affect the problems public welfare was intended to relieve as well as its ability to relieve it. Moreover, even the nature and causes of poverty have changed. At the time the Social Security Act established our present basic framework for public aid, the major cause of poverty was unemployment and economic depression. Today, in a year of relative prosperity and high employment, we are more concerned about the poverty that persists in the midst of abundance.

The reasons are often more social than economic, more often subtle than simple. Some are in need because they are untrained for work—some because they cannot work, because they are too young or too old, blind or crippled. Some are in need because they are discriminated against for reasons they cannot help. Responding to their ills with scorn or suspicion is inconsistent with our moral precepts and inconsistent with their nearly universal preference to be independent. But merely responding with a "relief check" to complicated social or personal problems—such as ill health, faulty education, domestic discord, racial discrimination, or inadequate skills—is not likely to provide a lasting solution. Such a check must be supplemented, or in some cases made unnecessary, by positive services and solutions, offering the total resources of the community to meet the total needs of the family to help our less fortunate citizens help themselves.

Public welfare, in short, must be more than a salvage operation, picking up the debris from the wreckage of human lives. Its emphasis must be directed increasingly toward prevention and rehabilitation—on reducing not only the long-range cost in budgetary terms but the long-range cost in human terms as well. Poverty weakens individuals and nations. Sounder public welfare policies will benefit the nation, its economy, its morale, and, most importantly, its people.

Under the various titles of the Social Security Act, funds are available to help the States provide assistance and other social services to the needy, aged and blind, to the needy disabled, and to dependent children. In addition, grants are available to assist the States to expand and strengthen their programs of child welfare services. These programs are essentially State programs. But the Federal Government, by its substantial financial contribution, its leadership, and the standards it sets, bears a major responsibility. To better fulfill this responsibility, the Secretary of Health, Education, and Welfare recently introduced a number of administrative changes designed to get people off assistance and back into useful, productive roles in society.

These changes provided for:

— the more effective location of deserting parents;

— an effort to reduce that proportion of persons receiving assistance through willful misrepresentation, although that proportion is only a small part of the 1.5% of persons on the rolls found to be ineligible;

   — allowing dependent children to save money for educational, employment or medical needs without having that amount deducted from their public assistance grants;

   — providing special services and safeguards to children in families of unmarried parents, in families where the father has deserted, or in homes in danger of becoming morally or physically unsuitable; and

   — an improvement in the training of personnel, the development of services and the coordination of agency efforts.

In keeping with this new emphasis, the name of the Bureau of Public Assistance has been changed to the Bureau of Family Services.

But only so much can be done by administrative changes. New legislation is required if our State-operated programs are to be fully able to meet modern needs.

I. Prevention and Rehabilitation

As already mentioned, we must place more stress on services instead of relief.

I recommend that the States be encouraged by the offer of additional Federal funds to strengthen and broaden the rehabilitative and preventive services they offer to persons who are dependent or who would otherwise become dependent. Additional Federal funds would induce and assist the States to establish or augment their rehabilitation services, strengthen their child welfare services, and add to their number of competent public welfare personnel. At the present time, the cost of these essential services is lumped with all administrative costs—routine clerical and office functions—and the Federal Government pays one-half of the total of all such costs incurred by the States. By separating out and identifying the cost of these essential rehabilitation, social work and other service costs, and paying the States three-fourths of such services—a step I earnestly recommend for your consideration—the Federal Government will enable and encourage the States to provide more comprehensive and effective services to rehabilitate those on welfare. The existing law should also be amended to permit the use of Federal funds for utilization by the State welfare agency of specialists from other State agencies who can help mount a concerted attack on the problems of dependency.

There are other steps we can take which will have an important effect on this effort. One of these is to expand and improve the Federal-State program of vocational rehabilitation for disabled people. Among the 92,500 disabled men and women successfully rehabilitated into employment through this program last year were about 15,000 who had formerly been receiving public assistance. Let me repeat this figure: 15,000 people, formerly supported by the taxpayers through welfare, are now back at work as self-supporting taxpayers. Much more of this must be done—until we are restoring to employment every disabled person who can benefit from these rehabilitation services.

The prevention of future adult poverty and dependency must begin with the care of dependent children — those who must receive public welfare by virtue of a parent's death, disability, desertion or unemployment. Our society not only refuses to leave such children hungry, cold, and devoid of opportunity — we are insistent that such children not be community liabilities throughout their lives. Yet children who grow up in deprivation, without adequate protection, may be poorly equipped to meet adult responsibilities.

The Congress last year approved, on a temporary basis, aid for the dependent children of the unemployed as a part of the permanent Aid to Dependent Children program. This legislation also included temporary provisions for foster care where the child has been removed from his home, and an increase in Federal financial assistance to the aged, blind and disabled. The need for these temporary improvements has not abated, and their merit is clear. I recommend that these temporary provisions be made permanent.

But children need more than aid when they are destitute. We need to improve our preventive and protective services for children as well as adults. I recommend that the present ceiling of $25,000,000 authorized for annual appropriations for grants to the States for child welfare services be gradually raised, beginning with $30,000,000 for 1963, up to $50,000,000 for the fiscal year ending June 30, 1969, and succeeding years.

Finally, many women now on assistance rolls could obtain jobs and become self-supporting if local day care programs for their young children were available. The need for such programs for the children of working mothers has been increasing rapidly. Of the 22 million women now working, about 3 million have children under 6, and another 4½ million have school-age children between 6 and 17. Adequate care for these children during their most formative years is essential to their proper growth and training. Therefore, I recommend that the child welfare provisions of the Social Security Act be changed to authorize earmarking up to $5,000,000 of grants to the States in 1963 and $10,000,000 a year thereafter for aid in establishing local programs for the day care of young children of working mothers.

II. Promoting New Skills and Independence

We must find ways of returning far more of our dependent people to independence. We must find ways of returning them to a participating and productive role in the community.

One sure way is by providing the opportunity every American cherishes to do sound and useful work. For this reason, I am recommending a change in the law to permit States to maintain with Federal financial help community work and training projects for unemployed people receiving welfare payments. Under such a program, unemployed people on welfare would be helped to retain their work skills or learn new ones; and the local community would obtain additional manpower on public projects.

But earning one's welfare payment through required participation in a community work or training project must be an opportunity for the individual on welfare, not a penalty. Federal financial participation will be conditioned upon proof that the work will serve a useful community or public purpose, will not displace regular employees, will not impair prevailing wages and working conditions, and will be accompanied by certain basic health and safety protections. Provisions must also be made to assure appropriate arrangements for the care and protection of children during the absence from home of any parent performing work or undergoing training.

Moreover, systematic encouragement would be given all welfare recipients to obtain vocational counseling, testing, and placement services from the United States Employment Service and to secure useful training wherever new job skills would be helpful. Close cooperative arrangements would be established with existing training and vocational education programs, and with the vocational and on-the-job training opportunities to be created under the Manpower Development and Training and Youth Employment Opportunities programs previously proposed.

III. More Skilled Personnel

It is essential that state and local welfare agencies be staffed with enough qualified personnel to insure constructive and adequate attention to the problems of needy individuals — to take the time to help them find and hold a job — to prevent public dependency and to strive, where that is not possible, for rehabilitation — and to ascertain promptly whether any individual is receiving aid for which he does not qualify, so that aid can be promptly withdrawn.

Unfortunately, there is an acute shortage of trained personnel in all our welfare programs. The lack of experienced social workers for programs dealing with children and their families is especially critical.

At the present time, when States expend funds for the training of personnel for the administration of these programs, they receive Federal grants on a dollar-for-dollar basis. This arrangement has failed to produce a sufficient number of trained staff, especially social workers. I recommend, therefore, that Federal assistance to the States for training additional welfare personnel be increased; and that in addition, the Secretary of Health, Education, and Welfare be authorized to make special arrangements for the training of family welfare personnel to work with those children whose parents have deserted, whose parents are unmarried, or who have other serious problems.

IV. Fitting General Conditions or Safeguards to Individual Needs

In order to make certain that welfare funds go only to needy people, the Social Security Act requires the States to take all income and resources of the applicant into consideration in determining need. Although Federal law permits, it does not require States to take into full account the full expenses individuals have in earning income. This is not consistent with equity, common sense or other Federal laws such as our tax code. It only discourages the will to earn. In order to encourage assistance recipients to find and retain employment, I therefore recommend that the Act be amended to require the States to take into account the expenses of earning income.

Among relatives caring for dependent children are a few who do not properly handle their assistance payments—some to the extent that the well-being of the child is adversely affected. Where the State determines that a relative's ability to manage money is contrary to the welfare of the child, Federal law presently requires payments to be made to a legal guardian or representative, if Federal funds are to be used. But this general requirement may sometimes block progress in particular situations. In order to recognize the necessity for each State to make exceptions to this rule in a very limited number of cases, I recommend that the law be amended to permit Federal sharing to continue even though protective payments in behalf of children—not to exceed ½ of 1% of ADC recipients in each State—are made to other persons concerned with the welfare of the family. The States would be required to reexamine these exceptions at intervals to determine whether a more permanent arrangement such as guardianship is required.

When first enacted, the aid to dependent children program provided for Federal sharing in assistance payments only to the child. Since 1950, there has been Federal sharing in any assistance given to one adult in the household as well as to the child or children. Inasmuch as under current law there may be two parents in homes covered by this program, one incapacitated or unemployed, I recommend in the interest of equity the extension of Federal sharing in assistance payments both to the needy relative and to his or her spouse when both are living in the home with the child.

V. More Efficient Administration

Under present public assistance provisions, States may impose residence requirements up to five of the last nine years for the aged, blind and disabled. Increased mobility, as previously mentioned, is a hallmark of our times. It should not operate unfairly on either an individual State or an individual family. I recommend that the Social Security Act be amended so as to provide that States receiving Federal funds not exclude any otherwise eligible persons who have been residents of the State for one year immediately preceding their application for assistance. I also recommend that the law be amended to provide a small increase in assistance funds to those States which simplify their laws by removing all residence requirements in any of their Federally aided programs.

In view of the changing nature of the economic and social problems of the country, the desirability of a periodic review of our public welfare programs is obvious. For that purpose I propose that the Secretary of Health, Education, and Welfare be authorized to appoint an Advisory Council on Public Welfare representing broad community interests and concerns, and such other advisory committees as he deems necessary to advise and consult with him in the administration of the Social Security Act.

No study of the public welfare program can fail to note the difficulty of the problems faced or the need to be imaginative in dealing with them. Accordingly, I recommend that amendments be made to encourage experimental, pilot or demonstration projects that would promote the objectives of the assistance titles and help make our welfare programs more flexible and adaptable to local needs.

The simplification and coordination of administration and operation would greatly improve the adequacy and consistency of assistance and related services. As a step in that direction, I recommend that a new title to the Social Security Act be enacted which would give to States the option of submitting a single, unified State plan combining their assistance programs for aged, blind and disabled, and their medical assistance programs for the aged, granting to such States additional Federal matching for medical payments on behalf of the blind and disabled.

These proposed far-reaching changes — aimed at far-reaching problems — are in the public interest and in keeping with our finest traditions. The goals of our public welfare programs must be positive and constructive — to create economic and social opportunities for the less fortunate — to help them find productive, happy and independent lives. It must stress the integrity and preservation of the family unit. It must contribute to the attack on dependency, juvenile delinquency, family breakdown, illegitimacy, ill health and disability. It must reduce the incidence of these problems, prevent their occurrence and recurrence, and strengthen and protect the vulnerable in a highly competitive world.

Unless such problems are dealt with effectively, they fester, and grow, sapping the strength of society as a whole and extending their consequences in troubled families from one generation to the next.

The steps I recommend to you today to alleviate these problems will not come cheaply. They will cost more money when first enacted. But they will restore human dignity; and in the long run, they will save money. I have recommended in the Budget submitted for fiscal year 1963 sufficient funds to cover the extension of existing programs and the new legislation here proposed.

Communities which have — for whatever motives — attempted to save money through ruthless and arbitrary cutbacks in their welfare rolls have found their efforts to little avail. The root problems remained.

But communities which have tried the rehabilitative road — the road I have recommended today — have demonstrated what can be done with creative, thoughtfully conceived, and properly managed programs of prevention and social rehabilitation. In those communities, families have been restored to self-reliance, and relief rolls have been reduced.

To strengthen our human resources — to demonstrate the compassion of free men — and in the light of our own constructive self-interest — we must bring our welfare programs up to date. I urge that the Congress do so without delay.

John F. Kennedy

These remarks were used as the basis of legislation which attempted to shift public assistance from financial aid to rehabilitation plans. The bill (H.R. 10032) also called for increased public assistance programs and better safeguards against welfare abuses. It provided a permanent solution to the ADC "suitable home" controversy by permitting states to discontinue aid to dependent children if a state statute provided other adequate care and assistance for such a child.

The bill prompted produced some of the most interesing hearings since 1935. The first witness was naturally HEW Secretary Abraham Ribicoff.

Public Welfare Amendments of 1962
Hearings on H.R. 10032 before the House Ways
and Means Committee
87th Cong., 2d Sess. (March, 1962)
(p. 63)

Statement of Abraham Ribicoff, Secretary of Health,
Education, and Welfare

I appear before you in support of H.R. 10032, which was introduced by Chairman Mills under the title of "Public Welfare Amendments of 1962."

This landmark bill will bring a new spirit in our public welfare program. Section 2 of the bill outlines the six new objectives of the legislation:

(1) Services: Services to help families become self-supporting and independent.

(2) Prevention: Prevention of dependency by dealing with the problems causing dependency.

(3) Incentives: Incentives to recipients of public assistance to improve their condition so as to make public assistance unnecessary and incentives to the States to improve their welfare programs.

(4) Rehabilitation: Services to rehabilitate recipients or those likely to become recipients of public assistance.

(5) Independence: Useful community work and training programs and other measures to assist recipients to become self-supporting and able to care for themselves.

(6) Training: Assistance in the provision of training in order to in-

crease the supply of adequately trained public welfare personnel, this being necessary for achieving the foregoing objectives.

In his demand for a new approach, the Secretary had the full support of the social work establishment. Miss Elizabeth Wichenden, Director of Project on Public Services for Families and Children, considered H.R. 10032 a major advance. Mr. Robert Bondy, the director of the National Social Welfare Assembly declared: "the provisions of this bill would represent a substantial advance toward the objectives spelled out in the Assembly position statement." Dr. Ellen Winston, a past president of the American Public Welfare Association was equally enthusiastic. Some legislators, however, still had doubts about the bill's effectiveness.

House Hearings
(p. 532)

Statement of the Honorable Neal Smith

Mr. Smith. Thank you, Mr. Chairman. I will try to be as brief as possible. First of all, due to the fact that I am going to say some things that may sound rather critical of the program, I want to make clear that I think the ADC program is needed and that it has been a needed program in spite of the shortcomings. . . .

There is a percentage — it may be 10 percent, it may be 15 percent — of the people that are on the program have been freeloaders [sic]. The problem is how to get rid of the freeloaders, because it is these freeloaders that take the money from the ones that need it.

In all this time, in Iowa at least, and I know this is the case in many States, we have never had enough money for the people that need it and it has been drained off by some of these freeloaders who should have become self-supporting.

This bill deals with rehabilitation and this is good as far as it goes, but about half of these freeloaders do not want to be rehabilitated and I cannot see that anything would be done in this bill to solve this situation. This is fine as far as those people are concerned that would like somehow to get off of the relief roll and become self-supporting, but I think something should be done about those that do not want to do anything to become self-supporting.

The first thing I would mention with regard to this is that enforcement is very important. Most States have laws that we call child desertion laws, or they are criminal laws of some kind, that make it a felony to desert the family. I found back when I was working as State's attorney assigned to the welfare board that some men that were in another State really were in close contact with the family; yet the wife would go down and make her application for ADC claiming the husband had deserted and she would get it and know that there was no danger of the husband being thrown in jail because the State would not extradite him.

I would point out in many States, and I found this through the national welfare conferences we had at that time, the Governors will pay for the extradition of a fellow that wrote a bad $10 check, but they usually won't extradite a child deserter even though the family is drawing a couple thousand dollars a year from the county, State, and Federal Governments.

In 1951, we extradited three deserters that were in other States and almost immediately a couple dozen women came down and said they no longer needed ADC and that their husbands suddenly had returned. We know in many of these cases the husbands just went to the other State and got a job and the wife applied for ADC because they knew they would get away with it. In our case, extradition seemed to work all right until one day the Governor looked at his extradition costs and saw that that account had been reduced. He stopped extraditing child deserters—and this is not unique to Iowa—the invitation was again extended to those who wanted to cheat.

This is going on in many States, so the first thing I think should be done in this area is to work with the States to encourage extradition of child deserters that go across to other States. Extradition and child desertion proceedings are purely within the police powers of the State. It has to be a cooperative venture of some kind and I do not think you can just pass a Federal law and that is the end of it. It has to be something cooperative with the States. But something should be done to encourage better enforcement of child desertion laws.

Another thing that helps is to have an attorney assigned to the board where you have a very large caseload. At least where there are 500 or 600 or more cases there should be an attorney assigned to the board to work day to day with the welfare workers to try to enforce the law on a case-to-case basis.

We had this for a while in Iowa, but then the State board of social welfare decided they did not want to do it any longer and as soon as this attorney was taken away from the board and these full-time services were not available, the caseload shot up again.

*   *   *

I would point out that, while some people say what we need is more welfare workers, in many, many States the welfare workers they have are not permitted to really be welfare workers. They could just as well be statisticians or computing machines. They send them out to find out how much income there is in the family, how many children they have, what they pay for rent, and they compute it down at the bottom and see how much the family has coming and that is the end of it. They are prohibited from doing anything else, or if they do do anything else or try to rehabilitate the family, the family can appeal to the State board and the welfare worker will be overruled; so, more than welfare workers, what we need is a State board to let the welfare workers be welfare workers, instead of being mere computing machines.

Another thing I would like to mention is that under the law as it is now from the very beginning day the Federal Government pays 50 percent and the State and local agency pays the other 50 percent. In Iowa and many States I think the State and the local governments split this half and half. This makes 50 percent for the Federal, 25 percent for the State, and 25 percent for the county.

The natural tendency is for people that are administering these funds to want to get people on to ADC as fast as possible because 50 percent is paid for by the Federal Government. As far as the local agency is concerned they have only a 25-percent stake instead of a 100-percent stake, and therefore if somebody comes in that is eligible they want to get them on ADC immediately instead of carrying them perhaps, if it looks like a temporary case for a month or two, on a local program.

In addition to this, the law at the present time seems to require this. It says that if eligible they immediately must be placed on ADC. That is not changed in this bill as far as I can see. I think that you ought to explore the possibility, at least, of requiring that before they are eligible for Federal funds they must have been carried on the State and local rolls at the amount that they would receive from Federal funds for perhaps a couple of months. I think that in many cases this will cause the local administrators and State agency to work harder during the first 2 months to get them rehabilitated and to see what they can do to help them.

I think that this would be a good thing, especially in view of the fact that we are now including families under the legislation where both the husband and wife are healthy but out of work. I would also like to suggest to the committee that a study be made, and I think that this has to be done by Congress. It should not be left to the administrative agencies, but we need a study of some kind by some committee of Congress to see just what regulations and interpretations have been made in these State and local agencies that prevent the carrying out of the law as it is intended and that, in fact, have caused the diversion of too many of these funds by a few, that do not want to be self-supporting. We need to know the extent to which State agencies have prevented local boards from properly administering these funds. The Intergovernmental Relations Commission is considering some aspect of this, but I think it needs a thorough investigation to the end that improvements can be obtained.

It seems to me that this kind of a study is very important and it must be done by some committee of Congress because you cannot expect the administrative agencies that have been administering the law to look at it the way that the Congress would.

Thank you very much.

When the bill emerged from the House Ways and Means Committee on March 10, the Administration's plan had been altered in several ways. ADC-UP was extended only for five years instead of permanently. The new

Kennedy formula for grants-in-aid under OAA, AB, and APTD ranging from $42.30 to $47.55 of the first $66 was rejected in favor of an arrangement for $46.50 to $51.75 of the first $70 a month. At the same time the committee rejected the Administration's attempts to limit the residence requirements in all public assistance programs to one year, and to make incentive payments to states which had none.

The House considered the bill on March 15 under a closed rule and it was eventually passed as reported.

The Senate Finance Committee began its hearings on May 14. and significantly highlighted the Greenleigh Report, a study of the ADC program in Cook County (Chicago).

Facts, Fallacies and Failures: A Study of the Aid to Dependent Children Program of Cook County, Illinois
Greenleigh Associates, Inc.
(New York, 1960)

*   *   *

XI

*Some Answers, Some Questions,
Some Clues to Deeper Answers*

These positive answers emerge, in summary, from this study:

ADC, through the 25 years of its existence, has helped Cook County children numbering hundreds of thousands—currently numbering some 81,000—who are doubly disadvantaged by the loss of support and by the death, incapacity or absence of one or both parents.

ADC has proved a vital force in keeping remnants of families together, in making it possible for children to be brought up in their own homes with at least one parent or relative rather than in a foster home or an institution.

ADC, by maintaining the child in his own home, costs the taxpayers much less than would foster home or institutional care.

ADC has made it possible for needy children to grow into self-supporting, useful adults now a part of the general community life.

A high proportion of ADC mothers—surprisingly high to this study staff—could be, and want to be, self-supporting. All they need is a certain amount of help.

Most ADC mothers are good mothers. Most are concerned about their children's future.

Juvenile delinquency is "startlingly low" among ADC children.

ADC children are a "good educational risk," more than half of them keeping up with their classmates. Their IQ tests are "average." Less than one-fifth of them are behavior problems in school.

The basic "Why" remains to be answered. "Why" dependency? What are its roots? "Why" so much illegitimacy, increasing in numbers?

These questions, beyond the scope of this study, need intensive investigation. This study sought light on the most pressing and immediate problems of ADC in Cook County. In the process it made limited studies of these deeper problems. These studies, while only scratching the surface, did uncover certain clues toward finding answers.

Why dependency? One common factor is the low economic level from which ADC parents come. Yet this does not explain dependency, since some ADC mothers have brothers and sisters who are not and never have been dependent. What makes one member of a family dependent but not others? Why do some families perpetuate dependency from generation to generation? Why do some families with very low income struggle along on their own when others can not?

To what extent is dependency due to personal defects – mental, emotional, physical; to unemployment or underemployment, to low wage rates? To what extent is it due to alcoholism, drug addiction, unmarried parenthood? How much does bad housing have to do with it? Discrimination?

Do social agency policies and practices prolong or shorten the period of dependency?

Why illegitimacy and its increase among ADC families? These are the figures:

Between 1950 and 1959 the number of illegitimate births recorded in Cook County increased 111 per cent. The rate of increase was higher among the Negro than the white population. Almost 70 per cent of the ADC families reported one or more illegitimate children. Numerically, it is estimated that of 81,000 children receiving ADC when this study was made, 52.9 per cent or 42,900 are illegitimate.

Some of the children born out of wedlock are likely to need ADC because there is apt to be no support from the fathers, and unmarried mothers may have less freedom to earn. There is also only a limited probability of adoption in the case of the Negro child.

By May 1960 illegitimacy had become the major factor of need in the ADC program in Cook County.

The staff interviewed at length 619 mothers whose youngest child was born out of wedlock. Findings discredited the commonly cited belief that ADC fosters and promotes illegitimacy, as well as the stereotype that Negro mothers accept illegitimacy as a way of life. ADC mothers, they found, do not have illegitimate children to get ADC benefits, because 90 per cent of the mothers did not want to have the child.

Specifically, of the 619 mothers interviewed, 552 did not want to have the baby. They suffered a great sense of guilt, and realized the extra handicap they were imposing on themselves and their children. Almost half had no information, or inadequate information, on how to prevent conception.

To many of these mothers, their husbands living—whereabouts unknown, —marriage to the new baby's father was impossible. In most cases they could not get support from the new father, a Negro with the typical job difficulty of his race, even if they could have married. To many of these women a man friend meant status, a little extra money, perhaps, to add to the minimum ADC budget, or the reassuring presence of a man in a home with children.

In only 10 per cent of the cases was the relationship a casual one. There appeared to be little promiscuity.

Once the illegitimate child is born, the Negro mother was found almost universally accepting and loving him as much as her other children. Even if she sought to have him adopted, her chances would be slim— 1.5 per cent, in Cook County, as compared to 99 per cent of illegitimate white children adopted.

Conditions contributing to illegitimacy are family breakdown, resulting in divorce and desertion; poor education and lack of ability to get work; family migration in search of work; overcrowded, slum housing; racial discrimination; lack of knowledge about ways of preventing conception.

But what are its basic causes? To what extent is illegitimacy confined to the lowest income group, to certain minorities? Does it grow out of social, economic and emotional deprivation; out of discrimination in employment and housing and other areas of rejection? Is lack of educational opportunity a reason? Does it come from generally lowered moral standards due to the prevalent portrayal of sex in advertising, motion pictures, radio and television? Is it due to the diminishing influence of the home, the school, or the church?

To what extent is it a result of family breakdown, divorce, separation or desertion? Does the absence of the father, and the resultant loneliness of the mother, contribute? What is the effect of inadequate relief allowances, harmful agency practices, feelings of worthlessness or hopelessness, or hostile community attitudes?

What can be done to check illegitimacy and reverse the trend? Would competent casework help? Family life education? Specialized child welfare services?

In some other places, notably Sweden and Puerto Rico, comprehensive programs have been undertaken to combat this problem. What success have these measures met?

The study found this encouraging fact: Almost two-fifths (38.1 per cent) of the ADC mothers have no illegitimate children, or they have an illegitimate child born a number of years ago and the problem has been resolved.

An additional 53.8 per cent need and want help in preventing unwanted pregnancies.

Remaining is the striking question of great current concern:

How do ADC children turn out? Whether a program is succeeding or failing depends on its product. ADC's product is the children who become adults. What about our grown-up ADC children? Are they self-maintaining, normal adults contributing to the welfare of the community, or are they, too, dependent? Have they been set apart, or do they feel set apart, from the rest of society? What is their health or emotional adjustment? How many are responsible adults raising their own families? How many are themselves mothers on ADC, and what could ADC have done to prevent this plight?

These are the key questions. The specialists making this Cook County study believe that the public—insufficiently informed and to a great extent misinformed about the ADC program as it is—should be given the answers. With more than one billion dollars of public funds involved across the nation, the intent of the Aid to Dependent Children program should be fulfilled.

The study report concludes:

By and large families receiving ADC have more strengths than weaknesses. The main strength is in their desire for help—a strong foundation on which to build. There are only a very few who do not need some help to become independent. On the other hand, few have many severe problems which will require intensive treatment.

Since the children are the reason ADC was established, let them be served, within their families, beyond subsistence alone. Give them the kind of help, according to their needs, that will let them grow into self-reliant, self-supporting adults—useful citizens of the community.

The record of the hearings included not only the Greenleigh Report, but a revealing publication by the National Travelers Aid Association, One Manner of Law—A Handbook on Residence Requirements in Public Assistance.

On June 14, the Finance Committee voted the bill out, without altering most of the House committee's amendments, although it did remove a plan to insure that parents would spend ADC payments on children.

Public Welfare Amendments of 1962
Senate Report No. 1589
87th Cong., 2d Sess.
(June 14, 1962)

II. SUMMARY OF THE PRINCIPAL PROVISIONS OF THE BILL

PUBLIC ASSISTANCE

A. Rehabilitative Services and Training in the Public Assistance Programs

A State, at its option, may now provide such services under all the public assistance programs except medical assistance for the aged. The Federal Government matches these expenditures on a 50–50 under the provision which governs administrative expenses.

Under the bill as passed by the House, States would be required to provide certain minimum services for applicants and recipients, which the Secretary would prescribe, to help them attain self-care (old-age assistance); self-supporting and self-care (the blind and the disabled); and to strengthen family life (aid to dependent children). There were no required services for medical assistance for the aged.

The committee's bill would leave the provision of such services optional with the States; but, if they are not provided by a State, the Federal matching of all administrative costs for that category of assistance (now 50 percent) would be reduced to 25 percent effective June 30, 1963.

The bill would authorize 75 percent Federal matching in all public assistance titles for certain services (including the minimum services) to be specified by the Secretary of Health, Education, and Welfare. These services (including the minimum services) could apply to applicants and recipients of assistance as well as to those likely to become or who have been recipients, on the request of such persons (within such periods as the Secretary may prescribe.)

The 75-percent matching would also be available for training personnel who are employed, or who are preparing to work, in State or local welfare agencies.

Other services which the Secretary does not designate would be continued at 50-percent matching, as would all other administrative costs. Cost: HEW estimate, $40.8 million[1] (with over half going into the ADC program).

B. Increase in Federal Matching Formula for the Aged, Blind, and Disabled

The Committee bill, as does the House bill, increases the Federal matching share in the case of the programs for the aged, the blind, and the disabled to twenty-nine thirty-fifths of the first $35 of the average monthly payment per recipient; the maximum for matching would be raised to $70 on a permanent basis effective October 1, 1962. The bill passed by the House makes the same increase in the matching formula on a permanent basis effective July 1, 1962. The temporary provision now in effect which uses matching on four-fifths of the first $31, with a maximum of $66 through June 30, 1962, was extended through September 30, 1962. Without such an extension the formula would revert to four-fifths of the first $30 with a maximum of $65. The change does not affect the special provision for medical care in the old-age assistance program. Cost: HEW estimate, $105.5 million[2] ($140.6 million for first full year of operation).

C. Changes in the Aid to Dependent Children (ADC) Program

1. Additional authority to States to prevent abuses in aid to dependent children payments. — The committee bill would provide that, beginning October 1, 1962, and ending June 30, 1967, payments (limited in number to 5 percent of recipients) would be authorized to be made to third parties interested in the welfare of the child where it is determined that the parent is so incapable of managing funds that the child's welfare is affected. Certain safeguards and standards would be prescribed. The committee eliminated the provision of the House bill which would have allowed the States to use voucher payments (payments directly to grocers, landlords, etc.). Cost: HEW estimate, negligible.[2]

2. Payments on the basis of the unemployment of the parent. — This temporary provision of existing law, which is effective May 1, 1961, to June 30, 1962, would be extended for 5 years by the House bill and the committee bill and be expanded to cover both parents instead of one as in existing law. A provision would be added which would deny aid to a parent for refusal to accept retraining without good cause.

Under prior law, ADC payments could be made only on the basis of the death, disability, or absence of the parent. Cost: HEW estimate, $85 million (of which $12 million is attributable to the second parent provision).

3. Payments on the basis of the disability of the parent. — Federal matching would be expanded to cover payments for both parents of children who are needy because of the disability of the parent. At the present time the Federal Government matches for one adult recipient only. Cost: HEW estimate, $22 million.

4. Community work and training programs. — The bill would provide that beginning October 1, 1962, for a period of 5 years, Federal matching funds would be available in cases where payments are made under work programs

[2]Cost figure for fiscal 1963.

which are a part of the ADC program and meet certain standards. Under interpretation of existing law there can be no matching as to payments made for work by a welfare agency; such payments currently are financed wholly by State and local funds. Under an amendment added by the committee, payments to individuals under these programs would be excluded from gross income for Federal income tax purposes. Cost: HEW estimate, negligible.[3]

5. Payments to children removed by court order into foster care. — Under temporary existing law, which is effective May 1, 1961, to June 30, 1962, payments can be made to ADC children removed by court order into foster home care. This provision would be made permanent under the House bill and the committee bill. Payments under prior law were limited to children living with specified relatives. The committee deleted the provision in the House bill which would have expanded the program to include children placed in private child care institutions as well as those receiving family home care as in existing law. The committee bill also includes an amendment which would allow States, for a 1-year period, under the foster care provisions of aid to dependent children program, to utilize the services of other public agencies in the placement and supervision of children in foster home care under agreements with the welfare agency. Cost: HEW estimate, $4.1 million.[3]

D. Other Changes in Public Assistance Programs

1. Incentive for employment through consideration of expenses. — The States would be required, in determining the amount of assistance to be provided for the needy aged, blind, disabled, and dependent children, to take into account necessary expenses that may reasonably be attributed to the earning of income. Under current administrative policy, the States may, at their option, consider such expenses.

Also, in determining need in the ADC program, the States would be allowed to disregard certain earned or other income put aside for the child's future need (for example, such items as education or preparation for employment). Cost: HEW estimate, negligible.[3][4]

2. Optional single State plan for aged, blind, disabled, and medical assistance for the aged. — States would be allowed to operate these programs under a single plan. States which select the single plan would become eligible for Federal matching for medical care for recipients of aid to the blind and to the disabled on the same basis as they are now available for recipients of old-age assistance (that is, up to $15 a month per recipient for vendor medical care). Such additional matching would not be available if States remained under their separate programs. Administration would be allowed,

[3]Cost figures for fiscal 1963.
[4]$7,000,000 a year after it goes into effect in July 1963.

however, by separate existing blind agencies. Cost: HEW estimate, $7.4 million.[3][5]

3. Training of public assistance workers. — Under the House bill, provisions of present law authorizing Federal grants to States to increase the number of adequately trained public welfare personnel to work in public assistance programs, which are due to expire June 30, 1963, would be made permanent, with dollar limitations on authorized appropriations for grants to States for training of public assistance workers — $3.5 million in fiscal 1963 and $5 million a year thereafter. Within the dollar limitations established by the House bill, the committee bill authorizes a program of direct Federal training and grant activity and of scholarships and stipends for persons preparing for employment in public welfare agencies. The committee bill would repeal existing provisions of law that authorize 100 percent Federal funds for expenditures made by States for training of staff. Cost: HEW estimate, negligible.[3]

4. Assistance to repatriated American citizens. — This provision of existing law, which was effective on June 30, 1961, and will expire on June 30, 1962, permits temporary assistance to citizens returning from foreign countries because of illness, destitution, or crisis. It would be extended for 2 years. Cost: HEW estimate, $400,000.[6]

5. Demonstration projects. — The bill would permit the Secretary of Health, Education, and Welfare to waive any State plan requirement which he deemed necessary (such as statewide applicability of plan) for pilot or demonstration projects designed to improve the public assistance programs and would provide alternative methods of financing such projects out of public assistance appropriations. Cost: HEW estimate, negligible.[3]

6. Aid-to-the-blind programs (Missouri and Pennsylvania). — The provision of the 1950 amendments, which granted an exemption to certain aid-to-the-blind programs (in effect at that time) from the income and resources test of Federal law, would be placed on a permanent basis. The temporary provision has been extended periodically and would, under existing law, expire in 1964.

7. Other committee amendments. — Two provisions were added by the committee which were not contained in the House bill. (a) The reported bill increases the dollar limitation which is applicable to public assistance expenditures in Puerto Rico from the present $9,500,000 to $10,500,000, and in the Virgin Islands from the present $320,000 to $400,000.[7] (b) The bill as reported also contains an amendment which provides that, in determining need for aid to the blind, a State shall, in addition to present ex-

---

[3]Cost figures for fiscal 1963.
[5]Increases to $16,000,000 in 1964 and subsequent years.
[6]Cost figures for 1963.
[7]The House bill would have increased these figures to $9,800,000 and $330,000, respectively, to reflect other changes made by the bill.

empted amounts ($85 a month in earnings plus one-half of the balance) exempt such other amounts of income or resources as may be necessary to fulfill a State-approved rehabilitation plan for a blind individual. Such additional exemptions cannot last for more than 1 year.

CHILD WELFARE SERVICES

*   *   *

ADVISORY COUNCIL

The bill provides for an advisory council, to be appointed by the Secretary of Health, Education, and Welfare in 1964, to review the status of the public assistance and child welfare services programs and report their findings to the Secretary. The power to appoint other advisory committees contained in the House bill was somewhat limited in the bill reported by the committee.

The bill was debated in the Senate for an unusual eleven days, although much of the discussion centered on the Anderson Amendment on medical care. In addition, amendments were accepted to extend federal participation in ADC payments to children in foster homes, and to allow those opposed to social security payments on religious grounds to opt out.

In a particularly significant step, the Senate voted to accept an amendment by Senator Paul H. Douglas encouraging OAA recipients' self-support by allowing them to earn a certain monthly sum before deductions were made from their OAA payments. Not only was the figure raised to $50, but the amendment passed unanimously by voice vote.

On July 17, the Senate passed the bill. The conference report accepted most of the Senate's more liberal amendments, but there was a successful effort to restore at least some state control over misuse of ADC funds. The Conference Committee also dropped the Senate amendment allowing persons to opt out of OASDI on religious grounds. Both houses accepted the compromise on July 19, and it was signed by the president one week later.

**Presidential Statement Upon Approving the
Public Welfare Amendments Bill**
(July 26, 1962)*

I have approved a bill which makes possible the most far-reaching revision of our Public Welfare program since it was enacted in 1935.

This measure embodies a new approach—stressing services in addition to support, rehabilitation instead of relief, and training for useful work instead of prolonged dependency. This important legislation will assist our

**Public Papers of the Presidents, John F. Kennedy, 1962,* p. 580.

states and local public welfare agencies to redirect the incentives and services they offer to needy families and children and to aged and disabled people. Our objective is to prevent or reduce dependency and to encourage self-care and self-support — to maintain family life where it is adequate and to restore it where it is deficient.

This measure encourages the states to expand their rehabilitation of the needy, increase their services to children and extend day-care services to the children of working mothers, establish useful community work and training projects, guard against misuse of welfare funds paid for the benefit of dependent children, and strengthen and improve welfare administration.

This bill also contains incentives for the training of additional skilled welfare workers; and I am hopeful that these incentives, along with the new constructive approach taken by this bill, will help to direct many more able men and women to the service of our severely handicapped welfare agencies.

The new law makes available additional Federal funds to the States for assistance to needy aged, blind, and disabled persons which amount to about $4 per recipient per month. The reports of both the Ways and Means Committee of the House of Representatives and of the Committee on Finance of the Senate make it clear that the States are expected to pass on these additional funds to the recipients under these programs. It would truly be a miscarriage of justice and a frustration of the legislative intent if these new Federal funds merely replaced existing state funds, and those for whom the increase was intended were denied the full benefit.

The problems which gave rise to this bill affect every community in the country — and this measure, I believe, marks a real turning point in this nation's efforts to cope realistically and helpfully with these pressing problems.

Critics have rightly been sceptical about the newness of the "new approach" but the new act was certainly important. The federal share of the cost of rehabilitation services was greatly increased, as were training possibilities. The ADC program, renamed aid to families with dependent children (AFDC) was, at least in theory, strengthened and better financed. (The unemployed father's program, for instance, was extended to five years.) Public assistance recipients were encouraged to earn some money without necessarily being penalized with reduced benefits.

Public Welfare Amendments of 1962
(July 25, 1962, 76 Statutes at Large 172)

TITLE I—PUBLIC WELFARE AMENDMENTS

*Part A—Improvement in Services To Prevent or
Reduce Dependency*

*SERVICES AND OTHER ADMINISTRATIVE COSTS UNDER
PUBLIC ASSISTANCE PROGRAMS*

Federal Financial Participation in Costs of Services

Sec. 101. (a) (1) Section 3(a) of the Social Security Act is amended by
striking out paragraph (4) and inserting in lieu thereof the following:
    "(4) in the case of any State, an amount equal to the sum of the fol-
    lowing proportions of the total amounts expended during such quarter
    as found necessary by the Secretary of Health, Education, and Wel-
    fare for the proper and efficient administration of the State plan—
        "(A) 75 per centum of so much of such expenditures as are
    for—

*   *   *

AID FOR BOTH PARENTS OF DEPENDENT CHILD

Sec. 109. Section 406(b) of the Social Security Act, as amended by section
108 of this Act, is amended by inserting "(and the spouse of such relative if
living with him and if such relative is the child's parent and the child is a dependent child by reason of the physical or mental incapacity of a parent or
is a dependent child under section 407)" after "relative with whom any dependent child is living" in clause (1) thereof.

*Part B—Improvement in Administration Through Demonstrations,
Training, and Public Advisory Groups*

ADVISORY COUNCIL ON PUBLIC WELFARE

Sec. 121. Title XI of the Social Security Act is amended by adding at the
end thereof the following new section:

*"APPOINTMENT OF ADVISORY COUNCIL AND OTHER
ADVISORY GROUPS*

*   *   *

*Part C — Improvement of Public Welfare Programs Through
Extension of Temporary Provisions and Increase in Federal
Share of Public Assistance Payments*

EXTENSION OF AID WITH RESPECT TO DEPENDENT CHILDREN OF UNEMPLOYED PARENTS OR IN FOSTER FAMILY HOMES

Extension With Respect to Children of Unemployed Parents

Sec. 131. (a) So much of the first sentence of section 407 of the Social Security Act as precedes paragraph (1) thereof is amended by striking out "1962" and inserting in lieu thereof "1967".

Extension With Respect to Foster Family Home Care

(b) So much of the first sentence of section 408 of such Act as precedes paragraph (a) thereof is amended by striking out ", and ending with the close of June 30, 1962".

INCREASE IN FEDERAL SHARE OF PUBLIC ASSISTANCE PAYMENTS

Sec. 132. (a) Paragraphs (1) and (2) of section 3(a) of the Social Security Act are amended to read as follows:

"(1) in the case of any State other than Puerto Rico, the Virgin Islands, and Guam, an amount equal to the sum of the following proportions of the total amounts expended during such quarter as old-age assistance under the State plan (including expenditures for insurance premiums for medical or any other type of remedial care or the cost thereof) —

"(A) $29/35$ of such expenditures, not counting so much of any expenditure with respect to any month as exceeds the product of $35 multiplied by the total number of recipients of old-age assistance for such month (which total number, for purposes of this subsection, means (i) the number of individuals who received old-age assistance in the form of money payments for such month, plus (ii) the number of other individuals with respect to whom expenditures were made in such month as old-age assistance in the form of medical or any other type of remedial care); plus

"(B) the Federal percentage (as defined in section 1101 (a) (8) of the amount by which such expenditures exceed the maximum which may be counted under clause (A), not counting so much of any expenditure with respect to any month as exceeds the product of $70 multiplied by the total number of such recipients of old-age assistance for such month; plus

"(C) the larger of the following: (i) the Federal medical per-percentage (as defined in section 6(c) of the amount by which such expenditures exceed the maximum which may be counted under clause (B), not counting so much of any expenditure with respect to any month as exceeds (I) the product of $85 multi-plied by the total number of such recipients of old-age assistance for such month, or (II) if smaller, the total expended as old-age assistance in the form of medical or any other type of remedial care with respect to such month plus the product of $70 multi-plied by such total number of such recipients, or (ii) 15 per centum of the total of the sums expended during such quarter as old-age assistance under the State plan in the form of medical or any other type of remedial care, not counting so much of any expenditure with respect to any month as exceeds the product of $15 multiplied by the total number of such recipients of old-age assistance for such month; . . .

*　　*　　*

Sec. 141. (a) The Social Security Act is amended by adding after title XV the following new title:

"TITLE XVI – GRANTS TO STATES FOR AID TO THE AGED, BLIND, OR DISABLED, OR FOR SUCH AID AND MEDICAL ASSISTANCE FOR THE AGED

"APPROPRIATION

"Sec. 1601. For the purpose (a) of enabling each State, as far as practicable under the conditions in such State, to furnish financial assistance to needy individuals who are 65 years of age or over, are blind, or are 18 years of age or over and permanently and totally disabled, (b) of enabling each State, as far as practicable under the conditions in such State, to furnish medical assistance on behalf of individuals who are 65 years of age or over and who are not recipients of aid to the aged, blind, or disabled but whose income and resources are insufficient to meet the costs of necessary medical services, and (c) of encouraging each State, as far as practicable under the conditions in such State, to furnish rehabilitation and other services to help individuals referred to in clause (a) or (b) to attain or retain capability for self-support or self-care, there is hereby authorized to be appropriated for each fiscal year a sum sufficient to carry out the purposes of this title. The sums made available under this section shall be used for making payments to States which have submitted, and had approved by the Secretary of Health, Edu-cation, and Welfare, State plans for aid to the aged, blind, or disabled, or for aid to the aged, blind, or disabled and medical assistance for the aged.

"STATE PLANS FOR AID TO THE AGED, BLIND, OR DISABLED, OR FOR SUCH AID AND MEDICAL ASSISTANCE FOR THE AGED

"Sec. 1602. (a) A State plan for aid to the aged, blind, or disabled, or for aid to the aged, blind, or disabled and medical assistance for the aged, must —

"(1) provide that it shall be in effect in all political subdivisions of the State, and, if administered by them, be mandatory upon them;

"(2) provide for financial participation by the State;

"(3) either provide for the establishment or designation of a single State agency to administer the plan, or provide for the establishment or designation of a single State agency to supervise the administration of the plan;

"(4) provide for granting an opportunity for a fair hearing before the State agency to any individual whose claim for aid or assistance under the plan is denied or is not acted upon with reasonable promptness;

"(5) provide such methods of administration (including methods relating to the establishment and maintenance of personnel standards on a merit basis, except that the Secretary shall exercise no authority with respect to the selection, tenure of office, and compensation of any individual employed in accordance with such methods) as are found by the Secretary to be necessary for the proper and efficient operation of the plan;

"(6) provide that the State agency will make such reports, in such form and containing such information, as the Secretary may from time to time require, and comply with such provisions as the Secretary may from time to time find necessary to assure the correctness and verification of such reports;

"(7) provide safeguards which restrict the use or disclosure of information concerning applicants and recipients to purposes directly connected with the administration of the plan;

"(8) provide that all individuals wishing to make application for aid or assistance under the plan shall have opportunity to do so, and that such aid or assistance shall be furnished with reasonable promptness to all eligible individuals;

"(9) provide, if the plan includes aid or assistance to or on behalf of individuals in private or public institutions, for the establishment or designation of a State authority or authorities which shall be responsible for establishing and maintaining standards for such institutions;

"(10) provide a description of the services (if any) which the State agency makes available to applicants for or recipients of aid or assistance under the plan to help them attain self-support or self-care, including a description of the steps taken to assure, in the provision of such services, maximum utilization of other agencies providing similar or related services;

"(11) provide that no aid or assistance will be furnished any individual under the plan with respect to any period with respect to which he is receiving assistance under the State plan approved under title I or aid under the State plan approved under title IV, X, or XIV;

"(12) provide that, in determining whether an individual is blind, there shall be an examination by a physician skilled in the diseases of the eye or by an optometrist, whichever the individual may select;

"(13) include reasonable standards, consistent with the objectives of this title, for determining eligibility for and the extent of aid or assistance under the plan;

"(14) provide that the State agency shall, in determining need for aid to the aged, blind, or disabled, take into consideration any other income and resources of an individual claiming such aid, as well as any expenses reasonably attributable to the earning of any such income; except that, in making such determination with respect to any individual who is blind, the State agency shall disregard (A) the first $85 per month of earned income plus one-half of earned income in excess of $85 per month and (B) for a period not in excess of twelve months, such additional amounts of other income and resources, in the case of an individual who has a plan for achieving self-support approved by the State agency, as may be necessary for the fulfillment of such plan, and in making such determination with respect to any other individual who has attained age 65 and is claiming aid to the aged, blind, or disabled, of the first $50 per month of earned income the State agency may, after December 31, 1962, disregard not more than the first $10 thereof plus one-half of the remainder; and

"(15) if the State plan includes medical assistance for the aged—

"(A) provide for inclusion of some institutional and some non-institutional care and services;

"(B) provide that no enrollment fee, premium, or similar charge will be imposed as a condition of any individual's eligibility for medical assistance for the aged under the plan;

"(C) provide for inclusion, to the extent required by regulations prescribed by the Secretary, of provisions (conforming to such regulations) with respect to the furnishing of such assistance to individuals who are residents of the State but are absent therefrom; and

"(D) provide that no lien may be imposed against the property of any individual prior to his death on account of medical assistance for the aged paid or to be paid on his behalf under the plan (except pursuant to the judgment of a court on account of benefits incorrectly paid on behalf of such individual), and that there shall be no adjustment or recovery (except, after the death of such individual and his surviving spouse, if any, from such indi-

vidual's estate) of any medical assistance for the aged correctly
paid on behalf of such individual under the plan.

Notwithstanding paragraph (3), if on January 1, 1962, and on the date on
which a State submits its plan for approval under this title, the State agency
which administered or supervised the administration of the plan of such
State approved under title X was different from the State agency which administered or supervised the administration of the plan of such State approved under title I and the State agency which administered or supervised
the administration of the plan of such State approved under title XIV, the
State agency which administered or supervised the administration of such
plan approved under title X may be designated to administer or supervise
the administration of the portion of the State plan for aid to the aged, blind,
or disabled (or for aid to the aged, blind, or disabled and medical assistance
for the aged) which related to blind individuals and a separate State agency
may be established or designated to administer or supervise the administration of the rest of such plan; and in such case the part of the plan which each
such agency administers, or the administration of which each such agency
supervises, shall be regarded as a separate plan for purposes of this title.

"(b) The Secretary shall approve any plan which fulfills the condition
specified in subsection (a), escept that he shall not approve any plan which
imposes, as a condition of eligibility for aid or assistance under the plan—

"(1) an age requirement of more than sixty-five years; or

"(2) any residence requirement which (A) in the case of applicants
for aid to the aged, blind, or disabled excludes any resident of the
State who has resided therein five years during the nine years immediately preceding the application for such aid and has resided therein
continuously for one year immediately preceding the application, and
(B) in the case of applicants for medical assistance for the aged, excludes any individual who resides in the State; or

"(3) any citizenship requirement which excludes any citizen of the
United States.

In the case of any State to which the provisions of section 344 of the Social
Security Act Amendments of 1950 were applicable on January 1, 1962, and
to which the sentence of section 1002(b) following paragraph (2) thereof is
applicable on the date on which its State plan for aid to the aged, blind, or
disabled (or for aid to the aged, blind, or disabled and medical assistance for
the aged) was submitted for approval under this title, the Secretary shall approve the plan of such State for aid to the aged, blind, or disabled (or for aid
to the aged, blind, or disabled and medical assistance for the aged) for purposes of this title, even though it does not meet the requirements of paragraph (14) of subsection (a), if it meets all other requirements of this title for
an approved plan for aid to the aged, blind, or disabled (or for aid to the aged,
blind, or disabled and medical assistance for the aged); but payments under
section 1603 shall be made, in the case of any such plan, only with respect to

expenditures thereunder which would be included as expenditures for the purposes of section 1603 under a plan approved under this section without regard to the provisions of this sentence.

Unemployment Compensation

The Kennedy Administration was concerned with two aspects of unemployment compensation during 1962. First, it emphasized a long-term revision of the unemployment insurance program permitting greater federal financial support. Second, the President pressed for a further extension of the temporary program.

Presidential Letter to the President of the Senate and to the Speaker of the House on the Unemployment Compensation System
(March 12, 1962)*

Dear Mr. _____: The imminent expiration of the Temporary Extended Unemployment Compensation program at a time whem unemployment is still high and there are large numbers of long-term unemployed makes enactment of the permanent improvements I have recommended in the existing Federal-State unemployment system especially urgent. This legislation is a vital part of the programs I believe essential to assure sustained prosperity and to strengthen our manpower base.

Although the February unemployment figures showed a heartening decline in the number out of work there are still 4,543,000 workers who need help. The number of long-term unemployed — those who have been jobless for 15 weeks or longer — totals 1,400,000. Unless prompt action is taken workers who exhaust their regular benefits after March 31, 1962, will no longer be able to receive any unemployment compensation. The serious crisis which compelled Congressional action last year has not abated for these workers, but the protection provided by the law will shortly expire unless the Congress acts.

Twice in recent years, in 1958 and again in 1961, the Congress has taken steps to provide unemployment compensation benefits for the long-term unemployed. As temporary stop-gap measures these Acts served a valuable purpose. They have also proven the need for a permanent modification in the system of benefits.

The merits of the proposals for permanent legislation I have recommended are well-established. The wider coverage, extended benefit periods and increased benefit amounts will lessen the hardship and suffering that

Ibid., p. 212.

accompany unemployment and will, at the same time, provide a stimulus to business.

When enacted, the legislation will exert a stabilizing effect upon our economy, helping to maintain consumer purchasing power and cushioning any economic reverses. It will make unnecessary the temporary stop-gap legislation sought each time a crisis develops, and modernize the system to better meet the needs of the worker, the community and the nation. Today, weekly benefits are often too low in relation to lost wages to enable the worker to meet his basic and non-deferrable expenses. Incentives to the various States to establish basic minimum payments equal, in most cases, to one-half the wages lost, would be provided. An additional 3,000,000 workers not now covered would be brought within the system. The burden of excessively high unemployment compensation taxes that exist in several States would be removed. The financial soundness of the system would be strengthened by increasing the amount of wages subject to taxation – the first increase in the history of the program. And finally, workers would not be denied benefits simply because they sought to develop another marketable skill through retraining.

It is estimated that 150,000 workers will exhaust their regular unemployment insurance in April 1962. The number will exceed 100,000 in all but one of the remaining months of the year. Many of these have a long work history but, because of automation or other technological developments, will find it difficult to obtain re-employment. We cannot, with the expiration of the present Temporary Extended Unemployment Compensation program, abdicate our responsibility to these workers. Adequate provision should be made for them.

I urge that early consideration be given to the legislation calling for permanent improvement of the Federal-State unemployment insurance system.

Sincerely,
John F. Kennedy

After a couple of weeks, a major revision seemed unobtainable; the President therefore made a special statement.

**Presidential Statement on the Need for Extending
the Unemployment Compensation Program**
(March 31, 1962)*

In my letter to the Congress on March 12, I expressed my concern about the effect on the large number of long-term unemployed of the imminent expiration of the Temporary Extended Unemployment Compensation

Ibid., p. 283.

program. I urged therefore that early consideration be given by the Congress to the legislation calling for permanent improvement of the Federal-State unemployment insurance system.

It is becoming increasingly apparent, however, that the Committees before whom this legislation is pending have such heavy schedules that they will be unable this year to give to this legislation the consideration it deserves.

In view of the fact that the present temporary program is expiring, and in view of the dire need of the large number of long-term unemployed, I believe that something must be done immediately to help them after they exhaust regular benefits. Accordingly, I shall shortly send to the Congress recommendations for appropriately extending the Temporary Extended Unemployment Compensation program, with retroactivity to those unemployed who exhaust their benefits after April 1 in order to prevent injustice pending prompt congressional action on the requested extension. About 1,500,000 long-term unemployed workers throughout the country would be aided by such an extension; and it would give the Congress the opportunity to consider my proposals for permanent improvements promptly after it convenes in January, 1963.

Two weeks later Kennedy accepted the fact that only short-term developments were possible.

Presidential Letter to the President of the Senate and to the Speaker of the House on Extension of Temporary Unemployment Compensation
(April 10, 1962)*

Dear Mr. _____: I am transmitting herewith, for the consideration of the Congress, a draft of the legislation which would extend the Temporary Extended Unemployment Compensation Program until April 1, 1963.

The present program expired April 1, 1962. But there are still large numbers of long-term unemployed, and I believe that immediate action is required so that the benefits of the program can continue. In my letter of March 12 you will recall I expressed concern about the effect of the termination of the temporary program upon these workers. I therefore urged early consideration by the Congress of legislation which called for permanent improvements in the Federal-State unemployment insurance system. However, in view of the heavy schedule faced by the committees of the Congress before whom that legislation is pending, it seems unlikely that the legislation will be able to receive the consideration it deserves this year. Under these circumstances, provision should be made for continuation of the temporary program.

The Temporary Extended Unemployment Compensation Program which expired April 1 did not cost as much as had been estimated. Accordingly,

*Ibid., p. 313.

$184 million will be available from the special taxes to be collected on 1962 and 1963 payrolls to help finance the extension I am proposing, and an increase of only 0.1 percent in the tax rate for 1964 is necessary to finance the remaining cost of the extended program.

The Secretary of Labor estimates that 1,500,000 long-term unemployed workers throughout the Nation will be benefited by the new extension of the Unemployment Compensation Program.

Sincerely,
John F. Kennedy

Congress slowly began to move. On June 13, Senator Eugene McCarthy introduced a bill to extend the temporary benefit program for one year, but nothing further happened until October 5. Senator McCarthy then offered an amendment to an unrelated House bill (H.R. 10117) extending the temporary program for four months. However, the Senate leadership feared a House rejection of the entire bill and therefore dropped it, attaching H.R. 10117's text—without the unemployment compensation provisions—to yet another piece of legislation. Both long-term and short-term changes in unemployment programs had failed in 1962.

Medical Care in 1962

Many regard 1962 as a turning point for medical care programs. President Kennedy remained as committed as ever to health services under social security while the AMA maintained its implacable hostility. However, such opposition did not prevent Administration pressure for the program.

Presidential Letter to the President of the American Medical Association
(June 5, 1962)*

Dear Mr. Larson: Your letter to me of May twenty-fifth—which I read with interest in the newspapers of May twenty-sixth—has been received in this office and deserves an appropriate reply.

I appreciate your confidence that I "would not intentionally give the American people incorrect information about the American Medical Association or any other organization or individual." Your letter objects to my news conference statement that the AMA was among the opponents of the original Social Security System. If your letter endorses the Social Security concept on behalf of the AMA—if it signifies a willingness on the part of the AMA to include doctors under its coverage—if it repudiates the statement made by Dr. Annis on May twenty-first which implies that Social Security "has to be bad to begin with" and is a "free ride (for) those who do

Ibid., p. 499.

not need these benefits" at the taxpayers' expense—then I am certain that your letter will be enthusiastically welcomed by the great majority of the American people.

On the other hand, if the AMA has never opposed Social Security, some questions may be asked in order to set the record straight:

—Why did Dr. Fishbein, the official spokesman for the AMA, make a statement in November 1939 at the request of the AMA Board of Trustees, and publish it in the Journal of the AMA in December 1939, with the following remarks about Social Security: "Indeed, all forms of security, compulsory security, even against old age and unemployment, represent a beginning invasion by the state into the personal life of the individual, represent a taking away of individual responsibility, a weakening of national caliber, a definite step toward either communism or totalitarianism." (*JAMA*, Vol. 113, No. 27, December 30, 1939, page 2428.)?

—Why did the AMA in 1949 send to every member of Congress a resolution adopted by the House of Delegates of the AMA containing the following statement: "So-called 'social security' is in fact a compulsory socialistic tax which has not provided satisfactory insurance protection for individuals where it has been tried but instead, has served as the entering wedge for establishment of a socialistic form of governmental control over the lives and fortunes of the people . . ." (*JAMA*, Vol. 140, No. 8, June 25, 1949, page 693; No. 9, July 2, 1949, pages 791–2.)?

—Why did the AMA House of Delegates in December 1953 state that it had "in the past registered its disapproval of the principle involved" in Social Security—and why is it I have repeatedly read critical references to Social Security in the Journal and Proceedings of the AMA?

I did not mean to imply that it was the AMA who had originally applied to the Social Security System the tern "cruel hoax" which Dr. Annis had used to describe our medical insurance program—but I am certain you will recall that this very phrase was used by the opponents of Social Security in the 1930's. If your organization did not oppose Social Security *before* its enactment—only *afterwards*—I will be glad to point out this unique distinction at my next press conference.

Sincerely,
John F. Kennedy

Special Presidential Message to the Congress on Health Care
(February 27, 1962)*

To the Congress of the United States:

The basic resource of a nation is its people. Its strength can be no greater than the health and vitality of its population. Preventable sickness, dis-

*Ibid., p. 165.

ability and physical or mental incapacity are matters of both individual and national concern.

We can take justifiable pride in our achievements in the field of medicine. We stand among the select company of nations for whom fear of the great epidemic plagues is long past; our life expectancy has already reached the biblical three score and ten; and, unlike so many less fortunate peoples of the world, we need not struggle for mere survival. But measured against our capability in the fields of health and medical care, measured against the scope of the problems that remain and the opportunities to be seized, this nation still falls far short of its responsibility.

Many thousands needlessly suffer from infectious diseases for which preventive measures are available. We are still tenth among the nations of the world in our infant mortality rate. Prolonged and costly illness in later years robs too many of our elder citizens of pride, purpose and savings. In many communities the treatment of the mentally ill and the mentally retarded is totally inadequate. And there are increasingly severe shortages of skilled personnel in all the vital health professions.

Basically, health care is a responsibility of individuals and families, of communities and voluntary agencies, of local and state governments. But the Federal Government shares this responsibility by providing leadership, guidance and support in areas of national concern. And the Congress last year recognized this responsibility in important ways.

Progress During 1961

Our states and communities have responded quickly and with impressive vigor to the invitation to cooperate action extended by the Community Health Services and Facilities Act passed by the Congress and signed into law only four months ago. As a result better care for the chronically ill and the aged will soon be available in many parts of the Nation, both inside and outside the hospitals and other institutions in this program.

There is also visible progress in the effort to control water pollution, resulting from the expanded legislation passed by the Congress in 1961. Last year construction was begun on more waste treatment plants than ever before in our history — 30 percent above the calendar year 1960 level.

There were, in addition, other important forward thrusts taken, with Federal help, in the protection of our nation's health. Medical research advanced at an accelerated pace. We are now better equipped than ever before to evaluate and deal with radiation perils. The incidence of polio has been reduced to the lowest levels ever recorded. We have engaged our most talented doctors and scientists in an intensified search for the cause and cure of cancer, heart disease, mental illness, mental retardation, environmental health problems and other serious health hazards.

But, of the four basic improvements in the Federal health program I recommended to the Congress last year, two urgent needs — health insurance for the aged and assistance to education for the health professions — have not yet been met. The passage of time has only served to increase their urgency; and I repeat those requests today, along with other needed improvements.

I. Health Insurance for the Aged

Our social insurance system today guards against nearly every major financial setback: retirement, death, disability and unemployment. But it does not protect our older citizens against the hardships of prolonged and expensive illness. Under our Social Security system, a retired person receives cash benefits to help meet the basic cost of food, shelter and clothing — benefits to which he is entitled by reason of the contributions he made during his working years. They permit him to live in dignity and with independence — but only if a serious illness does not overtake him.

For, compared to the rest of us, our older citizens go to the hospital more often — they have more days of illness — and their stays in the hospital are thus more costly. But both their income and the proportion of their hospital bill covered by private insurance are, in most cases, substantially lower than those of younger persons.

Private health insurance has made notable advances in recent years. But older people, who need it most but can afford it least, are still unable to pay the high premiums made necessary by their disproportionately heavy use of health care services and facilities, if eligibility requirements are to be low and the scope of benefits broad. Today, only about half of our aged population has any health insurance of any kind — and most of these have insufficient coverage.

To be sure, welfare assistance, and Federal legislation to help the needy or "medically indigent", will provide health services in some instances. But this kind of help is not only less appealing, coupled as it is with a means test, it reaches very few of those who are not eligible for public assistance but are still not able to afford the care they need.

I therefore recommend again the enactment of a health insurance program for the elderly under the Social Security system. By this means the cost of health services in later years can be spread over the working years — and every worker can face the future with pride and confidence. This program, of course, would not interfere in any way with the freedom of choice of doctor, hospital or nurse. It would not specify in any way the kind of medical or health care or treatment to be provided. But it would establish a means to pay for the following minimum levels of protection:

First — Inpatient hospital expenses for up to 90 days, in excess of $10 per day for the first 9 days (with a minimum payment by each person of $20), and full costs for the remaining 81 days.

Second — The cost of nursing home services up to 180 days immediately after discharge from a hospital. By providing nursing home care for twice as long as that in the hospital, the patient is encouraged to use the less expensive facilities when these will satisfy his requirements.

Third—the cost of hospital outpatient clinic diagnostic services in excess of $20. These benefits will reduce the need for hospital admissions and encourage early diagnosis.

Fourth—the cost of community visiting nurse services, and related home health services, for a limited number of visits. These will enable many older people to receive proper health care in their own homes.

It should be emphasized that we are discussing a gap in our self-financed, contributory social insurance system. These are all *insurance* benefits which will be available to everyone over 65 who is eligible for Social Security or Railroad Retirement benefits. They would be entirely self-financed by an increase in Social Security contributions of one quarter of one percent each on employers and employees, and by an increase in the maximum earnings base from $4800 a year to $5200 a year. No burden on the general revenues is involved. I am not unmindful of the fact, however, that none of our social insurance systems is universal in its coverage—and that direct payments may be necessary to provide help to those not covered for health insurance by Social Security. But the two problems should not be confused—and those who have made no contribution toward such a fund should not be regarded as in the same category as those who have—and because a minority lacks the protection of social security is no reason to deny additional self-financed benefits to the great majority which it covers.

The Administration's own Medicare Bill, H.R. 4222, was bottled up in the House Ways and Means Committee where Chairman Mills remained strongly opposed to the program. Then on June 29, Senator Clinton Anderson of New Mexico offered a compromise medical care measure as an amendment to the Public Welfare Amendments Bill, H.R. 10606. It was the work of Senators Anderson, Humphrey, and Javits, and despite alternative programs, took the political spotlight for several weeks.

Congressional Debates
108 Congressional Record, p. 12271
(June 29, 1962)

Senator Clinton P. Anderson [Dem., N. M.] . . . Unless favorable action is taken now, health insurance for the aged could become a major issue in the fall elections, and next year a bill will be passed. But the problem that confronts our aged people is so pressing that I hope we will not delay a solution another year.

The proposed amendment is a conscientious effort to meet the reasonable objections to S. 909, while at the same time preserving its essential points

—health insurance benefits for aged social security beneficiaries and railroad retirement annuitants without a means test and financed through the contributory social security system.

The Social Security Approach is Essential

On these essential social security features, I cannot compromise. Our proposed amendment would utilize the social security financing mechanism, for through this mechanism the health insurance needs of our people in their later years can be met by payments made during their working years.

Health insurance will go far to make retirement protection under social security truly adequate in a way that increased cash monthly payments can never achieve. Health costs of the aged are not evenly distributed from month to month or even from year to year. A person over 65 may have no appreciable health costs for several years and then in a short time have health costs running into thousands of dollars. It is clearly not possible to increase the cash benefit under OASI sufficiently to cover such large expenses.

The health insurance payments to which the elderly would be entitled would be paid as a right earned through the social security system which they have helped support by their contributions during their working years. There would be no means test.

The amendment would follow the same threefold attack on dependency in old age as that carried out by the present social security program. First, basic health insurance protection against hospital costs and certain alternatives to hospitalization would be afforded the elderly through social security; second, the existence of a program of basic protection would encourage the development of additional, private protection which the individual could purchase by his own means; third, all the States would be placed in a far better financial position to provide adequate medical assistance to help the relatively small group whose special needs and circumstances make it impossible for them to meet health costs that exceed those covered in this bill.

The proposed program would be financed on the same financially sound basis as the present social security program. Its cost over the longrun future has been carefully calculated, and sufficient income to meet both short-term and longrun program obligations is provided for.

Health Benefits for those not Insured
Under Social Security

It is estimated that by January 1964—the effective date of my proposed amendment—the total population age 65 and over in the United States will be 17.9 million. Of this number, over a quarter of a million, although not eligible for social security or railroad retirement protection, would have their health needs taken care of under various other governmental programs — including retired Federal employees who have governmental health insurance protection available to them. This leaves approximately 17½ million persons 65 and over, of which about 15 million would be eligible for health insurance under social security or railroad retirement. We have included in this amendment a provision for furnishing to these 2½ million aged people from general revenues, the same health benefits as provided to those insured under the social security and railroad retirement programs.

The gross cost of the provision would be about $250 million in calendar year 1964, the year the health benefits program would go into effect. This cost would be offset by savings in Federal medical care expenditures in 1964 that except for the passage of my bill would be made under public assistance and the veterans' programs. These savings would be about $200 million, leaving a net cost to general revenues of about $50 million in 1964. The annual cost of the provision would drop sharply in following years and eventually wash out altogether.

Improved Administrative Procedures

Since the introduction of S.909 last year I have had the benefit of many helpful suggestions from physicians and hospital administrators all over the country pointing out ways in which the administrative features of the bill could be improved. I have also studied the sincere concerns expressed by some that the Federal procedures might impose difficult requirements or administrative burdens on hospitals. Our proposed amendment meets each of the specific criticisms that some provisions of S.909 might possibly — though the possibility be remote — result in Government interference with the operation of hospitals or the practice of medicine.

Significant Administrative Role for Private Organizations

Under our proposed amendment the Secretary of Health, Education, and Welfare would be given specific statutory authority to delegate some of the more sensitive administrative functions to Blue Cross or to other similar voluntary organizations that are experienced in dealing with hospitals and other providers of health services. Any group of hospitals — or group of other providers of health services — could designate a private organization of their own choice to receive their bills for services and to pay these bills. If advantageous, additional administrative functions could be included in the contract between the Government and the organization. These administrative functions would include reviewing hospital fiscal records as a part of the determination of the cost of services, and acting as a center for communicating and interpreting payment procedures to hospitals.

I should point out that representatives of the American Hospital Association appearing before the Committee on Ways and Means last summer urged an approach that would utilize the services of voluntary organizations if a bill of this type were to be enacted, and I am convinced from numerous conversations with individuals in the field of hospital administration that the provisions I am now outlining will prove to be eminently satisfactory to them. The principal advantage hospitals and other providers of services would find in this arrangement would be that policies and procedures of the Federal program would be applied by the same organization administering the private, voluntary benefit program with which most of them deal.

The role that Blue Cross plans and similar expert organizations could play in carrying out the provisions of my proposed amendment would have advantages that go beyond the benefits that would be derived from their experience in dealing with hospitals and the working relationships already established. With such organizations serving as intermediaries between the Government and providers of services, those who are concerned that the Government might try to intervene in hospital affairs would feel much more comfortable.

Role of State Agencies

The Federal Government would use State agencies to determine whether hospitals which are not accredited by the Joint Commission on the Accreditation of Hospitals or skilled nursing facilities and other providers of health services are qualified to participate in the program. The conditions of participation for such providers are spelled out in my bill. State agencies would determine whether they are met. State health departments or other appropriate agencies designated by each State would also give professional consultation to providers of health services to assist them in meeting the conditions for participation and in establishing and maintaining necessary fiscal records and providing information necessary to derive operating costs which are the basis for payment for their services.

State governments are well fitted to perform these functions since they already license health facilities.

Conditions for Participation

Many people in the health field have applauded the intention—clearly reflected in S. 909—to be specific about any conditions that hospitals or other organizations would have to meet before they could participate in the proposed program. To make sure that the new program would not in any way undercut the efforts of the health profession and would not permit payment to substandard institutions, the participation requirements of S. 909 paralleled requirements of the health professions as they define and accredit institutions. A misunderstanding of the provision has produced the notion that the Government would impose additional requirements beyond those necessary for accreditation. The amendment we are offering makes very explicit that the requirements for participation may not go beyond the professionally set and professionally accepted standards established for hospitals, save for the requirement of a utilization review arrangement. The amendment even goes so far as to name the Joint Commission on the Accreditation of Hospitals and to require use of the Commission's provisions and findings; it provides that, with the one exception of the review arrangement, a hospital that is accredited by the Joint Commission would be conclusively presumed to meet the conditions for participation.

Our amendment would assure that participating nursing homes are of high quality by requiring that only nursing facilities affiliated with hospitals may participate.

Financing of the Program

The Chief Actuary of the Social Security Administration has assured me that the benefits of the proposal would be financed on a sound actuarial basis under the usual cost assumptions, which involve, among other things, level-earnings assumptions. The financing of both the cash benefits, including the higher ones that would result from raising the earnings base, and the new health benefits, would be accomplished by raising the maximum taxable earnings base to $5,200 per year and by an additional combined employer-employee tax of one-half percent. Whereas S. 909 provided for a separate Health Insurance Account to be maintained in the social security trust fund, our amendment would attach even more importance to separate accounting for health benefits by establishing a distinct and separate Health Insurance Trust Fund.

The proposed health benefits would be financed by an allocation to the Health Insurance Trust Fund from the total social security tax receipts — an allocation equal to what a combined employer-employee tax of 0.68 percent would yield. Part of this — 0.50 percent — comes from the increase in the scheduled contribution rates in all future years. The remainder comes from the net gain resulting in the cash-benefits portion of the system from raising the earnings base from $4,800 to $5,200. The health benefits of the proposal and those of the existing system as a whole would be on a sound actuarial basis under these proposed financial provisions.

Summary

Our amendment would embody all of the great merit of the social security approach and at the same time provide meaningful assistance for the relatively few older people who are not now protected by the social insurance system. It has strong safeguards against any possibility that Government would exert control over providers of services and established medical practices. It would have the additional advantage of not requiring Government and the doctors to come to agreement on fees and other sensitive matters that are best left to the private sector. It represents the vast area of agreement that has been reached by those of us who sincerely seek a way by which much needed protection against the cost of serious illness can be provided for our senior citizens.

These is no justification for further delay; we must not wait longer to provide an effective program of protection for the Nation's elderly people.

* * *

Mr. Javits. Madam President, I think it most significant that Republicans have played what I hope is a major role in redrafting the amendments submitted by the Senator from New Mexico [Mr. Anderson] and in bringing about a merger of the ideas in my medical care bill with those contained originally in the King-Anderson bill. It is this kind of bipartisan action which makes prospects for the measure so encouraging.

Despite the bipartisan nature of the proposal, opposition to medical care legislation remained strong. When the debates resumed on July 12, the amendment sponsors inserted a new section to make their program more acceptable.

Congressional Debates
108 Congressional Record, p. 13362
(July 12, 1962)

Senator Jacob Javits [Rep., N.Y.] The purpose of this amendment is to offer the individual an opportunity to purchase or continue a private health care plan which would give him the statutory benefit of 90 days of hospitalization with a deductible, or under group and similar plans 45 days of hospitalization with no deductible, in addition to other health care benefits.

The amendment permits any individual entitled to health insurance benefits for the aged, under proposed title XVII of the Social Security Act, at his option to elect to have payment for those benefits he uses be made to an eligible private carrier under an approved plan.

An approved plan must include the benefits under the statutory plan plus some other health care benefits to be provided by the private carrier. Except that as an option in place of the 90-day hospital benefit with a deductible of $10 a day for 9 days, specified private plans could offer a 45-day hospital benefit with no deductible.

Qualified to offer the option of either the 90-day hospitalization benefit with the deductible, or the 45-day hospitalization benefit paying "first costs," would be group insurance plans; prepayment group practice plans, nonprofit plans, and plans (generally "mass enrollment" plans) having acquisition costs comparable to those of approved group plans. Other non-group plans must offer the 90-day hospital benefit, and could qualify if the carrier did business in the 50 States and wrote at least 1 percent of the health insurance business, was determined by the Secretary to be otherwise national in scope, or did at least 5 percent of the health insurance business within a State in which it sought to write business under this bill.

Private plans must include medical or other health benefits in addition to those reimbursed by the Government. No fee, premium, or other charge to the individual could be made for the reimbursable benefits. The carrier would be paid the reasonable administrative costs of providing the reimbursable benefits, but not to exceed 150 percent of Government costs for the same functions.

An individual must make the election to continue a private health plan within 3 months after becoming entitled to health insurance benefits, and is permitted one such election; he may later revoke that election if he desires. He must have been covered by the approved plan for 1 year prior to becoming eligible for health insurance benefits in the case of group and non-profit plans, and for 2 years in the case of commercial individual policies (except that coverage for 90 days is sufficient for those becoming eligible prior to April 1965, and coverage beginning January 1, 1965, is sufficient for those becoming eligible in or after April 1965, if less than 1 or 2 years).

The private plan is required to include only the 90- or 45-day inpatient hospitalization benefit during the period before the individual becomes eligible under the program; after he becomes eligible, the plan must also provide all auxiliary benefits such as skilled nursing facility, home health, and outpatient hospital diagnostic services.

Despite this attempt at compromise, Senator Leverett Saltonstall of Massachusetts, put forward another amendment on the behalf of several other Senators.

Congressional Debates
108 Congressional Record, p. 13369
(July 12, 1962)

Mr. Saltonstall. Madam President, on behalf of myself and Senators Aiken, Scott, Fong, Boggs, Prouty, and Cotton, I have called up the amendment which we offer as a substitute for the Anderson amendments. Except for minor technical changes, this amendment is similar to S. 937 which nine Senators, including myself, joined in cosponsoring last session. The only significant change is that, on the basis of information furnished by the Department of Health, Education, and Welfare, the deductible feature applicable to one of the three options in the bill has been reduced from $250 to $175 for a single person and from $400 to $300 for a couple.

My colleagues and I offer this proposal because we believe it offers the most constructive approach to providing a sound, voluntary medical care program for our older citizens. It would supplement the Kerr-Mills plan which is geared to providing assistance to the medically indigent, by offering a medical program to those aged persons of modest incomes not eligible under Kerr-Mills.

* * *

Kerr-Mills is helpful legislation. I believe, however, that a further medical assistance program is needed to supplement it, to help persons who, although not meeting the "medically indigent" criteria of Kerr-Mills, possess modest incomes insufficient to enable them to meet their basic medical demands. The amendment presently before us, would, in my estimation, provide such a program.

Like the Eisenhower administration medicare bill, which I sponsored in 1960, this amendment embodies the following essential principles: First, it is a voluntary program and not one based on compulsory social security financing; Second, it involves Federal-State matching and State administration; Third, it offers benefits to meet the specific needs of an aged participant; and, Fourth, it requires some participation on the part of the individual participating in the program.

Our amendment provides 3 optional plans from which participants can select the one they best feel is suited to their individual needs. Total costs of $100 to $128 per person per year would include a modest enrollment fee paid by the individual participant and Federal-State matching based on the per capita income of the State.

Senator Saltonstall's amendment called for the preventive care program, the major illness program, and the private insurance program. It was narrowly defeated. The next Republican amendment, introduced by Senator Bush offered federal supplements to pay private hospital insurance premiums and it was overwhelmingly rejected. However, it was evident that both sides were fairly evenly paired and feelings were clearly aroused. The temper of the Senate may be judged from the following exchanges.

Congressional Debates
108 Congressional Record, p. 13672, 18574
(July 16, 1962)

Senator Douglas . . . The need for the Anderson proposal for health care protection for the aged is well demonstrated. The people are for it, and with the adjustments made recently, it is clear the private insurance industry can easily "live with" the proposal. But opposition to this legislation persists, mainly coming from the American Medical Association and assisting groups like the American Manufacturers Association and the American Farm Bureau. All of these groups have opposed social security plans in the past. The AMA has been opposed to group practice, and to prepayment plans for medical costs. After social security went into operation spokesmen for the AMA denounced it as "socialistic." Later, it opposed providing aid for the totally disabled through social security. It is now adopting a policy that is consistent with its universal past policy.

But there is nothing socialistic or foreign about this proposal. Actually the precedent for a prepaid social insurance system against health care costs was established in this country as early as 1798. For Congress in that year passed a bill providing that deductions would be made from the salary paid to U.S. marines to pay for medical care.

The United States is the last of the free Western nations to get around to providing social insurance for hospital care for its aged citizens who are most in need of this protection. The proposal before us is sound, conservative, and necessary. The Senate has before it an opportunity which it should not turn down. I hope we will defeat the motion to table and that we will send this essential legislation to the House for action.

                              *   *   *

Senator Allott . . . Much more is at stake here than a simple matter of administrative techniques. The whole doctrine of separation of governmental powers, as worked out by the Founding Fathers and reaffirmed by succeeding generations, is at issue.

Adoption of the Anderson-Javits approach would be more than a "foot in the door" for socialized medicine; it would be a long step toward the creation of a new and all-powerful Federal bureaucracy in Washington with a corollary destruction of significant authority and responsibility by State and local government.

In the field of health, itself, the present participation by the Federal Government is limited. If the principles in the Anderson-Javits bill are accepted, they could equally apply to public health measures. If the States are deemed incompetent in provision of medical care to individuals in need, why shouldn't they be deemed incompetent to conduct administration of public health activities? The latter much more clearly affect the total population. They far more certainly cross State lines in their several implications. Are State and local health departments to be replaced by a Federal health juggernaut?

This question is not confined solely to health or medical care. In its large implications, it must be viewed in the total context of possible changes in America's Government. There seems to be a substantial group of people who want to destroy the traditional division of powers, replacing them with centralized concentration of control far removed from the people.

The Kennedy administration has given encouragement to this point of view. Two recent examples should suffice: First, the unsuccessful recommendation that Congress surrender to the executive its control over taxes; and second, the unsuccessful effort to increase Federal involvement in local and State affairs through the proposed creation of a Department of Urban Affairs and Housing, which would have responsibility for certain types of activities in all communities of more than 2,500 population — using definition of "urban population" used by U.S. Bureau of the Census.

As the vote drew near the debate grew more and more vehement. Behind the scenes, it looked as if the Senate was evenly divided and Senator Everett M. Dirksen spoke out vigorously on behalf of the opponents, defending Kerr-Mills.

Congressional Debates
108 Congressional Record, p. 13867
(July 16, 1962)

Senator Everett M. Dirksen [Rep., Ill.] . . . The whole question is one of approach. It is for that reason that I contend that the motion to table, which will be made in 25 minutes, should prevail. I assign some reasons. First, with respect to Kerr-Mills, what kind of effort has been made to sell that act? If the former Secretary of Health, Education, and Welfare has been half as diligent in bringing the Kerr-Mills Act to the attention of the country as Orville Freeman was in bringing an agricultural program to the attention of the country, not only from Washington but through his field force, this would be a far different story.

There is a medicare program. I am astonished that the administration leaders have been so careful never to mention the Kerr-Mills Act, which went on the books in the fall of 1960.

The second reason I assign why the amendments should be tabled is that not a single critic has proposed to amend the Kerr-Mills Act with respect to the so-called pauper's oath or needs clause.

Where is the amendment from the critics which would take that out?

I have an amendment on my desk; and before too long I expect to offer it. But I am no critic of the Kerr-Mills Act.

Why does not someone trot out an amendment, if there is dissatisfaction with the means test and the need clause? It has not been done. The administration has failed to sell the Kerr-Mills Act. I have looked for literature; I have been unable to find it. I receive tons of printed matter, in all colors and illustrated. It is on the whole subject of social security. But try to find a piece of literature, which is the responsibility of HEW, to make manifest to the eligible citizens of the country what they are entitled to under the 1960 law. It is not available. If the administration were interested, this would have been provided long before now.

I assign another reason. There has been an inadequate study of the whole subject.

A few minutes later the vote on the Anderson-Javits Amendment was taken and the four vote margin of defeat meant the battle for medical care was over for 1962. The war, however, was still on. In October the President signed P.L. 87-863, which doubled the existing maximum tax deduction for medical expenses for those under sixty-five and increased such deductions by one-third for those over sixty-five or disabled.

Presidential Statement on the Defeat of
the Medical Care Bill
(July 17, 1962)*

The Medical Care for the Aged Bill was defeated in the United States Senate. A switch of two votes in the Senate would have provided, I believe, for its passage.

I believe this is a most serious defeat for every American family, for the 17 million Americans who are over 65, whose means of support, whose livelihood is certainly lessened over what it was in their working days, who are more inclined to be ill, who will more likely be in hospitals, who are less able to pay their bills.

I think they have suffered a serious setback today. But this issue is not confined to them. All those Americans who have parents, who are liable to be ill, and who have children to educate at the same time, mothers and fathers in their 30's and 40's, I believe they have suffered a serious setback. In 1960, with Senator Anderson, I introduced the Medical Care for the Aged. A change of four votes in the Senate in 1960 would have provided for its passage. This year we came closer.

I think the American people are going to make a decision in November as to whether they want this bill, and similar bills, to be passed, or whether they want it to be defeated. Nearly all the Republicans and a handful of Democrats joined with them to give us today's setback. The election in 1960 was very close. It has meant that nearly every vote in the House and Senate is close. Some we win by one or two votes; others we lose. We have to decide, the United States, in 1962, in November, in the Congressional elections, whether we want to stand still or whether we want to support this kind of legislation for the benefit of the people.

You are going to have a chance to make that judgment. I hope that we will return in November a Congress that will support a program like Medical Care for the Aged, a program which has been fought by the American Medical Association and successfully defeated. This bill will be introduced in January 1963. I hope it will pass. With your support in November, this bill will pass in 1963.

Sincerely,

John F. Kennedy

*Public Papers of the Presidents, John F. Kennedy, 1962, p. 560.

1963

Although the first session of the eighty-eighth Congress was one of the longest on record (January 9 — December 30, 1963), little was achieved in the area of income security legislation. The horror of President Kennedy's assassination (November 22) is only a partial explanation of a relatively fruitless session.

Because of the "new approach" to public assistance no fresh measures were demanded in 1963. Indeed, as far as public assistance was concerned, the period was dominated by recriminations relating to the study of AFDC in Washington D.C., commissioned by Senator Robert Byrd (Dem., W. Va.).

In unemployment compensation programs, President Kennedy continued to press for major long-term changes.

Presidential Letter to the President of the Senate and the Speaker of the House
(May 14, 1963)*

Dear Mr. President: (Dear Mr. Speaker:) I am transmitting herewith a bill designed to carry out a recommendation made in my Economic Report to the Congress for long-overdue permanent improvements in our Federal-State system of unemployment insurance. The bill would extend coverage of the system to over 3,000,000 more workers, increase the size and duration of the benefits, improve the financing of the system, and make certain technical changes.

I cannot emphasize too strongly the need and importance of strengthening our unemployment insurance system. These improvements will not only ease the burdens of involuntary unemployment, but will add to our built-in defenses against recession.

The deficiencies of the present system of restricted benefits and coverage have been amply demonstrated in recent years. Twice, in 1958 and again in 1961, Congress found it necessary to enact temporary stop-gap legislation to provide extended unemployment compensation benefits for the long-term unemployed. More and more workers have remained unemployed for long periods of time in the last few years. The percentage of the insured unemployed who were unemployed more than 26 weeks increased from 15 percent in 1956 to 29 percent in 1961, and remained at 21 percent in 1962.

The proposed bill would provide Federal extended benefits for those workers who have long work histories but who have exhausted their State benefits and remained unemployed for more than 26 weeks. The first 26 weeks of unemployment benefits would be left to the States. The Federal Government would assume responsibility for a maximum of 26 additional weeks for those with a much longer, firmer attachment to the labor force

*Public Papers of the President, John F. Kennedy, 1963, p. 400.

than is required under any State law. The maximum of 26 additional weeks of benefits is based on the fact that under the 1961 temporary extended benefit program nearly two-thirds exhausted the 13 additional weeks of benefits provided.

To qualify for extended benefits a worker would have to be employed in at least 78 of the 156 weeks preceding his unemployment, as well as in 26 of the last 52 weeks. In order to qualify for the maximum duration of 26 additional weeks of benefits, a worker must have 104 weeks of employment in the 3 year qualifying period.

Long periods of unemployment in the group of workers with firm attachment to the labor force involve a difficult period of personal adjustment to a changed situation. Unemployment insurance by itself is not a cure for such unemployment; nor is it the only measure necessary to deal with the problem. The Manpower Development and Training Act, the Public Works Acceleration Act, the 1962 Public Assistance amendments, the strengthening of the employment service, particularly the services to those over 45 and to those under 21, are all invaluable tools we have already acquired for this purpose. Other measures we have proposed include the Youth Employment Act, the Senior Citizens Community Planning and Services Act, and the National Education Improvement Act now pending before Congress.

Unemployment insurance is, however, an invaluable additional tool because of its automatic response to economic conditions. It provides the worker with income and the community with purchasing power while other more individualized programs are getting under way for those for whom they are suitable.

Another major provision of the bill encourages the States to raise their basic benefit payments. Under present-day conditions weekly benefits are often too low in relation to lost wages to enable the worker to meet his basic and nondeferrable expenses. Thus the bill establishes an initial Federal goal of individual weekly benefits of 50 percent of individual weekly wages, up to a State maximum of 50 percent of Statewide average weekly wages. This goal increases to 66-2/3 percent by 1970.

The financing of the system would also be strengthened by the bill. A system of equalization grants to States is provided in order to spread the burden of excessively high unemployment compensation costs; and the amount of wages subject to taxation would be increased to $5,200 in calendar year 1966. The new benefits will be financed by a 0.3 percent increase in the net Federal tax.

I am attaching an explanatory statement which describes these Administration proposals in detail. I urge that early consideration be given to this legislation. It will provide a much needed addition to the series of tools with which we can meet the unemployment problems of this country.

Sincerely,
John F. Kennedy

*His request received no more attention than it had in 1961 and 1962.
The idea of federal standards for state legislation was still unpopular; bills
likely to raise taxes were strongly opposed by employers' groups. Indeed,
the two bills enacted by Congress in 1963 relating to unemployment compensation both eased the tax burden on employers. Under the Temporary
Extended Unemployment Compensation Act of 1961, employers had had
to pay an extra .4 per cent federal tax. This percentage proved too large and
therefore H.R. 4655 called for a reduction from .4 per cent to .25 per cent
of the sum due on January 1, 1964. The House passed this bill on April 29
by a voice vote, but the Senate spread the reduction over a three-year period,
at the same time increasing the sum available to the states for administration of unemployment compensation laws. The second measure was related
to the Temporary Unemployment Compensation Act of 1958. The loans
made to the states under that measure were scheduled to be repaid before
January 1, 1963. Employers in the debtor states were to finance the repayment through a tax increase through 1966. H.R. 8821 froze this increase at
the 1964 rate. Similarly, the rate of tax on sums borrowed from the trust fund
account under Title XII of the Social Security Act was frozen at its 1961
rate of .15 per cent. Both houses passed the bill in the late autumn (P.L.
88 – 173).*

*The long-awaited breakthrough on medical care for the aged remained
unaccomplished, although the year began with a promising presidential
message.*

Special Presidential Message to the Congress on the Needs of the Nation's Senior Citizens
(February 21, 1963)*

To the Congress of the United States:

On the basis of his study of the world's great civilizations, the historian
Toynbee concluded that a society's quality and durability can best be
measured "by the respect and care given its elderly citizens". Never before
in our history have we ever had so many "senior citizens". There are present today in our population 17½ million people aged 65 years or over,
nearly one-tenth of our population—and their number increases by 1,000
every day. By 1980, they will number nearly 25 million. Today there are
already 25 million people aged 60 and over—nearly 6 million aged 75 and
over—and more than 10 thousand over the age of 100.

These figures reflect a profound change in the composition of our population. In 1900, average life expectancy at birth was 49 years. Today more
than 7 out of 10 new-born babies can expect to reach age 65. Life expectancy at birth now averages 70 years. Women 65 years old can now expect

*Ibid., p. 188.

to live 16 more years, and men 65 years old can expect to live 13 additional years. While our population has increased 2½ times since 1900, the number of those aged 65 and over has increased almost sixfold.

This increase in the life span and in the number of our senior citizens presents this Nation with increased opportunities: the opportunity to draw upon their skill and sagacity — and the opportunity to provide the respect and recognition they have earned. It is not enough for a great nation merely to have added new years to life — our objective must also be to add new life to those years.

In the last three decades, this Nation has made considerable progress in assuring our older citizens the security and dignity a lifetime of labor deserves. But "the last of life, for which the first was made . . ." is still not a "golden age" for all our citizens. Too often, these years are filled with anxiety, illness, and even want. The basic statistics on income, housing and health are both revealing and disturbing:

The average annual income received by aged couples is half that of younger two-person families. Almost half of those over 65 living alone receive $1000 or less a year, and three-fourths receive less than $2000 a year. About half the spending units headed by persons over 65 have liquid assets of less than $1000. Two-fifths have a total net worth, including their home, of less than $5000. The main source of income for the great majority of those above 65 is one or more public benefit programs. Seven out of 10 — 12.5 million persons — now receive social security insurance payments, averaging about $76 a month for a retired worker, $66 for a widow, and $129 for an aged worker and wife. One out of 8 — 2¼ million people — are on public assistance, averaging about $60 per month per person, supplemented by medical care payments averaging about $15 a month.

A far greater proportion of senior citizens live in inferior housing than is true of the houses occupied by younger citizens. According to the 1960 census, one-fourth of those aged 60 and over did not have house-holds of their own but lived in the houses of relatives, in lodging houses, or in institutions. Of the remainder, over 30 percent lived in substandard housing which lacked a private bath, toilet, or running hot water or was otherwise dilapidated or deficient, and many others lived in housing unsuitable or unsafe for elderly people.

For roughly four-fifths of those older citizens not living on the farm, housing is a major expense, taking more than one-third of their income. About two-thirds of all those 65 and over own their own homes — but, while such homes are generally free from mortgage, their value is generally less than $10,000.

Our senior citizens are sick more frequently and for more prolonged periods than the rest of the population. Of every 100 persons age 65 or over, 80 suffer some kind of chronic ailment; 28 have heart disease or high blood pressure; 27 have arthritis or rheumatism; 10 have impaired vision; and 17 have hearing impairments. Sixteen are hospitalized one or more times annually. They require three times as many days of hospital care every year as persons under the age of 65. Yet only half of those age 65 and over have any kind of health insurance; only one-third of those with incomes under $2000 a year have such insurance; only one-third of those age 75 and over have such insurance; and it has been estimated that 10% to 15% of the health costs of older people are reimbursed by insurance.

These and other sobering statistics make us realize that our remarkable scientific achievements prolonging the lifespan have not yet been translated into effective human achievements. Our urbanized and industrialized way of life has destroyed the useful and satisfying roles which the aged played in the rural and small-town family society of an earlier era. The skills and talents of our older people are now all too often discarded.

Place and participation, health and honor, cannot, of course, be legislated. But legislation and sensible, coordinated action can enhance the opportunities for the aged. Isolation and misery can be prevented or reduced. We can provide the opportunity and the means for proper food, clothing, and housing—for productive employment or voluntary service—for protection against the devastating financial blows of sudden and catastrophic illness. Society, in short, can and must catch up with science.

All levels of government have the responsibility, in cooperation with private organizations and individuals, to act vigorously to improve the lot of our aged. Public efforts will have to be undertaken primarily by the local communities and by the States. But because these problems are nationwide, they call for Federal action as well.

Recent Federal Action

In approaching this task, it is important to recognize that we are not starting anew but building on a foundation already well laid over the last 30 years. Indeed, in the last two years alone, major strides have been made in improving Federal benefits and services for the aged:

1. —The Social Security Amendments of 1961, which increased benefits by $900 million a year, substantially strengthened social insurance for retired and disabled workers and to widows, and enabled men to retire on Social Security at age 62. Legislation in 1961 also increased Federal support for old-age assistance, including medical vendor payments.

2. —The Community Health Services and Facilities Act of 1961 authorized new programs for out-of-hospital community services for the chronically ill and the aged, and increased Federal grants for nursing home construction, health research facilities, and experimental hospital and medical care facilities. Such programs are now underway in 48 States.

3. —The Public Welfare Amendments of 1962 authorized a substantial increase in Federal funds for old-age assistance, reemphasized restorative

services to return individuals to self-support and self-care, and provided encouragement for employment by permitting States to allow old-age assistance recipients to keep up to $30 of his first $50 of monthly earnings without corresponding reductions in his public assistance payments.

4. — The Housing Act of 1961 included provisions for the rapid expansion of housing for our elderly through public housing, direct loans and FHA mortgage insurance. Commitments in 1961 and 1962 were made for more than 1½ times the number of housing units for older citizens aided in the preceding 5 years.

5. — The Senior Citizens Housing Act of 1962 provided low-interest long-terms loans and loan insurance to enable rural residents over 62, on farms and in small towns, to obtain or rent new homes or modernize old ones.

6. — The new Institute of Child Health and Human Development, which was authorized last year, is expanding programs of research on health problems of the aging.

7. — Other new legislation added safeguards on the purchase of drugs which are so essential to older citizens — boosted railroad retirement and veterans benefits — helped protect private pension funds against abuse — and increased recreational opportunities for all.

8. — By administrative action we have (a) increased the quality and quantity of food available to those on welfare and other low-income aged persons and (b) established new organizational entities to meet the needs and coordinate the services affecting older people:

— a new Gerontology Branch in the Chronic Disease Division of the Public Health Service, the first operating program geared exclusively to meeting health needs of the aging and giving particular emphasis to the application of medical rehabilitation to reduce or eliminate the disabling effects of chronic illnesses (such as stroke, arthritis, and many forms of cancer and heart disease) which cannot yet be prevented; and

— a new Presidents' Council on Aging, whose members are the Secretaries and heads of eight cabinet departments and independent agencies administering in 1964 some $18 billion worth of benefits to people over 65. These and other actions have accelerated the flow of Federal assistance to the aged; and made a major start toward eliminating the gripping fear of economic insecurity. But their numbers are large and their needs are great and much more remains to be done.

1. Health

1. *Hospital Insurance.* Medical science has done much to ease the pain and suffering of serious illness; and it has helped to add more than 20 years to the average length of life since 1900. The wonders worked in a modern American hospital hold out new hopes for our senior citizens. But, unfortu-

nately, the cost of hospital care—now averaging more than $35 a day, nearly 4 times as high as in 1946—has risen much faster than the retired worker's ability to pay for that care.

Illness strikes most often and with its greatest severity at the time in life when incomes are most limited; and millions of our older citizens cannot afford $35 a day in hospital costs. Half of the retired have almost no income other than their Social Security payments—averaging $70 a month per person—and they have little in the way of savings. One-third of the aged family units have less than $100 in liquid assets. One short hospital stay may be manageable for many older persons with the help of family and savings; but the second—and the average person can expect two or three hospital stays after age 65—may well mean destitution, public or private charity, or the alternative of suffering in silence. For these citizens, the miracles of medical science mean little.

A proud and resourceful nation can no longer ask its older people to live in constant fear of a serious illness for which adequate funds are not available. We owe them the right of dignity in sickness as well as in health. We can achieve this by adding health insurance—primarily hospitalization insurance—to our successful social security system.

Hospital insurance for our older citizens on social security offers a reasonable and practical solution to a critical problem. It is the logical extension of a principle established 28 years ago in the Social Security system and confirmed many times since by both Congress and the American voters. It is based on the fundamental premise that contributions during the working years, matched by employers' contributions, should enable people to prepay and build earned rights and benefits to safeguard them in their old age.

There are some who say the problem can best be solved through private health insurance. But this is not the answer for most; for it overlooks the high cost of adequate health insurance and the low incomes of our aged. The average retired couple lives on $50 a week, and the average aged single person lives on $20 a week. These are far below the amounts needed for a modest but adequate standard of living, according to all measures. The cost of broad health insurance coverage for an aged couple, when such coverage is available, is more than $400 a year—about one-sixth of the total income of an average older couple.

As a result, of the total aged population discharged from hospitals, 49 percent have no hospital insurance at all and only 30 percent have as much as three-fourths of their bills paid by insurance plans. (Comparable data for those under 65 showed that only 30 percent lacked hospital insurance, and that 54 percent had three-fourths or more of their bills paid by insurance.) Prepayment of hospital costs for old-age by contributions during the working years is obviously necessary.

Others say that the children of aged parents should be willing to pay their bills; and I have no doubt that most children are willing to sacrifice to aid their parents. But aged parents often choose to suffer from severe illness rather than see their children and grandchildren undergo financial hardship. Hospital insurance under Social Security would make it unnecessary for families to face such choices—just as old-age benefits under Social Security have relieved large numbers of families of the need to choose between the welfare of their parents and the best interests of their children.

Others may say that public assistance or welfare medical assistance for the aged will meet the problem. The welfare medical assistance program adopted in 1960 now operates in 25 States and will provide benefits in 1964 to about 525,000 persons. But this is only a small percentage of those aged individuals who need medical care. Of the 111,700 persons who received medical assistance for the aged in November, more than 70,000 were in only three States, California, Massachusetts, and New York.

Moreover, 25 States have not adopted such a program, which is dependent upon the availability each year of State appropriations, upon the financial condition of the States, and upon competition with many other calls on State resources. As a result, coverage and quality vary from State to State. Surely it would be far better and fairer to provide a universal approach, through social insurance, instead of a needs test program which does not prevent indigency, but operates only after indigency is created. In other words, welfare medical assistance helps older people get health care only if they first accept poverty and then accept charity.

Let me make clear my belief that public assistance grants for medical care would still be necessary to supplement the proposed basic hospitalization program under social security—just as old-age assistance has supplemented old-age and survivors insurance. But it should be regarded as a second line of defense. Our major reliance must be to provide funds for hospital care of our aged through social insurance, supplemented to the extent possible by private insurance.

The hospital insurance program achieves two basic objectives. First, it protects against the principal component of the cost of a serious illness. Second, it furnishes a foundation upon which supplementary, private programs can and will be built. Together with retirement, disability, and survivors insurance benefits, it will help eliminate privation and insecurity in this country.

For these reasons, I recommend a hospital insurance program for senior citizens under the Social Security System which would pay (1) all costs of in-patient hospital services for up to 90 days, with the patient paying $10 a day for the first 9 days and at least $20, or, for those individuals who so elect, all such costs for up to 180 days with the patient paying the first $2\frac{1}{2}$ days of average costs, or all such costs for up to 45 days; (2) all costs of care in skilled nursing home facilities affiliated with hospitals for up to at least 180 days after transfer of the patient from a hospital; (3) all costs above the first $20 for hospital out-patient diagnostic services; and (4) all costs of up to 240 home health-care visits in any one calendar year by community visiting nurses and physical therapists. Under this plan, the individual will have the option of selecting the kind of insurance protection that will be most consistent with his economic resources and his prospective health needs — 45 days with no deductible, 90 days with a maximum $90 deductible, or 180 days paying a "deductible" equal to 2½ days of average hospital costs. This new element of freedom of choice is a major improvement over bills previously submitted.

These benefits would be available to all aged Social Security and railroad retirement beneficiaries, with the costs paid from new social insurance funds provided by adding one-quarter of one percent to the payroll contributions made by both employers and employees and by increasing the annual earnings base from $4,800 to $5,200.

Hospitals, skilled nursing facilities, and community health-service organizations would be paid for the reasonable costs of the services they furnished. There would be little difference between the procedures under the proposed program and those already set up and accepted by hospitals in connection with Blue Cross programs.

Procedures would be developed, utilizing professional organizations and State agencies, for accrediting hospitals and for assisting nonaccredited hospitals and nursing facilities to become eligible to participate.

I also recommend a transition provision under which the benefits would be given to those over 65 today who have not had an opportunity to participate in the social security program. The cost of providing these benefits would be paid from general tax revenues. This provision would be transitional inasmuch as 9 out of 10 persons reaching the age of 65 today have social security coverage.

The program I propose would pay the costs of hospital and related services but it would not interfere with the way treatment is provided. It would not hinder in any way the freedom of choice of doctor, hospital, or nurse. It would not specify in any way the kind of medical or health care or treatment to be provided by the doctor.

Health insurance for our senior citizens is the most important health proposal pending before the Congress. We urgently need this legislation — and we need it now. This is our number one objective for our senior citizens.

2. *Improvements in Medical Care Provisions under Public Assistance.* The public assistance medical aid program should, as I have said, serve as a supplement to health insurance. I have asked the Department of Health, Education and Welfare to continue its efforts to encourage those States that have not already established programs for the medically-indigent aged to do so promptly. I also urge those States which now have incomplete programs to expand them to give the medically needy aged all the help they need.

In addition, the basic welfare law authorizing medical care for those on old-age assistance should now be strengthened.

(a) First, in a few States — six at this time — the scope of medical care available to the neediest group of aged persons, those on old-age assistance is more limited than that which is available to the new category established by the Kerr Mills Act: the "medically indigent," those aged persons who only require assistance in meeting their medical care costs. This is unfair. Accordingly, I recommend that Federal law require the States to provide medical protection for their aged receiving old-age assistance at least equal to that provided to those who are only medically indigent.

(b) Secondly, under present law, Federal old-age assistance grants may be used by a State to provide medical care in a general hospital only up to 42 days for a person suffering from mental illness or tuberculosis. This forces transfer of individuals who need hospitalization for longer periods to State institutions, normally outside the community. In my recent message on mental illness and mental retardation, I proposed that mentally ill and mentally retarded persons should, insofar as possible, receive care in community hospitals and facilities — where their prospects for treatment and restoration to useful life are far better than in the often-obsolete, custodial State institutions. Accordingly, in order to help improve the States' financial capacity to provide these aged with care in their own communities for longer periods, I recommend that the 42 day limitation be eliminated.

3. *Nursing Homes.* As a larger proportion of our growing aged population reaches advanced ages, the need for long-term care facilities is rapidly rising. The present back-log of need is staggering. Enactment of the Hospital Insurance Bill will increase that need still further. In my Message on Improving American Health, I recommended — and again urge — amendment of the Hill-Burton Act to increase the appropriation authorization for high quality nursing homes from $20 million to $50 million.

4. *Other important health legislation.* We not only need a better way for the aged to pay for their health costs; we also need more physicians, dentists, and nurses, and more modern hospitals as well as nursing homes — so that our senior citizens, and all our people, can continue to have the best medical care in the world. Older people need and use more medical facilities and services than any other age group. For that reason, I again urge enactment of previously recommended legislation authorizing (1) Federal matching funds for the construction of new and the expansion or rehabilitation of existing teaching facilities for the medical, dental, and other health professions, (2) Federal financial assistance for students of medicine, dentistry, and osteopathy, (3) revision of the Hill-Burton hospital construction program to enable hospitals to modernize and rehabilitate their facilities, and (4) Federal legislation to help finance the cost of constructing and equipping group practice medical and dental facilities.

5. *Food and Drug Protection for the Elderly.* Measures which safeguard consumers against both actual danger and monetary loss resulting from frauds in sales of unnecessary or worthless dietary preparations, devices, and nostrums are especially important to the elderly. It has been estimated

that consumers waste $500 million a year on medical quackery and another $500 million annually on some "health foods" which have no beneficial effect. The health of the aged is in jeopardy from harmful and useless products and they are unable to bear the financial loss from worthless products.

Unnecessary deaths, injuries and financial loss to our senior citizens can be expected to continue until the law requires adequate testing for safety and efficacy of products and devices before they are made available to consumers. I therefore again urge that the Congress extend the provisions of the Food, Drug, and Cosmetic Act of 1938 to include testing of the safety and effectiveness of therapeutic devices, to extend existing requirements for label warnings to include house-hold articles which are subject to the Food, Drug, and Cosmetic Act, and to extend adequate factory inspection to foods, over-the-counter drugs, devices, and cosmetics.

Recent hearings conducted by Senator McNamara and his Special Committee on Aging have highlighted certain commercial practices of a small portion of industry which sold worthless and ineffective merchandise to all segments of our society, and particularly to the aged. This is an abuse of the public trust. Consequently, the Secretary of Health, Education, and Welfare will take necessary steps to expand measures to supply consumers, and particularly aged consumers, with information which will enable them to make more informed choices in purchasing foods and drugs.

II. Tax Benefits

*   *   *

III. Economic Security

1. *Improvements in Social Security Insurance.* The OASDI system is the basic income maintenance program for our older people. It serves a vital purpose. But it must be kept up-to-date.

My recommendation for financing hospital insurance under social security — by increasing the maximum taxable wage base, on which benefits are computed, from $4800 to $5200 a year — will automatically provide an improvement in future OASDI cash benefits for millions of workers, raising the ultimate maximum monthly benefits payable to a worker from $127 to $134, and for a family from $254 to $268.

For the average regularly employed man the Social Security wage base has become a smaller and smaller portion of his earnings, and his insurance against the loss of employment income upon retirement, death or disability is thus declining steadily. Today only 39 percent of all regularly employed men have all of their earnings counted under the $4,800 ceiling. It is generally agreed that the earnings base needs to be adjusted from time to time as earnings levels rise, and the Congress has done so in the past. Raising the wage base to $5,200 will still only cover the total wages of about 50 percent of regularly employed men. This increase in the Social Security wage base is sound, beneficial and necessary.

The entire relationship between benefits and wages, however, needs to be re-examined. As required by the Social Security Act, the Secretary of Health, Education, and Welfare will soon appoint an Advisory Council on Social Security Financing. I am directing him to charge this Council with the obligation to review the status of the social security trust funds in relation to the long-term commitments of the social security program, and to study and report on extensions of protection and coverage at all levels of earnings, the adequacy of benefits, the desirability of improving the present retirement test, and other related aspects of the social security system. The results of the Council's work should provide a sound basis for continued improvement of the program, keeping it abreast of changes in the economy.

2. *Improvements in Old-Age Assistance.* In the fiscal year 1964 the Federal Government will provide grants to the States of about $1.5 billion under the old-age assistance program. I recommend three improvements in the equity and effectiveness of this program, in addition to the two medical payments changes previously mentioned:

First, under existing Federal law, States are permitted to require up to 5 years residence for eligibility under the old-age assistance program. Currently, 20 States impose the maximum 5-year requirement, 3 States require fewer than 5 years but more than 1, and the remaining States require 1 year or less.

Lengthy residence requirements are an unnecessary restriction on elderly people receiving public assistance who would like to move to another State to be near a child or other relative. Others in need, not previously receiving such assistance, find themselves in a "no-man's land," with no aid at all and no place to turn because they have not lived long enough in the State of their present residence. To ensure that our Federal-State public assistance program can help all of our needy aged, I recommend that the maximum period of residence which may be required for eligibility be gradually reduced to 1 year by 1970. This change does not represent an expansion of the program or a significant cost to the Federal Government or any individual State; and it will simplify administration by eliminating many detailed investigations of residence.

Second, a problem of increasing proportions found among our needy citizens is the difficulty some have in properly handling the money which they receive from a public welfare agency. Of the more than 2 million recipients of old-age assistance, over half are 75 years or older, one in three is 80 or more, and one in eight is over 85. One-third are confined to their homes or require help from others because of physical or mental disability and almost 9 percent are in nursing homes and other institutions. Among this group some lose their assistance payments through forgetfulness; others are defrauded by unscrupulous persons. Obviously many of these aged beneficiaries who are not in need of legal guardians, should nevertheless have help in handling their money; yet current provisions of the Federal law tend to make it difficult for States to provide necessary protective services.

I therefore recommend that the old-age assistance program be modified to permit Federal participation in protective payments made to a third party in behalf of needy aged individuals. This would be comparable to provisions adopted last year for dependent children.

Third, many of our older people, with very limited income, live in rental housing which falls far short of any reasonable standard of health or safety. As mentioned earlier, among households headed by a person 65 years of age or over who live in rented housing, nearly 40 percent are in quarters classified as substandard. Yet they are frequently charged exorbitant rents for this housing.

*   *   *

Conclusion

Our aged have not been singled out in this special message to segregate them from other citizens. Rather, I have sought to emphasize the important values that can accrue to us as a nation if we would but recognize fully the facts concerning our older citizens — their numbers, their situation in the modern world, and their unutilized potential.

Our national record in providing for our aged is a proud and hopeful one. But it can and must improve. We can continue to move forward — by building needed Federal programs — by developing means for comprehensive action in our communities — and by doing all we can, as a nation and as individuals, to enable our senior citizens to achieve both a better standard of life and a more active, useful and meaningful role in a society that owes them much and can still learn much from them.

John F. Kennedy

The year 1963 also saw some minor developments in the cause of national health care. Title XVII was added to the Social Security Act, providing grants for research on mental retardation (P.L. 88-156). In addition two reports on the operation of Kerr-Mills programs were issued — both originating from the Senate's Special Committee on Aging. Both publications were highly critical and found the MAA plans ineffective and insufficient.

The Hospital Insurance Bill was introduced by Representative Cecil R. King of California and Senator Clinton Anderson on February 21 (H.R. 3920; S. 880). Most elements of the eighty-seventh Congress Administration bill were included as well as various provisions from the Javits-Anderson plan. A provision allowing beneficiaries to receive their payments through a fiscal intermediary was added by another bill. The House had just begun hearings on H.R. 3920 when the President was assassinated and the entire matter was postponed until 1964.

THE GREAT SOCIETY
1964-1968

THE GREAT SOCIETY
1964-1968

Undoubtedly a decade will have to pass before the Great Society—President Johnson's domestic policies—can be fairly evaluated. Without the benefit of hindsight, it is possible to record that during the first two, or perhaps three, years of the presidency, there was an unrivalled spate of social legislation, including extensive legislation in the field of income maintenance and medical care. Less obvious is whether the legislation of 1964 and 1965 responded more to the problems of the 1930's or to those of the 1960's, or whether any fundamental changes in approach had occurred. Whether the federal apparatus could grapple with the basic problems of a society apparently torn apart by racial strife at home and a war in Vietnam was an even more difficult question.

These are the long-term unanswered questions. Meanwhile advocates of an increased federal role could not help being impressed by the record.

1964

Income Security

Nineteen Sixty-four was an important year for social legislation in general, for President Johnson showed himself a forceful supporter of programs which had languished over the years. The Economic Opportunity Act, establishing the Poverty Program, was in many respects an attack on those factors which led to the need for an income security program. Instead of seeking to ensure that everyone had minimum financial protection, the new act sought to strike at the roots of poverty and help to eradicate them. Section two of that law summed up its purpose:

> *Although the economic well-being and prosperity of the United States have progressed to a level surpassing any achieved in world history, and although these benefits are widely shared throughout the Nation, poverty continues to be the lot of a substantial number of our people. The United States can achieve its full economic and social potential as a nation only if every individual has the opportunity to contribute to the full extent of his capabilities and to participate in the workings of our society. It is, therefore, the policy of the United States to eliminate the paradox of poverty in the midst of plenty in this Nation by opening to everyone the opportunity for education and training, the opportunity to work, and the opportunity to live in decency and dignity. It is the purpose of this Act to strengthen, supplement, and coordinate efforts in furtherance of that policy.*

Title I established the youth programs (including the Job Corps, work-training programs, work-study programs); Title II, the urban and rural community action programs, under which most of the poverty funds have been spent. Title III provided for special programs to combat poverty in rural areas; Title IV authorized employment and investment incentives; Title V covered work experience programs. (Incidentally, Section 502 allowed income to be ignored for the purposes of OASDI.)

It seemed logical that 1964 would also be an auspicious year for improvements in social security and a breakthrough in medical care. However, these did not occur. HEW needed an additional $159 million for public assistance programs which were out of congressional favor, but for OASDI, the year began brightly. The program had become sacrosanct. Theoretically Congress had less control over the social security trust fund than over the open-ended financing of public assistance programs, and besides, it was widely accepted that those who had "contributed" were entitled to have the benefits increased with the cost of living.

In 1964 there was more than usual public support for increasing benefits, because of a powerful report by the President's Council on Aging. Some idea of the tone of the document emerges in the introduction to the second chapter.

Action for Older Americans
1964 Annual Report of the President's Council on Aging
(p. 11)

*   *   *

Chapter II

ACTION FOR INCOME

". . . We are moving ahead to keep the older American from becoming a second-class citizen.
"Our programs in income maintenance . . . and other actions are bringing us closer to the time when elderly people generally can enjoy the independence and the sense of purpose and accomplishment that are their due . . ."

Lyndon B. Johnson
February 9, 1964

Our old people are quite frequently our poor people. As the economic mainstream has risen from scarcity to affluence, it has left millions of our aged stranded in the backwaters of poverty.

Fortunately, they have been aided by the broad scope, diversity, and magnitude of Federal income maintenance programs. Without these programs, the incidence and severity of poverty would be much greater.

Nevertheless, 3 million elderly families live on the wrong side of the "poverty line" with incomes of less than $3,000 a year. At least 1.9 million aged couples live on less than $2,500 a year, and 5.7 million aged individuals live on less than $1,800 a year.

The list of Federal income maintenance programs, topped by social security, represents an economic life preserver by replacing in part the income lost through retirement, disability, or death of the breadwinner. Last year, for example, these programs totaled more than $18 billion and buoyed up millions of older Americans. About 9 out of 10 persons age 65 and over were receiving payments from one of these income maintenance programs.

Representative of those receiving benefits under Federal income maintenance programs are:

A retired steel worker and his wife in Pittsburgh . . . a self-employed management consultant in Boston . . . a World War I veteran in Florida . . . a retired railroad conductor in Ohio . . . a former postal clerk and his wife in Dallas . . . a salesman's widow in San Francisco . . . a chronically ill tobacco farmer in Kentucky . . . a blind man in Philadelphia . . . a crippled woman in Arizona.

Since 1950, 80 percent of the increased income which Americans 65 and over achieved can be attributed to Federal income maintenance programs. At that time, the aged population numbered some 12 million and had an aggregate income of about $15 billion. The aged population is now up to about 18 million and their income has more than doubled to about $35 billion. But during the same span, Federal income maintenance payments have increased eight times from $2.1 billion to $18 billion.

While there was expansion in income maintenance programs administered by the Civil Service Commission, the Railroad Retirement Board, and the Veterans Administration, the major bulges in the growth curve were caused by the seven major Social Security Act amendments since 1950.

But direct payment programs were not the only kind of income programs bolstering the available income of older persons. Federal tax laws contain special provisions available to older persons which indirectly add to their income status. In 1964, for example, the special tax savings available to older persons ran about $850 million a year; enactment of the Revenue Act of 1964 further reduced the net tax liability of the aged by more than $675 million.

Another "extra" that benefited all Americans, but especially senior citizens, was the administration's ability to pursue successfully a policy of unprecedented peacetime economic growth while maintaining general price stability. By almost any economic measure, the last 4 years have seen real gains — the gross national product increased some 24 percent, employment expanded 4 percent, the unemployment rate fell 2 percent, and personal income rose 22 percent.

*　　*　　*

The report was made public by President Johnson in a dramatic announcement.

Presidential Statement Upon Making Public the Report
of the President's Council on Aging
(February 9, 1964)*

This administration will continue to build on the efforts of President Kennedy to make this a better country for its older citizens. Under my 1965 budget proposals the Federal Government will spend an estimated $19 billion from budget and trust funds for benefits and services for older persons. We are moving ahead to keep the older American from becoming a second-class citizen.

Our programs in income maintenance, our efforts in supporting private industry in the building of better housing for older people, our investments in research, our assistance in the provision of medical facilities — these and other actions are bringing us closer to the time when elderly people generally can enjoy the independence and the sense of purpose and accomplishment that are their due.

Much more meeds to be done to brighten the later years.

Longer life is both a major achievement and a major challenge of our time. Nearly 23 years have been added to the average lifetime in our century. A child born in 1900 could expect 47 years of life; his grand-children, born today, can look forward to 70. They will carry the continuity of America well toward the middle of the 21st century.

Today nearly 18 million men and women in the United States have reached or passed their 65th birthday. Approximately one-third of them are 75 or over. More than 12,000 have lived 100 years.

For these older Americans — and for those of us moving each year to join them — the lengthening of life gives an opportunity for a new dimension to living. The increased span of retirement provides time for self-realization, creative endeavor, and public service.

Old age is not a problem in itself. But the fact is, millions of older Americans face many problems. They face:

— The problem of poverty. There are 3 million elderly families with incomes of less than $3,000 a year, and two-thirds of all elderly persons, who live alone or with nonrelatives, have incomes below $1,500.

— The problem of housing. One out of each five dwelling units occupied by persons over 60 is substandard.

— The problem of health. Older people need much more medical service than younger. They have much less money to pay for it.

— The problem of employment. Age alone is a too-frequent excuse

*Public Papers of the Presidents, Lyndon B. Johnson, 1963–1964, Vol. 1, p. 273.

to remove men and women needlessly and arbitrarily from active participation in life.

We must attack all these problems all the time, if we are to achieve goals of security and opportunity for all older Americans.

To fall behind on one front is to fall behind on all fronts. Poverty is an all-pervasive blight. And so are miserable housing, poor health, and social banishment.

One of the most urgent orders of business at this time is the enactment of hospital insurance for the aged through social security to help older people meet the high costs of illness without jeopardizing their economic independence.

This program would not only be a major attack on health problems among older people but a major attack on poverty.

At the same time, I urge all States to adopt adequate programs of medical assistance for the aged under the Kerr-Mills legislation. This assistance is needed now, and it will be needed later as a supplement to hospital insurance to deal with those special problems that private insurance and the social insurance program will not cover.

On June 24, the House Ways and Means Committee, putting aside the Medicare Bill (H.R. 3920) reported out H.R. 11865, which called for a 5 per cent increase for twenty million social security beneficiaries. Among other things, the bill "blanketed in" some six hundred thousand elderly persons, included physicians in the social security system, again lowered the age limit for widows, and increased both tax rate and tax base for employers and employees.

With the traditional closed rule debate, the House passed the measure on July 29. Much of the discussion and even more concern was over medical care. Yet at least it aired some issues which had been glossed over in earlier years. A remarkable show of bi-partisan agreement opened the debate. Indeed, at first, the only breach in harmony came from the conservatives.

Congressional Debates
110 Congressional Record, p. 17267
(July 29, 1964)

Representative Curtis . . . I should like to discuss a little bit, if I may, the social security system itself. Many speeches have been made on the floor of the House since I have been here about the social security system having proved itself. I warned before, and I warn again, that everyone for the first 20 or 30 years of its existence, could say it is going to look good. It is much like the old gimmick of chain letters, whereby a person sends out letters asking others to send in a dollar. Those who are in first certainly believe it is a great system, because they pay out a dollar and get in 10, but as the circle widens a different picture develops.

I will say that those who have been under social security have paid in $1 and got $100. Of course they have thought it was good. The people going on social security right now will pay in $1 and get out $10, so they believe it is good.

For the next 10 years everyone in this room is going to benefit from this type of system.

The test of social security always has been with respect to what will happen in the next 30 years. This system will not mature for 90 years. This system must be kept intact and it must be kept responsible.

Yes, you have heard it is fiscally solvent. That is true, but it is on the assumptions which the actuarial people are given—and they are good people—in the Social Security Administration. They state it is on the assumptions given to them that they have been asked to make the judgment. However, we have a responsibility to look at those assumptions to see indeed how reliable they are and if there is something in the system which may be seeds of destruction. If there are, it is important that we pull them out if we can, because indeed I happen to think we can do it.

It was not long before medical care emerged as a major issue, but its support was not strong enough and H.R. 11865 emerged from the House without any reference to health provisions. However when the Senate Finance Committee began hearings on August 6, HEW Secretary Anthony Celebrezze made it clear that the Administration was now prepared to fight. Improvements in social security were important, but medical care, especially hospital insurance was even more crucial. Despite the Secretary's plea, the bill, reported by the Senate Finance Committee contained no medicare provision. Indeed, it was almost identical to the House version, except that the Senate committee refused to include tips in the wage base and excluded physicians from OASDI coverage. At the same time, the committee added an amendment to increase by five dollars the amount of the federal matching grant under OAA, AB, and APTD. The Finance Committee report explained the changes.

Social Security Act Amendments of 1964
Senate Report No. 1513
88th Cong., 2d Sess. (August 20, 1964)
(p. 5,7)

*　　*　　*

3. Changes in House bill provisions

The provision in the House bill extending coverage to self-employed physicians has been deleted because the national association representing

70 percent of the physicians in the United States has, once again, indicated to the committee its opposition to the inclusion of self-employed physicians.

The committee has also deleted the House provision which would have repealed the longstanding prohibition against the social security coverage of policemen and firemen under State and local retirement systems. The committee believes the present method of providing such coverage on a State-by-State basis offers both an opportunity for those who wish coverage to obtain it while it continues the safeguards which organizations representing policemen and firemen believe are necessary to preserve the integrity of their unique retirement systems.

Finally, the committee deleted the section of the House bill providing for the coverage of cash tips. The committee was not altogether convinced that this was a workable provision, and believes that it might unduly burden employers and employees and tend to disrupt traditional working relationships in industries where tipping plays a major role.

*   *   *

PUBLIC ASSISTANCE

A. Increase In Federal Matching Maximum

The committee added an amendment which would increase the maximum amount which will be matched by the Federal Government by $5 a month per individual in the State public assistance programs for the aged, the blind, and the disabled. The cost of this proposal will be about $35 million a year.

Senate debate began on August 31 with Senator Russell Long introducing the bill. He then moved to increase the benefits and earnings rules for those under social security, one way of undermining the advocates of medicare. Debate on the social security increases, however, eventually gave way to discussion of medical programs. On September 2, the Senate became the first house of Congress to enact a medical care bill by passing the Gore Amendment. (See next section)

Meanwhile, the Senate pressed on with discussion of the other issues in OASDI. Senator William Prouty of Vermont again tried to undermine the Medicare provisions with a social security increase but this was ultimately defeated. The bill with the Gore Amendment passed the next day, September 3. It included a flat $7 increase for all social security beneficiaries, and an increase of $5,600 in the tax base; it allowed widows to draw benefits at a reduced rate at sixty, permitted certain persons in their seventies to be blanketed in, and authorized beneficiaries to earn up to $1500 without loss of benefit and a further $500 with only partial reductions. It also enabled certain persons to opt out of OASDI on religious grounds. In the area *of public assistance, the $5 federal share increase remained, and states were authorized to exclude the first $50 per month earned in calculating OAA payments.*

Senate conferees were appointed and two weeks later, the House Medicare supporters agreed to the appointment of conferees.

It made little difference, however. The House conferees took a 3-2 position against a social security bill which included Medicare; the Senate conferees held 4-3 that they would accept no social security bill without Medicare. The impasse was obvious. On October 2, the conferees gave up any attempt to agree and Congress adjourned the following day. No major social security legislation was therefore enacted in 1964. However, a number of minor technical acts relating to the program were passed.

1964 was not a year for tackling unemployment or unemployment compensation. President Johnson did not ignore it, but in the Manpower Report of the President *(required under the Manpower Development and Training Act of 1962), unemployment compensation was considered as only one of various ways of alleviating unemployment. Developed in 1935 to help temporarily "laid off" workers, unemployment compensation was increasingly unsuited to the problems of the 1960's. Now finding employment for minority groups, older persons, and insufficiently skilled younger workers presented greater challenges. Existing programs did all too little for the hard-core unemployed.*

Medicare

The fight for Medicare came to a head in 1964. When the battle for the Administration proposal H. R. 3920 had begun in 1963. HEW Secretary Anthony Celebrezze had been the first witness to appear before the House Ways and Means Committee.

Social Security: Medical Care for the Aged Amendments
Hearings on H. R. 3920 before the House Ways and Means Committee
88th Cong., 1st Sess. (November, 1963)
(p. 26)

What are the dimensions of this problem?

It is widespread. The later years of life bring with them very high health costs on the one side and reduced incomes on the other. Few of the aged escape these pincers. Nine out of ten people are hospitalized at least once after reaching age 64. Almost two out of three will go to the hospital at least twice between age 65 and death. People over 65 use three times as much hospital care, on the average, as people under 65.

The facts about the income and assets of older people are no less disturbing. The aged have less than half the income of younger people in similar family situations. One-half the aged couples have less than $2800 in annual income and little in the way of assets other than equity in their homes.

The average aged person living alone now has an income of not much over $1,200 a year. But averages do not tell the whole story. At least two-fifths of the aged — including wives as sharing in the incomes of their husbands — have incomes of under $1,000 a year. Not more than 10 percent of the aged have incomes over $4,000, and most of them have not yet retired and will have much lower incomes when they do.

Moreover, a national average does not reflect the situation in particular localities. Where wages and living standards are well below the national average, the aged too will have comparably lower incomes.

The problem created by the combined effect of high health costs and low income in old age requires an approach that does not depend on payment of the cost after retirement but instead enables people to pay for their protection against these costs out of their earnings and over the course of their working lifetimes.

Why is hospital insurance under social security an important part of the solution?

The basic idea of social security is that people pay contributions over their working lifetimes (together with their employers) to provide benefits after retirement in old age. The proposal for hospital insurance for the aged is patterned after the same principle.

While earning, the worker would make small contributions to pay for protection against the high hospital costs that are a common occurrence in old age. He would have the protection at age 65 without need to make further contributions after retirement.

Protection against the cost of hospital care in old age is a logical and necessary extension of the retirement protection furnished by the present social security program. Monthly cash benefits can meet the regular recurring expenses of food, clothing, and shelter, but such benefits alone cannot give economic security in old age.

It is also necessary that older people have protection against the unpredictable and unbudgetable costs of expensive illness. A person may go on for a long time with little in the way of medical expenses and then, in a very short period, have a hospital bill running into thousands of dollars.

Cash benefits are not a practical way to meet this need. What is needed is a substantial measure of protection against the cost of major illness in addition to cash benefits. The administration's proposal, as embodied in H.R. 3920, does just this.

Why cannot the problem be solved through private voluntary insurance?

Briefly stated, the reason we believe private health insurance cannot do the job alone and I emphasize the word "alone," is that this insurance, if adequate and if paid for in old age, costs more than most older people can afford to pay.

Because old age is a time of life when health costs are high, therefore insurance costs are high. And as I have already pointed out, older people generally have low incomes. What makes matters more difficult is that older people usually are not in a position to obtain the cost advantages of group health insurance.

Let me illustrate the problem of costs to an aged individual by referring to the three main types of private, voluntary health insurance plans available to the aged.

Let us take first the four statewide plans being underwritten by groups of private companies. These plans have a basic portion and a major medical portion, which in combination cost an aged couple $456 a year in New York and Texas, $420 a year in Massachusetts, and $408 a year in Connecticut.

Premiums of this magnitude amount to about one-sixth of the median income of aged couples. And they would be still higher if benefit costs were not kept down through the exclusion of preexisting conditions, coinsurance, and other limitations.

Even so, all indications are that these premiums are bound to get higher. For example, the Connecticut plan, which went into effect in 1961, has already been forced by its substantial losses to ask for an 18-percent increase in premium rates.

Blue Cross plans for the aged represent a second type of approach. The premiums required under more than a third of these plans exceed $200 a year per couple. About three-fifths of the Blue Cross plans have dollar limits or coinsurance provisions on hospital room costs; only about one-half cover nursing-home care or visiting-nurse service.

Commercial 65 – Plus plans represent a third approach. Two of the most widely advertised and best known plans of this type provide a hospital room-and-board allowance of $10 per day, which is only about one-half of average charges for room and board in a hospital.

One plan covers a maximum of 31 days, the other a maximum of 60 days. The premium for the more limited plan is $156 a year per couple; for the other, $204 a year.

Because of limitations in all these policies the average aged person who has one must, in addition to paying the premiums on his policy, be prepared to pay from 50 to 80 percent of his total medical bill.

Although the percentage of aged persons with some kind of health insurance protection has risen, the absolute number without protection is nearly as large as it was 5 years ago. Despite the publicity given to the four State-65 plans and the new Blue Cross plans for the aged, less than half a million — about 3 percent of the aged — have been enrolled in these new plans.

Moreover, many have not been able to keep up their policies. Today there are over 8 million aged persons who have no health insurance protection at all. About 3 million more have inadequate policies of the $10-a-day type. Probably less than a million, 5 to 6 percent of the aged, have health insurance protection covering as much as 40 percent of average medical costs.

The best that private insurance has been able to do to solve the dilemma of high costs and low income is to offer either low-cost policies with inadequate protection or more adequate policies that are priced out of the reach of most of the aged.

Insurance companies necessarily use various devices to control the problem of risk selection, which together have the result of reducing protection available or, in some instances, denying it altogether.

The companies are understandably concerned lest a large proportion of their enrollment consist of those most likely to have high costs, such as those who are already very old or already ill or who have chronic conditions. Among the devices to control costs that are used in varying degrees, depending on the type of policy, are refusal of application on the basis of a health questionnaire or a physical examination, deductibles and coinsurance, cancellation provisions, and—in the case of major medical policies —annual limits and lifetime limits.

Characteristically, private insurance policies, including Blue Cross non-group-enrollment plans for the aged, have special provisions relating to preexisting conditions. They may impose waiting periods of from 6 to 24 months before covering costs resulting from such conditions, or they may permanently exclude costs arising from such conditions.

The effect of such exclusions is to limit the protection significantly in the case of the aged, since a considerable proportion of the conditions requiring hospital care among the aged are conditions that existed prior to enrollment in the plan.

As indicated, the only way to really meet the problem is through insurance paid for during working years. But the paid-up type of private insurance is very little. Only 6 carriers out of more than 850 commercial companies writing health insurance have offered this type of policy, and even these few companies have not found a market.

The number of people who own such a policy is very small. The cost is prohibitive for most people nearing retirement age. For most people who are young, the paid-up-at-retirement policies are hopelessly impractical. The fixed dollar payments that they provide become more and more inadequate if, as is very likely to be the case, health-care costs increase substantially between the time a person buys the policy and the time, after 65, when he has occasion to use it.

In our opinion, private insurance alone will not be able—in the foreseeable future—to meet effectively the needs of the aged. Most of the aged who are covered by private health insurance are those who are still working, those in better health, and those in the higher-income groups.

Extension of any kind of insurance coverage—even a poor and inadequate kind—to the remaining aged becomes increasingly difficult to achieve because these people are more likely to be in the low-income and poor-health-risk groups.

The industry and the nonprofit organizations have been imaginative and energetic in seeking solutions to the problems. But the dilemma created by high health costs and low incomes in old age cannot be solved by any plan that puts the full cost on the aged and tries to cover that cost through premiums paid in old age.

The Blue Cross Association—the organization whose members have sold half the health insurance policies held by the aged—and the American Hospital Association have jointly announced their belief that voluntary insurance alone and unsubsidized cannot meet the need.

Yet private insurance has a significant role to play in helping to meet the medical-care costs of older people. A large number of older people, slightly over half, have indicated a willingness and ability to pay something in old age toward health insurance protection by purchasing various types of policies.

We believe that with basic protection furnished on a paid-up basis under social security, additional people will want to buy complementary private insurance protection.

Why can't we rely on the program of medical assistance for the aged to solve the problem?

The welfare programs such as medical assistance to the aged and old age assistance do have an important supplementary role, but they cannot and should not play a primary role for the great majority of retired people.

Our objective should be to prevent poverty and dependency to the extent possible rather than try to provide relief for these unhappy conditions after they have occurred. We should do better than say to an aged person that, when he has become poor enough and when he can prove his poverty to the satisfaction of the appropriate public agency, he may be able to get help.

We should take into account the pride and independent spirit of our older people—the pride and independent spirit that lead many of them to suffer their illnesses in silence and to put off needed medical care rather than ask for help. What is required as the first line of defense is protection furnished as a right and in a way which fully safe-guards the dignity and independence of our older people.

The aged person does not know how long he is going to live and how many emergencies will arise during the rest of his lifetime. When a trip to the hospital has forced him to deplete his savings before he can get help through the means-test programs, he has lost heavily in his sense of security and independence.

Unlike the younger person whose savings are gone, the older person usually has no way of building them up again. His ability to meet later emergencies and the security that this ability gives him are gone, without hope of ever being restored.

This committee has taken the lead again and again in seeing to it that the Nation's attack on poverty is hinged on prevention and on the idea that people should contribute to their own security through social insurance.

It is of great importance that we continue our main reliance on social insurance and that the role of public assistance be one of a backstop, a last resort, not one in which it is made to serve as a primary defense.

MAA has another kind of deficiency which likewise cannot be over come: An adequate MAA program that is intended to be the main attack on the health-cost problem of the aged cannot be financed without a very large fiscal drain on the States as well as on the general revenues of the Federal Government.

A major problem in a program financed jointly by the Federal and State Governments is that the Federal offer of funds is meaningful only if the States are able to provide sufficient matching funds.

Low-income States may not be able to afford a program at all. Other States may be able to establish only inadequate programs. The wealthiest States will be able to establish the most comprehensive programs and will receive the lion's share of the Federal funds.

For example, 73 percent of the funds expended in September 1963 under MAA went to just five States – five of the industrialized, financially better off States – which have within their borders only 33 percent of the Nation's aged population.

So far the MAA program has not brought medical care to any large number of people with higher incomes and assets than old-age assistance receipients have. Actually, the majority of those receiving help under the MAA program could have met the eligibility tests under old-age assistance and are on MAA only because of the more liberal Federal matching formula. MAA does not help at all many of the aged who need help; and for many of those who do get some help, the help is very limited.

As indicated, there are inherent limitations in the Federal-State welfare programs that make them an undesirable and ineffective way of dealing with the problem we have before us.

On the other hand, there is a continuing function for MAA, and we hope that every State that has not done so will adopt an MAA program and that States which now have limited or inadequate programs will improve them.

With a basic program of hospital insurance under social security, many additional States, relieved of what would otherwise be a very heavy burden on their general revenues, would be able to afford an MAA program as a supplement to social security, and the States which now have inadequate medical programs will be able to improve them.

Why is social security hospital insurance the best answer to the problem of health costs in old age?

By allowing medical expense deductions for income tax purposes, the Government helps those among the aged who are relatively well off. The very wealthy person has 91 percent of his medical bills taken care of this way.

But only one-fifth of the aged have high enough incomes to pay income taxes and be helped at all by this provision — even at the 20-percent income tax rate. Governmental action has also been taken to help the very poor. It is the great majority of people, who are neither wealthy nor very poor, who have been left out. These are people who have been self-supporting all their lives and want to continue to be — who do not want welfare even if it were adequate.

What is needed is a system under which all workers can, during their productive years, pay contributions toward protection against the high health costs that will beset them in later years.

In our opinion social security, and only social security, offers a ready-built thoroughly tested mechanism that would make this desirable arrangement available to practically everybody.

The proposed program of hospital insurance for the elderly would follow the same kind of threefold attack on dependency in old age as that found under the present social security program.

First, basic protection against the cost of hospitalization and of certain alternatives to hospitalization would be afforded the elderly through social security.

Second, private protection would be built upon this social security base through employer plans and individually.

Third, for the members of the small group with such special needs and circumstances that they are unable to meet their health costs through the proposed social security plan and their private insurance and other resources, help could be available through medical assistance which all the States would be in a far better financial position to provide on an adequate basis.

Hospital insurance under the contributory social security program would offer all these advantages while affording protection in a way that is consistent with our respect for the independence, the dignity, and the privacy of the individual.

A similar grilling awaited the Secretary on hospital insurance and the Kerr-Mills Act as Medicare opponents implied that HEW had not made a serious effort to implement Kerr-Mills.

The five volumes of testimony resulting from the hearings before the House committee, contained almost every possible view of the medical care debate. At least four alternate proposals were made and Senators and Congressmen heatedly took sides.

Inevitably the AMA opposed the new bill and it was joined by the American Hospital Association as well as the insurance industry. However, some ad hoc *medical groups such as the Physicians' Committee for Health*

Care for the Aged through Social Security were prepared to press for the legislation and, as usual, the AFL-CIO could be relied on to support the measure.

While sentiment in the House Ways and Means Committee was fairly evenly divided on this legislation, Chairman Wilbur Mills remained opposed objecting mainly to the fiscal soundness of the bill. He ultimately withdrew his support and Representative King, sponsor of the bill, decided not to press for a committee vote, thus eliminating any Medicare Bill in 1964. However, President Johnson remained concerned with the problems of medical care under social security.

Special Presidential Message on Health
(February 10, 1964)*

To The Congress of the United States:

The American people are not satisfied with better-than-average health. As a Nation, they want, they need, and they can afford the best of health:
   not just for those of comfortable means
   but for *all* our citizens, old and young, rich and poor.
In America,
There is no need and no room for second-class health services.
There is no need and no room for denying to any of our people the
   wonders of modern medicine.
There is no need and no room for elderly people to suffer the personal
   economic disaster to which major illness all too commonly exposes
   them.
In seeking health improvements, we build on the past. *For in the conquest of ill health our record is already a proud one:*
   American medical research continues to score remarkable advances.
   We have mastered most of the major contagious diseases.
   Our life expectancy is increasing steadily.
   The overall quality of our physicians, dentists, and other health
workers, of our professional schools, and of our hospitals and laboratories is unexcelled.
   Basic health protection is becoming more and more broadly available.
Federal programs have played a major role in these advances:
Federal expenditures in the fiscal 1965 budget for health and health-
   related programs total $5.4 billion—about double the amount of 8
   years ago.

*Public Papers of the Presidents, Lyndon B. Johnson, 1963–1964, Vol. 1, p. 274.

Federal participation and stimulus are partly responsible for the fact that last year—in 1963—the Nation's total health expenditures reached an unprecedented high of $34 billion, or 6 percent of the gross national product.

But progress means mew problems:

As the life span lengthens, the need for health services grows.

As medical science grows more complex, health care becomes more expensive.

As people move to urban centers, health hazards rise.

As population, which has increased 27 percent since 1950, continues to grow, a greater strain is put on our limited supply of trained personnel.

Even worse, perhaps, are those problems that reflect *the unequal sharing of the health services we have:*

Thousands suffer from diseases for which preventive measures are known but not applied.

Thousands of babies die needlessly; 9 other nations have lower infant death rates than ours.

Half of the young men found unqualified for military service are rejected for medical reasons; most of them come from poor homes.

Clearly, too many Americans still are cut off by low incomes from adequate health services. Too many older people are still deprived of hope and dignity by prolonged and costly illness. The linkage between ill-health and poverty in America is still all too plain.

In its first session, *the 88th Congress made some important advances on the health front:*

It acted to increase our supply of physicians and dentists.

It began a Nation-wide attack on mental illness and mental retardation.

And it strengthened our efforts against air pollution.

But our remaining agenda is long, and it will be unfinished until each American enjoys the full benefits of modern medical knowledge.

Part of this agenda concerns a direct attack on that particular companion of poor health—poverty. Above all, we must see to it that all of our children, whatever the economic condition of their parents, can start life with sound minds and bodies.

My message to the Congress on poverty will set forth measures designed to advance us toward this goal.

In today's message, I present the rest of this year's agenda for America's good health.

1. Hospital Insurance for the Aged

Nearly thirty years ago, this Nation took the first long step to meet the needs of its older citizens by adopting the Social Security program. Today, most Americans look toward retirement with some confidence that they will be able to meet their basic needs for food and shelter.

But many of our older citizens are still defenseless against the heavy medical costs of severe illness or disability:

One-third of the aged who are forced to ask for old age assistance do so because of ill health, and one-third of our public assistance funds going to older people is spent for medical care.

For many others, serious illness wipes out savings and carries their families into poverty.

For these people, old age can be a dark corridor of fear.

The irony is that this problem stems in part from the surging progress in medical science and medical techniques — the same progress that has brought longer life to Americans as a whole.

Modern medical care is marvelously effective — but increasingly expensive.

Daily hospital costs are now four times as high as they were in 1946 — now averaging about $37 *a day.*

In contrast, the average Social Security benefit is just $77 a month for retired workers and $67 a month for widows.

Existing "solutions" to these problems are (1) private health insurance plans and (2) welfare medical assistance. *No one of them is adequate, nor are they in combination:*

Private insurance, when available, usually costs more than the average retired couple can afford.

Welfare medical assistance for the aged is not available in many States — and where it is available, it includes a needs test to which older citizens, with a lifetime of honorable, productive work behind them, should not be subjected.

This situation is not new.

For more than a decade we have failed to meet the problem.

There is a sound and workable solution. Hospital insurance based on Social Security payments is clearly the best method of meeting the need. It is a logical extension of the principle — established in 1935 and confirmed time after time by the Congress — that provision should be made for later years during the course of a lifetime of employment. *Therefore:*

I recommend a hospital insurance program for the aged aimed at two basic goals:

First, it should protect against the heaviest costs of a serious illness — the costs of hospital and skilled nursing home care, home health services, and outpatient hospital diagnostic services.

Second, it should provide a base that related private programs can supplement.

To achieve these goals:

1. *These benefits should be available to everyone who reaches 65.*
2. *Benefit payments should cover the cost of services customarily*

furnished in semi-private accommodations in a hospital but not the cost of the services of personal physicians.

3. *The financing should be soundly funded through the Social Security system.*

4. *One-quarter of one percent should be added to the Social Security contribution paid by employers and by employees.*

5. *The annual earnings subject to Social Security taxes would be increased from $4,800 to $5,200.*

6. *For those not now covered by Social Security, the cost of similar protection would be provided from the administrative budget.*

Under this proposal, the costs of hospital and related services can be met without any interference whatever with the method of treatment. The arrangement would in no way hinder the patient's freedom to choose his doctor, hospital, or nurse.

The only change would be in the manner in which individuals would *finance* the hospital costs of their later years. The average worker under Social Security would contribute about a dollar a month during his working life to protect himself in old age in a dignified manner against the devastating costs of prolonged hospitalization.

Hospitalization, however, is not the end of older people's medical needs. Many aged individuals will have medical expenses but will be covered neither by Social Security, hospital insurance nor by private insurance.

Therefore, I urge all States to adopt adequate programs of medical assistance under the Kerr-Mills Legislation. This assistance is needed now. And it will be needed later as a supplement to hospital insurance.

The need for health insurance provisions was stressed again and again in House debate; but as Representative King pointed out, there was no way to call for a vote on Medicare. The strict control exercised by the House Ways and Means Committee meant that the battle had to be fought in the Senate.

Although the bill had been sent to the Senate without any health insurance provisions, support for a medical care amendment was growing in that house. Secretary Celebrezze pressed strongly for medical care in the hearings, and most of the other witnesses reflected his concern on this issue.

Social Security: Medical Care for the Aged Amendments
Hearings on H.R. 11865 before the Senate Finance Committee
88th Cong., 2d Sess. (August, 1964)
(p. 69)

The Job Left Undone Under the House Bill

As I indicated earlier, H.R. 11865 fails completely in providing for the highest priority need: hospital insurance protection under social security.

The reasons the administration favors hospital insurance for older people under social security and the supporting evidence for our position have been documented in detail — most recently before the House Committee on Ways and Means and the Subcommittee on the Health of the Elderly, a subcommittee of the Senate Special Committee on Aging. Testimony on this subject was also presented to this committee in 1960. The recently completed Social Security Administration survey of the aged verifies our previous conclusions, and I am attaching a statement of findings from this survey.

The problem is: People after 65 have need of much more medical care than people at younger ages.

However, the Finance Committee reported H.R. 11865 much as the House had reported it; without any provisions for Medicare. Proponents of the health plan explained their views in a Senate report.

Social Security: Medical Care for the Aged Amendments
Senate Report No. 1513
88th Cong., 2d Sess. (August 24, 1964)

Conclusions

The older people of this country should not have to wait longer for hospital and nursing insurance protection through social security. This urgently needed program must be enacted now. No reasonable amount of cash benefits can make the social security program really adequate unless our older people can also have insurance protection against the crushing burden of hospital costs. Without such protection during the last 12 or 15 years of their life expectancy, older people will be without real economic security. The savings and retirement income they will have built up during their working years to provide an independent life in old age will be in jeopardy.

The wealthy now receive substantial assistance with their own medical bills by the generous allowances for income tax deductions for medical expenses. The very poor receive some help. But the great majority, those who are neither very rich nor extremely poor, have been left out. These are the people who have been self-supporting all their lives and want to continue to be — who do not want welfare even if it were adequate.

What is needed is a system under which all workers can, during their productive years, pay contributions toward protection against the high health costs that can be expected to beset them in later years. Social security, and only social security, offers a ready-built, thoroughly tested mechanism that would make this desirable arrangement available to practically everybody. Under this arrangement, it will be practicable for aged persons to supplement their basic hospital and nursing insurance protection with private insurance coverage for other medical expenses. And, under this arrangement, it will be practicable for the States to do far more than they can at present to finance adequate backstop programs for meeting medical costs through public assistance.

The need for a social security-based health insurance program for the aged has been stated and restated over the years. The undersigned, with the exception of Senator Ribicoff who was not then a member of the committee, expressed this view in 1960 in a similar minority statement.

The need for an effective health insurance program for the aged has grown more urgent over the years as the cost of health services has continued to rise more rapidly than any other item or service Americans purchase. If the social security system which was established in 1935 is not expanded to employ this kind of protection for the aged, large numbers of the aged will be left vulnerable to the threat of dependence and poverty. Those who believe in strengthening social security—and the majority of the committee must, since the bill has been favorably reported—and maintaining it as an effective deterrent to dependence and poverty should support a meaningful health insurance program.

> *Clinton P. Anderson*
> *Paul H. Douglas*
> *Albert Gore*
> *Eugene J. McCarthy*
> *Vance Hartke*
> *Abraham Ribicoff*

On the Senate floor the issue of Medicare slowly re-emerged as Senator Douglas tried to persuade Senator Long to withdraw his amendment increasing social security benefits by 7 per cent. While Senator Long was not prepared to yield as easily as that, the Douglas motion began serious debate on Medicare. The implications of the debate were extensive.

Congressional Debates
110 Congressional Record, p. 21092
(August 31, 1964)

Senator [Paul] Douglas [Dem., Ill.] . . . Mr. President, at a later time perhaps I shall address the Senate at greater length. In a sense, I have blundered into the present discussion. I had not anticipated speaking, but I was almost alone on the floor of the Senate when my good friend from Louisiana started to speak. He exercised his blandishments and introduced his amendments in such a way that I felt I should raise the flag of danger. Under the guise of an increase in insurance benefits, he would make it more difficult to provide the fundamental protection against the costs of medical care, which the vast majority of old people need.

After extensive debate early in September, 1964, the Gore Amendment favoring medical care under social security was eventually passed. Some opponents, such as Senator Carl T. Curtis (Rep., Neb.) argued that the Gore Amendment was misleading and that it "would be a great disappointment to older people." (110 Congressional Record, p. 21269, September 2, 1964). Senator Jack Miller argued against any program not established "on the basis of relative ability to pay." (Ibid., p. 21299) Senator Gordon Allott of Colorado made wide claims in favor of Kerr-Mills. Nevertheless, on September 2, 1964 the Senate voted 49-44 in favor of the amendment. However, the Conference Committee was hopelessly deadlocked and health proposals were put off till 1965.

The presidential elections of 1964 gave a good hint of what was to come. The Republican platform called for greater faith in the individual and demanded "a strong, sound system of social security," but at the same time sought a "revision of the social security laws to allow higher earnings. . . ." The platform also called for "full coverage of all medical and hospital costs for the needy elderly people, financed by general revenues through broader implementation of federal-state plans. . . ." The Republicans spoke of "enlargement of employment opportunities for urban and rural citizens" and vocational rehabilitation for the "chronically unemployed and the poverty-stricken" to ". . . effectively treat the needs of the poor, while resisting direct federal handouts that erode away individual self-reliance and self-respect and perpetuate dependency."

The Democrats, on the other hand, claimed that "we will continue to fight until we have succeeded in including hospital care for older Americans in the social security program" and that we will "carry the War on Poverty forward as a total war." They insisted that "the advancing years of life should bring not fear and loneliness, but security, meaning and satisfaction," and that "the unemployment insurance program must be basically revised to meet the needs of the unemployed."

On paper the two platforms did not offer the clear alternatives which their proponents claimed for them, but the voters made their wishes clear as President Johnson defeated Senator Goldwater by the biggest margin in the history of the presidency.

1965

From the point of view of the Department of Health, Education, and Welfare, 1965 was certainly a year of miracles. The Department even celebrated with a special publication: 1965-Year of Legislative Achievements, *a 214-page chronicle of new legislation in mental retardation, community health services, heart stroke and cancer centers, clean air, water resources, the arts and humanities, housing and urban development. Nineteen-hundred and sixty-five was also the year of the Elementary and Secondary Education Act (P.L. 89–10), the Higher Education Act (P.L. 89–329) and the Older Americans Act, but of greatest significance were Medicare and Medicaid.*

That some medical legislation would be passed in 1965 was clear as soon as the 1964 election returns came in. The Senate, after all, was already on record in favor of Medicare, and the forty-two new liberal Democrats made it certain that the House would favor passage. But there was still the issue of how Medicare should be financed. Could it be grafted on to the existing social security trust funds? The views of the Advisory Council on Social Security, published January 1, 1965, were significant.

Report of the Advisory Council on Social Security
1965

The Council's Position in Brief

Essentially the problem is this: Incomes decrease sharply upon old-age or disability retirement, but the incidence of costly illness increases. During their working years, when ill health is less frequent, employed workers can generally meet costs of current care for themselves and their families – directly or through insurance – out of their current employment income, often through an employee-benefit plan and with the help of their employers. The situation of the aged and disabled is quite different. Not only do they have the higher health costs associated with old age and disability but their incomes are greatly reduced because they are no longer working.

The solution, the Council believes,[12] is to apply the method of contributory social insurance, which underlies the present social security program, so that people can contribute from earnings during their working years and have protection against the costs of hospital and related services after age 65 and during disability without having to pay contributions at the time when income is generally curtailed. Contributory social insurance, the Council believes, offers the only practical way of making sure that almost everyone will have hospital protection in old age and during periods of long-term total disability.

It is not proposed, however, that social insurance cover all the costs of illness during old age and long-term total disability. The American approach to income security has traditionally involved a partnership of private effort and governmental measures. For example, old-age, survivors, and disability insurance is supplemented by employer and trade union plans, private insurance, and individual savings and investments. All contribute to the common goal of personal and economic independence. Backstopping this

[12]One member of the Council does not share in this belief; his reasons are given in Appendix A, pages 40–41.

combination of measures for individual self-support are the Federal-State public assistance programs.

We believe this same pluralistic approach can be used effectively in meeting the costs of illness during old age and disability. With social security meeting just about all of the costs of hospitalization, which, on the average, represent at least half the costs associated with the more expensive illnesses, the person who is old or totally disabled will be in a much better position than he is today to meet, on his own and through private insurance, the costs of physician services, drugs and the other elements of complete medical care. Also, with social security providing basic hospital protection, it should be practicable to improve the Federal-State public assistance programs to make them serve more effectively in meeting the health costs for older and disabled people whose needs are not met in other ways.

Millsmanship

President Johnson was anxious to see the passage of a bill bringing medical care for the elderly within the realm of the social security system. The elections of 1964 made this politically possible; the President's enthusiasm made it politically certain. The Administration bills, H.R. 1 and S. 1, called for medical care for the aged, coupled with an overall 7 per cent increase in social security benefits. From the beginning, 1965 looked like no other year. Although many regarded Congressman Mills as an avowed enemy of medical care, he took over sponsorship of the new bill as if it were his own. The House Ways and Means Committee now composed of seventeen northern liberal Democrats and eight Republicans eliminated any serious opposition.

H.R. 1 and S. 1 added hospital insurance to the social security system, generally increased social security benefits and changed the public assistance formulae. (The short title of the bill was the "Hospital Insurance, Social Security, and Public Assistance Amendments of 1965.") The bill, as adopted, was limited to those over sixty-five and covered only limited hospital and nursing home expenses, excluding physicians' services. Funding was exclusively within the OASDI program.

The Ways and Means Committee held no formal public hearings in connection with H.R. 1, since, as Chairman Mills put it, "we have had extensive public hearings in the subject of medical care for the aged in the last Congress. . . . We also have available the information which has been presented to us in the last several Congresses in public hearings on this subject—in the eighty-seventh Congress, the eighty-sixth Congress, and the eighty-fifth Congress." Thus, in 1965, only executive hearings were held, although Chairman Mills invited most of the customary organizations to attend and two volumes of testimony were published.

Again Secretary Celebrezze was the first witness and after his initial

*statement the questioning of HEW witnesses, particularly by minority
members of the committee, provided considerable insights into the changing
philosophy behind social insurance.*

Medical Care for the Aged
Executive Hearings on H.R. 1 before the House Ways and Means Committee
89th Cong., 1st Sess., (February, 1965)
(p. 1)

Secretary Celebrezze. H.R. 1, introduced by the distinguished gentleman
from California, Mr. King, incorporates the recommendations of the administration for changes in the Social Security Act.

The bill would establish a program of social insurance for hospital and
related care for the aged; it would provide a 7-percent increase in cash benefits and otherwise improve the benefit and coverage provisions and the
financing structure of the Federal old-age, survivors, and disability insurance
system; and it would provide for improvements in the Federal-State public
assistance programs.

The committee has heard many hours of public testimony on the proposed
hospital insurance in the last 15 months. And there have been a number of
studies of the problem by advisory groups, most recently by the Advisory
Council on Social Security.

Therefore, I will not go into great length on the data substantiating the
need for a program of hospital insurance for the aged. Rather, I will summarize the reasons why we support the plan. Basically we urge this program
because most elderly people have such modest financial resources that they
can neither afford to pay the large expenses accompanying the serious illnesses often occurring in old age nor afford the cost of adequate insurance
against large health expenses. Their incomes are typically one-half as large
as the incomes of people under 65 in families of the same size whereas the
reduction in the cost of living in retirement is only about 10 to 15 percent.

While their incomes are low, the health expenditures of people past 65
are very high—twice as high as those of younger people. In the case of expenditures for hospitalization, the ratio is 2¾ to 1. Because of their high
health costs and because it must usually be sold on an individual rather than
a group basis, health insurance for the elderly is necessarily expensive. This
can be seen from the rates charged by the "State-65" plans which are now
available in eight States.

Under the State-65 policies, administrative and other nonbenefit costs
are kept as low as possible. Yet the policies that provide relatively broad
coverage—perhaps 40 percent of all health costs of the aged are covered
under these policies compared with perhaps 20 percent under many widely
held commercial policies—are very expensive.

Under these plans the cost ranges from $420 per year for an elderly couple in Massachusetts to $552 in California, Ohio, and New York, amounts which equal 15 to 20 percent of the total income of the typical older couple. In most States, this type of relatively comprehensive protection furnished in as economical a manner as possible is not available at all.

In view of the disparity between their incomes and health insurance costs, it is not surprising that only a little over half of the elderly have any health insurance at all and that many of those who do have some protection have very inadequate protection covering, say, only 50 to 60 percent of hospital charges plus partial allowance for physicians' service in a hospital.

Over the past several years, a large and growing proportion of those applying for public aid have been forced to do so only because they cannot meet their health costs. Some three-fifths of the aged going on public assistance — old age assistance (OAA) and medical assistance for the aged (MAA) together — do so because of health costs. Today over one-third of all public assistance expenditures for the aged are for health costs.

We believe that prevention of dependency and destitution through social insurance is greatly to be preferred to confining governmental effort to the relief of poverty after older people, and in many cases their children, have demonstrated that they are no longer able to get along on their own.

It seems to us that this principle — the preference for the prevention of poverty — applies as well to providing protection against the high and unpredictable costs of hospital and related care as it does to the provision of regular cash benefits under social security.

The proposed program would follow the social security approach. People would contribute from earnings during their working years, when their incomes are highest, and have protection against the costs of hospital and related services after age 65 without having to pay contributions at the time when income is generally curtailed.

The proposal is a necessary extension of the monthly cash benefits of social security; adding this protection to cash benefits is the only practical way that economic security can be furnished in old age. Monthly cash benefits alone cannot do the whole job.

Such benefits can be effective in helping the elderly to meet the regular, recurring expenses of food, clothing, and shelter, but monthly cash benefits cannot practically be made high enough to meet the unbudgetable cost of expensive illness. For this purpose it is necessary to have an insurance program aimed directly at the cost of illness.

While neither private insurance nor public assistance, alone or together, can meet the pressing need the aged have for protection against the cost of expensive illness, the proposed program contemplates an important role for both. The proposed program will serve as a foundation on which people can build greater protection through private health insurance and employer retirement plans, just as the present social security cash benefit system is serving as a base on which people build additional protection through private means.

With basic protection furnished under social security, and taking into account the role of private insurance, public assistance will be able to assume the role most appropriate for it—that of a program intended for members of the relatively small group whose hospital needs and circumstances are such that they are unable to meet their health costs through a combination of social and private insurance and individual savings.

Hospital Insurance Provisions

The hospital insurance provisions of H.R. 1 are largely the same as those in the proposed Social Security Amendments of 1964 as passed last year by the Senate. The proposal however has been subjected to continuing study both within and outside Government. Helpful suggestions, leading to a number of changes, were made during the legislative consideration of the bill last year as well as by the Advisory Council on Social Security and other groups and individuals.

The current proposal follows a recommendation of the Advisory Council in providing a single package of benefits rather than having older people make a choice among alternative hospital benefit plans with different duration and deductible provisions.

Two of the options previously included had deductibles and one did not; in this bill there is a flat deductible for hospital insurance equal to the national average daily cost of hospital care and a deductible of one-half that amount for outpatient diagnostic services.

This average daily cost amounts to about $40. The maximum number of days provided for hospital care in this bill also follows the Advisory Council recommendation for a 60-day maximum.

The bill follows another recommendation of the Council in providing for financing that would cover a substantially larger increase in hospital costs in the next 10 years than had been contemplated in our previous discussion with this committee.

The current bill, through the device of designating the care as "post-hospital extended care," would also more clearly differentiate the post-hospital skilled nursing and rehabilitative care that is intended to be covered from the long-term custodial care furnished in many nursing homes. The bill would make it easier for these facilities to participate in the program.

It would do so by substituting for the requirement of affiliation with a hospital a new provision that would require only that the extended care facility have an agreement for the timely transfer of patients and medical information. The cost-sharing provision contained in the Senate bill last year has not been included in the new bill.

A new provision has been included that would result in the separate identification of the contributions made toward hospital insurance. Under this provision the W-2, or such other receipt as is required, would show the proportion of social security contributions going into the hospital insurance fund so that each employee would know the cost of the hospital coverage to him.

I may add that this requires an amendment to the Internal Revenue Act which is contained in the bill.

I would like now to discuss with you the major provisions of the hospital insurance title of H.R. 1.

Eligibility

Under the bill, hospital insurance protection would be provided for all people who are age 65 and over and entitled to monthly social security benefits or to benefits under the Railroad Retirement Act. In addition, with the cost borne by general revenues, protection would be provided under a special transitional provision of the plan for people now nearing or past age 65 who are not eligible for benefits under these systems.

Since Congress has already provided a health benefit plan for both active and retired Federal employees, these employees would not be included in this special provision. The few others not included in the transitional plan are aliens with less than 10 years of residence in the United States and members of subversive organizations.

Of the 19 million people over 65 in July 1966, just about all, therefore, would be protected against hospital costs: About 16⅔ million would be covered as persons eligible under the old-age survivors insurance or railroad retirement programs, about 400,000 would be eligible for protection under the civil service retirement plan, and about 2 million would be covered under the general revenue provisions in H.R. 1.

Benefits

The major focus of the protection under the bill is on the cost of hospitalization. In addition, the bill provides protection against the cost of three other types of services, which can in many cases be a less expensive substitute for inpatient hospital care. The four types of benefits that would be payable under the bill are—

(1) Inpatient hospital services for up to 60 days in a benefit period, subject to a flat deductible amount equal to the national average daily cost of hospital care—about $40 at the beginning, which is the average cost per day, with provision being made to adjust this to keep a constant relationship between the deductible and hospital costs;

(2) Posthospital extended care benefits for up to 60 days following hospitalization;

(3) Organized home health services for up to 240 visits in a year to a homebound patient; and

(4) Hospital outpatient diagnostic services furnished in a 30-day

period, subject to a deductible equal to one-half the deductible amount for inpatient hospital services — about $20 initially.

The provision of these four types of benefits will enable the aged beneficiary to have the kinds of services and levels of care most appropriate to his needs and will not create an economic incentive to use hospital bed care unduly.

Coverage of extended care will help to achieve prompt hospital discharges because the next appropriate step in the care of a person who has been hospitalized for a serious illness may be a period of convalescence and rehabilitation in an extended care facility rather than continued occupancy of a high-cost bed normally used by an acutely ill hospital patient.

In essence, the coverage of important alternatives to inpatient hospital care would help subordinate financial considerations to medical considerations in decisions on whether inpatient hospital care of some other form of care would be best for the patient.

One of the keys in determining the nature of the health services that will be paid for under the bill is the type of institution which may participate in the program. The requirements for hospital participation are fully in accord with the established principles and objectives of professional hospital organizations.

Hospitals accredited by the Joint Commission on Accreditation of Hospitals — an organization composed of representatives of the American Hospital Association, the American Medical Association, American College of Surgeons, and the American College of Physicians — would be conclusively presumed to meet all the statutory conditions for participation, save that for utilization review.

Moreover, if the Joint Commission should adopt a requirement for utilization review, accredited hospitals could be presumed to meet all the statutory conditions.

Unaccredited hospitals, mostly the smaller institutions, could also participate in the program on meeting certain conditions. They would have to meet the conditions set forth in the bill, which constitute the kind of minimum definition of what a hospital is that is used by the American Hospital Association for listing purposes rather than accreditation purposes, and any additional requirements found necessary with respect to health and safety. These health and safety requirements could be no more strict than those used by the Joint Commission on Accreditation. Linking the conditions for participation to the requirements of the Joint Commission provides assurance that only professionally established conditions would have to be met by providers of health services which seek to participate in the program.

The proposed program would not cover services furnished in nursing homes generally, many of which are not aimed at providing medical services for curing or rehabilitating the patient but at giving the patient merely custodial care. The benefits of this program are intended to cover medical services rather than personal care or housing.

Participating extended care facilities would therefore have to have adequate nursing care and physician supervision or care as well as to meet necessary health and safety conditions. Extended care facilities would also have to agree with a hospital for the timely transfer of patients and the timely interchange of medical and other information about patients transferred between the institutions. This would help to assure the proper level of care as the patient's needs change.

The chief actuary, Robert J. Myers, was examined about the nature of the trust fund and the size of the social security tax base.

House Hearings
(p. 8 – 10, p. 19)

Financing

Statement of Mr. Robert J. Myers

The hospital insurance program would be financed by allocating six-tenths of 1 percent of covered wages paid in 1966, 0.76 of 1 percent of covered wages paid in 1967 and 1968; and 0.90 of 1 percent of taxable wages paid thereafter, to a special hospital insurance trust fund that would be established for the program.

The allocations would be 0.45, 0.57, and 0.675 of 1 percent in the case of self-employment income. Contributions would be paid on annual earnings up to $5,600 — the proposed new contribution base.

The cost of the benefits for persons not insured under the social security or railroad retirement systems would be borne by general revenues. In the first year of the program, 1967, the cost of benefits to the uninsured is estimated to amount to $255 million, but the Federal savings in MAA and OAA resulting from hospital benefits to both the insured and uninsured is about $200 million, so that the net Federal general revenue cost is about $55 million.

Benefits would be payable for covered hospital and related health services furnished beginning July 1, 1966, except for posthospital extended care, for which the effective date would be January 1, 1967, in order to allow additional time for the provision of these benefits.

The allocations to the hospital insurance trust fund from social security contributions would begin on January 1, 1966. The allocation basis for 1966 would thus enable a contingency fund to be built up before benefits become payable in order to assure that from the very beginning the benefits can be paid as they become due.

Under the bill there would be a separate trust fund for the hospital insurance program, in addition to the present old-age and survivors insurance trust fund and the disability insurance trust fund. Under the bill, hospital insurance benefits could be paid only from the hospital insurance trust fund.

These financing provisions would cover fully the cost of the proposed program estimated on a basis which makes allowance for future increases in the cost of hospital care. The assumptions underlying the cost estimates are more conservative than those used in estimating the cost of the hospital insurance bill discussed in the executive sessions of this committee last year or the bill passed by the Senate last year.

We are following assumptions suggested by the Advisory Council on Social Security, which allow for a full 10 years of substantially greater increases in hospital costs than in wages and also for substantially greater increases in hospital costs than other prices indefinitely.

I would like to point out that the assumption underlying the cost estimates on the relation of future hospital costs and earnings is that the level of hospital costs will rise more rapidly over the next 10 years than the health insurance industry assumed in making their calculations of costs when they testified on the previous administration-sponsored hospital insurance bills.

The conservative nature of our assumptions is indicated by the fact that the cost estimates also anticipate some increase in hospital usage by the elderly after the bill is enacted. The plan is financed not only to meet the rates figures on these assumptions but also to build up and maintain the contingency reserve. . . .

*   *   *

A 7-percent Across-The-Board Increase in Benefit Payments

The bill would provide a 7-percent increase in cash benefits to take account of increases in the cost of living. Last year this committee approved a 5-percent across-the-board benefit increase.

The 7-percent increase that the bill would provide retains the percentage-increase principle and follows the general structure of last year's bill, taking into account the changes in the cost of living since 1958, including those which have taken place in the last year.

*   *   *

An increase in the contribution and benefit base to $5,600 (which is the figure in last year's Senate bill) would be comparable now to the $5,400 provision agreed to by this committee last year. Under that provision the base would have been increased, effective January 1965. Because of rising wages, a comparable figure for January 1966 is about $5,600.

As the Advisory Council on Social Security stated in its recent report, the the contribution and benefit base must be increased from time to time as earnings levels rise in order to maintain the wage-related character of the benefits, to restore a broad financial base for the program, and to distribute the cost of the system among low-paid and higher paid workers in the most desirable way.

A $5,600 earnings base will make it possible to provide, for workers at and above average earnings levels, benefits that are more reasonably related to their actual earnings, and by taxing a larger proportion of the Nation's growing payrolls will improve the financial base of the program.

* * *

Like the bill passed by the House last year, H.R. 1 also would extend coverage to the self-employment income of doctors of medicine, the only self-employed professional group not now covered under social security. A great many physicians, perhaps a majority, want to participate in the social security program, and the benefits provided under social security would be very valuable to them.

Since physicians, like all other Americans, benefit from the prevention of dependency through the social security program, they should also share in its support.

* * *

Mr. [John W.] Byrnes. [Rep., Wis.] What would that rate be if we were using the $4,800 base that we have today?

Mr. Myers. Mr. Byrnes, that would require an additional three-tenths of 1 percent.

Mr. Byrnes. 10.7 percent?

Mr. Myers. 10.7 percent; yes, sir.

Mr. Byrnes. What would it be at $5,400?

Mr. Myers. At $5,400 it would require an extra 0.06 percent; in other words, 10.46 percent for the employer and employee combined.

Mr. Byrnes. So if we buy this we are, no matter what base we use, exceeding the 10 percent that just a few years ago Secretary Ribicoff warned us against and which, Mr. Secretary, you concurred in or at least agreed to within the last 2 years.

Secretary Celebrezze. I think I said that we should keep our cost factors as low as possible, but I saw nothing magic in 10 percent.

Mr. Byrnes. As I say, you generally concurred with Secretary Ribicoff.

Secretary Celebrezze. Senator Ribicoff was saying that we have to stop at 10 percent. I said we had to analyze and keep our cost factors as low as possible, but there was no magic in the 10-percent figure.

Mr. Byrnes. No, but it was a caution point at which we should stop, look, and listen.

Secretary Celebrezze. You should stop, look, and listen no matter what your percentage is in any field.

Mr. Byrnes. I am not going to waste your time or mine quibbling over little things like that. You know that it was suggested as a danger signal that requires a careful look.

Secretary Celebrezze. I am trying to explain that to you. Senator Ribicoff said 10 percent. You asked me if I agreed with it, and—this is in the record —I said I saw nothing magic about 10 percent, but we should always be keeping our ratio as low as possible. That was my answer.

Mr. Byrnes. Your answer was a little more in keeping with Senator Ribicoff's.

Secretary Celebrezze. No; I didn't agree with Senator Ribicoff; he questioned me before the Senate committee on that 10 percent and I told him the same thing.

Mr. Byrnes. Let me ask about the matter of this prepayment aspect in this bill. You suggest on page 4 that people would contribute during their working years and have protection against costs of hospital and related service after 65.

How much of a reserve fund is ever contemplated here, Mr. Secretary? In other words, what will be the excess payment by the current workers over and above the cost of taking care of the currently over 65.

Secretary Celebrezze. Mr. Myers has those figures.

Mr. Myers. Mr. Byrnes, as to the estimated size of the Hospital Insurance Trust Fund, the figures are contained on page 39 of Actuarial Study No. 59. The fund is estimated at about $500 million at the end of the first year of operations, 1966, and is estimated to increase slowly in the next few years to a level of about $1½ billion by 1970.

The questioning from the committee's minority members raised customary issues.

House Hearings
(p. 291)

Mr. Byrnes. So that fundamentally what we are doing here is not prepaying, but what we are doing here is having the people who are currently working finance the benefits of those currently over 65?

Mr. Myers. I think it can be viewed that way, just as the old-age and survivors insurance trust fund can, or else you can also view that it is prepayment in advance on a collective group basis, so that the younger contributors are making their contributions with the expectation that they will receive the benefits in the future—and not necessarily with the thought that their money is being put aside and earmarked for them, but rather that later there will be current income to the system for their benefits.

Mr. Byrnes. In other words, on the theory that if I am going to be asked to pay for a tax today for a benefit that is available to people over 65, then when I get to be 65 somebody who is then working ought to do the same thing for me? Is that it?

Mr. Myers. Yes; I would say that is the way it is, and this is a reasonable group prepayment basis, I think you can call it, because of the compulsory nature of the tax for now and for all time to come on people in covered employment.

In a private insurance operation this would not be at all feasible as a prepayment basis under any concept because there is no assurance there will always be new policyholders.

The committee considered many other matters — the maximum possible social security tax, the relationship between different income security programs, the nature of social insurance, and inevitably medical care. There was obviously ill feeling about the report of the Advisory Committee.

House Hearings
(p. 33)

Mr. Curtis. Mr. Cohen, please don't make me put on the record what I said on the floor of the House about the manner in which this Council was selected.

Mr. [Wilbur] Cohen [Undersecretary of HEW]. I would be pleased to have you put it on the record, Mr. Curtis, because I don't agree with you at all. I think this was a distinguished group.

Mr. Curtis. They were distinguished individually, but every one of them was picked to do a specific thing.

Secretary Celebrezze. The Council strictly complied with the law, and the law says you have to have a broad representation.

Mr. Curtis. All right. We had had this out before.

Secretary Celebrezze. Two of the members were with the Eisenhower administration.

Mr. Curtis. Yes, because they were the two people that were for this kind of medicare program.

HEW representatives seemed vague about practical issues, such as the likely demand for facilities.

House Hearings
(p. 122)

Mr. [Herman T.] Schneebeli [Rep., Penn.]. I have one more question.

How many more hospital beds, percentagewise, will we need 3 years after the passage of H.R. 1, as a result of the passage of H.R.1?

Mr. [Robert] Ball. [Commissioner for Social Security] I don't know as I could answer your question in quite that form, but we have done some calculations along this line. It is, of course, assumed that there will be greater utilization of hospitals once this is passed than before. However, if you were to assume even as high an increase as 20 percent utilization by the aged—if you went even that high, which I think is double what we would really expect—that would mean an increase in total hospital utilization for the country of about 5 percent.

Mr. Schneebeli. They constitute one-quarter of the total.

Mr. Ball. Yes; about 20 to 25 percent of hospital utilization is in this age group. So the impact on total hospitalizations, although significant, I think can be easily exaggerated.

Mr. Schneebeli. Is it going to have more of an impact on your nursing home facilities?

Mr. Ball. Yes. As you know the hospital situation is very different in different parts of the country, and between rural and urban. There are many places, actually, where there are more beds in some parts of the country than are being used.

Mr. Schneebeli. Unfortunately it is not true in my section. You say roughly about a 5-percent increase.

Mr. Ball. I would think that would be an outside.

The hearings represented a grand finale for those who, for some thirty years, had lobbied so vigorously either for or against health care. The AMA representative, for example, made the traditional arguments.

House Hearings
(p. 742)

Statement of American Medical Association

The American Medical Association opposes H.R. 1 as it opposed the same legislation which was rejected by the last two Congresses.

The measure would be unpredictably expensive. It is unnecessary. It would represent a dangerous venture by the Federal Government in the field of health care.

Enactment of this program would impose an unfair burden on the Nation's wage earners and their employers to finance health care benefits for millions of older Americans who are self-supporting, even wealthy, and do not need Government benefits.

Further, Government regulation and control which would be established under this bill is not compatible with good medicine. The availability of medical service to the aged could be contingent upon the availability of tax money and not upon the medical needs of older citizens. With quantity thus restricted, quality would inevitably suffer.

Beyond these points, we are opposed to making older persons Federal wards.

We are opposed to Government undercutting and disrupting the continuing progress of private health insurance and prepayment plans, on which 145 million Americans of all ages today depend for protection from their illness costs.

We are opposed to offering false promises to the unfortunate who do need help. This bill would provide only a fraction of the care necessary in any serious illness, a fact which many of our aged do not realize.

Time today does not permit an extensive repetition of our voluminous arguments against federalized hospital care of the aged which we offered in 1961 and again in 1963 and 1964. Here are the points which merit your most urgent consideration as you evaluate the latest version of this legislation:

The bill is unnecessary. The great majority of Americans over 65 are not poor, ill, and without proper health care. Both the health and the finances of our senior citizens are far better than they have been pictured, and they will be improving constantly in the years ahead. The medical cost problems that do exist among the aged are problems of individuals and not of an entire age group.

The record of this committee contains hundreds of pages of detailed testimony which we have offered at past hearings to support these statements. Much of it comes from the Government's own files. Doubtless you will review these facts and figures in the course of your deliberations.

We believe this record demonstrates that the health and economic condition of the aged has been grossly misrepresented to the American people to secure enactment of H.R. 1 and earlier versions of the bill.

Means already exist for solving the problem: The Nation now has voluntary, flexible programs to provide health care for the aged.

More than half of the over-65 Americans, who are self-supporting, have protected themselves from illness costs through Blue Cross, Blue Shield, and health insurance. It is true that some policies may not be all that we would wish in the extent of coverage they provide, but we submit that the great majority of the plans and policies are providing ample protection for the elderly in meeting this problem.

Health insurance has made phenomenal advances in this country in recent years, and the coverage of the elderly is making the most spectacular growth. Persons over 65 are joining Blue Shield plans, for example, at a rate four times faster than all other age groups combined. Senior citizens are getting the protection they want and need; they are getting it in increasing numbers; in so doing, they are demonstrating their willingness and ability to take care of their own needs when they are financially able to do so.

This fact deals a heavy blow to the argument that the Nation's workers and their employers should pay a compulsory tax to finance Government benefits for the entire aged population.

There has always been universal agreement that those who cannot take care of themselves must receive help. This principle was the basis for the passage in 1960 of the Kerr-Mills Act which makes possible a wide range of health care benefits for all people over 65 who cannot take care of their own needs. Kerr-Mills provides help through Federal-State matching funds. Administration of this assistance is retained by the States and local communities.

All 50 States now have old age assistance programs under Kerr-Mills. Forty States and four other jurisdictions have medical assistance for the aged programs under the act.

The bill would not meet the problems of the needy aged: The restricted benefits in H.R. 1 — 60 days in a hospital, 60 days in a nursing home, so many units of home health services, some outpatient diagnostic services, et cetera—represent a financial limitation designed to hold the costs of the program down. The patient is the sufferer when the extent of services he receives depends upon financial considerations instead of his illness requirements. It has been estimated that the measure would cover approximately 25 percent of the annual health care expenses of the average person over 65. Where are the needy aged expected to get the other 75 percent?

Government meddling versus quality health care: The foundation of this country's unrivaled system of medical care is the voluntary relationship existing between the patient and his doctor. This would begin to disappear as the Government supplanted the individual as the purchaser of health care, and as the physician's medical judgment collided with regulations promulgated by the Secretary to control the movement of individuals in and out of medical institutions, and the "reasonable costs" for services to be paid those institutions

The bill would impose a heavy burden on taxpayers and result in a waste of public funds.

H.R. 1, as did its predecessors, provides for increased payroll taxes on workers and employers to pay for benefits for everyone over 65, regardless of financial need. The blow would fall the hardest on those at the low end of the income scale. The $5,600 a year employee would pay as much to support the program as the $56,000 executive.

The AMA opposes this tax on moral as well as practical grounds. There is no justification for compelling young taxpayers and their employers to pay taxes to buy health care for millions of other people simply because they happen to be over 65.

The money they would pay in taxes in their working years would not be set aside for their health care in their own later years. They would pay taxes today for today's beneficiaries. Tomorrow their benefits would be paid by tomorrow's taxpayers. It has been estimated that this bill may cost $35 billion to provide care for today's 18 million older beneficiaries during their lifetimes. Obviously, H.R. 1 would place an enormous mortgage on future generations.

The executive hearings ended on February 16, but the Ways and Means Committee continued meeting in executive session until March 23. In those few weeks the members rewrote not only the shape of the legislation, but also redrew the map of public medical care in this country.

What happened in these closed hearings is not easy to follow. First, the Republicans themselves were concerned that their defeat had sprung from a hostile attitude towards Medicare. The new House Minority Leader called for positive opposition and therefore, the Republicans introduced their own legislation, the Byrnes Bill (H.R. 4351). The bill set up a voluntary system of insurance coverage for medical expenses outside of social security, but including a direct federal subsidy.

The AMA also launched its own plan, Eldercare, using the Kerr-Mills machinery to pay federal and state subsidies in order to allow elderly persons to buy medical insurance coverage. Since H.R. 1 only covered hospital expenses while private policies could presumably cover any type of expense, the AMA announced that its program was far more generous than the Administration's.

There was, in addition to H.R. 1, another Administration proposal to expand and accelerate the Kerr-Mills program. This bill attracted some Republican support.

There were thus four bills before the House Committee on Ways and Means as it went into executive sessions: the Administration's H.R. 1, providing care for the elderly through social security; the Republican-supported Byrnes Bill, subsidizing a voluntary health insurance program for the elderly to cover a wide variety of medical expenses; the AMA's Eldercare program, and finally the Mills proposal for extending Kerr-Mills.

In mid-February, the committee began work on the bill, and by early March a remarkable political maneuver had taken place. Chairman Mills, the long-time opponent of medical care, did not choose between the competing plans but instead combined them. The Administration bill was to become Title XVIIIA; the Byrnes proposal became Title XVIIIB and a greatly extended Kerr-Mills program (including both the AMA and Mills' own bill) became Title XIX. This coup came as a surprise to all. It is reported to have amused President Johnson. It did not amuse the AMA. The committee bill, H.R. 6675, was voted out 17–8. The President's message expressed his excitement.

Presidential Statement Following Committee Action on the Medicare Bill
(March 23, 1965)*

The Medical care and social security bill voted out today by the House Committee on Ways and Means is a tremendous step forward for all of our

*Public Papers of the Presidents, Lyndon B. Johnson, 1965, p. 311.

senior citizens. It incorporates all of the major provisions of the administration's hospital insurance bill financed through social security which was introduced by Congressman Cecil King and Senator Clinton Anderson.

The Committee's action is an historic one — the first time that a House committee has acted favorably on a medical insurance bill for all of our older citizens. It is an action which all Americans can and should welcome.

Great credit goes to the hard-working Members of the Ways and Means Committee and especially to the distinguished Chairman, Wilbur D. Mills, for the many weeks of work to make medical care protection for the older people of our Nation a practical reality. Chairman Mills deserves special credit for his statesmanlike leadership in working out on a sound and practical basis a solution to one of the most important problems which has been pending before the Congress for nearly 15 years.

It is my hope that many Republicans will join with the Democrats in voting for this very fine bill. It is a bill which is financially sound and which will benefit the entire Nation.

Lyndon B. Johnson

House Report No. 213 on H.R. 6675 explained the breadth of the Mills proposal.

Social Security Amendments of 1965
House Report No. 213
89th Cong., 1st Sess.
(March 24, 1965)

*   *   *

II. SUMMARY OF PRINCIPAL PROVISIONS OF THE BILL

A. HEALTH INSURANCE AND MEDICAL CARE FOR THE AGED

Your committee's bill would add a new title XVIII to the Social Security Act providing two related health insurance programs for persons 65 or over:

> (1) A basic plan in part A providing protection against the costs of hospital and related care; and
> (2) a voluntary supplementary plan in part B providing protection against the costs of physicians' services and other medical and health services to cover certain areas not covered by the basic plan.

The basic plan would be financed through a separate payroll tax and separate trust fund. The plan would be actuarially sound under conservative cost assumptions. Benefits for persons currently over 65 who are not insured under the social security and railroad retirement systems would be financed out of Federal general revenues.

Enrollment in the supplementary plan would be voluntary and would be financed by a small monthly premium ($3 per month initially) paid by enrollees and an equal amount supplied by the Federal Government out of general revenues. The premiums for social security and railroad retirement beneficiaries who voluntarily enroll would be deducted from their monthly insurance benefits. Uninsured persons desiring the supplemental plan would make the periodic premium payments to the Government.

Your committee's bill would also add a new title XIX to the Social Security Act which would provide a more effective Kerr-Mills program for the aged and extend its provisions to additional needy persons. It would replace with a single uniform category the differing medical provisions for the needy which currently are found in five titles of the Social Security Act.

A description of these three programs follows:

1. Basic Plan—Hospital Insurance, etc.

General description. — Basic protection, financed through a separate payroll tax, would be provided by H.R. 6675 against the costs of inpatient hospital services, posthospital extended care services, posthospital home health services, and outpatient hospital diagnostic services for social security and railroad retirement beneficiaries when they attain age 65. The same protection, financed from general revenues, would be provided under a special transitional provision for essentially all people who are now aged 65, or who will reach 65 in the near future, but who are not eligible for social security or railroad retirement benefits.

Effective date. — Benefits would first be effective on July 1, 1966, except for services in extended care facilities which would be effective on January 1, 1967.

Benefits. — The services for which payment would be made under the basic plan include —

(1) inpatient hospital services for up to 60 days in each spell of illness with the patient paying a deductible amount of $40 for each spell of illness; hospital services would include all those ordinarily furnished by a hospital to its inpatients; however, payment would not be made for private duty nursing or for the hospital services of physicians except services provided by interns or residents in training under approved teaching programs;

(2) posthospital extended care (in a facility having an arrangement with a hospital for the timely transfer of patients and for furnishing medical information about patients) after the patient is transferred from a hospital (after at least a 3-day stay) for up to 20 days in each spell of illness; 2 additional days will be added to the 20 days for each day that the person's hospital stay was less than 60 days (up to a maximum of 80 additional days) — the overall maximum for posthospital extended care could thus be 100 days in each spell of illness;

(3) outpatient hospital diagnostic services with the patient paying a $20 deductible amount for each diagnostic study (that is, for diagnostic services furnished to him by the same hospital during a 20-day period; if, within 20 days after receiving such services, the individual is hospitalized as an inpatient in the same hospital, the deductible he paid for outpatient diagnostic services (up to $20) would be credited against the inpatient hospital deductible ($40); and

(4) posthospital home health services for up to 100 visits, after discharge from a hospital (after at least a 3-day stay) or extended care facility and before the beginning of a new spell of illness. Such a person must be in the care of a physician and under a plan established by a physician within 14 days of discharge calling for such services. These services would include intermittent nursing care, therapy, and the part-time services of a home health aide. The patient must be homebound, except that when certain equipment is used the individual could be taken to a hospital or extended care facility or rehabilitation center to receive some of these covered home health services in order to get advantage of the necessary equipment.

No service would be covered as posthospital extended care or as outpatient diagnostic or posthospital home health services if it is of a kind that could not be covered if it were furnished to a patient in a hospital.

A spell of illness would be considered to begin when the individual enters a hospital or extended care facility and to end when he has not been an inpatient of a hospital or extended care facility for 60 consecutive days.

The deductible amounts for inpatient hospital and outpatient hospital diagnostic services would be increased if necessary to keep pace with increases in hospital costs, but no such increase would be made before 1968. For reasons of administrative simplicity, increases in the hospital deductible will be made only when a $5 change is called for and the outpatient deductible will change in $2.50 steps.

Basis of reimbursement. — Payment of bills under the basic plan would be made to the providers of service on the basis of the "reasonable cost" incurred in providing care for beneficiaries.

Administration. — Basic responsibility for administration would rest with the Secretary of Health, Education, and Welfare. The Secretary would use appropriate State agencies and private organizations (nominated by providers of services) to assist in the administration of the program. Provision is made for the establishment of an Advisory Council which would advise the Secretary on policy matters in connection with administration.

Financing. — Separate payroll taxes to finance the basic plan, paid by employers, employees, and self-employed persons, would be earmarked in a separate hospital insurance trust fund established in the Treasury. The amount of earnings (wage base) subject to the new payroll taxes would be the same as for purposes of financing social security cash benefits. The same contribution rate would apply equally to employers, employees, and self-employed persons and would be as follows:

	Percent
1966	0.35
1967 – 72	.50
1973 – 75	.55
1976 – 79	.60
1980 – 86	.70
1987 and thereafter	.80

The taxable earnings base for the health insurance tax would be $5,600 a year for 1966 through 1970 and would thereafter be increased to $6,600 a year.

The schedule of contribution rates is based on estimates of cost which assume that the earnings base will not be increased above $6,600. If Congress, in later years, should increase the base above $6,600, the tax rates established can be reduced under the cost assumptions underlying the bill.

The cost of providing basic hospital and related benefits to people who are not social security or railroad retirement beneficiaries would be paid from general funds of the Treasury.

2. Voluntary Supplementary Insurance Plan

General description. — A package of benefits supplementing those provided under the basic plan would be offered to all persons 65 and over on a voluntary basis. Individuals who enroll initially would pay premiums of $3 a month (deducted, where possible, from social security or railroad retirement benefits). The Government would match this premium with $3 paid from general funds. Since the minimum increase in cash social security benefits under the bill for workers retiring or who retired at age 65 or older would be $4 a month ($6 a month for man and wife receiving benefits based on the same earnings record), the benefit increases would fully over the amount of monthly premiums.

Enrollment. — Persons who have reached age 65 before January 1, 1966, will have an opportunity to enroll in an enrollment period which begins on the first day of the second month after the month of enactment and ends March 31, 1966.

Persons attaining age 65 subsequent to December 31, 1965, will have enrollment periods of 7 months beginning 3 months before the month of attainment of age 65.

In the future, general enrollment periods will be from October to December 31, in each odd numbered year. The first such period will be October 1 to December 31, 1967.

No person may enroll more than 3 years after the close of the first enrollment period in which he could have enrolled.

There will be only one chance to reenroll for persons who are in the plan but drop out, and the reenrollment must occur within 3 years of termination of the previous enrollment.

Coverage may be terminated (1) by the individual filing notice during an enrollment period, or (2) by the Government, for nonpayment of premiums.

A State would be able to provide the supplementary insurance benefits its public assistance recipients who are receiving cash assistance if it chooses to do so.

Effective date. — Benefits will be effective beginning July 1, 1966.

Benefits. — The voluntary supplementary insurance plan would cover physicians' services, home health services, hospital services in psychiatric institutions, and numerous other medical and health services in and out of medical institutions.

There would be an annual deductible of $50. Then the plan would cover 80 percent of the patient's bill (above the deductible) for the following services:

(1) Physicians' and surgeons' services, whether furnished in a hospital, clinic, office, in the home or elsewhere;

(2) Hospital care for 60 days in a spell of illness in a mental hospital with a 180-day lifetime maximum;

(3) Home health service (with no requirement of prior hospitalization) for up to 100 visits during each calendar year;

(4) Additional medical and health services, whether provided in or out of a medical institution, including the following:

(a) Diagnostic X-ray and laboratory tests, electrocardiograms, basal metabolism readings, electroencephalograms, and other diagnostic tests;

(b) X-ray, radium, and radioactive isotope therapy;

(c) Ambulance services; and

(d) Surgical dressings and splints, casts, and other devices for reduction of fractures and dislocations; rental of durable medical equipment such as iron lungs, oxygen tents, hospital beds, and wheelchairs used in the patient's home, prosthetic devices (other than dental) which replace all or part of an internal body organ; braces and artificial legs, arms, eyes, etc.

There would be a special limitation on outside-the-hospital treatment of mental, psychoneurotic, and personality disorders. Payment for such treatment during any calendar year would be limited, in effect, to $250 or 50 percent of the expenses, whichever is smaller.

Administration by carriers: Basis for reimbursement. — The Secretary of Health, Education, and Welfare would be required, to the extent possible, to contract with carriers to carry out the major administrative functions relating to the medical aspects of the voluntary supplementary plan such as determining rates of payments under the program, holding and disbursing funds for benefit payments, and determining compliance and assisting in utilization review. No contract is to be entered into by the Secretary unless he finds that the carrier will perform its obligations under the contract efficiently and effectively and will meet such requirements as to financial responsibility, legal authority, and other matters as he finds pertinent. The contract must provide that the carrier take necessary action to see that where payments are on a cost basis (to institutional providers of service), the cost is reasonable cost. Correspondingly, where payments are on a charge basis (to physicians or others furnishing noninstitutional services), the carrier must see that such charge will be reasonable and not higher than the charge applicable, for a comparable service and under comparable circumstances, to the other policyholders and subscribers of the carrier. Payment by the carrier for physicians' services will be made on the basis of a receipted bill, or on the basis of an assignment under the terms of which the reasonable charge will be the full charge for the service.

Financing. — Aged persons who enroll in the supplemental plan would pay monthly premiums of $3. Where the individual is currently receiving monthly social security or railroad retirement benefits, the premiums would be deducted from his benefits.

The Government would help finance the supplementary plan through a payment from general revenues in an equal amount of $3 a month per enrollee. To provide an operating fund, if necessary, at the beginning of the supplementary plan, and to establish a contingency reserve, a Government appropriation would be available (on a repayable basis) equal to $18 per aged person estimated to be eligible in July 1966 when the supplementary plan goes into effect.

The individual and Government contributions would be placed in a separate trust fund for the supplementary plan. All benefit and administrative expenses under the supplementary plan would be paid from this fund.

Premium rates for enrolled persons (and the matching Government contribution) would be increased from time to time if medical costs rise, but not more often than once every 2 years. The premium rate for a person who enrolls after the first period when enrollment is open to him or who reenrolls after terminating his coverage would be increased by 10 percent for each full year he stayed out of the program.

Medical expense deduction. — The health care provisions of your committee's bill have a relationship to the medical expense deductions allowed under the Internal Revenue Code. In the past the 3-percent limitation in the case of medical care expenses and the 1-percent limitation applied to expenditures for medicines and drugs were waived for persons 65 or over in recognition of the fact that medical expenses generally constituted a heavy financial burden for older people. In the past, however, there was no broad-coverage health insurance plan for older persons. The health insurance provisions of your committee's bill are designed to meet these problems in a generally comprehensive manner. The historical basis for the special medical expense provisions in the tax law for the relief of older taxpayers, therefore, no longer appears to exist. For this reason the bill provides that the 3-percent floor on medical expense deductions, as well as the 1-percent limitation on medicines and drugs, is to apply to those age 65 or over in the same manner as it presently applies to those under age 65. This will have the effect of partially or fully recovering the $3 monthly premium paid from general funds of the Treasury from those aged persons who have taxable income, depending on the amount of their taxable income.

To encourage the purchase of hospital insurance by all taxpayers, the bill provides a special deduction, available to those who itemize their deductions, for one-half of any premiums paid for insurance of medical care expenses whether or not they have medical expenses in excess of the 3-percent floor, but this deduction may not exceed $250.

Another change limits the insurance premiums which may be taken into account to those which arise from coverage of medical care expenses. Still a further change treats as current, qualifying medical care expenses (subject to limitations) the prepayment before age 65 of insurance for medical care after age 65.

3. Improvement And Extension Of Kerr-Mills Medical Assistance Program

Purpose and scope. — In order to provide a more effective Kerr-Mills medical assistance program for the aged and to extend its provisions to additional needy persons, the bill would establish a single and separate medical care program to replace the differing provisions for the needy which currently are found in five titles of the Social Security Act.

The new title (XIX) would extend the advantages of an expanded medical assistance program not only to the aged who are indigent but also to needy individuals in the dependent children, blind, and permanently and totally disabled programs and to persons who would qualify under those programs if in sufficient financial need.

Medical assistance under title XIX must be made available to all individuals receiving money payments under these programs and the medical care or services available to all such individuals must be equal in amount, duration, and scope. Effective July 1, 1967, all children under age 21 must be included who would, except for age, be dependent children under title IV.

Inclusion of the medically indigent aged not on the cash assistance rolls would be optional with the States but if they are included comparable groups of blind, disabled, and parents and children must also be included if they need help in meeting necessary medical costs. Moreover, the amount and scope of benefits for the medically indigent could not be greater than that of recipients of cash assistance.

The current provisions of law in the various public assistance titles of the act providing vendor medical assistance would terminate upon the adoption of the new program by a State and must terminate no later than June 30, 1967

Scope of medical assistance. — Under existing law, the State must provide "some institutional and noninstitutional care" under the medical assistance for the aged program. There are no minimum benefit requirements at all under the other public assistance vendor medical programs.

The bill would require that by July 1, 1967, under the new program a State must provide inpatient hospital services, outpatient hospital services, other laboratory and X-ray services, skilled nursing home services, and physicians' services (whether furnished in the office, the patient's home, a hospital, a skilled nursing home, or elsewhere) in order to receive Federal participation. Coverage of other items of medical service would be optional with the States.

Eligibility. — Improvements would be effectuated in the program for the needy elderly by requiring that the States must provide a flexible income test which takes into account medical expenses and does not provide rigid income standards which arbitrarily deny assistance to people with large medical bills. In the same spirit the bill provides that no deductible, cost sharing, or similar charge may be imposed by the State as to hospitalization under its program and that any such charge on other medical services must be reasonably related to the recipient's income or resources. Also important is the requirement that elderly needy people on the State programs be provided assistance to meet the deductibles that are imposed by the new basic program of hospital insurance. Also where a portion of any deductible or cost sharing required by the voluntary supplementary program is met by a State program, the portion covered must be reasonably related to the individual's income and resources. No income can be imputed to an individual unless actually available; and the financial responsibility of an individual for an applicant may be taken into account only if the applicant is the individual's spouse or child who is under age 21 or blind or disabled.

Increased Federal matching. — The Federal share of medical assistance expenditures under the new program would be determined upon a uniform formula with no maximum on the amount of expenditures which would be subject to participation. There is no maximum under present law on similar amounts for the medical assistance for the aged program. The Federal share, which varies in relation to a State's per capita income, would be increased over current medical assistance for the aged matching so that States at the national average would receive 55 percent rather than 50 percent, and States at the lowest level could receive as much as 83 percent as contrasted with 80 percent under existing law.

In order to receive any additional Federal funds as a result of expenditures under the new program, the States would need to continue their own expenditures at their present rate. For a specified period, any State that did not reduce its own expenditures would be assured of at least a 5-percent increase in Federal participation in medical care expenditures. As to professional medical personnel used in the administration of the program, the bill would provide a 75-percent Federal share as compared with the 50-50 Federal-State sharing for other administrative expenses.

Administration. — The State agency administering the new program would have to be the same as that administering the old-age assistance program. As some States have done under existing law, such an agency could arrange for provision of medical care by or through the State health agency. The bill specifically provides as a State plan requirement that cooperative agreements be entered into with State agencies providing health services and vocational rehabilitation services looking toward maximum utilization of these services in the provision of medical assistance under the plan.

Effective date. — January 1, 1966.

4. Cost Of Health Care Plans

Basic plan. — Benefits and administrative expenses under the basic plan would be about $1 billion for the 6-month period in 1966 and about $2.3 billion in 1967. Contribution income for those years would be about $1.6 and $2.6 billion, respectively. The costs for the uninsured (paid from general funds) would be about $275 million per year for early years.

Voluntary supplementary plan. — Costs of the voluntary supplementary plan would depend on how many of the aged enrolled.

If 80 percent of the eligible aged enrolled, benefit costs (and administrative expenses) of the supplementary plan would be about $195 million to $260 million in the last 6 months of 1966 and about $765 million to $1.02 billion in 1967. Premium income from enrollees for those years would be about $275 and $560 million, respectively. The matching Government contribution would equal the premiums.

If 95 percent of the eligible aged enrolled, benefit costs of the supplementary plan would be about $230 to $310 million in 1966 and about $905 million to $1.22 billion in 1967. Premium income from enrollees for those years would be about $325 and $665 million, respectively. The Government contribution would equal the premiums.

Public assistance plan. — It is estimated that the new program will increase the Federal Government's contribution about $200 million in a full year of operation over that in the programs operated under existing law.

B. CHILD HEALTH AMENDMENTS

*   *   *

C. OLD-AGE, SURVIVORS, AND DISABILITY INSURANCE AMENDMENTS

I. Benefit Changes

(a) 7-percent across-the-board increase in old-age, survivors, and disability insurance benefits

The bill provides a 7-percent across-the-board benefit increase, effective retroactively beginning with January 1965, with a minimum increase of $4 for retired workers at age 65. These increases will be made for the 20 million social security beneficiaries now on the rolls.

Monthly benefits for workers who retire at or after 65 would be increased to a new minimum of $44 (now $40) and to a new maximum of $135.90 (now $127). In the future, creditable earnings under the increase in the contribution and benefit base to $5,600 a year (now $4,800) would make possible a maximum benefit of $149.90.

The maximum amount of benefits payable to a family on the basis of a single earnings record would be related to the worker's average monthly earnings at all earnings levels. Under present law, there is a $254 limit on family benefits which operates over a wide range of average monthly earnings. Under the bill, until 1971, the highest family maximum would be $312.

Under the second-step increase in the wage base to $6,600 to be effective in 1971, also provided in the bill, the worker's primary benefit would range from a minimum of $44 to a future possible maximum of $167.90 a month. Maximum family benefits up to $368 would also be payable.

(b) Payment of child's insurance benefits to children attending school or college after attainment of age 18 and up to age 22

H.R. 6675 includes the provision adopted by both House and Senate last year which would continue to pay a child's insurance benefit until the child reaches age 22, provided the child is attending a public or an accredited school, including a vocational school or a college, as a full-time student after he reaches age 18. Children of deceased, retired, or disabled workers would be included. No mother's or wife's benefits would be payable if the only child in the mother's care is one who has attained age 18 but is in school.

This provision will be effective January 1, 1965. It is estimated that 295,000 children will be able to receive benefits for a typical school month in 1965 as a result of this provision.

(c) Benefits for widows at age 60

The bill would provide the option to widows of receiving benefits beginning at age 60, with the benefits payable to those who claim them before age 62 being actuarially reduced to take account of the longer period over which they will be paid. Under present law, full widow's benefits and actuarially reduced worker's and wife's benefits are payable at age 62.

This provision, adopted by both Houses of Congress last year, would be effective for the second month after the month of enactment. It is estimated that 185,000 widows will be able to get benefits immediately under this provision.

(d) Amendment of disability program

(i) *Definition.* — H.R. 6675 would eliminate the present requirement that a worker's disability must be expected to result in dealth or to be of long-continued and indefinite duration, and instead provide that an insured worker would be eligible for disability benefits if he has been totally disabled throughout a continuous period of at least 6 calendar months. Benefits payable by reason of this change would be paid for the second month following the month of enactment.

(ii) *Payment period.* — The period during which an individual must be under a disability prior to entitlement of benefits is reduced by 1 month under the bill. Disability benefits would be payable beginning with the last month of the 6-month waiting period rather than with the first month after the 6-month waiting period as under existing law. This change would be applicable to all cases in which the last month of the waiting period occurs after the month of enactment.

It is estimated some 155,000 disabled workers and dependents will be benefited by these provisions.

Certain changes are also made in the provision terminating disability benefits and waiving subsequent waiting periods so as to make them more restrictive when applied to shorter term disabilities.

(iii) *Entitlement to disability benefits after entitlement to benefits payable on account of age.* — Under the bill, a person who becomes entitled before age 65 to a benefit payable on account of old age could later become entitled to disability insurance benefits.

(iv) *Allocation of contribution income between OASI and DI trust funds.* — Under the bill, an additional one-fourth of 1 percent of taxable wages and three-sixteenths of 1 percent of taxable self-employment income would be allocated to the disability insurance trust fund, bringing the total allocation to three-fourths of 1 percent and nine-sixteenths of 1 percent, respectively, beginning in 1966.

(e) Benefits to certain persons at age 72 or over

Your committee's bill adopts a provision approved by the House and Senate last year, which would liberalize the eligibility requirements by providing a basic benefit of $35 at age 72 or over to certain persons with a minimum of three quarters of coverage acquired at any time since the beginning of the program in 1937. To accomplish this, a new concept of "transitional insured status" is provided. Present law requires a minimum of six quarters of coverage in employment or self-employment.

(i) Men and women workers. — The concept of "transitional insured status" which would make an individual eligible for an old-age or wife's benefit provides that the oldest workers will receive benefits with only three quarters of coverage, under the bill. These three quarters may have been acquired at any time since the inception of the program in 1937. For those who are not quite so old, the quarters of coverage requirement would increase until the requirement merges with the present minimum requirement of six quarters.

The following table illustrates the operation of the "transitional insured status" provision for workers.

Transitional insured status requirements with respect to workers benefits[1]

Men		Women	
Age (in 1965)	Quarters of coverage required	Age (in 1965)	Quarters of coverage required
76 or over	3.	73 or over	3.
75	4.	72	4.
74	5.	71	5.
73 or younger	6 or more.	70 or younger	6 or more.

[1]Benefits will not be payable, however, until age 72.

(ii) Widows. — Any widow who is age 72 or over in 1966, if her husband died or reached age 65 in 1954 or earlier, could get a widow's benefit if her husband had at least three quarters of coverage. Present law requires six quarters.

If the husband died or reached 65 in 1955, the requirement would be four quarters. If he died or reached 65 in 1956, the requirement would be five quarters. If he died or reached 65 in 1957 or later, the minimum requirement would be six quarters, the same as present law.

For widows reaching age 72 in 1967 and 1968, there is a "grading-in" of the quarters of coverage requirement; which would be four or five quarters of coverage, respectively. Widows reaching age 72 in 1969 or after would be subject to the requirements of existing law of six or more quarters of coverage.

The table below sets forth the requirements as to widows:

Transitional insured status requirements with respect to widow's benefits

Year of husband's death (or attainment of age 65, if earlier)	Present quarters required	Proposed quarters required for widow attaining age 72 in —		
		1966 or before	1967	1968
1954 or before_____	6_____	3_____	4_____	5.
1955_____	6_____	4_____	4_____	5.
1956_____	6_____	5_____	5_____	5.
1957 or after_____	6 or more____	6 or more_____	6 or more___	6 or more.

(iii) Basic Benefits. — Men and women workers who would be eligible under the above-described provisions for workers would receive a basic benefit of $35 a month. A wife who is aged 72 or over (and who attains that age before 1969) would receive one-half of this amount, $17.50. No other dependents' basic benefits would be provided under these provisions.

Widows would receive $35 a month under the above-described provision.

These provisions would become effective for the second month after the month of enactment, at which time an estimated 355,000 people would be able to start receiving benefits.

(f) Retirement test

H.R. 6675 liberalizes the social security earned income limitation so that the uppermost limit of the "band" of a $1 reduction in benefits for each $2 in earnings is raised from $1,700 to $2,400. Under existing law the first $1,200 a year in earnings is wholly exempted, and there is a $1 reduction in benefits for each $2 of earnings up to $1,700 and $1 for $1 above that amount.

Your committee's bill would increase the $1 for $2 "band" so that it would apply between $1,200 and $2,400, with $1 for $1 reductions above $2,400. This change is effective as to taxable years ending after 1965.

The bill also exempts certain royalties received in or after the year in which a person reaches age 65 from copyrights and patents obtained before age 65, from being counted as earnings for purposes of this test, effective as to taxable years beginning after 1964.

(g) Wife's and widow's benefits for divorced women

Your committee's bill would authorize payments of wife's and widow's benefits to the divorced wife aged 62 or over of a retired, deceased, or disabled worker if she had been married to the worker for at least 20 years before the date of the divorce and if her divorced husband was making (or was obligated by a court to make) a substantial contribution to her support when he became entitled to benefits, became disabled, or died. H.R. 6675 would also provide that a wife's benefits would not terminate when the woman and her husband are divorced if the marriage has been in effect for 20 years. Provision is also made for the reestablishment of benefit rights for a widow or a wife who remarries and the subsequent marriage lasts less than 20 years. These changes are effective for the second month following the month of enactment.

(h) Adoption of child by retired worker

Your committee's bill would change the provisions relating to the payment of benefits to children who are adopted by old-age insurance beneficiaries to require that, where the child is adopted after the worker becomes entitled to an old-age benefit, (1) the child must be living with worker (or adoption proceedings have begun) in or before the month when application for old-age benefits is filed; (2) the child must be receiving one-half of his support for the entire year before the worker's entitlement; and (3) the adoption must be completed within 2 years after the worker's entitlement.

2. Coverage Changes

The following coverage provisions were included:

(a) Physicians and interns

Self-employed physicians would be covered for taxable years ending after December 31, 1965. Interns would be covered beginning on January 1, 1966.

(b) Farmers

Provisions of existing law with respect to the coverage of farmers would be amended to provide that farm operators whose annual gross earnings are $2,400 or less (instead of $1,800 or less as in existing law) can report either their actual net earnings or 66⅔ percent (as in present law) of their gross earnings. Farmers whose annual gross earnings are over $2,400 would report their actual net earnings if over $1,600, but if actual net earnings are less than $1,600, they may instead report $1,600. (Present law provides that farmers whose annual gross earnings are over $1,800 report their actual net earnings if over $1,200, but if actual net earnings are less than $1,200, they may report $1,200.)

(c) Cash tips

Coverage of cash tips received by an employee in the course of his employment as wages would be provided, effective as to tips received after 1965.

(i) Reporting of tips. — The employee would be required to report to his employer in writing the amount of tips received and the employer would report the employee's tips along with the employee's regular wages. The employee's report to his employer would include tips paid to him through the employer as well as those received directly from customers of the employer. Tips received by an employee which do not amount to a total of $20 a month in connection with his work for any one employer would not be covered and would not be reported.

(ii) Tax on tips. — The employer would be required to withhold social security taxes only on tips reported by the employee to him. Unlike the provision in last year's House bill, this provision requires the employer to withhold income tax on such reported tips.

The employer would be responsible for the social security tax on tips only if the employee reported the tips to him within 10 days after the end of the month in which the tips were received. The employer would be permitted to gear these new procedures into his usual payroll periods. The employer would pay over his own and the employee's share of the tax on these tips and would include the tips with his regular reports of wages. If at the time the employee report is due (or, in cases where the report is made earlier — if between the making of the report and the time it is due), the employer does not have unpaid wages or remuneration of the employee under his control sufficient to cover the employee's share of the social security tax applicable to the tips reported, the employee will pay his share of the tax with his report.

If the employee does not report his tips to his employer within 10 days after the end of the month involved, the employer would have no liability. In such a case the employee alone would be liable not only for the amount of the employee tax but also an additional amount equal to the employee tax.

For purposes of withholding income tax on tips, the employer is required to deduct and withhold only on the tips reported to him and only to the extent that the tax can be deducted and withheld before the close of the calendar year from wages (excluding tips, but including funds turned over to the employer by the employee for such purpose) under the control of the employer.

(d) State and local government employees

Several changes made by the bill would facilitate social security coverage of additional employees of State and local governments.

(e) Exemption of certain religious sects

Members of certain religious sects may be exempt from the tax on self-employment income and from social security coverage upon application which would be accompanied by a waiver of benefit rights.

An individual eligible for the exemption must be a member of a recognized religious sect (or a division of a sect) who is an adherent of the established teachings of such sect by reason of which he is conscientiously opposed to acceptance of the benefits of any private or public insurance, making payments in the event of death, disability, old-age, or retirement, or making payments toward the cost of or providing services for, medical care (including the benefits of any insurance system established by the Social Security Act).

The Secretary of Health, Education, and Welfare must find that such sect has such teachings and has been in existence at all times since December 31, 1950, and that it is the practice for members of such sect to make provision for their dependent members which, in the Secretary's judgment, is reasonable in view of their general level of living. The exemption for previous years (taxable years ending prior to December 31, 1965) must be filed by April 15, 1966.

The exemption would be effective as early as taxable years beginning after December 31, 1950.

*   *   *

4. Financing Of OASDI Amendments

The benefit provisions of H.R. 6675 are financed by (1) an increase in the earnings base from $4,800 to $5,600 (effective January 1, 1966), and $6,600 (effective 1971), and (2) a revised tax rate schedule.

The tax rate schedule under existing law and the revised schedule provided by the bill for the OASDI program follow:

[In percent]

Years	Employer-employee rate (each)		Self-employed rate	
	Present law	Bill	Present law	Bill
1965	3.625	3.625	5.4	5.4
1966	4.125	4.0	6.2	6.0
1967	4.125	4.0	6.2	6.0
1968	4.625	4.0	6.9	6.0
1969–72	4.625	4.4	6.9	6.6
1973 and after	4.625	4.8	6.9	7.0

5. Amount of additional benefits in the full year 1966

7 percent benefit increase ($4 minimum in primary benefit) _____ $1,430,000,000.
Child's benefit to age 22 if in school _____ $195,000,000.
Reduced age for widows _____ $165,000,000 (no long-range charge to system because of actuarial reduction).
Reduction in eligibility requirement for certain persons aged 72 or over _____ $140,000,000.
Liberalization of disability definition _____ $105,000,000.
Liberalization of retirement test _____ $65,000,000.

D. PUBLIC ASSISTANCE AMENDMENTS

1. Increased Assistance Payments

The Federal share of payments under all State public assistance programs is increased a little more than an average of $2.50 a month for the needy aged, blind, and disabled and an average of about $1.25 for needy children, effective January 1, 1966. This is brought about by revising the matching formula for the needy aged, blind, and disabled (and for the adult categories in title XVI) to provide a Federal share of $31 out of the first $37 (now twenty-nine thirty-fifths (29/35) of the first $35) up to a maximum of $75 (now $70) per month per individual on an average basis. The matching formula is revised for aid to families with dependent children so as to provide a Federal share of five-sixths (5/6) of the first $18 (now fourteen-seventeenths (14/17) of the first $17) up to a maximum of $32 (now $30). A provision is included so that States will not receive additional Federal funds except to the extent they pass them on to individual recipients. Effective January 1, 1966. Cost About $150 million a year.

2. Tubercular And Mental Patients

H.R. 6675 removes the exclusion from Federal matching in old-age assistance and medical assistance for the aged programs (and for combined program, title XVI) as to aged individuals who are patients in institutions for tuberculosis or mental diseases or who have been diagnosed as having tuberculosis or psychosis and, as a result, are patients in a medical institution. The bill requires as condition of Federal participation in such payments to, or for, patients in mental hospitals certain agreements and arrangements to assure that better care results from the additional Federal money. The States will receive additional Federal funds under this provision only to the extent they increase their expenditures for mental health purposes under public health and public welfare programs. The bill also removes restrictions as to Federal matching for needy blind and disabled who are tubercular or psychotic and are in general medical institutions.
Effective January 1, 1966. Cost: About $75 million a year.

3. Protective Payments to Third Persons

A provision for protective payments to third persons on behalf of old-age assistance recipients (and recipients on combined program, title XVI program) unable to manage their money because of physical or mental incapacity is added by H.R. 6675. Effective January 1, 1966.

4. Earnings Exemption Under Old-Age Assistance

Your committee's bill increases earnings exemption under old-age assistance program (and aged in combined program) so that a State may, at its option, exempt the first $20 (now $10) and one-half of the next $60 (now $40) of a recipient's monthly earnings. Effective January 1, 1966. Cost: About $1 million first year.

5. Definition Of Medical Assistance For Aged

H.R. 6675 modifies the definition of medical assistance for the aged so as to allow Federal sharing as to old-age assistance recipients for the month they are admitted to or discharged from a medical institution. Effective July 1, 1965. Cost: About $2 million.

6. Exemption Of Retroactive OASDI Benefit Increase

The bill adds a provision which would allow the States to disregard so much of the OASDI benefit increase (including the children in school after 18 modification) as is attributable to its retroactive effective date.

7. Economic Opportunity Act Earnings Exemption

H.R. 6675 also provides a grace period for action by States that have not had regular legislative sessions, whose public assistance statutes now prevent them from disregarding earnings of recipients received under the Economic Opportunity Act.

8. Judicial Review Of State Plan Denials

The bill provides for judicial review of the denial of approval by the Secretary of Health, Education, and Welfare of State public assistance plans and of his action under such programs or noncompliance with State plan conditions in the Federal law.

*   *   *

The committee report appeared on March 24. By April 6, the committee had cleared the bill for floor action under a closed rule and on the following day debate began. Although the new bill was partly a Republican measure, the Republican leadership found itself unable to support it.

Congressional Debates
111 Congressional Record, p. 7219
(April 7, 1965)

Representative Byrnes . . . If we pass the committee bill, we will be taking an unprecedented step in the field of social security. We will be tying into the social security system a service benefit. Not the payment of a specified amount of dollars at some future date, but payment for a specified service — hospitalization — regardless of what that service might cost.

That is why I am unalterably opposed to financing hospitalization through the social security system. You have been told that this is a separate tax with a separate fund, and everyone will know what the hospitalization program costs in terms of the payroll tax.

Once we embark on the program, will that make any difference?

Representative Joel T. Broyhill (Rep., Va.) described the horrors of socialized medicine in England and Saskatchewan and the advantages of Eldercare.

111 Congressional Record, p. 7405-06

Mr. Broyhill . . . Gentlemen, we have been given an awesome responsibility.

Will we be known as the body which admitted its hasty actions and came to honest grips with the problem?

Or will we be known as the House which opened the door to a new concept of welfarism which slowly but inexorably eroded the vitality of a great nation?

Certainly we can go along with what we mistakenly believe to be the majority view.

But will our consciences go with us?

I submit that the people have given us a mandate — not on specific legislation — but to use our minds for the best interest of our Nation.

In the past several months, I have detected a certain disdain among my colleagues regarding the views of the medical profession on this important matter.

Flushed with the November bounty, they have scarcely heeded the warnings of physicians regarding the inherent danger of social security medicine.

The medical profession — especially in the past 29 years — has brought us into a virtual "golden age of medicine." Indeed, there is general agreement that "there has been more medical progress in the past two decades than in the previous two centuries."

American physicians — educated in a tradition of freedom and excellence — have been the architects of this golden age.

Are we now—as in that childhood story—about to kill the goose that lays the golden egg?

Let us give this some thought.

Chairman Mills explained and defended the bill in rather measured tones, and then concluded with a political tour-de-force.

111 Congressional Record, p. 7214

Mr. Mills . . . Mr. Chairman, now very briefly—because it would take hours to discuss it all, but I have very briefly discussed even the medical portions of this bill—I would want you to know that finally it has been possible for us, after all these years, to develop a proposition that I could wholeheartedly and conscientiously, with every bit of the energy at my command, support. That has not been the case with reference to propositions in the past. Here, Mr. Chairman, I believe we have finally worked out a satisfactory and reasonable solution of an entire problem, not just a partial solution of a major problem. I feel that we have done it in a way, Mr. Chairman, that will commend it to the people for whom we do it and that they will realize that in spite of all that has been said in the past, in spite of all the ways that have been suggested in the past, finally the Committee on Ways and Means has produced the proper way to do it and that is the way that good legislation is developed.

Mr. Chairman, there is not a member of the Committee on Ways and Means whom I could not name today who has not made a major contribution to this bill by the inclusion of ideas of his own.

Mr. Chairman, where did we get the idea of the supplementary health benefits plan? Out of that fertile brain of the distinguished gentelman from Wisconsin [Mr. Byrnes].

Where did we get this idea and that idea? Out of the fertile brain of some other Democratic member or some other Republican member of the Committee on Ways and Means.

My distinguished friend, the gentleman from Virginia [Mr. Broyhill], right at the last moment called to our attention a situation about which none of us had thought. However, as a result of the gentleman's many years of experience on the Committee on the Post Office and Civil Service, he thought about it. It was fair and equitable, and we put it in.

Mr. Chairman, every member of the committee has made his contribution. On top of that, Mr. Chairman, the people in the Department of Health, Education, and Welfare worked with us faithfully from morning until night through all of these many days during which we have been in hearings and executive session and have made their contribution.

Mr. Chairman, those on the legislative counsel's staff of the House of Representatives and those who are staff members of both the joint committee and of the Committee on Ways and Means on both sides of the aisle have made their contribution.

Therefore, Mr. Chairman, I believe that there is sufficient ground within this bill for all of us to take pride and take credit.

I would suggest, therefore, that when tomorrow comes, we not toy with the bill by considering a motion to recommit, but that we take the bill as reported to the House from the Committee on Ways and Means and pass this bill as we have passed every other bill dealing with amendments to the Social Security Act in the past—by an overwhelming majority.

The House passed H.R. 6675 by a large majority, 313 to 115.

The Senate

It was the broader bill which reached the Senate Finance Committee and on which public hearings were held. The only Administration complaint concerned the removal of ancilliary medical services from the hospital insurance plan (Title XVIIIA) to the new voluntary (Title XVIIIB) program.

The public hearings gave an opportunity for various traditional protagonists and antagonists to reappear. The chambers of commerce directed their chief attack against the medical care provisions, as well as the extension of disability insurance. The trade union movement congratulated itself for the great coup it had scored. One of the most perceptive observations on the actual operational defeats of Title XVIII, came from the Teamsters, although the bluntness of their statement may have been distasteful to the medical profession.

Social Security
Hearings on H.R. 6675 before the Senate Finance Committee
89th Cong., 1st Sess. (April, 1965)
(p. 2693)

Statement of Sidney Zagri, Legislative Counsel, International Brotherhood of Teamsters

Our questions arise in three major areas:

1. Does the bill protect the retiree from the bilking practices of the medical profession—overcharges, unnecessary operations, uncalled for stays in the hospital, et cetera, which has been the experience under Teamster and other private health and welfare insurance programs? And I will expand somewhat on this point in just a moment, from our experience in New York City and the United Mine Workers' experience, and other labor unions, in the area where doctors have charged sums sometimes double the amount provided for in the insurance program, charging the patient separately, creating unnecessary admissions to the hospital to collect on insurance fees,

removing organs because there was a dollar sign and so forth. This is documented by a detailed study of Columbia University and Montefiore Hospital, and I will document this in just a moment. But this is the kind of question that I am raising: Does this bill provide the necessary machinery to curtain, to curb and protect the individual from this type of practice. I am afraid it does not. I am afriad that it provides that administrative machinery based upon traditional and customary lines, which is a little bit like the fox watching the henhouse, and I would like to have the committee bear with me a moment while I raise the second point.

2. Does the bill assure that the neediest of the retired citizens will receive the medical services and medical facilities that the bill seeks to provide him, or will the benefits go primarily to those who were already protected under private group insurance plans or individual private insurance plans.

3. What guarantees will the individual have in terms of maintenance of a quality standard of medical care consistent with the capabilities and resources made available to the practitioner through the progress of medical sciences?

The bilking practices of the medical profession as presently experienced under private insurance plans will continue under the administration provisions of H.R. 6675.

                              *   *   *

Recommendations

1. That the ascertainment of costs and fees be left within the exclusive jurisdiction of the Secretary of Health, Education, and Welfare and that his discretion to delegate this responsibility be limited to that of a public agency authority.

2. That all fees be fixed on the basis of prevailing rates in the areas for specific operations and other medical services.

3. That no reimbursement for doctor's fees be paid — and this is very important — unless the doctor certifies that the bill presented represents the total charge for his service. Any misrepresentation on this score will constitute a misdemeanor and be subject to criminal prosecution.

4. A fixed fee be established for the doctor's certification of a patient to a hospital, nursing home, or home care. As you know, under this bill, no one can go to a hospital or nursing home unless he would be certified. We do not know, no one has estimated the size of the bonanza that medicare promises for America's doctors, but two figures hint at it: the total cost of health care for Americans over 65 was more than $5 billion last year. Blue Cross, Government, and private insurance witnesses testified before the House Ways and Means Committee that the bill surely would increase the use of hospitals by the aged; estimates are varying from 10 to 40 percent in the first years.

5. Utilization review committees provided for in this bill — to check on abuses of administration as well as longevity of hospital stays — and this is very important — because we have 2½ more times need than we have hospital beds, and if the needy of this country are going to get into hospitals, we are going to have to have a speedier rotation system, and we cannot have that kind of bilking where the doctor will use the full term of the insurance to keep people in there in order to satisfy their particular financial necessities, not patient-doctor. So therefore I say that the committee reviewing these long stays or longevity stays should be comprised of doctors outside of the hospital, preferably a special committee of the county medical society or the deans of the local medical schools or a combination of the two.

Representatives of Blue Cross and Blue Shield, on the other hand, felt more than competent to undertake any burden which might be thrust on them under the new plans.

Senate Hearings
(p. 333, p. 391)

A major matter of public policy to be decided by the action on this bill is, "How should Government spend money for services to private individuals rendered by private institutions and practitioners?" There are two major alternatives. The Government can work through the privately financed health care system, of which Blue Cross is a part, or around it. The bill as presently written declares it to be the policy of Congress to distribute purchasing power through the system.

*   *   *

We will assist in the implementation of H.R. 6675, if requested. Blue Cross plans, like many hospitals, were started by thousands of public servants, many of whom were not professionally involved in health. They were labor leaders, businessmen, educators, legislators who saw a vital need to help their fellow citizens have access to health care. They organized hospitals. They wrote, sponsored, and passed enabling legislation authorizing Blue Cross plans. These laws declared public policy to include the functioning of these plans as a public pool, using some of the principles of insurance, but dedicated to obtaining total community membership.

Needless to say, the AMA and at least a part of the insurance industry remained hostile to the last.

With the hearings over, Senator Long tried to persuade the committee to accept a substitute for Title XVIII, increasing its coverage but reinstituting a means test. Neither the committee nor the press treated his attempt well. What lay behind Senator Long's motion is not clear. Some suspected the AMA was involved since the plan, which was generous in many ways, would *probably have produced a House-Senate stalemate. The amendments were first presented to the Finance Committee as a casual extension of the House bill, but on June 17 the liberals voted to substitute the Long Bill. The President when informed of this, swung into action. He was unable to persuade Senator Long to change his mind, but White House pressure on other liberal supporters was apparently more successful. On June 23, both amendments were defeated. A further sixty days of care with a $10 deductible was added to XVIIIA as a compromise.*

The Finance Committee reported out a bill with increased coverage under XVIIIA, an increased social security tax, and a right to earn more under OASDI. In the end the Senate accepted about one hundred changes recommended by the Finance Committee and some thirty amendments introduced in debate. Senator John J. Williams' motion that patients under either Medicaid or Medicare be guaranteed the same right to choose a physician was easily accepted as was Senator Byrd's amendment providing that social security benefits might be taken at sixty at an actuarily reduced rate. The Senate also accepted amendments to remove ceilings on tax deductions for medical bills.

Most surprising of all was the voice vote acceptance of Senator Hartke's amendment eliminating the time limitation under Title XVIIIA. Rejected amendments included a motion to abolish the time limits on coverage, an attempt to remove Title XVIII and substitute a heavily federally-financed Kerr-Mills program, and a proposal for a Medicare means test. Other rejected amendments included attempts to adjust social security benefits to the cost of living index and to blanket in persons over seventy or seventy-two. These attempts represented an important inroad into the self-funding nature of the OASDI Trust Fund. The Senate did, however, accept a Long Amendment allowing stages to disregard the $7 social security benefit increase in calculating public assistance payments.

The Senate debate also gave a number of Senators an opportunity to declare their views about social security and Medicare. Not all Republicans were enthusiastic—particularly about Medicare.

Congressional Debates
111 Congressional Record, p. 15904
(July 8, 1965)

Mr. John Tower. [Rep., Tex.] Mr. President, I have, in the past, indicated many reasons why the proposed medical care system is unwise. It is expensively inadequate, covering only very limited hospital costs and not dealing at all with the crucial problem of long-term illness. In addition, it provides, at taxpayer expense, this limited care for everyone—be he poverty stricken or millionaire.

But, the most pressing objection to medicare is that its enormous expense

will push social security taxation beyond 11 percent on employer and employee, perhaps even higher. Even then, funds likely will not be sufficient to
meet all the promises of care. There is a real danger the financial stability
of the entire social security system will be undermined.

Medicare can destroy social security as we know it.

*The bill was finally passed on July 9, with 513 changes from the House
version and an increased cost of $6 billion (from $1.5 billion to $7.5 billion).*

*The House-Senate conferees met six times before producing their report
— which generally accepted the House version of the bill. Payment of
auxiliary hospital services were returned to Title XVIIIB, and most of the
increased coverage under Title XVIIIA was rejected, as was the right to
take social security benefits at sixty. At the same time, the higher tax base
established by the Senate was accepted.*

*The conference report was accepted by both houses, and for the first
time, the United States appeared to have a national health program.
OASDI had been expanded to OASDHI, taking in the compulsory XVIIIA
and the voluntary XVIIIB (practitioner payments). This aspect of the program became known as Medicare. In addition, Title XIX extended Kerr-
Mills to cover those under sixty-five who were "medically indigent." This
aspect of the program, Medicaid, being a public assistance title, was, however, a voluntary federal-state program.*

President Johnson was obviously delighted with the success of his bill.

Presidential Remarks with President Truman at the Signing
in Independence of the Medicare Bill
(July 30, 1965)*

President Truman. Thank you very much. I am glad you like the President.
I like him too. He is one of the finest men I ever ran across.

Mr. President, Mrs. Johnson, distinguished guests:

You have done me a great honor in coming here today, and you have made
me a very, very happy man.

This is an important hour for the Nation, for those of our citizens who
have completed their tour of duty and have moved to the sidelines. These
are the days that we are trying to celebrate for them. These people are our
prideful responsibility and they are entitled, among other benefits, to the
best medical protection available.

Not one of these, our citizens, should ever be abandoned to the indignity
of charity. Charity is indignity when you have to have it. But we don't want
these people to have anything to do with charity and we don't want them to
have any idea of hopeless despair.

Public Papers of the Presidents, Lyndon B. Johnson, 1965, Vol. II, p. 811.

Mr. President, I am glad to have lived this long and to witness today the signing of the Medicare bill which puts this Nation right where it needs to be, to be right. Your inspired leadership and a responsive forward-looking Congress have made it historically possible for this day to come about.

Thank all of you most highly for coming here. It is an honor I haven't had for, well, quite awhile, I'll say that to you, but here it is:

Ladies and gentlemen, the President of the United States.

The President. President and Mrs. Truman. Secretary Celebrezze, Senator Mansfield, Senator Symington, Senator Long, Governor Hearnes, Senator Anderson and Congressman King of the Anderson-King team, Congressman Mills and Senator Long of the Mills-Long team, our beloved Vice President who worked in the vineyard many years to see this day come to pass, and all of my dear friends in the Congress—both Democrats and Republicans:

The people of the United States love and voted for Harry Truman, not because he gave them hell—but because he gave them hope.

I believe today that all America shares my joy that he is present now when the hope that he offered becomes a reality for millions of our fellow citizens.

I am so proud that this has come to pass in the Johnson administration. But it was really Harry Truman of Missouri who planted the seeds of compassion and duty which have today flowered into care for the sick, and serenity for the fearful.

Many men can make many proposals. Many men can draft many laws. But few have the piercing and humane eye which can see beyond the words to the people that they touch. Few can see past the speeches and the political battles to the doctor over there that is tending the infirm, and to the hospital that is receiving those in anguish, or feel in their heart painful wrath at the injustice which denies the miracle of healing to the old and to the poor. And fewer still have the courage to stake reputation, and position, and the effort of a lifetime upon such a cause when there are so few that share it.

But it is just such men who illuminate the life and the history of a nation. And so, President Harry Truman, it is in tribute not to you, but to the America that you represent, that we have come here to pay our love and our respects to you today. For a country can be known by the quality of the men it honors. By praising you, and by carrying forward your dreams, we really reaffirm the greatness of America.

It was a generation ago that Harry Truman said, and I quote him: "Millions of our citizens do not now have a full measure of opportunity to achieve and to enjoy good health. Millions do not now have protection or security against the economic effects of sickness. And the time has now arrived for action to help them attain that opportunity and to help them get that protection."

Well, today, Mr. President, and my fellow Americans, we are taking such action – 20 years later. And we are doing that under the great leadership of men like John McCormack, our Speaker; Carl Albert, our majority leader; our very able and beloved majority leader of the Senate, Mike Mansfield; and distinguished Members of the Ways and Means and Finance Committees of the House and Senate – of both parties, Democratic and Republican.

Because the need for this action is plain; and it is so clear indeed that we marvel not simply at the passage of this bill, but what we marvel at is that it took so many years to pass it. And I am so glad that Aime Forand is here to see it finally passed and signed – one of the first authors.

There are more than 18 million Americans over the age of 65. Most of them have low incomes. Most of them are threatened by illness and medical expenses that they cannot afford.

And through this new law, Mr. President, every citizen will be able, in his productive years when he is earning, to insure himself against the ravages of illness in his old age.

This insurance will help pay for care in hospitals, in skilled nursing homes, or in the home. And under a separate plan it will help meet the fees of the doctors.

Now here is how the plan will affect you.

During your working years, the people of America – you – will contribute through the social security program a small amount each payday for hospital insurance protection. For example, the average worker in 1966 will contribute about $1.50 per month. The employer will contribute a similar amount. And this will provide the funds to pay up to 90 days of hospital care for each illness, plus diagnostic care, and up to 100 home health visits after you are 65. And beginning in 1967, you will also be covered for up to 100 days of care in a skilled nursing home after a period of hospital care.

And under a separate plan, when you are 65 – that the Congress originated itself, in its own good judgment – you may be covered for medical and surgical fees whether you are in or out of the hospital. You will pay $3 per month after you are 65 and your Government will contribute an equal amount.

The benefits under the law are as varied and broad as the marvelous modern medicine itself. If it has a few defects – such as the method of payment of certain specialists – then I am confident those can be quickly remedied and I hope they will be.

No longer will older Americans be denied the healing miracle of modern medicine. No longer will illness crush and destroy the savings that they have so carefully put away over a lifetime so that they might enjoy dignity in their later years. No longer will young families see their own incomes, and their own hopes, eaten away simply because they are carrying out their deep moral obligations to their parents, and to their uncles, and their aunts.

And no longer will this Nation refuse the hand of justice to those who have given a lifetime of service and wisdom and labor to the progress of this progressive country.

And this bill, Mr. President, is even broader than that. It will increase social security benefits for all of our older Americans. It will improve a wide range of health and medical services for Americans of all ages.

In 1935 when the man that both of us loved so much, Franklin Delano Roosevelt, signed the Social Security Act, he said it was, and I quote him, "a cornerstone in a structure which is being built but it is by no means complete."

Well, perhaps no single act in the entire administration of the beloved Franklin D. Roosevelt really did more to win him the illustrious place in history that he has as did the laying of that cornerstone. And I am so happy that his oldest son Jimmy could be here to share with us the joy that is ours today. And those who share this day will also be remembered for making the most important addition to that structure, and you are making it in this bill, the most important addition that has been made in three decades.

History shapes men, but it is a necessary faith of leadership that men can help shape history. There are many who led us to this historic day. Not out of courtesy or deference, but from the gratitude and remembrance which is our country's debt, if I may be pardoned for taking a moment, I want to call a part of the honor roll: it is the able leadership in both Houses of the Congress.

Congressman Celler, Chairman of the Judiciary Committee, introduced the hospital insurance in 1952. Aime Forand from Rhode Island, then Congressman, introduced it in the House. Senator Clinton Anderson from New Mexico fought for Medicare through the years in the Senate. Congressman Cecil King of California carried on the battle in the House. The legislative genius of the Chairman of the Ways and Means Committee, Congressman Wilbur Mills, and the effective and able work of Senator Russell Long, together transformed this desire into victory.

And those devoted public servants, former Secretary, Senator Ribicoff; present Secretary, Tony Celebrezze; Under Secretary Wilbur Cohen; the Democratic whip of the House, Hale Boggs on the Ways and Means Committee; and really the White House's best legislator, Larry O'Brien, gave not just endless days and months and, yes, years of patience — but they gave their hearts — to passing this bill.

Let us also remember those who sadly cannot share this time for triumph. For it is their triumph too. It is the victory of great Members of Congress that are not with us, like John Dingell, Sr., and Robert Wagner, late a Member of the Senate, and James Murray of Montana.

And there is also John Fitzgerald Kennedy, who fought in the Senate and took his case to the people, and never yielded in pursuit, but was not spared to see the final concourse of the forces that he had helped to loose.

But it all started really with the man from Independence. And so, as it is fitting that we should, we have come back here to his home to complete what he began.

President Harry Truman, as any President must, made many decisions of great moment; although he always made them frankly and with a courage and a clarity that few men have ever shared. The immense and the intricate questions of freedom and survival were caught up many times in the web of Harry Truman's judgment. And this is in the tradition of leadership.

But there is another tradition that we share today. It calls upon us never to be indifferent toward despair. It commands us never to turn away from helplessness. It directs us never to ignore or to spurn those who suffer untended in a land that is bursting with abundance.

I said to Senator Smathers, the whip of the Democrats in the Senate, who worked with us in the Finance Committee on this legislation—I said, the highest traditions of the medical profession are really directed to the ends that we are trying to serve. And it was only yesterday, at the request of some of my friends, I met with the leaders of the American Medical Association to seek their assistance in advancing the cause of one of the greatest professions of all—the medical profession—in helping us to maintain and to improve the health of all Americans.

And this is not just our tradition—or the tradition of the Democratic Party—or even the tradition of the Nation. It is as old as the day it was first commanded: "Thou shalt open thine hand wide unto thy brother, to thy poor, to thy needy, in thy land."

And just think, Mr. President, because of this document—and the long years of struggle which so many have put into creating it—in this town, and a thousand other towns like it, there are men and women in pain who will now find ease. There are those, alone in suffering, who will now hear the sound of some approaching footsteps coming to help. There are those fearing the terrible darkness of despairing poverty—despite their long years of labor and expectation—who will now look up to see the light of hope and realization.

There just can be no satisfaction, nor any act of leadership, that gives greater satisfaction than this.

And perhaps you alone, President Truman, perhaps you alone can fully know just how grateful I am for this day.

Lyndon B. Johnson

Social Security Act Amendments of 1965
(July 30, 1965, 79 Statutes at Large 286)

HOSPITAL INSURANCE BENEFITS AND SUPPLEMENTARY MEDICAL INSURANCE BENEFITS

*   *   *

Sec. 102. (a) The Social Security Act is amended by adding after title XVII the following new title:

"TITLE XVIII – HEALTH INSURANCE FOR THE AGED

* * *

"Part A – Hospital Insurance Benefits for the Aged

"DESCRIPTION OF PROGRAM

"Sec. 1811. The insurance program for which entitlement is established by section 226 provides basic protection against the costs of hospital and re-lated post-hospital services in accordance with this part for individuals who are age 65 or over and are entitled to retirement benefits under title II of this Act or under the railroad retirement system.

"SCOPE OF BENEFITS

"Sec. 1812. (a) The benefits provided to an individual by the insurance program under this part shall consist of entitlement to have payment made on his behalf (subject to the provisions of this part) for—

"(1) inpatient hospital services for up to 90 days during any spell of illness;

"(2) post-hospital extended care services for up to 100 days during any spell of illness;

"(3) post-hospital home health services for up to 100 visits (during the one-year period described in section 1861(n)) after the beginning of one spell of illness and before the beginning of the next; and

"(4) outpatient hospital diagnostic services.

"(b) Payment under this part for services furnished an individual during a spell of illness may not (subject to subsection (c)) be made for—

"(1) inpatient hospital services furnished to him during such spell after such services have been furnished to him for 90 days during such spell;

"(2) post-hospital extended care services furnished to him during such spell after such services have been furnished to him for 100 days during such spell; or

"(3) inpatient psychiatric hospital services furnished to him after such services have been furnished to him for a total of 190 days dur-ing his lifetime.

"(c) If an individual is an inpatient of a psychiatric hospital or a tubercu-losis hospital on the first day of the first month for which he is entitled to benefits under this part, the days on which he was an inpatient of such a hospital in the 90-day period immediately before such first day shall be in-cluded in determining the 90-day limit under subsection (b) (1) (but not in determining the 190-day limit under subsection (b) (3)).

"(d) Payment under this part may be made for post-hospital home health services furnished an individual only during the one-year period described in section 1861(n) following his most recent hospital discharge which meets the requirements of such section, and only for the first 100 visits in such period. The number of visits to be charged for purposes of the limitation in the preceding sentence, in connection with items or services described in section 1861(m), shall be determined in accordance with regulations.

"(e) For purposes of subsections (b), (c), and (d), inpatient hospital services, inpatient psychiatric hospital services, post-hospital extended care services, and post-hospital home health services shall be taken into account only if payment is or would be, except for this section or the failure to comply with the request and certification requirements of or under section 1814(a), made with respect to such services under this part.

"(f) For definition of 'spell of illness', and for definitions of other terms used in this part, see section 1861.

"DEDUCTIBLES AND COINSURANCE

"Sec. 1813. (a) (1) The amount payable for inpatient hospital services furnished an individual during any spell of illness shall be reduced by a deduction equal to the inpatient hospital deductible or, if less, the charges imposed with respect to such individual for such services, except that, if the customary charges for such services are greater than the charges so imposed, such customary charges shall be considered to be the charges so imposed. Such amount shall be further reduced by a coinsurance amount equal to one-fourth of the inpatient hospital deductible for each day (before the 91st day) on which such individual is furnished such services during such spell of illness after such services have been furnished to him for 60 days during such spell.

"(2) The amount payable for outpatient hospital diagnostic services furnished an individual during a diagnostic study shall be reduced by a deduction equal to the sum of (A) one-half of the inpatient hospital deductible which is applicable to spells of illness beginning in the same calendar year as such diagnostic study and (B) 20 per centum of the remainder of such amount. For purposes of the preceding sentence, a diagnostic study for any individual consists of the outpatient hospital diagnostic services provided by (or under arrangements made by) the same hospital during the 20-day period beginning on the first day (not included in a previous diagnostic study) on which he is entitled to hospital insurance benefits under section 226 and on which outpatient hospital diagnostic services are furnished him.

"(3) The amount payable to any provider of services under this part for services furnished an individual during any spell of illness shall be further reduced by an amount equal to the cost of the first three pints of whole blood furnished to him as part of such services during such spell of illness.

"(4) The amount payable for post-hospital extended care services furnished an individual during any spell of illness shall be reduced by a coinsurance amount equal to one-eighth of the inpatient hospital deductible for each day (before the 101st day) on which he is furnished such services after such services have been furnished to him for 20 days during such spell.

"(b) (1) The inpatient hospital deductible which shall be applicable for the purposes of subsection (a) shall be $40 in the case of any spell of illness or diagnostic study beginning before 1969.

"(2) The Secretary shall, between July 1 and October 1 of 1968, and of each year thereafter, determine and promulgate the inpatient hospital deductible which shall be applicable for the purposes of subsection (a) in the case of any spell of illness or diagnostic study beginning during the succeeding calendar year. Such inpatient hospital deductible shall be equal to $40 multiplied by the ratio of (A) the current average per diem rate for inpatient hospital services for the calendar year preceding the promulgation, to (B) the current average per diem rate for such services for 1966. Any amount determined under the preceding sentence which is not a multiple of $4 shall be rounded to the nearest multiple of $4 (or, if it is midway between two multiples of $4, to the next higher multiple of $4). The current average per diem rate for any year shall be determined by the Secretary on the basis of the best information available to him (at the time the determination is made) as to the amounts paid under this part on account of inpatient hospital services furnished during such year, by hospitals which have agreements in effect under section 1866, to individuals who are entitled to hospital insurance benefits under section 226, plus the amount which would have been so paid but for subsection (a) (1) of this section.

*   *   *

"Reasonable Cost of Services

"(b) The amount paid to any provider of services with respect to services for which payment may be made under this part shall, subject to the provisions of section 1813, be the reasonable cost of such services, as determined under section 1861(v).

*   *   *

"USE OF PUBLIC AGENCIES OR PRIVATE ORGANIZATIONS TO FACILITATE PAYMENT TO PROVIDERS OF SERVICES

Sec. 1816. (a) If any group or association of providers of services wishes to have payments under this part to such providers made through a national, State, or other public or private agency or organization and nominates such agency or organization for this purpose, the Secretary is authorized to enter into an agreement with such agency or organization providing for the determination by such agency or organization (subject to such review by the Secretary as may be provided for by the agreement) of the amount of the payments required pursuant to this part to be made to such providers, and for the making of such payments by such agency or organization to such providers. Such agreement may also include provision for the agency or organization to do all or any part of the following: (1) to provide consultative services to institutions or agencies to enable them to establish and maintain fiscal records necessary for purposes of this part and otherwise to qualify as hospitals, extended care facilities, or home health agencies, and (2) with respect to the providers of services which are to receive payments through it (A) to serve as a center for, and communicate to providers, any information or instructions furnished to it by the Secretary, and serve as a channel of communication from providers to the Secretary; (B) to make such audits of the records of providers as may be necessary to insure that proper payments are made under this part; and (C) to perform such other functions as are necessary to carry out this subsection.

*   *   *

"FEDERAL HOSPITAL INSURANCE TRUST FUND

Sec. 1817. (a) There is hereby created on the books of the Treasury of the United States a trust fund to be known as the 'Federal Hospital Insurance Trust Fund' (hereinafter in this section referred to as the 'Trust Fund'). The Trust Fund shall consist of such amounts as may be deposited in, or appropriated to, such fund as provided in this part.

*   *   *

"Part B — Supplementary Medical Insurance Benefits for the Aged

"ESTABLISHMENT OF SUPPLEMENTARY MEDICAL INSURANCE PROGRAM FOR THE AGED

"*Sec. 1831.* There is hereby established a voluntary insurance program to provide medical insurance benefits in accordance with the provisions of this part for individuals 65 years of age or over who elect to enroll under such program, to be financed from premium payments by enrollees together with contributions from funds appropriated by the Federal Government.

"*Sec. 1832.* (a) The benefits provided to an individual by the insurance program established by this part shall consist of—

"(1) entitlement to have payment made to him or on his behalf (subject to the provisions of this part) for medical and other health services, except those described in paragraph (2) (B); and

"(2) entitlement to have payment made on his behalf (subject to the provisions of this part) for—

"(A)   home health services for up to 100 visits during a calendar year; and

"(B)   medical and other health services (other than physicians' services unless furnished by a resident or intern of a hospital) furnished by a provider of services or by others under arrangements with them made by a provider of services.

"(b) For definitions of 'spell of illness', 'medical and other health services', and other terms used in this part, see section 1861.

"PAYMENT OF BENEFITS

"*Sec. 1833.* (a) Subject to the succeeding provisions of this section, there shall be paid from the Federal Supplementary Medical Insurance Trust Fund, in the case of each individual who is covered under the insurance program established by this part and incurs expenses for services with respect to which benefits are payable under this part, amounts equal to —

"(1) in the case of services described in section 1832(a)(1) — 80 percent of the reasonable charges for the services; except that an organization which provides medical and other health services (or arranges for their availability) on a prepayment basis may elect to be paid 80 percent of the reasonable cost of services for which payment may be made under this part on behalf of individuals enrolled in such organization in lieu of 80 percent of the reasonable charges for such services if the organization undertakes to charge such individuals no more than 20 percent of such reasonable cost plus any amounts payable by them as a result of subsection (b); and

"(2) in the case of services described in section 1832(a)(2) — 80 percent of the reasonable cost of the services (as determined under section 1861(v)).

*　　*　　*

"PAYMENT OF PREMIUMS

"*Sec. 1840.* (a)(1) In the case of an individual who is entitled to monthly benefits under section 202, his monthly premiums under this part shall (except as provided in subsection (d) be collected by deducting the amount thereof from the amount of such monthly benefits. Such deduction shall be made in such manner and at such times as the Secretary shall by regulation prescribe.

*　　*　　*

"USE OF CARRIERS FOR ADMINISTRATION OF BENEFITS

"*Sec. 1842.* (a) In order to provide for the administration of the benefits under this part with maximum efficiency and convenience for individuals entitled to benefits under this part and for providers of services and other persons furnishing services to such individuals, and with a view to furthering coordination of the administration of the benefits under part A and under this part, the Secretary is authorized to enter into contracts with carriers, including carriers with which agreements under section 1816 are in effect, which will perform some or all of the following functions (or, to the extent provided in such contracts, will secure performance thereof by other organizations); and, with respect to any of the following functions which involve payments for physicians' services, the Secretary shall to the extent possible enter into such contracts:

"(1) (A) make determinations of the rates and amounts of payments required pursuant to this part to be made to providers of services and other persons on a reasonable cost or reasonable charge basis (as may be applicable);

"(B) receive, disburse, and account for funds in making such payments; and

"(C) make such audits of the records of providers of services as may be necessary to assure that proper payments are made under this part;

"(2) (A) determine compliance with the requirements of section 1861 (k) as to utilization review; and

"(B) assist providers of services and other persons who furnish services for which payment may be made under this part in the development of procedures relating to utilization practices, make studies of the effectiveness of such procedures and methods for their improvement, assist in the application of safeguards against unnecessary utilization of services furnished by providers of services and other persons to individuals entitled to benefits under this part, and provide procedures for and assist in arranging, where necessary, the establishment of groups outside hospitals (meeting the requirements of section 1861 (k) (2)) to make reviews of utilization;

"(3) serve as a channel of communication of information relating to the administration of this part; and

"(4) otherwise assist, in such manner as the contract may provide, in discharging administrative duties necessary to carry out the purposes of this part. . . .

*   *   *

"ADVISORY COUNCIL ON SOCIAL SECURITY

"*Sec. 706.* (a) During 1968 and every fifth year thereafter, the Secretary shall appoint an Advisory Council on Social Security for the purpose of reviewing the status of the Federal Old-Age and Survivors Insurance Trust Fund, the Federal Disability Insurance Trust Fund, the Federal Hospital Insurance Trust Fund, and the Federal Supplementary Medical Insurance Trust Fund in relation to the long-term commitments of the old-age, survivors, and disability insurance program and the programs under parts A and B of title XVIII, and of reviewing the scope of coverage and the adequacy of benefits under, and all other aspects of, these programs, including their impact on the public assistance programs under this Act.

*   *   *

Sec. 121. (a) The Social Security Act is amended by adding at the end thereof (after the new title XVIII added by section 102) the following new title:

"TITLE XIX – GRANTS TO STATES FOR MEDICAL ASSISTANCE PROGRAMS

"APPROPRIATION

"*Sec. 1901.* For the purpose of enabling each State, as far as practicable under the conditions in such State, to furnish (1) medical assistance on be-half of families with dependent children and of aged, blind, or permanently and totally disabled individuals, whose income and resources are insufficient to meet the costs of necessary medical services, and (2) rehabilitation and other services to help such families and individuals attain or retain capability for independence or self-care, there is hereby authorized to be appropriated for each fiscal year a sum sufficient to carry out the purposes of this title. The sums made available under this section shall be used for making payments to States which have submitted, and had approved by the Secretary of Health, Education, and Welfare, State plans for medical assistance.

"STATE PLANS FOR MEDICAL ASSISTANCE

"*Sec. 1902.* (a) A State plan for medical assistance must –
  "(1) provide that it shall be in effect in all political subdivisions of the State, and, if administered by them, be mandatory upon them;
  "(2) provide for financial participation by the State equal to not less than 40 per centum of the non-Federal share of the expenditures under the plan with respect to which payments under section 1903 are author-ized by this title; and, effective July 1, 1970, provide for financial participation by the State equal to all of such non-Federal share or pro-vide for distribution of funds from Federal or State sources, for carry-ing out the State plan, on an equalization or other basis which will assure that the lack of adequate funds from local sources will not re-sult in lowering the amount, duration, scope, or quality of care and services available under the plan;
  "(3) provide for granting an opportunity for a fair hearing before the State agency to any individual whose claim for medical assistance under the plan is denied or is not acted upon with reasonable prompt-ness;
  "(4) provide such methods of administration (including methods re-lating to the establishment and maintenance of personnel standards on

a merit basis, except that the Secretary shall exercise no authority with respect to the selection, tenure of office, and compensation of any individual employed in accordance with such methods, and including provision for utilization of professional medical personnel in the administration and, where administered locally, supervision of administration of the plan) as are found by the Secretary to be necessary for the proper and efficient operation of the plan;

"(5) either provide for the establishment or designation of a single State agency to administer the plan, or provide for the establishment or designation of a single State agency to supervise the administration of the plan, except that the determination of eligibility for medical assistance under the plan shall be made by the State or local agency administering the State plan approved under title I or XVI (insofar as it relates to the aged);

"(6) provide that the State agency will make such reports, in such form and containing such information, as the Secretary may from time to time require, and comply with such provisions as the Secretary may from time to time find necessary to assure the correctness and verification of such reports;

"(7) provide safeguards which restrict the use or disclosure of information concerning applicants and recipients to purposes directly connected with the administration of the plan;

"(8) provide that all individuals wishing to make application for medical assistance under the plan shall have opportunity to do so, and that such assistance shall be furnished with reasonable promptness to all eligible individuals;

"(9) provide for the establishment or designation of a State authority or authorities which shall be responsible for establishing and maintaining standards for private or public institutions in which recipients of medical assistance under the plan may receive care or services;

"(10) provide for making medical assistance available to all individuals receiving aid or assistance under State plans approved under titles I, IV, X, XIV, and XVI; and—

"(A) provide that the medical assistance made available to individuals receiving aid or assistance under any such State plan—

"(i) shall not be less in amount, duration, or scope than the medical assistance made available to individuals receiving aid or assistance under any other such State plan, and

"(ii) shall not be less in amount, duration, or scope than the medical or remedial care and services made available to individuals not receiving aid or assistance under any such plan; and

"(B) if medical or remedial care and services are included for any group of individuals who are not receiving aid or assistance under any such State plan and who do not meet the income and resources requirements of the one of such State plans which is appropriate, as determined in accordance with standards prescribed by the Secretary, provide—

"(i) for making medical or remedial care and services available to all individuals who would, if needy, be eligible for aid or assistance under any such State plan and who have insufficient (as determined in accordance with comparable standards) income and resources to meet the costs of necessary medical or remedial care and services, and

"(ii) that the medical or remedial care and services made available to all individuals not receiving aid or assistance under any such State plan shall be equal in amount, duration, and scope;

except that the making available of the services described in paragraph (4) or (14) of section 1905(a) to individuals meeting the age requirement prescribed therein shall not, by reason of this paragraph (10), require the making available of any such services, or the making available of such services of the same amount, duration, and scope, to individuals of any other ages;

"(11) provide for entering into cooperative arrangements with the State agencies responsible for administering or supervising the administration of health services and vocational rehabilitation services in the State looking toward maximum utilization of such services in the provision of medical assistance under the plan;

"(12) provide that, in determining whether an individual is blind, there shall be an examination by a physician skilled in the diseases of the eye or by an optometrist, whichever the individual may select;

"(13) provide for inclusion of some institutional and some non-institutional care and services, and, effective July 1, 1967, provide (A) for inclusion of at least the care and services listed in clauses (1) through (5) of section 1905(a), and (B) for payment of the reasonable cost (as determined in accordance with standards approved by the Secretary and included in the plan) of inpatient hospital services provided under the plan;

"(14) provide that (A) no deduction, cost sharing, or similar charge will be imposed under the plan on the individual with respect to inpatient hospital services furnished him under the plan, and (B) any deduction, cost sharing, or similar charge imposed under the plan with respect to any other medical assistance furnished him thereunder, and any enrollment fee, premium, or similar charge imposed under the plan, shall be reasonably related (as determined in accordance with standards approved by the Secretary and included in the plan) to the recipient's income or his income and resources;

"(15) in the case of eligible individuals 65 years of age or older who are covered by either or both of the insurance programs established by title XVIII, provide—

"(A) for meeting the full cost of any deductible imposed with with respect to any such individual under the insurance program established by part A of such title; and

"(B) where, under the plan, all of any deductible, cost sharing, or similar charge imposed with respect to any such individual under the insurance program established by part B of such title is not met, the portion thereof which is met shall be determined on a basis reasonably related (as determined in accordance with standards approved by the Secretary and included in the plan) to such individual's income or his income and resources;

"(16) provide for inclusion, to the extent required by regulations prescribed by the Secretary; of provisions (conforming to such regulations) with respect to the furnishing of medical assistance under the plan to individuals who are residents of the State but are absent therefrom;

"(17) include reasonable standards (which shall be comparable for all groups) for determining eligibility for and the extent of medical assistance under the plan which (A) are consistent with the objectives of this title, (B) provide for taking into account only such income and resources as are, as determined in accordance with standards prescribed by the Secretary, available to the applicant or recipient and (in the case of any applicant or recipient who would, if he met the requirements as to need, be eligible for aid or assistance in the form of money payments under a State plan approved under title I, IV, X, XIV, or XVI) as would not be disregarded (or set aside for future needs) in determining his eligibility for and amount of such aid or assistance under such plan, (C) provide for reasonable evaluation of any such income or resources, and (D) do not take into account the financial responsibility of any individual for any applicant or recipient of assistance under the plan unless such applicant or recipient is such individual's spouse or such individual's child who is under age 21 or is blind or permanently and totally disabled; and provide for flexibility in the application of such standards with respect to income by taking into account, except to the extent prescribed by the Secretary, the costs (whether in the form of insurance premiums or otherwise) incurred for medical care or for any other type of remedial care recognized under State law;

"(18) provide that no lien may be imposed against the property of any individual prior to his death on account of medical assistance paid or to be paid on his behalf under the plan (except pursuant to the judgment of a court on account of benefits incorrectly paid on behalf of such individual), and that there shall be no adjustment or recovery (except, in the case of an individual who was 65 years of age or older when he received such assistance, from his estate, and then only after the death of his surviving spouse, if any, and only at a time when he has no surviving child who is under age 21 or is blind or permanently and totally disabled) of any medical assistance correctly paid on behalf of such individual under the plan;

"(19) provide such safeguards as may be necessary to assure that eligibility for care and services under the plan will be determined, and such care and services will be provided, in a manner consistent with simplicity of administration and the best interests of the recipients;

"(20) if the State plan includes medical assistance in behalf of individuals 65 years of age or older who are patients in institutions for mental diseases—

"(A) provide for having in effect such agreements or other arrangements with State authorities concerned with mental diseases, and, where appropriate, with such institutions, as may be necessary for carrying out the State plan, including arrangements for joint planning and for development of alternate methods of care, arrangements providing assurance of immediate readmittance to institutions where needed for individuals under alternate plans of care, and arrangements providing for access to patients and facilities, for furnishing information, and for making reports;

"(B) provide for an individual plan for each such patient to assure that the institutional care provided to him is in his best interests, including, to that end, assurances that there will be initial and periodic review of his medical and other needs, that he will be given appropriate medical treatment within the institution, and that there will be a periodical determination of his need for continued treatment in the institution;

"(C) provide for the development of alternate plans of care, making maximum utilization of available resources, for recipients 65 years of age or older who would otherwise need care in such institutions, including appropriate medical treatment and other aid or assistance; for services referred to in section 3(a) (4) (A) (i) and (ii) or section 1603(a) (4) (A) (i) and (ii) which are appropriate for such recipients and for such patients; and for methods of administration necessary to assure that the responsibilities of the State agency under the State plan with respect to such recipients and such patients will be effectively carried out; and

"(D) provide methods of determining the reasonable cost of institutional care for such patients;

"(21) if the State plan includes medical assistance in behalf of individuals 65 years of age or older who are patients in public institutions for mental diseases, show that the State is making satisfactory progress toward developing and implementing a comprehensive mental health program, including provision for utilization of community mental health centers, nursing homes, and other alternatives to care in public institutions for mental diseases; and

"(22) include descriptions of (A) the kinds and numbers of professional medical personnel and supporting staff that will be used in the administration of the plan and of the responsibilities they will have, (B) the standards, for private or public institutions in which recipients of medical assistance under the plan may receive care or services, that will be utilized by the State authority or authorities responsible for establishing and maintaining such standards, (C) the cooperative arrangements with State health agencies and State vocational rehabilitation agencies entered into with a view to maximum utilization of and coordination of the provision of medical assistance with the services administered or supervised by such agencies, and (D) other standards and methods that the State will use to assure that medical or remedial care and services provided to recipients of medical assistance are of high quality.

Notwithstanding paragraph (5), if on January 1, 1965, and on the date on which a State submits its plan for approval under this title, the Stage agency which administered or supervised the administration of the plan of such State approved under title X (or title XVI, insofar as it relates to the blind) was different from the State agency which administered or supervised the administration of the State plan approved under title I (or title XVI, insofar as it relates to the aged), the State agency which administered or supervised the administration of such plan approved under title X (or title XVI, insofar as it relates to the blind) may be designated to administer or supervise the administration of the portion of the State plan for medical assistance which relates to blind individuals and a different State agency may be established or designated to administer or supervise the administration of the rest of the State plan for medical assistance; and in such case the part of the plan which each such agency administers, or the administration of which each such agency supervises, shall be regarded as a separate plan for purposes of this title (except for purposes of paragraph (10)).

"(b) The Secretary shall approve any plan which fulfills the conditions specified in subsection (a), except that he shall not approve any plan which imposes, as a condition of eligibility for medical assistance under the plan—

"(1) an age requirement of more than 65 years; or

"(2) effective July 1, 1967, any age requirement which excludes any individual who has not attained the age of 21 and is or would, except for the provisions of section 406(a) (2), be a dependent child under title IV; or

"(3) any residence requirement which excludes any individual who resides in the State; or

"(4) any citizenship requirement which excludes any citizen of the United States.

"(c) Notwithstanding subsection (b), the Secretary shall not approve any State plan for medical assistance if he determines that the approval and operation of the plan will result in a reduction in aid or assistance (other than so much of the aid or assistance as is provided for under the plan of the State approved under this title) provided for eligible individuals under a plan of such State approved under title I, IV, X, XIV, or XVI.

*   *   *

"*DEFINITIONS*

"*Sec. 1905.* For purposes of this title—

"(a) The term 'medical assistance' means payment of part or all of the cost of the following care and services (if provided in or after the third month before the month in which the recipient makes application for assistance) for individuals who are—

"(i) under the age of 21,

"(ii) relatives specified in section 406(b) (1) with whom a child is living if such child, except for section 406(a) (2), is (or would, if needy, be) a dependent child under title IV,

"(iii) 65 years of age or older,

"(iv) blind, or

"(v) 18 years of age or older and permanently and totally disabled, but whose income and resources are insufficient to meet all of such cost—

"(1) inpatient hospital services (other than services in an institution for tuberculosis or mental diseases);

"(2) outpatient hospital services;

"(3) other laboratory and X-ray services;

"(4) skilled nursing home services (other than services in an institution for tuberculosis or mental diseases) for individuals 21 years of age or older;

"(5) physicians' services, whether furnished in the office, the patient's home, a hospital, or a skilled nursing home, or elsewhere;

"(6) medical care, or any other type of remedial care recognized under State law, furnished by licensed practitioners within the scope of their practice as defined by State law;

"(7) home health care services;

"(8) private duty nursing services;

"(9) clinic services;

"(10) dental services;

"(11) physical therapy and related services;

"(12) prescribed drugs, dentures, and prosthetic devices; and eyeglasses prescribed by a physician skilled in diseases of the eye or by an optometrist, whichever the individual may select;

"(13) other diagnostic, screening, preventive, and rehabilitative services;

"(14) inpatient hospital services and skilled nursing home services for individuals 65 years or age or over in an institution for tuberculosis or mental diseases; and

"(15) any other medical care, and any other type of remedial care recognized under State law, specified by the Secretary;

*   *   *

Part 3 — Public Assistance Amendments Relating to Health Care

REMOVAL OF LIMITATIONS ON FEDERAL PARTICIPATION IN ASSISTANCE TO INDIVIDUALS WITH TUBERCULOSIS OR MENTAL DISEASE

*   *   *

TITLE III — SOCIAL SECURITY AMENDMENTS

SHORT TITLE

Sec. 300. This title may be cited as the "Old-Age, Survivors, and Disability Insurance Amendments of 1965".

INCREASE IN OLD-AGE, SURVIVORS, AND DISABILITY INSURANCE BENEFITS

Sec. 301. (a) Section 215(a) of the Social Security Act is amended by striking out the table and inserting in lieu thereof the following:

"TABLE FOR DETERMINING PRIMARY INSURANCE AMOUNT AND MAXIMUM FAMILY BENEFITS

*   *   *

DISABILITY INSURANCE BENEFITS

Sec. 303. (a) (1) Clause (A) of the first sentence of section 216(i) (1) of the Social Security Act is amended by striking out "or to be of long-continued and indefinite duration" and inserting in lieu thereof "or has lasted or can be expected to last for a continuous period of not less than 12 months".

*   *   *

(b) Section 3101 of the Internal Revenue Code of 1954 (relating to rate of tax on employees under the Federal Insurance Contributions Act) is amended to read as follows:

"SEC. 3101. RATE OF TAX.

"(a) *Old-age, Survivors, and Disability Insurance.* — In addition to other taxes, there is hereby imposed on the income of every individual a tax equal to the following percentages of the wages (as defined in section 3121(a)) received by him with respect to employment (as defined in section 3121(b))—

"(1) with respect to wages received during the calendar year 1966, the rate shall be 3.85 percent;

"(2) with respect to wages received during the calendar years 1967 and 1968, the rate shall be 3.9 percent;

"(3) with respect to wages received during the calendar years 1969, 1970, 1971, and 1972, the rate shall be 4.4 percent; and

"(4) with respect to wages received after December 31, 1972, the rate shall be 4.85 percent.

"(b.) *Hospital Insurance.*— In addition to the tax imposed by the preceding subsection, there is hereby imposed on the income of every individual a tax equal to the following percentages of the wages (as defined in section 3121(a)) received by him with respect to employment (as defined in section 3121(b), but without regard to the provisions of paragraph (9) thereof insofar as it relates to employees)—

"(1) with respect to wages received during the calendar year 1966, the rate shall be 0.35 percent;

"(2) with respect to wages received during the calendar years 1967, 1968, 1969, 1970, 1971, and 1972, the rate shall be 0.50 percent;

"(3) with respect to wages received during the calendar years 1973, 1974, and 1975, the rate shall be 0.55 percent;

"(4) with respect to wages received during the calendar years 1976, 1977, 1978, and 1979, the rate shall be 0.60 percent;

"(5) with respect to wages received during the calendar years 1980, 1981, 1982, 1983, 1984, 1985, and 1986, the rate shall be 0.70 percent; and

"(6) with respect to wages received after December 31, 1986, the rate shall be 0.80 percent."

(c) Section 3111 of the Internal Revenue Code of 1954 (relating to rate of tax on employers under the Federal Insurance Contributions Act) is amended to read as follows:

"*SEC. 3111. RATE OF TAX.* "(a) *Old-Age, Survivors, and Disability Insurance.* — In addition to other taxes, there is hereby imposed on every employer an excise tax, with respect to having individuals in his employ, equal to the following percentages of the wages (as defined in section 3121(a)) paid by him with respect to employment (as defined in section 3121(b))—

"(1) with respect to wages paid during the calendar year 1966, the rate shall be 3.85 percent;

*　　*　　*

TITLE IV—PUBLIC ASSISTANCE AMENDMENTS

INCREASED FEDERAL PAYMENTS UNDER PUBLIC ASSISTANCE TITLES OF THE SOCIAL SECURITY ACT

Sec. 401. (a) Section 3 (a) of the Social Security Act is amended (1) by striking out, in so much thereof as precedes clause (A), "during such quarter" and inserting in lieu thereof "during each month of such quarter"; (2) by striking out, in clause (A), "29/35", "any month", and "$35" and inserting in lieu thereof "31/37", "such month", and "$37", respectively; and (3) by striking out clauses (B) and (C) and inserting in lieu thereof the following:

"(B) the larger of the following:

"(i) (I) the Federal percentage (as defined in section 1101(a) (8)) of the amount by which such expenditures exceed the amount which may be counted under clause (A), not counting so much of such excess with respect to such month as exceeds the product of $38 multiplied by the total number of recipients of old-age assistance for such month, plus (II) 15 per centum of the total expended during such month as old-age assistance under the State plan in the form of medical or any other type of remedial care, not counting so much of such expenditure with respect to such month as exceeds the product of $15 multiplied by the total number of recipients of old-age assistance for such month, or

"(ii) (I) the Federal medical percentage (as defined in section 6(c)) of the amount by which such expenditures exceed the maximum which may be counted under clause (A), not counting so much of any expenditures with respect to such month as exceeds (a) the product of $52 multiplied by the total number of such recipients of old-age assistance for such month, or (b) if smaller, the total expended as old-age assistance in the form of medical or any other type of remedial care with respect to such month plus the product of $37 multiplied by such total number of such recipients, plus (II) the Federal percentage of the amount by which the total expended during such month as old-age assistance under the State plan exceeds the amount which may be counted under clause (A) and the preceding provisions of this clause (B) (ii), not counting so much of such excess with respect to such month as exceeds the product of $38 multiplied by the total number of such recipients of old-age assistance for such month;".

(c) Section 403(a) (1) of such Act is amended (1) by striking out "fourteen-seventeenths" and "$17" in clause (A) and inserting in lieu thereof "five-sixths" and "$18", respectively; and (2) by striking out "$30" in clause (B) and inserting in lieu thereof "$32".

(d) Section 1003 (a) (1) of such Act is amended (1) by striking out, in clause (A), "29/35" and "$35" and inserting in lieu thereof "31/37" and "$37", respectively; and (2) by striking out, in clause (B), "$70" and inserting in lieu thereof "$75".

(e) Section 1403 (a) (1) of such Act is amended (1) by striking out, in clause (A), "29/35" and "$35" and inserting in lieu thereof "31/37" and "$37", respectively; and (2) by striking out, in clause (B), "$70" and inserting in lieu thereof "$75".

*   *   *

DISREGARDING CERTAIN EARNINGS IN DETERMINING NEED UNDER ASSISTANCE PROGRAMS FOR THE AGED, BLIND, AND DISABLED

Sec. 403. (a) Effective October 1, 1965, section 2(a) (10) (A) of the Social Security Act is amended by striking out"; except that, in making such determination, of the first $50 per month of earned income the State agency may disregard, after December 31, 1962, not more than the first $10 thereof plus one-half of the remainder" and inserting in lieu thereof the following: "; except that, in making such determination, (i) the State agency may disregard not more than $5 per month of any income and (ii) of the first $80 per month of additional income which is earned the State agency may disregard not more than the first $20 thereof plus one-half of the remainder".

The President also wanted to plan for the increased demand for medical services and to placate the AMA at the same time.

Presidential Statement Announcing Plans for the White House Conference on Health
(August 13, 1965)*

We must constantly protect and improve the health of our people. The time has come to call upon our best scientific and administrative talents to help chart the future in this critical area. I hope that this Conference will formulate guidelines for developing creative programs that will bring better health to every American. The mandate of this Conference will not stop at the water's edge. I will call upon it to help develop international goals in the field of health.

Note: The statement was read by Bill D. Moyers, Special Assistant to the President, at his news conference at Austin, Tex., at 4 p.m. on Friday, August 13, 1965. It was not made public in the form of a White House press release.

In making the announcement Mr. Moyers added that the Conference would be held November 30 – December 1, 1965. He stated that Dr. George W. Beadle, President of the University of Chicago, would serve as Chairman, and that Boisfeuillet Jones, President of the Woodruff Foundation of Atlanta and

**Ibid.* p. 880.

former Special Assistant to the Secretary of Health, Education, and Welfare, would serve as Executive Vice Chairman.

President Johnson forgot few in his "fence-mending." He celebrated the thirtieth anniversary of social security with enthusiasm, and he reminded the younger voters, who were to pay for the new programs, how much they too would benefit.

Presidential Statement Commemorating the Thirtieth Anniversary of the Signing of the Social Security Act
(August 15, 1965)*

Thirty years ago yesterday—August 14, 1935—President Franklin D. Roosevelt signed into law the Social Security Act—an act which was to bring a better life to many millions of Americans then living and to countless generations yet unborn.

For millions of Americans the enactment of this legislation meant the beginning of a new era of hope and confidence, and the end of an era of bleak and bitter despair.

We pause now to remember that moment of great social renewal and to honor the memory of the man whose moral and political leadership brought this act into being, and who committed the Nation to the proposition that the man or woman who had labored over a lifetime was entitled to the grace and dignity of self-support in old age.

This anniversary is one of deep significance in the history of this country. For the act that was created on that August day, 30 years ago, became the foundation of a great new social structure built by all the people of this country for the protection of all the people.

— Here was the beginning of the world's largest social insurance program which today pays out benefits to more than 20 million people — the aged, the disabled, the widowed, and orphaned.

— Here were the social insurance programs which now provide a base on which our people can build, through their initiative, thrift, and hard work, the elements of a good life.

— Here was the start of our nationwide unemployment insurance program—a partnership of Federal and State Governments to protect workers and their families during periods of temporary joblessness.

— Here were the first threads of today's broad network of State and local public welfare agencies which, with the help of Federal funds, serve the blind, the destitute, the aged, and especially the needy children of this land.

Ibid., p. 880.

The 1935 law laid the foundation for all of these measures which are so vital to the strength of American society.

We are still building, still improving that great social structure that was started three decades ago.

Two weeks ago, in Independence, Mo., in the presence of President Harry Truman, another social pioneer, I signed the amendments that this Congress—the great 89th Congress—has fashioned for this law to help shield our elderly people from the economic burdens of illness and to update our social security programs in many other ways.

But we know, as President Roosevelt knew and said 30 years ago, that this structure is not yet complete. It will continue to grow as our needs grow—a living monument to the American ideal of health, prosperity, and happiness for all.

Some of these needs are clear to us today, and have been translated into national goals. Among these are:

— first, the assurance of a level of income for every citizen of this Nation who is too young or too old to work, or has become physically or mentally disabled, or who is unable to find work that is sufficient to assure health and decency.

— second, the rehabilitation for gainful employment of every disabled person for whom such rehabilitation is possible.

— third, opportunity for the pursuit of meaningful civic, cultural, and recreational activities in the retirement years.

These are immediate national goals for improved social well-being. We are working to fulfill them today. At the same time we know there will be other needs tomorrow.

This great, living law allows us to respond, as a Nation, to meet those needs. It is the instrument of a democratic society, engaged in a great and historic effort to secure the well-being and happiness of all of its people.

Presidential Statement Making Public a Report
on Benefits Available to Young People Under the
Social Security Act Amendments of 1965
(September 8, 1965)*

The Social Security Amendments of 1965, which provide urgently needed health insurance plans for the aged, reflect this administration's concern for the well-being of our more than 18 million older citizens.

Just as importantly, this historic legislation provides significant new and improved services and benefits for millions of our young people, from neglected infants to the sons and daughters of low-income families who are

*Ibid., p. 984.

working their way through college. Most importantly, it can do much to help eliminate sickness and disability as causes of lifelong poverty.

Because, as I have often said, our children are our most precious national resource, I want to call special attention to the many services and benefits available to young people—especially the children of the poor—under the new amendments. The Secretary of Health, Education, and Welfare has provided the attached summary of these provisions.

As Secretary Gardner has emphasized in a letter to the Governors of all the States, many of these additional benefits and services can be made available to those who need them only if the States take advantage of the Federal assistance offered by this legislation for the improvement of State health and welfare programs. I want to urge State and local officials in every part of the Nation to take prompt action to bring these benefits to the young people who hold in their hands the future well-being of our society.

1966

Unemployment Compensation

The story of the attempt at a wholesale reform of unemployment compensation began in 1965. On May 18 of that year, President Johnson sent a special message to Congress concerning labor and including a renewed call for revising the unemployment compensation programs.

On the following day Representative Mills introduced H.R. 8282, which embodied the Administration's proposals. Senator Eugene McCarthy introduced the same legislation as S. 1991 in the Senate. The bill provided for wide-ranging changes within the unemployment compensation system, but included a controversial section setting federal standards for the level and duration of state unemployment benefits. The bill also extended coverage to an additional 4.7 million workers and eliminated the "experience rating" tax reduction provision which allowed states to tax employers at a level determined by the experience of the particular employer or the posted experience of all employers, or through a combination of the two. The most politically explosive provision, Title II, revised the tax rates for unemployment compensation, and raised the tax base to OASDI level.

These changes were introduced by proposing two new titles for the social security legislation. Title XX established a "Federal Unemployment Adjustment Benefits Program"; Title XXI provided "Matching Grants for Excess Cost."

At the hearing state unemployment compensation officials objected to compulsory federal standards which would diminish the authority of the state agencies. Other opponents of the bill were various business groups, such as the Ohio Chamber of Commerce whose representative concluded with the observation that "doles and handouts will not vitalize the economy."

Secretary of Labor Willard Wirtz testified in support of the bill. He particularly stressed the programs for social workers' training, child welfare services, handicapped children, maternal and child health, and child dental care.

Various other Administration officials testified: Stanley Surrey, Assistant Secretary for Tax Policy, of the Treasury Department, appeared in connection with the suggested tax changes for elderly persons; Robert Ball, Commissioner for Social Security, explained the proposals for OASDHI. However, when the exhaustive hearings were completed, the Ways and Means Committee tabled any further action on H.R. 8282 for that year.

When Congress reconvened the following January, the Administration once again called for congressional action providing improvements in the unemployment compensation system. The Ways and Means Committee took no immediate action but decided to schedule two more days of public hearings in March before going into executive session to work out acceptable legislation. Although testimony was heard on March 15 and 16 it was not until June 17 that a clean bill, H.R. 15119, was finally reported out of the committee, including few of the proposals which the Administration considered necessary. The bill eliminated the controversial section establishing minimum federal standards for state unemployment compensation programs and substantially cut back on extension of coverage. It also retained the "experience rating" system which allowed substantial tax deductions for certain employers. Extended benefits were reduced from a twenty-six- to a thirteen-week period, during periods of recessions only. A provision was added to allow appeals to state courts in order to challenge Labor Department findings that state programs were operated contrary to federal regulations. The committee report included a concurring statement by seven of the eight Republican committeemen calling H.R. 15119 a sound bill because of its protection of state sovereignty.

The committee had eliminated most of the opposition to the bill by deleting all the controversial provisions. The main complaint was that the bill fell far short of the real needs of the unemployed. The removal of the standards provision caused criticism by several members during the debates, as did the elimination of the provision extending coverage to farmers. Such protests were to no avail. On June 22, the House overwhelmingly passed H.R. 15119 without amendments and with very little debate.

H.R. 15119 was then sent to the Senate, where the Finance Committee called hearings for the middle of July to consider both the House bill and the original Administration bill (S. 1991). Again Secretary of Labor Willard Wirtz was the first witness to appear. He advocated liberalization of almost every section of H.R. 15119 in line with the Administration's original proposals.

The witnesses for business interests who had opposed the original Ad-

ministration proposals now testified to support the bill which had passed the House, H.R. 15119.

Organized labor opposed the bill as totally inadequate. George Meany, President of the AFL-CIO, appeared and urged adoption of the Administration's original proposals rather than H.R. 15119, calling the latter a "completely unsatisfactory measure." At the conclusion of the union leader's testimony, Chairman Russell Long of Lousiana turned to him and said, ". . . I want to thank you for what I think is a truly great statement." This was a fair indication of the liberalization of the measure subsequently enacted by the Finance Committee.

When the bill was reported out by the committee, several of the Administration's original proposals had been reinserted. The most controversial section of the bill—providing federal standards for state programs—was again included. The Senate report discussed this change, along with the other provisions adopted by the Finance Committee and included a minority statement by six Republican members.

Unemployment Insurance Amendments of 1965
Senate Report No. 1425
89th Cong., 2d Sess. (July 28, 1966)

II. Summary of Committee Amendments

The Committee on Finance amended the House bill in six respects. Four of these, relating to benefit standards, extended benefits, coverage of small firms, and the taxable wage base, involve substantive changes. The fifth and sixth committee amendments are technical changes. They insure benefits for individuals engaged in multistate employment and provide uniform duration for extended benefits triggered by a national "on" indicator. These six amendments are outlined in this part. They are described more fully in other parts of this report.

(a) Benefit requirements. — The committee added benefit standards to the requirements of the Federal Unemployment Tax Act (FUTA) which must be complied with by the States if their employers are to receive the full Federal tax credit of 2.7 percent. The standards relate to benefit amount, duration, and eligibility.

  1. *Benefit amount.* — The amount of unemployment compensation payable must be at least 50 percent of the individual's average weekly wage up to 50 percent of the State average wage.

  2. *Duration.* — Benefits must be payable for at least 26 weeks to each individual who had 20 weeks of employment (or its equivalent).

3. *Eligibility.* — No worker may be required to have more than 20 weeks of employment (or its equivalent) in his base period to qualify for benefits.

(b) Extended benefits. — The structure of the House extended benefit plan is retained but the financing provisions are modified so that the Federal Government will pay the entire cost out of the Federal portion of the unemployment tax. Under the House bill the cost of this program would have been shared equally by the Federal Government and the States.

(c) Tax rate and wage base. — The Federal unemployment tax rate increase to 3.3 percent (from 3.1 percent) provided by the House bill is retained. However, the wage base increase to $3,900 is made effective for 1968 rather than 1969, as under the House bill, and the further increase in the wage base in 1972, under the committee amendment, is to $4,800 rather than to $4,200.

(d) Small firms. — The House provision extending coverage to employers of one or more workers during each of 20 weeks in a calendar year or employers with payrolls of $1,500 in a calendar quarter was deleted by the Committee on Finance. By this action, the provision of present law which limits coverage to employers of four or more workers during each of 20 weeks in a calendar year is retained.

H.R. 15119 was called for Senate debate on August 5, with Senator Russell Long acting as the floor manager of the bill. The most interesting aspect of the discussion was undoubtedly the parliamentary maneuvering it entailed.

Senator Long introduced the controversial federal standards amendment and noted that there were four requirements: (a) state law could not require more than twenty weeks of employment to qualify for benefits; (b) unemployment compensation benefits had to be equal to at least one-half of the individual's average weekly wage or the state maximum weekly benefit amount, whichever was less; (c) eligibility for receipt of benefits had to last a minimum of twenty-six weeks; (d) the state maximum benefit amount had to equal at least 50 per cent of the state-wide average weekly wage.

Senator Long precipitated the controversy by requesting unanimous consent that the four standards be voted on separately. When opposition arose, he forced a division of the question, causing separate votes to be taken on each standard.

The Senate adopted the first and least controversial requirement of the four proposed by the committee, by a vote of 44 – 39 (17 not voting). The floor leader then submitted the second committee amendment. Since forty-eight of the fifty states already paid minimum benefits meeting this standard, and the other two states, California and Massachusetts, would have to make adjustments of less than one-quarter of 1 per cent, there was little controversy over this proposal. With only a few minutes of discussion, the amendment was adopted.

Next, Senator Long called for passage of the amendment establishing a minimum of twenty-six weeks of benefits. By unanimous consent, the Senate amended this to exclude seasonal workers and after only a few minutes of debate, the proposal was defeated 38–44 (18 not voting).

The Senator reacted to his defeat by re-introducing the same provision in the form of an entirely new amendment but it was again rejected. Realizing that a favorable vote was not possible at the moment, Senator Long took the floor and moved for adjournment. The complicated parliamentary maneuvering continued when the Senate resumed debate on H.R. 15119 on August 8. After considering and adopting several committee amendments dealing with the financing of the programs, Senator Thruston Morton of Kentucky then offered a substitute amendment which was almost identical to the bill that had passed the House on June 22. Debate on that proposal ended with its rejection by a roll call vote of 36–51.

Senator Long followed with a revised edition of the federal standards proposal which called for the same twenty-six weeks of benefits, but increased the minimum duration of employment to thirty-nine weeks. This satisfied those opponents who had objected to paying benefits for more weeks than the number of required work weeks and the Long plan was then adopted.

Subsequent amendments restored the Finance Committee language and provided for minimum benefits and reduction of federal contributions when states failed to comply with the federal standards.

The bill as amended passed the Senate on August 8 by a 53–31 margin. There were no federal standards in the House version of the bill, so there were certain to be difficulties when the Conference Committee convened to work out a final version of the legislation.

It was over two months later that the House finally appointed members from the Ways and Means Committee to act as conferees. This long delay was probably the result of two factors. First, the House was strongly opposed to any bill that included federal standards for state unemployment compensation programs. By refusing to appoint conferees, no federal standards could be imposed, and the longer the delay, the more willing the Senate would be to drop the federal standards provision. Second, the conferees had to be appointed from the Ways and Means Committee, but these representatives were already pressed for time because of action on several other pieces of tax legislation.

The House finally appointed its conferees on October 12, only ten days before the Congress was to adjourn. The committee was unable to agree to any compromise and the bill finally died in conference.

Public Assistance and OASDHI

Although no major social security bills were enacted in 1966, one proposal did become law by being attached as a rider to the Tax Adjustment Act. The amendment struck a major blow at the philosophy of a contributory OASDHI program by calling for general blanketing in as well as for a subsidy to the trust fund out of general revenues.

The proposal was originally introduced on March 8 and caused immediate controversy on the Senate floor. It would have provided for minimum monthly benefits of $44 to all persons over seventy years of age who were not then eligible for OASDI benefits. Senator Prouty estimated the cost of his proposal at $600 million annually, to be paid out of the trust fund, which would then be reimbursed by general revenues. (This was by no means Senator Prouty's first attempt to enact such a provision. When the 1965 social security amendments were being debated, the Vermont Republican offered the same proposal, which was then overwhelmingly defeated.) One of the ironic aspects of the new program was that it was attached to a tax bill designed to raise revenue for the war in Vietnam. Many Senators opposed the amendment because it made no sense to pass a bill raising revenue for the war, and providing additional Social Security benefits to be paid out of the money raised by the new tax.

Senator Long led the fight against the proposal and moved to have it tabled but he was unsuccessful and the amendment was passed.

However, the Senator was not satisfied, and he temporarily blocked Senator Prouty's attempt to have the last recorded vote reconsidered, which is the customary parliamentary procedure for making a vote final. Once he obtained the floor, Senator Long refused to yield and instead repeated his earlier arguments against the amendment.

Eventually Senator Mike Mansfield of Montana moved to reconsider the earlier vote, and Senator Prouty moved to table Mansfield's motion, bringing the Prouty proposal again before the Senate for a vote. This time a one vote margin in favor of the plan attached the legislation as a rider to the tax bill.

When the bill went to conference, the Prouty Amendment was considerably modified, although the basic provision remained and was subsequently adopted by both houses. Only those persons who would be seventy-two before 1968 and who were not receiving public assistance payments were blanketed in. The benefits were $35 a month for a single person or head of a household and $17.50 for a spouse and unless the insured had three quarters of coverage the benefits would be paid out of the general revenues rather than the trust fund. These changes meant that instead of covering eighteen million persons at a cost of $790 million, only 370,000 benefited at a cost of $95 million.

The Prouty Amendment was a hint that OASDHI and public assistance were merging rather than drifting apart. However, public assistance was increasingly under attack. The Advisory Council on Public Welfare pub-lished its report and its recommendations in June, and its recommendations were typical of a different approach towards income security.

Having the Power, We have the Duty
Report of Advisory Council on Public Welfare
(Submitted to the Secretary of Health, Education, and Welfare)
June, 1966

The Council's Recommendations

Only comprehensive nationwide protections can meet this challenge. The Council, therefore, recommends the addition of a title to the Social Security Act to provide, in cooperation with the States, a new nationwide program of basic social guarantees on the following basis:

1. General Proposal

The new program would require that adequate financial aid and social services be available to all who need them as a matter of right. To make this possible a new pattern of Federal-State cooperation is proposed. The Federal Government would set nationwide standards, adjusted by objective criteria to varying costs and conditions among the States, and assume the total cost of their implementation above a stipulated State share. The States would thus be freed to concentrate their efforts on meeting human needs, relieved of the present multiple Federal program requirements and the constant pressure to find new sources of State financing. The required components for participation in this new program are described below.

2. Assistance Standards

A floor of required individual or family income would be established for each State in terms of the cost of a modest but adequate family budget for families of various sizes and circumstances as established by objective methods of budget costing. This would constitute the minimum level of assistance which must prevail in that State.

3. Eligibility for Aid

All persons with available income falling below this established budget level would be entitled to receive aid to the extent of that deficiency. Need would be the sole measure of entitlement and irrevelant exclusions such as those based on age, family composition or situation, degree of disability presumption of income not actually available to the applicant, low earning capacity, filial responsibility, or alleged employability would not conform with requirements of this program. Provision for immediate emergency aid when needed would also be required.

4. Eligibility Determination

Applicants for aid would establish their initial eligibility by personal statements or simple inquiry relating to their financial situation and family composition, subject only to subsequent sample review conducted in such manner as to protect their dignity, privacy, and constitutional rights.

5. Child and Youth Welfare Services

The Federal Government would also specify the required components for child and youth welfare services to be included within the comprehensive new program. These would include protective and social services for children in a vulnerable situation, foster care placement in homes and institutions at reasonable rates of reimbursement, adoptive placement services, services to unmarried mothers, homemaker services, day care, other types of group service, provisions for specialized institutional care, probation and school social service (where not otherwise available), special programs for young people, and services related to the licensing of nongovernmental programs. Special provisions would be required for young people coming to the attention of authorities for unlawful or antisocial acts or believed to be vulnerable to such activity.

It is the goal of the Council that adequate child welfare services should be available to all children in need of them as a matter of enforceable legal right. Recognizing, however, the practical difficulty of assuring the universal availability of a full range of services immediately, it is recommended that the Federal Government distinguish between services which must be available to all eligible children and those which may be included in the comprehensive program on a progressively expanding basis within the same financing pattern.

6. Other Social Services

The comprehensive State plan would also include other specified social services for families, older persons, individuals with special problems relating to health or other handicaps, and for a better ordering of community social resources. Again a distinction would be made between those to which individuals would be entitled by legal right on the basis of universal availability and those approved for inclusion within the State plan on a basis of progressive coverage. Examples of such social services would include the following: neighborhood advice and referral centers; services to assist the aged and home-bound in meeting their medical, housing, recreational, social and activity needs; supportive services for mothers with special problems; social services related to health needs including family planning; services to advance employability—including aid in moving to new locations promising employment opportunity; and community planning services.

7. Legal Rights

Entitlement to all benefits and services within this program would be protected by the following legally enforceable rights: (1) the right to apply and receive prompt, objective, and impartial determination of eligibility for and provision of benefit or service, (2) the right to be given a fair hearing against unacceptable judgments, by an impartial appeals agent, (3) the right to representation in appeals, by an attorney whose services and costs would be compensated by the agency if not otherwise provided for, (4) the right to court review, and (5) the obligation on the agency to publicize the conditions of entitlement to all benefits and services. The right to services would be conditioned on the need for service rather than income level.

8. Personnel

Because the fulfillment of all these objectives depends upon a dramatic increase in the present limited national pool of professional social workers, social work aides, and related auxiliary personnel, special legislation for Federal financial aid to encourage and expand the training of such workers is essential to this plan.

9. States' Share

The State's share in the financing of this comprehensive program would be established each year on a total dollar basis determined by objective criteria related to its fiscal capacity and effort.

10. Federal Share

For States operating under this program of basic social guarantees the Federal Government would assume the full financial responsibility for the difference in cost between the State's share and the total cost of the new program. This constitutes in effect a revolutionary reversal of roles of the Federal and State governments in the financing pattern. Under the present system it is assumed that the primary responsibility for determining the scope, level of benefits, and financing of the various components of a public welfare program rests with the States. Under the new proposal national standards of performance would be recognized as calling for an equivalent national assumption of financial responsibility by the Federal Government. Within this pattern, since no differentials would be applied among types of expenditures, Federal auditing would be limited to actual expenditures and program performance in terms of required Federal standards. States would, of course, be required either to finance their share by State funds or to make comparable financial arrangements with their political subdivisions to assure equitable and universal standards throughout the State.

11. Interim Option

States not yet prepared to participate in the new nationwide program could continue on a transitional but limited interim basis to operate under the existing titles. States' rights and State options would thus be protected during the period of accommodation but the fiscal, policy, and administrative advantages to the States of a plan which fixes and limits their total financial obligation in relationship to their fiscal capacity would be a powerful incentive to cooperate in this new plan of partnership. The simplification of accounting, reporting, and audit procedure alone would eliminate many of the complexities and confusions that presently plague Federal-State relationships.

The Advisory Council's recommendation for some form of guaranteed income supported the National Commission on Technology, Automation, and Economic Progress which had endorsed a national income maintenance program earlier in 1966. In addition, a paper by Wilbur Cohen, Undersecretary of Health, Education, and Welfare, called for adoption of a program assuring a minimum income to all and suggested other income maintenance proposals for the future. It seemed as if 1967 might be the year for real change, but President Johnson chose to harness the energies of the American people to fight an extensive war in Southeast Asia.

Almost all of the legislation submitted to Congress to change social security programs stimulated considerable controversy before it was adopted or rejected. The Medicare plan passed in 1965 was one of the most controversial pieces of legislation ever considered by Congress, yet there were numerous bills to amend it even before it went into effect. One revision did pass both houses with little opposition. The Medicare Extension Bill offered by the President, simply extended the deadline for persons to sign up for the program by two months. This would allow an additional 1.3 million persons to sign up for the doctor's fee-reimbursement feature of Medicare.

On October 12, in a speech at the Social Security Administration headquarters in Baltimore, President Johnson revealed the specific proposals he would ask Congress to enact. Among his suggestions was a 10 per cent average increase for all social security recipients.

Presidential Remarks at the Social Security Administration Headquarters
(October 12, 1966)*

Ladies and Gentlemen:

I am delighted to be here in Baltimore and to see on the platform a good many of my old and trusted friends.

Congressman Long came over here ahead of us, I think, because he wanted me to introduce him instead of Secretary Gardner. Congressman, we are delighted to have you and appreciate your meeting us here.

*Weekly Compilation of Presidential Documents, Vol. 2, No. 41, p. 1458–61.

I am almost as happy to be in the neighborhood of Baltimore as 54,000 Oriole fans were last Sunday.

But contrary to some rumors, I am not here to scout Dave McNally for the Washington Senators.

I came here this morning to discuss the very brilliant record of the social security system and to offer to the Nation and the world information about important proposals that your President will make concerning its future.

I want to pay a special tribute to one of the greatest Cabinet officers of all time—even if he is a Republican—John Gardner, the Secretary of Health, Education, and Welfare.

And Under Secretary Wilbur Cohen who has carried a very heavy load in this field through the years.

I want to pay a very special tribute to Commissioner Ball. When I commended him, I commended the thousands of dedicated, tireless social security employees who have served him diligently, capably, and well.

A few weeks ago, I heard a lot of dire predictions about how the system would fail when we inaugurated the new program. I have never seen such faultless administration. To each of you, whether you are at the bottom of the grade or at the top of the list, I want to say that your President appreciates the job that you have done and wants to publicly commend you for it.

Thirty years ago, President Franklin D. Roosevelt asked the Congress and the country to support him in the first social security legislation that America had ever passed. At that time I was a young man working as a Congressman's secretary in Washington. I remember that that proposal set off what we call down in Texas a "battle royal." There were prominent members of Congress who claimed that "social security meant socialism."

One of my most vivid memories is of the day—in 1935, when I had not yet become a Member of Congress, but was working there—when I stood in the Speaker's office urging the Congressman I worked for to say "yes" to the social security roll call when it was to be voted on a few minutes later in the House. He had reservations about the bill and its future, but he voted "aye." I have always been proud of that action.

But others did not vote "aye." Others voted to kill it through recommittal and some voted against it even on the final roll call. That seems impossible to believe in this year 1966 but it was easy to believe in 1935 and 1936.

Led by seven minority members of the Ways and Means Committee, the minority on this social security issue branded this vital bill "a crushing burden on industry and labor." They claimed that it would "destroy old age retirement systems set up in private industry."

They voted to recommit the bill. That is the way those of us who are against something try to kill it—to recommit it. That is a fancy term that the average layman doesn't understand. That is a politician's parliamentary device to stick a dagger in its heart. I think you can understand that.

That vote in the House of Representatives that day was 253 to oppose recommitment on the floor and send it back to 149. Then, they tried to hide their vote – the 149 that had voted to kill it – by helping to pass it. When they pulled back the curtain and let a little sunshine come in, and the vote was whether you are for or against social security, the vote on final passage was not 253 to 149 but it was 372 to 33.

When President Roosevelt signed that bill, he called it "the cornerstone in a structure which is by no means complete."

And how right he was – as he was on so many other matters, as we have seen.

In my 30 years, we have moved again and again to strengthen and expand social security. We broadened the coverage. We extended the benefits to widows, orphans and the disabled. And finally, after a 20-year struggle, we established a new social security landmark. Today, Medicare offers 19 million older Americans freedom from the nagging fear that illness will bankrupt them or their children.

This time, I had the privilege of leading that fight. I found myself pleading, not with one man but with many, to say "yes" to Medicare.

We had talked about it in our speeches and our platforms for more than 20 years but we had never gotten it reported from a committee.

And somehow I had the strange feeling that it had all happened before.

The "nay-sayers" dusted off their old speeches of 30 years ago. They revised them and rewrote them. But they said about the same thing – fear.

Once again they talked about socialism: about the destruction of free enterprise.

One minority Member of Congress – the minority on the Medicare issue – said it was "a political hodgepodge."

That was not designed to help the bill.

And a tired old voice from the past branded Medicare "a cruel hoax."

Once again they dusted off the old recommit weapon – to kill the bill by returning it to the committee. And the vote in the House was 236 to 191. And Medicare passed, 313 to 115.

And if the good Lord lets me live, I am going to spread the word out and let the information leak out all over this country about this parliamentary device called recommit.

Today, social security and Medicare stand as two of the most historic programs ever enacted by any Congress. They stand as two of the most far-reaching programs ever carried out by any governmental agency.

Every one of you has joined in this great drama. You can feel pride over what you have done for your country.

You have done it without regard to party just as many members of both parties voted for the passage of the bill and members of both parties voted against it.

But those who brought social security into the legislative history of this country and those who added Medicare to it, their children's children can always be proud of that role of honor to which they affixed their names.

I am not going to call the names of those who voted against social security or voted against Medicare, because we don't want to bring up unpleasant memories or deal in personalities.

This is no time to spend our talents on past subjects or failures. This is a day that we must look ahead—look ahead to the unfinished business of this country.

Far too many social security beneficiaries today—not only older citizens, but their widows and orphans and the disabled—are trying to live off of too little income.

Far too many citizens on social security—more than one-third of the total—exist on incomes below the poverty line. Most of them have social security as a main source of income. For some, it happens to be their only source of income.

The business of insuring a decent and dignified life for all of our citizens should be the unfinished business of all of our people.

The need for revision of social security and other benefits for the aged people of America has been widely felt by members of both parties in this country.

Last July the 10th the Republican National Committee released a 10-point program entitled "A Republican Approach to the Needs of the Aging." Four points were directed to revisions in the social security system, aged assistance, and Medicare. On April 9th of last year, I directed the Secretary of Health, Education, and Welfare, Secretary Gardner, to immediately organize a task force within the Government to bring forth a proposal for increasing social security benefits and make desirable improvements.

So the program which I announce today results from an intensive study begun by the Secretary and our experts last April and in some instances revisions that were urged by Members of Congress of both parties 6 months or more ago.

I plan to send to Congress next January four basic proposals to keep social security abreast of our times and in keeping with the 20th Century.

First, and foremost, and I think the most fundamental: I will recommend to the next Congress an average increase in social security benefits of at least 10 percent—to provide every beneficiary a higher standard of living.

I want to repeat for the benefit of the press—if you weren't listening yesterday or today I want you to listen now—at least 10 percent. That means an average of a minimum of 10 percent. It could be 12, it could be 14, it could be 15. If you are getting $44 now and you get $100, it will be considerably more than that. But not a specific, direct, irrevocable, precise 10 percent. At least 10 percent.

Now to further elaborate on that I will propose that those in the lowest brackets receive proportionately higher increases.

Second: I will propose that every worker who has been regularly employed under social security for 25 years or more shall be guaranteed a minimum monthly benefit of $100.

There are a good many of our senior citizens throughout the country. Some 22 million in social security will understand if we provide a minimum monthly benefit of $100, that it may exceed a good deal of the flat, specific 10 percent that so many are writing about.

Third: I will recommend specific proposals that will materially increase the income of those under social security who continue to work after reaching retirement age.

They are allowed to make $1500 per year now. We will have proposals that will not only help us alleviate the tight labor market in certain situations but will permit people to materially increase their income, if they continue working after retirement age.

Fourth: We will recommend that hospital and medical care coverage be provided not only to the aged but we will recommend that it cover more than one million disabled social security beneficiaries who may not now qualify under the age requirement.

We presently consider these four proposals the minimum toward a more modern and a more realistic social security system. Again, I emphasize the minimum. We will have other suggestions and proposals in the draft.

I will recommend ways to finance them so that the system will always remain actuarially sound.

In addition, I have requested the distinguished Secretary, Mr. Gardner, and the very able former Governor, Farris Bryant, who is on my White House staff, to head a special task force to develop a truly modern program, the latest in nursing home construction for every State in this Union.

I have asked them to call on the most modern and most imaginative architects in this land, and other experts, to begin making plans for nursing homes that are especially designed for our older people so that they can live their lives in places of beauty and comfort.

The program will call for Federal, State, local, and private participation in this exciting new enterprise for the benefit of older Americans.

Today I call upon each Governor, each mayor, each preacher, and each teacher to go about him and look at the nursing homes where our elder citizens are now spending their last days. Some of them are a national, State, and local disgrace and ought to be closed.

But any kind of a roof is better than no roof at all. For that reason, we not only must clean up the firetraps and we must brush up the mousetraps, but we must set in motion in this country a truly national home construction program for our elder citizens.

The Bible tells us to "honor thy father and thy mother." It enjoins us to "honor the face of the old man." We have not always been true to that trust. Too often we have ignored our older Americans—too often we have condemned them to live out their lives in want.

One of the most effective speeches I ever heard in behalf of our elder citizens I heard as a youngster in the early days of radio when Senator Huey

Long went on the radio one night and talked about the necessity of taking care of our older citizens.

And with the help of Congressman Mills, Senator Huey Long's young son, Russell Long, I predict, will lead this movement next year to get us the far-reaching, comprehensive social security legislation that this Nation ought to have.

I have visited the elderly citizens in various States in this Union. I have seen nursing homes so shabby and so badly run that they made me heartsick and stomach sick, too.

I have seen the old people there waiting for death in such poverty that it brought tears to my eyes.

And I thought — all of this in the midst of a gross national product of almost $750 billion a year. I have pledged to myself — and I now pledge to all my fellow Americans — that so long as I am your President, I will never rest until our senior citizens receive the honor and the treatment they deserve.

You, here at the Social Security Administration, are very central to that mission.

You are handling your great trust with care and efficiency and without regard to political development.

But despite your immense growth, your administrative cost cutting and your cost consciousness have brought savings to this Government of $23½ billion this year. The cost of administering your programs — the social security programs — is only 2.2 percent out of each dollar of social security contributions. That is a record that all Americans can be proud of.

So I came here today not only to honor your award winners and to pay tribute to your merit service. I came here to salute every single employee of the Social Security Administration in the United States of America through paying my respect and my compliments to you.

A great lady and a great friend of mine, Katy Loucheim, has just launched a new career in our State Department — and at the same time she launched a book of poems.

One of her verses — about a bureaucrat — ends with these words:

> The bureaucrat is seldom seen
> Without a pen — or with a dream.

Well, I believe that many of those who toil in government bureaus are equipped not only with their pens and their red tape, but they are equipped with dreams in their heads and their hearts; not only with efficiency, but with ideas and with a passion for public good.

And so today I ask each employee of the Social Security Administration of the United States to give us suggestion of new programs, new needs, new plans, and new forces that we should unleash and put into effect to make this a better America, a stronger America, a healthier America.

I should like for this period of the 20th century to be remembered as the period when we produced more food to feed more people – because food is the necessary sustaining ingredient for all the other things – the period when we spent more money and more effort on educating more people; the period when we spent more time and more dollars on providing health for our bodies; the time when we did more planning and added more acres for conservation, recreation and beautification.

Food, education, health, and conservation are the enemies of the real enemies of all people – these are diseases, illiteracy, ignorance, dirty air, dirty water, dirty parks, and dirty streets where the children cannot play.

Finally, I just want to observe this: That in the last 3 years we have produced and distributed more food through our Government programs in this country and the world than in any similar period in history. That means more people have eaten well.

This year we sent a billion dollars worth of food to India. I am told it helped feed 90 million people and kept 30 million people from starving to death. The trucks run up and down the streets every day in Bombay and other cities in India picking up the bodies of people who have died the night before.

In all the history of this country, since 1789, we passed only six education bills in the Federal Government. The first one was President Lincoln; the second one was President Wilson. It was 50-odd years before they got the second. The third one was President Truman; and President Eisenhower passed three more, making a total of six.

Well, the last 3 years we passed 18 from Head Start to PHD higher education. That is, there were three times as many bills passed in 3 years than were passed in 190 years of our history.

In all of these years since Abraham Lincoln passed the first bill to 1963, we spent $2 billion total on education. In the last 3 years we have spent $6 billion. Three times as much was spent in 3 years than in all of our history. And that is going to pay us very rich dividends down the road in an educated electorate in this country.

In your health programs, outside of the Hill-Burton hospital construction and a few minor health measures – we had no health program. But you inaugurated in July the most far reaching, most comprehensive health program affecting 20 million people now in Medicare and spending billions of dollars a year.

But that is just one of 24 health bills that we passed. Nurses training, modernization of hospitals, comprehensive health planning, heart, cancer, stroke – think of all the wonderful things. Twenty-four health bills in three years.

Conservation – when President Roosevelt launched the TVA the appropriation was $11 million and it committed the admiration of the entire world. Yet this year I sent a message to Congress on the TVA providing a bond issue of $750 million. That didn't even make the want-ad page of the paper.

So we are going places. We have our bright tomorrow. We have a great deal to be thankful for and a lot to look forward to, if we can just spend our time on constructive proposals instead of destructive proposals, if we can just spend our time in building instead of tearing down.

Mr. Rayburn served the Congress for 50 years. One of his favorite expressions was: "Judge a man not only by the company he keeps but by what he says. And always in judging him remember that any donkey can tear a barn down. It takes a good carpenter to build one."

There is a big donkey population in this country about this season of the year. There are a lot of them tearing barns down. But you men who are not seasoned in the political arena and don't have the obligations of putting your name on the ticket of the chance to build a barn and you are building. You built with social security, you built with Medicare, you are building with the improvements we are suggesting today. Now give us the benefit of your ideas, of your dreams, of your recommendations and let's leave this a better world for our children than we found it for ourselves.

On October 13, during the opening remarks at his news conference, President Johnson expressed gratitude for the Republican support which had greeted his social security programs.

Presidential News Conference
(October 13, 1966)*

*   *   *

Social Security Proposals

I am quite pleased with the apparent tremendous response to the proposals I made in Baltimore yesterday to increase social security benefits and to extend Medicare to the disabled.

I have had, as you know, as I stated last April, my top advisers in the Government working on improving a system for almost 6 months. And my speech yesterday reflected some of our thinking in that field.

I was particularly pleased to observe from the ticker today the really historic move on the part of my friends, the Republicans, in the Congress to support social security legislation.

I didn't have time to check all the record but in the first social security bill, 94 percent of the Republican Party voted to recommit the social security bill on the grounds it was socialism.

And only a few months ago, 93 percent of them voted to kill Medicare —another very important part of social security.

*Ibid., No. 41, p. 1474–75.

So now they seem to be in a big hurry to pass a bill as soon as they can. We welcome them to the vineyard. We're glad they have religion. I'll have our people work through the nights, if they care to act on it before going home. I will not insist on that, but I would welcome it. If they care to come back after the election, those of them that are coming back, I will be glad to have them act on it then.

I just refreshed my memory. I read what our dear friend, our late beloved Mr. Kaltenborn, and our friend, the news analyst, Mr. Harkness, said on the night of the election in 1948 about President Truman and how the President finally — after he heard that broadcast at 4 o'clock that said he is leading by a million but that can't be true, and he is leading by 2 million but that can't be true, and finally at five o'clock he heard it the last time — he said: "Well, I don't know about the polls, I don't know about the predictions, and I don't know about the columnists or the news analysists, but, boys, it looks like we are elected and we better get up and put on our clothes and get busy."

But for all the talk, Vietnam had consumed the initiative for restructuring the income security system which had developed in the preceding years.

1967

Presidential Recommendations

In his October 12, 1966, speech, the President had suggested an average 10 per cent increase for OASDHI congressional recipients and he was supported by leaders of both parties. In his State of the Union message early the next year President Johnson doubled the amount mentioned the previous fall and called instead for an overall average increase of 20 per cent.

President Lyndon B. Johnson
Fourth Annual Message
(January 10, 1967)*

Let us insure that older Americans, and neglected Americans, share in their Nation's progress.

We should raise social security payments by an overall average of 20 percent. That will add $4 billion 100 million to social security payments in the first year. I will recommend that each of the 23 million Americans now receiving payments get an increase of at least 15 percent.

Weekly Compilation of Presidential Documents, Vol. 3, No. 2, p. 29.

I will ask that you raise the minimum payments by 59 percent—from $44 to $70 a month, and to guarantee a minimum benefit of $100 a month for those with a total of 25 years of coverage. We must raise the limits that retired workers can earn without losing social security income.

Although the President did not elaborate his proposals in his speech, Congress had to wait only two weeks before receiving the Administration's plan. In his first special message to the ninetieth Congress, President Johnson detailed his extensive amendments to the social security system calling for change in five of the programs.

First, the President proposed across-the-board increases of at least 15 per cent for all OASDHI beneficiaries, with increases going as high as 59 per cent for those receiving the smallest benefits, and a minimum payment of $70 per month. Another increase in the OASDHI program provided for a minimum benefit of $100 a month if a worker had been covered for at least twenty-five years. The retirement test was also liberalized and coverage was extended to one-half million farm workers not yet covered. These additional benefits were to be financed by raises in both the payroll tax and the amount of wages taxable.

Second, President Johnson requested changes in the Medicare program, which had been operational only seven months. In particular he wanted extension of coverage to disabled workers who were receiving social security benefits but who were not yet sixty-five.

The third program slated for amendment was the Medicaid (Title XIX) plan providing federal grants to states for health care costs of medically needy persons. Since this program had greatly exceeded the original estimates, the Johnson proposal called for a limitation the costs which could be incurred by the Federal Government.

The Administration's plan also sweepingly changed the public assistance programs by increasing state public assistance payments to subsistence level at least. The establishment of a work incentive program for welfare recipients allowed additional monthly income without reduction of benefits. In addition certain temporary benefits were to be made permanent and a new, federally-financed, state work-training program was to be established.

Child-health and welfare programs were also to be amended, and the Internal Revenue Code would be revised. The tax reform proposal substituted a flat exemption for the elderly for the numerous and confusing exemptions applicable to persons over sixty-five.

Congressional Action

On February 20, 1967, Representative Wilbur Mills of Arkansas, chairman of the House Ways and Means Committee, introduced the Administration proposals as H.R. 5710. Hearings were scheduled for March and April.

Representatives of private insurance carriers, who were acting as fiscal intermediaries or carriers under Medicare testified and suggested several improvements. George Meany, president of the AFL-CIO, seemed to give tacit approval to the bill, but warned the committee that organized labor considered H.R. 5710 as only the first step towards boosting social security benefits by 50 per cent. The restriction of Title XIX Medicaid programs to those persons who had incomes of less than 50 per cent above public assistance programs, met strong opposition from Mr. Meany and he also rejected the plan to drop persons between twenty-one and sixty-five from Title XIX coverage.

The committee hearings entered the second week as George Cartmill, president of the American Hospital Association, appeared in order to explain the results of studies which had been conducted since Medicare had gone into effect. Congress was alarmed over the rapid rise in hospital costs since the program was adopted. Although the 1965 act had assumed an annual 7 per cent increase in hospital costs, representatives of the Association testified that increases during the previous year amounted to 18.6 per cent. They predicted the costs would continue to rise at a rate of 15 per cent for the next three to five years.

Representatives of the American Nursing Home Association testified against legislated standards for nursing homes, warning that these provisions would lead to federal control of health facilities.

When Wilbur Schmidt, chairman of the National Council of State Public Welfare Administrators, appeared, discussion switched from Medicare problems to the public assistance proposals. Mr. Schmidt discussed the broad new programs proposed by the Administration and advocated the concept of work-training programs for persons on welfare. However, he claimed that the objective could not be met by the Administration's amendments.

The committee heard a series of witnesses representing both insurance company associations and individual insurance companies. Their testimony emphasized that social security was designed only as a floor of protection for the elderly and that the Administration's benefit increases would push the program toward a framework of total protection. Most of the insurance spokesmen also supported the proposed reduction in Medicaid (Title XIX) and opposed expansion of Medicare to disabled persons.

The U.S. Chamber of Commerce testified in opposition to the pending bill. Although he voiced support for an across-the-board benefits increase, the group's spokesman found that 8 per cent was more reasonable than the Administration's 15 per cent figure. He also opposed the provision guaranteeing a minimum $100 benefit for workers with twenty-five or more years of coverage, stating that such a provision was contrary to the basic notions of social security and would destroy the benefit-wage relation principle.

The last two days of public testimony were devoted almost entirely to statements from members of Congress who not only appeared on behalf of H.R. 5710, but also sought support for their own social security bills.

On August 2, a clean bill, H.R. 12080, was reported out of committee to the full House. It followed the Johnson OASDHI proposals, but was considerably scaled down, calling for an across-the-board increase of 12.5 per cent and costing an additional $3.4 billion in the first year. The increased costs were to be financed by an increase in the payroll tax, effective in 1969, and a rise in the taxable wage base to $7600. The committee completely eliminated other Johnson proposals. H.R. 12080 did not, for instance, include a provision extending Medicare to the disabled, nor did it provide tax relief for the elderly.

The public assistance provisions of the bill generated outright hostility especially those sections covering aid to families with dependent children. H.R. 12080 established mandatory work-training programs for all AFDC recipients, including mothers, and provided federally-subsidized day-care centers for pre-school children. The committee estimated that this program would apply to three of the four million AFDC recipients. H.R. 12080 also froze the number of AFDC recipients in each state where federal participation was concerned.

The committee summarized the general purposes and major provisions of the bill in its report to the House.

Social Security Act Amendments of 1967
House Report No. 544
90th Cong., 1st Sess.
(August 10, 1967)

The proposals embodied in H.R. 12080[1] as reported by your committee would make major improvements and reforms in the provisions of the Social Security Act relating to the old-age, survivors, and disability insurance program, the hospital and medical insurance programs, the medical assistance program, the aid to families with dependent children and child welfare programs, and the child health programs.

Old-Age, Survivors, and Disability Insurance

First, the bill would increase social security benefits of the more than 23 million elderly and disabled people, widows and orphans receiving benefits and would improve the protection of the old-age, survivors, and disability insurance provisions of the social security program, by providing—

   (1) An across-the-board benefit increase of 12½ percent for persons on the rolls, with a minimum monthly primary insurance amount of $50;

[1]Introduced by Chairman Mills at the direction of the Committee and co-sponsored by Mr. Byrnes.

(2) An increase in the earnings base from $6,600 to $7,600 and, reflecting the higher payments made by people at the upper earnings levels, the retirement benefit of a man 65 and his wife would be at least 50 percent of his average earnings under the social security program;

(3) An increase from $35 to $40 in the special payments now provided for certain people age 72 and older who have not worked long enough to qualify for regular cash benefits;

(4) An increase in the amount an individual may earn and still get full benefits;

(5) New guidelines for determining when a disabled worker cannot engage in substantial gainful activities;

(6) An alternative insured-status test for workers disabled before age 31;

(7) Monthly cash benefits for disabled widows and disabled dependent widowers at age 50 at reduced rates;

(8) A new definition of dependency for children of women workers;

(9) Additional wage credits for military service; and

(10) Other improvements in the social security cash benefits program.

Health Insurance

Second, the bill would improve the health insurance benefits now provided to the aged under the medicare legislation of 1965, would extend the protection of health insurance, and would simplify administration, by providing—

(1) Coverage of additional days of hospital care;

(2) Elimination of the requirement that a physician certify to the medical necessity of admissions to general hospitals and of outpatient services;

(3) A new alternative procedure for payment of benefits provided under the supplementary medical insurance program where the patient has not paid the bill for the services;

(4) Simplified billing for hospitals by transferring coverage of outpatient hospital diagnostic services to the supplementary medical insurance program and eliminating the coinsurance provision applicable to inpatients for pathology and radiology services, and permitting hospitals to collect charges from outpatients for relatively inexpensive services (subject to final settlement in accordance with existing reimbursable cost provisions);

(5) Authority for experiments to achieve greater economy and efficiency, without reduction in quality of care, through various alternatives for reimbursement of hospitals and other providers of health services; and

(6) Other miscellaneous improvements.

Financing the Social Insurance Program

The cost of the changes would be met through the existing financing and through an increase in the earnings base from $6,600 to $7,600 and through a small increase in the tax rates. As a result, the system would be in actuarial balance.

Aid to Families with Dependent Children

Third, the bill would make reforms in the aid to families with dependent children programs:

(1) To give greater emphasis to getting appropriate members of families drawing aid to families with dependent children (AFDC) payments into employment and thus no longer dependent on the welfare rolls, the bill would require the States—

(a) To have plans for each adult and child 16 or over who is not in school which will stress the development of their work potential, provide basic education and vocational training, and provide day care for children of AFDC working mothers;

(b) To exempt a portion of earned income for members of the family who can work so that they will have an incentive to seek employment;

(c) To institute and strengthen community work and training programs in order to assure that they will be available to and utilized by all appropriate assistance recipients; and

(d) To modify the optional unemployed parents program to provide uniform eligibility requirements throughout the United States.

In order to enable the States to implement these requirements, the Federal Government would supply more favorable Federal matching for the services (including child welfare and day care) and training which the States would be required to furnish under the aid to families with dependent children program. Similar matching would be provided for training, supervision, materials, and other items and services which were previously not matched by the Federal Government under the community work and training program.

(2) To aid in the reduction of illegitimate births, and to prevent the neglect, abuse, and exploitation of children, the bill would require the States—

(a) To provide family planning services that are offered on a voluntary basis in all appropriate cases;

(b) To institute protective payments to an interested person to assure that the child rather than an incompetent or irresponsible parent or relative receives the benefit of assistance, or to provide direct vendor payments where it is determined that cash payments to the parent or relative would be detrimental to the welfare of the child;

(c) To bring unsuitable home conditions of children to the attention of the courts or law enforcement agencies; to develop a program through a single organizational unit to establish paternity of illegitimate needy children (in order to get support payments from the fathers); to utilize reciprocal support arrangements with other States to enforce court support orders for deserted children; and to enter into cooperative arrangements with the court to carry out these arrangements.

In order to enable the States to carry out these requirements, Federal matching would be provided for family planning services and child welfare services under the AFDC matching formula. The bill provides more favorable Federal matching and broadens eligibility for foster care for children removed from an unsuitable home by court order. Moreover, certain requirements that have restricted the use of protective payments would be removed and vendor payments would be authorized for the first time in the cash program. Finally, a new program optional with the States would authorize dollar-for-dollar Federal matching to provide temporary assistance to meet the great variety of situations faced by needy children in families with emergencies.

To further stimulate the States to carry out these new provisions effectively, the bill would provide that the largest and most rapidly increasing recipient category in this program (children qualifying on the basis of the absence of a parent from the home) will be frozen (insofar as Federal participation is concerned) at its present proportion of the child population of the State.

Child Welfare and Public Assistance

Fourth, to expand and improve the operation of the child welfare and public assistance programs, the bill would—

(a) Increase the authorization for child welfare services and combine them administratively within State and local agencies with welfare services under the aid to families with dependent children program;

(b) Extend and expand the public assistance demonstration grant program;

(c) Initiate a program of grants to educational institutions to expand undergraduate and graduate social work training; and

(d) Provide Federal matching for essential home repairs of a limited nature for public assistance recipients.

Medical Assistance (Medicaid)

Fifth, to modify the program of medical assistance to establish certain limits on Federal participation in the program and to add flexibility in administration, the bill would—

(a) Impose a limitation of Federal matching at an income level related to payments for families receiving aid to families with dependent children or to the per capita income of the State, if lower;

(b) Allow States a broader choice of required health services under the program;

(c) Exempt from the requirement of "comparability" for all recipients the benefits "bought-in" for the aged under the medicare supplementary medical insurance program;

(d) Allow recipients free choice of qualified providers of health services;

(e) Allow, at the option of the States, direct payments to medically needy recipients for physicians' services; and

(f) Establish an Advisory Council on Medical Assistance to advise on administration of the program.

Two days before the House debate began, HEW Secretary John Gardner clarified Administration opposition to the two controversial public welfare sections of the bill. Secretary Gardner said, "I do not believe that children should have to pay for the shortcomings and inequities of the society into which they are born. . . . I do not believe that children should have to pay for the real or supposed sins of their parents and I think it would be shortsighted of a society to produce, by its neglect, a group of future citizens very likely to be unproductive and characterized by bitterness and alienation."

On August 16 the House adopted a closed rule and provided for eight hours of debate for the bill. The discussion was opened the next morning by Wilbur Mills, chairman of the Ways and Means Committee, and chief draftsman of the bill's provisions, who justified the public welfare amendments in the bill.

Congressional Debates
113 Congressional Record, p. 10688
(August 16, 1967)

Mr. Mills . . .

Mr. Chairman, we have written into this bill certain requirements that a State must now meet. Those requirements are set out in the report in detail. We want the States to have a work and training program. We want the States to see to it that those who are drawing as unemployed fathers, or drawing as mothers, unless there is good cause for them not to be required to take it, that they take training and then work. Is there anything wrong with that? What in the world is wrong with requiring these people to submit themselves, if they are to draw public funds, to a test of their ability to learn a job? Is that not the way that we should go? Is that not the thing we should do?

Are you satisfied with the fact that illegitimacy in this country is rising and rising and rising? I am not. We have tried to encourage the States to develop programs to do something about it. Now we are requiring them to do something about it. We are not penalizing any child. We are not going to take a child off the rolls in any State nor fail to participate with Federal funds in the care of that child, regardless of what his parent does. But we are not going to continue to put Federal funds into States for the benefit of parents when they refuse to get out of that house and try to earn something.

What else have we done? We have taken what can be an expensive step because we tell the States that you must disregard certain earnings of these people in determining their needs as an inducement to get them out of their house and to work.

What do they say now? They say they cannot work. If they work, they lose their assistance payments. Maybe they are not qualified in all instances to earn very much, but to the extent that they can work and make something, we want them working. If there are any jobs available for them, we want them to have them. This is what we wanted to do in 1962. We left it to the option of the States, and they did not do it. Five years later, today, we are on the floor with a bill which requires that it be done.

We are being very generous with the States, on the other hand. We are saying to the States, since we are requiring this of you, we will not match these kinds of services, as we do through cash payments. We will see to it that the States do not have to pay more than 25 percent of the total cost of those services, and because we are requiring it of them, we are going to help them with this big additional load.

What does this do? We pointed it out in this report. In 1972, the Department tells us, in all probability they expect 400,000 fewer children on the rolls than there would have been under the existing law.

Is that not the way we should lead people? Is that not the way we lead people from a condition that I am sure they do not want to be in—of need —into a position of independence and self-support?

This has been too long in coming, Mr. Chairman, because, I believe, some day there is going to be a revolution, an upheaval, or something put on by the American taxpayers, if they can ever get organized. Whenever that happens, Mr. Chairman, we are going to find, in my opinion, unless the trends in these programs are reversed, and their administration made more sensible and more in the public interest, the taxpayer is going to insist that they be eliminated from the cost of government.

I do not think there is any question about it. If ever I heard anything in connection with a request for a tax increase—surcharge, or whatever it may be called—it is this. The letters have come from every State in the Union in truckloads: See to it, before we are taxed more, that the giveaway programs and programs that can pared to the bone are pared to the bone.

Mr. Chairman, what we have done in this bill will reduce the cost of these programs by approximately $713 million by 1972. If these provisions are not enacted, the programs will cost us $6.7 billion in 1972. These are items

over which no one, including the President, has any control—except the
Congress. The States send in their bills and we give them a check, after
the expenditures have been incurred. There is no way to reduce these in the
Appropriations Committee. It is our job today to get these programs on
the proper track.

*Criticism of the cutbacks in the federal share of Title XIX was voiced by
many members, particularly those from California and New York. (Both
states had developed extensive Medicaid programs.) However, bipartisan
support for the proposed increases in OASDHI benefits overwhelmed the
few liberal Congressmen who opposed the coercive elements in the public
assistance sections and the Title XIX cutbacks. These opponents finally
realized they could not block House passage of H.R. 12080, and therefore
voted in favor of the bill, preferring to carry their fight for deletion of the
controversial sections to the Senate. H.R. 12080 thus passed the roll call
with only three dissenting votes.*

*Senate hearings opened on August 22 with witnesses from the Depart-
ment of Health, Education, and Welfare, led by Secretary Gardner. He
reiterated the original Administration proposals by calling for a 15 per cent
across-the-board benefit increase and a minimum monthly benefit of $70.
He also urged restoration of a $100 minimum for long-term contributors,
approval of the original financing plans, and the expansion of Medicare
coverage to one and a half million disabled persons receiving social security
benefits. Although the Secretary approved of the congressional concern for
"getting families off welfare," he was opposed to the House solution to the
problem.*

*Senator Abraham Ribicoff, former Secretary of HEW, questioned Secre-
tary Gardner on the mandatory work provisions of the AFDC program and
also the AFDC freeze. Both committee members and Administration witnesses voiced particular concern over the relatively high rate of illegitimate
birth among those on public assistance.*

*After three days of testimony from Administration spokesmen, the com-
mittee began hearing statements from public witnesses. The American
Medical Association, represented by its new president, Dr. Milford Rouse,
continued to oppose Part B of Title XVIII, which provided supplementary
doctor-bill coverage under Medicare. The Association instead suggested
that a new program of subsidies for private health insurance systems be
adopted. It also went on record against proposed drug reimbursement
proposals.*

*Several Senators testified before the committee. Senator Robert Kennedy
of New York emphasized that the AFDC provisions in the general welfare
laws encouraged family breakups.*

Social Security Act Amendments of 1967
Hearings on H.R. 12080 before the Senate Finance Committee
90th Cong., 1st Sess. (August, 1967)
(p. 776)

Senator Kennedy. Mr. Chairman and members of the committee, in the midst of our great affluence, there remain 30 million poor people in this country today. That fact, more than anything else, is what these hearings are about.

For, despite the growth of our social security system over the years, a fifth of those living in poverty are over 65. These years should bring them a life of peaceful comfort and dignity—but instead retirement means a life beset with financial problems, burdened with dwindling savings and unpaid bills. Millions more approach 65 with apprehension—they know that when they stop work they begin not the golden years, but years of life in poverty.

And, despite the growth of our public welfare programs over the years, welfare at present aids less than a fourth of the 30 million poor. And, those who receive aid often do not get enough to satisfy even their barest minimum needs. For too many on welfare and for the rest of the poor, there are only days of misery without enough food for their children, and nights of fear in substandard housing, warding off marauding rats. And, for those receiving assistance, there are also complex and degrading procedures; there are rules designed to qualify eligible applicants which often serve to disqualify or discourage people in need; there are rules which force families to stay apart in order to receive aid. For too many, then, welfare is not only inadequate, but appears as a reluctant handout designed to screen the poor away from the rest of society.

These figures, these conditions, these procedures define the magnitude and importance of the task before your committee. And they also suggest the utter inadequacy of the legislation which the other body has sent over for us to consider. That legislation includes some good changes—the ideas of offering job training, day care, and work incentives to welfare recipients in order to enable them to seek productive employment; some changes that are not good enough—the increase in the minimum social security payment to $50 and the 12½ percent across-the-board increase in benefits; and far too many changes which can only be described as plainly regressive—a series of public welfare amendments which, taken together, reflect a punitive attitude reminiscent of medieval poor law philosophy and will result in reduced assistance for millions in need, and a ceiling on title XIX assistance that is unrealistic and unworkable. Let me, if I may, Mr. Chairman, discuss these matters briefly.

First, on social security. Our social security system has grown extensively over the years, so that 95 million people are now insured and 23 million receive benefits; but we have not yet succeeded in lifting millions of older

Americans into a retirement of security and selfrespect. Secretary Gardner told you last week that social security is the major source of income for nearly all retired beneficiaries, and the sole source for half. About 14 million retired workers and their dependents receive benefits. And last year these benefits averaged $84 a month—just $1,000 a year for individuals, and $142 a month—$1,704 annually—for couples. In light of these figures, it is not surprising that some 5 million to 7 million retired Americans live in poverty.

We in Congress must share the responsibility for the inadequacy of retirement benefits. The two increases of 7 percent which we enacted in 1958 and 1965 actually fell short of restoring the 1954 purchasing power of benefits—for the cost of living has risen about 25 percent since that time. Thus, four-fifths of the 12½-percent increase provided in the House bill would be taken up just to give beneficiaries as much real income as they would have had in 1954. Meanwhile, wages have risen about 50 percent in those 13 years. The wealth of our Nation has steadily increased but, because of our neglect, our older citizens have not shared in that affluence—instead, more elderly couples each year retire into a life of poverty.

With 10 Senators of both parties, I introduced legislation earlier this year to make up for the ground we have lost. That bill, S. 1009, would provide benefit increases averaging over 50 percent, and, crucially, would finance these increases by a gradual infusion of general revenues. It envisioned a leveling off of general revenue contribution at 35 percent of the costs of social security by the late 1970's.

At the moment, when we are engaged in a deepening war in Vietnam which saps our resources and consumes over $2 billion each month, it seems impractical to urge the full scope of these proposals.

I believe, however, that it is time we began a partial changeover to general revenue financing.

The payroll tax is scheduled under present law to increase to 4.85 percent each on employer and employee in 1973, plus a contribution for health insurance. The House bill would raise that to 5 percent each, plus 0.65 percent for each health insurance. As members of the committee well know, a tax on payrolls in highly regressive. For low-wage employees particularly, a required contribution beyond that contemplated in the House bill would be very burdensome. Many workers already pay more in payroll taxes than they do in income taxes.

General revenue financing would be a far more equitable way to raise revenues for the social security system, particularly revenues which would be used to provide additional benefits for low-income people—for those who worked either so irregularly or at such low wages that their contributions do not really finance the benefits they receive.

I emphasize this because the proposal I shall make this morning to broaden the scope of H.R. 12080 would give relatively more help to the poorest of our elderly, to those who have the most difficulty in finding dignity and comfort in their retirement. If we are to provide a meaningful floor of protection for older people as a matter of social insurance, I believe it is only fair to other workers that we finance it through general revenues.

I propose that the committee raise the across-the-board increase in benefits to 20 percent, weighting it, if possible, toward those beneficiaries at the lower end of the spectrum. I propose, in addition, that the minimum benefit be raised to $100 a month, $150 for couples. These proposals combined would produce an average benefit increase of 29 percent.

To finance this proposal, I suggest, first, that the contribution and benefit base be raised to $8,400 next January and to $10,800 on January 1, 1971; and second, that general revenue contributions be infused at the rate of 11 percent of the total financing of the system beginning in 1972.

This plan is feasible. I am assured by officials of the Social Security Administration that it is in long range actuarial balance. . . .

Almost equally compelling was the evidence of Senator Edward Brooke of Massachusetts, the newly elected Negro Senator, who told the committee that he favored getting as many poor persons as possible off welfare and back to work. But he stated that the plans for reaching that goal embodied in H.R. 12080 would only lead to greater poverty.

Senate Hearings
(p. 826 – 27)

Senator Brooke . . .

We have recently seen dramatic and horrifying examples of violence and disruption which can occur when one segment of our population lives for too long in poverty and despair. Newark, Detroit, Watts, and Roxbury were primarily reactions to continuing, longstanding, and relentless economic deprivation. They were the outbursts of the totally frustrated, the hopeless, the "internal aliens" in our Nation for whom the community accepted a responsibility, those who had no other means of support: the blind, the aged, the disabled, the unemployed. This is still the principal purpose of public welfare.

But welfare, in and of itself, is not desirable. For those who can work, there is something about relief – permanent relief – that cripples the spirit and violates the recipient's sense of honor and self-respect. It is a negation of the American dream. And, perhaps, more telling, it does not work, if by "working" we mean offering some promise for permanent solutions. Relief relieves desperate pressures, but it accomplishes little or nothing toward helping those who need it to escape from their unfortunate condition.

The elimination of this type of dependence on public welfare by those who are mentally and physically capable of becoming productive members of society is, I am sure, the objective of the legislation which you are considering today. The members of the House Ways and Means Committee have very wisely determined that the States and the local communities have, in all too many cases, confined their attentions to administering the relief rolls. Too little creative effort has been put into helping individuals on relief to break out of the cycle and to make their contribution to society. To correct this imbalance, the committee has seen fit to incorporate into the 1967 Social Security Amendments provisions requiring the States to make available, where appropriate, employment counseling, testing, and job training services for each adult and each child over 16 who is not attending school. The States would also be required to provide day care services for children whose mothers want to work to participate in job-training programs. Family planning services are to be made available by the States. Earning exemptions are to be granted by all States, to encourage individuals on welfare to become participants in the community without losing the opportunity to participate in welfare programs. All of these measures are good. They offer incentives to the States to provide the kinds of services without which the poor people of our country cannot begin to pull themselves out of the cycle of poverty.

I congratulate the authors of this legislation for including these provisions in H.R. 12080. But I ask you, what will we have accomplished if, in passing this legislation we help some of the poor while forcing others back into even greater poverty and despair.

Mayor John Lindsay of New York was even more outspoken.

Senate Hearings
(p. 1123, p. 1144)

Mr. John Lindsay . . .

Mr. Chairman and members of the committee, everybody talks about welfare, to paraphrase Mark Twain's observation about the weather, but everybody wants to do something about it.

Certainly few of the people involved with welfare would give unreserved endorsement to the system under which we now operate.

The recipients—among them the jobless, the handicapped, the poverty-stricken—don't like it, because almost no one truly wants to live on handouts. The administrators are appalled by the paperwork and disillusioned by the lack of constructive results. And the taxpayers are more and more resentful of the millions of dollars that are being spent on public assistance with no diminishment of the welfare rolls.

The legislation before you, H.R. 12080, reflects that national mood; it evolves from an understandable and energetic desire to redesign a social welfare program that in many ways has been a philosophic and financial flop.

We in New York City support the primary objective of this bill, insofar as that objective is to reduce dependency upon the government; to enable public welfare recipients to lead constructive, independent lives, free of government maintenance and supervision.

The goal is admirable. It is, however, one that has eluded us for decades, and experience alone should compel upon us a precise, realistic examination of the strategy by which the goal now is to be attained.

Our review of the amendments has convinced us that many of them will not work. Some will make our jobs more difficult. Others will make them more expensive.

In summary, this legislation contains elements that in our judgment may have the ultimate effect of converting a deeply troubling situation into a thundering crisis.

* * *

So, in conclusion, I would urge the Senate to adopt the positive features of H.R. 12080, to restore some of the excellent provisions of the administration bill, and to strike out the punitive, coercive measures that will move us even further down the road that is now clearly labeled as a deadend.

To remove the coercive provisions would encourage States to develop alternatives to welfare for their poor residents. It would also avoid contaminating the positive features with the atmosphere of threats and punishments.

I would also urge the Senate to strengthen the public assistance provisions by restoring H.R. 5710's requirement that States meet their own minimum standards by adding measures to simplify the terms of eligibility for public assistance and by separating the two functions of social service and income maintenance. This will enable social workers to spend all their efforts to strengthen family life, assist family members to retain capability for maximum self-support and personal independence, to use the words of the House Ways and Means Committee report itself.

The retrogressive provisions of 12080 on the contrary would lock social workers even further into the investigator's role, a role that has proven both futile and wasteful both of public funds and professional skill as Commissioner Ginsberg can tell you at great length.

My purpose here today has been to indicate that aside from the philosophy of 12080 with respect to public welfare, which is contrary to our growing understanding of the roots of poverty and its remedies, the bill's punitive and compulsory provisions simply will not work.

While these provisions will be costly and burdensome for the States and local communities, they will not achieve the goals of providing a minimum standard of living for all Americans and the opportunity for self-support for those who are able.

Other witnesses warned the committee of possible dangers. The former governor of Minnesota, the Honorable Elmer L. Anderson, testified in his capacity as president of the Child Welfare League of America, in opposi-

tion to the public assistance portions of the bill. He said, "A bill such as this (H.R. 12080) could only have come from the House of Representatives because those esteemed members did not fully understand the regressive proposals in this legislation and how they would ultimately harm the lives of millions of our children" (Senate Hearings, p. 1321). George Meany, of the AFL-CIO, urged adoption of the Administration's proposals rather than the House bill. He also voiced support for Medicare coverage for the cost of the drug as well as for drug price regulation.

After fifteen days of public hearings and over two thousand pages of testimony, the Finance Committee went into executive session. Regardless of decisions on the controversial public assistance provisions, there was certain to be lively debate on the bill when it reached the floor. On November 14, the Finance Committee issued its report, including almost all of the provisions President Johnson had originally requested. Only expansion of Medicare to disabled persons, and a revised tax plan for the elderly were deleted from major Administration requests.

The most significant changes in the House bill concerned the public assistance provisions. The freeze on federal participation in AFDC assistance was entirely deleted, and the committee exempted all AFDC mothers with pre-school children from mandatory participation in the work-training programs.

Social Security Act Amendments of 1967
Senate Report No. 744
90th Cong., 1st Sess.
(November 14, 1967)

*   *   *

II. SUMMARY OF PRINCIPAL PROVISIONS OF THE BILL

A. OLD-AGE, SURVIVORS, AND DISABILITY INSURANCE

1. Provisions of the House Bill Changed, and New Provisions Added, by the Committee

There are several provisions in the Committee's bill that affect the amount of benefits to be paid out. Overall, the increase in benefit payments for the first full year of operation, as compared with what payments would be under present law, would be 25 percent. This figure includes increases arising from the benefit formula change, a change in the retirement test, the addition of benefits for disabled widows, the payment of benefits on an actuarially reduced basis at age 60 and certain other, less important changes.

Increase in Social Security Benefits

By far the most important change proposed by the Committee is an across-the-board increase in benefit payments with a guaranteed increase in monthly cash benefits of 15 percent for all beneficiaries on the social security rolls and with a minimum primary insurance amount of $70.

The increased benefits would be first payable for March 1968. It is estimated that 23.8 million people would be paid increased benefits beginning early in April. As a result of the benefit increase, $4.3 billion in additional benefits would be paid out in the first 12 months.

The benefit increases proposed by the committee are the same as those recommended by the Administration and exceed those adopted by the House. The House bill would have provided for an increase in cash benefits of 12½ percent, with a minimum primary insurance amount of $50 per month. Under the provisions adopted by the committee, the average monthly benefit paid to retired workers and their wives now on the rolls would increase from $145 to $171 ($164 under the House bill). Monthly benefits would range from a new minimum of $70 to $163.30, for retired workers now on the social security rolls who began to draw benefits at age 65 or later, compared with $50 to $159.80 under the House bill. Under existing law, the benefit range for such retired people now receiving old-age benefits is $44 to $142 a month.

The amount of earnings which would be subject to tax and could be used in the computation of benefits would be increased from $6,600 to $8,000 in 1968, to $8,800 in 1969, and to $10,800 in 1972. The House bill provided for one increase in the base—to $7,600 a year, effective January 1, 1968.

The increase in the amount of earnings that can be used in the benefit computation would result in a maximum benefit of $288 (based on average monthly earnings of $900—$10,800 a year) in the future; the maximum benefit under the House bill would be $212 (based on average monthly earnings of $633—$7,600 a year). Under present law, the maximum benefit is $168 (based on maximum average monthly earnings of $550—$6,600 a year). Under the committee bill, the maximum benefits payable to a family on a single earnings record would be $540 ($423.60 under the House bill) rather than $368 as under present law.

These higher maximum retirement benefits just outlined will be payable to workers who are now young and who consequently will be paying contributions on these higher amounts of earnings over a considerable period of time before they retire. But because of the higher earnings base, benefit amounts would be increased significantly over those that would be payable under present law and under the House bill for workers who are much older now and who consequently pay on these higher amounts for a much shorter period. A man age 50 in 1968, for example, who earns $8,800 a year until he is 65 will get a benefit of $204 at age 65—31.6 percent higher than he could get under present law, and 9.9 percent higher than he would get under the House bill. If he earns $10,800 a year or more, his benefit will be $223 — 43.9 percent higher than he would get under present law, and 20.1 percent higher than under the House bill.

The special payments made to individuals aged 72 and over would be increased by the committee bill from $35 to $50 a month for a single person and from $52.50 to $75 a month for a couple. Under the House bill these payments would be increased to $40 and $60, respectively.

Reduced Benefits at Age 60

Under present law, full-rate widow's, widower's, and parent's insurance benefits are payable at age 62; and reduced old-age, wife's and dependent husband's benefits are payable at age 62; only widow's insurance benefits are payable as early as age 60 at a reduced rate.

Under the committee bill, the age of eligibility would be lowered to 60 for all categories of aged beneficiaries, with the benefits payable before age 62 reduced according to the principle which is applied under present law. The reduction rate in present law for a wife's (or a husband's) benefit is twenty-five thirty-sixths of 1 percent, and for an old-age or widow's benefit it is five-ninths of 1 percent, for each month that the beneficiary is under age 65 (age 62 for a widow) when he begins to get benefits. Thus, a worker coming on the rolls at the age 60 would receive two-thirds of his full benefit.

H.R. 12080, as passed by the House of Representatives, contained no comparable provision.

Monthly benefits would be payable under this provision beginning with the month of December 1968. An estimated 775,000 additional people are expected to claim benefits for December, and benefits amounting to $555 million would be paid during the first 12 months of operation. Because the benefit amount payable at age 60 would be reduced to take account of the longer period over which benefits would be paid, payment of these benefits would not result in any increase in the long-range cost of the program.

Retirement Test

The committee modified the provision of the House bill which would have increased from $1,500 a year to $1,680 the amount a person may earn without having some social security benefits withheld. The committee bill, like the House bill, provides an increase from $1,500 to $1,680 in the amount a person may earn in a year without having any social security benefits withheld for taxable years ending in 1968. The committee bill modifies the House bill by providing for an additional increase in this amount to $2,000 for taxable years ending in 1969 and later. The amounts to which the $1-for-$2 reduction would apply would range from $1,680 to $2,880 (as in the House bill) for taxable years ending in 1968. For taxable years ending in 1969 and later the $1-for-$2 reduction would apply from $2,000 to $3,200. The amount a person may earn in a month and still get full benefits for that month (regardless of how much he earns in a year) would be increased to $140 (as in the House bill) for taxable years ending in 1968 and would increase to $166⅔ (one-twelfth of $2,000) for taxable years ending in 1969 and later. About $175 million would be paid out in additional benefits with respect to calendar year 1968 to 760,000 people in calendar year 1968, and about $500 million would be paid out in additional benefits with respect to calendar year 1969 to 840,000 people in calendar year 1969.

Disabled Widows and Widowers

The committee bill would provide full-rate benefits for many totally disabled widows and widowers — the benefits equaling 82½ percent of the deceased spouse's primary insurance amount. Under the House bill, reduced benefits — ranging from 50 percent to 82½ percent of the spouse's primary insurance amount — would have been provided for disabled widows and widowers age 50 and over. The committee's bill would not only increase the benefit amounts provided by the House but would also eliminate the requirement that the disabled widow or widower be at least age 50. As in the House bill, benefits would be payable only to a widow or widower who became totally disabled not later than 7 years after the spouse's death, or in the case of a widowed mother, before her mother's benefits end or within 7 years thereafter. About 70,000 disabled widows and widowers would be eligible for benefits and about $71 million in benefits would be paid during the first 12 months of operation.

Benefits for the Blind

The committee added to the House bill a provision which would make blind people with at least six quarters of social security coverage eligible for disability insurance benefits without regard to their ability to work. In order to qualify for benefits a person would have to have vision of 20/200 or less, rather than 5/200 as in present law.

Child's Benefits for those Disabled Before Age 22

The committee added to the House bill a provision which would provide child's insurance benefits for an otherwise qualified disabled child if his disability began after age 18 and before age 22. Under present law, a person must have become disabled before age 18 to qualify for childhood disability benefits.

*   *   *

B. HEALTH INSURANCE BENEFITS

1. Provisions of the House Bill Changed, and New Provisions Added, by the Committee

Additional Days of Hospital Care

The committee bill modified the provision of the House bill which would extend the number of inpatient hospital days covered during a "spell of illness" from 90 to 120 days, with a $20 coinsurance requirement from the 91st day through the 120th day. Instead, each medicare beneficiary would be provided with a lifetime reserve of 60 days of added coverage of hospital care after the 90 days covered in a "spell of illness" have been exhausted. Coinsurance of $10 for each day would be applicable to such added days of coverage. Under the House bill persons who are more or less permanently institutionalized, and who therefore have only one spell of illness during their lifetime would have qualified for only 30 additional days of hospital care. Under the committee provision they would qualify for up to 60 additional days of care during their lifetime.

Payment of Physician Bills Under the Supplementary Medical Insurance Program

The committee bill modifies the provision in the House bill which provides for physician payment under the medical insurance program. Under present law, payment may be made only to the physician upon assignment or to the patient upon presentation of a receipted bill. The House bill provided for retention of present law provisions and added new alternatives for payment to the physician or patient on the basis of an unpaid bill. As modified and simplified by the committee, only two methods of payment would be provided: Payment either directly to the patient on the basis of an itemized bill (which could be either receipted or unpaid) or directly to the physician as under the present assignment method.

Payment for Services in Nonparticipating Hospitals

The committee added a provision to the House bill which would permit payment for services received in certain nonparticipating hospitals. At present, payments can be made to participating hospitals and, in an emergency case, to a nonparticipating hospital which meets certain standards only if the nonparticipating hospital agrees to accept reasonable cost reimbursement as full payment for the services rendered.

For a temporary period, almost all of which has already expired, the committee bill would permit direct reimbursement to be made to an individual who was furnished hospital services during the temporary transitional period in a nonparticipating hospital. This coverage would not extend to admissions to hospitals which occur after 1967. Payment would be limited to 60 percent of the room and board charges and 80 percent of the hospital ancillary charges, for up to 20 days in each spell of illness (subject to the $40 deductible and other statutory payment limitations in present law) if the hospital did not formally participate in medicare before January 1, 1969. If it did participate in medicare before that date and if it applied its utilization review plan to the services for which medicare benefits are being claimed and which it provided before its regular participation started, the full 90 days of coverage could be provided. Thus, there would be an incentive over and above existing incentives for presently nonparticipating hospitals to participate because participation is a condition for covering past services beyond 20 days as well as a condition for future coverage.

A similar provision relating only to emergency services would apply beginning with respect to admissions taking place on or after January 1, 1968, but only as an alternative to present coverage of emergency care. Hospitals could apply for payment on a reasonable-cost basis as under present law, or if the hospital did not apply, the patient could obtain payment directly under the new provisions on the basis of 60 percent of room and board charges and 80 percent of ancillary service charges.

A new definition would be used for hospitals eligible under these transitional and emergency care provisions. Under it, a qualifying hospital must have a full-time nursing service, be licensed as a hospital, and be primarily engaged in providing medical care under the supervision of a doctor of medicine or osteopathy. This definition would apply retroactive to July 1, 1966, so that some hospitals which today would be ineligible to receive payment for emergency services may receive such payments on behalf of beneficiaries back to the beginning of the program provided they apply for such payments. If they do not apply for reimbursement, the patient would be paid directly under the new payment provisions.

Coordination of Reimbursement With Health Facility Planning

The committee added to the House bill a provision under which the Secretary of Health, Education, and Welfare would take into account the specific disapproval by State agencies carrying on planning under the Partnership for Health Act, of certain expenditures by hospitals or other health facilities for substantial capital items. Depreciation and interest attributable to substantial capital items which are found not in accordance with a State's overall plan would not be includable as a part of the "reasonable cost" of the facilities covered services provided to individuals under title V, XVIII, and XIX. The provision would be effective with respect to capital expenditures made after June 30, 1970, or earlier at the request of a State.

Incentives for Economy while Maintaining or Improving Quality in the Provision of Health Services

The committee modified the House provision which would authorize the Secretary of Health, Education, and Welfare to experiment with various methods of reimbursement to organizations and institutions participating under medicare, medicaid, and the child health programs which would provide incentives for limiting costs of the program while maintaining quality care. Under the committee bill, the authorization would also cover similar experiments with respect to physicians' services, but only with respect to those physicians volunteering to participate in such experiments.

*   *   *

C. FINANCING OF SOCIAL SECURITY PROGRAM

*   *   *

D. PUBLIC ASSISTANCE

1. *Provisions of the House Bill Changed, and New Provisions Added, by the Committee*

Limitation on Federal Matching in AFDC Program

The House bill sets a limitation on Federal financial participation in the AFDC program related to the proportion of the child population that could be aided because of the absence from the home of a parent. Federal financial participation would not be available for any excess above the percentage of children of absent parents who received aid to the child population in the State as of January 1, 1967.

This limitation is not retained in the committee bill.

Work Incentive Program for AFDC Families

The committee modified the provisions of the House bill by establishing a new work incentive program for families receiving AFDC payments to be administered by the Department of Labor, and by defining more precisely than in the House bill those AFDC recipients who would be referred to the program. The State welfare agencies would decide who was appropriate for such referral but would not include (1) children who are under age 16 or going to school; (2) any person with illness, incapacity, advanced age or remoteness from a project that precludes effective participation in work or training; (3) persons whose substantially continuous presence in the home is required because of the illness or incapacity of another member of the household; (4) a mother who is in fact caring for one or more children of preschool age, if such mother's presence in the home is necessary and in the best interest of the children; (5) persons whose participation in the program would not (as determined by the State agency) be in their best interest and in the interest of the program. For all those referred the welfare agency would be required to assure necessary child care arrangements for the children involved. An individual who desires to participate in work or training would be considered for assignment and, unless the request was specifically disapproved, would be referred to the program.

People referred by the State welfare agency to the Department of Labor would be handled under three priorities of operations. Under priority I, the Secretary of Labor, through the over 2,000 U.S. employment offices, would establish an employability plan for each person and make arrangements for as many as possible to move into regular employment.

Under priority II all those found suitable would receive training appropriate to their needs and a weekly incentive payment of up to $20. After training, as many as possible would be referred to regular employment.

Under priority III, the employment office would make arrangements for special work projects to employ those who are found to be unsuitable for the training and those for whom no jobs in the regular economy can be found at the time. These special projects would be set up by agreement between the employment office and public agencies or nonprofit agencies organized for a public service purpose.

It would be required that workers receive at least the minimum wage (Federal or State) if the work they perform is covered under a minimum wage statute.

Moreover, the work performed under such projects could not result in the displacement of regularly employed workers and would have to be of a type which, under the circumstances in the local situation, would not otherwise be performed by regular employees.

The special work projects would work like this: The State welfare agency would make payments to the employment office equal to:

(1) The welfare benefit the family would have been entitled to if the relative did not work in the project, or, if smaller,

(2) That part of the welfare benefit equal to 80 percent of the wages which the individual receives on the special project.

The Secretary of Labor would arrange for the participants to work in a special work project. The amount of the funds paid by him into the project would depend on the terms he negotiates with the agency sponsoring the project. The amount of funds put into the projects by the Secretary of Labor could not be larger than the funds sent to the Secretary by the State welfare agency.

The extent to which the State welfare expenditures might be reduced would depend upon the negotiating efforts of the Secretary of Labor. If he is successful in placing these workers in work projects where the pay is relatively good, the contribution the State must make into the employment pool would be less.

Employees who work under these agreements would have their situations reevaluated by the employment office at regular intervals (at least every 6 months) for the purpose of making it possible for as many such employees as possible to move into regular employment or training.

An important facet of this suggested work program is that in most instances the recipient would no longer receive a check from the welfare agency. Instead, he would receive a payment from an employer for services performed. The entire check would be subject to income, social security, and unemployment compensation taxes, thus assuring that the individual would be accruing rights and responsibilities as he would in regular employment. In those cases where an employee receives wages which are insufficient to raise his income to a level equal to the grant he would have received had he not been in the project plus 20 percent of his wages, a welfare check equal to the difference would be paid. In these instances the supplemental check would be issued by the welfare agency and sent to the worker.

A refusal to accept work or undertake training without good cause by a person who has been referred would be reported back to the State agency by the Labor Department; and, unless such person returns to the program within 60 days (during which he would receive counseling), his welfare payment would be terminated. Protective and vendor payments would be provided to protect dependent children from the faults of others. Under the House bill, such payments would be optional with the States, but under the committee proposal the children must be given this protection.

Earnings Exemption

Under the present AFDC program, the States, at their option, may disregard not more than $50 per month of earned income of each dependent child under age 18 but not more than $150 per month in the same home in computing a family's income for public welfare purposes. The States also have the option of disregarding $5 of income from any source before applying the child's earned income exemption.

Under the House bill, all earned income of each child recipient under age 16, and of each child age 16 to 21 who is a full-time student attending school, would be excluded in determining need for assistance. In the case of a child over 16 who is not in school or an adult relative the first $30 of earned income of the group plus ⅓ of the remainder of such income for the month would also be exempt. The option of the States to disregard $5 a month of any type of income would be continued. The provision exempting $50 a month of a child's income would be superseded by these provisions.

Under the committee bill, the earnings exemption provision would be enlarged to require States to exempt the first $50 and one-half of family income over $50 rather than $30 and one-third of family earnings above $30. After July 1, 1969, the same earnings exemption would be extended to the old-age assistance program and the aid to the permanently and totally disabled program.

The exemption of all earnings would not be available to any child whether above or below age 16 unless he was attending school full time.

Unemployed Fathers Program

The committee bill removes certain provisions contained in the House bill which affect eligibility of children on AFDC when their father is unemployed. Specifically, the requirement that the father have six calendar quarters of work or have been entitled to unemployment compensation would be removed. In addition, the committee bill would restore present provisions of existing law under which a State may at its option make payments for a month in which the father received unemployment compensation. Under the House bill, receipt of any unemployment compensation would bar assistance for the month.

* * *

E. CHILD WELFARE SERVICES

* * *

F. MEDICAL ASSISTANCE (MEDICAID)

1. Provisions of the House Bill Changed, and New Provisions Added, by the Committee Bill

Limitation on Federal Participation in Medical Assistance

Under the House bill, States would be limited in setting income levels for Federal matching purposes to the lower of (1) 133⅓ percent of the AFDC payment level, or (2) 133⅓ percent of the States per capita income applied to a family of four.

In lieu of the House provisions the committee bill would apply *both* of the following provisions:

(1) Beginning July 1, 1968, the Federal Government would not participate in matching any of the cost of medical assistance to persons whose income exceeds 150 percent of the old-age assistance standards in a given state; *and*

(2) Beginning July 1, 1969, Federal participation will be at the rate of—

(a) The Federal medical assistance percentage (which varies according to State per capita income from 50 percent to 83 percent) applicable with respect to all cash assistance recipients and persons in medical institutions whose incomes are less than the applicable cash assistance standard in a State; *and*

    (b) The square of the Federal medical assistance percentage (which gives a result which varies between 25 percent and 69 percent) with respect to the medically needy (subject to the limitation in (1) above)

This formula results in a reduction in short-term costs to the Federal Government estimated as follows:

Fiscal Year:	*Amount* *(in millions)*
1969	$45
1970	701
1971	998
1972	1,294

After the squaring rule becomes effective in 1969 the long-term savings under the House bill and the committee amendment are approximately the same. The lower savings under the committee amendment estimated for 1969 results in large part from the fact that part (2) of the limitation would not go into effect until fiscal year 1970.

Skilled Nursing Home Standards Under Medicaid

The bill would require the States, as a condition to participation in the medicaid program, to place public assistance recipients only in those nursing homes which are licensed as meeting certain conditions. The conditions include requirements which relate to environment, sanitation, and housekeeping now applicable to extended care facilities under medicare, as well as the fire and safety standards of the Life Safety Code of the National Fire Protection Association (unless the Secretary finds that a State's existing fire code is adequate).

The committee amendment would also require the States to have a professional medical audit program under which periodic medical evaluations of the appropriateness of the kind and level of care provided title XIX patients in nursing homes, mental hospitals, and other institutions will be made.

Effective July 1, 1970, States which provide skilled nursing home care under medicaid will also be expected to provide home health care services.

Hospital Deductibles and Copayment for Medically Indigent

Under present law, States may not impose any deductibles or cost sharing with respect to hospital care provided under the medicaid program. Under the committee bill, the costs of hospital care received by the medically needy could be subject to deductibles or other cost sharing if a State desired to have such provisions in its program. As under existing law such deductible or cost sharing could not be imposed with respect to the money payment recipients.

* * *

Direct Billing

Under present law, the States are required to pay for health services provided under medical assistance programs directly to the provider of the services. The House bill would permit States to make payment directly to the recipient for physicians' services with respect to those medical assistance recipients who are not also receiving cash assistance. Under the committee bill, the provision is broadened to include dentists as well as physicians and to apply also to those recipients who are receiving cash assistance. The Secretary would establish safeguards to assure that charges by physicians to the recipients are reasonable, and that the State agency has methods and procedures to safeguard against the possibility of unnecessary utilization of care, and to assure the reasonableness of any charges paid by any recipient.

* * *

Required Services Under Medicaid

Under current law, States must provide, as a minimum, five basic services: inpatient hospital services, outpatient hospital services, other laboratory and X-ray services, skilled nursing home services, and physician's services. States may select a number of other items from an additional list in the law. The House bill provided that a State, as an alternative to the basic five items of services, may select any seven of the first 14 services listed in the law. In addition to the basic five, the services from among which States can make their selection are: (1) Medical care or any type of remedial care recognized under State law, furnished by a licensed practitioner within the scope of his practice as defined under State law; (2) home health care services; (3) private duty nurse services; (4) clinic services; (5) dental services; (6) physical therapy and related services; (7) prescribed drugs, dentures and prosthetic devices and eyeglasses; (8) other diagnostic, screening, preventive and rehabilitative services; and (9) inpatient hospital services and skilled nursing home services for individuals age 65 or older in an institution for mental diseases.

Under the committee bill, States would be required to continue to provide the basic five services for all money payment recipients, the most needy receiving help under the program. With respect to the medically indigent, States would be allowed to select either the first five, or at least seven out of 14, services authorized under present law, except that if nursing home or hospital care services are selected, a State must also provide physician's services in those institutions. Subsequent to July 1, 1970, a State would be required to also provide home health services for its assistance recipients who are eligible for skilled nursing home care.

* * *

G. CHILD HEALTH

* * *

The bill came before the Senate on November 15. Senator Long, the floor manager, had the Finance Committee's amendments adopted en bloc without floor objection.

Senator Winston Prouty of Vermont then introduced an amendment freezing the tax rate and the maximum taxable earnings at their existing levels. Under the Prouty proposal, costs for the increased benefits were to be financed through the general revenues. There was little debate on the issue and the amendment was subsequently rejected.

There were several successful amendments to the bill. Senator Thomas Kuchel of California introduced a measure easing severe cut-backs in Medicaid. Senator Lee Metcalf of Montana sponsored legislation excluding persons who were acting in the place of the mother (i.e., grandmother, sister, aunt) from mandatory work-training for AFDC recipients. He also introduced the amendment deleting restrictive requirements for disability benefits.

The Senate also adopted a consent order in order to complete action on H.R. 12080 as quickly as possible. Debate on all pending amendments was limited and discussion on the entire bill was restricted to six hours.

Senator Jacob Javits of New York attempted to establish advisory councils for state and local agencies composed of welfare recipients. This was to "provide for a voice by the recipients themselves in a way in which welfare is being administered," but the plan was rejected.

Senator Miller of Iowa then introduced his amendment creating a new program for reimbursing hospital and nursing homes for Medicare costs. The provider of the services would be able to determine which of several alternative formula should be used including either average per diem cost, or the Medicare patient's actual cost. The program, estimated at $200 million was adopted by voice vote.

Senator Fred Harris of Oklahoma submitted legislation requiring all states to provide AFDC to children of unemployed fathers (AFDC-UP). Under the existing law, federal grants were available if a state adopted such a program, but this amendment made state adoption mandatory. The controversial amendment drew strong responses but it was eventually carried on a close vote. Although the mandatory work-training provisions in H.R. 12080 had been substantially softened, several Senators from both parties wanted the provision deleted altogether. Senator Robert Kennedy and fifteen co-sponsors suggested a program exempting mothers from the work incentive program while their children were not in school. This amendment was the most controversial Senate change and provoked emotional and seemingly bitter debate. The tone was set by Senator Kennedy himself.

Congressional Debates
113 Congressional Record, p. 16945
(November 21, 1967)

Senator Kennedy . . .

Perhaps the greatest failure of welfare in this country has been its damage to the fabric of family life. Too often it has forced fathers to leave home so that their families might obtain assistance, such assistance being unavailable unless the home breaks up. Just yesterday, the Senate, recognizing how profoundly damaging and undesirable this is, adopted the Harris amendment to make aid to dependent children of unemployed fathers a mandatory part of each State's welfare plan.

Yet the work incentive plan which the committee has proposed, although constructive in its general purpose, takes a step in the direction of the broken home. It will force mothers who have children attending school to work, during or after school hours, during months when school is in session and during vacation period. School-age children will be forced to come home to an empty house, the proverbial latchkey children whose names so often are found on the rolls of the juvenile court.

As the legislation reads at the present time, we have accepted the idea that a mother with preschool children should remain at home and that the mother should not be forced to work under those conditions. I think that is important. But where the legislation falls down is where the mother has a child 8, 9, 10, 12, 14, or 15 years of age, and the mother is taking care of one or more such children, and she has a responsibility for those children. That legislation requires that the mother, despite the fact that she cares for those children and has a responsibility for them, has got to go out to work during a period of time that those children are off from school, or during the summer.

She is unnecessarily coerced. The idea of breaking up the family home, the family unit is not good. I believe that we should move in the opposite direction and encourage the mother to remain at home with the children.

My amendment accepts the idea that while children are in school, the mother can work during that period of time; but when the children are out of school, or on vacation, or during the summer, the mother, it seems to me, should remain at home to take care of the children.

Another part of the legislation which is a matter of concern to me, and is dealt with by this amendment, provides that where the mother does not participate in the work program, her welfare assistance is not only automatically cut off from her but she also no longer has the right to handle that money, there is then established a procedure where a third party is brought in and the money is handled through that third party.

Once again, it breaks down the concept of the home idea, of the family unit and the importance of the mother. Perhaps the mother is wrong. But, perhaps she is right, that a particular job has been established for her and that it does not make much sense. Perhaps she wants to stay home with the children and says, "That is more important for me to do." Here we are taking the step of cutting off aid to the mother but, it seems to me, it also destroys the mother's position in the home by saying that she is no longer going to receive welfare assistance and that it will be automatically handled through a third party, which I think is a bad mistake.

I recognize that there will be instances when it will be necessary to go through a third party. But it should be left to the State to make the judgment or determination; it should not be made by Congress. Congress should not decide that every mother who should refuses to work under our program should no longer be considered fit to handle funds under the welfare program.

The controversy over the public assistance amendments overshadowed the debates about OASDI benefits to some extent. A proposal to substitute the House-adopted 12.5 per cent OASDI benefit increase for the Finance Committee's 15 per cent figure was rejected 22–58. On the other hand the Senate rejected an amendment raising the permissible earnings of a social security recipient to $2,700 without any loss in benefits in favor of a similar plan increasing the earnings ceiling to $2,400.

It also passed a comprehensive twenty-one-page amendment, introduced by Senator Long, requiring that drugs bought under state Medicaid programs be purchased on a generic-name rather than brand-name basis.

It was close to midnight on November 21, 1967 before the Senate completed action on the numerous amendments; the members then adjourned until the following morning when final debate on the bill would begin. In a memorandum from Robert Myers, chief actuary of the Social Security Administration, it was estimated that the total cost of the Senate revision of H.R. 12080 would be $7.8 billion. This was more than double the estimated $3.2 billion of the House version, and substantially above the $6.3 billion the Finance Committee's bill would have cost. However, in spite of the expense of the expanded programs there was little doubt that the Senate would pass the bill. When the roll-call vote was recorded, seventy-eight Senators favored the bill and only six voted against it.

Because of substantial differences between the House and Senate versions of H.R. 12080, there was a serious question whether a compromise could be worked out before the first session of the ninetieth Congress ended. Even if a bill could be worked out, it was possible that either the House or Senate would reject the compromise.

However, less than three weeks after Senate passage, the Conference Committee issued its report and compromise bill. It closely resembled the House version, and virtually eliminated all the amendments attached in the Senate. For instance, the AFDC mandatory work-incentive provisions, which had been significantly modified by the Senate, were reinstated to their full force. This resulted in a threatened filibuster by Senate liberals in order to block final action on the bill until 1968, when the controversial sections could be reconsidered. The same Senators severely criticized the freeze provision which provided a ceiling on the proportion of dependent children who could receive AFDC benefits in individual states.

The compromise bill provided for a 13 per cent increase in overall OASDHI benefits, with the largest percentage increases for those receiving the smallest benefits. The minimum benefit was raised from $44 to $55 per month and the Long Amendment on drug purchases was entirely dropped. The bill also liberalized the retirement test by allowing an OASDI recipient to earn $140 per month, instead of $125, without the loss of benefits. To finance these increased benefits, the taxable wage base was raised from $6,600 to $7,800, and the payroll tax rate was increased from 4.4 per cent to 4.8 per cent in 1969 and eventually to 5.9 per cent in 1987.

The cost of the compromise bill was estimated to be $3.7 billion in 1969, the first full year of operation. This was only $400 million higher than the House bill—less than half of the Senate version's cost.

The most significant change in the Medicaid program was the restriction imposed on federal participation. The Federal Government could not furnish funds to any state with a Title XIX program covering persons with incomes of more than 133 per cent of the state's AFDC assistance standards. Thus, the level of income standards for AFDC recipients, would be binding on the determination of medically needy persons, if the state wanted to receive Title XIX funds.

There were also several non-controversial changes made in the Medicare programs. Under the new provisions, a Medicare patient covered by Title XVIII B could submit an itemized bill for reimbursement even though he had not yet paid it. This meant that an elderly patient did not have to pay the bill out of his own savings first and wait for the government to reimburse him.

Since the conference bill was so similar to the original House version there was no doubt that it would be overwhelmingly approved in the lower chamber. It passed after only one hour of debate.

In the Senate, a harder fight was expected. The majority leader, Senator Mike Mansfield, considered invoking cloture if liberal Senators tried to filibuster. All the strategy planning was unnecessary, however, as the re-

sult of a parliamentary coup engineered by Finance Committee Chairman Senator Russell Long. On December 14 when the bill's opponents happened to be absent, he immediately moved to bring the conference report before the Senate, referring to the piece of legislation only by its number (H.R. 12080) and not by its name. Senator Tydings of Maryland, who had been assigned by the liberals to block attempts at passage, later stated that he had no idea that the bill being adopted was the Social Security Amendments.

The bill passed by voice vote and Senator Long then moved to have the vote reconsidered. That motion was tabled. Thus, in a few moments, with only a handful of Senators on the floor, the conference report was adopted and the filibuster averted.

Senator Mansfield, however, quickly protested "the unfair treatment of a group of Senators" and ultimately it was agreed that another vote on the bill would be taken giving opponents of the bill an opportunity to voice their disapproval. The most the liberals could do was to promise to renew the fight to eliminate the bill's controversial welfare provisions in 1968. The final vote was 62 – 14 with 24 not voting.

President Johnson signed H.R. 12080 on January 2, 1968, and at the same time revealed the appointment of a commission "to look into all aspects of existing welfare and related programs to make just and equitable recommendations for constructive improvements, whenever needed and indicated."

Presidential Statement Upon Signing the Social Security Amendments of 1967
(January 2, 1968)*

This coming year will mark one-third of a century since social security became the law of the land.

Because of social security, tens of millions of Americans have been able to stand straighter and taller—unafraid of their future.

Social security has become so important to our lives, it is hard to remember that when it was first proposed it was bitterly attacked—much as Medicare was attacked and condemned before it came into being 2½ years ago.

Today, for the second time in 30 months, I am signing into law a measure that will further strengthen and broaden the Social Security System. Measured in dollars of insurance benefits, the bill enacted into law today is the greatest stride forward since social security was launched in 1935.

In March, 24 million Americans will receive increased benefits of at least 13 percent. In the years to come, as the 78 million American earners now

*Weekly Compilation of Presidential Documents, January 8, 1968, p. 28–29.

covered by social security become eligible, they will gain even greater benefits.

— For a retired couple, maximum benefits will rise from $207 to $234 and ultimately to $323 per month.

Minimum benefits for an individual will be increased from $44 to $55 a month.

— Outside earnings can total $140 a month with no reduction in benefits.

— 65,000 disabled widows and 175,000 children will receive benefits for the first time.

— Medicare benefits are expanded to include additional days of hospitalization.

Combined, the social security amendments of 1965 and 1967 bring an average dollar increase of 23 percent. Medicare protection amounts on the average to an additional 12 percent. This makes total increases of 35 percent in the past 30 months.

When the benefit checks go out next March, 1 million more people will be lifted above the poverty line. This means that 9 million people will have risen above the poverty line since the beginning of 1964.

Social security benefits are not limited to the poor. They go to widows, orphans, and the disabled who without them would be reduced to poverty. They relieve an awful burden from the young who would otherwise have to divert income from the education of their children to take care of their parents.

Franklin Roosevelt's vision of social insurance has stood the test of the changing times. I wish I could say the same for our Nation's welfare system.

The welfare system today pleases no one. It is criticized by liberals and conservatives, by the poor and the wealthy, by social workers and politicians, by whites and by Negroes in every area of the Nation.

My recommendations to the Congress this year sought to make basic changes in the system.

Some of these recommendations were adopted. They include a work incentive program, incentives for earning, day care for children, child and maternal health services, and family planning services. I believe these changes will have a good effect.

Other of my recommendations were not adopted by the Congress. In their place, the Congress substituted certain severe restrictions.

I am directing Secretary Gardner to work with State governments so that compassionate safeguards are established to protect deserving mothers and needy children.

The welfare system in America is outmoded and in need of a major change.

Commission on Income Maintenance Programs

I am announcing today the appointment of a Commission on Income Maintenance Programs to look into all aspects of existing welfare and related programs and to make just and equitable recommendations for constructive improvements, wherever needed and indicated. We must examine any and every plan, however unconventional, which could promise a constructive advance in meeting the income needs of all the American people.

That Commission of distinguished Americans will be chaired by Ben W. Heineman, chairman of the board, Chicago and Northwestern Railroads. Its membership will include Messrs. Thomas J. Watson, Jr., chairman of the board, IBM Corp., Donald C. Burnham, president, Westinghouse Electric Corp., James W. Aston, president, Republic National Bank, Dallas, Texas, Asa T. Spaulding, recently retired president, North Carolina Mutual Life Co., Durham, N.C., Henry S. Rowen, president, Rand Corp., Santa Monica, Calif., George E. Reedy, Jr., president, Struthers Research and Development Corp., Washington, D.C., Anna Rosenberg Hoffman, public and industrial relations consultant, New York City, Julian Samora, professor of sociology, University of Notre Dame, Robert M. Solow, professor of economics, MIT, Edmund G. "Pat" Brown, partner, law firm Bell, Hunt, Hart and Brown, and David Sullivan, general president, Building Service Employees International Union, New York.

Over the last third of a century in America we have proved that people who earn their living can make their lives better and more secure if they divert part of their incomes to protect themselves from the twists of fortune that face all men. Our challenge for the coming years is to see if we can extend that same human insurance and human dignity to persons who are not able to buy their own protection. Our challenge is to save children.

1968

The year 1968 opened like any other Johnson year, but the beginning was deceptive. Civil disturbances and the war in Vietnam were polarizing the country, and directly or indirectly affecting the issues of income maintenance. The cleavage between social security and welfare became even more marked. Welfare was a politically explosive issue, but both major presidential candidates advocated automatic cost-of-living escalations for OASDHI payments.

The mood of the country was ugly, and serious or meaningful legislative change could not be expected. Indeed, attacks on the Poverty Program indicated that the approach to income maintenance was moving back towards retributory measures. However, many ideas were being proposed to reform the income maintenance programs totally. Moreover, there were major steps toward the development of the concept of "welfare rights." These are perhaps best seen by breaking the year down into different "functions."

Legislative Action

President Johnson claimed that 1968 was a "normal" year and his budget message followed usual pattern. He promised, for instance, that "legislation will be proposed to update the unemployment insurance program," but there was no legislative action at all.

Rising medical care costs called attention to federal health programs, and considerable administrative reorganization occurred in HEW to better coordinate the provision of medical care. This approach was reflected in the presidential message of March 4, 1968.

Presidential Message to the Congress on Health in America
(March 4, 1968)*

To the Congress of the United States:

My health recommendations to the Congress this year include five major new goals:

First, to reduce sharply the inexcusably high rate of infant mortality in the United States.

Second, to meet the urgent need for more doctors, nurses, and other health workers.

Third, to deal with the soaring cost of medical care and to assure the most efficient use of our health resources.

Fourth, to lower the shocking toll of deaths caused by accidents in America.

Fifth, to launch a nation-wide volunteer effort to improve the health of all Americans.

Each of these goals—and others which I will discuss in this message —will require an unprecedented national commitment. Each will take years to achieve. But every one of them must be reached if we are to guarantee to every citizen a full measure of safety, health and good medical care.

The first generation of Americans built their dream of a new nation on the conviction that life, liberty and the pursuit of happiness are the inalienable rights of every man.

For nearly two centuries, our Nation has sought to make those rights a reality for more and more of our people.

It has fallen to this generation to assure that those rights have real meaning for every citizen. And this generation of Americans has made an historic commitment to open new opportunities—for economic advance, for educational fulfillment, for equality—for every citizen:

*Weekly Compilation of Presidential Documents, March 11, 1968, p. 423–34.

—Through unprecedented economic growth during the last 83 months and the war against poverty, nearly 12 million Americans have been lifted out of the depths of want and despair.

—Through more than 18 landmark education measures in the last four years, a tripling of the Federal investment in education, and a doubling of all public and private expenditures on education in the last six years, the Nation is moving rapidly to give every American child a real chance for full growth and development.

—Through the landmark Civil Rights Acts of 1964 and 1965, we have moved closer to the day when equal justice and opportunity will become a reality for all Americans.

We have sought also to make these basic rights meaningful to the older person stricken with arthritis, to the poor child with rheumatic fever, to the infant who in an earlier day might have suffered the ravages of polio.

In the last three years, the Federal Government enacted nearly 30 new health measures. We have increased its investment from $6 billion to nearly $14 billion annually to assure that the benefits of modern medicine are available to all our people:

—To make medical care available to those who need it most, the elderly and the poor, expenditures have risen from $1 billion to nearly $8 billion. Another $2.5 billion is spent each year to bring the finest health care to our servicemen and veterans.

—To build new laboratories, hospitals and health clinics, and to train the men and women to work in them, expenditures have risen from $2 billion to nearly $3 billion annually.

—To prevent and control disease, expenditures have risen from $450 million to nearly $700 million.

The real meaning of these statistics is found in the lives of people who have been helped:

— 19.5 million Americans, 65 and over, are now able to receive the medical care they need without suffering crushing economic burdens.

— 20 million children who have been vaccinated against measles, and 323,000 fewer children suffer from measles each year.

— 30 million have been protected against diphtheria, polio, tetanus and whooping cough, reducing by more than 50 percent the number of children who suffer from these diseases.

— 43,000 retarded children can now look forward to more productive lives because of the 150 special clinics built to serve them.

— 47 million Americans live in communities served by new mental health centers.

—The life expectancy of Americans continues to increase, promising millions a longer and fuller life. In 1920, it was 54.1 years; today it is over 70.

And the discoveries of modern science promise a better life for all citizens: the prevention of German measles, the advances in treating leukemia, the progress in understanding life's processes.

We must continue to build upon those proud achievements.

The Birthright of Sound Health

The American child is born into a land richer with promise than any nation in the history of the world.

But to share in that promise, he must survive the perils of birth and infancy. For too many American children, the hazards of survival are steep.

This great, wealthy, resourceful Nation—which should lead the world in saving its young—instead ranked 15th in infant mortality in 1965.

In that year, nearly 25 infants out of every 1,000 born in this country died before the age of one. Thousands more were handicapped for life because of inadequate health care in their first year.

The infant mortality rate among poor families was nearly double the national average. In certain city ghettos and pockets of rural poverty the rate was 7 times that in surrounding suburban areas.

Those figures shamed this enlightened Nation. And we acted to meet the problem.

Through the Maternal and Child Health program:

— 300,000 women are now receiving family planning services.

— 390,000 receive maternity care.

— 680,000 infants are getting the attention so crucial to their later development.

Through the Crippled Children's program, 460,000 children will be treated for handicapping conditions each year.

Through Medicaid, thousands of needy mothers and their infants are receiving the care vital to their health and well being.

The infant mortality rate in this country dropped from 25.2 deaths per thousand in 1963, to 22.1 per thousand in 1967—a 12% decline in four years.

The success of these programs in two cities demonstrates that the tragic rate of infant mortality can be reduced even faster. Last year, because of modern medicine and a concentrated effort, the rate in Washington, D.C. fell 8.5%; the rate in Chicago in the first 10 months of the year dropped 15%.

In 1963, 100,000 infants died. In 1967, that figure was reduced to 80,000. But this progress is not enough. For thousands more did not receive the medical care so vital to their future growth and development.

The Child Health Improvement and Protection Act of 1968

This Nation must accelerate its efforts. The cost of future care rises every time a child's disease or handicap is left unattended. A man's potential is diminished every time an affliction that could be cured in childhood causes permanent damage. Most important of all, America's conscience is scarred and her future dimmed every time a child dies needlessly.

We must now attack the problem of infant mortality on a nation-wide basis by providing essential medical care to the 700,000 needy mothers who give birth each year and to their infants.

To launch this effort, *I recommend a $58 million increase in appropriations for the maternal and child health care programs in fiscal 1969.* $25 million of this increase will provide for the expansion of maternity and infant care centers and clinics.

Our goal is to assure every needy American family:

— Adequate prenatal and postnatal care for the mother.

— A safe delivery by trained health professionals.

— Competent examination of the child at birth, and expert treatment when needed.

— The best of modern medical care for the infant during his first year to prevent disease, cure illness, and correct handicaps.

— An opportunity, on a voluntary basis, to plan the number and spacing of children.

To fulfill this objective, *I propose the Child Health Act of 1968.*

With this authority, the Nation will be able to provide comprehensive medical care for every needy mother and her infant.

For America's Young

As we launch a major new effort to improve health care for the very young, we must not lose sight of our responsibility for all of America's children. We are encouraged by the gains made under our pioneering efforts:

— Head Start and other preschool programs which have brought education and health care to more than 2 million children.

— Medicaid which will provide health care to more than 3 million children this year.

— 137 new mental retardation clinics have been built to serve over 40,000 retarded children.

Nevertheless, the dimensions of what remains to be done are seen in these grim statistics:

— 436,000 children are victims of cerebral palsy.

— 424,000 have epilepsy.

— 12.3 million have eye defects.

— 2.5 million have hearing impairments.

— 3.2 million have speech defects.

— 2.3 million have orthopedic handicaps.

— 4.8 million are emotionally disturbed.

To continue our efforts to meet the needs of America's children, *I recommend that the Congress provide $1.4 billion in fiscal 1969 — an increase* *of $215 million—for child health services under Medicaid and other Federal health programs.* These funds will provide:

—3.5 million poor children with health services under Medicaid.

—More than 1 million children with comprehensive health services at 56 Children and Youth Centers.

—500,000 Head Start children with medical examinations and follow-up treatment.

—460,000 children with treatment for handicapping conditions.

—200,000 children with family services at Neighborhood Health Centers.

The Benefits of Research

The history of our times is not solely a study in crisis. It is also one of hope: when polio was conquered; when other infectious diseases that had plagued man for centuries fell one after another; when breakthroughs in genetics brought a better understanding of the process of life.

These are the quiet successes achieved in countless laboratories, leaving their mark forever on the future of man.

1967 was a breakthrough year which brought many rich dividends:

1. Measles can now be completely prevented.
2. The creation of life in a California test tube startled the world.
3. The Minnesota-trained doctor's first heart transplant was an historic milestone.

But none of these achievements were the result of a single year's research. They came from the careful work of many years. They were made possible by the Federal Government's continuing support to scientists who seek to expand our store of fundamental knowledge. That support has grown from $1 billion in 1963, to nearly $1.5 billion today, and comprises 65 percent of the Nation's total expenditures for biomedical research.

Yet we have only begun to unlock the secrets of better health and a richer life.

Our understanding of disease and human development is woefully incomplete. We can control some types of cancer, but do not yet know their exact causes.

We are still groping to understand the causes and the cures of mental illness. We have only begun to discover the reasons for mental retardation.

The relentless search for knowledge must go on. To assure the breakthroughs of next year, and the years after, *I recommend that the Congress provide $1.5 billion for health research in fiscal 1969.*

Population and Human Reproduction

Two vital fields long neglected by research are population and human reproduction. Thousands of parents want help in determining how to plan their families. Thousands of others are unable to have the children they desire.

Our lack of knowledge impedes our effort to provide the help they need.

— Far too little is known about the physiology of reproduction and its effect on all aspects of human life.

— Searching studies are needed to determine the complex emotional, sociological, physiological and economic factors involved.

A wide range of scientists must bring to these problems their specialized disciplines — biologists, behavioral scientists, biochemists, pharmacologists, demographers, experts in population dynamics.

To launch this effort, *I have directed the Secretary of Health, Education, and Welfare to establish a Center for Population Studies and Human Reproduction in the National Institute of Child Health and Human Development.* The Center will serve to give new energy and direction to the research activities of all Federal Departments and Agencies in these fields.

I am asking the Congress to appropriate $12 million to support the research activities of the Center during its first year of operation.

As we move to expand our knowledge of population and human reproduction, we must make that knowledge available to those who want it. Last year, the Federal Government helped to bring information and counseling on a voluntary basis to more than 500,000 women. But there are millions more who want help.

I recommend that the Congress provide for an increase in funds from $25 million in fiscal 1968 to $61 million in fiscal 1969 so that three million women can have access to family planning help if they so desire.

Health Manpower

Several years ago, this Nation set out to encourage the training of more doctors, nurses and medical technicians.

As the result of the imaginative programs recommended by the Administration and approved by the Congress over the last five years,

— An additional 100,000 doctors, nurses, dentists, laboratory technicians, and other health workers are being trained this year to meet the health needs of our growing population.

— More than 850 medical, dental and nursing schools have enlarged their capacity or improved their instruction.

This rate of progress is encouraging. But our increasing population and the demand for more and better health care swell the need for doctors, health professionals and other medical workers.

Yet we lack the capacity to train today those who must serve us tomorrow.

To train more health workers and to train them better and faster, *I propose the Health Manpower Act of 1968.*

This Act will extend and strengthen five vital measures which are due to expire in June 1969:

(1) *The Health Educational Act of 1963* will be reinforced to:

— Provide new classrooms, laboratories and libraries needed to train more doctors and other health professionals.

— Authorize new operating and project grants which will encourage the schools to expand their enrollment, improve their curricula, and reduce the length of their training.

— Extend financial aid to thousands of students each year.

— Simplify procedures so that schools can obtain funds for joint research-teaching-library projects through one application.

(2) *The Nurse Training Act of 1964* will be improved to:

— Strengthen the loan, scholarship, and traineeship program so that nearly 50,000 nursing students can be helped through school in the first year of the program.

— Encourage nursing schools to expand enrollment and overcome high attrition rates by revamping their curicula and tailoring their courses to the needs of the students.

(3) *The Health Personnel Training Act of 1966* will be continued to speed the training of paramedical personnel and other health workers by

— Constructing new classrooms.

— Improving the quality of instruction.

— Developing new curricula and methods of training.

(4) *The Health Research Act of 1965* will be amended to permit greater emphasis on the development of research facilities meeting critical regional or national needs.

(5) *The Graduate Health Training Act of 1964* will be extended to increase the number of skilled administrators and public health workers.

I urge the Congress to appropriate $290 million in fiscal 1969 to carry forward our vital health manpower programs.

This effort will be bolstered by the Veterans in Public Service Act, which I recently proposed to the Congress. Under that Act, the talents of the veteran will be enlisted for service to his community. For whose who return to meet critical health manpower shortages, there will be special benefits while they are in training and on the job.

I urge the Congress to launch this program promptly so that we can bring the skills and experience of the veteran to bear on our pressing health needs.

Partnership for Health

In 1966 we launched the Partnership for Health. Its purpose was to support State and local efforts to:

— Identify the health needs of each State and city.

— Mobilize the resources of the State to meet those needs.

—Determine what additional resources, facilities, equipment and
manpower, are required.

In the brief period since its enactment, this great Partnership has pioneered
in the expansion of State and local responsibility for the health of our
citizens.

Every State and many communities have now created health planning
agencies which are at work developing and implementing bold new health
strategies. This planning, tailored to the special needs of each State, will
forge Federal, State and local efforts into an effective instrument to bring
better health care to the people.

This important work must continue — and it must be expanded.

*I recommend that the Congress appropriate $195 million for the Partnership For Health in fiscal 1969, an increase of $35 million over fiscal 1968
— an increase of 22 percent.*

The Regional Medical Program

In 1966, we began the Regional Medical Program to reduce the toll of
death and disability from heart disease, cancer, stroke and related illnesses.
Its purpose is to translate research into action, so all the people of our Nation can benefit as rapidly as possible from the achievements of modern
medicine.

Fifty-four regions, spanning the nation, have begun planning. Eight regions have already begun action programs. Most of the others will start by
the end of the year.

These programs are concentrating regional resources and developing
more effective ways to attack the three chief killers in this country. Thousands of Americans stricken by heart disease, cancer or stroke are already
receiving better care.

But these threats to our health and vitality remain stubborn and unyielding.

*I recommend that the Congress extend the Regional Medical Program
and increase — by almost 100 percent — to $100 million the funds available
for the program in fiscal 1969.*

Controlling Costs of Health Care

Virtually every family feels the burden of rising costs of medical care.

Thousands of Americans today are not getting urgently needed medical
care because they cannot afford it.

Others pay for it only by giving up necessities, postponing a long-held
dream, or mortgaging their futures.

The outlook is sobering. It has been estimated that between 1965 and
1975, the cost of living will increase by more than 20 percent. But the cost
of health care will increase by nearly 140 percent by 1975:

— Average payments per person will nearly double from about $200 a year to some $400 a year.

— Drug payments will rise by 65 percent.

— Dental bills will increase 100 percent.

— Doctor's bills will climb 160 percent.

— Payments for general hospital services will jump 250 percent.

Part of these increases will be for expanded and improved health services. But a large part of the increase will be unnecessary — a rise which can be prevented.

Last year I appointed a Commission of distinguished citizens — physicians, hospital officials, teachers, business executives, and other leaders — to make a comprehensive study of health manpower and medical care.

The Commission, which reported in November, cited three major deficiencies in present practices which contribute to unacceptable increases in medical costs:

— Most health insurance plans encourage doctors and patients to choose hospitalization even when other, less costly, forms of care would be equally effective.

— Health professions are generally paid in proportion to the amount of service they render. There are no strong economic incentives to encourage them to avoid providing care that is unnecessary.

— Hospitals charge on a cost basis, which places no penalty on inefficient operations. Moreover, present systems of hospital management make it very difficult to maintain effective control over hospital costs.

The Commission concluded:

"If the needs for health care are to be met, the health care system must be organized to employ its resources with more wisdom and effectiveness. The two areas which appear to offer the greatest potential for improvement are (1) reducing unnecessary (or unnecessarily expensive) medical care and (2) increasing efficiency in the provision of hospital care."

It will not be easy to carry out this recommendation.

But unless we do — unless we act now — health care will not improve as fast as it should.

Congress has recognized this problem of rising medical costs. Late last year it authorized the Secretary of Health, Education, and Welfare to test different types of payment systems under Medicare, Medicaid, and the Maternal and Child Health programs.

I have directed the Secretary of Health, Education, and Welfare to begin immediately extensive tests of incentives designed to reduce the cost of medical care.

First, we must explore ways to prevent unnecessary hospitalization. Our experience in Medicare can serve as a guideline. Under that plan, hospital stays are limited to periods which are clearly necessary, and payments are provided for other less expensive types of care which serve the patient equally well: outpatient clinic service, home treatment, nursing home care. We can also draw on the experience of new private prepaid comprehensive plans featuring incentives designed to reduce unnecessary hospitalization.

Second, we must test incentives designed to control the cost of hospital care itself. The Health Manpower Commission reported that costs among some of the Nation's best hospitals vary by as much as 100%, without significant differences in quality or scope of services. This shows that savings in hospital costs can be achieved. We must find ways to encourage efficiency and penalize waste.

These tests will call for the cooperation of doctors, hospitals and insurance companies.

They will be the pioneer efforts. If they are successful—and if they can be applied on a broad basis—they will hold much promise for the American people.

I recommend that the Congress authorize the Secretary of Health, Education, and Welfare, under Medicare, Medicaid and the Maternal and Child Health programs, to employ new methods of payment as they prove effective in providing high quality medical care more efficiently and at lower cost.

It is appropriate that the Government—which pays more than 20% of the nation's medical bill—take the lead in stemming soaring medical care costs.

But this can be only part of the effort. Ultimate success will depend on the ingenuity of our health profession and institutions, and the insurance systems allied with them.

The rewards of success—and the penalties of inaction—demand a dedicated effort by all. Unless the cost spiral is stopped, the Nation's health bill could reach a staggering $100 billion by 1975. The cost of providing adequate medical care to a family could double.

The Cost of Drugs

Beyond this, we must make certain that the American taxpayer does not pay needlessly high and exhorbitant prices for prescription drugs used in Federally-supported programs.

Recent surveys have shown, for instance, that 12 drugs of the same type range in retail price from $1.25 to $11 for 30 tablets. The taxpayer should not be forced to pay $11 if the $1.25 drug is equally effective. To do this would permit robbery of private citizens with public approval.

I recommend that the Congress authorize the Secretary of Health, Education, and Welfare to establish a reasonable cost range to govern reimbursement for drugs now provided under Medicare, Medicaid and the Maternal and Child Health programs.

This payment method will apply in all parts of these programs, except in those cases where hospitals and other health care institutions have established effective and reliable systems for cost and quality control.

The physician will be free to select more expensive drugs of the same quality and effectiveness, if he chooses, but reimbursement will be limited to the payment range established by the Secretary.

To Protect the American Patient

The wide array of medication available to the American patient is a tribute to modern science.

But the very abundance of drugs creates problems.

In our society, we normally demand that the consumer be given sufficient information to make a choice between products. But when the consumer is a patient, he must rely exclusively on his doctor's choice of the drug that can best treat his condition.

Yet the doctor is not always in a position to make a fully informed judgment. He has no complete, readily available source of information about the thousands of drugs now available.

He must nonetheless make a decision affecting the health, and perhaps the life, of his patient.

To make sure that doctors have accurate, reliable and complete information on the drugs which are available, *I recommend that the Congress authorize this year publication of a United States Compendium of Drugs.*

This Compendium would be prepared by the Secretary of Health, Education, and Welfare, in cooperation with pharmaceutical manufacturers, who would bear the cost of its publication, and with physicians and pharmacists.

It will give every doctor, pharmacy, hospital, and other health care insitution complete and accurate information about prescription drugs—use and dosage, warnings, manufacturer, generic and brand names, and facts about their safety and effectiveness.

The Tragedy of Accidents

More than 630,000 Americans died in accidents in the last six years.

This is a tragedy heightened by the fact that much of it is senseless and unnecessary.

Thousands of deaths will be prevented under the Highway and Traffic Safety laws passed by the Congress in 1966. Thousands more can be prevented by prompt medical attention.

The needed medical services are often available. But because of an inadequate rescue system, the victim dies before he reaches the hospital.

The compelling need is for modern, effective rescue systems to give immediate attention to accident victims—on the spot and while they are being speeded to the hospitals.

We have proven excellent rescue systems in action, saving fighting men injured in battle. First in Korea, and now in Vietnam, the military has shown and speed the effectiveness of helicopter crews, paramedical personnel and communications experts mobilized to save the lives of wounded men.

Few States and communities have drawn upon that experience. In many areas, ambulance crewmen are not even trained in first aid. Ambulances themselves are rarely well-equipped. Communications systems are inadequate, if they exist at all.

I have directed the Secretaries of Transportation, Health, Education, and Welfare, and Defense to devise a test program to help our States and communities develop effective rescue systems to fit their own needs.

In a previous message to the Congress this year, I proposed the Occupational Safety and Health Act of 1968, to safeguard 75 million American workers on the job.

Through this Act we can attack the conditions which cause nearly 15,000 deaths and 2.2 million injuries each year.

With these measures, we can move far toward reducing the tragic toll of accidental death and injury in America.

Physical Fitness

For more than a decade the Federal government has taken a direct interest in improving the physical fitness of Americans.

President Eisenhower, President Kennedy and I have taken steps to encourage our citizens — particularly the young — to pursue the active life.

Through these efforts, boys and girls across America have discovered the joys of exercise and sports competition.

But here — as in our health programs — we must look not only at the progress that has been made, but at the problems that remain.

— In tests of physical strength and stamina, American children still score substantially lower than children in other countries.

— 32 million children get less than the recommended physical fitness program in school; seven million get none at all.

— Only 50 percent of all college students meet accepted physical fitness standards.

Physical fitness activities and sports contribute to more than health. They teach self-discipline and teamwork. They offer excitement and a wholesome alternative to idleness. They combat delinquency. They permanently enrich the individual and his society by developing qualities of leadership and fair play.

To expand opportunities to engage in exercise, active recreation, and sports, I am establishing the President's Council on Physical Fitness and Sports, to be chaired by the Vice President.

The Council will be a Cabinet-level group, with an Advisory Committee of distinguished citizens, to develop national goals and programs to promote sports and fitness in America.

As a first step, the Council will call a national conference to explore the long-term requirements of physical fitness and sports in the nation.

Leadership and Efficient Management

Health expenditures in the United States are now nearly $50 billion a year. The Federal Government pays $14 billion of that amount, up from $5 billion four years ago to $16 billion in fiscal 1969.

The expanding Federal programs must be managed efficiently, with the most careful attention to the most urgent needs of the American people. *To that end, I am today directing the Secretary of Health, Education, and Welfare to submit to me a modern plan of organization to achieve the most efficient and economical operation of the health programs of the Federal Government.*

But better organization and leadership will be wasted if we cannot find and hold the quality of people essential for these great tasks.

I recommend the Health Personnel Act of 1968 to modernize the health personnel system within the Department of Health, Education, and Welfare. This act will provide:

— Pay increases and a flexible personnel to attract and retain professionals of the highest caliber.

— A new promotion system based upon quality of performance.

Mobilization for Health

In our drive toward a healthier America, Federal programs and Federal dollars have an important role to play. But they cannot do the job alone.

An even larger role belongs to State and local government, and to the private enterprise system of our Nation. The medical and hospital associations, the health care institutions, the health insurance industry, the communication media, voluntary civic associations, employers and labor unions, charities and church groups must join this effort. I call upon them to join in a 12-point volunteer effort to build a healthier America:

(1) To examine every child under the age of five to identify potentially crippling ailments and provide early and effective treatment.

(2) To use the public airways for public profit by offering regular health programs on television and radio to help every American preserve his cherished birthright of good health.

(3) To give prominent magazine and newspaper coverage to good health practices for our children and older Americans.

(4) To identify and reward new approaches by medical societies, group practice organizations and hospitals for delivering better health care at lower cost.

(5) To expand voluntary health insurance to those not now covered and include services not now included.

(6) To establish local systems of new incentives to recruit, train, retrain, license and effectively use nurses and medical corpsmen leaving the Armed Services, and other vital members of the health team.

(7) To make home health care part of the education of every young girl in all the schools of America.

(8) To encourage the opening of health centers to provide complete care in every community.

(9) To make physical fitness programs and recreational facilities available to people of all ages and in all walks of life.

(10) To alert teenagers and their parents to the danger of drug abuse.

(11) To develop better programs for health services for the one-third of the working poor who suffer from chronic illness.

(12) To mobilize a new spirit of public concern and private action to meet and master our health problems.

Great changes have taken place in the financing of medical care in this country. The Federal government will invest some $16 billion in the health field in fiscal 1969. We should now expect our Nation's great private resources, through volunteer and cooperative action, to step up their efforts to bring better health to all our citizens.

Health Care for All Americans

In the medical research laboratories of the world, a quiet revolution is changing the condition of man. Enemies which have held man in hostage throughout history are conquered each year. Hope turns daily to promise, and promise to practical achievement.

But progress cannot be measured in the laboratory alone. Triumph in a test tube is not triumph enough—if it remains there.

Success in a laboratory, however brilliant, is not complete if barriers of poverty, ignorance or prejudice block it from reaching the man who needs it, or the child who wastes away without it.

With the program I have outlined in this message, I believe we can move closer to our goal of decent health care for every American.

This is a program to assure that American medicine will continue to build on its great record, and that its benefits will enrich and improve the life of every citizen.

I urge the Congress to act promptly on this program.

Lyndon B. Johnson

The White House
March 4, 1968

The President could not carry out his programs and there was no important Administration-sponsored legislation concerning income security. Indeed, only one major piece of non-Administration legislation was passed.
The Department of Health, Education, and Welfare had moved to implement the mandatory provisions and AFDC freeze of the Social Security
Act of 1967, but opposition was growing. Senators Kennedy of New York
and Harris of Oklahoma introduced two bills on January 31, 1968 to repeal
the controversial sections.

No immediate action was taken on either of the Kennedy-Harris proposals, but the Senate Finance Committee later attached a portion of the
Harris legislation as a rider to the Excise Tax Bill which was reported out
on March 14. Instead of outright repeal of the controversial 1967 AFDC
changes, Wilbur Cohen, the newly-appointed Secretary of the Department
of Health, Education, and Welfare, recommended a one-year postpone-
ment of the freeze. This would allow time to determine the effects of the
other 1967 public assistance amendments. The final result was a compromise. The Tax Surcharge Act (P.L. 90–364) delayed the enforcement of
the AFDC freeze while the mandatory work programs began in mid-1968.

Despite inaction on Administration bills, Congressmen continued to promote their own income security legislation. Representative Conyers of
Michigan introduced H.R. 14496, the Family Allowances Act, to provide
$10 a month for every child in the country in addition to any existing in-
come maintenance payments. Representative William F. Ryan of New York
introduced H.R. 17331, the Income Maintenance Act.

A Bill (H.R. 17331) to Provide for a Comprehensive
Income Maintenance Program
90th Cong., 2d Sess. (1968)

"Sec. 1602. Income Maintenance Benefits.

*"Except as provided in section 1606, each eligible individual who makes
application for a benefit for a calendar month under section 1612 shall be
entitled to an income maintenance benefit payable with respect to such
month in an amount equal to the maximum benefit munder section 1603
less any reduction on account of income under section 1604.*

"Sec. 1603. Maximum Benefit.

"(a) General Rule. —
"(1) Computation of Benefit. — Except as provided in subsection (b),
     the maximum benefit for a month shall be equal to the sum of —
"(A) $50, plus

"(B) $39 multiplied by the number of additional allowances to which the eligible individual is entitled under paragraph (3) for such month, except that such benefit may not exceed $284 for a month in the case of an eligible individual other than an eligible spouse, or $142 for a month in the case of an eligible spouse.

"(2) Eligible spouse. – An eligible individual is an eligible spouse for a calendar month if at the close of such month –

"(A) he is married and has as his principal place of abode the home of his spouse, and

"(B) both he and his spouse are entitled to receive benefits under this chapter for such month.

"(3) Additional allowances. – An eligible individual shall be entitled to an additional allowance for each eligible dependent.

"(b) Special Rule for Residents or Rural Areas. – In the case of an eligible individual who resides in a rural area (as defined by section 520 of the Housing Act of 1949), the maximum benefit shall be equal to 90 percent of the amount determined under subsection (a), unless such individual's application for such benefit contains a statement by such individual that during such month he did not consume home-grown produce equal in value to 10 percent of the maximum benefit under subsection (a).

"Sec. 1604. Reduction On Account Of Income.

"(a) General Rule. – Except as provided in subsection (b), the reduction on account of income of an eligible individual's maximum benefit for a month shall be equal to 50 percent of income received by such individual and any eligible dependent of such individual during such month.

"(b) Special Rules For Persons Eligible for Certain Public Assistance."

Investigation

Although legislative action failed to produce dramatic breakthroughs on income maintenance programs, it was a significant year for investigation, and this seemed to indicate a change in social security tactics. The Presidential Commission on Income Maintenance Programs sat throughout the year, but its report was not expected until late in 1969. The report of the National Advisory Commission on Civil Disorders (the Riot Commission), however, was issued in March. It called for massive action by all levels of government to relieve ghettos pressures and observed that, "Our present system of public welfare is designed to save money instead of people, and tragically ends up doing neither." The report not only discussed the deficiencies of the existing welfare programs, but also made specific recommendations for immediate and long range changes.

Report of the National Advisory Commission on Civil Disorders
(p. 457)

The Commission believes that our present system of public assistance contributes materially to the tensions and social disorganization that have led to civil disorders. The failures of the system alienate the taxpayers who support it, the social workers who administer it, and the poor who depend on it. As Mitchell Ginsberg, head of New York City's Welfare Department, stated before the Commission, "The welfare system is designed to save money instead of people and tragically ends up doing neither."

The system is deficient in two critical ways:

First, it excludes large numbers of persons who are in great need, and who, if provided a decent level of support, might be able to become more productive and self-sufficient;

Second, for those who are included, it provides assistance well below the minimum necessary for a decent level of existence, and imposes restrictions that encourage continued dependency on welfare and undermine self-respect.

In short, while the system is indispensable because for millions — mostly children — it supports basic needs, drastic reforms are required if it is to help people free themselves from poverty.

The existing welfare programs are a labyrinth of federal, state and local legislation. Over 90 percent of national welfare payments are made through programs that are partly or largely federally funded. These reach an average of 7.5 million persons each month:

> 2.7 million are over 65, blind or otherwise severely handicapped. 3.6 million are children in the Aid for Dependent Children (AFDC), whose parents do not or cannot provide financial support.

> 1.2 million are the parents of children on AFDC. Of these, over one million are mothers and less than 200,000 are fathers; about two-thirds of the fathers are incapacitated. Only 60,000 fathers are in the special program called "Aid to Families with Dependent Children (Unemployed Parents)" (AFDC-UP) operating in 22 states.

Among all welfare programs, AFDC and AFDC-UP have clearly the greatest impact on youths and families in central cities areas; for this reason, it will be the principal focus for discussion here.

States and local governments contribute an average of about 45 percent of the cost of supporting the AFDC program, with each state setting the level of grants for its own residents. Monthly payments vary widely from state to state. They range from $9.30 per AFDC recipient monthly in Mississippi to a high of $62.55 in New York. In fiscal year 1967, the total annual cost of the AFDC program, including federal, state and local contributions, was approximately $2.0 billion, providing an average of about $36 monthly for each recipient.

This sum is well below the poverty subsistence level under any standard. The National Advisory Council on Public Welfare has commented:

> The national average provides little more than half the amounts admittedly required by a family for subsistence; in some low-income states, it is less than a quarter of that amount. The low public assistance payments contribute to the perpetuation of poverty and deprivation that extend into future generations.

Over the last six years, despite the longest sustained period of economic progress in the history of this country, the AFDC caseload has risen each year while the unemployment rate has fallen. Cases increased nationally by 319,000 during fiscal year 1967 and will, under present HEW estimates, increase by another 686,000 during fiscal year 1968. The burden of welfare — and the burden of the increases — will fall principally on our central cities. In New York City alone, 525,000 people receive AFDC support and 7,000 to 10,000 more are added each month. Yet, it has been estimated in 1965, nation-wide, over 50 percent of persons eligible to receive assistance under welfare programs were not enrolled.

In addition to the AFDC program, almost all states have a program of general assistance to provide minimum payments based largely or entirely on need. During calendar year 1966, the states spent $336 million on general assistance. No federal funds have ever been available for this program. In fact, no federal funds have ever been available for men or women, however needy, who are neither aged, severely handicapped nor the parents of minor children.

The dimension of the "pool" of poor but unassisted individuals and families — either ineligible under present programs or eligible but unenrolled — is indicated by the fact that in 1966 there were 21.7 million nonaged persons in the United States with incomes below the "poverty level" as defined by the Social Security Administration. Only a third of these received assistance from major public welfare programs:

> [T]he bulk of the nonaged poor live in families where there is a breadwinner who works either every day or who had worked a part of the year, so that the picture that people have of who the poor are is quite a different thing from an analysis of the poverty population. And what we have done in effect is carve out, because of our categorical approach to public assistance, a certain group of people within that overall poverty population to give help to.
>
> Seventy per cent of the nonaged poor families were headed by men, and 50 per cent of these held full-time jobs and 86 per cent of them worked at least part of the year, so that the typical poor family is much like the typical American family, except they don't make enough money. And they have been historically excluded from the AFDC program.[32]

The gaps in coverage and low levels of payments are the source of much of the long-term dissatisfaction with the system. The day-to-day administration of the system creates even sharper bitterness and dissatisfaction, be-

[32]Testimony before the Commission of Lisle C. Carter, Jr., Assistant Secretary for Individual and Family Services, Department of Health, Education and Welfare.

cause it serves to remind recipients that they are considered untrustworthy, ungrateful, promiscuous and lazy. Among the most tension-producing statutory requirements, administrative practices and regulations are the following:

First, in most states benefits are available only when a parent is absent from the home. Thus, in these states an unemployed father whose family needs public assistance in order to survive, must either abandon his family or see them go hungry. This so-called "Man-in-the-House" rule was intended to prevent payments to children who have an alternative potential source of support. In fact, the rule seems to have fostered the breakup of homes and perpetuated reliance on welfare. The irritation caused by the rule is aggravated in some states by regular searches of recipients' homes to ferret out violations.

Second, until recently *all* amounts earned by adult welfare recipients on outside jobs, except for small allowances for expenses, were deducted directly from the welfare payments they would otherwise have received. This practice, required by federal law, appears to have taken away from many recipients the incentive to seek part- or full-time employment. The 1967 amendments to the welfare laws permit retention of the first $30 earned by a recipient each month and one-third of all earnings about that amount. This is a start in the right direction but does not go nearly far enough. New York City has, for example, begun experimenting with a promising program that allows welfare mothers to keep the first $85 of earnings each month and a percentage of amounts above that.

Third, in most states, there is a residency requirement, generally averaging around a year, before a person is eligible to receive welfare. These state regulations were enacted to discourage persons from moving from one state to another to take advantage of higher welfare payments. In fact, they appear to have had little, if any, impact on migration and have frequently served to prevent those in greatest need — desperately poor families arriving in a strange city — from receiving the boost that might give them a fresh start.

Fourth, though large amounts are being spent on social service programs for families, children and young people, few of these programs have been effective. In the view of the Advisory Council on Public Welfare, the inadequacies in social services:

> are themselves a major source of such social evils as crime and juvenile delinquency, mental illness, illegitimacy, multi-generational dependency, slum environments, and the widely deplored climate of unrest, alienation, and discouragement among many groups in the population.

A final source of tension is the brittle relationship that exists between many welfare workers and the poor. The cumulative abrasive effects of the low levels of assistance, the complicated eligibility requirements, the continuing efforts required by regulations to verify eligibility — often by means that constitute flagrant invasions of privacy — have often brought about an adversary relationship between the case worker and the recipient family.

This is intensified by the fact that the investigative requirements not only force continuing confrontations but, in those states where the same worker performs both investigative and service functions, leave the worker little time to provide service.

As was stated by Lisle Carter, Assistant Secretary of Health, Education and Welfare, in testimony before the Commission:

> [W]e think [it] is extremely important that welfare recipients begin to feel that the welfare worker is on their side instead of on the side of the agency. There have been statements made that the welfare workers are among the most hated persons in the ghetto, and one of the studies shows that the recipients tend to feel that what the workers says is something that cannot be challenged. Nowhere do you get the feeling that . . . the worker is there to really go to bat for recipients in dealing with the other pressures that they face in the community. . . .

One manifestation of the tension and dissatisfaction created by the present system has been the growth of national and local welfare protest groups. Some are seeking to precipitate a national welfare crisis, in part by bringing on the welfare rolls so many new recipients that America will be forced to face the enormity of its poverty problem. Others, often composed of welfare recipients or welfare workers, seek expanded welfare programs and attack day-to-day inequities in the administration of the system.

On the other hand, many Americans who advocate better housing, better schools, and better employment opportunities for disadvantaged citizens oppose welfare programs of all kinds in the belief that they "subsidize" people who should be working. The fact is, as we have pointed out, that all but a small fraction of welfare recipients are disabled because of age, ill health or the need to care for their children. Even more basic is the fact that the heads of most poor families who can work are working, and are not on welfare. For both of these groups of people in need—those who cannot work and those who can and do—the problem in at least one vital respect is the same: lack of sufficient income to provide a base on which they can begin building a path out of poverty, if not for themselves, at least for their children.

An altered and expanded welfare system by extending support to more of those in need, by raising levels of assistance on a uniform national basis, and by eliminating demeaning restrictions, could begin to recapture the rich human resources that are being wasted by poverty.

Basic Strategies

In framing strategies to attack welfare problems, the Commission recognizes that a number of fundamental questions remain to be answered. Although many of the present inadequacies in the system can be identified, and specific changes recommended, long-term measures for altering the system are still untested.

A first strategy is to learn more about how welfare affects people and what its possibilities for creative use are. We endorse the recommendation of the Advisory Council on Public Welfare for greatly expanded research. We also commend the experimental incentive programs being carried out through the Department of Health, Education and Welfare and the Office of Economic Opportunity, as well as the Model Cities Program through which some cities hope to develop integrated programs of income supplementation, job training and education. We further commend the President's recent creation of a Commission on Income Maintenance Programs, which may provide answers to the complex problems here presented.

Despite the questions left open, we believe that many specific inadequacies in the present structure can and should be corrected.

The most important basic strategy we would recommend is to overhaul the existing categorical system to:

> (a) provide more adequate levels of assistance on the basis of uniform national standards.
>
> (b) reduce the burden on state and local government by financing the cost of assistance almost entirely with federal funds.
>
> (c) create new incentives to work and eliminate the features that cause hardship and dependency.
>
> (d) improve family-planning and other social services to welfare recipients.

Our longer-range strategy, one for which we can offer only tentative guides, is the development of a national system of income supplementation to provide a basic floor of economic and social security for all Americans.

Suggested Programs

Overhauling the Present System

To repair the defects in the existing categorical system is not simply a matter of changing one or two aspects. Major changes are needed in at least seven areas.

Standards of assistance

The federal government should develop a minimum income standard for individuals and families enrolled in AFDC. The standard should be at least as high as the subsistence "poverty" level periodically determined by the Social Security Administration. Only a few states now approach this "poverty" level, which is currently set at $3,335 for an urban family of four. The amending legislation should, if feasible, also permit cost of living variations among the states and within "high-cost" areas in each state.

As a critical first step toward raising assistance levels, the Commission recommends that the present provision under which the federal government pays fifteen-eighteenths of the first $18 of AFDC monthly payments be amended to provide that the federal government assume the entire first $15 and the same proportion of payments beyond $15 presently applied to that above $18. Taken together with existing legislation that requires the states to maintain levels of support when federal assistance rates are increased, the effect of this change would be to raise by over one-third the monthly welfare payments in eight states of the Deep South. In Mississippi, payments would be more than doubled.

Extension of AFDC-UP

The Commission strongly urges that the temporary legislation, enacted in 1961, which extends the AFDC programs to include needy families with two unemployed parents be made permanent and mandatory on all states and that the new federal definition of "unemployment" be broadened. This program, which reaches the family while it is still intact, has been put into effect in only 22 states. Even in states where it has been implemented, the numbers participating have been small, partly because many states have narrowly defined the term "unemployment" and partly because the number of broken homes makes many children eligible under the regular form of AFDC.

Financing

Because the states are unable to bear substantially increased welfare costs, the federal government should absorb a far greater share of the financial burden than presently. At least two methods are worth considering. The first would be to rearrange payment formulas so that, even at the highest levels of payments, the federal government absorbed 90 percent or more of the costs. A second method would be to have the federal government assume 100 percent of the increment in costs that would be encountered through raising standards of assistance and rendering AFDC-UP mandatory. Under either of these approaches, the share of costs presently imposed on municipal governments should be removed to release their limited resources for other uses.

Work incentives and training

In three important ways, steps were taken in the 1967 amendments to the Federal Welfare Act to encourage—or compel—welfare recipients to seek employment. Each of these controversial steps had some salutory aspects but each requires substantial further attention:

(a) *Job training.* The amendments provide substantially greater funds for job training. This was in principle a wise step. The amendments also, however, require the states to condition grants to "appropriate" adult welfare recipients on their willingness to submit to job training. Though the Commission agrees that welfare recipients should be encouraged to accept employment or job training, we strongly disagree with compelling mothers of small children to work or else lose welfare support. Many mothers, we believe, will want to work. A recent study of about 1,500 welfare mothers in New York indicated that 70 percent of all mothers—and 80 percent of Negro mothers —would prefer to work for pay than stay at home.

(b) *Day-care centers for children.* The 1967 amendments provide funds for the first time for day-care programs for children of working mothers. Further expansion is desirable to make centers an effective means of enabling welfare recipients to take advantage of training and employment opportunities. Efforts should be made to ensure that centers are open in the evening and that more education features are built into center programs. State and federal standards that prevent centers from employing subprofessional workers, including welfare recipient mothers, should be removed.

Welfare mothers themselves should be encouraged to set up co-operative centers with one or more mothers tending children of other mothers and with welfare funds available for salaries. Such "living room" day care can only be effective if the mother taking care of the children can be paid without losing any substantial portion of her welfare check.

(c) *Retention of part of earnings.* The amendments permit an AFDC or AFDC-UP recipient to retain the first $30 of earned income monthly and one-third of the balance. Both the sums that can be kept without penalty, and the percentage of the balance that can be retained, should be raised substantially to maximize incentive to work. To determine the appropriate level and, indeed, to determine how job training and welfare programs can best interrelate, call for experimental programs to test different combinations and approaches. These programs should be supported at all levels of government.

Removal of freeze on recipients

The 1967 welfare amendments freeze, for each state, the percentage of children who can be covered by federal AFDC grants to the percentage of coverage in that state in January 1968. The anticipated effect of this new restriction will be to prevent federal assistance during 1968 to 475,000 new applicants otherwise eligible under present standards. In the face of this restriction, states and cities will have to dig further into already depleted local resources to maintain current levels. If they cannot bear the increased costs, a second alternative, less feasible under existing federal requirements, will be to tighten eligibility requirements for everyone or reduce per capita payments. We strongly believe that none of these alternatives are acceptable.

Restrictions on eligibility

The so-called "Man-in-the-House" rule and restrictions on new residents of states should be eliminated. Though these restrictions are currently being challenged in the courts, we believe that legislative and administrative action should be taken to eliminate them now.

Other features of the program which can strengthen the capacity of welfare recipients to become self-sufficient and which deserve increased federal support are:

(a) *Clear and enforceable rights.* These include prompt determinations of eligibility and rights to administrative appeal with representation by counsel. A recipient should be able to regard assistance as a right and not as an act of charity.

Applicants should be able to establish initial eligibility by personal statements or affidavits relating to their financial situation and family composition, subject to subsequent review conducted in a manner that protects their dignity, privacy and constitutional rights. Searches of welfare recipients' homes, whether with or without consent, should be abandoned. Such changes in procedures would not only accord welfare recipients the respect to which they are entitled but also release welfare workers to concentrate more of their time on providing service. They would also release a substantial portion of the funds spent on establishing eligibility for the more important function of providing support.

(b) *Separation of administration of AFDC and welfare programs for the disabled.* The time that welfare workers have available for the provision of services would be increased further by separating the administration of AFDC and general assistance programs from aid to aged and physically incapacitated. The problems of these latter groups are greatly different and might better be handled, at the federal level, through the Social Security Administration. Any such change would, of course, require that programs for the disabled and aged continue to be paid out of general funds and not impair the integrity of the Social Security Trust Fund.

(c) *Special neighborhood welfare contact and diagnostic centers.* Centers to provide the full complement of welfare services should be combined into the multi-purpose neighborhood service facilities being developed by the Office of Economic Opportunity and the Department of Housing and Urban Development. Federal funds should be provided to help local welfare agencies decentralize their programs through these centers, which would include representatives of all welfare, social, rehabilitation and income-assistance services.

(d) *Expansion of family-planning programs.* Social workers have found that many women in poverty areas would like to limit the size of their families and are simply unaware of existing birth control methods, or do not have such methods available to them. Governments at all levels — and particularly the federal — should underwrite broader programs to provide family-planning information and devices to those who desire them. Through such programs, the Commission believes that a significant contribution can be made to breaking the cycle of poverty and dependency.

Toward a National System of Income Supplementation

In 1949, Senator Robert A. Taft described a system to provide a decent level of income for all citizens:

> I believe that the American people feel that with the high production of which we are now capable, there is enough left over to prevent extreme hardship and maintain a minimum standard floor under subsistence, education, medical care and housing, to give to all a minimum standard of decent living and to all children a fair opportunity to get a start in life.

Such a "minimum standard of decent living" has been called for by many other groups and individuals, including the AFL-CIO, major corporate executives, and numerous civil rights and welfare organizations. The study of the new Commission on Income Maintenance Programs, and the Model Cities Program will be of particular importance in providing direction. We believe that efforts should be made to develop a system of income supplementation with two broad and basic purposes:

> To provide for those who can work or who do work, any necessary supplements in such a way as to develop incentives for fuller employment;

> To provide for those who cannot work and for mothers who decide to remain with their children, a system that provides a minimum standard of decent living and to aid in saving children from the prison of poverty that has held their parents.

Under this approach, then, all present restrictions on eligibility—other than need—would be eliminated. In this way, two large and important groups not covered by present federal programs would be provided for: employed persons working at substandard hours or wages, and unemployed persons who are neither disabled nor parents of minor children.

A broad system of supplementation would involve substantially greater federal expenditures than anything now contemplated. The cost will range widely depending on the standard of need accepted as the "basic allowance" to individuals and families, and on the rate at which additional income above this level is taxed. Yet if the deepening cycle of poverty and dependence on welfare can be broken, if the children of the poor can be given the opportunity to scale the wall that now separates them from the rest of society, the return on this investiment will be great indeed.

The Commission also reported on infant mortality and life expectancy rates in the ghetto, as well as the lower utilization of health services. Unfortunately in the political climate of 1968 the report had no significant effect. The work of the Joint Economic Committee of the Congress was more mundane, but certainly more politically productive. In December,

*1967, the Subcommittee on Fiscal Policy published an influential com-
pendium entitled* Old Age Income Assurance, *covering all aspects of
income maintenance programs. In March, 1968, the Subcommittee on
Economic Progress, issued* Federal Programs for the Development of
Human Resources, *discussing income maintenance and family support,
and health care and improvement among other topics.*

*Similar subjects had already been debated in hearings held by the Sub-
committee on the Health of the Family, an offshoot of the Senate Special
Committee on Aging and it was clear that the health care problems of the
elderly (and their related income problems) were far from solved. In terms
of long-term, general solutions to the income maintenance problem, the
most important hearings were those held by the Subcommittee on Fiscal
Policy during June, 1968. Under the chairmanship of Representative Martha
Griffiths, the members insisted on a need for radical changes.*

**Income Maintenance Programs
Hearings before the Subcommittee on Fiscal Policy
of the Joint Economic Committee**
90th Cong., 2d Sess. (June, 1968)
(p. 1 – 2)

Criticisms of welfare are as old as welfare – perhaps older. In general,
criticism takes the form of assertions that welfare is not doing enough or
that it is doing too much. Such criticisms are directed toward the values
implicit in welfare programs. On rare occasions – unfortunately much too
rare – another kind of criticism emerges. This criticism runs to the effect
that, whatever the welfare system is trying to do, it is not doing it very well.

In recent years, criticism of this second sort has been mounting. It is
argued that the present system is neither economic nor equitable because
programs are badly coordinated, many people are denied access to assistance on arbitrary grounds, levels of assistance vary widely from one area
to another, attempts are made to maintain distinctions among individuals
which are expensive to administer and lack much in obvious fairness, the
administration of the systems entails a costly and oppressive surveillance
of beneficiaries, and assistance is given in ways that tend to assure continued dependency.

The Subcommittee on Fiscal Policy is holding these hearings from a conviction that this is high time to initiate a public review of the objectives and
operation of the welfare system. We are also concerned to demonstrate
that it is possible to conduct a rational discussion of welfare design. Given
that we are now deeply involved in maintaining incomes and there are no
reasonable indications that we will not continue to do so, what is a sensible
way to do the job? It is not that the subcommittee is unconcerned about
values – we are devoting the last 3 days of the hearings to these issues;

rather, we do believe that it is important first to get straight on the economics.

The economics of programs are questions of objectives and the best way to achieve them. In one view, the objective of welfare programs is to alter the distribution of income through transfers from those who have to those who have not. The economic way to effect these transfers

The hearings brought together leaders of welfare agencies and well-known economists who had taken an interest in income maintenance. Professor J. Tobin of Yale and Dr. J.A. Pechman of the Brookings Institution came to argue in favor of a negative income tax. Professor R.J. Lampman of the University of Wisconsin favored a similar scheme, and Mr. Robert Theobald advocated a guaranteed income, but on the whole the hearings were inconclusive. At least the Joint Economic Committee had seized the initiative in the development of new income maintenance programs and had even found a powerful new weapon in existing programs, the Welfare Rights Movement.

Some sense of the approach and force of the new pressure group became clear in the hearings. Professor R.A. Cloward of Columbia University described the movement's background.

Joint Committee Hearings
(p. 51)

Mr. Cloward. Madam Chairman, I have come to make what I think is a somewhat different criticism of the public welfare system in America than is usually heard.

Most critics of public welfare focus on the low levels of benefits, as well they might. The average family of four under the aid to dependent children category receives approximately $1,800 per annum in this Nation, ranging from a low of about $400 in Mississippi to a high of about $2,700 in northern States such as New York and New Jersey.

Critics also point to the myriad statutes and policies which legally keep hundreds of thousands of the poorest families in America from receiving any benefits at all. A prime example is the durational residence law—on the books in 40 States—though I am happy to say that these laws are being successfully challenged in the Federal courts. These laws prevent aid from being given to such categories as migratory workers who are periodically stranded without funds in a State far from home, or to the masses of southern sharecroppers and tenant farmers who are being driven into northern States by the inexorable march of agricultural mechanization.

There are many other examples of statutes which have the consequence of excluding from any aid whatsoever substantial portions of our population. In addition to the residence laws, one thinks of various relative responsibility provisions man-in-the-house rules, and substitute-father laws.

However, the most devastating criticism of public welfare is never made. It is that the system is designed to insure that most people do not succeed in obtaining even the meager benefits to which they are legally entitled. Poor Americans, in other words, are literally cheated out of billions of dollars by government—and this at a time when affluent Americans are receiving transportation subsidies, agricultural subsidies, housing subsidies, urban renewal subsidies, and other governmental benefits of unparallelled magnitude.

To combat this lawlessness by government, welfare recipients have found it necessary to form a national protest movement. Under the inspired leadership of Dr. George A. Wiley, who is testifying here today, the National Welfare Rights Organization is now successfully forcing welfare departments in many localities to distribute benefits in compliance with the law.

One form of lawlessness arises from various policies and practices which keep eligible people from getting on the welfare rolls in the first place.

For example, welfare administrators deliberately engender ignorance of entitlements among potential applicants by refusing to release copies of welfare regulations to them. Hence many people do not realize they are eligible and do not apply. Or, if they do apply and are declared ineligible, they have no independent means of knowing whether they are being lied to—as they very often are.

Ladies and gentlemen, welfare manuals are unclassified public documents, and welfare applicants are American citizens. There can be no explanation for governmental secrecy about benefits except that the intent is to give as few people as possible as little as possible, whatever their legal eligibility.

But even if applicants know of their rights, they find it exceedingly difficult to assert them. The steps involved in proving one's eligibility constitute a veritable bureaucratic obstacle course, replete with invasions of privacy and the necessity of producing birth, marriage, employment, and a multitude of other personal documents which even the most compulsive middle-class family could not be expected to have ready at hand. One must conclude that the poor are supposed to cultivate the habits of the packrat. Nevertheless, lacking appropriate documents they are turned away.

And even if all documents are available, welfare functionaries—under public pressure to keep costs down—may then reject the application, telling the victim to seek help from relatives or friends.

Ladies and gentlemen, our investigations of poverty in northern cities have led us to the terrible conclusion that, for every person on the welfare rolls, there is another who is probably legally eligible but not receiving benefits.

Governmental lawlessness has indeed succeeded in reaching its objective. Little wonder, then, that the National Welfare Rights Organization is now planning to mount a nationwide advertising campaign to recruit the eligible poor onto the welfare rolls.

But one should not suppose that lawlessness ends where benefits begin.

Many of those who do manage to get on the rolls are then cheated out of many allowances.

The calculation of budget allowances is extraordinarily detailed and complex—in New York, the few unemployed men who get on the rolls are eligible for 45 razor blades per year. Under pressure to save money, it is all too easy to forget one or another of these detailed allowances when computing a family budget. And the result is that underbudgeting is rampant.

In many jurisdictions, the law also prescribes special allowances for recipients to purchase heavy clothing or household furnishings. These grants are not ordinarily incorporated as part of the family's regular semi-monthly check, but are to be requested as needed.

However, people cannot request a grant that is kept secret, and even when they do inadvertently learn of their eligibility, their requests are often turned down or trimmed down. The resulting economy runs into hundreds of millions of dollars.

Across the country, the National Welfare Rights Organization has been mobilizing massive campaigns of recipients to obtain these special allowances. It prints and distributes the applications which welfare departments will not release, and it stages demonstrations in welfare centers until the completed forms are honored and checks issued.

The National Welfare Rights Organization is doing government's work —and doing it very well, indeed. In New York City, for example, more than $10 million in special grants have been obtained in just the last 5 weeks as a result of such campaigns.

Ladies and gentlemen, your deliberations on the inadequacies of the present public welfare system are timely, if somewhat tardy. The poor are also deliberating; more than that, they are acting. If you do not reform this system, it seems likely to me that they will.

Judicial Action

The National Welfare Rights Organization was only one part of the Welfare Rights Movement, an effort which gained enormous momentum after the establishment of OEO-funded neighborhood law offices. For example, cases involving welfare rights began to attract attention during 1967. Some of the state supreme courts, especially those in California, played an extremely significant role. In Parrish v. *Civil Service Commission of Alameda County, 57 Cal. 2d 623; 425 P.2d 223 (1967), mass raids on welfare recipients' homes to determine eligibility were held to be unconstitutional. Later, the same court became involved in Governor Reagan's attempts to cutback the Medic-Cal (California Title XIX) program. In* Morris v. *Williams, 63 Cal. 2d 689; 433 P.2d 697 (1967), the court prevented the California Health and Welfare Agency from reducing medical programs for those persons receiving public assistance unless other groups*

were similarly dealt with. Health programs for those persons deemed
medically indigent, but not eligible for public assistance, would also have to
be reduced.

The federal courts became involved in residence questions in public
assistance programs. A series of cases were heard in different parts of the
country: a three-judge district court in Connecticut struck down the Con-
necticut residence requirements in Thompson v. Shapiro, *270 F. Supp. 331*
(1967); and similar decisions were reached in Delaware in Green v. *Depart-*
ment of Public Welfare, *270 F. Supp. 173; and in Pennsylvania in* Smith v.
Reynolds, *277 F. Supp. 65. The best-known case was decided in a three-*
man district court for the District of Columbia, Harrell v. Tobriner, *279*
F. Supp 22 (1967).

In June, 1968, the Supreme Court decided King v. Smith *which achieved*
something which HEW regulations had proved powerless in doing.

King v. Smith
392 U.S. 309 (1968)

Mr. Chief Justice Warren delivered the opinion of the Court.

Alabama, together with every other State, Puerto Rico, the Virgin Islands,
the District of Columbia, and Guam, participates in the Federal Government's Aid to Families With Dependent Children Program (AFDC),
which was established by the Social Security Act of 1935.[1] 49 Stat. 620
(1935), as amended, 42 U.S.C. §§ 301–1394. This appeal presents the
question whether a regulation of the Alabama Department of Pensions and
Security, employed in that Department's administration of the State's
federally funded AFDC program, is consistent with Subchapter IV of the
Social Security Act, 42 U.S.C. §§ 601–609, and with the Equal Protection
Clause of the Fourteenth Amendment. At issue is the validity of Alabama's
so called "substitute father" regulation which denies AFDC payments to
the children of a mother who "cohabits" in or outside her home with any
single or married able-bodied man. Appellees brought this class action
against appellants, officers, and members of the Alabama Board of Pensions
and Security, in the United States District Court for the Middle District of
Alabama, under 42 U.S.C. § 1983,[2] seeking declaratory and injunctive

[1]The program was originally known as "Aid to Dependent Children." 49 Stat. 627 (1935).
Alabama's program still bears this title. In the 1962 amendments to the Act, however, the name
of the program was changed to "Aid and Services to Needy Families with Children," 76 Stat.
185 (1962). Throughout this opinion, the program will be referred to as "Aid to Families With
Dependent Children," or AFDC.
[2]"Every person who, under color of any statute, ordinance, regulation, custom, or usage, of
any State or Territory, subjects or causes to be subjected, any citizen of the United States, or
other person within the jurisdiction thereof to the deprivation of any rights, privileges, or immunities secured by the Constitution and laws, shall be liable to the party injured in an action
at law, suit in equity, or other proper proceeding for redress."

relief. A properly convened three-judge District Court[3] correctly adjudicated the merits of the controversy without requiring appellees to exhaust state administrative remedies,[4] and found the regulation to be inconsistent with the Social Security Act and the Equal Protection Clause.[5] We noted probable jurisdiction, 390 U.S. 903, 88 S.Ct. 821, 19 L.Ed.2d 869 (1968), and for reasons which will appear, we affirm without reaching the constitutional issue.

I.

The AFDC program is one of three major categorical public assistance programs established by the Social Security Act of 1935. See U.S. Advisory Commission Report on Intergovernmental Relations, Statutory and Administrative Control Associated with Federal Grants for Public Assistance 5–7 (1964) (hereafter cited as Advisory Commission Report). The category singled out for welfare assistance by AFDC is the "dependent child," who is defined in § 406 of the Act. 49 Stat. 629 (1935), as amended, 42 U.S.C. § 606(a), as an age-qualified[6] "needy child * * * who has been deprived of parental support or care by reason of the death, continued absence from the home or physical or mental incapacity of a parent, and who is living with" any one of several listed relatives. Under this provision, and insofar-as relevant here, aid can be granted only if "a

[3]Since appellees sought injunctive relief restraining the appellant state officials from the enforcement, operation and execution of a statewide regulation on the ground of its unconstitutionality, the three-judge court was properly convened pursuant to 28 U.S.C. § 2281. See Alabama Public Service Commission v. Southern R. Co., 341 U.S. 341, 343, n. 3, 71 S.Ct. 762, 95 L.Ed. 1002 (1951). See also Florida Lime & Avocado Growers v. Jacobsen, 362 U.S. 73, 80 S.Ct. 568, 4 L.Ed.2d 568 (1960); Allen v. Grand Central Aircraft Co., 347 U.S. 535, 74 S.Ct. 745, 98 L.Ed. 933 (1954). Jurisdiction was conferred on the court by 28 U.S.C. §§ 1343(3) and (4). The decision we announce today holds Alabama's substitute father regulation invalid as inconsistent with Subchapter IV of the Social Security Act. We intimate no views as to whether and under what circumstances suits challenging state AFDC provisions only on the ground that they are inconsistent with the federal statute may be brought in federal courts. See generally Note, Federal Judicial Review of State Welfare Practices, 67 Col.L.Rev. 84 (1967).

[4]We reject appellants' argument that appellees were required to exhaust their administrative remedies prior to bringing this action. Pursuant to the requirement of the Social Security Act that States must grant AFDC applicants who are denied aid "an opportunity for a fair hearing before the State agency," 42 U.S.C. § 602(a) (4), Alabama provides for administrative review of such denials. Alabama Manual for Administration of Public Assistance, Part I, § II, Parts V – 5 to V – 12. Decisions of this Court, however, establish that a plaintiff in an action brought under the Civil Rights Act, 42 U.S.C. § 1983, 28 U.S.C. § 1343, is not required to exhaust administrative remedies, where the constitutional challenge is sufficiently substantial, as here, to require the convening of a three-judge court. Damico v. California, 389 U.S. 416, 88 S.Ct. 526, 19 L.Ed.2d 647 (1967). See also McNeese v. Board of Education, 373 U.S. 668, 83 S.Ct. 1433, 10 L.Ed.2d 622 (1963); Monroe v. Pape, 365 U.S. 167, 180 – 183, 81 S.Ct. 473, 480 – 482, 5 L.Ed.2d 492 (1961). For a general discussion of review in the federal courts of state welfare practices, see Note, Federal Judicial Review of State Welfare Practices, 67 Col.L.Rev. 84 (1967).

[5]Smith v. King, 277 F.Supp. 31 (D.C.M.D. Ala.1967).

[6]A needy child, to qualify for the AFDC assistance, must be under the age of 18, or under the age of 21 and a student, as defined by HEW. 79 Stat. 422 (1965), 42 U.S.C. §§ 606(a) (2) (A) and (B).

parent" of the needy child is continually absent from the home.[7] Alabama considers a man who qualifies as a "substitute father" under its regulation to be a nonabsent parent within the federal statute. The State therefore denies aid to an otherwise eligible needy child on the basis that his substitute parent is not absent from the home.

Under the Alabama regulation, an "able-bodied man, married or single, is considered a substitute father of *all the children of the applicant * * * mother*" in three different situations: (1) if "he lives in the home with the child's natural or adoptive mother for the purpose of cohabitation"; or (2) if "he visits [the home] frequently for the purpose of cohabiting with the child's natural or adoptive mother"; or (3) if "he does not frequent the home but cohabits with the child's natural or adoptive mother elsewhere."[8] Whether the substitute father is actually the father of the children is irrelevant. It is also irrelevant whether he is legally obligated to support the children, and whether he does in fact contribute to their support. What is determinative is simply whether he "cohabits" with the mother.[9]

The testimony below by officials responsible for the administration of Alabama's AFDC program establishes that "cohabitation," as used in the regulation, means essentially that the man and woman have "frequent" or "continuing" sexual relations. With regard to how frequent or continual these relations must be, the testimony is conflicting. One state official testified that the regulation applied only if the parties had sex at least once a week; another thought once every three months would suffice; and still another believed once every six months sufficient. The regulation itself provides that pregnancy or a baby under six months of age is prima facie evidence of a substitute father.

Between June 1964, when Alabama's substitute father regulation became effective, and January 1967, the total number of AFDC recipients in the State declined by about 20,000 persons, and the number of children recipients by about 16,000 or 22%. As applied in this case, the regulation has caused the termination of all AFDC payments to the appellees, Mrs. Sylvester Smith and her four minor children.

Mrs. Smith and her four children, ages 14, 12, 11, and 9, reside in Dallas County, Alabama. For several years prior to October 1, 1966, they had received aid under the AFDC program. By notice dated October 11, 1966,

---

[7]The States are also permitted to consider as dependent children needy children who have an unemployed parent, as is discussed in n. 13, infra, and needy children without a parent who have under certain circumstances been placed in foster homes or child care institutions. See 42 U.S.C. §§ 607, 608.

[8]Alabama Manual for Administration of Public Assistance, Pt. I, c. II, § VI.

[9]Under the regulation, when "there appears to be a substitute father," the mother bears the burden of proving that she has discontinued her relationship with the man before her AFDC assistance will be resumed. The mother's claim of discontinuance must be "corroborated by at least two acceptable references in a position to know. Examples of acceptable references are: law-enforcement officials; ministers; neighbors; grocers." There is no hearing prior to the termination of aid, but an applicant denied aid may secure state administrative review.

they were removed from the list of persons eligible to receive such aid. This action was taken by the Dallas County welfare authorities pursuant to the substitute father regulation, on the ground that a Mr. Williams came to her home on weekends and had sexual relations with her.

Three of Mrs. Smith's children have not received parental support or care from a father since their natural father's death in 1955. The fourth child's father left home in 1963, and the child has not received the support or care of his father since then. All the children live in the home of their mother, and except for the substitute father regulation are eligible for aid. The family is not receiving any other type of public assistance, and has been living, since the termination of AFDC payments, on Mrs. Smith's salary of between $16 and $20 per week which she earns working from 3:30 a.m. to 12 noon as a cook and waitress.

Mr. Williams, the alleged "substitute father" of Mrs. Smith's children, has nine children of his own and lives with his wife and family, all of whom are dependent upon him for support. Mr. Williams is not the father of any of Mrs. Smith's children. He is not legally obligated, under Alabama law, to support any of Mrs. Smith's children.[10] Further, he is not willing or able to support the Smith children, and does not in fact support them. His wife is required to work to help support the Williams household.

II.

The AFDC program is based on a scheme of cooperative federalism. See generally advisory Commission Report, supra, at 1–59. It is financed largely by the Federal Government, on a matching fund basis, and is administered by the States. States are not required to participate in the program, but those which desire to take advantage of the substantial federal funds available for distribution to needy children are required to submit an AFDC plan for the approval of the Secretary of Health, Education, and Welfare (HEW). 49 Stat. 627 (1935), 42 U.S.C. §§ 601, 602, 603, and 604. See Advisory

---

[10]Under Alabama statutes, a legal duty of support is imposed only upon a "parent," who is defined as (1) a "natural legal parent," (2) one who has "legally acquired the custody of" the child, and (3) "the father of such child, * * * though born out of lawful wedlock." 34 Ala. Code §§ 89, 90; 27 Ala.Code §§ 12 (1), 12(4). Law v. State, 238 Ala. 428, 191 So. 803 (1939). The Alabama Courts have interpreted the statute to impose a legal duty of support upon one who has "publicly acknowledged or treated the child as his own, in a manner to indicate his voluntary assumption of parenthood" irrespective of whether the alleged parent is in fact the child's real father. Law v. State, 238 Ala. 428, 191 So. 803 (1939). It seems clear, however, that even a stepfather who is not the child's natural parent and has not acquired legal custody of him is under an obligation of support only if he has made this "voluntary assumption of parenthood." See Chandler v. Whatley, 238 Ala. 206, 189 So. 751 (1939); Englehardt v. Yung's Heirs, 76 Ala. 534, 540 (1884); Nicholas v. State, 32 Ala.App. 574, 28 So.2d 422 (1946). Further, the Alabama Supreme Court has emphasized that the alleged father's intention to support the child, requisite to a finding of voluntary assumption of parenthood, "should not be slightly nor hastily inferred * * *." Englehardt v. Yung's Heirs, 76 Ala. 534, 540 (1884).

Commission Report, supra, at 21–23.[11] The plan must conform with several requirements of the Social Security Act and with rules and regulations promulgated by HEW. 49 Stat. 627 (1935), as amended, 42 U.S.C. § 602. See also HEW, Handbook of Public Assistance Administration, Pt. IV, §§ 2200, 2300 (1967) (hereafter cited as Handbook). [12]

One of the statutory requirements is that "aid to families with dependent children shall be furnished with reasonable promptness to all eligible individuals * * * ." 64 Stat. 550 (1950), 42 U.S.C. § 602(a) (9). As noted above, § 406(a) of the Act defines a "dependent child" as one who has been deprived of "parental" support or care by reason of the death, continued absence or incapacity of a "parent." 42 U.S.C. § 606(a). In combination, these two provisions of the Act clearly require participating States to furnish aid to families with children who have a parent absent from the home, if such families are in other respects eligible. See also Handbook, Pt. IV, § 2200(b) (4).

The State argues that its substitute father regulation simply defines who is a nonabsent "parent" under § 406 (a) of the Social Security Act. 42 U.S.C. § 606(a). The State submits that the regulation is a legitimate way of allocating its limited resources available for AFDC assistance, in that it reduces the caseload of its social workers and provides increased benefits to those still eligible for assistance. Two State interests are asserted in support of the allocation of AFDC assistance achieved by the regulation: first, it discourages illicit sexual relationships and illegitimate births; second, it puts families in which there is an informal "marital" relationship on a par with those in which there is an ordinary marital relationship, because families of the latter sort are not eligible for AFDC assistance.[13]

We think it well to note at the outset what is *not* involved in this case. There is no question that States have considerable latitude in allocating their AFDC resources, since each State is free to set its own standard of need[14] and to determine the level of benefits by the amount of funds it de-

---

[11]Alabama's substitute father regulation has been neither approved nor disapproved by HEW. There has, however, been considerable correspondence between the Alabama and federal authorities concerning the regulation, as is discussed in n. 23, infra.

[12]Unless HEW approves the plan, federal funds will not be made available for its implementation. 42 U.S.C. § 601. Further, HEW may entirely or partially terminate federal payments if "in the administration of the [state] plan there is a failure to comply substantially with any provision required by section 602(a) of this title to be included in the plan." 42 U.S.C. § 604, as amended, § 245, 81 Stat. 918 (1968). See generally Advisory Commission Report, supra, at 61–80.

[13]Commencing in 1961, federal matching funds have been made available under the AFDC subchapter of the Social Security Act for a State which grants assistance to needy children who have two able-bodied parents living in the home, but who have been "deprived of parental support or care by reason of the unemployment * * * of a parent." 42 U.S.C. § 607. Participation in this program for aid to dependent children of unemployed parents is not obligatory on the States, and the Court has been advised that only 21 States participate. Alabama does not participate.

[14]HEW's Handbook, in Pt. IV, § 3120, provides that: "A needy individual * * * [under AFDC] is one who does not have income and resources sufficient to assure economic security, *the*

votes to the program.[15] See Advisory Commission Report, supra, at 30–59. Further, there is no question that regular and actual contributions to a needy child, including contributions from the kind of person Alabama calls a substitute father, can be taken into account in determining whether the child is needy.[16] In other words, if by reason of such a man's contribution, the child is not in financial need, the child would be ineligible for AFDC assistance without regard to the substitute father rule. The appellees here, however, meet Alabama's need requirements; their alleged substitute father makes no contribution to their support; and they have been denied assistance solely on the basis of the substitute father regulation. Further, the regulation itself is unrelated to need, because the actual financial situation of the family is irrelevant in determining the existence of a substitute father.

Also not involved in this case is the question of Alabama's general power to deal with conduct it regards as immoral and with the problem of illegitimacy. This appeal raises only the question whether the State may deal with these problems in the manner that it has here—by flatly denying AFDC assistance to otherwise eligible dependent children.

Alabama's argument based on its interests in discouraging immorality and illegitimacy would have been quite relevant at one time in the history of the AFDC program. However, subsequent developments clearly establish that these state interests are not presently legitimate justifications for AFDC disqualification. Insofar as this or any similar regulation is based on the State's asserted interests in discouraging illicit sexual behavior and illegitimacy, it plainly conflicts with federal law and policy.

---

standard of which must be defined by each State. The act recognizes that *the standard so defined depends upon the conditions existing in each State.*" (Emphasis added.) The legislative history of the Act also makes clear that the States have power to determine who is "needy" for purposes of AFDC. Thus the Reports of the House Ways and Means Committee and Senate Finance Committee make clear that the States are free to impose eligibility requirements as to "means." H.R.Rep. No. 615, 74th Cong., 1st Sess., 24 (1935); S.Rep. No. 628, 74th Cong., 1st Sess., 36(1935). The floor debates corroborate that this was Congress' intent. For example, Representative Vinson explained that "need is to be determined under the State law." 79 Cong.Rec. 5471 (1935).

[15]The rather complicated formula for federal funding is contained in 42 U.S.C. § 603. The level of benefits is within the State's discretion, but the Federal Government's contribution is a varying percentage of the total AFDC expenditures within each State. See H.R.Rep. No. 615, 74th Cong., 1st Sess., 12, 24 (1935); S.Rep. No. 628, 74th Cong., 1st Sess., 4, 36 (1935). The benefit levels vary greatly from State to State. For example, in May 1967, the average payment to a family under AFDC was about $224 in New Jersey, $221 in New York, $39 in Mississippi, $20 in Puerto Rico, and $53 in Alabama. Hearings on H.R. 12080 before the Senate Committee on Finance, 90th Cong., 1st Sess., pt. 1, 296–297 (1967). See generally, Harvith, Federal Equal Protection and Welfare Assistance, 31 Albany L.Rev. 210, 226–227 (1967).

[16]Indeed, the Act requires that in determining need the state agency "shall * * * take into consideration any other income and resources of any child or relative claiming aid to families with dependent children * * *." 42 U.S.C. § 602(a) (7). Regulations of HEW, which clearly comport with the statute, restrict the resources which are to be taken into account under § 602 to those "that are, in fact, available to an applicant or recipient for current use on a regular basis * * *." This regulation properly excludes from consideration resources which are merely assumed to be available to the needy individual. Handbook, Pt. IV, § 3131(7). See also §§ 3120, 3123, 3124, 3131(10), and 3131(11).

A significant characteristic of public welfare programs during the last half of the 19th century in this country was their preference for the "worthy" poor. Some poor persons were thought worthy of public assistance, and others were thought unworthy because of their supposed incapacity for "moral regeneration." Leyendecker, Problems and Policy in Public Assistance, at 45–57 (1955); Wedemeyer and Moore, The American Welfare System, 54 Calif.L.Rev. 326, 327–328 (1966). This worthy person concept characterized the mothers' pension welfare programs,[17] which were the precursors of AFDC. See Bell, Aid to Dependent Children, at 3–19 (1965). Benefits under the mothers' pension programs, accordingly, were customarily restricted to widows who were considered morally fit. See Bell, supra, at 7; Leyendecker, supra, at 53.

In this social context it is not surprising that both the House and Senate Committee Reports on the Social Security Act of 1935 indicate that States participating in AFDC were free to impose eligibility requirements relating to the "moral character" of applicants. H.R.Rep. No. 615, 74th Cong., 1st Sess., 24 (1935); S.Rep. No. 628, 74th Cong., 1st Sess., 36 (1935). See also 79 Cong.Rec. 5679 (statement by Representative Jenkins) (1935). During the following years, many state AFDC plans included provisions making ineligible for assistance dependent children not living in "suitable homes." See Bell, supra, at 29–136 (1965). As applied, these suitable home provisions frequently disqualified children on the basis of the alleged immoral behavior of their mothers. Ibid.[18]

In the 1940's, suitable home provisions came under increasing attack. Critics argued, for example, that such disqualification provisions undermined the mother's confidence and authority, thereby promoting continued dependency; that they forced destitute mothers into increased immorality as a means of earning money; that they were habitually used to disguise systematic racial discrimination; and that they senselessly punished impoverished children on the basis of their mothers' behavior, while inconsistently permitting them to remain in the alleged unsuitable homes. In 1945, the predecessor of HEW produced a state letter arguing against suitable home provisions and recommending their abolition. See Bell, supra, at 51. Although 15 States abolished their provisions during the following decade, numerous other States retained them. Ibid.

In the 1950's, matters became further complicated by pressures in numerous States to disqualify illegitimate children from AFDC assistance. Attempts were made in at least 18 States to enact laws excluding children on the basis of their own or their siblings' birth status. See Bell, supra, at 72–

[17]For a discussion of the mothers' pension welfare programs, see J. Brown, Public Relief 1929–1939, at 26–32 (1940).

[18]Bell quotes a case record, for example, where a mother whose conduct with men displeased a social worker was required, as a condition of continued assistance, to sign an affidavit stating that, "I * * * do hereby promise and agree that until such time as the following agreement is rescinded, I will not have any male caller coming to my home nor meeting me elsewhere under improper conditions." Bell, supra, at 48.

73. All but three attempts failed to pass the State legislatures, and two of the three successful bills were vetoed by the governors of the States involved. Ibid. In 1960, the federal agency strongly disapproved of illegitimacy disqualifications. See Bell, supra, at 73 – 74.

Nonetheless, in 1960, Louisiana enacted legislation requiring, as a condition precedent for AFDC eligibility, that the home of a dependent child be "suitable," and specifying that any home in which an illegitimate child had been born subsequent to the receipt of public assistance would be considered unsuitable. Louisiana Acts, No. 251 (1960). In the summer of 1960, approximately 23,000 children were dropped from Louisiana's AFDC rolls, Bell, supra, at 137. In disapproving this legislation, then Secretary of Health, Education, and Welfare Flemming issued what is now known as the Flemming Ruling, stating that as of July 1, 1961,

> *"a state plan * * * may not impose an eligibility condition that would deny assistance with respect to a needy child on the basis that the home conditions in which the child lives are unsuitable, while the child continues to reside in the home.* Assistance will therefore be continued during the time efforts are being made either to improve the home conditions or to make arrangements for the child elsewhere."[19]

Congress quickly approved the Flemming Ruling, while extending until September 1, 1962, the time for state compliance. 75 Stat. 77 (1961), as amended, 42 U.S.C. § 604(b).[20] At the same time, Congress acted to implement the ruling by providing, on a temporary basis, that dependent children could receive AFDC assistance if they were placed in foster homes after a court determination that their former homes were, as the Senate Report stated, "unsuitable because of the immoral or negligent behavior of the parent." S.Rep. No. 165, 87th Cong., 1st Sess., 6 (1961), U.S.Code Cong. & Admin.News 1961, p. 1721. See 75 Stat. 76 (1961), as amended, 42 U.S.C. § 608.[21]

In 1962, Congress made permanent the provision for AFDC assistance

---

[19]State Letter No. 452. Bureau of Public Assistance, Social Security Administration, Department of Health, Education, and Welfare. (Emphasis added.)

[20]The Senate Finance Committee Report explained the purpose of the amendment as follows:

"The Department of Health, Education, and Welfare in January 1961 advised the State agencies administering title IV of the Social Security Act – aid to dependent children – that after June 30, 1961, grants to States would not be available if the State terminated assistance to children in a home determined to be unsuitable unless the State made other provision for the children affected. Section 4 of your committee's bill would provide that the requirement made by the Department of Health, Education, and Welfare would not become effective in States which took the type of action described, as the result of a State statute requiring such action, before the 61st day after the end of the regular session of such State's legislature, such regular session beginning following the enactment of this section. One or two of the States affected by the Department's ruling do not have regular sessions of their legislatures in 1961 and would accordingly be safeguarded against the withholding of funds until such time as their legislatures have had regular sessions and have had an opportunity to modify the State statutes involved." S. Rep. No. 165, 87th Cong., 1st Sess., 6 (1961), U.S.Code Cong. & Admin.News 1961, p. 1720.

[21]For a discussion by then Secretary of HEW Ribicoff and now Secretary Cohen concerning the 1961 amendments in relation to the Flemming Ruling, see Hearing on H.R. 10032 before the House Committee on Ways and Means, 87th Cong., 2d Sess., 294 – 297, 305 – 307 (1962).

to children placed in foster homes and extended such coverage to include children placed in child-care institutions. 76 Stat. 180, 185, 193, 196, 207 (1962), 42 U.S.C. § 608. See S.Rep. No. 1589, 87th Cong., 2d Sess., 13 (1962), U.S.Code Cong. & Admin.News, p. 1943. At the same time, Congress modified the Flemming Ruling by amending § 404(b) of the Act. As amended, the statute permits States to disqualify from AFDC aid children who live in unsuitable homes, provided they are granted other "adequate care and assistance." 76 Stat. 189, 42 U.S.C. § 604(b) (1962). See S.Rep. No. 1589, 87th Cong., 2d Sess., 14 (1962), U.S. Code Cong. & Admin. News, p. 1943.

Thus, under the 1961 and 1962 amendments to the Social Security Act, the States are permitted to remove a child from a home that is judicially determined to be so unsuitable as to "be contrary to the welfare of such child." 42 U.S.C. § 608(a) (1). The States are also permitted to terminate AFDC assistance to a child living in an unsuitable home, if they provide other adequate care and assistance for the child under a general welfare program. 42 U.S.C. § 604(b). See S.Rep. No. 1589, 87th Cong., 2d Sess., 14 (1962). The statutory approval of the Flemming Ruling, however, precludes the States from otherwise denying AFDC assistance to dependent children on the basis of their mother's alleged immorality or to discourage illegitimate births.

The most recent congressional amendments to the Social Security Act further corroborate that federal public welfare policy now rests on a basis considerably more sophisticated and enlightened than the "worthy person" concept of earlier times. State plans are now required to provide for a rehabilitative program of improving and correcting unsuitable homes, 42 U.S.C. § 602(a), as amended, § 201(a) (1) (B) (14), 81 Stat. 877 (1968); 42 U.S.C. § 606, as amended, § 201(f), 81 Stat. 880 (1968); to provide voluntary family planning services for the purpose of reducing illegitimate births, 42 U.S.C. § 602(a), as amended, § 201(a) (1) (C) (15), 81 Stat. 878 (1968); and to provide a program for establishing the paternity of illegitimate children and securing support for them, 42 U.S.C. § 602(a), as amended, § 201(a) (1) (C) (17), 81 Stat. 878 (1968).

In sum, Congress has determined that immorality and illegitimacy should be dealt with through rehabilitative measures rather than measures that punish dependent children, and that protection of such children is the paramount goal of AFDC.[22] In light of the Flemming Ruling and the 1961, 1962,

---

[22]The new emphasis on rehabilitative services began with the Kennedy Administration. President Kennedy, in his 1962 welfare message to the Congress, observed that communities that had attempted to cut down welfare expenditures through arbitrary cutbacks had met with little success, but that "communities which have tried the rehabilitative road — the road I have recommended today — have demonstrated what can be done with creative * * * programs of prevention and social rehabilitation." See Hearings on S. 10606 before the Senate Committee on Finance, 87th Cong., 2d Sess., 109 (1962). Some insight into the mood of the Congress that

and 1968 amendments to the Social Security Act, it is simply inconceivable, as HEW has recognized,[23] that Alabama is free to discourage immorality and illegitimacy by the device of absolute disqualification of needy children. Alabama may deal with these problems by several different methods under the Social Security Act. But the method it has chosen plainly conflicts with the Act.

III.

Alabama's second justification for its substitute father regulation is that "there is a public interest in a State not undertaking the payment of these funds to families who because of their living arrangements would be in the same situation as if the parents were married, except for the marriage." In other words, the State argues that since in Alabama the needy children of married couples are not eligible for AFDC aid so long as their father is in the home, it is only fair that children of a mother who cohabits with a man not her husband and not their father be treated similarly. The difficulty with this argument is that it fails to take account of the circumstance that children of fathers living in the home are in a very different position from children of mothers who cohabit with men not their fathers: the child's father has a legal duty to support him, while the unrelated substitute father, at least in Alabama, does not. We believe Congress intended the term "par-

approved the Flemming Ruling in 1961 with respect to this matter is provided by an exchange during the debates on the floor of the House. Representative Gross inquired of Representative Mills, Chairman of the House Ways and Means Committee, concerning the AFDC status of illegitimate children. After a brief discussion in which Representative Mills explained that he was looking into the problem of illegitimacy, Representative Hoffman asked whether Representative Gross was taking the position that "these innocent children, no matter what the circumstances under which they were born are to be deprived of the necessities of life." Representative Gross replied, "Oh, no; not at all," and agreed with Representative Hoffman's subsequent statement that the proper approach would be to attempt to prevent illegitimate births. 107 Cong. Rec. 3766 (1961). See generally Bell, supra, at 152–173.

[23]Both before and after the Flemming Ruling, the Alabama and federal authorities corresponded with considerable frequency concerning the State's suitable home and substitute father policies. In April 1959, HEW by letter stated that "suitable home" legislation then being proposed by Alabama raised substantial questions of conformity with the Social Security Act, because it seemed to deprive children of AFDC assistance on the basis of illegitimate births in the family. In May 1959 and again in August 1959 new suitable home policies were submitted and were rejected by HEW. Negotiations continued, and in June 1961, HEW responded that the newest legislative proposal was inconsistent with Congress' statutory approval of the Flemming Ruling because (1) assistance would be denied to children on the basis that their homes were unsuitable but they would be permitted to remain in the homes; and (2) a home could be found unsuitable simply on the basis of the child's birth status. Still later, on June 12, 1963, HEW rejected another Alabama suitable home provision on the ground that it provided for denial of AFDC assistance while the child remained in the home without providing for other "adequate care and assistance," as required by the 1962 amendment to the Federal Act. The evidence below establishes that soon after appellant King's appointment as Commissioner, he undertook a study that led to the adoption of the substitute father regulation. When this regulation was submitted to HEW, it responded that the regulation did not conform with 42 U.S.C. § 604(b) for the same reasons as its predecessor legislative proposals. Additional correspondence ensued, but HEW never approved the regulation.

ent" in § 406(a) of the Act, 42 U.S.C. § 606(a), to include only those persons with a legal duty of support.

The Social Security Act of 1935 was part of a broad legislative program to counteract the depression. Congress was deeply concerned with the dire straits in which all needy children in the Nation then found themselves.[24] In agreement with the President's Commission on Economic Security, the House Committee Report declared, "the core of any social plan must be the child." H.R. Rep. No. 615, 74th Cong., 1st Sess., 10 (1935). The AFDC program, however, was not designed to aid all needy children. The plight of most children was caused simply by the unemployment of their fathers. With respect to these children, Congress planned that "the work relief program and * * * the revival of private industry" would provide employment for their fathers. S. Rep. No. 628, 74th Cong., 1st Sess., 17 (1935). As the Senate Committee Report stated: "Many of the children included in relief families present no other problem than that of providing work for the breadwinner of the family." Ibid. Implicit in this statement is the assumption that children would in fact be supported by the family "breadwinner."

The AFDC program was designed to meet a need unmet by programs providing employment for breadwinners. It was designed to protect what the House Report characterized as "one clearly distinguishable group of children." H.R.Rep. No. 615, 74th Cong., 1st Sess., 10 (1935). This group was comprised of children in families without a "breadwinner," "wage earner," or "father," as the repeated use of these terms throught the Report of the President's Commission,[25] Committee Hearings[26] and Reports[27] and the floor debates[28] makes perfectly clear. To describe the sort of breadwinner that it had in mind, Congress employed the word "parent." 49 Stat. 629 (1939), as amended, 42 U.S.C. § 606(a). A child would be eligible for assistance if his parent was deceased, incapacitated or continually absent.

The question for decision here is whether Congress could have intended that a man was to be regarded as a child's parent so as to deprive the child of AFDC eligibility despite the circumstances: (1) that the man did not in fact support the child; and (2) that he was not legally obligated to support the child. The State correctly observes that the fact that the man in question does not actually support the child cannot be determinative, because a natural father at home may fail actually to support his child but his pres-

---

[24]See H.R.Rep.No. 615, 74th Cong., 1st Sess., 9–10 (1935) (characterizing children as "the most tragic victims of the depression"); S.Rep.No. 628, 74th Cong., 1st Sess., 16–17 (1935) (declaring that the "heart of any program for social security must be the child").
[25]See H.R.Doc.No. 81, 74th Cong., 1st Sess., 4–5, 29–30 (1935).
[26]Hearings on H.R. 4120 before the House Committee on Ways and Means, 74th Cong., 1st Sess., 158–161, 166, 174, 262–264 (1935); Hearings on S. 1130 before the Senate Committee on Finance, 74th Cong., 1st Sess., 102, 181, 337–338, 647, 654 (1935).
[27]See H.R.Rep.No. 615, 74th Cong., 1st Sess., 10 (1935); S.Rep.No. 628, 74th Cong., 1st Sess., 17–18 (1935).
[28]See 79 Cong.Rec. 5468, 5476, 5491, 5786, 5861 (1935).

ence will still render the child ineligible for assistance. On the question whether the man must be legally obligated to provide support before he can be regarded as the child's parent, the State has no such cogent answer. We think the answer is quite clear: Congress must have meant by the term "parent" an individual who owed to the child a state-imposed legal duty of support.

It is clear, as we have noted, that Congress expected "breadwinners" who secured employment would support their children. This congressional expectation is most reasonably explained on the basis that the kind of breadwinner Congress had in mind was one who was legally obligated to support his children. We think it beyond reason to believe that Congress would have considered that providing employment for the paramour of a deserted mother would benefit the mother's children whom he was not obligated to support.

By a parity of reasoning, we think that Congress must have intended that the children in such a situation remain eligible for AFDC assistance notwithstanding their mother's impropriety. AFDC was intended to provide economic security for children whom Congress could not reasonably expect would be provided for by simply securing employment for family breadwinners.[29] We think it apparent that neither Congress nor any reasonable person would believe that providing employment for some man who is under no legal duty to support a child would in any way provide meaningful economic security for that child.

A contrary view would require us to assume that Congress, at the same time that it intended to provide programs for the economic security and protection of *all* children, also intended arbitrarily to leave one class of destitute children entirely without meaningful protection. Children who are told, as Alabama has told these appellees, to look for their food to a man who is not in the least obliged to support them are without meaningful protection. Such an interpretation of congressional intent would be most unreasonable, and we decline to adopt it.

Our interpretation of the term "parent" in § 406(a) is strongly supported by the way the term is used in other sections of the Act. Section 402(a)(10) requires that, effective July 1, 1952, a state plan must:

> "provide for prompt notice to appropriate law-enforcement officials of the furnishing of aid to families with dependent children in respect of a child who has been deserted or abandoned by a *parent*." 64 Stat. 550 (1950), 42 U.S.C. § 602(a) (10). (Emphasis added.)

The "parent" whom this provision requires to be reported to law enforcement officials is surely the same "parent" whose desertion makes a child

---

[29] As the Senate Committee Report stated, AFDC was intended to provide for children who "will not be benefited through work programs or the revival of industry." S.Rep.No. 628, 74th Cong., 1st Sess., 17 (1935).

eligible for AFDC assistance in the first place. And Congress obviously did not intend that a so-called "parent" who has no legal duties of support be referred to law enforcement officials (as Alabama's own welfare regulations recognize),[30] for the very purpose of such referrals is to institute non-support proceedings. See Handbook, Pt. IV, §§ 8100–8149.[31] Whatever doubt there might have been over this proposition has been completely dispelled by the 1968 amendments to the Social Security Act, which provide that the States must develop a program:

> "(i) in the case of a child born out of wedlock who is receiving aid to families with dependent children, to establish the *paternity of such child and secure support for him, and*

> "(ii) in the case of any child receiving such aid who has been deserted or abandoned *by his parent, to secure support for such child from such parent (or from any other person legally liable for such support)* * * *." 42 U.S.C. § 602(a), as amended, § 201(a) (1) (C) (17), 81 Stat. 878 (1968). (Emphasis added.)

Another provision in the 1968 amendments requires the States, effective January 1, 1969, to report to HEW any *"parent * * * against whom an order for the support and maintenance* of such [dependent] child or children has been issued by" a court, if such parent is not making the required support payments. 42 U.S.C. § 602(a), as amended, § 211(a) (21), 81 Stat. 896 (1968). (Emphasis added.) Still another amendment requires the States to cooperate with HEW in locating any *parent* against whom a support petition has been filed in another State, and in securing compliance with any support order issued by another State, 42 U.S.C. § 602(a), as amended, § 211(a) (22), 81 Stat. 897 (1968).

The pattern of this legislation could not be clearer. Every effort is to be made to locate and secure support payments from persons legally obligated to support a deserted child.[32] The underlying policy and consistency in statutory interpretation dictate that the "parent" referred to in these statutory provisions is the same parent as that in § 406(a). The provisions seek to secure parental support in lieu of AFDC support for dependent children. Such parental support can be secured only where the parent is under a

---

[30]Alabama's own welfare regulations state: "Report parents who are legally responsible under Alabama law. These are the *natural* or *adoptive* parents of a child. A natural parent includes the father of a child born out of wedlock, if paternity has been *legally* established. It does not apply to a stepparent." Alabama Manual for Administration of Public Assistance, Pt. I, c. II, p. 36.

[31]HEW requires States to give notice of desertion only with respect to persons who, "under State laws, are defined as parents * * * for the support of minor children, and against whom legal action may be taken under such laws for desertion or abandonment." Handbook, Pt. IV, § 8131(2). And, as discussed in n. 10, supra, the alleged substitute father in the case at bar is not legally obligated by Alabama law to support the appellee children. See also Handbook, Pt. IV, § 3412(4) (providing that a stepparent not required by state law to support a child need not be considered the child's parent).

[32]Another 1968 amendment provides for the cooperation of the Internal Revenue Service in locating missing "parents." §410, 81 Stat. 897 (1968).

state-imposed legal duty to support the child. Children with alleged substitute parents who owe them no duty of support are entirely unprotected by these provisions. We think that these provisions corroborate the intent of Congress that the only kind of "parent," under § 406(a), whose presence in the home would provide adequate economic protection for a dependent child is one who is legally obligated to support him. Consequently, if Alabama believes it necessary that it be able to disqualify a child on the basis of a man who is not under such a duty of support, its arguments should be addressed to Congress and not this Court.[33]

IV.

Alabama's substitute father regulation, as written and as applied in this case, requires the disqualification of otherwise eligible dependent children if their mother "cohabits" with a man who is not obligated by Alabama law to support the children. The regulation is therefore invalid because it defines "parent" in a manner that is inconsistent with § 406(a) of the Social Security Act. 42 U.S.C. § 606(a).[34] In denying AFDC assistance to appellees on the basis of this invalid regulation, Alabama has breached its federally imposed obligation to furnish "aid to families with dependent children * * * with reasonable promptness to all eligible individuals * * *." 42 U.S.C. § 602(a) (9). Our conclusion makes unnecessary consideration of appellees' equal-protection claim, upon which we intimate no views.

We think it well, in concluding, to emphasize that no legitimate interest of the State of Alabama is defeated by the decision we announce today. The State's interest in discouraging illicit sexual behavior and illegitimacy may be protected by other means, subject to constitutional limitations, including state participation in AFDC rehabilitative programs. Its interest in economically allocating its limited AFDC resources may be protected by its undisputed power to set the level of benefits and the standard of need, and by its taking into account in determining whether a child is needy all actual and regular contributions to his support.

All responsible governmental agencies in the Nation today recognize the enormity and pervasiveness of social ills caused by poverty. The causes of and cures for poverty are currently the subject of much debate. We hold

---

[33]We intimate no views whatsoever on the constitutionality of any such hypothetical legislative proposal.

[34]There is of course no question that the Federal Government, unless barred by some controlling constitutional prohibition, may impose the terms and conditions upon which its money allotments to the States shall be disbursed, and that any state law or regulation inconsistent with such federal terms and conditions is to that extent invalid. See Ivanhoe Irrigation District v. McCracken, 357 U.S. 275, 295, 78 S.Ct. 1174, 1185, 2 L.Ed.2d 1313 (1958); State of Oklahoma v. United States Civil Service Commission, 330 U.S. 127, 143, 67 S.Ct. 544, 553, 91 L.Ed. 794 (1947). It is equally clear that to the extent HEW has approved any so-called "man-in-the-house" provision which conflicts with §406(a) of the Social Security Act, 42 U.S.C. § 606(a), such approval is inconsistent with the controlling federal statute.

today only that Congress has made at least this one determination: that destitute children who are legally fatherless cannot be flatly denied federally funded assistance on the transparent fiction that they have a substitute father.

Affirmed.

APPENDIX: THE NIXON PROGRAM
1969

APPENDIX: THE NIXON PROGRAM

1969

In 1969 there were significant developments in both the judicial and executive branches concerning income security. In Shapiro v. Thompson *the United States Supreme Court decided on April 21, 1969 that residency requirements for welfare assistance on the state and federal level were unconstitutional. On August 8, 1969 President Richard M. Nixon introduced his new welfare program which contained a radically different approach to family assistance problems.*

Shapiro v. Thompson
394 U.S. 618 (1969)

Mr. Justice Brennan delivered the opinion of the Court.

These three appeals were restored to the calendar for reargument. 392 U. S. 920 (1968). Each is an appeal from a decision of a three-judge District Court holding unconstitutional a State or District of Columbia statutory provision which denies welfare assistance to residents of the State or District who have not resided within their jurisdictions for at least one year immediately preceding their applications for such assistance. We affirm the judgments of the District Courts in the three cases.

*   *   *

II

There is no dispute that the effect of the waiting-period requirement in each case is to create two classes of needy resident families indistinguishable from each other except that one is composed of residents who have resided a year or more, and the second of residents who have resided less than a year, in the jurisdiction. On the basis of this sole difference the first class is granted and the second class is denied welfare aid upon which may depend the ability of the families to obtain the very means to subsist — food, shelter, and other necessities of life. In each case, the District Court found that appellees met the test for residence in their jurisdictions, as well as all other eligibility requirements except the requirement of residence for a full year prior to their applications. On reargument, appellees' central contention is that the statutory prohibition of benefits to residents of less than a year creates a classification which constitutes an invidious discrimination denying them equal protection of the laws. We agree. The interests which appellants assert are promoted by the classification either may not constitu-

875

tionally be promoted by government or are not compelling governmental interests.

III

Primarily, appellants justify the waiting-period requirement as a protective device to preserve the fiscal integrity of state public assistance programs. It is asserted that people who require welfare assistance during their first year of residence in a State are likely to become continuing burdens on state welfare programs. Therefore, the argument runs, if such people can be deterred from entering the jurisdiction by denying them welfare benefits during the first year, state programs to assist long-time residents will not be impaired by a substantial influx of indigent newcomers.[7]

There is weighty evidence that exclusion from the jurisdiction of the poor who need or may need relief was the specific objective of these provisions. In the Congress, sponsors of federal legislation to eliminate all residence requirements have been consistently opposed by representatives of state and local welfare agencies who have stressed the fears of the States that elimination of the requirements would result in a heavy influx of individuals into States providing the most generous benefits. See, *e. g.*, Hearings on H. R. 10032 before the House Committee on Ways and Means, 87th Cong., 2d Sess., 309–310, 644 (1962); Hearings on H. R. 6000 before the Senate Committee on Finance, 81st Cong., 2d Sess., 324–327 (1950). The sponsor of the Connecticut requirement said in its support: "I doubt that Connecticut can and should continue to allow unlimited migration into the state on the basis of offering instant money and permanent income to all who can make their way to the state regardless of their ability to contribute to the economy." H. B. 82, Connecticut General Assembly House Proceedings, February Special Session, 1965, Vol. II, pt. 7, p. 3504. In Pennsylvania, shortly after the enactment of the one-year requirement, the Attorney General issued an opinion construing the one-year requirement strictly because "[a]ny other conclusion would tend to attract the dependents of other states to our Commonwealth." 1937–1938 Official Opinions of the Attorney General, No. 240, p. 110. In the District of Columbia case, the constitutionality of §3–203 was frankly defended in the District Court and in this Court on the ground that it is designed to protect

---

[7]The waiting-period requirement has its antecedents in laws prevalent in England and the American Colonies centuries ago which permitted the ejection of individuals and families if local authorities thought they might become public charges. For example, the preamble of the English Law of Settlement and Removal of 1662 expressly recited the concern, also said to justify the three statutes before us, that large numbers of the poor were moving to parishes where more liberal relief policies were in effect. See generally Coll, Perspectives in Public Welfare: The English Heritage, 4 Welfare in Review, No. 3, p. 1 (1966). The 1662 law and the earlier Elizabethan Poor Law of 1601 were the models adopted by the American Colonies. Newcomers to a city, town, or county who might become public charges were "warned out" or "passed on" to the next locality. Initially, the funds for welfare payments were raised by local taxes, and the controversy as to responsibility for particular indigents was between localities in the same State. As States — first alone and then with federal grants — assumed the major responsibility, the contest of nonresponsibility became interstate.

the jurisdiction from an influx of persons seeking more generous public assistance than might be available elsewhere.

We do not doubt that the one-year waiting-period device is well suited to discourage the influx of poor families in need of assistance. An indigent who desires to migrate, resettle, find a new job, start a new life will doubtless hesitate if he knows that he must risk making the move without the possibility of falling back on state welfare assistance during his first year of residence, when his need may be most acute. But the purpose of inhibiting migration by needy persons into the State is constitutionally impermissible.

This Court long ago recognized that the nature of our Federal Union and our constitutional concepts of personal liberty unite to require that all citizens be free to travel throughout the length and breadth of our land uninhibited by statutes, rules, or regulations which unreasonably burden or restrict this movement. That proposition was early stated by Chief Justice Taney in the *Passenger Cases*, 7 How. 283, 492 (1849):

> "For all the great purposes for which the Federal government was formed, we are one people, with one common country. We are all citizens of the United States; and, as members of the same community, must have the right to pass and repass through every part of it without interruption, as freely as in our own States."

We have no occasion to ascribe the source of this right to travel interstate to a particular constitutional provision.[8] It suffices that, as MR. JUSTICE STEWART said for the Court in *United States* v. *Guest*, 383 U. S. 745, 757–748 (1966):

> "The constitutional right to travel from one State to another . . . occupies a position fundamental to the concept of our Federal Union. It is a right that has been firmly established and repeatedly recognized.
>
> ". . . [T]he right finds no explicit mention in the Constitution. The reason, it has been suggested, is that a right so elementary was conceived from the beginning to be a necessary concomitant of the stronger Union the Constitution created. In any event, freedom to travel throughout the United States has long been recognized as a basic right under the Constitution."

---

[8]In *Corfield* v. *Coryell*, 6 F. Cas. 546, 552 (No. 3230) (C. C. E. D. Pa. 1825), *Paul* v. *Virginia*, 8 Wall. 168, 180 (1869), and *Ward* v. *Maryland*, 12 Wall. 418, 430 (1871), the right to travel interstate was grounded upon the Privileges and Immunities Clause of Art. IV, § 2. See also *Slaughter-House Cases*, 16 Wall. 36, 79 (1873); *Twining* v. *New Jersey*, 211 U. S. 78, 97 (1908). In *Edwards* v. *California*, 314 U. S. 160, 181, 183–185 (1941) (DOUGLAS and Jackson, JJ., concurring), and *Twining* v. *New Jersey, supra,* reliance was placed on the Privileges and Immunities Clause of the Fourteenth Amendment. See also *Crandall* v. *Nevada*, 6 Wall. 35 (1868). In *Edwards* v. *California, supra,* and the *Passenger Cases,* 7 How. 283 (1849), a Commerce Clause approach was employed.

See also *Kent* v. *Dulles*, 357 U. S. 116, 125 (1958); *Aptheker* v. *Secretary of State*, 378 U. S. 500, 505–506 (1964); *Zemel* v. *Rusk* 381 U. S. 1, 14 (1965), where the freedom of Americans to travel outside the country was grounded upon the Due Process Clause of the Fifth Amendment.

Thus, the purpose of deterring the in-migration of indigents cannot serve as justification for the classification created by the one-year waiting period, since that purpose is constitutionally impermissible. If a law has "no other purpose . . . than to chill the assertion of constitutional rights by penalizing those who choose to exercise them, then it [is] patently unconstitutional." *United States* v. *Jackson*, 390 U. S. 570, 581 (1968).

Alternatively, appellants argue that even if it is impermissible for a State to attempt to deter the entry of all indigents, the challenged classification may be justified as a permissible state attempt to discourage those indigents who would enter the State solely to obtain larger benefits. We observe first that none of the statutes before us is tailored to serve that objective. Rather, the class of barred newcomers is all-inclusive, lumping the great majority who come to the State for other purposes with those who come for the sole purpose of collecting higher benefits. In actual operation, therefore, the three statutes enact what in effect are nonrebuttable presumptions that every applicant for assistance in his first year of residence came to the jurisdiction solely to obtain higher benefits. Nothing whatever in any of these records supplies any basis in fact for such a presumption.

More fundamentally, a State may no more try to fence out those indigents who seek higher welfare benefits than it may try to fence out indigents generally. Implicit in any such distinction is the notion that indigents who enter a State with the hope of securing higher welfare benefits are somehow less deserving than indigents who do not take this consideration into account. But we do not perceive why a mother who is seeking to make a new life for herself and her children should be regarded as less deserving because she considers, among others factors, the level of a State's public assistance. Surely such a mother is no less deserving than a mother who moves into a particular State in order to take advantage of its better educational facilities.

Appellants argue further that the challenged classification may be sustained as an attempt to distinguish between new and old residents on the basis of the contribution they have made to the community through the payment of taxes. We have difficulty seeing how long-term residents who qualify for welfare are making a greater present contribution to the State in taxes than indigent residents who have recently arrived. If the argument is based on contributions made in the past by the long-term residents, there is some question, as a factual matter, whether this argument is applicable in Pennsylvania where the record suggests that some 40% of those denied public assistance because of the waiting period had lengthy prior residence in the State.[9] But we need not rest on the particular facts of these cases. Appellants'

[9]Furthermore, the contribution rationale can hardly explain why the District of Columbia and Pennsylvania bar payments to children who have not lived in the jurisdiction for a year regardless of whether the parents have lived in the jurisdiction for that period. See D. C. Code § 3–203; D. C. Handbook, EL 9.1, I (C)(1966); Pa. Stat. Tit. 62, § 432 (6) (1968). Clearly, the children who were barred would not have made a contribution during that year.

reasoning would logically permit the State to bar new residents from schools, parks, and libraries or deprive them of police and fire protection. Indeed it would permit the State to apportion all benefits and services according to the past tax contributions of its citizens. The Equal Protection Clause prohibits such an apportionment of state services.[10]

We recognize that a State has a valid interest in preserving the fiscal integrity of its programs. It may legitimately attempt to limit its expenditures, whether for public assistance, public education, or any other program. But a State may not accomplish such a purpose by invidious distinctions between classes of its citizens. It could not, for example, reduce expenditures for education by barring indigent children from its schools. Similarly, in the cases before us, appellants must do more than show that denying welfare benefits to new residents saves money. The saving of welfare costs cannot justify an otherwise invidious classification.

In sum, neither deterrence of indigents from migrating to the State nor limitation of welfare benefits to those regarded as contributing to the State is a constitutionally permissible state objective.

IV

Appellants next advance as justification certain administrative and related governmental objectives allegedly served by the waiting-period requirement. They argue that the requirement (1) facilitates the planning of the welfare budget; (2) provides an objective test of residency; (3) minimizes the opportunity for recipients fraudulently to receive payments from more than one jurisdiction; and (4) encourages early entry of new residents into the labor force.

At the outset, we reject appellants' argument that a mere showing of a rational relationship between the waiting period and these four admittedly permissible state objectives will suffice to justify the classification. See *Lindsley* v. *Natural Carbonic Gas Co.*, 220 U. S. 61, 78 (1911); *Flemming* v. *Nestor*, 363 U. S. 603, 611 (1960); *McGowan* v. *Maryland*, 366 U. S. 420, 426 (1961). The waiting-period provision denies welfare benefits to otherwise eligible applicants solely because they have recently moved into the jurisdiction. But in moving from State to State or to the District of Columbia appellees were exercising a constitutional right, and any classification which serves to penalize the exercise of that right, unless shown to be necessary to promote a *compelling* governmental interest, is unconstitutional. Cf. *Skinner* v. *Oklahoma*, 316 U. S. 535, 541 (1942); *Korematsu* v. *United States*, 323 U. S. 214, 216 (1944); *Bates* v. *Little Rock*, 361 U. S. 516, 524 (1960); *Sherbert* v. *Verner*, 374 U. S. 398, 406 (1963).

The argument that the waiting-period requirement facilitates budget predictability is wholly unfounded. The records in all three cases are utterly devoid of evidence that either State or the District of Columbia in fact uses

[10]We are not dealing here with state insurance programs which may legitimately tie the amount of benefits to the individual's contributions.

the one-year requirement as a means to predict the number of people who will require assistance in the budget year. None of the appellants takes a census of new residents or collects any other data that would reveal the number of newcomers in the State less than a year. Nor are new residents required to give advance notice of their need for welfare assistance.[13] Thus, the welfare authorities cannot know how many new residents come into the jurisdiction in any year, much less how many of them will require public assistance. In these circumstances, there is simply no basis for the claim that the one-year waiting requirement serves the purpose of making the welfare budget more predictable. In Connecticut and Pennsylvania the irrelevance of the one-year requirement to budgetary planning is further underscored by the fact that temporary, partial assistance is given to some new residents[14] and full assistance is given to other new residents under reciprocal agreements.[15] Finally, the claim that a one-year waiting requirement is used for planning purposes is plainly belied by the fact that the requirement is not also imposed on applicants who are long-term residents, the group that receives the bulk of welfare payments. In short, the States rely on methods other than the one-year requirement to make budget estimates. In No. 34, the Director of the Pennsylvania Bureau of Assistance Policies and Standards testified that, based on experience in Pennsylvania and elsewhere, her office had already estimated how much the elimination of the one-year requirement would cost and that the estimates of costs of other changes in regulations "have proven exceptionally accurate."

The argument that the waiting period serves as an administratively efficient rule of thumb for determined residency similarly will not withstand scrutiny. The residence requirement and the one-year waiting-period requirement are distinct and independent prerequisites for assistance under these three statutes, and the facts relevant to the determination of each are directly examined by the welfare authorities.[16] Before granting an application, the welfare authorities investigate the applicant's employment, hous-

[13]Of course, such advance notice would inevitably be unreliable since some who registered would not need welfare a year later while others who did not register would need welfare.

[14]See Conn. Gen. Stat. Rev. § 17–2d, now § 17–2c, and Pa. Pub. Assistance Manual § 3154 (1968).

[15]Both Connecticut and Pennsylvania have entered into open-ended interstate compacts in which they have agreed to eliminate the durational requirement for anyone who comes from another State which has also entered into the compact. Conn. Gen. Stat. Rev. § 17–21a (1968); Pa. Pub. Assistance Manual § 3150, App. I (1966).

[16]In Pennsylvania, the one-year waiting-period requirement but not the residency requirement is waived under reciprocal agreements. Pa. Stat., Tit. 62, § 432 (6) (1968); Pa. Pub. Assistance Manual § 3151.21 (1962).

1 Conn. Welfare Manual, c. II, § 220 (1966), provides that "[r]esidence within the state shall mean that the applicant is living in an established place of abode and the plan is to remain." A person who meets this requirement does not have to wait a year for assistance if he entered the State with a bona fide job offer or with sufficient funds to support himself without welfare for three months. *Id.*, at § 219.2.

HEW Handbook of Pub. Assistance Administration, pt. IV, § 3650 (1946), clearly distin-

ing, and family situation and in the course of the inquiry necessarily learn the facts upon which to determine whether the applicant is a resident.[17]

Similarly there is no need for a State to use the one-year waiting period as a safeguard against fraudulent receipt of benefits;[18] for less drastic means are available, and are employed, to minimize that hazard. Of course, a State has a valid interest in preventing fraud by any applicant, whether a newcomer or a long-time resident. It is not denied however that the investigations now conducted entail inquiries into facts relevant to that subject. In addition, cooperation among state welfare departments is common. The District of Columbia, for example, provides interim assistance to its former residents who have moved to a State which has a waiting period. As a matter of course, District officials send a letter to the welfare authorities in the recipient's new community "to request the information needed to continue assistance."[19] A like procedure would be an effective safeguard against the hazard of double payments. Since double payments can be prevented by a letter or a telephone call, it is unreasonable to accomplish this objective by the blunderbuss method of denying assistance to all indigent newcomers for an entire year.

Pennsylvania suggests that the one-year waiting period is justified as a means of encouraging new residents to join the labor force promptly. But this logic would also require a similar waiting period for long-term residents of the State. A state purpose to encourage employment provides no rational basis for imposing a one-year waiting-period restriction on new residents only.

We conclude therefore that appellants in these cases do not use and have no need to use the one-year requirement for the governmental purposes suggested. Thus, even under traditional equal protection tests a classifica-

---

guishes between residence and duration of residence. It defines residence, as is conventional, in terms of intent to remain in the jurisdiction, and it instructs interviewers that residence and length of residence "are two distinct aspects . . . ."

[17]See, e. g., D. C. Handbook, chapters on Eligibility Payments, Requirements, Resources, and Reinvestigation for an indication of how thorough these investigations are. See also 1 Conn. Welfare Manual, c. I (1967); Pa. Pub. Assistance Manual §§ 3170–3330 (1962).

The Department of Health, Education, and Welfare has proposed the elimination of individual investigations, except for spot checks, and the substitution of a declaration system, under which the "agency accepts the statements of the applicant for or recipient of assistance, about facts that are within his knowledge and competence . . . as a basis for decisions regarding his eligibility and extent of entitlement." HEW, Determination of Eligibility for Public Assistance Programs, 33 Fed. Reg. 17189 (1968). See also Hoshino, Simplification of the Means Test and its Consequences, 41 Soc. Serv. Rev. 237, 241–249 (1967); Burns, What's Wrong With Public Welfare?, 36 Soc. Serv. Rev. 111, 114–115 (1962). Presumably the statement of an applicant that he intends to remain in the jurisdiction would be accepted under a declaration system.

[18]The unconcern of Connecticut and Pennsylvania with the one-year requirement as a means of preventing fraud is made apparent by the waiver of the requirement in reciprocal agreements with other States. See n. 15, *supra.*

[19]D. C. Handbook, RV 2.1, I, II (B) (1967). See also Pa. Pub. Assistance Manual § 3153 (1962).

tion of welfare applicants according to whether they have lived in the State for one year would seem irrational and unconstitutional.[20] But, of course, the traditional criteria do not apply in these cases. Since the classification here touches on the fundamental right of interstate movement, its constitutionality must be judged by the stricter standard of whether it promotes a *compelling* state interest. Under this standard, the waiting period requirement clearly violates the Equal Protection Clause.[21]

V

Connecticut and Pennsylvania argue, however, that the constitutional challenge to the waiting-period requirements must fail because Congress expressly approved the imposition of the requirement by the States as part of the jointly funded AFDC program.

Section 402 (b) of the Social Security Act of 1935, as amended, 42 U. S. C. § 602 (b), provides that:

> "The Secretary shall aprove any [state assistance] plan which fulfills the conditions specified in subsection (a) of this section, except that he shall not approve any plan which imposes as a condition of eligibility for aid to families with dependent children, a residence requirement which denies aid with respect to any child residing in the State (1) who has resided in the State for one year immediately preceding the application for such aid, or (2) who was born within one year immediately preceding the application, if the parent or other relative with whom the child is living has resided in the State for one year immediately preceding the birth."

On its face, the statute does not approve, much less prescribe, a one-year requirement. It merely directs the Secretary of Health, Education and Welfare not to disapprove plans submitted by the States because they include such a requirement.[22] The suggestion that Congress enacted that directive to encourage state participation in the AFDC program is completely refuted by the legislative history of the section. That history discloses that Congress enacted the directive to curb hardships resulting from lengthy residence requirements. Rather than an approval or a prescription of the re-

[20]Under the traditional standard, equal protection is denied only if the classification is "without any reasonable basis," *Lindsley* v. *Natural Carbonic Gas Co.*, 220 U. S. 61, 78 (1911); see also *Flemming* v. *Nestor*, 363 U. S. 603 (1960).

[21]We imply no view of the validity of waiting-period *or* residence requirements determining eligibility to vote, eligibility for tuition-free education, to obtain a license to practice a profession, to hunt or fish, and so forth. Such requirements may promote compelling state interests on the one hand, or, on the other, may not be penalties upon the exercise of the constitutional right of interstate travel.

[22]As of 1964, 11 jurisdictions imposed no residence requirement whatever for AFDC assistance. They were Alaska, Georgia, Hawaii, Kentucky, New Jersey, New York, Rhode Island, Vermont, Guam, Puerto Rico, and the Virgin Islands. See HEW, Characteristics of State Public Assistance Plans under the Social Security Act (Pub. Assistance Rep. No. 50, 1964 ed.).

quirement in state plans, the directive was the means chosen by Congress to deny federal funding to any State which persisted in stipulating excessive residence requirements as a condition of the payment of benefits.

One year before the Social Security Act was passed, 20 of the 45 States which had aid to dependent children programs required residence in the State for two or more years. Ten other States required two or more years of residence in a particular town or county. And 33 States required at least one year of residence in a particular town or county.[23] Congress determined to combat this restrictionist policy. Both the House and Senate Committee Reports expressly stated that the objective of § 402(b) was to compel "[l]iberality of residence requirement."[24] Not a single instance can be found in the debates or committee reports supporting the contention that § 402(b) was enacted to encourage participation by the States in the AFDC program. To the contrary, those few who addressed themselves to waiting-period requirements emphasized that participation would depend on a State's repeal or drastic revision of existing requirements. A congressional demand on 41 States to repeal or drastically revise offending statutes is hardly a way to enlist their cooperation.[25]

But even if we were to assume, *arguendo*, that Congress did approve the imposition of a one-year waiting period, it is the responsive *state* legislation which infringes constitutional rights. By itself § 402 (b) has absolutely no restrictive effect. It is therefore not that statute but only the state requirements which pose the constitutional question.

Finally, even if it could be argued that the constitutionality of § 402 (b) is somehow at issue here, it follows from what we have said that the provision, insofar as it permits the one-year waiting-period requirement, would be unconstitutional. Congress may not authorize the States to violate the Equal Protection Clause. Perhaps Congress could induce wider state participation in school construction if it authorized the use of joint funds for

[23]Social Security Board, Social Security in America 235-236 (1937).

[24]H. R. Rep. No. 615, 74th Cong., 1st Sess., 24; S. Rep. No. 628, 74th Cong., 1st Sess., 35. Furthermore, the House Report cited President Roosevelt's statement in his Social Security Message that "People want decent homes to live in; they want to locate them where they can engage in productive work . . . ." H. R. Rep., *supra*, at 2. Clearly this was a call for greater freedom of movement.

In addition to the statement in the above Committee report, see the remarks of Rep. Doughton (floor manager of the Social Security bill in the House) and Rep. Vinson. 79 Cong. Rec. 5474, 5602-5603 (1935). These remarks were made in relation to the waiting-period requirements for old-age assistance, but they apply equally to the AFDC program.

[25]Section 402(b) required the repeal of 30 state statutes which imposed too long a waiting period and 11 state statutes (as well as the Hawaii statute) which required residence in a particular town or county. See Social Security Board, Social Security in America 235-236 (1937).

It is apparent that Congress was not intimating any view of the constitutionality of a one-year limitation. The constitutionality of any scheme of federal social security legislation was a matter of doubt at that time in light of the decision in *Schechter Poultry Corp.* v. *United States*, 295 U. S. 495 (1935). Throughout the House debates congressmen discussed the constitutionality of the fundamental taxing provisions of the Social Security Act, see, *e. g.*, 79 Cong. Rec. 5793 (1935) (remarks of Rep. Cooper), but not once did they discuss the constitutionality of § 402(b).

the building of segregated schools. But could it seriously be contended that Congress would be constitutionally justified in such authorization by the need to secure state cooperation? Congress is without power to enlist state cooperation in a joint federal-state program by legislation which authorizes the States to violate the Equal Protection Clause. *Katzenbach* v. *Morgan*, 384 U. S. 641, 651, n. 10 (1966).

VI

The waiting-period requirement in the District of Columbia Code involved in No. 33 is also unconstitutional even though it was adopted by Congress as an exercise of federal power. In terms of federal power, the discrimination created by the one-year requirement violates the Due Process Clause of the Fifth Amendment. "[W]hile the Fifth Amendment contains no equal protection clause, it does forbid discrimination that is 'so unjustifiable as to be violative of due process.' " *Schneider* v. *Rusk*, 377 U. S. 163, 168 (1964); *Bolling* v. *Sharpe*, 347 U. S. 497 (1954). For the reasons we have stated in invalidating the Pennsylvania and Connecticut provisions, the District of Columbia provision is also invalid—the Due Process Clause of the Fifth Amendment prohibits Congress from denying public assistance to poor persons otherwise eligible solely on the ground that they have not been residents of the District of Columbia for one year at the time their applications are filed.

Accordingly, the judgments are

Affirmed.

Presidential Address to the Nation on Welfare Reform
(August 8, 1969)*

Target: Reform

Since taking office, one of my first priorities has been to repair the machinery of government, and put it in shape for the 1970s. I have made many changes designed to improve the functioning of the executive branch. I have asked Congress for a number of important structural reforms: among others, a wide-ranging postal reform, a comprehensive draft reform, a reform of the unemployment insurance and antihunger programs, and reform of the present confusing hodge-podge of Federal grants-in-aid. Last April 21 I sent Congress a message asking for a package of major tax reforms, including both the closing of loopholes and the removal of more than 2 million

Weekly Compilation of Presidential Documents, 1969, p. 1103 (Aug. 11, 1969).

low-income tax-paying families from the tax rolls entirely. I am glad Congress is acting now on tax reform; I hope it acts soon on the other reforms as well.

The purpose of all these reforms is to eliminate unfairness; to make government more effective as well as more efficient; and to bring an end to its chronic failure to deliver the service that it promises.

My purpose tonight however, is not to review the past record, but to present a new set of reforms — a new set of proposals — a new and drastically different approach to the way in which government cares for those in need, and to the way the responsibilities are shared between the State and Federal governments.

I have chosen to do so in a direct report to the people because these proposals call for public decisions of the first importance; because they represent a fundamental change in the Nation's approach to one of its most pressing social problems; and because, quite deliberately, they also represent the first major reversal of the trend toward ever more centralization of government in Washington. After a third of a century of power flowing from the people and the States to Washington it is time for a New Federalism in which power, funds, and responsibility will flow from Washington to the States and to the people.

During last year's election campaign, I often made a point that touched a responsive chord wherever I traveled.

I said that this Nation became great not because of what government did for people, but because of what people did for themselves.

This new approach aims at helping the American people do more for themselves.

It aims at getting everyone able to work off welfare rolls and onto payrolls. It aims at ending the unfairness in a system that has become unfair to the welfare recipient, unfair to the working poor, and unfair to the taxpayer.

This new approach aims to make it possible for people — wherever in America they live — to receive their fair share of opportunity. It aims to ensure that people receiving aid, and who are able to work, contribute their fair share of productivity.

This new approach is embodied in a package of four measures: first, a complete replacement of the present welfare system; second, a comprehensive new job training and placement program; third, a revamping of the Office of Economic Opportunity; and, fourth, a start on the sharing of the Federal tax revenues with the States.

Next week — in three messages to the Congress and one statement — I will spell out in detail what these measures. contain. Tonight I want to explain what they mean, what they are intended to achieve, and how they are related.

Welfare

Whether measured by the anguish of the poor themselves, or by the drastically mounting burden on the taxpayer, the present welfare system has to be judged a colossal failure.

Our States and cities find themselves sinking in a welfare quagmire, as caseloads increase, as costs escalate, and as the welfare system stagnates enterprise and perpetuates dependency. What began on a small scale in the depression thirties has become a monster in the prosperous sixties. The tragedy is not only that it is bringing States and cities to the brink of financial disaster, but also that it is failing to meet the elementary human, social, and financial needs of the poor.

It breaks up homes. It often penalizes work. It robs recipients of dignity. And it grows.

Benefit levels are grossly unequal—for a mother with three children, they range from an average of $263 a month in one State, down to an average of $39 in another State. So great an inequality is wrong; no child is "worth" more in one State than in another. One result of this inequality is to lure thousands more into already overcrowded inner cities, as unprepared for city life as they are for city jobs.

The present system creates an incentive for desertion. In most States, a family is denied welfare payments if a father is present—even though he is unable to support his family. In practice, this is what often happens: a father is unable to find a job at all, or one that will support his children. To make the children eligible for welfare, he leaves home—and the children are denied the authority, the discipline and the love that come with having a father in the house. This is wrong.

The present system often makes it possible to receive more money on welfare than on a low-paying job. This creates an incentive not to work; it also is unfair to the working poor. It is morally wrong for a family that is working to try to make ends meet to receive less than the family across the street on welfare. This has been bitterly resented by the man who works, and rightly so—the rewards are just the opposite of what they should be. Its effect is to draw people off payrolls and onto welfare rolls—just the opposite of what government should be doing. To put it bluntly and simply—any system which makes it more profitable for a man not to work than to work, and which encourages a man to desert his family rather than stay with his family, is wrong and indefensible.

We cannot simply ignore the failures of welfare, or expect them to go away. In the past 8 years, 3 million more people have been added to the welfare rolls—all in a period of low unemployment. If the present trend continues, another 4 million will have joined the welfare rolls by 1975. The financial cost will be crushing; the human cost will be suffocating.

I propose that we abolish the present welfare system and adopt in its place a new family assistance system. Initially, this new system would cost more than welfare. But unlike welfare, it is designed to correct the condition it deals with and thus to lessen the long-range burden.

Under this plan, the so-called "adult categories" of aid—aid to the aged, the blind, and disabled—would be continued, and a national minimum standard for benefits would be set, with the Federal Government contributing to its cost and also sharing the cost of additional State payments above that amount.

But the program now called "Aid to Families with Dependent Children"—the program we normally think of when we think of "welfare"—would be done away with completely. The new family assistance system I propose in its place rests essentially on three principles: equality of treatment, a work requirement, and a work incentive.

Its benefits would go to the working poor, as well as the nonworking; to families with dependent children headed by a father, as well as to those headed by a mother; and a basic Federal minimum would be provided, the same in every State.

I propose that the Federal Government build a foundation under the income of every American family with dependent children that cannot care for itself—wherever in America that family may live.

For a family of four now on welfare, with no outside income, the basic Federal payment would be $1,600 a year. States could add to that amount and most would do so. In no case would anyone's present level of benefits be lowered. At the same time, this foundation would be one on which the family itself could build. Outside earnings would be encouraged, not discouraged. The new worker could keep the first $60 a month of outside earnings with no reduction in his benefits, and beyond that his benefits would be reduced by only 50 cents for each dollar earned.

By the same token, a family head already employed at low wages could get a family assistance supplement; those who work would no longer be discriminated against. A family of five in which the father earns $2,000 a year—which is the hard fact of life for many families—would get family assistance payments of $1,260 for a total income of $3,260. A family of seven earning $3,000 a year would have its income raised to $4,360.

Thus, for the first time, the government would recognize that it has no less of an obligation to the working poor than to the nonworking poor; and for the first time, benefits would be scaled in such a way that it would always pay to work.

With such incentives, most recipients who can work will want to work. This is part of the American character.

But what of the others—those who can work but choose not to?

The answer is very simple.

Under this proposal, everyone who accepts benefits must also accept work or training provided suitable jobs are available either locally or at some distance if transportation is provided. The only exceptions would be those unable to work, and mothers of preschool children. Even mothers of preschool children, however, would have the *opportunity* to work — because I am also proposing along with this a major expansion of day-care centers to make it possible for mothers to take jobs by which they can support themselves and their children.

This national floor under incomes for working or dependent families is not a "guaranteed income." Under the guaranteed income proposal, everyone would be assured a minimum income, regardless of how much he was capable of earning, regardless of what his need was, regardless of whether or not he was willing to work.

During the presidential campaign last year I opposed such a plan. I oppose it now, and will continue to oppose it. A guaranteed income would undermine the incentive to work; the family assistance plan increases the incentive to work. A guaranteed income establishes a right without responsibilities; family assistance recognizes a need *and* establishes a responsibility. It provides help to those in need, and in turn requires that those who receive help work to the extent of their capabilities. There is no reason why one person should be taxed so that another can choose to live idly.

In States that now have benefit levels above the Federal floor, family assistance would help ease the States' financial burdens. But in 20 States — those in which poverty is most widespread — the new Federal floor would be above present average benefit levels, and would mean a leap upward for many thousands of families that cannot care for themselves.

Manpower Training

*   *   *

The Commission on Income Maintenance Programs ultimately reported in November in favor of a negative income tax to which those in need would be entitled as of right.

Report of the Commission on Income Maintenance Programs
November 12, 1969

*   *   *

Our main recommendation is for the creation of a universal income supplement program financed and administered by the Federal Government, making payments based on income needs to all members of the population. The payments would vary by family size and would provide a base income for any needy family or individual.

The basic payments would be reduced by 50-cents for each dollar of income from other sources. This formula would encourage recipients to continue working or to seek employment and would not discourage continued development of private savings and insurance, and social insurance systems.

We propose that the program be initiated at a level providing a base income of $2,400 to a family of four. Families of four with other income up to $4,800 would receive some supplementation. This program would provide an estimated $6-billion of net added income to $10 million households in 1971.

Since $2,400 is below the poverty line for a family of four, the basic benefit would not meet the full income needs of families with no other income. This level was not chosen because we feel that it is an adequate income, but because it is a practical program that can be implemented in the near future. The level can be raised to an adequate level within a short period of time. Of the $6-billion added to disposable household income, $5-billion would go directly to the poor, and the remainder to those somewhat above the poverty line. Half of the income needs of the poor would be met by this program alone.

The commission strongly recommends that the benefit levels be raised as rapidly as is practical and possible in the future. To set payment levels at the poverty line immediately would cost an estimated $27-billion, and provide income transfers to a total of 24 million households. We believe that a program of that potential magnitude must be adopted in steps. We have recommended a feasible first step. . . .

INDEX

A

894

C

D

E

K

L

N

O

912

S

U